Discrimination at Work

Employment Law Handbook

May 2012

IDS

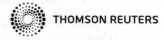

Discrimination at Work

Employment Law Handbook

Incomes Data Services
Finsbury Tower, 103-105 Bunhill Row, London EC1Y 8LZ
Tel: 0845 077 2911 Fax: 0845 310 5517
Email: ids@incomesdata.co.uk
Website: www.incomesdata.co.uk

ISBN 978 0 414 02985 9

IDS Employment Law Handbook, 'Discrimination at Work', is published by Thomson Reuters (Professional) UK Limited trading as Incomes Data Services Limited (Registered in England & Wales, Company No. 16790446). Registered Office: Aldgate House, 33 Aldgate High Street, London EC3N 1DL.

The information contained in this journal in not intended to be a substitute for specific legal advice and readers should obtain advice from a qualified adviser in relation to individual transactions or matters.

No natural forests were destroyed to make this product: only farmed timber was used and re-planted.

A CIP catalogue record for this book is available from the British Library.

Typeset by DC Graphic Design Ltd, Swanley Village, Kent BR8 7PA
Printed by St Austell Printing Co, 41 Truro Road, St Austell, Cornwall PL25 5JE

Contents

Part 4 Discrimination in the workplace

Part 7 Proving discrimination

36 Compensation: heads of damage

37 Equality and Human Rights Commission 1333

Part 9 Public sector equality duties

Introduction

On 1 October 2010 the majority of the provisions in the Equality Act 2010 (EqA) came into force, signalling a new era for discrimination law. The EqA – a single statute covering all the 'protected characteristics' of age, disability, gender reassignment, marriage and civil partnership, pregnancy and maternity, race, religion or belief, sex, and sexual orientation – replaced almost all the previous anti-discrimination legislation in Great Britain, including the Equal Pay Act 1970, the Sex Discrimination Act 1975, the Race Relations Act 1976, the Disability Discrimination Act 1995, the Employment Equality (Religion or Belief) Regulations 2003 SI 2003/1660, the Employment Equality (Sexual Orientation) Regulations 2003 SI 2003/1661 and the Employment Equality (Age) Regulations 2006 SI 2006/1031. However, the Equality Act 2006 remains in force, subject to various amendments set out in Schedule 26 to the EqA, in so far as it relates to the Equality and Human Rights Commission (EHRC).

The key aims of the new Act were to harmonise the previous provisions where appropriate, and to strengthen the law to support progress on equality. With regard to the first aim, the EqA sets out common definitions of unlawful discrimination that apply across all, or most, of the nine characteristics protected by the Act. In some cases, however, it has not been possible to harmonise the relevant provisions. For example, the provisions on equal pay are dealt with separately from the other discrimination provisions, while the unique nature of the protection afforded to employees with disabilities means that certain forms of discrimination apply only in that context. With regard to the second aim – strengthening anti-discrimination law – the EqA extended the scope of some provisions that previously applied only to certain strands of discrimination law and introduced some entirely new concepts, such as the prohibition on pre-employment health enquiries.

As a result of the harmonisation and consolidation of discrimination law, the same statutory provisions apply (with some exceptions) regardless of which 'strand' of discrimination is being relied upon. Thus, similar issues will arise whether the employee is alleging, for example, sex or age discrimination. For this reason, it now seems appropriate to consider the topic of discrimination in a single, overarching Handbook.

As readers will appreciate from the sheer size of this Handbook, discrimination law has become a vast topic with the capacity to affect every aspect of the employment relationship. The steady flow of cases through the employment tribunal system continues to provide diverse examples of the legislation in practice, while the appellate courts have never had so many discrimination issues to deal with.

Influence of European Law

Much of the EqA derives from, or is specifically designed to implement, the provisions of EU Equality Directives. For this reason, EU law has played, and will continue to play, a pivotal role in the development of discrimination law in this country. Throughout the Handbook, there are extensive considerations of EU case law and how it applies, or may apply, in the United Kingdom. The influence of EU law on domestic jurisprudence is discussed in depth in Chapter 2, 'European discrimination law'.

Code of Practice on Employment and Explanatory Notes

The employment provisions of the EqA are underpinned by a statutory Code of Practice on Employment, made under the EHRC's powers in S.14 of the Equality Act 2006. References in this Handbook to the EHRC Employment Code are to the version that was laid before Parliament on 12 October 2010. Although a failure to comply with the Code is not actionable in itself, the Code is admissible in legal proceedings and must be taken into account by courts and tribunals where it appears relevant.

The Government also published Explanatory Notes to accompany the EqA. These extensive Notes summarise the previous legislation and the background to the EqA, as well as giving further details about many of the Act's provisions. They are referred to, where appropriate, throughout this Handbook.

Scope of the Handbook

This Handbook covers all the strands of discrimination previously dealt with in individual IDS Employment Law Handbooks and Supplements. It replaces the IDS Employment Law Handbooks on 'Sex Discrimination' (2008), 'Race and Religion Discrimination' (2003), and 'Disability Discrimination' (2010), and the IDS Employment Law Supplements on 'Age Discrimination' (2006), and 'Sexual Orientation Discrimination' (2003). This Handbook does not, however, cover the provisions in the EqA dealing with sex discrimination in contractual terms, which are instead dealt with in IDS Employment Law Handbook, 'Equal Pay' (2011). Nor does it deal in any depth with the provisions concerned with discrimination on the ground of pregnancy or maternity, which are dealt with in IDS Employment Law Handbook, 'Maternity and Parental Rights' (2009), Chapter 13.

This Handbook focuses on discrimination in employment. It does not cover the other fields to which the EqA applies, such as education, the provision of goods and services, and the letting of premises. However, given that many of the same concepts apply across all fields covered by the Act, we refer to cases decided in other contexts where relevant.

Stop press – Government announces reforms to EqA and EHRC

Just as we were going to press, the Government announced a raft of changes to the EqA and the EHRC. The amendments to the EqA follow examination of the legislation as part of the Government's 'red tape challenge' and include a consultation on repealing employers' liability for third-party harassment. The Home Secretary and Minister for Women and Equalities, Theresa May, stated that 'bureaucracy and prescription are not routes to equality'.

The measures announced include:

- consultation on repealing employers' liability for third-party harassment under S.40 EqA (see Chapter 28, 'Liability of employers, employees and agents' under 'Employer's liability for harassment by third parties'). The Government argues that employees are already adequately protected against such behaviour by employers' common law duty to take reasonable care of the safety of their employees; employers' duty under Health and Safety legislation to ensure, so far as is reasonably practicable, their employees' health, safety and welfare at work; the Protection from Harassment Act 1997; constructive dismissal law; and, potentially, the protection from harassment provisions in S.26 EqA

- consultation on repealing employment tribunals' power in S.124(3) EqA to make recommendations that apply to all an employer's staff (see Chapter 34, 'Enforcing individual rights', under 'Remedies – recommendations'). The power was introduced into the EqA so that tribunals could make recommendations to address discrimination where a claimant had already left the workplace. However, the Government believes that the power is unlikely to serve a practical purpose or to be an appropriate or effective legal remedy

- consultation on repealing S.138 EqA, which contains the statutory questionnaire procedure (see Chapter 33, 'Proving discrimination', under 'Requesting information and disclosure of evidence – statutory questionnaires'). The Government believes that this procedure has failed to increase pre-hearing settlements and reduce tribunal workloads, and has instead created burdens and risks for employers

- reviewing the operation of the S.149 EqA public sector equality duty that requires public bodies to consider, among other things, the impact of their decisions on those who share a relevant protected characteristic such as sex or race (see Chapter 38, 'General public sector equality duty', and Chapter 39, 'Specific public sector equality duties')

- repealing the socio-economic duty contained in S.1 EqA, which would (if it had been brought into force) have obliged public bodies to have regard to the desirability of exercising their functions so as to reduce the inequalities of outcome which result from socio-economic disadvantage (see Chapter 40, 'Socio-economic duty'); and

- working with the British Chambers of Commerce to help small and medium-sized companies understand what they do and do not need to do to comply with the EqA.

The two consultations issued by the Government Equalities Office, 'Equality Act 2010: consultation on repeal of two enforcement provisions' and 'Equality Act 2010: consultation on employer liability for harassment of employees by third parties', close on 7 August 2012.

The Government's response to its 2011 consultation, 'Building a fairer Britain: Reform of the Equality and Human Rights Commission', sets out wide-ranging reforms to the EHRC, including scrapping some of its powers and duties under the Equality Act 2006 so that it can focus on its core functions. The Government believes the EHRC can 'add value' primarily as a national expert on equality and human rights issues and as a strategic enforcer of the law and guardian of rights. The EHRC will also be subject to tighter financial controls, and have a new Chairman and a new, smaller board. If the EHRC has not progressed sufficiently by autumn 2013 the Government will make further reforms, which may include splitting the EHRC's responsibilities across new or existing bodies. The current powers and duties of the EHRC are discussed in detail in Chapter 37, 'Equality and Human Rights Commission'.

Scheme of the Handbook

The scheme of the Handbook is as follows:

- Chapters 1, 2 and 3 look at the three sources of discrimination law: domestic legislation; EU Treaties and Directives; and the European Convention on Human Rights

- Chapters 4–13 discuss the characteristics that are afforded protection under the EqA: age (Chapter 5); disability (Chapter 6); gender reassignment (Chapter 7); marriage and civil partnership (Chapter 8); pregnancy and maternity (Chapter 9); race (Chapter 10); religion or belief (Chapter 11); sex (Chapter 12); and sexual orientation (Chapter 13)

- Chapters 14–22 are concerned with the types of conduct that are prohibited by the EqA. Chapter 14 deals with the general principles involved; Chapter 15 examines direct discrimination; Chapters 16 and 17 look at indirect discrimination; Chapter 18 focuses on harassment claims; Chapter 19 deals with the victimisation provisions; Chapter 20 examines the new provisions relating to discrimination arising from disability; Chapter 21 considers the duty to make reasonable adjustments; and Chapter 22 looks at other forms of prohibited conduct, including pregnancy and maternity discrimination and the rules relating to absence from work during the gender reassignment process

- Chapters 23–27 consider the circumstances in which discrimination is prohibited. Chapter 23 sets out the general principles relevant to discrimination in the workplace; Chapter 24 examines how discrimination can arise in the recruitment process, and explores the new rules on pre-employment health questions; Chapter 25 looks at discrimination occurring during the course of the employment relationship; Chapter 26 focuses on discrimination in the dismissal process, including redundancy and retirement; and Chapter 27 discusses post-employment discrimination, victimisation and harassment

- Chapters 28 and 29 address the question of liability under the EqA. Chapter 28 is concerned with the liability of employers, employees and agents, while Chapter 29 focuses on the liability of bodies such as trade unions that play a role in the workplace

- Chapters 30 and 31 explain the exceptions to the principle of non-discrimination that are allowed by the EqA. Chapter 30 deals with the general exceptions that apply across all, or most, of the protected characteristics, such as the occupational requirements exception, while Chapter 31 is concerned with specific exceptions, i.e. those that apply in respect of a particular characteristic

- Chapters 32 and 33 consider what a claimant needs to show in order to prove discrimination. Chapter 32 focuses on the special rules relating to the burden of proof in discrimination cases and Chapter 33 examines the circumstances in which a court or tribunal may infer discrimination from the facts before it

- Chapters 34–37 deal with enforcement under the EqA. Chapter 34 is concerned with the enforcement of individual rights and considers general matters such as tribunal jurisdiction, time limits and compromising claims, while Chapters 35 and 36 focus on compensation for discrimination. Chapter 37 discusses the role of the Equality and Human Rights Commission in combating unlawful discrimination and promoting equality of opportunity

- Finally, Chapters 38–40 look at the public sector equality duties provided for under the EqA. Chapter 38 examines the general public sector equality duty, Chapter 39 considers the specific public sector equality duties, and Chapter 40 explains the so-called socio-economic duty, which is not yet in force.

The law is stated as at 1 May 2012.

Part 1
Sources of discrimination law

1 UK discrimination law

Discrimination law in the United Kingdom has taken on an ever-increasing **1.1** prominence in the employment sphere since the first Race Relations Act was enacted in 1965. Over the years the number of personal characteristics protected from discrimination and similar conduct has grown, sometimes as a result of domestic initiatives and sometimes through the implementation of European Directives. Landmark pieces of anti-discrimination legislation include the Equal Pay Act 1970, the Sex Discrimination Act 1975 and the Race Relations Act 1976. These were followed some years later by the Disability Discrimination Act 1995 and, in the first few years of the 21st century, a wave of new discrimination rights covering religion or belief, sexual orientation and age.

UK discrimination law has been heavily influenced by European Union (EU) law. With the exception of the principle of equal pay, which is contained in Article 157 of the Treaty of the Functioning of the European Union (formerly Article 141 of the EC Treaty), EU discrimination law is mainly set out in various Directives.

The three key Directives in this field are: **1.2**

- the recast Equal Treatment Directive (No.2006/54), which relates to 'the implementation of the principle of equal opportunities and equal treatment of men and women in matters of employment and occupation'. It covers sex, pregnancy and maternity, marriage and civil partnership, and gender reassignment

- the Equal Treatment Framework Directive (No.2000/78), which sets out a general framework for eliminating employment or occupational inequalities based on age, disability, religion or belief, and sexual orientation

- the Race Directive (No.2000/43), which implements the principle of equal treatment between persons irrespective of racial or ethnic origin.

These Directives are discussed in Chapter 2, 'European discrimination law'.

1.3 Anti-discrimination legislation before Equality Act 2010

Prior to 1 October 2010, anti-discrimination legislation was found in a number of different pieces of legislation, including:

- the Equal Pay Act 1970
- the Sex Discrimination Act 1975
- the Race Relations Act 1976
- the Disability Discrimination Act 1995
- the Employment Equality (Religion or Belief) Regulations 2003 SI 2003/1660
- the Employment Equality (Sexual Orientation) Regulations 2003 SI 2003/1661
- the Employment Equality (Age) Regulations 2006 SI 2006/1031
- the Equality Act 2006.

1.4 On 1 October 2010 the majority of the provisions of the Equality Act 2010 (EqA) came into force, signalling a new era for discrimination law. The EqA replaces almost all the previous anti-discrimination legislation in Great Britain (as listed above), with the exception of the Equality Act 2006, which remains in force (subject to various amendments set out in Schedule 26 to the EqA) in so far as it relates to the Equality and Human Rights Commission (EHRC). The EHRC, a non-departmental public body set up in 2007, took over the functions of the Equal Opportunities Commission (in respect of sex discrimination and equal pay), the Commission for Racial Equality (in respect of race discrimination) and the Disability Rights Commission (in respect of disability discrimination), all of which were dissolved on 1 October 2007. The EHRC also adopted a similar role in respect of the 'new' discrimination strands of religion or belief, sexual orientation and age, as well as a wider role relating to the promotion of human rights.

The EHRC is discussed in Chapter 37, 'Equality and Human Rights Commission'. (Note that for some time there has been a separate single Equality Commission for Northern Ireland, established under the Northern Ireland Act 1998.)

1.5 Equality Act 2010

The EqA, which aims to harmonise discrimination law and strengthen the law to support progress on equality, is a vast statute, extending to 218 sections and 28 Schedules.

Legislative history

The EqA is the product of a long and uncertain legislative process that began in February 2005, when the then Labour Government announced the establishment of an Equalities Review and a Discrimination Law Review. Chaired by the then head of the Commission for Racial Equality (CRE), Trevor Phillips (now head of the EHRC, which has since assumed the functions of the CRE and the other equality bodies), the Equalities Review was established to investigate the causes of persistent discrimination and inequality in British society. The Discrimination Law Review, led by the Government's Women and Equality Unit (now part of the Government Equalities Office, which sits within the Home Office), was tasked with considering the fundamental principles of discrimination legislation and its underlying concepts, and the opportunities for creating a clearer, more streamlined framework of equality legislation.

The Equalities Review published 'Fairness and Freedom: The Final Report of the Equalities Review' in February 2007. Among other things, the Report called for transparency about progress towards equality, including a requirement that public bodies regularly publish employment data to a standard format; positive action measures to tackle persistent inequalities and improve representation; adoption of a simpler, more coherent legal framework through a single Equality Act and an outcomes-focused single equality duty on public sector bodies; and the use of procurement and commissioning to encourage private and voluntary sector organisations to adopt the same equality principles as the public sector.

In June 2007, the Government published the results of the Discrimination Law **1.7** Review in a Green Paper, 'A Framework for Fairness: Proposals for a Single Equality Bill for Great Britain'. In June 2008, this consultation process resulted in a number of key legislative proposals for an Equality Bill, set out in a White Paper, 'Framework for a Fairer Future – The Equality Bill' (Cm 7431). Proposals outlined in the White Paper included extending positive action so that employers could take under-representation into account when selecting between two equally qualified candidates; banning clauses in employment contracts that prevented employees from discussing their pay; introducing wider powers for employment tribunals to make recommendations in discrimination claims, so that recommendations could apply to the whole workforce and not just the successful claimant; and replacing the public sector race, disability and gender equality duties with a new single equality duty extending to gender reassignment, age, sexual orientation and religion or belief. In July 2008, the Government set out its detailed response to the consultation and gave more information about the content of the new Bill in 'The Equality Bill – Government response to the Consultation' (Cm 7454) – in effect, a second White Paper.

The Equality Bill was introduced in the House of Commons on 24 April 2009, and published three days later on 27 April. It was accompanied by a further White Paper, 'A Fairer Future – The Equality Bill and other action to make equality a reality', which explained what the Bill was intended to achieve. The Bill was subject to numerous changes during the Parliamentary process but finally received Royal Assent in the wash-up procedure on 8 April 2010, shortly before Parliament was dissolved prior to the General Election in May 2010.

1.8 Transitional arrangements and extent

Although the majority of the EqA's provisions came into force on 1 October 2010, the new Conservative-Liberal Democrat Coalition Government decided to postpone the implementation of several measures until a later date. Subsequently, on 17 November 2010, the Government announced that the socio-economic duty on certain public bodies contained in S.1 would not be brought into force (see further Chapter 40, 'Socio-economic duty'.) On 2 December 2010, the Government stated that it would not implement the gender pay reporting measures in S.78 while it was working with businesses to encourage the publication of equality workforce data on a voluntary basis. And in the 2011 Budget delivered on 23 March 2011, the Government announced that it would not pursue the combined (or dual) discrimination provisions contained in S.14.

In order to avoid confusion as to which Act applied in the immediate aftermath of the EqA coming into force, transitional provisions were introduced. The Equality Act 2010 (Commencement No.4, Savings, Consequential, Transitional, Transitory and Incidental Provisions and Revocation) Order 2010 SI 2010/2317 sets out relevant provisions. Article 7 stipulates that the enforcement provisions in Part 9 of the EqA apply where '(a) an act carried out before 1 October 2010 is unlawful under a previous enactment, and (b) that act continues on or after 1st October 2010 and is unlawful under the 2010 Act'. In other words, the provisions of the EqA apply with regard to any act of discrimination that commenced before 1 October 2010 but was continuing on or after that date. Obviously, any act of discrimination that occurred and was completed prior to 1 October 2010 will be subject to the provisions of the relevant antecedent legislation, while any discriminatory act that occurred on or after 1 October will be subject to the EqA.

1.9 By virtue of S.217 EqA, all of the provisions of the Act with which this Handbook is concerned apply to England, Scotland and Wales. In respect of Northern Ireland, however, none of the relevant provisions of the EqA apply save for the provisions dealing with offshore work set out in S.82.

1.10 The protected characteristics

As mentioned above, one of the key aims of the EqA was to harmonise the law across the different 'strands' or grounds of discrimination that existed under the previous legislation. These are now brought together in S.4 EqA as 'protected characteristics'. The nine characteristics are exactly the same as those that were protected by the anti-discrimination legislation in place immediately before the coming into force of the EqA. Listed alphabetically, they are:

- age
- disability
- gender reassignment
- marriage and civil partnership
- pregnancy and maternity
- race
- religion or belief
- sex (i.e. gender)
- sexual orientation.

These characteristics are discussed in detail in Chapters 4–13 of this Handbook.

Prohibited conduct   1.11

The forms of conduct prohibited under the EqA largely replicate the types of conduct made unlawful under the previous equality legislation, e.g. direct and indirect discrimination, harassment, victimisation and failure to make reasonable adjustments. They are collectively referred to as 'prohibited conduct' under the Act and are dealt with in Chapters 14–22 of this Handbook. When considering whether conduct is prohibited under the Act, it must be borne in mind that not all forms of discrimination apply to all the protected characteristics – see further Chapter 14, 'Prohibited conduct: general principles' under 'Potential claims under each characteristic'.

Discrimination at work   1.12

Having (or being perceived to have or associating with someone who has) a protected characteristic and being subjected to prohibited conduct on the ground of that characteristic is not enough to found a claim under the EqA. The discrimination must also take place in circumstances covered by the Act. The circumstances in which discrimination is unlawful in the work context are contained in Part 5 of the Act, which is entitled 'Work'. These circumstances, which are considered in depth in Chapters 23–27 of this Handbook, mirror those covered by the previous discrimination legislation and include recruitment, employment, dismissal and post-employment.

It is important to note that the EqA is not solely an employment statute. It extends beyond the work sphere and prohibits discrimination in a number of non-employment areas, such as the provision of goods and services, public procurement and education. These topics fall outside the scope of this Handbook.

1.13 Equal pay

The harmonised approach in the EqA to discrimination law has its limits. While it makes sense to have one definition of discrimination, harassment, etc, that can be applied across all characteristics covered by the Act, not all types of discrimination are amenable to this 'one-size-fits-all' approach. This is particularly true of equal pay, with the result that the provisions on equal pay in the EqA are dealt with separately in Part 5. Despite calls for fundamental reform, the changes in respect of what can still be termed 'equal pay law' have been minimal – the provisions of the Equal Pay Act 1970, as interpreted by three decades of case law, have effectively been transplanted wholesale into the EqA, albeit using slightly different wording on occasion. Thus, a claimant must still point to an actual, as opposed to hypothetical, comparator of the opposite sex who is doing like work, work of equal value or work rated as equivalent (S.65 EqA). A 'sex equality clause' operates to modify any contractual term which is less favourable than that of the comparator (S.66). The sex equality clause will not apply, however, if the employer shows that the difference in pay is due to a material factor, reliance on which does not involve either direct sex discrimination or unjustified indirect sex discrimination (S.69).

Equal pay law falls outside the scope of this Handbook. It is, however, the subject of detailed consideration in IDS Employment Law Handbook, 'Equal Pay' (2011).

1.14 Discrimination based on association or perception

The EqA has introduced a number of new provisions that were not found in the antecedent discrimination legislation. One of the key innovations of the 2010 Act was to provide a statutory basis for direct discrimination and harassment claims to be brought based on the complainant's association with someone who has a protected characteristic or where the complainant is wrongly perceived to have a protected characteristic. All the protected characteristics other than marital or civil partnership status are covered by these new forms of prohibited conduct (see S.13(4)).

Section 13(1) EqA states that it is unlawful to treat an individual less favourably because of 'a' protected characteristic. Thus, the individual does not need to possess the protected characteristic him or herself. The wording is wide enough to cover someone who *associates* with someone who has a protected characteristic or who is *perceived* to have a protected characteristic. This is an important extension of the principle of non-discrimination and, in some cases, will mean improved protection from discrimination by comparison with the previous equality enactments. In respect of age, disability, gender reassignment and sex, direct discrimination was previously defined in such a way as to require the complainant to have the protected characteristic him or herself, with the result that a claim would not generally succeed where the treatment was based on the protected characteristic of a third party. (In light of European case law,

8

however, the EAT in EBR Attridge LLP (formerly Attridge Law) and anor v Coleman 2010 ICR 242, EAT, interpreted the Disability Discrimination Act 1995 (DDA) so as to overcome that apparent limitation.) According to the Government's Explanatory Notes to the EqA, the effect of the new S.13 is to '[bring] the position in relation to those protected characteristics into line with that for race, sexual orientation and religion or belief in the previous legislation' (para 63).

The wide definition of discrimination in S.13 also encompasses discrimination **1.15** by perception: that is, discrimination because of a person's perceived characteristic. Under S.13, the perception that a person is disabled, for example, will be a potential ground of unlawful discrimination. The Explanatory Notes give the example of an employer who rejects a job application from a white man whom it wrongly thinks is black because the applicant has an African-sounding name. This would constitute direct race discrimination based on the employer's mistaken perception (para 63).

For further details, see Chapter 15, 'Direct discrimination' under 'Discrimination by association' and 'Discrimination by perception'.

Combined discrimination   1.16
Section 14 EqA makes provision for claims of 'combined discrimination' (sometimes called 'dual discrimination' or 'intersectional discrimination'). This is aimed at situations where people are discriminated against because of a particular combination of protected characteristics. For example, a black woman may suffer prejudice or harassment that a black man or a white woman would not experience. However, while the previous Labour Government had intended to bring S.14 into force in April 2011, the Coalition Government announced shortly before that date that the combined discrimination provisions would not be brought forward. Therefore, at the time of writing, *S.14 is not yet in force,* although the provision has not been repealed so the rules may take effect at some point in the future.

The absence of a right to bring discrimination claims combining protected characteristics has been perceived as a problem for some time and was highlighted by the Court of Appeal in Bahl v Law Society and ors 2004 IRLR 799, CA. At present, a person alleging combined discrimination must bring separate single-strand claims in respect of each protected characteristic. Such claims can be difficult to prove and may not reflect the reality of the discrimination experienced.

For further details on combined discrimination, see Chapter 15, 'Direct discrimination', under 'Combined discrimination'.

1.17 Disability discrimination changes

New provisions in the EqA have addressed some of the deficiencies of the DDA. Among other things, the Act attempts to overcome the so-called 'Malcolm gap' in disability-related discrimination and extends the scope of indirect discrimination to cover disability.

1.18 Discrimination arising from disability. Section 3A(1) DDA provided disabled employees with protection from discrimination 'for a reason which relates to' disability. To prove discrimination under that provision, the individual must have been treated less favourably than others to whom that disability-related reason did not, or would not, apply. The scope of this provision was initially construed widely but in Mayor and Burgesses of the London Borough of Lewisham v Malcolm 2008 IRLR 700, HL (a housing case), the House of Lords held that the appropriate comparator under S.3A(1) was a non-disabled person who was otherwise in the same circumstances as the disabled claimant. This threw the law into confusion and undermined the protection against disability-related discrimination in employment to which the long-standing comparator test set out in Clark v TDG Ltd t/a Novacold 1999 ICR 951, CA, had previously applied.

In Novacold, the Court of Appeal had held that the comparator need not be in the same or similar circumstances as the disabled complainant. So, for example, in a case where the employee was dismissed for sickness absence arising from a disability, the Novacold comparator would be a person who had not been absent from work (and would not have been dismissed), whereas the Malcolm comparator would be a non-disabled person who had also been absent, and who would accordingly have been treated in the same way as the disabled claimant.

1.19 After some doubt the Court of Appeal confirmed in Stockton on Tees Borough Council v Aylott 2010 ICR 1278, CA, that the narrower Malcolm approach applied equally in the employment field. Thus it went from being very easy to establish less favourable treatment under S.3A(1) to being almost impossible. The Government's response was to introduce a new provision into the EqA – S.15 – prohibiting 'discrimination arising from disability'. Unlike disability-related discrimination, which is not carried over into the EqA, S.15 does not require the disabled person to establish that his or her treatment is less favourable than that experienced by a comparator. As a consequence, the provision avoids the main issue in Mayor and Burgesses of the London Borough of Lewisham v Malcolm (above): namely, who that comparator should be. Under S.15(1), a person (A) discriminates against a disabled person (B) if:

- A treats B unfavourably because of something arising in consequence of B's disability, and

10

- A cannot show that the treatment is a proportionate means of achieving a legitimate aim.

The Explanatory Notes to the EqA state that S.15 is 'aimed at re-establishing **1.20** an appropriate balance between enabling a disabled person to make out a case of experiencing a detriment which arises because of his or her disability, and providing an opportunity for an employer or other person to defend the treatment' (para 70). The Notes give the example of an employee with a visual impairment who is dismissed because he or she cannot do as much work as a non-disabled colleague. This would potentially amount to discrimination arising from disability, and if the employer sought to justify the dismissal, it would need to show that it was a proportionate means of achieving a legitimate aim.

For further details of the scope of S.15, see Chapter 20, 'Discrimination arising from disability'.

Indirect discrimination. The Government also took the opportunity presented **1.21** by the EqA to include disability among the protected characteristics covered by the indirect discrimination provisions in S.19. In short, indirect discrimination is established where a policy that an employer applies puts those who share a protected characteristic at a particular disadvantage when compared with those who do not share it. S.6(3)(b) EqA clarifies that, in relation to disability, 'a reference to persons who share a protected characteristic is a reference to persons who have the same disability' (our stress). Accordingly, for indirect discrimination purposes, the 'particular disadvantage' must affect those who share the claimant's particular disability. This overlooks the fact that even people who have the same disability cannot easily be treated as a homogenous class, since the way in which the same disability manifests itself will vary from person to person, making it difficult for a disabled person to demonstrate a group disadvantage.

For further discussion of the potential application of S.19 in the context of disability, see Chapter 16, 'Indirect discrimination: proving disadvantage' under 'Indirect discrimination in context – indirect disability discrimination'.

Pre-employment health enquiries. Pre-employment enquiries about health **1.22** issues are thought to be one of the main reasons why disabled job applicants often fail to reach the interview stage. Evidence also suggests that they have a powerful deterrent effect on potential applicants who are disabled. In view of this, an entirely new provision governing the making of such enquiries was introduced by the EqA. This provides that, other than in specified circumstances, an employer must not ask a job applicant a question about his or her health:

- before offering work to the applicant – S.60(1)(a), or

11

- where the employer is not in a position to offer work, before including the applicant in a pool from which the employer intends, when in a position to do so, to select a person to whom to offer work – S.60(1)(b).

1.23 An employer does not commit an act of disability discrimination merely by asking about a job applicant's health, but the employer's conduct in reliance on information given in response may lead a tribunal to conclude that the employer has committed a discriminatory act. In these circumstances, the burden of proof will shift to the employer to show that no discrimination took place.

Section 60 does not impose a blanket ban on pre-employment health enquiries, however. It does not apply to questions that are necessary to establish whether the job applicant will be able to comply with a requirement to undergo an assessment (such as an interview or selection test); whether a duty to make reasonable adjustments will arise in connection with any such assessment; or whether the applicant will be able to carry out a function that is intrinsic to the work concerned. The employer is also entitled to ask questions necessary to monitor diversity in the range of job applicants; to enable it to take positive action; or to establish whether the applicant has a particular disability, where having that disability is an occupational requirement.

For more information on pre-employment health enquiries, see Chapter 24, 'Recruitment', under 'Pre-employment health questions'.

1.24 Public sector equality duty

The individual complaints-led approach to tackling discrimination in employment and other areas has been a part of UK law for decades. While that approach is still the main plank of the drive to eliminate unlawful discrimination, the last few years have seen the beginning of a more proactive approach to complement the enforcement of individual rights with the introduction of 'public sector equality duties'. The intention is to ensure that public authorities and bodies or persons exercising public functions promote equal opportunities with regard to all characteristics (race, sex, disability, etc) protected by law. This is in addition to the obligations imposed on those bodies or persons in their roles as employers and service-providers.

The EqA introduced a new single 'public sector equality duty', which came into force in April 2011. This single duty brought the pre-existing public sector equality duties on race, disability and gender together under one umbrella and went further by extending the duty to cover gender reassignment (which was only partially covered by the gender equality duty), sexual orientation, religion or belief, and age. The public sector equality duty is discussed in detail in Chapter 38, 'General public sector equality duty'.

1.25 In addition, the EqA confers on ministers a power to impose specific duties, i.e. legal requirements over and above the general public sector equality duty that are designed to ensure that public bodies meet their obligations under the general duty. Further details about the scope of these provisions are given in Chapter 39, 'Specific public sector equality duties'.

The EqA also includes a new duty on certain public bodies to consider socio-economic disadvantage when deciding how to exercise their functions. However, this duty has not been brought into force. For further details, see Chapter 40, 'Socio-economic duty'.

Explanatory Notes, Codes of Practice and other guidance

1.26

In addition to the Act itself, there are a number of statutory and non-statutory documents that are relevant and helpful when it comes to interpreting and applying the law.

Explanatory Notes to the EqA

1.27

The Government published Explanatory Notes to accompany the EqA. These extensive notes summarise the previous legislation and the background to the Act, as well as giving further detail about many of its provisions. They are referred to, where appropriate, throughout this Handbook.

Codes of Practice

1.28

The employment provisions of the EqA are underpinned by two statutory Codes of Practice made under the EHRC's powers contained in S.14 of the Equality Act 2006: the Code of Practice on Employment and the Code of Practice on Equal Pay. These Codes were issued in October 2010, but were technically in draft form until 6 April 2011, when they were formally brought into force by the Equality Act 2010 Codes of Practice (Services, Public Functions and Associations, Employment, and Equal Pay) Order 2011 SI 2011/857.

The Code of Practice on Employment covers discrimination in employment and work-related activities under Part 5 of the EqA. It replaces the various previous codes on different aspects of discrimination law, where necessary harmonising their content. Drawing on case law and precedent, it illustrates where and how the EqA can apply. The Code of Practice on Equal Pay also draws on case law to give guidance in relation to the equal pay provisions in the EqA. In addition, it covers equal pay reviews, identifies discriminatory elements in pay systems and provides guidance on drawing up an equal pay policy.

The Codes do not impose legal obligations, and nor are they authoritative statements of the law. While a failure to comply with the Codes is not actionable in itself, the Codes are admissible in legal proceedings and must be taken into account by courts and tribunals where they appear relevant. Relevant provisions

1.29

in the Codes are referred to, where appropriate, throughout both this Handbook and the IDS Employment Law Handbook, 'Equal Pay' (2011).

1.30 Guidance on the definition of disability

Section 6(5) EqA allows a Minister to issue guidance on matters to be taken into account in deciding whether a claimant is disabled. Part 2 of Schedule 1 to the EqA deals with the content of such guidance and the procedure for issuing, revising and revoking it. The guidance may give examples of effects that it would, or would not, be reasonable to regard as substantial adverse effects in relation to particular activities, and substantial adverse effects that it would, or would not, be reasonable to regard as long term – para 11, Sch 1. Guidance issued under S.6(5) does not impose any legal obligations in itself but courts and tribunals must take account of it, where relevant – para 12, Sch 1.

'Guidance on matters to be taken into account in determining questions relating to the definition of disability' came into force on 1 May 2011, replacing 2006 guidance on the same matters issued under the DDA. However, the 2006 guidance still remains relevant to the question of disability in respect of acts of discrimination occurring before 1 May 2011 – Article 3(5) Equality Act 2010 (Guidance on the Definition of Disability) Appointed Day Order 2011 SI 2011/1159. For a detailed examination of the definition of disability under the EqA, see Chapter 6, 'Disability'.

1.31 Other guidance

The Advisory, Conciliation and Arbitration Service (Acas) has worked with the Government Equalities Office (GEO) and the EHRC to produce a quick start guide for employers. This guide, 'The Equality Act – What's new for employers?', covers the main changes made by the EqA and outlines how employers can reassess and align their practices to remain compliant with the legislation. Acas has also prepared guidance on 'Delivering equality and diversity', which sets out useful information for employers on equality policies, equality training and key equality issues in the workplace.

In addition, the GEO, in partnership with the British Chambers of Commerce, Citizens Advice and the Equality and Diversity Forum, has produced various summary guides setting out what the provisions in the EqA mean for businesses, the public sector, the voluntary sector and the public. Details can be found on the Home Office website under 'Equalities'.

1.32 The EHRC has also published guidance and good practice on its website aimed at helping employers, workers, service users, service providers and education providers understand and use the new legislation.

Harmonisation

1.33

One of the key objectives of the EqA was to harmonise discrimination law across the various strands of discrimination (now called 'protected characteristics'). It achieved this by consolidating the plethora of different Acts of Parliament and Statutory Instruments that previously housed this area of law, as well as standardising various key concepts, terms and definitions across the discrimination strands. In this process, the EqA brought together areas of discrimination law that originally derived from EU law and other areas that have their origins purely in UK domestic law. From a constitutional point of view, this potentially poses a problem when it comes to making future amendments to the EqA.

Whereas amendments designed to implement EU law can be made by secondary legislation, amendments dealing with matters not covered by EU law or which go further than the specific requirements of EU law normally have to be made by primary legislation, i.e. an Act of Parliament. For the reasons explained below, this could eventually lead to different parts of the EqA becoming out of synch and thus undermining the principle of consistency between the different discrimination strands that was one of the main drivers of the single Equality Act in the first place. Anticipating this, the drafters of the EqA inserted two clauses into the EqA – Ss.203 and 204 – that enable all future harmonising provisions to be enacted by Ministerial Order.

The problem of lack of harmony

1.34

Virtually all mandatory provisions of EU law are implemented into UK domestic law via subordinate legislation. The constitutional and legal power to do this is contained in S.2(2) of the European Communities Act 1972. This allows subordinate legislation to be passed for the purposes of implementing any EU obligation or dealing with consequential matters arising out of or related to such an obligation. However, only matters falling strictly within the confines of an EU obligation can be implemented using the power under S.2(2). If the UK Government desires to enact a provision that goes beyond what EU law requires, then the normal constitutional rule is that it can only do this by means of primary legislation, unless some other express enabling power is available.

Owing to the pressure on the Parliamentary legislation timetable, it is often not possible for the Government to find time to pass primary legislation designed simply to effect desirable changes to existing legislation. It is apparent, therefore, that in the absence of a workable solution there would be considerable scope for the principle of harmonisation as it applies to the EqA to unravel across the various discrimination strands: for while alterations that are necessary to implement legislative developments at EU level could quickly be made via secondary legislation, the equivalent changes in respect of matters that are not

15

strictly covered by the EU law provisions might be delayed or possibly never implemented at all because the necessary primary legislation to enact those amendments would not be forthcoming.

1.35 This problem can be illustrated by the tensions that were laid bare when various legislative amendments were made to the Race Relations Act 1976 in 2003. Under that Act, there were five grounds on which it was possible to be discriminated against – colour, nationality, race, ethnic or national origins. However, in 2000 the EU enacted the Race Directive (No.2000/43) containing mandatory measures that required the RRA to be amended in certain ways. For example, the Directive provided for special rules to be implemented relating to the burden of proof, for a revised definition of 'indirect discrimination', and for a free-standing right not to be subjected to harassment on racial grounds. But the Directive itself only applied to race discrimination on grounds of race, ethnic or national origins. It did not cover the two additional elements covered by the RRA – namely, colour and nationality. This meant that when, in 2003, the Government decided to pass secondary legislation – in the form of the Race Relations Act 1976 (Amendment) Regulations 2003 SI 2003/1636 – in order to implement the amendments required by the EU Race Directive, those amendments could only be applied to the three grounds of discrimination specifically contemplated by the EU Directive. In consequence, a somewhat clumsy two-tier system under the RRA came into being, comprising a set of enhanced rights (as introduced by the 2003 amending Regulations) applicable to claims based on race, ethnic or national origins, and a set of more restrictive rights (i.e. those that pre-existed the amending Regulations) in respect of claims based on colour or nationality.

If sufficient Parliamentary time had been found to enable the changes prompted by the EU Race Directive to be enacted by primary legislation, it would have been possible to have harmonised the changes across all five of the grounds of race discrimination covered by the RRA. But no such time was found. The fact that Parliament proceeded by way of secondary legislation enacted under S.2(2) of the 1972 Act meant that different sets of rules applied to the different grounds. Indeed, because Parliament never did find sufficient time to deal with the problem, it took until 1 October 2010 with the coming into force of the fully harmonised provisions contained in the EqA for the unhappy two-tier system of rights to be dismantled.

1.36 Maintaining harmony across the EqA

It can be seen from the example discussed above that there could be considerable scope for provisions within the EqA to become inconsistent in the same way as the provisions dealing with the definition of racial grounds under the former RRA. In an attempt to head off this problem, the Act contains what is known as a 'Henry VIII clause' in S.203 – so called because of the provision enacted by Parliament in 1539 under the Statute of Proclamations, which conferred upon the King the power to legislate by proclamation instead of Act of Parliament. The key feature of such clauses in a modern context is that they confer a power to make future amendments to the very Act in which they are contained or to other primary legislation by means of secondary legislation, in the form of Ministerial Order or statutory regulations.

In this particular instance, S.203(1) and (2) EqA provides that a Minister may, by Order, make a 'harmonising provision'. The power to make such an Order will only be triggered if the Minister is required to implement into UK law a mandatory EU obligation affecting equality law by passing secondary legislation under S.2(2) of the European Communities Act 1972. The rather dense provisions of S.203(6)–(8) EqA go on to provide that, whenever this scenario arises, the Minister may enact by Order amendments (i.e. 'harmonising provisions') to sections of the EqA that are not themselves covered by EU law but which correspond to the implementing measure enacted under S.2(2) of the 1972 Act, or which the Minister thinks are necessary or expedient as a result of the EU-derived amendment.

So, for example, if the EU at some time in the future were to enact a mandatory **1.37** change to the definition of 'indirect discrimination' in the context of, say, sex discrimination, the UK Government would most likely opt to implement those particular changes by amending the EqA pursuant to S.2(2) of the 1972 Act. However, the appropriate Minister could also choose to enact an amending Order containing a relevant 'harmonisation provision' pursuant to S.203 that effects the same alterations to the definition of 'indirect discrimination' in respect of the other protected characteristics in order to ensure that consistency is maintained.

Certain provisions in the EqA cannot be made the subject of such an Order. These are set out in Schedule 24 to the EqA and currently include Part 1 of the Act, dealing with public sector duties with regard to socio-economic inequalities; Chapter 2 of Part 5, dealing with occupational pensions; S.78, dealing with the gender pay gap; Chapter 1 of Part 11, dealing with the public sector equality duty; and Schedule 1, containing supplementary provisions in respect of disability discrimination.

The harmonisation procedure
1.38

The so-called Henry VIII clauses that have become a common feature of many recent Acts of Parliament are not without controversy. And though it is fair to say that utilisation of the particular power under S.203 EqA to implement harmonisation provisions is unlikely to generate much of a constitutional rumpus, the legislature has nonetheless ensured that it is subject to a fairly robust Parliamentary procedure.

By virtue of S.203(3) and (4) EqA, a Minister may only use the power to make a harmonisation Order after consulting interested parties on the Government's

17

proposals. Where that consultation prompts the Minister to consider changes to those proposals, these changes must be the subject of such further consultation as he or she considers appropriate. Once the consultation has been concluded, the Minister may then decide to lay a draft order before Parliament, but he or she can only do so if at least 12 weeks have elapsed since the beginning of the consultation – S.204(5). The draft Order must be accompanied by an explanatory report detailing the consultation findings, and setting out the Minister's reasons for making the harmonising provision and why the conditions for using the power in S.203 are satisfied – S.204(2). The Order is then subject to what is known as the 'affirmative resolution procedure'. This requires that both the House of Lords and the House of Commons separately resolve to agree the Order before it can become law. This is in contrast to the more common and less stringent 'negative resolution procedure', which brings a draft Order or statutory instrument automatically into force 40 days after it has been laid unless one or other of the Houses specifically passes a resolution objecting to it.

1.39 Under S.203(11), the Minister responsible for the EqA must report to Parliament on the exercise of the power under S.203 two years after the date on which the section first came into force, and must provide a similar report on a continuing basis every two years thereafter.

1.40 Measures not covered by Equality Act

It should be noted that certain pieces of legislation containing what could be termed 'equality measures' have not been repealed and consolidated into the EqA. Such provisions, which are outlined briefly below, aim to prevent the less favourable treatment of part-time workers, fixed-term employees and agency workers.

1.41 Part-time workers

The Part-time Workers (Prevention of Less Favourable Treatment) Regulations 2000 SI 2000/1551, which came into force on 1 July 2000, implement the EU Part-time Work Directive (No.97/81). The Regulations make it unlawful for an employer to treat part-time workers less favourably than their full-time colleagues with regard to their terms and conditions of employment, unless the treatment can be justified on objective grounds. The right applies only if the treatment is on the ground that the worker is a part-time worker.

The Regulations generally apply to 'workers'. The definition of 'worker' in the Regulations is identical to the definition in S.230 of the Employment Rights Act 1996 and basically covers employees employed under a contract of employment and other workers who work under a contract personally to perform work for another party to the contract (who is not a client or customer of the worker's profession or business). However, certain provisions apply only to employees.

This is to take account of the fact that, under other pieces of employment protection legislation, employees have rights that do not apply to the wider category of 'workers'. For example, Reg 7 provides that only employees can claim that their dismissal for asserting a right under the Regulations is automatically unfair. Other workers must rely on the right not to be subjected to a detriment for asserting the same right under the Regulations.

In order to pursue a claim under the Regulations, part-time workers must be **1.42** employed on the 'same type of contract' as their full-time comparators. In addition, in order to be comparable the part-time workers and the full-time workers must be 'engaged in the same or broadly similar work having regard, where relevant, to whether they have a similar level of qualification, skills and experience' – Reg 2(4).

Fixed-term employees   1.43

The Fixed-term Employees (Prevention of Less Favourable Treatment) Regulations 2002 SI 2002/2034, which came into force on 1 October 2002, implement the EU Framework Directive on Fixed-term Work (No.99/70). The Directive is designed to prevent fixed-term employees being treated less favourably than permanent employees, and to promote the use of permanent contracts over fixed-term ones where possible. The Regulations apply only to *employees* rather than to the wider category of 'workers'.

Under the Regulations, a fixed-term employee has the right not to be treated less favourably by his or her employer as regards the terms of his or her contract or by being subjected to any other detriment by any act, or deliberate failure to act, of the employer. The right not to be treated less favourably applies only if the treatment is on the ground that the employee is a fixed-term employee and the treatment cannot be objectively justified. In order to determine whether a fixed-term employee has been treated less favourably, it is necessary to compare the way in which he or she has been treated with the treatment accorded to a 'comparable permanent employee'. 'Comparable employees' are dealt with in Reg 2, which sets out three criteria to be applied when determining the appropriate comparator – whether both employees are employed by the same employer; whether both employees are engaged in the same or similar work; and whether both employees work at the same establishment. All three must be met in order for Reg 2 to be satisfied.

Agency workers   1.44

The Agency Workers Regulations 2010 SI 2010/93, which came into force on 1 October 2011, implement the EU Temporary Agency Workers Directive (No.2008/104). The Regulations seek to improve the lot of agency workers through the provision of a right to 'equal treatment' with directly recruited permanent employees and workers of the hirer. As agreed in 2008 by the TUC

19

and the CBI, the Regulations give agency workers the right to the same pay, holidays and other basic working conditions as directly recruited staff after 12 weeks in a given job.

Note that under the Regulations agency workers do not acquire an entitlement to *all* the terms and conditions enjoyed by the hirer's permanent workers or employees. Entitlement only arises in respect of 'basic working and employment conditions', which, by virtue of Reg 6(1), are restricted to terms and conditions relating to pay, the duration of working time, night work, rest periods, rest breaks and annual leave.

1.45 The right in respect of equal pay applies not just to the basic hourly rate, but to all pay for work done, including bonuses that are directly related to the performance of the agency worker personally. However, it does not extend to some of the wider benefits that permanent staff may enjoy in the context of their longer-term relationship with the employer, such as occupational pensions and sick pay.

2 European discrimination law

Relationship between EU and UK law

EU equality measures

The Equality Act 2010 (EqA) gives wide-ranging protection to individuals in **2.1** the United Kingdom who have suffered discrimination in the workplace. However, discrimination law is not simply a domestic matter. European legislation and jurisprudence have had a significant influence on the development of discrimination law in this country. Both have necessitated amendments to domestic law in order to ensure that UK law does not fall short of the protection afforded to individuals under European law. Moreover, where European legislation provides a cause of action that is not (expressly) covered by domestic law, an individual may seek to rely directly on the European legislation.

Relationship between EU and UK law   2.2

To understand how European legislative measures have an effect on the development of discrimination law in the United Kingdom, it is first necessary to understand how EU law interacts with UK law. The starting point is the European Communities Act 1972, which came into force on 1 January 1973, the date on which the United Kingdom joined the European Union (EU) (then known as the European Communities). At that point, the United Kingdom ceded its sovereignty over certain areas, including employment and discrimination law, to the EU, and courts and tribunals became bound by the principle, established by the European Court of Justice (ECJ) in Van Gend en Loos v Nederlandse Administratie der Belastingen 1963 ECR 1, ECJ, that EU law has supremacy over domestic law. This supremacy is underlined by S.3(2) of the 1972 Act, which requires courts and tribunals to have regard to European Treaties, European legislation and decisions of the ECJ in deciding cases before them.

Before turning to specifics, it is helpful to say a little more about the EU Treaties, and the legislation made under them, that are relevant for our purposes. In the wake of the Lisbon Treaty (which came into force on 1 December 2009), two Treaties form the principal sources of EU law: the Treaty on the Functioning of the European Union (TFEU) (which started life as the Treaty of Rome), and the Treaty on European Union (TEU) (which is often referred to as the Maastricht Treaty). These are supplemented by a large number of Directives and Regulations that govern specific areas over which the EU has legislative competence, e.g. equality between men and women.

21

2.3 With the exception of the principle of equal pay, which is set out in Article 157 TFEU, most employment law measures have taken the form of a Directive. A Directive is directed at Member States and requires them to achieve a particular effect. Thus, the principal aim of a Directive is to require national Governments to create specific protections and corresponding remedies in domestic law. In the United Kingdom, Directives are implemented either by primary legislation (i.e. an Act of Parliament) or secondary legislation (i.e. a statutory instrument). Given the pressures on parliamentary time, the latter option is the most frequently used, since statutory instruments can usually be endorsed by Parliament without requiring lengthy debate. The authority to implement Directives by way of secondary legislation is contained in S.2 of the European Communities Act 1972, which created an enabling power allowing for the introduction of regulations necessary for the implementation of further developments in EU law. This power has been exercised numerous times in order to amend discrimination legislation in force prior to the introduction of the EqA. For example, the Disability Discrimination Act 1995 (Amendment) Regulations 2003 SI 2003/1673, which made a number of important amendments to the Disability Discrimination Act 1995 (DDA), were made under S.2 of the 1972 Act.

The main EU Directives outlawing discrimination in employment and occupation are:

- the *recast EU Equal Treatment Directive (No.2006/54)* ('the recast Directive'), which relates to 'the implementation of the principle of equal opportunities and equal treatment of men and women in matters of employment and occupation'. It covers sex, pregnancy and maternity, marriage and civil partnership and gender reassignment. The Directive consolidated previous Directives, such as the EU Equal Treatment Directive (No.76/207), which set out the principle of equal treatment for men and women in employment

- the *EU Equal Treatment Framework Directive (No.2000/78)* ('the Framework Directive'), which sets out a general framework for eliminating employment or occupational inequalities based on age, disability, religion or belief, and sexual orientation

- the *EU Race Equality Directive (No.2000/43)* ('the Race Equality Directive'), which implements the principle of equal treatment between persons irrespective of racial or ethnic origin.

2.4 These Directives are discussed in greater detail under 'EU equality measures' below.

Since October 2010, the EqA is, among other things, the legislative instrument by which the United Kingdom implements into domestic law the protections from discrimination guaranteed under EU law. Thus, tribunals and courts applying and interpreting the Act must do so by reference to the equal treatment provisions of the TFEU, the legislation made under it (e.g. Directives), and the case law of the European Court of Justice (ECJ). As will become clear in the rest of this chapter and throughout this Handbook, the application of EU law, as interpreted by the ECJ, has been critical to ensuring that individuals benefit from the full extent of their rights under EU law.

Direct effect   2.5

According to the ECJ in Van Gend en Loos v Nederlandse Administratie der Belastingen 1963 ECR 1, ECJ, the TFEU is not to be treated simply as an instrument governing relations between Member States. Rather, in those areas where the Community has legislative competence (such as discrimination law), the TFEU and the Directives made under it are capable of directly conferring upon individuals substantive rights the existence of which owe nothing to national laws. Where an individual enjoys such rights, he or she can rely on them in domestic proceedings, and the court or tribunal hearing those proceedings will be obliged (because of the supremacy of EU law) to disapply any national provision that conflicts with those rights. Where, in domestic proceedings, an individual is entitled to rely directly upon a provision of EU law in this way, that provision is said to have 'direct effect' in relation to that individual.

Conditions for direct effect. Not every provision of European law is intended 2.6 to confer rights on individuals, however. For one thing, some classes of EU legislation – e.g. Recommendations – are intended to provide voluntary guidance rather than create binding rights and obligations.

Secondly, it is important to understand that even where a provision is contained in a legally binding measure – such as a Directive – it will not necessarily have direct effect. In Van Gend en Loos (above) the ECJ explained that a provision of EU law will be capable of direct effect only where it is clear and precise; is unconditional and unqualified; and is not subject to the need for further implementing measures by Member States. Many Articles of the TFEU and the TEU are no more than statements of general principle and cannot have been intended to confer specific rights on individuals. Similarly, there are Articles of Directives that do no more than introduce, exhort or explain in a general way.

How direct effect works. In Biggs v Somerset County Council 1995 ICR 811, 2.7 EAT, the Appeal Tribunal adopted what came to be known as the 'conservative' interpretation of direct effect. That case concerned a claim for an unfair dismissal that had occurred some 18 years before. B, the claimant, had not applied to a tribunal when she was first dismissed because the unfair dismissal legislation then in force expressly excluded employees who, like her, had worked below a specified weekly hours threshold. She changed her mind in 1994 after the House of Lords (in R v Secretary of State for Employment ex parte EOC and anor 1994 ICR 317, HL) declared the hours threshold to be in

23

breach of the principle of equal pay for equal work now enshrined in Article 157 of the TFEU. An important aspect of B's case was her submission that she was entitled to rely on Article 157 as a 'free-standing' right, separate from her domestic claim for unfair dismissal. The advantage of relying on a separate EU cause of action, from B's perspective, was that this might not be subject to the same three-month time limit as the unfair dismissal claim.

However, the EAT rejected the existence of a separate EU cause of action outright. It stated that a tribunal's jurisdiction is limited to that granted to it by specific measures of national legislation. Although a tribunal is bound to apply relevant EU law 'within its jurisdiction', it has no jurisdiction to hear and determine disputes about EU law generally. The EAT was not prepared to accept that such jurisdiction could be inferred from the European Communities Act 1972.

2.8 In the EAT's view, the more radical approach previously adopted by the Scottish EAT in Secretary of State for Scotland and anor v Wright and anor 1991 IRLR 187, EAT – where a claim for redundancy payments was allowed to proceed even though it relied on Article 157 and the EU Equal Treatment Directive (No.76/207) (now incorporated into the recast Directive) – was based on a false legal premise. Directly effective EU rights do not create a separate cause of action, unconnected with the domestic legal framework. Rather, they allow a tribunal to disapply incompatible provisions of domestic law within its jurisdiction. Accordingly, a claim to a tribunal must always be based on the relevant domestic statutory cause of action – even if the claimant intends that the tribunal should disapply some provision of that cause of action on the ground of its incompatibility with his or her EU rights. Once the incompatible provision has been disapplied, the claim will proceed on the basis of the modified statutory cause of action.

The Court of Appeal approved the EAT's approach in the Biggs case (see Biggs v Somerset County Council 1996 ICR 364, CA) and it has been followed in several cases since – see, for example, Staffordshire County Council v Barber 1996 ICR 379, CA; Secretary of State for Employment v Mann and ors 1997 ICR 209, CA; and Barry v Midland Bank plc 1997 ICR 192, EAT. However, more recent decisions have cast doubt on whether this line of authority is strictly correct. Notably, the European Court's judgment in Impact v Minister for Agriculture and Food and ors 2008 IRLR 552, ECJ, suggests that domestic tribunals might acquire jurisdiction to hear claims based on the direct effect of EU law without such jurisdiction being expressly granted by legislation. There, Irish civil servants sought to rely on the direct effect of provisions of the EU Fixed-term Work Directive (No.1999/70) based on facts occurring after the deadline for transposition of the Directive had passed in July 2001 but before the implementing provisions of Irish law came into force in July 2003. They brought their complaints before a Rights Commissioner, whose jurisdiction was established under the domestic provisions from July 2003 but who enjoyed no express jurisdiction to hear claims based directly on the Directive. The employer challenged the Rights Commissioner's jurisdiction to hear claims based on facts occurring before 2003 and, after an appeal to the Labour Court, a reference was made to the ECJ.

The ECJ held that a specialised court (such as, in this instance, the Rights **2.9** Commissioner) which is granted jurisdiction in matters relating to transposing legislation must also have jurisdiction to hear claims arising directly from the Directive thereby transposed in respect of the period between the deadline for transposing the Directive and the date on which the transposing legislation entered into force. This is so provided it is established that the obligation on the claimant to bring before an ordinary court, at the same time, a separate claim based directly on the Directive would involve procedural disadvantages liable to render the exercise of the rights conferred on him or her by EU law excessively difficult.

It is noteworthy that Mr Justice Elias (then President of the EAT) made similar comments in Unison and anor v Brennan and ors 2008 ICR 955, EAT. There, Elias P agreed with the Advocate General's Opinion in Impact – later adopted by the ECJ – that to have to pursue two parallel sets of proceedings (in this case, one in the employment tribunal to claim equal pay and one in the High Court to obtain declaratory relief in respect of a discriminatory term in a collective agreement) in order to get the full protection conferred by EU law would inevitably breach the principle of effectiveness, which requires Member States to provide effective remedies in domestic law for breach of EU rights. Moreover, the principle of equivalence required that the remedies made available in domestic courts for breach of EU rights must be no less favourable than those afforded to similar claims of a purely domestic nature. In his view, it would be far more difficult and expensive to have the terms of a collective agreement declared void in the High Court than in the employment tribunal. Accordingly, it would be a breach of EU law if an application for a declaration could not be pursued in the employment tribunal. (Note that this decision is also mentioned under 'Indirect effect' below.)

In light of these more recent decisions, it is arguable that a claimant wishing to **2.10** rely directly on the effect of a Directive, or Article 157, should be able to do so in the employment tribunal even though, under the EqA, no express provision is made for such a claim to be heard there. This might be an option where the right to equal treatment under EU law is wider than that expressly provided for under the EqA. In practice, however, the most likely course of action for claimants who believe that their rights under the EqA fall short of the protection afforded to them by EU law is to bring a claim in the employment tribunal under the EqA and ask the tribunal – as happened in Unison and anor v Brennan and ors (above) – to interpret the relevant domestic provision so as to give effect to their rights under EU law. This principle is known as 'indirect effect' and is discussed below.

2.11 **'Horizontal' and 'vertical' direct effect.** Even where a provision has direct effect, it cannot always be relied upon by individuals in claims against other individuals or organisations. The courts have long recognised a distinction between 'vertical' and 'horizontal' direct effect. A provision that is said to have 'vertical' direct effect can only be relied upon by an individual against the state and emanations of the state, while a provision that is said to have 'horizontal' direct effect can also be relied upon by an individual against another private individual.

It is now well established that an Article of the TFEU which is found to be capable of conferring rights on individuals under the test established by the ECJ in Van Gend en Loos v Nederlandse Administratie der Belastingen 1963 ECR 1, ECJ (above), will have both horizontal and vertical direct effect – i.e. it can be relied upon by individuals in proceedings against either another individual or a Member State. However, there are actually very few Treaty articles that contain substantive rights that are relevant in the context of employment. The notable exception is Article 157 TFEU (formerly Article 141 of the Treaty of Rome), which lays down the principle of equal pay for equal work as between men and women, and can be relied on directly in an equal pay claim where the particular circumstances are not covered by the EqA.

2.12 Like a Treaty article, a provision contained in a Directive will also be capable of direct effect if it is clear and precise, unconditional and unqualified, and is not subject to the need for further implementing measures by Member States – Van Duyn v Home Office 1975 Ch 358, ECJ. It is a further condition that a provision in a Directive capable of direct effect will not in fact be directly effective until the deadline for Member States to implement the Directive has passed. However, the provisions of a Directive can usually only have vertical, not horizontal, direct effect – i.e. they can be relied upon by individuals in proceedings against a Member State but not against another individual. This is because (unlike Treaty articles) Directives are binding only on Member States and consequently the justification for vertical direct effect – that Member States should not benefit from their own default in implementing a Directive – does not apply to private employers (see Marshall v Southampton and South West Hampshire Area Health Authority (Teaching) 1986 ICR 335, ECJ).

Perhaps by way of compensation, the courts have adopted a reasonably broad view of what constitutes 'the state' for the purposes of vertical direct effect. It is not restricted simply to the Crown, government departments and local government, etc, but encompasses any organisation that can be said to be an 'emanation of the state'. The ECJ has held that it is for the national courts to determine whether a particular body constitutes an emanation of the state, but added that 'a body, whatever its legal form, which has been made responsible, pursuant to a measure adopted by the State, for providing a public service under the control of the State and has for that purpose special powers beyond those which result from the normal rules applicable in relations between individuals is included among the bodies against which the provisions of a Directive capable of having direct effect may be relied upon' – Foster and ors v British Gas plc 1991 ICR 84, ECJ.

In the context of anti-discrimination law, it is only the right to equal pay, being **2.13** derived from Article 157 TFEU, that can be relied on by an individual against another individual as well as the state. By contrast, the obligation on Member States to eliminate discrimination and inequality of opportunity based on sex, race, pregnancy and maternity, marriage and civil partnership, gender reassignment, age, disability, religion or belief and sexual orientation emanates from EU Directives – i.e. the Race Equality Directive, the Framework Directive and the recast Directive. Therefore, individuals seeking to rely on European law to further a case of unlawful discrimination on any of those protected grounds are restricted to the vertical direct effect of the relevant Directive. This means that only employees of the state and emanations of the state can rely directly on rights guaranteed under that Directive.

Indirect effect   2.14

Along with supremacy and direct effect, the third key concept pertinent to the applicability of EU law is 'indirect effect'. The ECJ has explained the principle of indirect effect in the following terms: 'In applying national law and in particular a national law specifically introduced to implement [a Community measure], national courts are required to interpret domestic law in the light of the wording and purpose of the Directive' – Von Colson and anor v Land Nordrhein-Westfalen 1984 ECR 1891, ECJ. S.2(4) of the European Communities Act 1972 contains a requirement to much the same effect. Importantly, this obligation is not limited to domestic law specifically designed to implement the Community measure in question – Webb v EMO Air Cargo (UK) Ltd 1993 ICR 175, HL, following Marleasing SA v La Comercial Internacional de Alimentación SA 1992 1 CMLR 305, ECJ.

The usefulness of indirect effect in an employment law context lies in the fact that it applies regardless of whether the party sued is an emanation of the state or an individual. Consequently, it may be relied upon by private sector employees who, as we have explained above, are unable to rely on the direct effect of Directives that have not been properly implemented into national law. An illustration of the principle of indirect effect in action is provided by the EAT's decision in Chessington World of Adventures Ltd v Reed 1998 ICR 97, EAT. In that case, the Appeal Tribunal was prepared to interpret the concept of discrimination 'on grounds of sex' broadly in order to bring discrimination against transsexuals within it, and thus reconcile the Sex Discrimination Act 1975 (SDA) with the original Equal Treatment Directive (No.76/207).

27

2.15 However, the principle of indirect effect does not impose an absolute duty on courts and tribunals to interpret domestic law in accordance with EU law, merely a duty to do this 'so far as possible' – Marleasing SA v La Comercial Internacional de Alimentacion SA (above). According to the House of Lords, where national law is clear and capable of only one meaning, it must not be distorted to make it comply with an EU Directive that has a different meaning – Webb v EMO Air Cargo UK Ltd (above).

That said, courts and tribunals should be prepared to go quite far in their attempt to reconcile national legislation with EU law. It might be assumed that it is not possible to read a domestic provision consistently with a Directive when the words of that provision, even on the broadest interpretation, are not capable of having the meaning required by the Directive. However, the courts and tribunals have shown themselves ready to insert words into legislation in order to achieve the required effect. One of the first examples of this was in Litster and ors v Forth Dry Dock and Engineering Co Ltd 1989 ICR 341, HL, where the House of Lords inserted additional wording into the Transfer of Undertakings (Protection of Employment) Regulations 1981 SI 1981/1794 in order to give effect to the EU Acquired Rights Directive (No.77/187). Another example is Redcar and Cleveland Borough Council v Bainbridge and ors (No.1) 2008 ICR 238, CA. There, women whose jobs had been given a higher value than a group of men's under a job evaluation study claimed equal pay with the higher-paid men on the basis that they were employed on 'work rated as equivalent' for the purposes of S.1(2)(b) of the Equal Pay Act 1970 (EqPA) (now S.65(1)(b) EqA). S.1(5) EqPA (now S.65(4) EqA) stated that a woman was employed on 'work rated as equivalent' to that of a man 'if, but only if, her job and their job have been given an equal value'. The Court of Appeal allowed the claims to proceed even though, strictly speaking, the men's jobs were not 'rated as equivalent' to the women's. In its view, the principle of equal pay for equal work – derived from what is now Article 157 and the recast Equal Treatment Directive – applied equally to the situation of the instant case where the female claimants were doing jobs of *higher* value than their comparators but earning less. Accordingly, it was necessary that S.1(5) EqPA should be read as including the words italicised below: 'A woman is to be regarded as employed on work rated as equivalent with that of any men if, but only if, her job and their job have been given an equal value *or her job has been given a higher value.*' (Note that the additional wording is not replicated in S.65(4) EqA, but there is no reason to suggest that the same principle will not apply.)

2.16 Courts and tribunals have also been able to achieve compatibility between UK and EU legislation by *ignoring* words in the domestic provision. So, for example, in Unison and anor v Brennan and ors 2008 ICR 955, EAT, the Appeal Tribunal felt justified in omitting words in S.6(4A) of the (now-repealed) Sex Discrimination Act 1986 (SDA) where it was necessary to do so in order to give full effect to the EU Equal Pay Directive (No.75/117) and the EU Equal Treatment Directive (No.76/207) (since consolidated in the recast Directive).

More recently, the courts have undertaken even more dramatic rewriting of legislation in an effort to give effect to EU law. In EBR Attridge LLP (formerly Attridge Law) and anor v Coleman 2010 ICR 242, EAT, the Appeal Tribunal determined that it was appropriate to insert whole subsections into the Disability Discrimination Act 1995 (DDA). This was done in order to give effect to the ECJ's decision in the same case – Coleman v Attridge Law and anor 2008 ICR 1128, ECJ – that the protection against disability discrimination in the Framework Directive is not limited to people who themselves have a disability. The fact that the clear wording of the DDA restricted the right to bring a disability discrimination claim to those who were disabled indicates the extent of the courts and tribunals' powers in this regard, given that the EAT was able to achieve a directly contrary effect.

Interestingly, the guidance on which the EAT in Coleman placed the greatest **2.17** reliance came not from a case dealing with the interpretation of EU law, but from a case – Ghaidan v Godin-Mendoza 2004 2 AC 557, HL – dealing with the courts' power of interpretation under S.3(1) of the Human Rights Act 1998. That provision obliges courts to read and give effect to UK legislation 'so far as it is possible to do so' in a way compatible with the European Convention on Human Rights and Fundamental Freedoms (ECHR) and the House of Lords accepted that this is the same in substance as the obligation of courts and tribunals to 'as far as possible' interpret UK legislation in a way that gives effect to obligations under EU law.

The Ghaidan v Godin-Mendoza case demonstrates that whether it is possible to read a statute consistently with either ECHR or EU rights depends not on the number of words that must be read into the statute by implication, but on whether the amendments would be consistent with the fundamental features of the legislation. If the insertion of one word would contradict the key principles and scope of the legislation, it would not be a permissible amendment, whereas the implication of dozens of words will be permissible if it is consistent with the principles and scope.

In Coleman v Attridge Law and anor (above), the legislation at issue was the **2.18** DDA, and the EAT concluded that it would be consistent with the principle that underpins the legislation – the elimination of discrimination on the ground of disability – to read the relevant statutory provisions so that both disabled and non-disabled people are protected. The consequences of this approach for employment law are that it will be a very rare case indeed where a tribunal or court, faced with an ECJ decision which indicates that, on a literal interpretation, a domestic provision does not give effect to an EU Directive, finds that it is not possible to interpret the UK provision consistently with the Directive. This is because the underlying principles of the legislation are bound to include the implementation of the Directive, and the Directive in turn will expound general principles, which its measures are intended to promote.

That said, there are still limits to courts' and tribunals' powers in this regard, as highlighted by the High Court's decision in Equal Opportunities Commission v Secretary of State for Trade and Industry 2007 ICR 1234, QBD. There, the EOC successfully challenged the United Kingdom's implementation of various provisions of the EU Equal Treatment Amendment Directive (No.2002/73) (now part of the recast Directive) relating to the right to bring claims for harassment and discrimination on the grounds of pregnancy or maternity leave. However, the High Court held that it was impossible to read the relevant provisions in the SDA in a way that would render them compliant with the Directive, while ensuring that the interpretation of the provisions was clear and comprehensible for employers and employees alike. As a result, the High Court stated that the Government would have to recast the relevant provisions of the SDA in order to remedy the situation. The changes were eventually effected by the Sex Discrimination Act 1975 (Amendment) Regulations 2008 SI 2008/656.

2.19 Reliance on 'fundamental principles' of EU law

As mentioned above, it is a long-established principle that rights derived from a Directive are not directly enforceable between private individuals, who must instead rely on the Directive's indirect effect and the court or tribunal's ability to interpret the domestic provision in line with EU law. Where such interpretation is not possible, it has been generally accepted that national law will prevail. However, a string of recent decisions from the ECJ has thrown this settled understanding of the interrelationship between UK and EU law into doubt. In effect, the ECJ has been prepared to find direct effect of a European measure, and disapply national legislation accordingly, on the basis of 'general principles' of European law.

The first significant decision in this context was Mangold v Helm 2006 IRLR 143, ECJ, in which the European Court held that a German law providing fixed-term workers aged 52 and over with fewer legal protections than their younger counterparts was incompatible with the prohibition on age discrimination laid down by the Framework Directive. This was the case even though the date for implementing the Directive into German law had not yet passed when the 56-year-old claimant entered into the fixed-term contract – Germany had been granted a three-year extension of the transposition period until 2 December 2006. In the Court's view, Article 18 of the Directive (which required Member States making use of the additional period to report annually on the steps taken and progress made towards implementation) implied that the Member State is required to take concrete measures to bring its own laws into line with the objectives of a Directive, and not adopt inconsistent legislation during the implementation period. The German law came into force on 1 January 2003, after the publication of the Framework Directive in the Official Journal of the Community on 2 December 2000.

More surprisingly, the Court went on to suggest that protection from age **2.20** discrimination is more than just a right derived from a Directive, holding that 'the principle of non-discrimination on grounds of age is to be regarded as a general principle of community law'. According to the ECJ, the Framework Directive simply set out the means for combating age (as well as religion or belief, disability and sexual orientation) discrimination and that the prohibition on such discrimination is 'a general principle of Community law', which is set out in a number of 'international instruments and in the constitutional traditions common to Member States'. Where national rules fall within the scope of Community law (for example, because they themselves implement a Directive – in this case, the EU Fixed-term Work Directive (No.1999/70)) and reference is made to the ECJ for a preliminary ruling, the ECJ must assist the national court in determining whether these rules are compatible with Community law. In this regard, observance of the general principles of Community law on equal treatment was not conditional on the expiry of the period allowed for implementing a Directive.

The Mangold decision seemed to suggest that it was possible to rely directly on 'general principles of Community law' to enforce rights derived from EU law in a dispute between private individuals. The implications, in real terms, of this decision were not immediately clear, however. One view was that the impact of the Court's ruling would be limited, as it restricted age claims based on general principles of Community law to circumstances where inconsistent domestic law was passed during the period of transposition for the Directive, i.e. claims in respect of laws in force since 2 December 2000 (the date of the Directive's publication). This was the approach taken by the EAT in Lloyd-Briden v Worthing College EAT 0065/07, where it upheld a tribunal's decision to strike out an unfair dismissal claim by an 82-year-old claimant. Applying Mangold, it accepted that non-discrimination on the ground of age is a fundamental principle of EU law which will, in certain circumstances, allow a court or tribunal to disregard a conflicting provision of national law. However, it referred to the decision in Adeneler v Ellinikos Organismos Galaktos 2006 IRLR 716, ECJ, where the ECJ, post-Mangold, noted that where a Directive is belatedly transposed into domestic law, national courts are only required to interpret national law to give effect to the Directive's aims from the date that the period for transposition into national law expires. That said, Member States are under a duty during the period between a Directive's entry into force and the final date for its transposition into national law to refrain from taking measures liable seriously to compromise the aim of the Directive in question. Relying on this, the EAT concluded that the Mangold decision was limited to cases where an age-discriminatory provision has been enacted during the Framework Directive's transposition period. Accordingly, the tribunal had not

31

been obliged to set aside the (now-repealed) statutory bar on persons over 65 claiming unfair dismissal which predated adoption of the Directive. However, the EAT went on to note that a court or tribunal could have directly applied the principle of non-discrimination on the ground of age and disregarded the law in question if the United Kingdom had failed to repeal it by the end of the transposition period (which it had not).

2.21 The ECJ subsequently had the opportunity to resolve any ambiguity over the effect of Mangold v Helm (above) when a similar issue came before it in Kücükdeveci v Swedex GmbH und Co KG 2010 IRLR 346, ECJ. The case concerned a German law which provided for a statutory notice period based on length of service, rising from one month after two years' service to four months after ten years. However, any periods of service where the employee was under the age of 25 were excluded. K, who was dismissed after ten years' service with only one month's notice because for most of her service she had been under 25, argued that the law was age discriminatory. The ECJ agreed, holding that it breached the Framework Directive as it amounted to direct age discrimination that could not be justified. Moreover, it was not possible to interpret the national provision so as to give effect to the Directive.

The question for the European Court that automatically followed from these findings was whether the German court was required to disapply the incompatible national provision, even though the case involved a dispute between private individuals. On this point, the ECJ referred to its earlier decision in Mangold v Helm (above), reiterating that non-discrimination on the ground of age is a 'general principle of EU law', to which the Framework Directive gives expression. The general principle applies in a case that falls within the scope of EU law.

2.22 Applying this approach to the facts of the instant case, the ECJ held that the Framework Directive had the effect of bringing the German law within the scope of EU law once the period for the Directive's transposition expired – which, in Germany's case, was 2 December 2006. Since K's dismissal had occurred after that date, the Court concluded that it was the responsibility of the German court to ensure that the principle of non-discrimination on the ground of age was fully effective. This meant that inconsistent domestic legislation, such as the German law at issue in the case, had to be disapplied, even in a dispute between private individuals. Furthermore, the German court could do so without first making a reference to the ECJ for a preliminary ruling. It followed that K could rely on the Directive in her claim against the employer, another legal individual.

Thus, in Kücükdeveci, the European Court confirmed, and expanded upon, the existence and application of 'general principles of EU law'. In the course of its judgment it made a number of interesting points which are worth reiterating. Notably, the Court acknowledged that a Directive does not have horizontal direct effect – i.e. it does not of itself impose obligations on an individual and cannot therefore be relied upon in a dispute against such an individual. That said, the Court held that where the Directive gives expression to a general principle of equal treatment in employment and occupation, the national court must provide the legal protection which individuals derive from EU law and ensure the full effectiveness of that law. This requires it, if need be, to disapply any provision of national legislation contrary to that principle.

Although both Mangold v Helm (above) and Kücükdeveci v Swedex GmbH **2.23** und Co KG (above) concerned age discrimination, there is no reason to believe that the principle of non-discrimination on the ground of age is the only general principle of Community law deserving wider protection than the confines of express European legislation currently allow. In X v Mid Sussex Citizens Advice Bureau and anor 2011 ICR 460, CA (a case on whether unpaid volunteers came within the protection of the DDA), Lord Justice Elias suggested that the prohibition on disability discrimination would attain the same status under the Kücükdeveci principle. It is also noteworthy that the ECJ in Hennigs v Eisenbahn-Bundesamt; Land Berlin v Mai 2012 IRLR 83, ECJ, recently described the principle of non-discrimination on the ground of age as 'enshrined in primary law' by Article 21 of the Charter of Fundamental Rights of the European Union. That same Article also prohibits discrimination on grounds of sex, race, colour, ethnic origin, religion or belief, disability and sexual orientation, which suggests that these grounds too will have similar status.

Suing the state
2.24

The final point to note is that, where a Government fails properly to implement a Directive, individuals who are thereby deprived of a remedy may bring a claim for damages against the state in respect of that failure. This principle was established in Francovich and ors v Italian Republic 1995 ICR 722, ECJ. This type of claim is of importance, as the limitations on the principles of direct and indirect effect (see 'Direct effect' and 'Indirect effect' above) mean that, for some private sector employees, a 'Francovich' claim against the state will be their only means of redress. However, the ECJ has made it clear that the remedy is not restricted to individuals in respect of whom a Directive is not directly effective. As a result, public sector employees may be able to choose between bringing a claim directly under a Directive or making a Francovich claim – (1) Brasserie du Pêcheur SA v Federal Republic of Germany (2) R v Secretary of State for Transport ex parte Factortame Ltd and ors 1996 IRLR 267, ECJ.

In Francovich and ors v Italian Republic (above) the ECJ ruled that state liability will depend on three conditions being satisfied:

- the Directive in question must confer rights upon individuals

- the content of those rights must be readily ascertainable by reference to the provisions of the Directive

33

- there must be a causal link between the failure of the Member State to fulfil its obligations under the Directive and the damage suffered by the person affected.

2.25 Where a Member State has failed to implement an EU Directive at all (e.g. where the deadline for implementation expires before relevant domestic legislation is passed), the conditions listed above are the only ones that need to be met – Dillenkofer and ors v Federal Republic of Germany 1997 IRLR 60, ECJ. Where, however, the complaint is not that a Member State has failed to implement a Directive at all but that it has implemented it inadequately, the ECJ has established a modified test for state liability. The first and third conditions identified in Francovich remain the same but, instead of applying the 'readily ascertainable' test, the question to ask is whether the Member State's failure to implement the Directive properly was a 'sufficiently serious' breach of its Treaty obligations, meaning that the state has 'manifestly and gravely disregarded the limits on its discretion' – (1) Brasserie du Pêcheur SA v Federal Republic of Germany (2) R v Secretary of State for Transport ex parte Factortame Ltd and ors (above). The indications are that this test establishes quite a high threshold of seriousness before the state will become liable – see, for example, R v HM Treasury ex parte British Telecommunications plc 1996 IRLR 300, ECJ.

The Court of Appeal has held that an individual wishing to proceed with a Francovich claim against the state in this country should commence proceedings in the ordinary civil courts rather than in an employment tribunal – Secretary of State for Employment v Mann and ors 1997 ICR 209, CA. The correct respondent will be the Attorney General in England and Wales, the Lord Advocate in Scotland, and the Attorney General for Northern Ireland in Northern Ireland.

2.26 EU equality measures

In this section we summarise the key EU equality measures. The impact of these measures on UK substantive law is discussed in greater depth in the relevant chapters of this Handbook where and when the need arises. We also briefly look at the Charter of Fundamental Rights of the European Union and consider its likely impact on UK discrimination laws in future.

As explained under 'Relationship between EU and UK law' above, EU discrimination law is to be found primarily in the following Directives:

- the *recast EU Equal Treatment Directive (No.2006/54)*, which relates to 'the implementation of the principle of equal opportunities and equal treatment of men and women in matters of employment and occupation'

- the *EU Equal Treatment Framework Directive (No.2000/78)*, which sets out a general framework for eliminating employment or occupational inequalities based on age, disability, religion or belief, and sexual orientation

- the *EU Race Equality Directive (No.2000/4)*, which implements the principle of equal treatment between persons irrespective of racial or ethnic origin.

Note that the EU Pregnant Workers Directive (No.92/85), and its impact on domestic law, is discussed in IDS Employment Law Handbook, 'Maternity and Parental Rights' (2009).

Recast Directive   2.27

Until recently, there were seven different Directives dealing with gender equality:

- No.75/117 on the application of the principle of equal pay for men and women ('the Equal Pay Directive')

- No.76/207 on equal treatment for men and women as regards access to employment ('the Equal Treatment Directive')

- No.2002/73, amending Directive No.76/207, on equal treatment for men and women as regards employment, vocational training and promotion and working conditions

- No.86/378 on equal treatment for men and women in occupational social security schemes

- No.96/97, amending Directive No.86/378, on the implementation of the principle of equal treatment for men and women in occupational social security schemes

- No.97/80 on the burden of proof in cases of discrimination based on sex ('the Burden of Proof Directive'), and

- No.98/52 on the extension of Directive No.97/80 to the United Kingdom.

However, in 2006 the European Parliament and the Council of Ministers **2.28** consolidated all seven measures, together with relevant case law from the ECJ, into the recast EU Equal Treatment Directive (No.2006/54) ('the recast Directive'), which relates to 'the implementation of the principle of equal opportunities and equal treatment of men and women in matters of employment and occupation'. The recast Directive came into force on 15 August 2006 and had to be implemented by Member States by 15 August 2008, although in most cases the measures were already implemented in order to comply with the original Directives. The seven consolidated Directives were repealed with effect from 15 August 2009 and references to those Directives elsewhere in EU legislation are now to be read as a reference to the relevant part of the recast Directive.

The recast Equal Treatment Directive is a consolidating measure rather than an extension or expansion of the principles of equal treatment, and has therefore had no impact on the scope of European discrimination law. It does, however, incorporate certain principles derived from case law that may not have been explicit in the existing Directives. For example, the Preamble notes that it is now established that, in certain circumstances, the principle of equal pay is not limited to situations in which men and women work for the same employer.

2.29 In addition to sex, the Directive also covers pregnancy and maternity and gender reassignment. However, there is some uncertainty over whether it extends to marital or family status. Article 2(1) of the now-repealed EU Equal Treatment Directive (No.76/207) specifically provided that 'there shall be no discrimination whatsoever on grounds of sex either directly or indirectly by reference in particular to *marital or family status*' (our stress). Clearly, the mention of 'marital status' indicated that married and unmarried persons came within the scope of the Directive. However, the actual discrimination prohibited by Article 2(1) was 'discrimination… on grounds of *sex*' (our stress), which meant that any complainant relying on that provision – whether married or not – had to show that he or she had suffered sex discrimination. It would seem that the recast Directive has not altered this position. Article 14(1) of that Directive (the provision correlating to Article 2(1) of the 1976 Directive) has dropped all reference to 'marital or family status'. Sex discrimination based on marital or family status would arguably be caught by the prohibitions against direct and indirect sex discrimination contained in the recast Directive, but that Directive confers no remedy for any discrimination on grounds of marital or family status that does not constitute sex discrimination. Rather, EU law leaves it to national governments to decide whether or not to enact specific prohibitions against such discrimination.

What follows is a brief description of the key provisions of the recast Directive, except for those relating to equal pay, which are found in IDS Employment Law Handbook, 'Equal Pay' (2009), Chapter 1, under 'EU gender equality measures'.

Note that the European Commission was obliged to conduct a review of the recast Directive by 15 February 2011 and, if appropriate, propose any amendments it deems necessary. As far as we are aware, no such amendments were proposed.

2.30 **Key definitions.** Article 2(1) of the recast Directive contains the following key definitions that were previously contained in the Equal Treatment Directive:

- *direct discrimination*: where one person is treated less favourably on the ground of sex than another is, has been or would be treated in a comparable situation

- *indirect discrimination*: where an apparently neutral provision, criterion or practice would put persons of one sex at a particular disadvantage compared with persons of the other sex, unless that provision, criterion or practice is objectively justified by a legitimate aim, and the means of achieving that aim are appropriate and necessary

- *harassment*: where unwanted conduct related to the sex of a person occurs with the purpose or effect of violating the dignity of a person, and of creating an intimidating, hostile, degrading, humiliating or offensive environment

- *sexual harassment*: where any form of unwanted verbal, non-verbal or physical conduct of a sexual nature occurs, with the purpose or effect of violating the dignity of a person, in particular when creating an intimidating, hostile, degrading, humiliating or offensive environment.

Article 2(2) states that discrimination includes harassment and sexual harassment, instructions to discriminate, and any less favourable treatment of a woman related to pregnancy or maternity leave.

Scope. Article 14 is the key provision setting out the principle of equal treatment **2.31** as regards access to employment, vocational training and promotion and working conditions. Article 14(1) provides that there shall be no direct or indirect discrimination on the ground of sex in relation to:

- access to employment, self employment or occupation, including selection criteria, recruitment conditions and promotion

- access to all types and to all levels of vocational guidance and vocational training, including work experience

- employment and working conditions, including dismissals, as well as pay within the meaning of Article 157 TFEU

- membership of, involvement in, or benefits afforded by an organisation of workers or employers, or any organisation whose members carry on a particular profession.

In respect of access to employment, including training leading to employment, **2.32** Article 14(2) permits Member States to introduce measures providing that 'a difference of treatment which is based on a characteristic related to sex shall not constitute discrimination where, by reason of the nature of the particular occupational activities concerned or of the context in which they are carried out, such a characteristic constitutes a genuine and determining occupational requirement, provided that its objective is legitimate and the requirement is proportionate'.

Articles 15 and 16 address what have become known as 'family-friendly rights'. Article 15 provides that a woman returning from maternity leave should be entitled to return to the same job or an equivalent post, on no less favourable conditions, and benefit from any improvement in working conditions to which she would have been entitled had she not been on maternity leave. Article 16 goes on to state that if a Member State has recognised rights to adoption and paternity leave, it should ensure that working men and women are protected against dismissal due to exercising those rights. In addition, on returning from such leave, workers are entitled to the same level of protection as a woman returning from maternity leave is afforded under Article 15.

2.33 **Remedies and enforcement.** Articles 17 and 18 impose obligations on EU Member States to put in place adequate judicial procedures for the enforcement of obligations under the Directive. Article 17 establishes that such procedures should not be limited in their application to persons who are still in the relationship in which the discrimination occurred, and should instead be available to all persons who consider themselves wronged by a failure to apply the principle of equal treatment. Para 3 of Article 17 goes on to state that this shall be without prejudice to national rules regarding time limits. Article 18 deals with the question of compensation, requiring Member States to introduce measures necessary to ensure that victims of sex discrimination are able to gain 'real and effective' compensation that reflects the loss and damage sustained and is both dissuasive and proportionate.

2.34 **Burden of proof.** The burden of proof provisions originally contained in the Burden of Proof Directive can now be found in Article 19 of the recast Directive. This provision states that, where a complainant who considers that the principle of equal treatment has not been applied to him or her establishes facts from which it may be presumed that there has been direct or indirect discrimination, it shall be for the respondent to prove that there has been no breach of that principle. This Article applies equally to complaints under Article 157 TFEU – Article 19(4).

2.35 **Equality bodies.** Article 20 places an obligation on Member States to create a body (or bodies) for the promotion, analysis, monitoring and support of equal treatment of all persons. Such bodies can – as is the case with the Equality and Human Rights Commission in the United Kingdom – be the national body with the responsibility for safeguarding human rights or individual rights. Their competences should include providing assistance to victims of discrimination in pursuing claims, conducting surveys concerning discrimination, and publishing reports and recommendations.

2.36 **Victimisation.** Article 24 requires measures to be put in place to protect employees, and employees' representatives, from dismissal or other adverse treatment by the employer as a reaction to a complaint aimed at enforcing compliance with the principle of equal treatment.

2.37 **Framework Directive**
The EU Equal Treatment Framework Directive (No.2000/78) ('the Framework Directive') lays down a general framework for Member States to combat discrimination in employment and occupation on the grounds of religion or

belief, disability, sexual orientation and age. Although the Directive was agreed on 27 November 2000, it did not need to be implemented into national law until 2 December 2003 (2 December 2006 with respect to age). In the United Kingdom the necessary changes were introduced by way of secondary legislation – the Employment Equality (Religion or Belief) Regulations 2003 SI 2003/1660, the Employment Equality (Sexual Orientation) Regulations 2003 SI 2003/1661, and the Employment Equality (Age) Regulations 2006 SI 2006/1031. In the case of disability, amendments were made to the DDA by the Disability Discrimination Act 1995 (Amendment) Regulations 2003 SI 2003/167. The protections can now be found in the EqA.

Key definitions. Article 2(2) of the Framework Directive contains the following **2.38** key definitions:

- *direct discrimination*: where one person is treated less favourably than another is, has been or would be treated in a comparable situation on grounds of religion or belief, disability, age or sexual orientation

- *indirect discrimination*: where an apparently neutral provision, criterion or practice would put persons having a particular religion or belief, a particular disability, a particular age, or a particular sexual orientation at a particular disadvantage compared with other persons, unless that provision, criterion or practice is objectively justified by a legitimate aim, and the means of achieving that aim are appropriate and necessary

- *harassment*: where unwanted conduct related to religion or belief, disability, age or sexual orientation takes place with the purpose or effect of violating the dignity of a person and of creating an intimidating, hostile, degrading, humiliating or offensive environment.

Discrimination includes harassment and instructions to discriminate – Article 2(3) and (4).

Scope. Articles 2(1) and 3(1) provide that there shall be no direct or indirect **2.39** discrimination whatsoever on the grounds of religion or belief, disability, age or sexual orientation in relation to:

- access to employment, self employment or occupation, including selection criteria, recruitment conditions and promotion

- access to all types and to all levels of vocational guidance and vocational training, including work experience

- employment and working conditions, including dismissals and pay

- membership of, involvement in, or benefits afforded by an organisation of workers or employers, or any organisation whose members carry on a particular profession.

However, Article 4(1) permits Member States to introduce measures providing that 'a difference of treatment which is based on a characteristic related to any of the grounds [protected by the Directive] shall not constitute discrimination where, by reason of the nature of the particular occupational activities concerned or of the context in which they are carried out, such a characteristic constitutes a genuine and determining occupational requirement, provided that its objective is legitimate and the requirement is proportionate'. Furthermore, Article 4(2) grants organisations with a religious ethos, such as churches, a specific exemption from the prohibition of discrimination by providing that 'a difference of treatment based on a person's religion or belief shall not constitute discrimination where, by reason of the nature of [the occupational] activities or of the context in which they are carried out, a person's religion or belief constitute a genuine, legitimate and justified occupational requirement'.

2.40 **Reasonable accommodation for disabled persons.** With regard to disabled persons, Article 5 requires employers to take appropriate measures to enable a person with a disability to have access to, participate in, or advance in employment, or to undergo training, unless such measures would impose a disproportionate burden on the employer.

2.41 **Justification of age discrimination.** Article 6(1) states that Member States may provide that differences of treatment on the ground of age shall not constitute discrimination, if 'they are objectively and reasonably justified by a legitimate aim, including legitimate employment policy, labour market and vocational training objectives, and if the means of achieving that aim are appropriate and necessary'. It goes on to give the following examples of different treatment on the ground of age:

- the setting of conditions on access to employment and vocational training, employment and occupation, including dismissal and remuneration conditions, for young people, older workers and persons with caring responsibilities in order to promote their vocational integration or ensure their protection

- the fixing of minimum conditions of age, professional experience or seniority in service for access to, or advantages linked to, employment

- the fixing of a maximum age for recruitment based on the training requirements of a post or the need for a reasonable period of employment before retirement.

The Directive further allows Member States to stipulate ages for admission or entitlement to retirement benefits, provided this does not result in discrimination on the ground of sex – Article 6(2).

40

Remaining provisions. The provisions dealing with remedies and enforcement **2.42** (Article 9), the burden of proof rules (Article 10) and victimisation (Article 11) are similar to those found in the recast Directive (see 'Recast Directive' above).

Race Equality Directive   2.43

The EU Race Equality Directive (No.2000/43) ('the Race Equality Directive'), which was adopted on 29 June 2000, lays down a framework for implementing the principle of equal treatment between persons irrespective of racial or ethnic origin. The necessary changes to UK domestic law – to what was then the Race Relations Act 1976 – were made by the Race Relations Act 1976 (Amendment) Regulations 2003 SI 2003/1626. However, the European Commission subsequently sent the United Kingdom a Reasoned Opinion, asserting that it had incorrectly implemented the Directive. To remedy the situation, the Government passed the Race Relations Act 1976 (Amendment) Regulations 2008 SI 2008/3008.

It is important to note that the Directive only applies to discrimination on grounds of race, ethnic and national origins. It does not cover the two additional grounds covered by the EqA (and previously by the RRA) – i.e. colour and nationality.

Key definitions. Article 2(2) of the Race Equality Directive contains the **2.44** following key definitions with regard to combating race discrimination:

- *direct discrimination*: where one person is treated less favourably than another is, has been or would be treated in a comparable situation on grounds of racial or ethnic origin

- *indirect discrimination*: where an apparently neutral provision, criterion or practice would put persons of a racial or ethnic origin at a particular disadvantage compared with other persons, unless that provision, criterion or practice is objectively justified by a legitimate aim, and the means of achieving that aim are appropriate and necessary

- *harassment*: where unwanted conduct related to racial or ethnic origin takes place with the purpose or effect of violating the dignity of a person, and of creating an intimidating, hostile, degrading, humiliating or offensive environment.

Discrimination includes harassment and instructions to discriminate – Article 2(3) and (4).

Scope. Articles 2(1) and 3(1) provide that there shall be no direct or indirect **2.45** discrimination based on racial or ethnic origin in relation to:

- access to employment, self employment or occupation, including selection criteria, recruitment conditions and promotion

- access to all types and to all levels of vocational guidance and vocational training, including work experience

- employment and working conditions, including dismissals and pay

- membership of, involvement in, or benefits afforded by an organisation of workers or employers, or any organisation whose members carry on a particular profession.

However, Article 4 permits a derogation from the principle of non-discrimination on racial and ethnic grounds. It states that Member States may introduce measures providing that 'a difference of treatment which is based on a characteristic related to racial or ethnic origin shall not constitute discrimination where, by reason of the nature of the particular occupational activities concerned or of the context in which they are carried out, such a characteristic constitutes a genuine and determining occupational requirement, provided that the objective is legitimate and the requirement is proportionate'.

2.46 **Remaining provisions.** The Directive also contains specific provisions instructing Member States to introduce measures to protect individuals from victimisation (Article 9); apply the burden of proof rules (Article 8); and set up a race equality body (Article 13).

2.47 **EU Charter of Fundamental Rights**
When the Treaty of Lisbon came into force on 1 December 2009, it put the Charter of Fundamental Rights of the European Union on a legal basis for the first time. The Charter, originally agreed in 2000, contains 54 Articles said to be the 'core values' of the EU, many of which could be significant in an employment context. Some of the rights contained in the Charter already exist in the European Convention on Human Rights and Fundamental Freedoms (ECHR) (discussed in detail in Chapter 3, 'Human rights law'), while others – such as protection from discrimination and the right to a safe working environment – are enshrined in existing Treaties and EU Directives. There are, however, some aspects of the Charter that seem to go beyond existing rights. For example:

- Article 15(1) states that everyone has the right to engage in work and pursue a freely chosen or accepted occupation

- Article 21(1) prohibits discrimination on a wider range of grounds than is currently covered in the equality Directives, including social origin, genetic features, political or any other opinion, property, and birth.

2.48 Although the Charter sets out these and many other rights, the extent to which an individual can rely on them has been a matter of fervent debate. Originally, it was suggested that public sector employees might be able to cite the Charter's provisions in claims against their employers – in much the same way that they can rely on Article 157 TFEU in equal pay claims. However, this now seems unlikely given the way the Charter has been integrated into EU law.

Article 6(1) of the amended TEU states that the Charter shall have the same legal value as the Treaties, but stipulates that Charter rights shall not extend the competence of the EU. Thus, the Charter cannot be used as a means of extending the EU's legal authority to act on a matter – such extensions can only come from further Treaties. Article 6(3) goes on to provide that fundamental rights – as derived from the ECHR and from 'constitutional traditions' of Member States – shall constitute general principles of EU law. Cases where individuals have been able to rely on general principles of EU law are discussed under 'Relationship between EU and UK law – reliance on "fundamental principles" of EU law' above.

According to the European Commission's website, the provisions of the Charter **2.49** are addressed to the EU institutions – the Commission, the Council, the ECJ, etc, and to Member States *but only when they are implementing EU law*. Thus, Member States must have regard to the fundamental rights enshrined in the Charter when transposing a Directive into national law, but are not bound by those rights in general. It should be remembered, however, that the Treaty provisions incorporating the Charter into EU law will be subject to interpretation by the ECJ, a body which is itself now bound by these fundamental rights.

UK opt-out. The Charter's effect in the United Kingdom is severely curtailed **2.50** as a result of the opt-out secured by the UK Government. During the negotiations on the Lisbon Treaty, the UK and Polish governments expressed concern about how the Charter might affect domestic laws and practices. The result of these concerns was a protocol on the application of the Charter to Poland and the United Kingdom. Article 1 of this protocol states that the Charter does not extend the ability of the ECJ, or any court or tribunal in the United Kingdom or Poland, to find that the laws, regulations or administrative provisions, practices or action of Poland or the United Kingdom are inconsistent with the fundamental rights, freedoms and principles that it reaffirms. Article 2 of the protocol goes on to state that, to the extent that a provision of the Charter refers to national laws and practices, it shall only apply to Poland or the United Kingdom to the extent that the rights or principles that it contains are recognised in the law or practices of those countries.

The effect of the protocol would seem to be that, while the Charter will guide both domestic courts and the ECJ in their interpretation of EU law, it will not override existing domestic law. That is not to say that the Charter is irrelevant. On the contrary, it has the potential to shape the future development of the European Union. The fact that the Charter is addressed to the EU institutions means, for example, that when proposing new EU legislation, the European

43

Commission will have to ensure that the fundamental rights of citizens would not be infringed by that legislation. Furthermore, the discrimination provisions of the Charter indicate the direction European law is likely to take when it comes to extending the range of characteristics covered by the EU equality measures.

3 Human rights law

Human Rights Act 1998

Human rights in discrimination context

Proposals for reform

Although the primary sources of anti-discrimination law in the United Kingdom **3.1** are the Equality Act 2010 (EqA) and European enactments, the issue of equality is also partially addressed in human rights legislation. In the United Kingdom this takes the form of the Human Rights Act 1998 (HRA), which incorporates the European Convention on Human Rights (ECHR) into domestic law. In this chapter, we look at how employees are able to assert their rights under the ECHR in UK courts and employment tribunals, before briefly considering an individual's right to petition the European Court of Human Rights directly. We then give an overview of the ECHR rights that have been, and continue to be, particularly relevant in a discrimination context. Finally, we consider the Government's proposals for reform in this area – in terms of the HRA itself and the role of the European Court of Human Rights.

Human Rights Act 1998
3.2

The HRA, which came into force on 2 October 2000, was designed to give effect in the United Kingdom to the rights and freedoms guaranteed under the ECHR – or, to give it its full title, the Convention for the Protection of Human Rights and Fundamental Freedoms. Since then, the ECHR has become an important part of the UK legal landscape, including discrimination law.

It took the better part of 50 years to transpose the ECHR into UK law. In 1950 the ECHR was adopted by the Council of Europe, an international organisation (separate from the European Union) which was set up in 1949 to promote democracy and human rights throughout Europe. It was brought into force three years later but, although the United Kingdom ratified it, successive post-war governments were reluctant to incorporate it into UK law. In 1966 the United Kingdom finally gave UK citizens who had exhausted all the available domestic remedies the right to present individual petitions to the European Court of Human Rights (ECtHR) based in Strasbourg, France, but stopped short of incorporating the ECHR into UK law. This situation changed when the Labour Party was elected in 1997. One of Labour's manifesto pledges was to incorporate the ECHR into UK law. The HRA was the result of that commitment.

The ECHR sets out fundamental rights and freedoms, including the right to **3.3** life, the prohibition of torture and slavery and the right to liberty and security, the majority of which are replicated in the HRA. How these rights are enforced depends on whether an individual works in the public or private sector. The HRA makes it unlawful for public authorities to act in a way that is incompatible with the ECHR and gives individuals whose rights have been infringed by public authorities the right *directly* to bring proceedings and obtain remedies. By contrast, individuals who work for private employers cannot rely directly on ECHR rights in UK courts, but the Act places a statutory duty on courts and tribunals to interpret, so far as it is possible to do so, Acts of Parliament and statutory instruments in a way that gives effect to those rights – see S.3(1) HRA. This duty on UK courts and tribunals to interpret legislation in line with the ECHR is effectively the way in which private individuals are able to 'enforce' their rights, albeit *indirectly*. We consider both routes by which individuals can assert their ECHR rights below, before briefly mentioning the remaining option for those who have exhausted all domestic avenues of legal redress, i.e. presenting an individual petition directly to the ECtHR.

Note that, pursuant to S.9(1) of the Equality Act 2006, the Equality and Human Rights Commission is responsible for promoting understanding of the importance of human rights (including ECHR rights), encouraging good practice in relation to them, and promoting the awareness, understanding and protection of human rights. In addition, it must encourage public authorities to comply with their duty to act in a way compatible with ECHR rights. However, the Commission will not generally undertake independent enforcement of human rights – apart from its power to seek judicial review, its functions in respect of human rights are largely promotional. For more information on the Commission's duties in respect of human rights, see Chapter 37, 'Equality and Human Rights Commission', under 'Duties'.

3.4 Interpreting UK law in accordance with ECHR rights

The principal way in which the HRA has an effect in discrimination cases is by the interpretation of existing law – i.e. the EqA and its antecedents – in a manner that complies with the ECHR. S.3(1) provides that UK courts and tribunals must interpret, so far as it is possible to do so, Acts of Parliament and statutory instruments in a way compatible with ECHR rights. This requirement applies to legislation regardless of when it was enacted – S.3(2)(a). The duty on courts and tribunals to interpret legislation in line with the ECHR is effectively the way in which employees working for private employers are able to assert their Convention rights – they bring a claim under the EqA upon which the court or tribunal can 'hang' the ECHR argument.

A key element of the HRA is to encourage Parliament to introduce legislation that is compatible with the ECHR. That said, Parliament retains the right to enact legislation that is incompatible. When a government-backed Bill is going through Parliament, the Minister in charge of the Bill must, before the second reading of the Bill, make a statement that the Bill's provisions are compatible with ECHR rights – this is known as a 'statement of compatibility' – S.19(1)(a) HRA. If the Minister is unable to give this assurance, he or she must make a statement that the Government wishes to proceed with the Bill regardless of the fact that it is not compatible with the ECHR – S.19(1)(b). The statement must be in writing and be published in a manner that the Minister considers appropriate – S.19(2). There is no corresponding requirement for Private Members' Bills. S.19 effectively preserves Parliamentary sovereignty by leaving open the possibility that the Government might at some point in the future introduce legislation that does not comply with the ECHR, although it would be expected to explain its reasons for doing so to Parliament.

The HRA's approach to statutory interpretation under S.3 is very similar to the **3.5** process that takes place when UK courts interpret EU Directives. Domestic courts already construe domestic legislation in line with EU law and will even read words into domestic legislation when necessary to give effect to EU law (see Chapter 2, 'European discrimination law', under 'Relationship between EU and UK law – indirect effect'). The same approach has been taken by courts and tribunals construing domestic legislation in line with the ECHR. In Ghaidan v Godin-Mendoza 2004 2 AC 557, HL, the House of Lords considered the courts' power of interpretation under S.3(1). In its view, whether it is possible to read a statute consistently with ECHR rights depends not on the number of words that must be read into the statute by implication, but on whether the amendments would be consistent with the fundamental features of the legislation. If the insertion of one word would contradict the key principles and scope of the legislation, it would not be a permissible amendment, whereas the implication of dozens of words will be permissible if it is consistent with the principles and scope.

When deliberating upon ECHR issues, S.2(1) HRA provides that courts and tribunals must take account of any relevant judgments, decisions, declarations or advisory opinions of the ECtHR and other opinions produced by the European Commission of Human Rights (which screened human rights complaints for the ECtHR until it was abolished in 1998) and the Committee of Ministers under the Convention (which monitors the execution of judgments). The obligation under S.2(1) arises where there is a 'clear and constant jurisprudence of the Strasbourg court' in relation to the issue under consideration, according to Lord Justice Rix in Copsey v WBB Devon Clays Ltd 2005 ICR 1789, CA. In this regard, there is a range of jurisprudence that domestic courts and tribunals are expected to consider and there is nothing in the HRA to suggest that courts are limited to considering cases that relate to the United Kingdom or emanate therefrom. Accordingly, employment tribunals can take account of rulings of the ECtHR in cases concerning any state that has ratified the ECHR.

47

3.6 Furthermore, one of the far-reaching effects of the HRA is that courts are able to disregard earlier rulings from domestic higher courts that are inconsistent with the ECHR. So, for example, it would theoretically be the case that the EAT is not obliged to follow a Supreme Court ruling on the meaning of a statute where the meaning ascribed by the Supreme Court is judged by the EAT to be incompatible with ECHR rights.

Where it is not possible to interpret primary legislation in line with the ECHR, UK courts are required to enforce unambiguous and incompatible primary legislation – S.3(2)(b) HRA. In these circumstances, they may also make a declaration of incompatibility – see below. The situation differs in relation to incompatible statutory instruments, which can be struck down by UK courts or simply disapplied unless primary legislation makes it impossible for a court to remove the incompatibility – S.3(2)(c).

3.7 **Declaration of incompatibility.** While much may be achieved to ensure that UK law complies with ECHR rights by interpretation of existing provisions, there may be circumstances where there is a direct conflict between a piece of UK legislation and the ECHR. In such circumstances there is a procedure for challenge, but the court is only given declaratory powers and – as such – the sovereignty of Parliament as the supreme law-making body in the United Kingdom is preserved. S.4(1) and (2) HRA provides that, if a court is satisfied that a provision in an Act of Parliament is incompatible with an ECHR right, it may make a declaration of incompatibility. Similarly, a declaration of incompatibility may be made in relation to a statutory instrument that is incompatible with an ECHR right and primary legislation prevents removal of the incompatibility – S.4(3) and (4).

Where a court is considering whether to make a declaration of incompatibility, S.5 HRA provides that the Crown has a right to intervene in the proceedings. Rule 19.4A of the Civil Procedure Rules 1998 SI 1998/3132 adds that the court may not make a declaration of incompatibility unless 21 days' notice, or such other period of notice as the court directs, has been given to the Crown. Where such notice has been given, a Minister, or other person permitted by the HRA, must be joined as a party on giving notice to the court.

3.8 However, it should be noted that employment tribunals and the EAT do not have the power to make a declaration of incompatibility as they are not listed in the 1998 Act as being courts empowered to do so – see Whittaker v P and D Watson (t/a P and M Watson Haulage) and anor 2002 ICR 1244, EAT (where the Appeal Tribunal suggested that a party seeking a declaration of incompatibility should have his or her case dealt with on paper only by the EAT President, with the President, in appropriate cases, simply adjourning or dismissing the appeal and giving leave to appeal to the Court of Appeal). The relevant courts that have this power include the High Court, the Court of

Appeal and the Supreme Court, and, in Scotland, the High Court of Justiciary (sitting otherwise than as a trial court) and the Court of Session – S.4(5).

Even if made, a declaration of incompatibility is of limited use to an individual, since it does not affect the validity, continuing operation or enforcement of the domestic provision in respect of which it is given, and it is not binding on the parties to the proceedings in which it is made – S.4(6) HRA. Such a declaration will prompt the Government to amend the law, however. The procedure for making the necessary amendments to remove the incompatibility is set out in S.10 and Schedule 2 to the 1998 Act.

Enforcing ECHR rights directly against public authorities 3.9
Section 6(1) HRA makes it unlawful for a public authority, including a court or tribunal, to act in a way that is incompatible with an ECHR right. An exception is made where the authority has no choice because it is bound to act in a certain way as a result of an Act of Parliament or a statutory instrument made under primary legislation that cannot be interpreted in a manner compatible with the ECHR – S.6(2). Crucially, public sector employees who believe that their employers are in breach of S.6(1) can assert their ECHR rights by bringing direct claims against them in employment tribunals and courts.

Note that the Equality and Human Rights Commission must encourage public authorities to comply with their S.6 duty to act in a way compatible with ECHR rights – see Chapter 37, 'Equality and Human Rights Commission', under 'Duties'.

Who is a 'public authority' for the purposes of S.6? A public authority 3.10 includes a court or tribunal – S.6(3)(a). A court or tribunal is therefore required to give effect to ECHR rights unless unable to do so. A public authority is also expressly stated to include 'any person certain of whose functions are functions of a public nature' – S.6(3)(b). However, S.6(5) adds that in relation to a particular act, 'a person is not a public authority by virtue only of [S.6(3)(b)] if the nature of the act is private'. Note that Parliament cannot be a public authority – S.6(3).

Public authorities can therefore be said to fall into two categories:

• 'pure' public authorities

• authorities with mixed public and private functions.

Section 6 is a complicated provision. During the 1998 Act's passage through 3.11 the House of Commons, Jack Straw, the Home Secretary at the time, expressed the view that the effect of S.6 was to create three categories, the first being 'obvious' public authorities, all of whose functions are public. In his view, the clearest examples of such authorities were government departments, local authorities and the police. The second category contained organisations with a mix of public and private functions. The effect of S.6(5) is that those organisations, unlike the 'pure' public authorities, are susceptible to the Act's direct application in relation to their public actions, but not their private ones. The third category consisted of organisations with no public functions – with the result that they fall outside the scope of S.6.

It follows from this that 'pure' public authorities, such as local authorities, are bound by the ECHR when carrying out all their functions, including any acts or omissions. If they fail to treat their employees in a manner compatible with ECHR rights (and they were not required to act in that way in order to give effect to incompatible primary legislation), employees can bring a direct claim under S.7 for any breach of these rights – see below.

3.12 Mixed public authorities include bodies that exercise public functions that the Government would otherwise have to undertake. Examples include Network Rail, doctors in general practice, public custodial aspects of the work of private security firms and the BBC. In respect of these hybrid bodies, the ECHR's impact on their employment functions may be more limited in comparison with pure public authorities. The key issue is the application of S.6(5). For example, the health and safety functions of Network Rail are public in nature, and therefore subject to the HRA; however, S.6(5) means that there is no obligation to apply ECHR rights when exercising any private acts. Accordingly, such acts are not caught by the requirements contained in the Act. So far as employment law is concerned, many branches of the law regard the act of employment as private in nature. Employers will therefore argue that, in relation to employment disputes with employees, claims based directly on the ECHR cannot be made. However, there may be counter-arguments that the employment of staff is part of the public function when those staff are carrying out work related to that function and employees will be able to bring claims directly.

Finally, there are the purely private employers, none of whose functions are caught by the HRA. In these circumstances, employees will not be able to bring claims based directly on ECHR rights, but this is not to say that the ECHR will not be relevant in respect of proceedings to enforce other claims. Employers who fall into the second and third categories will still be affected by the ECHR indirectly because, as discussed above, courts and tribunals are bound to apply domestic legislation in a manner compatible with the ECHR in all situations and with regard to all persons (public or private) unless the court or tribunal is prevented from doing so by primary legislation. As the Court of Appeal put it in X v Y 2004 ICR 1634, CA (an unfair dismissal case), 'the effect of [S.6] in the case of a claim against a private employer is to reinforce the extremely strong interpretative obligation imposed on the employment tribunal by [S.3]'. In the Court's view, this was particularly so where the ECtHR has found the ECHR right in question to impose a positive obligation on the state to secure the enjoyment of that right between private individuals, as it has done in relation to Articles 8 (the right to respect for private and family life), 9 (the right to freedom of religion) and 10 (the right to freedom of expression).

Claims to enforce ECHR rights. Section 7(1) HRA provides that a person **3.13** who claims that a public authority has acted (or proposes to act) in a way contrary to S.6(1) may bring proceedings against the authority under the HRA in the appropriate court or tribunal (S.7(1)(a)), or rely on the ECHR right or rights concerned in any legal proceedings (S.7(1)(b)), but only if he or she is (or would be) a victim of the unlawful act. An 'appropriate court or tribunal' means such court or tribunal as may be determined in accordance with rules, and proceedings against an authority include a counterclaim or similar proceedings – S.7(2) HRA. Rule 7.11 of the Civil Procedure Rules 1998 SI 1998/3132 supplements this provision by providing that a claim under S.7(1)(a) HRA can be brought only in the High Court in respect of a judicial act, but in respect of any other claim can be brought in any court. An employment tribunal or the EAT has no jurisdiction to hear a S.7(1)(a) claim.

If the proceedings are brought on an application for judicial review, the applicant is to be taken to have a sufficient interest (or, in Scotland, title and interest to sue) in relation to the unlawful act only if he or she is, or would be, a victim of that act – S.7(3) and (4) HRA. 'Legal proceedings' for the purposes of S.7(1)(b) include proceedings brought by or at the instigation of a public authority and covers an appeal against the decision of a court or tribunal in respect of such proceedings – S.7(6). An individual may rely on his or her ECHR rights under S.7(1)(b) in any proceedings brought by a public authority regardless of when the act in question took place – S.22(4).

Proceedings against a public authority under S.7(1)(a) must be brought before **3.14** the end of the period of one year beginning with the date on which the act complained of took place, or such longer period as the court or tribunal considers equitable having regard to all the circumstances, but that is subject to any rule imposing a stricter time limit in relation to the procedure in question – S.7(5). For example, applications for judicial review are subject to a three-month time limit – Rule 54.5 Civil Procedure Rules. The wording of S.7(5) for extending the time limit is very similar to that used in the equivalent provision in the EqA – S.123(1)(b) EqA allows tribunals to extend time where it is 'just and equitable' in the circumstances – and it seems that the approach taken in discrimination cases may inform courts and tribunals when exercising their discretion under S.7(5) – see, for example, the High Court's decision in A v Essex County Council 2007 EWHC 1652, QBD.

Where applicable, public authorities can defend a claim on the basis that they had no choice but to act in a way that was incompatible with the ECHR because of the effect of UK law. In such a case the only remedy open to a complainant would be a declaration of incompatibility from the High Court or Court of Appeal – see under 'Interpreting UK law in accordance with ECHR rights – declaration of incompatibility' above. It must be remembered, however, that employment tribunals and the EAT do not have the power to make such declarations.

3.15 *Victims.* As noted above, a public authority employee can only rely on ECHR rights directly in any legal proceedings if he or she is a victim of an unlawful act. S.7(7) HRA provides that the employee will be considered a 'victim' within the meaning of S.7, if he or she would be a victim for the purposes of Article 34 of the ECHR if proceedings were brought in the ECtHR in respect of the unlawful act. Article 34 states: 'The Court may receive applications from any person, non-governmental organisation or group of individuals claiming to be the victim of a violation by one of the High Contracting Parties of the rights set forth in the Convention or the Protocols thereto.' In addition, where a person relies on his or her ECHR rights in judicial review proceedings, that person must qualify as a victim – S.7(3) and (4).

The notion of who is a victim of an unlawful act is very wide and principles developed under ECHR case law on the meaning of 'victim' are directly relevant when considering whether a person has the right to bring a claim under the HRA. So, for instance:

- individual complainants do not need to show that their rights have actually been violated. It suffices that they run the risk of being directly affected by the measure of which complaint is made. For example, in Campbell and anor v United Kingdom 1982 4 EHRR 293, ECtHR, children attended a school where corporal punishment took place. These children were victims even though they had not yet been subjected to any punishment

- as a general rule, only those directly affected by an act or omission can claim to be a victim under the ECHR

- a claimant may also claim to be an indirect victim where the direct victim is unable to bring a complaint – for example, a close relative or spouse of an affected person

- a company may be the victim of a breach of its rights, but a shareholder can only claim to be a victim in exceptional circumstances – for example, where it is impossible for the company itself to make a complaint.

3.16 **Remedies.** In cases involving public authorities, S.8(1) HRA provides that tribunals and courts are able to grant the remedies and make orders within their powers as they consider 'just and appropriate'. The appropriate remedy will depend on the facts of the case and the powers of the court that is deciding the case. Relief such as damages, injunctions and declarations can be granted in cases involving public authorities.

Damages may be awarded only by a court that has power to do so in civil proceedings – S.8(2) HRA. No such award should be made unless, taking account of all the circumstances of the case, including any other relief or remedy granted, or order made, in relation to the act in question and the consequences of any decision in respect of that act, the court is satisfied that the award is necessary to afford 'just satisfaction' to the person in whose favour it is made – S.8(3). In deciding whether to award damages, or the amount that should be awarded, the court must take into account the principles applied by the ECtHR in relation to the award of compensation under Article 41 (which lays down the Court's duty, if necessary, to afford just satisfaction to the injured party) – S.8(4).

Interestingly, Article 13 of the ECHR – which gives an unqualified right to an **3.17** effective remedy in national courts for breaches of the Convention – has been omitted from the HRA's scope. However, S.2 requires courts and tribunals to take the case law of the European Court and Commission into account, including case law on Article 13, when determining questions that arise in connection with an ECHR right.

Individual petitions to ECtHR **3.18**

Finally, we should briefly mention that individuals retain the right to present a petition to the ECtHR directly where they believe that the UK has failed to respect their rights and freedoms set out in the ECHR. Prior to the introduction of the HRA, this was the only option for individuals to enforce their human rights, and it was a route that was cumbersome and expensive.

Article 34 provides that an individual who considers him or herself to be 'the victim of a violation by one of the [states bound by the ECHR] of the rights set forth in the Convention' may lodge an application directly with the Court. An application to the ECtHR can be lodged against the state and a public authority, but not against another individual or private institution.

In order for the application to be admissible, the following criteria must **3.19** be fulfilled:

- the applicant has exhausted all domestic remedies in the state concerned
- the application has been lodged within six months of the date of the final decision at domestic level
- the complaint is based on the ECHR; and
- the applicant has suffered a significant disadvantage.

Where the Court finds that a state has violated a right under the ECHR, it will deliver a judgment that is binding on the state concerned. If it finds against a state and observes that the applicant has sustained damages, it will award the applicant 'just satisfaction' – i.e. a sum of money by way of compensation for the damage.

3.20 As mentioned above, taking a case directly to Strasbourg is usually a slow and costly process. Nevertheless, where domestic avenues have been exhausted, presenting an individual petition to the ECtHR will be the last course of redress for a complainant. Currently, two sets of joined religious discrimination cases that were rejected by the UK courts are before the ECtHR. In Eweida v British Airways plc 2010 ICR 890, CA, and Chaplin v Royal Devon and Exeter NHS Trust Hospital ET Case No.1702886/09 the claimants were prevented from wearing a cross while at work, but their claims of indirect discrimination under the Employment Equality (Religion or Belief) Regulations 2003 SI 2003/1660 (now repealed and replaced by equivalent provisions in the EqA) failed domestically as they were unable to identify others with their beliefs who suffered particular disadvantage as a result of their employers' dress codes. Also separately before the ECtHR are the cases of Ladele v London Borough of Islington 2010 ICR 532, CA, and McFarlane v Relate Avon Ltd 2010 ICR 507, EAT, in which the claimants sought an exemption from having to provide services to same-sex couples. The domestic courts held that an employer's refusal to accommodate the manifestation of a discriminatory religious belief, in cases where discrimination in the provision of public services results, will generally be justified by reference to the legitimate aim of eliminating discrimination and advancing equality. The Equality and Human Rights Commission has intervened in both sets of proceedings. The cases, including details of the Commission's submissions before the ECtHR, are discussed in detail in Chapter 11, 'Religion or belief', under 'European Convention on Human Rights' and 'Manifestation of religion or belief – is UK approach compliant with Article 9?'.

Note that the procedure for petitioning the ECtHR is currently under review by the Council of Europe and, at the request of the UK Government, a group of experts in this country – see 'Proposals for reform – reform of the ECtHR' below. At European level, agreement was reached at a High Level Conference in Brighton in April 2012 to tighten the admissibility criteria for petitions to the Court. Measures agreed included reducing the time limit for claims from six months to four; rejecting any application raising an issue that has been duly considered by a domestic court having regard to Convention case law, unless it raises a 'serious question' of interpretation or application; and removing a restriction on the circumstances in which the Court may reject a claim where the applicant has not suffered a 'significant disadvantage'. The measures are envisaged to be in place by the end of 2013.

3.21 Human rights in discrimination context

Section 1 HRA incorporates most of the ECHR rights into domestic law. The most important in a discrimination context, set out in Schedule 1 to the Act, are the following:

- Article 8, which protects private and family life

- Article 9, which protects freedom of thought, conscience and religion

- Article 10, which protects freedom of expression

- Article 14, which provides that there shall be no discrimination in respect of the enjoyment of any Convention right.

Before considering each Article separately, it is worth making some general comments about the operation of these ECHR rights.

First, it is important to stress that the rights under Articles 8–10 are not **3.22** phrased in absolute terms and are subject to certain restrictions. For example, Article 8(1) guarantees an individual the right to respect for private and family life, home and correspondence but this is qualified by Article 8(2), which adds that public authorities must not interfere with the exercise of the right unless interference is in accordance with the law and necessary in a democratic society to protect a number of other interests, such as national security, the economic well-being of the country and the rights and freedoms of others. Accordingly, it is permissible for states and emanations of states (such as public authorities) to interfere with the rights guaranteed under Article 8(1) where this is in accordance with the law, is in pursuit of a legitimate aim and is necessary in a democratic society.

When considering restrictions on the exercise of an ECHR right, tribunals and courts will have regard to the principle of proportionality, which is concerned with finding a balance between the protection of the individual's rights and the interests of the community at large. A fair balance can only be achieved if the restriction adopted does not go beyond what is strictly necessary to achieve that purpose. So far as employers are concerned, if they adopt practices that are in breach of qualified ECHR rights, then they must ensure that the reasons given for denying those rights are substantiated in accordance with the wording of the Article. Otherwise, they risk either the court or tribunal finding direct liability for breach of the Convention (if the employer concerned is a public body) or, in the case of a private employer, interpreting the relevant domestic legal provision in accordance with S.3 HRA in a manner that establishes liability against the employer and secures the Convention rights of the claimant.

Secondly, it is worth noting at the outset that Article 14, which contains a **3.23** prohibition of discrimination on a number of grounds, does *not* provide a free-standing cause of action. Rather, the prohibition only applies in respect of the enjoyment of other ECHR rights. For example, an individual could claim that he or she has not enjoyed the same rights to freedom of expression under Article 10 as members of the opposite sex (for example, in relation to a dress code at work) as required by Article 14, but could not bring a claim directly under Article 14 in respect of less favourable treatment unrelated to another ECHR right. Some signatory states to the ECHR have adopted Protocol 12, which extends the broad prohibition on discrimination found in Article 14 to the

55

enjoyment of 'any right set forth by law' and the exercise of public authority. However, the United Kingdom has not signed up to the Protocol. For more details of this, see Chapter 13, 'Sexual orientation', under 'European Convention on Human Rights'.

Finally, it is important to recognise that the ECHR is a 'living instrument'. Accordingly, courts' and tribunals' interpretation of the rights is likely to change over time to reflect contemporary standards and democratic values.

3.24 Right to private and family life

Article 8(1) ECHR guarantees an individual the right to respect for private and family life, home and correspondence but this is qualified by Article 8(2), which adds that public authorities must not interfere with the exercise of the right unless interference is in accordance with the law and necessary in a democratic society to protect a number of other interests, such as national security, the economic well-being of the country, the protection of health or morals and the rights and freedoms of others.

This Article, which encompasses the right to privacy in relation to an individual's sexual orientation and gender identity, has been successfully invoked in a number of cases by homosexuals and transsexuals – particularly in the period prior to the United Kingdom introducing specific protections for these groups. For example, in Smith and anor v United Kingdom 1999 IRLR 734, ECtHR, the ECtHR held that where the British armed forces discharged four homosexuals on the ground of their sexuality because of the long-standing ban on homosexual service personnel, this amounted to a violation of the applicants' right to respect for private life under Article 8. The four applicants brought their claim under the ECHR after having sought a judicial review of the armed forces' decision to dismiss them as the only available form of redress in the domestic courts. Their application had been rejected by the High Court, a decision confirmed by the Court of Appeal. And in Goodwin v United Kingdom 2002 IRLR 664, ECtHR, the ECtHR held that the failure of UK law to recognise a post-operative transsexual person's new gender was incompatible with, among other things, the right to respect for private and family life in Article 8.

3.25 Case law under Article 8 that is relevant in a discrimination context is discussed in Chapter 7, 'Gender reassignment', under 'Protection under antecedent legislation' and Chapter 13, 'Sexual orientation', in the sections on 'European Convention on Human Rights' and 'Protection under the Equality Act' under 'Sexual practices and behaviour – approach under the ECHR'.

3.26 Right to freedom of religion

Under Article 9 ECHR, individuals have the right to freedom of thought, conscience and religion, which includes the freedom to manifest one's religion or belief, in worship, teaching, practice and observance. While the right to hold a religion or a belief is absolute, the right to manifest them is subject to limitations that are 'necessary in a democratic society in the interests of public safety, for the protection of public order, health or morals, or for the protection of the rights and freedoms of others'. The importance of Article 9 is underlined by S.13 HRA, which provides that where a court or tribunal determines any question under the Act that may affect the exercise by a religious organisation of the right under Article 9 to freedom of thought, conscience or religion, it must have particular regard to the importance of that right.

UK courts and tribunals have applied Article 9 restrictively and are generally reluctant to find that an employer has interfered with the right to manifest religious beliefs, especially when it conflicts with other protected rights. Many cases have been rejected by the courts on the basis that the individual concerned is free to practise their religion outside the workplace, with the result that Article 9 is not engaged.

3.27 In the well-publicised case of Eweida v British Airways plc 2010 ICR 890, CA, the Court of Appeal held that an employer's 'no visible jewellery' policy, which prevented a devout practising Christian employee from displaying a cross on a necklace while at work, had not suffered indirect discrimination under the Employment Equality (Religion or Belief) Regulations 2003 SI 2003/1660 (since repealed and re-enacted in the EqA). The Court also rejected the claimant's argument that Article 9 was relevant to her case. Referring to the decision of the ECtHR in Kalac v Turkey 1999 27 EHRR 552, ECtHR, it observed that Article 9 does not protect every act motivated or inspired by religion or belief. Furthermore, an individual's specific circumstances may have to be taken into account, with the result that, where a person has accepted a role that does not accommodate that right and there are other ways in which he or she can practise or observe his or her religion, it is unlikely that there will have been an interference with Article 9.

Similarly, in Ladele v London Borough of Islington 2010 ICR 532, CA, L, a registrar, refused to conduct civil partnership services because of her Christian belief that same-sex unions were contrary to God's law. The Court of Appeal agreed with the EAT's decision that the Council did not discriminate against her on the ground of religion when it threatened her with dismissal for refusing to carry out the services. Nor did the Court think that the claimant's claims would be assisted by relying on the right to manifest one's religion under Article 9. It noted that the ECtHR case law supported the conclusion that the claimant's proper and genuine desire to have her religious views relating to marriage respected should not override the Council's concern to ensure that all its registrars manifest equal respect for both the homosexual and the heterosexual communities. In support of this, the Court cited the ruling in Pichon and Sajous v France (Application No.49853/99), ECtHR – a case in which pharmacists refused to sell contraceptives for religious reasons. The ECtHR held that Article

9 did not protect the claimants as they could 'manifest [their] beliefs in many ways outside the professional sphere'. (Note that the Ladele and Eweida cases have now progressed to the ECtHR and a ruling in these joined cases is awaited with great interest – see 'Human Rights Act 1998 – individual petitions to ECtHR' above.)

3.28 Even where Article 9 is engaged, interference in a person's right to manifest their religion or belief is potentially justifiable in accordance with Article 9(2). The ECtHR has consistently confirmed that states have a wide margin of appreciation when it comes to limiting the right to manifest religion or beliefs in the public, as opposed to the private, sphere. In this regard, the Court almost invariably concludes that such restrictions pursue one or more of the permissible interests set out in Article 9(2) and that the interference with ECHR rights is a proportionate means of achieving the relevant interest(s).

The significance of Article 9 jurisprudence regarding the protected characteristic of religion or belief under the EqA is discussed in detail in Chapter 11, 'Religion or belief', in the sections on 'European Convention on Human Rights' and 'Manifestation of religion or belief'.

3.29 Right to freedom of expression
Article 10(1) ECHR provides that everyone has the right to freedom of expression, including the freedom to hold opinions and to receive and impart information and ideas without interference by a public authority. The right is in many ways more qualified than any other right in the ECHR, in that it is provided that, 'since it carries with it duties and responsibilities, [the right] may be subject to such formalities, conditions, restrictions or penalties as are prescribed by law and are necessary in a democratic society, in the interests of national security, territorial integrity or public safety, for the prevention of disorder or crime, for the protection of health or morals, for the protection of the reputation or rights of others, for preventing the disclosure of information received in confidence, or for maintaining the authority and impartiality of the judiciary' – Article 10(2).

The ECtHR has held that the right to freedom of expression may include the right of an individual to express his or her ideas by means of the way he or she dresses. Accordingly, dress codes that differentiate on the basis of, say, the sex of the employee, such as those that require men to have short hair or that prohibit women from wearing trousers, may be subject to claims under Article 10 together with Article 14. However, by virtue of Article 10(2), an employer may argue that the restriction is justified for the protection of the reputation or rights of others; the 'reputation or rights of others' would include those of the employer. The employer would also need to establish that the restriction was prescribed by law and was necessary in a democratic society.

In Moran v RBR International Ltd ET Case No.2302546/00 an employment **3.30** tribunal had to assess whether Articles 10 and 14 were engaged when applying the Sex Discrimination Act 1975 (now repealed and re-enacted in the EqA). It found that the employer, by prohibiting a female worker from wearing trousers, had unduly interfered with her freedom of expression under Article 10. Since the employer's approach mirrored conventional differences between the sexes rather than any commercial need for the dress code, this was also a breach of Article 14.

The right to freedom of expression under Article 10 is often relied on in conjunction with the right to private and family life under Article 8 – see, for example, Kara v United Kingdom 1999 27 EHRR 272, ECtHR (a dress code case involving a male transvestite).

Prohibition of discrimination
3.31

Article 14 ECHR provides that the enjoyment of the rights and freedoms set out in the Convention 'shall be secured without discrimination on any ground such as sex, race, colour, language, religion, political or other opinion, national or social origin, association with a national minority, property, birth or other status'.

As mentioned above, the important thing to note about Article 14 is that it is parasitic upon the exercise of another ECHR right: it is not a free-standing right not to be discriminated against. So, in order to challenge a workplace-based practice on the ground of discrimination under the ECHR, it is first necessary to show that the discrimination was in relation to an act which fell within the scope of one of the other ECHR rights. It is not necessary for there to be a breach of another Article, merely that the circumstances fall within the ambit of that Article.

It should also be noted that the list of characteristics in Article 14 is only a **3.32** starting point, not an exhaustive list. So, for example, 'other status' has been held to include sexual orientation, marital status, professional status and disability. However, it should also be borne in mind that there is only unlawful discrimination if there was 'no reasonable and objective justification' for that discrimination. In determining this, the court or tribunal would consider the aim and effect of the measure and whether the means adopted were proportionate to the aim sought.

For example, if an employer was carrying out a redundancy selection exercise and, as part of the exercise, all over-55s were required to undergo a medical examination, this act – which falls within the ambit of the right to privacy under Article 8 – would amount to unlawful discrimination on the ground of age unless the employer could demonstrate that there was a justifiable purpose behind the discrimination. If, however, all over-55s were required to undertake a written test, the alleged discrimination would not fall within the ambit of any ECHR right.

59

3.33 Proposals for reform

Prior to the 2010 General Election, the Conservative Party was highly critical of the HRA's impact in the domestic courts and the influence of case law emanating from the ECtHR in Strasbourg – particularly berating (non-employment) decisions such as the Supreme Court's ruling that the right to a private life under Article 8 required sex offenders to be given the right to appeal against their inclusion on the sex offenders list (R (on the application of F (by his litigation friend F)) and anor v Secretary of State for the Home Department 2011 1 AC 331, SC), and also the ECtHR's decision that the United Kingdom's blanket ban on convicted prisoners voting contravenes the right to regular, free and fair elections under Article 3 of Protocol 1 to the ECHR (Hirst v United Kingdom 2006 42 EHRR 41, ECtHR). Its election manifesto specifically contained a commitment to abolish the HRA and replace it with a UK Bill of Rights that would 'encourage greater social responsibility' among individuals. However, it seems unlikely that the Conservatives, who formed a Coalition Government with the Liberal Democrats in May 2010, would take the radical step of withdrawing from the ECHR completely, especially given the coalition agreement that a British Bill of Rights would 'incorporate and build on' the ECHR, which would continue to be enshrined in British law. Nevertheless, precisely what a proposed Bill of Rights might entail, and how it would differ from the HRA, remains unclear.

On 18 March 2011, the Coalition Government established a Commission to advise on the creation of a UK Bill of Rights and reform of the ECtHR. The Commission is not due to report on its conclusions until the end of 2012, which means it may be a while before the future of human rights in the United Kingdom is settled.

3.34 UK Bill of Rights

On 5 August 2011, the Commission on a Bill of Rights launched a public consultation on the need for such a Bill in the United Kingdom. The consultation document ('Do we need a UK Bill of Rights?', August 2011) provides a useful summary of current rights and protections under the HRA. However, it does not provide any information about what a Bill of Rights might involve or how such instruments work in other countries. The consultation closed on 11 November 2011.

3.35 Reform of the ECtHR

Another area in which the Commission has been asked to make recommendations is the role of the ECtHR. The Court, which was set up in 1959, has been struggling with a voluminous and ever-growing case-load that has put an unprecedented strain on its resources and its ability to provide effective legal redress to individuals whose ECHR rights have been violated. In 2011, the

ECtHR's backlog of cases stood at over 150,000, increasing at a rate of 20,000 each year. The need for reform of the Court has been recognised by the Council of Europe, which began looking into potential areas of change in 2010 to ensure that the Court continues to be able to fulfil its role as final arbiter of human rights.

In July 2011 the Commission published its interim advice on reform of the EctHR, in which it emphasised that the Court should be a court of last resort – not a first port of call for all human rights issues. Primary responsibility for securing ECHR rights and providing effective remedies for violations lies with the states and their national (legislative, executive and judicial) institutions. The ECtHR, in its view, should only be called upon to address a limited number of cases that raise serious questions affecting the interpretation or application of the ECHR and serious issues of general importance.

Accordingly, the Commission made the following initial recommendations to **3.36** restore the natural equilibrium between states' responsibilities under the ECHR and the role of the Court: first, to reduce very significantly the number of cases that reach the Court by introducing new screening mechanisms; secondly, to reconsider the relief that the Court is able to offer by way of 'just satisfaction' under Article 41; and thirdly, to enhance procedures for the selection of well-qualified judges of the Court. The Commission will explore these and other areas of reform, together with the modalities for achieving necessary reforms, and it is expected to be engaged in this work throughout the entirety of 2012.

Note that at a High Level Conference in Brighton in April 2012, which was initiated by the United Kingdom Government, agreement was reached between the State parties to the European Convention to tighten the admissibility criteria for petitions to the Court. Measures agreed included reducing the time limit for claims from six months to four; rejecting any application raising an issue that has been duly considered by a domestic court having regard to Convention case law, unless it raises a 'serious question' of interpretation or application; and removing a restriction on the circumstances in which the Court may reject a claim where the applicant has not suffered a 'significant disadvantage'. No doubt these measures, which are envisaged to be in place by the end of 2013, will inform the Commission's work.

Part 2

Protected characteristics

4 Characteristics covered by the Equality Act

Concept of 'protected characteristics'

Characteristics not covered by the Equality Act

Anti-discrimination law in the United Kingdom only applies to discrimination **4.1** on specific grounds set down by statute. It does not give individuals a general right not to be discriminated against for any reason. These grounds or 'strands' of discrimination, which were originally found in a myriad of different anti-discrimination statutes and statutory instruments, are now contained in S.4 of the Equality Act 2010 (EqA), which refers to them as 'protected characteristics'. It is by reference to these characteristics that the various forms of unlawful discrimination – 'direct', 'indirect', 'harassment' and 'victimisation' (now collectively termed 'prohibited conduct' under the EqA) – must be made out.

Listed alphabetically, the protected characteristics are:

- age
- disability
- gender reassignment
- marriage and civil partnership
- pregnancy and maternity
- race
- religion or belief
- sex (i.e. gender)
- sexual orientation.

These nine characteristics are exactly the same as those that were protected by **4.2** the anti-discrimination legislation in place prior to the coming into force of the EqA on 1 October 2010. As discussed under 'Characteristics not covered by the Equality Act' below, the Government rejected calls made during consultation on the Equality Bill for other characteristics or grounds of discrimination, such as genetic predisposition, to be added to the list.

Sections 5–12 EqA set out explicitly what is meant by each of the characteristics (except pregnancy and maternity, dealt with separately in S.18). On the whole, these definitions replicate those that applied under the antecedent legislation, albeit that in every case the relevant characteristic was previously expressed as

65

a 'ground' of discrimination. In some instances, however, the Government took the opportunity presented by the EqA to modify the relevant definition and thus alter the scope or 'reach' of the ground of discrimination in question. This applies in particular to disability, gender reassignment and race (for further details, see Chapters 6, 7 and 10 respectively).

4.3 Concept of 'protected characteristics'

After more than three decades during which the term 'grounds of discrimination' was consistently used in both UK anti-discrimination legislation and the various EU Directives, that term has been abandoned under the EqA in favour of 'protected characteristics'. The reasons for the change were never fully explained by the Labour Government during the debates on the Equality Bill or in the various public consultation papers. Even so, it remains fruitful to consider what might lie behind the change and, in particular, what is denoted by the word 'characteristics', as this can offer insights into the choices made as a matter of policy when deciding what types of discrimination should and should not be covered by the EqA.

4.4 Origin of the term 'protected characteristics'

The phrase 'protected characteristics' originally derives from decisions of courts in the United States interpreting various constitutional and federal codes incorporating a right to equal treatment. So, for example, in Willingham v Macon Telegraph Publishing Co 1975 USCA5 242, the United States Court of Appeals (Fifth Circuit) was required to decide whether S.703(a) of the Civil Rights Act 1964 made it unlawful for an employer to refuse to recruit a man on account of his having long hair. The Court (by a majority) rejected the plaintiff's claim on the basis that S.703(a) did not cover grooming rules, even if based upon stereotypical gender assumptions. In so holding, the Court observed: '[D]istinctions in employment practices between men and women on the basis of something other than immutable or protected characteristics do not inhibit employment opportunity in violation of S.703(a). Congress sought only to give all persons equal access to the job market, not to limit an employer's right to exercise his informed judgement as to how best to run his shop.' Equality jurisprudence in the United States has no doubt moved on since then, but it is notable for our purposes how this early explanation of the conceptual understanding of the phrase 'protected characteristics' implies that 'characteristics' are worthy of protection against discrimination inasmuch as they are 'immutable' features of a human being's identity, whereas transmutable features are not.

A similar approach was adopted in the seminal case of In the Matter of Acosta 19 I&N Dec. 211 (USBIA 1 Mar 1985) – a decision of the US Board of Immigration Appeals (BIA). This involved consideration of the plaintiff's application for refugee status in the context of US and international law under which a person is to be regarded as being a refugee if he or she has a well-founded fear of persecution on account of, inter alia, his or her 'membership of a particular social group'. The BIA applied the doctrine of *ejusdem generis* ('of the same kind') to construe the meaning of the phrase 'particular social group' in a manner consistent with the other grounds on which asylum can be claimed, i.e. sex, race, religion, nationality and political opinion. The BIA noted that 'each of these grounds describes persecution aimed at an immutable characteristic: a characteristic that either is beyond the power of an individual to change or is so fundamental to individual identity or conscience that it ought not be required to be changed'.

The influence of the Acosta decision has been so great that virtually all other **4.5** common law jurisdictions, including Canada, Australia, New Zealand and the United Kingdom, now adopt the same *ejusdem generis* approach to defining and refining the protected categories that comprise membership of 'particular social groups' for the purposes of international immigration law. In 2007, for example, the House of Lords in K v Secretary of State for Home Department 2007 AC 412, HL, ruled that a 15-year-old girl from Sierra Leone was entitled to asylum on account of her fear that as a member of a particular social group (namely young Sierra Leonean women) she would be subjected to genital mutilation if she were forced to return to her country of origin. Their Lordships unanimously held that a 'particular social group' within the meaning of Article 1A(2) of the 1951 Convention Relating to the Status of Refugees should be defined as a group of persons who shared a common characteristic, other than their risk of persecution, which distinguished the group from the remainder of the society of which they were part. The common characteristic in question had to be one that was innate and immutable, or so closely linked to identity, conscience or the exercise of a person's human rights that he or she should not be required to change it. This approach was termed by Baroness Hale in the K v Secretary of State case as 'the protected characteristics approach'.

'Immutability' and 'homogenous identity'   **4.6**
The term 'protected characteristics' had begun to be used in some employment law cases prior to the publication of the Equality Bill – see, for example, Saini v All Saints Haque Centre 2009 IRLR 74, EAT. Obviously, this new terminology resonated with the Government when it came to drafting the Bill and it is interesting that the same notion of 'immutability' or 'innateness' that underlies the decisions in the US jurisprudence (discussed under 'Origin of the term "protected characteristics"' above) was also significant when it came to deciding which characteristics should and should not receive protection. So, for example, the Government's rationale for rejecting calls to add caring responsibilities to the list of protected characteristics was that: 'The role of carer applies more to what a person does, than to what a person is (their innate or chosen

67

characteristics). A person may be in a caring role for only a very short period, or for a substantially extended period – but it is unlikely to be an unchanging situation. Furthermore, there may be large numbers of persons who do not identify themselves as "carers", even though they take care of another person from time to time. As such, being a carer is less appropriate as a separate specifically protected characteristic than the existing strands of race, age, disability, gender, etc' – 'The Equality Bill: Government Response to Consultation' (Cm 7454), paras 15.11–15.12.

We can deduce from this that there are two basic criteria for qualification as a 'protected characteristic': (i) immutability – i.e. the characteristic has to reflect something innate about the person which is not susceptible to whim or change; and (ii) homogenous identity – i.e. the characteristic should confer some sense of a shared identity or experience among those who possess the characteristic in question. Judged according to these criteria, it is easy to see why age, marital status, race, sexual orientation and sex (including matters associated with gender such as pregnancy and gender reorientation) comprise 'protected characteristics'. However, it is less clear why religion or belief and disability qualify.

4.7 **Special features of religion or belief and disability.** The two characteristics that, arguably, do not fulfil the criteria for qualification as a 'protected characteristic' outlined above are religion or belief and disability. Regarding the former, many argue that there is a fundamental difference between religious identity and innate characteristics such as ethnicity, gender and sexual orientation, in that it is self-chosen and self-assumed. While one can leave a religion or cease to hold a belief, one cannot abandon one's ethnicity or, in the vast majority of cases, one's gender or (although this is disputed in some quarters) sexual orientation. Therefore, the argument goes, these characteristics should be protected, whereas religion or belief, which is in essence a lifestyle choice, should not.

Critics of this position, however, contend that it takes a far too simplistic approach to the question of choice and to the relationship between personal identity and beliefs. From the perspective of a devout adherent, religion centres on the notion that one is called to that set of beliefs and particular way of life by God, often following a period of inner struggle. Furthermore, when religion is viewed as part of the life of a community within which the adherent lives, the consequences of ceasing to be an active member of that community can be too onerous for many adherents to contemplate. On this view, religion is not simply a matter of lifestyle choice but involves a deep attachment to a set of values that govern a person's life, the key choices they make and the way they interact with others. On this basis, adherents will argue that their religious identity, while different from their gender, ethnic and sexual identity, is still a basic form of identity that should be respected and protected in the same way.

Given that, in drafting the EqA, the Government chose to express religion or **4.8** belief as a 'protected characteristic', it can be assumed that it favoured the view that religion or belief is something innate to a person's identity in the psychological, social and cultural senses explained above (even if that characteristic is not entirely immutable). This is presumably one reason why this ground of discrimination is covered in the EqA in similar terms to the other protected characteristics. Another more pragmatic reason may be that the United Kingdom was in any event obliged to protect against religion or belief discrimination under the EU Equal Treatment Framework Directive.

Turning to disability as a protected characteristic, few would dispute that disabled people deserve protection. However, it could be argued that people with disabilities simply do not form a homogenous group in the same way as those possessing other protected characteristics such as age, race, gender or religious belief. This is partly because there are many different forms and degrees of disability and partly because medical intervention or aids can often diminish the adverse effect of a disability, sometimes to the point of making its outward signs virtually invisible. As a result, it is much less likely that the fact that a person suffers from a disability gives rise to a common and shared experience.

The implications of this difference reveal themselves most sharply when it **4.9** comes to seeking to prove indirect discrimination. Prior to the EqA, there was no provision in the Disability Discrimination Act 1995 covering indirect disability discrimination. However, in the interests of consistency, the Government decided to extend the standard definition of indirect discrimination to disability along with all the other protected characteristics (save pregnancy and maternity) – see S.19 EqA. Yet it is generally accepted that it will be much more difficult for disabled persons to make out indirect discrimination in view of the individual nature of disability. Those with other protected characteristics can usually establish indirect discrimination by pointing to evidence that the general application of a 'provision, criterion or practice' (PCP) has an adverse impact on other persons who share the same characteristic. Identifying the disadvantaged group is not usually a problem. In contrast, the lack of homogeneity among those who are disabled makes identifying a particular group that is disadvantaged by the PCP in the same manner and to the same extent as the complainant much more difficult.

These logistical difficulties are to a large extent offset by special provisions in the EqA dealing specifically with disability, including the imposition of a duty on employers (and others) to make reasonable adjustments where a PCP puts a disabled person at a substantial disadvantage in comparison with persons who are not disabled. However, the very fact that special measures are necessary testifies to the differences between disability and the other protected characteristics.

4.10 ## Characteristics not covered by the Equality Act

As already mentioned, anti-discrimination law in the United Kingdom only applies to discrimination on specific grounds set down by the EqA. It does not give individuals a general right not to be discriminated against for any reason. The same is true under the EU equality Directives. In contrast, the European Convention on Human Rights (ECHR) takes an inclusive approach that does not limit protection to a number of specified grounds. The relevant article, Article 14, provides that: 'The enjoyment of rights and freedoms set forth in this Convention shall be secured without discrimination *on any ground such as* sex, race, colour, language, religion, political or other opinion, national or social origin, association with a national minority, property, birth or other status' (our stress).

Restricting protection to a limited number of defined grounds or characteristics has two significant consequences. First, it means that any person suffering discrimination on any ground other than one of the nine covered by the EqA will not be protected. Secondly, the 'atomised' approach makes it far more difficult to guarantee protection where the reason for the discriminatory treatment is, in reality, an admix of two or more protected characteristics. For example, a pregnant lesbian who believes she has been discriminated against may find it difficult to pin the reason for the unequal treatment down to a single protected characteristic (pregnancy or sexual orientation), as the reason may in reality be the combination of the two. This concern was addressed by the previous Labour government via the insertion into the EqA of a specific provision covering combined discrimination (S.14). However, this provision has not been brought into force and the current Coalition Government has made it clear that it has no intention of ever bringing it into force. The issues of combined discrimination and how the problem of proving discrimination can be tackled where two or more protected characteristics may be involved are discussed in detail in Chapter 15, 'Direct discrimination', under 'Combined discrimination'.

During the public consultation on the Equality Bill, the Government considered but rejected calls for new grounds of discrimination to be included in the Bill. These grounds are outlined below.

4.11 ### Caring responsibilities

As already mentioned under 'Concept of "protected characteristics"' above, the Government specifically rejected calls for caring responsibilities to be added to the protected grounds covered by the EqA. The reasons for this were outlined as part of the earlier discussion.

Genetic predisposition 4.12

The Government decided not to extend specific protection on the ground of 'genetic predisposition' – i.e. less favourable treatment suffered by individuals based on genetic testing that reveals them to be more likely to develop serious health issues. Although the Government acknowledged that there was some genuine concern that employers and insurers may discriminate on this basis, it concluded that there was little reliable evidence of this at present and therefore that there was no pressing need to legislate in this area. Sufficient protection was in any event provided by the Data Protection Act 1998 in respect of the processing of personal and sensitive data, and, in the context of goods and services, by a concordat agreed between the Government and the insurance industry imposing a moratorium until at least 2014 on insurers' use of predictive genetic test results.

Language 4.13

Some respondents to the public consultation on the Equality Bill suggested that language should be included as a protected characteristic. The most vociferous was the Welsh Language Board, which sought protection specifically for Welsh language speakers. The Board contended that it had found evidence of firms preventing Welsh-speaking staff from communicating with each other in Welsh and, while conceding that there was no clear evidence of direct discrimination, sought protection against indirect discrimination for Welsh speakers in Wales. The Government, however, categorically rejected the case for an extension of the protected grounds to cover language in general, or Welsh language speakers in particular. Its reasons, as set out in 'The Equality Bill – Government response to the Consultation', July 2008 (Cm 7454), were that: 'There would be significant policy implications in introducing language generally as an additional protected ground because this would raise questions about the equivalence or otherwise of many languages spoken in this country. There would also be significant practical implications, given the number of different languages used... Nor does it seem appropriate to legislate in the discrimination field generally to protect Welsh speakers... It is more appropriate that duties relating to the use of the Welsh language in the provision of public services should continue to be provided through the Welsh Language Act 1993 or equivalent legislation' (para 15.33).

Parental status 4.14

The Government resisted calls for parental status to be included as a protected characteristic in addition to pregnancy and maternity on the ground that it had already done enough in this direction by extending the right to request flexible working to those responsible for children up to the age of 16 – 'The Equality Bill: Government response to the Consultation', July 2008 (Cm 7454), para 15.10. Parents (including adoptive parents) taking statutory paternity or parental leave are also protected against detrimental treatment under S.47C of

71

the Employment Rights Act 1996 (combined with Reg 19 of the Maternity and Parental Leave etc Regulations 1999 SI 1999/3312, Reg 28 of the Paternity and Adoption Leave Regulations 2002 SI 2002/2788 or Reg 33 of the Additional Paternity Leave Regulations 2010 SI 2010/1055). These provisions are discussed in detail in IDS Employment Law Handbook, 'Maternity and Parental Rights' (2009), Chapters 6, 7 and 9.

4.15 Caste

The one suggested new ground of discrimination that did make some headway with the Government during the passage of the Equality Bill was caste discrimination. The term 'caste' is defined in the Explanatory Notes accompanying the EqA as denoting 'a hereditary, endogamous (marrying within the group) community associated with a traditional occupation and ranked accordingly on a perceived scale of ritual purity. It is generally (but not exclusively) associated with South Asia, particularly India, and its diaspora. It can encompass the four classes (*varnas*) of Hindu tradition (the Brahmin, Kshatriya, Vaishya and Shudra communities); the thousands of regional Hindu, Sikh, Christian, Muslim or other religious groups known as *jatis*; and groups amongst South Asian Muslims called *biradaris*. Some jatis regarded as below the varna hierarchy (once termed "untouchable") are known as *Dalit*.'

Initially, in its formal response to the consultation, the Government rejected the case for including caste as an additional and separate ground of protection on the basis that: (i) there was little evidence of such discrimination in the United Kingdom, at least in respect of the fields covered by the EqA (i.e. employment, vocational training, education and the provision of goods, facilities and services); and (ii) in so far as there was anecdotal evidence that caste discrimination sometimes affected individual decision-making (such as choice as to whom to marry), this was not an appropriate matter for protection under discrimination law. However, during the Report Stage of the Bill, the Government suddenly and unexpectedly accepted an amendment moved by the Liberal Democrat Lord Avebury to include a power to make caste discrimination an aspect of race discrimination – a power that is now contained in S.9(5) and (6) EqA. During the debate at the Committee Stage, it was noted that the Equality and Human Rights Commission, among others, thought that the called-for power was unnecessary as there was a good case to be made that race discrimination already covered caste. However, Lord Avebury argued that in the absence of any specific mention of caste in domestic law, it would be a 'chancy and expensive business' for anyone to test this in the courts.

4.16 In acceding to the amendment, the Solicitor General gave a commitment to keep the matter of whether to activate the power conferred in S.9 EqA under review. To this end, the Government commissioned the National Institute of Economic and Social Research (NIESR) to produce a report on the extent to which caste discrimination is a real problem. That report, entitled 'Caste discrimination and harassment in Great Britain', was published in December 2010 and concluded that the EqA's current provisions dealing with race and religion or belief are not as effective in tackling such discrimination as specific caste-discrimination protections would be. In the specific context of work, the authors of the Report found evidence of cases of bullying, menial task allocation, exclusion from work social events and networks, and humiliating behaviour based on perceptions of relative superiority and inferiority taking place. Such behaviour was evidenced in a case where women from 'upper' castes refused to take water from the same tap as that used by 'lower' caste colleagues. In another case, a man reported that he and other similarly 'low' caste colleagues were treated by *Jatt* line managers (a specific occupational caste comprising agricultural workers from the Punjab) less favourably in terms of matters such as approving requests than Sikh employees who were of a 'higher' caste. That said, the same man acknowledged that sometimes the line managers treated people of their own caste badly. Even some white and black employees had problems. The Report states that this shows how difficult it can be to ascertain whether bullying and harassment, when widespread across a company, is linked to caste or not. However, where problematic behaviour is experienced more frequently by those of low caste, the authors suggest that this could indicate a caste element.

In other respects, instances of caste discrimination were found to be very rare – particularly in the contexts of recruitment and promotion. There was some suggestion from the case studies analysed by the authors that nepotism influenced by caste considerations may have played a part in some promotion decisions. As the Report makes clear, 'Under British law, nepotism is not in itself unlawful, so long as it does not particularly disadvantage people with a protected characteristic... [I]f caste discrimination were unlawful, nepotism would seem likely to result in potentially unlawful indirect discrimination, unless the recruitment policy could be justified' (NIESR Report, Ch 6, para 6.3).

The Coalition Government has yet to decide whether, in the light of the NIESR **4.17** Report and other representations, to make the necessary amendments to the definition of race discrimination in S.9 EqA so as to fold caste discrimination into this protected ground. A decision on this was originally expected in 2011 but it is possible that the Government is awaiting the outcome of what appears to be the first ever case alleging caste discrimination brought before an employment tribunal. That case, involving two former lawyers employed by the Coventry-based law firm Heer Makek, centres on an allegation by the claimants that they were treated less favourably because of their inter-caste marriage. This case – which has received widespread press attention – is of interest because the allegation of caste discrimination appears to be being made on the basis that such discrimination is already caught by the existing protections against race and/or religion or belief discrimination.

4.18 **Other suggested grounds**

During the passage of the Equality Bill through Parliament, the Government declined to add a number of other grounds to the list of protected characteristics. 'Paternity' was rejected on the basis that the Government had no evidence that fathers were discriminated against by employers. Explaining this during a House of Commons Committee debate, the Solicitor General observed: 'As my colleague put it to me last night, what the lads usually do is take a new father out for a drink; they do not start to discriminate against him. We have not found any evidence to suggest a new strand that needs protecting.'

Another rejected ground was 'socio-economic disadvantage'. Although the Government at the time declined to frame this as a protected characteristic, it acceded to a late amendment to the Bill that resulted in a clause being added which, if enacted, would impose a duty on public authorities to seek to reduce socio-economic disadvantage. In particular, the duty would require relevant public authorities 'when making decisions of a strategic nature about how to exercise its functions... to have due regard to the desirability of exercising them in a way that is designed to reduce the inequalities of outcome which result in socio-economic disadvantage' – S.1(1) EqA. However, the Coalition Government has made it clear that it has no intention of implementing this provision.

5 Age

The EU Equal Treatment Framework Directive (No.2000/78) (the 'Equal **5.1** Treatment Framework Directive'), which was passed on 27 November 2000, requires Member States to enact legislation to prohibit various forms of discrimination, including discrimination on the ground of age. Whereas the deadline for implementation of most of the grounds of discrimination covered by the Directive (i.e. disability, religion or belief and sexual orientation) was 2 December 2003, in the case of age discrimination Member States were given an option to delay implementation for an additional three years. The United Kingdom took full advantage of this concession with the result that the Employment Equality (Age) Regulations 2006 SI 2006/1031 (the 2006 Age Regulations) and the Employment Equality (Age) Regulations (Northern Ireland) 2006 SI 2006/261 did not come into force until 1 October 2006.

Prior to the enactment of the 2006 Age Regulations, several attempts had been made to bring aspects of age discrimination within the parameters of existing *sex* discrimination legislation, none of which met with much success. These included proceedings for judicial review of provisions contained in the Employment Rights Act 1996, which, at that time, excluded employees aged over 65 from claiming unfair dismissal and redundancy payments – see Secretary of State for Trade and Industry v Rutherford and anor (No.2) 2006 ICR 785, HL. The House of Lords, rejecting the argument that the statutory exclusion had a disproportionate effect on men and was therefore indirectly discriminatory, ruled that the indirectly discriminatory effect of the age provisions was objectively justified. A further case involved a sex discrimination claim brought against an airline challenging its retirement policy of permitting cabin crew employed prior to 1971 to retire at 60, whereas those employed after 1971 were required to retire at 55. The female claimants alleged that this was indirectly discriminatory because more men than women had the longevity of service necessary for the later retirement option, but the EAT ruled that the discriminatory effect was justified for legitimate business reasons, which included the cost to the employer of changing the terms and conditions on retirement so as to remove the discrimination in question – see Cross and ors v British Airways plc 2005 IRLR 423, EAT. (Note that this aspect of the EAT's decision was not considered when the case was unsuccessfully appealed to the Court of Appeal – see Cross and anor v British Airways plc 2006 ICR 1239, CA.)

5.2 Notwithstanding these failed attempts to import protection against age discrimination into UK law through the back door, it is nonetheless arguable that, on the basis of recent decisions of the European Court of Justice, age discrimination was in effect already rendered unlawful under European law even prior to the coming into force of the Equal Treatment Framework Directive. For a full consideration of this point, see under 'Protection under European law' below.

5.3 **Equality Act 2010.** With effect from 1 October 2010, most of the provisions of the 2006 Age Regulations were repealed and substituted by equivalent provisions in the Equality Act 2010 (EqA). However, for a while, Schedule 6 to the 2006 Age Regulations – which set out a statutory retirement procedure that employers needed to comply with in order to lawfully require employees to retire at 65 – continued to operate. This procedure, along with the default retirement age of 65 established by the 2006 Regulations, has now been abolished save in respect of certain transitional arrangements. For full details of what is now termed the 'protected characteristic of age' under the EqA, see 'Protection under the Equality Act' below.

5.4 Protection under European law

Although complex, the inter-relationship between EU Treaty Articles, EU Directives and UK legislation has long formed part of our settled understanding of constitutional law. (For full details, see Chapter 2, 'European discrimination law'.) However, a recent line of age discrimination cases in the ECJ has threatened to disrupt this settled understanding by suggesting that the prohibition against age discrimination is, in fact, a general principle of EU law to which the Equal Treatment Framework Directive merely gives expression. This is surprising given the orthodox view that it was the Directive and the Directive alone that first introduced protection against age discrimination (along with protection against disability, religion or belief, and sexual orientation discrimination) into European law.

In Mangold v Helm 2006 IRLR 143, ECJ, the European Court held that the prohibition on age discrimination did not just emanate from the Equal Treatment Framework Directive, but was rather a 'general principle of community law' to which the Directive merely gives expression. In that case, the ECJ applied this general principle to require the disapplication of a discriminatory German statutory provision that had been enacted *after* the Directive was published but *before* the deadline for its transposition had passed. In reaching its decision, the Court reasoned: 'Directive 2000/78 does not itself lay down the principle of equal treatment in the field of employment and occupation. Indeed, in accordance with Article 1 thereof, the sole purpose of the Directive is "to lay down a general framework for combating discrimination on the grounds of religion or belief, disability, age or sexual orientation", the source of the actual principle underlying the prohibition of those forms of discrimination being found, as is clear from the third and fourth recitals in the preamble to the Directive, in various international instruments and in the constitutional traditions common to the Member States. The principle of non-discrimination on grounds of age must thus be regarded as a general principle of Community law... [O]bservance of the general principle of equal treatment, in particular in respect of age, cannot as such be conditional upon the expiry of the period allowed the Member States for the transposition of a Directive intended to lay down a general framework for combating discrimination on the grounds of age... In those circumstances it is the responsibility of the national court, hearing a dispute involving the principle of non-discrimination in respect of age, to provide, in a case within its jurisdiction, the legal protection which individuals derive from the rules of Community law and to ensure that those rules are fully effective, setting aside any provision of national law which may conflict with that law.'

The precise implications of this ruling are open to debate, but the Court's **5.5** decision can certainly be read as disturbing the long-established principle that the rights derived from a Directive have vertical but not horizontal effect – i.e. they can be relied upon and enforced directly by individuals in proceedings against a Member State, or an emanation of the state, but not against another individual or private company. This is in contradistinction to sufficiently clear and precise rights enshrined in Treaty Articles (such as the right to equal pay for equal work in Article 157 of the Treaty on the Functioning of the European Union) which, as fundamental tenets of EU law, are treated as having both vertical and horizontal direct effect – see Van Gend en Loos v Nederlandse Administratie der Belastingen 1963 ECR 1, ECJ, and Marshall v Southampton and South West Hampshire Area Health Authority (Teaching) 1986 ICR 335, ECJ.

Prior to Mangold v Helm (above), the ECJ had never asserted that the principle of non-discrimination on the ground of age, or on any other ground, was to be regarded as an elevated principle of Community law equivalent to enforceable rights enshrined in a Treaty. Still less had this general principle been used as the basis for disapplying incompatible provisions of national law. The ECJ's ruling also appeared to undermine the assumption that Member States are not obliged to honour or implement the mandatory provisions of a relevant Directive until the deadline specified for the implementation of that Directive.

For a while, a measure of orthodoxy appeared to have been restored by two **5.6** subsequent decisions of the European Court, decided within months of Mangold, which established some limits to the scope of the ruling in that case. First, in Chacón Navas v Eurest Colectividades SA 2007 ICR 1, ECJ, the Court held that it did not follow from the general Community principle of non-discrimination that the scope of the Framework Directive could be extended to add less favourable treatment on the ground of sickness to the grounds of discrimination specifically listed in the Directive. This suggested that the so-called general principle could not be stretched to accord enforceable rights to protection on grounds of discrimination that were not themselves expressly contemplated by the Framework Directive. Secondly, in Adeneler v Ellinikos Organismos Galaktos 2006 IRLR 716, ECJ, while accepting that it was incumbent on Member States not to implement measures contrary to a Directive once the Directive had been published or notified to the relevant Member State, the Court concluded that whenever a Directive is belatedly transposed into domestic law, national courts are only required to interpret domestic law to give effect to the Directive's aims from the date that the period for transposition into national law expires.

However, in neither of these cases was the basic premise established in Mangold v Helm (above) – that equal treatment, being a cardinal principle of Community law, is capable of having both vertical and horizontal direct effect – impugned. And in any event such inroads as these cases made into limiting the effect of Mangold were seemingly blown apart by the ECJ's decision in Kücükdeveci v Swedex GmbH and Co KG 2010 IRLR 346, ECJ. In that case the ECJ went one step further than Mangold by applying the general principle of equal treatment articulated in Mangold to require the national court to disapply a German legislative provision passed in 1926 (more than 70 years before the Directive was even drafted). This was because the relevant provision under which periods of employment completed by the employee before reaching the age of 25 were not to be taken into account in calculating the notice period for dismissal constituted a difference of treatment on the ground of age and, as such, was prohibited by the general principle of equal treatment. The Court observed that: 'By reason of the principle of the primacy of EU law, which extends also to the principle of non-discrimination on grounds of age, contrary national legislation which falls within the scope of EU law must be disapplied.'

5.7 So, in summary, the decisions in Mangold and Kücükdeveci appear to establish that, notwithstanding that provisions derived from Directives can in general only be enforced as against the state and not horizontally against private citizens or bodies, anti-discrimination on the ground of age is a fundamental principle of EU law that is capable of being relied upon by one private individual claiming against another. In this context, all that the Equal Treatment Framework Directive does is flesh out the detail and scope of the general principle. It is worth observing that what is true of age discrimination must, by logical extension, be true of the other grounds covered by the Directive – disability, religion or belief, and sexual orientation – and possibly even grounds covered by other EU equality Directives (such as sex and race). Lord Justice Elias certainly thought so in X v Mid Sussex Citizens Advice Bureau and anor 2011 ICR 460, CA, although in that particular case it was unnecessary for the Court of Appeal to reach a decisive view on the 'Mangold issue'.

It is not readily apparent why the general principle of non-discrimination articulated in Mangold and approved – even augmented – in Kücükdeveci should warrant such a radical change of approach by the European Court. In this regard, the reasoning of Advocate General Mazák in the age discrimination case Palacios de la Villa v Cortefiel Servicios SA 2009 ICR 1111, ECJ, is worth noting, despite the fact that his Opinion was given prior to the ECJ's ruling in Kücükdeveci and that his conclusion on the substantive matter of law at issue in that case was not subsequently supported by the full Court. The Advocate General cautioned against allowing a general principle of EU law 'a degree of emancipation' such that it can be invoked independently of the implementing legislation. In his view, such an approach would compromise legal certainty and call into question the distribution of competence between the EU and Member States.

The ECJ will soon be presented with an opportunity to revisit the Mangold line **5.8** of cases to determine decisively whether the general principle of equal treatment has horizontal direct effect. In March 2011 an Austrian Court referred the following question to the ECJ for a preliminary ruling in Tyrolean Airways v Betriebsrat Bord der Tyrolean (ECJ Case No.C-132/11): 'Can a national court treat as void and disapply a clause of an individual employment contract which indirectly infringes Article 21 of the Charter of Fundamental Rights, the general legal principle of European Union law relating to the prohibition of age discrimination, and/or Articles 1, 2 and 6 of [EU Equal Treatment Framework Directive No.2000/78]... on grounds of the horizontal direct effect of the fundamental rights of the European Union?'

Pending a decision on this, it is difficult to offer categorical advice about the status in EU law of the principle of equal treatment as it applies to age discrimination in particular and to other grounds of discrimination protected by EU equality Directives in general. It is true that, in view of the fact that UK national law contains extensive statutory protection in respect of all the relevant grounds of discrimination, the issue is likely to be far less pressing than for some other Member States, particularly now that the controversial 'default retirement age' exception in the UK statutory provisions has been abolished – as to which, see under 'Protection under the Equality Act – abolition of the statutory retirement regime' below. Even so, it is possible to envisage circumstances where even UK courts would be very keen to know whether and to what extent the principle can be relied upon, especially in the context of claims brought against private employers.

While we await the ECJ's ruling in the Tyrolean Airways case, perhaps a sensible **5.9** and pragmatic approach would be to follow the narrow interpretation of Mangold v Helm (above) adopted by the EAT in Lloyd-Briden v Worthing College EAT 0065/07, while taking on board the caveat that this case was decided before the ECJ's express approval of the Mangold ruling in Kücükdeveci v Swedex GmbH and Co KG (above). In Lloyd-Briden, the Appeal Tribunal rejected the contention that the statutory upper age limit – which at the time still applied to claims of unfair dismissal by virtue of S.109 of the Employment Rights Act 1996 – should be disapplied on the basis that it was directly discriminatory on the ground of age and thus contrary to the general principle of equal treatment held to be directly effective in Mangold. After conducting a careful review of all the relevant ECJ case law, including the rulings in Chacón Navas v Eurest Colectividades SA and Adeneler v Ellinikos Organismos Galaktos discussed above, Mr Justice Wilkie observed: 'In my judgment, the combined effect of these decisions of the ECJ is that where, as here, the UK Government has complied with the provisions of Article 18 [of the Equal Treatment Framework Directive, which requires Member States to implement the provisions of the Directive into their national law by specified dates], there is no place for the direct operation in domestic UK law of the general principles so as to extend the provisions against discrimination, which are to be found in the Directive, so that they apply earlier than the timely transposition of the Directive into UK domestic law... Mangold is limited so as to require a domestic court only to disregard domestic legislation which has been enacted in breach of the Member State's obligations under Article 18 of the Directive.'

5.10 Protection under antecedent legislation

Age discrimination in employment is prohibited in the United Kingdom by the EqA, which came into force on 1 October 2010. Prior to the enactment of that Act, age discrimination was governed by the 2006 Age Regulations, which came into force on 1 October 2006. These Regulations prohibited direct and indirect discrimination, harassment and victimisation in an employment context. Although these basic concepts applied to age discrimination under the 2006 Regulations in exactly the same way as they applied to most of the other protected grounds of discrimination, the Regulations introduced several distinct features that were unique to age discrimination and which affected the scope of the protection available. The most notable of these were:

- the ability of an employer to justify *direct* as well as indirect age discrimination

- a blanket exception in respect of the compulsory retirement of employees at age 65 or above, provided that the employer followed a statutory retirement procedure under which the employee had the right to request to work beyond his or her intended retirement date.

5.11 Justification of direct age discrimination

The definition of 'direct discrimination' contained in Reg 3(1)(a) of the 2006 Age Regulations provided that 'a person (A) discriminates against another person (B) if on the grounds of B's age, A treats B less favourably than he treats or would treat other persons... and A cannot show the treatment... to be a proportionate means of achieving a legitimate aim'. Reg 2(3)(b) made it clear that the reference to B's age in this context included B's 'apparent age'. Thus, in stark contrast to all other strands of discrimination covered by the anti-discrimination legislation in place at the time, employers could seek to justify *direct* age discrimination. Until the enactment of the Regulations, it had only ever been possible to justify *indirect* discrimination.

The scope of the justification defence in Reg 3(1)(a) was exactly the same as that which applied to indirect discrimination under Reg 3(1)(b). The then Labour Government's explanation for allowing direct discrimination to be justified was that age can sometimes genuinely be a relevant factor for certain aspects of employment and vocational training, and that it was therefore necessary to give employers scope to justify less favourable treatment in this regard. It contended that this was perfectly lawful within the terms of the EU Equal Treatment Framework Directive (No.2000/78), Article 6(1) of which states that: 'Member States may provide that differences of treatment on grounds of age shall not constitute discrimination, if, within the context of national law, they are objectively and reasonably justified by a legitimate aim, including legitimate employment policy, labour market and vocational training objectives, and if the means of achieving that aim are appropriate and necessary.'

Notwithstanding Article 6(1), the lawfulness of Reg 3(1)(a) of the 2006 **5.12** Regulations was called into question when in 2008 the Incorporated Trustees of the National Council on Ageing (later renamed 'Age UK') applied to the High Court for judicial review of the Regulations based on its belief that they failed properly to transpose various provisions of the Directive into UK law. This resulted in the High Court making a reference to the ECJ to determine, inter alia, whether Article 6(1) of the Directive permits Member States to introduce legislation providing that direct discrimination on the ground of age does not constitute discrimination so long as it is justified as a proportionate means of achieving a legitimate aim, and whether the same provision of the Directive requires Member States to specify the kinds of differences of treatment that may be so justified. In R (Incorporated Trustees of the National Council on Ageing (Age Concern England)) v Secretary of State for Business, Enterprise and Regulatory Reform 2009 ICR 1080, ECJ, the European Court ruled that it was for the national court to ascertain whether the aims contemplated by Reg 3 were legitimate within the meaning of Article 6(1) in that they were covered by a social policy objective such as those related to employment policy, the labour market or vocational training. The ECJ also asserted that it was for the national court to determine, in the light of all the relevant evidence and taking account of the possibility of achieving by other means any legitimate social policy objectives relied upon, whether the measure set out in Reg 3 was 'appropriate and necessary' within the terms of Article 6(1). The ECJ went on to point out that Member States enjoy broad discretion in choosing the means capable of achieving their social policy objectives. However, it observed that Article 6(1) imposes on Member States the burden of establishing to a high standard of proof the legitimacy of the aim relied on for the differences in treatment on the ground of age, and therefore mere generalisations would not be enough to show that the aim of the national measure is capable of justifying the derogation from the principle of non-discrimination on the ground of age.

When the matter returned to the High Court for a decision on the judicial review challenge in the light of the ECJ's ruling, the judge, Mr Justice Blake, concluded that Reg 3 was compatible with the Equal Treatment Framework Directive – see R (on the application of Age UK) v Secretary of State for Business, Innovation and Skills 2010 ICR 260, QBD. Having regard to the explanatory notes to the Regulations and the elaborate publicly available consultation process, the Government had proved to the requisite high standard that its social policy concerns of protecting the confidence and integrity of the labour market underpinned its decision to enable direct discrimination to be justified. Those were legitimate concerns within the principles of the Directive and the case law of the ECJ. Blake J proceeded to reject the claimant's argument that the inclusion of broad social policy reasons that were left undefined in the Regulations infringed the principle of legal certainty. Once it was recognised that social policy justifications need not be precisely listed in the Regulations, but may be found in the legislative background, the fact that the aims are broad ones did not infringe legal certainty.

It continues to be possible to justify direct age discrimination under the EqA – see 'Protection under the Equality Act – justifying direct discrimination' below.

5.13 Default retirement age exception

Another controversial feature of the 2006 Age Regulations was the statutory exception covering retirement. Reg 30 provided that it was not discriminatory on the ground of age for an employer compulsorily to retire an employee aged 65 or over so long as the retirement procedure specified in Schedule 6 to the 2006 Age Regulations was complied with. In the absence of this exception, the compulsory retirement of an employee by reason of the fact that he or she had attained a specified 'retirement' age would self-evidently have constituted direct age discrimination, since the employee's treatment would clearly have been meted out solely or principally on the basis of the employee's age. In effect, Reg 30 created a 'default retirement age' (DRA) whereby the forced retirement of employees who had attained the age of 65 was permissible from a discrimination point of view. This was in contrast to employers who compulsorily retired employees before the age of 65: they would have to seek to show that the consequential age discrimination was objectively justified within the terms of Reg 3(1) to avoid liability for direct discrimination.

In addition to dealing with the discriminatory aspects of retirement, the Regulations also inserted provisions into the Employment Rights Act 1996 to cover unfair dismissal. These not only set out the procedural requirements that had to be complied with by employers seeking to rely upon the DRA of 65 for the purposes of Reg 30, but also laid down further procedural steps that had to be complied with to ensure that a retirement dismissal was not unfair for the purposes of unfair dismissal law. These steps were set out in Schedule 6 to the 2006 Age Regulations. At the time the 2006 Age Regulations were enacted, the Government acknowledged that retaining the retirement age exception was controversial, not least because it appeared to contradict the Government's broader social and economic policy initiatives directed towards increasing the state pension age in line with increased average life spans. The Government therefore sought to head off criticism by promising to review the operation of the DRA by 2011, and intimating that, if the overall conclusion was that the DRA was no longer necessary owing to a cultural and social change, it would be abolished.

However, prior to any review being conducted, the DRA exception in Reg 30 **5.14** was challenged as unlawful in the same judicial review proceedings brought by the Incorporated Trustees of the National Council on Ageing as those concerning the justification defence in Reg 3 – see under 'Justification of direct age discrimination' above. In R (on the application of Age UK) v Secretary of State for Business, Innovation and Skills 2010 ICR 260, QBD, the High Court held that Reg 30 was not incompatible with the Equal Treatment Framework Directive in that the decision to adopt a DRA was not a disproportionate means of giving effect to the social aim of labour market confidence. A DRA was not inherently arbitrary but rather entailed the making of a social choice in the light of a number of social and economic factors. Furthermore, the DRA was not a generalised statement of social worthlessness but a measure designed to give certainty and corresponding focus for planning purposes for employers and employees alike. On this basis, the decision to fix a DRA was not, in itself, outside the scope of the Directive.

However, the judge, Mr Justice Blake, expressed greater qualms about the actual choice of 65 as the DRA. Although that choice could not be regarded as disproportionate when the Regulations were first enacted in 2006, if Reg 30 had been adopted for the first time in 2009 (the date of the Court's decision), or if there had been no indication of an imminent review of the DRA, then the setting of the DRA at 65 would have been disproportionate and not capable of objective and reasonable justification. This was because it was clear from the available evidence that a DRA of 65 creates greater discriminatory effect than is 'necessary' on a class of people who are able to and want to continue in their employment, whereas a higher age would not have general detrimental labour market consequences or block access to high-level jobs by future generations. The judge reasoned that if the selection of 65 as the DRA was not 'necessary', it was not possible for it to be 'justified'. He ended his judgment by observing: 'I cannot presently see how 65 could remain as a DRA after the review.' These,

83

as it turned out, were prescient words given that the entire statutory retirement regime erected by the 2006 Age Regulations (including the DRA) was abolished shortly after the EqA was enacted – for details, see under 'Protection under the Equality Act – abolition of the statutory retirement regime' below.

5.15 Protection under the Equality Act

When the EqA came into force on 1 October 2006, most of the provisions of the 2006 Age Regulations were repealed and substituted by equivalent provisions in the later Act, including those governing justification of direct discrimination and the retirement exception (although the DRA has since been abolished – see 'Abolition of default retirement age' below).

Section 4 EqA lists 'age' as one of the protected characteristics covered by the Act. The scope of the protection accorded to the protected characteristic of age is set out in S.5 EqA. This section replaces the similarly worded Reg 3 of the 2006 Age Regulations, outlined under 'Protection under antecedent legislation' above. There is some difference in wording between the two provisions, but this does not reflect any change of substance. The main difference is the substitution of the phrase 'on the ground' for that of 'the protected characteristic' – a change of phraseology that is common across all the strands of discrimination covered by the EqA.

5.16 Definition of 'age group'

Section 5(1) EqA states that a reference in the 2010 Act to a person who has the protected characteristic of age is 'a reference to a person of a particular age group', and a reference to persons who share that characteristic is 'a reference to persons of the same age group'. An 'age group' is a group of persons defined by reference to age, whether to a particular age or to a range of ages – S.5(2). In other words, whenever the Act refers to the protected characteristic of age, it means a person belonging to a particular age group.

The definition of 'age group' in what is now S.5(2) EqA (previously Reg 3(3) of the 2006 Age Regulations) allows the claimant to define the disadvantaged age group as he or she wishes. The Explanatory Notes accompanying the EqA state that an 'age group' would include, for example, 'over-50s' or '21-year-olds'. While a person aged 21 does not share the characteristic of age with 'people in their 40s', the Notes state that a person aged 21 and people in their 40s can share the characteristic of being in the 'under-50' age range (para 37). According to the Code of Practice on Employment issued by the Equality and Human Rights Commission (EHRC), an age group can also be relative, consisting, for example, of people who are 'older than me' (para 2.4).

5.17   In certain contexts – most notably, indirect age discrimination – the EqA requires a comparison to be drawn between people of different age groups. As was previously the case under the 2006 Regulations, the Act does not stipulate the age group with which the comparison should be drawn. The EHRC Code suggests that the claimant may seek to draw a comparison with everyone outside his or her age group; often, however, the comparison will be more specific and will be led by the context and circumstances (para 2.7).

Justifying direct discrimination 5.18

It continues to be possible for employers to justify direct age discrimination (i.e. less favourable treatment) under the EqA in the same way as it was possible under the 2006 Regulations. This is a unique aspect of the protection against age discrimination in that it does not apply to any of the other protected characteristics. S.13(2) EqA states that: 'If the protected characteristic is age, A does not discriminate against B if A can show A's treatment of B to be a proportionate means of achieving a legitimate aim.' As we have seen, the availability of this defence was unsuccessfully challenged by way of judicial review in respect of the equivalent provision in the 2006 Age Regulations – see 'Protection under antecedent legislation – justification of direct age discrimination' above.

When the 2006 Age Regulations were first introduced, it was widely assumed that the threshold for justifying direct age discrimination was higher than that for justifying indirect discrimination but this assumption was thrown into doubt by the ECJ's decision in R (Incorporated Trustees of the National Council on Ageing (Age Concern England)) v Secretary of State for Business, Enterprise and Regulatory Reform 2009 ICR 1080, ECJ, where the Court intimated that there was no significance in the slight difference of wording between Article 6(1) of the EU Equal Treatment Framework Directive (No.2000/78), which covers direct age discrimination, and Article 2(2), which sets out the general justification defence to indirect discrimination. However, the Supreme Court in Seldon v Clarkson Wright and Jakes (A Partnership) 2012 UKSC 16, SC, has now confirmed that the justification test for direct age discrimination under the EqA is narrower than that for indirect age discrimination in that direct discrimination can only be justified by reference to legitimate objectives of a public interest nature, rather than purely individual reasons particular to the employer's situation. For a detailed discussion of the justification defence in the context of direct age discrimination, see Chapter 15, 'Direct discrimination', under 'Justifying direct age discrimination'.

Discrimination by perception and association related to age 5.19

One element of the 2006 Regulations that was not carried over – at least expressly – into the EqA was a specific provision in Reg 3(3)(b) making it clear that direct discrimination on the ground of age embraced direct discrimination caused by the perception of age. Reg 3(3)(b) stipulated that for the purposes of direct discrimination, the reference to the claimant's age included the claimant's 'apparent age'. Thus, a person had the right to claim discrimination on the ground of age if any less favourable treatment suffered was on account of a perception about their age, whether or not that perception was correct.

However, while this particular provision has no direct equivalent in the EqA, it remains the case that misperception about a person's age can found a direct discrimination complaint if it can be shown that less favourable treatment is causally linked to the misperception. Moreover, a person is now protected under the EqA if he or she is discriminated against because of his or her *association* with someone of a different age. This protection from discrimination by perception and association derives from the way in which direct discrimination is defined in S.13 EqA. S.13(1) stipulates that 'A person (A) discriminates against another (B) if, *because of* a protected characteristic, A treats B less favourably than A treats or would treat others' (our stress). Previously, direct discrimination was defined in Reg 3(1)(a) of the 2006 Age Regulations in terms of less favourable treatment 'on grounds of *B's age*' (our stress). The removal of the claimant's own age from the equation means that a person is now protected if they are directly discriminated against on account of age in general. In this way, discrimination by perception and association are woven into the very fabric of the definition of direct discrimination. For a more detailed discussion, see Chapter 15, 'Direct discrimination' under 'Discrimination by association' and 'Discrimination by perception'.

5.20 Abolition of the statutory retirement regime

As promised when the 2006 Age Regulations were first enacted, in 2010 the Government undertook a thoroughgoing review of the entire statutory retirement regime, including the provisions of Reg 30 entitling employers to compulsorily retire employees at 65. As a result of this review, it announced in July 2010 that the default retirement age would be phased out in 2011 and that the statutory retirement regime put in place by the 2006 Age Regulations would be abolished.

This abolition was effected by the Employment Equality (Repeal of Retirement Age Provisions) Regulations 2011 SI 2011/1069, which came into force on 6 April 2011. Subject to certain transitional arrangements, these Regulations removed the specific exception that applied to the default retirement age. As a result, requiring an employee to retire at a fixed retirement age will amount to direct age discrimination under S.13(1) EqA unless the employer can justify that requirement under S.13(2).

5.21 So far as unfair dismissal is concerned, the procedural requirements set out in Schedule 6 to the 2006 Age Regulations (which were preserved following the enactment of the EqA) have also been abolished (subject to transitional provisions). 'Retirement' is no longer treated as one of the potentially fair reasons for dismissal under S.98 ERA so an employer wishing to fairly dismiss an employee aged 65 or over who has sufficient qualifying service will need to show that the reason for dismissal falls within one of the other potentially fair reasons for dismissal – e.g. capability, conduct, redundancy, or 'some other substantial reason' – and that the dismissal was reasonable in all the circumstances. In other words, the dismissal will be treated in the same way as any other dismissal. For full details of the consequences of the abolition of the DRA from a discrimination law perspective, see Chapter 26, 'Dismissal', under 'Retirement'; and in relation to unfair dismissal, see IDS Employment Law Handbook, 'Unfair Dismissal' (2010), Chapter 9, 'Retirement', under 'Abolition of statutory retirement regime'.

Statutory exceptions   5.22
In addition to retirement, the 2006 Age Regulations contained a number of other exceptions that applied solely in the context of age discrimination. These exceptions, which concerned service-related benefits, the national minimum wage, enhanced redundancy payments, life assurance and contributions to personal pension schemes, have been retained in Schedule 9 to the EqA. In addition, the EqA has added another exception covering childcare benefits. The exceptions in Schedule 9 seek to cater for the fact that age considerations are invariably involved in the determination of conditions of entitlement to, and levels of benefit of, the benefits covered. Full details can be found in Chapter 31, 'Specific exceptions', under 'Age exceptions'.

6 Disability

Meaning of 'disability'

Physical or mental impairment

Substantial adverse effect

Normal day-to-day activities

Long-term effect

Effect of medical treatment

Medical evidence

The Disability Discrimination Act 1995 (DDA) introduced protection against **6.1** discrimination on the ground of disability into the law of the United Kingdom for the first time (although certain modifications applied to Northern Ireland). Prior to that, all that existed was a quota system – more often than not ignored – which sought to encourage rehabilitation, retraining and the creation of sheltered employment for disabled people. The 1995 Act imposed a duty on employers to make reasonable adjustments and outlawed 'disability-related' discrimination – a special form of indirect discrimination. The Act anchored the protection from discrimination on the definition of 'disability', which, following the repeal of the DDA and its substitution by the Equality Act 2010 (EqA) on 1 October 2010, remains the core of the legislative protection accorded to disabled persons.

As noted under 'Meaning of "disability"' below, the model of disability protection introduced by the DDA – and re-enacted by the EqA – is the 'medical model'. This focuses on whether the complainant's condition satisfies the definition of 'disability'. Under the DDA, the definition of disability gradually became more inclusive as a result of legislative amendments so that, for example, certain conditions such as HIV, multiple sclerosis and cancer automatically qualified as disabilities from the point of diagnosis and the requirement that a mental impairment had to be 'clinically well-recognised' was removed.

The legislation's reach in terms of the types of conduct prohibited has also been **6.2** extended over the years. As originally enacted, the DDA envisaged three forms of disability discrimination: (i) disability-related discrimination, being less favourable treatment for a reason related to a disabled person's disability, if such treatment could not be objectively justified; (ii) a failure to make reasonable adjustments where the physical features of the employer's premises, or the policies or practices that the employer applied, placed disabled people at a substantial disadvantage; and (iii) victimisation, being less favourable treatment for having done anything in relation to the DDA (such as bringing proceedings).

Amendments made in 2004 introduced a new form of disability discrimination – direct discrimination, i.e. less favourable treatment on the ground of a person's disability. Although this was, and remains, one of the key planks of protection under the other discrimination strands, e.g. sex and race discrimination, for a long time the Government took the view that, in relation to disability, disability-related discrimination provided adequate protection on this front. It had good reason for thinking this – disability-related discrimination, in referring to less favourable treatment for a reason related to a person's disability, covered a wider range of conduct than direct discrimination, which refers to treatment that occurs on the ground of that disability. On the other hand, disability-related discrimination could be objectively justified, a wide-ranging defence not available in respect of claims of direct discrimination. In any event, the enactment of the EU Equal Treatment Framework Directive (No.2000/78) ('the Framework Directive') on 1 December 2003 meant that express protection from direct discrimination was required as a matter of EU law and the Disability Discrimination Act 1995 (Amendment) Regulations 2003 SI 2003/1673 introduced the concept of direct discrimination into the DDA from 1 October 2004. The Regulations also inserted a free-standing cause of action for harassment, again to comply with requirements of the Framework Directive.

6.3 Therefore, from October 2004 until October 2010, there were five forms of discrimination prohibited under the DDA – direct discrimination, disability-related discrimination, failure to make reasonable adjustments, harassment and victimisation. For most of that time, these operated as five distinct heads. However, a case law development in June 2008 changed all that. The House of Lords in Mayor and Burgesses of the London Borough of Lewisham v Malcolm 2008 IRLR 700, HL, departed from established employment case law to interpret disability-related discrimination restrictively, so as to cover much the same ground as direct disability discrimination. This development, which is explained fully in Chapter 20, 'Discrimination arising from disability', was of such magnitude that it required a complete reformulation of the law governing disability-related discrimination when the EqA was enacted.

The 2010 Act maintains protection from direct discrimination, failure to make reasonable adjustments, harassment and victimisation. But in place of disability-related discrimination, it has introduced a new form of disability discrimination – 'discrimination arising from a disability' – and has extended the protection from indirect discrimination, which had previously applied to all strands of discrimination except disability, to disability. Furthermore, the EqA's definition of direct disability discrimination – less favourable treatment because of disability – covers a broader range of conduct than the equivalent provision in the DDA. Notably, the EqA has the potential to cover cases where a non-disabled person is discriminated against because of his or her association with a disabled person ('discrimination by association'), or where an individual is wrongly perceived to have a disability ('discrimination by perception'). These issues are examined in more detail in Chapter 15, 'Direct discrimination' under 'Discrimination by association' and 'Discrimination by perception'.

Under European law, the key legal measure relevant to disability discrimination **6.4** is the aforementioned Framework Directive, which requires Member States to outlaw discrimination in employment and occupation on the ground of disability, as well as on the grounds of religion or belief, sexual orientation and age. Although the Directive was agreed on 27 November 2000, it did not need to be implemented into national law until 2 December 2003 (2 December 2006 as regards age). Thus, protection from disability discrimination had been a feature of UK domestic law for some time before the European legislation was enacted (although, as noted above, the Framework Directive necessitated some changes to the DDA). It is now the EqA that purports to implement the mandatory provisions of the Directive into UK law.

Meaning of 'disability' 6.5

The protection from disability discrimination afforded by the EqA only applies in respect of those who fall within the Act's definition of a disabled person, and since this definition is crucial to the understanding and application of the Act, the first substantive issue for any tribunal is normally whether the claimant is a disabled person under the Act. The only exception to this is the protection against victimisation (see Chapter 19, 'Victimisation'), which is available to both disabled and non-disabled people. Where the claimant is bringing a claim on the ground of another person's disability ('discrimination by association') or on the ground that he or she is perceived to have a disability ('discrimination by perception'), the statutory definition of discrimination still applies, albeit in a slightly different context – see Chapter 15, 'Direct discrimination', under 'Discrimination by association' and 'Discrimination by perception'.

The EqA defines a 'disabled person' as a person who has a 'disability' – S.6(2). A person has a disability if he or she has 'a physical or mental impairment' which has a 'substantial and long-term adverse effect on [his or her] ability to carry out normal day-to-day activities' – S.6(1). The burden of proof is on the claimant to show that he or she satisfies this definition.

Section 6(3) EqA provides that a reference to a person who has the protected **6.6** characteristic of disability is a reference to a person who has a particular disability, and that persons share that characteristic if they have the same disability. It is not the case, therefore, that a person shares the protected characteristic with another person simply because both are disabled: there has to be commonality between them in respect of the nature or type of disability they have. This requirement may well have an impact when it comes to showing indirect discrimination, one element of which requires the claimant to show that a provision, criterion or practice 'puts, or would put, persons with whom [the claimant] shares the [protected] characteristic at a particular disadvantage when compared with persons with whom [the claimant] does not share it' (S.19(2)(b) EqA). Indirect discrimination in the context of disability is discussed in detail in Chapter 16, 'Indirect discrimination: proving disadvantage', under 'Indirect discrimination in context – indirect disability discrimination'.

The definition of disability in S.6(1) is similar in many respects to that previously contained in the DDA, although there are a few changes which we discuss below as and when they arise. The most significant of these is that the EqA no longer contains a list of eight specific 'capacities' (mobility, manual dexterity, continence, etc) which, under the DDA, determined whether an impairment had the potential to have a substantive adverse effect on the claimant's ability to carry out normal day-to-day activities. Instead, a non-exhaustive list of examples of how the effects of an impairment might manifest itself in relation to these capacities is now contained in the Appendix to the 'Guidance on matters to be taken into account in determining questions relating to the definition of disability' (see 'Regulations, guidance and Codes of Practice' below). The effect of this change will be to make it easier for a claimant to show that an impairment has a substantial adverse effect on normal day-to-day activities and thus satisfy a tribunal that he or she has the protected characteristic of disability.

6.7   The statutory definition of disability in what was S.1 DDA and is now S.6 EqA represents the 'medical model', focusing as it does on the functional limitations of a person. This approach to defining disability attracted a strong body of criticism when the DDA was in force. It was perceived to be too complex in other than very narrowly defined circumstances and a source of uncertainty in that it was often unclear whether a claimant was disabled or not. Where such uncertainty arose, the claimant would be 'put to proof' before an employment tribunal and this would inevitably lead to extensive witness statements and expert evidence to support the claimant's account of what he or she could and could not do. During the EqA's passage through Parliament, some organisations – including the Discrimination Law Association – advocated moving from the medical model to the 'social model' of disability, which focuses on the barriers placed in the way of disabled people rather than 'impairments'. Such barriers include the attitudinal, economic and environmental factors that prevent certain people from experiencing equality of opportunity because of an impairment or perceived impairment, and thus affect a much wider group of people than that which falls within the medical model definition. However, the Government chose to retain the medical model, arguing – among other things – that, as the DDA definition was relatively well known in UK law and by those using the court and tribunal system, there was some merit in not changing it unless for a very good reason.

It is important to note that among the nine protected characteristics covered by the EqA, disability is, in many respects, the most asymmetrical. Both under the antecedent legislation and now also under the EqA, disability protection looks and feels very different from the protection accorded to the other characteristics. Indeed, the higher courts have recognised this – see, for example, Stockton on Tees Borough Council v Aylott 2010 ICR 1278, CA, where Lord Justice Mummery observed: '[I]t is not sensible, or even legally correct, simply to carry across from the longer established fields of discrimination law (race and gender) their principles and precedents. The disability-related form of disability discrimination and the duty to make reasonable adjustments do not even appear in the earlier discrimination law, which, if used in deciding disability discrimination claims, may prove to be an obstacle to a proper understanding of the new law. As Baroness Hale explained in Archibald v Fife Council 2004 ICR 954, HL, the sex discrimination legislation and the race discrimination legislation are different from disability discrimination. The earlier legislation is based on the irrelevance of the identified differences between human beings, who are accordingly entitled to receive equal treatment and to protection from less favourable treatment on the proscribed ground of sex or race.'

Regulations, guidance and Codes of Practice 6.8

Although the definition in S.6(1) is the starting point for establishing the meaning of 'disability', it is not the only source that must be considered. The supplementary provisions for determining whether a person has a disability – previously found in Schedule 1 to the DDA – are largely retained in Part 1 of Schedule 1 to the EqA. Furthermore, a number of regulations were made under the DDA to supplement the statutory provisions and the Government has indicated an intention to replace them all in due course. For the purposes of this chapter the relevant regulations under the DDA were the Disability Discrimination (Meaning of Disability) Regulations 1996 SI 1996/1455 and the Disability Discrimination (Blind and Partially Sighted Persons) Regulations 2003 SI 2003/712, both of which have been consolidated into the Equality Act 2010 (Disability) Regulations 2010 SI 2010/2128.

In addition, the Government has issued 'Guidance on matters to be taken into account in determining questions relating to the definition of disability' (2010) ('the Guidance') under S.6(5) EqA. This Guidance, which came into force on 1 May 2011, replaces the previous Guidance on the same matters issued under the DDA in 2006. The Guidance does not impose any legal obligations in itself but courts and tribunals must take account of it where relevant – para 12, Sch 1 EqA. Indeed, in Goodwin v Patent Office 1999 ICR 302, EAT, the EAT's then President, Mr Justice Morison, stated that tribunals should refer to any relevant parts of the Guidance they have taken into account and that it was an error of law for them not to do so. However, more recently, in Ahmed v Metroline Travel Ltd EAT 0400/10, the EAT qualified the Goodwin approach, noting that the observations made in that case were now long-standing, well established and well understood by tribunals. Mrs Justice Cox said that it was especially important for the correct approach to using the Guidance to be understood in the early years of the DDA. However, it was more than 15 years since disability discrimination legislation had been introduced. In this particular case, the employment judge had understood the potential relevance of the Guidance and the importance of using it correctly, and no error of law was disclosed by his failure to refer to the Guidance in more detail, particularly when his attention had been drawn to it so extensively in written submissions. Furthermore, where, as in the instant case, the lack of credibility as to the claimant's evidence of his disability was the main reason for concluding he was not disabled within the meaning of the DDA, there could be no error of law if the tribunal fails to refer to the official Guidance.

6.9 (Note that references in this chapter to 'the Guidance' are to the new Guidance. However, the 2006 Guidance still applies where the alleged act of discrimination occurred before 1 May 2011 – Art 3(5) of the Equality Act 2010 (Guidance on the Definition of Disability) Appointed Day Order 2011 SI 2011/1159.)

Finally, the Equality and Human Rights Commission (EHRC) has published a Code of Practice on Employment ('the EHRC Employment Code') that has some bearing on the meaning of disability under the EqA. Like the Guidance, the Code does not impose legal obligations but tribunals and courts must take into account any part of the Code that appears to them relevant to any questions arising in proceedings.

6.10 **Material time for establishing disability**
The time at which to assess the disability (i.e. whether there is an impairment which has a substantial adverse effect on normal day-to-day activities) is the date of the alleged discriminatory act – Cruickshank v VAW Motorcast Ltd 2002 ICR 729, EAT. This is also the material time when determining whether the impairment has a long-term effect – see 'Long-term effect' (below). An employment tribunal is entitled to infer, on the basis of the evidence presented to it, that an impairment found to have existed by a medical expert at the date of a medical examination was also in existence at the time of the alleged act of discrimination – see John Grooms Housing Association v Burdett EAT 0937/03 and McKechnie Plastic Components v Grant EAT 0284/08.

Note that evidence of the extent of someone's capabilities some months after the act of discrimination may be relevant where there is no suggestion that the condition has improved in the meantime – Pendragon Motor Co Ltd t/a Stratstone (Wilmslow) Ltd v Ridge EAT 962/00. That case involved the admissibility of a video recording taken of the claimant six months after he had left work. The tribunal refused to admit the evidence but was overturned on appeal by the EAT, which remitted the case to a different tribunal for a rehearing on all the evidence, including any properly adduced and proved video evidence. In the EAT's view, video evidence taken at a later date may be relevant to the question of the extent of the claimant's actual capabilities at the time of the discriminatory act, especially where there is no suggestion that the condition has improved in the meantime. The video evidence may also be relevant when determining the reasonableness or otherwise of any adjustments that might need to be made. The duty to make reasonable adjustments is considered in detail in Chapter 21, 'Failure to make reasonable adjustments'.

Past disabilities
6.11

Note that the employment provisions of the EqA apply in relation to a person who has had a disability in the past in the same way as they apply in relation to a person who currently has a disability – S.6(4). This is discussed further under 'Physical or mental impairment – past disabilities' below.

Meaning of disability in other legislation
6.12

In this chapter we consider the meaning of 'disability' for the purposes of the EqA. The definition in S.6(1) is unique to the 2010 Act: the fact that a person may or may not come within a definition of disability used in another statute does not affect whether that person satisfies the definition of disability contained in the EqA. In McDougall v Richmond Adult Community College 2007 ICR 1567, EAT, M sought to argue that her compulsory admission (i.e. sectioning) under the Mental Health Act 1983 was itself conclusive evidence that her impairment had a substantial adverse effect on her day-to-day activities, meaning that she had a mental impairment within the meaning of the DDA. The EAT held that a person satisfying the conditions for compulsory admission under the Mental Health Act did not necessarily satisfy the conditions for disability under the DDA. However, it went on to say that, in practice, a mental impairment leading to sectioning limits a person's ability to carry out normal day-to-day activities, and has a substantial adverse effect thereon. Furthermore, in the circumstances of the case, the severity of M's condition – which left her unable to understand the real world – meant that she was disabled for DDA purposes. (Note that the EAT's judgment was overturned by the Court of Appeal on a different point – see 'Long-term effect – recurring conditions' below. However, this aspect of its decision was not appealed and therefore remains good law.)

Similarly, the fact that a person qualifies for a disability benefit does not automatically bring him or her within the definition of disability contained in the EqA. In Hill v Clacton Family Trust Ltd 2005 EWCA Civ 1456, CA, H worked as a care assistant at a home for young people with learning difficulties. She complained to her GP of feeling paranoid and anxious after taking a group of children to a stunt show event during which a stuntman riding a motorcycle crashed into and killed a volunteer. Prior to the hearing of her disability discrimination claim, H was awarded disability living allowance by the Social Security Appeals Tribunal (SSAT) on the basis that she was suffering from post-traumatic stress disorder (PTSD). The employment tribunal dismissed H's claim on the basis that she was not suffering from PTSD and therefore did not have a mental impairment falling within the definition of 'disability' contained in the DDA. Her appeal was dismissed by the EAT and she appealed to the Court of Appeal, arguing – among other things – that the tribunal had failed to take proper account of the fact that she had been awarded disability living allowance at the highest rate by the SSAT on the basis that she was suffering from PTSD. The Court rejected this contention. Although it was unfortunate that two public bodies – the employment tribunal and the SSAT – could reach different conclusions as to whether H was disabled, the SSAT's decision was in no way conclusive of the issue of whether she had a disability for the purposes of the DDA. There was no rule or principle of law that an employment tribunal is bound to follow the decisions of the SSAT, and it was for the employment tribunal to make up its own mind on the evidence before it.

6.13 Physical or mental impairment

The definition of disability in S.6(1) EqA requires that the adverse effects on a person's ability to carry out normal day-to-day activities arise from 'a physical or mental impairment'. Unfortunately there is no statutory definition of either a 'physical impairment' or a 'mental impairment', and nor is there any definition in the Guidance or the EHRC Employment Code, although both make clear that impairment includes a sensory impairment.

In McNicol v Balfour Beatty Rail Maintenance Ltd; Rugamer v Sony Music Entertainment UK Ltd 2002 ICR 381, EAT, the EAT suggested the following definition of physical or mental impairment under the DDA: 'some damage, defect, disorder or disease compared with a person having a full set of physical and mental equipment in normal condition'. And in McNicol v Balfour Beatty Rail Maintenance Ltd 2002 ICR 1498, CA, the Court of Appeal held that 'impairment' in this context bears 'its ordinary and natural meaning... It is left to the good sense of the tribunal to make a decision in each case on whether the evidence available establishes that the applicant has a physical or mental impairment with the stated effects.' It would seem therefore that the term is meant to have a broad application. Para A3 of the Guidance tends to support this view, as it states that in many cases there will be no dispute as to whether a person has an impairment, adding that any disagreement is more likely to be about whether the *effects* of the impairment are sufficient to fall within the S.6(1) definition.

96

Certain conditions, such as alcohol or drug addiction, are expressly excluded **6.14** from protection under the Act (see 'Excluded disabilities' below) but apart from these, almost any impairment is potentially capable of being a disability under the Act. The parameters are set by the additional requirement that the complaint must have a long-term substantial adverse effect on a person's ability to carry out normal everyday activities.

Thus, it is the *degree* to which a person is affected by a particular impairment that in most cases will determine whether that person is afforded the protection of the EqA. It is not enough to say that diabetes, for example, is a disability under the Act. Rather, it is for each claimant suffering from diabetes to show that he or she is affected by that condition to an extent that brings him or her within the Act's parameters. This prevents people with temporary conditions, such as a sprained ankle, or minor conditions (in the sense that the condition would not generally be regarded as a disability) such as infrequent bladder weakness, from seeking and benefiting from protection.

When the DDA first became law, the need for tribunals to determine whether **6.15** an individual had a medical complaint serious enough to amount to a disability introduced new concepts into tribunal deliberations and, not unnaturally, the application of those concepts brought a few teething problems as tribunals grappled with the inevitable complexity of medical issues. Some of these difficulties arose in the leading case of Goodwin v Patent Office 1999 ICR 302, EAT, in which the parties to the dispute asked the EAT to give tribunals guidance on the proper approach to adopt when applying the DDA's provisions. This guidance remains equally relevant today in interpreting the meaning of S.6 EqA.

The EAT said that the words used to define disability in S.1(1) DDA (now S.6(1) EqA) require a tribunal to look at the evidence by reference to four different questions (or 'conditions' as the EAT termed them):

- did the claimant have a mental and/or physical impairment? (the 'impairment condition')

- did the impairment affect the claimant's ability to carry out normal day-to-day activities? (the 'adverse effect condition')

- was the adverse condition substantial? (the 'substantial condition'); and

- was the adverse condition long term? (the 'long-term condition').

These four questions should be posed sequentially and not together – Wigginton v Cowrie and ors t/a Baxter International (a partnership) EAT 0322/09.

This 'step' approach has subsequently been approved in numerous cases. In J **6.16** v DLA Piper UK LLP 2010 ICR 1052, EAT, the then President of the EAT, Mr Justice Underhill, observed that it was good practice for employment tribunals to state their conclusions separately on the questions of impairment and adverse effect and, in respect of the latter, their findings on substantiality and long-term effect. However, in reaching those conclusions, tribunals should not feel compelled to proceed by rigid consecutive stages. Specifically, in cases where the existence of an impairment is disputed, it would make sense for a tribunal to start by making findings about whether the claimant's ability to carry out normal day-to-day activities is adversely affected on a long-term basis and then to consider the question of impairment in the light of those findings. Applying this guidance, the Northern Ireland Court of Appeal in Veitch v Red Sky Group Ltd 2010 NICA 39, NICA, held that an industrial tribunal had fallen into error when it failed to deal adequately, clearly and in a logical sequence with the 'Goodwin questions' when determining whether the claimant suffered from a mental impairment amounting to a disability for the purposes of the DDA. Furthermore, the tribunal appeared to have assumed that at every stage of the Goodwin inquiry the claimant bore the onus of producing medical evidence to underpin his case, so that in the absence of such evidence his claim was bound to fail. Such an approach overstated the true position. It was the responsibility of the tribunal to assess such medical evidence as was presented and then to conclude for itself whether the claimant suffered from a disability at the relevant time.

6.17 Identifying the impairment

In relation to the question of whether a person has a physical or mental impairment (the 'impairment condition'), the EAT in Goodwin v Patent Office 1999 ICR 302, EAT, advised the following:

- when determining whether an individual has a disability, the starting point for the tribunal must be the information stated on the employee's ET1 and the employer's response

- however, the parties might not identify the relevant issues clearly on these forms and it would not be satisfactory to allow the disability issue to remain unclear until the hearing itself. It would be good practice, therefore, either to design standard directions which would clarify the issue or to arrange a directions hearing for that purpose. Parties may well wish to put forward expert evidence. Where this is the case, proper advance notice must be given to the other party of such expert evidence and a copy of the report to be relied on

- tribunals are urged to exercise the inquisitorial powers accorded to them by what are now rules 14(2) and (3) of the Tribunal Rules, contained in Schedule 1 to the Employment Tribunals (Constitution and Rules of Procedure) Regulations 2004 SI 2004/1861. The 'interventionist' role, which is set out in Schedule 6 to the Tribunal Rules in relation to equal pay claims, would be a good model for disability cases. The reason for the interventionist approach is that some claimants may be unable to accept that they are disabled and, in others, denial of the disability may itself be a symptom of their condition

- tribunals should adopt a purposive approach to the interpretation of the legislation – i.e. give effect to the stated or presumed intention of Parliament. Regard must also be had to the ordinary and natural meaning of the words. Tribunals have been given assistance in this by the Guidance

- when considering the requirement that a physical or mental impairment is 'substantial' and 'long term', the tribunal must take the Guidance into account, and where it is clear that the person is disabled within the meaning of the DDA, the tribunal must not search the Guidance for new hurdles over which the claimant has to jump. (Note, however, that in the subsequent case of Vicary v British Telecommunications plc 1999 IRLR 680, EAT, the EAT held that in determining whether the effect of an individual's impairment is 'substantial' the Guidance is of assistance in marginal cases only. See below under 'Substantial adverse effect').

It will not always be essential for a tribunal to identify a specific 'impairment' **6.18** if the existence of one can be established from the evidence of an adverse effect on the claimant's abilities – J v DLA Piper UK LLP 2010 ICR 1052, EAT. In that case, J, a qualified barrister, was interviewed for a job and a post was offered to her subject to completion of a medical questionnaire. Before completing the questionnaire, J spoke to a manager in the firm's HR department and informed her of her history of depression. A few days later, the firm contacted J to tell her that it had decided to impose a recruitment freeze as a result of the credit crunch and that the job offer was accordingly withdrawn. J brought a claim under the DDA, asserting that the real reason for the withdrawal of the offer was her medical history. The tribunal struck out the claim on the basis that J was not disabled. It decided that she did not suffer from a sufficiently well-defined impairment and, in so doing, relied on medical evidence relating to J's previous job and a report from a consultant psychiatrist which stated that the evidence of adverse effect on J's everyday activities was weak. J appealed to the EAT. Among other things, she argued that only in exceptional cases need the tribunal identify a specific 'impairment'. She submitted that the existence of an impairment will, in most cases, be evident from the existence of an adverse effect on a claimant's ability to carry out day-to-day activities, and the tribunal should examine that issue first. The EAT agreed, up to a point. It accepted that there will be cases where identifying the nature of the impairment in question involves difficult medical questions and that in most such cases it will be easier, and legitimate, for a tribunal to 'park' that issue and first consider adverse effect. However, the EAT would not go so far as to say that the impairment issue can be ignored in all but exceptional cases, stating that the distinction between impairment and effect is built into the legislation and the statutory Guidance.

(Note that part of the reason why the tribunal did not accept that the claimant was disabled in the DLA Piper case (above) was that she was unable to show that her illness impacted on her in a way prescribed under the capacities listed in the DDA. For example, if a claimant's condition did not affect his or her 'memory or ability to concentrate, learn or understand', the claim would fall at the first hurdle under the DDA, notwithstanding that the condition affected the claimant's day-to-day activities in the ordinary sense. However, the definition of disability under the EqA is no longer confined to a list of specific capacities, making it easier to prove the existence of a disability – see under 'Normal day-to-day activities' below for more details.)

6.19 **Medical cause of impairment**
Appendix 1 to the EHRC Employment Code states that 'there is no need for a person to establish a medically diagnosed cause for their impairment. What is important to consider is the effect of the impairment, not the cause' – para 7. This endorses the decision in Ministry of Defence v Hay 2008 ICR 1247, EAT, where the EAT held that an 'impairment' under S.1(1) DDA could be an illness or the result of an illness, and that it was not necessary to determine its precise medical cause. The statutory approach, said the EAT, 'is self-evidently a functional one directed towards what a claimant cannot, or can no longer, do at a practical level'.

Applying the functional approach to the case before it, the EAT ruled that a tribunal was entitled to hold that an employee who had a range of respiratory impairments, including tuberculosis, which led to his absence from work from June 2004 until his dismissal at the end of March 2006, was disabled. Although expert medical evidence indicated that the impairments attributable to tuberculosis alone would have had a substantial adverse effect on his day-to-day activities for less than 12 months, the tribunal held that he was nonetheless disabled by reason of 'a constellation of symptoms' that lasted more than a year, even though they were not all medically attributed to tuberculosis. Upholding this decision, the EAT concluded that someone who suffered from a combination of impairments with different effects, to different extents, over periods of time which overlapped, could be regarded as disabled. This view is supported by the Guidance, which states that, although a person may have more than one impairment – any one of which alone would not have a substantial adverse effect – account should be taken of whether the impairments together have a substantial effect overall on the person's ability to carry out normal day-to-day activities – para B6.

6.20 There are limits, however. In Sawyer v Secretary of State for the Department of Work and Pensions (Job Centre Plus) EAT 0133/08, for example, the EAT held that a claimant who had a history of developing colds or chest infections whenever he was in a room in which the temperature dropped to below 27 degrees centigrade was unable to establish that he was disabled under the

100

DDA, and therefore could not argue that he was discriminated against when a heater he had been given by the employer was taken away. Although S submitted a medical certificate which stated that he developed 'recurrent colds and tonsillitis chest infections', and dressed in heavy garments and woolly hats to keep warm, the EAT pointed out that 'infections, by definition, come and go'. It went on to hold that the fact that S developed a cold or chest infection when the room temperature dropped below a certain point 'was not an impairment, or at least not an impairment within the meaning of the DDA'.

Physical impairments   6.21

As we have already mentioned, there is no definition of 'physical impairment' in the EqA but in College of Ripon and York St John v Hobbs 2002 IRLR 185, EAT, the EAT said that a person has a physical impairment if he or she has 'something wrong with them physically,' and in Millar v HM Commissioners for Revenue 2006 IRLR 112, Ct Sess (Inner House), the Court of Session noted that many forms of physical impairment result from conditions that cannot be described as an illness, such as a genetic deformity. Both para 2.12 of the EHRC Employment Code and para A5 of the Guidance confirm that sensory impairments, such as those affecting sight or hearing, are included.

Examples of potential physical impairments include problems connected with the back, neck or the use of limbs, diabetes and stomach, liver, kidney or digestive problems. Sensory impairments include deafness or other disorders related to hearing, blindness and partial sight. The Appendix to the Guidance gives examples of factors that might reasonably be regarded as having a substantial adverse effect on normal day-to-day activities. For example, in the case of colour blindness, it states that it would be reasonable to have regard to an inability to distinguish any colours at all, but that it would not be reasonable to regard a simple inability to distinguish between red and green, which is not accompanied by any other effect such as blurring of vision. In other words, a minor colour deficiency would not amount to a disability whereas a serious deficiency could.

While it is potentially possible for *any* physical impairment to constitute a **6.22** disability, it is open to a tribunal to find that a person's complaint is not serious enough to be covered. In Foord v JA Johnston and Sons ET Case No.S/200300/97, for example, F, a shop assistant in a bakery, refused to work extra hours to cover for a colleague who was on holiday because standing for too long meant she would suffer a lot of pain in her legs and feet. After F was dismissed she went to see a doctor, who diagnosed her as having fallen arches, which meant that she was unable to stand or be on her feet for prolonged periods of time. However, the tribunal did not accept that F had a physical impairment under the DDA. She was able to cope with her normal working hours of 8 am to 2 pm, six days a week, and had only experienced difficulties on one occasion, when she worked an extra two hours. In the tribunal's view, this was not sufficient to indicate that F had a disability. (Note that, by way of contrast, in Creese v Royal Mail Group Ltd ET Case No.1402524/08 an employment tribunal found that an employee who worked as a postman was disabled within the meaning of the DDA on account of his fallen arches. This condition caused bouts of severe leg pain that necessitated substantial periods of sickness absence.)

6.23 **Mental cause of physical impairment.** An impairment may not be regarded as a physical impairment if it has a mental cause rather than a physical one. In McNicol v Balfour Beatty Rail Maintenance Ltd; Rugamer v Sony Music Entertainment UK Ltd 2002 ICR 381, EAT, the EAT upheld the tribunals' findings that employees suffering from 'functional' or 'psychiatric overlay' – a condition where an individual claims to be suffering from physical injury but the doctor is satisfied that there is no organic physical cause for the symptoms and believes that they result from the individual's mental state – did not have a physical impairment for the purposes of the DDA. The EAT stressed the importance of determining whether an impairment is physical or mental since, prior to amendments made in 2005, the DDA required a claimant with a mental impairment resulting from, or consisting of, a mental illness to show that he or she had a clinically well-recognised illness, while there was no such requirement for a claimant alleging a physical impairment. The EAT stated that the difference between a physical and a mental impairment depended on whether the nature of the impairment itself was physical or mental, and not on whether a physical or mental activity was affected. The decision in McNicol was subsequently upheld by the Court of Appeal – McNicol v Balfour Beatty Rail Maintenance Ltd 2002 ICR 1498, CA – the Rugamer case having already been settled. The Court said that the appeal highlighted the importance of claimants making clear the nature of the impairment on which their claim is based.

However, in the later decision of College of Ripon and York St John v Hobbs 2002 IRLR 185, EAT, the EAT refused to interfere with the tribunal's conclusion that, on the basis of H's physical symptoms (progressive muscle weakness and wasting) and the effects of those symptoms, she suffered from a physical impairment under the DDA. This was despite the fact that the neurologist who examined her found that there was 'no organic disease process causing the symptoms' and that 'her disability [was] not therefore organic'. He declined to comment on whether H had a psychological disability and suggested that it might be appropriate to seek an opinion from a consultant psychiatrist (which was not done). In the EAT's view, the tribunal had been entitled to hold on the evidence before it that 'the dysfunction described by [H] is sufficient to bring her case within the expression of "physical impairment" and that it is not necessary for us to know precisely what underlying disease or trauma has caused the physical impairment'.

6.24 The inconsistency between the McNicol and College of Ripon cases is complicated by the fact that, even though the Court of Appeal in McNicol upheld the tribunal's decision on the basis that the employee in that case did not have a physical impairment because he could not show a physical cause for his symptoms, Lord Justice Mummery – who gave the lead judgment – endorsed the EAT's comments in College of Ripon and York St John that an impairment can be either the cause or an effect. This view was confirmed by the Court of Session in Millar v Inland Revenue Commissioners 2006 IRLR 112, Ct Sess (Inner House), where the Court was of the view that the question of whether a claimant had a physical impairment could be determined without reference to causation or to any form of illness. It noted that many forms of physical impairment result from conditions that cannot be described as an illness. An amputee, for example, does not have an illness but his or her physical condition should readily establish an impairment. Where there is an issue as to the nature of the impairment, it is a matter of fact whether it is physical or mental.

The EAT sought to reconcile the McNicol and College of Ripon decisions in Hospice of St Mary of Furness v Howard 2007 IRLR 944, EAT. It noted that in neither did the claimant put forward a case based on mental impairment – the difference was that in McNicol there was express evidence, which was accepted, that there was no physical impairment, while in Hobbs, no evidence as to a lack of a physical impairment was adduced. Viewed together with Millar, these two authorities indicated that:

- it is not necessary for a claimant to establish the cause of an alleged physical impairment, but

- where there is an issue as to the existence of a physical impairment it is open to a respondent to seek to disprove the existence of such impairment, including by seeking to prove that the claimed impairment is not genuine or is mental and not physical.

The Guidance states that 'it may not always be possible, nor it is necessary, to **6.25** categorise a condition as either a physical or a mental impairment. The underlying cause of the impairment may be hard to establish. There may be adverse effects which are both physical and mental in nature. Furthermore, effects of a mainly physical nature may stem from an underlying mental impairment, and vice versa' – para A6.

Where a claimant is suffering from an impairment that has both physical and mental effects, and that cannot be easily categorised, it would be advisable for him or her to mention both types of impairment in the claim form. This would avoid the claim failing if a single categorisation given initially later turns out to be incorrect.

Examples of physical impairments. The range of conditions that are capable **6.26** of constituting physical impairments within the meaning of the EqA is very

103

broad. Examples of fairly well known physical conditions that have been held to be physical impairments under the DDA include the following:

- ME (myalgic encephalomyelitis) or chronic fatigue syndrome – Shaw and Co Solicitors v Atkins EAT 0224/08

- club-foot – Tarling v Wisdom Toothbrushes Ltd t/a Wisdom ET Case No.1500148/97

- back injury (soft tissue injury) – Gamble v New Charter Housing Trust Ltd ET Case No.2408397/09

- epilepsy – Montgomery v David Stanley Optical Ltd and ors ET Case No.3301766/08

- irritable bowel syndrome – Ali v UK Border Agency ET Case No.2704215/09

- Crohn's Disease – Pratt v Heasell Ltd ET Case No.1502549/03

- incontinence – Rimmer-Clay v Brighton Housing Trust ET Case No.3102861/08

- photosensitive epilepsy – Ridout v TC Group 1998 IRLR 628, EAT

- cerebral palsy – Carden v Essex County Council ET Case No.3203154/06

- achondroplasia (dwarfism) – English v Somerfield Stores Ltd and ors ET Case Nos.1501565/03 and another

- multiple sclerosis – Pearce v Guardian Homecare UK Ltd ET Case No.2326394/09

- diabetes – Yaqoob v Institute of Chartered Accountants in England and Wales ET Case No.2409731/08

- 'cluster headaches' (migrainous neuralgia) and chronic migraine – Lowe v Komatsu (UK) Ltd ET Case No.2500775/07; Hampson v Cheshire East Community Health Primary Care Trust ET Case No.1301717/10

- dyslexia – Nicklin v Vicky Martin Concessions Ltd ET Case No.2406032/08

- visual impairment – Price v Solus (London) Ltd ET Case No.3302118/08.

6.27 It is important to remember, however, that in order for a condition to amount to a disability, the other criteria in the S.6(1) definition must also be satisfied. These are considered later in this chapter. The difference in the severity of a particular impairment and the particular effect it has on the individual concerned means that exactly the same condition can rightly be held to amount to a disability in one case but not to constitute a disability in another. Before examining the component parts of the statutory definition of disability, we shall first discuss three of the most common medical conditions in the United Kingdom: back injury, epilepsy and incontinence.

Back injury. Back problems are potentially capable of constituting a physical **6.28** impairment under the EqA but, as with all conditions, whether an individual's impairment does in fact amount to a disability will depend on the manner and degree to which it affects that person. An example of a case where an employee's back problems were held to be a disability is Friskney v Total Systems Services Processing Europe Ltd ET Case No.1800541/08. F suffered damage to a disk in his spine during a road traffic accident in August 2006 but he did not reveal this fact when he was recruited in December of that year. His pain was such that he could not sit at his desk for more than an hour without walking around for ten minutes, and he had trouble concentrating on his work. In November 2007, F was dismissed for incapability. Following a preliminary hearing to determine whether F was disabled, the tribunal believed that he had very substantially exaggerated the effect of his injury on his day-to-day activities. A consultant neurosurgeon had observed that F could manage his job without difficulty; could help his wife with vacuum-cleaning and washing-up; and had resumed cycling as a sporting activity. Notwithstanding this, the tribunal determined that F was disabled for the purposes of the DDA. A significant part of its decision was the fact that F had undergone spinal surgery, which carries the risk of serious repercussions if it were to go wrong. This demonstrated that F's back injury was having a substantial adverse effect on his day-to-day activities and in particular his mobility and his ability to concentrate.

Despite the fact that some back injuries are notoriously difficult to prove or disprove, cases will often turn on the medical evidence. For example, in Howlett v Hawes Signs Ltd ET Case No.1200301/98 H, a warehouseman, had a history of back problems and underwent surgery in April 1997. On 5 December 1997, H's doctor informed his employer that H had made excellent progress and would have no difficulty in moving small items, although he might need help in lifting larger ones. The employer had no other work for H to do and H brought a tribunal claim based on the employer's failure to remove heavy lifting from his job. The tribunal dismissed the claim because H had failed to establish that he was disabled within the meaning of the DDA. The doctor's report had given him the all-clear. Moreover, the report of H's consultant orthopaedic surgeon in June 1998 had stated that he had 'returned to driving and normal activities' several months previously and was ready to return to work in a non-lifting job. In the tribunal's view, those medical reports were wholly inconsistent with any claim that H was disabled.

It is important to remember that, although normal work-related activities **6.29** should be taken into account, the test for determining whether an individual has a disability relates to the person's ability to carry out normal *day-to-day* activities, not whether he or she can carry out specialist work (see further under 'Normal day-to-day activities' below). In Bourne v ECT Bus CIC EAT 0288/08 B was employed as a bus driver and suffered a soft-tissue injury to her back in a road traffic accident. The employer's occupational health doctor and B's own

GP certified her as fit to work but B was adamant that she was unable to do any work and she was eventually dismissed on the ground of incapacity. At a subsequent tribunal hearing, a jointly instructed expert concluded that B had exaggerated the effect of her injuries and it was noted that she had obtained work with another transport company as a bus driver just over one year after her dismissal. The tribunal held that B was not disabled under the DDA because, among other things, it was not satisfied that there was a substantial adverse effect on her ability to carry out normal day-to-day activities. Before the EAT, B argued that it was perverse for the tribunal to find that she was dismissed for incapacity but that there was not a substantial adverse effect on her day-to-day activities. However, the EAT dismissed her appeal. The tribunal did not find that B was unable to perform her job for a 12-month period and it was therefore not bound to consider her disabled simply because she was dismissed on the ground of incapacity. Further, even if B could not fully carry out her job of driving a bus for an eight-hour shift, that was not a normal day-to-day activity.

Even where employees are successful in showing that their back problem amounts to a disability, their claims may fail on the ground that the employer was justified in the less favourable treatment – usually dismissal. In Sillifant v North and East Devon Health Authority ET Case No.1401241/97 S, an office manager, injured her back in a fall while on holiday, resulting in frequent absences from work, for which she was dismissed. The medical evidence presented to the tribunal showed that S had suffered muscle and ligament tendon damage of the kind that generally takes two years to mend. The tribunal found that S was disabled under the DDA because her physical impairment had a substantial and long-term effect on her ability to carry out normal day-to-day activities. However, the tribunal dismissed her claim of disability-related discrimination because, although the Council may have treated her less favourably on account of her disability, its actions were justified in circumstances in which the employee's job was a key one in a small department and she could not say when she would return to work.

6.30 **Epilepsy.** Epilepsy is the second most common neurological condition in the United Kingdom after migraine. In the majority of cases, it can be effectively controlled by medication and causes few problems in the workplace. In some cases, however, it gives rise to legitimate concerns, particularly where an employee experiences epileptic seizures at work. These concerns become acute where the employee's job involves working with unguarded machinery or safeguarding the well-being of others. Even though there is some controversy about whether it is a physical or a mental impairment, epilepsy is clearly capable of constituting an impairment for the purposes of the EqA and, indeed, it was held to amount to a disability under the DDA.

Before dismissing any epileptic employee, even on safety grounds, an employer should apprise itself fully of the employee's medical history. For example, in

Hudson v Lincolnshire Partnership NHS Trust ET Case No.2602808/08 H suffered from epilepsy, which gave rise to a number of absences from work. He was also absent for a lengthy period as a result of a tooth abscess, caused when the drugs that the dentist gave him reacted with the drugs that he took to control the epilepsy. The Trust then put him on notice that further periods of absence would not be tolerated. The following year H began suffering from balance problems, meaning that at times he would fall down and have to crawl on all fours. This led to another absence from work and the Trust decided that he should be dismissed. Between notice of dismissal and the expiry of that notice, a change in H's drug regime had been implemented and his balance problems were resolved – it was believed that the build-up of his drugs over the years had had an adverse effect on H. Although the Trust's occupational health adviser cleared him to return to work, H was put on garden leave for the remainder of his notice period and the Trust refused to reconsider the issue of his dismissal. H's disability discrimination claims were upheld – in any ordinary case in which a clinician had indicated that there had been a cure which substantially altered an employee's future prognosis, any reasonable employer would have rescinded – or at the very least suspended – the decision to dismiss. The tribunal concluded that H was treated differently by the Trust because of his epilepsy.

However, there may be occasions when it is reasonable for an employer to send **6.31** an employee home on health and safety grounds while further investigations are made. In Yarrow v Thorn Lighting Ltd ET Case No.2500604/97, for instance, Y was recruited to work on a conveyor belt system at a busy factory where there were forklift trucks in operation. The company learnt from Y's previous employer that Y had had several blackouts or fits during the course of her employment. It was suggested that she did not always take her medication and that she regularly drank large amounts of alcohol, which exacerbated the problem. Following a medical examination by the company doctor, Y's employer decided that further information was necessary before she could be allowed to return to work. The tribunal was satisfied that Y had a disability and that her medical condition presented a health and safety risk either to herself or to others if she were to fail to take her medication. However, further medical investigations were necessary in order to assess the nature and extent of her condition. The tribunal concluded that the company was justified in sending Y home and asking her to satisfy it that it was safe to employ her before allowing her back to work.

Incontinence. Incontinence can be either a physical impairment in itself or a **6.32** side-effect of surgery to deal with another physical ailment or condition. If the former, then it is likely to be regarded as having an adverse effect on the ability to carry out normal day-to-day activities and the main issue for the tribunal will be whether, in the individual circumstances of the case, that effect is substantial. In Bonhomme v Communisis plc ET Case No.1801127/02, for

107

example, an employment tribunal held that a claimant who suffered from colitis resulting in occasional bouts of severe incontinence was disabled for the purposes of the DDA.

The Appendix to the 2010 Guidance, which is entitled 'An illustrative and non-exhaustive list of factors which, if they are experienced by a disabled person, it would be reasonable to regard as having a substantial adverse effect on normal day-to-day activities', includes 'difficulty carrying out activities associated with toileting, or caused by frequent minor incontinence'. However, infrequent minor incontinence is excluded.

6.33 In Rimmer-Clay v Brighton Housing Trust ET Case No.3102861/08 an employment tribunal held that R-C was disabled by reason of stress incontinence. Even though she had undergone a remedial surgical procedure, the tribunal was satisfied that the surgery was likely only to alleviate the symptoms rather than cure them and that, as a result, the claimant was suffering from a 'recurring condition' within the meaning of para 2(2) of Schedule 1 to the DDA (now para 2(2) of Schedule 1 to the EqA) – see 'Long-term effect – recurring conditions' below for more details. In deciding that the claimant's condition had a substantial adverse effect on her ability to carry out normal day-to-day activities, the tribunal held that the beneficial effects of surgical procedure fell to be disregarded by virtue of para 6(1) of Schedule 1 to the DDA (now para 6(1) of Schedule 1 to the EqA).

Where incontinence occurs as the *result* of surgery (or other medical treatment), the claimant is likely to be regarded as being disabled by another route. Under para 8 of Schedule 1 to the EqA, special provision is made for persons who are disabled by virtue of 'progressive conditions', which can include those conditions that have been successfully treated in themselves but where the effects of the treatment give rise to a further impairment the effects of which are already substantial or likely to become so in the future. In Kirton v Tetrosyl Ltd 2003 ICR 1237, CA, the Court of Appeal held that a claimant who suffered from urinary incontinence due to a sphincter deficiency as a result of surgery for prostate cancer had a 'progressive condition'. The Court reasoned that, as the surgery was a standard response to the discovery of the applicant's progressive cancer condition which, when undertaken, led to a real possibility of sphincter deficiency, the impairment of urinary incontinence was 'as a result of that condition' within the meaning of para 8(1)(b); and that, since the cancer was likely to result in an impairment, though of a different kind, which would have a substantial adverse effect, the applicant was to be taken, by virtue of para 8(1), to have an impairment which had a substantial adverse effect for the purposes of the definition of 'disability'.

6.34 Subsequent changes to the definition of disability would now mean that the claimant in the Kirton case would be deemed to have a disability simply by virtue of having cancer – see 'Deemed disabilities' below. However, the principle established in that case holds good. This is reflected in the Guidance which, at para B.22, offers the following example of a person who would be regarded as disabled under para 8 of Schedule 1 to the EqA: 'A man has an operation to remove the colon because of progressing and uncontrollable ulcerative colitis. The operation results in his no longer experiencing adverse effects from the colitis. He requires a colostomy, however, which means that his bowel actions can only be controlled by a sanitary appliance. This requirement for an appliance substantially affects his ability to undertake a normal day-to-day activity and should be taken into account as an adverse effect arising from the original impairment.'

Mental impairments

6.35

There is no definition of 'mental impairment' in the EqA but Appendix 1 to the EHRC Employment Code states: 'The term "mental impairment" is intended to cover a wide range of impairments relating to mental functioning, including what are often known as learning disabilities' – para 6.

Mr Justice Lindsay, then President of EAT, set out guidelines for parties seeking to establish the existence of a mental impairment under the DDA in Morgan v Staffordshire University 2002 ICR 475, EAT, and although this decision has less significance now in light of the changes introduced by the Disability Discrimination Act 2005 (see under 'Mental illness' below), it still contains some useful pointers:

- tribunal members cannot be expected to have anything more than rudimentary familiarity with psychiatric classification. Matters therefore need to be spelt out. Claimants should identify clearly and in good time before the hearing exactly what their impairment is and respondents should indicate whether that impairment is an issue and, if so, why. The parties will then be clear as to what has to be proved or rebutted, in medical terms, at the hearing

- tribunals are unlikely to be satisfied of the existence of a mental impairment in the absence of suitable expert evidence. However, this does not mean that a full consultant psychiatrist's report is required in every case. There will be many cases where the illness is sufficiently marked for the claimant's GP to prove it. Whoever deposes, it will be prudent for the specific requirements of the legislation to be drawn to that person's attention

- if it becomes clear that, despite a GP's letter or other initially available indication, an impairment is to be disputed on technical medical grounds, then thought will need to be given to further expert evidence (see 'Medical evidence' below)

- there will be many cases, particularly if the failure to make adjustments is in issue, where the medical evidence will need to cover not merely a description of the mental illness but when, over what periods, and how it can be expected to have manifested itself in the course of the claimant's employment

- the dangers of a tribunal forming a view on mental impairment from the way the claimant gives evidence on the day cannot be overstated. Tribunal members need to remind themselves that few mental illnesses are such that the symptoms are obvious all the time and that they have no training or, as is likely, expertise, in the detection of real or simulated psychiatric disorders. Furthermore, the date of the hearing itself will seldom be a date on which the presence of the impairment will need to be proved or disproved.

6.36 Below, we discuss four conditions that have given rise to a number of cases on the question of mental impairment: stress, post-traumatic stress disorder, depression and dyslexia. We also consider autism spectrum disorders, including Asperger's syndrome. First, however, it is useful to briefly explain the impact of the DSM-IV and to look at two general categories of mental impairment – mental illness and learning difficulties.

6.37 **DSM-IV.** Prior to changes introduced by the Disability Discrimination Act 2005, a mental illness could only amount to a mental impairment if it was a 'clinically well-recognised illness'. The version of the Guidance in force at the time stated that a clinically well-recognised illness was one that was recognised by 'a respected body of medical opinion'. It went on to state that it was very likely that this would include those illnesses specifically mentioned in publications such as the American Diagnostic and Statistical Manual of Mental Disorders, 4th Edition, 1994, called simply DSM-IV. This publication, a new edition of which is currently under consultation and is due to be published in May 2013, has attracted much criticism over the years with regard to the validity and reliability of its diagnoses. Furthermore, opponents argue that it bears no relation to an agreed scientific model of mental disorder and that the decisions taken about its categories were therefore not scientific ones.

Despite these criticisms, there is evidence that tribunals still have regard to DSM-IV when deciding whether or not a mental impairment exists, notwithstanding that they are no longer obliged to under the law. For example, in Hull v Tamar Science Park ET Case No.1702199/08 the tribunal noted the report of a chartered clinical psychologist, L, which stated that, following a car accident in May 2006, H suffered a sufficient number and range of symptoms to satisfy the DSM-IV criteria for post-traumatic stress disorder. The tribunal accepted L's diagnosis that H suffered from a stress-related disorder.

6.38 **Mental illness.** The DDA originally stated that a mental illness would only amount to a mental impairment if it was a 'clinically well-recognised illness'. However, a common problem, identified in research carried out for the former Department for Education and Employment, was that 'many people with quite severe mental illnesses may not have a clear diagnosis, or may have different diagnoses at different times', which made it difficult for them to satisfy that requirement. Consequently, the requirement was removed by S.18 of the Disability Discrimination Act 2005 as from 5 December 2005. The effect of this was to put mental illness on a par with physical impairments and other mental impairments, a parity now reflected in the EqA. It means, in practical terms, that the focus of the tribunal's inquiry is on the effect the mental impairment has on the employee's day-to-day activities.

Tribunals should be careful not to fall into the trap of applying too exacting a standard for determining whether a condition qualifies as a mental impairment. In Rayner v Turning Point and ors EAT 0397/10 one of the reasons given by the EAT for overturning a tribunal's decision that the claimant was not disabled was the tribunal's over-reliance on a medical report compiled by an eminent psychologist that had concentrated on the pre-2005 requirement to show a clinically well-recognised illness to establish that a person was suffering from a mental impairment. In the words of His Honour Judge McMullen, the former test required 'a more rigorous clinical diagnosis' than was the case following the 2005 amendments to the DDA.

6.39 In Goodwin v Patent Office 1999 ICR 302, EAT, G, a paranoid schizophrenic, was employed by the Patent Office as a patent examiner but he was not on proper medication during the eight months he worked there. He was dismissed following complaints from work colleagues about his odd behaviour and brought a complaint of disability discrimination under the DDA. The tribunal heard evidence from a doctor that G had a mental illness and that his symptoms – imagining that others could access his thoughts, putting a paranoid interpretation on the words and actions of others, and auditory hallucinations, which often caused him to leave his office or the building – impaired G's ability to sustain concentration for any period. However, the tribunal held that G did not have a disability because the effect of his mental illness on his ability to carry out normal day-to-day activities was not substantial.

The EAT overruled the tribunal, holding that the evidence inevitably led to the conclusion that an employee who had paranoid schizophrenia had a disability within the meaning of the DDA. The tribunal had overlooked the detailed reasons for G's dismissal that the Patent Office had set out in its response. On that form, it had related various incidents of G's odd behaviour at work and the warning G had been given about his behaviour towards two female employees. The Patent Office had added that it had sought the advice of the occupational health service, through which G had been examined by a doctor. The doctor advised that G did not have the ability to provide a regular and effective service. Furthermore, at the tribunal hearing the Patent Office produced a note from G's manager complaining that G was unable to hold a normal conversation. The EAT commented that this alone was good evidence that G's ability to concentrate and communicate had been adversely affected

111

to a significant degree. The EAT remitted the case to a differently constituted tribunal for it to determine whether the Patent Office was nonetheless justified in having dismissed G.

6.40 In McDougall v Richmond Adult Community College 2007 ICR 1567, EAT, M sought to argue that that her compulsory admission (i.e. sectioning) under the Mental Health Act 1983 was itself conclusive evidence that she had a mental impairment within the meaning of the DDA. The EAT held that, as a matter of law, a person satisfying the conditions for compulsory admission under the 1983 Act does not necessarily satisfy the conditions for disability under the DDA. It went on to say, however, that in practice, a mental impairment leading to sectioning limits a person's ability to carry out normal day-to-day activities and has a substantial adverse effect thereon. Furthermore, in the circumstances of the case, the severity of the employee's condition – which left her unable to understand the real world – meant that she was disabled for DDA purposes. Although the EAT's judgment was later overturned by the Court of Appeal, this aspect of its decision was not appealed and therefore remains good law (see 'Long-term effect – recurring conditions' below).

6.41 **Learning difficulties.** Appendix 1 to the EHRC Employment Code makes it clear that the term 'mental impairment' is intended to cover learning disabilities – see para 6. In Dunham v Ashford Windows 2005 ICR 1584, EAT, the EAT gave guidance on how tribunals should deal with mental impairment cases where the impairment is a learning difficulty, such as dyslexia, rather than a mental illness. D, who had difficulties reading and writing, was employed by AW as a fork-lift truck driver and yardman. Following his dismissal, he brought a complaint alleging that his employer had discriminated against him on the ground of disability by dismissing him and by failing to make reasonable adjustments to accommodate his difficulties. A preliminary issue arose as to whether D was disabled within the meaning of the DDA. The evidence before the tribunal consisted of a report compiled by C, a senior psychologist, which stated that D suffered from 'generalised borderline moderate learning difficulties'. Having considered the report, the tribunal accepted that D had obvious problems coping with matters of numeracy, literacy and memory. It concluded, however, that he failed to establish that he suffered from a mental impairment within the terms of the DDA. Part of the tribunal's reasoning was that C was a psychologist and not a medical practitioner. In overturning the decision, the EAT accepted that a claimant is unlikely to establish a mental impairment solely on the basis of 'difficulties at school' or because he or she 'is not very bright'. Expert evidence as to the nature and degree of the impairment is required, although in a case involving learning difficulties, evidence from a doctor is not essential. Medical evidence is not required in every case, especially where there is appropriate expert evidence as to the type and nature of impairment.

Stress. Since the late 1990s, stress has become one of the key employment law **6.42** issues. Although it is not a psychiatric injury or even a mental illness, stress can lead to feelings of anxiety and depression and may exacerbate other conditions such as dyslexia or epilepsy, or even physical conditions – see, for example, Walton v Nescot ET Case No.2305250/00, where an employee's diabetes was aggravated by his stressful working conditions. Furthermore, employees complaining of stress may in fact be suffering from a stress-related illness, such as clinical depression, which has been triggered or exacerbated by the levels of stress with which they have to cope. This is dealt with below under 'Depression'. Since the removal of the requirement in 2005 to show a clinically well-recognised illness in order for a mental impairment to qualify as a 'disability' for the purposes of what is now S.6(1) EqA (see 'Mental illness' above), it has become easier for claimants to show that depression and stress-related conditions comprise such impairments. But for the reasons outlined immediately below, this does not mean that these conditions will comprise a disability in every case.

It is not uncommon for employees who are absent from work to say that they are suffering from 'stress', 'work stress', 'anxiety', 'nervous debility' or 'depression'. But this does not necessarily mean that they are disabled for the purposes of the EqA. As noted above, they must demonstrate a physical or mental impairment. Because stress itself does not constitute a disability, a failure to recruit or a dismissal based on a person's propensity to suffer from stress will not amount to unlawful discrimination. In order for an individual to succeed in such a claim, he or she must show that the stress related to a disability. For example, in Hull v Tamar Science Park ET Case No.1702199/08 H was diagnosed in 2004 as suffering from moderately severe agitated depression and hypertension. She had endured a particularly stressful year in 2007, which included a car accident, two deaths and the end of a relationship. All this was compounded by ongoing work stress that left H suffering from low moods, poor sleep and difficulty in coping with everyday matters. Although she felt much better by the end of 2007, by January 2008 she was again experiencing stress – for example, she felt anxious about official letters and waited a day or two before a friend could open them for her. The tribunal accepted that H suffered from a stress-related illness and that she was disabled for the purposes of the DDA.

As the Hull case shows, the nature of stress is that it can occur in bouts, **6.43** separated by periods of stress-free good mental health. The fact that an employee can enjoy stress-free periods is no barrier to establishing that the stress condition is a disability provided he or he can show that the impairment has a substantial adverse effect on his or her ability to carry out day-to-day activities. So, for example, in Ahern v Republic Retail Ltd ET Case No.1404415/09 the claimant began working for the employer in September 2008, at which point she had suffered from chronic anxiety for seven or eight years. She requested that she be permitted to work four days a week,

113

enabling her to attend counselling one day a week. This was agreed, but shortly afterwards her manager left and she was required to explain her reasons for working part time to every subsequent manager. A felt she had to continually fight to retain the adjustments agreed at the outset. In July 2009 a new manager tried to change her days and hours of work and she was forced to bring a grievance to re-establish her originally agreed terms. The claim was upheld to the extent that, by failing to keep any adequate personnel records as to employees' disabilities, A suffered frustration and stress each time a new manager was appointed. That amounted to a failure to make reasonable adjustments.

6.44 **Post-traumatic stress disorder.** A severe stress reaction, such as post-traumatic stress disorder, is potentially capable of constituting a disability. This disorder arises as a result of an event of an exceptionally threatening or catastrophic nature, such as a serious accident, witnessing violent death or being the victim of torture, terrorism or rape. Furthermore, the effects may be delayed and/or protracted. An example:

- **Dunball v Glenkeir Whiskies Ltd** ET Case No.3201252/08: D, an assistant manager for GW Ltd, suffered from post-traumatic stress disorder following a road traffic accident in early 2007 and then became ill with depression. She returned to work in September only because her general manager told her that her job would otherwise be at risk. However, D was still unwell and in November – following a very difficult period of clumsiness at work, panic attacks, extreme anxiety, and reduced awareness of safety – she was admitted to a mental health facility where she remained for ten days. She was eventually dismissed. The tribunal found that D was a disabled person for the purposes of the DDA at the relevant time. She suffered a mental impairment, namely moderate depression and post-traumatic stress disorder, which was likely to last 12 months and recur. Also, the mental impairment had a substantial impact on D's normal day-to-day activities.

In Abadeh v British Telecommunications plc 2001 ICR 156, EAT, A, a telephone operator employed by BT, received a sudden blast of loud, high-pitched noise through the left earphone of his headset. The incident caused A to suffer permanent hearing loss, tinnitus and post-traumatic stress disorder. The tribunal accepted that post-traumatic stress disorder amounted to a mental impairment but held that it did not amount to a disability in A's case because it did not have a substantial adverse effect on his ability to carry out normal day-to-day activities. On appeal, the EAT found a number of errors in the tribunal's approach – such as failing to assess the beneficial effects of A's ongoing medical treatment – and remitted the case to another tribunal.

6.45 **Depression.** Depression affects a person's physical state, mood and thought processes, and is an illness that requires treatment. It can manifest itself in many different forms, with the most common types being mild, moderate and severe – or clinical – depression. Depression can affect anyone at any age and, according to the Mental Health Foundation, one in six people will experience it at some point in their life.

Tribunals and the EAT have no difficulty in holding that depression is potentially **6.46** capable of constituting a disability. Three examples:

- **Kapadia v London Borough of Lambeth** 2000 IRLR 14, EAT: in 1995 K was diagnosed by his general practitioner as having reactive depression and was referred to R, a consultant clinical psychologist, who gave K about 20 counselling sessions over the following two years. In 1997 the Council's medical adviser advised that K was permanently unfit to undertake his duties and K was retired on medical grounds. A tribunal found that K's depression was a mental impairment but held that it did not amount to a disability because it had no more than a trivial effect on his ability to carry out normal day-to-day activities. The EAT reversed this decision. The tribunal had disregarded medical evidence that clearly showed that the effect of K's depression was much more than trivial. For example, his general practitioner's report stated that K had considerable difficulty concentrating, that his sleeping pattern was affected and that he experienced 'degrees of agoraphobia'. The doctor's evidence also stated that without the counselling sessions, there was a very strong likelihood that he would suffer a total mental breakdown. (Note that this case was subsequently appealed to the Court of Appeal on other grounds – see 'Medical evidence' below)

- **Harris v Royal Mencap Society** ET Case No.2303029/09: H, a purchasing officer, was signed off work in February 2008. His GP reported that he was suffering from anxiety and depression, and put him on antidepressants. H came back to work in March and remained at work until October when, owing to capability issues, he was signed off sick again. He never returned. At a preliminary hearing the tribunal found that H was disabled for the purposes of the DDA. By July 2008 he had been taking antidepressants for four months and the tribunal was satisfied that, but for the medication, his depression would have had a substantial adverse effect on his concentration – a day-to-day activity. Furthermore, there was a significant risk that H's impairment would last 12 months

- **Ward v Signs by Morrell Ltd** ET Case No.2106342/97: W complained that he was dismissed in August 1997 because of the depression from which he had been suffering since the summer of 1996. The depression was brought on by matrimonial difficulties and problems at work and, without Prozac, his life would have been very difficult. He had trouble sleeping and lost concentration, especially when cooking, with the result, for example, that he would forget how long the potatoes had been boiling. W also claimed that he was generally forgetful and lacked confidence and although he still

115

enjoyed playing football, he lacked the enthusiasm to get into the team. At a preliminary hearing the tribunal accepted W's evidence and held that he was disabled, as his depression amounted to a mental impairment which had a substantial and long-term adverse effect on his normal day-to-day activities.

6.47 In many cases, however, employees fail to establish that their depression is serious enough to constitute a disability. It may be that their symptoms are not severe enough to amount to a physical or mental impairment; or that the depression does not have a substantial effect on their ability to carry out normal day-to-day activities; or that the illness does not last, or is not likely to last, for at least 12 months. In J v DLA Piper UK LLP 2010 ICR 1052, EAT, the EAT said that, when considering the question of impairment in cases of alleged depression, tribunals should be aware of the distinction between clinical depression and a reaction to adverse circumstances. While both can produce symptoms of low mood and anxiety, only the first condition should be recognised by the DDA. In practice, the requirement that any impairment must have long-term effects if it is to amount to a disability for the purposes of the EqA should assist in drawing a line between the two.

6.48 **Dyslexia.** According to the British Dyslexia Association, dyslexia is often referred to as a 'specific learning difficulty' and can affect reading, spelling, writing, memory and concentration, and sometimes maths, music, foreign languages and self-organisation. The Association estimates that around 4 per cent of the population are severely dyslexic and a further 6 per cent have mild to moderate problems. The accepted clinical view is that dyslexia is not a sign of low intelligence.

What an employer may perceive as poor written skills, slowness, forgetfulness, lack of concentration or poor organisational or time-management skills may in fact be the result of dyslexia. Therefore, an employer who takes such factors into account when selecting employees for job vacancies, redundancy, promotion or training opportunities, or relies on them to dismiss an employee on the ground of incapability, should exercise caution if it wishes to avoid liability under the EqA. (Note that the extent to which an employer's knowledge can affect liability under the Act is considered in Chapter 20, 'Discrimination arising from disability', under 'Employer's knowledge of disability'.) An example:

- **Bid v KPMG LLP** ET Case No.1300313/09: B, a graduate accountant trainee, was unaware that she was dyslexic. As part of her training, she was required to take regular exams and KPMG had a strict policy – which was contractual – that trainees were only allowed two attempts at a paper. In October 2008, B failed her first attempt at a knowledge paper and her course tutor alerted KPMG to the possibility that she might be dyslexic. B failed her second attempt at the paper and was dismissed. In subsequent tribunal proceedings, B claimed that KPMG had failed in its duty to make reasonable adjustments under the DDA. The employment tribunal agreed – it would have been a reasonable adjustment for KPMG to have avoided applying its exam policy until such time as it was established whether B was disabled and, if so, whether that had affected her performance.

Note that establishing that the effect of dyslexia is long term will not normally be a contentious issue, since it will generally have been present from an early age, even if undiagnosed until later in life.

Autism spectrum disorders. Disorders that fall within the term 'autism **6.49** spectrum' are currently classified as pervasive developmental disorders. These include autism, Asperger's syndrome and Rett syndrome, all of which are typically characterised by social deficits, communication difficulties, stereotyped or repetitive behaviours and interests, and/or cognitive delays. Although these disorders share some common features, sufferers are often described as being 'on the spectrum' because of differences in severity across these conditions. Asperger's syndrome (or Asperger disorder), which is one of the most common autism spectrum disorders (ASDs), is characterised by significant difficulties in social interaction, alongside restricted and repetitive patterns of behaviour and interests. Although not an invariable feature of the condition, people suffering from Asperger's often use language in an unusual way and display physical clumsiness.

In Hewett v Motorola Ltd 2004 IRLR 545, EAT, the EAT held that an employment tribunal erred in holding that an employee with Asperger's syndrome was not disabled within the meaning of the DDA because the difficulties in relation to communication and social interaction that his impairment caused were not specifically included in the 'capacities' listed in para 4(1) of Schedule 1 to the Act (which defined the circumstances in which an impairment was to be taken to affect a person's ability to carry out normal day-to-day activities). According to the EAT, the concept of 'understanding' – which was included in para 4(1) – was not limited simply to an ability to understand information, knowledge or instructions, and a person who has difficulty in understanding normal social interaction among people and/or the subtleties of human non-factual communication can be regarded as having his or her understanding affected.

The list of specified 'capacities' previously set out in para 4(1) has not been **6.50** included in the EqA, as the Government reasoned that it served little or no purpose in helping to establish whether someone is disabled and was an unnecessary extra barrier to disabled persons bringing claims of disability discrimination – see under 'Normal day-to-day activities' below for further details. It would therefore be surprising if any tribunal were now to find that a person diagnosed with an ASD was not disabled within the meaning of S.6(1) EqA. Certainly, since the Hewitt decision, there have been many instances of

117

tribunals upholding discrimination claims brought by those suffering from such disorders.

6.51 Three examples:

- **Isles v London Borough of Ealing** ET Case No. 3301433/04: I began working for the respondent Council in August 1999. In September of that year he was diagnosed as suffering from Asperger's syndrome and informed his employer about his condition. In March 2004 he applied for an internal post but was not shortlisted. He lodged a grievance, as a result of which the employer told him that neither of the two managers who had carried out the shortlisting were aware of his disability and that, had they been so aware, it might have affected their scoring and judgement. At that point the employer called in an independent consultant who obtained information from the internet about Asperger's syndrome and then assessed I's application for the post. The consultant confirmed the initial judgement that I would not be shortlisted. An employment tribunal upheld I's claim of disability on the basis that the reason that his grievance was rejected was the employer's perception of his disability and its impact on him if he were to be offered the post for which he had applied. The employer had failed to make reasonable adjustments in that there was no discussion with I regarding the way that his condition affected him and his work. I was awarded £7,500 for injury to feelings

- **Forsyth v Harris t/a The Sportsman** Case No.1100006/10: F, who was employed in July 2008 to wash up and provide cover for other kitchen workers in the employer's restaurant, suffered from an ASD that resulted in language and communication impairments. He was guaranteed three shifts of six hours per week but by the middle of August 2009 the number of shifts he was offered began to decrease. On 26 August he was late for work and on his arrival found that alternative cover had been arranged and he was sent home. The manager of the restaurant alleged that F had been rude to her. He denied this, but offered to apologise if he had upset her in any way and asked for a meeting so that he could discuss his disability and establish simple adjustments to ensure a successful working relationship. The employer failed to reply but thereafter excluded F from the rota. In October the employer accepted, in a phone call to F, that he had been dismissed, asserting that the reasons for this were F's lateness and the fact that he was incompetent in his job and had been rude to his manager. An employment tribunal found F to be disabled for the purposes of the DDA and upheld his claims of both disability discrimination and unfair dismissal. With regard to the former claim, the tribunal found that, as F had specifically referred to his condition, the employer either knew or ought to have known that F was disabled. He had been put at a disadvantage by the employer's required method of working since, as a result of his condition, he needed clear instructions, preferably in written form, yet the employer had never provided him with clear information about his performance and had never explained that he was at risk of dismissal if his performance did not show a consistent improvement. The employer had failed to make reasonable adjustments and F was accordingly awarded £3,000 for injury to feelings

• **Morgan v Northamptonshire Teaching Primary Care Trust** ET Case No.1201412/09: M had worked for the respondent Trust as an agency worker from April 2008 to January 2009. During this period he was diagnosed with Asperger's syndrome, which impaired his emotional understanding and caused difficulties with social interaction. In January 2009 he applied for a permanent post with the employer and informed it of his disability. He was shortlisted and did well at interview, as a result of which he was made a conditional offer of employment, subject to obtaining two satisfactory references and clearance from its occupational health department. However, a reference from M's former employer stated that it would not take him back, primarily because of his sickness and lateness. The reference acknowledged that the sickness and lateness were due to his recently diagnosed condition, which was now being treated. A second reference was also poor, remarking on the deterioration in M's emotional health and performance. The Trust decided to withdraw its job offer even before receiving the outcome of the occupational health report. An employment tribunal found that M was disabled and the employer ought to have been aware that this was the case. Rather than simply withdrawing the job offer, it should have made the reasonable adjustments of obtaining a more detailed occupational health assessment and discussing with M ways in which reasonable adjustments in the workplace could help him.

Deemed disabilities   6.52
Under para 7 of Schedule 1 to the EqA, regulations may be made prescribing descriptions of people who are to be treated as having disabilities and circumstances in which a person who has a disability is to be treated as no longer having it.

The Equality Act 2010 (Disability) Regulations 2010 SI 2010/2128 provide that people certified by a consultant ophthalmologist as:

• blind

• sight impaired or severely sight impaired, or

• partially sighted

are deemed to have a disability, and therefore be disabled, for the purposes of the Act – Reg 7.

6.53 In addition, para 6 of Schedule 1 to the EqA provides that certain specified medical conditions are to be treated as disabilities. These are:

- cancer

- HIV infection (defined as infection by a virus capable of causing the Acquired Immune Deficiency Syndrome), and

- multiple sclerosis.

This means that individuals with these conditions are effectively deemed to have a disability from the point of diagnosis without the need to satisfy the various elements of the statutory test. Under the equivalent provision in the DDA (para 6A, Sch 1 DDA), regulations could be made excluding certain types of cancer from the scope of the deeming provision. However, after consulting in 2005 on the use of this power, the Government concluded that it would be too difficult to exclude minor cancers without also risking the exclusion of more serious conditions. Accordingly, the power was not exercised and it has not been carried over into the EqA.

6.54 **Disabled Persons (Employment) Act 1944.** Paragraph 7 of Schedule 1 to the DDA also provided that a person would be deemed to be disabled for an 'initial period' if he or she was registered as a disabled person under the Disabled Persons (Employment) Act 1944 (or its Northern Ireland equivalent) on both 12 January 1995 and 2 December 1996. This provision continues to have effect despite the repeal of the DDA – see Article 19(d) of the Equality Act 2010 (Commencement No.4, Savings, Consequential, Transitional, Transitory and Incidental Provisions and Revocation) Order 2010 SI 2010/2317. The 'initial period' was the period of three years beginning on 2 December 1996, and during the initial period a person was deemed to be disabled. After the initial period (which has now expired) that person is deemed to have been disabled throughout that period and hence can claim protection against discrimination on the ground of past disabilities – see 'Past disabilities' below. A certificate of registration will be treated as conclusive evidence of a person's registration under the 1944 Act and, unless the contrary is shown, any document purporting to be a certificate of registration will be taken to be such a certificate and to have been validly issued.

In Quinlan v B&Q plc EAT 1386/97 Q underwent open-heart surgery in 1987 and was registered disabled as from March 1996. He was dismissed from his subsequent position as general assistant at a garden centre because he was unable to undertake heavy lifting, which would have been potentially injurious to his health. He was not disabled under the deeming provisions in para 7, Schedule 1 DDA because he had not satisfied the condition of being registered on both 12 January 1995 and 2 December 1996. In order to qualify for protection, Q therefore had to satisfy the DDA definition of a disabled person. However, the EAT upheld the tribunal's finding that Q's physical impairment did not amount to a disability under that Act as he was able to lift everyday objects and his ability to carry out normal day-to-day activities was therefore not affected.

Past disabilities   6.55

Section 6(4) and para 9 of Schedule 1 to the EqA contain the provisions on past disabilities previously found in S.2 and Schedule 2 to the DDA, with minor modifications. The effect of these provisions is to extend the protection afforded to those with current disabilities to those who have had a disability in the past.

Section 6(4) stipulates that most of the EqA's provisions (including the employment provisions) apply in relation to a person who has had a disability, and modifies the wording of the Act accordingly. It does not matter that the disability was experienced at a time before the provisions of the EqA (or, indeed, the DDA) were in force. By virtue of para 9(1) of Schedule 1 to the EqA, the question of whether a person had a disability at a particular time is determined 'as if the provisions of, or made under, this Act [that] were in force when the act complained of was done had been in force at the relevant time' – i.e. the time that the person had the alleged disability. Para 9(2) makes it clear that this may be a time before the EqA came into force. (Note: the word 'that', inserted into the above extract from para 9(1) in square brackets, does not appear in the text of the EqA but seems necessary to make the provision linguistically intelligible and it is apparent from the wording of the equivalent provision in the DDA that its omission is accidental.)

The previous legislation expressly stated that a past disability could only be 6.56 established if the substantial adverse effect of the impairment had actually lasted for at least 12 months – para 5, Sch 2 DDA. (This was subject to an exception where the substantial adverse effect ceased and then recurred, in which case it was treated as continuing – see 'Long-term effect – past disabilities that recur' below.) As that requirement has not been carried over into the EqA, it is arguable that a past impairment that was likely at the time to last for at least 12 months – even though in the event it did not do so – is now covered. However, according to the revised Guidance, the test for past disabilities has remained unchanged – see para C12. This appears persuasive, given that, if a person cannot show that their past disability 'has lasted' for at least 12 months under para 2(1)(a) of Schedule 1 to the Act, then he or she would have to show that it 'is likely' to last for at least 12 months – para 2(1)(b). The fact that this latter provision is expressed in the present tense strongly suggests that it cannot be used to establish a past disability.

Future disabilities   6.57

The EqA does not cover those with a latent genetic or other disposition to a disability in the future as their condition has no effect on their ability to carry out normal day-to-day activities – diagnosis does not itself bring someone

121

within the definition (save where the individual is diagnosed with cancer, HIV infection or multiple sclerosis – see 'Deemed disabilities' above). This means that someone diagnosed as having, for example, the Huntington's chorea gene will not be protected until he or she actually develops some symptoms. However, where a person has a progressive condition he or she will be covered by the Act from the moment that condition leads to an impairment which has some effect on his or her ability to carry out normal day-to-day activities, even if not substantial, provided that impairment is likely to have a substantial adverse effect in the future – see 'Substantial adverse effect – progressive conditions' below.

6.58 **Excluded disabilities**
Paragraph 1 of Schedule 1 to the EqA states that regulations may provide for a condition of a prescribed description to be, or not to be, an impairment. The current regulations – the Equality Act 2010 (Disability) Regulations 2010 SI 2010/2128 – specifically exclude from the scope of the EqA a number of conditions that otherwise might well constitute disabilities under the Act:

- addiction to alcohol, nicotine or any other substance, unless the addiction was originally the result of the administration of medically prescribed drugs or other medical treatment – Reg 3. 'Addiction' includes a dependency – Reg 2

- a tendency to set fires – Reg 4(1)(a)

- a tendency to steal – Reg 4(1)(b)

- a tendency to physical or sexual abuse of other persons – Reg 4(1)(c)

- exhibitionism – Reg 4(1)(d), and

- voyeurism – Reg 4(1)(e).

The condition known as seasonal allergic rhinitis – which includes, for example, hayfever – does not amount to an impairment either, although the condition can be taken into account for the purposes of the Act if it aggravates the effect of another condition – Reg 4(2)–(3).

6.59 Paragraph A7 of the Guidance states that it is not necessary to consider how an impairment was caused, even if the cause is a consequence of a condition which is excluded. Therefore, people with impairments *resulting from* addictions, such as liver damage following alcoholism, will still be protected. In Power v Panasonic UK Ltd 2003 IRLR 151, EAT, P, an area sales manager, suffered from depression and was drinking heavily. Following her dismissal, she complained to an employment tribunal that she had suffered disability discrimination. The tribunal dismissed the claim, holding that the core issue of the case was whether P became clinically depressed and turned to drink, or whether her alcohol addiction led to her depression. It concluded that the Regulations then in force (the Disability Discrimination (Meaning of Disability) Regulations 1996 SI 1996/1455 ('the Meaning of Disability Regulations')) and the contemporaneous version of the Guidance were in conflict – the former stating that an addiction is excluded from the definition of disability and the latter that it is not necessary to consider how an impairment was caused. The tribunal determined that the approach of the Regulations was to be preferred. In overturning this decision, the EAT found that the Regulations and the Guidance were different but not in conflict. The cause of the impairment in issue was not material when deciding whether a person was disabled within the meaning of the DDA. The tribunal should have considered whether the alleged disability fell within the definition contained in the DDA and then moved on to consider whether it was excluded by the Regulations. The tribunal's use of the phrase 'core issue' indicated that it had wrongly focused on the cause of P's impairment rather than on whether she was disabled within the meaning of the DDA.

In Murray v Newham Citizens Advice Bureau Ltd (No.2) 2003 ICR 643, EAT, **6.60** the EAT held that the excluded conditions which were then contained in the Meaning of Disability Regulations referred only to 'free-standing conditions', and not to those conditions that are the direct consequence of a physical or mental impairment. However, this view was doubted in the later decision of Edmund Nuttall Ltd v Butterfield 2006 ICR 77, EAT. In that case, B was employed as a mechanical and electrical coordinator. In 2003, he committed an offence of indecent exposure and, before he was sentenced, his solicitors produced medical evidence indicating that he was suffering from a moderately severe depressive illness at the time of the offence. When EN Ltd found out about this criminal conviction it dismissed B and he subsequently brought claims of, among other things, disability discrimination. The tribunal upheld the claim, holding that, when he committed the offences of indecent exposure, B was suffering from depression – a mental impairment that fell within S.1(1) DDA. It also took the view that he had committed offences of indecent exposure because of his underlying depression. Therefore, in dismissing B for committing those offences, EN Ltd had effectively treated him less favourably for a reason related to his disability. In considering the appeal, the EAT referred to Murray but was not persuaded by the concept of the excluded conditions as being 'free-standing'. In its view, the critical question was one of causation. In other words, what was the reason for the less favourable treatment? If, in this case, the legitimate impairment was the reason for B's dismissal, then there was prima facie discrimination that needed to be justified. If, on the other hand, the reason was the excluded condition, then the claim failed. Where both the legitimate impairment and the excluded condition form the employer's reason for the less favourable treatment, the legitimate impairment is thus an effective cause of the less favourable treatment, and discrimination is made out notwithstanding that the excluded condition also forms part of the employer's reason for that treatment. Applying this legal analysis to the instant case, the EAT concluded that B's depressive illness was not the reason for his less favourable treatment. It was only when EN Ltd learned that he had been convicted of offences of indecent exposure that it took the decision to dismiss him. Therefore, the sole reason for the less favourable treatment was the excluded condition.

Murray and Butterfield now represent conflicting decisions at EAT level. However, the later was preferred by the High Court in Governing Body of X Endowed Primary School v Special Educational Needs and Disability Tribunal and ors 2009 IRLR 1007, QBD, although this was not an employment case. The Butterfield view is also supported by the revised Guidance, which states that 'the exclusions apply where the tendency to set fires, tendency to steal, tendency to physical or sexual abuse of other persons, exhibitionism, or voyeurism constitute an impairment in themselves. The exclusions also apply where these tendencies arise as a consequence of, or a manifestation of, an impairment that constitutes a disability for the purposes of the Act' – para A13.

6.61 Substantial adverse effect

To amount to a disability, the impairment must have a 'substantial adverse effect' on the person's ability to carry out normal day-to-day activities – S.6(1)(b) EqA. If an impairment ceases to have a substantial adverse effect on a person's ability to carry out normal day-to-day activities but that effect is likely to recur, it is to be treated as continuing to have that effect – para 2(2), Sch 1 (see under 'Long-term effect – recurring conditions' below). Regulations may provide for an effect on a person's ability to carry out normal day-to-day activities to be treated as being, or not being, a substantial adverse effect – para 4, Sch 1 EqA. However, no regulations have been made under this power (or under the equivalent power in the DDA).

'Substantial' is defined in S.212(1) EqA as meaning 'more than minor or trivial'. This definition did not appear in the DDA but was used in the original Guidance and in the Code of Practice issued under the DDA (the 'Code of Practice for the elimination of discrimination in the field of employment against disabled persons or persons who have had a disability').

6.62 In Anwar v Tower Hamlets College EAT 0091/10 the EAT held that a tribunal had not erred when it found that the effect of an impairment was 'more than trivial' but still 'minor' as opposed to 'substantial'. In that case, the claimant claimed to have a disability by reason of suffering from headaches. The employment judge found that these, while 'no means negligible, did not give rise to a substantial adverse effect'. Referring to the Guidance, he accepted that the headaches could not be described as trivial and were undoubtedly unpleasant while they lasted, but they were, in his view, 'an example of the sort of physical condition experienced by many people which has what can fairly be described as a minor effect'. On appeal, the EAT rejected the argument that the 'substantial adverse effect' requirement must necessarily be satisfied if the adverse effect in question is found to be more than trivial. This suggests that there is a continuum and that something that is trivial may be of even less consequence than something that is minor. In any event, the EAT in Anwar pointed out that the employment judge had not simply baldly asserted that the effect of the claimant's headaches was minor though more than trivial: he had recorded the number and frequency of the headaches and the effect they had based on the evidence given by the claimant. This made it impossible to say that his decision was insufficiently reasoned or was perverse.

Appendix 1 to the EHRC Employment Code provides guidance on the meaning of 'substantial'. It states: 'The requirement that an effect must be substantial reflects the general understanding of disability as a limitation going beyond the normal differences in ability which might exist among people. Account should also be taken of where a person avoids doing things which, for example, cause pain, fatigue or substantial social embarrassment; because of a loss of energy and motivation' – paras 8 and 9.

In Goodwin v Patent Office 1999 ICR 302, EAT, the EAT said that, of the four **6.63** component parts to the definition of a disability in S.1 DDA (now S.6 EqA), judging whether the effects of a condition are substantial is the most difficult. The EAT went on to set out its explanation of the requirement as follows:

> 'What the Act is concerned with is an impairment on the person's ability to carry out activities. The fact that a person can carry out such activities does not mean that his ability to carry them out has not been impaired. Thus, for example, a person may be able to cook, but only with the greatest difficulty. In order to constitute an adverse effect, it is not the doing of the acts which is the focus of attention but rather the ability to do (or not do) the acts. Experience shows that disabled persons often adjust their lives and circumstances to enable them to cope for themselves. Thus a person whose capacity to communicate through normal speech was obviously impaired might well choose, more or less voluntarily, to live on their own. If one asked such a person whether they managed to carry on their daily lives without undue problems, the answer might well be "yes", yet their ability to lead a "normal" life had obviously been impaired. Such a person would be unable to communicate through speech and the ability to communicate through speech is obviously a capacity which is needed for carrying out normal day-to-day activities, whether at work or at home. If asked whether they could use the telephone, or ask for directions or which bus to take, the answer would be "no". Those might be regarded as day-to-day activities contemplated by the legislation, and that person's ability to carry them out would clearly be regarded as adversely affected.'

Whether a particular impairment has a substantial effect is a matter for the tribunal to decide. When considering this question, the EAT in Goodwin advised tribunals to take into account the version of the Guidance in force at the time, which – like the current version – contained a number of examples of 'substantial' effects. The EAT's advice is echoed by para 12(1) of Schedule 1 to the EqA, which provides that a tribunal must take into account 'such guidance as it thinks is relevant'. However, in Vicary v British Telecommunications plc 1999 IRLR 680, EAT, the EAT concluded that the Guidance is of assistance in marginal cases only. Also, in Leonard v Southern Derbyshire Chamber of Commerce 2001 IRLR 19, EAT, the EAT said that the Guidance should not be used too literally. This was because the examples it gives are illustrative only and should not be used as a checklist.

6.64 Three cases where tribunals considered that an impairment did *not* have a substantial adverse effect:

- **Hudson v Post Office** ET Case No.3100773/98: H was removed from his position as vehicle driver when the employer discovered that he had a congenital defect in his left eye. Normal vision is 6/6, which he had in his right eye, but he could only manage 6/24 with his left eye. The tribunal held that this sight impairment could not be said to have a substantial adverse effect on his ability to carry out normal day-to-day activities because he could rely on his good eye

- **Ashton v Chief Constable of West Mercia Constabulary** 2001 ICR 67, EAT: A, a police officer who was born a man, suffered bouts of depression while undergoing gender reassignment. She transferred from police patrol duties to a new role of communications operator for a six-month probationary period, which was later extended to 12 months, but was dismissed when those duties were not performed satisfactorily. The tribunal found that the 12-month probationary period in the new job coincided with the 'real life test' during which A lived and worked in the female role before undergoing irreversible surgery. The tribunal also found that the shortcomings in A's performance were due to a combination of factors: the depression she was suffering as a result of hormone therapy, the stressful environment of the communications operations room, the further stress of A having to prove herself and the stress of undergoing a major life change. The tribunal found that neither her depression nor her gender identity dysphoria (GID) were disabilities for the purposes of the DDA. Although the GID was long term, the impairment did not, in the tribunal's view, have a substantial adverse effect on A's ability to carry out normal day-to-day activities. The tribunal did not accept A's argument that her mobility had been impaired because her treatment for gender reassignment had caused her not to socialise outside work. The EAT upheld the tribunal's finding. The decision not to socialise was A's own choice, made because she preferred to keep herself to herself

- **Stafford v Focus Hotels Management Ltd** ET Case No.1200256/10: S injured her back in September 2009 when lifting a crate of soft drinks. In

January 2009 her GP reported that her condition was usually self-limiting and was 90 per cent likely to be resolved within 12 months. In April 2010 the GP reported that S's pain had improved and although she was unable to lift heavy loads her general mobility was not seriously affected. An employment tribunal held that although S had a physical impairment its effects were not substantial and so it did not amount to a disability within the meaning of the DDA.

Factors to be taken into account 6.65

In cases where it is not clear whether the effect of an impairment is substantial, the Guidance suggests a number of factors to be considered (see paras B1 to B17). These include the time taken by the person to carry out an activity (para B2) and the way in which he or she carries it out (para B3). A comparison is to be made with the time or manner that might be expected if the person did not have the impairment.

Cumulative effects of impairment. The cumulative effects of an impairment 6.66 are also relevant. An impairment might not have a substantial adverse effect on a person in any one respect, but its effects in more than one respect taken together could result in a substantial adverse effect on the person's ability to carry out normal day-to-day activities. The Guidance gives the example of a man with depression who experiences a range of symptoms, which include a loss of energy and motivation that makes even the simplest of tasks or decisions seem quite difficult. He finds it difficult to get up in the morning, get washed and dressed, and prepare breakfast. He is forgetful and cannot plan ahead. As a result he has often run out of food before he thinks of going shopping again. Household tasks are frequently left undone, or take much longer to complete than normal. Together, the effects amount to the impairment having a substantial adverse effect on carrying out normal day-to-day activities – para B5.

Two tribunal cases:

- **Stratton v Cauldwell Communications Ltd and anor** ET Case No.2400889/06: the tribunal held that S was disabled under the DDA because he had a physical impairment – diabetes – that had a substantial adverse effect on his ability to carry out normal day-to-day activities. S's diabetes affected his continence, so that he needed to urinate several times an hour and on occasion he had not been able to get to the toilet in time. Furthermore, his diabetes had an effect on his memory and concentration to the extent that he sometimes struggled, for example, to write a cheque. His speech was also affected and colleagues sometimes had to ask him to articulate more clearly. The tribunal found that, while the effects on his memory and concentration were not in themselves sufficiently substantial to constitute a disability, the cumulative effects of his continence and concentration problems had an adverse and substantial impact on his ability to carry out day-to-day activities

- **Brook v Leslie H Trainer and Sons Ltd** ET Case No.1604613/10: the tribunal held that the claimant, who suffered from vibration white finger, was disabled in view of the different impacts this condition had on his manual dexterity. He was prone to waking at night with numbness in his fingers, which affected his sleep. Although the symptoms came and went spontaneously, when affected he would often be unable to grip screwdrivers. Power of grip was reduced to 60 per cent and sensation to pin pricks was reduced in some fingers, but sensation to light touch was normal. The tribunal rejected the employer's contention that the degree of the claimant's impairment was minor: in its view, the case was finely balanced, but the loss of 40 per cent of grip was a significant functional deficit, and the cumulative effect of the claimant's impairment went beyond ordinary differences in people's general ability.

6.67 **Multiple impairments.** The Guidance states that, where a person has more than one impairment but none of the impairments considered in isolation has a substantial adverse effect on normal day-to-day activities, account should be taken of whether the impairments together have such a substantial adverse effect – para B6. The Guidance gives the example of a minor impairment that affects physical coordination and an irreversible but minor injury to a leg that affects mobility. Taken together, these two impairments might have a substantial adverse effect on the person's ability to carry out certain normal day-to-day activities.

In Ministry of Defence v Hay 2008 ICR 1247, EAT, the EAT ruled that a tribunal was entitled to hold that an employee who had a range of respiratory impairments, including tuberculosis, which led to his absence from June 2004 until his dismissal at the end of March 2006, was disabled. Although expert medical evidence was that the impairment attributable to tuberculosis alone would have had a substantial adverse effect on his day-to-day activities for *less* than 12 months, the tribunal held that he was nonetheless disabled by reason of a constellation of symptoms, not medically attributed to tuberculosis, which lasted more than a year.

6.68 **Effects of behaviour.** Another factor to be taken into account is 'how far a person can *reasonably* be expected to modify his or her behaviour, for example by use of a coping or avoidance stategy, to prevent or reduce the effects of an impairment on normal day-to-day activities. In some instances, a coping or avoidance strategy might alter the effects of the impairment to the extent that they are no longer substantial and the person would no longer meet the definition of disability. In other instances, even with the coping or avoidance strategy, there is still an adverse effect on the carrying out of normal day-to-day activities' – para B7 of the Guidance. The Guidance gives the example of a person who needs to avoid certain substances because of allergies who may find the day-to-day activity of eating substantially affected. Account should be taken of the degree to which a person can reasonably be expected to behave in such a way that the impairment ceases to have a substantial adverse effect.

In Liddington v Argos Ltd ET Case No.1901083/07 L suffered from lower back pain as a result of his obesity. He was unable to dig his garden and could only mow his lawn for a maximum of ten minutes. When walking his dogs, he needed to take frequent rests and he was also unable to carry out some household jobs. L lost 11 per cent of his total body weight but continued to be troubled by back pain and required a lot of time off work. An issue arose as to whether he was disabled for the purposes of the DDA. His employer argued that his impairment did not cause a significant adverse effect and that L should have modified his behaviour by losing weight. The tribunal disagreed, noting that L had tried to control his obesity but that it was long term and he was finding it difficult to help himself. It was therefore satisfied that the condition had a significant adverse effect, particularly during two periods, separated by over a year, when L was unable to work.

Consideration should be given to whether a person avoids doing things which, **6.69** for example, cause pain, fatigue or substantial social embarrassment. The Guidance states that it would not be reasonable to conclude that a person who employed an avoidance strategy was not a disabled person – para B9. In Goodwin v Patent Office 1999 ICR 302, EAT, the EAT cautioned against accepting claimants' assertions that they can cope with normal daily activities when in fact they may simply have developed avoidance or coping strategies.

Two other provisions in the Guidance are relevant here. The first is para B10, which states that if it is possible that a person's ability to manage the effects of an impairment will break down so that effects will sometimes still occur, this possibility must be taken into account when assessing the effects of the impairment. The Guidance gives the example of someone who has dyslexia and whose coping strategies cease to work when he or she is under stress. The second is para D22, which provides that an impairment may not directly prevent someone from carrying out one or more normal day-to-day activities, but it may still have a substantial adverse long-term effect on how he or she carries out those activities. Two examples are given. The first is where the impairment causes pain or fatigue in performing normal day-to-day activities. In these circumstances, the person may have the ability to carry out a normal day-to-day activity, but be restricted in the manner of carrying it out because of experiencing pain in doing so. Or the impairment might make the activity more than usually fatiguing so that the person might not be able to repeat the task over a sustained period of time. The second example is where a person has been advised by a medical practitioner, as part of a treatment plan, to change, limit, or refrain from a normal day-to-day activity on account of an impairment or only do it in a certain way or under certain conditions. This is considered further under 'Effect of medical treatment' below.

6.70 Determining whether a person still has a disability despite modifications to his or her behaviour is not always easy. Two contrasting examples:

- **Commissioner of Police of the Metropolis v Virdi** 2009 EWCA Civ 477, CA: V, a serving police officer, had lost 40 per cent of central vision in his left eye, thus meeting the World Health Organisation's definition of chronic visual impairment. He brought complaints of disability discrimination under the DDA, alleging that his employer had failed to make reasonable adjustments to accommodate his short reading span in certain examinations that he was required to take in order to be promoted from sergeant to inspector. The tribunal chair noted that in order to mitigate the adverse effects of his impaired vision, V had adopted coping strategies such as significantly reducing his driving, turning his head when crossing the road or trying to recognise someone, and resting for some time after reading or using a computer. She went on to find, however, that case law provided that such coping strategies could not be taken into account when determining whether a disability had a substantial adverse effect, and accordingly held that V was disabled within the meaning of the DDA. The EAT overturned the decision. It found that the tribunal chair had misread the relevant case law; the directions she had given herself in relation to coping strategies involved a clear error of law and contradicted the version of the Guidance then in force. Accordingly, the decision that V was disabled could not stand. However, when giving judgment, Mr Justice Elias – then President of the EAT – said that he had 'considerable doubts' as to whether V's taking rests after a period of reading or using a computer could properly be considered a coping strategy at all. In his view, these rests did not amount to a way in which V coped with his difficulty in reading; they simply defined the nature of the adverse impact of his impairment – i.e. he could not read for periods without a break. The EAT's decision was subsequently upheld by the Court of Appeal

- **Vicary v British Telecommunications plc** 1999 IRLR 680, EAT: V, who had lost strength in her arms, was unable to carry a washing basket, a bag of shopping, a suitcase, or a briefcase or handbag. The tribunal dismissed her complaints on the basis that she could reduce the impact of the impairment by using shoulder bags instead of hand-held ones and carry washing or shopping in small quantities. The EAT thought this was a misunderstanding of the task facing a tribunal, saying that the fact that a person is able to mitigate the effects of his or her disability does not mean that the person does not have a 'disability' within the meaning of the DDA. It seemed obvious to the EAT that it would indeed be a substantial impairment of an ability to carry out normal day-to-day activity if V could not use a hand-held bag or carry washing, other than in small quantities.

Environmental factors. Another factor that should be taken into account **6.71** when determining whether the effect of an impairment is substantial is the impact of environmental factors such as the temperature, humidity, time of day or night, how tired the person is or how much stress he or she is under, as these may exacerbate the effects of an impairment – para B11. In Ekpe v Commissioner of Police of the Metropolis 2001 ICR 1084, EAT, for example, E, who suffered from a muscle-wasting condition of her right hand, was unable to do a number of daily activities but in the winter months she also suffered a lot of pain, to the extent that she had difficulty opening doors with her right hand.

The environmental factors that affect an employee's impairment can arise from the employer's system of work. In Pears v Good Hope Hospital NHS Trust ET Case No.1304560/97 P worked as a nursing auxiliary. He developed an allergic reaction to latex dust. In one incident, his reaction was so severe that it resulted in anaphylactic shock and, over a period, he became so sensitive to the dust that he suffered a reaction if he just entered an area where someone had recently removed latex gloves. However, the tribunal determined that P was not disabled within the terms of the DDA. He suffered from a permanent physical impairment but it did not have a substantial adverse effect on his ability to carry out normal day-to-day activities. It simply involved a question of risk assessment and avoidance.

Effects of treatment. Paragraph 5(1) of Schedule 1 to the EqA provides that **6.72** an impairment is to be treated as having a substantial adverse effect on the ability of the person concerned to carry out normal day-to-day activities if measures are being taken to treat or correct it and, but for that, it would be likely to have that effect. In this regard, 'likely' means 'could well happen' – SCA Packaging v Boyle 2009 ICR 1056, HL (see 'Long-term effect – likely to last 12 months' below).

This means that, in assessing whether there is a substantial adverse effect on the person's ability to carry out normal day-to-day activities, any medical treatment which reduces or extinguishes the effects of the impairment should be ignored. This is further considered under 'Effect of medical treatment' below. In Carden v Pickerings Europe Ltd 2005 IRLR 721, EAT, the EAT held that the equivalent provision in the DDA – para 6(1) of Schedule 1 – applied in circumstances where a plate and pins had been surgically inserted in the claimant's ankle, which meant that he required no further treatment so long as his ankle received the continuing support or assistance that the pins and plate provided.

Appeals to the EAT
6.73

As already mentioned, it is the assessment of the effects of a disability on an individual that can cause particular difficulties for tribunals in disability discrimination cases. However, the EAT will only interfere with a decision of a tribunal as to whether or not a person's impairment has a substantial adverse effect if the tribunal has misdirected itself in law or the decision is perverse.

That said, the EAT has shown itself willing to scrutinise this aspect of a tribunal's reasoning and has overturned a number of decisions on appeal. In Chief Constable of Lothian and Borders Police v Cumming 2010 IRLR 109, EAT, for example, C, who worked as a special constable, applied to become a regular constable but was rejected following an occupational physician's advice that she did not meet the eyesight standard laid down by a statutory instrument for appointment to the regular police force. A consultant ophthalmic surgeon's report explained that C had a 'mild left-sided amblyopia', which restricted her ability to look up and left. She needed to take regular breaks when doing close reading work and she had a mild squint and scarring on her left eye. However, as C's binocular vision was normal, the consultant's report indicated that her problems should not impair her ability to train as a full-time officer. C brought a claim of disability discrimination. The tribunal took the view that, following the EAT's decision in Paterson v Commissioner of Police of the Metropolis 2007 ICR 1522, EAT (see below under 'Normal day-to-day activities'), participation in professional life is a normal day-to-day activity. The Chief Constable's refusal to allow C to go forward into her chosen career therefore had a substantial adverse effect on this day-to-day activity. In the alternative, the tribunal concluded that, even without taking into account the effect on C's career, there was a substantial adverse effect from her restricted ability to look up or left, her need to take breaks when doing close reading, and the effects on her appearance of the squint and the scarring. C therefore came within the definition of 'disabled'.

6.74 The EAT overturned this decision. The tribunal had erred in finding that the Chief Constable's refusal to accept C as a police officer was a relevant adverse effect on her ability to carry out normal day-to-day activities. Although applying for a profession is something many people do, it does not imply any particular physical activity, and the employer's refusal is not a physical effect. Also, the tribunal's finding that the other adverse effects of C's impairment were substantial was perverse. Not only had C been insistent that her impairment would not affect her in her duties, but the tribunal had also considered irrelevant factors. C's appearance was not said to have any effect on her so could not be of relevance when assessing the substantiality of adverse effects. Furthermore, without hearing evidence, the tribunal was not in a position to make comparisons between C's abilities and those of someone with no sight in one eye, or those of the general population. The EAT therefore substituted a finding that C was not a disabled person within the meaning of the DDA.

6.75 **Focus should be on what person *cannot* do**
When determining whether a person meets the definition of disability under the EqA, the Guidance emphasises that it is important to focus on what an individual

cannot do, or can only do with difficulty, rather than on the things that he or she can do – para B9. As the EAT pointed out in Goodwin v Patent Office 1999 ICR 302, EAT, even though the claimant may be able to perform a lot of activities, the impairment may still have a substantial adverse effect on other activities, with the result that the claimant is quite properly to be regarded as meeting the statutory definition of disability. Equally, where a person can carry out an act, but only with great difficulty, that person's ability has been impaired.

Three examples: **6.76**

- **Vicary v British Telecommunications plc** 1999 IRLR 680, EAT: the employment tribunal held that V's impairment did not have a 'substantial adverse effect' as regards her 'manual dexterity' because she was able to use both hands. It thought that a loss of strength could not be equated with a loss of function. It examined the functions which V could perform, observing that she could handle a knife and fork and that she could use a keyboard, albeit more slowly than before she developed her condition. The EAT held that the tribunal's decision was perverse on a number of grounds, one of which was that the tribunal should not have focused on the activities which V was able to perform but on those which she was not able to perform. An inability to prepare vegetables, cut up meat and carry a meal on a tray would obviously be regarded as a substantial impairment to an ability to carry out normal day-to-day activities

- **Leonard v Southern Derbyshire Chamber of Commerce** 2001 IRLR 19, EAT: L, who suffered from clinical depression, was dismissed in October 1998. She told the tribunal that the symptoms of her depression were tearfulness and difficulty in coping with stressful situations and relationships. She tired easily and slept for long periods. The employment tribunal found that L's tiredness affected her mobility in terms of the distances she could walk and drive, as well as her manual dexterity, because, when she was tired, her physical coordination went. Her vision also tended to blur. L could not maintain concentration and she suffered some memory loss. She tripped over pavement edges but could eat, drink and catch a ball. She had no difficulty in handling a knife and fork, or threading a needle, but her concentration went if she tried to sew. She could push a sofa but not lift it. The tribunal concluded that, looking at the evidence as a whole, L's depression did not have a substantial adverse effect on her ability to carry out normal day-to-day activities. On appeal, the EAT stated that, while it is essential that a tribunal consider matters in the round, the tribunal in the instant case had erred in its approach by focusing on the things that L could do instead of on those things that she could not do, or could do only with difficulty. In the words of Mr Justice Nelson: 'This focus of the [DDA] avoids the danger of a tribunal concluding that as there are still things that an applicant can do the adverse effect cannot be substantial.'

133

- **Kelsey v Retail Merchant Services Ltd** ET Case No.1200908/10: the claimant's dyslexia caused him to have difficulty with reading, remembering the spelling and meaning of words and following a short sequence of instructions such as a simple recipe or list of domestic tasks. An employment tribunal held that the claimant was disabled on the basis that he was unable to do things such as writing a short note that somebody of his ability would, but for the impairment, have been able to do easily.

6.77 In Ahmed v Metroline Travel Ltd EAT 0400/10 the EAT considered whether an employment tribunal's failure to concentrate on what the claimant could not do necessarily amounted to an error of law. The case involved a significant factual dispute between the parties as to the nature of the injury sustained and the effects of that injury. The claimant was a bus driver who suffered whiplash injury as the result of a road accident. Following a period of sick leave, a medical report was compiled by an expert consultant which concluded that the claimant was fit to return to work and that his condition would improve if he engaged in his usual activities. However, the claimant's own GP continued to sign him off sick as he was particularly concerned about the level of drowsiness caused by pain-relief medication prescribed to the claimant. Eventually, the employer convened a capability disciplinary procedure, which resulted in the termination of the claimant's employment. An employment tribunal rejected his disability discrimination claim on the ground that the claimant's soft tissue injury to his lower back was not a substantial injury and did not amount to a physical impairment that had a substantial effect on his ability to carry out day-to-day activities. On appeal, the claimant contended that in its judgement the employment tribunal had simply referred to the activities that he was able to do and not to those that he was unable to do as a result of his injury (such as lifting his young daughter, climbing stairs without using the banister or being able to drive for 15 to 20 minutes without discomfort). The EAT accepted that, in the light of the Goodwin and Leonard decisions (above), it would be impermissible for a tribunal to seek to weigh what a claimant could do against what he or she could not do, and then determine whether he or she had a disability by placing those matters in the balance. However, this was not an error into which the tribunal had fallen in this particular case. Findings of fact as to what a claimant actually can do may throw significant light on the question of what he or she cannot do, particularly in a case such as this where there is a factual dispute as to what the claimant is asserting he or she is unable to do. In this case, the tribunal had resolved that dispute by accepting the consultant's account of what the claimant said he could do and disbelieving the evidence as to what he said he could not do. There was no error of law in this approach.

6.78 **Tribunals' observations**

Tribunals will usually have before them the evidence of the claimant as to the extent of his or her impairment and they will often have medical evidence as well. In assessing the weight to be attached to the evidence, tribunals are entitled to take account of their own observations of the claimant as he or she appears before the tribunal. However, an individual's appearance in the unfamiliar legal setting of a tribunal hearing is not always a reliable guide to the extent to which the individual is suffering from an impairment in normal day-to-day activities and a tribunal will err if it allows its own observations to override the proper application of the Guidance in its assessment of that evidence. In Leonard v Southern Derbyshire Chamber of Commerce 2001 IRLR 19, EAT (see 'Focus should be on what person *cannot* do' above), the tribunal was so impressed with the claimant's performance before it that it decided that, despite her depression, she was managing to cope and did not have a disability. On appeal, the EAT stressed that while it is essential that tribunals consider matters in the round and make an overall assessment of whether the adverse effect of an impairment is substantial, the tribunal in this case had erred in the manner in which it had applied the Guidance and in its evaluation of the claimant's evidence. In the EAT's view, the claimant clearly had a disability under the DDA.

The EAT has recommended that, where a tribunal's own observations appear **6.79** to conflict with the evidence presented to it, the tribunal should raise the issue at the hearing – Ekpe v Commissioner of Police of the Metropolis 2001 ICR 1084, EAT. In that case, E suffered from a wasting of the intrinsic muscles of her right hand but the tribunal thought from its own observations that E had exaggerated the seriousness of her condition. The tribunal observed E using 'an extremely inconvenient style of ring binder containing over 330 pages with her right hand' and thought that this contradicted E's argument that there was very little indeed that she could do with that hand. The EAT held that the tribunal did not err when it considered the way in which E handled a ring binder. In its view, a decision as to whether an admitted disability does or does not have an adverse impact on normal day-to-day activities and whether that impact is substantial was quite properly going to be influenced by the behaviour of a claimant before the tribunal. The EAT added, however, that it would expect any tribunal considering whether to draw any conclusion from such behaviour to raise that possibility at the hearing, so that it could be dealt with. A tribunal should bear in mind that behaviour before a tribunal may not be representative of behaviour generally. In the case of some conditions, notably back conditions, there may be 'good days and bad days'. In other situations a claimant may put on a brave face, and this could be misinterpreted. Furthermore, where there is expert medical evidence available, any tentative conclusion to be drawn from observations of the claimant by the inexpert eyes of the members of the tribunal should ideally be raised with those experts to see whether there may not be some ready explanation for the claimant's behaviour. In the instant case, however, the EAT was unable to say that the tribunal's failure to take those steps amounted to an error of law. The tribunal was presented with a claimant who was apparently claiming that there was very little she could do with her right hand, yet it saw her doing a lot. In the EAT's view, the tribunal was entitled to take that into account in determining whether the other complaints made by her were exaggerated.

6.80 Progressive conditions

A person who has a progressive condition as a result of which he or she has an impairment that has (or had) some effect on his or her ability to carry out normal day-to-day activities but that effect is not (or was not) substantial will be taken to have an impairment which has a substantial adverse effect if the condition is likely to result in such an impairment – para 8(1) and (2), Sch 1 EqA. In this regard, 'likely' means 'could well happen' – SCA Packaging v Boyle 2009 ICR 1056, HL (see 'Long-term effect – likely to last 12 months' below).

The equivalent provision in the DDA listed cancer, multiple sclerosis, muscular dystrophy and HIV infection as examples of progressive conditions but this list has not been reproduced in the EqA. Instead, claimants who suffer from cancer, multiple sclerosis or HIV infection are deemed to have a disability from the point of diagnosis without the need to demonstrate any adverse effect on their normal day-to-day activities – see 'Physical or mental impairment – deemed disabilities' above. Regulations may provide for a condition of a prescribed description to be treated as being, or as not being, progressive – para 8(3), Sch 1. However, no regulations have yet been made under this power (or under the equivalent power in the DDA).

6.81 The effect of para 8 is that as soon as a person with a progressive condition experiences symptoms which have any effect on his or her normal day-to-day activities he or she will be taken as having a disability. This will remain the case even if the effects cease – for example, during a period of remission. To fall within this provision a claimant must show that the progressive condition: (a) has had some effect on his or her ability to carry out normal day-to-day activities (although it need not be continuous); and (b) is likely to have a substantial adverse effect in the future. The Guidance points out that a medical prognosis of the likely impact of a condition will be the normal route to establishing protection under this provision – para B19. It goes on to state, however, that the claimant will still need to show that the effect of the impairment is long term – see 'Long-term effect' below.

The Guidance makes it clear that the effect of the condition on the claimant's ability to carry out normal day-to-day activities need not be continuous or substantial. Indeed, a person will be taken as having a disability even where the adverse effect is a result of treatment for a progressive condition – see Kirton v Tetrosyl Ltd 2003 ICR 1237, CA, where the claimant suffered minor incontinence caused by an operation for prostate cancer.

Examples of progressive conditions given in the Guidance include systemic **6.82** lupus erythematosis, various types of dementia and motor neurone disease – para B20. And in Kerrigan v Rover Group Ltd ET Case No.1401406/97 it was accepted that acute and chronic asthma and asthma-related illnesses could be progressive conditions. Three further examples:

- **Hickling v Caterpillar (UK) Ltd** ET Case No.1900692/09: H experienced heart problems in 2007 and was diagnosed with a defective heart valve. He went on sick leave in June 2008 and had an operation to repair the valve. He remained on sick leave until the end of the year when the employer commenced a redundancy exercise that led to H being dismissed. The employment tribunal made a preliminary decision that H was disabled for the purposes of the DDA. He suffered from a progressive condition and was experiencing a degree of adverse effect from April 2007

- **Hargreaves v Lloyds TSB Bank plc** ET Case No.2403408/08: H was employed in managerial roles at the bank until his dismissal in February 2008. In July 2005 he had been diagnosed with type 2 diabetes melitus but a medical report prepared for him in September 2008 stated that he did not, as yet, suffer from any diabetic complications, although these would inevitably occur eventually. The tribunal held that H was not disabled under the DDA. While diabetes was a progressive condition, the medical evidence did not suggest that H was as yet experiencing any adverse effects from the impairment

- **O'Donnell v Ministry of Defence** ET Case No.3103421/97: O'D was refused a job with the MoD because a medical showed that he suffered from Ankylosing Spondylitis (AS), an incurable condition causing some pain and stiffness in the back. O'D had learnt to cope with the condition, which tends to affect male adults and be progressive until the age of 40, when it levels out. O'D was 39. The tribunal found that O'D's condition was not progressive since the medical evidence showed that the majority of pathological changes relating to his condition had probably already occurred. Even if the tribunal was wrong about that, it did not think that the AS was 'likely to result' in O'D having an impairment which had a substantial adverse effect on his ability to carry out normal day-to-day activities. Accordingly, the tribunal held that he did not have a disability.

Paragraph 8 of Schedule 1 will only apply where 'the condition is likely to **6.83** result' in the person having an impairment which has a substantial adverse effect. In Mowat-Brown v University of Surrey 2002 IRLR 235, EAT, the EAT emphasised this point, stating that 'the question to be asked is whether, on the balance of probabilities, the claimant has established that the condition *in his case* is likely to have a substantial adverse effect. It is not enough simply to establish that he has a progressive condition and that it has or has had an effect on his ability to carry out normal day-to-day activities... In some cases it may

137

be possible to produce medical evidence of his likely prognosis. In other cases it may be possible to discharge the onus of proof by statistical evidence' (our stress).

As the EAT made clear in that case, a tribunal may well have to rely on medical evidence in determining whether a condition is likely to deteriorate and whether it is likely to have a substantial adverse effect on a person's ability to carry out normal day-to-day activities. It is also possible that the same condition will give rise to different prognoses as to future deterioration, depending on the facts. For example, in Mowat-Brown the tribunal held that the claimant's multiple sclerosis was not a progressive condition under the DDA. A medical expert stated that it was difficult to give an accurate prognosis for an individual with multiple sclerosis, but that there were grounds on which to be optimistic in the claimant's case. The EAT found no error in the tribunal's decision and dismissed the appeal.

6.84 **Severe disfigurement**

An impairment that consists of a severe disfigurement is deemed to have a substantial adverse effect on the ability of the person concerned to carry out normal day-to-day activities – para 3(1), Sch 1 EqA. There is no need to demonstrate such an effect. This means that people with disfigurements such as scars, birthmarks, limb or postural deformation or diseases of the skin are potentially covered by the Act. The provision is necessary as such people would otherwise fall outside the definition in the EqA and would be unable to seek redress for the discrimination they suffer on the basis of their appearance.

The Act does not give any indication as to what factors should be considered when deciding whether a disfigurement is severe enough to come within the provisions of para 3(1). However, para B25 of the Guidance states that assessing severity will mainly be a matter of the degree of the disfigurement, although it may be necessary to take account of factors such as its nature, size, and prominence, as well as where it is. So, for example, a facial disfigurement may be considered more severe than a disfigurement on a person's back. Two examples:

- **Hudson v Post Office** ET Case No.3100773/98: the tribunal held that the peripheral scarring and deformity of H's upper and lower eyelids as a result of surgery to remove a cyst from his eye constituted a severe disfigurement which, by virtue of para 3(1) of Schedule 1 to the DDA (now para 3(1) of Schedule 1 to the EqA), was to be treated as having a substantial adverse effect on his ability to carry out normal day-to-day activities

- **Griffiths v Lancashire County Council** ET Case No.2408001/08: G brought a claim under the DDA, citing his disability as a hare lip and cleft palate which, he argued, constituted a severe disfigurement under the Act. An employment judge dismissed the claim. Having observed G over a number of hours, he could not observe any facial disfigurement. It was not obvious that G ever had a hare lip or that his teeth and the way he spoke were affected by it as claimed.

Paragraph 3(2) and (3) of Schedule 1 allow regulations to be made prescribing **6.85** circumstances in which certain severe disfigurements (in particular, deliberately acquired disfigurements) will *not* be treated as having a substantial adverse effect. Reg 5 of the Equality Act 2010 (Disability) Regulations 2010 SI 2010/2128 excludes:

* tattoos (which have not been removed), and

* body piercings for decorative or other non-medical purposes, including any object attached through the piercing for such purposes.

Normal day-to-day activities **6.86**

The EqA, like the DDA before it, only protects individuals whose ability to carry out 'normal day-to-day activities' is impaired. This criterion may seem strange given that the discrimination claims with which we are concerned here arise in the context of employment, but the requirement ensures that 'disability' under the EqA reflects a general understanding of the term in day-to-day situations rather than specific work situations requiring specific skills.

Previously under the DDA, for an impairment to be treated as affecting a person's ability to carry out normal day-to-day activities, it had to affect one or more specified 'capacities' – namely: mobility; manual dexterity; physical coordination; continence; ability to lift, carry or otherwise move everyday objects; speech, hearing or eyesight; memory or ability to concentrate, learn or understand; or perception of the risk of physical danger (see para 4(1), Sch 1 DDA). However, this requirement has now been dropped as, in the Government's view, the list of capacities 'served little or no purpose in helping to establish whether someone is disabled in the eyes of the law, and was an unnecessary extra barrier to disabled people taking cases in courts and tribunals' (para 11.53, 'The Equality Bill – Government response to the Consultation', July 2008 (Cm 7454)). According to the Explanatory Notes to the EqA, 'this change will make it easier for some people to demonstrate that they meet the definition of a disabled person. It will assist those who currently find it difficult to show that their impairment adversely affects their ability to carry out a normal day-to-day activity which involves one of these capacities' – para 682.

Appendix 1 to the EHRC Employment Code states that 'normal day-to-day **6.87** activities' are activities that are carried out by most men or women on a fairly regular and frequent basis, and gives examples such as walking, driving, typing and forming social relationships. The Code adds: 'The term is not intended to include activities which are normal only for a particular person or group of

139

people, such as playing a musical instrument, or participation in a sport to a professional standard, or performing a skilled or specialised task at work. However, someone who is affected in such a specialised way but is also affected in normal day-to-day activities would be covered by this part of the definition' – paras 14 and 15.

6.88 Meaning of 'normal'

The Guidance emphasises that the term 'normal day-to-day activities' is not intended to include activities that are normal only for a particular person or a small group of people. Account should be taken of how far the activity is carried out on a daily or frequent basis. In this context, 'normal' should be given its ordinary, everyday meaning – para D4.

Tribunals have sometimes drawn a distinction between an activity that in general terms can be regarded as 'normal' and the degree of performance of that activity alleged to be affected by the claimant's impairment. For example, while driving and gardening are readily accepted as being normal day-to-day activities, an impairment (such as a hiatus hernia or gastritis) that prevents a claimant from driving 200 miles without a break or from gardening continuously for two or three hours does not have an effect on 'normal' day-to-day activities – Tucker v Aid Call Ltd ET Case No.2351282/10. Similarly, a bus driver suffering from a whiplash injury was unable to show that his impairment amounted to a disability on the basis of evidence that he was unable to work a nine-hour bus-driving shift – Ahmed v Metroline Travel Ltd EAT 0400/10.

6.89 In Goodwin v Patent Office 1999 ICR 302, EAT, the EAT took the view that there was no need to specify what constitutes a day-to-day activity on the basis that, while it is difficult to define, it is easily recognised. The EAT stressed that the enquiry is focused on normal daily activities, not on particular circumstances. The effect of para D4 is that the fact that a person cannot demonstrate a special skill, such as playing the piano, is not relevant as it is not a normal day-to-day activity, even if the individual concerned is a musician. Similarly, if a person has organised his or her home in such a way as to accommodate a disability, the fact that that person is able to manage at home is not determinative of the issue. If the person is unable to perform any normal daily activity, he or she has an impairment. The EAT also stressed that it followed that the fact that a person with an impairment is able to carry out many functions is not a relevant consideration and tribunals will err if they focus on the things that a person can do instead of on the things that he or she cannot do.

The indirect effects of an impairment must also be taken into account when assessing whether the impairment falls within the statutory definition. Indirect effects might include, for example, where a person has been advised by a doctor to limit or refrain from a normal day-to-day activity on account of an impairment or where an impairment causes pain or fatigue so that, while the normal day-to-day activity can still be performed, the person might not be able to repeat the task over a sustained period of time – para D22 of the Guidance. The EAT in Goodwin (above) gave the example of a person with exceptionally acute hearing, whose ability to hear is obviously not adversely affected. However, the condition may well adversely affect other capacities; for example, it may give rise to difficulties in coping with conversation in a group, or a person's ability to concentrate, or the ability to go into a busy shop, all of which are normal day-to-day activities.

Regard should also be given to the fact that physical impairments can have **6.90** mental effects and vice versa. The Guidance gives the example of a person with a physical impairment who, because of pain and fatigue, may experience difficulties in carrying out normal activities that involve mental processes. Similarly, mental impairments or learning difficulties can have physical manifestations, such as a person with a mental impairment having difficulty in carrying out physical activities – para D15.

Normal for who? In Vance v Royal Mail Group plc EAT 0003/06 the question **6.91** arose of whether a claimant was disabled where, as a result of his impairment, he would have been unable to perform certain normal activities but which, in practice, he was not actually required to perform in his day-to-day life. The claimant had osteoarthritis as a result of which, had he been required to do so, he would have experienced great difficulty undertaking housework. An employment tribunal decided that, since he was not required to perform housework and similar activities, his impairment was not such as to have a substantial effect on his ability to carry out normal day-to-day activities and that he was not therefore disabled within the meaning of the DDA. On appeal, the EAT upheld the tribunal's decision, ruling that a person who would not be able to carry out an activity that was normal for others was not to be treated as disabled if he did not, in fact, carry it out as part of his or her daily life. Lady Smith (presiding in the EAT) reasoned that, if this were not so, the reference in S.1 DDA (now re-enacted in S.6(1) EqA) to the extent of a person's impairment – '*substantial* and long-term adverse effect' – would be otiose. The EAT distinguished the claimant's situation in the instant case from that of people who did not carry out a particular day-to-day activity because they had adjusted their lifestyle so as to accommodate an impairment from which they suffered in a way which, by the relevant date, had come to exclude that activity.

The EAT's decision in the Vance case (above) is open to question. It is notable that the wording of the relevant statutory provision does not define disability in terms of an impairment having a substantial adverse effect on the claimant's ability 'to carry out *his* normal day-to-day activities'. Rather, the focus is on the kind of activities that the claimant's impairment has an effect on and there is nothing to suggest that these have to be activities actually undertaken by the claimant.

141

6.92 **Gender-focused activities.** Any suggestion that activities are not normal activities if one sex performs them to a much greater extent than the other was dispelled by the EAT in Ekpe v Commissioner of Police of the Metropolis 2001 ICR 1084, EAT. In that case, the tribunal held that putting make-up on and putting rollers in hair were not normal day-to-day activities as they were carried out almost exclusively by women. The EAT said that this was plainly wrong because it would exclude anything done by women rather than men, or vice versa, as not being normal. The Guidance supports this view by stating that a normal day-to-day activity is not necessarily one that is carried out by a majority of people – para D5.

6.93 **Work-related activities.** The Guidance makes it clear that the term 'normal day-to-day activities' does not include work of any particular form because no particular form of work is 'normal' for most people. The EqA only covers effects which go beyond the normal differences which may exist among people – para B1. This means that the inability to perform a particular task at work would not bring a person within the definition of a disabled person unless there was also an adverse impact on the person's normal day-to-day activities. The Guidance states as an example that carrying out delicate work with specialised tools may be a normal working activity for a watch repairer, whereas it would not be normal for a person employed as a semi-skilled worker – para D8. However, other activities such as preparing invoices and counting takings carried out by the watch repairer would be normal day-to-day activities – D.10.

The concept of 'disability' under European law was considered in Chacón Navas v Eurest Colectividades SA 2007 ICR 1, ECJ, where the European Court focused on the effect of the impairment on an employee's professional life. In light of that decision, the EAT in Paterson v Commissioner of Police of the Metropolis 2007 ICR 1522, EAT, concluded that 'normal day-to-day activities' must be interpreted as including activities relevant to professional life. It accordingly held that taking high-pressure examinations for the purpose of gaining promotion constituted a 'normal', if irregular, everyday activity. It followed that the claimant police officer, who had dyslexia and was at a disadvantage when sitting examinations for promotion, was disabled within the meaning of the DDA. The EAT's decision gives useful guidance on the phrase 'normal day-to-day activities', emphasising that the phrase is to be given a broad definition that can include irregular but predictable activities which occur in professional life.

6.94 In Chief Constable of Dumfries and Galloway Constabulary v Adams 2009 ICR 1034, EAT, the EAT held that the ECJ's use of the term 'professional life' in Chacón Navas referred to activities that were found across a range of employment situations. It was not, in the EAT's view, meant to cover a specialist skill, even though such a skill might be normal within the particular industry (for example, a skilled watchmaker using specialised tools to craft fine objects of precision). Applying this reasoning, the EAT held that while the special skills required specifically of a policeman would not be a 'normal day-to-day activity', it did qualify as such where the activity was a common one across a range of industries. It followed that in the instant case, a policeman suffering from chronic fatigue was able to argue that the activities of walking, stair climbing and driving were normal day-to-day activities even when carried out on night shifts between 2 and 4 am. There were enough people carrying out night work for it to be a normal day-to-day activity.

Although a person's ability to carry out work-related activities is not relevant to determining whether that person is disabled, the fact that he or she can carry out normal day-to-day activities in all circumstances save the very special ones of his or her particular employment does not prevent a finding that the employee is disabled – Cruickshank v VAW Motorcast Ltd 2002 ICR 729, EAT. In that case C's asthma was triggered by exposure to fumes at work but improved when he was away from work. C's employer decided that there were no vacancies in either the offices or the yard to which C could be moved and he was dismissed. The tribunal dismissed C's disability discrimination claim on the ground, inter alia, that although he did have an impairment that was long term, he was not a disabled person within the meaning of the DDA because his impairment did not have a substantial and long-term adverse effect on his ability to carry out normal day-to-day activities. C appealed to the EAT.

6.95 Before the EAT, the employer argued that the Act was limited to offering protection to people who have an incapacity with a near-constant effect on their ability to carry out normal day-to-day activities. The employer contended that a person who could carry out day-to-day activities in all circumstances except the very special circumstances of his or her job could not be disabled within the meaning of the DDA. The EAT rejected this argument, holding that 'normal day-to-day activities' in S.1 DDA was 'only a yardstick' for deciding whether an impairment was serious enough to qualify for protection under that Act. It therefore followed that in assessing whether a disability has a significant and long-term effect on the ability to perform everyday tasks, it was not appropriate to confine the evaluation to the extent to which the claimant is disabled in a 'normal day-to-day' environment. Accordingly, the EAT thought that if a person's symptoms were such that they had a significant and long-term effect on his or her ability to perform everyday tasks at work, those symptoms should not be ignored simply because the work itself may be specialised and unusual. The EAT allowed the appeal against the tribunal's decision that C was not disabled within the meaning of the DDA and remitted the case to a fresh tribunal for rehearing.

Thus it would seem that where the effects of an impairment are exacerbated by conditions at work, the tribunal must consider the claimant's ability to carry out day-to-day activities both at work and outside work. The term 'normal

143

day-to-day activities' is a measure of seriousness; it does not dictate the actual environment in which the symptoms are to be judged.

6.96 Note that evidence as to how an employee carries out his or her duties at work can be relevant when a tribunal is assessing an employee's credibility, provided those work duties are also normal day-to-day activities – Law Hospital NHS Trust v Rush 2001 IRLR 611, Ct Sess (Inner House). For example, if an employee asserted that he or she could not lift a kettle with his or her right hand at home, evidence that the employee regularly lifted heavy weights with his or her right hand at work could be relevant to that employee's credibility as a witness. Equally, evidence that an employee could not carry out such activities at work, or could only do so with considerable difficulty, could support his or her case.

6.97 **Evidence.** In Goodwin v Patent Office 1999 ICR 302, EAT, the EAT cautioned against accepting claimants' assertions that they can cope with normal day-to-day activities when in fact they may simply have developed avoidance or coping strategies. One such coping mechanism is to 'play down' the effect of the disability. In such a situation, the medical evidence, if available, may help the tribunal determine whether the claimant is employing such strategies. 'Coping' strategies are dealt with more fully under 'Substantial adverse effect' above, while medical evidence is deal with under 'Medical evidence' below.

6.98 **Activities**
The Guidance states that it is not possible to provide an exhaustive list of day-to-day activities. However, in general, day-to-day activities are things people do on a regular or daily basis. The examples given are: shopping, reading and writing, having a conversation or using the telephone, watching television, getting washed and dressed, preparing and eating food, carrying out household tasks, walking and travelling by various forms of transport, and taking part in social activities. Normal day-to-day activities can also include general work-related activities, and study and education-related activities, such as interacting with colleagues, following instructions, using a computer, driving, carrying out interviews, preparing written documents, and keeping to a timetable or a shift pattern – D3.

Paragraphs D11–22 of the Guidance advise on what should be taken into account in deciding whether a person's ability to carry out normal day-to-day activities might be restricted by the effects of a person's impairment. The Appendix to the Guidance then gives examples of circumstances where it would (or would not) be reasonable to regard the adverse effect on the ability to carry out a normal day-to-day activity as substantial. However, these examples are 'indicators and not tests. They do not mean that if a person can do an activity listed then he or she does not experience any substantial adverse effects: the person may be affected in relation to other activities, and this instead may indicate a substantial effect. Alternatively, the person may be affected in a minor way in a number of different categories, and the cumulative effect could amount to a substantial adverse effect' – D13. The examples in the Appendix describe the effect that would occur when the various factors described under 'Substantial adverse effect' above and 'Long-term effect' below have been allowed for. These include, for example, the effects of a person making such modifications of behaviour as might reasonably be expected, or of disregarding the impact of medical or other treatment – para D14. Tribunals will fall into error if they ignore the Guidance, as happened in Coca Cola Enterprises Ltd v Shergill EAT 0003/02 where, in the tribunal's opinion, the Guidance did not reflect current society.

6.99 As noted earlier, the indirect effects of an impairment must also be taken into account when considering its adverse effects on normal day-to-day activities – see para D22 of the Guidance. In Leonard v Southern Derbyshire Chamber of Commerce 2001 IRLR 19, EAT, for example, L's clinical depression caused tiredness which in turn affected her mobility in terms of the distances she could walk and drive, as well as her manual dexterity, because, when she was tired, her physical coordination went. Her vision also tended to blur and she could not maintain concentration and suffered memory loss. She was found to be disabled within the meaning of the DDA.

Below we consider the types of factor that should be taken into account in deciding whether a person's ability to carry out normal day-to-day activities has been restricted by the effects of an impairment by reference to the examples set out in the Appendix to the Guidance. For ease of use we have adopted as headings the capacities that previously existed in para 4(1) of Schedule 1 to the DDA. However, these are not exhaustive and reference should be made to the Guidance for a broader consideration of day-to-day activities.

6.100 **Mobility.** The Appendix to the Guidance gives the following examples of factors which it would be reasonable to regard as having a substantial adverse effect on normal day-to-day activities:

- difficulty going out of doors unaccompanied; for example, because the person has a phobia, a physical restriction, or a learning disability

- difficulty waiting or queuing; for example, because of a lack of understanding of the concept, or because of pain or fatigue when standing for prolonged periods

- difficulty using transport; for example, because of physical restrictions, pain or fatigue, a frequent need for a lavatory or as a result of a mental impairment or learning disability

- difficulty in going up or down steps, stairs or gradients; for example, because movements are painful, fatiguing or restricted in some way

145

- a total inability to walk, or an ability to walk only a short distance without difficulty; for example, because of physical restrictions, pain or fatigue.

6.101 The Guidance gives the example of a woman with Down's syndrome who is only able to understand her familiar local bus route. This means that she is unable to travel unaccompanied on other routes, because she gets lost and cannot find her way home without assistance. This has a substantial adverse effect on her ability to carry out the normal day-to-day activity of using public transport – D15.

Examples given in the Appendix of where there would be no substantial adverse effect on mobility include where a person experiences some discomfort as a result of travelling, for example by car or plane, for a journey lasting more than two hours, or some tiredness or minor discomfort as a result of walking unaided for a distance of about 1.5 kilometres or one mile. In Bimpson v Close Motor Finance Ltd ET Case No.2400739/08 B started working for CMF Ltd on 2 January 2008 but his employment only lasted six days. In determining whether B was disabled, the tribunal accepted that he had a problem with motorway driving in that it triggered anxiety. He therefore drove on A-roads instead. However, B was not disabled for the purposes of the DDA. The tribunal considered it debatable whether an inability to drive had a substantial adverse effect on day-to-day activities, but found that it did not have such an effect when the inability related only to motorways, particularly in circumstances where a person is able to drive on A-roads.

6.102 According to the Appendix, it would be reasonable to regard difficulty in using transport – for example, because of physical restrictions, pain or fatigue – as having a substantial adverse effect on normal day-to-day activities. A person's inability to travel by public transport was considered in Abadeh v British Telecommunications plc 2001 ICR 156, EAT, where the EAT held that a tribunal had erred in finding that travelling by underground and by aeroplane were not day-to-day activities for the claimant because he did not live or work in London and his work did not involve his having to travel by aeroplane. The tribunal had failed to have regard to the version of the Guidance then in force, which stated that, in deciding whether an activity is a normal day-to-day activity, account should be taken of how far it is normal for most people and carried out by most people on a daily or frequent and fairly regular basis. The EAT stated that travelling by car or public transport was a normal day-to-day activity for most people carried out by them on such a basis. The tribunal had erred in considering what was a normal activity for the particular claimant. The issue to be determined was whether the claimant's inability to use a particular form of transport such as the underground, which he never in fact used, had a substantial adverse effect on him.

In Aderemi v London and South Eastern Railway Ltd ET Case No.2300599/11 an employment tribunal held that the claimant (who was employed as a railway station assistant and who suffered from back pain making it difficult for him to stand for long periods) was not disabled for the purposes of S.6(1) EqA. In so concluding the tribunal noted that, in relation to mobility, the examples given in the Appendix of where it would be reasonable to regard an impairment as having substantial adverse effect included 'total inability to walk, or difficulty walking other than at a slow pace or with unsteady or jerky movements'. The tribunal was satisfied that the claimant's back pain did not prevent him from walking, sitting or standing provided it was not for prolonged periods. Although the effects of back pain were not to be underestimated, the tribunal concluded that the low back pain experienced by the claimant in this case had not crossed the threshold into the statutory definition of disability, namely that his condition had a substantial and adverse effect on his ability to carry out day-to-day activities. (Note that the current Guidance uses the phrase 'a total inability to walk, or an ability to walk only a short distance without difficulty'.)

Manual dexterity. The Appendix gives the following examples of factors which **6.103** it would be reasonable to regard as having a substantial adverse effect on normal day-to-day activities:

- difficulty in getting dressed; for example, because of physical restrictions

- difficulty preparing a meal; for example, because of restricted ability to do things like open cans or packages

- difficulty eating; for example, because of an inability to coordinate the use of a knife and fork

- difficulty operating a computer; for example, because of physical restrictions in using a keyboard

- difficulty accessing and moving around buildings; for example, because of inability to open doors, or grip handrails on steps or gradients.

Examples given in the Appendix of where there would be no substantial adverse **6.104** effect on manual dexterity include the inability to reach typing speeds standardised for secretarial work and the inability to undertake activities requiring delicate hand movements, such as threading a small needle or picking up a pin.

Loss of manual dexterity was considered in Savage v Robinson Plastic Packaging Ltd ET Case No.2602802/06. Part of the ring finger of S's left hand had to be amputated as a result of an accident at work. At a preliminary hearing the tribunal found that he was not disabled for the purposes of the DDA. S's work was highly skilled and required a high degree of manual dexterity, and, in the tribunal's opinion, he coped very well with his impairment. He was right handed and although he found using his left hand difficult for some tasks, he managed.

147

6.105 **Physical coordination.** According to the Guidance, 'a person's impairment may have an adverse effect on day-to-day activities that require an ability to co-ordinate their movements, to carry everyday objects such as a kettle of water, a bag of shopping, a briefcase, or an overnight bag, or to use standard items of equipment' – para D18. The example given is that of a young man who has dyspraxia and experiences a range of effects which include difficulty coordinating physical movements. He is frequently knocking over cups and bottles of drink and cannot combine two activities at the same time, such as walking while holding a plate of food upright without spilling the food.

In Howden v Capital Copiers (Edinburgh) Ltd ET Case No.400005/97 H experienced sharp, gripping pains which forced him to lie down, as well as having other adverse effects on his well-being. He was admitted to hospital on several occasions and was operated on three times but no satisfactory cause was found for his pain. The tribunal accepted that H's condition amounted to a physical impairment under the DDA notwithstanding the absence of an exact diagnosis. The condition had a substantial long-term adverse effect on his ability to carry out normal day-to-day activities, including loss of mobility, manual dexterity and physical coordination, and that was sufficient to bring it within the ambit of the Act.

6.106 **Continence.** The Appendix gives the following examples of factors which it would be reasonable to regard as having a substantial adverse effect on normal day-to-day activities:

- difficulty carrying out activities associated with toileting, or caused by frequent minor incontinence

- difficulty using transport; for example, because of a frequent need for a lavatory.

However, the Appendix states that infrequent minor incontinence would not be regarded as having such an effect.

6.107 Account should therefore be taken of the frequency and extent of the loss of control when considering whether a person's ability to carry out normal day-to-day activities is adversely affected. The example given in the Guidance is of a young woman who has developed colitis, an inflammatory bowel disease. The condition is a chronic one that is subject to periods of remission and flare-up. During a flare-up she experiences severe abdominal pain and bouts of diarrhoea which makes it very difficult for her to drive, including for the purposes of her job, as she must ensure she is always close to a lavatory – D22.

In Rimmer-Clay v Brighton Housing Trust ET Case No.3102861/08 R-C suffered from stress incontinence. She underwent a surgical procedure to help women with this problem. A leaflet about the procedure stated that 80–90 per cent of women felt that their stress incontinence improved after the operation and that, for the majority of patients, it continued to work well after 10–15 years. However, the leaflet continued that the procedure did not cure symptoms of passing urine frequently and rushing to the toilet with urgency. The tribunal held that R-C's operation should be disregarded for the purposes of the DDA. Since the information about the operation did not state that it was a permanent cure, only that it continued to work after 10–15 years, it was likely to recur. Accordingly, R-C was disabled under the DDA.

Ability to lift, carry or otherwise move everyday objects. The Appendix 6.108 states that it would be reasonable to regard a difficulty in picking up and carrying objects of moderate weight, such as a bag of shopping or a small piece of luggage, with one hand as having a substantial adverse effect on normal day-to-day activities. In contrast, an inability to move heavy objects without assistance or a mechanical aid, such as moving a large suitcase or heavy piece of furniture without a trolley, should not be regarded as having such an effect. The example in the Guidance is of a man with achondroplasia who has an unusually short stature and whose arms are disproportionate in size to the rest of his body. He has difficulty lifting everyday items like a vacuum cleaner, and he cannot reach a standard height sink or washbasin without a step to stand on. This has a substantial adverse effect on his ability to carry out normal day-to-day activities, such as cleaning, washing up and washing his hands – D18.

In Vicary v British Telecommunications plc 1999 IRLR 680, EAT, the tribunal found that V's inability to lift a chair should be disregarded because lifting chairs was not a 'normal day-to-day activity'. The EAT held that the tribunal's finding flew in the face of the version of the Guidance then in force, which stated that a chair was an 'everyday object' for the purposes of lifting, carrying or otherwise moving everyday objects. In Quinlan v B&Q plc EAT 1386/97, on the other hand, the fact that a gardening centre assistant (who had undergone open heart surgery) could lift everyday objects meant that he was not disabled under the DDA, even though he was dismissed for his inability to lift heavy bags at work.

Similarly, in Redhead v St John's Ambulance Service ET Case No.3101427/09 6.109 an employee employed as an ambulance person was held not to be disabled within the meaning of the DDA. A medical report stated that it would be unwise for the claimant to return to work which might involve lifting heavy objects and concluded that the claimant had a substantial impairment in relation to his mobility. However, the tribunal pointed out that 'heavy lifting is not a normal day-to-day activity', and concluded that the claimant had failed to discharge the onus on him to show that he had a disability.

149

6.110 **Speech, hearing or eyesight.** The Appendix gives the following examples of factors which it would be reasonable to regard as having a substantial adverse effect on normal day-to-day activities:

- inability to converse, or give instructions orally, in the person's native spoken language

- difficulty hearing and understanding another person speaking clearly over the telephone (where the telephone is not affected by bad reception)

- persistent and significant difficulty in reading or understanding written material where this is in the person's native written language; for example, because of a visual impairment (except where that is corrected by glasses or contact lenses).

In relation to speech, consideration should be given to the ability to speak clearly at a normal pace and rhythm and to understand other people speaking normally in their native language – D17. Consideration should also be given to any effects on speech patterns or which impede the acquisition or processing of a person's native language; for example, by someone who has had a stroke. In Goodwin v Patent Office 1999 ICR 302, EAT, the EAT held that the evidence of G's manager that G was unable to hold a normal conversation with work colleagues was good evidence that G's ability to concentrate and communicate had been adversely affected to a significant degree by his schizophrenia.

6.111 The Appendix states that it would not be reasonable to regard the following as having a substantial adverse effect:

- inability to speak in front of an audience simply as a result of nervousness

- some shyness and timidity

- inability to articulate certain sounds due to a lisp

- inability to be understood because of having a strong accent

- inability to converse orally in a language which is not the speaker's native spoken language

- inability to sing in tune.

With regard to hearing, the Guidance gives the example of a man with a hearing impairment which has the effect that he cannot hold a conversation with another person even in a quiet environment. He has a hearing aid which overcomes that effect. However, it is the effect of the impairment without the hearing aid that needs to be considered (see 'Effect of medical treatment' below). In this case, the impairment has a substantial adverse effect on the day-to-day activity of holding a conversation – D23. However, the fact that someone cannot hold a conversation in a very noisy place, such as a factory floor, a pop concert, sporting event or alongside a busy main road, would not be regarded as evidence of 'substantial adverse effects'.

With regard to sight, the example given in the Guidance of an impairment that **6.112** has an adverse effect on normal day-to-day activities is of a man who has retinitis pigmentosa, a hereditary eye disorder which affects the retina. He has difficulty seeing in poor light and experiences a marked reduction in his field of vision. As a result, he often bumps into furniture and doors when he is in an unfamiliar environment, and can only read when he is in a very well-lit area – para D20.

If a person's sight is corrected by glasses or contact lenses, or could be corrected by them, what needs to be considered is any adverse effect that the visual impairment has on the ability to carry out normal day-to-day activities which remains while he or she is wearing such glasses or lenses – para 5(3)(a), Sch 1 EqA (see 'Long-term effect – effect of medical treatment' below).

The Appendix states that the inability to read very small or indistinct print **6.113** without using a magnifying glass; to distinguish a known person across a substantial distance (e.g. across the width of a football pitch); or to distinguish between red and green (where this is not accompanied by any other effect such as blurring of vision) is not to be regarded as having a substantial adverse effect. In Hudson v Post Office ET Case No.3100773/98 poor vision in one eye was held not to be a disability: there would be no adverse effect on day-to-day activities because the individual could rely on his good eye.

Note that the Equality Act 2010 (Disability) Regulations 2010 SI 2010/2128 provide that people certified by a consultant ophthalmologist as blind, sight impaired or severely sight impaired, or partially sighted are deemed to have a disability, and therefore be disabled, for the purposes of the Act – see 'Physical or mental impairment – deemed disabilities' above.

Memory or ability to concentrate, learn or understand. Paragraph D19 of **6.114** the Guidance states that 'a person's impairment may adversely affect the ability to carry out normal day-to-day activities that involve aspects such as remembering to do things, organising their thoughts, planning a course of action and carrying it out, taking in new knowledge, and understanding spoken or written information'. Consideration should also be given to whether the person has cognitive difficulties or learns to do things significantly more slowly than a person who does not have an impairment.

The Appendix gives the following examples of factors which it would be reasonable to regard as having a substantial adverse effect on normal day-to-day activities:

- difficulty preparing a meal; for example, because of an inability to understand and follow a simple recipe

151

- difficulty understanding or following simple verbal instructions

- persistent difficulty in recognising, or remembering the names of, familiar people such as family or friends

- persistent distractibility or difficulty concentrating.

6.115 The Guidance gives the example of a woman with bipolar affective disorder who is easily distracted. This means that she is frequently unable to concentrate on performing an activity like making a sandwich or filling out a form without being distracted from the task. Consequently it takes her significantly longer than a person without the disorder to complete such tasks. However, the inability to concentrate on a task requiring application over several hours would not be regarded as a substantial adverse effect. For examples of cases dealing with memory and learning difficulties, see under 'Physical or mental impairment – mental impairments' above.

The Guidance recognises that an impairment of this kind can have an adverse effect on a person's ability to understand human non-factual and non-verbal communication such as body language and facial expressions and that account should be taken of how such factors can have an adverse effect on normal day-to-day activities – D17. The example given is of a man with Asperger's syndrome, a form of autism. He finds it hard to understand non-verbal communications such as facial expressions, and non-factual communication such as jokes. He is given verbal instructions during office banter with his manager, but his ability to understand the instruction is impaired because he is unable to isolate the instruction from the social conversation. This has a substantial adverse effect on his ability to carry out normal day-to-day communication.

6.116 In Hewett v Motorola Ltd 2004 IRLR 545, EAT, H – who worked as a firmware engineer – had Autistic Spectrum Disorder (ASD) and/or Asperger's syndrome. He brought a disability discrimination claim against M Ltd, alleging that it had failed to make reasonable adjustments. Before the tribunal, H contended that his impairment had a substantial effect on his memory or ability to concentrate, learn or understand. He was persistently unable to remember names of familiar people or to adapt to minor changes in work routine, which made it hard for him to make and keep friends, and he was largely excluded from social interaction. However, the tribunal made a preliminary determination that, while H's ability to concentrate might on occasion have been impaired by the difficulty he faced in social situations, this impairment was not substantial. Accordingly, he was not disabled for the purposes of the DDA. The EAT overturned this decision. The tribunal had erred in its approach to the concept of 'understanding'. It had failed to acknowledge that someone who has difficulty in understanding normal social interaction among people, and/or the subtleties of human non-factual communication can be regarded as having their understanding affected and that the concept of understanding is not limited to an ability to understand information, knowledge or instructions. For other examples of cases dealing with ASD conditions, see 'Physical or mental impairment – mental impairments' above.

According to the Appendix, it would not be reasonable to regard the following factors as having a substantial adverse effect on normal day-to-day activities:

- inability to fill in a long, detailed, technical document, which is in the person's native language, without assistance
- occasionally forgetting the name of a familiar person, such as a colleague
- inability to concentrate on a task requiring application over several hours.

Perception of the risk of physical danger. The Guidance states that 'normal **6.117** day-to-day activities also include activities that are required to maintain personal well-being or to ensure personal safety, or the safety of other people. Account should be taken of whether the effects of an impairment have an impact on whether the person is inclined to carry out or neglect basic functions such as eating, drinking, sleeping, keeping warm or personal hygiene; or to exhibit behaviour which puts the person or other people at risk' – D16.

According to the Appendix, persistent difficulty crossing a road safely, for example, because of a failure to understand and manage the risk, would be regarded as a substantial adverse effect. However, consciously taking a higher than normal risk, such as persistently crossing a road when the signals are adverse, or driving fast on highways for pleasure, would not. Nor would an occasional apprehension about significant heights.

The Guidance example refers to a woman who has had anorexia for two years and the effects of her impairment restrict her ability to carry out the normal day-to-day activity of eating – para D16.

Long-term effect   6.118

The substantial adverse effect of an impairment has to be *long term* to fall within the definition of 'disability' in the EqA, whether the disability is a current one under S.6(1) or a past disability under S.6(4). This requirement ensures that temporary or short-term conditions do not attract the Act's protection, even if they are severe and very disabling while they last, such as acute depression or a strained back.

Under para 2(1) of Schedule 1 to the EqA the effect of an impairment is 'long term' if it:

- has lasted for at least 12 months

- is likely to last for at least 12 months, or

- is likely to last for the rest of the life of the person affected.

6.119 This last option means that someone who is terminally ill and is not expected to live for 12 months will be considered to have a long-term impairment. Under para 2(4), regulations may prescribe circumstances in which, despite para 2(1), an effect is to be treated as being, or as not being, long-term. No regulations have yet been made under this provision (or under the equivalent provision in the DDA).

An employment tribunal will commit an error of law if it fails to have regard to all three scenarios envisaged by para 2(1) and to make the necessary findings of fact to determine the matter. In McKechnie Plastic Components v Grant EAT 0284/08 the EAT held that a tribunal should have considered all three alternative grounds – rather than simply whether the effect of the claimant's impairment had lasted 12 months – and it remitted the case on this basis.

6.120 Likely to last 12 months

For current impairments that have not lasted 12 months the tribunal will have to decide if the substantial adverse effects of the condition are likely to last for at least 12 months. The word 'likely' is also used in other related contexts – namely, for determining whether an impairment has a recurring effect, whether adverse effects of a progressive condition will become substantial, and how an impairment should be treated for the purposes of the EqA when the effects of that impairment are controlled or corrected by medical treatment. In all four contexts, the Guidance stipulates that an event is likely to happen if it 'could well happen' – para C3 of the Guidance. This definition of the word 'likely' reflects the House of Lords' decision in SCA Packaging Ltd v Boyle 2009 ICR 1056, HL. In that case, B suffered from nodules on her vocal cords, which resulted in her experiencing chronic hoarseness when speaking. At a pre-hearing review to determine whether B was in fact disabled, the tribunal found that she suffered from a physical impairment and that, but for coping strategies which she used in her daily life, it was 'more likely than not' that the substantial adverse effect of the impairment would have continued. Therefore B was disabled for the purposes of the DDA. On appeal, the Northern Ireland Court of Appeal upheld the tribunal's finding on disability but held that, in addressing the degree of likelihood required under the DDA, the tribunal should have asked whether the substantial adverse effect 'could well happen'. Dismissing the employer's appeal, the House of Lords unanimously decided that the Court of Appeal had been correct in endorsing the 'could well happen' over the 'more probable than not' approach. According to Baroness Hale, the word 'likely' in each of the relevant provisions of the DDA (now EqA) simply meant something that is a real possibility, in the sense that it 'could well happen', rather than something that is probable or 'more likely than not'. This decision clearly

154

makes it much easier for individuals with certain conditions to satisfy the statutory test for disability, in that their Lordships' construction of the word 'likely' represents a significantly lower hurdle than the probability test that was formerly thought to apply.

Prior to the decision in the SCA case (above) the Guidance had asserted that the word 'likely' in the context of determining whether the adverse effects of an impairment were likely to last more than 12 months meant 'more probable than not', based on the EAT's decision in Latchman v Reed Business Information Ltd 2002 ICR 1453, EAT. However, as stated above, that test was disapproved by the House of Lords in SCA in favour of one defining 'likely' as simply meaning 'could well happen'. Not surprisingly, tribunals that reference the old test when concluding that the effects of a claimant's condition were not likely to last more than 12 months have been held by the EAT to have erred in law – see Wigginton v NJ Cowie and ors t/a Baxter International (a Partnership) EAT 0322/09 and Anwar v Tower Hamlets College EAT 0091/10.

It is important to note that the issue of how long an impairment is likely to last **6.121** should be determined *at the date of the discriminatory act* and not the date of the tribunal hearing – Richmond Adult Community College v McDougall 2008 ICR 431, CA (see below). Para C4 of the Guidance stresses that anything that occurs after the date of the discriminatory act will not be relevant. It also states that account should be taken of both the typical length of such an effect on an individual and any relevant factors specific to this individual, such as general state of health and age.

The requirement that an impairment be long term clearly applies to all impairments but in practice seems to have been particularly relevant in the case of depression. Three examples:

- **Heverin v Halton Borough Council** ET Case No.2104489/07: H was employed as a home care assistant until she resigned in July 2007. Before the tribunal, she claimed that she was disabled by reason of her depression and her consultant psychiatrist had provided a report stating that her episode of depression had lasted longer than 12 months and had substantially affected her day-to-day activities. The tribunal disagreed. H had produced no evidence to show how her depression affected her normal day-to-day activities and there was no hint that she was unable to concentrate on various tasks in the way she conducted herself before the tribunal

- **Butler v Eastleigh Housing Association Ltd** ET Case No.3101121/97: B, a finance manager, became depressed following an incident during which he took exception to remarks made to him by a colleague in front of other staff. B's GP diagnosed B as having reactive depression. B continued to be affected by stress and was signed off sick for two weeks. He was eventually dismissed in January 1997. A couple of months later he secured another

155

finance position that he held down initially on a part-time basis, and later full time. The tribunal held that at the time of his dismissal B was suffering from acute depression, which started in about October 1996, but the effects were not long-lasting as in less than two months from his dismissal he had started another job. Accordingly, B was not disabled within the terms of the DDA

- **Jobling v Corporate Medical Management Ltd** EAT 703/01: J suffered from depression between November 1998 and February 1999 and was prescribed medication which she continued to take for some time thereafter. Her claim of disability discrimination failed on the ground that she did not have a continuing depressive illness after February 1999 despite her continued use of medication after that date. The tribunal accepted medical evidence that her continued use of medication was 'almost a placebo effect'. The EAT saw no reason to interfere with the tribunal's decision.

6.122 **Consecutive short-term impairments.** In deciding whether the duration of the effects of two different consecutive impairments – which each lasted less than 12 months – can be aggregated, it is necessary to consider whether the second impairment had developed from the first – Patel v Oldham MBC 2010 ICR 603, EAT. This is reflected in the Guidance, which states that the cumulative effect of related impairments should be taken into account when determining whether the person has experienced a long-term effect for the purposes of meeting the definition of a disabled person – para C2.

6.123 **Fluctuating effects.** The effect of an impairment does not have to remain the same during the 12-month period. As the Guidance points out in para C7, some activities may initially be very difficult but become easier. The main adverse effect may even disappear temporarily, or disappear altogether while another effect may develop into a substantial adverse effect.

6.124 **Recurring conditions**

People with some conditions, such as rheumatoid arthritis and epilepsy, experience periods of remission and good health during which they would not be able to satisfy the definition of disability. To ensure that such people are protected, para 2(2) of Schedule 1 to the EqA provides that if an impairment ceases to have a substantial adverse effect on a person's ability to carry out normal day-to-day activities, it is treated as continuing to have that effect if the effect is 'likely to recur'. 'Likely to recur' means that 'it could well happen' – see para C3 of the Guidance and SCA Packaging Ltd v Boyle 2009 ICR 1056, HL (discussed under 'Likely to last 12 months' above).

Paragraph C6 of the Guidance states that the effects are to be treated as long term if they are likely to recur beyond 12 months after the first occurrence. This is to ensure that the total period during which a person has an impairment with recurring effects is at least 12 months. The example is given of a young man with bipolar affective disorder, a recurring form of depression. His first episode occurred in months one and two of a 13-month period. The second episode took place in month 13. This will satisfy the requirements of the definition of disability in respect of the meaning of 'long term' because the adverse effects have recurred beyond 12 months after the first occurrence and are therefore treated as having continued for the whole period – in this case, a period of 13 months.

In Swift v Chief Constable of Wiltshire Constabulary 2004 ICR 909, EAT, the **6.125** EAT emphasised that the question for the tribunal is not whether the impairment itself is likely to recur, but whether the substantial adverse effect of the impairment is likely to recur. The tribunal must therefore identify the effect of the impairment with a degree of precision, since a substantial adverse effect resulting from a different impairment that was not the consequence of the condition initially diagnosed would not qualify as a recurrence.

When the EqA was at the Commons Committee stage, an amendment was proposed whereby depression would automatically be treated as 'likely to recur' if the claimant had, within the last five years, experienced an episode lasting at least six months that had had a substantial adverse effect on his or her ability to carry out normal day-to-day activities. This amendment – designed to protect individuals who experience short-term, recurrent episodes of depression – was rejected. The Solicitor-General expressed the view that para 2(2) of Schedule 1 already provides sufficient protection in these circumstances.

Under para 2(3) of Schedule 1 to the EqA, regulations may provide that in **6.126** certain circumstances the likelihood of an effect recurring is to be disregarded. No regulations have been made under this provision (or under the equivalent provision in the DDA). Note, however, that seasonal allergic rhinitis (e.g. hayfever) is not to be treated as an impairment under the Act, except where it aggravates the effects of an existing condition – Reg 4(2) and (3) Equality Act 2010 (Disability) Regulations 2010 SI 2010/2128.

Likelihood of recurrence. The Guidance states that the likelihood of recurrence **6.127** should be considered taking all the circumstances of the case into account, including what the person could reasonably be expected to do to prevent the recurrence – para C9. An example of preventative action might be to avoid substances to which the person is allergic. However, the Guidance cautions that the way in which a person controls or copes with the effect of a condition may break down in certain situations, e.g. an unfamiliar environment. If there is an increased likelihood that the control will break down, it will be more likely that there will be a recurrence, and this possibility should be taken into account – C10.

In assessing the likelihood of a claimant's impairment recurring – and thus qualifying as 'long term' – an employment tribunal should disregard events taking place after the alleged discriminatory act but prior to the tribunal hearing

157

– Richmond Adult Community College v McDougall 2008 ICR 431, CA. M suffered from a history of depression and between November 2001 and February 2002 she was sectioned under the Mental Health Act 1983. On 1 April 2005 the College offered M employment, subject to references and health clearance. However, three weeks later the offer was withdrawn as a result of an occupational health report that deemed M unfit to work. M lodged a disability discrimination claim under the DDA against RACC but in August 2005 her mental health problems returned and she was sectioned once more in December of that year. The employment tribunal rejected M's claim, concluding that she had not been disabled for DDA purposes at the time of the alleged discriminatory act. In this regard, the tribunal accepted that M had suffered from a 'persistent delusional disorder' and a 'schizo-affective disorder', and that in the circumstances she had a 'mental impairment' within the meaning of S.1(1) DDA. In its view, however, M failed to satisfy other aspects of the definition of disability, in that her impairment did not have a long-term substantial adverse effect on her ability to carry out normal day-to-day activities. In reaching its decision as to the long-term effect, the tribunal noted that the effects of M's disorder had lasted (at most) for eight months up to February 2002, and had not recurred by the time of the alleged discriminatory act. Furthermore, the evidence at the time of that act – April 2005 – failed to suggest that a recurrence was likely. M appealed to the EAT, arguing that in assessing whether, as at April 2005, her disorder was likely to recur – and hence whether it could be categorised as having a long-term effect – the tribunal should have taken into account the fact that the disorder did, in the event, recur in August 2005. The EAT agreed. The tribunal should have asked itself what, in April 2005, was the likelihood of M's condition recurring given what was known at the date of the hearing. On appeal, however, the EAT's decision was overturned. Lord Justice Pill, who gave the leading judgment, stated that the central purpose of the DDA was to prevent employers making discriminatory decisions, and to provide sanctions if such decisions are made. Whether an employer has committed a wrong under the DDA must be judged on the basis of the evidence available at the time of the action complained of. Accordingly, the tribunal's decision to reject M's DDA claim was reinstated.

6.128 The Court of Appeal's decision in McDougall – which is endorsed by the Guidance – resolved the confusion as to when the existence of a disability should be assessed, especially when determining the 'likelihood' of a substantial adverse effect lasting for 12 months or recurring in the future. However, the Court of Appeal's decision appears to leave something of a hole in the protection afforded to disabled workers by the EqA. It seems somewhat artificial to require an employment tribunal, when deciding whether a claimant has a condition that is likely to recur, to ignore conclusive evidence that the condition did in fact recur in the period between the date of the act complained of and the tribunal hearing. How far tribunals will be able to ignore such evidence in practice remains to be seen.

(Note that S.60 EqA now provides that an employer must not ask about a job applicant's health (including any disability) before offering him or her work or, where the employer is not in a position to offer work immediately, before including the applicant in a pool of persons to whom it intends to offer the work in the future – see Chapter 24, Recruitment', under 'Pre-employment health questions'.)

The likelihood of recurrence can be an issue in cases involving epilepsy where, **6.129** except in the most severe instances, the condition is symptomless between seizures. For example, in Alexander v Driving Standards Agency ET Case No.2601058/98 A, a driving test examiner, was diagnosed as having had an epileptic seizure in April 1997. She advised the Driving and Vehicle Licensing Agency, which suspended her driving licence, and her employer then suspended her from her duties. The tribunal found that A's epilepsy did not fall within the definition of a disability under the DDA. She had had only two epileptic seizures, both of which occurred during the night while she was asleep. The chances of her having a seizure during the day were rated as extremely small by medical advisers and the tribunal thought it unlikely that any substantial adverse effect that A had experienced in the past would recur. It followed that the effect of the impairment was not long term. The tribunal added that the only effects of a nocturnal seizure on day-to-day activities were the side effects, which could last for up to 24 hours. They included a severe headache, memory loss and some speech impediment. In the tribunal's view, these effects, although adverse, were not substantial.

Medical treatment. The effect of medical treatment is only relevant where the **6.130** treatment would permanently cure the person without the need for any further treatment, thereby removing the impairment. If the treatment merely delays or prevents a recurrence, and a recurrence would be likely if the treatment stopped, as is the case with most medication, then the treatment should be ignored and the effect of the impairment regarded as likely to recur – para C11 of the Guidance. This is considered in more detail in 'Effect of medical treatment' below.

Past disabilities
6.131
Section 6(4) EqA and para 9 of Schedule 1 to the EqA contain the provisions on past disabilities previously found in S.2 DDA and Schedule 2 to the DDA, with minor modifications. The effect of these provisions is to extend the protection afforded to those with current disabilities to those who have had a disability in the past, even if he or she has since recovered or the effects have become less than substantial.

Section 6(4) stipulates that most of the EqA's provisions (including the employment provisions) apply in relation to a person who has had a disability,

159

and modifies the wording of the Act accordingly. It does not matter that the disability was experienced at a time before the provisions of the EqA (or, indeed, the DDA) were in force.

6.132 Note that para 5 of Schedule 2 to the DDA expressly stated that a past disability could only be established if the substantial adverse effect of the impairment had actually lasted for at least 12 months (unless the substantial adverse effect ceased and then recurred, in which case it was treated as continuing – see below). As that requirement has not been carried over into the EqA, it is arguable that a past impairment that was likely at the time to last for at least 12 months – even though in the event it did not do so – is now covered. However, according to the revised Guidance, the test for past disabilities has remained unchanged – see para C12. This appears persuasive, given that, if a person cannot show that their past disability 'has lasted' for at least 12 months under para 2(1)(a) of Schedule 1 to the Act, then he or she would have to show that it 'is likely' to last for at least 12 months – para 2(1)(b). The fact that this latter provision is expressed in the present tense strongly suggests that it cannot be used to establish a past disability.

6.133 **Past disabilities that recur**
Paragraph 5 of Schedule 2 to the DDA provided that, with respect to past disabilities, where an impairment ceased to have a substantial adverse effect on a person's ability to carry out normal day-to-day activities, it was to be treated as continuing to have that effect if that effect recurred. It was immaterial that the effect was not likely to recur; it was sufficient that it did in fact do so. However, this provision has not been carried forward into the EqA. The test under the EqA focuses on the likelihood of recurrence, even in a case where the effect has actually recurred. Thus, if an impairment ceased to have a substantial adverse effect and such an effect was unlikely to recur, but did in fact recur, the individual will be unable to 'bridge the gap' during the period of good health and, as a result, may be unable to establish that his or her impairment lasted for 12 months. The consequence will be that that person will not be regarded as being a 'disabled person' within the meaning of the Act.

Given the lack of commentary on this point in the Explanatory Notes or in the Hansard debates, it is not altogether clear that this apparent change of test was the deliberate intention of the Government when it omitted to carry through the provisions previously contained in para 5 of Schedule 2 to the DDA. Certainly, the new Guidance assumes that the same test still applies – see para C12, which states that 'in deciding whether a past condition was a disability, its effects count as long term if they lasted 12 months or more after the first occurrence, or *if a recurrence happened or continued until more than 12 months after the first occurrence*' (our stress). What the highlighted words seems to be saying is that a past condition will comprise a disability if it recurs more than 12 months after its first occurrence or within 12 months but continues beyond 12 months after the first occurrence. If, contrary to our preferred view, the test has indeed changed, the effect may well be to increase the burden on tribunals to establish – through consideration of available medical evidence – whether a particular condition was likely to recur. The fact that the condition in question has actually recurred will not of itself be sufficient evidence on which the tribunal can draw the conclusion that it was a recurrent condition.

In Rimmer-Clay v Brighton Housing Trust ET Case No.3102861/08 an **6.134** employment tribunal decided on the basis of the test that applied under the DDA that an employee was disabled owing to an impairment – stress incontinence – that was likely to recur. The claimant had undergone a surgical procedure to assist with her condition. The medical evidence suggested that between 80 and 90 per cent of women who have the surgical procedure experience a substantial improvement in their condition and for the majority the operation continued to work well for a period of at least 10–15 years. However, the procedure was unable to cure all symptoms of passing urine frequently or the need to rush off to the lavatory with urgency. In those circumstances, the tribunal reasoned that the effects of the medical intervention had to be disregarded for the purposes of what is now para 5(1) of Schedule 1 to the EqA, and that, since the operation had not effected a permanent cure, the claimant's impairment was 'likely to recur' within the meaning of what is now para 2(2) of Schedule 1 to the EqA.

Effect of medical treatment
6.135

In determining whether a person's impairment has a substantial effect on his or her ability to carry out normal day-to-day activities, the effects of medical treatment or corrective aids on the impairment should be ignored. If an impairment would be likely to have a substantial adverse effect but for the fact that measures are being taken to treat or correct it, it is to be treated as having that effect – para 5(1), Sch 1 EqA. This is so even where the measures taken result in the effects of the impairment being completely under control or not at all apparent – para B13 of the Guidance.

The 'measures' envisaged by para 5(1) of Schedule 1, the effects of which are to be ignored, include 'medical treatment and the use of a prosthesis or other aid' – para 5(2), Sch 1. Examples of impairments that might be covered by this provision include epilepsy that is controlled by taking medication, diabetes that is controlled by taking insulin, or hearing loss that is improved by wearing a hearing aid. Thus, for example, the substantial adverse effects of a hearing impairment must be judged by reference to the person's ability to hear without a hearing aid and the effects of diabetes by reference to what the condition would be without being controlled by medication or diet – para B14.

161

6.136 The 'medical treatment' referred to in para 5(2) is not defined in the EqA but in Abadeh v British Telecommunications plc 2001 ICR 156, EAT, the EAT made it clear that psychotherapy was medical treatment for the purposes of the equivalent provision in the DDA. And in Kapadia v London Borough of Lambeth 2000 IRLR 14, EAT, the EAT held that medical treatment includes counselling by a consultant clinical psychologist. In that case, the EAT gave short shrift to the Council's arguments that counselling sessions did not constitute 'medical treatment' under the DDA because they were directed at the reduction of the employee's symptoms rather than the correction of the mental impairment. In the EAT's view, it could not seriously be argued that a series of counselling sessions that prevents the patient from needing drug treatment for his or her condition does not amount to treatment. (Note that this case was appealed to the Court of Appeal on separate grounds – see Kapadia v London Borough of Lambeth 2000 IRLR 699, CA.)

In determining the effects of an impairment without medication, the EAT has stated that: 'The tribunal will wish to examine how the claimant's abilities had actually been affected at the material time, whilst on medication, and then to address their minds to the difficult question as to the effects which they think there would have been but for the medication: the deduced effects. The question is then whether the actual and deduced effects on the claimant's abilities to carry out normal day-to-day activities [are] clearly more than trivial' – Goodwin v Patent Office 1999 ICR 302, EAT.

6.137 In Abadeh v British Telecommunications plc (above) the EAT noted that para 6 of Schedule 1 to the DDA (the equivalent provision to para 5, Sch 1 EqA) required measures that 'are being taken' to treat or correct an impairment to be ignored. The EAT stated that it followed that para 6 applied only to continuing treatment, not to treatment that has ceased, where the effects of the treatment can be more readily assessed. The reason for its application to continuing treatment is that the treatment may mask or ameliorate a disability so that it does not have a substantial effect. Thus, if the outcome of the treatment cannot be ascertained, or if it is known that the removal of the treatment would result in a relapse or deterioration, that treatment must be disregarded – see para B13 of the Guidance.

On the other hand, where the continuing treatment has produced a *permanent* improvement, the EAT said that that improvement must be taken into account in determining the effects of the individual's impairment. The EAT gave two examples. The first is where physiotherapy has resulted in an improvement in a person's movement so that he or she no longer needs a stick to aid walking. Where the physiotherapy is continuing, the permanent improvement already achieved must be taken into account. However, the residual problems requiring the continuing treatment must be taken into consideration in assessing disability without regard to the continuing treatment if the outcome of that treatment is not known. If, on the other hand, the medical prognosis is that the continuing treatment will resolve the residual problems, that recovery may be taken into account. The second example given by the EAT involves the treatment of depression by medication. The EAT said that if the final effects of the medication are not known, or there is a substantial risk of a relapse when the treatment ceases, the effects of the medication are to be disregarded.

Applying those principles to the facts of the case before it, the EAT noted that **6.138** the medical evidence showed that the psychotherapeutic treatment which the claimant had been receiving for post-traumatic stress disorder had achieved some improvement in his condition. However, it was not clear on the evidence available to the tribunal at that time whether the improvement was likely to be permanent or temporary, and return when the treatment ceased. The EAT found that the tribunal had misdirected itself in law by failing to deal with the medical treatment and directed the tribunal to which the case was to be remitted to assess the medical evidence available at the time of that hearing. If the medical evidence showed that a permanent improvement had been made, that improvement would have to be taken into account. If the improvement was considered to be temporary, or it was unclear whether it was permanent or not, then the treatment would have to be ignored.

Similarly, in Kapadia v London Borough of Lambeth (above) the EAT held that the tribunal had erred in law in failing to consider the effects of an individual's reactive depression without the counselling that he had been receiving from a consultant clinical psychologist. The tribunal had not taken account of the medical evidence which showed that, but for the counselling sessions, there was a very strong likelihood that he would suffer a total mental breakdown.

The evidence of an expert medical practitioner as to the degree to which medical **6.139** treatment or corrective aids have an impact on the adverse effects of an impairment can sometimes be important. In Barnes v Thorpe Underwood Services Ltd ET Case No.1803539/10 the claimant was injured following a horse riding accident as a result of which she suffered ongoing back pain. She was prescribed pain relief patches, which she claimed had a considerably beneficial effect. The claimant contended that without these the effects of her impairment would have been substantial. However, a medical consultant gave evidence that the claimant's condition had only a trivial impact on her ability to carry out day-to-day activities and that, in his experience, the behavioural pattern of a motivated individual was not so transformed by the patches as to turn a person who would otherwise be disabled into someone with no disability at all. In the light of the consultant's evidence, the tribunal concluded that the claimant had exaggerated the impact of her condition and that even if the medical aids were to be taken out of account, the extent of her impairment was not such as to make her disabled within the meaning of the DDA.

6.140 **Exception for spectacles and contact lens wearers.** Paragraph 5(1) does not apply in the case of sight impairments that can be corrected by spectacles or contact lenses – para 5(3)(a). This means that short- or long-sightedness that corrects to good vision cannot amount to a disability under the EqA, regardless of how 'disabled' an individual may feel without the corrective lenses. There are some occupations, such as the police force, that require a person not only to have good vision using spectacles or contact lenses, but also a minimum standard of unaided vision. Since a person whose sight is correctable by spectacles or contact lenses is not a disabled person under the Act, a person who is refused entry into such an occupation cannot claim to have been discriminated against under the EqA on this ground.

The Guidance states that the only effects on a person's ability to carry out normal daily activities to be considered are those which remain, or would remain, if spectacles or contact lenses are used – para B15. Thus, a person is only disabled under the Act if his or her vision with the best spectacles or contact lenses is still impaired to a degree that substantially affects normal daily activities. Para B15 goes on to say that the use of devices to correct sight which are not spectacles or contact lenses are not included in the exception. Presumably, this means that people who, even with the best spectacles or contact lenses, still have a sight impairment and rely on devices such as magnifying glasses or telescopic lens systems to improve their vision will be regarded as disabled for the purposes of the Act.

Note that the Disability Regulations provide that blind, sight impaired or severely sight impaired, and partially sighted people certified by a consultant ophthalmologist are deemed to be disabled – Reg 7.

6.141 **Further exceptions.** There is a power in para 5(3)(b) to extend the exception to other impairments. However, no regulations have yet been made under this provision (or under the equivalent provision in the DDA).

6.142 Medical evidence

Medical evidence plays an important role in tribunal proceedings involving disability discrimination claims. Tribunals frequently have to consider medical evidence, not only in relation to the nature of the impairment suffered by the claimant, but also as to its effects and, if the condition has not lasted 12 months, whether it is likely to last that long. Sometimes there may be conflicting medical reports presented by either side. Sometimes the medical reports might simply reflect differing views within the medical profession itself. For example, doctors' opinions are divided as to whether ME (myalgic encephalomyelitis) – or chronic fatigue syndrome – is an illness and, if it is, whether the cause is physical, mental, or a combination of both. Tensions are also created where the legal concepts of impairment and disability for the purposes of the EqA are different from the accepted medical concepts of those terms. Clearly, it is important that tribunals attach the correct weight to medical evidence and that they know what they are free to accept and free to reject.

It is the employment tribunal's task to determine the question of whether a claimant's impairment has a long-term adverse effect on his or her ability to carry out normal day-to-day activities according to such medical evidence as is presented. The fact that there is little if any evidence of these matters does not necessarily mean that the tribunal will be unable to reach a proper conclusion, although the presence or absence of such evidence may be a matter of relevance to be taken into consideration when deciding what weight should be put on the claimant's account of the difficulties caused by his or her impairment – see Veitch v Red Sky Group Ltd 2010 NICA 39, NICA. In that case, the Northern Ireland Court of Appeal observed that the absence of medical evidence may become of central importance in considering whether there is evidence of long-term adverse effects arising from an impairment, and frequently, in the absence of such evidence, a tribunal would have insufficient material from which it could draw the conclusion that long-term effects had been demonstrated.

6.143 Unless they have good reason to do so, tribunals should not reject uncontradicted medical evidence – Kapadia v London Borough of Lambeth 2000 IRLR 699, CA. In that case K's general practitioner, Dr N, diagnosed K as suffering from reactive depression in April 1995 and referred him to a consultant clinical psychologist, R, who saw K about 20 times over the next two years. In early 1996 K obtained promotion to the post of senior accountant but subsequently began to take an increasing amount of time off work for illness. In June 1997 K retired on medical grounds on the recommendation of the Council's medical adviser, who reported that K was permanently unfit for work. The tribunal held that K was not disabled within the meaning of the DDA. Although K's reactive depression was a mental impairment, in the tribunal's view it had no more than a trivial effect on his ability to carry out normal day-to-day activities and therefore was not 'substantial'.

The EAT found that the tribunal had erred in holding that there was no evidence that K's impairment had a substantial adverse effect. R's report stated that K's symptoms of anxiety and depression 'constituted a mental impairment of sufficient duration and severity to have had a substantial and long-term effect on his ability to carry out normal day-to-day activities'. Dr N's report stated that K had considerable difficulty concentrating, that his sleeping pattern was affected and that he experienced 'degrees of agoraphobia'. None of this evidence had been contradicted by the Council. The EAT stated that although it could foresee situations where a tribunal might, for a good reason, reject uncontradicted medical evidence, this was not such a case. In the instant case the tribunal had simply disregarded the medical evidence, which the EAT said was a 'wholly impermissible' approach to take. The Court of Appeal upheld the EAT's

165

decision. In its view, one example of a situation in which a tribunal would not be obliged to accept uncontested medical evidence would be where it was clear that the medical witness has misunderstood the evidence that he or she has been invited to consider. However, this was not the case here.

6.144 Similarly, in Mahon v Accuread Ltd EAT 0081/08 the EAT expressed surprise that the tribunal had departed from the view of the medical expert and that of the Social Security Appeals Tribunal without explaining why. Furthermore, in a case where the claimant had been medically examined by an expert witness who had concluded that the symptoms of his disability were genuine but was not called to appear at the hearing, it was unfair for the claimant to be cross-examined as to whether he was exaggerating those symptoms.

Another issue that arose in Kapadia was whether the Council was entitled to adduce a medical report from an independent expert whom it had commissioned. K had consented to the examination but did not consent to the doctor disclosing the report to the Council. Lord Justice Pill in the Court of Appeal pointed out that the report should have been disclosed and that no further consent was required from the claimant. By consenting to an examination at the request of the Council, the claimant was consenting to the disclosure to it of the resulting report. It may be that the confusion over the disclosure of the medical report arose because of the position of medical reports under the Access to Medical Reports Act 1988. Under that Act an employee does have the right to prevent a report from being supplied to the employer once the employee has seen it. However, the Act only applies to reports prepared by a medical practitioner who is or has been responsible for the clinical care of the individual. It does not apply to independent doctors or company doctors.

6.145 While tribunals must consider all the medical evidence presented to them, they must not delegate to doctors their responsibility for determining whether a claimant is disabled or not. They must make their own assessment of the evidence and not be overawed by the opinion of a medical expert as to whether or not a claimant's condition falls within the statutory definition. In Vicary v British Telecommunications plc 1999 IRLR 680, EAT, the claimant suffered from an upper arm condition which caused her to lose strength in her arms. The tribunal found that she was unable to perform a number of normal day-to-day activities involved in cooking, washing, shopping, DIY and housework, and accepted that the adverse effects on the claimant's abilities to carry out such activities were long term, but held that these effects were not substantial. In reaching this conclusion the tribunal referred to the evidence of the employer's regional medical officer. That doctor had a special qualification in occupational health and had attended seminars on the application of the DDA. In her opinion, the claimant's impairment was not 'substantial' within the meaning of the DDA.

The EAT held that the tribunal's decision was perverse for a number of reasons, one of which was that the tribunal had misdirected itself in respect of the medical evidence from the company doctor. In particular, the EAT held that the tribunal should not have had regard to the doctor's attendance at DDA seminars, which was irrelevant. Furthermore, the EAT ruled that it was not for a witness to determine whether or not impairments were 'substantial' and whether or not an activity was a 'normal day-to-day activity' for the purposes of the DDA. These were matters solely for the tribunal to determine. In the instant case, the tribunal had effectively delegated this responsibility to the company doctor. On the facts, the EAT felt bound to conclude that V suffered from a 'disability' within the meaning of the DDA.

A similar conclusion was reached by the EAT in McKechnie Plastic Components **6.146** v Grant EAT 0284/08. In that case the claimant suffered from a mixed state of anxiety and depressive disorder. A jointly commissioned medical report concluded that the impairment was not substantial and did not have an adverse effect on the claimant's ability to carry out day-to-day activities. However, the employment tribunal judge found it difficult to reconcile this with compelling evidence he heard from the claimant, her son and a friend, which painted a picture of the claimant as a recluse who was virtually imprisoned by her own anxiety from any contact with people without the support of her family. The employment judge decided that, despite the medical evidence, the claimant was disabled. On appeal, the EAT held that this was a conclusion that had been open to the employment tribunal, although it was unfortunate that the medical expert had not been called upon to provide oral testimony at the tribunal hearing. The EAT stressed that it was not suggesting that tribunals should feel completely free to substitute their own view for that of a jointly instructed medical expert, but ultimately the issue of whether a claimant was suffering from a medical impairment that amounts to a disability was one for the tribunal to determine.

7 Gender reassignment

It has been estimated by the Gender Identity Research and Education Society **7.1** (GIRES) that approximately 10,000 transsexual people in the United Kingdom have sought medical care regarding gender variance, and 6,000 of them have actually undergone gender transition – see 'Gender Variance in the UK: Prevalence, Incidence, Growth and Geographic Distribution' (2009, updated 2011). According to the GIRES Report, 80 per cent of transsexuals were assigned as boys at birth and 20 per cent as girls. The Report states that gender variant people can seek medical treatment at any age, but the median age is 42. It also points out that the implications of the above figures are that organisations should assume that 1 per cent of their employees and service users may be experiencing some degree of gender variance, and that, at some stage, about 0.2% of these may undergo transition.

In the International Classification of Diseases ICD-10, published by the World Health Organisation, transsexualism is currently recognised to be a psychiatric disorder, known as 'gender dysphoria' or 'gender identity disorder'. The disorder is defined as 'a desire to live and be accepted as a member of the opposite sex, usually accompanied by a sense of discomfort with, or inappropriateness of, one's anatomic sex and a wish to have surgery and hormonal treatment to make one's body as congruent as possible with one's preferred sex'. The question of whether, in the United Kingdom, transsexualism is a mental illness as opposed to a mental disorder has been extensively debated by medical practitioners and by Parliament in connection, for example, with the funding of care and treatment under the Mental Health Act 1983. The general conclusion is that the condition is a mental disorder rather than an illness, and is a recognised medical condition that usually attracts a specified physical treatment regime, including hormones and surgery.

Protection under antecedent legislation   7.2

Prior to the Equality Act 2010 (EqA), statutory protection from discrimination against transsexuals was found in relevant amendments to the Sex Discrimination Act 1975 (SDA), which came into force on 1 May 1999. These amendments were prompted by the European Court of Justice decision P v S and anor 1996

169

ICR 795, ECJ, where it was held that discrimination on the basis of transsexualism comprised discrimination on the ground of sex and was therefore unlawful under the EC Equal Treatment Directive (No.76/207). In P v S the claimant – a male-to-female transsexual – was dismissed by her employer shortly before undergoing the final stages of gender reassignment surgery that would have given her the physical attributes of a woman. She complained of sex discrimination but an employment tribunal held that she had no redress under domestic law. It found that the reason P lost her job was the fact that she proposed to undergo gender reassignment, but that the SDA at that point protected only those who were treated differently because they belonged to one or other of the sexes: it did not extend to those who changed from one sex to the other, or wished to do so.

When the issue was referred to the ECJ, the Court ruled that it was a fundamental principle of European law and a requirement in Articles 2(1) and 3(1) of the Equal Treatment Directive (now Article 14(1) of the recast Equal Treatment Directive (No.2006/54)) that there should be 'no discrimination whatsoever on grounds of sex'. Moreover, the right not to be discriminated against on the ground of sex was one of the fundamental human rights that the Court was obliged to protect. In these circumstances, the scope of the Directive could not be confined simply to discrimination based on the fact that a person is of one or other sex, but should also include protection for those who had undergone or were undergoing gender reassignment, discrimination against whom was based 'essentially if not exclusively upon the sex of the person concerned'.

7.3 In the light of the ECJ's decision, the UK Government moved to remedy the gap in domestic law by introducing the Sex Discrimination (Gender Reassignment) Regulations 1999 SI 1999/1102, which inserted S.2A into the SDA. That provision prohibited direct discrimination and victimisation on the ground of gender reassignment. In 2005, the SDA was further amended when the Employment Equality (Sex Discrimination) Regulations 2005 SI 2005/2467 inserted a new S.4A into the SDA to provide for a free-standing right to be protected against harassment. S.4A(3) specifically extended this protection to anyone who was intending to undergo, was in the process of undergoing or had undergone gender reassignment.

Another important development that broadly coincided with the legal changes described above was the decision of the European Court of Human Rights in Goodwin v United Kingdom 2002 IRLR 664, ECtHR. In that case it was held that the failure of UK law to recognise a post-operative transsexual person's acquired gender was incompatible with, among other things, the right to respect for private and family life found in Article 8 of the European Convention on Human Rights. In light of this decision, the Gender Recognition Act 2004 was passed to enable transsexuals who have undergone, or are in the process of undergoing, gender reassignment to have their 'new' gender legally

170

recognised. Further details of this Act, and the procedure for applying for full legal recognition under it, are discussed under 'Legal recognition of acquired gender' below.

Protection under the Equality Act 7.4

The law governing discrimination against transsexual people is now contained in S.7(1) EqA, which provides that a person has the protected characteristic of gender reassignment 'if the person is proposing to undergo, is undergoing or has undergone a process (or part of a process) for the purpose of reassigning the person's sex by changing physiological or other attributes of sex'. This re-enacts the similar provisions contained in Ss.2A(1) and 82(1) SDA, but with one important difference. Whereas, under the SDA, 'gender reassignment' was defined in S.82(1) as a process 'which is undertaken under medical supervision', this condition has been dropped from the definition in S.7 EqA. This means that persons who, without medical supervision, have undergone, are undergoing or are intending to undergo a process to effect their gender reassignment will now be regarded as having the protected characteristic of gender reassignment. The significance of this point is discussed under 'The gender reassignment process' below.

By virtue of S.7(2) and (3) EqA, a reference in the EqA to a transsexual person is a reference to a person who has the protected characteristic of gender reassignment, and vice versa, while a reference to persons who share that protected characteristic is a reference to transsexual persons. The Explanatory Notes to the 2010 Act clarify that a woman making the transition to being a man and a man making the transition to being a woman share the characteristic of gender reassignment, as does a person who has only just started out on the process of changing his or her sex and a person who has completed the process (para 42).

As with the other protected characteristics, a person who falls within the scope 7.5 of S.7 qualifies for protection against direct discrimination, indirect discrimination, victimisation and harassment. Under the SDA there was no express provision extending the definition of indirect discrimination to transsexuals as such, although it was widely accepted that the general definition of indirect *sex* discrimination conferred the necessary protection to this particular protected group. Under the EqA, by contrast, the definition of indirect discrimination in S.19 specifically applies to all of the protected characteristics, which means that each of the protected groups – including transsexuals – are protected from indirect discrimination in their own right.

It is important to note that the definition in S.7 focuses on gender reassignment, not gender identity. At the House of Commons Committee stage on the Equality Bill, the Government rejected a proposed amendment couching this protected

171

characteristic in terms of 'gender identity'. The proposal was fuelled by concerns that some individuals deserving of protection against discrimination do not identify with either gender and have not embarked on any process of gender reassignment, medical or otherwise. However, the Solicitor General took the view that there was no evidence of discrimination against such persons. In any event, she considered that they would be able to rely on the protections against direct discrimination and harassment given that these are now defined in such a way as to cover discrimination based on misperception. For a more detailed discussion of 'discrimination by perception', see Chapter 15, 'Direct discrimination', under 'Discrimination by perception', and Chapter 18, 'Harassment', under 'Related to a relevant protected characteristic – harassment by association or perception'.

7.6 Application to transvestites

Under the SDA, the rights covering transsexual people did not apply to transvestites – i.e. people who wear clothes that are normally associated with the opposite sex (except in so far as transvestism is a manifestation of transsexualism). The same position continues to obtain under the EqA. As was made clear during the public consultation on the Equality Bill, the new definition of gender reassignment is not intended to protect transvestites or others who choose temporarily to adopt the appearance of the opposite gender (see para 9.42, 'The Equality Bill – Government response to the Consultation', July 2008 (Cm 7454)). Since transvestism does not entail a process of reassignment of gender through the changing of physiological or other attributes of sex, it does not meet the definition of gender reassignment in S.7 EqA.

That said, if the decision to cross-dress is part of the process of gender reassignment, then a person will be protected against any discrimination or harassment in relation to that decision. A helpful illustration of this is provided in para 2.27 of the Equality and Human Rights Commission's Code of Practice on Employment ('the EHRC Employment Code'). Suppose that before a formal dinner organised by the employer, a worker tells his colleagues that he intends to come to the event dressed as a woman 'for a laugh'. His manager tells him not to do this, as it would be bad for the company's image. Because the worker has no intention of undergoing gender reassignment, he would not have a claim for discrimination under the EqA. On the other hand, if the employer had said the same thing to a worker driven by his gender identity to cross-dress as a woman as part of the process of reassigning his sex, this could amount to direct discrimination because of gender reassignment.

7.7 Furthermore, a transvestite will be protected from direct discrimination and harassment if he or she is *perceived* – wrongly as it turns out – to be proposing to undergo gender reassignment. For further discussion of 'discrimination by perception', see Chapter 15, 'Direct Discrimination', under 'Discrimination by perception', and Chapter 18, 'Harassment', under 'Related to a relevant protected characteristic – harassment by association or perception'

The gender reassignment process   7.8

Section 7 EqA applies to anyone who is 'proposing to undergo, is undergoing or has undergone a process (or part of a process) for the purpose of reassigning the person's sex'. It therefore covers the entire process of gender reassignment, which can take many months and sometimes even years. In Bellinger v Bellinger 2003 2 AC 467, HL, Lord Nicholls identified the four typical stages of gender reassignment as psychiatric assessment, hormonal treatment, a period of living as a member of the opposite sex subject to professional supervision therapy ('the real-life test') and, in suitable cases, gender reassignment surgery.

No requirement to be 'under medical supervision'. In contrast with the 7.9
position under the SDA, S.7 EqA does not stipulate that the gender reassignment process must be conducted under medical supervision. The removal of this precondition was intended to reflect the fact that gender reassignment is not so much a medical process as a personal transition involving a change in the attributes traditionally assigned to a particular gender. The EHRC Employment Code makes this clear when stating that: 'Under the Act "gender reassignment" is a personal process, that is, moving away from one's birth sex to the preferred gender, rather than a medical process. The reassignment of a person's sex may be proposed but never gone through; the person may be in the process of reassigning their sex; or the process may have happened previously. It may include undergoing the medical gender reassignment treatments, but it does not require someone to undergo medical treatment in order to be protected' (paras 2.23–2.24).

So, to take the example given in the Code, if a person who was born physically female decides to spend the rest of his life as a man, and then starts and continues to live as a man without seeking medical advice because he successfully 'passes' as a man without the need for any medical intervention, he would be protected as someone who has the protected characteristic of gender reassignment.

Meaning of 'proposing to undergo'. A related point is that, because the 7.10
protected characteristic is defined in terms of a transition *process*, there is not necessarily a clear date when it can be said that a person acquires the protected characteristic in question. Unlike pregnancy and maternity, which is defined in terms of a 'protected period' in respect of which the start and end dates are delineated, the start of the period of protection in the case of gender reassignment is far from clear-cut. All we have to go on are the words of S.7, which is expressed in terms of a person having the protected characteristic of gender reassignment if 'the person is *proposing to undergo*' (our stress) a process of gender reassignment. The words in italics intimate that the key to establishing the start of the statutory protection is to define when it can be said that a person first proposes to undergo a process leading to reassignment of his or her gender. In this regard, the Solicitor General observed during Parliamentary

173

consideration of the Equality Bill at the House of Commons Committee stage that 'proposing' suggests 'a more definite decision point' than simply 'considering'. It may be manifested by the person making his or her intention known, or by a change in dress or behaviour. Other possible indications that a person has reached a definitive decision point are cross-dressing (but only if prompted by the person's gender identity) and/or attendance at counselling sessions relating to the commencement of gender reassignment.

The following case provides an example of when a person can be said to be 'proposing to undergo' gender reassignment:

- **Sims v Le Boutillier Estates Ltd t/a Hearnes Estate Agents** ET Case No.3102370/04: S was the manager of one of LBE Ltd's estate agency branches. In 2001 he was diagnosed as having gender dysphoria and by Christmas 2003 he had decided that he needed to live full time as a woman in order to feel happy and fulfilled. He informed L, the managing director of LBE Ltd, and was assured of his support. It was agreed that they would meet staff together to inform them that S would be absent for a couple of months during the summer and would return as a woman. However, on the day planned for the meeting, L told S that it had to be postponed because a member of his church had informed him that transsexuality was contrary to the Christian faith, and he wished to seek further guidance from his church minister on this issue. L was concerned about the position he and his wife would be placed in if they supported S in committing what might be seen as a sin for which S was likely to go to hell. As a result, S resigned and successfully brought claims for gender reassignment discrimination and unfair constructive dismissal. In relation to the S.2A SDA (now S.7 EqA) claim, the employment tribunal held that S had suffered discrimination because of his intention to undergo gender reassignment.

7.11 Difficulties can arise in relation to individuals who decide to undergo gender reassignment but keep the matter entirely private. The EHRC Employment Code makes the important point that 'in order to be protected under the Act, there is no requirement for a transsexual person to inform their employer of their gender reassignment status' – para 2.27. But while this is undoubtedly correct given the wording of S.7, the Solicitor General acknowledged during the Parliamentary debates on the Equality Bill that 'it is difficult to see how this can work practically'. An analogous difficulty could arise where a person has a disability but there are no outward signs of the physical or mental impairment in question. But in a disability context the EqA contains specific provisions providing employers with a defence if they did not know, and could not reasonably be expected to know, that the complainant was disabled – see S.15(2) and para 20(1) of Schedule 8 to the EqA. No equivalent provision is made in the case of gender reassignment. In practice, however, it is unlikely – except in a case of misperception – that someone would be subjected to any form of discrimination prompted by the person's gender reassignment before there is any external indication of his or her having begun the gender transition process.

Protection during the reassignment process. It was acknowledged during the **7.12** debates on the Equality Bill at the House of Commons Committee stage that the process of transitioning gender can be protracted, and that during this process a person can have a disorienting sense that they are operating as both genders or as neither. This is particularly true during the 'real-life test stage' of the transition when, typically following hormone treatment, the trans-person begins to live consistently as a member of the opposite sex, including when out in public and within the workplace. During this stage, it is clear that S.7 will apply to ensure that the person is protected from discrimination and harassment.

It is often just before the start of the real-life test stage that a person begins to reveal his or her intentions to people beyond the members of his or her immediate family circle and close friends. In practical terms, it is advisable that prior to starting the real-life stage the employee discusses the prospect of his or her imminent gender change with the employer. At this point logistical issues should be raised, such as when to inform colleagues and, if necessary, customers and clients; dress codes and uniform requirements; and use of lavatory or changing room facilities.

In Croft v Royal Mail Group plc (formerly Consignia plc) 2003 ICR 1425, CA, **7.13** Lord Justice Pill gave useful guidance on the complex issues that can arise during an employee's 'real-life test'. On the one hand, he said, S.2A SDA (now S.7 EqA) provided that transsexual people have the right not to be discriminated against on the ground of gender reassignment. On the other hand, they are not immediately entitled to be treated as members of the sex to which they aspire. For instance, in the case of a male-to-female transsexual, the right to be treated as a woman is acquired by making progress in the gender reassignment process (as described by Lord Nicholls in Bellinger v Bellinger above). It falls to the tribunal to make a judgement as to when the transsexual person becomes a woman and thus becomes entitled to the same facilities as other women. The person's self-definition will aid the tribunal in this decision but it is not decisive.

Lord Justice Pill observed that, for most purposes, the application of S.2A created few practical problems. However, the provision of lavatory facilities for pre-operative transsexuals was far from straightforward because Reg 20 of the Workplace (Health, Safety and Welfare) Regulations 1992 SI 1992/3004 required the employer to provide separate toilet facilities for men and women. Having said that, the fact that the male-to-female transsexual person is still biologically a man when undergoing the real-life test did not mean that the employer could simply escape liability. A permanent refusal to allow use of the female lavatories could amount to discrimination, even if the transsexual person had not undergone the final surgical intervention. However, in a

175

situation in which two sets of facilities, male and female, are required by law and in which a category of persons changing from one sex to the other is recognised, there is a period during which the employer is entitled to make separate arrangements for persons undergoing that change. The moment at which a person is entitled to use female lavatories depends on all the circumstances, including her conduct and that of the employer. The employer must take into account the stage of treatment reached, including the employee's own assessment and presentation. The employee's self-definition was less important with regard to the use of lavatory facilities because of the legal requirement that employers provide separate facilities for men and women. The employer is also entitled to take into account, though not to be governed by, the susceptibilities of other members of the workforce.

7.14 *Gender reassignment-related absences.* A transgender person undergoing the gender reassignment process is likely to have to take time off work to attend medical appointments and undergo surgical procedures; or he or she may be too ill to attend work as a result of complications associated with the gender reassignment treatment or surgery. S.16 EqA provides specific protection against discrimination in these circumstances, full details of which are discussed in Chapter 22, 'Other forms of prohibited conduct', under 'Gender reassignment discrimination due to absence'.

7.15 **Continuing protection where transition process is abandoned.** Once begun, a person will continue to be protected even if he or she does not go through the entire gender reassignment process. This is made clear by the wording of S.7(1) EqA, which speaks in terms of someone who 'has undergone a process (*or part of a process*) for the purposes of reassigning the person's sex' (our stress). The point has already been made that someone who was born physically as one sex will have the protected characteristic of gender reassignment if he or she decides to live as the opposite sex and starts to do so, even if this entails no medical intervention. Such a person will have started the process by proposing to do it in the first place. The statutory protection continues at all times while he or she continues to live according to his or her preferred gender. But it would also continue even if the person has started but withdrawn from the process, thereby reverting to living according to his or her birth gender. So, for example, a person born physically male may let friends know that he intends to reassign his sex and begin to attend counselling sessions to start the process. If, however, he then decides to go no further, he remains protected under the EqA as a result of having undergone at least part of the process of reassigning his sex.

7.16 Overlap with disability

Suffering from gender dysphoria without more is unlikely to amount to a disability for the purposes of the disability discrimination provisions in the EqA. Unless long-term complications arise, the fact that a person is undergoing or has undergone a process of gender reassignment is unlikely to have a substantial adverse effect on his or her ability to carry out normal day-to-day activities (the definition of disability set out in S.6(1) EqA) – see Chapter 6, 'Disability', under 'Meaning of "disability"', for more details.

In Ashton v Chief Constable of West Mercia Constabulary 2001 ICR 67, EAT, a police officer who was born male suffered bouts of depression while undergoing gender reassignment. She transferred from police patrol duties to a new role of communications operator on a six-month probationary period, which was later extended to 12 months, but was dismissed when those duties were not performed satisfactorily. She brought, inter alia, a claim under the Disability Discrimination Act 1995 (DDA) (now subsumed into the EqA). An employment tribunal found that the 12-month probationary period in the new job coincided with the 'real-life test' during which the claimant lived and worked in the female role before undergoing irreversible surgery. The tribunal also found that the shortcomings in her performance were due to a combination of factors: the depression A was suffering as result of hormone therapy, the stressful environment of the communications operations room, the further stress of having to prove herself and the stress of undergoing a major life change. The tribunal found neither her depression nor her gender identity dysphoria (GID) were disabilities for the purposes of the DDA. Although the GID was long term, the impairment did not, in the tribunal's view, have a substantial adverse effect on the claimant's ability to carry out normal day-to-day activities. The tribunal did not accept her argument that her mobility had been impaired because her treatment for gender reassignment had caused her not to socialise outside work. On appeal, the EAT upheld the tribunal's findings. In its view, the decision not to socialise was the claimant's own choice, made because she preferred to keep herself to herself.

If, however, a person who had undergone gender reassignment suffered long- **7.17** term complications arising out of surgical procedures, then, depending upon the degree of suffering, it is possible that the employee would be regarded as disabled for the purposes of S.6(1) EqA. The same might apply if long-term serious depression was triggered by the transition process.

Legal recognition of acquired gender   **7.18**

On 4 April 2005, the Gender Recognition Act 2004 came into force enabling transsexual people – so long as they satisfy certain conditions – to have their acquired gender legally recognised. Previously, a transsexual person's sex remained his or her biological sex at birth. So, a male-to-female transsexual who had fully completed gender reassignment would always legally remain a male. It followed from this that, under domestic law, a male-to-female transsexual would not be eligible for a state retirement pension at the age of 60 – the age at which women born before April 1950 become eligible – but would

177

have to wait until the age of 65 – the age men born at the same time become eligible (see, for example, Richards v Secretary of State for Work and Pensions 2006 ICR 1181, ECJ, and Grant v United Kingdom 2007 44 EHRR 1, ECtHR). Similarly, a transsexual was prevented from marrying a partner of the same biological birth gender, as UK law regarded this as a marriage between two people of the same sex, which is not permitted under domestic law (see, for example, Bavin v NHS Trust Pensions Agency and anor 1999 ICR 1192, EAT, and KB v NHS Pensions Agency and anor 2004 ICR 781, ECJ).

In Goodwin v United Kingdom 2002 IRLR 664, ECtHR, a post-operative male-to-female transsexual challenged the United Kingdom's refusal to legally recognise a transsexual person's acquired gender as being in breach of Articles 8 (respect for private life) and 12 (right to marry) of the European Convention on Human Rights. The European Court of Human Rights agreed. In its view, 'the unsatisfactory situation in which post-operative transsexuals live in an intermediate zone as not quite one gender or the other is no longer sustainable'. The following year, the House of Lords was asked to adjudicate on this issue in Bellinger v Bellinger 2003 2 AC 467, HL. There, B, a male-to-female transsexual, was seeking legal recognition of her marriage to a man. Their Lordships were sympathetic to B's plight but ruled that the marriage was void. However, they declared that S.11(c) of the Matrimonial Causes Act 1973, which provides that a marriage is void where the parties are not respectively male and female, was incompatible with the Human Rights Act 1998 but were of the view that it was for Parliament to legislate in this area. On 1 July 2004, just over a year after the decision in Bellinger, the Gender Recognition Act 2004 (GRA) entered the statute books.

7.19 Procedure for obtaining legal recognition

An individual who has been living in the other gender, and who is at least 18 years of age, can apply for a gender recognition certificate – S.1(1) GRA. Any such application is determined by a Gender Recognition Panel (GRP), which consists of lawyers and medical practitioners or registered psychologists – S.1(3) and Schedule 1.

The Panel must grant the application if it is satisfied that the applicant:

- has or has had gender dysphoria
- has lived in the acquired gender throughout the preceding two years
- intends to continue to live in the acquired gender until death, and
- complies with the requirements imposed by and under S.3 – S.2(1).

7.20 During the 12 months from April 2010 to March 2011, a total of 316 applications were dealt with by the GRP, with a full Gender Recognition Certificate being granted in 260 cases (82 per cent) – see Ministry of Justice Statistics Bulletin – Gender Recognition Certificate Statistics (January to March 2011).

It is important to note that neither surgical procedures nor an intention to undergo such procedures are a prerequisite for obtaining a gender recognition certificate. So, for example, a male-to-female transsexual can live as a woman and apply for a certificate legally recognising her as female without ever undergoing the final surgical procedures for the sex change.

Once the certificate has been issued, the person is recognised in his or her **7.21** acquired gender – S.9(1) GRA. For instance, a male-to-female transsexual will become a female and will benefit from any rights and responsibilities associated with that gender. The person will also be entitled to a new birth certificate reflecting the acquired gender (provided a UK birth register entry already exists for the person), will be able to marry someone of the opposite gender to his or her acquired gender and will be eligible for the state retirement pension and other benefits at the age appropriate to that acquired gender. Employers should amend personal records accordingly.

8 Marriage and civil partnership

Meaning of 'marriage' and 'civil partnership'

Protection under the Equality Act

Overlap with other protected characteristics

Prior to the coming into force of the Equality Act 2010 (EqA), S.3 of the Sex **8.1** Discrimination Act 1975 (SDA) made it unlawful to discriminate, either directly or indirectly, against married persons and civil partners on the ground of their marital/civil partnership status. Civil partners for this purpose were defined as two people of the same sex who have registered their relationship under the Civil Partnership Act 2004 (CPA) – S.1 CPA.

The same protection against discrimination in respect of married persons and civil partners is now contained in the EqA, which came into force on 1 October 2010. S.8 of the Act defines the protected characteristic of marriage and civil partnership, stipulating that a 'person has the protected characteristic of marriage and civil partnership if the person is married or is a civil partner'. A reference to a person who has that protected characteristic is to be read accordingly, and a reference to persons who share the characteristic is a reference to persons who are married or are civil partners – S.8(2). The Explanatory Notes accompanying the EqA give the example of a married man and a woman in a civil partnership, who would share the protected characteristic of marriage and civil partnership (para 45).

Meaning of 'marriage' and 'civil partnership' 8.2

Strangely, neither 'marriage' nor 'civil partnership' is specifically defined in the EqA, not even by reference to the statutory provisions governing these relationships at law. However, marriage is commonly understood to mean 'the voluntary union for life of one man and one woman, to the exclusion of all others' – per Lord Penzance in Hyde v Hyde and Woodmansee (1865–69) LR 1 P&D 130, Ct for Divorce and Matrimonial Causes. That union obviously has to be solemnised at a religious service or ceremony within the terms of the various marriage statutes in force.

A civil partnership is defined in S.1 CPA as a relationship between two people of the same sex where the partnership has been registered either in the United Kingdom or overseas at a British consulate. In addition, same-sex couples are regarded under the CPA as civil partners where they have registered an 'overseas relationship' that is treated as a civil partnership within the terms of Chapter 2 of Part 5 of the CPA. Essentially, this allows for same-sex relationships registered under the laws of certain other countries to be deemed 'civil partnerships', so that such persons working or living in the United Kingdom will be entitled to the protection accorded to civil partners under the EqA. Subject to various conditions and exceptions, an 'overseas relationship' will fall within the definition of a 'civil partnership' in S.1 CPA if either (a) it is a 'specified relationship' referred to in Schedule 20 (which lists the equivalents of civil partnerships under the law of specified countries both within and outside the United Kingdom), or (b) it is registered with a responsible authority in a country or territory outside the United Kingdom and meets the 'general conditions' set out in S.214 – i.e. the couple are not already married or in a civil partnership or similar; the relationship is of indeterminate duration; and its effect is that they are treated as a couple (either generally or for specified purposes) or as being married.

8.3 Protection under the Equality Act

The protection from discrimination on the ground of marriage or civil partnership status in the EqA only applies to claims brought under Part 5 of that Act, which covers 'work'. Unlike all the other protected characteristics (with the limited exception of age), claims of discrimination on the ground of marriage and civil partnership status cannot be brought under Part 3 (provision of services and public functions), Part 4 (disposal, management and occupation of premises), Part 6 (education) or Part 7 (membership of associations).

Furthermore, even within the context of discrimination at work, the protection against harassment set out in S.26 EqA does not apply to married persons and civil partners – see S.26(5). In written evidence to the House of Commons and House of Lords Joint Committee on Human Rights explaining the Government's reasons for this limitation, the Solicitor General stated: 'Responses to the consultation did not provide any evidence to show that extension of protection was warranted beyond the current range of protection. As one of the principles in the development of the Equality Bill was not to legislate where there is no evidence of need, the Government decided not to expand protection further than the current provision. While the original reasons for introducing marriage protection in employment may no longer exist, we consider continued protection in this discrete area is warranted' (26th Report of 2008–09 Session, para 67).

8.4 It was in fact a close run thing whether marriage and civil partnership would continue to receive any specific protection under the EqA at all, even in the context of work. During the early consultation stages of the Equality Bill, the Government's initial stance had been that there was no longer a need to provide protection against employment discrimination for married persons and civil partners. It pointed out that the original justification for providing protection from marital discrimination in the Sex Discrimination Act 1975 (SDA) was to prevent women having to leave their jobs on getting married. The Government's view was that social circumstances had so significantly changed since then as to make the need for protection otiose. It also expressed concern that the provision preventing discrimination on the ground of marriage and civil partnership was in fact having a counterproductive effect in the light of case law preventing employers from operating sensible workplace policies banning the employment of married couples or civil partners within the same workplace or management chain. However, upon further reflection and in response to public consultation feedback – which was split almost 50/50 for and against retention of the existing protection – the Government decided to retain the provision, noting that to remove it might run the risk of discrimination against married couples and civil partners re-emerging. In its response to the consultation, the Government commented that there is nothing in any case to prevent employers from adopting rules preventing married couples and civil partners from working together within the same workplace or for the same employer, provided this is a proportionate means of achieving a legitimate aim (para 15.40, 'The Equality Bill – Government response to the Consultation', July 2008 (Cm 7454)).

Application to single and divorced people and cohabitees 8.5

It is important to note that the protected characteristic of marriage and civil partnership as framed in S.8 EqA only protects persons against discrimination so long as they are currently married or have civil partnership status. There is no provision providing equivalent protection to people who are single, cohabiting, widowed or divorced (or, in the case of a civil partnership, where that partnership has been dissolved). This is exactly the same position as obtained under the SDA.

During the consultation stage of the Equality Bill, the Government rejected calls to extend protection to single people and unmarried couples. As regards the latter, it took the view that the legislation would have difficulty in drawing a line reflecting the permanence or otherwise of any particular relationship (para 15.41 of the Government response). Moreover, at the Report stage in the House of Lords, the Government rejected an amendment to change the protected characteristic of marriage to 'marital status', the effect of which would have been to extend coverage of the characteristic to single people, cohabitees and the divorced. It considered that there was no evidence to suggest that anyone is discriminated against by an employer or prospective employer simply because he or she is unmarried, widowed or divorced, despite suggestions from some quarters that this was a problem in some Asian communities.

Position under EU law. At one point, it might have been legitimate to contend 8.6 that EU law required a broader protection than that provided previously by the SDA and now by the EqA. Article 2(1) of the now-repealed EU Equal Treatment Directive (No.1976/207) specifically provided that 'there shall be no discrimination whatsoever on grounds of sex either directly or indirectly by reference in particular to *marital or family status*' (our stress). Clearly, the

183

mention of 'marital status' indicated that married and unmarried persons came within the scope of the Directive. However, the discrimination prohibited by Article 2(1) was 'discrimination… on grounds of *sex*' (our stress), which meant that any complainant relying on that provision – whether married or not – had to show that he or she had suffered sex discrimination as well as marital discrimination. This proposition was confirmed by the High Court in Ireland in Hyland v Minister for Social Welfare and Attorney-General 1989 2 CMLR 44, High Ct (Ireland), in the context of the equivalent provision contained in the EC Social Security Directive (No.79/7). The Court accepted that the 1979 Directive prohibited sex discrimination, including sex discrimination that was disguised as discrimination based on marital status. However, if married men or married women were treated worse than their unmarried equivalents but equally in respect of each other, the Directive was irrelevant.

This interpretation appears by implication to have been accepted when it came to drafting the recast Equal Treatment Directive (No.2006/54), which consolidated, updated and replaced the seven existing Directives on gender equality in employment (including the 1976 Equal Treatment Directive) with effect from 15 August 2009 – see further Chapter 2, 'European discrimination law'. Article 14(1) of the recast Directive (the provision correlating to Article 2(1) of the 1976 Directive) dropped all reference to 'marital or family status'. The upshot of this appears to be that any sex discrimination based on marital or family status would be caught by the prohibitions against direct and indirect sex discrimination contained in the 2006 recast Directive, but that the Directive confers no remedy for any discrimination on the ground of marital/family status that does not constitute sex discrimination. Rather, EU law leaves it to national governments to decide whether or not to enact specific prohibitions against such discrimination.

8.7 Forthcoming marriages and civil partnerships

Based on the wording of S.8 EqA, it is clear that a mere intention to marry or become a civil partner in the near future is not sufficient to engage the protection afforded by the EqA against discrimination because of the protected characteristic of marriage and civil partnership. This is apparent from S.8(2), which states: 'In relation to the protected characteristic of marriage and civil partnership – (a) a reference to a person who has a particular protected characteristic is a reference *to a person who is married or is a civil partner*' (our stress).

Exactly the same position applied under the antecedent provision in S.3 SDA. In Bick v Royal West of England Residential School for the Deaf 1976 IRLR 326, EAT, the employment tribunal said that it was in no doubt that Parliament had intended S.3 to apply to discrimination against a complainant who announces his or her intention of getting married. However, the wording of the section meant that protection was only provided to those who were actually married at the time the alleged discriminatory act took place. On the particular facts of that case, the claimant – who was dismissed by her employer because she was about to get married – was unable to succeed with a marital discrimination claim because at the time the act of discrimination – i.e. the dismissal – took place she was still single and therefore fell outside the protection of the section.

In McLean v Paris Travel Service Ltd 1976 IRLR 202, ET, the claimant was **8.8** able to circumvent this problem by claiming direct *sex* discrimination as opposed to marital discrimination under the SDA. M was dismissed after informing her employer that she intended to marry one of the assistant managers. The employer had a policy of not employing married couples. The employment tribunal held that M's dismissal amounted to direct sex discrimination as she had been treated less favourably than the employer treated or would have treated a man in these circumstances.

Analogous reasoning could presumably be applied in the case of an employee who is dismissed or treated less favourably on account of his or her forthcoming civil partnership or declared intention to enter into such a partnership. The employee could contend that the discrimination was because of sexual orientation and bring a claim on that basis. Success or failure would then depend upon whether the claimant was able to satisfy the tribunal that the employer would not have treated a heterosexual employee in similar circumstances (for example, someone who was planning to get married) more favourably.

Impact of the Human Rights Act 1998. In Turner v Turner ET Case **8.9** No.2401702/04 an employment tribunal suggested that where an employee has been dismissed as a result of indicating an intention to marry, S.3 SDA (now S.8 EqA) could be interpreted in accordance with the Human Rights Act 1998 (HRA) to provide a cause of action. In that case, T began working for the employer in September 2000 as the deputy manager of a residential care unit caring for adolescents. In October 2002, she began a relationship with D, the employer's son, who was then 20 years of age. The employer found out about the relationship in April 2003 and at a meeting with T expressed concerns about her having a relationship with someone of roughly the same age as those in her care and said that her position as deputy manager could be compromised if she was seen with a young boyfriend. However, no further action was taken by the employer. On 25 December D told the employer that he and T were to be married in January 2004 and, on 29 December 2003, T was summarily dismissed for 'gross misconduct... and conduct which is detrimental to the interests of the company'. She subsequently brought various claims, including a claim for marital discrimination under S.3. The tribunal found that the reason for her dismissal had been her intention to marry the employer's son. However, the difficulty T had to surmount in relation to her S.3 claim lay in the fact that, although T and D were married in January 2004, T was unmarried at the time of her dismissal. In this respect, the tribunal referred to the decision in Bick v Royal West of England Residential School for the Deaf (above) but decided to depart from it as it was decided prior to the introduction of the HRA. In the tribunal's view, S.3 HRA required S.3 SDA to be interpreted so far as possible in accordance with the European Convention on Human Rights. The tribunal referred to Articles 8 (the right to respect for private and family life) and 12 (the right to marry) of the Convention and concluded that it would 'drive a coach and horses through the right enshrined in Article 12 were a narrow interpretation of S.3 to be maintained'. In order to give effect to the HRA in general and Articles 8 and 12 in particular, it followed that S.3 SDA had to be interpreted as encompassing not only discrimination against married persons but also against those about to marry. The tribunal also found it significant that D and T had a very short engagement and that a definite date for the marriage had been fixed. For these reasons, T's claim succeeded.

Both Bick and Turner are decisions of first instance and are therefore not binding on other courts or tribunals. As a result, until the EAT adjudicates on this issue, doubts will remain. One final point should be noted in this context. The reasoning adopted in the Turner case is unlikely to apply to people indicating their intention to enter into a civil partnership. European and domestic jurisprudence has made it clear that Article 12 – on which the tribunal in Turner had principally relied – does not apply to same-sex relationships: see Wilkinson v Kitzinger and ors (No.2) 2006 HRLR 36, Fam Div, and Schalk v Austria 2011 2 FCR 650, ECtHR.

8.10 Marriage to or civil partnership with a particular person

One question that has arisen is whether it is possible to bring a claim of marital or civil partnership discrimination where the discrimination relates not to the claimant's marital or civil partnership status as such but to the fact that the claimant is married to or in a civil partnership with a particular person. The two schools of thought on this issue are aptly illustrated by the following tribunal decisions:

• **Ganhao v ICM Support Services Ltd** ET Case No.2600651/05: C and her husband worked for ICM Ltd, which treated them for all practical purposes as a single 'unit', so that when the husband was transferred to a different workplace, C was expected to go as well. Her husband subsequently resigned and C went off work sick with a pregnancy-related ailment at the same time. When she returned to work she discovered that her job had been given to someone else because ICM Ltd assumed she had left at the same time as her husband. An employment tribunal upheld C's claims of sex and marital discrimination, concluding that the way in which she had been treated appeared to owe everything to the fact that she was her husband's wife. Without analysing S.3 SDA in any great detail, the tribunal thought that there was the clearest possible prima facie case of discrimination on the ground of C's marital status and a very strong inference that it was because she was the woman within the marriage that she was treated in this way. In the tribunal's words, the employer treated C as her husband's 'appendage'

- **John v Neath Borough Council** ET Case No.7257/90: an employment tribunal rejected the claim of marital discrimination by J, a female job applicant, who was turned down as an environmental health officer solely because her husband worked in the part of the Council where the job was based. Although the tribunal readily sympathised with J's resentment at the way in which she was treated not as a professional but as a sort of appendage of her husband, it reluctantly concluded that the treatment she suffered was not because she was married but because of the identity of the person to whom she was married. The tribunal reasoned that, for the purpose of comparing the treatment meted out to persons of different marital status, the question that had to be asked was: 'Have the respondents treated the applicant less favourably than they would have treated an unmarried person who had a close relationship with another person, of whatever sex, in the same section of the employer's establishment?' The tribunal found that it was the employer's policy never to allow employees in a small section to be closely related, whatever the nature of the relationship, and it accepted that this policy had been applied fairly to other individuals. In that sense, the policy was not specifically directed against married people.

A similar conclusion to that reached by the tribunal in the John case was **8.11** reached by the High Court in Glanvill v Secretary of State for Health and Social Services *The Times* 29 July 1978, HC. In that case – a judicial review against the Secretary of State's refusal to reimburse a GP for the wages paid to his wife in the conduct of the practice – the Court held that S.3 applied to protect married people on the ground that they were married, and did not cover Mrs Glanvill on the ground that she was married to Dr Glanvill.

However, two subsequent decisions of the EAT have, in effect, rejected the narrow construction of S.3 SDA found in the John and Glanvill cases in favour of the broader and more generous construction preferred by the tribunal in Ganhao. In Chief Constable of Bedfordshire v Graham 2002 IRLR 239, EAT, a Chief Constable rescinded an offer of promotion to a female police officer primarily because she would not be a competent and compellable witness in the event of any criminal proceedings being taken against her spouse – who would have been her Divisional Commander had the promotion taken place. Upholding the decision of the employment tribunal, the EAT ruled that the reason for the rescission of the promotion offer had been 'marriage-based'. The issue of competence and compellability would not have arisen had the female officer been in a close relationship other than a marital one with the Divisional Commander. It followed that the Chief Constable had, on the ground of marital

187

status, treated the female officer less favourably than he had treated or would treat an unmarried person of the same sex contrary to S.3 SDA.

8.12 This reasoning was expressly approved by the EAT in Dunn v Institute of Cemetery and Crematorium Management EAT 0531/10. In that case, a female claimant complained, inter alia, of discrimination contrary to S.3 SDA when she was allegedly treated less favourably in the way a number of grievances were investigated because of the employer's unhappiness with her husband, who was employed in the same organisation. An employment tribunal rejected the claimant's claim of marital discrimination on the basis of very similar reasoning to that adopted by the employment tribunal in the John case (see above). On appeal, the EAT (His Honour Judge McMullen presiding) summarised the issue in the case as being whether S.3 covered discrimination against a person because of some characteristic of the particular individual he or she was married to (or in a civil partnership with) or because of some specific connection between the act of discrimination complained of and that individual. The EAT acknowledged that the claimant might have been treated in the same way if she had been in a close relationship other than marriage with her partner, but suggested that this would not have defeated her marriage discrimination claim. Essentially, in the EAT's view, a person who is married or in a civil partnership is protected against discrimination under S.3 SDA (and now under S.8 EqA) both on the ground of his or her marital or civil partnership status per se and on the ground of his or her relationship with the other partner. On this basis, any less favourable treatment which is 'marriage-specific' is unlawful. Although the EAT did not deal with the comparator question in any depth, it did emphasise that the statutory comparison was 'between a married person and an unmarried person, and nobody else'.

The most recent consideration of this issue was given by another division of the EAT in Hawkins v Atex Group Ltd and ors EAT 0302/11. In that case, the EAT's then President, Mr Justice Underhill, took issue with HHJ McMullen's approach in the Dunn case, suggesting that it failed to grapple sufficiently with the subtleties of marital discrimination. In Hawkins, Underhill J ruled that less favourable treatment based not on the mere fact that the claimant is married but on the fact that he or she is in a close relationship with another employee (which would include marriage) does not comprise marital discrimination within the meaning of what is now S.8 EqA. In the particular case, H was married to the chief executive of AG Ltd. For some years she provided her services through a service company jointly owed by her and her husband, but from January 2010 she became directly employed by AG Ltd as its marketing director. In June 2010 she was suspended pending an investigation of allegations, including that she and her husband, contrary to the express concerns of AG Ltd, had employed themselves and their daughter. When H was dismissed along with her husband and daughter, she claimed that her dismissal comprised direct marital discrimination contrary to S.3 SDA. However, an employment judge struck out that claim on the basis that it had no reasonable prospect of success, reasoning that there was no evidence to suggest that AG Ltd was motivated specifically by the fact that she and her husband were married, rather than simply by the closeness of their relationship. On appeal, the EAT upheld the tribunal judge's decision. In Underhill J's words: 'It is impossible to conceive of a "marriage-specific" reason for the conduct complained of, and none is alleged in the Particulars of Claim: whether or not the suspicions of conflicts of interest or nepotism which plainly led the respondents to act as they did were justified, they would as a matter of common sense have arisen equally whether [the claimant] and Mr Hawkins were married or not.'

In effect, the EAT is saying that the question in these cases is not whether the **8.13** claimant suffered the treatment in question because he or she is married to a particular spouse, but whether the claimant suffered it because he or she was married. Tribunals must therefore distinguish between cases where the close relationship between the employee and his or her spouse is the reason for the treatment, and those where the fact of the relationship being one of marriage (or civil partnership) is the true reason. In the former case, if it can be said that the employer would have treated the claimant in the same way even if he or she were not married to the person in question but were merely 'common law spouses', then this cannot comprise marital discrimination, since the treatment in question is not 'marriage-specific'. The Hawkins case fell into this category: the claimant's dismissal was not one specifically motivated by the fact that the CEO and his wife were married, but by the closeness of their relationship, which gave rise to the employer's concerns about nepotism and which was the true reason for the dismissal. Accordingly, there was no 'marriage-specific' treatment. Underhill J intimated that the same was true of the treatment of the claimant in the Dunn case.

In view of the detailed consideration given to the issue by Underhill J in Hawkins v Atex Group Ltd and ors, it is likely that the approach adopted in that case will be preferred by tribunals in subsequent cases to that adopted by HHJ McMullen in Dunn v Institute of Cemetery and Crematorium Management EAT 0531/10.

HHJ McMullen also addressed a further argument in Dunn that was not **8.14** considered at all in the Hawkins case: that Articles 8 (the right to respect for private and family life) and 12 (the right to marry) of the European Convention for the Protection of Human Rights and Fundamental Freedoms (together with Article 14, which provides that the enjoyment of rights and freedoms under the Convention must be secured without discrimination on any ground, including sex, birth or other status) meant that S.3 SDA would, in any case, have had to be interpreted in such a way as to protect a person from being discriminated against by reason of the particular person to whom he or she was married. Although, strictly speaking, it was not necessary for the EAT to deal with this point in the light of its conclusion that the wording of S.3 was clear enough to confer such protection in any event, the EAT nonetheless stated that it would have been minded to hold that S.3 – and by extension S.8 EqA – had to be interpreted to give effect to Convention rights and that Article 8 precluded an employee from being discriminated against on account of the person to whom he or she is married (or with whom he or she has a civil partnership). Given that this obiter reasoning was not imposed by the EAT in Hawkins, it will be interesting to see if it is relied upon in subsequent cases to confer marital discrimination protection on those who are treated less favourably on account of the particular person to whom they are married or in a close relationship with.

8.15 Overlap with other protected characteristics

As we have already seen, considerable overlap exists between the protected characteristic of marriage and civil partnership and the protected characteristics of sex, sexual orientation and, to a lesser extent, gender reassignment. We consider this overlap briefly below.

8.16 Sex discrimination

Sex discrimination as well as marital discrimination can arise if two colleagues in the same workplace marry in circumstances where the employer operates a policy that restricts the employment of married couples. Such a policy is not unlawful per se, but if the employer treats one of the married partners less favourably than the other this may constitute sex discrimination as well as discrimination on the ground of marriage. In Chief Constable of Bedfordshire v Graham 2002 IRLR 239, EAT, the claimant was a female police inspector who married a divisional commander and a year later was appointed area inspector in the same division. However, her appointment was rescinded by the Chief Constable due to his concern that if criminal proceedings were taken against the claimant's husband the claimant would be neither competent nor compellable as a witness. G was subsequently assigned the post of area inspector of another division. An employment tribunal upheld her claims of sex and marital discrimination under Ss.1 and 3 SDA. On appeal, the EAT upheld the tribunal's decision, confirming that the employer's treatment comprised both sex and marital discrimination on the following bases:

- the policy restricting the ability of a female officer to work alongside her spouse amounted to indirect sex discrimination on the ground that such a policy would be likely to affect women more than men

- the claimant was also indirectly discriminated against on the ground of marital status, since the proportion of married female officers who could comply with the employer's policy was considerably smaller than the proportion of unmarried female officers who could comply with it; and

- since the employer's decision to post the claimant to a different location was based on the fact that the claimant and her husband were spouses, the employer had directly discriminated against the claimant on the ground of her marital status by treating her less favourably.

Another scenario where a claimant may be able to bring discrimination claims **8.17** on the grounds of both marriage and sex is where the discriminatory treatment has been prompted by the employer's attitude towards working mothers. In Hurley v Mustoe 1981 ICR 490, EAT, for example, a married woman with four young children was dismissed on the first day of her employment as a waitress when the owner of the restaurant discovered she had children. The reason for this treatment was that the employer believed that women who had care of young children were unreliable when it came to evening work. The claimant brought claims of both direct sex discrimination and indirect marital discrimination under Ss.1 and 3 SDA respectively (now Ss.11 and 8). An employment tribunal rejected both claims. Regarding the sex discrimination complaint, the tribunal found that the employer's policy regarding employment of people who were parents of young children applied equally to men and women, which meant that the claimant had not shown that she had been treated less favourably by reason of her sex. As for the indirect marital discrimination complaint, although the tribunal accepted that more married than unmarried people had care of young children and so would find it more difficult to meet the employer's 'requirement or condition' of not having young children, the indirectly discriminatory effect of this requirement or condition was justifiable on the basis that it was necessary in the context of a small business.

On appeal, the EAT overturned the tribunal's decision on both counts. In respect of direct sex discrimination, it ruled that, contrary to the tribunal's finding, there was absolutely no reliable evidence that the employer's policy was not to employ men with small children. This meant that the policy in effect discriminated against women with small children only, thus demonstrating that the claimant had been treated less favourably than a man would have been on the ground of sex contrary to S.1 SDA (now S.11 EqA). Turning to the indirect marital discrimination claim, the EAT ruled that the tribunal's finding on justification was fundamentally flawed. In order to justify the indirect discriminatory effect of the employer's requirement or condition, it was necessary for the employer to show that the requirement not to have young children was necessary for both men and women. But it was simply impossible to show this where that requirement was only ever, in reality, applied to married women and not to married men. As Mr Justice Brown-Wilkinson observed: 'There was no evidence that men with small children are unreliable and not even popular prejudice suggests that they are. Therefore, in our view there was no evidence on which the [employment] tribunal could find that the relevant condition was justifiable.'

8.18 The Hurley decision was reached in 1981 and the dramatic rise in the incidence of children born outside marriage since then may now make it difficult to show that a provision, criterion or practice of not having children has a disproportionate impact upon married people when compared with unmarried people. Nevertheless, Hurley remains a useful illustration of how, in some circumstances, marital discrimination can also give rise to potential claims of sex discrimination.

8.19 Sexual orientation

There is obviously a very close link between civil partnership and sexual orientation since only persons of the same sex are legally entitled to enter into such partnerships. At the time of writing we are unaware of any cases brought by civil partners relying solely upon the protection accorded to them by virtue of S.8 EqA (or by its predecessor, S.3 SDA). This is not entirely surprising given that any complainant in a position to rely on S.8 would be far more likely to have brought his or her claim on the basis of sexual orientation discrimination. This point is elaborated further in Chapter 13, 'Sexual orientation', under 'Overlap with other protected characteristics'.

8.20 Transsexuals

A person who has undergone a process of gender reassignment is entitled to apply for a gender reassignment certificate conferring full legal recognition of his or her acquired gender and anyone holding such a certificate is entitled to get married or enter into a civil partnership – see Chapter 7, 'Gender reassignment' under 'Legal recognition of acquired gender' for more details. For present purposes, the significance of the right to marry or enter into a civil partnership is that if, say, a male-to-female transsexual employee were to be treated less favourably because of her marriage to a man or civil partnership with a woman, she could seek to bring a direct discrimination claim based on both protected characteristics – i.e. gender reassignment and marriage/civil partnership. However, should the claim be for harassment, the claimant would only be able to base her claim on gender reassignment because marriage/civil partnership is excluded from the scope of harassment protection under the EqA – see under 'Protection under the Equality Act' above.

9 Pregnancy and maternity

The protected period

Overlap with sex discrimination

9.1 Section 4 of the Equality Act 2010 (EqA) lists pregnancy and maternity as one of the nine protected characteristics covered by the Act but curiously, unlike the other protected characteristics, it is not defined further in Chapter 1 of Part 2 of the Act (headed 'Protected characteristics'). However, the scope of the protection afforded to a woman during pregnancy and maternity is apparent from S.18 EqA. This section is contained in Chapter 2 of Part 2 of the Act (headed 'Prohibited conduct'), which sets out the forms of discrimination prohibited under the Act (e.g. direct and indirect discrimination, harassment and victimisation). S.18 prohibits 'pregnancy and maternity discrimination' and sets out the circumstances in which such discrimination will be said to occur.

Section 18 concerns pregnancy and maternity discrimination in the employment context only and is designed to replicate the effect of S.3A of the Sex Discrimination Act 1975 (SDA). It provides that an employer discriminates against a woman if it treats her unfavourably:

- during the 'protected period' of her pregnancy because of the pregnancy or an illness resulting from the pregnancy – S.18(2)

- because she is on compulsory maternity leave – S.18(3), or

- because she is exercising or seeking to exercise, or has exercised or sought to exercise, the right to ordinary or additional maternity leave – S.18(4).

For further details of these grounds of protection, see IDS Employment Law Handbook, 'Maternity and Parental Rights' (2009), Chapter 13, 'Discrimination and equal pay', under 'Direct discrimination'.

The protected period

9.2

The special protection accorded to those who are pregnant or who have a pregnancy-related illness under S.18(2) is temporally confined to the 'protected period'. This is defined as beginning at the start of the woman's pregnancy – S.18(6) EqA. If she has the right to ordinary and additional maternity leave, it ends on the expiry of the additional maternity leave period or when she returns to work after the pregnancy, if that is earlier – S.18(6)(a). Ordinary and additional maternity leave are provided for in Ss.71 and 73 of the Employment Rights Act 1996 (ERA) respectively (see S.213 EqA, which defines references to maternity leave in the Act by reference to the ERA), and in the Maternity and Paternity Leave etc Regulations 1999 SI 1999/3312 – see IDS Employment Law Handbook, 'Maternity and Parental Rights' (2009), Chapter 3, 'Maternity leave'.

If the woman does not have the right to ordinary and additional maternity leave (typically, because she is not an employee), the protected period ends two weeks after the end of her pregnancy, i.e. at the end of the period of compulsory maternity leave referred to in S.72 ERA – S.18(6)(b) EqA.

9.3 Note that S.18(5) EqA provides that, where unfavourable treatment because of pregnancy or a related illness is in implementation of a decision taken during the protected period, that treatment is to be regarded as occurring in that period, even if the implementation is not until after the end of that period (i.e. after the woman has returned to work).

Where the discrimination in question relates to unfavourable treatment because the woman is on compulsory maternity leave or because she is exercising or seeking to exercise, or has exercised or sought to exercise, the right to ordinary or additional maternity leave, the special protection accorded by S.18 EqA can be relied upon whether or not the discrimination occurs during the protected period.

9.4 Overlap with sex discrimination

Outside of the protected period, it remains open to a woman to argue that any treatment meted out to her because of her pregnancy amounted to less favourable treatment because of sex contrary to S.13 EqA (i.e. direct discrimination) (see Chapter 15, 'Direct discrimination'), or to indirect sex discrimination under S.19 EqA (see Chapters 16 and 17, 'Indirect discrimination: proving disadvantage' and 'Indirect discrimination: objective justification').

The key difference between the special protection from pregnancy and maternity discrimination in S.18 and the general protection from direct discrimination under S.13 EqA (see Chapter 15) is that S.18 does not require that a complainant compare the way she has been treated with the way a male comparator has been or would have been treated. For the purpose of a S.13 claim, a comparator, who may be real or hypothetical, must be in circumstances that are not materially different to those of the complainant – S.23(1). In contrast, S.18 requires simply that the complainant show she has been treated 'unfavourably' – no question of comparison arises. This recognises the fact – as confirmed by the case law of the European Court of Justice – that pregnancy is a condition unique to women, such that it makes no sense for a claimant to be required to compare her treatment with the treatment that would have been accorded to a man in similar circumstances – see Dekker v Stichting Vormingscentrum voor

Jong Volwassenen (VJV-Centrum) Plus 1992 ICR 325, ECJ, and Handels-og Kontorfunktionærernes Forbund i Danmark v Dansk Arbejdsgiverforening 1992 ICR 332, ECJ.

9.5 Whenever a claim can be brought under S.18, then it should and must be: S.18(7) stipulates that no claim of direct sex discrimination may be made under S.13 based on treatment of a woman that is caught by S.18. The effect of this is that claims of pregnancy discrimination during the protected period of a woman's pregnancy and discrimination based on maternity leave must be brought under S.18, and cannot be framed instead as a direct sex discrimination claim under S.13. However, a claim for direct sex discrimination under S.13 will remain available for pregnancy and maternity cases that fall outside the scope of the special protection in S.18 – for example, because the alleged pregnancy discrimination takes place outside the protected period, or stems from an incorrect perception that a woman is pregnant, or from the claimant's association with a pregnant woman. In such cases the comparator approach will, on the face of it, apply. However, it is open to question whether this accords with EU law, at least in a case where the treatment complained of is based on pregnancy (or perceived pregnancy) as distinct from the consequences of pregnancy (such as a pregnancy-related illness extending beyond the protected period of the woman's maternity leave).

It is notable that, as well as prohibiting direct sex discrimination, S.13 appears to cover direct discrimination because of the protected characteristic of pregnancy and maternity. This follows from the fact that S.13(1) refers to less favourable treatment 'because of a protected characteristic', and pregnancy and maternity appear in the list of protected characteristics in S.4. It is curious that, in a case falling within S.18, S.18(7) disapplies S.13 only 'so far as relating to sex discrimination'; it does not expressly preclude a S.13 claim based on the protected characteristic of pregnancy and maternity. On the face of it, therefore, there is nothing to prevent a S.18 claimant from also bringing a S.13 claim of direct discrimination because of pregnancy or maternity, as distinct from sex – although, given that S.13 requires a comparator whereas S.18 does not, it is unclear what she would gain from doing so.

10 Race

Section 9 of the Equality Act 2010 (EqA) deals with the protected characteristic **10.1** of 'race'. Previously, the Race Relations Act 1976 (RRA) used the expression 'racial grounds' to cover the same terrain now covered by S.9. Under the RRA, 'race' was simply one of the five specific grounds that were embraced by the collective term 'racial grounds' as defined in S.3(1) RRA. The others were colour, nationality, ethnic origins and national origins.

Before examining the scope of the protected characteristic of race in detail under the EqA, it is appropriate first to outline the nature and scope of the protection against discrimination on the ground of race accorded by the RRA.

Protection under antecedent legislation   10.2

Formerly, direct discrimination was prohibited if it was carried out on *racial grounds*, which meant any of the following five grounds: colour, nationality, race, or ethnic or national origins – Ss.1(1)(a) and 3(1) RRA.

Until 2003, 'indirect discrimination' under the RRA focused solely on whether a uniformly applied 'requirement or condition' adversely affected persons in the same *racial group* as the complainant – defined by reference to the same elements that made up the definition of 'racial grounds' (i.e. colour, nationality, race, or ethnic or national origins) – S.1(1)(b). The fact that in some cases a racial group could comprise two or more distinct racial groups did not prevent it from constituting a single racial group for the purposes of a particular claim – S.3(2). However, as discussed immediately below, amendments made to the RRA in 2003 prompted by mandatory provisions contained in the EU Race Equality Directive (No.2000/43) ('the Race Equality Directive') significantly changed and complicated the picture in this regard.

The 2003 amendments   10.3
In 2000 the European Union enacted the Race Equality Directive, which contained mandatory measures that required the RRA to be amended in certain respects. Most notably, the Directive provided for special rules to be implemented relating to the burden of proof, for a revised definition of 'indirect discrimination', and for a free-standing right not to be subjected to harassment on racial grounds. However, the Directive itself only applied to race discrimination on

197

grounds of race, ethnic origins or national origins. It did not cover the two additional grounds already covered by the RRA – namely, colour and nationality.

For reasons principally to do with lack of Parliamentary time, the then Labour Government opted to make the necessary amendments to the RRA by way of secondary rather than primary legislation. This meant that the resulting statutory instrument (the Race Relations Act 1976 (Amendment) Regulations 2003 SI 2003/1636) was enacted under the powers conferred by S.2(2) of the European Communities Act 1972 and was limited to simply introducing those amendments that were strictly necessary to implement the mandatory provisions of the Race Equality Directive. The upshot was that the amendments could only be applied to the three grounds of discrimination specifically contemplated by that Directive. In consequence, as from 19 July 2003 a clumsy two-tier system came into being. This comprised a set of enhanced rights (i.e. those introduced by the 2003 amending Regulations) applicable to claims based on race, or ethnic or national origins, and a set of more restrictive rights (i.e. those that pre-existed the amending Regulations) in respect of claims based on colour or nationality.

10.4 This two-tier system, which threw up a number of anomalies that are discussed below, remained in force until October 2010 when it was eventually overhauled by the EqA. To avoid similar problems occurring in the future, special provisions – Ss.203 and 204 – were included in the 2010 Act that were designed to ensure more joined-up thinking should the Act ever need to be amended in the light of EU case law or legislative developments. These so-called 'harmonisation powers' are discussed in detail in Chapter 1, 'UK discrimination law', under 'Harmonisation'.

10.5 **Indirect discrimination and harassment claims.** One of the consequences of the 2003 amendments was that, at the point when those amendments came into force on 19 July 2003, the definition of 'indirect discrimination' under the RRA was split into two. This meant that different definitions applied depending upon which of the particular racial grounds was at issue in any particular case. The existing definition in S.1(1)(b) was retained in the case of discrimination on the grounds of colour and nationality. However, in order to reflect the definition of 'indirect discrimination' in the Race Equality Directive, an entirely new definition – phrased in terms of whether the application of a 'provision, criterion or practice' (PCP) puts or would put persons of the 'same race or ethnic or national origins' as the claimant at a particular disadvantage – was inserted into the RRA as new S.1(1A) to cover the three racial grounds specifically covered by the Directive (i.e. race, ethnic origins and national origins).

A further anomaly was created by the insertion of new S.3A RRA – which imported a free-standing right to claim harassment into the RRA for the first time, but only in so far as such harassment was perpetrated by reason of race, or ethnic or national origins. Harassment based on colour or nationality was not covered by the new provision so anyone alleging harassment on one of those grounds continued to have to bring the claim in the form of a direct discrimination complaint under S.1(1). The problem here was that proving that harassment amounted to less favourable treatment as required by that section was more difficult than proving harassment under the new right conferred by S.3A. As a matter of policy, it made no sense whatsoever to have different remedies and varying levels of protection depending simply upon what particular racial ground the complainant was relying on.

Application of the 'reverse burden of proof' rule. Prior to the entry into force **10.6** of the EqA, it was generally thought that the burden of proof provisions inserted into the RRA in order to implement the equivalent provisions in the Race Equality Directive applied only to the grounds of race discrimination specifically covered by that Directive (i.e. race, or ethnic or national origins). New S.54A RRA provided for a two-stage test under which a claimant bringing a race discrimination or harassment claim had to prove primary facts from which an inference of discrimination could be drawn (stage 1), otherwise the claim would fail. If, however, the claimant proved primary facts, the burden of proof would shift to the employer to provide a non-discriminatory explanation for the treatment in question (stage 2). Should the employer fail in this task, the claim would succeed. It was assumed that this 'reverse burden of proof' rule would not apply where the grounds relied on were colour or nationality as these were not covered by the Directive. And that, indeed, was the stance taken by the EAT in Okonu v G4S Security Services (UK) Ltd 2008 ICR 598, EAT.

However, a contrary view was taken by the EAT in Abbey National plc and anor v Chagger 2009 ICR 624, EAT, at least with regard to discrimination based on colour. In that case, the Appeal Tribunal ruled that it was inconceivable that the Race Equality Directive was not intended to apply to colour discrimination, since such discrimination is in practice an integral aspect or outward manifestation of discrimination based on 'racial or ethnic origins' – two grounds indubitably covered by the Directive. The EAT therefore concluded that an employment tribunal's decision that the claimant had been subjected to race discrimination when he was selected for redundancy on the ground of colour or national origins was not vitiated by its application of the reverse burden of proof provision in S.54A. This approach was subsequently approved by another division of the EAT in Milton Keynes General Hospital NHS Trust and anor v Maruziva EAT 0003/09. (Note that the EAT's decision in Chagger was subsequently reversed in part on appeal, but on an entirely different issue – see Abbey National plc and anor v Chagger 2010 ICR 397, CA.)

The position was clearer – but no more satisfactory – in respect of claims of **10.7** victimisation. In Oyarce v Cheshire County Council 2008 ICR 1179, CA, the Court of Appeal held that the reverse burden of proof rule in S.54A did not apply *at all* to victimisation claims irrespective of the particular ground of race

199

discrimination relied upon. This was because S.54A(1) made it clear that the whole of that section only applied where the respondent 'has committed an act of discrimination on grounds of race or national origins'. The Court interpreted 'discrimination' in this context to be restricted to discrimination as defined under S.1 RRA (i.e. direct and indirect race discrimination) and not under S.2 (discrimination by way of victimisation). This was in contradistinction to victimisation claims brought under the various pre-EqA provisions dealing with other strands of discrimination (e.g. sex, religion or belief, and sexual orientation) in respect of which the reverse burden of proof rule applied without exception.

In reaching its conclusion, the Court of Appeal rejected the argument that a purposive construction was required to ensure that the statutory burden of proof rules applied to victimisation in the same way as they applied to other types of discrimination claim brought under the RRA. It pointed out that S.54A had only been inserted because of the need to transpose the requirements of the Race Equality Directive and that that Directive contained no express provision extending the burden of proof rules to victimisation cases. Therefore, in addressing S.54A, a purposive construction had to proceed on the basis that the draftsman's purpose was to transpose the terms of the Directive, but *only* those terms.

10.8 Position under the Equality Act

The EqA accords protection against workplace discrimination – i.e. direct and indirect discrimination, harassment and victimisation – because of a person's 'race'. S.9(1) makes it clear that the term 'race' for this purpose includes colour, nationality, and ethnic or national origins.

Two things should be noted about S.9(1). First, the race provisions in the 2010 Act cover the same five racial grounds previously covered by the RRA. In fact, 'race' itself – which was one of the specific racial grounds listed in S.3(1) RRA – is now simply used as a generic term, a kind of shorthand reference for the other four grounds. Notwithstanding this, it is certain that, in so far as 'race' stands for anything distinct and unique compared to the other four grounds (which is doubtful for the reasons outlined under 'Grounds of "race"' below), it will continue to be covered under the EqA.

10.9 Secondly, the relevant definition of 'race' in S.9(1) is clearly not intended to be exhaustive. Use of the word 'includes' shows that it is not limited to the four grounds specifically mentioned. This non-exclusive definition contrasts with the equivalent provision in the RRA, which, as we have seen, defined 'racial grounds' exclusively in terms of race, colour, nationality, ethnic origins and national origins. Accordingly, there is now scope for including other appropriate grounds into the definition of 'race' and thereby extending the ambit of the protected characteristic of race. For example, it has been speculated that 'caste' discrimination might be included on the basis that a person's caste tends to be an admixture of personal issues concerning their ethnic origins and social class. However, it will be necessary for a test case to be run to establish whether or not this is so. (Note that, in any event, the EqA contains a specific power enabling the Government to amend the EqA to extend the protections for race discrimination to ensure that they cover caste – see Chapter 4, 'Characteristics covered by the Equality Act', under 'Characteristics not covered by the Equality Act – caste', for further details.)

Previous anomalies remedied   10.10

One beneficial effect of the EqA is that it has ironed out the anomalies created by the amendments made to the RRA in 2003 – see 'Protection under antecedent legislation' above. Most notably, the 2010 Act has harmonised the two alternative definitions of indirect discrimination that previously applied. Now, a standard definition of indirect discrimination – as set out in S.19 EqA – applies to all race discrimination claims regardless of the racial ground or group at issue. This definition is discussed in detail in Chapters 16, 'Indirect discrimination: proving disadvantage', and 17, 'Indirect discrimination: objective justification'.

Similarly, the free-standing right to protection against harassment introduced into the RRA by the 2003 amendments now applies irrespective of the particular racial group into which the claimant falls. This right, which is contained in S.26 EqA and applies to all protected characteristics, is discussed in detail in Chapter 18, 'Harassment'.

Finally, the 'reverse' burden of proof rule – which under the RRA only applied   10.11 to race discrimination claims based on race, or ethnic or national origins but not to colour or nationality – is now codified in S.136 EqA and applies to every single case in which it is alleged that there has been a contravention of the 2010 Act (see Chapter 32, 'Burden of proof', for further details). It therefore no longer matters which of the racial groups or grounds pertains to the claimant.

The discrepancy exposed by the Court of Appeal in Oyarce v Cheshire County Council 2008 ICR 1179, CA, regarding the non-application of the reverse burden of proof rule to race victimisation claims, has also been addressed. S.136(2) and (3) EqA, which encapsulates the reverse burden of proof rules (albeit using different wording from that used in the RRA and other antecedent equality legislation), applies 'to any proceedings relating to a contravention of this Act' – S.136(1). Since claims of 'victimisation' – as defined in S.27 – self-evidently comprise 'proceedings relating to a contravention of [the EqA]', it is clear that the rule now applies as much to race victimisation claims as to any other victimisation claim related to one of the other protected characteristics. For further discussion of victimisation claims, see Chapter 19, 'Victimisation'.

201

10.12 Protected racial groups

Section 9(2) EqA makes it clear that any reference in the Act to a person who has the 'protected characteristic of race' is a reference to 'a person of a particular racial group', while a reference to 'persons who share [that] protected characteristic' is a reference to 'persons of the same racial group'. A 'racial group' is a group of persons defined by reference to 'race' (as defined in S.9(1)); and a reference to 'a person's racial group' is a reference to 'a racial group into which the person falls' – S.9(3). The effect of these provisions is that the protected characteristic of race is defined in terms of the racial group(s) to which a person belongs. Just as under the RRA, a racial group for these purposes can be made up of two or more distinct racial groups – S.9(4) EqA. Thus, 'black Britons' – encompassing people who are both black and who are British citizens – would, for example, be protected as a racial group.

In Orphanos v Queen Mary College 1985 IRLR 349, HL, the House of Lords accepted that persons of 'non-British' origin could form a single racial group in the context of a claim of indirect race discrimination brought under the RRA concerning the application of a three-year EEC residency condition for access to lower college fee tariffs. A contrary view was taken by the Court of Appeal – albeit without any apparent consideration of the Orphanos case – in Tejani v Superintendant Registrar for the District of Peterborough 1986 IRLR 502, CA. There the Court held that a person who was a British national born in Uganda had not been directly discriminated against on the ground of his national origins when asked by a marriage registrar to produce his passport in circumstances in which such a request would not have been made to a person born in the United Kingdom. Since the registrar had treated everybody who came from abroad exactly alike, and the claimant had been asked for his passport simply on the ground that he had come from abroad without reference to any particular country or place of origin, he was held not to have been treated less favourably on the ground of nationality or national origin.

10.13 In R v Rogers 2007 2 AC 62, HL, the House of Lords in effect resolved the tension between these two cases by coming down decisively in favour of the Orphanos approach. The Rogers case arose in the context of a criminal prosecution whereby a road user was charged with an offence of racially aggravated abuse contrary to S.3(1)(a) of the Crime and Disorder Act 1998 (CDA). An offence is committed under that Act if the offender demonstrates hostility towards the victim based on the victim's membership (or presumed membership) of a racial or religious group – S.28(1) CDA. By virtue of S.28(4), 'racial group' is defined in very similar terms to the definition found in S.9 EqA (and previously in S.3(1) RRA), i.e. as a group of persons defined by reference to race, colour, nationality (including citizenship), or ethnic or national origins. The abuse in the instant case took the form of the defendant shouting 'bloody foreigners' to three young Spanish women on the pavement as he passed by and telling them to 'go back to your own country'. The defendant sought to argue that the words used were not capable of demonstrating hostility based on membership of a racial group because 'foreigners' – without reference to any specific nationality or national origin – was too general a categorisation to constitute a racial group as defined by S.28(4). The trial judge and, subsequently, the Court of Appeal rejected this defence, holding that 'foreigners' did constitute a racial group for the relevant purposes.

On further appeal, the House of Lords upheld the defendant's conviction. When considering whether the parameters of a 'racial group' should be capable of being so widely drawn, Baroness Hale remarked: '[I]t is argued by the appellant that the [CDA] requires that the group be defined by what it is rather than by what it is not. Hence it is argued that Spaniards are covered but foreigners, that is the non-British, are not. The same argument would presumably be made about a person who showed hostility towards all non-whites irrespective of the particular racial group to which they belonged. This cannot be right as a matter of language. Whether the group is defined exclusively by reference to what its members are not or inclusively by reference to what they are, the criterion by which the group is defined – nationality or colour – is the same… Fine distinctions depending upon the particular words used would bring the law into disrepute. This case shows that only too well but it is easy to think of other examples. "Wogs begin at Calais" demonstrates hostility to all foreigners, whereas "bloody wogs" might well be thought to have specific racial connotations. "Tinted persons" could in certain circumstances demonstrate hostility to all non-Caucasians, while "blacks" might refer to a particular racial group. But "black" might equally refer to several different racial groups whose members have very black skin. All are defined by reference to their race, colour, nationality, or ethnic or national origins, whether there are many, several, or only one such group encompassed by the words used.'

10.14 Although the decision in Rogers arose in a criminal law context, the relevant statutory definition under scrutiny was almost identical to those used in the RRA and the EqA. We would therefore suggest that Baroness Hale's reasoning – though strictly-speaking obiter with regard to its application in a race discrimination context – should be used to determine the proper meaning of 'racial group' in S.9 EqA. This is particularly so given that her reasoning is consistent with the stance taken by the House of Lords in the Orphanos case.

Grounds of 'race'   **10.15**

As previously mentioned, the EqA now uses 'race' as the umbrella term for the different facets that, individually or in combination, give expression to a person's 'race' or 'racial group'. S.9(1) EqA defines the protected characteristic of race by reference to 'colour', 'nationality', 'ethnic origins' and 'national origins' but makes it clear that this is not an exhaustive list. It should perhaps be pointed out at this stage that, in contrast to the RRA, the term 'ground' is not actually used in the EqA. However, for ease of understanding we continue to use it to describe the elements or aspects of race that are covered by the Act.

The four grounds specifically listed in S.9(1) are – with the addition of 'race' itself – identical to those previously used to define the meaning of 'racial group' in S.3(1) RRA. Under that Act a substantial body of case law developed in which the appellate courts illuminated the scope and meaning of these terms. Undoubtedly, these decisions will continue to be relevant when considering the identical terms used in S.9(1) EqA.

We now examine each of these grounds in turn.

10.16 Race

The ground of 'race' itself – although listed in S.3(1) RRA as a specific basis on which a 'racial group' could be defined – was not, as far as we are aware, separately considered by the courts in any cases decided under the RRA. This may have been because it is difficult to define in any meaningful way. The word is commonly used, and indeed is perhaps best understood, as an umbrella term embracing a number of diverse and overlapping elements such as ancestry, culture, history, language and physical characteristics – all of which are included in the definition of race in the New Oxford Dictionary of English. It is probably because 'race' is a generic term in this sense that the drafters of the EqA chose it in preference to the RRA's concept of 'racial grounds' as the means of describing the relevant protected characteristic for the purposes of the new Act.

It is interesting to note that the New Oxford English Dictionary draws attention to the fact that the use of the word 'race' has become problematic due to its association with a number of now discredited ideologies and theories developed during the 19th and 20th centuries concerning racial superiority and social Darwinism. This may help explain why courts and tribunals have focused more on colour, nationality and ethnic or national origins, than on race and racial origins.

10.17 Furthermore, it is possible that the determination of what is meant by 'race' and 'racial origins' has become virtually irrelevant in light of the decision in Mandla and anor v Dowell Lee and ors 1983 ICR 385, HL (discussed in detail under 'Ethnic origins' below). In that case the House of Lords held that the term 'ethnic' has 'come to be commonly used in a sense appreciably wider than the strictly racial or biological', although it 'retains a racial flavour'.

10.18 Colour

'Colour' is an aspect of race that, like 'race' itself, has not been specifically defined by the courts. This is probably because its meaning is axiomatic. Prejudice based ostensibly on the colour of someone's skin may itself merely be an outward manifestation of an underlying prejudice based on wider actual or perceived cultural differences. Therefore, an employment tribunal that finds that a person has been discriminated against or harassed because of his or her colour will often find it hard in practice to resist concluding that ethnic or national origins was also a reason – often the *real* reason – for that treatment.

The above point was forcefully made by Mr Justice Underhill in Abbey National **10.19** plc and anor v Chagger 2009 ICR 624, EAT, when considering whether the 'reverse burden of proof' in S.54A RRA applied to a race discrimination claim advanced on the basis of the claimant's colour. In the course of deciding that the rule did apply, Underhill J concluded that 'colour' was in any event intimately wrapped up in the concepts of 'race' and 'ethnic origins', both of which were elements of the definition of 'racial grounds' in S.3(1) RRA to which the reverse burden of proof rule did indisputably apply. His Lordship observed: 'We recognise that conceptually there is a difference between discrimination on the ground of colour on the one hand and discrimination on the ground of race or ethnic or national origin on the other. But in the real world the different kinds of discrimination referred to in S.3(1) overlap to a very considerable extent; and in many, perhaps most, cases they will be practically indistinguishable. That is all the more so because "race" and "ethnic origin" are themselves not neat scientific concepts but "rubbery and elusive" in their meaning: see the speech of Lord Fraser of Tullybelton in Mandla and anor v Dowell Lee and ors 1983 ICR 385, HL. When an employer is prejudiced on racial grounds against an employee from a "visible ethnic minority", it will often be not only impracticable but meaningless to seek to establish whether his prejudice is based on the colour of the employee's skin or his race (however defined) or his ethnic or national origin – or simply on the fact that he is evidently not "native English": the different factors will generally meld into one another indistinguishably. The overlap is particularly pronounced in the case of colour. While it is of course common enough to find discrimination on the ground of race or ethnic origin without discrimination on the ground of colour, the reverse is not the case: it is very hard to conceive of a case of discrimination on the ground of colour which cannot also be properly characterised as discrimination on the ground of race and/or ethnic origin. It could indeed be said that colour is significant primarily as an outward and visible manifestation of race or ethnic origin. An employer who said "I discriminated against you because of the colour of your skin but not because of your race or ethnic origin" would hardly be understood, let alone believed.'

The EAT's decision in Chagger was subsequently reversed in part on appeal – see Abbey National plc and anor v Chagger 2010 ICR 397, CA – but on an entirely different issue. Nothing in the Court of Appeal's decision suggested any disagreement with Underhill J's remarks quoted above.

Ethnic origins   10.20
While the meanings of 'race' and 'colour' have attracted little comment in the courts, a considerable body of case law has built up on the meaning of 'ethnic

205

origins'. Many people regard themselves as members of a distinct group, whether religious, social or cultural. However, this is only relevant for the purposes of S.9 EqA if the group can be defined in terms of its ethnic origins – i.e. can properly be called an 'ethnic group'.

The leading case on what constitutes an ethnic group is Mandla and anor v Dowell Lee and ors 1983 ICR 385, HL. In that case M's son, a Sikh, was refused a place at an independent school because he insisted on wearing his turban in contravention of the school's uniform rules. The Birmingham County Court dismissed M's claim of race discrimination and this was initially upheld by the Court of Appeal, which ruled that 'ethnic origins' was synonymous with 'racial origins' and that Sikhs were a group defined by religion, not race. However, the Court of Appeal was overturned by the House of Lords, which unanimously decided that, although the term 'ethnic' retains a 'racial flavour', it has come to be commonly used in a sense 'appreciably wider than the strictly racial or biological'. Ethnic origins may therefore include religious and cultural factors as well as racial factors.

10.21 In giving the leading speech, Lord Fraser quoted with approval the New Zealand case of King-Ansell v Police 1979 2 NZLR 531, NZCA, in which Judge Richardson said: '[A] group is identifiable in terms of its ethnic origins if it is a segment of the population distinguished from others by a sufficient combination of shared customs, beliefs, traditions and characteristics derived from a common or presumed common past, even if not drawn from what in biological terms is a common racial stock. It is that combination which gives them an historically determined social identity in their own eyes and in the eyes of those outside the group. They have a distinct social identity based not simply on group cohesion and solidarity but also on their belief as to their historical antecedents.'

Applying these principles, Lord Fraser identified two essential characteristics of an ethnic group:

- a long shared history, of which the group is conscious as distinguishing it from other groups, and the memory of which it keeps alive

- a cultural tradition of its own, including family and social customs and manners.

10.22 In addition to these essential characteristics, his Lordship identified others which – although not essential – could be expected to be displayed by the group, namely:

- either a common geographical origin or descent from a small number of common ancestors

- a common language, not necessarily peculiar to the group

- a common literature peculiar to the group

- a common religion different from that of neighbouring groups or from the general community surrounding it

- being a minority or being an oppressed or a dominant group within a larger community.

Lord Fraser was of the view that a group that shared a sufficient number of **10.23** these characteristics would be capable of including converts – for example, persons who marry into the group – and of excluding those who have left or renounced the group. In his Lordship's view, 'provided a person who joins the group feels himself or herself to be a member of it, and is accepted by other members, then he [or she] is, for the purposes of the Act, a member'.

Since the Mandla case was decided, the principles it established have been used in many cases to determine whether a particular group can claim to have a common ethnic origin. For example, in Commission for Racial Equality v Dutton 1989 IRLR 8, CA, the Court of Appeal held that Romany Gypsies had a common ethnic origin and were protected by the RRA. They are a group of Hindu origin who could trace their presence in Great Britain to the beginning of the sixteenth century. The following groups have also been held to comprise distinct ethnic groups:

- Irish travellers – O'Leary v Allied Domecq Inns Ltd, unreported 29/8/00, Central London County Court

- Scottish travellers – MacLennan v Gypsy Traveller Education and Information Project ET Case No.13272/07

- European Roma – R (European Roma Rights Centre and ors) v Immigration Officer at Prague Airport and anor 2005 2 AC 1, HL.

In Gwynedd County Council v Jones and anor 1986 ICR 833, EAT, the Appeal **10.24** Tribunal appeared to support an employment tribunal's conclusion that the English and the Welsh were separate ethnic groups as distinct from having separate nationalities or national origins. But this view should now be treated with caution in light of the more recent decisions in Northern Joint Police Board v Power 1997 IRLR 610, EAT, and BBC Scotland v Souster 2001 IRLR 150, Ct Sess (Inner House). In those cases it was decided that the English and the Scots could not be viewed as distinct ethnic groups. As Lord Cameron said in the Souster case, 'for the English just as for the Scots, the cultural tradition which underpins them as a racial group is far broader and less coherent than that which is required... for the constitution of an ethnic group'. He went on to say that 'the cohesiveness which in each case serves to identify them as a separate racial group is largely, but not exclusively, derived from history and geography but lacks that particular and individual distinctiveness of community which is a mark of the characteristics which Lord Fraser viewed as relevant to

207

the constitution of an ethnic group'. However, the English and the Scots could be seen as distinct racial groups on the basis of national origins – see under 'Nationality and national origins' below.

Although the Gwynedd County Council case may be unreliable authority in respect of the English and Welsh being distinct ethnic groups, the EAT's decision correctly highlights that a common language is not sufficient on its own to create a distinct ethnic group. While language was one of the factors mentioned by Lord Fraser in the Mandla case that might be expected to characterise an ethnic group, the EAT in the Gwynedd case held that language could not be the sole determining factor and that English-speaking Welsh people therefore do not constitute their own ethnic subgroup within the wider ethnic group of Welsh people.

10.25 **Religion as ethnic group.** The decision in Mandla and anor v Dowell Lee and ors (above) is of particular relevance to the question of whether groups which share a common religion attract protection from race discrimination under the EqA in addition to any separate protection accorded to them on the basis of 'religion or belief'. A body of case law decided under the RRA established that a religious group with a common *ethnic origin* came within the protection of the RRA – and the same rationale would undoubtedly apply for the purposes of the EqA. In view of this, the key question is: which religions can be said to have a sufficient number of the characteristics of an ethnic group to qualify?

In general, it would seem from the case law (some of which is outlined below) that the central difference between a religious group that falls within the definition of a 'racial group' and one that does not lies in the *history* of the group itself. If it has an evangelical history, in that it has grown and developed by persuading members of other groups to adopt its customs and beliefs, then it is unlikely to be regarded as an ethnic group even though its members may have a very strong sense of their own identity and regard themselves as a repressed minority. If, on the other hand, the group has spread and grown through migration rather than by influence and conversion, then it is much more likely that the group will be capable of being defined by reference to its ethnic origins.

10.26 *Jews.* When Mandla and anor v Dowell Lee and ors (above) was before the Court of Appeal, Lord Denning MR expressed the view that Jewish people constituted precisely the sort of group that the RRA was designed to cover. This confirmed the reasoning of the EAT in Seide v Gillette Industries Ltd 1980 IRLR 427, EAT, which held that Jews constituted a racial group and that discrimination against a person because he or she is Jewish amounted to race discrimination. In that case, however, the EAT drew a distinction between discrimination against someone because he or she belongs to the Jewish 'race' and discrimination against someone because he or she holds to the Jewish faith. While the former is unlawful direct discrimination on racial grounds, the latter is not – although it may well constitute indirect race discrimination if it can be established that people of that faith are put at a particular disadvantage by the general application of a provision, criterion or practice.

While there is now no doubt that Jewish people comprise an ethnic group for the purposes of what is now S.9 EqA, the observations of the EAT in the Seide case hint at how difficult it can be to determine whether discrimination in relation to matters of Jewish faith comprises 'race' discrimination in addition to discrimination on the ground of religion or belief. This is particularly true if the alleged discrimination in question concerns 'interdenominational' tensions and issues. The leading case on this is R (on the application of E) v Governing Body of JFS and anor 2010 IRLR 136, SC. There, the Supreme Court held (by a majority of five to four) that a Jewish school's oversubscription admissions policy directly discriminated contrary to the RRA by giving priority to children recognised as being Jewish according to the Office of the Chief Rabbi. The criteria necessary for such recognition were either matrilineal descent (i.e. proof that the child seeking admission has an Orthodox Jewish mother or ancestress in the matrilineal line) or that the child's mother had converted to the Orthodox faith before the child was born. On the facts, M – whose mother had converted to non-Orthodox Judaism – was turned down by the JFS (formerly known as the Jews' Free School) and his father sought judicial review of the school's admission criteria. The outcome hinged on whether those criteria treated people differently because of their 'ethnic origins' or because of their 'religion status'. If the former, then the RRA was engaged, meaning that any less favourable treatment on the ground of such origins would be unlawful; if the latter, then the school, being one that was designated under the School Standards Framework Act 1998 as having a 'religious character', was exempt by virtue of Ss.45 and 47 of the Equality Act 2006 (now para 5 of Schedule 11 to the EqA 2010) from the prohibitions against discrimination on the ground of religion or belief that would otherwise have applied.

10.27 Five of the Supreme Court Justices concluded that the definition of 'racial grounds' in S.3(1) RRA, in that they included 'ethnic origins', required a focus on *descent*. In the instant case, the test of matrilineal descent applied by the school comprised a test of 'ethnic origin', and, since that was the specific reason for rejecting the claimant's child's application for admission, the school's treatment constituted unlawful direct race discrimination for the purposes of the RRA. In so concluding, Lord Phillips pointed out that, in Mandla and anor v Dowell Lee and ors (above), Lord Fraser had identified a shared religion among the criteria that can define a person's ethnicity, and that, in the case of Jews, this was in fact the dominant criterion. This meant that in their case it was almost impossible to distinguish between ethnic status and religious status – the two concepts being virtually co-extensive. As the religious test of matrilineal descent in this case focused on the race or ethnicity of the woman from whom the child is descended, that test, in Lord Phillips' view, was a test

209

of ethnic origin. It followed that the school's discriminatory admissions policy – notwithstanding that the discrimination was unintentional – amounted to discrimination on racial grounds contrary to the RRA.

In contrast, the four Supreme Court Justices who dissented reasoned that the school's decision was taken not on racial but solely on religious grounds, and therefore the statutory exemption from religion or belief discrimination liability under Ss.45 and 47 of the Equality Act 2006 (now para 5 of Schedule 11 EqA 2010) applied. In Lord Rodger's words: '[The] mother could have been as Italian in origin as Sophia Loren or as Roman Catholic as the Pope for all that the [school's] governors cared: the only thing that mattered was that she had not converted to Judaism under Orthodox auspices... Faced with a boy whose mother had converted under Orthodox auspices, the governors would have considered him for admission without pausing for a single second to inquire whether he or his mother came from Rome, Brooklyn, Siberia or Buenos Aires, whether she had once been Roman Catholic or Muslim, or whether she was from a close-knit Jewish community or had chosen to assimilate and disappear into secular society. In other words, the "ethnic origins" of the child or his mother... would not have played any part in the governors' decision to admit him... [T]he only grounds for treating M less favourably than the comparator is the difference in their respective mothers' conversions – a religious, not a racial, ground.'

10.28 The JFS case illustrates just how complex the interlinking between religious status and ethnicity origins can be. However, most religious faiths do not have the same overlap with ethnic origins as Orthodox Judaism does. Accordingly, the scope for bringing claims of race discrimination in respect of any alleged discriminatory application of the tenets of other faiths is more limited – see, for example, the discussion concerning Muslims below. In practice, any such discrimination is likely to be 'prosecuted' as a claim based on the protected characteristic of religion or belief – see Chapter 11, 'Religion or belief'. In this regard, it is worth pointing out that, even in the JFS case, the school specifically conceded that its admissions policy was discriminatory on the ground of religion or belief. The inability of the applicant to obtain judicial review on that basis was simply down to the statutory immunity the school enjoyed from liability for that particular type of discrimination.

10.29 *Rastafarians.* The principles set out in Mandla and anor v Dowell Lee and ors (above) were applied in Crown Suppliers (Property Services Agency) v Dawkins 1993 ICR 517, CA, to determine whether Rastafarians were an ethnic group. In that case, D was a Rastafarian who was refused a job because he insisted on wearing his hair in dreadlocks. The Court of Appeal held that although Rastafarians were a distinct separate group with identifiable characteristics, they did not have a separate identity based on their ethnic origins and were not, therefore, an 'ethnic group' directly protected by the RRA. The Court reasoned that the word 'ethnic' as applied by the House of Lords in Mandla had a 'racial flavour'. When compared with the rest of the Afro-Caribbean community in England, there was nothing to set Rastafarians apart as a separate ethnic group. Nor did they have a long shared history – the history of the movement went back only some 60 years.

More recent cases have tended to be brought on the basis that Rastafarianism is a 'philosophical belief' protected under the Employment Equality (Religion or Belief) Regulations 2003 SI 2003/1660 (now S.10 EqA). This protection from religion/belief discrimination would seem to provide a more plausible basis for remedying less favourable treatment or indirect discrimination because of a person's Rastafarian beliefs than do the statutory provisions prohibiting race discrimination.

Muslims. The approach adopted in Crown Suppliers (Property Services Agency) **10.30**
v Dawkins (above), with its emphasis on the racial characteristics of the group in question, suggest that Muslims as a whole are unlikely to constitute a distinct and separate ethnic group. This question has not yet been addressed by the higher courts head on – although in Niazi v Rymans Ltd EAT 6/88 it is notable that the EAT did not call into question an employment tribunal's finding that Muslims were not an ethnic group.

The matter was considered in some detail, however, by an employment tribunal in Commission for Racial Equality v Precision Manufacturing Services Ltd ET Case No.4106/91. In that case the employer was alleged to have told a job centre not to send any Muslims as potential employees. After hearing extensive expert evidence on the nature of Islam, the tribunal applied the criteria set out in Mandla and anor v Dowell Lee and ors (above) and held that Muslims did not constitute an ethnic group. It accepted that Islam had a long history with a geographical origin, but drew a distinction between a group of people who trace their descent from a common geographical origin (who could be regarded as an ethnic group) and a group who trace their belief to a common origin (who could not). Islam, the tribunal noted, is an evangelical faith and the history of Islam is a history of the spreading of that faith and not the spreading of the people who first shared it. (In Mahomed v Guy Leisure Ltd ET Case No.1901952/02 a different employment tribunal reached the same conclusion based on similar reasoning.)

That said, some Muslim claimants have successfully secured protection against **10.31**
indirect race discrimination where they have been able to define themselves as belonging to a racial group comprising a sub-group of those who share their Islamic faith but who also have some specific aspect of race (such as nationality or colour) in common. For example, in JH Walker v Hussain and ors 1996 ICR 291, EAT, Muslim employees were disciplined for taking a day off work to celebrate the Islamic festival of Eid in breach of the employer's policy that non-statutory holidays would not be permitted during the company's busiest

211

months of May, June and July. The employees brought race discrimination claims contending: (i) that they had been treated less favourably on racial grounds by reference to their ethnic origins as Muslims, and (ii) that they had suffered indirect discrimination because, as a group, they were disproportionately disadvantaged by the employer's holiday policy. The EAT upheld the employment tribunal's decision to dismiss the direct discrimination complaint on the basis that Muslims did not comprise a distinct ethnic group for the purposes of Ss.1(1) and 3(1) RRA. However, it upheld the tribunal's decision that there had been unjustifiable indirect discrimination. The tribunal had correctly concluded that, for the purposes of determining whether the employer's policy had a disproportionate adverse effect, the relevant pool for comparison comprised two distinct racial groups – the group originating from the Indian subcontinent and the remaining workforce, consisting chiefly of Europeans. As the number of people from the Asian group who could comply with the direction to work during Eid was considerably smaller than the proportion of Europeans who could so comply, the employer's requirement constituted indirect discrimination.

It is worth noting that, on the facts of the JH Walker case, the Muslim complainants all happened to be Asian from the Indian sub-continent (i.e. had the same national origins), so it was possible to define the racial group to which they belonged by reference to something other than and in addition to their shared Islamic faith. Had the complainants all been white Muslims, then logic dictates that they would not have had a remedy under the RRA. Similarly, if both the Muslims and the rest of the workforce employed by the employer had belonged to a variety of different ethnic groups, they would again have been left without remedy since it would have been impossible to view the claimants as belonging to a separate ethnic group. Of course, since 2003, employees have had recourse to statutory protection against discrimination on the ground of religion or belief – see Chapter 11, 'Religion or belief'. This protection offers a far more transparent and straightforward basis on which to challenge the kind of discrimination encountered by the Muslim employees in the JH Walker case.

10.32 **Nationality and national origins**
The meanings of 'nationality' and 'national origins' were first judicially considered in London Borough of Ealing v Race Relations Board 1972 AC 342, HL (a case decided under the old Race Relations Act 1968). The House of Lords held that national origins meant something other than (and was not apt to cover) nationality in the legal sense of citizenship. Since the 1968 Act prohibited discrimination on the grounds of colour, race or ethnic or national origin, but not on the ground of nationality, a requirement that an applicant must be 'a British subject' was ruled not to be unlawful. This loophole was later closed when the 1968 Act was repealed and replaced by the RRA 1976, at which point both national origins and nationality were included in the definition

of 'racial grounds' in S.3(1) of that Act. The position remains the same under the EqA, where S.9 includes both nationality and national origins in the definition of 'race'.

Birthplace not determinative of national origins. Even though Parliament **10.33** chose to expand the ambit of race discrimination protection to include nationality in direct response to the Ealing decision (above), that decision continues to impose a restrictive meaning on the words 'national origins'. This is evident from the Court of Appeal's decision in R (Elias) v Secretary of State for Defence 2006 IRLR 934, CA (the 'Elias case'), where it was held that the eligibility criteria of a scheme designed to compensate people who had been interned by the Japanese in World War II were not discriminatory even though the criteria precluded compensation to anyone who was not born in the United Kingdom or had a parent or grandparents born there. The Court of Appeal accepted that, taken at face value, such 'birth-link criteria' appeared to be related to a person's 'national origins' and, on that basis, should be regarded as discriminatory on 'racial grounds' as defined in S.3(1) RRA. However, the Court held that it was unable to reach this conclusion since it was constrained by the Ealing decision (and subsequent cases applying that decision) to decide the contrary. In Ealing, the House of Lords had said that the word 'national' in the context of the term 'national origin' was used in the sense of, or was analogous to, race, lineage or descent. On this basis, their Lordships had specifically concluded that one's place of birth was not necessarily determinative of one's national origins.

Lord Justice Longmore in the Elias case accepted that an important part of one's origins is the place where one is born, and that this would usually determine an individual's national origin. He also thought that just because, in a few cases, a person's birthplace is not the same as his or her place of origin, this was no sound basis for concluding that an explicit birthplace criterion is non-discriminatory. Accordingly, had the matter been free from binding authority, he would have concluded that the application of the criteria in question amounted to direct discrimination under the RRA in that it constituted discrimination on 'racial grounds' – in particular, the ground of national origin. However, the matter was not free of authority in the light of the Ealing case. The upshot was that the Court in the Elias case was driven to the view that the claimant – a British subject who, having been born in Hong Kong, was interned by the Japanese in World War II and on being freed had subsequently lived most of her life in the United Kingdom, but whose parents and grandparents were born outside the United Kingdom – had not been directly discriminated against on the ground of her national origin by being refused a payment under the compensation scheme.

Distinction between 'nationality' and 'national origins'. In Northern Joint **10.34** Police Board v Power 1997 IRLR 610, EAT, the Appeal Tribunal sought to clarify the distinction between 'nationality' and 'national origins'. In that case an English police officer applied for the advertised post of Chief Constable of a Scottish police authority but was not shortlisted for the post. He claimed that he had been discriminated against on racial grounds. An employment tribunal decided that the English and Scots were separate racial groups by reference to their national origins on the basis that Scotland and England are both nations in the popular (i.e. non-legal) sense. This was attributed mainly to the fact that the two countries were separate sovereign nations before the Act of Union in 1707 and that, despite having been absorbed into the United Kingdom, each country had retained a separate status and identity. The police authority appealed on the ground that England and Scotland are both parts of the same nation.

The EAT held that the employment tribunal had correctly decided that the RRA covered discrimination against an English person by a Scot. An English person can be regarded as a member of a 'racial group' as defined by reference to his or her English national origins. In this regard, 'nationality' and 'national origins' have different meanings, since the former referred to a person's citizenship of an existing and recognised state, whereas a person's national origins may be embedded in a nation which no longer exists.

10.35 The historical reasons for 'nationality' and 'national origins' being treated as two distinct racial grounds in S.3(1) RRA and now S.9 EqA have been outlined in the discussion above. The question remains: what (if any) are the practical/ legal implications of the distinction so far as the EqA is concerned? It will be a relatively unusual case where discrimination is alleged to be on the ground of nationality but the facts of the case could not equally support an allegation of discrimination on the ground of national origins. One such case, however, was R (Mohammed) v Secretary of State for Defence 2007 EWCA Civ 1023, CA. This concerned the eligibility criteria relating to special compensation payments for surviving members of British groups who were held captive by the Japanese during World War II. These criteria essentially required claimants to be British, since payments were excluded in respect of nationals from countries such as India and Pakistan, which, under an International Treaty, had already made their own compensation arrangements with Japan. The claimant, a Pakistani national, had served in the British-Indian army during World War II and had been captured by the Japanese. He claimed that the eligibility criteria for compensation were discriminatory on the ground of race or colour. The MoD, on the other hand, while conceding that the criteria were discriminatory, contended that this was on the ground of nationality rather than race or colour, which meant that S.41(2)(a) RRA (now paras 1(1) and (2) of Schedule 23 to the EqA) applied. This provision precluded liability where discrimination was on the basis of a person's nationality and occurs pursuant to a legislative enactment or arrangements made by or with the approval of a Minister of the Crown.

The Court of Appeal upheld a High Court judge's decision that the discrimination in this case was based on nationality and, in so concluding, rejected the claimant's argument that, by favouring Europeans (i.e. 'whites') over non-Europeans, the criteria were effectively tainted by other racially discriminatory grounds. The eligibility criteria, in fact, operated in favour of *British* prisoners of war and were thus discriminatory by reason of 'nationality', not colour or race. As such, the MoD was able to rely upon the S.41(2)(a) exemption to escape liability.

Countries of the United Kingdom. According to the EAT in Northern Joint **10.36** Police Board v Power (above), the proper approach to the question of 'nationality' in the context of England, Scotland, Northern Ireland and Wales is to categorise all of them as falling under the umbrella of 'British' and to regard the population as citizens of the United Kingdom. So far as 'national origins' are concerned, what has to be ascertained are identifiable elements, both historical and geographical, which at least at some point in time reveal the existence of a nation. On this basis, there could be no doubt that the constituent countries of Great Britain were once separate nations and that the peoples of those countries therefore have separate national origins. The EAT accordingly confirmed that the employment tribunal had jurisdiction to entertain a complaint of race discrimination based on English or Scottish national origins.

In BBC Scotland v Souster 2001 IRLR 150, Ct Sess (Inner House), the Court of Session considered the Power case when a similar matter came before it – the case involving an English TV presenter who complained of race discrimination when he was replaced by a Scottish presenter. The Court confirmed the stance taken by the EAT in the earlier case, ruling that the claimant could bring a claim of race discrimination under the 'national origins' umbrella on the basis that he was English. It made clear, however, that the English and the Scottish were not distinct 'ethnic groups', which was the alternative basis on which the claimant had advanced his discrimination complaint.

To complete the picture so far as the constituent parts of the United Kingdom **10.37** and Eire are concerned, an employment tribunal has held that an Irish employee who had been subjected to a constant barrage of Irish jokes had been discriminated against on racial grounds by reference to his national origins – McAuley v Auto Alloys Foundry Ltd and anor ET Case No.62824/93. Given that the whole of Ireland was once a single nation, it was legitimate for an Irish employee to contend that his or her national origins were Irish and to complain of race discrimination on this basis.

It is irrelevant whether or not the employee is a citizen of Eire or Northern Ireland since, as was made clear in Northern Joint Police Board v Power (above) and BBC Scotland v Souster (above), citizenship is not the determining factor so far as national origins are concerned. That factor would be far more germane if the alleged discrimination in question were to be based on the employee's

215

nationality. In this regard, it should be noted that S.78 RRA stipulated that 'nationality includes citizenship'. However, that stipulation has not been carried across to the EqA. But this should not necessarily be interpreted as implying a narrowing of the scope of 'nationality' under the EqA. Given that that Act was primarily aimed at harmonising, and strengthening, the previous law, it is our view that a person's nationality will continue to be defined, inter alia, by his or her citizenship, including any new citizenship that has been acquired since birth – see the discussion immediately below.

10.38 **Changes of nationality and/or citizenship.** Another noteworthy aspect of the Court of Session's decision in BBC Scotland v Souster (above) was its consideration of whether a person's 'nationality' can be changed or adopted. On this point, the Court took a slightly wider view of 'nationality' and 'national origins' than the EAT had done in Northern Joint Police Board v Power (above), accepting that 'nationality' may refer to present nationality and so can encompass a change in an individual's nationality after his or her birth. Furthermore, just as it is possible to adhere to, and thus become a member of, a racial group defined by reference to 'ethnic origins' (as in Mandla and anor v Dowell Lee and ors 1983 ICR 385, HL – see 'Ethnic origins' above), so it is possible to adhere to and thus to become a member of a group defined by reference to 'national origins' – for example, through adoption or marriage. In this context, the perception of others may be important. A person can be discriminated against because he or she is perceived (wrongly) to have become a member of a racial group (e.g. become English). In Souster, the Court said that it would be for the claimant 'to prove that he is English, whether that be because his national origins are English or because he has acquired English nationality or that he is perceived to be English'.

10.39 **Multiple national origins.** In some circumstances, an employee's national origins may derive from different countries – for example, where he or she has an English mother and a Scottish father – in which case that person can be properly regarded as belonging to both racial groups. This is reflected in the wording of S.9(3) and (4) EqA (formerly S.3(1) and (2) RRA). S.9(3) states that 'a reference to a person's racial group is a reference to a racial group into which the person falls'; and S.9(4) goes on to clarify that 'the fact that a racial group comprises two or more distinct racial groups does not prevent it from constituting a particular racial group'. Taken together, these provisions ensure that the English/Scottish employee in the example given above would be able to claim that he or she has been discriminated against as a result of his or her Scottish origins or English origins, as the case may be.

In Orphanos v Queen Mary College 1985 IRLR 349, HL, the House of Lords held that an individual was entitled to place him or herself in a different racial group depending on the circumstances of the claim – e.g. the same person might claim to have been discriminated against as an Indian, as an Asian, or as a non-British person, depending on the circumstances. In that particular case O, a Greek Cypriot, claimed indirect discrimination when he was classed as an overseas student and charged much higher university fees than UK or EC nationals. The Government defined 'home students' as those who had been ordinarily resident in the United Kingdom or European Community (now European Union) for at least three years at the start of the academic year – a requirement that O claimed was much more difficult for people of his national group to comply with than those not of that group. On appeal to the House of Lords, their Lordships held that O belonged to three different national groups – 'Greek Cypriot', 'non-UK' and 'non-EC'. For the particular purposes of his claim the appropriate group was one of the latter two as he was seeking to compare himself with UK or EC students, and it was the fact that he was from outside the EC that resulted in the alleged discrimination. Their Lordships noted that if he had been confined to relying only on membership of the Greek Cypriot national group, then in order to have established indirect discrimination he would have had to make a comparison with the way every other single national group was treated, which was a wholly impracticable option.

Immigration control. Current UK immigration legislation significantly curtails **10.40** the ability of non-EU citizens to obtain employment in this country. In this regard, the Immigration, Asylum and Nationality Act 2006 (IANA 2006) makes it: (i) a civil offence to inadvertently employ a person who is subject to immigration control but who does not have permission to live or work in the United Kingdom, and (ii) a criminal offence to knowingly do so. However, an employer who has made appropriate checks on prospective employees has a defence, at least so far as the civil offence is concerned. One potential danger that employers face when making these immigration checks is that any discrimination based on a person's nationality or national origins will be unlawful under the EqA. Thus, employers must tread a very careful path through what is a legislative minefield. To aid employers, the UK Border Agency has issued a statutory Code of Practice pursuant to S.21 IANA 2006 entitled 'Guidance for Employers on the Avoidance of Unlawful Discrimination in Employment Practice While Seeking to Prevent Illegal Working'. Although a breach of the Code will not render a person liable to civil or criminal proceedings, its provisions must be taken into account by an employment tribunal where relevant – S.23(4) IANA.

As discrimination in these circumstances usually takes place in the context of recruitment, issues relevant to compliance with the IANA 2006 are addressed in more detail in Chapter 24, 'Recruitment', under 'Arrangements for deciding to whom to offer employment – immigration issues'.

Freedom of movement for workers within the EU. Nationality as a ground **10.41** of discrimination is excluded from the scope of the EU Race Equality Directive by virtue of Article 3(2). However, Article 45 of the Treaty on the Functioning

217

of the European Union (TFEU) is concerned to ensure freedom of movement for workers within the EU and does so by outlawing discrimination based on nationality between workers who are citizens of the Member States with regard to employment, remuneration and other conditions of employment. This includes indirect discrimination, which may occur if one Member State imposes conditions on employment or other benefits of employment and these conditions are harder for other EU nationals to comply with than they are for the nationals of that Member State.

In Bossa v Nordstress Ltd and anor 1998 ICR 694, EAT, the Appeal Tribunal held that an Italian national who alleged that he had been refused employment by an employer in Great Britain on account of his nationality was entitled to bring a claim under the RRA despite the fact that the employment in question was 'wholly or mainly outside Great Britain' within the meaning of S.8(1) of that Act. The EAT accepted that the provisions in the RRA that excluded claims in respect of employment outside Great Britain were deficient and failed to give supremacy to 'freedom of movement' requirements in the Treaty of Rome (the precursor of the TFEU). Accordingly, it was the duty of the employment tribunal to override any provisions of the RRA that were in conflict with the Treaty provisions. Although it was not spelled out in the ruling, it would also appear that the discriminatory act complained of must amount to discrimination on the ground of nationality. The EAT's decision means that if, for example, a French national living in France were to apply for a job advertised in a London newspaper and not be shortlisted on the ground of nationality – with the decision being made in Great Britain – the applicant would be entitled to bring a race discrimination claim even though he or she had never been in Great Britain and the job was to take place entirely in France.

10.42   (Note that the restriction on the territorial scope of the RRA contained in S.8 of that Act was not replicated in the EqA, which is entirely silent as to its territorial scope. This has left it up to the tribunals and courts to determine who has a sufficient connection to the United Kingdom to be entitled to bring a discrimination claim under the EqA. We consider the Act's territorial scope in Chapter 34, 'Enforcing individual rights', under 'Jurisdiction of tribunals – territorial jurisdiction'. See also IDS Employment Law Handbook, 'Employment Tribunal Practice and Procedure' (2006), Chapter 1, 'Tribunals' jurisdiction', under 'Limits to tribunals' jurisdiction – territorial jurisdiction'.)

A more detailed analysis of the interplay between race discrimination and the right to freedom of movement falls outside the scope of this Handbook. Suffice it to say that there have been few cases on the scope of Article 45 TFEU (or its predecessor, Article 39 of the Treaty of Rome). It was, however, established by the EAT in Birchall v Secretary of State for Education and anor EAT 605/95 that 'freedom of movement' protection is not concerned to ensure that a Member State treats its own nationals just as favourably as other Member

States treat theirs, but rather that each Member State does not discriminate between its own nationals and those of other EU Member States. And in R v Immigration Appeal Tribunal and Surinder Singh ex parte Secretary of State for Home Department 1992 3 All ER 798, ECJ (an immigration case), the European Court of Justice ruled that the denial of a right or benefit is only objectionable under what is now Article 45 if it is an impediment to the right of free movement. Accordingly, there must be a causal connection or nexus between the denial of a right or benefit and the exercise of the right of free movement.

11 Religion or belief

Protection against discrimination on the ground of religion or belief was first **11.1** introduced into Great Britain by the Employment Equality (Religion or Belief) Regulations 2003 SI 2003/1660 ('the 2003 Religion or Belief Regulations'). Prior to this, only Northern Ireland had any statutory protection against religious discrimination, in the form of the Fair Employment and Treatment (Northern Ireland) Order 1998 SI 1998/3162. This Order continues to govern the law relating to workplace discrimination on the grounds of religion and political opinion in the Province.

The 2003 Religion or Belief Regulations, which came into force on 2 December 2003, were introduced to implement the religious discrimination aspects of the EU Equal Treatment Framework Directive (No.2000/78). Under the Regulations, direct and indirect discrimination, harassment and victimisation were prohibited in an employment context where the discrimination was on the ground of religion or belief. As originally enacted, Reg 2(1) simply defined 'religion or belief' as 'any religion, religious belief, or similar philosophical belief'. However, it was subsequently amended by the Equality Act 2006 (with effect from 30 April 2007) to provide that: '(a) "religion" means any religion, (b) "belief" means any religious or philosophical belief, (c) a reference to religion includes a reference to lack of religion, and (d) a reference to a belief includes a reference to lack of belief'. The significance of these changes were two-fold: first, the requirement that, to gain protection, a 'belief' had to comprise a 'similar philosophical belief' – i.e. similar to a religious belief – was dropped, the definition of belief becoming simply 'any religious or philosophical belief'; and secondly, it was made clear that protection under the Regulations would be accorded equally to those of no religion or lacking a belief.

On 1 October 2010 the 2003 Regulations were repealed and replaced by **11.2** equivalent provisions in the Equality Act 2010 (EqA). S.10 of that Act defines the protected characteristic of religion or belief in virtually identical terms to the amended version of Reg 2(1). This means that the case law on what constitutes a 'religion or belief' decided under the antecedent legislation remains relevant under the 2010 Act – see further 'Protection under the Equality Act' below.

221

Given the lack of any detailed definition of 'religion', 'religious belief' or 'philosophical belief' in the legislation, it has been left to the national courts and tribunals to determine their exact scope. One significant influence in this regard has been the jurisprudence developed in the context of Article 9 of the European Convention for the Protection of Human Rights and Fundamental Freedoms (commonly known as the European Convention on Human Rights), which protects the fundamental right to 'freedom of thought, conscience and religion'. As explained below, UK courts and tribunals are expected to pay heed to Article 9, and the case law decided under it, when determining cases under national law, as there is a direct correlation between the concepts underlying the right guaranteed by that Article and the protection against religion or belief discrimination provided for under the EqA.

11.3 European Convention on Human Rights

The protected characteristic of religion or belief, as set out in S.10 EqA, gives expression to the mandatory requirement in the EU Equal Treatment Framework Directive for Member States to provide protection in national law to combat discrimination on the ground of, inter alia, religion or belief. The Recitals to the Directive assert that the European Union 'respects fundamental human rights, as guaranteed by the European Convention for the Protection of Human Rights and Fundamental Freedoms' (ECHR) and state that 'the right of all persons to equality before the law and protection against discrimination constitutes a universal right recognised by the [ECHR], to which all Member States are signatories'. This, in effect, provides a 'read across' between the EU Directive – which does not itself contain any definition of 'religion or belief' – and the ECHR, in particular Article 9, as it is clear that the Framework Directive needs to be interpreted consistently with relevant provisions of the ECHR. In turn, the UK's domestic legislative provisions must be interpreted so far as possible consistently with both the mandatory provisions of EU law – see Marleasing SA v La Comercial Internacional de Alimentación SA, 1992 1 CMLR 305, ECJ – and, by virtue of S.3 of the Human Rights Act 1998, European Convention rights. Accordingly, the jurisprudence of the European Court of Human Rights (ECtHR) on the scope and meaning of Article 9 provides an important framework for establishing what is meant by 'religion' and 'belief' for the purposes of the EqA.

The significance of Article 9 is reflected in the Explanatory Notes accompanying the EqA, which specifically refer to that Article when giving guidance as to the meaning and scope of the protected characteristic of religion or belief. Para 51 of the Notes states: 'This section [S.10] defines the protected characteristic of religion or religious or philosophical belief, which is stated to include for this purpose a lack of religion or belief. It is a broad definition in line with the freedom of thought, conscience and religion guaranteed by Article 9 of the

[ECHR].' Similarly, the Equality and Human Rights Commission's Code of Practice on Employment (the EHRC Employment Code) references Article 9 when providing guidance on S.10 EqA – see paras 2.51 and 2.60. Both the Explanatory Notes and the Code briefly consider the case law developed by the ECtHR when seeking to identify the factors that might be relied upon to demonstrate that a person subscribing to a particular system of belief would be protected under the EqA.

Scope of Article 9   11.4
Article 9(1) of the ECHR provides that:

> 'Everyone has the right to freedom of thought, conscience and religion; this right includes freedom to change his religion or belief and freedom, either alone or in community with others and in public or private, to manifest his religion or belief, in worship, teaching, practice and observance.'

Article 9(2), however, inserts a proviso in respect of the right to manifest the freedoms enshrined in Article 9(1). This provides that: 'Freedom to manifest one's religion or beliefs shall be subject only to such limitation as are prescribed by law and are necessary in a democratic society in the interests of public safety, for the protection of public order, health or morals, or for the protection of the rights and freedoms of others.'

In addition to Article 9, there are two other provisions in the Convention that 11.5 impact upon a person's freedom of thought, conscience and religion. These are Article 2 of Protocol No.1 – which, in guaranteeing a general right to education, stipulates that the 'State shall respect the right of parents to ensure education and teaching in conformity with their own religious and philosophical convictions'; and Article 14, which requires that the enjoyment of the rights and freedoms guaranteed under the Convention 'shall be secured without discrimination on any ground such as... religion'.

'**Religion**'. Outside the human rights context, the meaning of 'religion' has 11.6 been tackled by courts dealing with diverse matters such as whether a charity's objects were for the advancement of religion – see In re South Place Ethical Society 1980 1 WLR 1565, ChD – or whether a conscientious objector in the USA was entitled to exemption from conscription on the ground of religion – see United States v Seeger (1965) 380 US 163, US Supreme Ct. However, in the context of Article 9, the ECtHR has not sought to provide any absolute definition of 'religion', probably because the ambit of the rights guaranteed under that Article is far wider than even the most expansive definition of 'religion' could be. Article 9(1) protects not just an individual's religious beliefs but freedom of thought and conscience. This has enabled the Court to hold, for example, that pacifism (whether based on religious precepts or on ethical convictions such as humanism) falls within the scope of Article 9 – see Arrowsmith v United Kingdom 1980 3 EHRR 218, ECtHR.

223

Clearly, the principal world religions such as Buddhism, Christianity, Hinduism, Islam and Judaism will readily be accepted as belief systems falling within the scope of Article 9, as will minority variants of such faiths. Less mainstream 'religions' such as Druidism probably also qualify (in Chappell v United Kingdom 1989 EHRR CD543, ECtHR, the European Commission of Human Rights assumed that this was the case). More recent religious movements such as Jehovah's Witnesses (Kokkinakis v Greece 1994 17 EHRR 397, ECtHR), Scientology (Church of Scientology and anor v Sweden 1979 ECC 511, ECtHR), and even the Divine Light Zentrum (Omkarananda and the Divine Light Zentrum v United Kingdom 1981 DR 25, ECtHR), have all been held to qualify for protection under Article 9, even though in few, if any, of these cases has actual interference in a claimant's Convention rights been found to have occurred.

11.7 **'Beliefs/convictions'.** A person's beliefs – whether religious or otherwise – are also protected under Article 9. This is clear not only from the fact that the Article guarantees freedom of thought and conscience in addition to religion, but also from the express references to the right to 'manifest religion or belief'. However, not every belief qualifies for protection. In Campbell and anor v United Kingdom 1982 4 EHRR 293, ECtHR, the European Court of Human Rights established that, to come within the scope of the Article, a person's belief must:

- be worthy of respect in a democratic society

- concern a weighty and substantial aspect of human life and behaviour, and

- attain a certain level of cogency, seriousness, cohesion and importance.

11.8 The Campbell case was, in fact, mainly concerned with Article 2 of Protocol 1 to the ECHR, which 'guarantees the right of parents to ensure education and teaching in conformity with their own religious or philosophical convictions'. Interpreting the term 'philosophical convictions' in this context, the ECtHR held that this 'is not synonymous with the words "opinions" and "ideas", such as are utilised in Article 10 of the Convention guaranteeing freedom of expression; it is more akin to the term "beliefs" (in the French text: "*convictions*") appearing in Article 9'.

Applying the guidance outlined above, the ECtHR has accepted that value-systems such as pacifism (Arrowsmith v United Kingdom (above)), atheism (Angelini v Sweden (App. No.10491/83), ECtHR) and veganism (W v United Kingdom (App. No.18187/91) ECtHR) are encompassed by Article 9, as are political ideologies such as communism (Hazar and ors v Turkey 1990 72 DR 200, ECtHR). Non-belief is covered in the same way as positive belief. This was made clear by the ECtHR in Kokkinakis v Greece (above) when it said: 'As enshrined in Article 9, freedom of thought, conscience and religion is one of the foundations of a "democratic society" within the meaning of the Convention.

It is, in its religious dimension, one of the most vital elements that go to make up the identity of believers and their conception of life, but *it is also a precious asset for atheists, agnostics, sceptics and the unconcerned*' (our stress).

However, a mere 'consciousness' of belonging to a minority group and the public expression of such does not qualify for protection. In Sidiropoulos and ors v Greece 1999 27 EHRR 633, ECtHR, the Court suggested that if such consciousness or expression engaged any rights under the Convention at all, it would be in the sphere of the right to freedom of expression under Article 10 and/or the right to freedom of assembly under Article 11. Similarly, Article 9 does not protect a belief in the right to euthanasia or assisted suicide – see Pretty v United Kingdom 2002 35 EHRR 1, ECtHR. In that case, which was brought by a woman dying of an incurable degenerative disease, the ECtHR observed: 'The Court does not doubt the firmness of the applicant's views concerning assisted suicide but would observe that not all opinions or convictions constitute beliefs in the sense protected by Article 9(1) of the Convention. Her claims do not involve a form of manifestation of a religion or belief, through worship, teaching, practice or observance as described in the second sentence of the first paragraph. As found by the Commission, the term "practice" as employed in Article 9(1) does not cover each act which is motivated or influenced by a religion or belief.' The Court was, however, prepared to accept that the applicant's views – inasmuch as they concerned personal autonomy – engaged Article 8, which guarantees the right to respect for private and family life. **11.9**

Decisions of the UK courts have also helped shed light on the meaning and scope of Article 9, thereby offering insight into how 'religion or belief' is to be interpreted for the purposes of S.10 EqA. The most important of these is the House of Lords' decision in R (Williamson and ors) v Secretary of State for Education and Employment 2005 2 AC 246, HL. That case concerned a judicial review brought by teachers and parents of children at independent schools established to provide a Christian education in respect of a statutory ban on the use of corporal punishment. The claimants alleged that the ban was incompatible with their Convention rights, and in particular Articles 9 and 2 of the First Protocol. They contended that it was part of their fundamental Christian beliefs that such discipline should be administered, when appropriate, as an integral part of the teaching and education of children. In rejecting the application for judicial review, the House of Lords unanimously concluded that the interference in the claimants' freedom of religious or other belief – which was otherwise protected under Article 9 – was justified under Article 9(2). The ban on corporal punishment was necessary in a democratic society for the protection of the rights and freedoms of others (namely, children); it pursued the legitimate aim of promoting the welfare of children by protecting them from the deliberate infliction of physical violence that might have harmful

225

effects on them; and the means chosen to achieve that aim were appropriate and not disproportionate in their adverse impact on parents who believed in corporal punishment in schools.

11.10 In the course of his speech, Lord Nicholls emphasised the broad reach of Article 9(1) by observing that it protects 'the subjective belief of an individual... [R]eligious belief is intensely personal and can easily vary from one individual to another. Each individual is at liberty to hold his own religious beliefs, however irrational or inconsistent they may seem to some, however surprising.' His Lordship noted that in Metropolitan Church of Bessarabia v Moldova 2002 35 EHRR 13, ECtHR, the ECtHR had 'rightly noted that "in principle, the right to freedom of religion as understood in the Convention rules out any appreciation by the State of the legitimacy of religious beliefs or of the manner in which these are expressed"'. But drawing on the Convention case law, Lord Nicholls set out some basic criteria that any belief – religious or otherwise – must satisfy to be protected under Article 9. The belief must:

- be consistent with basic standards of human dignity or integrity

- relate to matters more than merely trivial

- possess an adequate degree of seriousness and importance, and be concerned with a fundamental problem

- be coherent in the sense of being intelligible and capable of being understood.

11.11 However, his Lordship warned against setting the bar too high when assessing whether a belief satisfies these criteria. Overall, they were not to be set at a level that would deprive minority beliefs of the protection they are intended to have under the ECHR.

While the Williamson case was clearly not decided under the EqA or the 2003 Religion or Belief Regulations, its relevance lies in the fact that it considers and distils the guidance to be found in the case law on the scope of Article 9 and – even more importantly – maps out an approach that broadly translates to the protection of 'religion or belief' discrimination under the 2003 Religion or Belief Regulations and the EqA. As we shall see, courts and tribunals have adopted a similar 'inclusive' stance to the one sanctioned by the House of Lords when determining what constitutes 'a religious or philosophical belief', while also applying the similar 'threshold requirements' (to use Lord Walker's phrase for Lord Nicholls' criteria) to weed out beliefs that lack seriousness, coherence and importance, or are incompatible with human dignity.

11.12 **Right to manifest religion or belief.** It is important to note that the right to 'freedom of thought, conscience and religion' in Article 9 is expressed to include a freedom to *manifest* religion or belief. In Kokkinakis v Greece 1994 17 EHRR 397, ECtHR, the Court took the view that the right to adhere to a religion and hold religious beliefs embraces the freedom to bear witness in words and deeds. And in Kalac v Turkey 1999 27 EHRR 552, ECtHR, the Court made it clear that, 'while religious freedom is primarily a matter of individual conscience, it also implies, inter alia, freedom to manifest one's religion not only in community with others, in public and within the circle of those whose faith one shares but also alone and in private'. Article 9(1) spells out the forms that manifestation of one's religion or belief may take – i.e. worship, teaching, practice and observance. But, crucially, the Court in the Kalac case concluded that Article 9 does *not* protect every act motivated or inspired by a religion or belief. Moreover, in exercising freedom to manifest one's religion, an individual may need to take his or her specific situation into account. The restrictions are particularly relevant in an employment context. For a more detailed discussion, see under 'Manifestation of religion or belief' below.

Limitations on scope of Article 9   11.13
In R (Williamson and ors) v Secretary of State for Education and Employment 2005 2 AC 246, HL (discussed under 'Scope of Article 9 – "beliefs/convictions"' above), the House of Lords observed that, when interpreting Article 9, it was necessary to apply some limitation on the broad range of religions and beliefs that fall within the scope of that Article. Otherwise, the operation of the relevant rights would become unmanageable and unpredictable. In Lord Walker's view, two 'filters' applied to ensure that not all beliefs secure protection under the ECHR. The first was to be found in the notion of 'manifestation' of religion or belief. This was particularly relevant to those who held religious beliefs as most religions require or encourage communal acts of worship, preaching, public professions of faith, and practices and observances of various sorts (including habits of dress and diet). His Lordship held that, to come within the protection of Article 9(1), any manifestation of a religious belief had to satisfy 'the implicit (and not over-demanding) threshold requirements of seriousness, coherence and consistency with human dignity'. Lord Walker's second 'filter' was found in the provisions of Article 9(2). These serve to qualify an individual's freedom to manifest his or her religion or beliefs by providing that interference with that right can be justified if the restrictions imposed are prescribed by law and are necessary in a democratic society in the interests, inter alia, of the protection of the rights and freedoms of others.

As we shall see, similar 'filters' operate in cases concerned with workplace religion or belief discrimination. Notwithstanding that the concepts of religion and belief are widely drawn for the purposes of acquiring the protected characteristic of religion or belief, this does not mean that everyone who shows that they subscribe to a protected religion or belief will successfully make out a case of discrimination. The cases demonstrate that the freedom to manifest one's religious or philosophical beliefs at work is considerably more limited than the basic freedom to hold such beliefs – see under 'Manifestation of religion or belief' below. A further filter is applied by requiring complainants

227

who bring direct discrimination complaints under the EqA to prove that the reason for any less favourable treatment was actually the protected characteristics in question. And in the context of indirect discrimination claims, the filter takes the form of a justification defence analogous to that in Article 9(2). Thus, even if an employee can show that a provision, criterion or practice (PCP) is applied which disproportionately affects persons sharing the same protected characteristic, it is open to the employer to show that the discriminatory effect of the PCP is justifiable as a 'proportionate means of achieving a legitimate aim'.

11.14 Protection under the Equality Act

Section 10 EqA defines the protected characteristic of religion or belief in very similar terms to those used in Reg 2(1) of the 2003 Religion or Belief Regulations. Under S.10(1) EqA 'religion' means 'any religion and a reference to religion includes a reference to a lack of religion'. And 'belief' is defined as 'any religious or philosophical belief and a reference to belief includes a reference to a lack of belief' – S.10(2). Any reference in the Act to a person who has the protected characteristic of religion or belief 'is a reference to a person of a particular religion or belief', while a reference to 'persons who share that characteristic' is a reference to persons of the same religion or belief – S.10(3).

It is apparent that the relevant definitions are fairly minimalist, and certainly fall a long way short of providing a prescriptive list of the religions or beliefs that qualify for protection. As a result, it has been left to the courts and tribunals to determine on a case-by-case basis which religions, religious beliefs and philosophical beliefs qualify for protection. The cases interpreting these concepts were decided under the 2003 Religion or Belief Regulations but they remain relevant to the EqA, since the definitions – though worded slightly differently – remain identical for all practical purposes.

11.15 Meaning of 'religion'
In R (Williamson and ors) v Secretary of State for Education and Employment 2005 2 AC 246, HL, Lord Walker doubted whether, in the context of Article 9, it was necessary or useful to reach a precise definition of 'religion'. He noted that the trend of authority was towards a more expansive reading of religion than traditionally applied. As we have seen, many belief-systems outside the established world religions have been held to fall within the protection guaranteed by Article 9 – see 'European Convention on Human Rights – scope of Article 9' above. And since the EqA must, so far as possible, be interpreted harmoniously with the rights enshrined in the Convention, it would probably be a mistake to apply too theistic an emphasis when approaching the question of what constitutes a 'religion' for the purposes of S.10 EqA.

The Acas Guide on 'Religion or Belief and the Workplace' (2010) anticipates that employment tribunals will generally have little difficulty determining whether a belief system constitutes a religion. In rare cases where the matter is disputed, the Guide suggests that tribunals are likely to consider factors such as collective worship, a clear belief system, and whether there is evidence of a profound belief affecting way of life or view of the world. The Guide points out that protection extends beyond the more well-known religions and faiths to include non-mainstream beliefs such as paganism and humanism. An appendix to the Guide provides a useful potted account of the practices and festivals associated with ten of the most commonly practised religions and faiths in Great Britain. These are: Baha'i, Buddhism, Christianity, Hinduism, Islam, Jainism, Judaism, Rastafarianism, Sikhism and Zoroastrianism. Even in the absence of confirmatory case law, it is certain that all of these would be regarded as a 'religion' for the purposes of S.10 EqA – a point confirmed by the EHRC Employment Code (see para 2.53 of the Code).

During the third reading of the Equality Bill, the House of Lords debated **11.16** whether cults should be excluded from the scope of religion or belief protection after the Conservative Party sought to insert an amendment to that effect. However, the proposal was rejected, in part because of the difficulty in defining a cult and the absence of any consensus of opinion as to what constitutes one. In this context, Baroness Thornton stated (on behalf of the then Labour Government): 'It is not our intention that the religion or belief provisions of the [Act] should extend protection against discrimination to any inappropriate groups whose activities would give cause for concern.' In reality, a court or employment tribunal faced with having to decide such a matter would be likely to rule that any religion or belief which specifically attracts adherents who are a threat to society or whose tenets focus on unlawful conduct would not qualify for protection under the EqA. Since such a religion or belief would not be worthy of respect in a democratic society, it would not satisfy the basic requirement for protection under Article 9 as interpreted in Campbell and anor v United Kingdom 1982 4 EHRR 293, ECtHR – see further under 'European Convention on Human Rights – scope of Article 9' above.

What is a 'belief'? 11.17

The protected characteristic as defined in S.10 EqA embraces not only religion but also belief. In determining the meaning of 'belief' in the 2003 Religion or Belief Regulations, the tribunal in Williams v South Central Ltd ET Case No.2306989/03 noted a dictionary definition of belief as 'persuasion of the truth of anything or opinion or doctrine or recognition of an awakened sense of a higher being, controlling power or powers and the morality connected therewith, rights of worship or any system of such belief or worship'. In that case, the claimant alleged that he was constantly abused at work because he wore an American flag patch on his uniform and that he was sacked because he had stood up for his belief as an American citizen. He maintained that his loyalty to his national flag amounted to a religious belief as defined in the Regulations. The tribunal rejected his claim on the basis that loyalty to one's national flag or to one's native country could not possibly fit in with the definition of 'belief' contained in the 2003 Religion or Belief Regulations.

Although only a first instance decision, the Williams case has been relied upon as guidance in subsequent cases. For example, in Sethi v Accord Operations Ltd ET Case No.3201823/06 the claimant alleged among other things that he was harassed on the ground of religion for refusing to accept his line manager's belief in hypnotism. He claimed that his religion was 'anti-hypnotism', a position closely aligned to the Hindu faith, although he did not actually describe himself as a Hindu. The tribunal rejected the claim. The claimant's belief in 'anti-hypnotism', as he described it, did not satisfy any definition of religion or religious or philosophical belief, and certainly did not meet with the relevant definitions set out by the tribunal in Williams or in the Acas Guide on 'Religion or Belief and the Workplace' (2010).

11.18 However, a note of caution needs to be sounded about these two cases as they were decided under the unamended version of Reg 2(1) of the 2003 Religion or Belief Regulations, when the protection against discrimination applied to religion and to 'religious belief or *similar philosophical belief*'. Following amendments introduced by the Equality Act 2006 the word 'similar' was dropped, with the consequence that 'philosophical beliefs' became protected irrespective of whether they had any similarity to religious beliefs. Thus, in so far as the dictionary definition of 'belief' cited by the tribunal in Williams incorporates a theistic slant, that definition may no longer fully encompass the range of beliefs now covered by S.10. But this is not to say that each and every belief will secure protection, since certain basic criteria still have to be met – as to which see under 'Philosophical belief' below. It may be, therefore, that the kind of patriotic fervour exhibited by the claimant in the Williams case, or the belief in 'anti-hypnotism' held by the claimant in the Sethi case, would still not qualify for protection under the EqA.

11.19 **Difference between 'religion' and 'religious belief'?** Under Reg 2(1) of the 2003 Religion or Belief Regulations (as amended), a person was protected both on the ground of his or her religion and on the grounds of his or her religious beliefs. The same is true of S.10 EqA, which defines the protected characteristic in terms of 'a person of a particular religion or belief' (S.10(3)(a)), with 'belief' being defined for this purpose as 'any religious or philosophical belief' (S.10(2)). The EHRC Employment Code suggests that the notion of religious belief 'goes beyond beliefs about and adherence to a religion or its central articles of faith and may vary from person to person within the same religion' (para 2.56 of the Code). On this basis, one of the more obvious examples of where discrimination might be related to religious belief as opposed to religion would be in the context of workplace tensions between members of the same faith where an individual alleges that he or she has been treated less favourably on the grounds of his or her particular beliefs within that religion. An example would be an inter-denominational dispute between Sunni and Shia Muslims or between Catholics and Protestants.

It would seem that, in interpreting 'religious belief', tribunals will not normally seek to distinguish between beliefs that are mandatory as part of a religion and those that are based upon or derived from cultural practices and tradition within a particular religious creed. In Hussain v Bhullar Bros t/a BB Supersave ET Case No.1806638/04 the key question was whether attendance at home following bereavement was actually part of the Muslim faith – i.e. a religion-based practice or belief. The facts were that immediately after his grandmother's death, the claimant (a Muslim) wanted to take a few days off work to be at home in order to fulfil his duties, in his father's absence, as the eldest son. These involved meeting male relatives and friends attending to pay their respects. His employer, however, was unable to arrange the necessary cover and required the claimant to come to work for at least part of the following day. He subsequently brought a religious discrimination claim under the 2003 Religion or Belief Regulations on the basis that he was not allowed to take time off in the mourning period following his grandmother's death. Applying a wide and liberal meaning to 'religion' and 'religious belief', the tribunal held that if a person genuinely believes that his or her faith requires a certain course of action, then that is sufficient to make it part of his or her religion. In its view, attempting to differentiate between cultural manifestation, traditions and religious observance would lead 'to unnecessary complications and endless debate'. Accordingly, attendance at home for bereavement purposes formed part of H's religion or religious belief. However, on the facts of the particular case, his claim of direct discrimination failed because he was unable to prove that his employer would have treated non-Muslims in the same situation any differently.

'Philosophical belief'   11.20

As previously mentioned, when the 2003 Religion or Belief Regulations first came into force, they prohibited discriminatory treatment in the workplace on the ground of 'any religion, religious belief, or *similar philosophical belief*' (our stress). This definition clearly limited the kinds of views and opinions for which an employee or worker could claim protection, the word 'similar' protecting only those beliefs that could be equated with beliefs based upon a religious creed. However, as the EU Equal Treatment Framework Directive (No.2000/78) refers to prohibiting discrimination based simply on 'religion or belief', there was concern that UK law was not fully compliant in that the inclusion of the word 'similar' implied a narrower approach. In consequence, Reg 2(1) was replaced in 2007 with a new version that dropped the word

231

'similar', thereby widening the reach of the Regulations to cover any philosophical belief without limitation or qualification. Substantially the same definition has been maintained in S.10(2) EqA.

The significance of the removal of the word 'similar' can be demonstrated by the different outcomes of two tribunal claims brought at different times by a claimant who was a vegan and an active member of the League Against Cruel Sports. He maintained that his belief in animal rights constituted a protected philosophical belief. His first claim was brought in 2006 under the original version of Reg 2(1), while his second (against a different employer) was brought in 2009 under the amended version. In respect of the 2006 claim – Hashman v Shaftesbury Town Council ET Case No.3102953/06 – a tribunal held that H's claim of religion or belief discrimination could not get off the ground because his belief – even if it was a philosophical one – was not 'similar' to a religious belief as then required by the 2003 Religion or Belief Regulations. However, in respect of the second claim – Hashman v Milton Park (Dorset) Ltd ET Case No.3105555/09 – an employment judge accepted that, as the Regulations no longer required a philosophical belief to be analogous to a religious belief, the claimant's belief in animal welfare and the immorality of blood sports did qualify for protection: his particular belief acted as a guiding moral principle of his entire life and it exhibited sufficient cogency, seriousness, cohesiveness and importance to qualify as a philosophical belief.

11.21 In the subsequent case of Grainger plc and ors v Nicholson 2010 ICR 360, EAT, the Appeal Tribunal provided important guidance of general application on the meaning and ambit of 'philosophical belief'. It held that an employee's belief that mankind is heading towards catastrophic climate change, and that human beings all come under a moral duty to lead a life that could help to mitigate or avoid this catastrophe, was capable of constituting a 'philosophical belief' under the 2003 Religion or Belief Regulations (as amended). In so holding, Mr Justice Burton (presiding) expressed the view that there is nothing in the make up of a philosophical belief that would disqualify beliefs based on political philosophies. Nor is there any reason to disqualify from the statutory protection a philosophical belief based on science, as opposed to religion. While it was necessary for the belief to have a similar status or cogency to a religious belief, it does not need to constitute or allude to a fully fledged system of thought.

In the course of the EAT's judgment, Burton J drew heavily on case law decided under Article 9 ECHR (discussed in detail under 'European Convention on Human Rights – scope of Article 9' above) and distilled from this the basic criteria that must be met in order for a belief to be protected under what is now S.10 EqA. As he himself recognised, there had to be some limitations: he quoted with approval the observation of a legal commentator that 'no system could countenance the right of anyone to believe anything and to be able to act accordingly'. Thus a belief can only qualify for protection if it:

- is genuinely held

- is not simply an opinion or viewpoint based on the present state of information available

- concerns a weighty and substantial aspect of human life and behaviour

- attains a certain level of cogency, seriousness, cohesion and importance, and

- is worthy of respect in a democratic society, is not incompatible with human dignity and is not in conflict with the fundamental rights of others.

These criteria have now been replicated in para 2.59 of the EHRC Employment Code as official guidance on what comprises a 'religious or philosophical' belief for the purposes of the protected characteristic of religion or belief. **11.22**

Although somewhat abstract, the criteria set out in Grainger have served to exclude extreme or 'crackpot' claims. It is fairly easy to think of examples of beliefs or convictions that would fail to meet the criteria. The Explanatory Notes to the EqA cite a passionate football fan's belief in his football club as an example of a 'belief' that would not be protected. And during the Parliamentary debates on the 2003 Religion or Belief Regulations a Government spokesperson cited a belief in the supreme nature of Jedi knights (characters from the well-known *Star Wars* films) as one that would not qualify for protection. But more informative are actual examples of where beliefs have been judged by employment tribunals to lack sufficient 'cogency, seriousness, cohesiveness and importance', or to be insufficiently concerned with a weighty and substantial aspect of human life and behaviour. Two examples:

- **Hannay v Professional Language Solutions Ltd** ET Case No.2203682/07: H applied for a job in the Middle East as a foreign language teacher but was turned down. He blamed this on, among other things, his religion or philosophical belief, which he described as a personal aspiration to be polite and civil to other people at all times and not to be forceful unless it became necessary. The employment tribunal struck out the claim, holding that H's personal aspirations did not qualify as a philosophical belief within the meaning of the 2003 Religion or Belief Regulations because they were not organised or written about in any way. Furthermore, they were not recognised by any particular group or philosophical movement

- **Farrell v South Yorkshire Police Authority** ET Case No.2803805/10: F was employed as a principal intelligence analyst by a Police Authority. He claimed he was discriminated against on the ground of his religion or belief when he was sacked following a report he presented on a strategic risk assessment. In the report he dismissed well-recognised crime analyses and counter-crime strategies as irrelevant and instead focused on what he saw as the truth about 7/7 and 9/11 – that they were 'false flag' operations, authorised by the US and British governments to gain support for foreign wars and to establish a

233

New World Order. All other threats, he said, paled into insignificance when compared to corruption in high places. An employment tribunal dismissed F's claim on the basis that his views, linked to his theological views about the 'end time', and his belief that this new world order was satanic, did not amount to protected beliefs. F's beliefs failed to meet even the bare minimum standards of cogency and cohesiveness required by case law.

11.23 In contrast, a belief in spiritualism held by an adherent of the Spiritualist Church was found to be protected under the 2003 Religion or Belief Regulations – Power v Greater Manchester Police Authority (No.1) EAT 0434/09. In that case, the EAT upheld the tribunal's decision that an employee's beliefs that there is life after death and that the dead can be contacted through mediums were worthy of respect in a democratic society and had sufficient cogency, seriousness, cohesion and importance. In so holding, His Honour Judge Peter Clark expressly referred to and endorsed the reasoning of Burton J in Grainger plc and ors v Nicholson (above).

An employment tribunal reached a similar conclusion in Maistry v BBC ET Case No.1313142/10 when deciding that a journalist could proceed with his claim for religion or belief discrimination against the BBC on the basis of his belief that 'public service broadcasting has the higher purpose of promoting cultural interchange and social cohesion'. In support of his claim, the claimant referred to the work of academics and statements of senior BBC executives, including those of the Director General, who, in a public debate on the purpose of public service broadcasting, asserted that it provides a 'public space' which everyone is free to enter and within which they can encounter culture, education and debate. According to the tribunal, the concept of public space as a venue for cultural dialogue and the possibility of enhanced citizenship had been imbued with cogency, seriousness, cohesion and importance by philosophers such as Jürgen Habermas and John Dewey. The tribunal's decision was also influenced by evidence about how the claimant's experience as a journalist and trade unionist in South Africa during the apartheid era had shaped his belief that committed and concerned journalism is essential to democracy.

11.24 The interpretation of 'philosophical belief' applied by Burton J in Grainger plc and ors v Nicholson (above) (and applied in subsequent cases) might be regarded as fairly liberal. It is certainly true that the decision has been criticised in some quarters as likely to open the floodgates to all sorts of beliefs being deemed worthy of statutory protection. Although a belief must meet the modest criteria spelled out in that case, Burton J accepted that a philosophical belief does not need to constitute or allude to a fully-fledged system of thought or be shared by others; and it can relate to a 'one-off' or single issue that does not necessarily govern the entirety of the believer's life. He also stated that there is no basis for excluding science-based philosophical beliefs or beliefs that form

234

part of a political philosophy (while ruling out mere adherence to a political party) – see 'Political beliefs' and 'Scientific/evidence-based beliefs' below.

In reality, however, the floodgates have remained closed and tribunals are not awash with religion or belief claims. Recent statistics reveal that, of the 880 discrimination claims presented during the year March 2010 to March 2011, religion or belief claims ranked second lowest (after sexual orientation claims) in terms of the number of cases brought. It is also worth noting that all that the EAT decided in Grainger was that the employee's asserted belief was *capable* of constituting a philosophical belief. The case was remitted to the employment tribunal to determine, first, whether the employee did have the philosophical belief in question, and, secondly, whether the employer had treated him less favourably because of that belief.

Analogy with religious beliefs. Rather enigmatically, Burton J in Grainger plc **11.25** and ors v Nicholson (above) observed: 'I am satisfied that, notwithstanding the amendment to remove "similar", it is necessary, in order for the belief to be protected, for it to have a similar status or cogency to a religious belief.' Clearly, the judge was not seeking to re-import the specific requirement in the original version of the 2003 Religion or Belief Regulations that a philosophical belief be 'similar' to a religious belief, since he specifically acknowledged that that requirement no longer applied. So what did he have in mind?

We take the view that Burton J's observation does little more than sum up the general quality of non-religious beliefs that satisfy the criteria necessary to comprise a 'philosophical belief'. Something of the same sweep that religious beliefs typically possess is implied by the adjective 'philosophical': philosophical thought tends to contain consistent internal logic and structure (i.e. cogency) and provide guiding principles for behaviour (i.e. status). On that basis, Burton J accepted at various points in his judgment that pacifism, Darwinism and Marxism, for example, would be likely to comprise a 'philosophical belief', while at the same time approving the intimation in an earlier decision – McClintock v Department of Constitutional Affairs 2008 IRLR 29, EAT – that a fact-based opinion or viewpoint centred simply on the present state of information available would not.

Objectionable beliefs. In Grainger plc and ors v Nicholson (above) Burton J **11.26** suggested that 'a political philosophy which could be characterised as objectionable' – such as concerted racism or homophobia – is unlikely to be protected because it would fall foul of the criterion that a protected belief must be worthy of respect in a democratic society and not incompatible with human dignity (as required by Article 9 ECHR – see, for example, Campbell and anor v United Kingdom 1982 4 EHRR 293, ECtHR).

It is interesting that Burton J, without explaining his reasoning in detail, viewed the exclusion of objectionable beliefs as axiomatic. Yet in neither the 2003

235

Religion or Belief Regulations nor the EU Equal Treatment Framework Directive was there any express exception in respect of obnoxious beliefs and philosophies. Both measures speak of '*any* religion' and '*any* religious or philosophical belief' – terminology that has been retained in S.10 EqA. Even so, we respectfully take the view that Burton J was right to apply the Article 9 jurisprudence in this area as a guide to the meaning and scope of the phrase 'religious or philosophical belief'. As we have previously pointed out, the Directive contains express reference in its Recitals to Article 9 – see under 'European Convention on Human Rights – scope of Article 9' above. Furthermore, S.3 of the Human Rights Act 1995 requires courts and tribunals to interpret domestic law in conformity with Convention rights so far as it is possible to do so. These provide the necessary juridical basis for applying the same limitation to domestic discrimination law as applies to Article 9.

11.27 In practice, however, tribunals have rarely been faced with claims where the beliefs at issue were so objectionable as to disqualify them from protection under the 2003 Religion or Belief Regulations or the EqA. In the two cases below – both of which concerned alleged discrimination in relation to beliefs associated with the British National Party – the issue might have arisen but, in fact, the respective tribunals dismissed the claims without having to rely on the proviso outlined by Burton J:

- **Marsden I'Anson v Chief Constable of West Yorkshire Police** ET Case No.1804854/09: M, a civilian staff member, was employed as an imaging officer. He was also a singer and songwriter. In March 2007, he was suspended for devoting an excessive amount of work time to using the employer's equipment for his personal material. The employer also believed that some of the material was racist and that M had links with the BNP. Following his eventual dismissal, M brought proceedings under the 2003 Religion or Belief Regulations. He described his philosophical belief as 'a belief in my cultural identity and ancestry, including the promotion and celebration of English culture and history'. The tribunal dismissed the claim. M's belief only manifested itself in the songs that he wrote and performed – it did not impact upon any other aspect of his life. Therefore, in accordance with the EAT's decision in Grainger plc and ors v Nicholson (above), M's belief had not attained a certain level of 'cogency, seriousness, cohesion and importance'

- **Wingfield v North Cumbria Mental Health and Learning Disabilities NHS Trust** ET Case No.2510953/05: W – a graduate primary care worker – was dismissed allegedly because the Trust discovered that she was a member of the BNP. She claimed, among other things, that this amounted to direct discrimination in contravention of the 2003 Religion or Belief Regulations. The tribunal stated that the definition of 'belief' in Reg 2(1)(b) was intended to refer to something that had a considerable impact on the behaviour of the individual. It noted that the 'fundamental core values' of the BNP were its commitment to the principle of national sovereignty, ensuring that the British Isles 'remain our homeland for all time and that all economic and social structures, institutions and legislation must be built or developed around the fundamentals of ensuring the freedoms and security of our people and maintaining our unique cultural and ethnic identity'. The tribunal held that these values did not amount to a protected belief. They did not necessarily have any impact on the way that BNP members lived their lives – they were political commitments used to gain support for a political party. Accordingly, W's claim was dismissed.

However, in Kelly and ors v Unison ET Case No.2203854/08 an employment **11.28** tribunal did hold that certain beliefs were not protected by the 2003 Religion or Belief Regulations because they were not worthy of respect in a democratic society and/or were incompatible with human dignity. The claimants in that case subscribed to an extreme version of socialism that was dedicated to revolution and the overthrow of the state. The tribunal decided that the essentially non-democratic nature of their beliefs deprived them of protection against discrimination on the ground of religion or belief. For more details, see 'Political beliefs' below.

Political beliefs. Although Burton J in Grainger plc and ors v Nicholson **11.29** (above) observed that support of a political party would not meet the description of a philosophical belief, he made it clear that beliefs based on political philosophies or doctrines, such as socialism, Marxism, communism and free-market capitalism, were likely to qualify. They are, after all, grand in scale, aspire to influence entire states or populations, and have internal cogency, seriousness, cohesiveness and importance.

However, in Kelly and ors v Unison (above) an employment tribunal reached the somewhat surprising conclusion that the Marxist/Trotskyite views held by the claimants – trade union officials who were disciplined by their union for the way they conducted themselves at a national conference – were not protected beliefs. The tribunal held that the view expressed by Burton J in Grainger regarding political beliefs was merely obiter and therefore not binding. It concluded that the statutory protection was not intended to provide 'a universal protection of political opinion'. One of the reasons given for its decision was that, as part of the claimants' personal political beliefs as members of the Socialist Party, they countenanced revolution, embraced the overthrow of the political system, and the replacement of all personal property with residency and sustenance allocations made according to the dictate of government. In the tribunal's view, 'Parliament did not pass a law which affords protection to those with extreme political views, whether in the workplace or in trade unions, from trenchant criticism even expressed in a manner which in any other context would be regarded as discrimination or harassment'. Such views conflicted

237

with the fundamental rights of others – including the right to freedom of speech – and the dignity of the individual, and therefore were not, according to the tribunal, worthy of respect in a democratic society.

11.30 The decision in Kelly is, to say the least, controversial. The tribunal's detailed reasoning in many places in its judgment is rather difficult to follow and should perhaps be treated with some caution. Indeed, in Maistry v BBC ET Case No.1313142/10 – a case in which a belief in the 'higher purpose' of public service broadcasting was held to be a philosophical belief (see under 'Philosophical beliefs' above) – another tribunal expressed serious reservations about the correctness of the conclusion reached in Kelly. It will be interesting to see if the same rationale for excluding extreme political beliefs is approved in future cases.

11.31 **Scientific/evidence-based beliefs.** In Grainger plc and ors v Nicholson (above) Burton J rejected the contention that science- or evidence-based beliefs were incapable of amounting to a philosophical belief. The issue stemmed from remarks made by Elias J in McClintock v Department of Constitutional Affairs 2008 IRLR 29, EAT, where he said: '[T]o constitute a belief there must be a religious or philosophical viewpoint in which one actually believes; it is not enough "to have an opinion based on some real or perceived logic or based on information or lack of information available".' In reality, the claimant's case in McClintock failed not so much because his was not a belief capable of amounting to a philosophical belief as because his stated objection to same-sex adoptions was in fact not a belief that derived from his Christian faith – for further details, see 'Genuineness and proof of actual adherence' below. Burton J thought that nothing in McClintock actually precluded science-based beliefs so long as they met the criteria set out in his judgment. In effect, he concluded that an ethical stance based on a science-based belief in potentially catastrophic climate change was perfectly capable of amounting to a 'philosophical belief'. Whether or not it actually did so depended upon the tribunal being satisfied that the claimant actually lived according to the precepts of such a belief and that the employer's actions were attributable to the fact that the claimant held that belief.

11.32 **Genuineness and proof of actual adherence**

In Grainger plc and ors v Nicholson 2010 ICR 360, EAT (see '"Philosophical belief"' above), Mr Justice Burton stated that for a religious or philosophical belief to be protected under the 2003 Religion or Belief Regulations and the EqA it must be genuinely held by the claimant. This implies that an employment tribunal must be satisfied that the claimant actually adheres to the belief and that that adherence forms something more than merely the assertion of a causal view or opinion.

In Devine v Home Office (Immigration and Nationality Directorate) ET Case No.2302061/04 the claimant complained of religious discrimination following the Home Office's rejection of his application for a job as an executive officer because of a potential conflict of interest arising from his previous work, which included giving advice on immigration issues, and his personal interest in providing accommodation for asylum seekers. An employment tribunal dismissed the claimant's argument that his sympathy for underprivileged asylum seekers and disadvantaged people was a demonstration of the Christian virtue of charity and, as such, should be protected by the 2003 Religion or Belief Regulations. In its view, the claim was 'too vague and ill-defined'. Furthermore, at no point had the claimant specifically advanced the case that he was a Christian.

The requirement that the claimant actually subscribes to the religion or belief **11.33** in issue was reinforced in McClintock v Department of Constitutional Affairs 2008 IRLR 29, EAT. In that case the EAT upheld an employment tribunal's decision that a Christian Justice of the Peace was not discriminated against by reason of his religion or belief when he was refused permission to excuse himself from sitting on family cases that might lead to the adoption of a child by a same-sex couple. Since the claimant had not put his objections to same-sex adoption on the basis of any religious or philosophical belief, the provisions of the 2003 Religion or Belief Regulations were not engaged. In so holding, the EAT noted that, to constitute a belief, there must be a religious or philosophical viewpoint in which one actually believes. It is not enough to have an opinion based on some real or perceived logic or on information or lack of information available. The outcome in this particular case essentially turned on its facts in that the tribunal had found that the basis of the claimant's objections to same-sex adoptions was not his Christian beliefs but his view that such adoptions were not in the interests of the child. As the tribunal pointed out, the claimant could not be considered to be against same-sex adoption as a matter of principle because he had stated in evidence that he would not be against same-sex adoption if there were evidence to show that it was not contrary to the interests of the child (although the claimant was clearly very sceptical that any such evidence would be found). Presumably, had he stated that he was against same-sex adoption per se as being contrary to his religious convictions, and if he had simply used his evidence-based arguments as to the effect of such adoptions on the child to reinforce his objection, his claim would not have fallen at the first hurdle.

As a general rule, tribunals should not impose too high a hurdle when it comes to the question of genuineness and to the need for proof of actual adherence, particularly in cases based on the assertion of religious beliefs. In R (Williamson and ors) v Secretary of State for Education and Employment 2005 2 AC 246, HL – a case concerned with the interpretation of Article 9 ECHR (see discussion under 'European Convention on Human Rights – scope of Article 9' above) –

239

Lord Nicholls observed: 'When the genuineness of a claimant's professed belief is an issue in the proceedings, the court will enquire into and decide this issue as a question of fact. This is a limited enquiry. The court is concerned to ensure an assertion of religious belief is made in good faith... But, emphatically, it is for not the court to embark on an enquiry into the asserted belief and judge its "validity" by some objective standard such as the source material upon which the claimant founds his belief or the orthodox teaching of the religion in question or the extent to which the claimant's belief conforms to or differs from the views of others professing the same religion. Freedom of religion protects the subjective belief of an individual.' In other words, while the courts can legitimately be concerned with whether or not the claim of religious belief is made *in good faith*, they should not concern themselves with whether the religious belief in question *is a good faith* in terms of judging the validity of that faith.

11.34 Having said that, if adherence to a particular faith affords access to a particular concession or advantage, it would seem the ECtHR is prepared to condone a more penetrating inquiry into the extent to which the claimant actually adheres to the faith in question. In Kosteski v Former Yugoslav Republic of Macedonia 2007 45 EHRR 31, ECtHR, an employee was fined for taking a day off work without permission to celebrate a Muslim religious holiday. The employer doubted the extent to which the employee was a devout Muslim and therefore entitled under domestic law to time off work to attend the festival. For his part, the employee contended that both the fine and the fact that he had been required to prove his religious affiliation violated his right to freedom of religion. In rejecting his claim, the ECtHR observed that: 'In so far as the applicant has complained that there was an interference with the inner sphere of belief in that he was required to prove his faith, the Court recalls that the [domestic] courts... made findings effectively that the applicant had not substantiated the genuineness of his claim to be a Muslim and that his conduct on the contrary cast doubt on that claim in that there were no outward signs of his practising the Muslim faith or joining collective Muslim worship. While the notion of the State sitting in judgment on the state of a citizen's inner and personal beliefs is abhorrent and may smack unhappily of past infamous persecutions, the Court observes that this is a case where the applicant sought to enjoy a special right bestowed by [domestic] law which provided that Muslims could take holiday on particular days... In the context of employment, with contracts setting out specific obligations and rights between employer and employee, the Court does not find it unreasonable that an employer may regard absence without permission or apparent justification as a disciplinary matter. Where the employee then seeks to rely on a particular exemption, it is not oppressive or in fundamental conflict with freedom of conscience to require some level of substantiation when that claim concerns a privilege or entitlement not commonly available and, if that substantiation is not forthcoming, to reach a negative conclusion.'

The extent of a court or tribunal's inquiry into genuineness may need to be even more robust when it comes to establishing whether a claimant subscribes to a philosophical as opposed to a religious belief. In Grainger plc and ors v Nicholson (above), Burton J thought that Lord Nicolls' remarks in R (Williamson and ors) v Secretary of State for Education and Employment (above) did not apply to the same extent to 'philosophical' beliefs. He observed: 'To establish a religious belief, the claimant may only need to show that he is an adherent to a particular religion. To establish a philosophical belief... it is plain that cross-examination is likely to be needed.' It is notable that in cases based on non-religious beliefs such as climate change and the sanctity of animal life, employment tribunals have engaged in extensive inquiries into the nature of those beliefs and the impact they have on the particular claimants' lives when determining whether the protection from discrimination on the ground of religion or belief applies.

Lack of religion or belief   11.35

When the 2003 Religion or Belief Regulations were originally introduced, the Government intended that a *lack* religion or belief would be encompassed by the definition of 'religion or belief' in Reg 2(1). This was reflected in the Explanatory Notes accompanying the original version of the Regulations, which expressly stated that a lack of belief would come within the definition. However, the actual wording of the Regulations left room for doubt and as a result the Equality Act 2006 introduced an amendment to Reg 2(1), which stated unambiguously that references to 'religion' and 'belief' encompassed references to lack of religion and lack of belief. The same clarification is reproduced in S.10(1) and (2) EqA, which states that a lack of religion or belief falls within the ambit of the protected characteristic of religion or belief. This ensures consistency with the right to freedom of thought, religion and conscience protected under Article 9 ECHR, which has been interpreted to encompass not only the right to belong to a religion but also the right 'not to believe' and/or to hold unconventional beliefs not subscribed to by others – see Kokkinakis v Greece 1994 17 EHRR 397, ECtHR.

Manifestation of religion or belief   11.36

As already noted, Article 9 ECHR expressly covers the right to *manifest* one's religion or belief in the form of worship, teaching, practice and observance – see 'European Convention on Human Rights' above. Case law interpreting this right has shown that the freedom to manifest one's religion is exercisable alone or in community with others, in private or within the circle of those whose faith one shares – Sahin v Turkey 2007 44 EHRR 5, ECtHR. The freedom extends, in principle, to the right to attempt to convince others of the tenets of one's religion or belief – Kokkinakis v Greece (above).

241

Having the freedom to *manifest* religious beliefs is important for two reasons. First, without the right to express and practise beliefs, the freedom of religion guaranteed by Article 9 would be emasculated. Adherents of religious faiths usually have to do more than simply believe: they are required or encouraged to act in certain ways, most obviously and directly in forms of communal or personal worship, supplication and meditation. Secondly, beliefs often comprise the *'forum internum'* – i.e. an individual's conscience and sense of self. Thus, the way in which a person expresses or manifests his or her religious beliefs in private and in public through speech, ritual, observance and practice can often be intrinsic to that person's sense of their own identity.

11.37 But the freedom to manifest one's religion or belief as guaranteed by Article 9 is qualified, first by restrictions placed on the scope of Article 9(1) by the courts, and secondly by the limitations on its application contained in Article 9(2). The rationale for this is that, in democratic societies where a plurality of religions and belief systems co-exist, it may be necessary to place restrictions on the freedom to manifest one's religion or belief in order to reconcile the interests of the various groups and ensure that everyone's beliefs are respected – see Kokkinakis v Greece and Sahin v Turkey (above).

11.38 **Limits to Article 9(1).** When it comes to the freedom to manifest one's religion or religious belief in public, decisions of the ECtHR appear to draw a subtle but crucial distinction between an activity that is central to the expression of a religion or belief on the one hand, and one that is merely inspired or encouraged by it on the other. The Court has held that whereas restrictions in relation to the former do engage rights guaranteed by Article 9(1) and therefore fall to be justified within the terms of Article 9(2), restrictions in respect of the latter do not engage Article 9 rights at all. In Arrowsmith v United Kingdom 1980 3 EHRR 218, ECtHR, for example, a pacifist sought to challenge her conviction for handing out leaflets to soldiers by bringing legal proceedings asserting a breach of Article 9. Her leaflets aimed to persuade the soldiers to decline to serve in Northern Ireland. However, they focused not upon the promotion of non-violent means for resolving political disputes but upon government policy in respect of Northern Ireland. The European Commission of Human Rights accepted that any public declaration proclaiming the idea of pacifism and urging acceptance of a commitment to the belief in non-violence would have amounted to a 'normal and recognised manifestation of pacifist belief'. But, as the leaflets had not specifically expressed the claimant's own pacifist values, their distribution was not a 'manifestation' of her pacifist belief within the terms of Article 9(1). This was despite the fact that the content of the leaflets and the action in disseminating them had been motivated by the claimant's belief.

A similar conclusion was reached in Kosteski v Former Yugoslav Republic of Macedonia 2007 45 EHRR 31, ECtHR (discussed under 'Genuineness and proof of actual adherence' above). In that case, a Muslim employee complained of a breach of Article 9 when he was penalised for taking a day's unauthorised leave in order to participate in a religious festival. The European Commission of Human Rights accepted that the employee's absence from work may well have been motivated by his intention to celebrate the Muslim festival but it was 'not persuaded that this was a manifestation of his beliefs in the sense protected by Article 9'. The Commission did not elaborate further on this ground for rejecting the applicant's case, but presumably it took the view that, as attendance at the festival was not a central requirement of the employee's faith, it was not protected as a 'manifestation of his religion or belief' in the narrow sense in which manifestation has been interpreted.

Application of Article 9(2). Even where Article 9 is engaged, interference in a **11.39** person's right to manifest their religion or belief is potentially justifiable in accordance with Article 9(2). This provides that restrictions on the right to manifestation of thought, conscience or religion are permissible so long as they 'are prescribed by law and are necessary in a democratic society in the interests of public safety, for the protection of public order, health or morals, or for the protection of the rights and freedoms of others'.

The ECtHR has consistently confirmed that states have a wide margin of appreciation when it comes to limiting the right to manifest religion and beliefs in the public, as opposed to the private, sphere. In this regard, the Court almost invariably concludes that such restrictions pursue one or more of the permissible interests set out in Article 9(2) and that the interference with Convention rights is a proportionate means of achieving the relevant interest(s). So, for example, in Sahin v Turkey (above) the ECtHR upheld a ban on the wearing of Islamic headscarves by Muslim women in Turkish universities pursuant to what it accepted was the legitimate aim of promoting secularism as a means of ensuring religious and gender equality in a pluralistic society. In Switzerland, where a similar ban covering teachers of small children was found to be a proportionate means of achieving a legitimate aim, the ECtHR suggested in a preliminary decision that wearing an Islamic headscarf might be viewed as having some kind of proselytising effect in that it appeared to be imposed on women by a religious precept that was hard to reconcile with the principle of gender equality – Dahlab v Switzerland (Application No.42393/98), ECtHR.

Article 9 and employment. It is interesting that one of the spheres in which the **11.40** right to manifest one's religion or beliefs has been most restricted is the workplace. The justification for this is the voluntary nature of employment. Decisions of the European Commission of Human Rights and the ECtHR have consistently emphasised the fact that employees have the freedom to resign if they choose to prioritise their right to manifest their religious beliefs through worship, practice and observance over their obligations to comply with their contractual duties and obligations while in the workplace. So for example,

243

there has been no recognition of any positive obligation on the part of employers to take steps to facilitate the manifestation of religious belief by relieving employees of work responsibilities at particular times in order to accommodate worship. Employees have a duty to observe the rules governing their working hours, and applying disciplinary penalties for failing to attend work on account of religious observance does not give rise to an issue falling within the scope of Article 9 – see, for example, Stedman v United Kingdom 1997 23 EHRR CD168, ECtHR. Similarly, a member of the clergy employed by a Christian church can be expected to discharge not only religious but also secular duties. He therefore cannot complain of a breach of Article 9(1) if he is dismissed for refusing to carry out such duties (e.g. offering pastoral advice to women undergoing abortions) because he finds that they conflict with his religious beliefs – Knudsen v Finland (1985) 42 DR 247, ECtHR.

In R (SB) v Governors of Denbigh High School 2007 1 AC 100, HL, Lord Bingham summarised the trend revealed by the above cases in the following way: 'The Strasbourg institutions have not been at all ready to find an interference with the right to manifest religious belief in practice or observance where a person has voluntarily accepted an employment or role which does not accommodate that practice or observance and there are other means open to the person to observe his or her religion without undue hardship or inconvenience.' We examine this restrictive approach in more detail under 'Time off for religious observance' below. Suffice it to say here that the choice to resign is, it would seem, all that Article 9 demands by way of protecting the rights of employees who voluntarily sign up to employment terms that constrain their ability to manifest their beliefs during working time.

11.41 Is a right to manifest protected by S.10 EqA?

When it comes to protection from religion or belief discrimination under S.10 EqA, domestic courts and tribunals have generally accepted that the right to manifest religion or religious belief within the workplace can be restricted. In practice, workplace disputes concerning religious or belief discrimination tend to arise not from the mere holding of particular beliefs, but from the way in which those beliefs are manifested in public. Particular beliefs can, for example, lead to conflict over matters such as dress codes, dietary requirements, food and drink preparation, holiday leave and workplace absence. In such circumstances, where, as is often the case, the dispute arises as a result of a policy or practice that is applied uniformly across the entire workforce irrespective of employees' particular religions or beliefs, any ensuing claim will be based on allegations of *indirect* rather than direct discrimination, with the consequence that the employer can seek to justify the application of the policy or practice notwithstanding the disproportionately adverse impact it has upon those who share the claimant's particular religion or beliefs. And once the rights of the employer and other employees are taken into account, the incidence of tribunals finding that an employer's actions in these circumstances are justified is very high.

Some legal commentators have argued that many of the decisions reached by UK courts and tribunals have failed to pay proper heed to Article 9, even when taking into account the constraints on the right to manifest religion to which that Article is itself subject. We address this argument under 'Is UK approach compliant with Article 9?' below. First, however, it is appropriate to consider in more detail how particular manifestations of religion and belief have been dealt with.

Dress and jewellery. In one of the first appellate cases to be decided under the **11.42** 2003 Religion or Belief Regulations – Azmi v Kirklees Metropolitan Borough Council 2007 ICR 1154, EAT – a devout Muslim teaching assistant brought claims of direct and indirect discrimination after being suspended from work for her persistence in wearing a full veil while teaching. Both claims were rejected by an employment tribunal. On appeal, the EAT held that the employer's instruction not to wear a veil did not constitute direct discrimination (i.e. less favourable treatment) contrary to Reg 3(1)(a) of the 2003 Religion or Belief Regulations because the employer would have treated in the same way any woman, whether Muslim or not, who for a reason other than religious belief covered her face. The EAT said it was not possible to accept the claimant's argument that the appropriate hypothetical comparator should have been another Muslim woman who covered her head but not her face.

Turning to the claimant's indirect discrimination complaint, the EAT accepted that the employer's apparently neutral requirement that employees not wear clothing that covered the face or which interfered unduly with his or her ability to communicate properly with pupils was clearly a provision, criterion or practice that put persons of the claimant's belief at a particular disadvantage when compared with others. However, the EAT ruled that the discriminatory effect of the provision, criterion or practice (PCP) was justified as a proportionate means of achieving the legitimate aim of raising the level of the educational achievements of the school children.

In the Azmi case Mr Justice Wilkie said there was no *a priori* reason why a case **11.43** of the kind at issue could only be properly brought as an indirect discrimination claim. However, where there is a clash between an employer's policy or practice and an employee's desire to manifest an aspect of his or her religion or belief, it is difficult to see how a direct discrimination claim could get off the ground provided that the employer's policy does not specifically target the complainant individually or the religious group to which he or she belongs. This proposition is amply demonstrated by the Court of Appeal's much-publicised decision in Eweida v British Airways plc 2010 ICR 890, CA. There, the claimant – who was a devout and practising Christian employed as part of BA's check-in staff – refused to conceal her silver cross necklace in breach of the company's strict

245

dress code prohibiting customer-facing employees from wearing any visible item of adornment. The only exception allowed by the dress code related to items of clothing or jewellery, the wearing of which was a mandatory requirement of the employee's religion (e.g. the hijab, turban and skull cap, which some Muslims, Sikhs and Jews respectively believe they are obliged to wear). The employer took the view that wearing a crucifix or cross was a matter of personal choice and did not fall within the stated exception, with the consequence that the claimant ended up being sent home without pay. Later, the employer altered its dress code to allow for the wearing of a cross, but this did not prevent the claimant from bringing claims of direct and indirect discrimination under the 2003 Religion or Belief Regulations in respect of her initial treatment.

An employment tribunal rejected both grounds of complaint. On subsequent appeal to the EAT and then the Court of Appeal, the claimant conceded that there had been no direct discrimination, but contended that there had been indirect discrimination in that the dress code disproportionally affected those of the Christian faith who wished to manifest their religious beliefs at work in the form of dress or jewellery. The Court of Appeal unanimously concluded that there was no evidence that the employer's policy put Christians at a particular disadvantage within the terms of the indirect discrimination provisions contained in the 2003 Religion or Belief Regulations. It pointed out that the tribunal had found that no other employee in a uniformed workforce of 30,000 had ever made a request to visibly wear a cross, much less refused to work if such a request was not met. In view of this, there was no reason whatever why the tribunal should have inferred that there were others whose religiously motivated choice – not of whether but of where they should wear a symbol of their faith – was of such importance to them that being unable to exercise it constituted a 'particular disadvantage'.

11.44 Dress and appearance codes have featured prominently in other cases where the right to manifest a religion or belief within the workplace has been at issue. Three further examples:

- **Chaplin v Royal Devon and Exeter NHS Foundation Trust** ET Case No.1702886/09: C, a practising Christian, was employed as a nurse. The Trust's uniform policy stated that no necklaces should be worn in order to reduce the risk of injury when handling patients. Since being a teenager, C had always visibly worn a cross on a chain. On several occasions she was asked to remove it but refused on the basis that this was disrespectful to her religion. Nor would she consider a number of proposals by the Trust such as pinning the chain inside her uniform or inside a pocket. After being redeployed, C brought claims of direct and indirect discrimination. The tribunal held that there was no direct discrimination – the Trust was prepared to reach an agreement with C that enabled her to carry out her duties while wearing a cross in the same way that agreement had been reached with Muslim doctors who wanted to wear the Hijab. C's indirect discrimination claim also failed because the PCP applied by the Trust did not put persons of the same religion or belief as C at a particular disadvantage. Even if it did, the indirectly discriminatory effect of uniform policy was objectively justified as a proportionate response to a legitimate aim, which in this case principally comprised protecting health and safety but also took into account the need to present a polished corporate image and for senior staff to be role models to more junior staff

- **Germain v Home Office** ET Case No.2306431/06: G, an ordained minister of the Corinthian Church, was employed as a human resources business partner. On a few occasions she wore her clerical collar together with a purple shirt to work. G's line manager queried whether this was appropriate given G's senior position, as it could be seen as a sign of authority. However, he did not ask her to remove it. G nonetheless took offence, resigned, and subsequently brought – among other things – direct and indirect discrimination claims under the 2003 Religion or Belief Regulations. Both claims were rejected. On direct discrimination, the tribunal found that G had not been subject to less favourable treatment, noting that a minister of another faith wearing a clerical collar or other distinctive article of clothing representing authority would have been treated in the same way. It rejected the argument that the appropriate comparator was a Muslim woman wearing the veil, or a Sikh man wearing a turban. It was the impression of authority within the church that caused the employer concern. G's claim of indirect discrimination failed on the basis that the employer's dress policy helped pursue the legitimate aim of preserving the neutrality of its HR professionals so they did not appear in any uniform laying claim to authority within the community, whether spiritual or otherwise. The insistence on neutral dress was found to be a proportionate means of achieving that aim

- **Dhinsa v Serco and anor** ET Case No.1315002/09: D was baptised an Amritdhari Sikh in 2008. One of the articles of faith of the Sikh religion is the wearing of a 'kirpan' – a ceremonial sword. The Prison Service operated a policy of restricting all staff except Sikh chaplains from wearing the kirpan at work. Amritdhari Sikhs, those Sikhs who are baptised, are committed to a strict code of discipline and the significance of carrying a kirpan is profound – it is a solemn duty to wear it at all times. However, the Prison Service asserted that it had to take note of the fact that, regardless of its religious significance, the kirpan could be used as a knife or dagger to attack staff or other prisoners, and therefore it was banned within prisons, other than for Sikh chaplains. D was dismissed because he refused to stop wearing the kirpan. He claimed this amounted to religious discrimination. An employment tribunal found that the belief of an Amritdhari Sikh to honour the necessity to wear a kirpan was a religious belief that qualified

247

for protection under the 2003 Religion or Belief Regulations and that D was put at an actual disadvantage by being dismissed as a direct result of the application of the PCP. However, the tribunal went on to conclude that actions in maintaining and applying the security policy were an appropriate, necessary and proportionate means of achieving a legitimate aim, and the policy was therefore justified.

11.45 Note that the claimants in both the Eweida v British Airways plc and Chaplin v Royal Devon and Exeter NHS Foundation Trust cases (discussed above) have commenced legal proceedings before the European Court of Human Rights contending that these decisions failed to comply with Article 9 ECHR. Both cases have been consolidated into a single set of proceedings in respect of which the Equality and Human Rights Commission has successfully applied to intervene in order to make general representations. For further details, see 'Is UK approach compliant with Article 9?' below.

11.46 **Time off for religious observance.** One context in which the right to manifest religion or belief has often arisen is in respect of time off during normal working hours to worship or attend religious festivals. From an Article 9 perspective, a line of decisions of the European Commission of Human Rights (which, prior to 1998, determined whether cases should proceed to a full hearing before the ECtHR) provide little support for employees seeking to manifest their religious beliefs in this way. While it is fully acknowledged in these cases that Article 9 embraces the right to worship alone or in community with others, the Commission consistently adopted the view that there is no interference with Article 9 rights where an employee is refused permission to take time off as he or she always has the option to resign in order to gain the necessary time and space to observe his or her religious beliefs – see, for example, Ahmad v United Kingdom 1982 4 EHRR 126, ECtHR, and Stedman v United Kingdom 1997 23 EHRR CD168, ECtHR.

This approach is well illustrated by the Commission's decision in Kontinnen v Finland 1996 87 DR 68, ECtHR. In that case the applicant worked on the Finnish Railways. After five years he became a Seventh-day Adventist and declared that he could not work after sunset on Fridays. After several incidents when he left with the early setting of the Finnish winter sun, his employer dismissed him. In rejecting the application to the ECtHR on the ground that there had been no infringement of the applicant's rights under Article 9, the Commission observed: 'In these particular circumstances [we] find that the applicant was not dismissed because of his religious convictions but for having refused to respect his working hours. This refusal, even if motivated by his religious convictions, cannot as such be considered protected by Article 9(1). Nor has the applicant shown that he was pressured to change his religious views or prevented from manifesting his religion or belief. The Commission would add that, having found his working hours to conflict with his religious convictions, the applicant was free to relinquish his post. The Commission regards this as the ultimate guarantee of his right to freedom of religion.'

The Commission's decisions have been criticised in some quarters, not least by **11.47** the Court of Appeal. In Copsey v WBB Devon Clays Ltd 2005 ICR 1789, CA, the Court reluctantly upheld an employment tribunal's decision rejecting the unfair dismissal claim of an employee who was dismissed following his refusal on religious grounds to agree to a variation in his contractual terms that could have resulted in his being required to work on Sundays. (It should be noted that this case arose before there was specific protection against discrimination on the ground of religion or belief.) Although the tribunal had not considered the impact of Article 9, the Court of Appeal concluded that the result would have been no different even if it had. Lord Justice Mummery, however, expressed his profound disagreement with the Commission's decisions in Ahmad v United Kingdom and Stedman v United Kingdom (above), stating that they were difficult to square with the supposedly fundamental character of Article 9 rights. He also added that, if it were not for them, he would have held that the employee's Article 9 rights had been interfered with (albeit that on the facts found by the tribunal he would have regarded the employer's actions to be justified under Article 9(2)). Lord Justice Rix adopted a slightly different tack. He concluded that, while he was prepared to accept the Commission's 'general thesis that contracts freely entered into may limit an applicant's room for complaint about interference with his rights', the body of the Commission's decisions in this area did not constitute such a 'clear and constant jurisprudence' that the UK courts should be required to follow.

Tribunals have tended to deal with analogous claims under the 2003 Regulations in a slightly different way. While accepting that an employee has the right to bring such a claim, the main question is usually whether the employer's decision not to allow the employee time off constitutes indirect discrimination. It does not matter for this purpose that the employee has freely signed up to contractual terms that do not allow time off to worship, etc; the issue is whether the employer's general application of the holiday or time off policy disproportionately affects persons who share the employee's religion or belief and, if so, whether the discriminatory effect is justified as a proportionate means of achieving a legitimate aim. In practice, most of the decided cases have turned on the question of justification, and the conclusions reached by tribunals demonstrate that, in this context as well as others, there is no absolute right to manifest one's religion or religious beliefs.

Three examples: **11.48**

- **Williams-Drabble v Pathway Care Solutions Ltd and anor** ET Case No.2601718/04: W-D was employed as a residential social worker by PCS Ltd in November 2003. When applying for the position, she stated

249

on her application form that she was a practising Christian. In addition, she pointed out at her interview that she could not work on Sunday as she attended the local church's Sunday service and had done so for the last two years. In April 2004, W-D's rota was changed and this prevented her from attending church. She subsequently claimed that she had been both directly and indirectly discriminated against by PCS Ltd in contravention of the Regulations. An employment tribunal dismissed the direct discrimination claim but upheld the indirect discrimination claim. By imposing a permanent rota change that required her to work on Sunday, PCS Ltd had applied a provision, criterion or practice (PCP) that put Christians like W-D at a particular disadvantage. Furthermore, PCS Ltd had failed to justify the rota change as a proportionate means of achieving a legitimate aim

- **James v MSC Cruises Ltd** ET Case No.2203173/05: J was a practising member of the Seventh-day Adventist Church, and as such she abstained from secular work on the Sabbath in order to worship, teach, learn and celebrate. In September 2005 she successfully applied for a position with MSC Ltd, which sold and marketed cruise holidays. However, on receiving the offer letter, she explained that she could not work on Saturday as this was the Sabbath. MSC Ltd responded that if J could not work on Saturdays then she would be unable take up the offer of employment. J brought an indirect discrimination claim under the 2003 Religion or Belief Regulations. An employment tribunal found the relevant disadvantage caused by the PCP of Saturday working but decided that it was justified. It accepted the employer's evidence that trading on Saturdays was an essential feature of the tourism industry, since this was when couples were most likely to be available jointly to explore holiday opportunities and make immediate decisions. It also had regard to the fact that Saturday working was not popular among existing staff; that a rota had been put in place to share the burden equally; and that the employer reasonably believed that any exceptions would create tension among colleagues

- **Cherfi v G4S Security Services Ltd** EAT 0379/10: C, a Muslim, worked for G4S as a security guard in Highgate, where the client required all security officers to remain on site throughout their shifts. Consequently, he was refused permission to travel to Friday prayers at a mosque in Finsbury Park. However, there was a prayer room on site and C had the option of working on Saturday or Sunday rather than Friday. C claimed that the PCP of requiring him to remain at work during Friday lunchtimes constituted indirect religious discrimination under the 2003 Regulations. An employment tribunal held that, although the PCP did place C at a disadvantage as a practising Muslim by not allowing him to attend prayers in congregation, G4S would be in danger of financial penalties or even losing its contract with its client if a full complement of security staff was not on site throughout the day. C had refused a variety of arrangements offered to accommodate his requirements. Thus, the tribunal found that the PCP was a proportionate means of achieving a legitimate aim – i.e. meeting the operational needs of the business. On appeal, the EAT upheld this decision. In its view, the tribunal had carried out the necessary balancing act, having considered both the reason why G4S refused to allow C to leave the site on Friday lunchtimes and the impact of this on C. The discriminatory effect of the PCP was limited to preventing C from attending congregational prayers during working hours. C was not prevented from praying at the Highgate site, and nor was he prevented from working on a Friday or pressured to accept work on a Saturday or Sunday. In view of this, and also having regard to the alternatives that had been open to C, the conclusion as to justification was one that the tribunal was entitled to reach.

Conflict between different protected rights. Another area in which issues **11.49** concerning the right to manifest religion or belief in the workplace have arisen is where the expression of an employee's religion clashes with a basic aspect of their job. The problem here is that the religious belief in question often conflicts with the rights of others within the workplace, or within sectors of the wider community, whom the employee is expected to serve. In such cases, employees may be faced with a personal dilemma: should they prioritise their religious beliefs over their contractual obligation to perform their job duties? And if they do, will they be protected from disciplinary action by the EqA?

The leading case is Ladele v London Borough of Islington and anor 2010 ICR 532, CA. There, the claimant, a registrar, refused to conduct civil partnership services because of her Christian belief that same-sex unions were contrary to God's law. The Court of Appeal agreed with the EAT that the Council did not directly discriminate against her on the ground of religion when it threatened her with dismissal for refusing to carry out the services. The reason for its treatment was not her religious belief but her refusal to carry out her duties – the Council required all registrars to carry out marriages and civil partnerships, and the claimant was treated no differently in this regard to anyone else. Nor was there unlawful indirect discrimination since the Council had a legitimate aim, which was to provide its services in a non-discriminatory way in accordance with its 'Dignity for All' policy. Requiring the claimant to perform civil partnerships was a proportionate means of achieving that aim. The effect on her of implementing that policy was held not to impinge on her religious beliefs, since she remained free to hold those beliefs and to worship as she wished.

The Court of Appeal in Ladele specifically considered the extent to which the **11.50** right to manifest religion and religious belief under Article 9 ECHR assisted the claimant's contention that she had been discriminated against. It noted that the ECtHR case law supported the conclusion that the claimant's proper and genuine desire to have her religious views relating to marriage respected should not override the Council's concern to ensure that all its registrars manifest

251

equal respect for both the homosexual and the heterosexual communities. For example, in Pichon and Sajous v France (Application No.49853/99), ECtHR – a case in which pharmacists refused to sell contraceptives for religious reasons – the ECtHR held that Article 9 did not protect them as they could 'manifest [their] beliefs in many ways outside the professional sphere'.

Very similar conclusions were reached by the EAT in McFarlane v Relate Avon Ltd 2010 ICR 507, EAT – a case decided just a couple of weeks before the Court of Appeal published its decision in Ladele. In McFarlane the Appeal Tribunal upheld the decision of an employment tribunal that the dismissal of an employee (a relationship counsellor) for refusing to counsel homosexuals about sexual matters was not direct religious discrimination, as the dismissal was based on the employee's refusal to comply with the employer's equal opportunities policy rather than on his Christian beliefs. Nor did the dismissal constitute unlawful indirect discrimination as it was a proportionate means of achieving a legitimate aim – namely, that of serving the community in a non-discriminatory manner. In so concluding, the EAT (Mr Justice Underhill presiding) considered and rejected the argument that the tribunal's conclusion was out of synch with the protections accorded by Article 9. It pointed to the fact that, in Kalac v Turkey 1999 27 EHRR 552, ECtHR, the European Court of Human Rights held that 'Article 9 does not protect every act motivated or inspired by a religion or belief'.

11.51 In an unusual move, the Court of Appeal subsequently gave a detailed judgment when dismissing an application by Mr McFarlane for leave to appeal against the EAT's decision – see McFarlane v Relate Avon Ltd 2010 IRLR 872, CA. In the course of this judgment, Lord Justice Laws dealt with a witness statement of the former Archbishop of Canterbury, Lord Carey, in support of the claimant's leave application. Lord Carey criticised, among other things, the outcomes of recent religion or belief discrimination cases (including Ladele v London Borough of Islington and anor (above)) and suggested that they displayed reasoning 'that is dangerous to the social order and represents clear animus to Christian beliefs'. Rejecting these observations as misplaced, Laws LJ stated: 'In a free constitution such as ours there is an important distinction to be drawn between the law's protection of the right to hold and express a belief and the law's protection of that belief's substance or content. The common law and Article 9 offer vigorous protection of the Christian's right (and every other person's right) to hold and express his or her beliefs. And so they should. By contrast they do not, and should not, offer any protection whatever of the substance or content of those beliefs on the ground only that they are based on religious precepts. These are twin conditions of a free society... So it is that the law must firmly safeguard the right to hold and express religious belief; equally firmly, it must eschew any protection of such a belief's content in the name only of its religious credentials. Both principles are necessary conditions of a free and rational regime.'

The conflict between the right to manifest religion and belief and the right not to be discriminated against on the ground of sexual orientation has also arisen in the context of the provision of goods, facilities and services. In Bull and anor v Hall and anor 2012 EWCA Civ 83, CA, two civil partners successfully complained of direct sexual orientation discrimination under Reg 3 of the Equality Act (Sexual Orientation) Regulations 2007 SI 2007/1263 (which extended protection against sexual orientation discrimination to non-work areas, including goods, facilities and services). The claimants brought a claim for damages after having been prevented from taking up their booking of a double room in a guesthouse because the owners (who were devout Christians) had a policy of allowing only married heterosexual couples to stay in the same bedroom. The county court judge held that the refusal to allow the claimants to occupy the double room they had booked was because of their sexual orientation and this amounted to direct discrimination. The Court of Appeal agreed. It rejected the argument that Reg 3 breached Article 9 of the ECHR to the extent that it limited the right of the owners to manifest their religious beliefs. In the words of Lady Justice Rafferty: 'Any interference with religious rights, specifically identified in Article 9 and listed in Article 14 of the ECHR, must satisfy the test of "anxious scrutiny". However, in a pluralist society it is inevitable that from time to time, as here, views, beliefs and rights of some are not compatible with those of others. As I have made plain, I do not consider that the [owners] face any difficulty in manifesting their religious beliefs, they are merely prohibited from so doing in the commercial context they have chosen.'

Note that the claimants in both the Ladele and McFarlane cases have commenced legal proceedings before the ECtHR contending that the decisions in their cases fail to comply with Article 9 ECHR– see 'Is UK approach compliant with Article 9?' below.

Proselytising. It is striking that the claimants in Ladele v London Borough of **11.52** Islington and anor and McFarlane v Relate Avon Ltd (above) wrestled with a profound personal dilemma, having found that their jobs put them in conflict with their deeply held religious convictions. In both cases, the employees behaved with circumspection, neither demanding a general change to their employers' policies nor seeking to foist their views onto other colleagues. However, in other cases, tribunals have had to deal with claims by employees who have proselytised their personal religious beliefs in an inappropriate way.

For example, in Chondol v Liverpool City Council EAT 0298/08 a committed Christian employee was employed as a social worker on secondment to Mersey Care NHS Trust. The Trust became concerned by what it perceived as the claimant's failure to recognise professional boundaries. For instance, he gave a copy of the Bible to a service user, who subsequently complained. Following his eventual dismissal, he brought proceedings claiming, among other things, that his dismissal constituted an act of direct religion or belief discrimination. The

253

EAT held that an employment tribunal had not erred in holding that the claimant had not been less favourably treated on the ground of religion or belief, as it had been entitled to find that his treatment was not because of his religion per se, but because he had been improperly foisting his religion on service users, and that the employer would have acted in precisely the same way regardless of the religion or view being promoted. The distinction between the claimant's religious beliefs as such and the inappropriate promotion of those beliefs was entirely valid in principle (although, of course, in any case in which such a distinction is relied on, it will be necessary to be clear that it reflects the employer's true reason for the treatment at issue).

11.53 Two other examples of where employees have been disciplined for crossing the boundaries of acceptable conduct when expressing their religious views:

- **Maitland v Wilmott and anor** ET Case No.1301020/07: M was a supply teacher who taught religious education (RE). She allegedly referred to some of her pupils as 'devils' and told one girl that she was not good enough to be a Christian, and that if she ever got married it would end in divorce. M's assignment was eventually terminated because she was seen as too 'evangelical'. The tribunal rejected her direct discrimination claim under the 2003 Religion or Belief Regulations. M's assignment was terminated because, among other things, she was attempting to impose her own religious views rather than teach RE in a factual and objective way

- **Rao v University Hospitals of Leicester NHS Trust** ET Case No.1901029/09: R, who had a strong Christian faith, began working for the Trust as a nurse in 2005. He enrolled for a course in palliative care in May 2008. During one session, students were asked to participate in a simulation where they were expected to discuss the effect of advanced illness on sexual relations with other students acting as patients. R declined to do this because he did not believe that it was appropriate. Instead, he suggested to the 'patient' that she might find visiting a church for an hour helpful, even when she told him that she did not go to church. R also told her that the doctor could not say when she would die as only God could do that. R resigned midway through a disciplinary process for breaching the Nursing and Midwifery Council's Code of Conduct. R's direct discrimination claim under the 2003 Religion or Belief Regulations was rejected by the employment tribunal. The treatment that he had been subjected to was not on the ground of his religion but on the ground of the inappropriate manifestation of his religion and the reasonable expectation that this would reoccur in the future.

11.54 Is UK approach compliant with Article 9?
Concern has been expressed by some legal commentators and religious groups and by the Equality and Human Rights Commission (EHRC) that the approach

254

taken by UK courts and tribunals when interpreting the religion or belief provisions in the 2003 Religion or Belief Regulations and the EqA contravenes the fundamental rights guaranteed by Article 9 ECHR. There are currently two sets of proceedings before the ECtHR seeking to clarify the scope of Article 9 in the context of claims by employees that they have been discriminated against for manifesting their Christian beliefs while at work. Each set of proceedings comprises two separate cases that have been consolidated for the purpose of the hearing before the ECtHR.

The first set of proceedings – Eweida and Chaplin v United Kingdom (Application Nos.48420/10 and 59842/10) – concerns employees disciplined by their respective employers for persisting in wearing crosses that were open to view. As outlined under 'Is a right to manifest protected by S.10 EqA? – dress and jewellery' above, their claims of religion or belief discrimination under the 2003 Religion or Belief Regulations were unsuccessful. The second set of proceedings – Ladele and McFarlane v United Kingdom (Application Nos.51671/10 and 36516/10) – concerns two employees who were disciplined for refusing to carry out particular job duties because those duties conflicted with their personal religious convictions. Again, as previously discussed, their claims of discrimination under the 2003 Religion or Belief Regulations were unsuccessful – see 'Is a right to manifest protected by S.10 EqA? – conflict between different protected rights' above. In both these sets of proceedings the EHRC has successfully applied to intervene so as to be able to make representations to the ECtHR. The EHRC has now published its full written submissions to the Court, the details of which are summarised below.

EHRC's submissions to ECtHR. Having been permitted to intervene in the **11.55** two sets of proceedings mentioned above, the EHRC published its formal written submissions to the ECtHR in September 2011. In the Eweida and Chaplin case (involving the right of employees to wear crosses visible to all), the EHRC submits that, on the basis of recent ECtHR case law such as Jakobski v Poland 2010 30 BHRC 417, ECtHR, Article 9 can be engaged not only where a particular religion compels an adherent to manifest his or her convictions in a particular way but also where the adherent follows non-prescribed religious practices. In other words, Article 9 can protect decisions to express or manifest religious convictions that are merely 'motivated or inspired by a religion' rather than being a mandatory requirement of the religion, provided the form of manifestation or expression is 'reasonable'. The EHRC acknowledges that this recent trend marks a departure from the stance adopted by the ECtHR and the European Commission of Human Rights in many previous cases (including Arrowsmith v United Kingdom 1980 3 EHRR 218, ECtHR).

The Jakobski case concerned a legal challenge brought by a Buddhist prisoner in respect of the Polish prison authorities' refusal of his request to be served vegetarian food. The ECtHR held that the applicant's wish to adhere to a

255

vegetarian diet could be regarded as having been motivated or inspired by his religion and was not unreasonable. The refusal to provide him with vegetarian meals fell within the scope of Article 9(1). The Court concluded that his rights had been unjustifiably violated because a fair balance had not been struck between the interests of the institution and other prisoners, and the particular interests of the applicant. Applying this rationale, the EHRC contends that the fact that not all Christians choose to wear a cross should not necessarily undermine the rights of those for whom the display of the cross is an essential and reasonable aspect of their autonomous interpretation of their faith. In its submissions, the EHRC criticises the fact that UK courts have sometimes concluded – for example, in Eweida v British Airways plc 2010 ICR 890, CA – that Article 9 is not engaged if a claimant's complaint relates to a restriction on a particular form of manifestation which is not an actual requirement of the religion in question. This means that the courts in such cases never reach the point of having to consider whether the interference in the right enshrined by Article 9(1) is proportionate within the terms of Article 9(2). In the EHRC's view, this betrays a failure of UK law to pay proper regard to the overarching requirements of Article 9 when considering matters of religion and belief.

11.56 The EHRC further contends that the extent to which there is a substantive interference in the fundamental right to manifest religion or belief should include consideration of the extent to which the particular manifestation is not a requirement of the religion or belief in question. In an employment context, the question of whether there has been an interference with a person's Article 9 rights is not to be determined solely by reference to the choices the person has made in accepting particular employment but also by reference to the actions of the employer. In this regard, where a person has accepted a job knowing their manifestation of religion or belief will conflict with the job, this is a factor that should be carefully considered at the interference stage, i.e. when determining whether an interference with Article 9 has occurred. Whether or not a person has accepted particular restrictions on their beliefs and whether accommodations could or should have been made are issues that should also be considered in the context of proportionality.

The EHRC also questions the extent to which the UK approach to deciding whether there has been unlawful indirect discrimination fails to comply with Article 9. It criticises the fact that UK courts have held (as in Eweida v British Airways plc (above)) that, in order to prove that a provision, criterion or practice (PCP) has an adverse disparate impact, it is necessary to show that those who share the same religious belief as the claimant are placed at a disadvantage by the PCP. In other words, the focus is on group rather than individual disadvantage. The EHRC contends that group disadvantage may be particularly difficult to demonstrate in the context of diverse religious beliefs which (unlike other protected characteristics such as race or national origin) are legitimately subject to autonomous interpretation by individual adherents.

In Eweida, for example, the Court of Appeal relied on the fact that no other employee had ever made a request to wear a crucifix over their uniform in order to find that the claimant's desire to wear the crucifix was merely 'a personal choice'. The necessary group disadvantage was thus lacking. In the EHRC's view this reasoning overlooks or underplays the serious individual detriment that can be caused by a general rule prohibiting a manifestation of religious belief.

In general, the Commission contends that cases such as Eweida v British **11.57** Airways plc (above) and Chaplin v Royal Devon and Exeter NHS Foundation Trust ET Case No.1702886/09 demonstrate a failure of the UK courts rigorously to assess the question of proportionality and to strike a fair balance between an employee's and an employer's legitimate aims. In its view, there is a difference between being permitted to wear a religious symbol that does not have an adverse effect on doing a job, and not being permitted to wear such a symbol that does have an adverse effect. This difference should be properly reflected when it comes to considering proportionality.

Turning to the submissions made in Ladele and McFarlane v United Kingdom, the EHRC reiterates its view that: (i) Article 9 can be engaged to protect a person who seeks to manifest religious beliefs in a way that is not a mandatory requirement of the religion in question; and (ii) the question of whether there has been an interference with a person's Article 9 rights is not to be determined solely by reference to the choices the person has made in accepting particular employment but also by reference to the actions of the employer. However, the EHRC is cognisant of the fact that Ladele v London Borough of Islington and anor 2010 ICR 532, CA, and McFarlane v Relate Avon Ltd 2010 ICR 507, EAT (both discussed under 'Is a right to manifest protected by S.10 EqA? – conflict between different protected rights' above), concern claims brought by employees responsible for providing public services – a registrar employed by a local authority to carry out marriages and civil partnerships in the former case, and a Relate counsellor responsible for providing relationship counselling in the latter – and that both these employees felt unable to offer their services to same-sex couples owing to their private religious beliefs. This resulted in a clash between the rights of those who sought to manifest their religious beliefs and the rights of gay people not to be discriminated against.

The EHRC points out that the ECtHR has recognised that interference with **11.58** some rights will require particularly strong justification and that the right to equal treatment on the ground of sexual orientation is one such right – see, for example, Salgueiro da Silva Mouta v Portugal 2001 31 EHRR 47, ECtHR. In view of this, the EHRC contends that public sector employees cannot expect their public functions to be shaped to accommodate their personal religious beliefs, and that it should generally be regarded as proportionate for an employer to refuse to make an accommodation where a public-facing employee

257

seeks to be exempted from performing his or her job duties or supplying services on discriminatory grounds. The employer's refusal will normally be justified by reference to the legitimate aim of eliminating discrimination and advancing equality.

11.59 **General conclusion.** The two sets of proceedings currently before the ECtHR raise interesting issues about the extent to which UK protection against discrimination on the ground of religion or belief is out of synch with the levels of protection required by Article 9.

Pending the actual decisions of the ECtHR in these cases, it is worth speculating whether the general approach taken by UK courts and tribunals is likely to be found wanting. In reality, it would require a sea-change in the ECtHR's traditional approach if it were to start substituting its own view for that of national courts concerning what is a proportional interference with the right to manifest religious belief. This is particularly so given that the Court has consistently held that this right is susceptible to strict limitations within the workplace. In view of its previous case law, it is difficult see on what grounds the ECtHR could impugn the approaches adopted by the tribunals in Chaplin v Royal Devon and Exeter NHS Foundation Trust, Ladele v London Borough of Islington and anor and McFarlane v Relate Avon Ltd (all above). Indeed, it is arguable that Article 9(1) rights are not even engaged in these cases given that the respective employers clearly did not apply less favourable treatment to the claimants because of their particular religious beliefs. But assuming for the moment that an interference in Article 9(1) rights did occur, there is a strong possibility that the approach adopted by the various tribunals was fully compliant with what Article 9(2) demands. The correct approach is essentially one of proportionality. Did the employer pursue a legitimate aim in restricting the claimant's (limited) right to manifest his or her religion or belief and, if so, was the restriction proportionate in the circumstances?

11.60 Applying this test to the Chaplin case, even though the tribunal accepted that the employer's policy on the wearing of jewellery constituted a particular disadvantage to those who shared the claimant's Christian belief, it ruled that the policy was a 'proportionate means of achieving a legitimate aim'. A similar conclusion was reached in the Ladele and McFarlane cases, where the justification defence was, if anything, even stronger. In those cases, the respective employers' requirements that the employees comply with their contractual duties was found to be manifestly proportionate given that the fundamental rights of others were at risk. The claimants were effectively seeking, because of their personal convictions, to be exempted from their duty to deliver public services free from discrimination to all. Given that the ECtHR itself has previously gone out of its way to stress that interference with the rights of others is a weighty consideration when determining the proportionality of any interference with rights guaranteed by Article 9(1), it is unlikely, in our view, that the ECtHR will conclude that there is anything amiss with the conclusions reached by the tribunals (and upheld on appeal by the higher courts) in these cases.

We would respectfully argue that only in respect of Eweida v British Airways plc (above) is there any reasonable doubt that the UK approach is fully compliant with Article 9. In that case, the principal basis on which the claimant's indirect discrimination case was rejected was that she was unable to show that the employer's restriction on wearing visible neck adornments caused disadvantage to those who shared the same religious belief. The particular way in which the claimant framed her complaint was that fellow Christians as a whole would be put at a substantial disadvantage by the employer's dress code. However, the tribunal found that there was no evidence that other practising Christians would have been unable to comply with the dress code given that the wearing of a cross was a matter of personal preference rather than a mandatory requirement of Christian scripture or faith. Both the EAT and the Court of Appeal upheld this finding. Lord Justice Sedley, giving the main judgment in the Court of Appeal, held that the definition of indirect discrimination in Reg 3(1)(b) of the 2003 Religion or Belief Regulations (now replicated in S.19 EqA) required some identifiable section of the workforce (even if only a small one) that would also suffer the same disadvantage as the claimant. His Lordship pointed out that there was no indication that the EU Equal Treatment Framework Directive (No.2000/78) intended either that solitary disadvantage should be sufficient or that any requirement of plural disadvantage must be dropped. The use of the conditional 'would put persons... at a particular disadvantage' in both the Regulations and the Directive did not have either the purpose or the effect of requiring the tribunal to aggregate the claimant with what may be an entirely hypothetical peer-group to whom the same disadvantage is to be attributed. Such an argument loaded far too much on the word 'would'.

Given this finding, it was not strictly necessary to consider the issue of **11.61** proportionality. However, the employment tribunal did intimate that it would have found the employers' dress code requirement not to be proportional had it held that indirect discrimination had occurred. But the Court of Appeal by a majority concluded that it would have overturned that decision had it been necessary to do so. The claimant's objection to concealing her cross was an entirely personal decision, neither arising from any doctrine of her faith nor interfering with her observance of it, and the issue had not been raised by any other employee. In fact, the claimant had complied with the uniform policy for seven years before raising it as a concern. The employer had generally sought to accommodate staff diversity and had dealt conscientiously with her complaint (even offering her a non-customer-facing role, which she had declined). These considerations, when weighed against the impact on the claimant of not being permitted to wear a cross in open view at work, meant that any indirect discrimination resulting from the employer's dress code was objectively justified.

It may be that the Court of Appeal's interpretation of when indirect discrimination arises is overly restrictive. Arguably, in view of the statutory phrase '*would* put persons… at a particular disadvantage' (our stress) in Reg 3(1)(b) of the 2003 Religion or Belief Regulations (now S.19 EqA), it should have been enough for the claimant simply to show that application of the employer's policy 'would' have caused disadvantage to anyone who, along with Ms Ladele herself, believed that the cross should be visibly worn. But even if, for the sake of argument, it is assumed that the Court of Appeal got this wrong, would this make UK law non-compliant with Article 9? In our view, on balance, it would not. Employers have been given every reason by the decisions of the European Commission of Human Rights and the ECtHR to believe that the scope for employees to manifest their religious beliefs within the workplace is limited. Additionally, when it comes to the forms that such manifestation can take, the ECtHR has drawn a distinction between the requirements of a religion that are mandatory and those that are not. It is indisputable that wearing the cross for a Christian falls into the latter category. It is therefore difficult to discern any clear basis on which the ECtHR would be willing to narrow the margin of appreciation that it has always accorded to signatory states when determining how Convention rights should be secured under national laws. When it comes to proportionality in the context of indirect discrimination, it is even more difficult to see any basis for the ECtHR to assume responsibility for making the required assessment. In the Eweida case, the Court of Appeal said that it would have held that it was proportional to deprive the claimant of the right visibly to wear an item of symbolic jewellery under the terms of a dress code which applied equally to 30,000 other employees regardless of their religion or beliefs. This seems, on its face, to be a perfectly fair conclusion in view of the particular factors that the Court held to be relevant.

12 Sex

In 1919 the large contribution made by women to the war effort during the **12.1** First World War (1914–18) resulted in the Government of the day making the first significant legislative foray into the field of sex equality: the Sex Disqualification (Removal) Act 1919. That Act provided that a person could not be disqualified by sex or marriage from exercising any public function, holding any civil or judicial office or post, entering any civil profession or vocation, or being admitted to any incorporated society. However, the 1919 Act did not protect women from discrimination once they had entered an office or profession. Such protection only came into being on 29 December 1975 with the coming into force of both the Sex Discrimination Act 1975 (SDA) and the Equal Pay Act 1970 (EqPA).

For 35 years, the SDA and the EqPA, together with the relevant EU measures (see 'European and human rights law' below), formed what Lord Denning MR described as 'a single code' dealing with gender discrimination – see Shields v E Coomes (Holdings) Ltd 1978 ICR 1159, CA. The distinction between the two Acts is discussed under 'Protection under antecedent legislation' below, but, briefly, the EqPA was aimed primarily at discriminatory terms in an employment contract while the SDA covered discrimination in the formation, variation and termination of such a contract, together with harassment. Both the SDA and the EqPA (and, indeed, the 1919 Act, which suprisingly continued in force even though its provisions were overtaken by the 'recruitment' provisions in the SDA) were repealed on 1 October 2010 and replaced by the Equality Act 2010 (EqA).

European and human rights law   12.2

No discussion of UK sex discrimination pay law would be possible without reference to European law – in particular, to the various equality Directives that have been enacted since 1976 dealing with equal treatment on the ground of gender in the context of employment and social security (which embraces occupational pension membership and benefits).

Article 2 of the Treaty on the Functioning of the European Union (TFEU) – the successor to the Treaty of Rome, which established the European Community – speaks of the promotion of 'equality between men and women' as one of the primary functions of the EU. Article 3(1) sets out a long list of the various 'activities' in which the EU is lawfully entitled to engage, with Article 3(2) expressly stipulating that '[i]n all the activities referred to in this Article, the Community shall aim to eliminate inequalities, and to promote equality, between men and women'. However, until recently, there has never been any question of this principle of equal treatment attracting the same elevated status that applies to the right to equal pay for equal work between men and women as enshrined in what was originally Article 199 of the Treaty of Rome and is now Article 157 TFEU. The latter has, ever since 1976, been consistently recognised by the European Court of Justice (ECJ) as conferring directly enforceable rights on those employed by private as well as public employers, and it is accordingly a principle that has been relied upon to provide a right to equal pay in the face of incompatible national law and even in the absence of any relevant national law provisions at all – see Defrenne v Sabena 1976 ICR 547, ECJ. In contrast, the orthodox view has been that the general references to equal treatment in Articles 2 and 3 of what is now the TFEU merely provide a legal basis for the adoption of more detailed measures to ensure the application of the principle of equal treatment. As a result, the issue of sex discrimination and gender equality has largely been dealt with by way of Directives.

12.3 However, this orthodoxy has recently been called into question in the context of EU provisions outlawing age discrimination in employment contained in the EU Equal Treatment Framework Directive (No.2000/78). In at least two cases, the ECJ appears to have ruled that the principle of equal treatment is so fundamental that it has direct effect in the same way as Article 157, and that the accompanying Directive merely 'gives expression' to that principle – see Mangold v Helm 2006 IRLR 143, ECJ, and Kücükdeveci v Swedex GmbH and Co KG 2010 IRLR 346, ECJ. As yet, it remains uncertain whether this is the correct interpretation of these cases and whether, in any event, the ECJ's rulings are confined to age discrimination (which admittedly seems unlikely) or whether they extend to the principle of equal treatment in other contexts (including sex/ gender). However, it would seem that a case currently waiting to be heard by the ECJ – Tyrolean Airways v Betriebsrat Bord der Tyrolean (Case No.C-132/11) – may well help resolve the conundrum. This case, together with a more detailed consideration of whether the principle of equal treatment has general direct effect, is discussed in Chapter 5, 'Age', under 'Protection under European law'.

12.4 Recast Equal Treatment Directive

In practice, it is unlikely that individuals seeking to complain of sex discrimination will need to rely on the general principle of equal treatment contained in the TFEU given the wide protection afforded by the recast EU Equal Treatment Directive (No.2006/54) ('the recast Directive').

Until 2006, there were seven Directives dealing with gender equality:

- No.75/117 on the application of the principle of equal pay for men and women (the Equal Pay Directive)

- No.76/207 on equal treatment for men and women as regards access to employment (the Equal Treatment Directive)

- No.2002/73, amending Directive No.76/207, on equal treatment for men and women as regards employment, vocational training and promotion and working conditions

- No.86/378 on equal treatment for men and women in occupational social security schemes

- No.96/97, amending Directive No.86/378, on the implementation of the principle of equal treatment for men and women in occupational social security schemes

- No.97/80 on the burden of proof in cases of discrimination based on sex (the Burden of Proof Directive)

- No.98/52 on the extension of Directive No.97/80 to the United Kingdom.

12.5 However, in 2006 the European Parliament and the Council of Ministers consolidated all seven measures, together with relevant case law from the ECJ, into the recast Directive, which is concerned with 'the implementation of the principle of equal opportunities and equal treatment of men and women in matters of employment and occupation'. The Directive came into force on 15 August 2006 and its provisions had to be implemented by Member States by 15 August 2008. However, in the case of the United Kingdom, most of the mandatory measures had already been implemented, principally by the SDA and the EqPA. The seven consolidated Directives were repealed with effect from 15 August 2009 and, following the repeal of the SDA and EqPA on 1 October 2010, it is the EqA that now serves to implement the provisions of the recast Directive into UK national law.

12.6 **Definitions.** Article 2(1) of the recast Directive contains the key definitions that were previously contained in the Equal Treatment Directive (as amended). These include the various forms of discrimination that have become familiar not only in the context of sex discrimination but across all the discrimination strands governed by EU law. The relevant definitions are:

- 'direct discrimination': where one person is treated less favourably on the ground of sex than another is, has been or would be treated in a comparable situation

- 'indirect discrimination': where an apparently neutral provision, criterion or practice would put persons of one sex at a particular disadvantage compared

263

with persons of the other sex, unless that provision, criterion or practice is objectively justified by a legitimate aim, and the means of achieving that aim are appropriate and necessary

- 'harassment': where unwanted conduct related to the sex of a person occurs with the purpose or effect of violating the dignity of a person, and of creating an intimidating, hostile, degrading, humiliating or offensive environment

- 'sexual harassment': where any form of unwanted verbal, non-verbal or physical conduct of a sexual nature occurs, with the purpose or effect of violating the dignity of a person, in particular when creating an intimidating, hostile, degrading, humiliating or offensive environment.

Article 2(2) states that discrimination includes harassment and sexual harassment, instructions to discriminate, and any less favourable treatment of a woman related to pregnancy or maternity leave.

12.7 **Meaning of 'equal treatment'.** Chapter 1 of Title II of the recast Directive consolidates the provisions of the Equal Pay Directive, while Chapter 2 deals with the principle of equal treatment in occupational pension schemes. It is, however, Chapter 3 (Articles 14–16), 'Equal treatment as regards access to employment, vocational training and promotion and working conditions', which is of most significance to sex discrimination. Article 14(1) provides that there shall be no direct or indirect discrimination on the ground of sex in relation to:

- access to employment, self-employment or occupation, including selection criteria, recruitment conditions and promotion

- access to all types and to all levels of vocational guidance and vocational training, including work experience

- employment and working conditions, including dismissals, as well as pay within the meaning of Article 157 TFEU

- membership of, involvement in, or benefits afforded by an organisation of workers or employers, or any organisation whose members carry on a particular profession.

12.8 In respect of access to employment, including training leading to employment, Article 14(2) permits Member States to introduce measures providing that 'a difference of treatment which is based on a characteristic related to sex shall not constitute discrimination where, by reason of the nature of the particular occupational activities concerned or of the context in which they are carried out, such a characteristic constitutes a genuine and determining occupational requirement, provided that its objective is legitimate and the requirement is proportionate'.

Chapter 3 of the recast Directive also addresses what have become known as 'family-friendly rights'. Article 15 provides that a woman returning from maternity leave should be entitled to return to the same job or an equivalent post, on no less favourable conditions, and benefit from any improvement in working conditions to which she would have been entitled had she not been on maternity leave. Article 16 goes on to state that if a Member State has recognised rights to adoption and paternity leave, it should ensure that working men and women are protected against dismissal due to exercising those rights. In addition, on returning from such leave, workers are entitled to the same level of protection as a woman returning from maternity leave is afforded under Article 15.

European Convention on Human Rights 12.9

There is no free-standing right to gender equality under the European Convention on Human Rights and Fundamental Freedoms. However, Article 14 of the Convention prohibits discrimination on a number of grounds, including sex, in respect of the enjoyment of *other* Convention rights. So, for example, an individual may claim that he or she has not enjoyed the same rights to freedom of expression (Article 10) or the right to marry (Article 12) as members of the opposite sex as required by Article 14, but could not bring a claim directly under Article 14 in respect of less favourable treatment unrelated to another Convention right. Some signatory states to the Convention have adopted Protocol 12, which extends the broad prohibition on discrimination found in Article 14 to the enjoyment of 'any right set forth by law' and the exercise of public authority. However, the United Kingdom has thus far declined to sign up to the Protocol and there is no prospect of that position changing in the near future.

Protection under antecedent legislation 12.10

Prior to the introduction of the EqA on 1 October 2010, the principal sex discrimination statutes in the United Kingdom were the EqPA and the SDA, both of which came into force on 29 December 1975. (Note that equivalent protection in Northern Ireland was, and still is, provided by the Equal Pay Act (Northern Ireland) 1970 and the Sex Discrimination (Northern Ireland) Order 1976 SI 1976/1042, both of which are unaffected by the EqA and remain in force). The EqPA was concerned with *contractual* sex discrimination, i.e. less favourable treatment of women compared to men (or vice versa) in the terms of employment. Despite its name, the Act was never limited to equality in pay but did not offer a remedy for sex discrimination that was not rooted in the contract of employment. So, for example, an employer's refusal to recruit or promote a woman because of her sex was not covered, as it was not a contractual matter; nor was the dismissal of an employee for alleged sex discriminatory reasons. Such discrimination was left to the SDA, which prohibited any less

265

favourable treatment on the ground of sex in the formation, operation, variation and termination of the employment relationship. In contrast to the EqPA, unequal treatment falling within the scope of the SDA could be proved either by reference to an actual comparator, or by consideration of how a hypothetical comparator would have been treated. Moreover, the SDA had a far broader reach than the EqPA as it applied not only to the employment field but also to the supply of goods and services, education and vocational training.

The SDA made it unlawful to discriminate directly or indirectly in the arrangements made for the purposes of determining who should be offered employment; in the terms on which an applicant is offered employment; by refusing or deliberately omitting to offer employment; in the way an employee is afforded access to opportunities for promotion, transfer or training, or to any other benefits, facilities or services; by refusing or deliberately omitting to afford an employee access to those opportunities, benefits, facilities or services; by dismissing an employee; by subjecting an employee to any other detriment; or by subjecting a former employee to a detriment. The Act also made it unlawful to subject a job applicant, employee or former employee to sex-based or sexual harassment. It applied to both women and men, with the exception of the special treatment accorded to women in connection with pregnancy or childbirth.

12.11 The SDA was amended on numerous occasions, usually to comply with the mandatory provisions of European Directives. Notable amendments were introduced by the following Regulations:

- Sex Discrimination (Indirect Discrimination and Burden of Proof) Regulations 2001 SI 2001/2660: these Regulations inserted S.63A into the SDA, providing that once a complainant has established a prima facie case of sex discrimination before an employment tribunal, the burden of proof shifts to the employer to show that there is a non-discriminatory reason for its actions. The Regulations also altered the definition of 'indirect discrimination' for the purposes of employment, replacing the phrase 'requirement or condition' with 'provision, criterion or practice'

- Employment Equality (Sex Discrimination) Regulations 2005 SI 2005/2467: these Regulations were enacted to implement the EU Equal Treatment Amendment Directive (No.2002/73). They introduced a number of amendments to the SDA, including further changes to the definition of 'indirect discrimination'; express prohibitions on harassment on the ground of a victim's sex or of a sexual nature; a prohibition on discrimination on the ground of pregnancy or maternity leave; and an extension of the Act's territorial scope

- Sex Discrimination Act 1975 (Amendment) Regulations 2008 SI 2008/656: these Regulations were enacted to rectify failings identified by the High

Court in judicial review proceedings concerning the 2005 amendments outlined immediately above – see R (Equal Opportunities Commission) v Secretary of State for Trade and Industry 2007 ICR 1234, QBD. In that case the Court found that a number of the 2005 amendments did not adequately implement the corresponding provisions of the Equal Treatment Amendment Directive and as a result further amendments to the SDA were introduced. The definition of harassment was altered to substitute the phrase 'on the ground of her sex' with the phrase 'related to her sex or that of another person', which meant that a person complaining of harassment under the SDA was no longer required to show that the alleged treatment took place because the complainant was a woman (or a man). The Regulations also inserted a new S.6(2B)–(2D) into the SDA to provide that an employer who failed to take reasonably practicable steps to protect employees from third-party harassment related to sex after being made aware that such harassment had occurred on at least two other occasions would be treated as subjecting the woman to harassment. In addition, S.3A was amended to remove the requirement for a woman alleging unfavourable treatment on the ground of pregnancy or maternity leave to compare how she would have been treated had she not been pregnant or on maternity leave, and S.6A was amended to, inter alia, eliminate any distinction between ordinary maternity leave and additional maternity leave in respect of the protection of non-pay benefits under the contract of employment.

Meaning of 'sex'   12.12

Case law under the SDA established that the notion of 'sex' discrimination was limited to gender, and could not be extended or interpreted to embrace discrimination on the ground of a person's sexual orientation – see (1) Macdonald v Ministry of Defence (2) Pearce v Governing Body of Mayfield Secondary School 2003 ICR 937, HL. The House of Lords held in that case (which concerned two joined appeals) that there was no discrimination on the ground of sex when a male officer was forced to resign from the armed forces because he was homosexual, or when a female schoolteacher was subjected to a campaign of verbal abuse by pupils because she was a lesbian. In both cases the appropriate comparator was a person of the opposite sex who shared with the claimant the characteristic of homosexuality, and it was accepted that such a person would have been treated in the same way.

However, a different conclusion was reached in respect of transsexuals. In P v S and anor 1996 ICR 795, ECJ, the European Court of Justice held that it was contrary to the Equal Treatment Directive to treat an individual less favourably because he or she intended to undergo, or has undergone, gender reassignment. The scope of the Directive could not be confined simply to discrimination based on the fact that a person is of one or the other sex. Where a person is dismissed on the ground that he or she has undergone gender reassignment, that person

267

has been treated unfavourably by comparison with persons of the sex to which he or she was deemed to belong before undergoing gender reassignment.

12.13 Subsequently, the EAT held in Chessington World of Adventures Ltd v Reed 1998 ICR 97, EAT, that it was possible to read S.1(1)(a) SDA – which prohibited direct discrimination (i.e. less favourable treatment on the ground of sex) – in a way consistent with the Directive as interpreted in P v S. The Appeal Tribunal ruled that discrimination on the basis of gender reassignment was essentially discrimination based on the sex of the person concerned and so was covered by the provisions of the 1975 Act. (Note, that as a result of these decisions, the SDA was amended in 1999 by the Sex Discrimination (Gender Reassignment) Regulations 1999 SI 1999/1102 to provide express and free-standing protection to transsexuals.)

12.14 ## Protection under the Equality Act

On 1 October 2010 the EqA replaced the SDA and the EqPA, which were repealed. In common with the other strands of discrimination, instead of the previous terminology which referred to discrimination *'on the ground of'* sex, the new Act has substituted the phrase *'protected characteristic of'* sex – S.11. This characteristic is protected from all forms of discrimination previously prohibited by the SDA, including direct and indirect discrimination, harassment, and victimisation. As was previously the case, the protection against sex discrimination under the EqA extends beyond the employment field (Part 5) to cover services and public functions (Part 3), premises (Part 4), education (Part 6) and associations (Part 7).

As explained in more detail under 'Demarcation between sex discrimination and equality of terms' below, the distinction between claims of sex discrimination and equal pay previously maintained by the SDA and the EqPA is preserved under the EqA. Accordingly, claims relating to equality of contractual terms (including equal pay) are governed not by the protected characteristic of sex as defined by S.11 EqA but by specific provisions contained in Chapter 3 of Part 5 of the Act.

12.15 It is noteworthy that the drafters of the EqA did not take the opportunity to substitute the word 'gender' for 'sex' in recognition of the increasingly popular use of the phrase 'gender discrimination' to describe discrimination based on sex. It may have been felt that the word 'sex' connotes the physiology of being male or female, whereas the word 'gender' imports wider connotations such as societal assumptions about the roles of the sexes, thus giving the term a political and social dimension. This distinction between 'sex' and 'gender' is observed, for example, in the Glossary to the World Health Organisation's 'Department of Gender and Women's Health Biennial Report 2002–2003', which defines the respective terms as follows: 'Gender is used to describe those characteristics of women and men, which are socially constructed, while sex refers to those which are biologically determined. People are born female or male but learn to be girls and boys who grow into women and men. This learned behaviour makes up gender identity and determines gender roles.' The EqA opts for the word 'sex' when referring to discrimination between males and females. However, it uses the word 'gender' when dealing with discrimination against transsexuals or those undergoing the process of sex change ('gender reassignment') – see Chapter 7, 'Gender reassignment'. The EqA also contains provisions relating to the 'gender pay gap' in the context of the right to equal pay – see S.78.

Section 11(a) EqA provides that a reference to a person who has the protected characteristic of sex is a reference to a man or a woman. A 'man' means a male of any age, and a 'woman' means a female of any age – S.212(1). A reference to persons who share the protected characteristic of sex is a reference to persons of the same sex – S.11(b). This provision differs slightly (although not in substance) from the approach taken by the SDA. Instead of affording equal protection to both sexes, S.1 SDA prohibited direct and indirect discrimination against women. However, by virtue of S.2 SDA that provision had to be read as applying equally to men, with an exception to accommodate the special treatment afforded to women in connection with pregnancy or childbirth.

Demarcation between sex discrimination and equality of terms   12.16
Under the EqA the demarcation between sex discrimination claims and claims related to equality of contractual terms (including equal pay) imposed by the SDA and the EqPA has been maintained in much the same form (albeit with one important difference noted below). Different parts of the EqA govern the different types of claim:

- Part 2 (read with Chapter 1 of Part 5) covers sex discrimination in employment generally (equivalent to the scope of the old SDA)

- Chapter 3 of Part 5 covers contractual terms and provides for the insertion of a 'sex equality clause' (equivalent to the 'equality clause' formerly inserted by the EqPA) into every contract of employment.

The division between the two regimes is enforced by Ss.70 and 71 EqA. S.70(1) provides that S.39(2) (found in Chapter 1 of Part 5) – which prohibits discrimination in terms of employment, among other things – has no effect in relation to a term that is modified or included by virtue of a sex equality clause, or that would be so modified were it not for a successful 'material factor' defence under S.69 EqA. (A similar exclusion applies in relation to Ss.49(6) and 50(6), which cover discrimination against office-holders.) Furthermore, neither the inclusion of a less favourable term (compared with that of an actual comparator doing equal work) in the employee's terms, or the failure to include in the employee's terms a term equal to that enjoyed by such a comparator, is

269

to be treated as sex discrimination under Part 2 – S.70(2). This replicates old S.8(5) SDA, with the same effect, i.e. if all the elements for an equal pay claim are there (equal work, actual comparator, etc), then the claimant cannot choose to bring a sex discrimination claim instead – it is the 'equal pay' route or nothing. If the claim is defeated by the employer's 'material factor' defence, there will be no prospect of a sex discrimination claim in the alternative.

12.17 The specific exclusion of contractual pay claims from the sex discrimination legislation by virtue of S.6(6) SDA is replicated in S.71(1) EqA. This states that S.39(2) does not apply to a term of a person's work that relates to pay but in relation to which a sex equality clause has 'no effect'. Thus, the default position – as previously – is that pay claims are excluded from the sex discrimination provisions, *regardless* of whether the elements of an equal pay claim are present. However, S.71(2) goes on to provide that this exclusion applies 'except in so far as treatment of the person amounts to a contravention of [S.39(2)] by virtue of S.13 [direct discrimination]'. (S.71(2) also refers to S.14, which covers combined discrimination, but this provision has not yet been brought into force.) This represents a key difference between the position set out in S.71 EqA and the position under the old law as set out in S.6(6) SDA as it specifically allows for a claim of sex discrimination in pay to be brought under the sex discrimination provisions in limited circumstances. The significance of this is that sex discrimination in pay may, for the first time, be established on the basis of a hypothetical comparison. The scope and implications of this new provision are discussed in detail in IDS Employment Law Handbook, 'Equal Pay' (2011), Chapter 4, 'Comparators', under 'Hypothetical comparators'.

13 Sexual orientation

European Convention on Human Rights
Protection under the Equality Act
Overlap with other protected characteristics

Protection against discrimination on the ground of sexual orientation was first **13.1** introduced into the national law of Great Britain by the Employment Equality (Sexual Orientation) Regulations 2003 SI 2003/1661 ('the 2003 Sexual Orientation Regulations'). These Regulations – which came into force on 1 December 2003 – were introduced to implement the relevant aspects of the EU Equal Treatment Framework Directive (No.2000/78). Under them, direct and indirect discrimination, harassment and victimisation were prohibited in an employment context where the discrimination was on the ground of sexual orientation. In April 2007 the 2003 Sexual Orientation Regulations were supplemented by the Equality Act (Sexual Orientation) Regulations 2007 SI 2007/1263, which made it unlawful to discriminate on the ground of sexual orientation in the provision of goods, facilities and services, education, disposal and management of premises and exercise of public functions.

With effect from 1 October 2010 both the 2003 Regulations and the 2007 Regulations were repealed and replaced by the Equality Act 2010 (EqA). S.12 of that Act defines the protected characteristic of sexual orientation in virtually identical terms to the way in which it was defined under Reg 2(1) of the 2003 Sexual Orientation Regulations. The scope of S.12 EqA is discussed in detail under 'Protection under the Equality Act' below.

Prior to the introduction of the 2003 Sexual Orientation Regulations, several **13.2** attempts were made (without success) to interpret existing legislation in a way that would afford some measure of protection against discrimination on the ground of sexual orientation. In Grant v South West Trains Ltd 1998 ICR 449, ECJ, the European Court of Justice rejected the contention that the right to equal pay for equal work enshrined in what was then Article 119 of the Treaty of Rome (now Article 157 of the Treaty on the Functioning of the European Union) and EC Equal Pay Directive (No.75/117) (now consolidated into the recast EU Equal Treatment Directive (No.2006/54) precluded discrimination in relation to remunerative benefits on the ground of sexual orientation. In order to be protected, the discrimination had to be shown to be on the ground of sex (i.e. gender). So where both male homosexual employees and women homosexual employees were denied access to a benefit – in this particular case, travel concessions – that the employer made available to the spouses of employees, this was not discriminatory within the terms of European law as it

271

stood at the time. Under domestic UK law, a similar conclusion was reached with regard to the Sex Discrimination Act 1975 (SDA) (now incorporated into the EqA). In (1) MacDonald v Ministry of Defence (2) Pearce v Governing Body of Mayfield School 2003 ICR 937, HL, the House of Lords ruled that the SDA did not protect individuals against discrimination on the ground of their sexual orientation alone. Where the reason for the treatment complained of was the complainant's homosexuality, the correct comparator for the purposes of determining whether the complainant had been treated less favourably was a homosexual person of the opposite sex. On this basis, their Lordships ruled that there had been no discrimination on the ground of sex when a male officer was forced to resign from the armed forces because he was homosexual, nor when a female schoolteacher was subjected to a campaign of verbal abuse by pupils because she was a lesbian. In both cases it was accepted that a homosexual person of the opposite sex would have been treated in exactly the same way.

If nothing else, the patent injustice revealed by the decisions in these cases demonstrated the pressing need for legislative reform. That need was answered with the enactment of the EU Equal Treatment Framework Directive (No.2000/78), which required Member States to introduce into their domestic law measures to combat discrimination on the ground of, inter alia, sexual orientation. The relevant provisions of the Directive came into force on 2 December 2003. On the previous day, the 2003 Sexual Orientation Regulations implementing the mandatory provisions of that Directive into UK law came into effect.

13.3 European Convention on Human Rights

Although S.12 EqA implements into domestic law the mandatory provisions of the EU Equal Treatment Framework Directive (No.2000/78), the Directive does not itself contain any definition of 'sexual orientation'. However, paragraphs 2 and 4 of its Recitals refer to the European Convention for the Protection of Human Rights and Fundamental Freedoms (commonly known as the European Convention on Human Rights (ECHR)), Articles 8 and 14 of which have been interpreted so as to provide protection against discrimination to homosexual and bisexual people. It is a cardinal principle of EU law that EU Directives must be interpreted harmoniously with the provisions of the ECHR. And it is a principle of domestic law that UK domestic legislative provisions must be interpreted so far as possible consistently with both the mandatory provisions of EU law – see Marleasing SA v La Comercial Internacional de Alimentación SA, 1992 1 CMLR 305, ECJ – and, by virtue of S.3 of the Human Rights Act 1998, Convention rights. This means that the jurisprudence of the European Court of Human Rights (ECtHR) on the scope and meaning of Articles 8 and 14 provides an important framework for establishing the scope of the protection to be accorded to gay and bisexual people under the EqA. Accordingly, before turning to a detailed examination of S.12 EqA, it is first appropriate to provide an overview of the case law interpreting the relevant Convention provisions.

Article 8 ECHR provides that: '(1) Everyone has the right to respect for his private and family life, his home and his correspondence. (2) There shall be no interference by a public authority with the exercise of this right except such as is in accordance with the law and is necessary in a democratic society in the interests of national security, public safety or the economic well-being of the country, for the prevention of disorder or crime, for the protection of health or morals, or for the protection of the rights and freedoms of others.'

13.4 Article 14 ECHR prohibits discrimination in the exercise and enjoyment of Convention rights, including those guaranteed by Article 8. It states that: 'The enjoyment of the rights and freedoms set forth in this Convention shall be secured without discrimination on any ground such as sex, race, colour, language, religion, political or other opinion, national or social origin, association with a national minority, property, birth or other status.'

Two things should be noted about Article 14. First, it is not an autonomous, free-standing anti-discrimination measure, but one that seeks to protect against discrimination only in conjunction with substantive Convention rights. Secondly, although sexual orientation is not one of the specific grounds listed, that list is clearly not intended to be exhaustive and sexual orientation has consistently been held to fall within the scope of Article 14 – see, for example, Salgueiro da Silva Mouta v Portugal 2001 31 EHRR 47, ECtHR.

13.5 Taking Articles 8 and 14 together, the courts has held that a person's sexual orientation and sexual life are matters that attract the protection accorded to private and family life, and that this encompasses a person's sexual behaviour – see X v Y 2004 ICR 1634, CA. While emphasising that the term 'private life' is broad and is not susceptible to exhaustive definition, the ECtHR has held that 'elements such as gender identification, name and sexual orientation and sexual life are important elements of the personal sphere protected by Article 8' – PG v United Kingdom 2008 46 EHRR 51, ECtHR. Crucially, the protection accorded by Article 8 goes much further than simply prohibiting discrimination in respect of what goes on in the privacy of the home. Rather, it extends to a right to identity and personal development, including the right to establish relationships with other human beings and with the outside world, stretching even to embrace activities of a professional or business nature. In this sense, the zone of interaction between an individual and others – even when this operates in a public context (such as a workplace) – is capable of being covered by the concept of 'private life' – see Peck v United Kingdom 2003 36 EHRR 41, ECtHR; and Niemietz v Germany 1993 16 EHRR 97, ECtHR.

273

However, as is made expressly clear by Article 8(2), the right to respect for private and family life is not absolute. In common with other Convention rights, it is permissible for states and emanations of states (such as public employers) to interfere with the rights guaranteed under Article 8(1) where this is in accordance with the law, is in pursuit of a legitimate aim, and is necessary in a democratic society. The latter requirement has been interpreted as meaning that any interference must be shown to be proportionate in respect of the legitimate aims sought to be achieved. That said, the ECtHR has held with specific regard to sexual orientation that particularly serious reasons must be shown to exist before any interference will be held to satisfy the requirements of Article 8(2) – see, for example, Smith and Grady v United Kingdom 2000 29 EHRR 493, ECtHR.

13.6 The first successful cases relating to sexual orientation brought under Article 8 concerned the privacy of same-sex relationships. In Dudgeon v United Kingdom 1982 4 EHRR 149, ECtHR, for example, the ECtHR ruled that the criminalisation of homosexual acts was an unjustified violation of the protection enshrined in Article 8. Privacy arguments were also successfully invoked in cases concerning a ban on the recruitment of homosexuals in the armed forces – Smith and Grady v United Kingdom (above) and Lustig-Prean and Beckett v United Kingdom 2000 29 EHRR 548, ECtHR. The Court has also ruled that differing ages of consent for gay and straight people comprised a violation of Article 8 – see L and V v Austria 2003 36 EHRR 55, ECtHR.

A helpful summary of the scope of legal protection accorded to individuals on the ground of their sexual orientation was provided by the High Court in R (Amicus and ors) v Secretary of State for Trade and Industry 2007 ICR 1176, QBD. In that case – a judicial review of the genuine occupational requirements exclusions contained in the 2003 Sexual Orientation Regulations – Mr Justice Richards (as he then was) observed: 'Sexual orientation is a most intimate aspect of private life and personal identity. It is protected under the Convention, in particular under Articles 8 and 14... Such protection extends to the employment context. The Convention case law also shows that weighty reasons are required to justify any interference with an individual's Convention rights not to be discriminated against on grounds of sexual orientation.'

13.7 The main controversy revealed by the case law in this context concerns the extent to which a person's sexual behaviour is protected. While Convention jurisprudence accepts that sexual behaviour and sexual orientation are inextricably intertwined, certain types of conduct have been held not to be protected in view of the circumstances in which it takes place and/or the nature of the conduct in question. This issue – which is also relevant in the context of protection under the EqA – is discussed in detail under 'Protection under the Equality Act – sexual practices and behaviour' below.

274

Protection under the Equality Act

The term 'sexual orientation' in the 2003 Sexual Orientation Regulations was defined as meaning 'sexual orientation towards (a) persons of the same sex; (b) persons of the opposite sex; or (c) persons of the same sex and of the opposite sex' – Reg 2(1). S.12 EqA defines the protected characteristic of sexual orientation in virtually identical terms, save for the fact that a small tweak has been made to the wording of category (c) to make the statutory wording a little more fluent. Accordingly, S.12(1) states that sexual orientation means 'a person's sexual orientation towards (a) persons of the same sex; (b) persons of the opposite sex; or (c) persons of either sex'.

Section 12(2) stipulates that a reference to a person who has the protected characteristic of sexual orientation is a reference to a person of a particular sexual orientation; while a reference to persons who share that protected characteristic is a reference to persons of the same sexual orientation. Thus, a heterosexual man and heterosexual woman are to be regarded as sharing a sexual orientation for the purposes of the Act, and the same is true of a homosexual (gay) man and a homosexual (lesbian) woman. Furthermore, a gay man, for example, is to be regarded as sharing the same protected characteristic as other gay men and lesbians. This is particularly relevant to claims of indirect discrimination in respect of which, by virtue of S.19 EqA, it is necessary to show that a provision, criterion or practice has been applied that puts persons who share the same protected characteristic as the claimant at a particular disadvantage compared with persons who do not share it.

Who is covered?

It is clear from the wording of S.12(1) EqA that homosexuals (gay males and lesbians), bisexual males and females, and heterosexuals ('straight' males and females) are all covered by the protected characteristic of sexual orientation. It is a moot point, however, whether persons who are asexual would similarly be covered, given that the protected characteristic presupposes an orientation based on sexual attraction of one kind or another.

Claimant and comparator having the same sexual orientation. Given the way in which direct discrimination is defined in S.13 EqA, a gay employee would not be entitled to complain that he or she has been subjected to less favourable treatment because of the protected characteristic of sexual orientation in comparison with another gay person. That is because, since both the advantaged and disadvantaged persons are homosexual, it would be impossible to show that the reason for the less favourable treatment was the disadvantaged person's sexuality. However, if, for example, the disadvantaged employee was a gay man and the advantaged person was a gay woman, then, depending on the evidence as to the nature of and reason for the less favourable

275

treatment in question, it might be possible to bring a claim of unlawful direct *sex* (i.e. *gender*) discrimination.

13.11 **Transsexuals.** Section 12 does not cover discrimination on the ground of gender reassignment. Despite a common misconception that transsexualism and sexual orientation are in some way connected, they are in fact entirely separate issues. Transsexuals are covered by specific provisions in the EqA, including S.7, which confers protection on any person who is proposing to undergo, is undergoing or has undergone a process or part of a process for reassigning the person's sex – for more details, see Chapter 7, 'Gender reassignment'.

13.12 **Persons whose sexual orientation is misperceived.** It is clear from the wording of S.12 EqA that the definition of 'sexual orientation' applies as much to heterosexual people as it does to homosexual and bisexual people. This means that if an employee is discriminated against for being heterosexual, he or she will be entitled to bring a claim under the EqA relying on the protected characteristic of sexual orientation.

But what is the position in respect of an employee who suffers discrimination not on account of his or her actual sexual orientation but because of what the discriminator perceives (wrongly) to be his or her sexual orientation? Under the 2003 Sexual Orientation Regulations, such a person was protected from direct discrimination under Reg 3(1)(a), which defined direct discrimination as less favourable treatment 'on grounds of sexual orientation', not on the ground of *the claimant's* sexual orientation. An employee who suffered harassment on account of a misperception about his or her sexual orientation was similarly protected under Reg 5(1). So, for example, in Williams v Ransu Ltd ET Case No.2507210/08 an employment tribunal held that the claimant – a female heterosexual – had been harassed contrary to Reg 5 of the 2003 Sexual Orientation Regulations when, having become friendly with a lesbian colleague, she was subjected to innuendo and speculation emanating from other colleagues about the nature of the friendship. The tribunal held that there was a dimension to the gossip – which it described as 'bigotry' – that plainly had the effect of violating the claimant's dignity and creating a degrading and humiliating environment that was 'on grounds of sexual orientation' within the meaning of Reg 5(1).

13.13 Exactly the same position would now obtain under the EqA. Under S.13(1) direct discrimination occurs where a person treats another less favourably '*because of* a protected characteristic' (our stress). As is explained in detail in Chapter 15, 'Direct discrimination', under 'Discrimination by perception', the substitution of the words 'because of' for the words 'on the grounds of' makes it even clearer than it was before that less favourable treatment on account of a person's perceived sexual orientation (or other protected characteristic) is unlawful.

276

The same is true with regard to harassment claims: S.26 EqA now defines 'harassment' as occurring where a person 'engages in unwanted conduct *related to* a relevant protected characteristic' and the conduct has the purpose or effect of creating an intimidating, hostile, degrading, humiliating or offensive environment for the claimant. Clearly, where such conduct is shown to have been perpetrated on account of a misperception about the claimant's sexual orientation, that conduct will be regarded as 'relating to' the protected characteristic of sexual orientation and will therefore constitute harassment.

The position was less clear-cut under the 2003 Sexual Orientation Regulations **13.14** in relation to a person who was known to be straight but who was nevertheless subjected to harassment in the form of jibes and insults as if he or she was gay. Could such a person claim to have been harassed 'on grounds of sexual orientation' as required by the Regulations? This question arose for consideration in English v Thomas Sanderson Blinds Ltd 2009 ICR 543, CA. In that case, E alleged that he had been subjected to homophobic banter by work colleagues over several years, which started when a colleague discovered that he had attended a boarding school in Brighton. E was not homosexual, nor was he mistakenly thought to be so by his tormentors, and he himself fully accepted that they did not believe him to be homosexual. On these admittedly unusual (and assumed) facts both the employment tribunal and the EAT held that E had no claim under Reg 5 of the 2003 Sexual Orientation Regulations because the homophobic banter, though an unacceptable vehicle for teasing the claimant, was not based on his colleagues' perception (or even their incorrect assumption) that he was homosexual. The banter was not therefore conduct 'on the grounds of sexual orientation' within the meaning of Reg 5(1). On further appeal, however, the Court of Appeal by a majority overturned that decision. It ruled that all that was required was that the claimant's sexual orientation – whether real or imagined – was the basis or ground of unwanted conduct directed at him. On the assumption that E was – as he alleged – repeatedly tormented as being gay, the calculated insult to his dignity, which did not depend at all upon his true sexuality or upon what the tormentors believed it to be, and the consequently intolerable working environment created, brought his case within the scope of Reg 5(1). Lord Justice Laws delivered a dissenting judgment in which he concluded that a person's actual, perceived, or assumed sexual orientation had to be the operative cause of the conduct in question.

The English case concerned a particular set of facts that are unlikely to occur very often – namely, where the claimant is not gay, and his or her colleagues do not believe him or her to be so, and he or she is aware of this fact. But were a similar case to arise again, the same result would undoubtedly be achieved under the EqA. Clearly, banter of the kind that occurred in the English case would be regarded as being 'related to' the protected characteristic of sexual orientation within the terms of S.26, even though the perpetrator is under no illusion about the reality of the claimant's actual sexual orientation.

277

13.15 Sexual practices and behaviour

In guidance notes produced by the Department of Trade and Industry (DTI) – now the Department of Business, Innovation and Skills – that accompanied the 2003 Sexual Orientation Regulations ('Explanation of the provisions of the Employment Equality (Sexual Orientation) Regulations 2003 and Employment Equality (Religion or Belief) Regulations 2003'), the Government asserted that the definition of sexual orientation given in Reg 2(1) – which, as already noted, is virtually identical to the definition in S.12 EqA – did not cover 'sexual practices or sexual conduct'. The DTI provided the example of a person who engages in a sexual act with a colleague at work. Any less favourable treatment by reason of such conduct would not in itself be sexual orientation discrimination. However, it would be direct discrimination 'on the ground of sexual orientation' if, say, a heterosexual person engaging in a sexual act with a colleague were treated less favourably than a gay person had been treated after engaging in a similar act with a colleague of the same sex. This suggests that a man who has been discriminated against because he engages in sadomasochism, for example, would not be covered, since the discriminatory treatment does not relate to his sexual orientation towards persons of the same sex, the opposite sex, or both sexes.

This particular point about sexual practices and conduct has not been restated in respect of S.12 EqA. However, an early first instance decision brought under the 2003 Sexual Orientation Regulations in effect confirmed the view of the DTI, and, because of the similarity of wording of S.12, there is, at least on the face of it, no reason why the approach taken in that case could not apply equally to cases brought under the EqA. In XY v AB Bank ET Case No.3200440/05 a highly paid gay banker claimed direct sexual orientation discrimination against a large City bank following his dismissal for gross misconduct. An employment tribunal found that his dismissal, which occurred after a male colleague alleged that he had performed a lewd sexual act in the work gym, did not constitute less favourable treatment on the ground of sexual orientation for the purposes of the 2003 Sexual Orientation Regulations. Rather, he was dismissed because the employer genuinely and legitimately believed him guilty of the alleged conduct. Although the manner in which the employer initially investigated the allegation was discriminatory, this did not taint the subsequent formal disciplinary investigation and hearing, as the latter procedure involved a thorough reappraisal of the case.

13.16 Approach under the ECHR. Although sexual practices or conduct are not of themselves covered by the definition of sexual orientation, it would be wrong, in our view, to say that they are entirely irrelevant to a claim of sexual orientation discrimination to the extent that they offer an *indication* of a person's actual or perceived sexual orientation. This is certainly the position that has been adopted under Article 8 ECHR. The relevant jurisprudence in this context shows that respect for 'private life' encompasses both *sexual* *orientation* and *sexual life* as being important elements of the personal sphere protected by Article 8 – see PG v United Kingdom 2008 46 EHRR 51, ECtHR. In R (on the application of Amicus and ors) v Secretary of State for Trade and Industry 2007 ICR 1176, QBD, Mr Justice Richards observed: 'As regards the protection conferred by the Convention… I do not consider there is any material difference between [sexual orientation and sexual behaviour]. Sexual orientation and its manifestation in sexual behaviour are both inextricably connected with a person's private life and identity.'

However, as pointed out under 'European Convention on Human Rights' above, the right to respect for private and family life is not absolute. States and public authorities are entitled under Article 8(2) to seek to justify interferences with that right in order to strike a fair balance between the competing interests of individuals and the community as a whole. This sometimes results in courts making decisions under Article 8 that stop short of affording protection to individuals where the nature of the sexual conduct or the circumstances in which it has occurred is such as to justify interference with the rights enshrined in Article 8(1). For example, in Laskey and ors v United Kingdom 1997 24 EHRR 39, ECtHR, the ECtHR held that criminal charges brought against members of a group of homosexual men who participated in private, consensual but extreme sadomasochistic practices did not amount to a violation of Article 8 because the interference in their right to respect for private life was necessary in a democratic society and proportionate. The prosecuting authorities were entitled to resort to the criminal law in regulating the infliction of physical harm, and could consider the potential for serious harm that might have resulted from the extreme activities of the men, which could not be viewed as purely a matter of their own private morality.

13.17 Significantly, in the Laskey case the ECtHR went out of its way to stress that its decision involved no discriminatory prejudice against gay men. In rejecting the applicants' contention that they had been singled out partly because they were homosexuals, the Court found no evidence to support this, and, in fact specifically took into account the trial judge's comment when passing sentence that 'the unlawful conduct now before the court would be dealt with equally in the prosecution of heterosexuals or bisexuals if carried out by them'.

The sort of factors generally taken into account when deciding whether particular activities or conduct fall within the protected sphere of a person's private or family life include:

- the nature of the activity or conduct in question. The more extreme it is, the more likely it will be that any interference with Article 8(1) rights will be justified within the terms of Article 8(2) – see Laskey and ors v United Kingdom (above)

279

- whether or not the individual has a reasonable expectation of privacy – Campbell v MGN Ltd 2004 2 AC 457, HL; Halford v United Kingdom 1997 24 EHRR 523, ECtHR

- whether the relevant activity or conduct took place in private or in public (see the case law discussed immediately below).

13.18 As the decision in Laskey and ors v United Kingdom (above) demonstrates, the mere fact that sexual conduct or a particular sexual practice takes place in private is no absolute guarantee that it will be protected under Article 8. It is, however, a highly relevant consideration. If the sexual activity or conduct occurs in public, the crucial consideration will be whether the circumstances are such that it can still be regarded as falling within the zone of interaction protected by Article 8(1). In the particular context of employment, case law generally suggests that the termination of employment as a response to an employee's sexual conduct or behaviour is unlikely to infringe Articles 8 and 14. Furthermore, such dismissals tend to be upheld as fair under Ss.94 and 98 of the Employment Rights Act 1996, provided that proper procedures have been followed. So, for example, in X v Y 2004 ICR 1634, CA, the dismissal of an employee after he had received a police caution for gross indecency with another man in a transport café lavatory was held not to be unfair and did not involve a violation of the employee's right to privacy under Article 8. The Court of Appeal conceded that that right covers a person's sexual orientation and sex life, and that a reasonable expectation of privacy may well extend beyond the confines of the home. However, in this particular case, the employee's conduct had occurred in a public place, was a criminal offence, and had led to a caution that was relevant to his employment (as a charity worker working with young offenders). The Court emphasised that the commission of a criminal offence is normally a matter of legitimate concern to the public and – depending on the details – to an employer, rather than being merely a private matter. The fact that the claimant wished to keep the matter private did not make it part of his private life.

In Pay v United Kingdom 2009 IRLR 139, ECtHR, the ECtHR rejected a claim alleging, inter alia, breach of Article 8 as it was clear that any interference with the applicant's right to respect for his private life was proportionate within the terms of Article 8(2). That case concerned a probation officer (P) whose job involved working with sex offenders. However, in his private life, he was also the director of a company selling products connected with bondage, domination and sadomasochism via the internet. Photographs and videos of him dressed in fetishist gear appeared on the company's promotional website. His refusal to acknowledge the relevance of this activity in terms of the sensitive nature of the job he did led to his being dismissed. An employment tribunal, and subsequently the EAT, held that the dismissal fell within the range of reasonable responses and had not breached P's Article 8 rights (or, for that matter, his rights under Article 10 ECHR guaranteeing freedom of expression). P launched proceedings before the ECtHR contending that his activities fell within the scope of 'private life' as they were an important and integral part of his sexual expression and sexual orientation, and that his dismissal was disproportionate to his employer's legitimate aim of protecting the reputation of the probation service. However, the Court ruled his application to be inadmissible. It accepted that P's video performances took place in a nightclub that was likely to be frequented only by like-minded people and that the published photographs were anonymised. On this basis, it could be assumed (without actually deciding the matter) that Article 8 was engaged and that dismissal amounted to an interference with P's rights under that provision. However, the Court observed that it was important that, as a probation officer, P maintained the respect of the offenders placed under his supervision and also the confidence of the public in general and victims of sex crime in particular. Given that he had not accepted that his activities could be damaging, the nature of his work with sex offenders and the fact that the dismissal resulted from his failure to curb even those aspects of his private life most likely to enter the public domain, the Court ruled that dismissal was not a disproportionate interference with his right to respect for private life.

The ECtHR also considered the argument that P had been discriminated against **13.19** in the enjoyment of his Article 8 rights contrary to Article 14. In this regard, the Court observed that the P 'was not dismissed because of his sexual orientation as such, but because of concerns that knowledge of his participation in [sadomasochistic] nightclub performances would come more fully into the knowledge of the general public and hinder the effectiveness of his work with sex offenders. In these circumstances, the Court considers that the reasons given for finding that the complaints under Articles 8 or 10 are manifestly ill-founded also afford a reasonable and objective justification under Article 14.'

Approach under the EqA. It is appropriate to consider to what extent the case **13.20** law regarding sexual behaviour, conduct and practices in the context of Article 8 should also inform the approach to be taken to defining the meaning of 'sexual orientation' in S.12 EqA. It is safe to assume that for this purpose an individual's sexual orientation may be manifested by his or her conduct or behaviour, and so, as in the case of Article 8, such conduct or behaviour should be taken on board when defining the scope and meaning of the protected characteristic as it applies to the particular individual. But what is the position where an employee is subjected to less favourable treatment by an employer on account of the sexual conduct or behaviour and then claims to have been directly discriminated against because of sexual orientation? Under the EqA, there is no justification defence available for direct discrimination (other than in relation to age). So, unlike proceedings brought directly under Article 8, tribunals are deprived of any opportunity to conduct a balancing exercise between the individual's right to respect for private life and the interests of the

281

employer and/or community as a whole. Such a balancing exercise is only possible under the EqA in respect of indirect discrimination. On the face of it, therefore, an employer could potentially be faced with hard justice. Take a scenario similar to that in Pay v United Kingdom (see 'Approach under the ECHR' above): if, say, a male school teacher was involved in extreme sexual activities or conduct such as acting as a male escort outside work hours, one might have thought that it would be open to the employer to take action against the employee on the basis that his activities were inappropriate to his job as a teacher. But if the employee claims that the activities in question reflect his sexual orientation, the employer would be unable to defend a claim of sexual orientation discrimination simply by seeking to show that its treatment of the employee was a proportional response in all the circumstances.

In practice, this problem is likely to be more theoretical than real. A direct discrimination claim can only succeed if the employee establishes that he or she was treated less favourably than someone of a different sexual orientation. This means that an employee who, for example, was dismissed because of inappropriate sexual conduct at work would have to prove that another employee of a different sexual orientation would not have been treated in the same way. On this basis, it is most unlikely that the employee in the Pay case, for example, would have fared any better had statutory protection against sexual orientation discrimination been available to him at the time of his dismissal. In that particular case, there was no evidence that a probation officer of a different sexual orientation who engaged in the same sexual behaviour would have been treated more favourably.

13.21 However, it is not so easy to be confident about the outcome had a discrimination claim been available to the employee in X v Y 2004 ICR 1634, CA (see under 'Approach under the ECHR' above). The particular criminal offence for which he was cautioned was 'gross indecency' contrary to S.13 of the Sexual Offences Act 1956. S.13 defined that offence solely in terms of sexual acts between men (whether in public or private), and it was therefore only gay men (or at least men engaging in homosexual sexual activities) who could be prosecuted. It is therefore likely that, had he been in a position to do so, the claimant in X v Y would have contended that the employer's decision to dismiss in view of the police caution he received amounted to less favourable treatment because no heterosexual employee engaging in sexual acts in a public lavatory would have been liable to be charged with the same or an equivalent offence. In view of the reasons given for the dismissal, it is difficult to see any basis on which the employer would have escaped liability for direct discrimination. (Note, however, that the offence of gross indecency has now been repealed by the Sexual Offences Act 2003 and replaced by a specific offence of 'sexual activity in a public lavatory' – S.71 SOA 2003. Significantly, this offence applies to both heterosexual and homosexual activity, meaning that an employer faced with similar facts today would find it easier to contend that exactly the same treatment would have been meted out to any employee convicted or cautioned for an offence under S.71, irrespective of his or her sexual orientation.)

Other public manifestations of sexual orientation 13.22

Sometimes a person's sexual orientation (or apparent orientation) is manifested not so much through their sexual behaviour as through other external indicators such as accent or physical appearance. There is no reason why a person who manifests their sexual orientation in this way should not be protected from direct discrimination or harassment. So, for example, a gay man with an effeminate demeanour who is harassed or less favourably treated by reason of his effeminacy will be able to claim that the harassment or direct discrimination was because of his sexual orientation. The same would be true of a lesbian with a mannish physical appearance who is harassed because of her looks.

The following decisions made under the 2003 Sexual Orientation Regulations illustrate this point:

- **Mann v BH Publishing Ltd and anor** ET Case No.2203272/04: C, an openly gay South African, began working for BHP Ltd on 24 May 2004. He spoke with what he described as a gay South African accent. His manager (H) mimicked his accent from the outset of his employment. After two days, C told him that he objected to the mimicry and said that he thought it constituted harassment on the ground of his sexual orientation. Despite this conversation, H continued to mimic his accent, and from this time on his colleagues began to tease and taunt C about his sexual orientation, including during an after-work social gathering at the local pub. After just ten days' employment, C resigned and claimed direct discrimination and harassment on the ground of his sexual orientation. An employment tribunal held that there had been no discrimination for the first two days of C's employment on the basis that H was a natural and talented mimic and his mimicry of C's accent was not connected with C's sexuality. However, from the time that C put his concerns to H, the mimicry violated his dignity and amounted to discrimination on the ground of his sexual orientation. The behaviour of his colleagues also amounted to unlawful discrimination

- **Black v Royal Mail Group Ltd** ET Case No.1101668/08: B, an openly gay man, was employed as a postman by RMG Ltd. He became very friendly with a female colleague, H, but their friendship broke down. In 2008, H raised a grievance about B's mother, who also worked for the employer, under RMG Ltd's bullying and harassment policy. As part of the investigation T, a manager, was interviewed. He said that B was very 'effeminate and immature' and that H and B had a 'girly' relationship, and when they fell out it 'got quite bitchy'. An employment tribunal upheld B's claim that these comments amounted to harassment on the ground of sexual

283

orientation. Each of the terms 'effeminate', 'girly' and 'bitchy' were – when used in respect of a man – a direct reference to that man having female characteristics. Where the words were used to describe a man known to be gay, they were clearly derogatory. Although the tribunal accepted that T was not homophobic, his choice of words was clearly influenced, subconsciously, by his knowledge that B was gay.

13.23 Overlap with other protected characteristics

The protected characteristic of sexual orientation has considerable overlap with that of marriage and civil partnership. It may also come into direct conflict with the protected characteristic of religion or belief. These interrelationships are discussed below.

13.24 Marriage and civil partnership

There is an obvious correlation between the protected characteristic of sexual orientation set out in S.12 EqA and the protected characteristic of marriage and civil partnership set out in S.8 (discussed in Chapter 8, 'Marriage and civil partnership'). Civil partnerships, by definition, entail the legal union of same-sex couples. Thus, any direct discrimination occurring because of civil partnership status, or any indirect discrimination taking the form of the application of a provision, criterion or practice that puts civil partners at a particular disadvantage, is also likely to comprise sexual orientation discrimination. To take an example drawn from the field of goods, facilities and services:

• **Bull and anor v Hall and anor** 2012 EWCA Civ 83, CA: two civil partners successfully complained of direct sexual orientation discrimination under the Equality Act (Sexual Orientation) Regulations 2007 SI 2007/1263 (which extended protection against sexual orientation discrimination to non-work areas, including goods, facilities and services). The claimants brought a claim for damages after having been prevented from taking up their booking of a double room in a guesthouse because the owners (who were devout Christians) had a policy of allowing only married heterosexual couples to stay in the same bedroom. The owners sought to defend the claim of direct discrimination on the basis that any less favourable treatment of the claimants was not because of the claimants' sexual orientation but because of their own religious-based objection to sex outside marriage, and that the same objection would have equally applied to non-married heterosexuals. Rejecting this argument, the county court judge drew attention to Reg 3(4) of the 2007 Regulations – equivalent to Reg 3(3) of the 2003 Sexual Orientation Regulations and now re-enacted as S.23(3) EqA. This clarified that, in making a like-for-like comparison for the purpose of determining whether there has been less favourable treatment, the fact that one person is a civil partner and the other person is married does not constitute a 'material difference'. In other words, what is now S.23(3) entitles a civil partner to make a comparison with the treatment that has been or would be meted out to a married person in similar circumstances (or vice versa). With this in mind, the judge reasoned: 'It seems to me that a correct analysis of the position of the defendants is that they discriminate on the basis of marital status… [O]n a proper analysis of the defendants' position on the facts of this particular case, the only conclusion which can be drawn is that the refusal to allow [the claimants] to occupy the double room which they had booked was because of their sexual orientation and that prima facie the treatment falls within the provisions of Reg 3(1) [of the 2007 Regulations] and that this is direct discrimination.' The Court of Appeal agreed, holding that the criterion at the heart of the restriction – that the couple should be married – was necessarily linked to the characteristic of heterosexual orientation and was directly discriminatory. The Court rejected the argument that Reg 3 breached Article 9 of the ECHR ('Freedom of thought, conscience and religion') to the extent that it limited the right of the guesthouse owners to manifest their religious beliefs. In the words of Lady Justice Rafferty: 'I do not consider that the [owners] face any difficulty in manifesting their religious beliefs, they are merely prohibited from so doing in the commercial context they have chosen.'

It should be noted that the claimants in the Hall case were unable to bring a **13.25** claim based on civil partnership discrimination as this was not a protected ground in the context of the provision of goods and services at the time. Indeed, this remains the case under the EqA since, by virtue of S.28(1), the provisions of Part 3 of the 2010 Act (i.e. those dealing with services and public functions) do not apply to this particular protected characteristic. Even so, as the decision shows, the non-availability of any specific protection against civil partnership discrimination is no handicap in practice because the claimants succeeded in obtaining damages by 'prosecuting' their claim as one of sexual orientation discrimination. This demonstrates just how much the two protected characteristics – sexual orientation and marriage and civil partnership – are interlinked. Indeed, even in the context of work and employment where workers who are civil partners are protected from discrimination on account of their civil partnership status, most cases are likely to be brought on the basis of sexual orientation, rather than civil partnership, discrimination. This is because it will usually be easier in practice for an employee to show that he or she has been subjected to less favourable treatment compared with a person of a different sexual orientation than it will be to show less favourable treatment compared with a person who is married or who is single. Furthermore, if a person suffers harassment on account of his or her civil partnership status, then his or her only remedy will be to bring a complaint of discrimination based on sexual orientation. That is because, for reasons fully explained in Chapter 8,

285

'Marriage and civil partnership', under 'Protection under the Equality Act', the free-standing right to complain of harassment is expressly excluded in relation to the protected characteristic of marriage and civil partnership.

13.26 Religion or belief

The interplay between the protected characteristics of sexual orientation and religion or belief can sometimes result in a tension between the two sets of rights, especially within the workplace. The clash usually stems from the fact that some religions regard homosexuality (or, more particularly, the sexual practice of homosexuality) as sinful and/or incompatible with the proprieties of family life and human relations.

There are two areas in which the right not to be discriminated against on the ground of sexual orientation is prone to come into conflict with the right not to be discriminated against on the ground of religion or belief. The first of these is reflected in the series of high-profile cases brought by employees who, as part of their job functions, found themselves obliged to act in ways that clashed with their deeply held religious convictions. This case law has been discussed in detail in Chapter 11, 'Religion or belief', under 'Manifestation of religion or belief'. Suffice it to say here that in the two leading cases – Ladele v London Borough of Islington and anor 2010 ICR 532, CA (concerning a registrar who refused on grounds of conscience to perform civil partnership ceremonies), and McFarlane v Relate Avon Ltd 2010 ICR 507, EAT (concerning a Christian counsellor who was dismissed for refusing to counsel same-sex couples on sexual matters) – the courts held that claims of direct religion or belief discrimination failed because the respective employers had not treated the claimants unfavourably on the ground of religion or belief. Furthermore, their claims of indirect discrimination were also dismissed on the basis that any disadvantage suffered by the claimants was justified. In both cases, the courts held that the employers' policy of promoting equality on the ground of sexual orientation constituted a legitimate aim. In Ladele, the Court of Appeal specifically observed that the employer's policy was 'of general, indeed overarching, policy significance to Islington, and it also had fundamental human rights, equality and diversity implications, whereas the effect on Ms Ladele of implementing the policy did not impinge on her religious beliefs: she remained free to hold those beliefs, and free to worship as she wished'.

13.27

The outcomes in these cases have led some commentators to suggest that the obligations on employers not to discriminate on the ground of sexual orientation trump the rights of the employee not to be discriminated against on the ground of religion or belief. This is arguably an over-simplification of the complex and nuanced reasoning that courts and tribunals have to engage in when determining indirect discrimination claims. For a more detailed discussion of these issues, see Chapter 11, 'Religion or belief', under 'Manifestation of religion or belief – is UK approach compliant with Article 9?'

The second area of controversy concerns the existence and scope of the 'genuine occupational requirements' exceptions previously contained in Reg 7(2) and (3) of the 2003 Sexual Orientation Regulations and now re-enacted in paras 1 and 2 of Schedule 9 to the EqA. These provisions provide for both a general exception where being of a particular sexual orientation is an occupational requirement of the job in question and a specific exception where, in the context of employment for the purposes of an organised religion, an employee fails to meet a requirement related to sexual orientation imposed by the employer in order to comply with the doctrines of a religion or to avoid conflicting with the strongly held religious convictions of a significant number of the religion's followers. Full details of these exceptions can be found in Chapter 30, 'General exceptions', under 'Occupational requirements', and Chapter 31, 'Specific exceptions', under 'Religion or belief exceptions'. Suffice it to say here that in 2004 the Amicus trade union sought a judicial review of both the general and 'organised religion' exceptions on the basis that they gave employers scope to discriminate in a manner not permitted by the EU Equal Treatment Framework Directive (No.2000/78) or by the ECHR. In dismissing the case, Mr Justice Richards concluded that the scope of the exceptions was sufficiently narrow to be compliant with Article 4(1) of the Equality Framework Directive – see R (on the application of Amicus and ors) v Secretary of State for Trade and Industry 2007 ICR 1176, QBD.

13.28 However, this may not be the end of the controversy surrounding the occupational requirements (OR) exceptions. In 2009 the European Commission sent a Reasoned Opinion to the UK Government suggesting that the OR defence went further than was permissible under EU law. This is probably what prompted the Government to propose amendments to the Equality Bill during its passage through Parliament aimed at 'clarifying' the scope of the OR exceptions generally. However, opponents saw these amendments as narrowing the terms of the exceptions and successfully sought to defeat them in order to retain the status quo. Accordingly, the wording of the exceptions in Schedule 9 EqA – in relation to both the general exception in para 1 and the specific exception concerning organised religion in para 2 – is to all intents and purposes identical to the wording of the antecedent legislative provisions. Although the European Commission does not appear to have followed up its opinion by bringing infraction proceedings against the Government, the question of whether the OR exceptions are fully compatible with EU law would seem to be still at large, notwithstanding the Amicus ruling.

Part 3

Prohibited conduct

14 Prohibited conduct: general principles

'Prohibited conduct' under the Equality Act

Elements of claim

Potential claims under each characteristic

In the previous ten chapters (Chapters 4–13) we consider the nine protected **14.1** *characteristics* covered by the prohibition on workplace discrimination in the Equality Act 2010 (EqA). These are age, disability, gender reassignment, marriage and civil partnership, pregnancy and maternity, race, religion or belief, sex and sexual orientation. In the next eight chapters (Chapters 15–22), we look at the *forms* of conduct made unlawful under the Act, e.g. direct and indirect discrimination, harassment, victimisation and failure to make reasonable adjustments. As with the antecedent discrimination legislation, some of these forms of discrimination – such as direct and indirect discrimination – apply to all the protected characteristics, whereas others are confined to a single characteristic – for example, only a disabled person can complain of an alleged failure to comply with the duty to make reasonable adjustments. In this chapter, we give a general overview of the forms of unlawful conduct covered by the EqA – now termed 'prohibited conduct' – before briefly explaining the *circumstances* in which prohibited conduct because of a protected characteristic is actionable under the EqA, e.g. recruitment and dismissal. For ease of reference, we list the types of claim that can be brought in relation to each protected characteristic at the end of the chapter.

'Prohibited conduct' under the Equality Act   14.2

As discussed in the preceding chapters, the EqA gives wide protection from discrimination to employees. However, it does not provide a blanket right not to be discriminated against – it is intended to offer protection to those who have, or are perceived to have, a particular characteristic that requires specific protection ('a protected characteristic'), or who associate with someone who has a protected characteristic. Furthermore, the treatment complained of must be of a kind made unlawful under the Act. In other words, if the treatment in question is not prohibited under the Act, then however heinous that treatment may be, the discrimination claim is bound to fail.

The types of conduct made unlawful under the EqA are spelled out in Ss.13–27 and largely replicate the provisions contained in the previous equality legislation.

291

They are collectively referred to as 'prohibited conduct' under the Act. The main types of prohibited conduct are:

- 'direct discrimination': less favourable treatment of a person because of a protected characteristic (S.13) – see Chapter 15, 'Direct discrimination'

- 'indirect discrimination': the employer applies a provision, criterion or practice which is discriminatory in relation to a person's protected characteristic (S.19) – see Chapter 16, 'Indirect discrimination: proving disadvantage', and Chapter 17, 'Indirect discrimination: objective justification'

- 'harassment': a person is subjected to unwanted conduct related to a protected characteristic that has the purpose or effect of violating his or her dignity, or creating an intimidating, hostile, degrading, humiliating or offensive environment for him or her (S.26) – see Chapter 18, 'Harassment'

- 'victimisation': a person suffers a detriment because he or she has done, or may do, a protected act, such as bringing proceedings under the Act (S.27) – see Chapter 19, 'Victimisation'. (Note that victimisation is no longer treated as a form of direct discrimination under the EqA – as it was under the antecedent legislation – but rather, is regarded as a stand-alone form of prohibited conduct.)

14.3 The provisions that outlaw direct and indirect discrimination apply to all the protected characteristics. However, the protected characteristics of marriage and civil partnership and pregnancy and maternity are excluded from the harassment provisions. A claim of victimisation – being linked to the doing of (or the possibility of doing) a protected act under the Act – is not dependent on the claimant possessing a protected characteristic.

The Act contains four additional forms of prohibited conduct that are specific to a particular protected characteristic:

- 'discrimination arising from disability': unfavourable treatment of a disabled person because of something arising from his or her disability (S.15) – see Chapter 20, 'Discrimination arising from disability'

- 'failure to comply with the duty to make reasonable adjustments': the employer fails to comply with the duty to make reasonable adjustments in relation to a disabled person (S.21) – see Chapter 21, 'Failure to make reasonable adjustments'

- 'gender reassignment discrimination because of absence from work': less favourable treatment of a transsexual person because of absence from work relating to gender reassignment (S.16) – see Chapter 22, 'Other forms of prohibited conduct', under 'Gender reassignment discrimination due to absence'

- 'pregnancy and maternity discrimination': unfavourable treatment of a woman because of her pregnancy or a pregnancy-related illness, or in relation to her maternity leave (S.18) – see Chapter 22, 'Other forms of prohibited conduct', under 'Pregnancy and maternity discrimination'.

We set out the types of claim that can be brought in relation to each **14.4** of the protected characteristics under 'Potential claims under each characteristic' below.

Note that Ss.111 and 112 add two further types of prohibited conduct: instructing, causing and inducing discrimination, and aiding discrimination. These are discussed in Chapter 28, 'Liability of employers, employees and agents' under 'Instructing, causing and inducing discrimination'.

Combined discrimination
14.5

It should be noted that there is a further form of prohibited conduct not listed above: 'combined discrimination' (sometimes called 'dual discrimination' or 'intersectional discrimination'). This type of discrimination, which covers less favourable treatment of a person because of a combination of two protected characteristics, is expressly outlawed under S.14 EqA. However, that provision has not yet been brought into force and is unlikely to become law in the foreseeable future.

Combined discrimination is discussed in greater detail in Chapter 15, 'Direct discrimination', under 'Combined discrimination'.

Elements of claim
14.6

As mentioned above, there are certain prerequisites that need to be met in order to bring a discrimination claim under the EqA. For a start, a complainant must have, be perceived to have or be associated with a person who has, a protected characteristic. Furthermore, the treatment complained of must be unlawful under one of the prohibited conduct provisions of the Act (i.e. Ss.13–27). For example, a woman bringing a direct sex discrimination complaint must produce evidence from which it is possible to conclude that she was treated less favourably than a man was, or would have been, treated in similar circumstances. But having a protected characteristic and being subjected to prohibited conduct on the ground of that characteristic is not enough. The reason for this is that Ss.13–27 are, in effect, 'definition provisions', and must be read alongside the substantive provisions in Part 5 that outlaw discrimination in the work context (Ss.39–60). The most relevant provisions in Part 5 for our purposes are Ss.39 and 40, which make it unlawful for employers to discriminate against, harass or victimise employees and job applicants.

So, to continue with the above example, the woman would also have to show that the alleged discrimination took place in the work context. If she is a current

293

employee, she would have to show that she was discriminated against in one of the ways described in S.39(2), which provides that an employer must not discriminate against an employee as to his or her terms of employment; in the way it affords him or her access, or by not affording access, to opportunities for promotion, transfer or training or for receiving any other benefit, facility or service; by dismissing him or her; or by subjecting him or her to any other detriment.

14.7 The various ways in which discrimination can occur in the employment context – during recruitment, in contractual terms, during employment, on termination of employment, and after the employment relationship has ended – are discussed in depth in Chapters 23–27 of the Handbook.

14.8 Potential claims under each characteristic

Below, we set out the potential claims that can be brought under the EqA in relation to each protected characteristic:

- *age*
  - direct discrimination (S.13)
  - combined discrimination (S.14) (not in force)
  - indirect discrimination (S.19)
  - harassment (S.26)
  - victimisation (S.27)
- *disability*
  - direct discrimination (S.13)
  - combined discrimination (S.14) (not in force)
  - discrimination arising from disability (S.15)
  - indirect discrimination (S.19)
  - failure to make reasonable adjustments (S.21)
  - harassment (S.26)
  - victimisation (S.27)
- *gender reassignment*
  - direct discrimination (S.13)
  - combined discrimination (S.14) (not in force)

- — direct discrimination: absence from work (S.16)
- — indirect discrimination (S.19)
- — harassment (S.26)
- — victimisation (S.27)
- *marriage/civil partnership*
  - — direct discrimination (S.13)
  - — indirect discrimination (S.19)
  - — victimisation (S.27)
- *pregnancy/maternity*
  - — direct discrimination (S.13)
  - — pregnancy and maternity discrimination (S.18)
  - — victimisation (S.27)
- *race*
  - — direct discrimination (S.13)
  - — combined discrimination (S.14) (not in force)
  - — indirect discrimination (S.19)
  - — harassment (S.26)
  - — victimisation (S.27)
- *religion/belief*
  - — direct discrimination (S.13)
  - — combined discrimination (S.14) (not in force)
  - — indirect discrimination (S.19)
  - — harassment (S.26)
  - — victimisation (S.27)
- *sex*
  - — direct discrimination (S.13)
  - — combined discrimination (S.14) (not in force)
  - — indirect discrimination (S.19)
  - — harassment (S.26)
  - — victimisation (S.27)

- *sexual orientation*
  - direct discrimination (S.13)
  - combined discrimination (S.14) (not in force)
  - indirect discrimination (S.19)
  - harassment (S.26)
  - victimisation (S.27).

15 Direct discrimination

Preliminary matters

Less favourable treatment

Comparator

'Because of' protected characteristic

Justifying direct age discrimination

Discrimination by association

Discrimination by perception

Combined discrimination

The proscription of direct discrimination, being the less favourable treatment **15.1** of an individual because of a protected characteristic, is generally seen as the most important plank of the protection from discrimination in employment. S.13(1) of the Equality Act 2010 (EqA) provides that direct discrimination occurs where 'a person (A) discriminates against another (B) if, because of a protected characteristic, A treats B less favourably than A treats or would treat others'. The wording is reminiscent of that used in the antecedent equality legislation such as the Sex Discrimination Act 1975 (SDA) and the Race Relations Act 1976 (RRA) (both now repealed) and incorporates many of the same elements necessary for finding direct discrimination. Case law under the previous legislation therefore remains relevant under the EqA, with such caveats as are noted in this chapter where relevant.

That said, S.13(1) differs from its predecessors in some important respects. It states that it is unlawful to treat an individual less favourably because of 'a' protected characteristic. Thus, the individual does not need to possess the protected characteristic him or herself. The wording is wide enough to cover someone who is *perceived* to have a protected characteristic or who *associates* with someone who has a protected characteristic. This is an important extension of the reach of the principle of non-discrimination. In addition, the EqA makes provision for combined, also referred to as 'dual', discrimination in that complaints can be based on the *combined* effect of two protected characteristics. However, at the time of writing, this provision (S.14) is not yet in force.

In this chapter, we first deal with some preliminary issues before turning to **15.2** discuss the individual elements that make up a finding of direct discrimination, that is: (i) less favourable treatment (2) because of a protected characteristic. In the final sections, we consider the new forms of conduct caught by S.13 – i.e.

297

associative and perceptive discrimination, and the scope of S.14, that covers combined discrimination.

References in this chapter to 'the EHRC Employment Code' are to the statutory Code of Practice on Employment issued by the Equality and Human Rights Commission. The Code does not impose legal obligations but courts and tribunals must take into account any part of the Code that appears to them relevant to any questions arising in proceedings. References to 'the Explanatory Notes' are to the Explanatory Notes of the EqA.

15.3 Preliminary matters

Before examining the definition of direct discrimination in detail, it is important to make some preliminary observations about the operation of S.13: which protected characteristics are covered by the section; what a claimant must establish in order to prove direct discrimination; and what defences, if any, are available to an employer faced with a claim under S.13.

15.4 Protected characteristics covered by S.13

Section 13 prohibits direct discrimination 'because of a protected characteristic'. This implies that the section applies to all nine protected characteristics listed in S.4 EqA: age, disability, gender reassignment, marriage and civil partnership, pregnancy and maternity, race, religion or belief, sex and sexual orientation. Indeed, unlike indirect discrimination and harassment, there is no subsection within S.13 limiting its scope to only some of the protected characteristics.

However, on the face of it S.25(5) appears to exclude the protected characteristic of pregnancy and maternity from the scope of S.13, stating that: 'Pregnancy and maternity discrimination is discrimination within... S.18' (which covers pregnancy and maternity discrimination against a pregnant woman or a woman on statutory maternity leave). But S.25 would appear simply to clarify what is meant by 'pregnancy and maternity discrimination' whenever the phrase occurs in the Act and we would argue that the prohibition on direct discrimination in S.13 *does* apply to the protected characteristic of pregnancy and maternity, albeit that its scope is more restrictive than S.18 as no comparator is required under the latter section. As stated above, S.18 is concerned with pregnancy and maternity discrimination against a pregnant woman or a woman on statutory maternity leave (i.e. during what is known as the 'protected period'). However, it has long been established that less favourable treatment of a woman on the grounds of her pregnancy, or the consequences of that pregnancy, during the protected period amounts to direct *sex* discrimination without the need for a comparison with a man in similar circumstances – Webb v EMO Air Cargo (UK) Ltd 1994 ICR 770, ECJ. Thus there is potential for overlap between pregnancy and maternity discrimination on the one hand and sex discrimination on the other. To avoid this, S.18(7) EqA stipulates that '[S.]13, so far as relating

298

to sex discrimination, does not apply to treatment of a woman in so far as' that treatment is in the protected period and is because of the woman's pregnancy; because of illness suffered by her as a result of her pregnancy; because she is on compulsory maternity leave; or because she is exercising or seeking to exercise, or has exercised or sought to exercise, the right to ordinary or additional maternity leave. Instead, such claims should be brought under S.18, which specifically caters for pregnancy and maternity discrimination claims.

The effect of S.18(7) is to preclude pregnancy and maternity claims being **15.5** brought as direct sex discrimination claims when they could be brought under the specific pregnancy or maternity discrimination provisions in S.18. Where, however, unfavourable treatment because of pregnancy or maternity is *not* covered by S.18 (for example, because it falls outside the protected period), a woman can still bring a sex discrimination claim under S.13. In this situation, it is arguable that – for the reasons discussed above – she would also be able to claim direct discrimination under S.13 because of the protected characteristic of pregnancy and maternity.

If S.13 does indeed cover direct pregnancy and maternity discrimination, this would also permit claims – by a man or woman – based on association and perception, which cannot be brought under S.18. Furthermore, there would be nothing to prevent a woman whose claim fell within S.18 from pursuing a claim of direct pregnancy and maternity discrimination under S.13 in relation to an act occurring during the protected period (either instead of, or in addition to, a S.18 claim). This is because S.18(7) only disapplies S.13 'so far as relating to *sex* discrimination' (our stress) in cases falling within S.18; it does not preclude claims of pregnancy and maternity discrimination under S.13. However, if it is possible to bring a S.13 claim alleging discrimination because of pregnancy or maternity during the protected period, S.13 would appear to require a comparison with a man or a (non-pregnant) woman in similar circumstances, which does not accord with the European case law eschewing a comparative approach in this context.

Pregnancy and maternity discrimination claims under S.18 are discussed in Chapter 22.

What is direct discrimination? **15.6**

Section 13(1) provides that an employer directly discriminates against a person if:

- it treats that person *less favourably* than it treats or would treat others, and

- the difference in treatment is *because of* a protected characteristic.

Tribunals often deal with these two stages in turn, and, for convenience, that is how we examine the definition in this chapter (see 'Less favourable treatment' and '"Because of" protected characteristic' below). However, as discussed

————— **299**

below, it is not always possible to separate the two issues. As Lord Nicholls commented in Shamoon v Chief Constable of the Royal Ulster Constabulary 2003 ICR 337, HL (a sex discrimination case), in some cases the 'less favourable treatment issue cannot be resolved without, at the same time, deciding the reason why issue. The two issues are intertwined.' In that case S, a Chief Inspector, claimed that she was treated less favourably than two male Chief Inspectors when she was relieved of her counselling responsibilities. However, she had been the subject of complaints and representations, whereas the male Chief Inspectors had not. According to Lord Nicholls: 'Whether this factual difference between their positions was in truth a material difference is an issue which cannot be resolved without determining why she was treated as she was. It might be that the reason why she was relieved of her counselling responsibilities had nothing to do with the complaints and representations. If that were so, then a comparison between her and the two male Chief Inspectors may well be comparing like with like, because in that event the difference between her and her two male colleagues would be an immaterial difference.'

15.7 It has long been established that direct discrimination is incapable in law of being justified. The only exception to this is direct age discrimination. Any attempts to relax the general rule have been forcefully rejected by tribunals. Take, for example, the case of Moyhing v Barts and London NHS Trust 2006 IRLR 860, EAT, in which a male nurse, M, was required, pursuant to hospital policy, not to carry out certain intimate duties involving women without being chaperoned by a female member of staff. M brought a claim of sex discrimination before an employment tribunal. It was common ground that he had been treated less favourably on the ground of his sex, in that female trainee nurses were not required to be chaperoned when performing intimate procedures on male patients. The tribunal held that the hospital's policy was logical and there were good and sound reasons for adopting it. Therefore, M's objection was unjustifiable and the policy could not be regarded as having given rise to a detriment. The EAT, however, held that the tribunal had erred in finding that M's claim that he had suffered a detriment was undermined by his 'unjustified objection' to the Trust's policy on chaperoning. Direct discrimination, it reiterated, could not be justified, and the fact that there may be good and sound reasons for distinguishing between men and women was no defence. The tribunal's assumption that, where the reason for a discriminatory policy is cogent and rational, that policy cannot lead to a detriment was clearly wrong, and would have the effect of allowing justification for direct discrimination in through the back door.

15.8 Proving discrimination

Direct discrimination is rarely blatant. As Lord Browne-Wilkinson observed in Glasgow City Council v Zafar 1998 ICR 120, HL, claims brought under the discrimination legislation present special problems of proof, since those who discriminate 'do not in general advertise their prejudices: indeed they may not even be aware of them'. For this reason, the burden of proof rules that apply to claims of unlawful discrimination in employment are more favourable to the claimant than those that apply to claims brought under most other employment rights and protections. The burden of proof rules are discussed in Chapter 32, 'Burden of proof'. Suffice it to say here that once a claimant shows prima facie evidence from which the tribunal could conclude, in the absence of any other explanation, that an employer has committed an act of discrimination, the tribunal is obliged to uphold the claim unless the employer can show that it did not discriminate – S.136 EqA.

Where the employer behaves *unreasonably*, that does not mean that there has been discrimination, but it may be evidence supporting that inference if there is nothing else to explain the behaviour – Anya v University of Oxford and anor 2001 ICR 847, CA (a race discrimination case). Thus, an employer can escape a finding of direct discrimination by arguing, before the tribunal, 'I'm a bastard to everyone', but only if it can show evidence that the unreasonable behaviour was not directed at the claimant alone. However, the rationality of an employer's decision to treat a person in a particular way may be taken into account. The Northern Ireland Court of Appeal held in Nelson v Newry and Mourne District Council 2009 IRLR 548, NICA, that a difference in treatment between a man and a woman disciplined for related misconduct did not support a finding of sex discrimination. In the Court's view, the fact that the employer's decision-making was not irrational or perverse must be very relevant in deciding whether there was evidence from which it could be inferred that the decision-making was motivated by an improper discriminatory intent. Drawing inferences from unreasonable behaviour is discussed in Chapter 33, 'Proving discrimination'.

Employer's defences   15.9

In the majority of cases, a tribunal finding that an individual was treated less favourably because of a protected characteristic will mark the successful end to his or her claim. However, there are some circumstances in which employers may still avoid liability. Below is a brief outline of the relevant provisions – more detailed consideration of the defences available to employers is provided elsewhere in this Handbook.

Justifying direct age discrimination. Where the protected characteristic is **15.10** age, it is open to the employer to justify any directly discriminatory treatment. S.13(2) provides that 'if the protected characteristic is age, A does not discriminate against B if A can show A's treatment of B to be a proportionate means of achieving a legitimate aim'. We discuss this defence under 'Justifying direct age discrimination' below.

Occupational requirements and specific exceptions. The widest category of **15.11** exception to the prohibition of direct discrimination covers 'occupational requirements'. As the name suggests, these are requirements related to characteristics that, although protected, are necessary for the job at issue. Such a requirement might apply if, for example, a black actor is required for a theatrical role to ensure that the performance is authentic. Occupational requirements are dealt with in Chapter 30, 'General exceptions', under 'Occupational requirements'. In addition, the EqA contains a number of specific exceptions; for example, in respect of religion or belief discrimination where the employment is of a religious nature. These exceptions are discussed in Chapter 31, 'Specific exceptions'.

15.12 **Positive action.** The EqA allows employers to take active steps to tackle disadvantage and persistent under-representation of certain groups within the workplace. For example, they may direct training at, and encourage applications from, groups they reasonably consider to be under-represented in their particular sector – see Chapter 30, 'General exceptions', under 'Positive action'. Accordingly, where an employer has adopted positive action measures, it will not be open to those who have not benefited from those measures to complain of unlawful discrimination.

15.13 Less favourable treatment

In order to claim direct discrimination under S.13, the claimant must have been treated less favourably than a comparator who was in the same, or not materially different, circumstances as the claimant. We consider the identification of the correct comparator for the purpose of S.13 under 'Comparator' below. In this section, we turn our attention to the question of what can amount to 'less favourable' treatment of the claimant. In the majority of cases, this will be fairly obvious. For instance, he or she may have been rejected for promotion or dismissed from his or her job. In others, however, less favourable treatment may be more difficult to establish.

The circumstances in which less favourable treatment in the field of work is unlawful – on recruitment, during employment and once employment has ended – are discussed in detail in Chapters 23–27, which cover 'Discrimination in the workplace'.

15.14 **What amounts to less favourable treatment?**
A successful direct discrimination claim depends on a tribunal being satisfied that the claimant was treated less favourably than a comparator because of a protected characteristic. It is for the tribunal to decide as a matter of fact what is less favourable. The fact that a claimant believes that he or she has been treated less favourably does not *of itself* establish that there has been less favourable treatment. In Burrett v West Birmingham Health Authority 1994 IRLR 7, EAT, for example, the Appeal Tribunal upheld a tribunal's decision that a nurse had not been less favourably treated simply because she felt

302

demeaned by the uniform that she, as a woman, was obliged to wear. Similarly, in HM Land Registry v Grant (Equality and Human Rights Commission intervening) 2011 ICR 1390, CA, the Court of Appeal rejected the claimant's submission that he was directly discriminated against when, following an office move, he was 'outed' by his new manager. In the Court's view, it was 'very difficult to see how revealing his sexual orientation [could] be held to be less favourable treatment' when he had already made his sexual orientation public at his previous workplace and there was therefore no reason to suppose that he would object to his manager's conduct. The Court thought this to be the case regardless of whether his new manager knew that he had come out at his old office. By putting facts into the public domain, the claimant took the risk that he might become the focus of conversation and, provided there was no ill intent, there was no discrimination.

That said, the claimant's *perception* of the effect of treatment upon him or her **15.15** is likely to significantly influence the tribunal's conclusion as to whether, objectively, that treatment was less favourable. Three examples:

- **R v Birmingham City Council ex parte Equal Opportunities Commission** 1989 IRLR 173, HL: the EOC claimed, by way of judicial review, that the Council treated girls less favourably than boys by providing fewer places in selective education for them. The House of Lords held that the EOC did not need to show that selective education was 'better' than non-selective education in order to establish that the girls had received less favourable treatment. It was enough that, by denying the girls the same opportunity as the boys, the Council was depriving them of a choice which, as the facts showed, was valued by them, or at least by their parents, and which (even though some might take a different view) was a choice obviously valued, on reasonable grounds, by many others

- **Royal Bank of Scotland plc v Morris** EAT 0436/10: C, who was black, was employed by RBS. He complained about his manager (T) to another manager (A). With no basis whatsoever, A suggested that C was alleging that T was racially motivated. C was offended by the suggestion that he was 'playing the race card' and resented that A was not seeing this as a straightforward complaint by one colleague against another, requiring to be treated on its merits, but as a complaint by a black employee against a white employee, which he found genuinely demeaning. A tribunal found that A's comment amounted to direct race discrimination and RBS appealed. On appeal, the EAT held that A's comment was based on a stereotypical assumption about a black employee complaining about a white colleague and was thus directly discriminatory. It rejected the argument that A would have asked the same question if a white employee had been complaining of his or her treatment by a black manager. According to the EAT: 'It is a matter of common experience that it is members of ethnic minorities who are

303

generally regarded as the principal victims of, and therefore complainants about, racial discrimination. Of course, white employees may sometimes be the victims of racial discrimination by black colleagues, but there is no stereotype to that effect.' However, the EAT went on to say that A's comment was, as acts of discrimination go, by no means grave. It was a single tactless remark, betraying an almost certainly unconscious racial stereotype of a rather subtle kind. Although the EAT could fully understand why C was upset by it, it was not otherwise offensive. The EAT hoped and expected that in the great majority of cases a comment of this kind would never form the subject of a tribunal claim and would be dealt with (assuming the employee wanted it dealt with at all) by an informal apology or through the grievance procedure

- **Home Office v Saunders** 2006 ICR 318, EAT: S, a female prison officer, was required by prison rules to carry out rub-down searches of male inmates. Male prison officers, however, were not permitted to search female inmates, because of a perceived risk that female inmates would object to being searched by a man on grounds of privacy and decency. S claimed that her employer had directly discriminated against her on the ground of sex in requiring her to carry out such searches. In upholding the tribunal's finding of direct sex discrimination, the EAT concluded that the tribunal was entitled to accept S's evidence regarding the feelings of distaste and indecency she felt when having to conduct a cross-gender search. Evidence was also given by other female prison officers. The employer did not dispute this evidence 'in any meaningful way' at the tribunal and it was therefore not open to the employer to challenge the tribunal's conclusion as to less favourable treatment.

15.16 In the EOC case above, the House of Lords accepted that denying the girls the choice of selective education meant that they had been treated less favourably without having to demonstrate that attendance at such a school would have been beneficial to their educational development. In Chief Constable of the West Yorkshire Police v Khan 2001 ICR 1065, HL (a victimisation case), the House of Lords went even further when it held that the claimant was treated less favourably when the employer refused, for allegedly discriminatory reasons, to provide him with a reference. It was almost certain that, had he been given a reference, it would have been very unfavourable and that from an objective point of view he was better off without one. Nonetheless he was held to have been treated less favourably than a comparator. There is, according to Lord Hoffmann, 'a distinction between the question of whether treatment is less favourable and the question of whether it has damaging consequences'. It is not enough, however, simply to show that the complainant has been treated differently. As Lord Scott said, 'there must also be a quality in the treatment that enables the complainant reasonably to complain about it. I do not think, however, that it is appropriate to pursue the treatment and its consequences down to an end result in order to try and demonstrate that the complainant is, in the end, better off, or at least no worse off, than he would have been if he had not been treated differently. I think it suffices if the complainant can reasonably say that he would have preferred not to have been treated differently.' Here, the claimant wanted a reference to be given, even though he knew that it would be likely to contain adverse remarks about him, and withholding it meant that he had suffered less favourable treatment.

Racial segregation. Section 13(5) states that, if the protected characteristic is **15.17** race, less favourable treatment includes segregating B from others. This provision is worded in similar terms to S.1(2) RRA. It avoids, for example, any argument from employers that although employees of different races were kept apart in the workplace, they were all treated equally.

Case law under S.1(2) RRA has shown that segregation must be distinguished from congregation. In FTATU v Modgill and ors and other cases 1980 IRLR 142, EAT, the Appeal Tribunal overruled a tribunal's finding of unlawful segregation on racial grounds where only Asian workers were employed in the employer's paint shop. The evidence showed that when vacancies arose in the shop they were filled by persons introduced by those already working there – a case of congregation, not segregation. (Note, however, that word-of-mouth recruitment can lead to claims of indirect discrimination by potential applicants who are excluded from the process – see Chapter 16, 'Indirect discrimination: proving disadvantage', and Chapter 24, 'Recruitment', under 'Arrangements for deciding to whom to offer employment – method of recruitment'.)

It is unclear why the Government did not use the opportunity presented by the **15.18** enactment of the EqA to extend the explicit protection under S.13(5) to all forms of segregation, e.g. gender segregation. However, despite the absence of any express provision, it is strongly arguable that such segregation would nonetheless give rise to less favourable treatment.

'Different' v 'less favourable' treatment. In the course of giving judgment in **15.19** Chief Constable of the West Yorkshire Police v Khan 2001 ICR 1065, HL, Lord Scott stressed that a claimant who simply shows that he was treated *differently* than others in a comparable situation were, or would have been, treated will not, without more, succeed with a complaint of unlawful direct discrimination. The EqA outlaws less favourable, not different, treatment, and the two are not synonymous.

One area where the distinction between different and less favourable treatment has come to the fore time and time again is where employers apply different rules to different groups of employees – usually along gender lines – in an attempt to enforce common standards of appearance in the workplace. Requiring a smart standard of business dress, particularly among those who work in customer-facing jobs, can involve different requirements for men and

305

for women where these reflect differences in conventional dress. However, merely treating men and women differently will not necessarily mean that men are treated less favourably than women, or vice versa.

15.20 In Schmidt v Austicks Bookshops Ltd 1978 ICR 85, EAT, the Appeal Tribunal adopted a 'swings and roundabouts' approach to assessing dress codes: it advocated considering an employer's clothing rules as a whole rather than 'garment by garment', and assessing whether the general effect of the rules is more restrictive for one sex than the other. Thus if the employer enforces rules even-handedly, so far as comparison is possible, it will have treated men and women alike. In the Schmidt case, although female shop assistants could not wear trousers, men were also subject to restrictions, such as a ban on t-shirts. As a result, a female employee could not show less favourable treatment. This approach was endorsed by the Court of Appeal in Smith v Safeway plc 1996 ICR 868, CA, where it held that a uniform policy will not be sex discriminatory if, as a whole, it applies a conventional standard of appearance for men and women.

However, treatment that is genuinely less favourable cannot be excused as being 'gender appropriate', even in the context of rules regulating clothing and appearance at work. In Lloyd v British Midland Airways Ltd ET Case No.2405288/98, for example, L obtained a job as a customer services agent. She attended a uniform fitting but was unable to fit into the largest uniform BMA provided and was dismissed. The tribunal found that BMA had directly discriminated against L in that, whereas the largest uniform provided for women was size 18, the only size requirement for men was that they should have no more than a 46" chest. Thus, while a woman's dimensions had to conform to a given size, a man could be any shape or size so long as he met the single chest-size criterion, which, the tribunal found, was itself larger than the equivalent chest size of a size 18 woman. This amounted to less favourable treatment of women on the ground of their sex.

15.21 Dress and appearance codes should be kept under review, as conventional standards of dress may change with time. In Hinchliffe v Reed Personnel Services Ltd and anor ET Case No.2407618/09, for example, the tribunal accepted that the employer was entitled to require a smart standard of business dress and appearance but did not consider that requiring women to wear make-up reflected conventional appearance standards. Dress codes are discussed further in Chapter 25, 'Discrimination during employment', under '"Any other detriment" – dress codes and appearance'.

15.22 **Less favourable treatment cannot be offset.** Once it has been established that the claimant suffered less favourable treatment, it is not possible to offset the effect of the treatment by offering some benefit to him or her in return; for example, extra pay. This point is illustrated by the decision in Ministry of Defence v Jeremiah 1980 ICR 13, CA. J worked as a quality examiner supervising factory production work. Overtime was optional for both male and female employees but, if the men volunteered for overtime, they were required to do 'dirty work' that the women were not required to do. There was no option for women to choose to do the dirty work, or for men to choose not to; however, the men were given extra pay because of it. The Court of Appeal confirmed that J, as a man, had been treated less favourably on the ground of his sex and had suffered a detriment – it was not for the tribunal to decide whether the extra money made the dirty work worthwhile. The Court of Appeal therefore rejected a 'whole package' approach to discrimination law – i.e. weighing up all the factors in the balance in determining whether there was less favourable treatment. Were it otherwise, employers would be able lawfully to discriminate because of a protected characteristic and frustrate the EqA's purpose.

'Trivial' differences. It has been held that where differences in treatment are 15.23 trivial, they may be disregarded under the 'de minimis' principle – Peake v Automotive Products Ltd 1977 ICR 968, CA, as explained in Ministry of Defence v Jeremiah 1980 ICR 13, CA. In practice, however, tribunals are reluctant to disregard any less favourable treatment, however minor, although the extent of the difference is likely to be reflected in the level of compensation awarded.

Less favourable treatment *of claimant*   15.24
Section 13(1) EqA defines direct discrimination in the following terms: 'A person (A) discriminates against another (B) if, because of a protected characteristic, A treats B less favourably than A treats or would treat others.' Some might think it self-evident from this definition that it is the claimant who must be adversely affected for the provision to apply, but there have been cases that have fallen at this first hurdle.

In two cases, brought under Reg 3(1)(a) of the Employment Equality (Age) Regulations 2006 SI 2006/1031, the EAT rejected discrimination claims because the job applicants had no genuine interest in the job they had applied for. Consequently, they could not argue that they had suffered less favourable treatment when they were not offered the job (in fact, one of them had not even sent in an application before bringing his claim). In Keane v Investigo and ors EAT 0389/09 the claimant, a woman in her late forties, unsuccessfully applied for a number of junior accountancy roles for which she was overqualified. She conceded that she had not been genuinely interested in the jobs, but nonetheless argued that she had suffered discrimination. The Appeal Tribunal, presided over by its then President, Mr Justice Underhill, noted that the definition of direct discrimination requires some kind of 'less favourable' treatment of the complainant. This element is commonly and usefully referred to as 'detriment'. An applicant, such as the claimant, who is not considered for a job in which he or she is not interested, cannot in any ordinary sense of the word be said to have suffered a detriment – or, to be more precise, to have been (comparatively) unfavourably treated.

307

15.25 K sought to rely on the European Court of Justice's decision in Centrum voor Gelijkheid van Kansen en voor Racismebestrijding v Firma Feryn NV 2008 ICR 1390, ECJ, that a Belgian employer who publicly stated that it would not recruit Moroccans because to do so would damage its business had committed an act of direct discrimination contrary to the EU Race Directive (No.2000/43) despite the absence of an identifiable victim. However, the EAT did not think that Centrum advanced K's case. The claim had not been brought by an individual and there was nothing in the ECJ's ruling to suggest that an individual claimant not affected by the employer's declaration of intent to discriminate could bring a claim. The judgment assumed that the mischief in the employer's conduct lay in the fact that the public statement that it would not recruit people from a certain ethnic or racial origin would, as the ECJ put it, 'strongly dissuade' such candidates from applying and thus deprive them of the chance of getting a job. Accordingly, the reasoning in Centrum did not address the position of candidates who did not want the job in the first place.

Underhill P was again presiding over the EAT in the second case, Berry v Recruitment Revolution and ors EAT 0190/10. There B, a man in his fifties, had brought a number of age discrimination claims against employers and employment agencies, even though he had not even applied for the jobs which he claimed were advertised in a discriminatory manner. The EAT held that since B had no intention of applying for the jobs in question, the terms of the advertisements could not be said to have deterred him from doing so, with the result that he suffered no detriment. Interestingly, Underhill P noted that B had apparently contacted numerous employers about alleged age-discriminatory job advertisements, reaching out-of-court settlements with some of them. While not expressing a view on B's motivation, he emphasised that discrimination legislation is not intended to provide a source of income to people who complain about discriminatory job advertisements but who have no desire to fill the vacancies in question. Underhill P added that those who try to exploit the legislation for financial gain were liable to have costs awarded against them, as indeed had happened to the claimant in Keane v Investigo and ors (above). For details on the award of costs in tribunal claims, see IDS Employment Law Handbook, 'Employment Tribunal Practice and Procedure' (2006), Chapter 18.

15.26 Although both cases in effect add an additional requirement that potential complainants must satisfy before they can bring a direct discrimination claim under S.13, the majority of complainants will have little difficulty in clearing this initial hurdle by showing that they genuinely wanted the job in question. The cases also seem to suggest that, provided the applicant can show a genuine interest in the job at issue and that he or she was deterred from applying as a result of the terms of the advert, a claim can be brought for unlawful discrimination without the claimant having formally applied.

308

Note that the EHRC has the power to institute legal proceedings in relation to unlawful advertising – see Chapter 37, 'Equality and Human Rights Commission', under 'Investigation of unlawful acts'.

Treatment complained of must have occurred. In Baldwin v Brighton and **15.27** Hove City Council 2007 ICR 680, EAT, a transsexual employee feared that he would suffer less favourable treatment when he discovered that someone whom he perceived to be prejudiced against transsexuals would sit on the interview panel that was to consider his application for transfer to a new post. The EAT held that it was not sufficient for his direct discrimination claim on the ground of gender reassignment that he merely suspected that the person *would* treat him less favourably.

Exceptions   15.28

The EqA makes specific provisions allowing for *more* favourable treatment in the context of disability and pregnancy or childbirth. Where these apply, it is not open to an employee who does not benefit to complain of less favourable treatment. So if, for example, a disabled person receives more favourable treatment than a non-disabled person, the latter is precluded from bringing a claim under S.13.

Disability. The EqA retains the asymmetric approach to disability discrimination **15.29** found in the antecedent legislation by providing that it is not discrimination to treat a disabled person *more* favourably than a person who is not disabled. This is achieved by S.13(3), which states: 'If the protected characteristic is disability, and B is not a disabled person, A does not discriminate against B only because A treats or would treat disabled persons more favourably than A treats B.' This would cover a situation where, for example, an employer has made reasonable adjustments to a disabled employee's working hours. An employee who does not have a disability could not argue that he or she has suffered less favourable treatment, because of disability, by not being allowed to work the same hours.

Pregnancy or childbirth. Section 13(6)(b) EqA provides that, if the protected **15.30** characteristic is sex, in a case where the complainant is a man, 'no account is to be taken of special treatment afforded to a woman in connection with pregnancy or childbirth'. This derives from an almost identical provision in S.2(2) SDA. The EHRC Employment Code gives the example of a man who is given a warning for being repeatedly late to work in the mornings. S.13(6)(b) would prevent him from alleging that he had been treated less favourably than a pregnant woman who had also been repeatedly late for work for a reason related to her pregnancy (such as morning sickness), and who was not given a warning (para 8.43).

A challenge to special measures adopted for employees who are pregnant or on maternity leave is not necessarily doomed to failure, however. In Eversheds

309

Legal Services v De Belin 2011 ICR 1137, EAT – decided under S.2(2) SDA – the EAT upheld a tribunal's decision that favouring a woman on maternity leave in a redundancy scoring was sex discrimination against a man in the selection pool. In the EAT's view, the obligation to protect employees who are pregnant or on maternity leave cannot extend to favouring such employees beyond what is 'reasonably necessary to compensate them for the disadvantages occasioned by their condition'. Where a maternity or pregnancy benefit is disproportionate – as it was here, since less discriminatory alternatives were available – a disadvantaged (male) colleague may claim sex discrimination.

15.31 Comparator

The key to establishing direct discrimination is often the construction of the correct comparator. S.13 EqA focuses on whether an individual has been treated 'less favourably' because of a protected characteristic. The question that naturally follows is: treated less favourably than whom? S.13(1) in its entirety states: 'A person (A) discriminates against another (B) if, because of a protected characteristic, A treats B less favourably than A treats or would treat others.' This, in itself, gives little indication of the identity of the appropriate comparator, although the use of the words 'would treat others' makes it clear that it is possible to construct a purely hypothetical comparison. Accordingly, it is not necessary for the claimant to point to an actual person who has been treated more favourably in comparable circumstances.

Whether the comparator is actual or hypothetical, the comparison must help to shed light on the reason for the treatment. However, the comparator test – i.e. asking whether someone without the claimant's protected characteristic would have been treated in the same way as the claimant – will only help the tribunal in determining whether there was direct discrimination if the situation of the claimant resembles that of the comparator in material respects. For this purpose, S.23(1) stipulates that there must be 'no material difference between the circumstances relating to each case' when determining whether the claimant has been treated less favourably than a comparator. In other words, in order for the comparison to be valid, 'like must be compared with like'.

15.32 The Explanatory Notes conveniently summarise the comparator as an actual or hypothetical person who:

- does not share the claimant's protected characteristic, and

- is in not materially different circumstances from him or her – para 91.

The fact that the comparator must not share the claimant's protected characteristic, alleged to be the reason for any adverse treatment suffered, does not generally pose any problems for tribunals. If the claimant alleges discrimination because he or she is Asian, the correct comparator will be an

310

individual who is not Asian. Similarly, if the claimant claims to have suffered discrimination because he or she is gay, the comparator will be someone who is not gay. The same approach applies where the protected characteristic is age – i.e. the comparator is someone who is not of the claimant's age. However, it is worth adding that, although the EqA allows a 60-year-old to compare his or her treatment to that meted out to a 59-year-old, such a small difference in age is unlikely to be sufficient for the tribunal to infer age discrimination. In Superquinn v Freeman AEE/02/8, for example, the Labour Court in Ireland overturned the Equality Tribunal's finding that a 31-year-old claimant had been the victim of age discrimination when her application for promotion was rejected in favour of a 28-year-old applicant. The Court held that, in the absence of other factors, a three-year difference in age was not significant enough to establish a presumption of age discrimination.

Note that there is no requirement for a comparator in cases of racial segregation and pregnancy or maternity discrimination – see Ss.13(5) and 18(2)–(4).

No materially different circumstances 15.33
As mentioned above, S.23(1) provides that on a comparison for the purpose of establishing direct discrimination there must be 'no material difference between the circumstances relating to each case'. On the face of it, this appears to suggest that *all* the circumstances relating to the case must be the same before a comparison between the claimant's treatment and that of a comparator can be made. However, para 3.23 of the EHRC Employment Code makes it clear that this is not necessary. It expressly states that the circumstances of the claimant and the comparator need not be identical in every way. Rather, 'what matters is that the circumstances which are *relevant to the [claimant's treatment]* are the same or nearly the same for the [claimant] and the comparator' (our stress) – para 3.23. This reflects the wording used in the antecedent discrimination legislation, which provided for the 'relevant circumstances' in the claimant's case to be the same as, or not materially different to, those in the comparator's case (see, for instance, S.5(3) SDA and S.3(4) RRA). Case law decided under the previous legislation is therefore still applicable in determining the relevant circumstances in a direct discrimination case under the EqA.

In the pivotal case of Shamoon v Chief Constable of the Royal Ulster Constabulary 2003 ICR 337, HL (a sex discrimination case), Lord Rodger said that the 'circumstances' relevant for a comparison include those that the alleged discriminator takes into account when deciding to treat the claimant as it did. He gave the example of a woman dismissed for being persistently late for work over a three-month period. The relevant circumstances will be her persistent lateness over a three-month period and the employer's treatment of her must be compared with how it treats or would treat a man in the same or not materially different circumstances, i.e. where he too has been persistently late for work over a three-month period. According to his Lordship, the Northern Ireland

311

Court of Appeal had been wrong to treat the question as being whether a reasonable person would attach some weight to a particular factor. The lower court had said that the fact that complaints had been made against the claimant, whereas no complaints had been made against the proposed comparators, was a relevant circumstance because no reasonable employer would have failed to take account of such a factor in determining how to treat the claimant. This was the wrong test. In his Lordship's judgment, a circumstance may be relevant if the employer in fact attached some weight to it, whether or not the tribunal thinks a reasonable employer ought to have done so. This approach was reaffirmed by the House of Lords in Macdonald v Ministry of Defence; Pearce v Governing Body of Mayfield Secondary School 2003 ICR 937, HL (another sex discrimination case), where Lord Hope held that, with the exception of the prohibited factor (be it sex, race or otherwise), 'all characteristics of the complainant which are relevant to the way his case was dealt with must be found also in the comparator'. This applies regardless of whether the comparator that is used is actual or hypothetical – Shomer v B and R Residential Lettings Ltd 1992 IRLR 317, CA.

15.34 Some cases where material differences were found to exist:

- **Wakeman and ors v Quick Corporation and anor** 1999 IRLR 424, CA: British nationals employed in the United Kingdom by a Japanese corporation complained that they were discriminated against on racial grounds in that they were paid less than employees seconded from Japan, who were all Japanese. The company argued that people of any nationality, even Japanese, who were recruited in the United Kingdom, would have been paid the same as the British employees. The seconded employees were paid more because of their expatriate status, to encourage them to move to the United Kingdom and to compensate them for the additional expenditure of living abroad. The Court of Appeal held that the difference in treatment was due to secondment, which was not a racial ground. In the circumstances, the Court held that the fact of secondment could be treated as being a material difference in the relevant circumstances of the claimants and the secondees with whom they wished to be compared

- **London Underground Ltd v Famakinwa and anor** EAT 1488/01: F and other members of staff, including G, were on a residential 'team building' exercise. G alleged that F had followed her into her bedroom where he made unwanted sexual overtures and assaulted her. G ran to another staff member's room to seek help. When the matter was reported, F was disciplined and ultimately dismissed. He claimed his dismissal was racially discriminatory. Part of F's complaint was that G had previously been disciplined for acts of harassment against fellow staff members and had not been dismissed. The EAT held that there was no comparison between the circumstances of the two cases

312

- **Balamoody v United Kingdom Central Council for Nursing, Midwifery and Health Visiting** 2002 ICR 646, CA: B was a nurse from Mauritius who ran a nursing home in the United Kingdom. He was struck off the professional register for various criminal offences relating to drug administration and record keeping at the nursing home. When his application for reinstatement to the register was unsuccessful, he complained of race discrimination. He cited as a comparator L, the matron at the nursing home, who, he argued, was responsible for the offences but had not been struck off. He also cited numerous newspaper reports of other nurses who had not been struck off for what he argued were instances of equal or more serious misconduct. The tribunal found that L was not a true comparator as she had not been convicted of any criminal offences and B had not previously brought up this complaint against her. The nurses in the newspaper reports were not true comparators as there was insufficient information as to the circumstances of their cases: B had no personal knowledge of them and had relied only on newspaper reports

- **Shamoon v Chief Constable of the Royal Ulster Constabulary** 2003 ICR 337, HL: a Chief Inspector, S, whose duties included performing staff appraisals, was removed from that duty by her Superintendent following complaints about the manner in which she carried them out. She complained that the decision to remove her from that duty was discriminatory on the ground of sex. The House of Lords held that two male chief officers, against whom S sought to compare her treatment, were directly comparable with her position in several respects: they were of the same rank; they served in the same branch; and they had similar responsibilities, including the responsibility for staff appraisals. However, the male officers were not appropriate comparators as there were two material differences that precluded such a direct comparison: there had been no complaints made against them and they were under the managerial control of a different Superintendent. The correct task for the tribunal was to consider how the claimant's Superintendent would have treated a male officer against whom similar complaints had been made

- **Cordell v Foreign and Commonwealth Office** 2012 ICR 280, EAT: C, who was profoundly deaf, worked for the FCO in Warsaw supported by a team of professional lipspeakers. The FCO subsequently offered her a role in Kazakhstan, subject to an assessment of whether, and at what cost, her disability could be accommodated there. Following this assessment, it withdrew the offer, having concluded that even if support could be found, which was uncertain, it would be prohibitively expensive. C complained of, among other things, direct disability discrimination, arguing that there was no material distinction between her circumstances, as a person needing financial support in order to be able to work in an overseas posting, and those of colleagues with children who benefit from the FCO's policy of providing

313

a continuity of education allowance (CEA), for school fees and associated costs, capped at around £25,000 per year per child. The EAT disagreed, and dismissed her complaint. While both C and the CEA beneficiaries might indeed need financial support to be able to accept an overseas posting, there was no general FCO policy of affording assistance in all such cases. The need for assistance with educational costs is a particular kind of need, met in a particular way, and the circumstances of a person with that need are materially different from those of a person without it. The EAT noted that the point was illustrated by the fact that C would also qualify for CEA allowances if she had school-age children.

15.35 By contrast, in O'Reilly v British Broadcasting Corporation and anor ET Case No.2200423/10 the tribunal found that O, a female TV presenter, suffered age discrimination when she was dropped from BBC's *Countryfile* in favour of younger presenters after a decision was made to move the programme to a primetime slot. O, who was aged 51, was informed that she would not be presenting on the new programme as the network wanted to 'refresh' the presenter line-up. Three other female presenters in their mid-forties were also told that they would no longer be used. Before the tribunal, the BBC argued that age was not a factor when deciding to drop O from the programme. In support of this, it pointed to a male presenter who continued to work on the new programme and who was aged 68. The tribunal, however, decided that he was not an appropriate comparator. O's treatment had to be compared with other 'second-tier' presenters like her. The new second-tier presenters were aged 38, 36 and 26. The tribunal concluded that, had O been 10 to 15 years younger, she would have been given proper consideration for a presenter role on the new *Countryfile*.

Cases under the antecedent legislation stressed the fact that the 'relevant circumstances' provision – e.g. S.5(3) SDA – was interpretive only, directed to ensuring that like was compared with like when an allegation of discrimination had been made. It could not be used by the employer to defend an act of unlawful discrimination. In Bain v Bowles and ors 1991 IRLR 356, CA, a magazine refused to place an advertisement for a housekeeper on behalf of B – a Scottish man living alone in Tuscany – based on a long-standing editorial policy of only including advertisements by female employers for female employees outside the United Kingdom. Previous experience had indicated that the risk of sexual harassment for those answering advertisements was greater in the case of an advertisement placed by a man living abroad on his own than in the case of a woman. When B brought his claim for sex discrimination, the magazine argued that the perceived risk of sexual harassment meant that the 'relevant circumstances' of B's advertisement were 'materially different' from those of a woman such as to provide a defence to the claim of discrimination under S.5(3). The Court of Appeal rejected this argument outright. As the provision could not be used as a defence, the magazine's perceived risk of sexual harassment was merely the *motive* for its action, which was irrelevant to determining whether or not it had discriminated against B.

Similarly, in Chief Constable of Greater Manchester Police and anor v Hope **15.36** 1999 ICR 338, EAT, the claimant, a white male police sergeant, formed a brief sexual relationship with a 17-year-old female civilian YTS trainee of Asian origin. A superior officer informed him that this relationship may have compromised his authority, and that the position was more serious because he was white and the trainee was Asian, given that the community to which the trainee belonged would not approve of a white sergeant forming a relationship with an Asian girl. H successfully claimed in the tribunal that these allegations amounted to direct discrimination against him on the ground of his race and sex, on the basis that they would not have been put to him but for his race, and he would not have faced an allegation of blameworthiness but for his sex. On appeal to the EAT, the police force argued that the correct comparison should be with a black or female officer whose conduct, however innocent, raised policy implications, as the relevant circumstances in the case included an issue relevant to police/community relations. The EAT held, however, that for the purpose of establishing the correct comparator, the policy could not rely upon the motive, however well meaning, behind the superior officer's questioning. The point was simply that a question was put to H which would not, on the tribunal's findings, have been put to an Asian male police sergeant. (The role of motive in direct discrimination claims is discussed below in the section on '"Because of" protected characteristic' under 'Determining the reason for the treatment – motive is irrelevant'.)

Hypothetical comparator. Early cases on determining the relevant **15.37** circumstances for the comparison exercise held that, while a claimant may be compared with a hypothetical person who does not share his or her protected characteristic, the comparison must be by reference to the same employment and not a hypothetical employment with different personnel. In Grieg v Community Industry and anor 1979 ICR 356, EAT, G's job application was rebuffed at the eleventh hour because she would have been the only female member of the work team. The employer argued that, for the relevant circumstances to be the same, the proper approach was to ask whether a man would have been treated differently if he had applied for a job on an all-female team. On appeal, the EAT rejected this argument, holding that the relevant employment for the purposes of making the appropriate comparison was the one for which the woman had applied. This approach was followed by the tribunal in Gallagher v Home Office and anor ET Case No.11832/84 where a female laundry instructor was told that she would not be allowed to do voluntary overtime in an all-male prison. The tribunal upheld her claim – because a male instructor would not have been similarly treated – and, in doing so, rejected the 'mirror-image' argument of the Home Office that a male in a woman's prison would have been identically treated.

315

While the overall conclusion in both decisions is undoubtedly correct, more recently, tribunals have tended to focus on the substance of the claimant's grievance in order to throw light on the material circumstances in a particular case. In Home Office v Saunders 2006 ICR 318, EAT, S, a female prison officer, was required by prison rules to carry out rub-down searches of male inmates. Male prison officers, however, were not permitted to search female inmates, because of a perceived risk that female inmates would object to being searched by a man on the grounds of privacy and decency. S claimed that her employer had directly discriminated against her on the ground of sex in requiring her to carry out such searches. The EAT held that the tribunal had been entitled to find that the hypothetical comparator was a male prison officer who was required to conduct a rub-down search of a female. In other words, the overarching principle was the requirement for a prison officer to conduct a rub-down search of a prisoner of the opposite sex. It followed that S was subject to direct sex discrimination in being required to carry out a rub-down search of a male prisoner, when a male colleague was specifically prohibited from carrying out a rub-down search of a female prisoner. The EAT rejected the employer's argument that changing the gender of both the prison officer and the inmate caused the relevant circumstances to be materially different.

15.38 In Kettle Produce Ltd v Ward EAT 0016/06, W, a female cleaner, was upbraided in the women's toilets by her male manager, G, who believed she was trying to avoid working. W complained of direct sex discrimination, but the Scottish EAT dismissed her claim. In its view, the central offence in W's case was that the incident took place in the women's toilets when she was confronted by a male manager. In constructing the hypothetical comparator, the invasion of a space reserved for the opposite sex had to be envisaged in order to make the circumstances not materially different. On the facts, the EAT concluded that a female manager with G's robust management style, bursting into the men's toilets, would have treated a male cleaner, having the same sensitivity as W and whom she believed to be avoiding work, in the same way as W was treated by G. The discrimination complaint was therefore not made out.

15.39 **Disability.** Where the protected characteristic that forms the basis of the discrimination complaint is disability, the EqA makes further provision in respect of the proper comparison to be made. Not only must the comparator be in the same material circumstances as the claimant but, according to S.23(2)(a), those circumstances must include the disabled person's abilities. Accordingly, when making a comparison for the purpose of establishing direct disability discrimination, a tribunal must take account of how a person with the same abilities as the claimant would have been treated.

The same requirement applied to direct discrimination under the Disability Discrimination Act 1995 (DDA), where the appropriate comparator was 'a person not having that particular disability whose relevant circumstances, including his abilities, are the same as, or not materially different from, those of the disabled person' – see S.3A(5). When, in 2001, the Government consulted on the implementation of the EU Equal Treatment Framework Directive (No.2000/78) with regard to disability, it acknowledged that direct discrimination had to be specifically excluded from the scope of the justification defence that then applied to disability-related discrimination. However, it noted that employers would still be able to justify not employing people who could not do the job even with a reasonable adjustment. This is what the 'material circumstances' requirement achieves with regard to disability. If a disabled person simply cannot do a particular job and the employer refuses to employ on that basis, this will not be direct discrimination. Even though the disabled person's disability is the reason why he or she cannot do the job, he or she has been treated no less favourably than a non-disabled person who also, for a non-disability-related reason, was unable to do the job.

Although in disability cases the claimant's abilities will be highly relevant, they **15.40** are not the only consideration for a tribunal when making a comparison. The leading case on the scope of the comparison envisaged by S.3A(5) DDA – and hence by Ss.13 and 23 EqA – is High Quality Lifestyles Ltd v Watts 2006 IRLR 850, EAT. There, a tribunal had decided that an employee who was HIV positive was directly discriminated against when his employer dismissed him on account of the risk of transmission of HIV to others. The employee had been employed as a support worker by a company providing specialist services to people with learning difficulties, autistic spectrum disorders and challenging behaviour. It was not unknown for support workers to be injured by service users – incidents of scratching, biting, kicking and punching, some drawing blood, had been reported. Thus, there was an appreciable risk of transmission, if not a very high one. The tribunal, in effect, assumed that once it was established that the risk of transmission was behind the dismissal, direct discrimination was necessarily made out.

On appeal, the EAT criticised the tribunal for this approach. In taking this causal connection as sufficient to establish liability, the tribunal had overlooked the issue of 'less favourable treatment', which can only be established by means of a comparison, taking into account relevant material circumstances. The tribunal ought to have imputed relevant circumstances to the hypothetical comparator; namely, a communicable disease, which was not HIV but which carried the same risk of causing illness or injury to others of the same gravity. If such a comparator would also have been dismissed, then the claimant had not been less favourably treated.

The Court of Appeal had the opportunity to review the EAT's exposition of the **15.41** law in Stockton on Tees Borough Council v Aylott 2010 ICR 1278, CA. It observed that while a tribunal must attribute the same abilities and other relevant circumstances to the comparator, and that failure to do so may be an error of law, the comparator is not required to be a 'clone' of the claimant. More importantly, however, the Court held that there is no obligation on the tribunal to construct a hypothetical comparator in every case, and that failure to do so does not necessarily lead to an error of law in the tribunal's decision. In the present case, the tribunal had concluded that the claimant's mental disability was the reason for his dismissal, given the stereotypical view of mental illness taken by the employer in its reaction to his disability. It followed that he had received less favourable treatment for the purposes of S.3A(5), and the hypothetical comparator added little to the process. According to Lord Justice Mummery: 'In this case the issue of less favourable treatment of the claimant, as compared with the treatment of the hypothetical comparator, adds little to the process of determining the direct discrimination issue. I am not saying that a hypothetical comparator can be dispensed with altogether in a case such as this: it is part of the process of identifying the ground of the treatment and it is good practice to cross check by constructing a hypothetical comparator. But there are dangers in attaching too much importance to the construct and to less favourable treatment as a separate issue, if the tribunal is satisfied by all the evidence that the treatment (in this case the dismissal) was on a prohibited ground.' Thus it seems that, although considering the treatment of a comparator will often be the most straightforward way of determining whether discrimination has occurred, the issue may sometimes take a back seat to a common-sense appreciation of the facts.

15.42 Stereotypical assumptions about a person's mental illness also arose for consideration in Aitken v Commissioner of Police of the Metropolis 2012 ICR 78, CA. In that case, A, who had been diagnosed with depression and obsessive compulsive disorder (OCD), brought a claim of direct discrimination based, among other things, on the force's handling of an investigation into reasonable adjustments and its decision to medically retire him. He claimed that the force had been influenced by a perception that he was 'dangerous', based on his offensive conduct at a work party and an incident when he became extremely agitated in a meeting to the extent that an occupational health physician feared for her safety. He asserted that the force had acted on assumptions about mental illness without objective medical evidence. The tribunal disagreed. It found that A had given the impression of having difficulty controlling his temper and scared his colleagues and, in these circumstances, the force's response was understandable and even mild. As for A's assertion that the force acted on the basis of assumptions about mental illness, the tribunal thought it irrelevant to consider whether the force's response to A's behaviour was justified by reference to what it then knew about the condition of OCD. The fact was that, at the time, A's behaviour was frightening, and reasonable people, including the occupational health physician, were scared of him. Thus, the force did not act on the basis of assumptions about mental illness but on the basis of how A appeared to others. This did not amount to direct discrimination. On appeal, both the EAT and the Court of Appeal refused to interfere with the tribunal's decision.

Another useful example of how a like-for-like comparison should be made in a direct disability discrimination case is the decision in Eagle Place Services Ltd and ors v Rudd 2010 IRLR 486, EAT. There, the Appeal Tribunal had to consider the appropriate comparator in the case of a solicitor working for a large law firm who had detached retinas. He benefited from adjustments to accommodate his condition, including a reduction in his working hours from eight to seven per day, the opportunity to take frequent breaks and leave the office to rest his eyes, adjustments to the lighting and air conditioning in his office, and being able to spend some time working from home. However, during negotiations over a permanent homeworking arrangement, R and the firm's head of HR got into a disagreement. R did not want to accept a reduction in salary commensurate with any reduction in hours and threatened to resign and claim constructive dismissal if any were imposed on him. He refused to allow a health and safety inspection of his home for homeworking purposes, and requested that his salary be artificially inflated so that he could benefit from a higher level of permanent health insurance. The firm dismissed him, citing breakdown of the working relationship based on these incidents. A tribunal, hearing R's claims of unfair dismissal and direct disability discrimination, noted that none of these incidents had been the subject of a proper investigation. It noted that there was 'a large credibility gap' between the firm's stated reasons for acting and the end result, dismissal. In those circumstances, it felt entitled to draw inferences from the paucity of the material justifying the dismissal to conclude that the real reason was that the firm was concerned that it would not get an appropriate return in terms of chargeable hours from R. This reason flowed from the firm's concerns over R's medical condition, meaning that direct discrimination was established. In so finding, the tribunal considered that the appropriate hypothetical comparator would be a lawyer of the same grade and skills as the claimant and who shared a similarly good relationship with the client (R worked solely for one client). The comparator would also need to work from home for two days per week but would not have to do so because of a sight disability. Such an employee, in the tribunal's view, would not have been dismissed.

The EAT dismissed the firm's appeal against that decision. It was satisfied that **15.43** the tribunal sufficiently set out the reasons for R's treatment, namely the perceived unprofitability of continuing to employ him with reasonable adjustments in place, and that the tribunal was entitled to conclude that this was direct discrimination. The EAT did, however, offer some refinement of the hypothetical comparator created by the tribunal. It thought that the appropriate comparator would be a fellow lawyer of the same grade and skills as R, who shared a similarly good relationship with the client, who for reasons other than disability required adjustments to be made to enable him to work, and in

319

respect of whom reasonable adjustments had been agreed to the satisfaction of both employer and employee, and in respect of whom commercial performance, even having regard to the proposed adjustments, was not an issue. Such a hypothetical employee would not have been dismissed by reason that he or she was considered to be an inconvenient liability, which would inhibit or damage the firm's commercial objectives. A decision to dismiss the comparator on those grounds would have been wholly unreasonable and it was simply not open to the firm to say that it did not discriminate against R because it would have acted equally unreasonably and dismissed the comparator. It is unreasonable to suppose that it would in fact have dismissed the comparator for what amounts to an irrational reason.

The refinement made by the EAT in the above case is an important one. It was clearly a relevant circumstance that the arrangements that were in place for R were satisfactory to all affected parties. The client on whose file R worked was happy with his work and so there was no question of the arrangements damaging the firm's business. If working arrangements required to accommodate an individual's disability do have a detrimental impact on the business, then, so long as the same would be true of a non-disabled comparator working under the same arrangements, the employer will be entitled to dismiss without thereby directly discriminating (although consideration would then need to be given as to whether the employer had complied with the S.20 EqA duty to make reasonable adjustments – see Chapter 21, 'Failure to make reasonable adjustments').

15.44 **Sexual orientation.** Section 23(3) EqA states that, where the protected characteristic is sexual orientation, the fact that one person is a civil partner while another is married is not a material difference between the circumstances relating to each case. The example given in the EHRC Employment Code states: 'A worker who is gay and in a civil partnership complains that he was refused promotion because of his sexual orientation. His married colleague is promoted instead. The fact that the worker is in a civil partnership and the colleague is married will not be a material difference in their circumstances, so he would be able to refer to his married colleague as a comparator in this case' – para 3.31.

15.45 **Discriminatory circumstances**
It has generally been held that the 'circumstances' of a comparator in a discrimination case must not be tainted in any way by discriminatory criteria, since this would have the effect of allowing discrimination because of a protected characteristic. The point is illustrated by the leading sex discrimination case of James v Eastleigh Borough Council 1990 ICR 554, HL. The complainant and his wife were both aged 61. However, the complainant was charged admission to a public swimming pool while his wife was admitted free of charge. The Council sought to argue that since the complainant had not reached pensionable age and his wife had, she could not be a valid comparator. The House of Lords held that the expression 'pensionable age' was no more

than a convenient shorthand which referred to the age of 65 in a man and 60 in a woman (the pension age at the relevant time), and was in itself discriminatory. It therefore could not be a relevant circumstance in identifying a comparator, and thus the complainant's lack of pensionable status was not a material difference between him and his wife. The complaint of sex discrimination succeeded.

Race discrimination and nationality. While the principle in James v Eastleigh **15.46** Borough Council (above) applies equally to other protected characteristics, courts and tribunals have departed from it in a number of cases concerned with discrimination based on nationality where the discrimination arose out of legal restrictions placed on the employment of foreign nationals – for example, the need for a work permit. It has been held that such matters could give rise to a material difference in circumstances and prevent a valid comparison being made between two groups. Three examples:

- **Dhatt v McDonalds Hamburgers Ltd** 1991 ICR 238, CA: an Indian national was sacked because he failed to produce a work permit when requested. He had produced his passport which was endorsed to show that he had indefinite leave to remain in the United Kingdom, which in practice meant that he did not need a permit as there were no restrictions on his right to work. The employee sought to compare his treatment with that of non-Indian citizens, including British citizens and EU nationals (who were also under no restrictions as to work in the United Kingdom). However, the Court of Appeal held that the comparison must be made with persons who were neither Indian nor British nor EU nationals. In reaching this decision the Court rejected arguments that a factor which is itself racially discriminatory (such as nationality) cannot qualify as a 'relevant circumstance' for the purposes of choosing a comparator whose 'relevant circumstances... are the same, or not materially different' (under what was then S.3(4) RRA). Parliament had legislated so as to create a distinction on the basis of nationality between those who were entitled to work without restriction in the United Kingdom and those who were not. Any discrimination involved in the choice of comparator was therefore 'sanctioned by statute'

- **Choux v Royal College of Veterinary Surgeons** EAT 668/95: C, a Swiss veterinary surgeon, applied to the Royal College of Veterinary Surgeons for registration to enable her to practise in the United Kingdom. Under S.5A of the Veterinary Surgeons Act 1966, an EU national with C's qualifications from the University of Parma in Italy would have automatically been entitled to be registered. However, the statute provided that non-EU nationals, such as C, could not be registered unless they sat an examination. The tribunal and the EAT held, following the Dhatt case, that for the purposes of S.3(4) RRA C could not compare herself with an EU national holding a similar qualification. EU nationals did not form a valid group for comparison

321

purposes because the respondent was required by statute to afford greater rights to EU nationals over non-EU nationals

- **Ice Hockey Super League Ltd v Henry** EAT 1167/99: H, a hockey player from the EU, complained that his contract was less favourable than the contracts of those employees who came from non-EU countries. H and other players from the EU had probationary periods in their contracts, whereas the contracts of non-EU hockey players did not contain a probationary period because it was difficult to obtain a work permit without a permanent contract. The tribunal and the EAT, following the Court of Appeal's decision in Dhatt, held that the correct comparator was another person within the group who did not require work permits, i.e. players from the EU. The requirement of a work permit, although based on nationality, was a relevant circumstance that precluded a comparison with a person who did not require a work permit.

15.47 The decisions in Dhatt and Henry in effect provided the employers with a convenient route around the narrow interpretation applied by the courts to the employer's defence under S.41(1) RRA, which excused discriminatory acts done under statutory authority. The Court of Appeal in Dhatt held that the employer had a 'public duty to assist in the enforcement of the immigration laws', and therefore had 'no alternative' but to enquire as to the applicant's right to work. The discrimination was 'sanctioned by statute' and the situation could not be likened to James v Eastleigh Borough Council (above), in which the Council had applied its discriminatory policy 'voluntarily', albeit 'for sensible reasons'. However, what the Court of Appeal appeared to ignore was the true substance of the applicant's complaint: he was not challenging the employer's ability to enquire as to his right to work, so much as challenging its decision not to accept what was, in law, a valid proof of his right to work. That, we would suggest, was not something which was 'sanctioned by statute'.

The Henry case is a clearer example of the Dhatt quantum leap. Although the immigration legislation required EU and non-EU nationals to be treated differently in certain respects, it did not require the League to discriminate in the manner it did. There was no necessity in law to impose a probationary period into H's or anyone else's contract. They were arguably acting 'voluntarily', albeit that they had 'sensible reasons' (to borrow the words used in Dhatt), in the same way that the policy of the Council in the James case was imposed voluntarily but for sensible reasons.

15.48 We are not aware of any successful challenges to the principles in Dhatt and Henry. However, we have serious doubts as to whether there were sufficient grounds in either case to disapply the House of Lords' ruling in James v Eastleigh Borough Council (above). But it is pertinent to note here that when the EqA came into force, S.41(1) RRA was repealed and no equivalent provision was put in its place. Thus, irrespective of whether the decision was correct on its facts, it is certainly arguable that the test applied in Dhatt – whether the discrimination involved in the choice of comparator was 'sanctioned by statute' – will continue to apply in cases that would previously have been caught by S.41(1). A good example of such a case would be Choux v Royal College of Veterinary Surgeons (above), where the respondent's hands were clearly tied by statute and the EAT did in fact find that the S.41 defence was also made out.

Hypothetical comparators   15.49
In the absence of a statutory comparator – i.e. an actual comparator who is in materially the same circumstances as the claimant and who has not suffered the same treatment – the question of less favourable treatment needs to be determined by reference to a hypothetical comparator who resembles the claimant in all material respects. But how should a tribunal go about constructing a hypothetical comparator and assessing whether the employer would have treated him or her any differently to the claimant? In the absence of an actual comparator, the process will necessarily involve drawing inferences from surrounding circumstances, and one way of doing this is to look at the treatment of people whose circumstances are not sufficiently similar to warrant their being treated as actual comparators, but which are sufficiently relevant for inferences to be drawn from the way they have been treated. Chief Constable of West Yorkshire v Vento (No.1) 2001 IRLR 124, EAT, involved a sex discrimination claim brought by a female police constable. The tribunal considered the circumstances of four other police constables (not all of whom were male) whose situations were not identical but were not wholly dissimilar either. It concluded that the claimant had been treated less favourably than a hypothetical male comparator. The EAT held that this was a permissible way of constructing a picture of how a hypothetical male comparator would have been treated. This approach was later approved by the House of Lords in Shamoon v Chief Constable of the Royal Ulster Constabulary 2003 ICR 337, HL, where their Lordships rejected the Court of Appeal's ruling that the claimant had to be able to point to at least one actual person whose treatment had been more favourable.

Another way of assessing whether a hypothetical comparator would have been treated differently is to call witnesses to answer questions about how such a hypothetical person would have been treated, although in the Vento case the EAT warned that tribunals must take great care in assessing the answers to such questions since they will be almost impossible to disprove and a witness would know, by the time of the hearing, what answer might be the most helpful or convenient to the side he or she wished to support.

The Court of Appeal has ruled that where there is no actual comparator, not **15.50** only is it permissible for the tribunal to consider how a hypothetical comparator would have been treated, it is incumbent on the tribunal to do so – Balamoody v United Kingdom Central Council for Nursing, Midwifery and Health Visiting

323

2002 ICR 646, CA (a race discrimination case). In that case the Court held that a tribunal had erred in failing to consider whether a nurse was treated less favourably than a hypothetical comparator when her applications to be restored to a professional register were rejected. In Chief Constable of Cambridgeshire Constabulary v McLachlan EAT 0562/02 a tribunal fell into a similar trap. M took maternity leave and returned to the police force in 1996 on a part-time basis. One afternoon M disobeyed an order requiring her to interview a complainant so that she could conclude her shift promptly at six o'clock and go home to her children. As a result, she was called to a disciplinary hearing and asked to resign. She did so and subsequently brought a claim for direct discrimination, which was upheld by a tribunal. On appeal, the EAT found that there was no helpful actual comparator in the case, and that the tribunal had erred in failing to construct a hypothetical comparator against which it could test her case. The force's apparent unreasonableness in the tribunal's eyes did not preclude the need to test whether the treatment meted out to the claimant was in fact less favourable than would have been afforded a comparable male. The obvious hypothetical comparator, the EAT thought, was a male part-timer with small children to care for who had disobeyed an order so that he could go home on time in order to look after them.

That said, there may be circumstances in which the construction of a hypothetical comparator adds little. In Stockton on Tees Borough Council v Aylott 2010 ICR 1278, CA, Lord Justice Mummery was of the view that where it was clear that the treatment at issue was on a prohibited ground, the need to construct a comparator was less of an issue. There, the tribunal had concluded that the claimant's mental disability was the reason for his dismissal, given the stereotypical view of mental illness taken by the employer in its reaction to his disability. It followed that he had received less favourable treatment and a hypothetical comparator added little to the process. Mummery LJ did acknowledge, however, that a hypothetical comparator should not be dispensed with altogether in such cases as 'it is part of the process of identifying the ground of the treatment and it is good practice to cross check by constructing a hypothetical comparator'.

15.51 Where a comparison with an actual comparator is possible, there is no obligation on the tribunal to construct a hypothetical comparator. In Williams v HM Prison Service EAT 1236/00 the EAT considered the Balamoody case (above) but rejected the suggestion that it is incumbent on a tribunal to construct a hypothetical comparator in circumstances where a comparison with an appropriate actual comparator had revealed no discrimination. The EAT could not see how, in such a case, any different result could be achieved by looking at a sensibly constructed hypothetical comparator.

324

Evidential comparators   15.52

In many cases there will be no actual comparator who satisfies the statutory criteria in S.23(1) of being in not materially different circumstances as the claimant and a hypothetical comparator will have to be used. However, in Shamoon v Chief Constable of the Royal Ulster Constabulary 2003 ICR 337, HL, Lord Scott pointed out that actual comparators also have a quite separate *evidential role* to play. The fact that a particular comparator cannot, because of material differences, qualify as the 'statutory comparator' does not disqualify him or her from an evidential role. Such comparators may be used as evidential tools that may or may not justify the tribunal in drawing an inference of discrimination and their usefulness will, in any particular case, depend on the *extent to which their circumstances are the same as those relating to the complainant*. On the facts of the Shamoon case, where the comparators were under the control of a different Superintendent and no complaints had been made against them, Lord Scott was of the opinion that those differences not only precluded the male officers from constituting the statutory comparators, they also deprived them of any significant evidential value in assessing whether a hypothetical comparator would have been treated any differently.

In the absence of comparators of sufficient evidential value, a claim may still succeed but some other material must be identified that is capable of supporting the requisite inference of discrimination. Discriminatory comments made by the alleged discriminator about the claimant might, in some cases, suffice. So might unconvincing denials of discriminatory intent given by the alleged discriminator, coupled with unconvincing assertions of other reasons for the allegedly discriminatory treatment. See further Chapter 33, 'Proving discrimination'.

Relevance of reason for treatment   15.53

In Shamoon v Chief Constable of the Royal Ulster Constabulary (above) the House of Lords took the view that, by tying themselves in knots attempting to identify an appropriate actual or hypothetical comparator, tribunals run the risk of failing to focus on the primary question; namely, why was the complainant treated as he or she was? If there were discriminatory grounds for that treatment then, as Lord Nicholls pointed out, there will 'usually be no difficulty in deciding whether the treatment... was less favourable than was or would have been afforded to others'. His Lordship viewed the issue as essentially boiling down to a single question: did the complainant, because of a protected characteristic, receive less favourable treatment than others? Similar comments were made in Stockton on Tees Borough Council v Aylott 2010 ICR 1278, CA, where Lord Justice Mummery stated: 'I think that the decision whether the claimant was treated less favourably than a hypothetical employee of the council is intertwined with identifying the ground on which the claimant was dismissed. If it was on the ground of disability, then it is likely that he was treated less favourably than the hypothetical comparator not having the

325

particular disability would have been treated in the same relevant circumstances. The finding of the reason for his dismissal supplies the answer to the question whether he received less favourable treatment.'

Therefore, where the identity of the comparator is in issue, tribunals may find it helpful to consider whether they should postpone the question of less favourable treatment until after they have decided why the particular treatment was afforded to the claimant. As pointed out by Mr Justice Elias (as he then was) in Law Society and ors v Bahl 2003 IRLR 640, EAT, one of the consequences of this approach is that where the tribunal has addressed the primary question, it will not generally be necessary for it actually to formulate the precise characteristics of the hypothetical comparator. Once it is shown that race, sex, age, etc had a causative effect on the way the complainant was treated, it is almost inevitable that the effect will have been adverse, and therefore the treatment will have been less favourable than that which an appropriate comparator would have received. Similarly, if it is shown that race, sex, age, etc played no part in the decision-making, then the complainant cannot succeed and there is no need to construct a comparator.

15.54 In Islington London Borough Council v Ladele 2009 ICR 387, EAT, Mr Justice Elias, then President of the EAT, returned to this issue. In his view, where the characteristics of the statutory comparator are in dispute, a tribunal is in practice unlikely to be able to identify the comparator without first answering the question why the claimant was treated as he or she was. To illustrate this point, he cited as an example a claimant who alleges that he did not get a job because of his race. The employer defends the race discrimination complaint by saying that he was not appointed because he was not academically clever enough, and there is evidence to show that the person appointed to the job had better academic qualifications. The claimant alleges that this was irrelevant to the appointment; it was not therefore a material difference. The employer disputes this. If, Elias P continued, the tribunal is satisfied that the real reason is race, then the academic qualifications are irrelevant. The relevant circumstances are not therefore materially different and it is plain that the statutory comparator was treated differently. However, if the tribunal is satisfied that the real reason is the difference in academic qualifications, then that provides a material difference between the position of the applicant and that of the comparator. So a finding of discrimination can be made without the tribunal needing specifically to identify the precise characteristics of the comparator at all.

Elias P went on to identify a particular situation where, in his view, a strict reliance on the comparator test can be positively misleading. This arises in cases where the protected characteristic contributes to, but is not the sole or principal reason for, the employer's act or decision (discussed in the section '"Because of" protected characteristic' under 'Determining the reason for the treatment – protected characteristic need not be only reason for treatment' below). The claimant will therefore have a claim for unlawful discrimination, even though he or she would have been subject to precisely the same treatment if there had been no discrimination, because the protected characteristic merely reinforces a decision that would have been taken for lawful reasons. In these circumstances the statutory comparator would have been treated in the same way as the claimant was treated and relying solely on the comparator test would give the wrong answer. Elias P did not give a practical example of when this particular situation might arise but we think it could occur where, say, the employer already has a strained relationship with the employee and has considered dismissal but the ultimate decision is influenced by the employee's protected characteristic – for instance, his or her age or sexual orientation. Not asking why the employee was dismissed would mean that the employer's discriminatory motivation is likely to go unnoticed.

Two recent decisions where the focus on the 'reason why' issue proved **15.55** determinative of the claimant's case:

- **Chondol v Liverpool City Council** EAT 0298/08: C, a social worker, was dismissed after the Council became concerned about what it perceived as his failure to recognise professional boundaries when dealing with service users. C's religious discrimination complaint was rejected by the tribunal. He appealed, arguing that the tribunal had failed to construct the correct comparator. The EAT disagreed, holding that the tribunal had found that C was dismissed partly because he improperly promoted his religious beliefs to service users, and not on account of those beliefs per se. Consequently, the question of how to define the comparator became academic

- **Cordell v Foreign and Commonwealth Office** 2012 ICR 280, EAT: C, who is profoundly deaf, worked for the FCO in Warsaw supported by professional lipspeakers. The FCO subsequently offered her a role in Kazakhstan, subject to an assessment of whether, and at what cost, her disability could be accommodated there. Following this assessment, it withdrew the offer, having concluded that even if support could be found, which was uncertain, it would be prohibitively expensive. Approaching the question of direct discrimination from the 'reason why' angle, the EAT held that C's direct discrimination claim must necessarily fail because the reason for her non-appointment was not her disability per se but a reason related to it – namely, the cost of providing the necessary support, coupled with the uncertainty over whether it would be available.

These cases show that it is now well-recognised that debating the correct **15.56** characterisation of the comparator is often less helpful than focusing on the fundamental question of the reason why the claimant was treated in the manner complained of. However, this does not mean that tribunals can ignore the comparator issue altogether. As Lord Justice Mummery emphasised in Stockton

327

on Tees Borough Council v Aylott (above), the identification of a comparator, whether real or hypothetical, is still an important step in the process of reasoning when the tribunal addresses the primary issue of why the respondent treated the complainant in a particular way. According to the EAT in Law Society and ors v Bahl (above), while it is no longer necessary for tribunals to specify with precision the hypothetical comparator, they may find it helpful to do so provisionally in order to identify any potentially relevant explanations which might account for the difference in treatment. Failure to do so, at least in a provisional way, may raise doubts as to whether the tribunal has properly considered all potentially relevant explanations when identifying whether unlawful discrimination exists.

The decision in B v A 2007 IRLR 576, EAT, is a useful example of a tribunal falling into this trap. In that case, B, a solicitor, dismissed his assistant, A, with whom he was in a personal relationship, after discovering her apparent infidelity. A brought a sex discrimination claim, which was upheld by the tribunal. On appeal, the EAT overturned the decision. The tribunal had found that the dismissal was 'driven by jealousy or the discovery of A's relationship with [someone else]'. A had therefore been dismissed because of the breakdown of her relationship with B, not because of her sex. That being so, it was simply not open to the tribunal to uphold her sex discrimination claim. In the EAT's view, the tribunal's error in relation to A's sex discrimination claim may well have been compounded by its failure to carry out a comparison between the claimant's treatment and how a man would have been treated. Although it is not an error of law to fail to construct a hypothetical comparator in a sex discrimination case, it is vital that a proper comparison be made, given that the advancement of a non-discriminatory reason will almost inevitably involve the assertion that someone of the opposite sex would have been treated the same way. The correct comparison here was with a homosexual male employer and a homosexual male employee. On the tribunal's findings, such an employee would have received exactly the same treatment; that is, the employer, driven by feelings of jealousy, would have dismissed him upon discovering his apparent infidelity.

15.57 ## 'Because of' protected characteristic

The definition of direct discrimination in the EqA requires the complainant to show that he or she received less favourable treatment 'because of a protected characteristic'. The phrase 'because of' was not found in the antecedent discrimination legislation, which required claimants to show that they had been treated less favourably 'on grounds of' or 'on the ground of' a particular characteristic (see, for example, S.3A DDA and S.1 SDA). Obviously, this change in wording raises the question of whether Parliament intended to alter the legal meaning of direct discrimination. All indications are that it did not.

328

According to the Explanatory Notes, the wording in the EqA was chosen for the sake of clarity, in order to make it 'more accessible to the ordinary user' (para 61). The view that the previous and new formulations are 'absolutely synonymous' was taken by the Solicitor General at the Public Bill Committee in the House of Commons. The EHRC Employment Code corroborates this, stating that the phrase 'because of' has the same meaning as the phrase 'on grounds of' a protected characteristic (see para 3.11). Furthermore, a comment made by the (then) President of the EAT, Mr Justice Underhill, in Amnesty International v Ahmed 2009 ICR 1450, EAT (a case brought under the RRA), is worth noting in this regard. In a footnote to his judgment, Underhill P expressed the view that there could be no objection to tribunals using 'because of' as a synonym for 'on grounds of' under the old statutory provisions on direct discrimination, provided the phrase was not used to import a test of causation.

15.58 Thus, the general principles on establishing the link between less favourable treatment and the reason for the treatment – set down in a number of cases interpreting the phrase 'on grounds of' or 'on the ground of' under the discrimination legislation in force prior to October 2010 – will continue to be relevant following the introduction of the EqA. We discuss these principles under 'Determining the reason for the treatment' below.

Scope of 'because of'

15.59 As with the antecedent legislation, the protection afforded by S.13 extends to cases where the claimant does not possess the relevant protected characteristic but is nonetheless less favourably treated 'because of' that characteristic – for example, where a white employee alleges that he has been dismissed for refusing to carry out the employer's instruction to discriminate against black customers. In Showboat Entertainment Centre Ltd v Owens EAT 1984 ICR 65, EAT, it was held that such treatment amounted to less favourable treatment 'on racial grounds' for the purposes of the RRA. And in Lisboa v Realpubs Ltd and ors EAT 0224/10 L, a gay employee, resigned and claimed discrimination and constructive dismissal because he was uncomfortable implementing a rebranding policy which he felt had the effect of making the pub he worked in (formerly a gay pub) less welcoming to gay customers. The EAT held that the way the rebranding policy was implemented constituted discrimination against gay customers and also against L, and that this gave rise to constructive dismissal.

In addition, the wider wording of S.13 EqA means that two new categories of would-be claimants are now covered: those who associate with a person who has a protected characteristic and those who are mistakenly thought to have a protected characteristic. We consider each of these categories separately below – see 'Discrimination by association' and 'Discrimination by perception' respectively.

329

15.60   However, the protection afforded by S.13 is not completely open-ended. In Redfearn v Serco Ltd 2006 ICR 1367, CA, for example, the Court of Appeal rejected a direct discrimination claim brought by R, who had been dismissed from a job working with persons of Asian origins following his election as a British National Party councillor. The Court concluded that R had not been dismissed 'on racial grounds' in these circumstances, even though the employer's decision to dismiss involved racial considerations.

15.61   **Determining the reason for the treatment**
A complaint of direct discrimination will only succeed where the tribunal finds that the protected characteristic was the reason for the claimant's less favourable treatment. Unfortunately, judicial guidance on the question of how to establish the necessary connection between the 'less favourable treatment' and the 'protected characteristic' has not been as instructive as it perhaps could have been. That said, recent decisions have provided some much-needed clarity.

There are a number of leading authorities on when conduct will be 'on grounds of' – and now, by analogy, 'because of' – a protected characteristic. One of the earliest is James v Eastleigh Borough Council 1990 ICR 554, HL (a sex discrimination case). That case involved a claim brought under S.29(1) SDA, which prohibited sex discrimination in the provision of facilities to the public, by a man who was charged 75p entry to a public swimming pool, while his wife was allowed in free. The difference in treatment was the result of the Council's policy of giving free entrance to those who had reached state pensionable age (being, at that time, 65 for men and 60 for women). The House of Lords held that the Council had discriminated against the claimant on the ground of his sex, within the meaning of S.1(1)(a) SDA, because he would have received the same treatment as his wife but for his sex. In reaching this conclusion, their Lordships considered that cases of direct discrimination can be established by asking the simple question: would the claimant have received the same treatment as a man but for her sex? This has become known as the 'but for' test.

15.62   However, subsequent cases did not universally apply the 'but for' test. In O'Neill v Governors of St Thomas More Roman Catholic Voluntarily Aided Upper School and anor 1997 ICR 33, EAT, for example, the EAT preferred to express the basic question as: 'What, out of the whole complex of facts before the tribunal, is the "effective and predominant cause" or the "real or efficient cause" of the act complained of?'

In Nagarajan v London Regional Transport 1999 ICR 877, HL, a case concerned with the definition of direct discrimination under the RRA (which referred to treatment 'on racial grounds' as compared to 'on the ground of [the complainant's] sex' or 'on the ground of the disabled person's disability'), the House of Lords endeavoured to bring matters back to first principles. According to Lord Nicholls, 'a variety of phrases, with different shades of meaning, have

330

been used to explain how the legislation applies in such cases: discrimination requires that racial grounds were a cause, the activating cause, a substantial and effective cause, a substantial reason, an important factor. No one phrase is obviously preferable to all others, although in the application of this legislation legalistic phrases, as well as subtle distinctions, are better avoided so far as possible. If racial grounds… had a *significant influence* on the outcome, discrimination is made out' (our stress). The crucial question, in every case, was 'why the complainant received less favourable treatment… Was it on grounds of race? Or was it for some other reason, for instance, because the complainant was not so well qualified for the job?'

While Lord Nicholls in Nagarajan sidestepped the issue of whether the 'but for' **15.63** test was still appropriate in cases of direct discrimination in the employment field, Lord Browne-Wilkinson, dissenting, took the view that 'the "but for" test is not a rule of law but a rule of convenience depending on the circumstances of the case'. In Chief Constable of West Yorkshire Police v Khan 2001 ICR 1065, HL, Lord Nicholls seemed to take the argument a stage further. He argued that the phrases 'on racial grounds' (direct discrimination under S.1(1)(a) RRA) or 'by reason that' (victimisation under S.2 RRA) denote a *subjective* test, namely: why did the alleged discriminator act as he or she did? What, consciously or unconsciously, was his or her reason? (Note that Khan was a victimisation case under S.2 RRA, so any comments their Lordships made in respect of direct discrimination were, strictly speaking, obiter, i.e. non-binding.)

The tension between the 'but for' and 'reason why' tests led to confusion at tribunal level as to the correct approach to adopt when identifying the reason for any less favourable treatment. That said, recent decisions have stressed that any apparent incompatibility between the leading authorities on this point is misplaced. In R (on the application of E) v Governing Body of JFS and the Admissions Appeal Panel of JFS and ors 2010 IRLR 136, SC, the Supreme Court was asked to determine whether a Jewish school directly discriminated against a pupil on racial grounds when it refused him a place because his mother was not recognised as Jewish by the Office of the Chief Rabbi. The school was designated as having a religious character and allowed to use faith-based oversubscription criteria to give priority to children who are members of, or who practise, their faith or denomination. However, the pupil's father argued that those criteria breached S.17 RRA, which prohibited discrimination by educational establishments when applying their admission procedures. The school submitted that its admissions policy was based on religious considerations.

By a five-to-four majority, the Supreme Court found the school's admissions **15.64** policy in breach of the prohibition on race discrimination. (In contrast, the four Supreme Court Justices who dissented reasoned that the school's decision was taken not on racial but on religious grounds, and therefore the statutory exemption from religion or belief discrimination liability under Ss.45 and 47 of the Equality Act 2006 – now para 5 of Schedule 11 to the EqA 2010 – applied.) In the course of giving judgment, the majority summarised the principles that apply in cases of direct discrimination under S.1(1)(a) RRA and gave valuable guidance on how to determine the reason for the claimant's treatment. Lord Phillips, President of the Supreme Court, emphasised that in deciding what were the 'grounds' for discrimination, a court or tribunal is simply required to identify the *factual criteria applied by the respondent as the basis for the alleged discrimination*. Depending on the form of discrimination at issue, there are two different routes by which to arrive at an answer to this factual inquiry. Crucially, the respondent's *motive* for discriminating according to the factual criteria, however benign, is not relevant in this context – see under 'Motive is irrelevant' below.

In some cases, Lord Phillips explained, there is no dispute at all about the factual criterion applied by the respondent. In other words, it will be obvious why the complainant received the less favourable treatment. If the criterion, or reason, is based on a prohibited ground, direct discrimination will be made out. To illustrate this type of case, Lord Phillips referred to the Council's policy in James v Eastleigh Borough Council (above) allowing pensioners free entry to its swimming pools. This criterion was *inherently discriminatory* because men and women had different state pensionable ages, with the result that men had to wait five years longer than women before they could benefit from the policy. Accordingly, the Council discriminated against the claimant on the ground of sex. Lord Phillips added that their Lordships in that case had identified the factual criterion applied by the Council by using the 'but for' test – a test he did not himself find helpful. Instead, he preferred to simply ask: 'What were the facts that the discriminator considered to be determinative when making the relevant decision?'

15.65 Next, Lord Phillips referred to cases where the reason for the less favourable treatment is not immediately apparent – i.e. the act complained of is not inherently discriminatory. Here, he opined, it is necessary to explore the *mental processes*, conscious or subconscious, of the alleged discriminator to discover what facts operated on his or her mind. He gave the following example to illustrate this type of case: 'A fat black man goes into a shop to make a purchase. The shop-keeper says "I do not serve people like you". To appraise his conduct it is necessary to know what was the fact that determined his refusal. Was it the fact that the man was fat or the fact that he was black? In the former case the ground of his refusal was not racial; in the latter it was.' Accordingly, the subjective test, described by Lord Nicholls in Chief Constable of West Yorkshire Police v Khan (above), 'is only necessary as a seminal step where there is doubt as to the factual criteria that have caused the discriminator to discriminate.' Thus, direct discrimination can arise in one of two ways: where a decision is taken on a ground that is inherently discriminatory or where it is taken for a reason that is subjectively discriminatory. As Lord Clarke put it in the JFS case, it is unfortunate that 'until now this distinction has not perhaps been as clearly identified in the authorities as it should be'.

To be fair, however, a few months before judgment was handed down in the JFS case, the EAT summarised the above principles in much the same way in Amnesty International v Ahmed 2009 ICR 1450, EAT. There, the employer was found guilty of direct race discrimination when it denied promotion to an employee on the basis that her ethnic origin exposed her, and others with her, to increased safety risks while travelling and potentially compromised the employer's impartiality. Mr Justice Underhill, then President of the EAT, succinctly summarised the 'James-type' and the 'Nagarajan-type' approach to determining the reason for the treatment as depending on the form of discrimination at issue.

Underhill P also commented on the 'but for' test recommended in the earlier **15.66** authorities. In his view, the test could be applied to both types of direct discrimination case, but its real value lay in its application to the latter: it is a simple shorthand for determining whether the proscribed factor operated on the alleged discriminator's mind, without getting tangled up in complex questions with regard to the employer's motivation. However, while it was a useful gloss on the statutory test, he stressed that it was not intended as an 'all-purpose substitute for the statutory language'. Indeed, if it were, there would be cases in which it was misleading, since the fact that a claimant's race or sex was part of the circumstances in which the treatment complained of occurred, or of the sequence of events leading up to it, did not necessarily mean that it formed part of the ground of, or reason for, that treatment.

This point was clearly made by the EAT in Martin v Lancehawk Ltd t/a European Telecom Solutions EAT 0525/03. In that case, M, a female employee of L Ltd, was having an affair with L, the male managing director. However, by October 2002 problems arose in the relationship and M decided to tell her husband about it, despite having told L that she would not do so. L dismissed M on 28 October, allegedly for gross misconduct, and M brought claims of unfair dismissal and direct sex discrimination. The tribunal upheld her unfair dismissal claim but dismissed the discrimination claim. On appeal, M, relying on the House of Lords' decision in James v Eastleigh Borough Council (above), argued that the only reason L had an affair with her was that she was a woman, as he would not have had an affair with a heterosexual man. Therefore, 'but for' her sex there would have been no relationship, from which it followed inexorably that 'but for' her sex she would not have been dismissed.

Rejecting M's appeal, the EAT noted that the decision in James is 'not one **15.67** which provides the most helpful assistance to the resolution of the type of problem raised by the present case' and that the situation in James was 'very different from the type of sex discrimination issue which most commonly arises in the workplace, namely one involving an inquiry as to whether the employer's treatment of a particular employee amounted to discrimination against her on the ground of her sex. In such cases there will usually be no scope for assessing from a supposed objective standpoint whether the employer's acts have been relevantly discriminatory. It will instead be essential to enquire why the employer acted as he did, a question which, once answered, will usually show whether there has been any unlawful discrimination.' On the facts of the case before it, the EAT concluded that the tribunal had not erred in dismissing M's discrimination claim. The crucial question was why had M been dismissed? In answering that question the tribunal had considered and accepted L's evidence that the reason was based not in any way on M's sex, but on the breakdown of their personal relationship.

Thus it seems that the 'but for' test remains one way of showing direct discrimination. However, in the majority of cases, the best approach to deciding whether allegedly discriminatory treatment was 'because of' a protected characteristic is to focus on the reason why, in factual terms, the employer acted as it did.

15.68 **Motive is irrelevant.** The EHRC Employment Code makes the point, at para 3.14, that the motive or intention behind the treatment complained of is irrelevant. In other words, it will be no defence for an employer, faced with a claim under S.13(1), to show that it had a 'good reason' for discriminating. In James v Eastleigh Borough Council (above) the House of Lords held that the Council's policy to allow those who had reached pensionable age free entry to its swimming pools discriminated against the male claimant on the ground of his sex. Lord Goff acknowledged that the Council had the best of intentions in adopting the policy, which was to give financial assistance to retired people, whether male or female. However, the Council's benign motive was no answer to a claim of direct discrimination.

Similarly, in Amnesty International v Ahmed (above), the employer's genuine concerns for employees' health and safety could not prevent the RRA from applying, since all the relevant elements of S.1(1) were present. Once the tribunal had found that race was the ground for the less favourable treatment – in this case, refusing the claimant promotion to the post of Sudan researcher – that was the end of the matter and the employer's reasons or motives, however legitimate or laudable, were irrelevant.

15.69 In R (on the application of E) v Governing Body of JFS (above) M's application for a place at JFS was rejected because he was not considered to be Jewish according to the criteria adopted by the Office of the Chief Rabbi (OCR). None of the Supreme Court Justices doubted that the OCR honestly and sincerely believed it was applying criteria that were demanded of it by Jewish religious law. However, as the majority of the Supreme Court held, the crucial question was why M's application to attend the school was rejected and the answer was that it was his ethnicity. The school's motive for discriminating against him

334

because of his ethnic origin did not impact on that conclusion. As Lord Kerr put it, 'the reason why the school refused M admission was, if not benign, at least perfectly understandable in the religious context. But that says nothing to the point. The decision was made on grounds which the [RRA] decreed are racial.'

In the course of his judgment, Lord Phillips commented that, in contrast with the law in many countries, direct discrimination under English law provides no defence of justification (with the exception of age discrimination). However, he could conceive of circumstances, such as the instant case, where discriminating against a minority racial group may be justified. He therefore concluded that 'there may well be a defect in our law of discrimination'. Baroness Hale had the same train of thought, suggesting that there may be a good case for allowing Jewish schools to adopt criteria which they believe to be required by religious law even if they are ethnically based. However, that should be for Parliament to decide.

15.70 It is worth pointing out here that, while the discriminator's motive and intention are irrelevant when determining whether the elements of a direct discrimination claim have been made out, they may well be relevant to the question of *remedy*. In O'Neill v Governors of St Thomas More Roman Catholic Voluntarily Aided Upper School and anor (above) the EAT noted that although the subjective mental processes of the respondents were not relevant to the question of their liability for discrimination, such considerations might be relevant to remedies for discrimination. It was for the tribunal to decide, having regard to all the circumstances, what remedies it considered just and equitable. This principle was applied by the EAT in Chief Constable of Greater Manchester Police and anor v Hope 1999 ICR 338, EAT (the facts of which are outlined under 'Comparator – no materially different circumstances' above). At first instance, a tribunal found that the police force had discriminated against the claimant by subjecting him to questioning over his relationship with a young Asian female trainee. It awarded the claimant £750 for injury to feelings, which was at the lower end of the scale. The majority of the EAT, however, having upheld the finding of discrimination, overturned the award of compensation (Judge Peter Clark dissenting). It found that given the difficulty of the police force's situation, 'presented with a community reaction which may be discriminatory but is connected with culture or beliefs genuinely held by a significant group of people' and needing to attempt to create good relations with communities as a whole – combined with the unattractive aspects of the claimant's conduct – meant that the limited detriment in the case should attract no remedy at all.

15.71 **Protected characteristic need not be only reason for treatment.** The Court of Appeal in Owen and Briggs v James 1982 ICR 618, CA, held that while the protected characteristic (in that case, race) need not be the only reason for the treatment, it must have been a substantial reason. However, the EAT went one step further in O'Neill v Governors of St Thomas More Roman Catholic Voluntarily Aided Upper School and anor (above), taking the view that the protected characteristic need not even be the main reason for the treatment, so long as it was an 'effective cause'. The EHRC Employment Code confirms this, noting that 'the [protected] characteristic needs to be a cause of the less favourable treatment, but does not need to be the only or even the main cause' – para 3.11. An example:

- **Bourke and anor v Secure Guard Ltd** ET Case Nos.1401986–7/05: B and G, who were gay, started working for SG Ltd as security guards and B was soon promoted. B then wrote a memo, purporting to represent the views of both claimants, in which he criticised company practices and procedures. Their manager, T, made it known to B that he was unhappy with the memo. A few days later, there was a misunderstanding and G failed to return keys to SG Ltd. T phoned the claimants' home and a heated discussion took place between him and G during which both lost their tempers. In the course of the discussion, T repeatedly used offensive epithets referring to G's sexual orientation. On discovering that B was at home in bed rather than at work (as, unknown to B, his shift had been due to start earlier that day), T dismissed both of them. B and G complained of direct discrimination on the ground of their sexual orientation, which was upheld by the tribunal. The tribunal acknowledged that there were several reasons for T's decision to dismiss the claimants, including G's failure to return the keys and B's challenging behaviour towards him. However, it decided that, due to T's use of insulting epithets directed at the claimants' sexuality at the point of dismissal, their sexual orientation affected T's decision 'at least to some degree'. Furthermore, there was no evidence of any other employee having been dismissed for a one-off offence of this kind; rather, T had previously adopted a relatively relaxed approach to disciplinary matters in similar circumstances. The discrimination claim was accordingly made out.

15.72 In determining whether the protected characteristic was an underlying reason for – as opposed to the immediate cause of – the less favourable treatment, the tribunal may need to look beyond the superficial answer to the question why the employer treated the employee less favourably. In O'Neill v Governors of St Thomas More Roman Catholic Voluntarily Aided Upper School and anor (above) O was a religious studies teacher at a Roman Catholic school who was not permitted to return to work after giving birth to a child she had conceived with a priest. The tribunal accepted that there were two distinct causes operating when the governors of the school decided not to allow O to return. One was the pregnancy itself, but the circumstances surrounding the pregnancy were, it believed, the 'dominant' cause – namely, the identity of the child's father, the publicity the story had attracted, and the untenability of O's position at the school. For this reason the tribunal concluded that O's dismissal had not been 'on grounds of sex'. The EAT overturned this decision. The critical question, it said, was whether, on an objective consideration of all the surrounding circumstances, O's dismissal had been on the ground of pregnancy (and hence her sex). It need not have been only on that ground. It need not even have been mainly on that ground. All that was required was that O's pregnancy be 'an effective cause' of her dismissal. There were always 'surrounding circumstances' to a pregnancy. For example, the fact that an employer's reason for dismissing a pregnant woman was that she would become unavailable for work did not make it any the less a dismissal on the ground of pregnancy. In the instant case, the other circumstances relied upon by the tribunal as the 'dominant' cause were all causally related to the fact that O was pregnant. Her pregnancy precipitated and permeated the decision to dismiss her. She had, consequently, been discriminated against on the ground of her sex. (Arguably, had O been dismissed for having an affair with the priest that had not resulted in pregnancy, she may have had more difficulty establishing that the dismissal was discriminatory – assuming the employer could establish that a male teacher who had a relationship with a nun would also have been dismissed, or that the dismissal was on the ground of the affair and not of her sex.)

Protected characteristic shared by discriminator. Section 24(1) EqA states **15.73** that: 'For the purpose of establishing a contravention of this Act by virtue of section 13(1), it does not matter whether A has the protected characteristic.' Thus, for the purposes of a direct discrimination claim, it is irrelevant that the alleged discriminator shares the claimant's protected characteristic. Previously, this was explicitly stated only in the case of religion or belief: Reg 3 of the Employment Equality (Religion or Belief) Regulations 2003 SI 2003/1660 provided that 'a person ("A") discriminates against another person ("B") if... on the grounds of the religion or belief of B or of any other person except A (*whether or not it is also A's religion or belief*) A treats B less favourably than he treats or would treat other persons' (our stress). S.24(1) makes it clear that this principle now applies across all the protected characteristics in direct discrimination cases. The Explanatory Notes to the Act give the example at para 95 of an employer who rejects a job application from a gay man because of the applicant's sexual orientation. It would not be open to the employer to argue that, as a gay man himself, he cannot be liable for discrimination.

Section 24(2) extends the principle to combined discrimination (see 'Combined discrimination' below), but not to other forms of discrimination, such as harassment. However, we would suggest that there is nothing to prevent its application in that context, even though the EqA does not make express provision to that effect.

Knowledge of protected characteristic. An employer may be able to **15.74** successfully fend off a direct discrimination claim if it can show that it was genuinely unaware of the claimant's protected characteristic. Some examples:

337

- **Crouch v Mills Group Ltd and anor** ET Case No.1804817/06: C worked in one of the employer's convenience stores. He was assumed to be heterosexual. Indeed, he regularly made comments to his manager, R, about wanting to have sex with her, and claimed to others that he could 'pull her' and other women. C contended that, during a conversation with R, he revealed his homosexuality and that, in response, she refused to talk to him. She also allegedly shortened his lunch break entitlement from one hour to half an hour. C was eventually dismissed for incapability and brought a number of complaints in the employment tribunal, including direct discrimination on the ground of his sexual orientation. The tribunal dismissed the claim. It rejected C's contention that he had told R of his homosexuality, and found that MG Ltd was not aware of his sexual orientation. Furthermore, C was not unreasonably ostracised, and nor did he have his lunch break shortened. C had not proved any facts or raised any inferences from which the tribunal could conclude that MG Ltd had committed an act of discrimination

- **Cook v Rock Steady Security Ltd** ET Case No.2801808/06: RSS Ltd advertised for part-time event security staff. The job involved providing assistance and safety advice to people attending a range of outdoor events. C applied and was invited to an interview, at which he was asked to fill out an application form, but he said he was unable to write. When RSS Ltd checked to see if C could read, and discovered that he could not, it explained that it could not give C the job as he needed to be able to read and write, and had to be able to read and understand safety instructions for each event. Although C suggested that he could memorise them in advance, RSS Ltd terminated the interview. C claimed that he had been directly discriminated against, in being denied the opportunity to apply for the post, on the ground of his dyslexia. A tribunal rejected his claim, finding that C did not make it clear at the time that his difficulties in reading and writing were caused by dyslexia. (Note, however, that the tribunal in Cook went on to find that C had been discriminated against for a reason related to his dyslexia under S.3A(1) DDA. This reflects the state of the law at the time that the employer's knowledge was generally irrelevant to the question of whether disability-related discrimination was established under S.3A(1) DDA. The current law is discussed in Chapter 20, 'Discrimination arising from disability').

- **McClintock v Department of Constitutional Affairs** 2008 IRLR 29, EAT: M, a Justice of the Peace, asked to be excused from cases that might lead to the adoption of a child by a same-sex couple. The DCA refused the request, reminding him of his judicial oath and of his duty to adjudicate on any case that came before him. He resigned, but his religious discrimination claim failed because he had never made it clear that he objected on religious grounds.

Inherently discriminatory treatment

15.75

In some cases, the 'reason why' question poses little difficulty for tribunals. These are cases where the act complained of is inherently discriminatory. In Amnesty International v Ahmed 2009 ICR 1450, EAT, Mr Justice Underhill, then President of the EAT, said that if an owner of premises puts up a sign saying 'no blacks permitted', it cannot be doubted that race is the reason why a black person is excluded from the premises. In cases of this kind, it is irrelevant what was going on in the mind of the discriminator. The reason for the action is inherent in the act itself and no further inquiry is needed and direct discrimination will be made out. The EHRC Employment Code gives the example at para 3.12 of an employer which states in a job advertisement that 'Gypsies and Travellers need not apply'. A gypsy or traveller eligible to apply for the job, but deterred from doing so because of the statement in the advert, will be able to complain of direct discrimination because of race. The discriminatory basis of the treatment is obvious from the treatment itself.

Three case examples:

15.76

- **James v Eastleigh Borough Council** 1990 ICR 554, HL: J, who was 61, was charged 75p entry to a public swimming pool, while his wife, who was the same age, was allowed in free. The difference in treatment was the result of the Council's policy of giving free entrance to those who had reached state pensionable age (being, at that time, 65 for men and 60 for women). The House of Lords held that the Council had discriminated against the claimant on the ground of his sex, within the meaning of S.1(1)(a) SDA. The discriminatory treatment resulted from the fact that women reached state pensionable age five years before men did. In other words, the discriminatory rule could have been expressed as 'free entry for women at 60 and men at 65'. Clearly, this rule was inherently discriminatory on the ground of sex

- **Amnesty International v Ahmed** (above): A, a UK national of northern Sudanese origin, worked for AI in the United Kingdom as a campaigner on issues relating to Sudan. She applied for the post of Sudan researcher but AI refused to promote her because it believed that the fact that A was herself of Sudanese origin would compromise its reputation for impartiality and could also expose both A and those who worked with her to a greater danger of violence than would be faced by a non-Sudanese person performing the job. A succeeded before the tribunal with a complaint of direct race discrimination and that decision was upheld on appeal. Since the reason for AI's concerns about impartiality and health and safety was A's ethnic identity, the reason for the refusal to appoint her was her ethnic origin (a protected characteristic under the RRA). Direct race discrimination was accordingly made out

- **R (on the application of E) v Governing Body of JFS and the Admissions Appeal Panel of JFS and ors** 2010 IRLR 136, SC: the school's admissions

339

policy, when oversubscribed, was to only admit children recognised as Jewish by the Office of the Chief Rabbi (OCR). M applied for a place at the school but was rejected because the OCR did not recognise him as of Jewish descent because his mother's conversion to Judaism was not recognised under OCR rules. M's father applied for judicial review of the school's decision, arguing that the admissions policy constituted unlawful race discrimination. A majority of the Supreme Court agreed, holding that as the admissions policy clearly focused on the ethnicity of the claimant's mother, the school had applied an inherently discriminatory criterion when it refused M a place. M had therefore been directly discriminated against on ethnic grounds contrary to S.1(1)(a) RRA.

15.77 Subjectively discriminatory treatment

It is unusual nowadays to find direct evidence of an intention to discriminate. Generally, those who discriminate do not advertise their prejudices. In fact, they may not even be aware of them. As Lord Nicholls explained in Nagarajan v London Regional Transport 1999 ICR 877, HL (a race discrimination case), 'many people are unable, or unwilling, to admit even to themselves that actions of theirs may be racially motivated. An employer may genuinely believe that the reason why he rejected an applicant had nothing to do with the applicant's race. After careful and thorough investigation of a claim members of an employment tribunal may decide that the proper inference to be drawn from the evidence is that, whether the employer realised it at the time or not, race was the reason why he acted as he did.' (The way in which tribunals go about deciding whether to draw an inference of discrimination is examined in Chapter 33, 'Proving discrimination'.

In Chief Constable of Cumbria v McGlennon 2002 ICR 1156, EAT, M, a police constable in the Cumbria force, was posted to a remote and unpopular police station. He claimed that this posting amounted to direct sex discrimination, on the basis that relatively few female officers had been posted to the station over the years, and that women were given more favourable postings. The tribunal upheld his claim. It found that the decision to impose the unpopular posting on M and another male officer even though no female officers were posted to the station and given that there were other officers available (both male and female) who could have been selected to transfer, coupled with the previous pattern of postings, justified the inference that M, as a male officer, had been selected for the posting instead of an equally suitable female officer because it was 'easier to post a man'. His selection therefore amounted to unlawful discrimination. The EAT agreed, recognising that discrimination may include 'even an unconscious (or what in other contexts might be viewed as merely benevolent) allowance for women's assumed family responsibilities and other difficulties which is not automatically accorded to men'.

340

Stereotypical assumptions. Where an assumption, often erroneous, about the **15.78** claimant can be shown to have influenced the employer's less favourable treatment of him or her, direct discrimination will usually be made out. It is no defence in this context that the stereotype may very likely be true – see, for example, R (on the application of European Roma Rights Centre and ors) v Immigration Officer at Prague Airport and anor 2005 2 AC 1, HL (an immigration case). In essence, an employer should refrain from assuming that an individual possesses (or lacks, as the case may be) certain characteristics because he or she has a particular protected characteristic. For instance, it should not be assumed that, because the claimant is a woman, she will not be able to do a job that requires heavy lifting. If strength is a requirement for the job, all applicants should be able to demonstrate whether or not they are capable of satisfying that condition, regardless of their gender. Nor would it be legitimate for an employer to assume that an individual will not 'fit in' because of his or her age or race.

The EHRC Employment Code, at para 3.15, gives the example of an employer who believes that someone's memory deteriorates with age. It assumes – wrongly – that a 60-year-old manager can no longer be relied on to undertake the role competently. When an opportunity for promotion arises, the employer fails to mention it to the manager. The employer's conduct is influenced by a stereotyped view of the competence of 60-year-olds and is likely to amount to less favourable treatment because of age (although, in principle, it remains open to the employer to objectively justify the discriminatory treatment – see under 'Justifying direct age discrimination' below). In Wilkinson v Springwell Engineering Ltd ET Case No.2507420/07 a teenage employee was dismissed because she was too young for the job. The employer's view of her performance was based upon a stereotypical assumption that youth and lack of capability go hand in hand. Age was the predominant reason for W's dismissal and, as the employer failed to put forward a justification defence, her discrimination claim succeeded.

Where the protected characteristic is disability, stereotypical assumptions about **15.79** an individual's capabilities seem to be particularly prevalent. In Stockton on Tees Borough Council v Aylott 2010 ICR 1278, CA, the Court of Appeal agreed with a tribunal's finding that the dismissal of an employee with bipolar disorder was direct discrimination, based on evidence that the employer had a stereotypical view of mental illness. The tribunal found that the employer's imposition of strict deadlines and performance monitoring following a period of stress-related absence, culminating in dismissal, betrayed the employer's fear of the claimant's return to work and a desire to manage him out. Although the claimant had been involved in a heated meeting with his line manager, his behaviour had never been threatening, and there was medical evidence that he could continue to work in a low-key and non-stressful role rather than in a managerial position. The tribunal had been entitled to conclude that a non-disabled comparator with a similar sickness record would not have been treated

341

in the same way and that the less favourable treatment was based on a 'stereotypical view of mental illness'.

Lord Justice Mummery, giving the judgment of the Court of Appeal, noted that 'direct discrimination can occur, for example, when assumptions are made that a claimant, as an individual, has characteristics associated with a group to which the claimant belongs, irrespective of whether the claimant or most members of the group have those characteristics'. However, he went on to warn that a tribunal can err in law if it concludes that direct discrimination has been established simply by relying on an unproven assertion of stereotyping. Direct discrimination claims must be decided in accordance with the evidence, not by making use, without requiring evidence, of a verbal formula such as 'institutional discrimination' or 'stereotyping'. There must be evidence (as there was in this case) from which the tribunal can properly infer that wrong assumptions were being made about that person's characteristics and that those assumptions were operative in the detrimental treatment, such as a decision to dismiss.

15.80 The Aylott case can be contrasted with City of Edinburgh Council v Dickson EAT 0038/09, where the EAT held that the employer was clearly not motivated by any assumptions or misgivings about a particular disability. D was employed as a community learning and development worker based at the community wing of a school. He had 'type one' diabetes, which was poorly controlled and meant that he was at risk of falling into a hypoglycaemic state, particularly around mealtimes. A person undergoing a hypoglycaemic episode can behave wholly out of character and have no recollection of what he or she has done. D was suspended after a visiting youth club organiser reported having seen him in the school's computer suite watching pornographic images. In the ensuing disciplinary investigation D insisted that he had no recollection of the incident, but that if it had occurred (which, he accepted, the evidence appeared to show) his behaviour must have been a result of his diabetes. F, the manager conducting the hearing, did not accept this explanation, despite notes submitted by the Council's occupational health doctor stating that D's inappropriate behaviour could have been caused by a hypoglycaemic episode, but that there was no evidence to indicate whether it had been. D brought claims of unfair dismissal and direct disability discrimination. A tribunal upheld his discrimination claim, deciding that F's failure to attach any weight to D's explanation – which the tribunal described as a 'disability explanation' – amounted to less favourable treatment on the ground of disability. The tribunal reasoned that an employee who had put forward a 'non-disability explanation' for the same conduct, such as sleepwalking, would not have had the explanation rejected in the same way.

The EAT overturned this part of the tribunal's decision. It noted that, following Nagarajan v London Regional Transport (above), what needs to be determined is what was influencing the mind of the decision-taker. In the instant case, there was no reason to suppose that F was influenced by the fact that D had diabetes. D's medical condition was irrelevant unless it explained his conduct, and F believed that it did not. The fact that D's explanation related to his disability did not mean that the Council's rejection of it was on the ground of disability, and nor did the fact that an employer treated a disabled person unreasonably – even in a matter related to his or her disability – mean that it did so because the person was disabled.

Accordingly, while tribunals must be alive to the fact that an employer may be **15.81** influenced by stereotypical views, there must still be sufficient reason to find that it was in fact influenced by such views. In B and anor v A 2010 IRLR 400, EAT, the Appeal Tribunal held that a tribunal was wrong to find that an employer had committed sex discrimination when it summarily dismissed a male employee accused of rape on the basis that he was likely to carry out further violence towards staff. There was no evidence that the employer was swayed by a stereotypical view that men are more likely to be violent than women. Similarly, in Live Nation (Venues) UK Ltd v Hussain and other cases EAT 0234–6/08, the Appeal Tribunal said that, although a finding that management believed the employee to be 'too old to change' was, in an appropriate case, capable of giving rise to an inference of age discrimination, there was no such evidence in this case. And in Haritaki v South East England Development Agency 2008 IRLR 945, EAT, the Appeal Tribunal held that a manager had not discriminated against the claimant when he suggested that her communication difficulties might be due to her 'Mediterranean' background. Although the reference to 'Mediterraneans' did 'at first sight indicate a stereotypical approach to people', the tribunal was entitled to find that the manager concerned was dealing sensitively with issues that had arisen about the claimant's style of communication.

Stereotypical assumptions underpinning a tribunal's decision to infer discrimination in a particular case are further discussed in Chapter 33, 'Proving discrimination'.

Justifying direct age discrimination

15.82

Unlike the other protected characteristics covered by S.13, there is a 'justification defence' available to employers facing claims of direct *age* discrimination. S.13(2) EqA provides: 'If the protected characteristic is age, A does not discriminate against B if A can show A's treatment of B to be a proportionate means of achieving a legitimate aim.' This is the test previously found in Reg 3(1) of the Employment Equality (Age) Regulations 2006 SI 2006/1031 ('the Age Regulations') and so the case law on objective justification that developed under those Regulations is instructive as to the circumstances in which direct age discrimination may be justified under S.13(2) EqA.

343

The phrase 'proportionate means of achieving a legitimate aim' in S.13(2) differs from the wording found in the EU Equal Treatment Framework Directive (No.2000/78) ('the Framework Directive') from which the test derives. In order for less favourable treatment to be justified for the purposes of Article 6(1) of the Directive, the difference in treatment must be 'objectively and reasonably justified by a legitimate aim' and the means of achieving that aim must be 'appropriate and necessary'.

15.83 When drafting the Equality Bill the Government chose to retain the old test of objective justification, which also applies in cases of indirect discrimination under S.19(2) EqA and discrimination arising from disability under S.15(1). Giving its reasons for the decision not to use the European wording in the context of indirect discrimination, the Government stated in its consultation response: 'We consider that the wording "appropriate and necessary" is problematic in domestic discrimination legislation because of the extreme exigency associated with "necessity" in domestic law. If this wording were to be used there might be a risk that this would be interpreted by the courts as an overly-strict requirement' ('The Equality Bill – Government response to the Consultation', July 2008 (Cm 7454), para 7.26). That said, the EHRC Employment Code uses the words 'appropriate' and 'necessary' to describe the second stage of the objective justification test and the Supreme Court in Homer v Chief Constable of West Yorkshire Police 2012 UKSC 15, SC, has made it clear that, although domestic legislation refers only to a 'proportionate means of achieving a legitimate aim', this has to be read in the light of the Directive. According to Baroness Hale, 'to be proportionate, a measure has to be *both* an appropriate means of achieving the legitimate aim *and* (reasonably) necessary in order to do so'. For further consideration on this point, see Chapter 17, 'Indirect discrimination: objective justification', under 'Background and overview – legislative history'.

The Code gives examples at paras 3.40–3.41 of the operation of the justification defence in the context of direct age discrimination. However, these should be treated with some caution as the Code was written at a time when the prevailing view was that the justification test was the same for both direct and indirect discrimination. The Supreme Court has now made it clear that this is not the case, despite the fact that the two tests are worded identically. According to their Lordships in Seldon v Clarkson Wright and Jakes (A Partnership) 2012 UKSC 16, SC, the justification test for direct discrimination is narrower than that for indirect discrimination: direct discrimination can only be justified by reference to legitimate objectives of a public interest nature, rather than purely individual reasons particular to the employer's situation, such as cost reduction or improving competitiveness – see below. For discussion of the objective justification in the context of indirect discrimination, see Chapter 17, 'Indirect discrimination: objective justification'.

Legitimate aims

15.84

Section 13(2) is silent as to what may amount to a legitimate aim for the purpose of justifying unlawful age discrimination (as indeed were the Age Regulations before it). The EHRC Employment Code states that for an aim to be legitimate it must be 'legal, should not be discriminatory in itself, and must represent a real, objective consideration' – para 4.28. In the wake of the ECJ's decision in Incorporated Trustees of the National Council on Ageing (Age Concern England) v Secretary of State for Business, Enterprise and Regulatory Reform 2009 ICR 1080, ECJ, on the legality of the United Kingdom's default retirement age (which has since been repealed), it was suggested that direct age discrimination could only be justified by reference to a social policy objective, such as those related to employment policy, the labour market or vocational training. This view has now been endorsed by the Supreme Court in Seldon v Clarkson Wright and Jakes (A Partnership) 2012 UKSC 16, SC, where their Lordships held that direct discrimination can only be justified by reference to legitimate objectives of a public interest nature, rather than purely individual reasons particular to the employer's situation, such as cost reduction or improving competitiveness. Having considered the jurisprudence of the ECJ, Baroness Hale (giving the leading judgment) identified two broad categories of legitimate social policy objective:

- 'inter-generational fairness' – which could include facilitating access to employment by young people; enabling older people to remain in the workforce; sharing limited opportunities to work in a particular profession fairly between the generations; promoting diversity and the interchange of ideas between younger and older workers

- 'dignity' – which would cover avoiding having to dismiss older workers on the grounds of incapacity or underperformance and avoiding divisive disputes about capacity or underperformance.

The legitimate aim need not have been articulated or even realised at the time **15.85** the measure was first adopted – it could provide rationalisation retrospectively.

Simply establishing an aim that falls within one of the above categories will not be sufficient, however. The employer must then go on to show that it is legitimate in the particular circumstances of the employment concerned. Baroness Hale gave two examples. First, the aim of improving the recruitment of young people in order to achieve a balanced and diverse workforce. 'This is in principle a legitimate aim. But if there is in fact no problem in recruiting the young and the problem is in retaining the older and more experienced workers then it may not be a legitimate aim for the business concerned.' Her second example was the aim of avoiding the need for performance management. This may be a legitimate aim, but if in fact the business already has sophisticated performance management measures in place, it may not be legitimate to avoid them for only one section of the workforce.

345

15.86 One question that remains is whether cost can ever be a legitimate aim. In Woodcock v Cumbria Primary Care Trust 2011 ICR 143, EAT, Mr Justice Underhill was of the view that an employer should be entitled to justify discriminatory treatment simply on the basis that the cost of avoidance would be 'disproportionately high'. However, when the case progressed to the Court of Appeal – Woodcock v Cumbria Primary Care Trust 2012 EWCA Civ 330, CA – Lord Justice Rimer stressed that an employer cannot justify discriminatory treatment 'solely' because the elimination of such treatment would involve increased costs. This approach was endorsed in Seldon v Clarkson Wright and Jakes (above), where the Supreme Court emphasised that cost reduction, or improving competitiveness, are not social policy objectives capable of amounting to legitimate aims for the purpose of justifying direct age discrimination. However, it should be pointed out that in reaching this conclusion, the Court relied on the direct age discrimination case of Fuchs and anor v Land Hessen 2012 ICR 93, ECJ, where the European Court held that a German law stipulating a retirement age of 65 for civil servants was potentially justified under the Framework Directive. In so holding, the ECJ reiterated the well-established doctrine that budgetary considerations can underpin the chosen social policy of a Member State and influence the nature or extent of the measures adopted, although such considerations cannot in themselves constitute a legitimate aim. Thus, it appears that while a desire to save costs cannot, of itself, amount to a legitimate aim, it may possibly be relied upon to support a legitimate social objective.

15.87 Proportionality

For discriminatory treatment to be justified under S.13(2), it must not only pursue a legitimate aim, but must also be a proportionate means of achieving that aim. Essentially, proportionality requires a balancing exercise, with the importance of the legitimate aim being weighed against the discriminatory effect of the treatment. In Homer v Chief Constable of West Yorkshire Police 2012 UKSC 15, SC, Baroness Hale stressed that to be proportionate, a measure must be *both* an appropriate means of achieving the legitimate aim *and* (reasonably) necessary in order to do so. The EHRC Employment Code states that: 'EU law views treatment as proportionate if it is an appropriate and necessary means of achieving a legitimate aim. But applying a provision, criterion or practice may be "necessary" in this context without being the only possible way of achieving the legitimate aim; it is sufficient that less discriminatory measures could not achieve the same aim. A balance must be struck between the discriminatory effect of the practice and A's reasons for applying it, taking into account all the relevant facts' – para 4.31. Although this was written in relation to justifying indirect discrimination, it is equally applicable in the context of direct age discrimination.

346

Below we discuss some areas where tribunals have frequently had to grapple with the justification defence. It should be noted, however, that all the cases referred to were decided before the Supreme Court gave judgment in Seldon v Clarkson Wright and Jakes (A Partnership) 2012 UKSC 16, SC. As a result, they should be considered in the light of that decision, which restricted the circumstances in which objective justification can apply in direct age discrimination cases – see 'Legitimate aims' above.

Compulsory retirement age   15.88

While the justification question is ultimately one of fact for the tribunal, there is a small yet significant body of case law at domestic and European level that can be drawn on for guidance in respect of compulsory retirement ages (which, since April 2011, require objective justification).

Domestic tribunals have adopted a rigorous approach to the issue and have been unwilling to accept bare assertions that a retirement age is justified, demanding to see cogent evidence that a retirement age is a proportionate means of achieving the employer's aims. In Hampton v Lord Chancellor and anor ET Case No.2300835/07 the employment tribunal had to consider whether a compulsory retirement age of 65 for Recorders was a proportionate means of achieving the aim of opening up vacancies for new Recorders. (Recordership is perceived as the first step on the path to appointment to the full-time judiciary.) In his capacity as Recorder, H was an office holder and afforded protection by the Age Regulations. When he turned 65 he was compulsorily retired. A tribunal agreed that H had suffered direct discrimination but held that compulsory retirement was a legitimate aim to maintain a reasonable flow of new appointments to the office of Recorder.

Turning to the question of whether proportionate means had been used to **15.89** achieve this legitimate aim, the respondent argued that the presence of Recorders between 65 and 70 would prevent the recruitment of younger Recorders who would then enter the pool for appointment to other judicial roles. The tribunal rejected this argument for a number of reasons, including the fact that the respondent had ignored statistics showing that a retirement age of 70 would still leave a pool of at least 1,138 Recorders eligible for promotion, which is a large pool given that only 3 per cent of Recorders are appointed judges each year. There was no evidence that a pool of that size would be unlikely to produce enough suitable candidates. The tribunal also rejected the argument that the presence of Recorders aged over 65 would reduce the availability of more challenging cases, holding that 'steps could be taken to ensure that those in the pool are allocated the right type of case for them to gain experience'. The tribunal therefore concluded that the imposition of a retirement age of 65 for Recorders was not a proportionate means of achieving the respondent's legitimate aim.

347

A law firm's policy of retiring partners at 65 was subjected to judicial scrutiny in Seldon v Clarkson Wright and Jakes (A Partnership) 2012 UKSC 16, SC. In accordance with this policy, S retired at the end of 2006 and subsequently claimed direct age discrimination in the employment tribunal. Since it was conceded by the respondent that compulsory retirement was an act of direct discrimination on the ground of age, the only issue left to consider was the justification defence. The tribunal accepted that the following were legitimate aims: (i) ensuring that associates were given the opportunity of partnership after a reasonable period, thereby ensuring that they would not leave the firm; (ii) facilitating the planning of the partnership and workforce across individual departments by having realistic long-term expectations as to when vacancies would arise; and (iii) limiting the need to expel partners on performance grounds, thus contributing to the congenial and supportive culture in the firm. The tribunal also agreed that the compulsory retirement age was a proportionate means of achieving these aims. S's direct age discrimination claim was accordingly dismissed.

15.90 S appealed to the Supreme Court. In dismissing his appeal and confirming the decision of the EAT to remit the case to the tribunal, Baroness Hale – with whom Lords Hope, Brown, Mance and Kerr were all in agreement – held that, contrary to the tribunal's view, the justification test for direct discrimination is narrower than that for indirect discrimination: direct discrimination can only be justified by reference to legitimate objectives of a public interest nature, rather than purely individual reasons particular to the employer's situation, such as cost reduction or improving competitiveness. In this respect, the ECJ had identified two broad categories of legitimate social policy objective: 'inter-generational fairness' and 'dignity'. Applying the ECJ jurisprudence to the instant case, Baroness Hale held that the staff retention and workforce planning aims were not, as S contended, simply individual aims of the business, but instead fell within the category of 'inter-generational fairness'. Furthermore, the aim of limiting the need to use performance management to expel partners clearly fell within the 'dignity' category of legitimate aim. As a result, all three aims had the requisite 'social policy/public interest' dimension and were thus legitimate.

On the question of proportionality, Baroness Hale stressed that this requires an employer or partnership to show that the means adopted to achieve the aim are both appropriate and necessary. Noting that the case was already being remitted to the tribunal as a result of the EAT's ruling on the performance management aim, Baroness Hale stated that she would not rule out the tribunal considering whether the choice of age 65 was a proportionate means of achieving the first two aims, as 'there is a difference between justifying *a* retirement age and justifying *this* retirement age'. Lord Hope added that it would be proper for the tribunal to take into account the fact that, when the clause was agreed and when S was retired under the clause, there existed a designated retirement age of 65 for employees. As a final matter, Baroness Hale held that where it is justified to have a general rule – such as a compulsory retirement age – the existence of that rule will usually justify the treatment which results from it. However, she stressed that while it will not be necessary to justify the application of a retirement age to a particular employee (for that would negate the purpose of having such a rule), it is necessary to justify the rule in the particular circumstances of the business. She concluded by warning that 'businesses will now have to give careful consideration to what, if any, mandatory retirement rules can be justified'.

The European Court of Justice has taken a relatively liberal stance when it **15.91** comes to justifying retirement ages. A number of commentators have been surprised at the willingness of the Court to accept that retirement ages are a proportionate response to the need to share employment between the generations. For example, Rosenbladt v Oellerking Gebäudereinigungsgesellschaft mbH 2011 IRLR 51, ECJ, concerned a German law that allows employment contracts to terminate automatically on the employee's 65th birthday, so long as the employee is entitled to a state pension and the automatic termination is provided for by collective agreement. The ECJ held that this was justified direct age discrimination under Article 6 of the Framework Directive. The national law making provision for termination at 65 was supported by the legitimate aims of sharing employment between generations and avoiding capability dismissals. Furthermore, the collective agreement implementing the policy offered workers foreseeable retirement, and employers flexibility in staff management. The availability to the employee of another source of income (e.g. a pension) and the fact that the law had been agreed between partners of equal standing also seemed to influence the court.

It must be noted, however, that the ECJ cases all concerned a Member State's justification for a national or regional law providing for a fixed retirement age. The liberal approach of the ECJ could, therefore, be viewed as in keeping with the margin of appreciation that a Member State has in implementing a Directive – in this case, the Framework Directive.

Retirement benefits

15.92

The question in Bloxham v Freshfields Bruckhaus Deringer ET Case No.2205086/06 was whether the transitional arrangements for the reform of a law firm's pension scheme amounted to a proportionate response to the need to tackle the problem of 'intergenerational unfairness' that beset the scheme. The employer amended the pension scheme so that those aged 50–55 could take early retirement, subject to consent and a reduction in pension entitlement. Transitional arrangements meant that partners retiring at 54 (which included B) would have to accept a 20 per cent reduction and those retiring at 53 a 25 per cent reduction.

349

The tribunal found direct discrimination. On the question of justification, it held that the employer's aim in reforming the pension scheme was to provide for a more sustainable pension arrangement and to reduce the effect of the intergenerational unfairness on younger partners. On the issue of proportionality, it found that the reforms were aimed at stopping the younger partners becoming increasingly disadvantaged; that removing the 20 per cent discount would have improved B's position at the expense of others; and that even after lengthy consultation with staff, a less discriminatory alternative was not proposed. Therefore, although the 20 per cent discount applied to B was discriminatory, it was objectively justified.

15.93 **Contractual redundancy schemes**

Enhanced payments made under contractual redundancy schemes that vary according to the employee's age must generally be objectively justified (unless the scheme closely mirrors the statutory redundancy payment scheme and falls under the age exemption in para 13 of Schedule 9 to the EqA – see Chapter 31, 'Specific exceptions' under 'Age exceptions – enhanced redundancy payments'). In MacCulloch v Imperial Chemical Industries plc 2008 ICR 1334, EAT, for example, the contractual enhanced redundancy scheme favoured older employees. M was 36 when she was made redundant by ICI after seven years' service. ICI's redundancy policy gave employees entitlement to a severance payment based on a combination of age and length of service. M's payment amounted to 55 per cent of gross annual salary. By contrast, an employee with ten years' service who had reached the age of 50 would receive 175 per cent of gross annual salary. M claimed direct age discrimination and the tribunal agreed. However, it accepted that encouraging and rewarding loyalty was a legitimate aim. Furthermore, it was legitimate to try to protect older employees by giving them a larger financial payment, as they were particularly vulnerable on losing their job compared to younger employees. The tribunal went on to find that the discrimination was objectively justified as a proportionate means of achieving a legitimate aim and dismissed M's claim.

15.94 The EAT held that the decision could not stand, as the tribunal had failed to undertake a proper analysis of the defence of justification. Remitting the claim for reconsideration, Mr Justice Elias, then President of the EAT, endorsed the employer's objective of rewarding loyalty as the reason for linking payments to length of service. He also approved the tribunal's findings that encouraging turnover and creating opportunities for junior staff are, in principle, capable of being legitimate aims that might be furthered by increasing payments for older workers and that it could be legitimate to pay more to older workers as they are particularly vulnerable in the job market.

On remission (ET Case No.2700083/07), the tribunal conducted the proportionality exercise and found that the scheme was justified. It particularly noted ICI's acknowledgement that the scheme was discriminatory on the ground of age and its attempts to try to change it. However, the workforce as a whole rejected the proposed changes because a number of people would be worse off under the new scheme. Abolishing the scheme would have led to poor industrial relations and undermine the commercial viability of the business. In these circumstances, the tribunal concluded that the discriminatory impact of the scheme was justified.

In Loxley v BAE Systems Land Systems (Munitions and Ordnance) Ltd 2008 **15.95** ICR 1348, EAT, BAE Ltd's redundancy scheme gave an entitlement to a redundancy payment based mainly on length of service. However, entitlement to the scheme was restricted to employees under 60 years of age, and those aged between 57 and 60 had their payments reduced according to tapering provisions. BAE Ltd explained that this was to prevent those close to retirement from receiving a windfall in the event that they were made redundant. L, who was 61 at the time he agreed to take redundancy and was therefore not entitled to a contractual redundancy payment, brought a claim of direct age discrimination. The tribunal found the redundancy scheme justified by the need to prevent employees close to retirement from receiving a windfall. The tribunal also thought that the fact that the scheme had been agreed in consultation with trade unions went some way to support the contention that it was justified.

On appeal, the EAT held that the tribunal's analysis was defective and it had erred in its approach to the question of justification. The case would be remitted for reconsideration by a fresh tribunal. Elias P, again presiding, went on to make some comments on the aims of the scheme at issue. He expressly rejected L's assertion that preventing employees from receiving a windfall cannot be a legitimate aim. Such an aim could be legitimate in relation both to the exclusion of over-60s and the tapering provisions adopted in the present case. Although excluding from a redundancy scheme those entitled to immediate receipt of a pension would not inevitably be justified, Elias P considered that an employee's entitlement to pension benefits would be a 'highly relevant factor' in determining what, if any, redundancy rights he or she ought to receive. Finally, he endorsed the tribunal's view that the fact that a scheme has been agreed with trade unions is potentially relevant. While 'plainly the imprimatur of the trade union does not render an otherwise unlawful scheme lawful... any tribunal will rightly attach some significance to the fact that the collective parties have agreed a scheme which they consider to be fair'. Elias P cautioned, however, against 'the risk that the parties will have been influenced, consciously or unconsciously, by traditional assumptions relating to age'.

A tribunal cannot, therefore, simply rely on the fact that a scheme has been **15.96** agreed with a trade union without more. In Pulham and ors v London Borough of Barking and Dagenham 2010 ICR 333, EAT, for example, the tribunal had relied on the fact that age discriminatory pay protection arrangements had

351

been agreed with the unions and had failed to conduct a proper balancing exercise. The issue of justification was remitted for reconsideration.

15.97 Age limits in safety-critical roles

Employers in safety-critical industries frequently operate age restrictions to ensure the health and safety of employees or the general public. In these circumstances, success or failure of the justification defence will often depend on the cogency of the evidence produced to demonstrate a link between age and physical or mental capability.

In Evans v Civil Aviation Authority ET Case No.201672/07 E, aged 60, had worked as a commercial helicopter pilot for 30 years. In the 1970s, the International Civil Aviation Organisation (ICAO) imposed an upper age limit of 60 on all commercial pilots as a safety measure, and the United Kingdom complied with the rule in January 1978. In November 2006, the ICAO amended the rule so that in multi-crew operations one pilot could be over the age of 60 provided he or she had not reached the age of 65 and the other pilot was under 60. This, however, was of little assistance to E as multi-pilot commercial transport operations for helicopters are extremely rare and the CAA had made no recommendation to the Department of Transport that the age limit for pilots in single crew operations be increased. As a consequence, E was prevented from flying helicopters commercially when he reached 60 and subsequently made a claim for direct discrimination in the employment tribunal.

15.98 As the CAA is a qualifications body it was subject to the provisions of the Age Regulations. It conceded that it had directly discriminated against E on the ground of age, but defended the claim on the basis that such treatment was a proportionate means of achieving the legitimate aim of safer public helicopter transport. It produced expert evidence demonstrating an increased risk of pilots over the age of 60 suffering from 'sudden cardiovascular incapacitation'. The tribunal agreed; the employer's policy was not out of step with the majority of other countries and international organisations and, on the evidence, the age limit for single pilot operations was a proportionate means of achieving the respondent's aim.

15.99 # Discrimination by association

As noted in the introduction to this chapter, the definition of direct discrimination in S.13 EqA makes no reference to the protected characteristic of any particular person – it simply states that 'a person (A) discriminates against another (B) if, because of a protected characteristic, A treats B less favourably'. In respect of some protected characteristics, this formulation provides greater protection than that afforded under the previous equality enactments. For the protected characteristics of age, disability, gender reassignment and sex, direct discrimination was previously defined in such a way as to require the *complainant* to possess the protected characteristic at issue, with the result that a claim would not generally succeed where the treatment was based on the protected characteristic of a third party (note, however, that in EBR Attridge LLP (formerly Attridge Law) and anor v Coleman 2010 ICR 242, EAT, the EAT interpreted the Disability Discrimination Act 1995 (DDA) so as to overcome this limitation – see below.) The effect of S.13, according to the Explanatory Notes, was to '[bring] the position in relation to those protected characteristics into line with that for race, sexual orientation and religion or belief in the previous legislation' – para 63.

Take, for example, the protected characteristic of age. Under the Age Regulations, direct age discrimination occurred where A treated B less favourably than others 'on grounds of B's age'. S.13, on the other hand, applies where A treats B less favourably 'because of [age]'. This removes the need to consider whether the complainant's age was the reason for the treatment complained of, thereby extending protection to 'discrimination by association'. So if, for example, A treats B less favourably because B has an elderly partner, A will have discriminated against B because of age, even though B's age is not the reason for the treatment. The EHRC Employment Code states that this form of discrimination can occur in various ways – for example, where the worker is parent, son or daughter, partner, carer or friend of someone with a protected characteristic – para 3.19. It adds that the association with the other person need not be a permanent one.

The Code goes on to suggest that discrimination by association could also occur **15.100** where an individual has campaigned to help someone with a particular protected characteristic or refused to act in a way that would disadvantage a person or people who have (or whom the employer believes to have) a protected characteristic. It gives the following example: 'An employer does not short-list an internal applicant for a job because the applicant – who is not disabled himself – has helped to set up an informal staff network for disabled workers. This could amount to less favourable treatment because of disability' – para 3.20.

The revised wording in S.13 takes account of the ECJ's ruling in Coleman v Attridge Law and anor 2008 ICR 1128, ECJ, that the Framework Directive protects those who, although not themselves disabled, nevertheless suffer direct discrimination or harassment owing to their association with a disabled person. In EBR Attridge LLP (formerly Attridge Law) and anor v Coleman 2010 ICR 242, EAT, the EAT held that the DDA, despite its apparent limitations, was in fact capable of being interpreted in line with the ECJ's decision. However, that decision did not affect the position in respect of age, gender reassignment or sex.

The Government's intention to include discrimination based on association **15.101** (and perception – see below) within the scope of S.13 is apparent from the wording of the provision itself and from the Explanatory Notes. During the consultation on the Equality Bill, certain bodies expressed concern at the

353

absence of any explicit provision prohibiting discrimination by association or perception. However, the Solicitor General resisted a Liberal Democrat amendment designed to meet that concern. In her view, the meaning of 'because of' was clear. She also pointed out that to include express protection in cases of discrimination by association or perception might imply that S.13 does not extend to other cases in which the claimant does not possess the relevant protected characteristic – for example, the situation where a white employee alleges that he or she has been dismissed for refusing to carry out the employer's instruction to discriminate against black customers. We discuss the wide category of potential complainants under the EqA under '"Because of" protected characteristic – scope of "because of"' above.

15.102 **Parents and carers.** It should be noted that, in 'The Equality Bill – Government response to the consultation', July 2008 (Cm 7454), the Government stated that it had not been persuaded of the need to create broad-based freestanding discrimination protection for carers, or, for that matter, parents acting in the capacity of parents. Instead, it considered the better approach was 'to continue with targeted provisions and specific measures'. The Government specifically saw the proposed extension of the protection against discrimination on the ground of 'association' as a specific measure in this regard. In its subsequent publication, 'A Fairer Future: The Equality Bill and other action to make equality a reality', July 2009, the Government Equalities Office intimated that the protection against discrimination by association would, for example, now mean that an employer could not refuse to promote a member of staff just because he or she cares for an older relative. It is certainly true that the revised definition of direct discrimination in S.13 supports the stance taken by the Equalities Office. In the context of caring for a disabled person, for instance, carers will enjoy protection from less favourable treatment they suffer at the hands of their employers on account of the disability of the person they are caring for – although not, it is important to note, because of the carer's caring responsibilities per se.

This point is aptly demonstrated by the case of Perrott v Department for Work and Pensions ET Case No.1600205/11. There, the employer operated a special leave policy for employees who wanted to take periods of care leave. However, this time was treated as unreckoned service and employees did not accrue annual leave in respect of it. P took two periods of special or unpaid leave under the policy – between 1 October 2008 and 3 April 2009 and 1 October 2009 and 5 April 2010 – to care for his disabled sister. He was dissatisfied that he did not accrue any leave while away from work, and complained of direct disability discrimination by association under the Disability Discrimination Act 1995. The tribunal dismissed his claim as being out of time. However, in the event that it was wrong on this point, it went on to consider the substantive merits of his claim.

354

In the tribunal's view, P's disability discrimination by association claim would **15.103** have failed in any event. The special leave policy benefited innumerable employees who wanted to take time off to care for someone, such as a child or elderly parents. The policy, by definition, would equally apply to those people in that they were granted special leave without that period being treated as reckoned service and without accruing annual leave. There was therefore no less favourable treatment in P's case because all employees who were granted special leave were treated identically. The same outcome would no doubt have been reached if the claim had been brought under S.13 EqA.

Exceptions **15.104**
A direct discrimination claim based on the claimant's association with a person having a protected characteristic is specifically excluded in the case of marital and civil partnership discrimination, and in respect of age discrimination in relation to the provision of childcare.

Marital or civil partnership discrimination. Section 13(4) EqA provides that, **15.105** as was previously the case under S.3 SDA, an individual may only claim direct discrimination in employment on the basis of marriage or civil partnership if the treatment is because the claimant him or herself is married or is a civil partner. Accordingly, the claimant's association with someone who has married or civil partnership status will not suffice.

Age discrimination. By way of a specific exception to the prohibition on age **15.106** discrimination by association, the EqA permits employers to restrict benefits relating to the provision of childcare to children of a particular age group – para 15, Sch 9. For further details, see Chapter 31, 'Specific exceptions', under 'Age exceptions – childcare benefits'.

Discrimination by perception **15.107**

The wide definition of discrimination in S.13 EqA also encompasses discrimination by perception: that is, discrimination because of a person's perceived characteristic. Under S.13, the perception that a person is disabled, for example, will be a potential ground of unlawful discrimination. The EHRC Employment Code gives two examples at para 3.21 of when this form of discrimination may arise. First, where an employer rejects a job application form from a white woman whom it wrongly thinks is black, because the applicant has an African-sounding name. Secondly, where an employer rejects a masculine-looking female job applicant who performs best at interview because, due to her appearance, it wrongly believes she is a transsexual. In this situation, the woman would have a claim for direct discrimination under S.13 because of perceived gender reassignment, even though she is not in fact transsexual.

Previously, the wording of the various anti-discrimination provisions was wide enough to prohibit discrimination by perception in the case of sexual orientation, race, and religion or belief, while Reg 3(3)(b) of the Age Regulations expressly covered discrimination by perception (but not by association). However, protection against discrimination by perception did not extend to the other protected characteristics. In Aitken v Commissioner of Police of the Metropolis EAT 0226/09 the EAT rejected the claimant's argument that, following the decision of the ECJ in Coleman v Attridge Law and anor 2008 ICR 1128, ECJ (see under 'Discrimination by association' above), the DDA should be interpreted so as to include discrimination on the ground of perceived disability. (When the case subsequently went to the Court of Appeal – Aitken v Commissioner of Police of the Metropolis 2012 ICR 78, CA – Lord Justice Mummery held that it was not appropriate for the Court to consider the discrimination by perception point because the tribunal had found as a matter of fact that the respondent did not have a mistaken perception of A's disability.)

15.108 The Government did not originally intend protection under the EqA against discrimination by perception to extend to cases where the protected characteristic was gender reassignment. In 'The Equality Bill – Government response to the Consultation', July 2008 (Cm 7454), it stated: '[O]ur intention is not to protect a wider group such as transvestite people or others who have no intention or commitment to live life permanently in the sex opposite to their birth sex. Extending protection to perceived gender reassignment would encompass that wider group' – para 9.10. However, the Government reviewed its stance in the light of the ECJ's ruling in Coleman v Attridge Law and anor (above) and announced that the prohibition on discrimination by perception would apply across all strands (except marriage and civil partnership – see 'Marriage and civil partnership exception' below).

It is not immediately clear how the prohibition on discrimination by perception fits with the complex statutory definition of disability (discussed in Chapter 6, 'Disability'). Must an employer wrongly suppose that all the elements of the definition (including the fact that the person perceived to be disabled has a substantial and long-term effect on the person's ability to carry out normal day-to-day activities) are satisfied in order for S.13 to apply? Given that most employers in this position will not have addressed their minds to the legal definition of disability, it would be surprising if this had been Parliament's intention. At the Commons Committee stage, however, the Government rejected a proposed amendment that would have gone some way towards clarifying the position.

15.109 ## Marriage and civil partnership exception
As with discrimination by association, discrimination by perception cannot be claimed in respect of the protected characteristic of marriage or civil partnership. S.13(4) stipulates that 'if the protected characteristic is marriage

and civil partnership, [S.13] applies to a contravention of Part 5 (work) only if the treatment is because it is [the claimant] who is married or a civil partner'. In other words, the claimant must be married or have civil partnership status in order to claim direct discrimination in employment on the basis of that protected characteristic: a perception that the complainant is married or a civil partner will not suffice for the purpose of bringing a claim. (Note, however, that in the case of civil partnership, the claimant may have grounds to bring a claim of sexual orientation discrimination by perception – see Chapter 13, 'Sexual orientation'.)

Combined discrimination

15.110

There are situations in which people are discriminated against because of a particular combination of protected characteristics – sometimes referred to as 'intersectional discrimination'. For example, a black woman may suffer prejudice or harassment that a black man or a white woman would not experience. The absence of a right to bring discrimination claims combining protected characteristics has been perceived as a problem for some time and was highlighted by the Court of Appeal in Bahl v Law Society and ors 2004 IRLR 799, CA. At present, a person alleging intersectional discrimination must bring separate single-strand claims in respect of each protected characteristic. Such claims can be difficult to prove and do not reflect the reality of the discrimination experienced.

The Government first considered introducing protection from multiple discrimination in its June 2007 consultation document ('A Framework for Fairness: Proposals for a Single Equality Bill for Great Britain'), and in April 2009 the Government Equalities Office published a discussion document, 'Equality Bill: Assessing the impact of a multiple discrimination provision', which sought views as to how such a provision would work in practice. The result is S.14 EqA, which allows a claim to be brought in relation to a combination of two protected characteristics – making 'combined discrimination' or 'dual discrimination' a more appropriate term than 'multiple discrimination'.

Section 14(1), which is headed 'Combined discrimination: dual characteristics', **15.111** provides that: 'A person (A) discriminates against another (B) if, because of a combination of two relevant protected characteristics, A treats B less favourably than A treats or would treat a person who does not share either of those characteristics.' The relevant protected characteristics for these purposes are age, disability, gender reassignment, race, religion or belief, sex and sexual orientation – S.14(2). The use of the phrase 'because of' means that discrimination by association and perception are covered (see 'Discrimination by association' and 'Discrimination by perception' above).

357

15.112   **Not yet in force.** The previous Labour Government intended to bring S.14 into force in April 2011 but the Coalition Government announced shortly before that date that it would not be implementing the section. Thus, at the time of writing, *S.14 is not in force* and there is no prospect of it coming into force in the near future. It is nevertheless useful to briefly set out the scope of that section and the procedure for bringing a complaint.

15.113   ## Excluded protected characteristics

Not all protected characteristics are covered by S.14 – marriage and civil partnership, and pregnancy and maternity, are excluded (by virtue of not being listed in S.14(2)). During consultation, the Government received no evidence of problems arising in practice from a combination of these characteristics and others. Another relevant consideration was that, as pregnancy and maternity claims do not involve a comparator (see the section 'Preliminary matters' above, under 'Protected characteristics covered by S.13 – pregnancy and maternity discrimination'), it would be difficult to combine them with a claim based on a protected characteristic which does entail such a requirement. However, where less favourable treatment occurs because of a combination of pregnancy or maternity and another characteristic, this may constitute combined discrimination because of sex and that other characteristic.

15.114   ## Combination of two protected characteristics only

The Government originally canvassed the idea of claims being brought on more than two combined grounds. In the Public Bill Committee in the House of Commons, however, the Solicitor General stated: 'We have evidence of people experiencing discrimination because of a combination of two protected characteristics, but there is insufficient evidence of cases involving more than two for us to feel that further regulation is warranted.' In a leaflet issued by the Government Equalities Office, 'Explaining the Equality Bill: Dual Discrimination', the Government referred to evidence compiled by the Citizens Advice Bureau suggesting that 90 per cent of cases of intersectional discrimination would be addressed by S.14 (that evidence was also cited at para 4.9 of the April 2009 discussion document). Another consideration was that to extend protection to combinations of three or more protected characteristics would make the law unduly complex and increase the burden on employers (see para 2.7, 'Equality Bill: Assessing the impact of a multiple discrimination provision').

15.115   ## Direct discrimination only

Section 14 only allows claims of direct combined discrimination to be brought; indirect discrimination, harassment and victimisation are not covered. In the Public Bill Committee in the House of Commons, the Solicitor General stated that there was insufficient evidence of a need to extend the combined discrimination provisions to indirect discrimination and harassment. With regard to indirect discrimination, she added: 'We think that including indirect

358

discrimination within the provision would mean businesses and employers having to consider the impacts of their policies and procedures on every possible combination of protected characteristic, which is not proportionate given the lack of evidence of need.'

However, the judgment in Ministry of Defence v DeBique 2010 IRLR 471, EAT – a case brought under the indirect discrimination provisions in the SDA and the RRA – suggests that a tribunal hearing an indirect discrimination claim that involves two or more protected characteristics is not necessarily limited to viewing each complaint in isolation, and may be entitled to take into account the fact that the claimant has suffered a combined disadvantage. In that particular case, the EAT held that the tribunal had not erred in considering the combined effect of two different provisions, criteria or practices (PCPs) that were alleged to be indirectly discriminatory and unjustifiable when taken together. The claimant (a female serving soldier in the UK army) alleged that the disadvantage about which she complained arose because she was a female soldier with a child and because she was a woman of Vincentian national origin for whom childcare assistance from a Vincentian live-in relative was not available because of immigration restrictions. The EAT upheld the tribunal's view that although, viewed in isolation, a PCP that she be available for active service on a 24/7 basis was justified, viewing this in isolation from the operation of the additional PCP concerning the immigration rules that prevented her (unlike most other male and female serving soldiers) from bringing a family member in to assist with childcare failed to reflect her particular disadvantage. On an analysis of the combined effect of the two PCPs, the tribunal had correctly concluded that the claimant was put to disadvantage by reason of her sex and race and that this could not be justified as a proportionate means of achieving a legitimate aim. If this decision is correct, it shows that there may be scope in an appropriate case to take into account the effect of a PCP in relation to more than one protected characteristic, even though S.14 (if it should ever come into force) does not apply to indirect discrimination claims.

Relationship with single-strand claims

15.116

For a claim under S.14 to succeed, it is not necessary that there be sufficient evidence to support a claim of direct discrimination under S.13 'because of *each of* the characteristics in the combination (taken separately)' – S.14(3) (our stress). This provision was originally phrased 'in relation to *either of* the characteristics in the combination', but it was amended at the Commons Report stage. Arguably, the revised wording could be taken to imply that there must be sufficient evidence to establish direct discrimination based on one or the other of the protected characteristics, though not necessarily both, in order for a claim under S.14 to succeed.

It is clear, however, that this was not the Government's intention. The Explanatory Notes indicate that the prohibition on combined discrimination

359

applies in circumstances 'where the single-strand approach may not succeed' – para 68. They give the example of a black woman who has been passed over for promotion to work on reception because her employer thinks black women do not perform well in customer service roles. Because the employer can point to equally qualified white female and black male employees in the same or a similar role, the woman may be unable to succeed in a direct race or sex discrimination claim under S.13 and may need to rely on S.14 to demonstrate that she has been subjected to less favourable treatment because of the combined characteristics of race and sex.

15.117   The EHRC Employment Code, which was laid before Parliament on 11 October 2010, does not deal with combined discrimination. This was because, at the time, S.14 was not expected to come into force before April 2011, and the Government was still considering if and how best to implement it. However, the draft version of the Code that was previously issued for consultation did set out detailed guidance in this area. It stated: 'To complain about combined discrimination, B does not need to show that each characteristic was individually an effective cause of the less favourable treatment. She need only show that the combination of characteristics was an effective cause of the treatment.' The consultative draft version of the Code went on to give various examples, including that of a manager at a child care centre who does not employ a gay man because she assumes that the safety of the children who attend the centre will be compromised. This treatment is based on the manager's prejudice and assumptions about gay men, rather than any preconceptions about gay women or straight men. The treatment will be an act of combined discrimination based on the combined characteristics of sexual orientation and sex.

It should be noted, however, that the single-strand approach may already offer adequate protection to the claimants in both of the above examples. According to existing case law, all the claimant has to do in order to succeed in a direct discrimination claim is show that the relevant characteristic was an *effective* cause of the alleged treatment. It need not be the only cause, or even the main cause – Nagarajan v London Regional Transport 1999 ICR 877, HL (discussed in the section, '"Because of" protected characteristic' above, under 'Determining the reason for the treatment – protected characteristic need not be only reason for treatment'). Thus, the gay man in the second example might argue that the manager would not have applied the same preconceptions to a gay woman or a straight man. On that basis, he might be able to establish both sex discrimination (based on a comparison with a gay woman) and discrimination because of sexual orientation (based on a comparison with a straight man). In these circumstances, it is difficult to see how a claim under S.14 would advance his case.

15.118   If S.14 does come into force at some time in the future, there is nothing to prevent a claimant from bringing separate single-strand claims on the same grounds alongside a claim of combined discrimination. Para 66 of the Explanatory Notes states: 'A claimant is not prevented from bringing direct discrimination claims because of individual protected characteristics and a dual discrimination claim simultaneously (or more than one dual discrimination claim).' The Government concluded that it would be 'neither compatible with EU law nor appropriate in policy terms' to include such a restriction (see para 4.11, 'Equality Bill: Assessing the impact of a multiple discrimination provision' (April 2009)). In practice, this could lead to multiple claims arising from one alleged incident. For example, a black woman subjected to less favourable treatment could bring a S.14 claim based on race and sex, as well as separate race and sex discrimination claims in the alternative.

Identifying a comparator   15.119

For the purposes of the S.14 comparison, there must be 'no material difference between the circumstances relating to each case' – S.23(1) EqA. If one of the protected characteristics in the combination is disability, the relevant circumstances include the abilities of the individuals to whom the comparison is applied – S.23(2)(b). If one of the protected characteristics is sexual orientation, the fact that one person is a civil partner while another is married is not a material difference between the circumstances relating to each case – S.23(3). Furthermore, it is irrelevant that the alleged discriminator has one or both of the protected characteristics in the combination – S.24(2).

One unanswered question concerning S.14 relates to the choice of actual or hypothetical comparator. In the example given above of the gay man applying to work at a childcare centre, it is strongly arguable that the appropriate comparator would be a person who does not have either of the relevant characteristics, i.e. a straight woman. This is the approach envisaged in para 91 of the Explanatory Notes, which states: 'The treatment of the claimant must be compared with that of an actual or a hypothetical person – the comparator – who does not share the same protected characteristic as the claimant (*or, in the case of dual discrimination, either of the protected characteristics in the combination*) but who is (or is assumed to be) in not materially different circumstances from the claimant' (our stress).

In the childcare example, however, the fact that a straight woman would have   15.120
been offered employment does not demonstrate conclusively that the claimant was discriminated against because of the *combination* of sex and sexual orientation: it could be that he was discriminated against solely on one of those grounds. Hence it is possible that, in order to shed light on the treatment that would have been afforded to a hypothetical comparator who shared neither of the claimant's relevant characteristics, two comparisons would have to be made – one with a gay woman, and one with a straight man. This was the approach suggested by the consultative draft version of the EHRC Employment Code, which stated: 'The way in which A treats persons who have one but not both

361

of the protected characteristics in question may enable an inference to be drawn as to how A would treat a hypothetical comparator who has neither protected characteristic.' As noted above, however, if the claimant can show that two such individuals would both have been recruited, it is arguable that he would succeed in single-strand claims of sex and sexual orientation discrimination – in which case, there would be no need to rely on S.14. This approach also sits uneasily with S.14(3), which appears to mean that a claim of combined discrimination can succeed even where there is insufficient evidence to support a single-strand claim (see under 'Relationship with single-strand claims' above).

In our view, the only way in which these conceptual difficulties can be avoided is if the employment tribunal sidesteps the issue of comparators, asking itself instead: what was the reason for the treatment afforded to the claimant? This was supported by the consultative draft version of the EHRC Employment Code, which stated: 'In considering whether a hypothetical comparator would have been treated more favourably, it may be simpler to concentrate on the reason for B's treatment. The facts may suggest that the reason for B's treatment is a prejudice or an assumption relating to the combination of characteristics. When it is clear that the reason for A's treatment of B is the combination of characteristics, it will follow that a hypothetical comparator without the characteristics would have been treated more favourably.' This 'reason why' approach is supported by some of the authorities – notably, Shamoon v Chief Constable of the Royal Ulster Constabulary 2003 ICR 337, HL – and discussed under 'Comparator – relevance of reason for treatment' above. In many cases, however, it must be acknowledged that the reason why the claimant was treated in a particular way is not immediately apparent, and that the comparator exercise is required precisely in order to answer that question.

15.121 **Employer's defence**
An employer has a defence to a combined discrimination claim if it can show, in reliance on another provision of the EqA or any other enactment, that the treatment in question 'is not direct discrimination [under S.13] because of either or both of the characteristics in the combination' – S.14(4). This provision is intended to cover the situation in which at least one of the protected characteristics is covered by an occupational requirement or other statutory exception (as to which, see Chapter 30, 'General exceptions', and Chapter 31, 'Specific exceptions') or, in the case of age discrimination, by the justification defence (see under 'Justifying direct age discrimination' above).

The draft version of the EHRC Employment Code that was put out to consultation gave the example of a nursing home that refuses to employ a black man to look after female patients. At first glance, this might appear to be combined discrimination because of race and sex. However, if the nursing home is able to show that being female is an occupational requirement, it would have a defence to a direct sex discrimination claim and S.14 will not apply.

Power to amend

A Minister of the Crown may make orders specifying further what a claimant does or does not need to show to prove combined discrimination, or further restricting the circumstances in which combined discrimination is prohibited by the EqA – S.14(6). According to a leaflet published by the Government Equalities Office, 'Explaining the Equality Bill – Dual Discrimination', this power has been included because 'combined discrimination is a new and untested concept; it is therefore prudent to provide flexibility to address any undesirable results and accommodate future changes'. Given the Government's decision to 'shelve' S.14 for the foreseeable future, it is unlikely that the power in S.14(6) will be used any time soon.

16 Indirect discrimination: proving disadvantage

Legislative history

Relevant protected characteristics

Provision, criterion or practice

Pool for comparison

'Particular disadvantage'

Indirect discrimination in context

Indirect discrimination is a concept that has been part of domestic discrimination **16.1** law since the sex and race discrimination legislation was first introduced in the 1970s. The subsequent equality enactments prohibiting discrimination on grounds of religion or belief, sexual orientation and age similarly provided for indirect discrimination claims. The definition of indirect discrimination has undergone substantial changes over the years and is now found in S.19 of the Equality Act 2010 (EqA), which came into force on 1 October 2010. S.19 EqA extends the scope of indirect discrimination to include disability and gender reassignment, which were not previously covered, and harmonises the various definitions of indirect discrimination found in the previous equality legislation (which had already been substantially brought into line with each other in the employment field following the wording of the relevant EU Directives).

Section 19(1) EqA defines indirect discrimination as occurring when a person (A) applies to another (B) a provision, criterion or practice ('PCP') that is discriminatory in relation to a relevant protected characteristic of B's. A PCP has this effect if the following four criteria are met:

- A applies, or would apply, the PCP to persons with whom B does not share the relevant protected characteristic

- the PCP puts, or would put, persons with whom B shares the characteristic at a particular disadvantage when compared with persons with whom B does not share the characteristic

- the PCP puts, or would put, B at that disadvantage, and

- A cannot show that the PCP is a proportionate means of achieving a legitimate aim – S.19(2).

365

16.2 This reflects the definition of indirect discrimination that previously applied in most employment cases. All four conditions have to be met before indirect discrimination can be established. The burden of proof lies with the claimant to establish the first, second and third of these elements as confirmed by the EAT in Dziedziak v Future Electronics Ltd EAT 0271/11. S.136 EqA, which applies to any proceedings brought under the Act, requires the claimant to show 'prima facie evidence' from which the tribunal could conclude, in the absence of any other explanation, that an employer has committed an act of discrimination. S.136 goes on to provide that once the claimant has shown a prima facie case, the tribunal is obliged to uphold the claim of discrimination unless the respondent can show that no discrimination occurred. Thus, if the tribunal is satisfied that the claimant has discharged the burden of establishing a prima facie case, it then falls to the employer to justify the PCP as a proportionate means of achieving a legitimate aim – see Chapter 17, 'Indirect discrimination: objective justification'. It should be noted that, as with direct discrimination, the intention of the discriminator is irrelevant. The discriminator does not even have to be aware that he is discriminating; it is sufficient that a PCP is applied that brings the other elements listed above into play.

16.3 This chapter begins by outlining the legislative history of indirect discrimination, with particular reference to the amendments made over the years to the original tests in the Sex Discrimination Act 1975 (SDA) and Race Relations Act 1976 (RRA). An understanding of this area is essential in order to make sense of the terminology and concepts used in some of the older authorities. We then outline the eight 'relevant protected characteristics' to which S.19 EqA applies before examining the main elements of the statutory definition of indirect discrimination. These are:

- the identification of a 'provision, criterion or practice' (PCP)

- the construction of a 'pool for comparison' comprising those individuals who are potentially affected by the PCP at issue, and

- the test of 'particular disadvantage', including the various methods of establishing that such disadvantage has occurred.

Having dealt with the general principles of indirect discrimination, we then highlight some of the main themes specific to each of the relevant protected characteristics, with illustrations drawn from case law and the Code of Practice on Employment issued by the Equality and Human Rights Commission ('the EHRC Employment Code').

16.4 Legislative history

The current definition of indirect discrimination is contained in S.19(1) EqA, which states: 'A person (A) discriminates against another (B) if A applies to B a

366

provision, criterion or practice which is discriminatory in relation to a relevant protected characteristic of B's.' S.19(2) goes on to provide: 'For the purposes of subsection (1), a provision, criterion or practice is discriminatory in relation to a relevant protected characteristic of B's if:

(a) A applies, or would apply, it to persons with whom B does not share the characteristic,

(b) it puts, or would put, persons with whom B shares the characteristic at a particular disadvantage when compared with persons with whom B does not share it,

(c) it puts, or would put, B at that disadvantage, and

(d) A cannot show it to be a proportionate means of achieving a legitimate aim.'

The 'relevant protected characteristics' for these purposes are age, disability, **16.5** gender reassignment, marriage and civil partnership, race, religion or belief, sex and sexual orientation (S.19(3)) – see under 'Relevant protected characteristics' below.

This chapter and Chapter 17 ('Indirect discrimination: objective justification') examine each element of the above definition in turn. However, it can be stated at the outset that this definition is almost identical in substance to that which applied under the equality enactments that S.19 EqA replaced, including S.1(2)(b) SDA and S.1(1A) RRA. Accordingly, most of the principles developed by case law in relation to those sections will apply equally to S.19 EqA. This chapter draws on the old cases for the principles that will guide indirect discrimination under the EqA; where there are differences, this is made clear.

Nevertheless, it is worth bearing in mind that the most recent definitions of **16.6** indirect discrimination in the SDA and RRA had only been in force since 2005 and 2003 respectively. The original definitions of indirect sex and race discrimination were significantly different and the relevant statutory provisions underwent a series of changes over the years. An understanding of the legislative history of indirect discrimination is therefore essential in order to appreciate the relevance of the older authorities to the new test.

Sex Discrimination Act 1975   16.7

There were no fewer than three definitions of indirect discrimination under the SDA. The first of these was in force from 1975 to 2001. This was contained in S.1(1)(b) SDA and provided: 'A person discriminates against a woman in any circumstances relevant for the purposes of any provision of this Act if... he applies to her a requirement or condition which he applies or would apply equally to a man but – (i) which is such that the proportion of women who can comply with it is considerably smaller than the proportion of men who can

367

comply with it, and (ii) which he cannot show to be justifiable irrespective of the sex of the person to whom it is applied, and (iii) which is to her detriment because she cannot comply with it.' The fact that an individual was physically capable of complying with a requirement or condition did not necessarily defeat a claim of indirect discrimination; in Price v Civil Service Commission and anor 1978 ICR 27, EAT, it was held that 'can comply' meant can comply *in practice*.

The definition then underwent two important sets of changes. The first of these came about when a new test was introduced under the Sex Discrimination (Indirect Discrimination and Burden of Proof) Regulations 2001 SI 2001/2660, which implemented the EU Burden of Proof Directive relating to sex discrimination (No.97/80) (now recast in the EU Equal Treatment Directive (No.2006/54)) and came into effect on 12 October 2001. The 2001 Regulations inserted a new S.1(2)(b) into the SDA, which provided that indirect discrimination occurs when:

- the employer applies to a woman a provision, criterion or practice (PCP) which he applies or would apply equally to a man

- the PCP is such that it would be to the detriment of a considerably larger proportion of women than of men

- the employer cannot show the PCP to be justifiable irrespective of the sex of the person to whom it is applied, and

- the PCP is to the woman's detriment.

16.8 It can be seen from this definition that the 2001 Regulations altered the previous definition in two ways. First, the phrase 'requirement or condition' was replaced by 'provision, criterion or practice'. This arguably made it easier to establish indirect sex discrimination because disputes about whether practices amounted to requirements or conditions were no longer necessary. Secondly, the terms 'can comply' and 'cannot comply' were removed and instead it became necessary that the PCP would be to the detriment of a 'considerably larger proportion of women than of men'.

A third amended definition came into force on 1 October 2005. It was effected by the Employment Equality (Sex Discrimination) Regulations 2005 SI 2005/2467 and implemented the EU Equal Treatment Amendment Directive (No.2002/73) (since replaced by the recast EU Equal Treatment Directive (No.2006/54)). This definition made two changes of note. First, whereas under the 2001 test the disparate impact of a PCP was measured in terms of 'detriment' to 'a considerably larger proportion of women than of men', this was replaced by a test of whether the PCP 'puts or would put women at a particular disadvantage when compared with men', and additionally whether it 'puts [the claimant] at that disadvantage'. The new wording recognised that it was not

368

always possible or necessary to use detailed statistical calculations to show disparate impact. As we shall see, however, despite this shift in emphasis, statistical calculations continue to be relevant in many cases as they provide one means of establishing particular disadvantage. Nor, it would seem, has the replacement of the word 'detriment' with 'disadvantage' made much difference to the way in which indirect sex discrimination claims are decided – see under '"Particular disadvantage"' below. The second change effected by the 2005 Regulations concerned the 'justification' element of the statutory test. The test of justification was altered to a formula derived from EU law; namely, that the PCP must be shown to be a 'proportionate means of achieving a legitimate aim' – see further Chapter 17, 'Indirect discrimination: objective justification'.

The current definition of indirect discrimination under S.19 EqA, which came **16.9** into force on 1 October 2010 and replaced the various definitions found in the previous equality enactments, is substantially similar to the 2005 definition of indirect sex discrimination. The main difference of substance is that S.1(2)(b)(ii) SDA required that the relevant PCP actually put the claimant at the disadvantage to which other women were subject. By contrast, it is now sufficient under S.19(2)(c) EqA that the PCP 'puts, *or would put*, [the claimant] at that disadvantage' (our stress). This reflects a 2008 amendment to the RRA (see below), making it clear that the EqA protects a person who is deterred by a discriminatory PCP from seeking employment for which he or she is otherwise qualified.

Immediately prior to the entry into force of the EqA, indirect discrimination on the ground of a person's marital or civil partnership status was dealt with in S.3(1)(b) and (2) SDA, which had been inserted into the SDA from 5 December 2005 by the Civil Partnership Act 2004. This provision was almost identical to the post-2005 definition of indirect sex discrimination contained in S.1(2) SDA (as to which, see above). The definition of indirect marital discrimination had been subject to two previous amendments in October 2001 and October 2005 along the same lines as the changes to the definition of indirect sex discrimination outlined above.

Race Relations Act 1976   16.10

The original test of indirect race discrimination in S.1(1)(b) RRA provided that indirect discrimination occurs when:

- A applies to B a requirement or condition which he applies or would apply equally to persons of a different racial group but

- the proportion of B's racial group who can comply with it is considerably smaller than the proportion of persons not of B's racial group who can comply with it, and

369

- A cannot show that the requirement or condition is justifiable irrespective of the colour, race, nationality or ethnic or national origins of the person to whom it is applied, and

- the requirement or condition is to B's detriment because he or she cannot comply with it.

16.11 This definition applied to all types of indirect race discrimination from the Act's commencement in 1977 until 2003, when a two-tier test came into effect (see further below). Thus, until 2003, 'indirect discrimination' under the RRA focused on whether a uniformly applied 'requirement or condition' adversely affected persons in the same *racial group* as the complainant – defined in S.3(1) by reference to colour, race, nationality, or ethnic or national origins. Tribunals were required to consider whether a considerably smaller proportion of the claimant's racial group could comply with the relevant requirement or condition. This test was very similar to the original test of indirect sex discrimination under the SDA (see above). In Mandla and anor v Dowell Lee and ors 1983 ICR 385, HL, the House of Lords held that a person 'can comply' with a requirement only if he or she can comply 'consistently with the customs and cultural conditions of the racial group'.

Amendments made to the RRA with effect from 19 July 2003 by the Race Relations Act 1976 (Amendment) Regulations 2003 SI 2003/1626 significantly changed and complicated the picture. The changes were prompted by mandatory provisions contained in the EU Race Equality Directive (No.2000/43), which provided for a revised definition of 'indirect discrimination'. In order to reflect this, an entirely new definition – phrased in terms of whether the application of a PCP puts or would put persons of the 'same race or ethnic or national origins' as the claimant at a particular disadvantage – was inserted into the RRA to cover the three racial grounds specifically covered by the Directive (i.e. race, ethnic origins and national origins). The new definition set out in S.1(1A) RRA provided that indirect discrimination occurs when:

- A applies to B a PCP which he applies or would apply equally to persons not of the same race or ethnic or national origins as B but

- the PCP puts or would put persons of B's race or ethnic or national origins at a particular disadvantage when compared with other persons, and

- the PCP puts B at that disadvantage, and

- A cannot show that the PCP is a proportionate means of achieving a legitimate aim.

16.12 Following a Reasoned Opinion from the European Commission to the effect that the United Kingdom had incorrectly implemented the Race Equality Directive, this new definition of indirect race discrimination was further amended with effect from 22 December 2008 by the Race Relations Act 1976

(Amendment) Regulations 2008 SI 2008/3008. Those Regulations extended the definition in S.1(1A) RRA to cover a PCP that puts *or would put* the claimant at that disadvantage. This was to ensure that a person who was deterred by a discriminatory PCP from seeking employment for which he or she was otherwise qualified (sometimes referred to as a 'deterred applicant') could claim indirect race discrimination.

Prior to the entry into force of the EqA, it was generally thought that the post-2003 definition of indirect discrimination (along with the various other provisions inserted into the RRA to implement the Race Equality Directive) did not apply to claims of discrimination on the ground of nationality, as distinct from race, or ethnic or national origins. The logic behind this was that the Directive did not extend to this form of discrimination, and that since the amendment to the RRA was made by way of regulations issued under the European Communities Act 1972, rather than by an Act of Parliament, the changes could do no more than was strictly necessary to implement the Directive. The upshot was that, when the amendments came into force on 19 July 2003, a clumsy two-tier system came into being comprising a set of enhanced rights (i.e. those introduced by the 2003 amending Regulations) applicable to claims based on race, or ethnic or national origins, and a set of more restrictive rights (i.e. those that pre-existed the amending Regulations) in respect of claims based on nationality. It was arguable that colour also fell outside the scope of the Directive, but domestic case law suggested that the Directive, and hence the new definition of indirect discrimination, did in fact apply in that context – see, for example, Abbey National plc and anor v Chagger 2009 ICR 624, EAT.

16.13 The EqA removed this anomaly by extending protection against the various forms of discrimination – including indirect discrimination – to all the components covered by the protected characteristic of 'race' (i.e. colour, nationality and ethnic or national origins – see S.9 EqA). The standard definition of indirect discrimination set out in S.19 EqA now applies to all race discrimination claims regardless of the racial ground or group at issue. Accordingly, indirect race discrimination occurs where A applies to B a PCP that applies (or would apply) to persons not of the same racial group as B; puts (or would put) persons of B's racial group at a particular disadvantage when compared to other persons; puts (or would put) B at that disadvantage; and cannot be justified as a proportionate means of achieving a legitimate aim. This is very similar to the post-2003 test that applied in respect of race and ethnic or national origins, and many cases decided under the RRA therefore remain relevant.

Other antecedent provisions
16.14

The other antecedent provisions on indirect discrimination – covering age, religion or belief, and sexual orientation – came into force more recently than

371

the original provisions in the SDA and RRA and closely followed the wording of the relevant EU Directive. As such, they did not differ significantly in scope from the definition of indirect discrimination now set out in S.19 EqA, and the previous body of case law in respect of these grounds of discrimination remains highly relevant.

Indirect discrimination on the ground of religion or belief was originally dealt with in Reg 3(1)(b) of the Employment Equality (Religion or Belief) Regulations 2003 SI 2003/1660, while indirect discrimination on the ground of sexual orientation was covered by Reg 3(1)(b) of the Employment Equality (Sexual Orientation) Regulations 2003 SI 2003/1661. Both these sets of Regulations came into force on 1 December 2003. Indirect age discrimination was previously dealt with in Reg 3(1)(b) of the Employment Equality (Age) Regulations 2006 SI 2006/1031, which came into force on 1 October 2006. All three sets of Regulations were designed to implement the relevant aspects of the EU Equal Treatment Framework Directive (No.2000/78), which sets out a framework for eliminating employment or occupational inequalities based on religion, belief, disability, age and sexual orientation.

16.15 The main substantive difference between these antecedent provisions and S.19 EqA is that the latter encompasses a PCP that *would put* the claimant at the relevant disadvantage, as well as one that actually has that effect. As noted above, this reflects a 2008 amendment to the RRA and makes it clear that protection against indirect discrimination extends to a claimant who is deterred by a discriminatory PCP from seeking employment for which he or she is otherwise qualified.

16.16 ## Relevant protected characteristics

In order for a provision, criterion or practice (PCP) to give rise to indirect discrimination under S.19 EqA, it must be discriminatory 'in relation to a relevant protected characteristic' of the claimant – S.19(1). The relevant protected characteristics for these purposes are:

- age
- disability
- gender reassignment
- marriage and civil partnership
- race
- religion or belief
- sex
- sexual orientation – S.19(3).

372

Section 25 EqA makes it clear that references in the Act to discrimination in **16.17** relation to any of the relevant protected characteristics include references to indirect discrimination within S.19.

It should be noted that *pregnancy and maternity* are omitted from the list of characteristics in S.19(3) (see further below). All the other protected characteristics dealt with in the EqA are covered by the provisions on indirect discrimination. Prior to the coming into force of the EqA, there was no prohibition on indirect discrimination in relation to disability or gender reassignment – see below. For a detailed commentary on these particular protected characteristics, reference should be made to Chapters 4–13.

Disability
16.18

The Government's decision to include disability among the protected characteristics in respect of which a claim of indirect discrimination under the EqA can be brought was somewhat controversial. This change was originally proposed in an attempt to plug the gap created by the House of Lords' decision in London Borough of Lewisham v Malcolm 2008 IRLR 700, HL, which had the effect of significantly narrowing the types of conduct caught by the definition of disability-related discrimination in the Disability Discrimination Act 1995 (DDA) – for detailed commentary, see Chapter 20, 'Discrimination arising from disability', under 'Previous protection under the DDA'. However, the Government subsequently decided to address the effects of Malcolm head-on by introducing a new form of disability discrimination, discrimination arising from disability, which is contained in S.15 EqA. For full details of the Malcolm case and the scope of S.15, see Chapter 20, 'Discrimination arising from disability'.

Some respondents to the Government's consultation exercise on the Equality Bill expressed the view that the complex nature of indirect discrimination is not suited to disability. In short, indirect discrimination is established where a policy that an employer applies puts those who share a protected characteristic at a particular disadvantage when compared with those who do not share it. S.6(3)(b) EqA clarifies that, in relation to disability, 'a reference to persons who share a protected characteristic is a reference to persons who have the *same* disability' (our stress). Accordingly, for indirect discrimination purposes, the 'particular disadvantage' must affect those who share the claimant's particular disability. This overlooks the fact that even people who have the same disability cannot easily be treated as a homogenous class, since the way in which the same disability manifests itself will vary from person to person, making it difficult for a disabled person to demonstrate a group disadvantage.

In any event, it is difficult to envisage a situation in which the application of an **16.19** employer's policy would be indirectly discriminatory, but would not also be caught by either the new definition of discrimination arising from disability (see

373

Chapter 20) or the duty to make reasonable adjustments (see Chapter 21, 'Failure to make reasonable adjustments'), which are substantially less complex than indirect discrimination, arguably easier to prove, and specifically tailored to the disability strand of discrimination. For these reasons, we envisage that few successful indirect disability discrimination claims will be brought.

For further discussion of the potential application of S.19 in the context of disability, see under 'Indirect discrimination in context – indirect disability discrimination' below.

16.20 Gender reassignment

Prior to the entry into force of the EqA, statutory protection against discrimination on the ground of gender reassignment was found in relevant amendments to the Sex Discrimination Act 1975 (SDA). These amendments came into force on 1 May 1999 and were prompted by the European Court of Justice's decision in P v S and anor 1996 ICR 795, ECJ, where it was held that discrimination on the basis of transsexualism comprised discrimination on the ground of sex and was therefore unlawful under the EU Equal Treatment Directive (No.76/207) (now consolidated into the recast Equal Treatment Directive (No.2006/54)). Under the SDA there was no express provision extending the definition of *indirect* discrimination to transsexuals as such, although it was widely accepted that the general definition of indirect *sex* discrimination conferred the necessary protection on this particular protected group. By contrast, the EqA now explicitly prohibits indirect discrimination on the ground of gender reassignment.

It is worth bearing in mind that some of the complaints that were previously framed as claims of direct discrimination on the ground of gender reassignment under the SDA might now, following the enactment of S.19 EqA, be pleaded instead (or in the alternative) as instances of indirect discrimination. For further discussion, see under 'Indirect discrimination in context – indirect gender reassignment discrimination' below.

16.21 Pregnancy and maternity

As noted above, there is no explicit protection in the EqA against indirect discrimination in pregnancy and maternity cases, and it is notable that specific protection against this form of indirect discrimination is not required by EU law. Accordingly, indirect pregnancy and maternity discrimination continues to be dealt with as indirect *sex* discrimination. Responding to a question at Committee stage of the Equality Bill as to why pregnancy and maternity are omitted from the list of relevant protected characteristics for indirect discrimination, the Solicitor General said: 'A woman who is indirectly discriminated against because she is pregnant, or is a new mother, would, by definition, be able to make a claim of indirect sex discrimination, since any provision or practice which disadvantages pregnant women or new mothers is disadvantageous to women. That is the current position and we are not aware of any difficulty, so we just go forward with the law as it is.'

For a discussion of the key issues in indirect sex discrimination claims, see under 'Indirect discrimination in context – indirect sex discrimination' below.

Provision, criterion or practice   16.22

The first stage in showing that indirect discrimination has occurred is for the claimant to demonstrate that a provision, criterion or practice (PCP) has been 'applied' to him or her – S.19(1) EqA. In Bhudi and ors v IMI Refiners Ltd 1994 ICR 307, EAT, the EAT rejected the contention that, in the light of certain decisions of the European Court of Justice, it was no longer necessary to show that a requirement or condition (now a PCP) had been applied.

An employee must identify the PCP capable of supporting his or her case. However, once it has been identified, it is no defence for the employer to be able, with equal cogency, to derive from the facts a different and unobjectionable PCP – Allonby v Accrington and Rossendale College and ors 2001 ICR 1189, CA (a case decided when the relevant statutory language was 'requirement or condition' but the principle of which still applies). In this regard, it should be borne in mind that the way in which a PCP is defined is crucial, since a failure to correctly identify a PCP could result in the defeat of what would otherwise be a good claim – see under 'Identifying the PCP with precision' below.

First, we consider what kind of matters are capable in principle of constituting **16.23** a PCP. We then discuss the need to identify the relevant PCP with precision; the distinction between 'direct' and 'indirect' discrimination; the importance of identifying the material time at which the PCP is applied; and the application of PCPs to hypothetical comparators. It should be noted that claimants may on occasion seek to challenge the combined effect of two or more PCPs; this is discussed in the section '"Particular disadvantage"' under 'Defining "disadvantage" – combined disadvantage' below.

What constitutes a PCP?   16.24
As noted under 'Legislative history' above, the statutory test for indirect discrimination underwent a number of changes before S.19 EqA came into force. In particular, the words 'requirement or condition' that previously appeared in both the Sex Discrimination Act 1975 (SDA) and the Race Relations Act 1976 (RRA) were replaced in 2001 and 2003 respectively by 'provision, criterion or practice' (PCP). The words 'provision, criterion or practice' are not defined by the EqA. On the face of it, they appear wider than the old test in that they cover discriminatory 'practices' as well as strict requirements or conditions. However, the Government, when introducing the change in wording to the SDA, took the view that the change would make very little difference – what

375

passed for a requirement or condition under the original test would amount to a PCP, although the change might have an impact in 'marginal cases'.

This (correct) reasoning was based on the fact that the words 'requirement or condition' were interpreted very widely by the courts, which held that there was no significant difference between them and took a broad view as to what they meant. For instance, in Clarke and anor v Eley (IMI) Kynoch Ltd 1983 ICR 165, EAT, the EAT ruled that the phrase 'requirement or condition' should be construed as widely as possible to help eliminate more subtle, covert discriminatory practices. This view was supported in Briggs v North Eastern Education and Library Board 1990 IRLR 181, NICA, where the Northern Ireland Court of Appeal confirmed that the words 'requirement or condition' were capable of including any obligation of service. It followed that any policy, rule, practice, criterion, prerequisite, qualification or provision applied by an employer was capable of constituting a requirement or condition.

16.25 In Hampson v Department of Education and Science 1988 ICR 278, EAT, the EAT also accepted that any test or yardstick applied by an employer was capable of being a requirement or condition. That conclusion was not challenged on subsequent appeal to the Court of Appeal and the House of Lords. What is more, the requirement or condition could be framed in a positive or a negative way. For example, requiring a person to work full time was the equivalent of not permitting him or her to work part time. The phrase 'requirement or condition' did not necessarily imply positive action: it also embraced omissions, denials, refusals, disqualifications and other negative decisions.

The EHRC Employment Code confirms that the term 'provision, criterion or practice' is capable of covering a wide range of conduct, noting: 'The phrase… is not defined by the Act but it should be construed widely so as to include, for example, any formal or informal policies, rules, practices, arrangements, criteria, conditions, prerequisites, qualifications or provisions' – para 4.5. Thus, it is not only written and clearly applied rules and regulations that are potentially caught by S.19 EqA but also a broad range of more informal matters.

16.26 **Sources of PCPs.** Common sources of PCPs include job descriptions, contracts of employment, staff handbooks, letters, notices and memos, collective agreements, redundancy and retirement policies, and union rules and procedures. Although PCPs are often expressly imposed, they can also be deeply embedded in workplace practices, grading structures and employment policies. There is no necessity for a PCP to be explicitly stated: it can be challenged even though it is not of a formal nature or expressed in writing – Cast v Croydon College 1998 ICR 500, CA. In Thorndyke v Bell Fruit (North Central) Ltd 1979 IRLR 1, ET, for example, a requirement not to have young children was sufficient to establish indirect sex discrimination even though the employer had not articulated it as such to female candidates but had revealed that it was in his mind by making a note on the successful candidate's application form that she was unable to have children. And in Watches of Switzerland Ltd v Savell 1983 IRLR 141, EAT, a 'vague, subjective, unadvertised' promotion procedure was held to amount to a requirement or condition (now a PCP).

No need for absolute bar. A PCP need not impose an absolute bar on the **16.27** affected employee in order to be caught by S.19 EqA. In its guidance on the Sex Discrimination (Indirect Discrimination and Burden of Proof) Regulations 2001 SI 2001/2660, which replaced the phrase 'requirement or condition' in the SDA with 'provision, criterion or practice', the Government made it clear that the change in wording was intended to remedy the mischief created by Perera v Civil Service Commission and anor (No.2) 1983 ICR 428, CA, in which the Court of Appeal held that a 'requirement or condition' was something that must be complied with in the sense that failure to meet it would be an absolute bar to whatever the claimant was seeking. In Perera an interviewing board, in declining to offer the claimant a post, took account of factors such as UK experience, command of the English language and age. Although these factors were capable of being indirectly discriminatory on the ground of race, the Court took the view that none amounted to a 'requirement' or 'condition' since a poor assessment under one or more of the heads would not be an absolute bar to employing an otherwise highly suitable employee.

The effect of Perera was that mere preferences were not caught by the discrimination legislation. Tribunals in both sex and race cases were required to dismiss complaints where, for example, a qualification for a job or a promotion was stated to be 'preferable' or 'desirable', despite the fact that it might be just as disadvantageous to members of the affected group as it would be if it were an absolute requirement. So, arguably, an employer could apply a criterion which was discriminatory but avoid a claim of indirect discrimination by showing that the criterion was not absolute and that someone who did not satisfy it would still be selected in exceptional circumstances.

Although the rigour of the Perera rule was to some extent mitigated by **16.28** subsequent case law, the change of wording to 'PCP' removed any doubt as to which approach to take. As the Government stated in its guidance on the change in relation to the SDA, a claimant 'still has to prove, for example, that an employer is applying a specific practice to their disadvantage but she will no longer have to prove that there was a rigid rule in place which was to her disadvantage'. The adoption of the new wording in the more recent equality enactments, and its re-enactment in the EqA, means that the less stringent test now applies to all of the discrimination strands to which the definition of indirect discrimination in S.19 applies.

One-off or discretionary decisions. Case law has established that a PCP can **16.29** arise from a one-off or discretionary decision. This is confirmed in para 4.5 of the EHRC Employment Code. For example, in British Airways plc v Starmer 2005 IRLR 862, EAT, the employer refused to allow a female pilot to work

377

50 per cent of her full-time hours following her return from maternity leave. It did, however, offer to reduce her hours to 75 per cent of full time. The employer argued that this decision could not amount to a PCP because it was a one-off discretionary management decision. The EAT held that although the decision might not amount to a criterion or a practice, the tribunal had been entitled to find that it was a provision. This conclusion was not undermined by the fact that, as a one-off discretionary decision, the same provision was not applied to anyone else. The relevant statutory provision – S.1(2)(b) SDA – referred to a PCP that the employer applied *or would apply* equally to members of the opposite sex. S.19(2)(a) EqA adopts the same language, requiring that the employer 'applies, *or would apply*' the PCP to persons who do not share the relevant protected characteristic (our emphasis). Thus, the same result would be achieved under the 2010 Act.

16.30 **Changes of policy.** The EAT's decision in ABN Amro Management Services Ltd and anor v Hogben EAT 0266/09 suggests that a change of policy is not, of itself, capable of constituting a PCP. H was made redundant in August 2008 when two business units were merged following a takeover. The employer took a 'tiered' approach to the integration of the two units, with the more senior employees being considered for redundancy first, in late 2007 and early 2008. At that time, the company's practice was to award redundant employees a discretionary bonus pro-rated to the number of months they had served at their termination date. Before the restructuring was complete, the employer changed its policy so that, from April 2008, redundant employees had to show 'exceptional circumstances' in order to receive a bonus. H was among the group of less senior employees considered for redundancy after April 2008, with the result that the new policy applied to him and he did not receive a bonus when he was made redundant. He argued that the change of policy amounted to indirect age discrimination under Reg 3(1)(b) of the Employment Equality (Age) Regulations 2006 SI 2006/1031 (which has since been substantially re-enacted in S.19 EqA).

H's case before the EAT was that the criterion for the payment of a bonus varied depending on whether the individual's redundancy terms were formulated before or after April 2008. The employees who benefited from the more generous pre-April 2008 policy were more senior, and typically older, than the later group. However, the EAT rejected the claim on the basis that it was 'artificial and unnatural' to describe the change from one substantive PCP to another as itself constituting a policy or criterion. What was 'applied' to the claimant in such a case was not the change itself but the new substantive policy brought about by the change. Unless that policy was itself discriminatory, Reg 3(1)(b) was not engaged. The EAT went on to consider whether the different age profile of the two groups was capable of raising a presumption of indirect age discrimination, but concluded that it was not. The state of affairs of which H complained was demonstrably the result of the intersection of two practices

– the tiered approach to redundancy selection and the introduction of the new policy in April 2008 – neither of which was alleged to be discriminatory.

Although this was sufficient to dispose of the appeal, the EAT noted that **16.31** another reason for rejecting the claim was that there was no moment at which some employees were treated one way and some another. Both before and after April 2008, everyone was treated the same, and the difference in treatment complained of was only established by comparing the situation that existed prior to April 2008 with that which existed after that date. (The importance of timing is discussed under 'Identifying the time a PCP is applied' below.) The EAT added that the fact that different policies applied at different times meant that the material circumstances of the two groups were not the same and no valid comparison could be drawn (see under 'Pool for comparison – "no material difference" in circumstances' below). It seemed likely to the EAT, in any event, that the employer would have been able to justify the change in policy in light of market conditions (see Chapter 17, 'Indirect discrimination: objective justification' for full details of the defence).

The EAT in Hogben took the view that the measure complained of was the employer's change in policy, which it concluded was not capable of amounting to a PCP. However, it may be significant that the claimant did not identify the alleged PCP in his pleadings, simply stating that the change in policy gave rise to indirect discrimination. A better way of putting it might have been that there was a PCP whereby, in order to receive a bonus without proof of exceptional circumstances, an employee affected by the restructuring had to be given notice of redundancy before April 2008. Arguably, such a PCP applied to all redundant employees but put younger staff (who tended to be less senior, and were therefore considered for redundancy in the second round) at a particular disadvantage, with the result that the employer would have to justify it as a proportionate means of achieving a legitimate aim. It is unclear whether the formulation of the alleged PCP in these terms would ultimately have persuaded the EAT to reach a different conclusion; the employer might still have argued that the alleged PCP was being applied to the advantaged and disadvantaged groups at different points in time. However, this underlines the need for claimants in indirect discrimination cases to give careful thought to the way in which their claim is framed.

Identifying the PCP with precision   16.32

It is crucial that the claimant identifies the PCP with precision, since otherwise his or her claim will fall at the first hurdle. Francis and ors v British Airways Engineering Overhaul Ltd 1982 IRLR 10, EAT – a case on the old formula of 'requirement or condition' – illustrates the importance of identifying with precision the nature of the PCP that is alleged to have been applied. In that case the EAT rejected a claim of indirect sex discrimination on the basis that the claimants' specific formulation of the discriminatory requirement did not

379

amount to a requirement or condition for the purposes of the indirect discrimination provision formerly set out in the SDA. However, the EAT acknowledged that a different version of the requirement or condition would have been sufficient to bring the case within the ambit of the indirect discrimination provisions.

In Francis F and 13 other women were employed as aircraft corporation workers (ACWs). As ACWs, they were placed on Schedule VI of the employer's grading structure. Unlike Schedules I to V, which were each divided into two sub-grades, Schedule VI consisted of only one grade, which meant that there was no opportunity for internal promotion. No women were employed in jobs graded under Schedules I to V, whereas employees in Schedule VI jobs were almost all women. This led F and her colleagues to contend that they had been indirectly discriminated against on the ground of sex by being denied opportunities for promotion. They argued that the requirement or condition being applied to them was 'the implicit requirement that [they] move to other grades of employment in order to seek promotion'. An employment tribunal held that no such requirement or condition had actually been applied to Schedule VI employees. On appeal, the EAT upheld that finding. The lack of any opportunity for promotion within Schedule VI was the consequence of the structure of the job of an ACW: it was a job that did not provide opportunities for promotion. Therefore, it could not be said that a requirement or condition had been applied that had the effect of restricting access to promotion. However, Mr Justice Browne-Wilkinson suggested the following alternative formulation: '[L]ooking at the employees in Schedules I to VI as one class, in order to be eligible for promotion... an employee must be employed under Schedules I to V.' That formulation would have increased the appropriate pool for comparison and necessitated a consideration of whether a requirement or condition had been applied that effectively required the complainant to be employed in one of the male-dominated jobs in order to be eligible for promotion.

16.33 In general terms, identifying the exact PCP that has been applied is important because of its implications for the other elements of the test for proving indirect discrimination. In particular, the extent of the disproportionate impact (if any) may have to be determined in relation to the proportions of people in the claimant's group and in the comparator group who are advantaged or disadvantaged by the particular PCP that has been applied. Also, the specific nature of the PCP will be crucial when it comes to testing the validity of the employer's arguments on justification.

In most cases the nature of the PCP applied is obvious. For instance, a refusal to allow an employee to work part time amounts to the same thing as a requirement to work full time, so the appropriate formulation in this context is quite straightforward. Similarly, PCPs based on physical attributes, hours of work, etc, can usually be formulated without much difficulty. However, in

380

some cases the formulation will present problems. This is especially so if, instead of arising out of a specific express decision of the employer, the cause of the discrimination is embedded within a workplace custom or practice. The more covert and indirect the nature of the discrimination in question, and the more general its application across different constituent parts of the workforce, the more taxing the task of defining the PCP involved is likely to be.

Distinction between 'direct' and 'indirect' discrimination   16.34

It is important for a claimant to identify whether the claim is based on direct or indirect discrimination. One of the reasons for this is that where direct discrimination is made out, the respondent will not be able to escape liability by justifying it (except in the case of direct age discrimination – see Chapter 15, 'Direct discrimination', under 'Justifying direct age discrimination'), whereas in a case of indirect discrimination that possibility exists.

In R (on the application of E) v Governing Body of JFS and the Admissions Appeal Panel of JFS and ors 2010 IRLR 136, SC, Baroness Hale took the opportunity to explore the difference between direct and indirect discrimination. In that case, the Supreme Court held by a majority that a Jewish Orthodox school directly discriminated against a pupil on the ground of his ethnic origins when it refused him a place because his mother was not recognised as Jewish by the Office of the Chief Rabbi. However, the claimant had also advanced a claim of indirect discrimination, arguing that the school's admissions policy placed pupils who did not satisfy the test of matrilineal descent at a particular disadvantage. In the course of her judgment, Baroness Hale commented as follows: 'The rule against direct discrimination aims to achieve formal equality of treatment: there must be no less favourable treatment between otherwise similarly situated people on grounds of colour, race, nationality or ethnic or national origins. Indirect discrimination looks beyond formal equality towards a more substantive equality of results: criteria which appear neutral on their face may have a disproportionately adverse impact upon people of a particular colour, race, nationality or ethnic or national origins. Direct and indirect discrimination are mutually exclusive. You cannot have both at once... The main difference between them is that direct discrimination cannot be justified. Indirect discrimination can be justified if it is a proportionate means of achieving a legitimate aim.' These comments were approved in the same case by Lord Walker. If direct and indirect discrimination are indeed mutually exclusive, as Baroness Hale suggests, this has important implications. It means that, while claimants may plead direct and indirect discrimination in the alternative, it is not open to an employment tribunal to find that the same factual matrix gives rise to both types of discrimination simultaneously.

In some cases where an employer applies a PCP, the reality is that he is treating   16.35
the claimant's group and the comparator group differently (rather than in a neutral way). Thus, where an employer applies a rule or implements a policy

with which the claimant's group as a whole can never comply, such treatment comprises direct rather than indirect discrimination. A PCP that has the effect of precluding compliance by all members of one sex, for example, can hardly be said to apply equally to both sexes, which is one of the defining characteristics of indirect discrimination.

The difference between 'direct' and 'indirect' discrimination was brought into sharp focus in James v Eastleigh Borough Council 1990 ICR 554, HL – a case brought under S.29 SDA, which prohibited discrimination in the provision of goods, facilities or services (see now S.29 EqA). In that case, free admission to a municipal swimming pool was given to all persons of state pensionable age. At that time women were eligible for a state pension at 60 and men at 65, and the claimant (a man aged 61) found himself denied the concession whereas his wife (also aged 61) was granted free admission. By a majority, the House of Lords ruled that the man had been discriminated against on the ground of sex since, but for the fact that he was a man, he would have been entitled to free admission to the swimming pool at the age of 61. The application of 'state pensionable age' as the criterion for granting the concession meant that no men in the general population between the ages of 60 and 65 qualified, whereas all women in the population between those ages did so. Their Lordships reasoned that where an alleged discriminator applies a gender-based criterion such as the attainment of state pensionable age, the issue for consideration in a sex discrimination claim will be whether direct as opposed to indirect discrimination has occurred. This followed from the fact that a 'requirement or condition' (now a PCP) had to be capable of being applied equally to persons of either sex. A gender-based criterion cannot be applied in this way precisely because it is itself discriminatory between the sexes. Furthermore, their Lordships held that it was difficult to see how indirect sex discrimination could arise in the case of a gender-based criterion since the conditions necessary for the application of the relevant provision in the SDA presupposed that the requirement or condition applied was gender-neutral but that it had an adverse impact on one sex compared to the other. This same reasoning still holds good for the indirect discrimination provision in S.19 EqA.

16.36 A good way of illustrating the two different forms of discrimination is to take an example. If an employer were to apply a requirement that all candidates for a job must have attended a girls-only school as part of their education, then that requirement would be directly discriminatory against men, since only women would be able to comply with it. The requirement would be gender-tainted. However, if the obverse requirement was applied – i.e. that only candidates who have never attended a girls-only school would be considered – that would be indirectly discriminatory against women, since all men and some women would be able to comply with the requirement, leaving many but not all women unable to comply with it.

It follows from all that has been said above that the fact that a PCP is applied equally to everyone does not mean that an indirect discrimination claim will fail. This may seem an obvious point, but the issue arose in McClintock v Department of Constitutional Affairs 2008 IRLR 29, EAT – a case brought under the indirect discrimination provision in the Employment Equality (Religion or Belief) Regulations 2003 SI 2003/1660, which was in all material respects identical to S.19 EqA. There, the EAT held (correctly) that the very concept of indirect discrimination is premised on the assumption that a PCP applies to all but adversely affects a particular group. It followed that the tribunal had erred in rejecting the claim on the basis that the relevant PCP applied to everyone.

Identifying the time a PCP is applied   16.37

Section 19 EqA requires the claimant to show that the alleged discriminator applies a PCP to him or her which he applies, or would apply, equally to persons with whom the claimant does not share the relevant protected characteristic (the 'comparator group') – S.19(2)(a). It is obvious from the wording of S.19 that it is crucial for the claimant to show that a PCP was actually applied to him or her. Less obvious but equally important is the need for the claimant to identify the time (the 'material time') when the PCP was applied, because the claimant has to show that its application caused him or her to suffer a particular disadvantage – S.19(2)(c). Pinpointing the material time is also relevant when considering the situation of other people who share the relevant protected characteristic (including hypothetical people) who will also need to be shown to have been put at a disadvantage by the PCP at the same time (the 'protected group') – S.19(2)(b). As will be seen under 'Why is timing so important?' below, it does not follow that an indirectly discriminatory PCP puts a claimant and/or the protected group at a disadvantage all of the time, given that people's circumstances can change.

The cases on the original test of indirect discrimination provide guidance on how to identify the material time a PCP is applied under the new test. In Commission for Racial Equality v Dutton 1989 IRLR 8, CA (a race discrimination case on the provision of goods, facilities and services), the Court of Appeal ruled that the point in time at which ability to comply with a requirement or condition must be judged is the date on which it has to be fulfilled or complied with by the claimant. In reaching this conclusion, the Court of Appeal approved the reasoning in Clarke and anor v Eley (IMI) Kynoch Ltd 1983 ICR 165, EAT, in the context of a complaint by a part-time employee that a redundancy procedure making part-timers more vulnerable to selection than full-timers was indirectly discriminatory. In that case the EAT held that, for the purposes of indirect sex discrimination, the relevant point in time is the date on which the claimant alleges that she has suffered a detriment (a 'particular disadvantage' under the new test), which in that case was the date

383

on which the employee was dismissed for redundancy. It was irrelevant that the claimant could have avoided the detriment at some earlier date by transferring to full-time work.

16.38 **Anticipatory discrimination.** The Clarke case (above) is an example of a requirement or condition (now a PCP) being invoked against the claimant. However, a discriminatory term in a contract can be challenged even before it is invoked and will be unenforceable by virtue of S.142(1) EqA if it purports to allow something that would be unlawful under the Act. In such a case the county court (or, in Scotland, a sheriff court) has the power to remove or modify the contractual term – S.143(1). In this regard, it should be borne in mind that contractual terms can be express or implied and located in a variety of places, including company policies and collective agreements that form part of the contract of employment.

The possibility of challenging anticipatory indirect discrimination by bringing an action in the county court – as opposed to an employment tribunal – was established in Meade-Hill and anor v British Council 1995 ICR 847, CA, a case dealing with the original wording of indirect sex discrimination. There, the claimant's terms and conditions were altered to include a wide-ranging mobility clause requiring that all employees on her grade and above 'shall serve in such posts in the United Kingdom... as the Council may in its discretion require'. Fearful that the mobility clause might be invoked at some point in the future, the claimant brought county court proceedings seeking a declaration pursuant to S.77(2) SDA (the then equivalent of S.142(1) EqA) that the mobility clause was unenforceable on the ground that it gave rise to unlawful indirect sex discrimination. She contended that, with regard to the pool of employees who were on the relevant grades (i.e. those to whom the clause applied), a greater proportion of women than men were secondary wage earners (i.e. they earned less than their spouses or partners) and fewer women could therefore comply with a direction to relocate. The county court judge dismissed the application on the ground that it was impossible to say whether the mobility clause was discriminatory in the absence of specific circumstances in which the employer actually sought to invoke it. Whether or not any particular woman could comply with a direction to relocate would depend upon the actual location to which the business was being moved.

16.39 The Court of Appeal by a majority overturned that decision. It identified the relevant issue as being whether the employee was entitled to commence proceedings in respect of a contractual mobility clause alleged to be indirectly discriminatory in circumstances where that clause was not actually being invoked by her employer. This depended upon the true construction of the original test of indirect sex discrimination in the SDA, and in particular on the meaning of the word 'applies' in the phrase 'applies to her a requirement or condition'. The claimant asserted that the particular requirement in her case was that she work in whatever location in the United Kingdom her employer might direct pursuant to the mobility clause. In the Court of Appeal's view, the inclusion of a contractual term that imposes an obligation on a party to the contract amounts to an application of a requirement or condition against that party. On this basis, the mobility clause was 'applied' at the time the contract was made, and the employee did not have to wait until it was invoked in order to challenge it.

In reaching this conclusion, one of the judges, Lord Justice Waite, held that the same broad approach to the issue of timing should be applied to the then in force 'detriment' (now 'disadvantage') requirement that forms part of the definition of indirect discrimination. In his view, 'it would seem to me to be quite wrong (and inconsistent with the scheme and purpose of the Act) to attribute to Parliament any intention that the detriment requirement should be interpreted restrictively, so as to apply only in cases where an applicant can show that in the particular circumstances obtaining at the date of the contract – or at any subsequent date – she is unable to comply with the requirement in question'. In his opinion, it was sufficient for the claimant to show for the purposes of bringing county court proceedings that the clause had the potential to operate as a requirement or condition with which she could not comply. However, Lord Justice Millett expressed the view, obiter, that at this stage the degree of justification which the employer would have to prove would not be as high as that required when he actually sought to invoke the clause. All he would have to do would be to justify the need to be in a position, at any point in the future, to invoke such a clause should the circumstances so require. For more detail on the employer's defence of justification, see Chapter 17, 'Indirect discrimination: objective justification'.

A strict reading of the previous tests of indirect discrimination (see under **16.40** 'Legislative history' above) did not lend obvious support to the notion that claims could be based on the anticipatory impact of a PCP (previously a requirement or condition). Those tests all specified that the employer 'applied' a PCP (or a requirement or condition) to the claimant, and prior to the entry into force of the EqA the claimant actually had to suffer a disadvantage (previously a detriment) in all cases except indirect race discrimination. Note, however, that S.19 now extends to a PCP that *would put* the claimant at a disadvantage. This may make it easier to challenge anticipatory discrimination.

The Court in Meade-Hill, however, was prepared to apply a very wide interpretation to the old definition of indirect discrimination. Meade-Hill has not been overturned and its reasoning could therefore be applicable to the current test where a contractual term is being challenged in a county or sheriff court as being indirectly discriminatory. It should be noted, however, that the ruling in Meade-Hill is arguably limited to claims brought where the county/ sheriff court has jurisdiction; it is unclear whether it applies to claims in

385

employment tribunals. For further discussion of this potential qualification to the principle in Meade-Hill, see the section '"Particular disadvantage"' under 'Defining "disadvantage" – anticipatory disadvantage' below.

16.41 **Why is timing so important?** The issue of when the PCP is applied is critical for several reasons. First, it affects the question of whether the protected group has suffered a 'particular disadvantage' by reference to the comparator group – S.19(2)(b). Fluctuating demographic factors (such as the relative proportions of male and female part-timers in the workforce in an indirect sex discrimination claim) may make the question of timing crucial.

Secondly, as noted above, in order to rely on S.19 EqA the claimant must show that the application of the PCP puts, or would put, him or her at that disadvantage – S.19(2)(c). Once again, the relevant time at which this is judged can be crucial, since the claimant's personal circumstances may change (or become capable of change) in such a way as to affect the issue of whether individual disadvantage has been sustained. For more detail on disadvantage, see under '"Particular disadvantage"' below.

16.42 Thirdly, there is the question of time limits for commencing proceedings in an employment tribunal. The limitation period in discrimination claims runs from 'the date of the act to which the complaint relates' – S.123(1) EqA. In the context of indirect discrimination, ascertaining that date can be difficult. In most cases the PCP will be applied by the employer at a specific point in time and it will be immediately apparent to the claimant that he or she is at a disadvantage. In such circumstances, the act complained of will be the application of the PCP. The picture, however, is more complicated if the PCP is part of an ongoing policy or practice amounting to a continuing act of discrimination. In that case, application of the PCP will be treated as conduct extending over a period within the meaning of S.123(3)(a) and regarded as having been done at the end of that period. For a detailed discussion of this point and of time limits generally, see Chapter 34, 'Enforcing individual rights', under 'Time limits'.

Finally, consideration may need to be given to the kind of situation that arose in the Meade-Hill case (discussed above), where the PCP does not actually affect the claimant until some time in the future. As noted above, the mobility clause in that case was found to have been 'applied' from the date the claimant agreed to it.

16.43 **Application of PCP to hypothetical comparators**
As noted above, S.19(2)(a) EqA requires the claimant to show that the PCP applies *or would apply* equally to persons with whom he or she does not share the relevant protected characteristic (the 'comparator group'). The wording of the section makes it clear that there is no statutory requirement that a PCP actually apply to members of the comparator group because it allows for the

creation of a hypothetical comparator. This point was confirmed in British Airways plc v Starmer 2005 IRLR 862, EAT. There, the employer argued unsuccessfully that its refusal to allow the claimant – a full-time airline pilot with childcare responsibilities – to work 50 per cent of full time did not amount to a PCP because it was a decision related only to her personally and had not actually been applied to others. Mr Justice Burton, the then President of the EAT, pointed to the specific wording of S.1(2)(b) SDA (the then equivalent of S.19(2)(a) EqA), and in particular to the fact that the provision referred to a PCP that applied or 'would apply' equally to a man. The provision allowed for the creation of a hypothetical comparator pool and thus also for any adverse disparate impact to be measured by reference to that pool. There was therefore no statutory requirement that a PCP actually apply to others.

Pool for comparison 16.44

The purpose of indirect discrimination legislation is to challenge those employment practices that, while ostensibly applied in a neutral way, nonetheless have a greater disadvantageous effect on one protected group than on other people – in other words, a PCP that 'puts, or would put, persons with whom B shares the characteristic at a particular disadvantage when compared with persons with whom B does not share it' – S.19(2)(b) EqA. This is substantially the same definition that applied under the separate equality enactments that were replaced by the EqA.

However, that definition has been introduced relatively recently. Prior to amendments made to the SDA in 2005, a claimant had to show that the application of a PCP was 'such that it would be to the detriment of a considerably larger proportion of women than of men'. Before that, the original test provided that the claimant had to show that a requirement or condition was 'such that the proportion of women who can comply with it is considerably smaller than the proportion of men who can comply with it'. Similarly, before 2003 the test for indirect discrimination under the RRA required that the proportion of the claimant's racial group who could comply with the relevant requirement or condition was 'considerably smaller than the proportion of persons not of that racial group' who could comply. This means that much of the case law on the appropriate comparison was decided under the old wording, rather than under the 'particular disadvantage' test now applicable. For further details of the antecedent provisions, see under 'Legislative history' above.

Under the old wording, the usual approach was to construct a 'pool for **16.45** comparison', comprising all those potentially affected by the requirement or condition (now PCP) at issue. The tribunal would then compare how the requirement or condition affected two discrete groups within that pool: on the one hand, the group of persons who shared the relevant protected characteristic with the claimant; and, on the other, the group of persons who did not share

387

that protected characteristic. Looking at the proportion of each group that could and could not comply with the requirement or condition, the tribunal could then come to a decision as to whether (for example) a considerably larger proportion of women was disadvantaged than of men – see under '"Particular disadvantage" – the statistical approach: relative proportions' below.

In Eweida v British Airways plc 2010 ICR 890, CA (a religious discrimination case), Lord Justice Sedley noted that the task of defining the pool for comparison under the old test of indirect discrimination 'defeated three decades' judicial attempts to find a workable formula', and that the EU Equal Treatment Framework Directive (No.2000/78), which introduced the new definition, attempted to avoid this snare. However, cases decided under the new definition continued to adopt the pool approach, and the EHRC Employment Code endorses it as a method (although not the only one) of establishing particular disadvantage under the EqA. Therefore the established case law principles on the pool for comparison remain relevant, despite the change of wording. Essentially, the key is to identify a hurdle that has been placed in the way of the complainant and consider the range of persons affected by it. This will direct attention on the 'pool for comparison', which is the focus of this section. The next step – discussed under '"Particular disadvantage"' below – is to consider whether those persons within the selected pool who share the relevant protected characteristic are more likely to fall at the hurdle than those who do not.

16.46 The pool should generally encompass all those affected by the PCP about which complaint is made, including people who are disadvantaged and advantaged by it. As para 4.18 of the Code puts it: 'In general, the pool should consist of the group which the provision, criterion or practice affects (or would affect) either positively or negatively, while excluding workers who are not affected by it, either positively or negatively.' The Code gives the following example:

> 'A marketing company employs 45 women, 10 of whom are part-timers, and 55 men who all work full time. One female receptionist works Mondays, Wednesdays and Thursdays. The annual leave policy requires that all workers take time off on public holidays, at least half of which fall on a Monday every year. The receptionist argues that the policy is indirectly discriminatory against women and that it puts her at a personal disadvantage because she has proportionately less control over when she can take her annual leave. The appropriate pool for comparison is all the workers affected by the annual leave policy. The pool is not all receptionists or all part-time workers, because the policy does not only affect these groups.'

16.47 A question of fact or law?

Ascertaining the appropriate pool is not always a straightforward process, but the pool must be identified before any assessment of disparate impact can take place. The selection of the appropriate pool was originally treated as a question of fact for the employment tribunal and, as such, its discretion could not readily be interfered with by the appellate courts unless it had chosen a pool that was irrational – see, for example, Kidd v DRG (UK) Ltd 1985 ICR 405, EAT. However, in Allonby v Accrington and Rossendale College and ors 2001 ICR 1189, CA, Lord Justice Sedley characterised the identification of the pool as 'a matter neither of discretion nor of fact-finding but of logic... Logic may on occasion be capable of producing more than one outcome, especially if two or more conditions or requirements are in issue. But the choice of pool is not at large.' So, once the PCP has been defined, 'there is likely to be only one pool which serves to test its effect'. Thus, it is now easier for the EAT to overturn a tribunal's definition of the pool.

The ruling in Allonby does not mean that there can never be more than one candidate for the designation of the appropriate pool. Indeed, the Court of Appeal acknowledged that there may be 'more than one outcome'. In a subsequent decision of the Court of Appeal – Grundy v British Airways plc 2008 IRLR 74, CA – Sedley LJ had the opportunity of considering further the difficulty frequently faced by tribunals of identifying the appropriate pool for comparison. He observed: 'The correct principle, in my judgment, is that the pool must be one which suitably tests the particular discrimination complained of: but this is not the same thing as the proposition that there is a single suitable pool for every case.' The EHRC Employment Code echoes these principles, stating at para 4.18: 'In most situations, there is likely to be only one appropriate pool, but there may be circumstances where there is more than one. If this is the case, the Employment Tribunal will decide which of the pools to consider.'

The issue, according to the Allonby and Grundy decisions, is whether the **16.48** employment tribunal's choice of pool is logical. In Ministry of Defence v DeBique 2010 IRLR 471, EAT, the Appeal Tribunal stated, with reference to Grundy, that no universal principle of law dictates what the pool should be in any particular case, and that a tribunal should take a flexible approach to disparity, having regard to the circumstances of the case and the underlying purpose of the legislation. In reaching its decision as to the appropriate pool, a tribunal should undoubtedly consider the position in respect of different pools within the range of decisions open to it, but it is entitled to select from that range the pool which it considers will realistically and effectively test the particular allegation before it. On that basis, the EAT concluded that the tribunal had been entitled to find that the Ministry of Defence had indirectly discriminated against a female soldier and single mother from St Vincent on grounds of sex and race when it required her to be available for duty 24 hours a day, seven days a week ('the 24/7 PCP'), while also applying to her a restriction in the immigration rules which prevented Foreign and Commonwealth soldiers from inviting their relations to live with them in their army barracks for the purpose of looking after their children ('the immigration PCP'). The tribunal had not erred in identifying the relevant pool for comparison in relation to the immigration PCP as being those in the British Army of Vincentian national origin and of British national origin who were (or might become) single parents. Within that pool, the Vincentian soldiers (who the tribunal found would also be predominantly women) were at a particular disadvantage because their extended families and, therefore, their potential child carers were more likely to be foreign nationals subject to immigration restrictions. The EAT did not accept that the pool should have included all soldiers in the British Army who were or might become single parents, regardless of their national origin. The tribunal had chosen a pool that was logical, permissible and effective for the purpose of testing the particular allegation of indirect race discrimination. In the EAT's view, the selected pool did not predetermine the answer, but reflected the realities of the complaint.

16.49 **'No material difference' in circumstances**
The pool for comparison must be drawn up in accordance with S.23(1) EqA, which states that 'on a comparison of cases for the purposes of [S.19] there must be no material difference between the circumstances relating to each case'. (Note that if the protected characteristic is sexual orientation, the fact that one person is a civil partner while another is married is not a material difference for this purpose – S.23(3).) Although, as we have seen, the language of the test of indirect discrimination has changed several times over the years, the overarching requirement that proof of discrimination – both direct and indirect – requires a comparison of people in the same relevant circumstances has been constant.

The case of Spicer v Government of Spain 2005 ICR 213, CA, illustrates the importance of comparing like with like. S was a British teacher working at a Spanish school in London. Some of the other teaching staff were Spanish civil servants recruited in Spain and seconded to work at the school. Although the Spanish secondees received lower basic pay than the British teachers, they also received relocation allowances which meant that their total remuneration was substantially greater. S claimed that, in paying him less than his Spanish colleagues, his employer had indirectly discriminated against him on the ground of race contrary to the RRA. The employment tribunal dismissed his claim and, on appeal, the EAT held that there was no basis for making a like-for-like comparison between the Spanish and British teachers at the school. The EAT took the view that, since the relocation allowance was paid solely to Spanish civil servants recruited in Spain, the circumstances of the two groups were materially different.

16.50 The Court of Appeal overturned that decision. It held that the tribunal had correctly identified the relevant requirement or condition in the instant case as being that, in order to receive a higher pay package involving a large monthly payment in respect of living expenses, an individual had to be a Spanish civil servant recruited in and posted from Spain. As a matter of logic, once that requirement or condition had been identified, the only possible pool for comparison in order to assess disparate impact consisted of all the teachers in the school. The 'relevant circumstances' of both the British and the Spanish groups were the same in that they were all teachers at the school. Any other analysis would produce the absurd result that the only people in the pool would be either all the British teachers or all the Spanish teachers, and on that basis a claim of indirect discrimination would never succeed.

It is significant that the employer in Spicer had failed to comply with an order to set out the details of any objective justification on which it sought to rely, and was therefore barred by the tribunal from raising that defence. As Lord Justice Wall put it in his judgment, this 'highly unusual feature' of the case had 'a profound effect on the outcome of these proceedings'. For what the employer's arguments effectively amounted to was, as Wall LJ noted, an attempt to reintroduce the justification defence by other means. In arguing that there was no basis for a like-for-like comparison between the British teachers and the Spanish teachers seconded to work at the school because of the difference in the pay situation of the two groups, the employer was effectively trying to avoid a finding of indirect discrimination by relying on the very same factor about which the claimant was complaining, i.e. the fact that one group was paid the relocation allowance and the other was not. Had the justification defence been available, the employer could have argued that the difference in pay was due to the fact that the Spanish civil servants had relocated, and was thus unrelated to race. However, this factor could not be relied upon for the purpose of determining the appropriate pool for comparison.

Scope of the pool   16.51
The scope of the selected pool for comparison can have a profound effect on the outcome of an indirect discrimination claim. As we have seen, however, identifying the appropriate pool is not always a straightforward process and is likely to depend to a large extent on the nature of the PCP at issue. In some cases, the pool may consist of the entire national workforce; in others, it may be appropriate to look at an 'internal pool' consisting of the whole of the respondent's organisation, or even a particular workplace or section of the workforce within that organisation. Tribunals should seek to avoid artificial limitations on the scope of the pool, while at the same time being careful not to distort the pool by bringing into the equation individuals who are not potentially affected – either positively or negatively – by the relevant PCP.

'Access to benefit' cases. Where a claimant alleges indirect discrimination in 16.52 relation to access to a job or other benefit, case law suggests that the discriminatory impact of a PCP may generally be ascertained by analysing a pool consisting of all persons who would qualify for the job or benefit in question if the PCP were not taken into account – University of Manchester v Jones 1993 ICR 474, CA. Essentially, the disputed PCP should be ignored for this purpose.

391

It follows that, in the case of a PCP applied to job applicants, the pool is likely to include all those who might be interested in applying for the job, or perhaps those who would meet the eligibility criteria, *were it not for the PCP*. In Grundy v British Airways plc 2008 IRLR 74, CA, Lord Justice Sedley illustrated the point by using the case of Price v Civil Service Commission and anor 1978 ICR 27, EAT (another sex discrimination case), as a practical example of a sensible approach. There, the rule at issue excluded those over the age of 28 from applying to the Civil Service. The EAT rejected the Civil Service Commission's argument that the pool for determining whether the rule discriminated indirectly against women was the entire national workforce (in which the proportion of women to men was about equal). It considered that the pool comprised those men and women who were otherwise qualified for Civil Service employment. That made sense of the question of whether a significantly smaller proportion of women than of men were able to comply with the requirement to be under 28 in order to be a candidate for a Civil Service job. Sedley LJ stated: 'To have taken the national workforce would have been to empty the issue of reality; and to have taken only those who were 28 or over would have assumed the legitimacy of the very rule that was in issue. There was therefore a logical reason to take neither, and a sound reason to take a pool – potential applicants both over and under 28 – which enabled like to be compared with like, but excluding the disputed criterion.'

16.53 Another example is Sargeaunt-Thomson v National Air Traffic Services Ltd ET Case No.3100109/05, in which S-T was turned down for a post as a trainee air traffic controller because his height (he was 6 ft 10 in, and still growing) affected his ability to do the job. He claimed indirect sex discrimination. The PCP in that case was a requirement that job applicants who might have difficulty in operating the employer's equipment because they were less than 5 ft or over 6 ft 1½ in tall or had certain disabilities complete a practical test to assess their ability to operate the employer's equipment without discomfort. It was agreed by the parties that, in this case, the correct pool was all those with appropriate qualifications for the post who, ignoring the disputed requirement, would otherwise be qualified for the job.

Similarly, in Webster v Chief Constable of Hertfordshire Constabulary ET Case No.2200687/99, W, who was male and a serving police officer, was permanently removed from operational duties because he failed a colour vision test. At the time of his recruitment W disclosed his vision problems but was put onto operational duties by mistake. Instead, he should have been placed on non-operational duties in accordance with Home Office guidelines on medical fitness for recruits. Concerns about his vision came to the fore when he was selected to attend an advanced driving course for response driving and failed a colour vision test. W brought an indirect sex discrimination claim based on the fact that colour blindness affects more men than women. Five different pools were canvassed before the tribunal, including the general population at large.

That pool was rejected because the general public might not qualify for entry to the police force on account of other police entry requirements unrelated to colour vision deficiency. The pool deemed appropriate was all those who, but for the entry requirement relating to colour vision, would be suitably qualified for service in the force.

Geographical scope. Sometimes the pool will consist of a single workplace, or **16.54** it might include the whole organisation or all employees of a particular type within an organisation. Sometimes, but not often, the appropriate pool will embrace the entire 'economically active population of the United Kingdom', as in Greater Manchester Police Authority v Lea 1990 IRLR 372, EAT. There, a requirement not to be in receipt of an occupational pension was imposed on all candidates for a job. The claimant successfully showed that the proportion of men who could comply with that requirement was considerably smaller than the proportion of women. The employer contended that the pool was drawn too widely in that it wrongly included people who did not possess the right qualifications for the post as well as those who were over-qualified and so would not realistically be interested in the job. This, they argued, distorted the statistics as to the proportion of each sex that could comply with a condition of not being in receipt of a pension. The EAT's decision to uphold the tribunal's choice of pool was largely influenced by the fact that the employer had not advanced any better suggestion for determining the scope of the pool; nor had it undermined the statistical basis upon which the claimant had relied in showing that the application of the requirement had an adverse impact on men.

National demographics will be of relevance in cases where Government legislative policy is being challenged. This was so, for example, in R v Secretary of State for Employment ex parte EOC and anor 1994 ICR 317, HL (in respect of the challenge to part-time qualifying thresholds for unfair dismissal rights and redundancy pay), and in R v Secretary of State for Employment ex parte Seymour-Smith and anor 1995 ICR 889, CA, and 1997 ICR 371, HL (in respect of the challenge to the two-year qualifying period for unfair dismissal rights and redundancy payments). Where, however, the national population at large is not subjected to the PCP, a narrower pool will usually be appropriate. So, as we have already noted under '"Access to benefit" cases' above, if the context in which the particular PCP applied is recruitment, then a job requiring specific skills or qualifications should usually lead to the pool being restricted to persons with those skills and qualifications. This may or may not be limited to a particular geographical area (such as the likely 'catchment area' for a factory). If the recruitment policy being challenged is applied by a national company with many branches up and down the country, then it would seem appropriate to include in the pool all employees of the trade or profession potentially covered by that policy. The same would apply if the advertisement for the post is carried in the national media, including internet job sites. But if the company is a local one and/or the job advertisement is confined to local media or posted

393

in the local job centre, it would make sense for the pool to be confined to persons within a specified area who qualify for the position.

16.55　So, for example, if a local optician with branches in Hampstead and Highgate in North London advertises for a full-time ophthalmist in the local press, it would be appropriate for a female claimant wishing to work part time to base her claim of indirect sex discrimination on a pool consisting of 'all qualified ophthalmists within the North London area' or 'all qualified ophthalmists within one hour's travelling distance of Hampstead'. If, however, Moorfields Eye Hospital advertises in the national and medical press for a specialist eye surgeon, the pool would be much wider, at least in terms of geographical extent.

16.56　**Internal pools.** Determining the scope of the pool can be problematic where the case concerns a PCP applied to a current employee or across an existing workforce. This will happen, for example, when a woman who had previously worked full time asks to return after maternity leave on a part-time or job-share basis. It will also occur when a challenge is made to an allegedly discriminatory redundancy selection procedure or to a grading system upon which promotion decisions are based or to changes in working patterns such as shift arrangements or job locations. The question then arises whether an 'internal' pool will be appropriate.

It would seem that in most such cases the appropriate pool will be drawn from all the persons employed within the company who are affected, or potentially affected, by the PCP in question. In Fulton and ors v Strathclyde Regional Council EAT 949/83 certain posts for full-time qualified social workers were advertised internally within a Regional Council. When four female social workers employed on temporary part-time contracts with the Council applied to job-share in respect of one of the full-time posts they were told that only applications for full-time work would be considered. They complained of indirect sex discrimination. A tribunal ruled that the appropriate pool was qualified social workers employed by the Council and that, within that pool, the evidence did not disclose that the proportion of women who could comply with the requirement to work full time was 'considerably smaller' than the proportion of men. On appeal, the EAT upheld the tribunal's choice of pool. It rejected the claimants' argument that, this being a case of recruitment, the appropriate pool was either all qualified social workers in Scotland or the whole of the adult population in Scotland. In the claimants' view, such a pool would have enabled 'judicial cognisance' to be taken of the fact that, owing to their greater responsibilities for raising children, the proportion of women in general who can comply with a requirement to work full time is considerably smaller than the proportion of men. The EAT, however, held that this was not a case like Price v Civil Service Commission and anor (above), where the vacancy was advertised in the national press, so that a wider pool of potential employees could reasonably be considered. Since the vacancies had been internally advertised, the pool had been properly confined to qualified social workers already employed by the Council.

A different view of a similar situation was taken by the EAT in United Distillers **16.57** v Gordon EAT 12/97. In that case the employer turned down a request by an employee that she be permitted to return after maternity leave on a job-share basis. In her claim of indirect discrimination, a tribunal used as the appropriate pool all persons likely to apply for the post of a personnel officer. On appeal, the employer argued that, since the claimant was already employed as a personnel officer, the pool for comparison should have been confined to personnel officers within the company. The EAT rejected that argument. In its view, it was entirely proper for the pool to include all those who would be eligible to be considered for the job if the requirement to work full time was not applied. In Lord Johnston's words: '[T]he tribunal did not fall into an error by comparing the position of the [claimant], hypothetically, with those who might apply for the job. The decision to insist on full-time working discriminates against any woman with childcaring responsibilities who applies for the job.'

As a general rule, it would seem that tribunals prefer the approach taken in the Fulton case to that taken in United Distillers. Indeed, it is highly arguable that the Court of Appeal requires such an approach to be adopted. The case of London Underground Ltd v Edwards (No.2) 1999 ICR 494, CA, was concerned with the alleged discriminatory effect of imposing changes to the rostering arrangements of train operators employed by London Underground. When considering the proper pool for comparison, Lord Justice Potter observed: 'The identity of the appropriate pool will depend upon identifying that sector of the relevant workforce which is affected or potentially affected by the application of the particular requirement or condition in question and the context or circumstances in which it is sought to be applied. In this case, the pool was all those members of the LU workforce, namely train operators, to whom the new rostering arrangements were to be applied... It did not include all LU employees. Nor did the pool extend to include the wider field of potential new applicants to LU for a job as a train operator. That is because the discrimination complained of was the requirement for existing employees to enter into a new contract embodying the rostering arrangement; it was not a complaint brought by an applicant from outside complaining about the terms of the job applied for.'

The case of Whiffen v Governing Body of Milham Ford Girls' School and anor **16.58** EAT 864/97 is a further example of the adoption of an 'internal' pool for comparison. W was a female basic grade teacher employed by a particular school on a succession of fixed-term contracts. The local education authority produced a model redundancy policy that contemplated, inter alia, the non-renewal of such contracts as a means of implementing redundancies. However, the authority left it to the discretion of each school's governors as to whether and to what extent that policy was followed. In 1996 W's school, faced with a

395

redundancy situation, chose to select her for redundancy because she was employed on fixed-term contracts. She complained that more women than men were employed on such contracts and that she had therefore been indirectly discriminated against on the ground of sex. At a preliminary hearing to decide the appropriate pool, W contended that this comprised all teachers employed on the basic grade across the entire education authority. The employment tribunal ruled, however, that since the redundancy policy was adopted not by the local education authority but by the governors of the particular school, and applied only to the particular grade on which the claimant was employed (i.e. basic grade), the appropriate pool was all teachers on basic grade employed by the governors. On appeal, the EAT upheld the tribunal's decision, saying that 'it has wisely selected a pool for comparison which meets both the requirements of the [SDA] and the justice of the case'.

The Whiffen case shows that it may be appropriate to narrow the pool beyond employees employed by a company or organisation and confine it to just those employed in a particular department or job or on a specific grade. But such a restriction will only be proper if the PCP in question is applied to a defined section of the workforce. Note that the Whiffen case went to the Court of Appeal, but on a different point relating to objective justification – Whiffen v Milham Ford Girls' School and anor 2001 ICR 1023, CA.

16.59 The extent to which a pool is confined to existing employees (or even to employees on specific grades) can be highly significant, since this can have a substantial impact on whether the claimant is able to demonstrate that persons with whom she shares the relevant protected characteristic are placed at a particular disadvantage. Tribunals should be careful to ensure that chance circumstances within a particular organisation are not used as a basis for rejecting complaints of indirect discrimination that would succeed if a larger pool for comparison were adopted. For further discussion of this point, see under 'Problem areas – unrepresentative pools' below.

16.60 **Avoiding artificial limitations.** As we have seen, the adoption of an internal pool for comparison will often be appropriate, but can sometimes make it more difficult for claimants to establish a particular disadvantage to the protected group. More generally, tribunals need to be wary of placing any artificial limitations on the pool that serve to exclude people who might be affected by the PCP in question. In University of Manchester v Jones 1993 ICR 474, CA, J was a 47-year-old female graduate who had obtained her degree as a mature student. She was turned down for a job because she fell outside the age range of 25–37 specified by the employer. The tribunal upheld her indirect sex discrimination claim on the ground that the proportion of female graduates who had obtained their degrees as mature students (i.e. at 25 years or older) and who could comply with the requirement to be aged between 25 and 37 was considerably smaller than the proportion of male graduates who had been mature students. On appeal, however, the EAT and the Court of Appeal held that the tribunal had fallen into error: the pool could not be restricted to graduates who had obtained their degrees at age 25 or older (i.e. mature graduates) since the job advertisement was not just directed at mature graduates but to all graduates aged 25–37 who had the requisite qualifications and experience irrespective of when they graduated. Nor was it correct to say that the pool was all female and male graduates in the national population, since the employer would have had no occasion to apply the disputed age requirement to any graduate who did not possess the other necessary qualifications and experience for the job. Nor was the pool merely those graduates in a position to comply with the requirement (i.e. those aged 25–37): in simply identifying the numbers of men and women who could comply with the requirement, such a choice of pool would fail to allow a comparison to be made of the relative proportions of men and women who could comply in relation to the total numbers of men and women to whom the requirement is or would be applied. Finally, it would not be permissible to limit the pool to graduates in a particular subject (e.g. the subject in which the claimant held a degree) since that would distort the pool by failing to include all persons – male and female – to whom the PCP is or would be applied. The appropriate pool comprised all those persons – male and female – who satisfied (or would satisfy) all the relevant criteria, apart from the PCP in question – i.e. all graduates with the relevant experience.

Excluding irrelevant individuals. While ensuring that all relevant individuals **16.61** are included in the pool, the tribunal must also take care not to bring irrelevant individuals into the equation. In Pike v Somerset County Council 2010 ICR 46, CA, the Court of Appeal interpreted the guidance given in the leading indirect sex discrimination case, Rutherford v Secretary of State for Trade and Industry (No.2) 2006 ICR 785, HL, in the context of a rule governing pension scheme access for employees who had retired and returned to work. The rule was that, of those who returned to work and were already in receipt of a teacher's pension, only those who returned to work full time would accrue further pension contributions – those who returned to work part time and were already in receipt of a pension would not. The Court of Appeal had to decide whether this gave rise to indirect sex discrimination and had to choose between two possible pools. Either the Court could look at all teachers, including those who had retired and returned to work and those who had not yet retired; or it could look only at those who had retired and were in receipt of a pension. The Court considered that the latter pool was the more appropriate. It noted Baroness Hale's observation in Rutherford that 'indirect discrimination cannot be shown by bringing into the equation people who have no interest in the advantage or disadvantage in question'. It would distort the comparison to include in the pool those in employment pre-retirement, who were 'uninterested' in the post-retirement rules.

The Court of Appeal had the opportunity to consider the issue again in R (on the application of Bailey and ors) v London Borough of Brent Council 2011 EWCA Civ 1586, CA. There, the Court dismissed an appeal brought by residents of Brent in a judicial review challenge concerning library closures. Brent Council was found to have had 'due regard' to its equality duties under S.149 EqA – in particular, to the risk of indirect discrimination against Asian residents – when deciding to close several libraries in the Borough. In the course of his judgment, Lord Justice Pill referred to Baroness Hale's dictum in Rutherford and concluded that it was legitimate to take, as the local authority did, the pool of library users rather than a pool comprising the entire population of its area in making an assessment of disparate impact. Adopting that pool, the figures accepted by the judge below did not support a claim that there was indirect discrimination. For further details of the case, see Chapter 38, 'General public sector equality duty', under 'Compliance – "due regard"'.

16.62 However, Baroness Hale's observation can give rise to difficulties. If the pool includes only those people with an interest in the relevant benefit, and the PCP at issue operates as an 'absolute bar' that none of those individuals can satisfy, the pool will comprise only those individuals who are disadvantaged by the PCP in question. This can make it difficult, if not impossible, to show disparate impact. For full discussion of this point, see under 'Problem areas – entire pool subject to disadvantage' below.

There is some flexibility over the identity of the pool, as in many cases it will not be possible to determine the precise number of people to whom the PCP would apply. In the context of recruitment, for example, it may not be possible to determine what proportion of the economically active population would otherwise be qualified for a particular job – especially when less precise factors such as experience and aptitude are involved. In such circumstances, tribunals are entitled to draw conclusions from imperfect statistics that may, for example, include within the pool some people who are overqualified and some who are underqualified. In Greater Manchester Police Authority v Lea 1990 IRLR 372, EAT, the PCP in question was that the claimant must not have an occupational pension. The pool for comparison chosen by the tribunal was the whole of the economically active population, and the tribunal looked at statistics showing the numbers of men and women in that group who had pensions, regardless of whether they fitted any of the other recruitment criteria. The EAT accepted that statistical perfection was not required and, as the employer had been unable to suggest a more appropriate pool or show that the statistics used were in any way misleading, the tribunal's decision was upheld.

16.63 **Problem areas**
We have already seen that the identification of the appropriate pool can involve a difficult balancing act for tribunals, which must avoid drawing the pool too narrowly while at the same time not bringing into the equation individuals who

are unaffected by the relevant PCP. This section focuses on some specific difficulties that have arisen in this regard. As we have already indicated, where the group of individuals who share the relevant protected characteristic with the claimant is so small as to be unrepresentative of the larger population, this can distort the comparison. Tribunals should also be aware of the dangers of defining the pool so as to import an element of discrimination (discriminatory taint), or in such a way that the PCP appears to place every single member of the chosen pool at a disadvantage. Finally, case law has established that special considerations may apply in so-called 'closed recruitment' cases, in which the employer applies a PCP whereby the successful job candidate must be personally known to him or her.

Unrepresentative pools. Where there is a large disparity between the number **16.64** of individuals in the protected group and in the comparator group within a selected pool, it may be very difficult to make the necessary comparison between the proportions of people within those groups who are adversely affected by a PCP. Such disparity can result in the pool being unreliable. This was acknowledged by the Court of Appeal in London Underground Ltd v Edwards (No.2) 1999 ICR 494, CA, where the claimant was one of only 21 women in a total pool comprising 2,044 train operators. All 2,023 men were able to comply with a requirement for flexible working hours, as were all the women save for the claimant herself. An employment tribunal held that the claimant had nonetheless been indirectly discriminated against on the ground of sex. Given the background of the disparity in numbers between male and female train operators, it was appropriate to go beyond the specifics of the pool in question and take account of common knowledge that women are more likely to be single parents and have primary responsibility for childcare. The tribunal accordingly held that the requirement for flexible working was one with which the proportion of women who could comply was considerably smaller than the proportion of men.

Both the EAT and the Court of Appeal upheld the tribunal's decision. In doing so, the courts specifically sanctioned the right of tribunals to use their general knowledge and expertise to look outside the pool for comparison and take into account national statistics showing that ten times as many women as men are single parents or look after children. In the words of Lord Justice Potter: '[T]he comparatively small size of the female component [in the pool] indicated... without the need for specific evidence, both that it was either difficult or unattractive for women to work as train operators... and that the figure of 95.2 per cent of women [able] to comply was likely to be a [maximum] rather than a [minimum] figure.'

The question confronting the Court of Appeal in the Edwards case was really: **16.65** 'Is it enough that only one employee in a small pool is unable to comply with a requirement when her reason for not being able to do so is one that is common

399

among more women in the general working population than men?' The Court's answer, that a tribunal ought to take a wider view of the situation when the affected group is too small to be representative, has the effect not only of protecting existing employees but of easing the way for potential recruits of the same sex. It means that where women begin to encroach on those fields of work traditionally carried out by men, or vice versa, the first arrivals and potential new recruits cannot be discouraged from doing so by the imposition of PCPs with which their sex can less easily comply.

16.66 **Importing discrimination into the relevant circumstances.** An ever-present danger when identifying the relevant circumstances is that of incorporating (or 'importing') an act of discrimination into the definition of the pool for comparison. This was emphasised by the High Court in R v Secretary of State for Education ex parte Schaffter 1987 IRLR 53, QBD. In that case a female unmarried lone parent challenged the statutory rules for the conferring of hardship grants on full-time students. These, although available to married persons with children and to parents who had divorced or lost their spouses, were unavailable to lone parents who had never married. The claimant, as an unmarried lone parent in full-time education, claimed she had been discriminated against on account of sex and marital status and sought a declaration that the non payment of the hardship grant was in breach of the EU Equal Treatment Directive (No.76/207) (now consolidated into the recast Equal Treatment Directive (No.2006/54)). For the purposes of her claim, certain demographic facts were not disputed: (i) that of all lone parents, about 80 per cent were female and about 20 per cent were male; (ii) that when lone parents were subdivided into two groups – 'married' (i.e. those who were once married) and 'single' (i.e. those who had never been married) – about 80 per cent of both of the subgroups were female; (iii) that of the total population of female lone parents, about 20 per cent were single; and (iv) that of the total population of male lone parents, about 20 per cent were single.

The Secretary of State argued that, in order to determine whether there was indirect discrimination against women in respect of the denial of hardship grants to single lone parents, a like-with-like comparison had to be made entailing a comparison of single lone parents. The claimant was a single lone parent and that fact was, therefore, the relevant circumstance. Since the proportion of female lone parents who were single was the same as the proportion of male lone parents who were single (i.e. 20 per cent), the Secretary of State contended that the impact of the denial of hardship grants fell equally on men and women. The fallacy of that argument, however, was that, although there was no significant difference between the percentage of female lone parents who were single and the percentage of male lone parents who were single, there was a decisive difference between the percentage of lone parents as a whole who were female and the percentage of lone parents who were male. Consequently, four times as many female lone parents as male lone parents were ineligible for hardship grants because they were single. In the light of this, the High Court ruled that the appropriate pool for comparing the proportions of women and men who could comply with the eligibility requirement was a pool of all students with dependent children claiming grants. Mr Justice Schiemann rejected the Secretary of State's submissions that the appropriate pool for comparison should be restricted to single lone parents and that it was irrelevant that, in absolute numbers, substantially more women than men were adversely affected by the eligibility test. The judge warned that, in determining whether a PCP is indirectly discriminatory, care should be taken not to limit the pool for comparison in such a way as to incorporate discrimination into the pool itself. The pool should be wide enough to include all those, both male and female, who are affected by the PCP under consideration.

Entire pool subject to disadvantage. A similar problem to the one discussed **16.67** above – namely, the danger of importing discrimination into the definition of the pool – arises where the pool for comparison is defined by reference to the nature of the PCP at issue, with the result that the PCP places every single member of that pool at a disadvantage. Consequently, there is no comparative advantage or disadvantage and the claim appears bound to fail. An example of this arose in Secretary of State for Trade and Industry v Rutherford and anor (No.2) 2006 ICR 785, HL (an equal pay claim). In that case the employees challenged the rules that used to provide that employees who are over 65 or who have reached normal retirement age cannot claim compensation for unfair dismissal and redundancy, on the basis that the rules had a disparate impact on men because more men than women want to work beyond that age. The employment tribunal sought to limit the pool to 'those for whom retirement had some meaning', choosing those who were within ten years either side of 65. The pool therefore consisted of persons aged 55–74 who were active in the labour market in Britain. The EAT held that there were no measurable criteria to identify 'those for whom retirement had some meaning' and so this limitation was too subjective. A broad, expansive concept of the pool was required and, in the EAT's view, the correct pool was all those aged 16–79 (in effect, all those members of the whole economically active population).

This decision was upheld by the Court of Appeal (correctly in our view), but when the case reached the House of Lords, their Lordships applied a different limitation on the scope of the pool for comparison and held (by a majority) that the pool was the entire national workforce over 65. In Baroness Hale's view, the pool – at least in an 'access to benefit' case – should not include those 'who have no interest in the advantage or disadvantage in question'. The problem with the pool selected by the House of Lords was that no one (man or woman) over the age of 65 qualified for unfair dismissal and redundancy rights. As all employees over 65 were denied these rights, there was no discrimination. In effect, the majority of the Lords appeared to be saying that the very existence of the statutory bar (the PCP about which complaint was being made) which

401

was alleged to cause disparate impact prevented a comparison being made with younger members of the workforce (i.e. that the pool for comparison was restricted to the over-65s) with the result that the claimants' legal challenge could not get off the starting blocks. Everyone in the pool regardless of gender was shut out by the material condition, namely the cut-off age of 65. In our view, there was nothing to suggest that the working population under 65 was not in the same relevant circumstances (leaving aside the statutory bar, which was the subject of the complaint) as older members of the workforce, and by limiting the pool to those over 65, their Lordships selected a pool which would result in the claim failing.

16.68 Be that as it may, the majority decision in Rutherford was approved and applied by the Court of Appeal in a case concerned with race discrimination – British Medical Association v Chaudhary 2007 IRLR 800, CA. C, an Indian doctor, felt that he had been discriminated against by the Royal College of Surgeons (RCS) and subsequently alleged before a tribunal that the British Medical Association (BMA), a professional body, indirectly discriminated against and victimised him in declining to support his race discrimination claims against the RCS. The employment tribunal drew an inference that the BMA was not prepared to contemplate supporting a case against the RCS or its regulatory officials – that is, the BMA had applied a criterion that, to be eligible for support in a race discrimination claim, the member had to be bringing the claim against someone other than the RCS. Since a considerably smaller proportion of Asian members of the BMA than non-Asian members could comply with this requirement, and since C himself could not comply with it, the tribunal concluded that the BMA had indirectly discriminated against C on the ground of his race.

The Court of Appeal, however, found that the BMA had had sound reasons for believing that C's case was being dealt with according to the RCS's rules, and that there was no basis for suspecting discrimination. In those circumstances, the finding that the BMA had a closed mind with regard to C was nothing short of perverse. Moreover, it was this finding that had led the tribunal to infer that the BMA imposed a PCP that a member seeking its support in a discrimination claim could not be bringing such a claim against the RCS or its officials. As a consequence, this inference was also unsustainable, meaning that the tribunal had no basis for finding indirect discrimination. Although it was not strictly necessary given the perversity finding, the Court also expressed views on the tribunal's approach in finding that a significantly smaller number of Asian BMA members could comply with the supposed requirement that to be eligible for support, the claim must be against someone other than the RCS. In its view, in the light of the House of Lords' decision in Rutherford, the appropriate 'pool for comparison' was not all BMA members, but one which was defined by reference to the nature of the rule, condition or requirement (i.e. the PCP) at issue. Accordingly, the pool in this case comprised all BMA members who wanted that organisation's advice and support in respect of race discrimination claims against the RCS and other regulatory medical bodies. Not a single member of that pool, continued the Court, could comply with the PCP allegedly imposed by the BMA, meaning that there was no comparative disadvantage or advantage for any racial group.

As with the majority of their Lordships in the Rutherford case, the Court of **16.69** Appeal in Chaudhary appears to be stating that if a PCP constitutes an absolute bar in the sense that it applies to everyone regardless of race (or sex, etc), there can be no indirect discrimination at all. This view clearly gains support from the definition of indirect discrimination in force at the time these respective judgments were made, which concentrated on whether 'a considerably smaller' proportion of persons of the claimant's ethnic group 'can comply' with the requirement or condition. If nobody in the relevant pool for comparison can comply with the requirement or condition, then it seems logical that there cannot be any comparative disadvantage to any particular racial group or gender. The problem with this approach, however, is that it seems to ignore the relevance of the fact that one protected group may, in practice, be significantly more disadvantaged by an absolute bar than another, and, in this regard, it is important to note that the new definition of indirect discrimination – which was introduced into the RRA and SDA in accordance with the relevant EU Equality Directives, and carried over into the EqA – concentrates on whether the employer's PCP places persons of one sex, ethnic group, etc, at a 'particular disadvantage' compared with persons who do not share the relevant protected characteristic.

We would argue that if the BMA's blanket refusal to support a certain type of claim had a disparate impact upon one particular racial group, that would seem to amount to a prima facie case of indirect discrimination, which would then have to be justified. To put it another way, if the pool for comparison contains a significantly higher proportion of one racial group that is disadvantaged by the policy, that would be capable of amounting to adverse disparate impact, notwithstanding that everyone else in the pool was also disadvantaged by the policy. On the facts of Chaudhary, it seemed fairly clear that Asian doctors would be far more likely to bring race discrimination claims than white doctors. Accordingly, there were more Asian than white doctors who, in the words of the Court of Appeal, would 'want the advice and support of the BMA for race discrimination claims against the specific regulatory medical bodies'. That fact, we would argue, gives rise to a clear case of indirect discrimination, which an employer should not be allowed to defeat simply by showing that other ethnic groups, who by comparison had little or no interest in the benefit in question, would also not be able to receive that benefit.

Support for this analysis can, to some extent, be gleaned from the remarks of **16.70** Lord Justice Sedley in Grundy v British Airways plc 2008 IRLR 74, CA. In that case, his Lordship criticised the actual pool identified as appropriate by the Court of Appeal in Chaudhary when he observed: '[I]t is arguable that the single proper pool in Chaudhary was neither of the pools which were canvassed: it was members seeking support for legal claims. If within that pool there was a blanket refusal to support race discrimination claims, it might well have had a substantial adverse impact on ethnic minority members; but it would have been open to the BMA to justify this on the ground – for example – that experience showed the ratio of cost to success in race discrimination cases to be so poor that funds could legitimately be withheld from these cases (apart possibly from exceptionally strong ones) as a class.' The Court of Appeal in Grundy took the view that the House of Lords' decision in Rutherford was confined to its own facts and was not intended to lay down a general principle.

The issue was revisited more recently in Hacking and Paterson and anor v Wilson EATS 0054/09, where the EAT in Scotland attempted to take a different route around the problems caused by Rutherford. W, who was employed as a property manager by HP, made a formal request for flexible working on her return from maternity leave. However, HP's policy was to refuse any requests for flexible working put in by property managers and it therefore rejected her request. Unable to combine working full time with her childcare arrangements, W resigned and brought a tribunal claim for indirect sex discrimination. HP applied for the claim to be struck out on the basis that W had no reasonable prospect of establishing that it had applied to her a PCP which placed her at a particular disadvantage when compared with men. The employer relied on the House of Lords' decision in Rutherford, as interpreted by the Court of Appeal in Chaudhary (above), for the proposition that the pool for comparison in an indirect discrimination claim must be defined by reference to the PCP at issue and was therefore confined to those property managers at HP who wanted flexible working. Since all such managers (whether male or female) would be refused any request to work flexibly, there could, in HP's view, be no indirect discrimination.

16.71 At a pre-hearing review, an employment tribunal sitting in Scotland rejected HP's contention that the claim should be struck out. It considered that W had put forward an arguable case both that the pool should extend to all the company's property managers and that consideration of this pool indicated prima facie indirect discrimination. The tribunal considered that the decision in Chaudhary did not mean that the pool was necessarily confined to those managers who were affected by its flexible working policy. Chaudhary could be distinguished in that it was a race discrimination case and concerned access to a benefit, whereas the instant case concerned the imposition of an obligation: namely, the requirement to work full time. Furthermore, the remarks in Chaudhary were obiter and were not, in the tribunal's view, of general application in the context of requests for flexible working following maternity leave. HP appealed to the EAT.

404

In the EAT's view, the tribunal had erred in holding that the appropriate pool for comparison should be all property managers in the company. The approach of the House of Lords in Rutherford was relevant and binding. It was not possible to accept the tribunal's view that the instant case could be distinguished on the ground that it involved the imposition of an obligation rather than access to a benefit. The contract into which the claimant had willingly entered remained unchanged; the employer was not seeking to change it or to impose any new obligation. The subsistence of terms and conditions which were agreed years before could not properly be characterised as the imposition of an obligation. As in Rutherford, the complaint in the instant case was concerned with the adverse outcome of being denied a benefit. According to the claimant, she could not accommodate her chosen childcare arrangements with working full time and so she could not carry on working for the respondent employer unless she was granted flexible working.

Applying the Rutherford approach, the EAT considered that the appropriate **16.72** pool was such of the employer's property managers as, at the relevant time, wanted flexible working to be available. Those who had no interest in flexible working ought not, for the reasons explained in Rutherford, to be included in the pool. However, it did not follow that, if the pool was made up only of those persons, the inevitable answer would be that there was no indirect discrimination. The fact that all of them would have received a negative response to a request for flexible working did not mean that all would have suffered what could properly be characterised as a disadvantage or that the disadvantage to them would necessarily have been the same. It was important to look at the nature of the consequences of the negative response. On that basis, the EAT upheld the tribunal's decision that the claim should not be struck out. When the case returned to the tribunal, the claimant would have to address the issue of whether or not the refusal of the request for flexible working put women at a 'particular disadvantage'.

There might have been a strong argument for the EAT in Hacking and Paterson to conclude that Rutherford simply had no application to the facts of the case. The EAT, however, took a different approach. Lady Smith accepted that the House of Lords' decision had set down a general principle that – at least in cases where the PCP involves the denial of a benefit – the pool should include only those affected (or potentially affected) by the PCP, and that this meant that no one in the appropriate pool in the instant case qualified for the benefit of flexible working. She nevertheless went on to state that, although the absolute bar meant that no one (or everyone) was placed at a disadvantage, a claim of indirect discrimination might still be made out if the claimant could show that the PCP placed women at a 'particular disadvantage'. Thus a prima facie case of discrimination might be established if more women than men were inconvenienced by the absolute bar, or even if the disadvantage the bar caused to women was in some way more severe. As Lady Smith put it, it is 'important

405

to look at the nature of the consequences of the [employer's] negative response'. However, her comments on whether a refusal of flexible working does in fact cause a particular disadvantage to women are likely to be the most controversial aspect of her judgment. This aspect is examined in the sections '"Particular disadvantage"', under 'Defining "disadvantage" – nature of the disadvantage' and 'Indirect discrimination in context – indirect sex discrimination' below.

16.73 **'Closed recruitment' cases.** The discussion above concerns the situation where, by virtue of the fact that the PCP is in the nature of an absolute bar, no one within the relevant pool is capable of complying with it. As we have seen, the higher courts so far have adopted the stance that a claimant in those circumstances cannot get a claim of indirect discrimination off the ground as he or she is unable to show that persons with whom he or she shares the relevant protected characteristic are disproportionately adversely affected by the application of the PCP (although the EAT in Hacking and Paterson (above) took a different approach, holding that the adoption of a Rutherford-style pool did not necessarily lead to the conclusion that there was no indirect sex discrimination). But what of the situation where, within the relevant pool, just one single member can satisfy the PCP? This typically occurs in 'closed recruitment' cases, where the employer selects and appoints a person already known to him or her without undertaking a recruitment exercise. Is it possible that a claimant of the opposite sex to that of the advantaged person – for example – can claim that his or her sex is disproportionately affected?

This is the question that arose in Lord Chancellor and anor v Coker and anor 2002 ICR 321, CA. In that case the then Lord Chancellor appointed H, a white male solicitor, as his special adviser on government policy issues. The post was never advertised and H was a close acquaintance of the Lord Chancellor. O, a black female solicitor, considered that she could have qualified for the job and was aggrieved at being denied the opportunity to apply. She claimed indirect sex and race discrimination on the basis that the Lord Chancellor had imposed a PCP that the special adviser must be someone from his close circle of acquaintances and that those acquaintances were overwhelmingly white and male. An employment tribunal held that the pool for comparison consisted of those people who possessed the qualities that the Lord Chancellor had set out in a letter to the Prime Minister in order to justify his appointment of H: first class common sense, judgement and ability to assess situations; a profound knowledge of how a broad area of government works in practice; a commitment to New Labour; a comprehensive knowledge of the whole politics of the law; and all the qualities and experience of the law necessary to offer sound political advice across the whole range of the work of the Lord Chancellor's Department. The tribunal went on to find the appointment had been indirectly discriminatory in that the Lord Chancellor had applied the requirement that the successful applicant be well known to him, which had a disproportionate impact as between men and women.

406

On appeal, the EAT reversed the decision, holding that this was a unique **16.74** situation and that there was no relevant pool because of the nature of the post of special adviser, and because the Lord Chancellor was determined to appoint a particular person. The Court of Appeal reinstated the tribunal's original decision on the pool for comparison, but went on to hold that there was no disproportionate impact on women or ethnic minorities within that pool. It concluded that the application of a requirement that job applicants be personally known to the Lord Chancellor had led to the successful candidate being the only person within the appropriate pool who could comply with that requirement. In the Court's view, making an appointment from within a circle of family, friends and personal acquaintances would rarely constitute indirect discrimination. This was because those known to the employer are likely to represent a minute proportion of the number of people who would otherwise be qualified to fill the post, with the consequence that the PCP of personal knowledge would exclude the majority of the pool, be they men, women, white or another racial group. Thus, where the Lord Chancellor appointed a special adviser from within his circle of (mainly white male) acquaintances, there was no indirect discrimination.

Although the facts of Coker appear to make this an unusual case, it should be remembered that instances of 'closed recruitment' do occur and, in light of the Court's reasoning, will apparently be difficult to challenge as indirectly discriminatory. Nevertheless, the Court was careful to qualify some of its statements and it may be that the decision is limited to its particular facts. For further discussion, see Chapter 24, 'Recruitment', in the section 'Arrangements for deciding to whom to offer employment', under 'Method of recruitment – personal acquaintance'.

'Particular disadvantage' 16.75

Once the appropriate pool for comparison has been ascertained, it is necessary to determine whether the application of the PCP to the members of that pool discloses indirect discrimination. Under the current formulation of the test of adverse disparate impact in the EqA, it is for the claimant to show that the PCP:

- puts, or would put, persons with whom B (the claimant) shares the relevant protected characteristic at a particular disadvantage when compared with persons with whom B does not share it – S.19(2)(b) – and

- puts, or would put, B at that disadvantage – S.19(2)(c).

Unlike its predecessors in the SDA and RRA prior to redrafting, this test makes no explicit reference to a comparison between the proportions of persons of different groups that are adversely affected by the practice in question, and nor does it mention numbers or statistics. It merely states that there must be a group which suffers or would suffer a 'particular disadvantage' without

407

specifying how that disadvantage must be shown. This is left to the UK courts and tribunals to interpret, aided by relevant decisions of the European Court of Justice.

16.76 When the old tests of indirect discrimination were in force, it was usual for disadvantage to be proved by statistical evidence concerning the proportions of disadvantaged and advantaged people in the relevant pool. As noted under 'Legislative history' above, a claim of indirect sex discrimination prior to October 2005 required evidence that a PCP had an adverse disparate impact on a 'considerably larger' (or smaller) proportion of women than men, while a claim of indirect race discrimination prior to July 2003 required the claimant to establish that the proportion of his or her racial group which could comply with the relevant requirement or condition was 'considerably smaller' than the proportion of persons not of that racial group which could comply. This entailed a statistically-driven comparative exercise and generated a huge amount of case law addressing the tricky issue of how to establish disproportionate impact – i.e. what amounts to a considerably larger or a considerably smaller proportion? While tribunals were occasionally prepared to apply their 'industrial knowledge' to the question of adverse disparate impact, detailed statistical evidence was usually required.

When the Government amended the SDA and RRA by introducing the new test of 'particular disadvantage', it took the view that the new wording would make it easier to establish indirect discrimination. Nevertheless, the EHRC Employment Code makes it clear that the old statistical approach is still a useful tool, stating: 'The way that the comparison is carried out will depend on the circumstances, including the protected characteristic concerned. It may in some circumstances be necessary to carry out a formal comparative exercise using statistical evidence' (para 4.20). Thus, it appears that tribunals assessing particular disadvantage will, at least in some cases, continue to apply the statistical approach, and the old case law therefore continues to be relevant. Clearly, any PCP that was held to have a disproportionate impact under the old test would satisfy the new test – for a tribunal to decide otherwise would offend against the principle that changes introduced to comply with EU Directives cannot amount to a regression in protection from discrimination. It is, therefore, the marginal cases that failed under the old tests where the new test is most likely to alter matters.

16.77 The Code also confirms that statistical analysis is not the only method of establishing disparate impact. Claimants may rely on evidence from expert and other witnesses, and tribunals will continue to take 'judicial notice' of certain matters that are well known, such as the adverse impact caused to women by a refusal to allow part-time working. Where statistical evidence is finely balanced or simply not available, these non-statistical means of establishing adverse disparate impact may be the only method open to claimants, and they may well

408

assume greater significance in the future as the case law on 'particular disadvantage' evolves.

This section starts by examining what amounts to a 'disadvantage' for the purposes of S.19 EqA. It then looks at group disadvantage, including the possibility of basing a claim on the disadvantage to a *hypothetical* group of persons sharing the relevant protected characteristic. Next, it examines the methods of establishing particular disadvantage outlined above – the statistical approach, use of expert and other evidence, and the doctrine of judicial notice. Finally, it explores the requirement for the claimant to suffer an individual disadvantage through the application of the relevant PCP.

Defining 'disadvantage'

16.78

As noted above, the claimant must show that the PCP applied by the employer both puts (or would put) persons with whom he or she shares the relevant protected characteristic at a *particular disadvantage*, and puts (or would put) him or her at *that disadvantage* – S.19(2)(b) and (c) EqA. The concept of 'particular disadvantage' is not new: it applied in the vast majority of employment cases before S.19 EqA came into force. While 'disadvantage' is not defined by the Act, the concept is similar to 'detriment', a term found in the original definitions of indirect discrimination in the SDA and RRA. Indeed, in a number of older cases the words 'detriment' and 'disadvantage' were used interchangeably – see, for example, De Souza v Automobile Association 1986 ICR 514, CA, and Ministry of Defence v Jeremiah 1980 ICR 13, CA (race and sex cases respectively). Accordingly, it would seem that decisions on the meaning of 'detriment' are relevant when considering the concept and scope of 'disadvantage'.

The EHRC Employment Code states at para 4.9 that 'disadvantage' is to be construed as 'something that a reasonable person would complain about – so an unjustified sense of grievance would not qualify. A disadvantage does not have to be quantifiable and the worker does not have to experience actual loss (economic or otherwise). It is enough that the worker can reasonably say that they would have preferred to be treated differently.' This, in effect, summarises the House of Lords' decision in Shamoon v Chief Constable of the Royal Ulster Constabulary 2003 ICR 337, HL, which considered discriminatory detriment under the Northern Irish equivalent of what was then S.6(2)(b) SDA. The equivalent provision is now S.39(2)(d) EqA, which provides that an employer (A) must not discriminate against an employee (B) 'by subjecting B to any other detriment'.

In Shamoon the House of Lords held that the test was whether 'a reasonable **16.79** worker would or might take the view that he had… been disadvantaged in the circumstances in which he had thereafter to work'. In that case the House of Lords held that a female Chief Inspector had been subjected to a detriment

409

when her responsibility for making appraisals was taken away. Lord Hope thought that once it was known, as it was bound to be, that she had had this part of her normal duties taken away from her following a complaint to the Police Federation, her standing among her colleagues was likely to be diminished. A reasonable employee in her position might well feel that she was being demeaned in the eyes of those over whom she was in a position of authority.

The House of Lords in Shamoon also endorsed the view of the Court of Appeal in the earlier case of Barclays Bank plc v Kapur and ors (No.2) 1995 IRLR 87, CA (a race case), that an unjustified sense of grievance cannot amount to a detriment. That case involved a claim of indirect race discrimination brought by four East African Asians who had worked at Barclays Bank in Kenya until they were forced to leave the country in 1970 as a result of changes in Kenyan immigration laws. All four accepted posts in the United Kingdom with the same bank under terms and conditions which provided that previous service with Barclays in Kenya would be credited for pension purposes. However, the Kenyan bank had already made ex gratia payments to the claimants to compensate them for their loss of accrued pension rights. As a result, the bank required all ex-Kenyan Asian recruits to waive their rights in respect of that past service in order to prevent their receiving credit for their years of service in Kenya in addition to compensation for loss of those pensionable years. European employees had not been paid such compensation on leaving Kenya and so were not required to waive their rights. The Court of Appeal held that the claimants had suffered no loss other than their loss of pension benefits, and that the total sum paid to them by way of compensation for that loss should be taken into account. On this basis, they had suffered no detriment. The claimants argued that they had suffered a detriment in that they had feelings of grievance at the way they had been treated. The Court held, however, that this was an unjustified sense of grievance that could not amount to a detriment.

16.80 Shamoon v Chief Constable of the Royal Ulster Constabulary 2003 ICR 337, HL, is also authority for the fact that the notion of detriment does not require the complainant to demonstrate any physical or economic consequence. As noted above, the detriment in that case was the removal of responsibility from the claimant. In accepting that this amounted to a 'detriment', the House of Lords disapproved of the view taken by the Court of Appeal in Lord Chancellor and anor v Coker and anor 2002 ICR 321, CA – a case on the original tests of indirect sex and race discrimination – that there had to be a physical or economic consequence for the complainant that was material and substantial. There, the claimant, a black woman, complained that she had suffered indirect sex and race discrimination by being excluded from the selection process for the position of special adviser to the Lord Chancellor, since the latter had recruited his special adviser from his circle of close friends and acquaintances, who were disproportionately white and male. The Court of Appeal held that there was no detriment, since there was no way the claimant would have met all the other criteria for selection even if the Lord Chancellor had opened up the selection process.

Nature of the disadvantage. While the test of 'particular disadvantage' appears **16.81** to allow a certain degree of latitude, it raises a number of questions. Does 'particular disadvantage' mean particular to the protected group in the sense of exclusive to it? Or does the term simply refer to an identifiable – i.e. distinct – disadvantage? In Chaplin v Royal Devon and Exeter NHS Foundation Trust ET Case No.1702886/09 – a religious discrimination case concerning a uniform policy that prevented a practising Christian from wearing a cross – the employment tribunal noted that the definition of 'particular' in the Oxford English Dictionary is 'noteworthy, peculiar or singular', and stated that the disadvantage to those sharing the claimant's belief did not meet that threshold because it was 'slight'. (For details of that case, see Chapter 11, 'Religion or belief', in the section 'Manifestation of religion or belief', under 'Is a right to manifest protected by S.10 EqA? – dress and jewellery'.) It may be the case that tribunals will, where appropriate, be able to look not only at the quantitative effects of a disadvantage (i.e. the proportions of the protected group and the comparator group that are affected) but also at its qualitative nature. Perhaps an extreme hardship will in some cases require less of a statistical difference than a mere inconvenience.

The indirect sex discrimination case of Hacking and Paterson and anor v Wilson EATS 0054/09 addresses some of these issues. W, who was employed as a property manager by HP, made a formal request for flexible working on her return from maternity leave. HP's policy was to refuse any requests for flexible working put in by property managers and it therefore rejected her request. Unable to combine working full time with her childcare arrangements, W resigned and claimed indirect sex discrimination. The main issue concerned the composition of the pool for comparison. On this point, the EAT in Scotland held that the appropriate pool was limited to such of the employer's property managers as, at the relevant time, wanted flexible working to be available. (This aspect of the decision is discussed in the section 'Pool for comparison' above, under 'Problem areas – entire pool subject to disadvantage'.) In the EAT's view, however, it did not follow that, if the pool was made up only of those persons, the inevitable answer would be that there was no indirect sex discrimination. The fact that all of them would have received a negative response to a request for flexible working did not mean that all would have suffered what could properly be characterised as a disadvantage or that the disadvantage to them would necessarily have been the same. It was important to look at the nature of the consequences of the negative response.

It followed that, when the case returned to the employment tribunal, the **16.82** claimant would have to address the issue of whether or not the refusal of the

411

request for flexible working put women at a 'particular disadvantage'. In this regard, the EAT commented that it was not inevitable that women would be disproportionately adversely affected by a refusal to grant flexible working. Society has changed dramatically: many women now return to full-time work after childbirth and more men take on childcare responsibilities. Although the childcare arrangements available to some women are such that they cannot work full time, the position of others is that, while they are able to access childcare arrangements that would enable them to work full time, they do not want to do so; for them, part-time working is a matter of choice rather than necessity. Moreover, people (both male and female) seek flexible working for different reasons, which include, for instance, enabling them to combine jobs, pursue other interests or follow educational courses. A negative response to the request for flexible working may, accordingly, give rise to differing effects. Where the effect is on an employee who is able to work full time but does not wish to do so, it is difficult to see that it would be correct to talk in terms of that employee being disadvantaged. Where the effect does amount to a disadvantage, the question of whether it amounts to a particular disadvantage that is liable to be experienced by women as opposed to men arises.

The decision in Hacking and Paterson suggests that, even if the PCP operates as an absolute bar that disadvantages the entire pool, the claimant may still establish a prima facie case of discrimination if more individuals in the protected group (i.e. those who share the claimant's protected characteristic) are inconvenienced by the absolute bar, or even if the disadvantage the bar causes to that group is in some way more severe. As Lady Smith put it, it is 'important to look at the nature of the consequences of the [employer's] negative response'. However, her comments on whether a refusal of flexible working does in fact cause a particular disadvantage to women are likely to be the most controversial aspect of her judgment. This aspect is examined under 'Indirect discrimination in context – indirect sex discrimination' below.

16.83 **Compliance does not preclude disadvantage.** A disadvantage is not limited to instances where an individual is refused or barred from something that he or she wants. In Eweida v British Airways plc 2009 ICR 303, EAT, Mr Justice Elias, then President of the EAT, refused to rule out the possibility that a policy with which the claimant has complied may yet give rise to a disadvantage. That case was brought under the indirect discrimination provisions of the Employment Equality (Religion or Belief) Regulations 2003 SI 2003/1660, which were in substantially the same form as S.19 EqA. E, a devout practising Christian, was employed by BA plc from 1999 as a member of the check-in staff. BA's uniform policy, from 2004 to February 2007, prohibited customer-facing members of staff from wearing any visible item of adornment. Only an item worn because of a mandatory religious requirement – and which could not be concealed under the uniform – was permitted to be visible if, and in the manner that, BA plc approved. Between May and September 2006 E visibly wore a silver cross on a chain around her neck on three occasions. On two of those occasions, she complied with management requests to conceal the necklace. On 20 September, however, she refused such a request, and was consequently sent home without pay. When she complained of indirect discrimination to an employment tribunal, it found that there was no particular disadvantage, since the visible wearing of the cross was E's personal decision and was not required by scripture or as an article of faith. It further found that there was no evidence that Christians, as a group, were or would be disadvantaged by the policy.

E's appeal to the EAT was rejected, the EAT holding that there was no evidence of anyone other than her being adversely affected, or potentially adversely affected, by the policy. However, there was no doubt that E herself suffered a particular disadvantage. It was readily accepted that being sent home from work for refusal to comply with the employer's policy was a disadvantage. Furthermore, Elias P was prepared to accept in principle that E could have suffered relevant disadvantage even when she complied with the uniform policy. Elias P thought there to be some merit in the argument that the policy caused particular disadvantage to all those who would otherwise have wished to display a religious symbol on their person, and that just because E was the only employee to complain, that did not mean no others considered themselves to have suffered a detriment. However, he cautioned that the disadvantage would still have to stem from the religious belief – those who wanted to wear jewellery for personal, non-religious reasons could not also be said to be particularly disadvantaged. (Note that the EAT's decision was upheld on appeal by the Court of Appeal – Eweida v British Airways plc 2010 ICR 890, CA. Although the Court expressed some doubts over the wording of some of the EAT's remarks, that did not undermine its approach to particular disadvantage. In particular, the Court endorsed the EAT's rejection of E's claim on the basis that there was no evidence that any identifiable group was, or would be, similarly disadvantaged by the uniform policy.)

Solitary disadvantage. The Eweida case (above) is also illuminating as to the **16.84** evidential problems inherent in showing particular disadvantage. E failed in her claim because she could not show that there were others who shared her admittedly personal view on the need to manifest one's religious belief. In effect, she was asking the employment tribunal to find indirect discrimination against a solitary individual. When the case reached the Court of Appeal, Lord Justice Sedley noted that indirect discrimination can only be established where an ostensibly neutral PCP adversely affects an identifiable group. Solitary disadvantage, therefore, does not give rise to indirect discrimination. Although – as noted under 'Group disadvantage – hypothetical group disadvantage' below – indirect discrimination permits consideration of how a PCP *would* affect people sharing the same protected characteristic as the claimant, in Sedley LJ's view this did not mean that a claimant may construct an entirely hypothetical

413

peer group to whom the disadvantage is to be attributed. In some cases it will be relatively simple, and in keeping with the purpose of the legislation, to aggregate a solitary employee with others known to have the same characteristic, and known to be potentially affected in the same way – a lone female worker, for example, could claim indirect discrimination on the basis of the way a particular policy would affect a hypothetical group of female staff. However, Sedley LJ considered that it would be 'forensically difficult, even impossible' to do the same for a solitary believer whose fellow believers, if they existed, might accord different degrees of importance to the same manifestation of faith.

16.85 **Combined disadvantage.** The EAT's decision in Ministry of Defence v DeBique 2010 IRLR 471, EAT – a case brought under the indirect discrimination provisions in the SDA and RRA – suggests that a tribunal hearing an indirect discrimination claim that involves two or more protected characteristics is not necessarily limited to viewing each complaint in isolation, and may be entitled to take into account the fact that the claimant has suffered a combined disadvantage. In that case, the EAT upheld a tribunal's decision that the Ministry of Defence had indirectly discriminated against a female soldier and single mother from St Vincent on grounds of sex and race when it required her to be available for duty 24 hours a day, seven days a week ('the 24/7 PCP'), while also applying to her a restriction in the immigration rules which prevented Foreign and Commonwealth soldiers from inviting their overseas relations to live with them in their army barracks for the purpose of looking after their children ('the immigration PCP').

The EAT upheld the tribunal's decision that although, on the face of it, the 24/7 PCP was justified, viewing it in isolation from the immigration PCP failed to reflect the claimant's particular disadvantage. The tribunal had been entitled to consider the combined effect of the 24/7 requirement, which was alleged to discriminate against the claimant on the ground of sex, and the immigration requirement, which discriminated against her on the ground of race. In general, the nature of discrimination is such that it cannot always be sensibly compartmentalised into discrete categories. While some complainants will raise issues relating to only one or other of the prohibited grounds, attempts to view others as raising only one form of discrimination for consideration will result in an inadequate understanding and assessment of the complainant's true disadvantage. Discrimination is often a multi-faceted experience. The particular disadvantage to which the claimant in the instant case was subject arose both because she was a 24/7 female soldier with a child and because she was a woman of Vincentian national origin, for whom childcare assistance from a live-in Vincentian relative was not permitted. The tribunal had recognised that this double disadvantage reflected the factual reality of her situation.

16.86 The EAT concluded that, on an analysis of the combined effect of the two PCPs, the tribunal had correctly concluded that the claimant was put to disadvantage by reason of her sex and race and that this could not be justified as a proportionate means of achieving a legitimate aim. When considering the 24/7 PCP in the context of the allegations, the relevant pool consisted of male and female soldiers in the British army whose potential child carers were foreign nationals. The women in this pool were at a particular disadvantage because they were more likely than the men to be single parents requiring assistance with childcare. With regard to the immigration PCP, the tribunal had identified the pool as those in the British Army of Vincentian national origin and of British national origin who were (or might become) single parents. Within that pool the Vincentian soldiers (who the tribunal found would also be predominantly women) were put at a particular disadvantage because their extended families and, therefore, their potential child carers were more likely to be foreign nationals subject to immigration restrictions. The tribunal's conclusions accurately reflected, in the EAT's judgment, the particular disadvantage caused to women of Vincentian origin in the British Army who were single parents.

If the EAT's decision is correct, it shows that there may be scope in an appropriate case to take into account the effect of a PCP in relation to more than one protected characteristic. It should be noted that DeBique sits uneasily with Bahl v Law Society and ors 2004 IRLR 799, CA, in which the Court of Appeal held that discrimination experienced as a result of a number of characteristics must be considered on each individual ground separately and its own right. However, in the high-profile case of O'Reilly v British Broadcasting Corporation and anor ET Case No.2200423/10 – a direct age and sex discrimination claim brought by a female presenter in her early fifties who was dropped from a primetime television slot – an employment tribunal took the view that, on a proper analysis, the Court of Appeal's decision in Bahl did not preclude the possibility of combined discrimination.

16.87 Note that the EqA contains a provision – S.14 – which would allow *direct* discrimination claims to be brought in relation to a combination of two protected characteristics, sometimes referred to as 'dual' or 'combined' discrimination. Although the vast majority of the Act's provisions came into force on 1 October 2010, S.14 was not given effect at the same time. The previous Labour Government intended to bring S.14 into force in April 2011 but when the new Coalition Government published its 2011 Budget and accompanying 'Plan for Growth' in March 2011, it announced that it would not bring the provision into force. In any event, there are two major differences between the EAT's approach in DeBique and that in S.14 EqA. First, S.14 applies only to direct discrimination, whereas the EAT's decision applies to indirect discrimination (direct discrimination not being an issue in the case). During the Equality Bill's passage through Parliament, the Solicitor General took the view that there was insufficient evidence of a need to extend the combined discrimination provision to indirect discrimination, adding: 'We

415

think that including indirect discrimination within the provision would mean businesses and employers having to consider the impacts of their policies and procedures on every possible combination of protected characteristic, which is not proportionate given the lack of evidence of need.' Secondly, S.14 allows only two protected characteristics to be combined, whereas there would appear to be no such limitation in the EAT's judgment in DeBique.

16.88 **Anticipatory disadvantage.** The issue of how to identify the point at which a PCP causes a disadvantage to a claimant has been discussed under 'Provision, criterion or practice – identifying the time a PCP is applied' above. However, the potential for challenging the anticipatory discriminatory effect of contractual terms should be borne in mind given the ruling of the Court of Appeal in Meade-Hill and anor v British Council 1995 ICR 847, CA. There, the Court held that a mobility clause was 'applied' from the date when the claimant agreed to it even though it had not been invoked. The majority of the Court of Appeal appeared to come close to saying that it was sufficient for the complainant to show that she would suffer a disadvantage *at some point in the future*. But such an approach, taken to its logical limits, would be surprising. It would enable, for example, women who at present face no impediment to working full time to claim indirect discrimination against an employer who insists on full-time working merely on the basis that they might be unable to comply with that requirement if they were to have children in the future.

In deciding just how far the Meade-Hill decision can be stretched to deal with potential or hypothetical as opposed to actual and present disadvantage suffered by a claimant, it should be borne in mind that the case was not decided in the context of an indirect discrimination claim brought before an employment tribunal. Instead, it arose out of county court proceedings in respect of that court's jurisdiction under S.77(5) SDA (now S.143 EqA) to exclude or modify discriminatory contractual terms. In view of this, the scope of the Court of Appeal's decision might best be seen as being confined to the county court's powers in that regard. If so, then the point of general principle arising from the decision in Meade-Hill could be summarised in this way: in an application to the county court to have a contractual term excluded or modified on the ground that it is indirectly discriminatory, it will be sufficient in order to prove disadvantage for the complainant to show that the discriminatory clause in question is contained in the contract of employment and that, if applied or enforced by the employer, the complainant's present circumstances are such that he or she would be put at a disadvantage by that term.

16.89 In cases falling within the jurisdiction of employment tribunals, it was clear under the antecedent equality legislation that the claimant must show that he or she was actually put at a disadvantage by the PCP at the time it was applied and that the courts would not engage in speculation as to whether the complainant would suffer disadvantage by a PCP that had to be satisfied at some point in the future. This was illustrated by the Court of Appeal's decision in Turner v The Labour Party and anor 1987 IRLR 101, CA. In that case an unmarried woman claimed that a rule in her employer's pension scheme that provided for pensions for surviving spouses but did not allow pension rights to be passed on to children was to the detriment of single divorced parents, the greater proportion of whom were women. A majority of the Court of Appeal ruled that, as the conditions for entitlement to a pension have to be satisfied at a future date and not at a date when a particular contribution is paid, the claimant had suffered no detriment on the ground that she could not comply with the requirement to be married. It could not be said that a woman who is presently single could not comply with being married at some time in the future; she might not want to marry but, at the time of the claim, no detriment had been shown as a result of her being unmarried. Lord Justice Ralph Gibson, however, dissented on this point. In his judgement, if a divorced woman is not married and has no immediate intention of marrying, she should be treated as a person who cannot at the date of her complaint comply with a condition of being married. In his Lordship's view, the detriment in the particular case consisted of the expense of paying for additional pension cover to secure for the claimant's children a pension equivalent to that payable to a surviving spouse.

It is important to note, however, that the Turner case was decided under the old wording of the SDA. In addition to covering claimants who are put at a particular disadvantage by the relevant PCP, the new definition of indirect discrimination extends to claimants who *would be* put at such a disadvantage – S.19(2)(c) EqA. This reflects a 2008 amendment to the RRA, making it clear that the EqA protects a person who is deterred by a discriminatory PCP from seeking employment for which he or she is otherwise qualified – a point that was not previously clear in relation to protected characteristics other than race. Arguably, this amendment might also allow an individual to claim that he or she *would* suffer a particular disadvantage by virtue of a PCP that might be applied at some future date. This argument has not yet been tested and it remains to be seen what view the tribunals and courts will take.

Is a causal link needed between protected characteristic and disadvantage? 16.90
Recent cases have raised the issue as to whether, in order for an indirect discrimination claim to succeed, the relevant protected characteristic must actually have caused the particular disadvantage complained of. In Homer v Chief Constable of West Yorkshire Police 2010 ICR 987, CA, the Court of Appeal suggested that the PCP complained of must place the claimant's group at a disadvantage *on account of the relevant protected characteristic* and not because of some other factor. Applying that principle to the circumstances of the particular case before it, the Court ruled that the claimant (who was aged 61) had not been indirectly discriminated against in relation to the protected characteristic of age when the employer introduced a PCP whereby legal advisers employed on its top grade must have a law degree. In particular, the

417

Court rejected the argument that the employer's degree requirement amounted to indirect age discrimination because the claimant's age prevented him from completing the degree before his enforced retirement at 65 (which was lawful at the relevant time). In the Court's view, what accounted for the disadvantage suffered by the claimant was not his age or the age group to which he belonged but his impending withdrawal from the workplace. In that sense he was no more disadvantaged than any person in the comparator age group (those aged 30–59) would have been if he or she had also stopped working before qualifying (e.g. for family reasons).

On further appeal, the Supreme Court overturned the decision of the Court of Appeal and held that the claimant had indeed suffered disadvantage on account of the age group to which he belonged – see Homer v Chief Constable of West Yorkshire Police 2012 UKSC 15, SC. Baroness Hale (with whom the other Supreme Court Justices all agreed) held that the degree requirement placed the claimant, as a 61-year-old, at a disadvantage in view of his impending retirement at 65. As 'age' and 'retirement' were inextricably interlinked, any particular (or disproportionate) disadvantage suffered by virtue of the application of a general PCP by people in the 60–65 age group must, by definition, be related to age. In other words, a requirement that works to the comparative disadvantage of a person approaching compulsory retirement age is indirectly discriminatory on the ground of age. It was not right to equate leaving work because of impending retirement with other reasons for doing so (such as family reasons), since in the latter situation a person generally had some choice in the matter, whereas someone coming up to a mandatory retirement age did not. The outcome was that the Supreme Court remitted the case to the employment tribunal to establish whether the indirect discrimination at issue was objectively justified.

16.91 So where does that leave us regarding the Court of Appeal's intimation in Homer that a causal link had to be shown between the disadvantage suffered by the claimant and the protected characteristic at issue? It is clear from the Supreme Court's decision that the Court of Appeal got the *application* of that principle wrong since, contrary to its conclusion, the particular disadvantage suffered by the claimant and other members of his age group by the employer's degree stipulation was found by the Supreme Court to be causally connected to the protected characteristic at issue, i.e. age. But what of the validity of the basic principle itself? Unfortunately, this issue was not the subject of scrutiny by the Supreme Court. Its decision cannot therefore be cited as direct authority for concluding that the entirety of the Court of Appeal's reasoning has been overturned. Having said that, the notion that the necessary causal link has to be shown in indirect discrimination cases is, as explained below, not without its difficulties and, on balance, we would suggest that it is probably erroneous in law.

In the first place, it should be noted that one of the specific reasons given by Lord Justice Mummery in the Court of Appeal for rejecting the claimant's indirect discrimination claim was that the particular disadvantage suffered by him was 'not the result of applying the law degree provision to his age'. This suggestion that the apparently neutral PCP must be specifically 'applied' to the claimant's age group is open to the criticism that it creates an extra hurdle for the claimant which is not contained in the legislation and which, moreover, arguably imports an element of direct discrimination into the statutory test for indirect age discrimination. In this regard, it may be relevant to note that Baroness Hale, in her judgment in the Supreme Court, drew attention to the current definition of indirect discrimination, which speaks in terms of the application of a 'provision, criterion or practice' that 'puts or would put persons with the same protected characteristic as the claimant at a particular disadvantage when compared with other persons'. In her judgment, this formulation was intended to make it easier, not harder, for claimants to show indirect discrimination in comparison with the old test of indirect discrimination that required the claimant to show that the application of a requirement or condition had a disproportionate adverse effect on those with the protected characteristic. In Baroness Hale's words, under the revised formulation, 'all that is needed is a particular disadvantage when compared with other people who do not share the characteristic in question. It [is] not intended to lead us to ignore the fact that certain protected characteristics are more likely to be associated with particular disadvantages'. So although, as previously stated, the Supreme Court's decision does not expressly deny the need to establish a causal link between the disadvantage suffered and the relevant protected characteristic, it supports the contention that the wording of what is now S.19 EqA should not be interpreted in a way that introduces barriers to making out a claim of indirect discrimination that did not exist before.

In the second place, it would seem that the Court of Appeal, in another case **16.92** decided *after* its decision in Homer, eschewed the notion that causal link has to be shown, albeit without any apparent consideration of its earlier decision in Homer. In R (on the application of Bailey and ors) v London Borough of Brent Council 2011 EWCA Civ 1586, CA, the Court dismissed an appeal brought by Brent residents in a judicial review challenge concerning library closures. Brent Council was found to have had 'due regard' to its equality duties under S.149 EqA – in particular, to the risk of indirect discrimination against Asian residents – when deciding to close several libraries in the Borough. In reaching that decision, the Court rejected the local authority's argument that, in order to establish indirect discrimination, it was necessary to show a causal relationship, or 'intrinsic link', between the relevant protected characteristic (in that particular case, race) and the particular disadvantage suffered (loss of library services) – although Lord Justice Davis accepted that, where such a link exists, no further statistical support may be needed. So, in that particular case, it would have been sufficient to show, by reference to appropriate statistics, that the local authority's policy put Asian residents at a

419

particular disadvantage compared with persons of other races. However, the evidence relied on by the appellants did not support that assertion. For further details of the case, see Chapter 38, 'General public sector equality duty', under 'Compliance – "due regard"'.

16.93 Group disadvantage

Section 19(2)(b) EqA provides that the claimant (B) must show that the PCP 'puts, or would put, persons with whom B shares the characteristic at a particular disadvantage when compared with persons with whom B does not share it'. Thus, the disadvantage must adversely affect an actual or hypothetical group that shares the relevant protected characteristic with the claimant. There are several possible methods of establishing such disparate impact; these are discussed under 'The statistical approach: relative proportions', 'Expert and other evidence' and 'Judicial notice of particular disadvantage', all below.

In the case of some of the protected characteristics, it may not be straightforward for the claimant to establish the identity of the disadvantaged group. Individuals within a particular religion often manifest their religious beliefs in different ways, while in the context of disability it is well known that people who have the same disability cannot easily be treated as a homogenous class. Indirect age discrimination can also be problematic: the relevant PCP must put persons of the claimant's 'age group' at a particular disadvantage and there appears to be a large degree of flexibility in defining that group. For discussion of the way in which group disadvantage operates in relation to these protected characteristics, see under 'Indirect discrimination in context' below.

The remainder of this section focuses on the possibility of establishing disadvantage by reference to a *hypothetical* protected group.

16.94 Hypothetical group disadvantage. The wording of S.19(2)(b) EqA makes it clear that there is no need to point to persons of a particular group on whom there is in fact a disproportionate impact. Where there is no such group, the test requires proof only that the PCP *would put* persons of a particular group at a particular disadvantage. For example, if there are no other persons of B's sex, race, etc, in the workplace (or in whatever pool the employment tribunal may choose for the purposes of a comparison), B can still succeed in an indirect discrimination claim by arguing that such persons, if they did exist, would be more susceptible than other people to the disadvantage of which he or she is complaining.

The possibility of hypothetical group disadvantage was first introduced into the SDA in 2001, and similar changes were made to the RRA in 2003 – see under 'Legislative history' above. The 2001 test for indirect sex discrimination required tribunals to look at whether the PCP *'would be* to the detriment of a considerably larger proportion of women than of men'. In appropriate cases this change of wording meant that tribunals could assess disparate impact by using a hypothetical pool of comparison, as in British Airways plc v Starmer 2005 IRLR 862, EAT. There, the employer argued unsuccessfully that its refusal to allow S (a full-time airline pilot with childcare responsibilities) to work 50 per cent of full-time hours did not amount to a PCP because it was a decision related only to S and had not actually been applied to others. Dismissing this argument, the EAT noted that the 2001 test allowed for the creation of a hypothetical comparator pool and thus also for any detrimental impact to be measured by reference to that pool. There was therefore no statutory requirement that a PCP actually apply to others.

There are limits, however, to the extent to which S.19 EqA permits consideration **16.95** of a hypothetical pool. In the religious discrimination case of Eweida v British Airways plc 2010 ICR 890, CA (discussed under 'Defining "disadvantage" – solitary disadvantage' above), Lord Justice Sedley stated that, although indirect discrimination permits consideration of how a PCP *would* affect people sharing the same protected characteristic as the claimant, this did not mean that a claimant may construct an entirely hypothetical peer group to whom the disadvantage is to be attributed. In some cases it will be relatively simple, and in keeping with the purpose of the legislation, to aggregate a solitary employee with others known to have the same characteristic, and known to be potentially affected in the same way – a lone female worker, for example, could claim indirect discrimination on the basis of the way a particular policy would affect a hypothetical group of female staff. However, Sedley LJ considered that it would be 'forensically difficult, even impossible' to do the same for a solitary believer whose fellow believers, if they existed, might accord different degrees of importance to the same manifestation of faith.

It has been argued that the revised wording allows PCPs to be challenged at an early stage before they have a significant impact. The type of circumstances that might form the basis of a challenge to such prospective disadvantage include those that occurred in Meade-Hill and anor v British Council 1995 ICR 847, CA. That case concerned a challenge to a general mobility clause in a contract of employment requiring certain employees to work in any part of the United Kingdom. The claimant argued that this clause amounted to indirect sex discrimination because, as a married woman earning less than her husband, she would have found it difficult to move her place of work. Even though the mobility clause had not been invoked against the claimant, the Court of Appeal held that the clause was indirectly discriminatory because a greater proportion of women than men were secondary earners and therefore less able or willing to move and that the clause was to her detriment. The Meade-Hill case has been discussed in some detail at other points in this chapter – see the sections 'Provision, criterion or practice', under 'Identifying the time a PCP is applied – anticipatory discrimination' and '"Particular disadvantage"', under 'Defining "disadvantage" – anticipatory disadvantage' above.

421

16.100   The following examples demonstrate this:

EXAMPLE 1	EXAMPLE 2
TOTAL POOL = 10,000	TOTAL POOL = 20
Men = 9,000 Women = 1,000	Men = 12 Women = 8
Number of men who can comply with requirement = 700	Number of men who can comply with requirement = 9
Number of women who can comply with requirement = 50	Number of women who can comply with requirement = 7
Proportion of men who can comply with requirement = 7.7%	Proportion of men who can comply with requirement = 75%
Proportion of women who can comply with requirement = 5%	Proportion of women who can comply with requirement = 87.5%

When very large total populations in a pool are compared, and the gender ratio of the pool is more or less equal, then small percentage differences between the proportions of men and women that can comply with a PCP can mask considerable differences in the absolute numbers of men who can comply compared with women. If 2 per cent of men can comply and 1 per cent of women, then twice as many men as women can comply (assuming the total number of men and women in the pool to be roughly equal). If the pool is a large one – say, the economically active national population – then a difference of just +1 per cent of a total population of 15 million men would mean 150,000 more men being able to comply than women.

16.101   By contrast, if the total pool is small – say, comprising only 16 persons equally divided between men and women – then if 62.5 per cent of the men can comply with the PCP in question but only 37.5 per cent of the women, this means that in actual figures five men and three women can comply. The 25 per cent difference between the proportions of men and women who can comply may seem substantial. Yet it would only take one of the men who can comply to leave and one woman who is capable of complying to be recruited for the differential impact to be entirely eradicated.

All this demonstrates how important it is for tribunals to look behind the actual percentage differences to determine the true story. In doing so, it is permissible for tribunals to call upon their common knowledge and experience: see under 'Judicial notice of particular disadvantage' below.

16.102   **Should focus be on advantaged or disadvantaged groups?** In the earlier cases, such as R v Secretary of State for Education ex parte Schaffter (above), the courts only looked at the advantaged groups of men and women (i.e. those who *could* comply with a PCP) as a percentage of the whole pool and compared those figures. In later cases, it was accepted that it may be instructive to look at the disadvantaged groups as well (i.e. those who could *not* comply with a PCP)

424

as a percentage of the whole pool and compare those figures with each other. This led to a debate as to whether the focus of the comparison should be on the advantaged or disadvantaged groups (the 'qualifiers' or 'non-qualifiers').

This debate became the central focus of the Rutherford litigation as the case progressed through the courts. In that case two male claimants had been dismissed by their (different) employers at the ages of 67 and 73 respectively. They brought employment tribunal claims for unfair dismissal and redundancy payments but came up against the statutory upper age limit contained in Ss.109(1)(b) and 156(1)(b) of the Employment Rights Act 1996 (ERA). These used to bar employment tribunals from hearing such claims if, at the date of dismissal, the employee had attained the 'normal retiring age' (NRA) for the job or the statutory default retirement age of 65. They argued that excluding them from these payments, which constituted 'pay' for the purposes of the Equal Pay Act 1970 (now replaced by the pay discrimination provisions of the EqA), was discrimination contrary to the principle of 'equal pay for equal work' enshrined in Article 141 of the EC Treaty (now Article 157 of the Treaty on the Functioning of the European Union) because the material reason for the difference in pay – the statutory bar – indirectly discriminated against men. In the absence of objective justification, the relevant legislation should be disapplied and their claims allowed to proceed.

16.103 The employment tribunal ruled that it had jurisdiction to entertain the claims as the upper age exclusion was indirectly discriminatory against men and was not objectively justifiable. Following the decision of Mr Justice Lindsay in Harvest Town Circle Ltd v Rutherford 2001 IRLR 599, EAT, the case was remitted to the tribunal, which, when once again assessing disparate impact, chose to focus on the disadvantaged groups by confining the pool for comparison to those who could not comply with the requirement to be under 65 in order to claim unfair dismissal. This approach was not approved when the matter came before the EAT a second time (under the name Secretary of State for Trade and Industry v Rutherford and ors (No.2) 2003 IRLR 858, EAT). There, the EAT held that the tribunal had erred in focusing on the disadvantaged groups in the labour force aged over 65, rather than on those who qualified for statutory unfair dismissal and redundancy rights and who were under 65. The disadvantaged group in 2001 between the ages of 65 and 79 comprised 190,500 men and 115,200 women, whereas there was no significant difference (98.88 per cent of men and 99.0 per cent of women) between the proportions of men and women under 65 who qualified. According to Mr Justice Wall, the wider pool (which consisted of the qualifiers or advantaged group) unequivocally showed that there was no disparate impact. In his opinion, the figures for the disadvantaged group were very small and in 'borderline country', with the result that the disadvantaged group represented an unsound basis on which to find disparate impact.

425

The case went to the Court of Appeal, which rejected the claimants' argument that the primary focus in indirect discrimination cases is on the disadvantaged rather than on the advantaged group. The Court of Appeal explained that concentration on the disadvantaged group can lead to seriously misleading results, especially in cases where most people in the pool are advantaged. Lord Justice Mummery gave the following example: where 99.5 per cent of men and 99 per cent of women can comply with a PCP, if the focus is shifted to the proportions of men and women who cannot comply (i.e. 1 per cent of women and 0.5 per cent of men) the result would be that twice as many women as men cannot comply with the requirement. In Mummery LJ's opinion, this 'would not be a sound or sensible basis for holding that the disputed requirement, with which the vast majority of both men and women can comply, had a disparate impact on women'.

16.104 Unfortunately, a conclusive opinion on the issue of where the focus should be when assessing disparate impact was not delivered when the claimants appealed further to the House of Lords – Rutherford and anor v Secretary of State for Trade and Industry (No.2) 2006 ICR 785, HL. Their Lordships unanimously held that the upper age exclusion on unfair dismissal and redundancy rights in the ERA was not indirectly discriminatory against men. However, they reached this conclusion on different grounds, meaning, as Lord Walker acknowledged, that it was not possible to extract 'a single easily stated principle' from the other four opinions by which employment tribunals could be guided in the future. The speeches of Lords Walker, Nicholls, and Rodger do, though, lend some support (even though they are obiter on the particular point and thus not binding) to the view that the primary focus in most cases should be on an advantage-led approach to statistical comparisons. Lord Walker, whose judgment is the most fully reasoned, advocated precisely this approach while noting that there may be circumstances in which some element of 'disadvantage-led' analysis might be helpful. Even so, he stressed that the more extreme the majority of the advantaged in the relevant pool, the more difficult it will be to pay much attention to the result of a 'disadvantage-led' approach.

Lord Walker went on to say that he could imagine some improbable cases in which a disadvantage-led approach would serve as an alert to the likelihood of objectionable discrimination. If, for example, in a pool of 1,000 persons the advantaged 95 per cent were split equally between men and women, but the disadvantaged 5 per cent were all women, the very strong disparity of disadvantage would make it a special case, and the fact that the percentages of the advantaged were not greatly different (100 per cent men and 90.5 per cent women) would not be decisive. But this was not the case here. The proportion for the disadvantaged group (men to women) was 1.44:1, whereas the proportion for the advantaged was 1:1.004. The latter figure did not reveal a significant disparity between men and women, and the former did not reveal such an extraordinary disparity as to make it necessary to resile from focusing on the advantaged group.

Lord Nicholls found no evidence of indirect sex discrimination in the statistics **16.105** either. However, he was silent on whether he favoured an 'advantage-led' or 'disadvantage-led' approach when determining whether there was indirect sex discrimination. In a brief judgment he looked at both groups and concluded that there was no disparate effect on men, and for this reason dismissed the appeal. Rather confusingly, he then stressed that this issue was explored more fully by Lord Walker and implicitly appeared to endorse Lord Walker's judgment.

Lord Rodger stated that he did not consider the issue of statistics as they were not relevant to the issue of indirect discrimination in this case, but that if they had been he would have placed the emphasis on those who could comply with the preconditions for having rights to unfair dismissal compensation and redundancy pay – namely, the advantaged group.

Although the ruling of the Court of Appeal and the obiter views of three of **16.106** their Lordships in the House of Lords focus the comparison exercise on the advantaged group, it should always be borne in mind that there is no one-size-fits-all approach to assessing disparate impact. This was made clear in Grundy v British Airways plc 2008 IRLR 74, CA (an equal pay case). There, the key question was whether a tribunal had carried out an inappropriate analysis of disparate impact when concluding that the genuine material factor relied upon by the employer – namely, historical pay arrangements – had an adverse disparate impact on women and thus fell to be objectively justified. The Court of Appeal, having trawled through all of the relevant case law, including Rutherford, held that it had not. In the circumstances of the case, the employment tribunal had been entitled to focus on those disadvantaged by the arrangements in question – a group in which women outnumbered men by 14 to one. There was, in Lord Justice Sedley's view (with which the other members of the Court agreed), no legal principle that tribunals must always focus on the advantaged group.

It is difficult to know where all this case law leaves tribunals on the issue of how to assess disparate impact. It appears that one method of comparison is not appropriate in all cases, but that in most cases the focus will be on the advantaged groups, especially where the statistics are conclusive. Other comparisons, however, should not be ruled out, including looking at the disadvantaged groups, especially bearing in mind that figures can be misleading when applied to small pools – see, for example, the discussion of misleading figures under 'Looking behind the percentage differences' above. Interestingly, the EHRC Employment Code seems to support a primarily disadvantage-led approach (see para 4.21), but we would argue that this does not override the principles established by the relevant case law.

427

In general, tribunals may find the guidance given in Harvest Town Circle Ltd v Rutherford (above) of some assistance. According to Mr Justice Lindsay in that case, there will be some cases where, on the statistics, a disparate impact is so obvious that a look at numbers alone or proportions alone will suffice. However, it will never be wrong for a tribunal to look at more than one form of comparison, if only to confirm that the case remains as obvious as it had first appeared. Moreover, if there is any doubt as to the obviousness of the case, the tendency should always be to look at a second or further form of comparison. Thus in less obvious cases it will be proper for the tribunal to look not merely at proportions, as proportions alone can be misleading, but also at numbers, and to look at both disadvantaged and non-disadvantaged groups and even to the respective proportions in the disadvantaged groups expressed as a ratio of each other. Finally, after looking in detail at such figures as should have been laid before it, the tribunal in less obvious cases must then stand back and, assimilating *all* the figures, judge whether the apparently neutral PCP in issue has a disparate impact that could fairly be described as considerable or substantial.

16.107 **National statistics.** National statistics were commonly used to establish disparate impact under the old tests for indirect sex and race discrimination and they continue to be relevant under the more recent test of 'particular disadvantage'. The EHRC Employment Code confirms that 'it may... be possible to use national or regional statistics to throw light on the nature and extent of the particular disadvantage' (para 4.12). In securing the necessary statistical evidence, a good source of official statistics for the general working population is the Labour Market Statistics published by the Office for National Statistics (ONS). A summary of the latest statistical data is available without charge on the internet in the form of releases (www.ons.gov.uk). Other sources of official statistics about the working population include the Department for Business, Innovation and Skills website (www.bis.gov.uk), which periodically publishes the Workplace Employment Relations Study – a national survey of people at work. The last such survey was conducted in 2004 and the next is due to be completed by mid-2012. Information is also available on the Equality and Human Rights Commission's website (www.equalityhumanrights.com).

National statistics have been relied upon frequently by claimants in indirect sex discrimination cases concerning part-time and flexible working. Statistics published by the Equal Opportunities Commission – which has since been merged into the EHRC – were relied upon in Trainer v Penny Plain Ltd ET Case No.2510846/05. There, in accepting the argument that a PCP to work full time has a disparate impact on women, the tribunal took into account the EOC's 'Investigation into Flexible and Part-Time Working' (2005), which found that 'flexible and part-time working is female dominated'. Similarly, in Clarke v Telewest Communications plc ET Case No.1301034/04, a claimant was entitled to rely on statistics compiled by the EOC to successfully argue that a requirement that she work evenings and weekends indirectly discriminated against her. The

428

first set of statistics in question was published in 'Facts about Women and Men in Great Britain 2004', and supported the widely accepted conclusion that a greater proportion of women in the workforce work part time owing to their childcare responsibilities. The second report, 'Evening and Weekend Working – 2000 and 2004', highlighted that in 2004 11 per cent of female employees with dependent children worked evenings and weekends in their main job, compared with 18 per cent of male employees with dependent children.

Workplace statistics. Where the appropriate pool comprises employees within **16.108** a particular organisation or a part thereof, workplace statistics are likely to be relevant in establishing indirect discrimination. The claimant may be dependent upon the employer for the supply of relevant statistical data. A particularly useful source of evidence will be data deriving from monitoring undertaken by the employer of its own workforce, where such information is gathered. To obtain the relevant data, it will often be necessary to make use of the written answers or statutory questionnaire procedures, or to apply to the tribunal for an order for disclosure. For further details, see IDS Employment Law Handbook, 'Employment Tribunal Practice and Procedure' (2006), Chapter 6.

An example of the use of workplace statistics is the race discrimination case of Perera v Civil Service Commission and anor 1982 IRLR 147, EAT. There, the claimant was prevented from gaining promotion to the grade of Higher Executive Officer with the Civil Service because he was over the age limit for applications of 32. The claimant's point was that the age limit of 32 operated to the detriment of people of Asian origin because many of them did not come to the United Kingdom until adulthood and thus might already be too old. He produced statistical evidence to show that there were no Executive Officers (from whose ranks promotions to Higher Executive Officer were made) of Asian origin under the age of 32 in the particular VAT office where he worked. The Commission also made available evidence showing a similar picture at two other London VAT offices. An employment tribunal held that this evidence was not sufficient to show that a smaller number of Asian than white Executive Officers in the *whole* Civil Service could comply with the age limit. The EAT allowed the claimant's appeal because, it said, even though the evidence before the tribunal was unsatisfactory and drawn from a very small sample, it would be 'most undesirable' if elaborate statistics were needed to prove a case (because of the time and expense involved). As in Greater Manchester Police Authority v Lea 1990 IRLR 372, EAT, an important factor in the EAT's decision was that the Commission had not put forward any evidence suggesting that the statistics before the tribunal were anything other than typical of the whole Civil Service.

When considering disparate impact, tribunals need to assure themselves that **16.109** the statistics they are considering are not merely fortuitous or short term – this requirement follows from the decision of the ECJ in the equal pay case of Enderby v Frenchay Health Authority and anor 1994 ICR 112, ECJ. Where the

429

pool is very small – a few employees at a relatively small workplace, for example – then figures taken solely from the pool may present an inaccurate picture and tribunals should be prepared to look externally for guidance. In White v Timbmet Ltd EAT 1125/99 the employment tribunal found that the correct pool was the employer's telemarketing department, comprising four workers: the claimant, two other women, and one man. With the exception of the claimant, everyone in the pool was able to comply with the requirement to work full time. The tribunal was loath to conclude on the basis of these figures that a considerably smaller proportion of women than men in the pool could work full time and consequently found that there was no indirect sex discrimination. On appeal, the EAT had no such qualms, holding that the tribunal should not have restricted its assessment to an analysis of the way in which the numbers fell within the particular pool because the pool was too small and the alteration of one person's circumstances would have fundamentally altered the figures. Instead, the tribunal should have considered statistics nationally, and its knowledge of women in society generally, as well as the statistics within the pool.

Another example of a tribunal looking beyond the statistics pertaining to a small pool is Venkatasamy v Dhillon and Co Solicitors ET Case No.3203381/04 – a case decided under the 2001 test of indirect sex discrimination. The claimant was a 'fee earner' in the immigration department of a solicitors' firm and was dismissed when she made it clear that she had no option but to leave work at 2.30 pm each day to collect her son from school. A tribunal found that the employer had applied a PCP that fee earners work until 5 pm. The selected pool for comparison was made up of eight fee earners (five women and three men). All the men (100 per cent) and four of the women (80 per cent) could comply with the PCP. In holding that such disproportionate impact was more than merely fortuitous, the tribunal took into account 2003 statistics from the Equal Opportunities Commission showing that 82 per cent of part-time workers are women and that more women with children work part time than men. The tribunal also applied its judicial knowledge to conclude that the PCP to work until 5 pm would be to the detriment of a considerably larger proportion of women than of men.

16.110 **Degree of disparate impact required.** Under the original tests for indirect sex and race discrimination, once the relative proportions of individuals who were able to comply with the requirement or condition within the selected pool had been ascertained, the final step in determining the extent of any disparate impact was to decide whether the proportion of the claimant's group who could comply was 'considerably smaller' than the proportion of the comparator group who could comply. Similarly, following the 2001 amendments to the SDA, the relevant PCP had to be to the detriment of a 'considerably larger' proportion of women than of men. The 'considerably larger/smaller' proviso ensured that the degree of disparate impact resulting from the application of the PCP was not merely marginal but was significant and substantial. It also ensured that discrimination was shown to be inherent in the PCP being applied rather than being simply the product of unreliable statistics or mere chance.

As we have already seen, the current definition of indirect discrimination does not adopt the 'considerably larger/smaller' terminology. Nevertheless, where statistical evidence is used as a means of demonstrating that the claimant's group is placed at a 'particular disadvantage', the old case law may still provide useful guidance as to the degree of disparate impact required to establish a claim. The EHRC Employment Code states that, when deciding whether the protected group experiences a 'particular disadvantage' in comparison with others, 'whether a difference is significant will depend on the context, such as the size of the pool and the numbers behind the proportions. It is not necessary to show that the majority of those within the pool who share the protected characteristic are placed at a disadvantage' (para 4.22).

The old case law did not lay down a benchmark as to what percentage difference **16.111** counted as considerably larger or smaller. It depended on the facts and circumstances of the case. Principles such as the 'four fifths' rule adopted by the US Equal Employment Opportunity Commission have not been favoured in UK or European courts – see McCausland v Dungannon District Council 1993 IRLR 583, NICA. Ultimately, whether one figure is considerably smaller or larger than another is a question of fact for the tribunal to decide and, provided no error of law has been made and the decision is not perverse, it is not readily interfered with on appeal – see London Underground Ltd v Edwards (No.2) 1999 ICR 494, CA. There, Lord Justice Potter said that the wide variety of different situations applicable in the employment field made it impossible to come up with a figure which could be applied in all cases. 'If a figure were to be selected... it would be likely to vary according to the context, and in particular as between a case where the requirement or condition is applied on a national scale in respect of which reliable supporting statistics are available and those where it is applied in relation to a small firm or an unbalanced workforce where the decision may have to be made on far less certain evidence and to a large degree upon the basis of the... tribunal's own experience and assessment as applied to such figures as are available.'

The meaning of 'considerable' should not be exaggerated, according to the House of Lords in R v Secretary of State for Employment ex parte Seymour-Smith and anor (No.2) 2000 ICR 244, HL. However, in Harvest Town Circle Ltd v Rutherford 2001 IRLR 599, EAT, Mr Justice Lindsay held that it would be a mistake to conclude that anything that was merely not 'trivial or de minimis' is sufficient. He also said that 'those seeking a simple and universal touchstone' as to what could be regarded as a considerable or substantial disparity must be disabused, and that 'it would be a mistake... to think that any disparity of less than 8.5 per cent [which the ECJ and House of Lords thought

431

insufficient in the Seymour-Smith case] must necessarily be found not substantial or not considerable'. And in London Underground Ltd v Edwards (No.2) (above), Potter LJ said that, while a percentage difference of no more than 5 per cent or thereabouts is not inherently likely to amount to a considerable disparity, such a conclusion need not inevitably follow in every case. Thus, a disparity of 5.1 per cent was enough to establish disparate adverse impact on women in Chief Constable of West Midlands Police v Blackburn and anor 2008 ICR 505, EAT (an equal pay claim about special payments for 24/7 working). There, statistical evidence showed that 96.6 per cent of men could comply with a requirement to be available 24/7, compared to only 91.5 per cent of women. (Note that the Blackburn case subsequently went to the Court of Appeal, which held that the special payments were objectively justified – see Chapter 17, 'Indirect discrimination: objective justification', under 'Proportionality – asessing the alternatives'.)

16.112 An even smaller percentage difference was accepted as being 'considerable' in Chief Constable of Avon and Somerset Constabulary v Chew EAT 503/00 – a case based on the original SDA test for indirect discrimination. There, the employment tribunal came to the conclusion that of 2,581 men and 453 women, all except one man and ten women could comply with the shift pattern required by the company – in other words 99.96 per cent of men and 97.7 per cent of women, a difference of 2.26 per cent. The tribunal held that there was a sufficient disparate impact on women and the EAT refused to intervene. In so ruling, the EAT accepted that the percentage difference of 2.26 in the instant case did not amount, on the face of it, to a sufficiently disparate effect. However, it held that the tribunal had been correct to adopt a flexible approach and to have regard to factors other than the identified percentage difference. The tribunal had been entitled to note that the statistics included the bare minimum number of officers who could not comply with the condition. Furthermore, it had been entitled to conclude that an inherently likely effect of the condition was that it would disadvantage officers with childcare responsibilities, and to note that the overwhelming burden of such responsibilities falls on women.

This case is a good illustration of the idea, set out later by Lindsay J in Harvest Town Circle Ltd v Rutherford (above), that more than one form of comparison may be appropriate. As noted previously, his Lordship specifically sanctioned an approach of looking 'not merely at proportions, as proportions alone can be misleading, but also at numbers' in circumstances where the tribunal senses that the headline statistics may not present a reliable picture. Also, although the tribunal in Chew did not appear to have explicitly considered this, the figures in that case provide a good illustration of how looking at both disadvantaged and non-disadvantaged groups may help to show up a less obvious disparity. While the difference between 99.96 per cent and 97.7 per cent seems relatively minor, the difference between 0.04 per cent and 2.3 per cent (the disadvantaged groups) is huge when those figures are looked at relative to each other (as recommended by the High Court and Northern Ireland Court of Appeal in R v Secretary of State for Education ex parte Schaffter 1987 IRLR 53, QBD, and McCausland v Dungannon District Council 1993 IRLR 583, NICA, respectively) rather than relative to the whole pool.

A similar multi-faceted approach was adopted in London Underground Ltd v **16.113** Edwards (No.2) (above), where, although only one female driver within the pool for comparison was actually disadvantaged by the requirement to move to rostered working, the Court of Appeal deemed it appropriate for the tribunal to take account of the number of male drivers in the pool (2,023) – none of whom was disadvantaged by the requirement – contrasted with the low number of female drivers (21). The comparatively small size of the female component indicated both that it was difficult or unattractive for women to work as train operators and that the percentage of women unable to comply was likely to be a minimum rather than a maximum figure. The Court also took into account the effect any amendment to the statistics would have in the event that they were either inaccurate or incomplete, The addition of one extra woman unable to comply with the PCP would raise the proportion of women who could not comply to 10 per cent whereas the addition of one further male employee who could not comply would scarcely alter the proportional difference at all.

Expert and other evidence   16.114
So far we have focused on the statistical approach to obtaining evidence of particular disadvantage, which is familiar from the extensive body of case law on the original definitions of indirect discrimination in the SDA and RRA. If statistical evidence is unlikely to be available, however, claimants alleging indirect discrimination will need to draw on other sources for evidence of particular disadvantage. Expert evidence may assist: tribunals should also be prepared to hear evidence from 'ordinary' witnesses, such as the employer's HR representatives, who can speak to the effect of policies, criteria and practices in a particular workplace.

In its response to the consultation on the Equality Bill, the Government said that it believed 'the concept of "a particular disadvantage"… opens up the possibility of expert evidence or witness evidence being used rather than detailed statistical analysis to show particular disadvantage to a particular group of people. This is important for strands such as sexual orientation and religion or belief, where reliable statistics are not available, and where there are issues of privacy involved in gathering data which might provide statistics.' The EHRC Employment Code reflects this view, stating: '[A] statistical analysis may not always be appropriate or practicable, especially when there is inadequate or unreliable information, or the numbers of people are too small to allow for a statistically significant comparison. In this situation, the employment tribunal may find it helpful for an expert to provide evidence as to whether there is any disadvantage and, if so, the nature of it. There are other cases where it may be

433

useful to have evidence (including, if appropriate, from an expert) to help the employment tribunal to understand the nature of the protected characteristic or the behaviour of the group sharing the characteristic – for example, evidence about the principles of a particular religious belief' (paras 4.13–4.14).

16.115 An example of a religious discrimination case in which the claimant relied on expert evidence is Chatwal v Wandsworth Borough Council EAT 0487/10, discussed in the section 'Indirect discrimination in context', under 'Indirect religion or belief discrimination – group disadvantage in indirect religious discrimination claims' below. C was an Amritdhari Sikh and a member of a particular branch known as Guru Nanak Nishkam Sewak Jatha ('GNNSJ'), which was a revivalist organisation within the broader Sikh community. He refused to participate in a kitchen-cleaning rota, claiming that his religious beliefs forbade him from touching meat or meat products. There was nothing in the Sikh scriptures to prohibit the touching of meat and the constitution of the GNNSJ was silent on the matter. An employment tribunal concluded that C had not discharged the burden of showing group disadvantage but the EAT overturned this decision and remitted the case to the tribunal. The tribunal had found that there was no statistical material to support C's claim and, in those circumstances, it was crucial to deal with the other evidence as to whether there were sufficient others of the same belief as C to constitute a 'group'. In particular, the tribunal had heard evidence from two experts on Sikh religious matters, and C had also produced letters from an Amritdhari Sikh official and a GNNSJ member supporting his claim. This evidence should have been properly addressed.

16.116 **Judicial notice of particular disadvantage**

Judicial notice is the name given to common knowledge that is accepted as such by a court or tribunal, without need for formal proof. It is a familiar concept in indirect sex discrimination, where it is accepted that, for example, policies that affect those with childcare responsibilities disproportionately affect women – for further details, see under 'Indirect discrimination in context – indirect sex discrimination' below. The EHRC Employment Code notes that some PCPs are intrinsically liable to disadvantage a group with a particular protected characteristic, and that in some cases the link between the protected characteristic and the disadvantage might be obvious; for example, dress codes create a disadvantage for some workers with particular religious beliefs (paras 4.10–4.11).

Even under the old tests of indirect discrimination, claimants were not necessarily expected to adduce statistical proof of disparate impact. This was particularly true where the effect of the application of a PCP necessitated an examination of social attitudes and practices. In London Underground Ltd v Edwards (No.2) 1999 ICR 494, CA, Lord Justice Potter remarked, when rejecting the employer's contention that the employment tribunal should have confined itself to a consideration of the evidence of adverse effect on the members of the pool in question, that: '[A] tribunal does not sit in blinkers. Its members are selected in order to have a degree of knowledge and expertise in the industrial field generally. The high preponderance of single mothers having care of a child is a matter of common knowledge.'

In the context of indirect sex discrimination, judicial notice has been taken of **16.117** the following:

- that women aged in their mid-20s to mid-30s are likely to be more responsible for childcare than men – Price v Civil Service Commission and anor 1978 ICR 27, EAT

- that a higher proportion of women than men work part time – Home Office v Holmes 1984 IRLR 299, EAT

- that women are more likely to be secondary earners – Meade-Hill and anor v British Council 1995 ICR 847, CA.

The willingness of the courts to dispense with formal proof of the general facts mentioned above is commonplace in cases where the PCP in question has been applied to a large pool (such as the workforce as a whole, or a sector of industry). It might be thought that where the PCP is applied to a much narrower pool (such as a particular department within a company), tribunals would require more detailed statistical proof of adverse disproportionate impact. Much will depend on the particular PCP at issue and the reason why it is alleged to have a discriminatory impact on one sex or the other or whoever comprises the alleged disadvantaged/advantaged. There are, however, many examples of tribunals faced with small pools and inconclusive statistics taking judicial notice of 'common knowledge' about the position of, for example, women in society generally.

Advisers may also want to bear in mind the dangers of not putting any statistics **16.118** forward in cases involving less well tested waters and just relying on judicial notice. In Brymer v Essex Police ET Case No.3202894/01 – a case decided under the original SDA test of indirect discrimination – B claimed that she could not comply with a 24-hour shift system because she was a carer for dependent parents and that, accordingly, she had suffered indirect sex discrimination. B did not put forward any statistics in support of her claim, but instead asserted on the basis of London Underground Ltd v Edwards (No.2) (above) that the caring responsibilities of women were so well known that no additional proof was required. The employment tribunal did not feel able to find, based on a pooling of its knowledge and expertise, that significantly more women than men are carers, and made an award of wasted costs against her.

435

16.119 **Individual disadvantage**

The final step in making out a case of indirect discrimination (prior to consideration of objective justification) requires the claimant to show not only that the PCP at issue puts or would put persons with whom he or she shares the relevant protected characteristic at a particular disadvantage (as to which, see under 'Group disadvantage' above) but also that 'it puts, or would put, [the claimant] at that disadvantage' – S.19(2)(c) EqA. The necessity of showing individual disadvantage is a means of ensuring that the claimant has a direct interest in bringing the claim of indirect discrimination – in other words, that he or she has 'standing' (or locus standi) to bring the claim.

Under the above definition, the claimant has to prove that the PCP puts (or would put) him or her at '*that* disadvantage', i.e. the *same* disadvantage as those others who share the relevant protected characteristic. This point was not spelt out under the original definition in the SDA or RRA. It is illustrated by McClintock v Department of Constitutional Affairs 2008 IRLR 29, EAT, a religion or belief case, in which the Appeal Tribunal held that a Christian Justice of the Peace who resigned from office following the rejection of his request to be excused from cases that might lead to the adoption of a child by a same-sex couple was not indirectly discriminated against on the ground of religion or belief. The relevant PCP was the requirement that magistrates honour the judicial oath, which involves adjudicating on any case that comes before them. One of the EAT's reasons for upholding the employment tribunal's rejection of the claim was that even if that PCP disadvantaged persons by reason of their religious or philosophical beliefs – and there was no evidence that it did – the claimant was unable to show that he had himself been disadvantaged for that reason. At no stage had he indicated that his objections were connected to his religion: rather, he stated that there was insufficient evidence for him to conclude that placements with same-sex couples were in children's best interests.

16.120 **Recruitment and 'access to benefit' cases.** In the context of recruitment and other cases involving denial of a benefit, case law suggests that there will be no personal disadvantage to the claimant if he or she does not genuinely want the job applied for or the benefit in question. In Keane v Investigo and ors EAT 0389/09 K, an accountant in her late forties, unsuccessfully applied for a number of junior accountancy roles for which she was overqualified and subsequently lodged claims of age discrimination. At the employment tribunal hearing, K's representative conceded that if K was found not to have been genuinely interested in the jobs she applied for, then she suffered no detriment or disadvantage when her applications for those jobs were rejected, even if the recruitment process potentially gave rise to discrimination on the ground of age. The tribunal dismissed K's claims, finding that there was no act that would constitute either direct or indirect age discrimination. It also found that these had not been genuine applications and so, in accordance with K's concession, this was an additional reason why the claims should fail. K appealed to the EAT against the tribunal's decision. She also sought to withdraw the concession in respect of detriment on the basis that her representative had made it without her consent.

The Appeal Tribunal, presided over by its then President, Mr Justice Underhill, held that there were no exceptional circumstances that would allow K to withdraw the concession made at the tribunal hearing. In any event, the concession was plainly right. The definition of direct discrimination requires some kind of 'less favourable' treatment of the claimant, while the definition of indirect discrimination requires the claimant to have been treated to his or her 'disadvantage'. Those elements are commonly and usefully referred to together as 'detriment'. An applicant who is not considered for a job in which he or she is not interested cannot in any ordinary sense of the word be said to have suffered a detriment – that is, to have been comparatively unfavourably treated (for the purpose of direct discrimination) or put at a disadvantage (for the purpose of indirect discrimination). The Keane case and another case in which the EAT reached a similar conclusion – Berry v Recruitment Revolution and ors EAT 0190/10 and others – are discussed further in Chapter 24, 'Recruitment', in the section 'Arrangements for deciding to whom to offer employment', under 'Advertisements – claimant must have genuine interest in job'.

Conditional disadvantage. In addition to covering claimants who are put at a particular disadvantage by the relevant PCP, the definition of indirect discrimination extends to claimants who *would be* put at such a disadvantage – S.19(2)(c) EqA. This reflects a 2008 amendment to the RRA, making it clear that the EqA protects a person who is deterred by a discriminatory PCP from seeking employment for which he or she is otherwise qualified. This was not previously clear in relation to protected characteristics other than race. The new wording does not, however, cover purely hypothetical situations, such as where an individual has no intention of seeking employment or is not qualified to undertake the job in question. This is because a person who had no intention of applying for a job, or was not otherwise qualified for it, would be unable to demonstrate a disadvantage – see Keane v Investigo and ors (above). **16.121**

Note that if no individual suffers actual disadvantage by the application of an indirectly discriminatory PCP, it may still be open to the Equality and Human Rights Commission to conduct an investigation into any discriminatory practices in accordance with its enforcement powers in Ss.20–24A of the Equality Act 2006, as amended by Schedule 26 to the EqA. For further details of these powers, see Chapter 37, 'Equality and Human Rights Commission'.

Indirect discrimination in context **16.122**

The preceding sections of this chapter explain the general principles of indirect discrimination law, which are applicable across all eight protected characteristics covered by the definition of indirect discrimination in S.19 EqA. Nevertheless,

437

each protected characteristic generates its own legal and factual issues. This section highlights some of the main themes specific to each of the relevant protected characteristics, with illustrations drawn from case law and the EHRC Employment Code. For further examples and detailed commentary, reference should be made to Chapter 24, 'Recruitment', and Chapter 25, 'Discrimination during employment'.

16.123 Indirect age discrimination

The original definition of indirect age discrimination, contained in Reg 3(1)(b) of the Employment Equality (Age) Regulations 2006 SI 2006/1031 ('the Age Regulations'), has been substantially re-enacted in the EqA. S.19 EqA requires a comparison to be drawn between people of different age groups to ascertain whether the relevant PCP puts the claimant's age group at a particular disadvantage. This follows from S.5(1), which states that a reference in the 2010 Act to a person who has the protected characteristic of age is 'a reference to a person of a particular age group', and a reference to persons who share that characteristic is 'a reference to persons of the same age group'. An 'age group' is 'a group of persons defined by reference to age, whether by reference to a particular age or to a range of ages' – S.5(2). In other words, whenever the Act refers to the protected characteristic of age, it means a person belonging to a particular age group.

In the context of indirect discrimination, there appears to be a large degree of flexibility in defining both the disadvantaged age group and the age group with which the comparison should be drawn. The Explanatory Notes accompanying the EqA state that an 'age group' would include, for example, 'over-50s' or '21-year-olds'. While a person aged 21 does not share the characteristic of age with 'people in their 40s', the Notes state that a person aged 21 and people in their 40s can share the characteristic of being in the 'under-50' age range (para 37). For further details, see Chapter 5, 'Age', under 'Protection under the Equality Act – definition of "age group"'.

16.124 The following are examples of employment policies that may fall foul of the prohibition on indirect age discrimination unless they can be objectively justified:

- an employer requires all employees to attain a certain level of physical fitness. This is potentially indirectly discriminatory against older workers, who, generally, are less likely to be physically fit than their younger colleagues

- an employer stipulates that job applicants must be prepared to work late or socialise after working hours. If members of a particular age group are demonstrably more likely to have, for example, childcare commitments, they could claim that this requirement indirectly discriminates against them on the ground of age (as well as sex, in the case of women)

438

- an employer adopts 'last in first out' (LIFO) or 'first in first out' (FIFO) as a redundancy selection criterion. This potentially indirectly discriminates against younger or older workers respectively.

Experience and qualifications. Cases brought under the Age Regulations have **16.125** provided numerous examples of indirect age discrimination claims arising from PCPs relating to experience or qualifications. In Rainbow v Milton Keynes Council ET Case No.1200104/07, for instance, an employer who advertised for teachers 'in the first five years of their career' committed an act of indirect age discrimination by failing to shortlist a 61-year-old job applicant. It was clear that people of her age were likely to have had far more teaching experience and, accordingly, to be put at a particular disadvantage. For further details of the case, see Chapter 24, 'Recruitment', in the section 'Arrangements for deciding to whom to offer employment,' under 'Advertisements – wording of advertisements'. Stipulating a minimum level of experience, on the other hand, is likely to discriminate against younger workers. For example, an employer seeks an employee with at least ten years' experience in the relevant sector. This is potentially indirectly discriminatory against workers aged, say, under 28, who will not have had the opportunity to gain the experience required.

It is commonplace for employers to ask job candidates to give examples from personal experience of how they have dealt with various situations. Although younger applicants are likely to have less work experience, the adoption of such a line of questioning is unlikely to amount to indirect age discrimination because younger candidates can give examples from other areas of their life – see Keen v Greater Manchester Fire and Rescue Service ET Case No.2405911/10, discussed in Chapter 24, 'Recruitment', in the section 'Arrangements for deciding to whom to offer employment', under 'Interviews – questions related to age and experience'.

In other cases, employers require that relevant experience must have been **16.126** gained within a specific timeframe. This is more likely to give rise to indirect discrimination. For example, in Foster v Stafford College ET Case No.1301144/07 F was made redundant from his post as a lecturer in computing. One of the criteria in the scoring matrix was 'recent and relevant business experience'. F and one other employee in the computing department, both aged over 55, scored no points for this criterion. F had taught for 21 years; prior to that, he had been in business for 17 years but that experience, not having been gained in the past 20 years, was ignored by his employer. Taking as the relevant pool the nine members of staff in the computing department, the tribunal found that the application of this criterion placed people in F's age group at a particular disadvantage. This amounted to indirect discrimination which, in the circumstances, was not justified.

Another common source of indirect age discrimination claims is where an employer requires employees to have a degree-level qualification. This is

439

potentially indirectly discriminatory against older workers, since far more school-leavers go to university now than did in the past, and has been the subject of several claims – see, for example, McCluskey v Edge Hill University ET Case No.2405206/07, discussed in Chapter 24, 'Recruitment', in the section 'Arrangements for deciding to whom to offer employment', under 'Qualifications – requirement to have a degree'.

16.127 The EHRC Employment Code gives a further example of indirect discrimination relating to qualifications: 'If an employer were to advertise a position requiring at least five GCSEs at grades A to C without permitting any equivalent qualifications, this criterion would put at a particular disadvantage everyone born before 1971, as they are more likely to have taken O level examinations rather than GCSEs. This might be indirect age discrimination if the criterion could not be objectively justified' (para 4.16). Similarly, an employer who requires job applicants to have a degree in media studies, a course that has only come to be widely offered in the last 25 years or so, would be likely to discriminate against older candidates.

16.128 **Proximity to retirement.** In some indirect age discrimination claims, the detriment complained of arises not simply from the claimant's age but from his or her proximity to retirement. For example, some employers operate a cut-off point for access to training set close to the retirement age, based on the assumption that older workers are soon to leave the world of work and are therefore less in need of training. Given the close relationship between age and retirement, such policies potentially give rise to indirect discrimination unless they can be objectively justified.

Indeed, it would seem to follow from the Supreme Court's decision in Homer v Chief Constable of West Yorkshire Police 2012 UKSC 15, SC, that any PCP that places the claimant's age group at a disadvantage on account of their proximity to retirement will constitute indirect age discrimination in that 'retirement' and 'age' are inextricably interlinked. In that particular case, H was ineligible for promotion to a senior grade of legal adviser to the police because he did not hold a law degree, which was an 'essential' requirement for the post. He argued that this requirement amounted to indirect age discrimination because his age – 61 – prevented him from completing a law degree before his impending compulsory retirement at 65 (which at the time was lawful). Although the employment tribunal held that H had been indirectly discriminated against, the EAT and the Court of Appeal overturned that decision, holding that the particular disadvantage of which he complained was not linked to his age but to his imminent withdrawal from the workforce. That factor, which left him without the necessary time to study for and obtain a law degree, meant that he was no more disadvantaged than any person in his comparator age group (those aged 30–59) would be who also stopped working before qualifying, on account of personal or family reasons, for example. Overturning that decision on appeal, the Supreme Court held that it was unrealistic to differentiate between age and retirement because they were interlinked. The general application of a PCP that in practice operates to the comparative disadvantage of a person approaching retirement age is indirectly discrimination on the ground of age. It was not right to equate leaving work for some other reason (such as family reasons) with impending compulsory retirement: in the former situation, a person generally has a choice in the matter, whereas someone facing compulsory retirement does not. The upshot was that the case was remitted to the employment tribunal to determine whether the indirect discrimination at issue was objectively justified.

The Supreme Court's decision in the Homer case is discussed further in the section '"Particular disadvantage"', under 'Defining "disadvantage" – is a causal link needed between protected characteristic and disadvantage?' above; in Chapter 17, 'Indirect discrimination: objective justification', under 'Background and overview – legislative history'; in 'Chapter 24, 'Recruitment', in the section 'Arrangements for deciding to whom to offer employment', under 'Qualifications – requirement to have a degree'; and in Chapter 25, 'Discrimination during employment', in the section 'Promotion, transfer and training', under 'Promotion – qualifications needed for promotion'. **16.129**

An analogous situation to the one that arose in the Homer case is where employers choose to cap redundancy payments by reference to the amount employees would have earned if they had worked until their normal retirement age, and this can have an impact on older employees. In Ormerod v Cummins Engine Company Ltd ET Case No.2508268/09 O had been employed as a production operator since 1974. He was made redundant in 2008 at the age of 63. His redundancy payment, according to his employer's agreement with the relevant unions, would have been £45,697, but the employer decided that in view of its economic situation, all redundancy payments would be capped at the level of the gross earnings that the employee would have received had he or she remained in employment until the normal retirement date. This meant that O's payment was capped at £24,461, further reduced by his notice payment to £17,497. An employment tribunal held that the employer's decision to cap redundancy payments amounted to a PCP which put persons of O's age group at a particular disadvantage. As such, it gave rise to indirect age discrimination which, on the facts, was not justified by reference to the aim of preventing older workers from receiving a windfall. A similar factual scenario arose in Kraft Foods UK Ltd v Hastie 2010 ICR 1355, EAT. In that case, however, the EAT held that the imposition of a cap was objectively justified. For further details, see Chapter 25, 'Discrimination during employment', under 'Benefits, facilities and services – enhanced redundancy schemes'.

Service-related benefits. Note that an exemption from the age discrimination provisions exists under para 10 of Schedule 9 to the EqA. In certain **16.130**

441

circumstances, this provision precludes an indirect age discrimination claim where length of service is used to determine a worker's benefits. It provides an absolute exemption for 'benefits' awarded with reference to a length-of-service criterion of up to five years, and allows a length-of-service criterion of over five years where the employer 'reasonably believes that doing so fulfils a business need'. In Rolls Royce plc v Unite the Union 2010 ICR 1, CA, the Court of Appeal held that a potentially indirectly discriminatory length of service criterion contained in a redundancy selection procedure fell within the equivalent exemption under the Age Regulations, as well as being objectively justified. For further details, see Chapter 31, 'Specific exceptions', under 'Age exceptions'.

16.131 Indirect disability discrimination

Prior to the entry into force of the EqA, there was no specific prohibition on indirect discrimination in relation to disability. Unlike the other equality enactments replaced by and consolidated into the EqA, the DDA did not cover indirect discrimination, although it did protect against disability-related discrimination.

The Government's decision to include disability among the protected characteristics in respect of which a claim of indirect discrimination can be brought was somewhat controversial. The change was originally proposed in an attempt to counter the effects of the House of Lords' decision in Mayor and Burgesses of the London Borough of Lewisham v Malcolm 2008 IRLR 700, HL, which had the effect of narrowing the scope of disability-related discrimination to the point that the DDA only outlawed conduct that could be characterised as direct discrimination. In response to concerns raised at the consultation stage of the Equality Bill, however, the Government subsequently decided to address the effects of Malcolm head-on by introducing a new form of disability discrimination, discrimination arising from disability, which is contained in S.15 EqA. This apparently leaves indirect disability discrimination with a limited role to play. For further details of the Malcolm case, see Chapter 20, 'Discrimination arising from disability', under 'Previous protection under the DDA'.

16.132 Some respondents to the Government's consultation exercise on the Equality Bill expressed the view that the complex nature of indirect discrimination is not suited to disability. In short, indirect discrimination is established where a policy that an employer applies puts those who share a protected characteristic at a particular disadvantage when compared with those who do not share it. S.6(3)(b) EqA clarifies that in relation to disability, a reference to persons who share a protected characteristic is a reference to persons who have the *same* disability. Accordingly, for indirect discrimination purposes, the 'particular disadvantage' must affect those who share the claimant's particular disability. This overlooks the fact that even people who have the same disability cannot easily be treated as a homogenous class, since the way in which the same disability manifests itself will vary from person to person, making it difficult for a disabled person to demonstrate a group disadvantage – see further under 'Particular disadvantage' below.

In any event, it is difficult to envisage a scenario where the application of an employer's policy would be indirectly discriminatory, but would not also be caught by either the new definition of discrimination arising from disability or the duty to make reasonable adjustments, which are substantially less complex than indirect discrimination, arguably easier to prove, and specifically tailored to the disability strand of discrimination – see Chapter 20, 'Discrimination arising from disability', under 'Overlap with indirect discrimination' for details. An example of indirect disability discrimination given in the original draft version of the EHRC Employment Code was that of an employee with depression who takes short-term absences over a number of years, and who is eventually dismissed (after reasonable adjustments have been made) in accordance with the employer's attendance management policy. However, this example – which is not reproduced in the final version of the Code – would potentially also amount to discrimination arising from disability under S.15 EqA.

16.133 One rare instance in which S.19 may be the only means of redress for a disabled claimant is where the individual has not brought his or her disability to the employer's attention. There is nothing in S.19 to indicate that the employer must be aware of the disability in order to be liable for indirect discrimination. By contrast, actual or constructive knowledge of the disability is required under both S.15 (discrimination arising from disability) and S.21 (failure to make reasonable adjustments) – see, respectively, S.15(2) EqA and para 20(1) of Schedule 8 to the Act. If, however, the employment tribunal finds that a PCP was not applied with the intention of discriminating against the claimant, it must not award compensation without first considering whether to make a declaration or a recommendation – S.124(4) and (5). In practical terms, therefore, a complaint under S.19 may provide only limited redress in this situation.

For these reasons, we envisage that few successful indirect disability discrimination claims will be brought, Indeed, we are unaware of any such claims to date. Below, we outline the potential application of S.19 in relation to disability and the considerations that arise in this context concerning the various elements of the statutory definition of indirect discrimination.

16.134 **Provision, criterion or practice.** In most disability cases involving allegations of indirect discrimination, the nature of the PCP applied is likely to be obvious. For instance, refusing to employ an individual who fails a physical capability test is the same thing as applying a criterion of a particular standard of physical capacity. Similarly, suspending an employee for offensive or violent conduct caused by a mental impairment can be characterised as the application of a disciplinary policy to that employee.

16.135 **Pool for comparison.** As with indirect discrimination claims generally, the pool for comparison in an indirect disability discrimination claim will depend on the facts of the case. The key is to identify a hurdle that has been placed in the way of the complainant and consider the range of persons – disabled and non-disabled – who come up against that hurdle. This will focus attention on the 'pool for comparison'. The next step is to consider whether more persons with the complainant's disability within the selected pool fall at the hurdle than do those without that disability.

When making the comparison, it is important to bear in mind that the claimant's group is restricted to those having the *same* disability. This is made clear by S.6(3) EqA, which provides that 'in relation to the protected characteristic of disability – (a) a reference to a person who has a particular protected characteristic is a reference to a person who has a particular disability; [and] (b) a reference to persons who share a protected characteristic is a reference to persons who have the same disability'. Thus, as the EHRC Employment Code notes at para 4.16: 'In relation to disability, [those with the particular protected characteristic] would not be disabled people as a whole but people with a particular disability – for example, with an equivalent level of visual impairment.' This means, by implication, that the 'others', by reference to whom advantage and disadvantage must be established, are necessarily a mixture of those without any disability and those with different disabilities. This may well skew the comparison, underlining concerns, raised by some respondents to the consultation on the Equality Bill, that the complex nature of indirect discrimination is not suited to disability.

16.136 The new definition of indirect discrimination, now re-enacted in S.19 EqA, allows for disadvantage to be established purely on the basis of a hypothetical comparison – the reference to a PCP that 'would put' a particular group at a disadvantage makes this clear. Accordingly, it is not necessary to prove that there are actual persons of a particular group on whom there is in fact a disproportionate impact – see '"Particular disadvantage"', under 'Group disadvantage – hypothetical group disadvantage' above. This principle is likely to be of particular importance to indirect disability discrimination, given that disabilities can be highly specific to the individual, and that the same disability can affect different people in different ways. A disabled employee will not be prevented from bringing a claim based on his or her employer's practices simply because there are no other disabled employees affected in the same way. However, the disabled employee will need to show some evidence that his or her disability, and its relevant effects, are, in fact, shared by others – see under 'Particular disadvantage' below.

444

Particular disadvantage. In the religious discrimination case of Eweida v **16.137** British Airways plc 2010 ICR 890, CA, Lord Justice Sedley noted that indirect discrimination can only be established where an ostensibly neutral PCP adversely affects an identifiable group. Solitary disadvantage, therefore, does not give rise to indirect discrimination. Although indirect discrimination permits consideration of how a PCP *would* affect people sharing the same protected characteristic as the claimant, in Sedley LJ's view, this did not mean that a claimant may construct an entirely hypothetical peer group to whom the disadvantage is to be attributed. In some cases it will be relatively simple, and in keeping with the purpose of the legislation, to aggregate a solitary employee with others known to have the same characteristic, and known to be potentially affected in the same way – a lone female worker, for example, could claim indirect discrimination on the basis of the way a particular policy would affect a hypothetical group of female staff. However, Sedley LJ considered that it would be 'forensically difficult, even impossible' to do the same for a solitary believer whose fellow believers, if they existed, might accord different degrees of importance to the same manifestation of faith.

This obstacle to establishing indirect discrimination is likely to loom large in disability cases. Given the broad definition of disability set out in S.6 and Schedule 1 to the EqA (explained in detail in Chapter 6, 'Disability'), very rare and person-specific conditions can be protected. Following the rationale in Eweida, a claimant with a very particular combination of impairments will need to show evidence that there are others who are potentially affected by the PCP complained of in the same way. The EHRC Employment Code notes that there may be circumstances where 'it may be useful to have evidence (including, if appropriate, from an expert) to help the employment tribunal to understand the nature of the protected characteristic or the behaviour of the group sharing the characteristic' – para 4.14. At the very least, the evidence will need to show that the claimant's disability is not unique. Sedley LJ's comment, noted above, that it would be forensically difficult to attribute a religious believer's personal convictions to a notional group of individuals and be confident that they would be affected in the same way by a particular PCP, applies equally to attributing a disabled person's particular symptoms to another and assuming that that other would be similarly disadvantaged.

This difficulty arises from the fact that people who have the same disability **16.138** cannot easily be treated as a homogenous class, since the way in which the disability manifests itself will vary from person to person. For example, multiple sclerosis can give rise to a variety of debilitating physical and mental symptoms, ranging from short-term memory problems to muscle weakness. An MS sufferer experiencing the former might be adversely affected by a policy relating to the way in which work is organised, but that same policy might have no impact on MS sufferers who are experiencing predominantly physical, rather than mental,

445

symptoms. Thus, it will not be self-evident that MS sufferers as a group face a particular disadvantage when compared to non-disabled people (or people with a different disability).

16.139 **Evidence.** Although the EHRC Employment Code makes it clear that statistics remain a useful tool in establishing indirect discrimination under the EqA, we consider that statistical evidence is likely to be of limited use in relation to disability. The approach set out in the Employment Code is much more appropriate to cases involving large numbers of potentially affected individuals, such as claims of indirect sex discrimination. As noted above, the effects of a disability can be particular to the individual, and so indirect disability discrimination claims will often involve very small numbers in the 'people with the PCP' group. Indeed, the Code makes it clear that 'a statistical analysis may not always be appropriate or practicable, especially when there is inadequate or unreliable information, or the numbers of people are too small to allow for a statistically significant comparison' – para 4.13.

If statistical evidence is unlikely to be available, claimants alleging indirect disability discrimination will need to draw on other sources for evidence of particular disadvantage. As noted above, the EHRC Employment Code indicates that expert evidence may help the tribunal understand the particular disability or the behaviour of the group with the same disability. Employment tribunals should also be prepared to hear evidence from 'ordinary' witnesses, such as the employer's HR representatives, who can speak to the effect of policies, criteria and practices in a particular workplace. Finally, tribunals should be prepared to take judicial notice of the fact that some PCPs are intrinsically liable to disadvantage a group with a particular protected characteristic, including those with a specific disability.

16.140 **Indirect gender reassignment discrimination**
Prior to the entry into force of the EqA, statutory protection against discrimination on the ground of gender reassignment was found in relevant amendments to the Sex Discrimination Act 1975 (SDA), which came into force on 1 May 1999. These amendments were prompted by the European Court of Justice's decision in P v S and anor 1996 ICR 795, ECJ, where it was held that discrimination on the basis of transsexualism comprised discrimination on the ground of sex/gender and was therefore unlawful under the EU Equal Treatment Directive (No.76/207) (now consolidated into the recast Equal Treatment Directive (No.2006/54)). Under the SDA there was no express provision extending the definition of *indirect* discrimination to transsexuals as such, although it was widely accepted that the general definition of indirect *sex* discrimination conferred the necessary protection on this particular protected group. For further details, see Chapter 7, 'Gender reassignment', under 'Protection under antecedent legislation'.

By contrast, the EqA explicitly prohibits indirect discrimination on the ground of gender reassignment. S.7(1) EqA provides that a person has the protected characteristic of gender reassignment 'if the person is proposing to undergo, is undergoing or has undergone a process (or part of a process) for the purpose of reassigning the person's sex by changing physiological or other attributes of sex' – see Chapter 7, 'Gender reassignment', under 'Protection under the Equality Act'. The definition of indirect discrimination in S.19 EqA specifically applies to all of the protected characteristics (with the exception of pregnancy and maternity – see under 'Relevant protected characteristics' above), which means that each of the relevant protected groups – including transsexuals – are now protected from indirect discrimination in their own right.

To date, we are unaware of any S.19 cases relating to the protected characteristic **16.141** of gender reassignment. However, the EHRC Employment Code contains the following example of indirect gender reassignment discrimination: 'An employer starts an induction session for new staff with an ice-breaker designed to introduce everyone in the room to the others. Each worker is required to provide a picture of themselves as a toddler. One worker is a transsexual woman who does not wish her colleagues to know that she was brought up as a boy. When she does not bring in her photo, the employer criticises her in front of the group for not joining in. It would be no defence that it did not occur to the employer that the worker [might] feel disadvantaged by the requirement to disclose such information' (para 4.24).

Some of the complaints that were previously framed as claims of direct discrimination on the ground of gender reassignment under the SDA might now, following the enactment of S.19 EqA, be pleaded instead (or in the alternative) as instances of indirect discrimination. For example, in Croft v Royal Mail Group plc 2003 ICR 1425, CA, the Court of Appeal held that an employer's denial of access to female lavatories to an employee who, as part of the process of male-to-female gender reassignment, was presenting herself as a woman in a 'real-life test' prior to surgery, did not constitute an act of direct discrimination contrary to S.2A SDA. The Court took the view that there must be a period during which the employer, taking into account the susceptibilities of other members of the workforce, is entitled to make separate arrangements for the employee. In this case, the employer was entitled, for a period of time, to rely on a unisex disabled lavatory as a sufficient facility for the claimant. A pre-operative transsexual employee faced with similar circumstances might now argue that the employer had applied a PCP whereby employees were required to use the toilet facilities appropriate to their biological sex, and that this requirement put transsexuals at a particular disadvantage. The outcome of such a case would be likely to turn on whether the PCP was objectively justified in the circumstances.

Absence from work. A transsexual person undergoing gender reassignment is **16.142** likely to have to take time off work to attend medical appointments and

447

undergo surgical procedures; or may be too ill to attend work where complications have arisen as a result of the gender reassignment treatment. S.16 EqA makes special provision for absences that arise because of gender reassignment. In short, it provides that an employer (A) discriminates against a transsexual employee (B) if, in relation to such an absence, A treats B less favourably than he would if B's absence was because of sickness or injury; or B's absence was for some other reason and it is not reasonable to treat B less favourably. For further details, see Chapter 22, 'Other forms of prohibited conduct', under 'Gender reassignment – absence from work'.

It is apparent that an employer who dismisses a transsexual person undergoing gender reassignment after, say, six months' absence will not fall foul of S.16 if he can show that an employee on sick leave (or, indeed, any other type of leave) for six months would also have been dismissed. Nevertheless, there may be scope in this situation for a claim of indirect discrimination under S.19. The individual might argue that the employer applied an apparently neutral PCP whereby six months' absence from work would result in dismissal; that this PCP puts individuals undergoing gender reassignment at a particular disadvantage owing to the greater likelihood of long-term absences arising in their case; and that the PCP cannot be objectively justified. It remains to be seen whether such an argument would be likely to succeed.

16.143 **Indirect marriage and civil partnership discrimination**
The protection previously afforded by S.3 of the Sex Discrimination Act 1975 (SDA) against indirect discrimination on the ground of a person's marital or civil partnership status has been carried over into S.19 EqA. S.8 EqA defines the protected characteristic of marriage and civil partnership, stipulating that a 'person has the protected characteristic of marriage and civil partnership if the person is married or is a civil partner'. A reference to a person who has that protected characteristic is to be read accordingly, and a reference to persons who share the characteristic is a reference to persons who are married or are civil partners – S.8(2). The Explanatory Notes accompanying the EqA give the example of a married man and a woman in a civil partnership, who would share the protected characteristic of marriage and civil partnership (para 45). For a detailed commentary on this protected characteristic, see Chapter 8, 'Marriage and civil partnership'.

In this context, the definition of indirect discrimination in S.19 EqA requires the application of an apparently neutral PCP which puts (or would put) married people or civil partners at a particular disadvantage; which puts (or would put) the claimant at that disadvantage; and which cannot be justified as a proportionate means of achieving a legitimate aim. It should be noted that, under the original wording in S.3 SDA, the relevant requirement or condition (now PCP) had to be such that the proportion of married persons who could comply with it was considerably smaller than the proportion of unmarried persons *of the same sex* who could do so. Thus, it was necessary to compare married men with unmarried men, and married women with unmarried women, when assessing disparate impact. The requirement for the comparator group to be of the same sex as the complainant was removed with effect from 5 December 2005. Therefore, in order to ascertain whether the PCP disadvantages married persons and civil partners, the tribunal will look at the impact the PCP has or would have on persons who are not married or civil partners *irrespective of their sex*. However, some of the cases discussed below pre-date the 2005 amendment and therefore take unmarried persons of the same sex as the complainant as the appropriate comparator group. This should be borne in mind when considering their impact. Similarly, many cases refer to a 'requirement or condition' imposed by the employer (as opposed to a PCP), which was the terminology used in the SDA until 12 October 2001.

Numerous cases concerning indirect discrimination against married persons **16.144** were brought under the SDA, and similar principles would apply to S.19 EqA. For example, in Leavers v Civil Service Commission ET Case No.2195/85 L (who was 34) answered an advertisement for a post in the Civil Service administrative grade which stipulated an age limit of 32. She asked for exemption from the age requirement on the ground that she had gained her degree relatively late in life because of childcare responsibilities. On being turned down as ineligible, she was told that she could apply for posts at the lower executive grade. L complained that she had been indirectly discriminated against on the ground of her marital status. Having found that the age limit was a requirement or condition (now a PCP), the employment tribunal focused on the appropriate pool for comparison. This, it held, comprised all 'economically active female graduates in Great Britain (under 60)'. It accepted the figures offered by L from the 1981 census that 37 per cent of all economically active married female graduates were under 32 whereas 62 per cent of unmarried woman graduates were under that age. Accordingly, the proportion of married women who could comply was considerably smaller than the proportion of unmarried women who could do so. The tribunal decided, however, that the age requirement was justifiable as it was necessary for the posts to be filled by high-flyers, and the years of training needed before such people could become diplomats meant that 32 was a reasonable age limit. (Although the tribunal noted that L had suffered a detriment by being considered for the executive grade only – as it offered a much lower salary and lesser status – this question was not relevant to the tribunal's decision.)

Policies restricting employment of couples. Some employers operate **16.145** workplace policies prohibiting the employment of married and/or cohabiting couples within the same workplace or management chain. Depending on their precise formulation and operation in practice, such rules are capable of giving rise to direct discrimination on the grounds of marriage, civil partnership or

449

sex. They may also indirectly discriminate on the ground of marital or civil partnership status unless they can be objectively justified as a proportionate means of achieving a legitimate aim.

For example, in Chief Constable of Bedfordshire Constabulary v Graham 2002 IRLR 239, EAT, G, an Inspector in the Bedfordshire Force, married a Chief Superintendent, who was also a member of the Force, in 1998. In May 1999, G was appointed to the post of Area Inspector of D Division, the Division which her husband commanded, but a month later she was told by the Chief Constable that her appointment had been rescinded. The Chief Constable stated that G's appointment was inappropriate since, by virtue of her relationship with her Division commander, she would not be a competent and compellable witness against her husband in criminal proceedings; her colleagues would find it difficult to bring a grievance against her; and it would be difficult for the Force to discipline her should she underperform. G complained to an employment tribunal that she had been discriminated against directly and indirectly on the ground of her marital status.

16.146 The employment tribunal upheld both claims. In relation to the indirect discrimination claim, it accepted G's argument that 65.9 per cent of married officers in the Bedfordshire Force could comply with the requirement or condition of not being in a cohabiting relationship with another member of the Force, whereas 94.2 per cent of unmarried officers could comply with it. The tribunal held that the proportion of married persons who could comply with the requirement or condition (now PCP) was considerably smaller than the proportion of unmarried officers who could comply, and that the imposition of the requirement or condition was not justified. Before the EAT, the Chief Constable argued, among other things, that the tribunal had erred in failing to identify precisely the requirement or condition that had been applied to the officer. The EAT gave short shrift to this approach, holding that the tribunal had been entitled to reach its conclusions, and dismissed the Chief Constable's appeal.

16.147 **Parental responsibilities.** Another situation in which an indirect marital discrimination claim may succeed is where the treatment has been prompted by the employer's attitude towards working parents. In Thorndyke v Bell Fruit (North Central) Ltd 1979 IRLR 1, ET, for example, T, a married woman with three young children, was interviewed for a position as collection supervisor. The director who interviewed her later wrote a rejection letter in which he said: 'I was unaware that you had three children and I do feel that with the job involvement necessary for this particular type of work it could prove difficult for you to run your home and also give full justice to the job.' T claimed successfully that she had been indirectly discriminated against on the ground of her marital status. The employment tribunal found that the director had clearly applied an implicit condition that an appointee should not have young or

450

dependent children. Such a condition was indirectly discriminatory on the ground of marital status, since a considerably smaller proportion of married women than of unmarried women could comply with it. T's inability to comply with the condition was to her detriment because she was denied the opportunity of competing on equal terms with other candidates for the job, and the employer had brought no evidence that the condition was justifiable irrespective of the marital status of the person to whom it was applied.

Similarly, in Hurley v Mustoe 1981 ICR 490, EAT, a married woman with four young children was dismissed on the first day of her employment as a waitress when the owner of the restaurant discovered she had children. The reason for this treatment was the employer's belief that women who had care of young children were 'unreliable'. A tribunal rejected her indirect marital discrimination claim. Although it accepted that more married than unmarried people had care of young children and so would find it more difficult to meet the employer's 'requirement or condition' of not having young children, the indirectly discriminatory effect of this requirement or condition was justifiable on the basis that it was necessary in the context of a small business. On appeal, the EAT overturned that decision on the basis that there was no evidence to support the tribunal's conclusion that the relevant condition was justifiable.

Need for statistical evidence. It should be noted that the Hurley case was **16.148** decided in 1981. The dramatic rise in the incidence of children born outside marriage since then may now make it difficult to show that a PCP of not having children has a disproportionate impact upon married people when compared with unmarried people. Figures compiled by the Office for National Statistics (ONS) show that in 2010 only 53 per cent of births in England and Wales occurred within marriage or civil partnership, compared with 61 per cent in 2000 and 88 per cent in 1980. The ONS also estimates that, of the 44.9 million adults usually resident in England and Wales in mid-2010, 48.2 per cent were married. The position is further complicated by the breakdown of marriages, which would tend to increase the proportion of unmarried people with dependent children, and by subsequent remarriages, which would have the opposite effect.

At the very least, it should not be simply assumed that the relevant PCP puts or would put persons who are married at a particular disadvantage when compared with persons who are not. Some evidence must be produced; claimants should not simply assume that such factors are self-evident. For example, in Kidd v DRG (UK) Ltd 1985 ICR 405, EAT, the employer at an all-female factory selected part-time workers for redundancy first. K was a married part-timer who claimed indirect discrimination on the ground of marital status. Her claim failed, however, when the EAT decided that the employment tribunal had been entitled to limit the pool for comparison to persons whose need to care for young children created a potential obstacle to full-time work. K had offered no evidence that married women in such a situation would be considerably less able to comply with the full-time requirement than unmarried women.

16.149 The views expressed in Kidd were echoed in Butler v Cannon Transport Ltd ET Case No.2500150/06. In that case a married man unsuccessfully alleged that his employer's requirement that he work a day shift without a guarantee of finishing in time to collect his son from school amounted to indirect discrimination on the ground of his marital status. The employment tribunal was of the opinion that the claimant had incorrectly merged two concepts: that married men are more likely than unmarried men to have children, and that married men are more likely than unmarried men to have responsibility for childcare. There was no evidence that the requirement to work beyond school leaving time would have a disproportionate impact on married men, and it was unsafe to make any assumptions as to disparate impact.

In Simpson v Whitehouse Group Ltd ET Case No.3202287/05, on the other hand, the claimant produced statistical evidence to support his claim. S, a married man with children, was employed as a local business development manager at a car dealership. His contract provided that he was employed to work from 9.30 am to 6 pm, Monday to Friday, and such additional hours as were reasonably necessary for the proper fulfilment of his duties. The company ran into financial difficulties and asked S to work either for half a day every Saturday or for the whole day on alternate Saturdays. He refused to do so and claimed indirect marital discrimination. The employment tribunal accepted statistical evidence that a considerably larger proportion of married men then unmarried men have children. The PCP relating to Saturday working would prevent those men from being able to spend time with their children at the weekend, and was therefore to their detriment (and would have been to S's detriment, had he complied with it). In the circumstances, however, the PCP was justified because it had been introduced in response to the employer's dire financial situation.

16.150 Statistical evidence was also an important factor in Gleed v Pricewaterhouse Coopers ET Case No.6400323/01. G, who had a young family, was rejected for a post as a management consultant, ostensibly because he did not have enough experience. The successful candidate was a married woman with no children who, in G's view, had less experience than him. G claimed that the employer had applied a requirement or condition (now a PCP) whereby the successful candidate should not have a young family, and that this amounted to indirect discrimination on the ground of marital status. The employer relied on statistics for the year 2000 showing that 40 per cent of children were born outside marriage and that 40 per cent of marriages broke down. On that basis, it argued that G's claim was that he suffered discrimination because he had children, not on the ground of marital status, and that this was outside the scope of the SDA. At a preliminary hearing, the employment tribunal held (without examining the merits) that it had jurisdiction to hear the claim. The statistics relied on by the employer showed that 60 per cent of children were born within marriage. Accordingly, the proportion of married people who could comply with a requirement of not having children was considerably smaller than the proportion of unmarried people who could comply.

Pool for comparison. It is worth noting that, in the context of childcare **16.151** responsibilities, the success or otherwise of an indirect marital discrimination claim will often turn on the identification of the pool for comparison. If the relevant pool is a national one, it may be easier to obtain supporting statistical evidence, whereas if the pool is confined to the particular workplace this may not be as straightforward. Two examples:

- **Sanger v The Great Trade Centre Ltd** ET Case No.2204324/00: S, a sales manager, took time off work when his wife and new baby were ill. When he returned to work his employer suggested that he accept a demotion to the post of sales executive until his domestic situation eased. This would allow him to take time off more easily and relieve the pressure on the company. S claimed he had suffered indirect discrimination on the ground of his marital status. However, the employment tribunal did not accept his argument that the employer had imposed a requirement or condition whereby sales managers must not have family responsibilities that might require them to take leave at short notice. It seemed more likely that the employer had simply put forward a proposal that would have enabled S to take unpaid leave more easily without causing problems to the business. Furthermore, even if a requirement or condition had been applied, an examination of the relevant pool disclosed no indirect discrimination. The business employed ten sales managers, of whom seven were married, two were cohabiting and one was single. Two of the married managers did not have dependent children; all the other managers did. Thus, there was no disparate impact on married men and it was purely fortuitous that S was married

- **Shepherd v Boots the Chemist Ltd** ET Case No.1700444/99: S worked as a shop assistant from 8 am to 1.30 pm, from Monday to Friday. The hours enabled her to take her 14-year-old daughter to school in the morning and pick her up at the end of the school day at 3 pm. The employer decided to restructure the working day to ensure that tasks such as shelf-filling were done outside shop opening hours. S was told she would have to work from 7 am to 12.30 pm. She objected on the basis that she could not expect her daughter to get up at 5.30 am, and to hang around for an hour or more waiting for the school to open. She was then offered the alternative option of working from 12 noon to 5.30 pm but rejected both options and resigned. She claimed indirect discrimination on the ground of her marital status. The employment tribunal took judicial notice of the fact that married women are more likely than unmarried women to have childcare responsibilities,

453

and accepted that the proportion of married women nationally who could comply with a requirement to work early mornings was considerably smaller than the proportion of unmarried women who could comply. However, the same was not true of the hours of 12 noon to 5.30 pm. Many 14-year-olds are unsupervised after school, and S's daughter could have stayed with family or friends, or gone to the public library to do her homework. Furthermore, if the relevant pool were confined to that particular branch, there was no evidence of disparate impact because all the shop assistants who could work the revised hours were women and a considerable majority were married. For those reasons the tribunal rejected S's claim.

16.152 Indirect race discrimination

Section 9 EqA deals with the protected characteristic of race. 'Race' includes colour, nationality, and ethnic or national origins – S.9(1). Unlike the equivalent provision in the Race Relations Act 1976 (RRA) – which defined 'racial grounds' exclusively in terms of colour, race, nationality or ethnic or national origins – this is not an exhaustive definition. For a detailed examination of this protected characteristic, see Chapter 10, 'Race'.

Until 2003, indirect discrimination under the RRA focused on whether a uniformly applied 'requirement or condition' adversely affected persons in the same *racial group* as the complainant – defined by reference to the same elements that made up the definition of 'racial grounds' (i.e. colour, race, nationality, or ethnic or national origins). Tribunals were required to consider whether a considerably smaller proportion of the claimant's racial group could comply with the relevant requirement or condition. However, on 19 July 2003 an entirely new definition – phrased in terms of whether the application of a PCP puts or would put persons of the 'same race or ethnic or national origins' as the claimant at a particular disadvantage – was inserted into the RRA to cover the three racial grounds specifically dealt with by the EU Race Equality Directive (No.2000/43). The upshot was that a clumsy two-tier system came into being comprising a set of enhanced rights (i.e. those introduced by the 2003 amending Regulations) applicable to claims based on race, or ethnic or national origins, and a set of more restrictive rights (i.e. those that pre-existed the amending Regulations) in respect of claims based on nationality (and arguably colour – although domestic case law suggested otherwise). The EqA removed this anomaly by applying the S.19 definition of indirect discrimination to all the components of race covered by S.9. For further details, see under 'Legislative history' above.

16.153 The standard definition of indirect discrimination set out in S.19 EqA now applies to all race discrimination claims regardless of the racial ground or group at issue. Accordingly, indirect race discrimination occurs where A applies to B a PCP that applies (or would apply) to persons not of the same racial group as B; puts (or would put) persons of B's racial group at a particular disadvantage when compared to other persons; puts (or would put) B at that disadvantage; and cannot be justified as a proportionate means of achieving a legitimate aim. This is very similar to the post-2003 test that applied in respect of race and ethnic or national origins, and many cases decided under the RRA therefore remain relevant.

The following example from early case law provides a good illustration of the concept of indirect race discrimination. In Hussein v Saints Complete House Furnishers 1979 IRLR 337, ET, a firm of household furnishers in Liverpool stipulated that it did not want job applicants from the city centre area because experience had shown that their unemployed friends tended to gather around the shop and discourage customers. As a result of this stipulation H was refused an interview because he lived in the 'Liverpool 8' postal district. An employment tribunal held that the employer had unjustifiably discriminated against H. Since 50 per cent of the city centre population was black, as against 2 per cent in Merseyside as a whole, the employer's condition excluded a significantly higher proportion of black applicants than white applicants.

Many of the cases examined in the earlier sections of this chapter concerning the general principles of indirect discrimination, and in Chapter 24, 'Recruitment', and Chapter 25, 'Discrimination during employment', involve claims of indirect race discrimination. For that reason, this section aims only to highlight some of the recurrent factual issues that arise in this context. Where appropriate, reference is made to other sections where the relevant case law is explored in greater depth.

Dress and appearance. As well as potentially discriminating on grounds of **16.154** sex, religion and/or gender reassignment (as to which, see Chapter 25, 'Discrimination during employment', under '"Any other detriment" – dress codes and appearance'), an employer who seeks to dictate employees' standards of dress or appearance risks placing certain racial groups at a particular disadvantage.

For example, in the non-employment case of G v Head Teacher and Governors of St Gregory's Catholic Science College 2011 EWHC 1452, QBD, the High Court held that it amounted to indirect race discrimination against a boy of African-Caribbean ethnicity for a school to impose a uniform policy preventing boys from wearing their hair in cornrows. On the evidence, the High Court was satisfied that there is a group of African-Caribbeans, who for reasons based on their culture and ethnicity believe cutting their hair to be wrong, that could be particularly disadvantaged by the school's policy. As the complainant was not prepared to have his hair cut in order to be able to attend the school and had suffered the traumatic experience of being turned away, the court was satisfied that he had suffered a particular disadvantage. Although the policy pursued the legitimate aim of suppressing gang culture, it could not be justified

455

given that an exception could be made where the ban caused a detriment to those from a particular ethnic background.

16.155 **Immigration issues.** Employers face potentially conflicting obligations where immigration is concerned, since they must balance their statutory responsibility for checking a person's eligibility to work in the United Kingdom with the need to avoid race discrimination. For further details see Chapter 24, 'Recruitment', under 'Arrangements for deciding to whom to offer employment – immigration issues'.

Although there are a number of restrictions on the right of nationals of countries outside the European Economic Area (EEA) to work in the United Kingdom, a blanket refusal to consider applications from people requiring a work permit is likely to amount to indirect race discrimination. In Osborne Clarke Services v Purohit 2009 IRLR 341, EAT, the employer refused to consider an Indian national's application to become a trainee solicitor on account of its policy of not recruiting anyone for such a post if they would require a work permit. An employment tribunal found this policy to be indirect discrimination on the ground of nationality, and rejected the employer's argument that, since Government guidance indicated that work permits were unlikely to be granted for trainee solicitors, the policy was justified. Upholding that decision on appeal, the EAT held that since there was no evidence of a dialogue between the employer and the immigration authorities, the employer could not begin to establish the level of evidence required to prove objective justification for its policy.

16.156 Indirect race discrimination may also arise where an employee is placed at a particular disadvantage by the operation of the immigration rules. In Ministry of Defence v DeBique 2010 IRLR 471, EAT, it was held that the Ministry of Defence had indirectly discriminated against a female soldier and single mother from St Vincent on grounds of sex and race when it required her to be available for duty 24 hours a day, seven days a week ('the 24/7 PCP'), while also applying to her a restriction in the immigration rules which prevented Foreign and Commonwealth soldiers from inviting their overseas relations to live with them in their army barracks for the purpose of looking after their children ('the immigration PCP'). With regard to the immigration PCP, the employment tribunal had identified the pool for comparison as those in the British Army of Vincentian national origin and of British national origin who were (or might become) single parents. Within that pool the Vincentian soldiers were put at a particular disadvantage because their extended families and, therefore, their potential child carers were more likely to be foreign nationals subject to immigration restrictions. The immigration PCP was not objectively justified because the difficulty experienced by a person in the claimant's position was foreseeable but the MoD had failed to make appropriate arrangements to deal with it, either by providing childcare or by taking steps to secure a relaxation of the relevant immigration policy.

Language requirements. A language requirement imposed by an employer **16.157** may indirectly discriminate on the ground of race unless it is necessary for the satisfactory performance of the job. The following example is given in the EHRC Employment Code: 'A superstore insists that all its workers have excellent spoken English. This might be a justifiable requirement for those in customer-facing roles. However, for workers based in the stock room, the requirement could be indirectly discriminatory in relation to race or disability as it is less likely to be objectively justified' (para 6.44).

The Code acknowledges that, in some circumstances, using a language other than English might be more practical for a line manager dealing with a particular group of workers with limited English language skills, but states that this should not be permitted to result in indirect discrimination. It gives the following example: 'A construction company employs a high number of Polish workers on one of its sites. The project manager of the site is also Polish and finds it more practical to speak Polish when giving instructions to those workers. However, the company should not advertise vacancies as being only open to Polish-speaking workers as the requirement is unlikely to be justified and could amount to indirect race discrimination' (para 6.49).

For further examples of potentially indirectly discriminatory language **16.158** requirements in the context of application forms and selection and aptitude tests, see Chapter 24, 'Recruitment', under 'Arrangements for deciding to whom to offer employment'.

Indirect religion or belief discrimination
16.159
The Employment Equality (Religion or Belief) Regulations 2003 SI 2003/1660 ('the Religion or Belief Regulations'), which came into force on 2 December 2003, were introduced in order to implement the religious discrimination aspects of the EU Equal Treatment Framework Directive (No.2000/78). They prohibited various forms of discrimination on the ground of religion or belief – including indirect discrimination – in the employment context. On 1 October 2010 the Religion or Belief Regulations were repealed and replaced by broadly similar provisions in the EqA. S.10 EqA deals with the protected characteristic of religion or belief and the indirect discrimination provisions in S.19 apply in this context. Thus, indirect religion or belief discrimination arises where A applies to B a PCP that:

- applies (or would apply) to persons not of the same religion or belief as B

- puts (or would put) person's of B's religion or belief at a particular disadvantage

- puts (or would put) B at that disadvantage, and

- cannot be justified as a proportionate means of achieving a legitimate aim.

457

16.160 In practice, workplace disputes concerning religion or belief discrimination tend to arise not from the mere holding of particular beliefs but from the ways in which those beliefs are manifested in public. Particular beliefs can, for example, lead to conflict over matters such as dress codes, dietary requirements, food and drink preparation, holiday leave and workplace absence. In such circumstances, where, as is often the case, the dispute arises as a result of a policy or practice that is applied uniformly across the entire workforce irrespective of employees' particular religions or beliefs, any ensuing claim will be based on allegations of *indirect* rather than direct discrimination, with the consequence that the employer can seek to justify the application of the policy or practice notwithstanding the disproportionately adverse impact it has upon those who share the claimant's particular religion or beliefs.

Below we discuss the requirement for group disadvantage, an issue that frequently arises in indirect religious discrimination claims, before briefly highlighting the main areas in which claims of indirect religious discrimination have tended to arise in the workplace. For a detailed discussion of this protected characteristic and the case law on indirect religious discrimination, reference should be made to Chapter 11, 'Religion or belief'.

16.161 **Group disadvantage in indirect religious discrimination claims.** One particular difficulty that arises in the context of indirect religious discrimination stems from the fact that individuals within a particular religion often manifest their religious beliefs in different ways. It seems clear that the religious belief in question need not be shared by adherents of the religion as a whole – see, for example, Dhinsa v Serco and anor ET Case No.1315002/09, discussed in Chapter 11, 'Religion or belief', in the section 'Manifestation of religion or belief', under 'Is a right to manifest protected by S.10 EqA? – dress and jewellery'. But how many others must share the relevant belief in order for the claimant to establish group disadvantage? As we have seen, solitary disadvantage is not sufficient – Eweida v British Airways plc 2010 ICR 890, CA, discussed in the section '"Particular disadvantage"', under 'Defining "disadvantage" – solitary disadvantage' above. In that case, it was held that an employer's policy prohibiting the wearing of jewellery did not indirectly discriminate against a devout Christian, whose wish to wear a silver cross on open view at work was denied by the policy, because there was no evidence that the policy put Christians at a particular disadvantage. The Court of Appeal identified a range of views as to how large a cohort it might be necessary to identify in order to establish indirect discrimination, without deciding which view was correct.

It may be significant, however, that S.19(2)(b) EqA requires only that the relevant PCP puts, or would put, 'persons with whom B shares the characteristic' at a particular disadvantage. There is no express reference to 'group disadvantage' as such, and nor is there any requirement for the disadvantaged group to be a large one. The EAT in Eweida expressed the test as follows: 'In our judgement, in order for indirect discrimination to be established, it must be possible to make some general statements which would be true about a religious group such that an employer ought reasonably to be able to appreciate that any particular provision may have a disparate adverse impact on the group' – Eweida v British Airways plc 2009 ICR 303, EAT. This statement was subsequently endorsed by the Court of Appeal in the same case – although it must be acknowledged that the reference to constructive knowledge on the employer's part sits uneasily with the principle that indirect discrimination can be unintentional.

Arguably, it is sufficient to show an adverse impact on a *small but significant* **16.162** group of individuals sharing a particular religious belief. Support for that proposition can be derived from Chatwal v Wandsworth Borough Council EAT 0487/10. There, C was employed by the Council as a customer services adviser. He was an Amritdhari Sikh and a member of a particular branch known as Guru Nanak Nishkam Sewak Jatha ('GNNSJ'), a revivalist organisation within the broader Sikh community. In May 2008, the Council adopted a new kitchen policy that required all employees to participate in a rota to clean the fridge and kitchen surfaces. C claimed that his religious beliefs forbade him from touching meat or meat products, and as meat was kept in the fridge he would not clean it. As a result, he was not allowed to use the kitchen. An employment tribunal dismissed C's religious discrimination claim on the basis that he had failed to establish any significant number of Sikhs who shared his belief. There was nothing in the Sikh scriptures to prohibit the touching of meat and the constitution of the GNNSJ was silent on the matter. The tribunal concluded that C had not discharged the burden of showing group disadvantage. At best, he had established that his belief was a personal and subjective religious belief, which was not sufficient for the purpose of an indirect discrimination claim.

However, the EAT overturned this decision on appeal and remitted the case to the tribunal. The tribunal had found that there was no statistical material to support C's claim and, in those circumstances, it was crucial to address and weigh the other evidence as to whether there were sufficient others of the same belief as C to constitute a 'group'. The tribunal had heard evidence from two experts on Sikh religious matters, and C had obtained letters from an Amritdhari Sikh official and a GNNSJ member. In the light of this, the EAT concluded that the tribunal had failed to explain why – on the evidence before it – C had not met the burden of proving that there was a significant group of others holding the same religious belief as to the handling of food.

In some cases, it will not be possible to point to a significant group that shares **16.163** the claimant's particular belief. For example, in Moise v Strettons Ltd ET Case No.3203326/09 M, a property management accountant, was a practising Catholic with a strong belief in devotion to the Divine Mercy. S Ltd did not permit employees to take annual leave during the busy two- or three-week period following each 'quarter day' when commercial tenants traditionally pay the next quarter's rent in advance. M asked to take leave around the Easter weekend in April 2009 in order to attend a Divine Mercy religious pilgrimage in Poland. S Ltd rejected her request because this fell during a 'quarter day' period, and subsequently dismissed her for taking unauthorised leave. An employment tribunal found that M had not been indirectly discriminated against on the ground of religion or belief. The rule whereby leave could not be taken during quarter-day periods did not put Catholics working for S Ltd at a disadvantage because – having regard to Eweida (above) – attending pilgrimages was 'very much a matter of choice for the claimant and not one of religious obligation'. The tribunal observed that there was no expert evidence to support the proposition that attending the Divine Mercy pilgrimage on an annual basis was 'an essential part of Catholicism or even of a subset of Catholicism'. In any event, the rule was justified as a proportionate means of achieving the legitimate aim of maintaining an essential service for S Ltd's clients.

16.164 **Dress codes and religious attire.** Indirect religious discrimination can arise where a dress code prevents an employee from wearing an item that is a manifestation of his or her religious beliefs. Two examples taken from the EHRC Employment Code:

- a hairdresser refuses to employ stylists who cover their hair, believing it is important for them to exhibit their flamboyant haircuts. It is clear that this criterion puts at a particular disadvantage both Muslim women and Sikh men who cover their hair. This may amount to indirect discrimination unless the criterion can be objectively justified (para 4.11)

- an employer introduces a 'no jewellery' policy in the workplace. This is not for health and safety reasons but because the employer does not like body piercings. A Sikh worker who wears a Kara bracelet as an integral part of her religion has complained about the rule. To avoid a claim of indirect discrimination, the employer should consider allowing an exception. A blanket ban on jewellery would probably not be considered a proportionate means of achieving a legitimate aim in these circumstances (para 6.40).

16.165 In one of the first appellate cases to be decided under the Religion or Belief Regulations – Azmi v Kirklees Metropolitan Borough Council 2007 ICR 1154, EAT – a devout Muslim teaching assistant was suspended from work for her persistence in wearing a full veil while teaching. The EAT accepted that the employer's apparently neutral requirement not to wear clothing that covered the face or which interfered unduly with the employee's ability to communicate properly with pupils was clearly a PCP that put persons of the claimant's belief at a particular disadvantage when compared with others. However, the EAT ruled that the discriminatory effect of the PCP was justified as a proportionate means of achieving the legitimate aim of raising the educational achievements of the schoolchildren.

460 ——————————————————————————

Another high-profile case concerning dress codes is Eweida v British Airways plc 2010 ICR 890, CA. There, the claimant – a devout and practising Christian employed as part of BA's check-in staff – refused to conceal her silver cross necklace in breach of the company's strict dress code prohibiting customer-facing employees from wearing any visible item of adornment. The claimant contended that there had been indirect discrimination in that the dress code disproportionately affected those of the Christian faith who wished to manifest their religious beliefs at work in the form of dress or jewellery. The Court of Appeal unanimously concluded that there was no evidence that the employer's policy put Christians at a particular disadvantage within the terms of the indirect discrimination provisions contained in the Religion or Belief Regulations. It pointed out that the employment tribunal had found that no other employee in a uniformed workforce of 30,000 had ever made a request to visibly wear a cross, much less refused to work if such a request was not met. In view of this, there was no reason whatever why the tribunal should have inferred that there were others whose religiously motivated choice – not of whether but of where they should wear a symbol of their faith – was of such importance to them that being unable to exercise it constituted a 'particular disadvantage'.

16.166 For a detailed discussion of these cases, and for further examples, see Chapter 11, 'Religion or belief', in the section 'Manifestation of religion or belief', under 'Is a right to manifest protected by S.10 EqA? – dress and jewellery'. Note that the claimant in Eweida has commenced legal proceedings before the European Court of Human Rights, contending that the employer's decision failed to comply with Article 9 of the European Convention on Human Rights, which concerns the right to freedom of thought, conscience and religion. The Equality and Human Rights Commission has successfully applied to intervene in order to make general representations. For further details, see Chapter 11 under 'Manifestation of religion or belief – is UK approach compliant with Article 9?'.

16.167 **Conflict between different protected rights.** A further potential source of indirect religious discrimination claims is where the expression of an employee's religion clashes with a basic aspect of his or her job. The leading case is Ladele v London Borough of Islington and anor 2010 ICR 532, CA. There, the claimant, a registrar, was threatened with dismissal when she refused to conduct civil partnership services because of her Christian belief that same-sex unions were contrary to God's law. The Court of Appeal held that the Council did not indirectly discriminate by insisting that all registrars must carry out marriages and civil partnerships. The Council had a legitimate aim, which was to provide its services in a non-discriminatory way in accordance with its 'Dignity for All' policy, and requiring the claimant to perform civil partnerships was a proportionate means of achieving that aim. The effect on her of implementing that policy was held not to impinge on her religious beliefs, since she remained free to hold those beliefs and to worship as she wished.

461

Very similar conclusions were reached by the EAT in McFarlane v Relate Avon 2010 ICR 507, EAT – a case decided just a couple of weeks before the Court of Appeal published its decision in Ladele. In McFarlane the Appeal Tribunal upheld the decision of an employment tribunal that the dismissal of a Christian relationship counsellor for refusing to counsel homosexuals about sexual matters did not constitute unlawful indirect discrimination. The employer's stance amounted to a proportionate means of achieving a legitimate aim – namely, that of serving the community in a non-discriminatory manner. The Court of Appeal subsequently dismissed an application by Mr McFarlane for leave to appeal against the EAT's decision – McFarlane v Relate Avon 2010 IRLR 872, CA.

16.168 Note that the claimants in both the Ladele and McFarlane cases have commenced legal proceedings before the ECtHR contending that the decisions in their cases fail to comply with Article 9 ECHR. The Equality and Human Rights Commission has successfully applied to intervene in order to make general representations. For further details, see Chapter 11, 'Religion or belief', under 'Manifestation of religion or belief – is UK approach compliant with Article 9?'.

In McClintock v Department of Constitutional Affairs 2008 IRLR 29, EAT, the Appeal Tribunal held that a Christian Justice of the Peace, who resigned from office following the rejection of his request to be excused from cases that might lead to the adoption of a child by a same-sex couple, was not indirectly discriminated against on the ground of religion or belief. The relevant PCP was the requirement that magistrates honour the judicial oath, which involves adjudicating on any case that comes before them. One of the EAT's reasons for upholding the employment tribunal's rejection of the claim was that even if that PCP disadvantaged persons by reason of their religious or philosophical beliefs – and there was no evidence that it did – the claimant was unable to show that he had himself been disadvantaged for that reason. At no stage did he indicate that his objections were connected to his religion; rather, he stated that there was insufficient evidence for him to conclude that placements with same-sex couples were in children's best interests.

16.169 A similar factual scenario arose in Matthews v Northamptonshire County Council ET Case No.1901629/09. There, a Christian member of an adoption panel believed that it was wrong for same-sex couples to be adoptive parents and abstained from voting whenever such an application came before the panel. The Council terminated her appointment. The parties agreed that the relevant PCP was one whereby panel members must actively participate in and vote on all adoption applications. In the tribunal's view, it had not been shown that this PCP put Christians at a particular disadvantage compared with others, since same-sex adoption was 'a practice to which non-Christians as well as Christians might well equally take exception'. In addition, the evidence suggested that the claimant's stance was based not on her Christian beliefs but on her understanding of the relevant medical and scientific literature.

For a detailed consideration of this area, see Chapter 11, 'Religion or belief', in the section 'Manifestation of religion or belief', under 'Is a right to manifest protected by S.10 EqA? – conflict between different protected rights'.

Expressing views about religion. In several cases, tribunals have had to deal **16.170** with claims by employees who have been disciplined or dismissed for proselytising or otherwise expressing their personal religious beliefs in an inappropriate way. This frequently gives rise to direct, as opposed to indirect, religious discrimination complaints. In such a case, it is open to an employment tribunal to find that the claimant has been less favourably treated not on the ground of religion or belief but because of the improper manifestation of his or her beliefs – for various examples, see Chapter 11, 'Religion or belief', in the section 'Manifestation of religion or belief', under 'Is a right to manifest protected by S.10 EqA? – proselytising'. However, an employer who relies on a workplace policy to support the decision to take disciplinary action may risk claims of *indirect* discrimination.

For example, in Amachree v Wandsworth Borough Council ET Case No.2328606/09 A, a committed Christian, was employed by the Council as a homelessness prevention officer, interviewing people in need of housing advice. He told X, a service user with an incurable disease, that doctors did not have all the answers and that she should put her faith in God. When X complained, A was suspended on full pay pending an investigation. Subsequently, A's legal adviser released a press statement with A's consent from which X could be identified. At a disciplinary hearing the Council found that A had made comments to X that were offensive and inappropriate and which could have a damaging effect on the Council's reputation. It also found that A had released to the media personal information relating to X that she had given to A in his capacity as a Council officer – an act which could have a similar effect. The Council found that both actions amounted to gross misconduct and summarily dismissed A.

A claimed that his dismissal constituted direct and indirect discrimination on **16.171** the ground of his religion. The employment tribunal rejected the direct discrimination claim on the basis that his treatment was not on the ground of his religion but was for inappropriately promoting that religion in a conversation with a service user, in conjunction with later breaching her confidentiality. As for the claim of indirect discrimination, A asserted that the Council's disciplinary code amounted to a PCP that applied equally to all but which put him and would put other Christians at a particular disadvantage when compared with others not of the same religion. The tribunal found that there was no evidence to support this claim, and nor was there evidence that any other Christians felt unfairly constrained by the code.

463

The second PCP that A relied on was that no religious discussion whatsoever could take place during an interview with a service user. The tribunal was not satisfied that the Council had a policy preventing proselytising – rather, there was a practice that Council officers should only discuss relevant matters during an interview. Furthermore, there was no evidence that this practice would have an adverse disparate impact on those of A's religion. In this regard, A argued that because Christians have to live out the teachings of the bible in word and deed, they more than anyone else would fall foul of a policy where no reference to religion could be made. The tribunal rejected this line of reasoning, holding that other major religions would be affected in the same way. Even if there had been evidence of disparate impact, the tribunal considered that a practice of not allowing irrelevant matters to be discussed at interview was legitimate in order to ensure the delivery of a professional and cost-effective service, and that this was achieved proportionately by preventing staff from discussing irrelevant topics.

16.172　Similarly, in Haye v London Borough of Lewisham ET Case No.2301852/09 a tribunal found that H, a Christian, was not discriminated against on the ground of her religious beliefs when she was dismissed for sending an e-mail containing offensive and aggressive language regarding her views about homosexuality to the Lesbian and Gay Christian Movement via her work account. This breached the Council's 'wired working policy' and its commitment to diversity and equality. H's dismissal was found not to be direct discrimination as the Council would have treated an employee not of the same religion who sent offensive correspondence in the same way. The tribunal also rejected H's indirect discrimination complaint. Although the 'wired working policy' was accepted by the Council to be a PCP, there was no evidence to show that it put Christians, or H herself, at a particular disadvantage. Even if it did, the tribunal found that the Council had a legitimate aim of controlling views expressed in the course of employment and this policy was a proportionate means of achieving that aim because it did not interfere in H's right to 'minister' outside work.

As we saw in Chapter 11, 'Religion or belief', the EqA does not just protect those who hold religious beliefs. It also covers certain philosophical beliefs, such as atheism, and non-belief is protected in the same way as positive belief. This means that those who are disciplined for expressing *anti-religious* views in the workplace may claim that they have been unlawfully discriminated against. For example, in Brown v Secretary of State for Energy and Climate Change ET Case No.2200545/10 B, an atheist, was engaged through an agency as a health and safety consultant. During an informal chat with two colleagues, he made a number of inflammatory remarks about Islam. He said that the Koran advocated violence and that Mohammed was a paedophile and a rapist who had encouraged rape and murder. The employer's harassment and bullying policy, which applied to contractors as well as employees, defined harassment as including actions or comments related to religion that were viewed as demeaning or unacceptable by the recipient. The respondent carried out an investigation and terminated B's contract. B claimed that he had been discriminated against on the ground of his atheism but an employment tribunal dismissed his claims of direct and indirect discrimination. With regard to the latter, the tribunal found that, while the respondent did not have a policy prohibiting religious discussion as such, it had applied a PCP whereby it would terminate the engagement of any contractor who made offensive remarks about the key characters or adherents of any religion or philosophical belief. There was no evidence that this PCP put atheists and non-believers at a particular disadvantage. While atheists should be entitled to express their views on the non-existence of God, the respondent's PCP did not prevent them from doing so and there was no requirement for them to be offensive and derogatory in the workplace. Furthermore, the PCP was a proportionate means of achieving a legitimate aim. It represented a very limited curtailment on freedom of speech and, in the tribunal's view, was a small price to pay for promoting diversity, harmony and good working relationships.

Time off for religious observance. Another situation that tends to generate **16.173** indirect religious discrimination cases is where employees are refused time off during normal working hours to worship, observe days of rest or attend religious festivals. For instance, stipulating that work must be done on a Friday, Saturday or Sunday could give rise to indirect religious discrimination against Muslims, Jews and Christians respectively. The issue here is whether the employer's general application of the holiday or time off policy disproportionately affects persons who share the employee's religion or belief and, if so, whether the discriminatory effect is justified as a proportionate means of achieving a legitimate aim.

Two examples of indirect discrimination claims brought under the Religion or Belief Regulations:

- **Edge v Visual Security Services Ltd** ET Case No.1301365/06: the employment tribunal held that a requirement to undertake occasional Sunday working 'would put people of the same religion as the claimant (Christians) at a particular disadvantage when compared with other persons because they would not be able to attend church service on Sunday, quite apart from the narrower, but perhaps equally important requirement, to observe Sunday as a day of rest'. The tribunal went on to find that the claimant was in fact put at that disadvantage as he could not attend Church owing to the requirement for occasional Sunday working

- **Fugler v MacMillan – London Hair Studios Ltd** ET Case No.2205090/04: the employer had a policy of discouraging employees from taking holidays on Saturday as this was the busiest day of the week. An employment tribunal held that this put the claimant, who was of Jewish faith, at a disadvantage as the Jewish Sabbath is on a Saturday and in 2004 the Jewish festival of Yom

465

held that, in determining whether a shift system was indirectly discriminatory, it was legitimate for an employment tribunal to take into account the fact that women were far more likely than men to be lone parents with childcare responsibilities. And more recently, in Blackburn and anor v Chief Constable of West Midlands Police 2008 ICR 505, EAT (an equal pay case), Mr Justice Elias, then President of the EAT, suggested that an employment tribunal was entitled, in considering the disparate impact of a measure, to rely on the 'common knowledge' that women have greater childcare responsibilities than men. This suggests that a claimant will not necessarily be expected to provide statistical evidence to show that the PCP places women at a particular disadvantage.

However, there have been cases where the EAT has been less willing to endorse the assumption that full-time working or certain shift patterns place women at a disadvantage without more. In Sinclair Roche and Temperley and ors v Heard and anor 2004 IRLR 763, EAT, for example, the Appeal Tribunal held that an employment tribunal had not been entitled to conclude that women have the greater responsibility for childcare in our society and that as a consequence a considerably larger proportion of women than men are unable to commit themselves to full-time working. The EAT suggested that it was not appropriate to make such a generalisation in relation to men and women solicitors, or men and women working in high-powered and highly paid jobs in the City.

16.178   More recently, in Hacking and Paterson and anor v Wilson EATS 0054/09, the EAT sitting in Scotland commented that it was not inevitable that women would be disproportionately adversely affected by a refusal to grant flexible working. Society has changed dramatically; many women now return to full-time work after childbirth and more men take on childcare responsibilities. Furthermore, although the childcare arrangements available to some women are such that they cannot work full time, the position of others is that, while they are able to access childcare arrangements which would enable them to work full time, they do not want to do so; for them, part-time working is a matter of choice rather than necessity. Moreover, people (both male and female) seek flexible working for different reasons, which include, for instance, enabling them to combine jobs, pursue other interests or follow educational courses. A negative response to the request for flexible working may, accordingly, give rise to differing effects. Where the effect is on an employee who is able to work full time but does not wish to do so, it is difficult to see that it would be correct to describe that employee as being disadvantaged. Where the effect does amount to a disadvantage, the question of whether it amounts to a particular disadvantage that is liable to be experienced by women as opposed to men arises.

It should be noted that the EAT in Hacking and Paterson also held that, where the employer operated a policy of refusing all requests for flexible working from its property managers, the correct pool for comparison in determining disparate impact was restricted to such of the property managers as, at the relevant time, wanted flexible working to be available. This aspect of the case is dealt with in the section 'Pool for comparison', under 'Problem areas – entire pool subject to disadvantage' above.

The EAT's assertion in Hacking and Paterson that women suffer no disadvantage at all (never mind a *particular* disadvantage) when an employer rejects part-time working if they choose to work part-time in order to bring up a child – as opposed to being forced to do so – is controversial to say the least, and raises a number of unanswered questions. At what point can it be said that part-time working is a matter of choice rather than necessity? How much effort should women be expected to make to ensure alternative childcare arrangements? If there are willing grandparents close at hand, does that mean that the woman is not forced to work part time? What if a woman's partner works from home, is unemployed or earns less than she does – should he be expected to provide the childcare? And what if full-time childcare, although available, is expensive, or the woman considers that it would not be in her child's best interests? No doubt these questions will be addressed by future case law.

We would respectfully suggest that, contrary to the EAT's views in Hacking and **16.179** Paterson, and despite recent changes in social attitudes, primary childcare responsibility still falls overwhelmingly on women. As more and more men take on childcare responsibilities, stereotypical assumptions about traditional male and female roles might become outdated. Arguably, the time will come when tribunals can no longer assume that women will be disproportionately adversely affected by requirements to, for example, work anti-social hours. However, we would argue that this is not yet the case.

If we are incorrect in this view, and specific proof of disparate impact is required in this context, it is worth noting that the choice of relevant pool can have a significant impact on the outcome. For example, it is generally a good deal easier to establish that a requirement to work full time places women at a particular disadvantage if the pool consists of all potential applicants for a job rather than merely a cross-section of a particular workforce. In the latter case, the proportion of women who are put at a disadvantage by the PCP may be so small in number that it becomes impossible to say that the application of the requirement has any discriminatory effect in practice. Where the selected pool happens to include a relatively small number of women, it may be that none of these, apart from the claimant, has childcare responsibilities or faces other impediments to full-time working.

Nevertheless, there are numerous cases in which claimants have succeeded in **16.180** establishing, on the basis of statistics relating to a relatively small pool, that a PCP relating to working patterns places women at a particular disadvantage. Two examples:

- **Savva v Hillgate Travel** ET Case No.2200525/06: S, a divorced mother, was employed as an account executive by a travel company on a fixed shift that fitted in with her childcare arrangements. The company decided that fixed shifts no longer suited its purposes and that it needed its workforce to be more flexible. S was unable to work a flexible shift. She claimed indirect sex discrimination when her employment was terminated on the ground of redundancy. On the issue of disparate impact, the employment tribunal limited the pool for comparison to the employer's workforce, of which 75 per cent were account executives doing the same job as the claimant and, of these, 75 per cent were women and 25 per cent men. Only four of the account executives worked fixed shifts and were women with childcare responsibilities. The tribunal concluded that these figures demonstrated that any request to work flexible shifts would put women in the workforce at a particular disadvantage in comparison to men. On the evidence, the employer had failed to show that the requirement that S work a flexible shift was justified

• **Bradley v West Midlands Fire and Rescue Authority** ET Case No.1304700/06: B was a single mother who worked as a firefighter. A new shift pattern was introduced making it harder, and, in her opinion, all but impossible on some occasions, to organise her childcare. Although B's family was able to provide some support, she submitted a request for flexible working, which was refused. Before the employment tribunal, the employer disputed the extent of the difficulties that B was experiencing with the new shift system. The tribunal referred to statistical evidence concerning applications for flexible working and exemption from the new shift pattern among the relevant section of the workforce. It also took judicial notice of the fact that a significant majority of single parents are women. On that basis, it held that the new shift pattern put women at a particular disadvantage compared to men, and that it had put B at that disadvantage. In reaching this conclusion, it reminded itself that the statutory test only requires the claimant to prove a 'disadvantage' and that it was not the case that she must show that compliance with the PCP was impossible. B's indirect discrimination claim was, however, ultimately dismissed on the ground that the application of the discriminatory PCP was a proportionate means of achieving a legitimate aim and was therefore justified.

16.181 The Scottish EAT's judgment in Hacking and Paterson (above) casts doubt on whether a woman who is denied part-time working can establish either *group* disadvantage or *individual* disadvantage. Even if she succeeds in establishing the former – whether by means of judicial notice, by reference to appropriate statistics or by a combination of the two – she will still have to demonstrate the latter. This is illustrated by Shackletons Garden Centre Ltd v Lowe EAT 0161/10. L worked as a sales assistant at a garden centre. Following her return from maternity leave, she objected to the employer's requirement that all employees must work rotational shifts involving some weekend working. A tribunal upheld her claim of indirect sex discrimination, stating: 'It is well recognised that significantly more women than men are primarily responsible for the care of their children. Accordingly, the ability of women to work particular hours is substantially restricted because of those childcare commitments in contrast to that of men.' On appeal, the EAT held that the employment tribunal had been entitled to conclude that the PCP relating to weekend working put women at a particular disadvantage. However, it had failed to identify the specific disadvantage caused to L. There was insufficient evidence that childcare arrangements would be unavailable if she worked the rota system required by her employer. In those circumstances, it was unclear that she had suffered an individual disadvantage as distinct from a 'self-inflicted detriment', and the case was remitted to a differently constituted tribunal.

For further discussion of this area, see Chapter 25, 'Discrimination during employment', in the section 'Terms of employment', under 'Working hours – childcare responsibilities'.

Experience and qualifications. An apparently neutral requirement relating to **16.182** experience or qualifications can place women with childcare commitments at a particular disadvantage. For example, in the Northern Irish case of Crilly v Ballymagroarty Hazelbank Community Partnership IT Case No.242/11 C applied for the position of neighbourhood regeneration officer with BHCP, which required two years' relevant paid experience in a community development capacity gained within the last five years. Although C had not had paid work for six years owing to her childcare responsibilities, she had extensive high-level voluntary involvement in community development and neighbourhood regeneration. She was not shortlisted for the post and claimed that the paid work experience requirement constituted indirect sex discrimination. BHCP argued that the requirement was underpinned by legitimate business reasons – both the project manager and previous two neighbourhood regeneration officers had left, and it wanted someone who could begin work immediately with minimal training and supervision.

The industrial tribunal found that the five-year requirement had a disproportionate adverse impact on women. This was evidenced, among other things, by the Northern Ireland Labour Force survey for January to March 2011, which showed that 90.6 per cent of those economically inactive owing to the fact that they were 'looking after family and home' were women. As the statistical disparity was so large, the tribunal felt able to draw the inference that women who were otherwise suitably qualified for the post were discouraged from applying and consequently were disproportionately adversely affected compared to suitably qualified men. The requirement also put C at a personal disadvantage since she was denied the opportunity to be interviewed and was not appointed. While the tribunal found that the aims underpinning the requirement could be said to be legitimate, they were not proportionate. For example, the need to employ someone who could do the job without extensive

471

training was not necessarily met by a requirement that allowed a potential three-year gap since a candidate's last paid employment. In any event, there was a two-month induction period, during which any issues concerning specific experience could have been addressed.

16.183 **Other caring responsibilities.** Statistics suggest that more women than men are responsible for the care of elderly relatives. Managers should therefore take as much care with requests for flexible working from eldercarers as with those from childcarers in order to avoid claims of indirect sex discrimination. In a report from the Office for National Statistics, 'Carers 2001 Census' (available at www.ons.gov.uk), it was found that women were more likely to be carers of sick, disabled and elderly people than men. The age group in which the largest proportion of people provided care was the fifties. More than one in five of people aged 50–59 were providing some unpaid care. About one in four women in this age group (24.6 per cent) were providing some care compared with 17.9 per cent of men. Another survey from the ONS found that 18 per cent of women were carers compared with 14 per cent of men – 'Carers 2000'. It should be noted that these figures are now somewhat out of date; the headline population estimates from the 2011 census are expected to be released in mid-2012, with more detailed estimates to follow in 2013.

16.184 **Pregnancy and maternity.** As noted under 'Relevant protected characteristics – pregnancy and maternity' above, there is no specific protection in the EqA against indirect pregnancy and maternity discrimination, which continues to be dealt with as indirect sex discrimination. An example of a pregnancy claim brought under the antecedent indirect discrimination provision in the SDA is Kelly v National Policing Improvement Agency ET Case No.2329773/10. K, a police constable, sought promotion to the rank of sergeant and applied to take the relevant examination. The exam took place once a year, in early March. No other dates were offered and no one was permitted to sit it on an alternative date. K took the exam in March 2010, four days before she gave birth. She was in considerable discomfort as a result of her pregnancy, had to take several toilet breaks, and failed by one mark. She claimed indirect sex discrimination against the qualifying body, alleging that women were placed at a particular disadvantage by two PCPs: one whereby the exam was only run once a year and had to be taken then without exception; and another whereby it had to be taken in a single three-hour sitting. K invited the employment tribunal to take judicial notice of the 'real chance that women generally will be unwilling or unable to take the exam by reason of pregnancy or maternity leave or, even if they take it, will not be able to perform to the best of their ability'. The tribunal rejected her claim, noting that there was no evidence that any women police constables seeking promotion had been adversely affected by either of the provisions relied upon. If the claimant's submissions as to judicial notice were correct, the tribunal would have expected concrete evidence of at least *some* other women who had experienced such disadvantage.

Indirect sexual orientation discrimination 16.185

Protection against workplace discrimination on the ground of sexual orientation was introduced into national law by the Employment Equality (Sexual Orientation) Regulations 2003 SI 2003/1661 ('the Sexual Orientation Regulations'). Under these Regulations, the customary forms of discrimination – including indirect discrimination – were prohibited. With effect from 1 October 2010, the Sexual Orientation Regulations were repealed and replaced by the EqA. S.12 of that Act defines the protected characteristic of sexual orientation in virtually identical terms to the old definition under Reg 2(1) of the Sexual Orientation Regulations.

Section 12(1) EqA defines sexual orientation as 'a person's sexual orientation towards (a) persons of the same sex, (b) persons of the opposite sex, or (c) persons of either sex'. S.12(2) stipulates that a reference to a person who has the protected characteristic of sexual orientation is a reference to a person of a particular sexual orientation; while a reference to persons who share that protected characteristic is a reference to persons of the same sexual orientation. Thus, a heterosexual man and a heterosexual woman are to be regarded as sharing a sexual orientation for the purposes of the Act, and the same is true of a homosexual (gay) man and a homosexual (lesbian) woman. This is particularly relevant to claims of indirect discrimination in respect of which, by virtue of S.19 EqA, it is necessary to show that a PCP has been applied that puts persons who share the same protected characteristic as the claimant at a particular disadvantage compared with persons who do not share it.

Under S.19 EqA, indirect sexual orientation discrimination occurs where A 16.186 applies to B a PCP that:

- applies (or would apply) to persons of a different sexual orientation

- puts (or would put) persons of B's sexual orientation at a particular disadvantage when compared to other persons

- puts (or would put) B at that disadvantage, and

- cannot be justified as a proportionate means of achieving a legitimate aim.

It should be noted that S.19(2)(b) merely requires that the PCP 'puts, or would put, persons with whom B shares the [protected] characteristic' at a particular disadvantage, without specifying how that disadvantage must be shown. As noted under '"Particular disadvantage"' above, a claimant does not necessarily have to produce statistical evidence to satisfy this test. This is especially important in the area of sexual orientation discrimination, as in many cases reliable statistics will not be available. It should also be noted that the test is satisfied if the PCP *would put* others who share the protected characteristic at a particular disadvantage. This means that where, for example, there are no other persons of the complainant's sexual orientation in the workplace, he or

473

she can still succeed in a claim of indirect discrimination by arguing that such persons, if they did exist, would be more susceptible than other people to the disadvantage complained of. This test thereby allows policies or practices to be challenged at an early stage before they have had a significant impact.

16.187 Most of the reported decisions relating to sexual orientation involve direct discrimination and/or harassment; cases involving indirect sexual orientation discrimination are relatively uncommon. However, an example of this form of discrimination would be if a brewery were to seek a couple to run a pub and expressed a preference that they be married. The preference for a married couple would be a PCP which, although not explicitly discriminatory, would put homosexual couples at a particular disadvantage since they cannot marry. Another example would be a policy or practice favouring employees with children. Such a policy or practice would put homosexual employees at a particular disadvantage if it could be shown that they were less likely than heterosexual employees to have children. To avoid liability for indirect discrimination, the employer would then have to demonstrate that the policy or practice was a proportionate means of achieving a legitimate aim.

Reference should be made to Chapter 13, 'Sexual orientation', for a detailed discussion of this protected characteristic, including the relevant EU legislation and the interrelationship of sexual orientation with other protected characteristics (notably, marriage and civil partnership).

17 Indirect discrimination: objective justification

In Chapter 16, 'Indirect discrimination: proving disadvantage', we examine **17.1** how an employee establishes a case of indirect discrimination under S.19 of the Equality Act 2010 (EqA). This involves the employee (B) proving, on the balance of probabilities:

- that the employer (A) has applied to him or her a provision, criterion or practice (PCP) that it applies, or would apply, to persons with whom B does not share the relevant protected characteristic

- that the PCP puts, or would put, persons with whom B shares the characteristic at a particular disadvantage when compared with persons with whom B does not share it, and

- that the PCP puts, or would put, B at that disadvantage.

It is then for the employment tribunal to consider the final element in the statutory test – whether the PCP is justified in accordance with S.19(2)(d) EqA, which provides that it will be discriminatory if 'A cannot show it to be a *proportionate means of achieving a legitimate aim*' (our stress). This is commonly referred to as 'objective justification' and is the focus of this chapter.

Despite the complexity of the other elements of the statutory test, which **17.2** necessitated a detailed consideration in Chapter 16, the focus of argument in many indirect discrimination claims is the issue of justification. S.19(2)(d) EqA operates, in effect, as an escape clause, in that it provides employers with the opportunity to show that, even though a PCP may have had an adverse impact on a particular protected group, it was implemented for reasons unconnected with the relevant protected characteristic and was therefore lawful. The employment tribunal must carry out a balancing exercise, weighing the organisation's need to impose the PCP against the PCP's discriminatory effect. Having an apparently sound reason for imposing the relevant PCP is not enough in itself: the employer must also demonstrate that the reasons for its

475

imposition are strong enough to overcome any indirectly discriminatory impact. The more discriminatory the PCP, the more difficult it will be for the employer to show that it was justified.

The Equality and Human Rights Commission's Code of Practice on Employment ('the EHRC Employment Code') contains guidance on objective justification in the context of indirect discrimination that largely reflects existing case law in this area (see paras 4.25–4.32). In short, the aim pursued should be legal, should not be discriminatory in itself, and must represent a real, objective consideration – para 4.28. Although business needs and economic efficiency may be legitimate aims, the Code states that an employer simply trying to reduce costs cannot expect to satisfy the test – para 4.29. As to proportionality, the Code notes that the measure adopted by the employer does not have to be the only possible way of achieving the legitimate aim; it is sufficient that the same aim could not have been achieved by less discriminatory means – para 4.31.

17.3 The concept of objective justification has its origins in the relevant EU equality Directives, and the case law of the European Court of Justice has played a critical part in establishing the key elements of the defence. In addition, European and domestic case law in the field of equal pay is highly significant in the context of claims brought under S.19 EqA. That is because it is generally accepted that an employer who relies on an indirectly discriminatory 'material factor' to justify a difference in pay between men and women must demonstrate that his actions were objectively justified as a proportionate means of achieving a legitimate aim – essentially the same test that applies under S.19 EqA. For further details, see IDS Employment Law Handbook, 'Equal Pay' (2011), Chapter 8, 'Material factor defence'.

The defence of objective justification arises in two other types of discrimination claim that fall outside S.19 EqA. An identically worded defence, requiring the employer to show that the relevant treatment is a 'proportionate means of achieving a legitimate aim', is available in claims of direct age discrimination and discrimination arising from disability – Ss.13(2) and 15(1)(b) EqA. There are specific considerations that apply in these contexts, and, certainly in the case of age discrimination, the burden of proving that a directly discriminatory measure or decision is objectively justified is greater than in the case of indirect discrimination – see Seldon v Clarkson Wright and Jakes (A Partnership) 2012 UKSC 16, SC. For further details of the operation of the justification defence under Ss.13 and 15, see Chapter 15, 'Direct discrimination', under 'Justifying direct age discrimination', and Chapter 20, 'Discrimination arising from disability', under 'Elements of S.15 claim – objective justification'.

17.4 This chapter begins by examining the legislative history of the objective justification defence and the relationship between the domestic provisions and the relevant EU Directives. We also give an overview of the main elements necessary to establish justification, outlining the key principles derived from European and domestic case law, the role of employment tribunals and the operation of the burden of proof. Next, we explore the need to establish a 'legitimate aim' and the extent to which certain types of aim, such as cost considerations, are capable in principle of justifying indirect discrimination. We then look at the all-important test of proportionality before focusing on some of the most common factual situations in which the justification defence arises. Finally, we explore the specific considerations that apply in connection with the justification of social policy measures by an EU Member State.

Background and overview 17.5

As noted above, the test of justification under S.19(2)(d) EqA requires the employer to demonstrate that the relevant PCP was a 'proportionate means of achieving a legitimate aim'. In most cases, the same wording was used in the previous anti-discrimination legislation. A different test previously applied to indirect discrimination on the ground of nationality, and arguably of colour, but the EqA has removed that anomaly. The relevant EU Directives, however, employ different wording, stating that the PCP must be 'objectively justified by a legitimate aim' and that the means of achieving that aim must be 'appropriate and necessary'. The significance of that difference in wording is discussed below. This section also contains a general overview of the justification defence and its operation in practice.

Legislative history 17.6
The definitions of indirect sex and race discrimination in the Sex Discrimination Act 1975 (SDA) and Race Relations Act 1976 (RRA) underwent a series of changes over the years prior to enactment of the EqA. For a full account of these changes, see Chapter 16, 'Indirect discrimination: proving disadvantage', under 'Legislative history'. The current test of justification came into effect in 2003 for most indirect race discrimination claims brought under the RRA, and in 2005 in relation to claims of indirect sex discrimination under the SDA. It was carried over into the EqA when that Act came into force on 1 October 2010, replacing the previous provisions.

The original test of indirect race discrimination under the RRA required the employer to show that the requirement or condition alleged to be discriminatory (now replaced by the term 'provision, criterion or practice' (PCP)) was 'justifiable irrespective of the colour, race, nationality or ethnic or national origins of the person to whom it is applied' – S.1(1)(b)(ii) RRA. The new definition – requiring the employer to show that the PCP is a 'proportionate means of achieving a legitimate aim' – was introduced into the RRA with effect from 19 July 2003 by the Race Relations Act 1976 (Amendment) Regulations 2003 SI 2003/1626, which implemented the EU Race Equality Directive

477

(No.2000/43). However, the revised definition in S.1(1A)(c) RRA applied only to the three racial grounds specifically covered by the Directive – namely, race, ethnic origins and national origins. Thus, the original test of justification continued to apply to claims of indirect race discrimination based on nationality (and arguably colour – although domestic case law suggested that the Directive, and hence the new definition of justification, did in fact apply in that context). This anomaly was finally resolved by S.19 EqA, which applies the newer definition of justification to all indirect race discrimination claims regardless of the racial ground or group at issue.

17.7 Similarly, the original test of justification under the SDA required the employer to show that the relevant requirement or condition was 'justifiable irrespective of the sex of the person to whom it is applied' – S.1(1)(b)(ii) SDA. This was amended on 1 October 2005 by the Employment Equality (Sex Discrimination) Regulations 2005 SI 2005/2467, which implemented the EU Equal Treatment Amendment Directive (No.2002/73) (since replaced by the recast EU Equal Treatment Directive (No.2006/54)). The amended test of justification in S.1(2)(b)(iii) SDA, which applied in employment cases, required the employer to demonstrate that the PCP was a 'proportionate means of achieving a legitimate aim' – the test that was subsequently carried over into S.19 EqA.

The other antecedent domestic provisions on indirect discrimination – covering age, religion or belief, and sexual orientation – came into force much later than the SDA and RRA. They were designed to implement the relevant aspects of the EU Equal Treatment Framework Directive (No.2000/78) and required the employer to show that the relevant PCP was a 'proportionate means of achieving a legitimate aim' from the outset. Accordingly, the previous body of case law relating to these strands remains highly relevant to claims brought under S.19 EqA.

17.8 For completion, we should point out that no provision was made for indirect disability discrimination under the former Disability Discrimination Act 1995. It is only with the passing of the EqA that this form of discrimination was extended to apply to the protected characteristic of disability – see further Chapter 16, 'Indirect discrimination: proving disadvantage', under 'Relevant protected characteristics – disability'.

17.9 **Differences between EU and domestic wording.** As noted above, the test of justification in S.19 EqA – which requires the employer to show that the PCP is a 'proportionate means of achieving a legitimate aim' – derives from the relevant EU Directives. However, those Directives employ different wording, requiring the employer to show that the PCP is '*objectively justified* by a legitimate aim and the means of achieving that aim are *appropriate and necessary*' (our stress).

When the Government introduced the new test of justification into the RRA in 2003, it believed that the words 'objectively justified' in Article 2(2)(b) of the

EU Race Equality Directive (No.2000/43) added nothing and therefore omitted them from the RRA for reasons of simplicity. However, its reasons for replacing 'appropriate and necessary' with 'proportionate' were not quite so clear. Apparently the Government was concerned that the UK courts and tribunals would interpret the word 'necessary' in too strict a manner. In its view, the test under European law was not one of absolute necessity but must incorporate an element of 'proportionality', whereby the tribunal performs a balancing exercise between the importance of the employer's aim and the discriminatory effect of the means chosen to achieve it (see statements by Beverley Hughes, Minister for Citizenship and Immigration, on the amendments to the RRA in the House of Commons Standing Committee on Delegated Legislation (11 June 2003, col 24)). Similar considerations underpinned the subsequent amendments to the SDA and the introduction of the other antecedent equality measures – the Employment Equality (Religion or Belief) Regulations 2003 SI 2003/1660, the Employment Equality (Sexual Orientation) Regulations 2003 SI 2003/1661, and the Employment Equality (Age) Regulations 2006 SI 2006/1031.

17.10 There have been concerns that the Government's decision to sacrifice 'appropriate and necessary' in favour of 'proportionate' may result in tribunals applying a diluted test, which could lead to accusations that it has failed properly to implement the relevant Directives. In 2005, when the Government amended the SDA, a number of the organisations that commented on its draft proposals during public consultation, such as the TUC and the EOC (now part of the EHRC), objected to the new test on the ground that the omission of the words 'appropriate and necessary' rendered the test of objective justification weaker than that envisaged by the EU Equal Treatment Amendment Directive (No.2002/73) (since replaced by the recast EU Equal Treatment Directive (No.2006/54)). However, the Government rejected the view that 'proportionate' is weaker than 'appropriate and necessary'. In its view, the case law of the European Court of Justice demonstrated that the term 'appropriate and necessary' sets out a 'test of proportionality involving balancing between the discriminatory effects of a measure and the importance of the aim pursued'.

The difference in wording was again the subject of debate during the consultation leading up to the enactment of the EqA, which (as we have seen) replicated the test found in the antecedent equality enactments. Giving its reasons for the decision not to adopt the European wording, the Government stated: 'We consider that the wording "appropriate and necessary" is problematic in domestic discrimination legislation because of the extreme exigency associated with "necessity" in domestic law. If this wording were to be used there might be a risk that this would be interpreted by the courts as an overly-strict requirement (for example, in order to satisfy the test the [PCP] would have to be the only possible means of achieving the legitimate aim)' – 'The Equality Bill – Government response to the Consultation', July 2008 (Cm 7454), para 7.26. For the same reason, the Government chose to retain the existing test of objective justification in S.13(2) EqA (direct age discrimination) and adopted the same test in S.15(1)(b) (discrimination arising from disability) – see Chapter 15, 'Direct discrimination', under 'Justifying direct age discrimination', and Chapter 20, 'Discrimination arising from disability', under 'Elements of S.15 claim – objective justification'.

17.11 The Government's long-standing concern that the term 'appropriate and necessary' might import a more stringent test appears to be misplaced, however, given that the case law of the European Court of Justice demonstrates that the term requires a balancing test between the discriminatory effects of a measure and the importance of the aim pursued. The 'appropriate and necessary' wording used in the EU Directives that prompted the 2003 and 2005 changes to domestic legislation codified the existing decisions of the ECJ on justification, in particular Bilka-Kaufhaus GmbH v Weber von Hartz (an equal pay case) – see further under 'The "Hampson test"' below. Domestic courts and tribunals are bound to assess the issue of justification according to the principles set out by the ECJ. Indeed, even before the amendments to the RRA and SDA in 2003 and 2005, the UK courts and tribunals had for some time been assessing the issue of justification according to EU principles.

Helpfully, the Supreme Court has now confirmed that the test of proportionality as set out in what is now S.19(2)(d) EqA has to be read in the light of the EU equality Directives which that provision implements, and must thus comply with the jurisprudence of the European Court interpreting those Directives. In Homer v Chief Constable of West Yorkshire Police 2012 UKSC 15, SC – an age discrimination case – the Supreme Court conducted a detailed analysis of this jurisprudence and stressed on the basis of it that, in order to be proportionate, an indirectly discriminatory PCP had to be *both* an appropriate means of achieving a legitimate aim *and* 'reasonably necessary'. Baroness Hale (with whom the other Justices agreed) made it clear that it would be a mistake to approach the matter as if the terms 'appropriate', 'necessary' and 'proportionate' were interchangeable. This shows that the Government's quibbles and qualms regarding using these words in the test for objective justification was substantially misplaced and that it might have been better simply to have included them expressly when framing the objective justification defence. As it is, employment tribunals that are misled by the fact that S.19(2)(d) simply refers to proportionality and therefore fail to approach the question of justification in a suitably structured way by considering the issues of 'appropriateness' and 'necessity' risk falling into error. As Baroness Hale explained, some measures may simply be inappropriate to the legitimate aim in question; or they may be appropriate, but go further – in terms of the discriminatory impact – than is reasonably necessary and so be disproportionate. Furthermore, when considering the impact of the discriminatory measure on the affected group as against the importance of the aim to the employer, the degree of the impact might be found to be too great to be justifiably offset by the employer's need for the measure, and thus disproportionate on that count. It is this degree of scrutiny of the legitimate aims relied upon by the employer and the discriminatory effect that must be applied by employment tribunals when considering whether the discriminatory effect of a PCP is proportional and thus justifiable.

The 'Hampson test'   17.12

The key elements of the test of objective justification derive from the case law of the European Court of Justice. In the equal pay case of Bilka-Kaufhaus GmbH v Weber von Hartz 1987 ICR 110, ECJ, the ECJ held that, to justify an objective which has a discriminatory effect, an employer must show that the means chosen for achieving that objective:

- correspond to a *real need* on the part of the undertaking

- are *appropriate* with a view to achieving the objective in question, and

- are *necessary* to that end.

Bilka-Kaufhaus became firmly rooted in UK sex discrimination law when it was applied by the House of Lords in Rainey v Greater Glasgow Health Board 1987 ICR 129, HL (another equal pay case). There, their Lordships were concerned with establishing whether a 'genuine material factor' (the defence that employers need to put forward in equal pay claims) existed and whether that justified a discriminatory pay differential. Citing Bilka-Kaufhaus, their Lordships held that a genuine material factor had to be based on 'objectively justified grounds' and confirmed that the same test was appropriate for justifying indirect sex discrimination.

Although both Rainey and Bilka-Kaufhaus were concerned with equal pay, **17.13** their far-reaching consequences for indirect discrimination claims under both the SDA and the RRA were confirmed by the Court of Appeal in a race discrimination case – Hampson v Department of Education and Science 1989 ICR 179, CA. In that case justification was not strictly at issue because a majority of the Court held that the claim could not proceed anyway because the defence of statutory immunity applied. However, Lord Justice Balcombe disagreed on this point, and so was able to go on to consider justification. In his opinion the true test involved striking 'an objective balance between the discriminatory effect of the condition and the reasonable needs of the party who applies the condition'. This signalled a retreat from a line of earlier cases that set a lower standard of justification, culminating in the Court of Appeal's decision in Ojutiku and anor v Manpower Services Commission 1982 ICR 661, CA, where Lord Justice Eveleigh had said that it was sufficient for the employer to demonstrate that the reasons for the discriminatory action would be 'acceptable to right-thinking people as sound and tolerable'.

The Hampson case subsequently went to the House of Lords, where their Lordships overruled the majority decision of the Court of Appeal on grounds

481

that did not concern the issue of justification – Hampson v Department of Education and Science 1990 ICR 511, HL. Balcombe LJ's formulation of the test for justification has, however, gone on to secure the widespread approval of the higher courts. As a result, the objective 'Hampson test' is now firmly established. It was followed by the Northern Ireland Court of Appeal in Briggs v North Eastern Education and Library Board 1990 IRLR 181, NICA, and expressly approved by the Court of Appeal in University of Manchester v Jones 1993 ICR 474, CA, and by the House of Lords in Webb v EMO Air Cargo (UK) Ltd 1993 ICR 175, HL (all sex discrimination cases).

17.14 Role of tribunals and burden of proof
The burden of establishing the defence of justification on the balance of probabilities lies squarely on the employer. In Dziedziak v Future Electronics Ltd EAT 0270/11 the Appeal Tribunal held that the reverse burden of proof rule under S.136 EqA only bites in an indirect discrimination claim after the claimant has demonstrated adverse disparate impact. Only then is the employer required to provide objective justification for the relevant PCP, and at that stage 'the provision as to reversal of the burden of proof makes sense; that is, a burden is on the employer to provide both explanation and justification'. For further details of the burden of proof in discrimination claims, see Chapter 32, 'Burden of proof'.

'Justification' is given no further definition in the EqA; nor is there any indication of the factors that can be relied upon to justify an indirectly discriminatory practice. The standard for justification is and always has been left to the courts and tribunals, and case law suggests that it is a high one. The EHRC Employment Code confirms that it is up to the employer to produce evidence: generalisations will not be sufficient – para 4.26. However, in Chief Constable of West Yorkshire Police and anor v Homer 2009 ICR 223, EAT, the EAT stated: 'It is an error to think that concrete evidence is always necessary to establish justification... Justification may be established in an appropriate case by reasoned and rational judgement. What is impermissible is a justification based simply on subjective impression or stereotyped assumptions.' In assessing any justification put forward, employment tribunals are under a duty to conduct a rigorous assessment of the organisation's requirements or rationale for imposing the PCP. (Note that the Homer case was subsequently appealed all the way to the Supreme Court – see Homer v Chief Constable of West Yorkshire Police 2012 UKSC 15, SC. However, although that Court held that the EAT and the Court of Appeal had erred in respect of certain aspects of their approach to the test of indirect discrimination, nothing in the Supreme Court's decision suggests it took issue with the EAT's observations just quoted.) It remains for the tribunal to decide whether justification has in fact been established and its findings on this point will not be interfered with by the EAT unless they can be said to be perverse – British Airways plc v Starmer 2005 IRLR 862, EAT.

482

It should be noted that a particularly stringent standard of scrutiny of the **17.15** justification defence may be appropriate where the discrimination, although indirect in form, is very closely related in substance to the direct form of the discrimination, since the latter can never be justified (save in the case of direct age discrimination) – R (on the application of Elias) v Secretary of State for Defence 2006 IRLR 934, CA (a race case involving a successful challenge to the Government's non-statutory compensation scheme for British civilians who were interned by the Japanese during World War II). In that case, the dispute centred on birth-related criteria that needed to be satisfied in order for former prisoners of war to be eligible for compensation. In holding that the eligibility criteria were not proportionate, the Court of Appeal stated that the trial judge had correctly adopted a rigorous standard in scrutinising the reasons advanced by the Secretary of State in justifying the criteria. A stringent standard of scrutiny of the justification was appropriate because the discrimination, though indirect in form, was closely related in substance to the direct form of race discrimination on the ground of national origins. In that particular case, the right to compensation was confined to 'British civilians', who for these purposes were defined as those who had been born in the United Kingdom or one of whose parents or grandparents had been born in the United Kingdom.

The same argument about a more stringent standard of proof was deployed (unsuccessfully) by the claimants in Blackburn and anor v Chief Constable of West Midlands Police 2009 IRLR 135, CA. There, the claimants failed to convince either the EAT or the Court of Appeal that the form of discrimination they had suffered – where they could not qualify for special '24/7' working payments owing to their childcare responsibilities – was 'closely related' to direct discrimination and that the task of establishing objective justification was therefore particularly onerous.

Timing of justification

17.16

The need to identify the material time at which the PCP was applied is discussed in Chapter 16, 'Indirect discrimination: proving disadvantage', under 'Provision, criterion or practice – identifying the time a PCP is applied'. The justification put forward by the employer for an indirectly discriminatory PCP falls to be judged *at the time when the measure was applied to the claimant*, not at the time when the PCP was introduced – Schönheit v Stadt Frankfurt am Main and another case 2004 IRLR 983, ECJ, and Cross and ors v British Airways plc 2005 IRLR 423, EAT.

It does not follow that the employer is prevented from relying on considerations that were not in his mind at the time of the PCP's application. In the equal pay case of Health and Safety Executive v Cadman 2005 ICR 1546, CA, the Court of Appeal confirmed that there is no rule of law whereby the justification must have consciously and contemporaneously featured in the employer's decision-making processes. This principle was applied in British Airways plc v Starmer

2005 IRLR 862, EAT, where the employer applied a PCP that pilots who had completed fewer than 2,000 flying hours would not be permitted to reduce their contractual hours below 75 per cent of full time. The EAT held that an employment tribunal had directed itself correctly when conducting the balancing exercise by taking account of safety considerations that had not been in the employer's mind at the time when the PCP was applied to the claimant. However, the tribunal had found that notwithstanding its right to adduce such evidence, the employer had not 'given any cogent evidence as to why it would be unsafe or in any way unsuitable for [the claimant]... to fly at 50 per cent of full time'. The tribunal therefore upheld the claim of indirect sex discrimination.

17.17 However, in R (on the application of Elias) v Secretary of State for Defence 2006 IRLR 934, CA (discussed under 'Role of tribunals and burden of proof' above), the Court of Appeal held that the burden of proving that a particular aim was legitimate becomes more onerous when the reasons for the aim were not in the mind of the discriminator at the time the discriminatory act was committed. In that case the Government had failed to realise at the relevant time that a compensation scheme for former prisoners of war was potentially discriminatory and sought during the course of litigation to rely on the aim of reducing the budgetary implications of the scheme by limiting it to persons who had a close connection with the United Kingdom.

17.18 **Relevance of monitoring.** Employers should periodically review their employment policies and practices, as a PCP can start off life as being justified only for this to change over the course of time. Indeed, the most effective way to ensure that a measure continues to be justified is for employers to undertake proactive monitoring. The EHRC Employment Code recommends that all employers carry out equality monitoring and sets out guidance in this regard – see paras 18.32–18.34.

In Chief Constable of West Midlands Police v Blackburn and anor 2008 ICR 505, EAT, the claimants argued in the context of an equal pay claim that the employer's failure to monitor the effect of a special priority payments scheme made the justification defence harder to sustain as it demonstrated that the issue of proportionality was not specifically addressed by the employer. While accepting that the issue of monitoring was one that the tribunal was entitled to take into account in weighing up proportionality, the EAT held that this was not one of those cases where the employer's contemporaneous reason for adopting a certain scheme differed from the one put before the tribunal. While the employer may not have appreciated that the scheme might have a small adverse impact on women, the objectives of the scheme were always transparently clear. Accordingly, the requirement that police officers work anti-social hours in order to receive a supplement was proportionate despite the lack of monitoring. The EAT's decision was subsequently upheld by the Court of Appeal but the monitoring point was not addressed.

The Government is obliged to conduct monitoring of legislation. In R v **17.19** Secretary of State for Employment ex parte Seymour-Smith and anor (No.2) 2000 ICR 244, HL, the House of Lords considered the lawfulness of the legislative measure ('the 1985 Order') introducing the two-year qualifying period for unfair dismissal rights between its introduction in 1985 and 1991 – the latter being the date the claimants were dismissed. In reaching the decision that the Government had discharged the burden of showing that the 1985 Order was still objectively justified in 1991, Lord Nicholls stated that if the Government introduces a measure that proves to have a disparate adverse impact on women, then it is under a duty to review the matter. The greater the degree of disparate impact, 'the greater the diligence which can reasonably be expected of the Government'. For a detailed discussion of this case, see under 'Government justification of social policy' below.

Legitimate aim
17.20

The justification test in S.19(2)(d) EqA requires that the application of the PCP is a 'proportionate means of achieving a *legitimate aim*' (our stress). This means that unless the aim behind the imposition of a PCP is regarded as 'legitimate', the employer's defence will not get off the ground and there will be no need for the employment tribunal to examine the issue of proportionality. According to the EHRC Employment Code, for an aim to be legitimate it must be 'legal, should not be discriminatory in itself, and it must represent a real, objective consideration' – para 4.28. However, there is no statutory definition of what amounts to a legitimate aim; nor is there any list of potentially relevant factors.

A wide range of matters are capable, in practice, of amounting to legitimate aims, although whether in fact they do so in any particular case will be a question for the employment tribunal. The Code states that the health, welfare and safety of individuals may qualify as a legitimate aim – para 4.28. This might cover, for example, the imposition of health checks or medical requirements that potentially discriminate against older workers or those with relevant disabilities. Other legitimate aims that could justify indirect discrimination include operational integrity and client needs. For example, policies specifying inconvenient hours of working (such as night working) have been held capable of justification, despite their adverse impact on women, on the ground of operational integrity. Similarly, clients' needs for a business's services at a particular time may justify requirements of full-time working or 24-hour availability.

For further details of the most commonly cited legitimate aims and the way in **17.21** which they operate in practice, see under 'Justification in context' below. This section focuses on whether and to what extent three types of aim – discriminatory aims, social policy aims and cost considerations – are capable in principle of amounting to legitimate aims for the purpose of justifying indirect discrimination.

485

17.22 **Discriminatory aims**

If the aim behind a PCP is discriminatory, it is generally accepted that it can never be legitimate and is incapable of justifying indirect discrimination – R v Secretary of State for Employment ex parte EOC and anor 1994 ICR 317, HL. In Allonby v Accrington and Rossendale College and ors 2001 ICR 1189, CA, a college dismissed its part-time lecturers in order to avoid paying them certain benefits in accordance with employment legislation. An employment tribunal rejected a claim that this was unlawful indirect sex discrimination, finding that the college had provided sound business reasons for looking to control the costs of part-time employment. However, the Court of Appeal found that the aim was itself discriminatory. The tribunal had shown no recognition of the fact that the aim was to deny part-time workers, a predominantly female group, benefits that Parliament had legislated to give them. Therefore, the aim could not provide justification.

17.23 **Social policy aims**

The Government can rely on social policy aims when implementing aspects of employment policy – see under 'Government justification of social policy' below. But to what extent can private employers cite social policy aims to justify the imposition of an apparently discriminatory PCP? Case law has established that it is not enough for an employer to show that an indirectly discriminatory measure was imposed in pursuance of an intrinsically laudable and otherwise reasonable policy – Greater Manchester Police Authority v Lea 1990 IRLR 372, EAT. In that case, the employer sought to justify a policy of excluding those holding an occupational pension from consideration for a job by reference to the social aim of providing employment for individuals with no other source of income. Such an aim was not related to the needs of the employer in discharging its function as a police authority and so the EAT held that it could not justify the indirect discrimination. There has to be a nexus established between the functional needs of the employer and the imposition of the PCP. Without showing this connection, it would be impossible, in the EAT's view, to carry out the objective balancing exercise that the proportionality test entails (see under 'Proportionality' below).

It should be noted that the position may be different in respect of direct age discrimination (which, as explained above, is uniquely subject to an objective justification defence). In this context, it appears that social policy considerations may amount to legitimate aims, even when relied on by an employer as opposed to a Member State. In MacCulloch v Imperial Chemical Industries plc 2008 ICR 1334, EAT, for example, the EAT (in the context of an enhanced redundancy scheme that favoured older employees) approved the employment tribunal's findings that encouraging turnover and creating opportunities for junior staff are, in principle, capable of being legitimate aims that might be furthered by increasing payments for older workers and that it could be

486

legitimate to pay more to older workers as they are particularly vulnerable in the job market. However, in R (on the application of Age UK) v Secretary of State for Business, Innovation and Skills 2010 ICR 260, QBD, the High Court held that an individual employer seeking to justify particular practices or treatment in reliance on social aims has a much more rigorous task than a Member State introducing legislation designed to implement a Directive. For further details, see Chapter 15, 'Direct discrimination', under 'Justifying direct age discrimination'.

Costs
17.24

The question of whether, and to what extent, cost considerations can constitute a legitimate aim is a perennially thorny one. According to the established 'cost plus' principle, which has been endorsed on a number of occasions by the EAT, cost can be cited by an employer as one of a number of factors justifying indirect discrimination but cannot be relied on in isolation. However, recent case law has called that principle into question and there are likely to be further judicial developments in this area – see further under 'The cost plus principle' below.

The EAT's decision in HM Land Registry v Benson and ors 2012 IRLR 373, EAT, sheds light on the extent to which cost savings (assuming they are combined with other factors) are capable of justifying indirect discrimination. The case suggests that an employer's decision about how to allocate financial resources will constitute a 'real need' or legitimate aim, even if the employer could have afforded to make a different allocation with a lesser impact on the disadvantaged class of employee in question. However, this is not the end of the matter because it will then be necessary to consider the proportionality issue, which involves balancing the reasonable needs of the enterprise against the measure's discriminatory impact – see under 'Proportionality' below.

In Benson the employer, HMLR, needed to reduce headcount and offered a 17.25 voluntary redundancy/early retirement scheme. It had more applicants than could be accommodated within the budget it had allocated to the project (£12 million) and so it undertook a selection exercise. Its principal (but not sole) criterion was to choose those whom it would cost least to dismiss so as to maximise the redundancies achievable within the budget. HMLR conceded that this had a disproportionate adverse impact on employees in the 50–54 age group. It was inherently more expensive, all other things being equal, to release such employees than to release their younger or older colleagues, because those aged 50–54 would have been entitled to early retirement on an unreduced pension. As a result, proportionately fewer applications from this age group were successful. An employment tribunal upheld indirect age discrimination claims brought by five such employees, finding that HMLR could have afforded to accept all the applications, albeit that it would have cost an extra £19.7 million to do so. However, the EAT (presided over by its then President, Mr Justice Underhill) allowed HMLR's appeal.

487

The EAT held that the tribunal had erroneously treated the £12 million budget as an aspect of the 'means' adopted by HMLR to achieve more broadly defined aims – namely, the aims of reducing headcount, reducing payroll costs, and leaving an appropriate balance of grades in place across the relevant offices. Instead, the employer's decision about the allocation of resources should have been accepted as a legitimate aim and been balanced against the discriminatory impact complained of. According to the EAT, HMLR's aim was to reduce the number of applicants at a cost that came within the £12 million budget, or alternatively to reduce headcount in such a way that its costs did not exceed its revenue. Both of these aims were legitimate. It was clearly legitimate for an employer to seek to break even year-on-year by making redundancies, to impose a budget, and to make decisions about the allocation of resources. The EAT noted that imposing a 'maximum spend' was not inherently discriminatory against particular age groups; any discriminatory impact was the result of the particular selection criterion chosen rather than of the aim pursued.

17.26 Turning to the issue of proportionality, the EAT referred to the tribunal's unchallenged finding that, if HMLR chose to carry out a selection exercise, it had no real alternative to imposing the cost criterion. In those circumstances, the EAT felt constrained to conclude that use of the criterion was justified. (It was not convinced, however, that this finding had been inevitable and suggested that the evidence in other cases might produce a different result.) In reaching this decision, the EAT rejected an argument based on Pulham and ors v Barking and Dagenham London Borough Council 2010 ICR 333, EAT, where the EAT had stated that an employer 'cannot automatically justify a failure to eliminate discrimination by allocating the costs of doing so to a particular budget and then declaring that budget to be exhausted'. That was a case of a directly discriminatory pay practice, which the employer wished to continue on the basis that it would cost too much to eliminate. Here, by contrast, the budget was for a particular project (the redundancy programme) that was not directly discriminatory, but which, as it turned out, required a selection exercise that could only practicably be done on an indirectly age discriminatory basis.

17.27 **The 'cost plus' principle.** It is significant that in the Benson case (above) there was a specific finding by the employment tribunal that cost was not the sole criterion relied on by the employer. In Cross and ors v British Airways plc 2005 IRLR 423, EAT (a sex discrimination case), the Appeal Tribunal held that it is open to a tribunal to find that cost is a factor justifying indirect discrimination, provided it is combined with other factors – i.e. cost cannot be a legitimate aim on its own. This is sometimes referred to as the 'cost plus' principle, and derives from an interpretation of European case law concerning justification in the context of equal pay and indirect gender discrimination. As we shall see, however, obiter (i.e. non-binding) comments in recent EAT and Court of Appeal decisions have cast doubt on this principle, paving the way for employers to argue before an appellate court that cost considerations *alone* may amount to a legitimate aim. There has as yet been no definitive ruling on this point and further litigation seems inevitable.

In Cross the female claimants complained about a retirement policy allowing employees recruited before November 1971 to retire at 60 instead of 55 – the age applied to most of the workforce. The claimants pointed out that in a workforce of 13,127 in 2002, there remained only 536 employees with a contractual retirement age of 60, the vast majority of whom – 406 – were male, whereas the workforce as a whole was predominantly female. In holding that the policy was justified, the employment tribunal found that its discriminatory impact weighed lightly, given the small number of individuals affected. With this in mind, the tribunal took into account the cost implications for BA of altering the retirement age and the knock-on detrimental impact this would have for the majority of the cabin crew, whose pension benefits would be reduced if their retirement age were increased to 60 and they took early retirement at 55.

On appeal to the EAT, the claimants argued that the tribunal had erred in **17.28** taking into account the issue of cost. They relied on a number of decisions of the European Court of Justice, culminating in Schönheit v Stadt Frankfurt am Main and another case 2004 IRLR 983, ECJ, which appeared to confirm that budgetary considerations can never justify sex discrimination. The appeal was heard by the then President, Mr Justice Burton. In the EAT's view, the ECJ decisions had established that an EU Member State, with its notionally bottomless purse, cannot rely on budgetary considerations to justify a discriminatory social policy. On the other hand, an employer seeking to justify a discriminatory PCP, while unable to rely *solely* on considerations of cost, is entitled to put cost into the balance along with other justifications if there are any. However, the EAT added that when it comes to the weighing exercise, 'costs justifications may often be valued less, particularly if the discrimination is substantial, obvious and even deliberate'. In the instant case, the tribunal had not relied solely on the cost issue in its finding of objective justification and there were no grounds for overturning its decision.

The 'cost plus' principle was endorsed by a later President of the EAT, Mr Justice Elias, in Redcar and Cleveland Borough Council v Bainbridge and ors 2008 ICR 249, EAT (an equal pay case that subsequently went to the Court of Appeal on another point). It is supported by the EHRC Employment Code, which puts it in this way: 'The greater financial cost of using a less discriminatory approach cannot, by itself, provide a justification for applying a particular provision, criterion or practice. Cost can only be taken into account as part of the employer's justification for the provision, criterion or practice if there are other good reasons for adopting it' – para 4.32. The Code also states: 'Although reasonable business needs and economic efficiency may be legitimate aims, an employer solely aiming to reduce costs cannot expect to satisfy the test. For

489

example, the employer cannot simply argue that to discriminate is cheaper than avoiding discrimination' – para 4.29.

17.29 Two examples of the application of the 'cost plus' rule by employment tribunals:

- **Rainbow v Milton Keynes Council** ET Case No.1200104/07: the employment tribunal found that an employer who advertised for teachers 'in the first five years of their career' committed an act of indirect age discrimination by failing to shortlist a 61-year-old job applicant. It was clear that people of her age were likely to have had far more teaching experience and, accordingly, to be put at a particular disadvantage. The case turned on the issue of objective justification. In this regard, the Council argued unsuccessfully that the PCP relating to experience was justified by reference to the increased cost of employing a more experienced teacher. It submitted that the law relating to age discrimination was 'in effect a blank canvas', having been introduced relatively recently, and therefore that the tribunal had scope to recognise bare economic considerations as forming the basis of a justification defence. However, the tribunal preferred to follow the EAT's guidance in Cross and ors v British Airways plc (above), concluding that cost can properly be a factor justifying indirect discrimination if combined with other reasons. In this case, the Council had not provided detailed evidence of the school's budgetary position, nor had it balanced 'the question of cost against the effects of an otherwise age discriminatory PCP'. In the tribunal's view, if cost were to be used as a justification for an otherwise discriminatory practice, the evidence had to be such that the respondent was 'more or less compelled' to take the discriminatory decision for 'cost plus' reasons

- **Sudlow v Thomson Airways Ltd** ET Case No.1201242/10: S began working as a pilot in 1988 but had to stop flying on health grounds in March 2006. He became entitled to benefits under a permanent health insurance (PHI) scheme from September of that year. The PHI scheme had been agreed at a time when his normal retirement age was 60 and, accordingly, the benefits payable under it ceased when he reached that age. The International Civil Aviation Authority subsequently amended its rules so that pilots could continue in employment until age 65, and S's normal retirement age was amended accordingly. S's employer, TA Ltd, brought in a new PHI scheme from October 2006. Under the new scheme, the company made income protection payments out of its own funds to employees between the ages of 60 and 65. However, the new scheme did not cover employees currently receiving benefits under the old PHI scheme. Thus, pilots in S's position only received income protection payments between the ages of 60 and 65 if they could come off PHI benefits, go back to their normal duties, and then stop work again and claim under the new scheme. This was not a route open to S since he was not fit to resume flying. The employment tribunal found that TA Ltd had applied a PCP whereby employees who were already receiving

PHI benefits before October 2006 were not eligible to benefit from the new scheme, and this put S's age group at a particular disadvantage compared with younger employees. Furthermore, the PCP was not justified. The tribunal acknowledged that it was a legitimate aim for a company to seek to manage its costs in connection with PHI benefits; however, costs in themselves were not a legitimate reason to justify an otherwise discriminatory PCP. In any event, the employer had produced insufficient evidence to establish that the costs of maintaining benefits to age 65 out of TA Ltd's own funds were prohibitive or would have resulted in a smaller budget being available for general pay increases.

The retreat from the 'cost plus' rule. In recent years, there have been indications **17.30** from both the EAT and the Court of Appeal that the 'cost plus' rule set out in the Cross case (above) may be open to challenge, although there has been, as yet, no definitive ruling on this point. In Woodcock v Cumbria Primary Care Trust 2011 ICR 143, EAT – a direct age discrimination case that subsequently went to the Court of Appeal (see below) – Mr Justice Underhill, then President of the EAT, cast doubt on the cost plus orthodoxy by expressing the view that there was no principled basis for a rule that cost considerations can never *by themselves* constitute sufficient justification for discrimination. In his view, the 'cost plus' principle was not, in fact, an absolute requirement of European case law and was apt to involve parties and tribunals in an artificial game of 'find the other factor', producing arbitrary and complicated reasoning. Moreover, he noted that deciding where 'cost' stops and other factors start is not a straightforward exercise.

Ultimately, the 'cost plus' approach is derived from Hill and anor v Revenue Commissioners and anor 1999 ICR 48, ECJ, in which the European Court noted that 'an employer cannot justify discrimination... solely on the ground that avoidance of such discrimination would involve increased costs'. Underhill P in Woodcock questioned the orthodox interpretation of this bald and seemingly unsupported statement. He reasoned that not only is it explicable in the way that it was understood by the EAT in Cross (above), but that 'it need mean no more than that it was not enough for an employer to say that avoiding discrimination would involve increased expenditure: he must show that the extent to which it would do so would indeed be disproportionate to the benefit in terms of eliminating the discriminatory impact'. In other words, the ECJ's guidance can be read in two ways: (1) the saving or avoidance of costs alone cannot amount to a legitimate aim and must always be linked to another factor; or (2) while cost alone can amount to a legitimate aim, an employer cannot succeed in establishing justification simply by citing cost considerations and must go on to demonstrate proportionality.

Underhill P clearly favoured the second interpretation, expressing the view that **17.31** an employer should be entitled to justify discriminatory treatment simply on

491

the basis that the cost of avoidance would be 'disproportionately high'. However, his comments were obiter (i.e. non-binding) since, in the EAT's view, the employment tribunal had been entitled to hold that the act of alleged discrimination in Woodcock – accelerating the employee's redundancy dismissal in order to avoid his remaining in the Trust's employment on his fiftieth birthday and becoming entitled to enhanced early retirement benefits that would have cost the Trust an additional £500,000 – was underpinned not only by budgetary considerations but also by a desire to prevent the employee from receiving a benefit that he had no legitimate right to expect. The prevention of that windfall, and the avoidance of the corresponding loss to the Trust, was a legitimate aim going beyond the mere wish to reduce costs, and the Trust's decision to give notice of dismissal before the employee's formal redundancy meeting was a proportionate means of achieving that aim.

Underhill P's comments in Woodcock were approved (albeit also on an obiter basis) in the indirect religious discrimination case of Cherfi v G4S Security Services Ltd EAT 0379/10, discussed further in the section 'Justification in context', under 'Operational needs – time off for religious observance' below. There, the EAT upheld an employment tribunal's decision that an employer's refusal to allow a security guard to leave work to attend Friday prayers at a mosque was a proportionate means of achieving a legitimate aim – namely, meeting the operational needs of the business. In reaching its decision, the EAT stated that, if the case had been one in which cost alone had been cited to justify discrimination, it would have supported the obiter views expressed in Woodcock.

17.32 A case that appeared to present an opportunity for re-examination of the cost plus principle was HM Land Registry v Benson and ors 2012 IRLR 373, EAT (discussed above), in which the EAT held that an employer was justified in selecting employees for voluntary redundancy/early retirement on the basis of whom it would cost least to dismiss, despite the fact that this resulted in a disparate impact on employees aged 50–54. Unfortunately, the EAT did not find it necessary to revisit the relevant authorities. This was because the employment tribunal had found that, although cost was the main criterion, the early retirement applications were not determined on the ground of cost alone; HMLR had also made adjustments designed to maintain an appropriate balance of experience among retained staff. The EAT opined that since this finding was not challenged by the claimants on appeal, there was no need to 'become embroiled in the question about the validity of the costs plus approach raised in Woodcock'. However, the EAT also commented that the selection of candidates on the basis of cost was the only factor that produced a disparate impact between age groups. Arguably, therefore, the other factors identified by the employment tribunal were irrelevant to the alleged discrimination and the 'cost plus' issue should have been addressed.

In March 2012, the Court of Appeal handed down its decision in the Woodcock case – Woodcock v Cumbria Primary Care Trust 2012 EWCA Civ 330, CA. Dismissing an appeal against the EAT's decision (see above), it held that the age discrimination inherent in the Trust's decision to dismiss W before he became entitled to a substantial enhanced pension on his fiftieth birthday was justified as a proportionate means of achieving a legitimate aim. Like the tribunal and the EAT, the Court considered that the aim of serving notice on W was to give effect to the Trust's genuine decision to terminate his employment by reason of redundancy. That was a legitimate aim, and it was a legitimate part of that aim for the Trust to time the dismissal so as to save the additional costs of benefits that W had no legitimate expectation of receiving. Thus, the Trust's actions had not been based solely on cost. Although the Trust had cut a procedural corner in issuing notice of dismissal before the redundancy consultation process had taken place, that consideration went only to the question of proportionality. There were no grounds for interfering with the tribunal's decision that, in the circumstances, the treatment was proportionate because the dismissal process had already been subject to a lengthy delay and consultation would have achieved nothing.

Nevertheless, the Court went on to consider the 'cost plus' rule on an obiter **17.33** basis, expressing its own doubts as to the continued correctness of the principle. Echoing the views of Underhill P in the EAT, Lord Justice Rimer stated that there was 'some degree of artificiality' in an approach to justification that renders cost inadmissible as a factor on its own, but admissible if linked to a non-cost factor. The Court observed that almost every decision an employer takes will have regard to costs, and that the wording of the discrimination legislation in force at the relevant time did not exclude cost considerations – it merely required the treatment to be a 'proportionate means of achieving a legitimate aim', as S.19 EqA does now. With regard to the ECJ's guidance in Hill and anor v Revenue Commissioners and anor 1999 ICR 48, ECJ, to the effect that 'an employer cannot justify discrimination... solely on the ground that avoidance of such discrimination would involve increased costs', Rimer LJ took the view that this 'cannot mean more than that the saving or avoidance of costs will not, without more, amount to the achieving of a "legitimate aim"'. Thus, if the Trust's treatment of W were correctly characterised as no more than treatment aimed at saving or avoiding costs, Rimer LJ would have accepted that it was not a means of achieving a 'legitimate aim' and was incapable of justification. However, the Court did not characterise the Trust's actions in that way. It accepted that the Trust was trying to bring about the dismissal of a redundant employee and that doing so without incurring excessive cost was a key consideration. That was a 'cost plus' reason.

Where does this leave us? Although Rimer LJ in Woodcock questioned the 'cost plus' orthodoxy, he ultimately appears to have left the principle intact. Accordingly, while the wider implications of the EAT's decision in Cross (above)

493

may now have been doubted at a high level, the general principle lives on and for the time being Cross remains the leading authority on cost as a legitimate aim. It seems prudent, therefore, for employers to continue to follow the Cross decision by identifying another justifying factor in addition to cost. Nevertheless, the views expressed by both the EAT and the Court of Appeal in Woodcock regarding the artificiality of the 'cost plus' approach – although strictly obiter – are likely to have high persuasive value. It is strongly arguable that cost factors should be relevant to the question of whether the means deployed to achieve the employer's aim are proportionate, rather than to whether that aim is legitimate in the first place.

17.34 Given this state of affairs, it is almost inevitable that there will be further developments in this area. Even if the 'cost plus' orthodoxy is judicially rejected at some point in the future, however, employers will not always be able to avoid liability simply by pointing to the cost of avoiding or correcting the discriminatory impact on the relevant protected group. Applying the principle of proportionality, if the discriminatory impact is great, the employer must avoid or correct it whatever the cost. Nevertheless – as Underhill P pointed out in Woodcock – 'there may equally be cases where the impact is trivial and the cost of avoiding or correcting it enormous; and in such cases we cannot see why the principle of proportionality should not be applied in the ordinary way' – see under 'Proportionality' below.

17.35 **Flexible working claims.** Finally, it is worth noting that the burden of additional costs is, on its own, enough to justify an employer's refusing a statutory request for flexible working – S.80G(1)(b)(i) Employment Rights Act 1996 (ERA). Accordingly, where a claimant has brought claims under both the EqA and the ERA in relation to the refusal of a flexible working request, an employer could find itself in the peculiar position of losing an indirect sex discrimination claim on the basis of the 'cost plus' rule while successfully defending a claim based on the flexible working provisions contained in the ERA.

17.36 # Proportionality

It is clear from the general approval given to Lord Justice Balcombe's test as set out in Hampson v Department of Education and Science 1989 ICR 179, CA (discussed under 'Background and overview – the "Hampson test"' above), that consideration of the employer's defence of justification in claims of indirect discrimination requires an objective balance to be struck between the discriminatory effect of the PCP and the reasonable needs of the party who applies it. The Hampson test still represents an accurate summary of the state of the law, despite the reformulation of the definition of indirect discrimination in the intervening years. This balancing exercise is often referred to as the test of 'proportionality' and is now codified in S.19(2)(d) EqA.

The EHRC Employment Code puts it in slightly (although not materially) different terms: 'Even if the aim is a legitimate one, the means of achieving it must be proportionate. Deciding whether the means used to achieve the legitimate aim are proportionate involves a balancing exercise. An employment tribunal may wish to conduct a proper evaluation of the discriminatory effect of the provision, criterion or practice as against the employer's reasons for applying it, taking into account all the relevant facts' – para 4.30.

In Pulham and ors v Barking and Dagenham London Borough Council 2010 **17.37** ICR 333, EAT, the then President of the EAT, Mr Justice Underhill, commented that the test of proportionality 'necessarily involves identifying the "legitimate aim" which the employer is seeking to achieve by taking the measure complained of – that measure being the "means". But the dichotomy of "aim" and "means" is not always clearcut and the two elements can sometimes reasonably be formulated in more than one way… Tribunals need not cudgel their brains with metaphysical inquiries about what count as aims and what count as means as long as the underlying balancing exercise is carried out.'

Assessing the needs of the employer   17.38
At first glance, the test of objective justification set out by the ECJ in Bilka-Kaufhaus GmbH v Weber von Hartz 1987 ICR 110, ECJ – see under 'Background and overview – the "Hampson test"' above – seems to present a formidable hurdle for an employer seeking to justify indirect discrimination: the employer is required to show to the satisfaction of the employment tribunal that the policy alleged to be discriminatory corresponds to a real need on the part of the employer; that the policy is appropriate with a view to achieving the employer's objective; and – on its face, the most difficult of all – that the policy is 'necessary' for this purpose. However, case law has to some extent tempered the apparent stringency of this requirement.

'**Real need**'. As previously discussed, it is not enough to show that the measure **17.39** was imposed in pursuance of an intrinsically laudable and otherwise reasonable policy. As the EAT explained in Greater Manchester Police Authority v Lea 1990 IRLR 372, EAT (see under 'Legitimate aim – social policy aims' above), in order to carry out the proper balancing exercise there has to be a nexus established between the function of the employer and the imposition of the requirement or condition (now PCP). It is not enough that the discriminator has a desire – however worthy – to further some social need or otherwise reasonable policy. In the Lea case the employer was unable to justify a policy of excluding those holding an occupational pension from consideration for a senior post by reference to the social aim of providing employment for individuals with no other source of income. However laudable, that aim was not related to the needs of the employer in discharging its function as a police authority.

495

In HM Land Registry v Benson and ors 2012 IRLR 373, EAT (discussed under 'Legitimate aim – costs' above), one of the issues was whether the employer had established a 'real need' based on cost considerations. In that case, HMLR offered a voluntary redundancy/early retirement scheme in an attempt to reduce headcount. It had more applicants than could be accommodated within the budget it had allocated to the project (£12 million) and so it undertook a selection exercise. Its principal (but not sole) criterion was to choose those whom it would cost least to dismiss so as to maximise the redundancies achievable within the budget. HMLR conceded that this had a disproportionate impact on employees in the 50–54 age group. It was inherently more expensive, all other things being equal, to release such employees than to release their younger or older colleagues, because those aged 50–54 would have been entitled to early retirement on an unreduced pension. As a result, proportionately fewer applications from this age group were successful. An employment tribunal upheld indirect age discrimination claims brought by five such employees, finding that HMLR could have afforded to accept all the applications, albeit that it would have cost an extra £19.7 million to do so. However, the EAT (presided over by its then President, Mr Justice Underhill) allowed HMLR's appeal.

17.40   The EAT held that the budget of £12 million represented a legitimate aim, or real need, on the part of HMLR. The tribunal had erroneously treated the £12 million limit as an aspect of the 'means' adopted by the employer to achieve more broadly defined aims. The tribunal's finding that the extra £19.7 million was not 'unaffordable' implied that it thought HMLR could find the funds without becoming insolvent. That was to treat the language of 'real need', in the context of objective justification, as connoting a requirement of absolute necessity. This was the wrong approach. In the EAT's view, the task of the employment tribunal is to accept the employer's legitimate decision as to the allocation of its resources as representing a genuine 'need', but to balance it against the discriminatory impact complained of. Had the tribunal done that here, it would have found HMLR's means proportionate. The EAT referred to the tribunal's unchallenged finding that, if HMLR chose to carry out a selection exercise, it had no real alternative to imposing the cost criterion. In those circumstances, the EAT felt constrained to conclude that use of the criterion was justified.

17.41   **'Reasonably necessary'.** As noted above, the Bilka-Kaufhaus test requires the employer to show that the PCP is 'necessary' to achieve the relevant objective. However, the word 'necessary' in this context has not been given its strictest possible interpretation: an employer is not required to prove that there was no other way of achieving its objectives. In Hardys and Hansons plc v Lax 2005 ICR 1565, CA (a race discrimination case), Lord Justice Pill stated: 'I accept that the word "necessary" used in Bilka is to be qualified by the word "reasonably"… The presence of the word "reasonably" reflects the presence and applicability of the principle of proportionality. The employer does not have to demonstrate that no other proposal is possible. The employer has to show that the proposal, in this case for a full-time appointment, is justified objectively notwithstanding its discriminatory effect.'

Nevertheless, Pill LJ went on to state that this 'reasonably necessary' test is much stricter than the 'range of reasonable responses' test applicable in unfair dismissal law. He accepted that the principle of proportionality requires an employment tribunal to take into account the reasonable needs of the employer's business. However, that was not to suggest that the tribunal is confined to considering whether the employer's views as to those needs fell within the band of reasonable responses available. Instead, the tribunal has to make its own judgement, upon a fair and detailed analysis of the working practices and business considerations involved, as to whether the discriminatory proposal or measure is reasonably necessary. Upholding the tribunal's decision that the employer had discriminated against the claimant when it refused to allow her to work part time or to job-share following her return from maternity leave, the Court held that the tribunal had carried out the necessary critical evaluation of the employer's requirement that the claimant work full time. It had been entitled to find that the employer had not sufficiently explored the feasibility of job sharing and had exaggerated the difficulties that would be caused by allowing the employee to return to work on a part-time basis.

The reasonable needs of the employer to impose a discriminatory PCP came **17.42** under particular scrutiny by the Court of Appeal in Allonby v Accrington and Rossendale College and ors 2001 ICR 1189, CA. In that case the claimant was a lecturer in office technology. From 1990–96 she was employed part time by a college, ARC, on a continuous succession of one-year contracts of service under which she was paid by the hour. In 1996, legislative changes required part-time lecturers to be accorded benefits equal or equivalent to those of full-time lecturers. ARC decided to terminate the contracts of its 341 hourly paid part-time lecturers and retain their services as subcontractors. One reason for this decision was to save an estimated £13,000 a year. The claimant's contract was terminated with effect from 29 August 1996 but she was offered re-engagement through ELS, a limited company operating as an employment business. ELS operated a database of available lecturers on whom colleges could call, by name if desired, for lecturing services. The claimant registered with ELS and her pay became a proportion of the fee agreed between ELS and ARC. Her income fell and she lost a series of benefits ranging from sick pay to access to a defined career structure. An employment tribunal decided that the dismissal by ARC constituted indirect discrimination, but that it was justifiable. The case came before the Court of Appeal, which held that the tribunal had erred in uncritically accepting ARC's reasons for the dismissals without attempting to evaluate objectively whether they were reasonably necessary. Furthermore,

497

there was no recognition by the tribunal that if the aim of a measure – in this case dismissal – was itself discriminatory it could never afford justification (see under 'Legitimate aim – discriminatory aims' above).

The principles and guidance set out in the Hardys and Allonby cases have been applied in a number of subsequent cases, including British Airways plc v Starmer 2005 IRLR 862, EAT. There, the then President of the EAT, Mr Justice Burton, stated: 'The decision of the respondent and its business reasons will be respected, but they must not be uncritically accepted.' Another example is Craddock v Cornwall County Council and anor EAT 0367/05, where a primary school teacher complained of indirect discrimination when her employer refused to allow her to return to work on a job-share basis following her maternity leave. Although the employer had put forward a number of cogent reasons for not allowing the claimant to undertake a job share, the EAT held that the tribunal had not subjected these reasons to sufficient scrutiny. It was not clear from the tribunal's judgment that it had weighed the discriminatory effect of the employer's actions against the justification for that action. In indirect discrimination claims there will often be cogent reasons for the discrimination, otherwise a tribunal might draw an inference of direct discrimination. Accordingly, the issue is whether the justification *outweighs* the disparate impact. In the instant case it was not clear that the tribunal had carried out the required balancing act rather than assuming that a cogent argument against the employment of a part-time employee was to be equated with a finding that the grounds relied upon as justification were of sufficient importance to override the disparate impact of the difference in treatment, in whole or in part.

17.43 Similarly, in Mitchell v David Evans Agricultural Ltd EAT 0083/06, the EAT held that the employment tribunal had failed to undertake a full analysis of the justification put forward by the employer as to why it needed a part-time administrator to go full time. The claimant was dismissed after her employer decided it required a full-time employee. Her request to work as part of a job-share so that she could accommodate her childcare responsibilities was rejected. The tribunal held that the company had justified its need for a full-time member of staff on the basis that a new computer system had been introduced, which the employer expected would take it to another level of business operation and efficiency. It had a justifiable requirement for greater administrative efficiency and required one individual who could assist with the bespoke service offered to clients. On appeal, the EAT held that it was not enough for the tribunal to identify in relatively cursory form the factors that it found to amount to objective justification and it was not clear from the tribunal's reasoning that it had adopted the correct approach. It should have assessed the reasonable needs of the business and made its own judgement upon a fuller analysis than was carried out as to whether the proposal was reasonably necessary and whether it could be justified notwithstanding its discriminatory effect.

The cases outlined above demonstrate and put into practice the guidance given by Lord Justice Sedley in Allonby v Accrington and Rossendale College and ors (above) as to the responsibility of the tribunal to scrutinise the alleged business needs put forward by the employer to justify indirect discrimination. His Lordship explained: 'In this situation it is not enough that the tribunal should have posed, as they did, the statutory question "whether the decision taken by the [employer] was justifiable irrespective of the sex of the person or persons to whom it applied"... [T]here has to be some evidence that the tribunal understood the process by which a now formidable body of authority requires the task of answering the question to be carried out, and some evidence that it has in fact carried it out. Once a finding of a [PCP] having a disparate and adverse impact on women had been made, what was required was at the minimum a critical evaluation of whether the [employer]'s reasons demonstrated a real need to dismiss the applicant; if there was such a need, consideration of the seriousness of the disparate impact of the [PCP] on women including the applicant; and an evaluation of whether the former were sufficient to outweigh the latter.'

Assessing the discriminatory effect   17.44

In performing the required balancing exercise, an employment tribunal must assess not only the needs of the employer, but also the discriminatory effect on those who share the relevant protected characteristic. In University of Manchester v Jones 1993 ICR 474, CA, the Court of Appeal held that this involved both a *quantitative* assessment of the numbers or proportions of people adversely affected and a *qualitative* assessment of the amount of damage or disappointment that may result to those persons, and how lasting or final that damage is. The particular hardships suffered by the claimant may also be taken into account provided proper attention is paid to the question of how typical those hardships are of others who are adversely affected.

The principle of proportionality had been held, in the context of an equal pay claim, to require a tribunal to carry out a balancing exercise between the discriminatory effects of an employer's pay practice and the reasonable needs of the employer in applying that practice – Hampson v Department of Education and Science 1989 ICR 179, CA. Extrapolating from this and applying the same principle in a non-pay discrimination context, it would therefore seem that the greater the discriminatory effect, the greater the burden on the employer to show that the PCP corresponds to a real commercial objective and is appropriate for achieving that objective. The House of Lords in Barry v Midland Bank plc 1999 ICR 859, HL, noting that the ECJ in Enderby v Frenchay Health Authority and anor 1994 ICR 112, ECJ, drew attention to the need for national courts to apply 'the principle of proportionality', explained the principle thus: '[T]he ground relied upon as justification must be of sufficient importance for the national court to regard this as overriding the disparate impact of the difference in treatment, either in

499

whole or in part. The more serious the disparate impact on women, or men as the case may be, the more cogent must be the objective justification.' In other words, the degree of justification required is 'proportionate' to the degree of disparate impact caused by the employer's practice or policy. It follows from Barry that stringent scrutiny of the justification defence may be appropriate where the discrimination, although indirect in form, is very closely related in substance to the direct form of the discrimination – for further details, see under 'Background and overview – role of tribunals and burden of proof' above.

17.45   It should be noted that the House of Lords' explanation of the 'principle of proportionality' in the Barry case – in essence, that justification must be proportionate to the seriousness of the disparate impact – was questioned by Lord Justice Sedley in British Airways plc v Grundy (No.2) 2008 IRLR 815, CA. His Lordship indicated that he had found it impossible to know how to gauge the seriousness of the disparate impact of a particular practice or term, and concluded that such an exercise was not necessary in any event. He stated: 'Ex hypothesi the disparity is substantial, not marginal, otherwise justification would not be needed. It cannot matter that it affects a relatively small number of employees, for the right which it invades is a personal contractual right. Nor can it matter that the amount involved is small: for an employee who is unlawfully underpaid 50p an hour, the difference may be between subsistence and poverty.' This analysis enabled the Court to uphold a tribunal's decision that an employer's pay practice had not been objectively justified, despite the tribunal's failure to follow the Barry proportionality test to the letter. Sedley LJ concluded: 'If... the tribunal have not tried to measure the disparate impact which they have found, it seems to me, with respect, that they have avoided an elephant trap rather than committed an error of law.' It remains to be seen what effect these words will have on future cases. However, to the extent that they conflict with the test laid down by the House of Lords in the Barry case, that established test should be preferred.

17.46   **Assessing the alternatives**
As previously mentioned, the test of justification in S.19(2)(d) EqA purports to implement the relevant EU equality Directives, which provide that a PCP will be indirectly discriminatory unless it 'is objectively justified by a legitimate aim and the means of achieving that aim are appropriate and *necessary*' (our stress) – see the section 'Background and overview', under 'Legislative history – differences between domestic and EU wording' above. The word 'necessary' in this context has not been interpreted so strictly as to require employers to prove that there was no other way of achieving their objectives. As already noted, in Hardys and Hansons plc v Lax 2005 ICR 1565, CA, the Court of Appeal stated that the employer, in showing objective justification, does not have to demonstrate that there was no route other than the discriminatory practice by

which the legitimate aim could have been achieved – see under 'Assessing the needs of the employer' above. However, the availability of a less discriminatory but equally effective measure will undermine the argument that a particular measure was proportionate.

If the claimant puts forward a non-discriminatory alternative for achieving the same objective, the employment tribunal may well decide that that alternative ought reasonably to have been adopted and find that, because it was ignored, the defence has not been made out – Cobb and ors v Secretary of State for Employment and anor 1989 ICR 506, EAT. A similar stance was taken by the ECJ in Kutz-Bauer v Freie und Hansestadt Hamburg 2003 IRLR 368, ECJ, where it held that national courts should take into account the possibility of achieving by other means the aims pursued by the provisions in question. And in its 'Coming of Age' consultation document concerning the Employment Equality (Age) Regulations 2006 SI 2006/1031 (now replaced by the age discrimination provisions in the EqA), the Government summed matters up thus: where a legitimate aim can be achieved equally well by a measure that has a big discriminatory effect and one that has a small discriminatory effect (or that does not discriminate at all), the latter should be used.

17.47 The fact that there are no alternatives will obviously weigh in the balance in favour of the employer's defence of justification for indirect discrimination. In Azmi v Kirklees Metropolitan Borough Council 2007 ICR 1154, EAT, the EAT upheld an employment tribunal's decision that a female Muslim teaching assistant had not been indirectly discriminated against on the ground of her religion or belief by a requirement that she remove her full face veil while teaching. Any indirect discrimination was justified as a proportionate response to the legitimate aim of providing effective tuition to young children. The employer had investigated alternative means of achieving the aim – including suggestions that the claimant could use a screen, remain with her back to a male teacher, remove children from the classroom or use more hand and body gestures – and had been entitled to conclude that none of these would work.

17.48 **Alternatives that undermine the legitimate aim.** When considering less discriminatory alternatives that might have been available, employment tribunals need to keep in mind the aim that the employer was seeking to achieve in the first place. In Barry v Midland Bank plc 1999 ICR 859, HL (an equal pay case), the issue was whether an employer was discriminating against women in the way redundancy payments were calculated. This was done in the same way as under the statutory redundancy scheme, by focusing on their salary at the time of dismissal. Some women who had earlier worked full time but who, at the time of their dismissal, were working part time contended that this meant that they were not getting the full reward for their service.

It was accepted that the reason for fixing the payment by reference to final salary was in part to cushion the redundant workers from the loss of income

501

that would flow from their being made redundant. To give effect to that objective, the focus necessarily had to be not on past service but on future loss. In the House of Lords, four of their Lordships held that there was no discrimination at all on these facts. Lord Nicholls, on the other hand, considered that there was prima facie indirect discrimination but concluded that the method of determining pay was objectively justified. Once the aim of cushioning against future loss was seen as legitimate, relating compensation to the actual pay received at the date of termination was inevitable. The way in which the women said the pay should be calculated – namely, by reference to the service over the whole period of employment – would have involved adopting a different scheme and would have undermined that particular objective. In so deciding, Lord Nicholls agreed with the Court of Appeal that to compel the employer to abandon its scheme and substitute a scheme where severance pay was treated and calculated not as compensation for loss of a job but as additional pay for past work would not be right.

17.49 Similarly, in Blackburn and anor v Chief Constable of West Midlands Police 2009 IRLR 135, CA (another equal pay case), an employment tribunal was held to have undermined the employer's legitimate aim when accepting that there was a non-discriminatory alternative available. There, the West Midlands Police Force (WMP) introduced special priority payments (SPPs) to reward police officers working unsocial hours. One of the qualifying criteria for SPPs was '24/7 working', which required officers to work a rotating shift pattern involving nights. Officers with childcare responsibilities were excused from 24/7 working and consequently did not receive the SPPs. This scheme had a disparate adverse effect on women. Although the tribunal accepted that rewarding night-time work was a legitimate aim, it thought that the same objective could have been achieved by less discriminatory means – for example, by simply paying the female claimants as if they had worked at night. It therefore concluded that the pay disparity at issue in this case was not objectively justified.

Allowing WMP's appeal, the EAT held that the tribunal had failed to engage with the actual aim behind the scheme. WMP's purpose was to single out and reward those working nights – an objective that would not be achieved if those not working nights were paid the same amount as those who were. Furthermore, the fact that WMP could afford to pay the bonus to those who could not work 24/7 was irrelevant. It was no answer to a defence of justification for a difference in pay to say that there was no need for the difference in the first place. The EAT pointed out that, if this were followed to its logical conclusion, there would be no reason in principle why a woman whose childcare commitments were specifically accommodated by being allowed to work part time should not be paid as if she worked full time.

17.50 The EAT's decision was upheld on further appeal by the Court of Appeal, which emphasised that, in a case such as this, the focus must be on the employer's aim. WMP's considered view that 24/7 working should be rewarded by the extra payments was both rational and within the parameters of the national police scheme for the making of SPPs. The fact that some other police forces might have adopted schemes that had no or less disparate impact was irrelevant. It was other means of achieving the employer's legitimate aim that were relevant, not the means of achieving different aims. Thus, providing SPPs to those who were excused from 24/7 working for childcare reasons was not a means of achieving WMP's legitimate aim of rewarding 24/7 working. It was difficult to see how that objective would be furthered if those who did not work 24/7 were paid the same amount as those who did.

The decision in Blackburn suggests that, where a PCP applied by an employer disadvantages a particular protected group, there is no need to make an exception to accommodate that group if doing so would undermine the employer's legitimate aim. This appears to be borne out by a line of high-profile cases in which it has been held that employers are not required to accommodate an employee's religious beliefs concerning homosexuality where they conflict with aims that are fundamental to the ethos of the organisation, such as the need to promote equal opportunities – see, in particular, Ladele v London Borough of Islington and anor 2010 ICR 532, CA, and McFarlane v Relate Avon 2010 ICR 507, EAT, discussed under 'Justification in context – promoting equal opportunities' below.

In other cases, however, employers have been expected to introduce a limited **17.51** exception to accommodate the needs of a protected group, provided this can be done without undermining the legitimate aim underpinning the policy. For example, where a dress code that seeks to promote an organisation's corporate image has a detrimental impact on employees of a particular religion, employment tribunals have sometimes been prepared to accept that an exception should be made – see under 'Justification in context – corporate image' below. Another example is the non-employment case of G v Head Teacher and Governors of St Gregory's Catholic Science College 2011 EWHC 1452, QBD. There, the High Court held that it amounted to indirect race discrimination against a boy of African-Caribbean ethnicity for a school to impose a uniform policy preventing boys from wearing their hair in cornrows. Although the policy pursued the legitimate aim of discouraging gang culture, it was not proportionate because of the blanket nature of the prohibition. The school could have allowed for exceptions to accommodate a genuine cultural or family practice; the Court did not accept that this would have had the effect of undermining the whole policy.

Conduct of the employer
17.52

The Court of Appeal's decision in GMB v Allen and ors 2008 ICR 1407, CA, suggests that where the means adopted by the employer to achieve a legitimate aim are manipulative or otherwise inappropriate, they will be disproportionate

503

and the justification defence will fail. In that case the GMB trade union entered into negotiations with Middlesbrough Metropolitan Borough Council over the implementation of a new pay structure. The union decided to focus on securing pay protection for those who would otherwise lose out as a result of the new scheme and on its ideal of achieving pay equality for the future, rather than on furthering the interests of its female members with backdated equal pay claims. In line with this approach, it advised some of its female members to settle their equal pay claims against the Council for approximately 25 per cent of their potential value. It told the women that this was the best that could be achieved by way of settlement and emphasised that lengthy legal proceedings could lead to loss of jobs. Feeling aggrieved at what they perceived to be the union's policy of sacrificing their interests to those of other members, five women brought a test case before an employment tribunal. They argued that the union had indirectly discriminated against them on the ground of sex contrary to the SDA (now replaced by the EqA) by failing fully to support their equal pay claims. The tribunal upheld the claims and the union appealed.

The EAT overturned the employment tribunal's finding that the union had failed to objectively justify the claimants' treatment. Somewhat controversially, it held that the concept of proportionality was not concerned with whether an employer conducted itself appropriately, and the fact that a legitimate aim might be achieved by using unlawful, even dishonest, practices did not necessarily mean that the means were disproportionate. The tribunal had correctly found that the union's aims – such as securing the best possible pay protection and avoiding job losses – were legitimate. In the EAT's view, however, it had fallen into error in deciding that the union's means of achieving those legitimate aims were not proportionate. It might be that the union misled some of its members into accepting its priorities without a full understanding of the sacrifices involved but that did not necessarily suggest that other, more proportionate, means could have been used. Rather, had the union acted 'properly', its legitimate objective might not have been achieved at all. In the light of these considerations, the EAT concluded that the negotiating policy adopted by the union was objectively justified, and hence that no indirect sex discrimination had occurred.

17.53 The EAT's decision was overturned by the Court of Appeal. A central issue was whether the union's attempts to manipulate the women into settling their claims against the Council could be characterised as the means to the attainment of an admittedly legitimate aim. The Court noted that the PCP which the union applied, and which was to the detriment of a considerably larger proportion of women than of men, was the deal that was done with the Council as a result of the union's policy of striking a balance between back pay, future pay and the need for pay protection of members. The EAT, in identifying the means as being, in effect, the balance that was struck between members' competing interests in the deal with the Council, had accorded too narrow an ambit to the concept of 'means'. If the adoption of the PCP assumed that steps would have to be taken with a view to persuading the female claimants to make sacrifices, including forbearance from litigation to enforce their perceived statutory rights, such steps were part of the means by which the achievement of the aim was to be pursued. The concept of 'means' was not inherently narrow and a number of different actions might each be a necessary, if not equal, part of the means of achieving the aim.

The Court went on to decide that, although the union's aims of protecting workers' pay and ensuring future equality were legitimate, the employment tribunal had been entitled to find that its manipulative methods of persuading the claimants to sacrifice their back pay entitlement were not a proportionate means of achieving those aims. If the union's aims were achievable only by disproportionate means, they could not be susceptible to justification; to conclude otherwise would be to license disproportionality. In the instant case the tribunal had concluded that the PCP had involved persuading the claimants and others in a similar position to sacrifice their back pay claims. Such persuasion, and the form it had taken (i.e. manipulation), was part of the means. That was a permissible and correct approach. Having taken it, the tribunal had not fallen into any legal error when, on the basis of the facts found, it had concluded that the means were disproportionate to the achievement of the overall aim.

Justification in context

17.54

The preceding sections of this chapter explain the general principles applicable in establishing objective justification. Despite the plethora of authorities, the question of whether the defence is made out is essentially one of fact for the employment tribunal. So long as there is sufficient evidence for the tribunal's conclusion, its decision will be difficult to challenge on appeal – Mandla and anor v Dowell Lee and anor 1983 ICR 385, HL (a race case). Not surprisingly, therefore, the circumstances in which the defence has succeeded have varied enormously, and it would be unwise to regard the outcome of cases that turn largely on their own facts as constituting precedents of any sort.

Bearing that in mind, it may nonetheless be helpful to set out some examples of factual situations in which the justification defence has been at issue. This section focuses on the aims that are most commonly cited in an attempt to justify indirect discrimination, with illustrations drawn from case law and the EHRC Employment Code. While some of these aims are potentially applicable across the range of protected characteristics covered by S.19 EqA, others (as we shall see) tend to be cited in respect of one or two specific characteristics. For example, an employer's need to present a corporate image is particularly relevant in the context of dress codes that have a disparate impact on people of a particular religious belief.

505

For further examples of the practical operation of the justification defence, reference should be made to Chapter 24, 'Recruitment', and Chapter 25, 'Discrimination during employment'.

17.55 Operational needs

Operational needs and/or organisational efficiency are relied on to justify indirect discrimination in a wide range of circumstances. In particular, they are frequently cited in connection with an employer's refusal to grant flexible working arrangements to women with childcare responsibilities or to allow time off for religious observance. Having an apparently sound business reason for denying a female employee's application to work part time, for example, or a Jewish employee's request to leave work early on a Friday, is not sufficient in itself – the employer must also consider whether the reasons for insisting on a particular working pattern are strong enough to overcome any indirectly discriminatory impact (i.e. whether the discriminatory PCP is a proportionate means of achieving the legitimate aim in question).

17.56 Childcare and flexible working. Many women request part-time or other flexible working arrangements to accommodate their childcare commitments and it is well established that an employer's rejection of such a request can give rise to a claim of indirect sex discrimination. The issues surrounding the need to demonstrate disparate adverse impact in this context are dealt with in Chapter 16, 'Indirect discrimination: proving disadvantage', in the section 'Indirect discrimination in context', under 'Indirect sex discrimination – part-time and flexible working'. If the claimant overcomes that hurdle, the employer will typically seek to justify the imposition of the particular working pattern by reference to the operational needs of the organisation.

Two examples of flexible working cases in which the justification defence succeeded:

- **Burston v Superior Creative Services Ltd** ET Case No.72892/95: the employer's refusal to allow B to work three days a week was found by the employment tribunal to be justified. B had wanted to reduce her role from five to three days a week by carrying out sales work only while a part-time replacement was employed to carry out the general administration that had previously taken up two days of her working week. However, sales had been poor before B's maternity leave and the employer was entitled to demand that she spend more than three days per week on sales in future

- **Conway v Dairy Crest Ltd** ET Case No.2312942/10: DC Ltd was a national business with 131 depots. It employed seven auditors to ensure that the depots complied with its operations standards. Auditors could be sent anywhere in the United Kingdom and were required to stay away from home for significant periods of time. Following her return from maternity leave, one of the auditors, C, applied to work part time at sites within reasonable travelling distance of her home to fit in with nursery opening hours. She made it clear that she was no longer willing to stay away overnight except on rare occasions. DC Ltd refused her request and C claimed indirect sex discrimination. It was not disputed that the PCP of staying away overnight put women at a particular disadvantage, and the employment tribunal accepted that C had suffered a personal disadvantage. However, the legitimate aim of the PCP was to maximise the time that auditors spent on site and to ensure that the small team of auditors could be sent anywhere in the country. If C only worked within reasonable daily travelling distance of her home, there would not be enough work for her. Furthermore, if she did not stay away overnight she would be unable to maximise her time on site and it would take her longer to complete an audit. The tribunal concluded that the discriminatory effect of the PCP was justified by the needs of the business.

An employer is unlikely to succeed in establishing objective justification if it **17.57** fails to give serious consideration to a woman's request for flexible working or to conduct a proper assessment of its operational needs. This is illustrated by the following cases:

- **McGarr v Ministry of Defence** ET Case Nos.2300464/02 and another: Lieutenant Colonel M, a barrister serving with the Adjutant General's Corps within the Army Legal Service (ALS), sought permission from the Director of the ALS to apply for an appointment as a part-time Chair of the Appeals Service Tribunal. Her request was rejected on the basis of the Army's historical practice of permitting only those members of the ALS holding the rank of colonel or above to undertake the duties of part-time judicial office. The MoD argued that the policy was justified on the ground that it was necessary to preserve 'operational effectiveness'. Dismissing this argument, the employment tribunal held that the MoD's reaction to M's wish to undertake judicial duties 'has throughout borne all the hallmarks of an institutional knee-jerk reaction to what it saw as a threat to its established way of doing things'. The tribunal found that no proper assessment had been made by the MoD 'as to the extent to which its operational requirements, including overseas deployment, might be adversely affected by permitting officers below the rank of colonel to undertake part-time judicial duties. No real attempt was made to gauge the numbers of officers likely to take advantage of such a policy and no sensible consideration given to the practical reality that, however high the degree of interest in part-time judicial office amongst officers below colonel rank, appointment to it is far from guaranteed and follows a lengthy selection process'

- **Littlejohn v Transport for London** ET Case No.2200224/07: L, who held a managerial position at TfL, put in a flexible working request before her return to work from maternity leave, seeking a change from full time to two days in the office and one day working from home. TfL refused her request, taking the view that a job share would not work. L resigned and succeeded before the tribunal with her indirect sex discrimination claim (as well as an unfair constructive dismissal claim). The employment tribunal found that TfL had not provided justification for refusing L's request. In reaching this conclusion, it took into account the following matters: (i) TfL did not believe that a job share would work but it had not actually considered whether it was workable in practice; (ii) it was concerned about its ability to recruit to a part-time position but the evidence showed that L's was a popular job and finding someone part time could have been explored; (iii) the tribunal did not accept that L's management function was incapable of being performed by two individuals; (iv) TfL had failed to look into alternatives that would have allowed L to remain in her job; and (v) L was only asking for part-time work for one year and TfL could have allowed this for a trial period

- **Stone v Cineworld Cinemas plc** ET Case No.1804043/11: S was employed as an operations manager at a cinema. She was required to work shifts starting at various times between 8.30 am and 4 pm. In June 2010 S asked to work a restricted shift pattern following her return from maternity leave. Her partner's working pattern involved three weeks away followed by three weeks at home. Since childcare was not available in the evenings, S wanted to restrict her availability to daytime shifts during the three weeks when her partner was working away. She would be available to work any shifts during the following three weeks, when he was at home to look after their child. She offered to work this pattern on either a full-time or a job-share basis but her request was refused. The employment tribunal accepted that, while the requirement to work the full range of shifts across each working week placed women at a particular disadvantage, the employer had a legitimate aim – namely, the smooth, efficient and economic running of the business. S's proposal to restrict her shift availability while continuing to work full time would require her colleagues to work more evening shifts and would limit her ability to provide cover at short notice. The employer was therefore justified in requiring S to work across all shift patterns if she remained a full-time operations manager. However, S's proposal to work the restricted shift pattern in a job-share had a more limited impact on the company because the job-sharer would be available to discharge the role in the evenings during the three-week periods when S was restricted to daytime hours. Any detrimental effect on the business would be minimal, whereas the discriminatory impact of refusing the proposal was very severe, meaning in practice that S could no longer continue in her job. The company had never seriously considered the job-share suggestion, nor had it explored the practical possibility of finding a suitable job-share partner. In those circumstances, the means adopted by the company to fulfil its legitimate aim were not proportionate.

For further discussion of this area, see Chapter 25, 'Discrimination during **17.58** employment', in the section 'Terms of employment', under 'Working hours – childcare responsibilities'. Additional examples of the operation of the justification defence in this context can be found in IDS Employment Law Handbook, 'Maternity and Parental Rights' (2009), Chapter 13, 'Discrimination and equal pay', under 'Indirect sex discrimination – justification'.

Time off for religious observance. Another situation that tends to generate **17.59** indirect discrimination claims arises where employees are refused time off during normal working hours to worship, observe days of rest or attend religious festivals. For instance, stipulating that work must be done on a Friday, Saturday or Sunday could give rise to indirect religious discrimination against Muslims, Jews and Christians respectively. In practice, most of the decided cases in this area have turned on the question of justification, with the operational needs of the organisation being relied on to justify refusing time off.

The following cases illustrate that insisting on a particular pattern of work may be justified where the employer can point to compelling business or organisational reasons in support of its policy:

- **Mayuuf v Governing Body of Bishop Challoner Catholic Collegiate School and anor** ET Case No.3202398/04: M was a mathematics teacher and a follower of the Maliki School of Islam. It was an essential requirement of his religion that he attend Friday prayers at a mosque. Following his appointment in April 2002, M was free during period five on a Friday afternoon, permitting him to attend mosque. However, in 2003 mathematics was identified as a priority area for improvement and it was decided that year 11 students would all be taught at the same time so that they could move up or down a set according to their ability. A new timetable was issued to reflect this strategy and thereafter M was required to teach on Friday afternoons. He brought a claim of indirect religious discrimination. The employment tribunal took into account the fact that there had been a decline in GCSE mathematics results; that there was a real and genuine need to teach year 11 classes at the same time to facilitate transfer between sets; that rewriting the timetable to accommodate M would have been practically impossible; and that engaging a supply teacher would have damaged continuity and entailed significant costs to the school (although, in the tribunal's view, cost was a secondary consideration). The tribunal balanced those factors against the discriminatory effect on M, for whom missing Friday prayers was a 'most serious matter', and concluded that the PCP of teaching period five on Fridays was justified as a proportionate means of achieving a legitimate aim

- **James v MSC Cruises Ltd** Case No.2203173/05: J was a practising member of the Seventh-day Adventist Church. As such, she abstained from secular work on the Sabbath in order to worship, teach, learn and celebrate. In September 2005 she successfully applied for a position with MSC Ltd, which sold and marketed cruise holidays. However, on receiving the offer letter, she explained that she could not work on Saturday as this was the Sabbath. MSC Ltd responded that if J could not work on Saturdays then she would be unable to take up the offer of employment. J brought an indirect religious discrimination claim. An employment tribunal found the relevant disadvantage caused by the PCP of Saturday working but decided that it was justified. It accepted the employer's evidence that trading on Saturdays was an essential feature of the tourism industry, since this was when couples were most likely to be available jointly to explore holiday opportunities and make immediate decisions. It also had regard to the fact that Saturday working was not popular among existing staff; that a rota had been put in place to share the burden equally; and that the employer reasonably believed that any exceptions would create tension among colleagues

- **Patrick v IH Sterile Services Ltd** ET Case No.3300983/11: P was employed as a technician by IHSS Ltd, which provided a round-the-clock instrument sterilisation service to hospitals. He was a committed Jehovah's Witness and at the beginning of his employment came to an arrangement with his managers that he would not be required to work on Sundays. Following a business decision to minimise reliance on agency staff, taken with a view to reducing costs and maintaining quality, the company required its employees to work weekend shifts. From January 2011, P was required to work at least one in every two Sundays and this affected his ability to worship and perform other duties at the Kingdom Hall. He brought a claim of indirect religious discrimination. The employment tribunal accepted that P was placed at a particular disadvantage compared with non-religious people by the requirement to work on Sundays. However, the company had the legitimate aim of fulfilling its contractual obligation to its customers to provide sterile laboratory services on a Sunday. Assuming the obligation to work on Sundays was distributed equitably among the small pool of staff, it was a proportionate means of achieving that aim. The tribunal added: 'We do not think it would be appropriate to exempt someone who wishes to practise worship on a Sunday from the obligation to cover Sunday work provided the requirement to do so was shared out equally.'

17.60 However, the following cases illustrate that it is not enough for employers simply to cite business or operational needs. They should also be prepared to demonstrate that, before insisting on the relevant PCP, they explored ways of accommodating the employee's request:

- **Edge v Visual Security Services Ltd** ET Case No.1301365/06: the employment tribunal ruled that a committed Christian who made it clear to his employer prior to being employed that he did not wish to work on Sundays for religious reasons was indirectly discriminated against on the ground of religion when he was required to do so from time to time. The requirement to undertake occasional Sunday working was a PCP and could not be objectively justified in this case. In the tribunal's view, although the employer could show a legitimate aim – i.e. 'the need of the business to carry out security work on Sundays' – it could not show that the requirement was a proportionate means of achieving that aim. The principal reason why the employer was not willing to rearrange its affairs to enable E to avoid working on Sundays 'was that it was simply too much trouble'

- **Estorninho v Jokic t/a Zorans Delicatessen** ET Case No.2301487/06: E, a practising Catholic, was employed as a chef. He followed the Catechism of the Catholic Church, which obliged him to abstain from work on Sundays, and he had been recruited on the basis that his religious beliefs ruled out Sunday working. The business became increasingly busy and, several months after his employment began, E was told that he would in future be required to work on Sundays. When he refused to do so, he was dismissed. The employment tribunal held that the PCP of Sunday working put Catholics at a particular disadvantage and could not be shown to be a proportionate means of achieving a legitimate aim. The increase in business potentially gave rise to a legitimate business need and it was proportionate to ask E to work extra shifts. However, the employer had produced no evidence that requiring E to work on Sundays was the only way in which the upturn in business could be dealt with. It was neither proportionate nor legitimate to issue such an instruction without first discussing the matter with the other chef or looking at other ways of providing cover

- **Fugler v Macmillan-London Hairstudios Ltd** ET Case No.2205090/04: F, who was Jewish, argued that his employer applied a PCP of discouraging employees from taking holidays on Saturdays. The employment tribunal accepted that, since the Jewish Sabbath is on a Saturday, and in 2004 Yom Kippur, an important Jewish festival, was also on a Saturday, this PCP put Jewish employees at a disadvantage. With regard to justification, the tribunal noted that the employer had a legitimate aim to serve clients on a Saturday, which was its busiest day. It was necessary, however, to perform a balancing exercise between the importance of the employer's aim and the discriminatory effect. Given that Yom Kippur is such an important day in the Jewish calendar, the tribunal concluded that the employer should have considered how it could rearrange F's duties and customers for that particular Saturday. It therefore upheld F's claim.

Where the employer has given serious consideration to the employee's request **17.61** and explored alternative ways of accommodating his or her religious beliefs, the justification defence is more likely to succeed. For example, in Cherfi v G4S Security Services Ltd EAT 0379/10 C, a Muslim, worked for G4S as a security guard in Highgate, where the client required all security officers to remain on site throughout their shifts. Consequently, he was refused permission to travel

— 511

to Friday prayers at a mosque in Finsbury Park. However, there was a prayer room on site and C had the option of working on Saturday or Sunday rather than Friday. C claimed that the PCP of requiring him to remain at work during Friday lunchtimes constituted indirect religious discrimination. An employment tribunal held that, although the PCP placed C at a disadvantage as a practising Muslim by preventing him from attending prayers in congregation, G4S would be in danger of financial penalties or even losing its contract with its client if a full complement of security staff was not on site throughout the day. It was not practicable to obtain cover for C's lunch break because this would have entailed paying the replacement for a whole shift. Furthermore, C had refused a variety of arrangements offered to accommodate his requirements. Thus, the tribunal found that the PCP was a proportionate means of achieving a legitimate aim – namely, meeting the operational needs of the business.

On appeal, the EAT upheld this decision. In its view, the tribunal had carried out the necessary balancing act, having considered both the reason why G4S refused to allow C to leave the site on Friday lunchtimes and the impact on C. The discriminatory effect of the PCP was limited to preventing C from attending congregational prayers during working hours. C was not prevented from praying at the Highgate site, and nor was he prevented from working on a Friday or pressured to accept work on a Saturday or Sunday. In view of this, and also having regard to the alternatives that had been open to C, the conclusion as to justification was one that the tribunal was entitled to reach.

17.62 For further discussion of this area, see Chapter 11, 'Religion or belief', in the section 'Manifestation of religion or belief', under 'Is a right to manifest protected by S.10 EqA? – time off for religious observance'.

17.63 **Dress and appearance.** Employers frequently seek to justify dress codes and other instructions relating to appearance, which might otherwise indirectly discriminate against certain protected groups, by reference to the need to promote their business image – see under 'Corporate image' below. Occasionally, however, an employer may be justified in insisting on a particular standard of dress to promote the effective delivery of its services. That was held to be the case in Azmi v Kirklees Metropolitan Borough Council 2007 ICR 1154, EAT, where the EAT upheld an employment tribunal's decision that a female Muslim teaching assistant had not been indirectly discriminated against on the ground of her religion or belief by a requirement that she remove her full face veil while teaching. Any indirect discrimination was justified as a proportionate response to the legitimate aim of providing effective tuition to young children.

17.64 **Food and drink.** The religious beliefs of some employees can lead to conflict over the handling of food and drink at work. Operational reasons were successfully relied on in Ahmed v Tesco Stores Ltd and ors ET Case Nos.1301492/08 and another to justify requiring a Muslim warehouse operative to handle alcohol, a PCP which he claimed indirectly discriminated against him on the ground of his religious beliefs. The employment tribunal found that, while the employer had sought to minimise the claimant's contact with products containing alcohol, it was an inevitable consequence of the nature of his job that he would be required to handle them from time to time. The aim of supplying stores with products containing alcohol was legitimate and it was not possible to maintain that supply without exposing operatives to contact with such products. The tribunal concluded that the employer's business needs outweighed the discriminatory impact on the individual.

Policies restricting employment of couples. Some employers operate **17.65** workplace policies prohibiting the employment of married and/or cohabiting couples within the same workplace or management chain – see further Chapter 16, 'Indirect discrimination: proving disadvantage', in the section 'Indirect discrimination in context', under 'Indirect marriage or civil partnership discrimination – policies restricting employment of couples'. Depending on their precise formulation, such rules may indirectly discriminate on the ground of sex and/or marital or civil partnership status unless they can be objectively justified as a proportionate means of achieving a legitimate aim.

In Faulkner v Chief Constable of Hampshire Constabulary EAT 0505/05 the EAT upheld a tribunal's decision that a 'Working Together' policy, which prevented 'staff in a partner, family or emotional relationship' from working together as supervisor and subordinate, was justified on the basis of the need to ensure actual and apparent correctness in working relationships. Although this case demonstrates how relationship at work policies could result in claims of indirect sex discrimination, it is important to bear in mind that the employment tribunal's decision in this respect was very much influenced by the specific issues of trust and public duty surrounding police officers. Accordingly, employers who introduce a partnerships policy should ensure that it is appropriate and necessary in the particular circumstances.

Client needs   17.66

Closely allied to the demands of operational efficiency are the needs of clients and customers. Employers sometimes seek to justify requirements of full-time working or 24-hour availability on the ground that clients need one key point of contact within the organisation. In Sullivan v John S Braid and Co Ltd ET Case No.2302098/03 the claimant had specifically been recruited to work as a shipping coordinator on a contract that her employer had with a cruise line company. This company was responsible for 75 per cent of the employer's revenue, and the employer had contracted with the cruise line to provide a full-time coordinator to work exclusively on that contract. The coordinator was also expected to deal with the queries of other clients based outside the United Kingdom, with the result that the coordinator was required to work across different time zones throughout the day so that any queries could be dealt with by the close of business at 5.30 pm.

The employment tribunal held that the employer was justified in dismissing the claimant who, having agreed to work full time, then announced that she could only work part time. The requirement that the position be full time was necessary to meet the specific need of the contract to have a dedicated shipping coordinator assigned to it, and to meet the needs of the employer's clients generally, as the coordinator had to be available for work at a time which coincided with various time zones. In reaching this conclusion, the tribunal noted that the employer had considered whether it was possible for the claimant to work at home, but had rejected the idea because she was still being trained. It also took account of the significant value of the main contract to the employer's business.

17.67 Similarly, client needs were successfully relied upon as a basis for justifying indirect discrimination by a marketing/design agency in Edgley v Oliver and Graimes Design Associates Ltd ET Case No. 3101782/05. In that case the employer refused to allow E – a senior account manager – to return to work three days a week following her maternity leave. The employment tribunal was satisfied that there was a legitimate ethos, essential to the survival of the business, whereby an immediate and personal service was provided by employees to clients, and that this required E's post to be full time. The delegation of urgent client enquiries to other employees and the need to resort to returning calls by mobile telephone were anathema to the service ethos on which the employer depended. Those reasons outweighed the discriminatory effect on E of refusing to allow her to return on a part-time basis.

In some businesses, creative continuity will be an important aspect of client needs. In Trainer v Penny Plain Ltd ET Case No.2510846/05, a women's clothing retailer turned down a request by its senior graphic designer to work three days a week following her return from maternity leave. Although the employee offered to provide additional flexibility during busy periods, this offer was always subject to the availability of childcare. An employment tribunal held that the employer's refusal to accommodate the employee's proposed working arrangements was objectively justified. The business was going through a period of rapid expansion and the tribunal was of the opinion that a business of its size and type – employing around 120 people – needed to have one individual in control of creative output. Although parts of the claimant's job could be compartmentalised, 'creative continuity' was vital: the creative output essential to the employer's business would be lost by splitting the design and conceptual work between two individuals.

17.68 Two further examples of cases in which employers successfully relied on client needs to justify their insistence on a particular pattern of work:

- **Pal v Secretary of State for Work and Pensions (Jobcentre Plus)** ET Case No.2405030/11: P worked at a telephone call centre answering benefits queries from members of the public. She asked to change her working pattern to term-time working only so that she could look after her child during the school holidays. Her employer refused and placed her on a waiting list, stating that a number of staff already worked this pattern and that it could not immediately accommodate any additional requests without a deterioration in customer service. The parties agreed that the employer had applied a PCP whereby staff would not be allowed to work term-time only unless they came within the quota allowed to do so, and the employer conceded that this placed women at a particular disadvantage. However, the employment tribunal held that the employer had established a legitimate aim – namely, the need to provide a reasonable level of service to members of the general public and to meet government targets – and that the PCP was objectively justified. In the tribunal's view, it was reasonable for any employer who had to provide service for 52 weeks of the year not to allow term-time working to an open-ended number of employees. Although this meant that P used up all her annual leave to cover part of the school holidays and had no guarantee that leave would always be granted during these periods, she had other options in the form of paid childcare

- **Danso v 1SC Guarding Ltd** ET Case No.3301845/09: the employer provided security services to a number of companies. All but three of its contracts required employees to work rolling 12-hour shifts over days, nights and weekends, and at the clients' insistence security officers had to work all of the shifts in succession so they were familiar with the range of issues likely to arise. D began working for the company in May 2008 and was aware of the requirements as to working hours. Her oldest daughter, who was 18, looked after the younger daughters, aged 11 and 14, when D worked nights, but in October 2008 she left home to go to university. D asked to be allowed to work only day shifts until she was able to make alternative arrangements. The employer refused but offered to provide her with work on an 'as and when' basis, to suit her personal circumstances, and said that it could provide her with day-shift work for a few weeks on a site scheduled for demolition. D accepted that offer, but when the job came to an end and she refused to work nights her employment was terminated. The employment tribunal dismissed her claim of indirect sex discrimination. Although the requirement to work nights was a PCP that impacted more heavily on women than men, since they bear the greater responsibility for childcare, the requirement was justified. The contracts that did not require night working were already staffed by permanent employees and it did not seem to the tribunal that those employees should be expected to give up their assignments, and nor was it reasonable for the employer to put at risk its contracts with its other clients by proposing changes to the shift system against their wishes. In those circumstances, the requirement to work nights was a proportionate means of achieving a legitimate aim.

515

17.69 **Corporate image**

Instructions regarding an employee's personal appearance are capable of giving rise to indirect discrimination. In particular, indirect religious discrimination can arise when a dress code prevents an employee from wearing an item that is a manifestation of his or her religious beliefs – see Chapter 16, 'Indirect discrimination: proving disadvantage', in the section 'Indirect discrimination in context', under 'Indirect religion or belief discrimination – dress codes and religious attire'. It may be open to an employer to justify such a policy by reference to the need to promote its corporate image. However, it is difficult to discern any overriding principle from the relevant case law.

In Eweida v British Airways plc 2010 ICR 890, CA, E – a devout and practising Christian employed as part of BA's check-in staff – refused to conceal her silver cross necklace in breach of the company's strict dress code prohibiting customer-facing employees from wearing any visible item of adornment. The Court of Appeal unanimously concluded that there was no evidence that the employer's policy put Christians at a particular disadvantage. This meant that it was not strictly necessary to consider the employment tribunal's finding that, if the employer's policy on the wearing of jewellery had indirectly discriminated against E, the employer would not have been able to establish a defence of objective justification. Nevertheless, the majority of the Court of Appeal indicated that, had the point arisen for consideration, it would have been inclined to allow the employer's cross-appeal on this point.

17.70

Lord Justice Sedley (with whom Lady Justice Smith agreed) expressed the view that, when considered on the footing that the indirect discrimination claim was advanced in the Court of Appeal – i.e. the disadvantage to a single individual stemming from the employer's policy – the tribunal's finding of facts showed that the policy was a proportionate means of achieving a legitimate aim. E's objection to concealing her cross was an entirely personal decision, neither arising from any doctrine of her faith nor interfering with her observance of it, and had not been raised by any other employee. In fact, E had complied with the uniform policy for approximately seven years before raising it as an issue. The employer had generally sought to accommodate staff diversity and had dealt conscientiously with her complaint (even offering her a non-customer facing role, which she had declined). E, however, had continued to act in breach of the policy while the matter was still being considered. Sedley LJ added that the instant case 'perhaps illustrated some of the problems which can arise when an individual (or equally a group) asserts that a provision, criterion or practice adopted by an employer conflicts with beliefs which they hold but which may not only not be shared but may be opposed by others in the workforce. It is not unthinkable that *a blanket ban may sometimes be the only fair solution*' (our stress).

Note that the claimant in Eweida has commenced legal proceedings before the European Court of Human Rights, contending that the employer's decision failed to comply with Article 9 of the European Convention on Human Rights, which concerns the right to freedom of thought, conscience and religion. The Equality and Human Rights Commission has successfully applied to intervene in order to make general representations. For further details, see Chapter 11, 'Religion or belief', under 'Manifestation of religion or belief – is UK approach compliant with Article 9?'.

Lord Justice Sedley's obiter comments on objective justification in Eweida – in **17.71** particular, his suggestion that a blanket ban may sometimes be the only fair solution – should be treated with a degree of caution. His comments appear to have been influenced by the fact that the claimant, in the somewhat unusual circumstances of the case, was unable to demonstrate group disadvantage. When the adverse impact on a particular group is more apparent, it may be appropriate for the employer to consider making an exception to its dress code in order to accommodate religious beliefs. The following is an example taken from the EHRC Employment Code: 'An employer introduces a "no jewellery" policy in the workplace. This is not for health and safety reasons but because the employer does not like body piercings. A Sikh worker who wears a Kara bracelet as an integral part of her religion has complained about the rule. To avoid a claim of indirect discrimination, the employer should consider allowing an exception to this rule. A blanket ban on jewellery would probably not be considered a proportionate means of achieving a legitimate aim in these circumstances' (para 6.40).

Similarly, in Noah v Desrosiers (t/a Wedge) ET Case No.2201867/07 an employment tribunal concluded that a hair salon owner was not justified in rejecting a Muslim job applicant because she wore a headscarf. While the requirement to display their hair at work amounted to a PCP that put persons of the applicant's religion at a disadvantage, the salon owner's desire to promote the salon's brand image was a legitimate aim. However, the tribunal considered that not wearing a headscarf in a hairdressing salon did not amount to an 'intrinsic element of a core function of the job'. (This was in contrast to Azmi v Kirklees Metropolitan Borough Council 2007 ICR 1154, EAT, where requiring a Muslim teaching assistant to remove her veil while teaching was held to be a necessary part of delivering effective teaching and support to the children concerned – see under 'Operational needs – dress and appearance' above.) In those circumstances, the treatment afforded to the claimant was not a proportionate means of achieving the employer's aim, especially since no less discriminatory options for promoting the business were ever explored. The tribunal added that the degree of risk caused by hiring the claimant should not be assumed to be as great as the employer believed, particularly as the owner could still have promoted the business's style herself, and customers would have been well aware why the claimant was not displaying her own hair.

For a detailed discussion of these cases, and for further examples, see Chapter 11, 'Religion or belief', in the section 'Manifestation of religion or belief', under 'Is a right to manifest protected by S.10 EqA? – dress and jewellery'.

17.72 **Promoting equal opportunities**

A number of high-profile indirect religious discrimination cases have explored the conflict that arises between different protected rights when an employee's religious beliefs concerning homosexuality prevent that individual from carrying out a basic aspect of his or her job. In this situation, an employer who insists on the employee carrying out the full range of duties appropriate to the post may be able to justify any indirect religious discrimination by reference to the need to promote equal opportunities both within and outside the organisation, and/or the need to provide a service to the public on a non-discriminatory basis. For a detailed consideration of this area, see Chapter 11, 'Religion or belief', in the section 'Manifestation of religion or belief', under 'Is a right to manifest protected by S.10 EqA? – conflict between different protected rights'.

The leading case is Ladele v London Borough of Islington and anor 2010 ICR 532, CA. There, the claimant, a registrar, was threatened with dismissal when she refused to conduct civil partnership services because of her Christian belief that same-sex unions were contrary to God's law. The Court of Appeal held that the Council did not indirectly discriminate by insisting that all registrars must carry out marriages and civil partnerships. The Council's actions were a proportionate means of achieving the legitimate aim of providing a service which was not merely effective in terms of practicality and efficiency, but which also complied with its policy of being an employer and a public authority wholly committed to promoting equal opportunities and requiring all its employees to act in a way which did not discriminate against others. Once it was accepted that the aim of providing the service on a non-discriminatory basis was legitimate, it followed that the only way the Council could achieve that aim was by requiring all its registrars to conduct civil partnerships. The aim of the Council's equal opportunities policy was of general, indeed overarching, significance to the Council, and it also had fundamental human rights, equality and diversity implications, whereas the effect on the claimant of implementing the policy did not impinge on her religious beliefs, since she remained free to hold those beliefs and to worship as she wished.

17.73 Very similar conclusions were reached by the EAT in McFarlane v Relate Avon 2010 ICR 507, EAT – a case decided just a couple of weeks before the Court of Appeal published its decision in Ladele. In McFarlane the Appeal Tribunal upheld the decision of an employment tribunal that the dismissal of a Christian relationship counsellor, M, for refusing to counsel homosexuals about sexual matters did not constitute unlawful indirect discrimination. The employer's stance amounted to a proportionate means of achieving a legitimate aim –

namely, that of serving the community in a non-discriminatory manner. The Court of Appeal subsequently dismissed an application by M for leave to appeal against the EAT's decision – McFarlane v Relate Avon 2010 IRLR 872, CA.

It should be noted that, in both Ladele and McFarlane, there existed alternative ways of providing a full range of services to members of the public while at the same time accommodating the religious views of the claimants. In Ladele, this could have been achieved by not designating those registrars who shared the claimant's beliefs as civil partnership registrars; and, in McFarlane, by arranging for gay couples to be referred to a different counsellor. However, the Court of Appeal and the EAT refused to engage in a balancing exercise between the competing rights of different protected groups. The EAT's view in McFarlane was that questions concerning the practicability of accommodating the claimant's beliefs were irrelevant. The employment tribunal had reasoned that the key question was whether the employer could legitimately refuse to accommodate views that contradicted its fundamental principles. In this situation, detailed evaluations of the possible alternatives open to the employer were out of place: the question was whether the employer was entitled to treat the issue as one of principle, in which case compromise was inappropriate. This suggests that employers are not required to accommodate an employee's religious beliefs where they conflict with aims that are fundamental to the ethos of the organisation. If that is correct, it appears to operate as an exception to the general rule that considering ways of avoiding or mitigating the discriminatory impact of the relevant PCP on the claimant is relevant to the issue of proportionality (see under 'Proportionality – assessing the alternatives' above).

17.74 The claimants in both the Ladele and McFarlane cases have commenced legal proceedings before the European Court of Human Rights, contending that the decisions in their cases fail to comply with Article 9 of the European Convention on Human Rights, which concerns the right to freedom of thought, conscience and religion. The Equality and Human Rights Commission has successfully applied to intervene in order to make general representations. For further details, see Chapter 11, 'Religion or belief', under 'Manifestation of religion or belief – is UK approach compliant with Article 9?'.

It is worth bearing in mind that in some cases an individual may be subject to an overriding legal or professional obligation to provide a service on a non-discriminatory basis. This is illustrated by McClintock v Department of Constitutional Affairs 2008 IRLR 29, EAT, in which the Appeal Tribunal held that a Christian Justice of the Peace, who resigned from office following the rejection of his request to be excused from cases that might lead to the adoption of a child by a same-sex couple, was not indirectly discriminated against on the ground of religion or belief. The relevant PCP was the requirement that magistrates honour the judicial oath, which involves adjudicating on any case that comes before them. The claim failed because the magistrate had produced

519

no evidence that he had been disadvantaged by reason of his religious beliefs. However, the EAT also stated that any indirect discrimination would have been objectively justified as a proportionate means of achieving a legitimate aim. The Department for Constitutional Affairs was fully justified in insisting that magistrates must, regardless of their moral or other principled objections, apply the law of the land as their oath required. Even though the Department had, in the past, made administrative exceptions with regard to particular cases, there was no legal obligation to make a general exception to cater for religious or other philosophical beliefs.

17.75 Health, welfare and safety

The EHRC Employment Code states at para 4.28: 'The health, welfare and safety of individuals may qualify as legitimate aims provided that risks are clearly specified and supported by evidence.' In practice, this aim is relied on to justify a variety of potentially discriminatory PCPs across the range of protected characteristics covered by S.19 EqA. It might cover, for example, the imposition of physical capability tests or eyesight tests for machine operators in factories which, although they might disadvantage older workers or those with relevant disabilities, would pursue the aim of minimising the risk of accident through operator error.

17.76 Some examples of employment tribunal cases in which health and safety considerations were cited in an attempt to justify a potentially indirectly discriminatory PCP:

- **Sargeaunt-Thomson v National Air Traffic Services Ltd** ET Case No.3100109/05: a 6ft 10in male applicant for a place as a trainee air traffic control officer had his job offer withdrawn because a display screen equipment (DSE) test revealed that his 38-inch legs were cramped under his desk. As a result, S-T was forced to sit further away from the display screen than would be normal and, as a consequence, was required to stretch further in order to reach the controls. In the company's view this could cause eye fatigue and problems with the neck, shoulders and upper back. Owing to the fact that the equipment was fixed and could not be adjusted, the company concluded that there were serious health and safety risks, with S-T's inevitable discomfort affecting his concentration and thereby his ability to undertake the job safely. An employment tribunal held that there was no evidence that a considerably larger proportion of men than women were very tall, but that if it was wrong on this point, the practice of requiring certain candidates to undertake a DSE assessment when it considered that there could be a risk to health and safety in operating the equipment was justifiable, especially given the safety-critical nature of the respondent's business

520

- **Webster v Chief Constable of Hertfordshire Constabulary** ET Case No.2200687/99: when W was recruited as a police constable in 1989 the employer knew that he had a colour visual deficiency. In 1999 it came to the employer's attention that he should not have been recruited, as he did not meet the colour vision standards issued by the Home Office. W was permanently removed from operational duties because it decided he could not be put in a position in which he might be required to give evidence in court where colour formed part of the prosecution case. It was also concerned that W's condition might pose a risk to safety when driving. W claimed that a requirement that he pass a colour vision test was indirectly discriminatory against men as hereditary defective colour vision is more common in men than in women. On the issue of justification, the employment tribunal held that the employer had failed to justify the requirement that W pass a colour vision test. There was no evidence that W's condition posed a safety hazard – indeed, there was no evidence that the requirement to pass the test served the Constabulary's reasonable needs. The tribunal also concluded that the risk to W's credibility in court was remote since the risk was limited to his ability to distinguish between shades of green. Accordingly, the discriminatory impact on W outweighed the reasonable needs of the Constabulary

- **Bradley v West Midlands Fire and Rescue Authority** ET Case No.1304700/06: the employer introduced a new shift pattern to ensure that firefighting crew cover was available when required. WMF's aim had had two elements: to comply with a mandatory requirement of central government to devise an integrated risk management plan, and to ensure the most efficient deployment of the Fire Service's resources in the interests of public safety and well-being. Although the employment tribunal accepted that the new arrangements were to the disadvantage of B – a single mother – it held that WMF had demonstrated that they were a proportionate means of achieving a legitimate aim. In reaching this conclusion, the tribunal took account of the fact that the attitude of WMF to the implementation of the new shift system had not been inflexible. At a strategic level it had amended the system once evidence based on the experience of its operation had become available. In addition, so far as B was concerned, WMF had put forward a number of alternatives which she had declined for reasons that were less than convincing. Furthermore, because B would only have been required to work late shifts for six consecutive nights three or four times a year, the tribunal felt that she would have been able to accommodate these shifts by a combination of paid child care and family support

- **Bamber v Greater Manchester Police** ET Case Nos.2401829/09 and another: B was an inspector with Greater Manchester Police (GMP). GMP operated a requirement that, before officers could undergo level 2 public order training, they must complete a 'shield run' – a timed 500-metre run wearing full public order kit and carrying a shield – within two minutes and

45 seconds. In November 2008 B failed the shield run and was not allowed to proceed with the training course. She claimed that the requirement was indirectly discriminatory on grounds of age and sex. GMP conceded that it put persons of the claimant's age group (45–55) and women officers at a particular disadvantage but argued that it was justified by operational needs. The employment tribunal accepted that GMP had the legitimate aim of ensuring an appropriate level of fitness to allow a response officer to function safely in a public order situation. With regard to the timed shield run, however, GMP's justification argument was undermined by the fact that it had recently increased the time required to complete the test to three minutes, and by evidence that other forces performed the shield run in a variety of ways or did not use it at all. Alternative fitness tests were available which might have had a better relationship to the demands of the role and been better validated. Accordingly, GMP had not discharged the burden of showing that the application of the PCP was a proportionate means of achieving its legitimate aim.

17.77 **Dress and appearance.** Employers commonly seek to justify workplace codes on dress and appearance in terms of promoting their corporate image and other business needs – see under 'Operational needs – dress and appearance' and 'Corporate image' above. However, such a policy may also be justified on health and safety grounds. The EHRC Employment Code gives the following example at para 4.32: 'A food manufacturer has a rule that beards are forbidden for people working on the factory floor. Unless it can be objectively justified, this rule may amount to indirect religion or belief discrimination against the Sikh and Muslim workers in the factory. If the aim of the rule is to meet food hygiene or health and safety requirements, this would be legitimate. However, the employer would need to show that the ban on beards is a proportionate means of achieving this aim. When considering whether the policy is justified, the Employment Tribunal is likely to examine closely the reasons given by the employer as to why they cannot fulfil the same food hygiene or health and safety obligations by less discriminatory means, for example by providing a beard mask or snood.'

17.78 Two further examples drawn from case law:

- **Dhinsa v Serco and anor** ET Case No.1315002/09: D, a prison officer, was baptised an Amritdhari Sikh in 2008. One of the articles of faith of the Sikh religion is the wearing of a 'kirpan' – a ceremonial sword. The Prison Service operated a policy of restricting all staff except Sikh chaplains from wearing the kirpan at work. Amritdhari Sikhs, those Sikhs who are baptised, are committed to a strict code of discipline and the significance of carrying a kirpan is profound – it is a solemn duty to wear it at all times. However, the Prison Service asserted that it had to take note of the fact that, regardless of its religious significance, the kirpan could be used as a knife or dagger, and therefore it was banned within prisons, other than for Sikh chaplains. D was dismissed because he refused to stop wearing the kirpan. He claimed this amounted to religious discrimination. An employment tribunal found that the belief of an Amritdhari Sikh to honour the strict requirement to wear a kirpan was a religious belief that qualified for protection and that D was put at an actual disadvantage by being dismissed as a direct result of the application of the PCP. However, the tribunal went on to conclude that actions in maintaining and applying the security policy were an appropriate, necessary and proportionate means of achieving a legitimate aim, and the policy was therefore justified

- **Chaplin v Royal Devon and Exeter NHS Foundation Trust** ET Case No.1702886/09: C, a practising Christian, was employed as a nurse. The Trust's uniform policy stated that no necklaces should be worn in order to reduce the risk of injury when handling patients. Since she was a teenager, C had always visibly worn a cross on a chain. On several occasions she was asked to remove it but refused on the basis that this was disrespectful to her religion. Nor would she consider a number of proposals by the Trust such as pinning the chain inside her uniform or inside a pocket. After being redeployed, C claimed indirect religious discrimination. The employment tribunal rejected her claim on the basis that the PCP applied by the Trust did not put persons of the same religion or belief as C at a particular disadvantage. Even if it did, the policy would have been objectively justified because it pursued the legitimate aim of protecting the health and safety of staff and patients and the Trust had engaged in reasonable dialogue with C in an attempt to resolve the issue.

17.79 The claimant in Chaplin has commenced legal proceedings before the European Court of Human Rights, contending that the employer's decision failed to comply with Article 9 of the European Convention on Human Rights, which concerns the right to freedom of thought, conscience and religion. The Equality and Human Rights Commission has successfully applied to intervene in order to make general representations. For further details, see Chapter 11, 'Religion or belief', under 'Manifestation of religion or belief – is UK approach compliant with Article 9?'.

17.80 **Sikhs and safety helmets.** The Employment Act 1989 (EA) (as amended by para 15 of Schedule 26 to the EqA) contains special provisions concerning Sikhs and construction sites. S.12(1) EA provides that if an employer applies a PCP relating to the wearing of a safety helmet by a Sikh on a construction site, then – unless the employer has reasonable grounds to believe that he would not wear a turban at all times on such a site – the PCP cannot be justified in the context of an indirect race discrimination claim.

523

17.81 Rewarding length of service or experience

Criteria based on length of service, loyalty or experience are frequently invoked by employers to support a wide range of decisions but may be subject to challenge as giving rise to indirect age or sex discrimination. For example, employers who specify a minimum (or, indeed, maximum) level of experience when recruiting for a post may leave themselves open to indirect age discrimination claims unless the requirement can be objectively justified – see Chapter 16, 'Indirect discrimination: proving disadvantage', in the section 'Indirect discrimination in context', under 'Indirect age discrimination – experience and qualifications'. As a general rule, employment tribunals tend to accept that recruiting, rewarding or retaining employees with longer service or a certain level of experience is a potentially legitimate aim, and most cases turn on the issue of proportionality.

The principles on justification in Handels-og Kontorfunktionaerernes Forbund i Danmark v Dansk Arbejdsgiverforening (acting for Danfoss A/S) 1991 ICR 74, ECJ (the equal pay case known as 'Danfoss'), are relevant in this context. There, the European Court of Justice held that it was acceptable for an employer to put a premium on experience and to reward it appropriately, with the result that an 'employer does not have to provide special justification for using the criterion of length of service when determining pay'. This ruling appeared to create a blanket justification for employers basing employment-related decisions on a length of service criterion, but was later qualified in another equal pay case – Cadman v Health and Safety Executive 2006 ICR 1623, ECJ – in which the European Court ruled that employees may challenge service-related pay where they raise 'serious doubts' that greater length of service actually enables job holders to perform their duties better, in which case the employer will be required to provide detailed justification. For further discussion of the relevant case law, see IDS Employment Law Handbook, 'Equal Pay' (2011), Chapter 8, 'Material factor defence', under 'Specific material factors – length of service'.

17.82 The demarcation between claims of sex discrimination and equal pay, which was previously reflected by the fact that separate Acts of Parliament governed these respective claims, is maintained under the EqA. It follows that contractual benefits based on length of service, in so far as they indirectly discriminate against women, should normally be challenged under the equal pay provisions in the EqA. However, non-contractual benefits and discretionary decisions based on a length-of-service criterion may be subject to challenge as giving rise to indirect sex discrimination under S.19 EqA.

It should be noted that an exemption from the age discrimination provisions exists under para 10 of Schedule 9 to the EqA. In certain circumstances, this provision precludes an indirect age discrimination claim where length of service is used to determine a worker's benefits. It provides an absolute exemption for 'benefits' awarded with reference to a length-of-service criterion of up to five years, and allows a length-of-service criterion of over five years where the employer 'reasonably believes that doing so fulfils a business need'. In Rolls Royce plc v Unite the Union 2010 ICR 1, CA, the Court of Appeal held that a potentially indirectly discriminatory length of service criterion contained in a redundancy selection procedure fell within the equivalent exemption under the Employment Equality (Age) Regulations 2006 SI 2006/1031, as well as being objectively justified. For further details, see Chapter 31, 'Specific exceptions', under 'Age exceptions – service-related benefits'.

Redundancy selection. The adoption of length of service as a redundancy **17.83** selection criterion may have a disparate adverse impact on women, who are statistically less likely than men to attain long service, and on younger employees. An employer's wish to retain employees with a certain level or type of experience may amount to a legitimate aim. However, the employment tribunal must go on to consider the issue of proportionality.

In Rolls Royce plc v Unite the Union (above), the Court of Appeal held that a length of service criterion used as part of a redundancy selection process was objectively justified as a proportionate means of achieving the legitimate aim of rewarding loyalty and the overall desirability of achieving a stable workforce. The proportionate means were amply demonstrated by the fact that length of service was only one of a substantial number of criteria for measuring employees' suitability for redundancy and was by no means determinative. To reward long service by employees in any redundancy selection process was, viewed objectively, an entirely reasonable and legitimate employment policy, and one that a conscientious employer would readily and properly negotiate with a responsible trade union.

However, in Foster v Stafford College ET Case No.1301144/07 an employer **17.84** failed to demonstrate that a redundancy selection criterion based on experience was proportionate in the circumstances. F, a lecturer in computing, was made redundant. One of the criteria in the redundancy scoring matrix was 'recent and relevant business experience'. F had taught for 21 years; prior to that, he had been in business for 17 years but that experience, not having been gained in the past 20 years, was ignored by his employer. The employment tribunal found that the application of this criterion placed people in F's age group (the over-55s) at a particular disadvantage. This amounted to indirect age discrimination which, in the circumstances, was not objectively justified. While accepting that the need to retain staff with recent business experience could be a legitimate aim, the tribunal noted that the college had produced no real evidence to demonstrate the impact and benefit of such experience on the lecturers' ability to do their jobs. Furthermore, the level of business experience required was a low one that could have been achieved by simply sending staff on regular work placements. The tribunal concluded that the discriminatory effect of the criterion was not outweighed by the relatively low importance of

525

the employer's aim. By allowing F to attend a one-week placement after his provisional redundancy scoring, the college could have enabled him to achieve maximum marks against this criterion, thereby avoiding dismissal.

17.85 **Enhanced redundancy payments.** Enhanced redundancy schemes often use length of service to determine the sum an employee will receive upon redundancy, and are capable of giving rise to indirect age discrimination unless they can be objectively justified. In MacCulloch v Imperial Chemical Industries plc 2008 ICR 1334, EAT, M, who was aged 36 and had been employed by ICI plc for seven years, received a severance payment based on a combination of age and length of service. Her payment amounted to 55 per cent of gross annual salary. By contrast, an employee with ten years' service who had reached the age of 50 would have received 175 per cent of gross salary. An employment tribunal found that the redundancy scheme directly and indirectly discriminated against M but that the discrimination was justified. Upholding M's appeal, the EAT held that while the tribunal had identified certain legitimate aims of the scheme – including the need to encourage and reward loyalty – it had not properly determined whether the measures adopted were proportionate ways of achieving those aims. However, Mr Justice Elias, then President of the EAT, considered that the tribunal had been entitled to accept the employer's objective of rewarding loyalty as the reason for linking payments to length of service.

For further discussion of the operation of the justification defence in the context of enhanced redundancy payments, see Chapter 25, 'Discrimination during employment', under 'Benefits, facilities and services – enhanced redundancy schemes'.

17.86 **Preventing a windfall**

Employers sometimes choose to cap enhanced redundancy payments by reference to the amount employees would have earned if they had worked until their normal retirement date, and this can have a detrimental impact on older employees, who will thereby receive a lower payment than they might otherwise have done. In such cases, employers have sought to justify the cap by reference to the aim of preventing older workers from receiving a windfall.

In Ormerod v Cummins Engine Company Ltd ET Case No.2508268/09 (also discussed in Chapter 16, 'Indirect discrimination: proving disadvantage', in the section 'Indirect discrimination in context', under 'Indirect age discrimination – proximity to retirement') an employment tribunal held that an employer's decision to cap redundancy payments in this way gave rise to indirect age discrimination which, on the facts, was not justified. The employer argued that it was inappropriate that the claimant, O, should be disproportionately better off on being made redundant than if he had worked up to his normal retirement date. However, the tribunal noted that O had a clear contractual entitlement to an enhanced redundancy payment and that there was no express provision entitling the company to impose a cap. In those circumstances, the cap was not proportionate because it effectively amounted to a breach of O's employment contract. In any event, the employer had failed to demonstrate that O would, in fact, have achieved a windfall had the cap not been applied. To show that the provision achieved a legitimate aim and was proportionate, the employer should have considered the financial position that O would have been in but for the application of the cap and, indeed, had he not been made redundant. In this regard, he had given evidence that his redundancy would result in a loss of some £20,000 in pension benefits and that he would suffer financially by losing the opportunity to work overtime, to earn bonuses and to request continued working beyond the age of 65.

A similar factual scenario arose in Kraft Foods UK Ltd v Hastie 2010 ICR **17.87** 1355, EAT, where an employer's redundancy scheme provided that the maximum amount payable on redundancy should not exceed the amount the employee would have earned, at his or her current rate of pay, if he or she had remained in employment until the normal retirement age of 65. In that case, however, the EAT held that the imposition of a cap was objectively justified as a proportionate means of achieving the legitimate aim of preventing the employee from receiving a windfall. Having examined the scheme in question, Mr Justice Underhill (then President of the EAT) considered that its purpose was to compensate employees who took voluntary redundancy for the loss of the earnings which they had a legitimate expectation of receiving if their employment had continued. Although redundancy schemes – whether contractual or statutory – do not directly link the payments to the loss, Underhill P considered that this anomaly is long-established and rooted in industrial practice. Given the scheme's purpose, unless a cap was incorporated into the scheme, payments to employees who were close to retirement would exceed what was necessary to cover the amount of their future loss of earnings. By way of illustration, an employee with the claimant's earnings and length of service, who was made redundant at the age of 64 years and 11 months, would receive £90,000 compensation for the loss of the chance to earn some £3,000 in the remaining month of his or her employment. It necessarily followed that it was a legitimate aim to prevent such excess compensation.

On the question of whether the cap was a proportionate means of achieving the aim of preventing a windfall, the claimant argued that it essentially performed the same role as a taper, such as had existed in the statutory redundancy scheme prior to the introduction of the Employment Equality (Age) Regulations 2006 SI 2006/1031 (now replaced by the EqA). Since the taper had been removed at the time unjustified age discrimination in employment was outlawed, the claimant contended that the Government had recognised that a practice of this kind could not be justified. Underhill P acknowledged that there were similarities between the cap and a taper. However, he did not accept the claimant's argument for two reasons. First, looking at the consultation papers that preceded the Age

527

Regulations, it was not safe to infer that the Government had considered the practice of tapering to be unjustifiable. Secondly, he thought that the cap was a more accurate means of preventing a windfall than a taper. Since a cap and a taper were the two common means of achieving this aim, it followed that the more accurate means – the cap – was proportionate. The imposition of the cap was therefore justified.

17.88 For further discussion of indirect discrimination and the operation of the justification defence in the context of redundancy schemes, see Chapter 25, 'Discrimination during employment', under 'Benefits, facilities and services – enhanced redundancy schemes'. Note that the jurisprudence is still in its infancy, and its future development will no doubt be heavily influenced by the fact that, as of 1 October 2011, the default retirement age of 65 has been abolished – for details, see Chapter 5, 'Age', under 'Protection under the Equality Act – abolition of the statutory retirement regime'. This development could prove particularly important to questions of proportionality.

17.89 ## Government justification of social policy

In recent years, one of the most important developments in discrimination law has been the use of the indirect discrimination provisions to attack planks of Government employment policy. In R v Secretary of State for Employment ex parte EOC and anor 1994 ICR 317, HL, the former Equal Opportunities Commission (now subsumed within the Equality and Human Rights Commission) challenged the continuous service thresholds for claiming statutory employment rights, which were more onerous for part-time than for full-time employees. The House of Lords accepted, in accordance with the ECJ's ruling in Rinner-Kühn v FWW Spezial-Gebäudereinigung GmbH and Co KG 1989 IRLR 493, ECJ (an equal pay case), that if the State can show that its legislative provisions are designed to meet a necessary aim of social policy and that they are suitable and necessary for attaining that aim, then the mere fact that the provision in question affects a greater number of one sex than the other does not constitute an infringement of EU equality law. The Secretary of State sought to justify the discriminatory threshold provisions for part-timers on the ground that these increased the availability of part-time work by lessening the burdens on employers in respect of redundancy and unfair dismissal liability. As to whether the measures in question were 'suitable' to achieve the desired aim, the Secretary of State claimed that the purpose of the thresholds was to reduce the costs of part-time employment for employers.

The House of Lords ruled that the differential thresholds were unlawful. Although the stated aim of bringing about an increase in the availability of part-time work was a legitimate aim, it had not been shown, by reference to objective factors, that the thresholds were suitable and requisite for achieving that aim. The Secretary of State's principal evidence consisted of an affidavit setting out the views of the Department of Employment and, as such, contained nothing capable of being regarded as factual evidence demonstrating the correctness of those views. As regards the argument that the thresholds were a suitable means of achieving a reduction in costs for employers, their Lordships pointed out that a similar reduction of costs could be achieved by paying a lower basic rate of pay to part-time employees than that paid to full-time employees. Yet legislation permitting a differential of that kind would undoubtedly constitute a gross breach of the principle of equal pay given that the vast majority of part-time workers are women. Any such legislation could not possibly be regarded as a suitable means of achieving an increase in part-time employment. In their Lordships' view, similar considerations applied to legislation that sought to reduce the indirect cost of employing part-time labour. No objective justification of the part-time thresholds had therefore been established.

17.90 As a result, the Government was forced to make the period of continuous employment needed to claim statutory employment rights two years for all employees, irrespective of whether they worked full or part time.

A further challenge was subsequently made in respect of the two-year rule itself. In R v Secretary of State for Employment ex parte Seymour-Smith and anor 1999 ICR 447, ECJ, the ECJ laid down a three-part test for assessing whether or not a discriminatory legislative provision was justified:

- the Member State must show that the allegedly discriminatory rule reflects a legitimate aim of its social policy

- this aim must be unrelated to any discrimination based on sex – mere generalisations concerning the capacity of a specific measure are not enough to show that this is the case

- the Member State could reasonably consider that the means chosen are suitable for attaining that aim. Mere generalisations will not amount to evidence in support of an argument that the means chosen were suitable.

17.91 When the case returned to the House of Lords – R v Secretary of State for Employment ex parte Seymour-Smith and anor (No.2) 2000 ICR 244, HL – their Lordships applied this test and held that all three requirements had been satisfied: the aim of the two-year threshold was to encourage employers to recruit more employees; this was a legitimate aim unrelated to sex discrimination; and there was some supporting factual evidence that the two-year qualifying period reduced the reluctance of employers to take on more staff (for further discussion of this case, see under 'Background and overview – timing of justification' above).

It should be noted that the qualifying threshold for claiming unfair dismissal was reduced to one year with effect from 1 June 1999 but increased to two years again by virtue of the Unfair Dismissal and Statement of Reasons for

529

Dismissal (Variation of Qualifying Period) Order 2012 SI 2012/989 in respect of periods of continuous employment beginning on or after 6 April 2012. The Government's stated reasons for this increase were to alleviate the burden on the employment tribunal system and to increase business confidence in order to create jobs. If the increase were to be challenged on the grounds of indirect sex or age discrimination – women and younger employees being arguably less likely to have attained two years' continuous service – the Government would be expected to produce supporting evidence, in line with the ECJ's judgment in Seymour-Smith (above), to demonstrate that the increase was a suitable means of attaining those aims.

17.92 **Social policy aims**
We have already seen that a private employer may not rely on a social policy aim to justify the imposition of an apparently discriminatory PCP – see under 'Legitimate aim – social policy aims' above. However, the Government can rely on social policy aims when implementing aspects of employment policy. The case of Secretary of State for Employment and anor v Chandler 1986 ICR 436, EAT, concerned a Government scheme providing temporary work for the long-term unemployed. C, although suited for a post on a Community Programme in every other way, did not qualify for entry because neither she nor her husband received any state benefits. C claimed that the requirement to be in receipt of unemployment benefit indirectly discriminated against married people in that it excluded: (i) married women who had elected to pay reduced National Insurance contributions and so were ineligible for unemployment benefit; and (ii) married persons disqualified from entitlement to claim such benefit because their spouses were in paid employment. The defendants conceded that they had applied a condition which was such that a considerably smaller proportion of married persons could comply with it. They argued, however, that the criterion was justifiable because of the overriding objective of benefiting those most in need of employment. The EAT accepted this argument on appeal.

A similar conclusion was reached in Cobb and ors v Secretary of State for Employment and anor 1989 ICR 506, EAT. There, the Appeal Tribunal upheld an employment tribunal's conclusion that the conditions of entry to the Community Programme, although conceded by the Secretary of State to have a disparate impact on married persons and/or women, were justified. The Secretary of State had decided, for cogent and logical reasons, to target younger unemployed people, and the employment tribunal had been entitled to conclude that the entry criterion of being in receipt of social security benefits achieved that end while making the most economic and effective use of resources.

17.93 **Cost considerations**
A long line of ECJ decisions has established that an EU Member State, with its notionally bottomless purse, cannot rely on budgetary considerations to justify

a discriminatory social policy. For example, in Jørgensen v Foreningen af Speciallæger and Sygesikringens Forhandlingsudvalg 2000 IRLR 726, ECJ – a case in which a female doctor argued that a scheme introduced in Denmark to regulate specialised medical care indirectly discriminated against female medical practitioners – the Court ruled that budgetary considerations cannot in themselves justify discrimination on the ground of sex by a Member State. Otherwise, the application of the principle of equal treatment between men and women might vary according to the state of the public finances of Member States. However, the Court added that budgetary considerations may underlie a Member State's choice of social policy and influence its adoption of social protection measures, and said that Member States enjoy a reasonable margin of discretion as regards the nature of social protection measures. In conclusion, the Court found that measures intended to ensure the sound management of public expenditure on specialised medical care and to guarantee people's access to such care may be justified if they meet a legitimate objective of social policy, are appropriate to attain that objective, and are necessary to that end.

For another decision of the ECJ to the effect that cost considerations alone cannot amount to justification when relied on by a Member State, see Kutz-Bauer v Freie und Hansestadt Hamburg 2003 IRLR 368, ECJ. There, the Court held that a German collective agreement was in principle indirectly discriminatory against women where it refused to allow employees of over pensionable age to have access to a scheme enabling older workers to work part time with enhanced pay. According to the ECJ, neither the cost to the State nor the cost to the employer was sufficient on its own to make out the case for objective justification.

17.94 More recently, in the direct age discrimination case of Fuchs and anor v Land Hessen 2012 ICR 93, ECJ, the European Court held that a German law stipulating a retirement age of 65 for civil servants was potentially justified under the EU Equal Treatment Framework Directive (No.2000/78). In so holding, the Court reiterated the well-established doctrine that budgetary considerations can underpin the chosen social policy of a Member State and influence the nature or extent of the measures adopted, although such considerations cannot in themselves constitute a legitimate aim. It appears clear, then, that a desire to save costs cannot, of itself, amount to a legitimate aim capable of justifying an indirectly discriminatory measure enacted by a Member State. The position in respect of costs justifications relied on by private employers is more nuanced and is discussed above under 'Legitimate aim – costs'.

Burden of proof

17.95 The burden of proof for establishing justification of discriminatory legislation is on the State – Hockenjos v Secretary of State for Social Security 2005 IRLR 471, CA. In that case the Court of Appeal held that regulations denying an unemployed man entitlement to a child premium on top of the jobseekers

531

allowance contravened the EU Social Security Directive (No.79/7) because they were indirectly discriminatory. Although this was a social security case, the Court of Appeal's approach to objective justification is relevant in the context of indirect discrimination generally, and, importantly, is a reminder of the stringent standards of proof applied to Member States seeking to justify indirectly discriminatory measures in social policy legislation. In accordance with the three-stage test in R v Secretary of State for Employment ex parte Seymour-Smith and anor 1999 ICR 447, ECJ (see under 'Government justification of social policy' above), the Court of Appeal held that the Secretary of State had to show that the discriminatory rule reflected a legitimate aim of the United Kingdom's social policy, that the aim was unrelated to any discrimination on the ground of sex, and finally that he could reasonably consider that the means chosen were suitable for attaining that aim. Built into this final question was the balance between holding fast to the Community's fundamental principles on the one hand and the Member State's freedoms to achieve its own social policy on the other.

With this balance in mind, the Court rejected an argument by the Secretary of State that the Member State's broad margin of discretion on social policy meant that he was entitled to succeed unless there was an alternative means of achieving the policy aim that was so obviously better that no reasonable Secretary of State could have avoided choosing it. Such an approach, held the Court, focused solely on the means of achieving the policy aim and did not allow for any balancing consideration to be given to the need not to frustrate a fundamental principle of Community law: namely, the equal treatment of men and women. Proportionality had to be taken into account and that meant balancing the importance of the principle of equality and the Member State's freedom to achieve its own social policy. In the instant case, there was no evidence that the Secretary of State, or anyone on his behalf, ever applied their mind to the question of whether there was a better or different way of achieving the policy aim that would avoid, or diminish, the considerable discrimination against fathers. Further, where there might be unexplored alternatives that did not offend a fundamental principle of Community law, the Secretary of State could not be held to have discharged the burden of establishing justification. It was not up the claimant to show that there was an obviously better alternative.

17.96 Timing of justification

When defending a claim, it is not necessary as a matter of law for a Member State to have analysed the proportionality question at the time of adopting the rule or policy. However, as we have previously seen, in such a situation a court will scrutinise closely whether the defendant had a legitimate aim – see R (on the application of Elias) v Secretary of State for Defence and anor 2006 IRLR 934, CA (discussed under 'Background and overview – timing of justification' above).

18 Harassment

Forms of harassment

Unwanted conduct

Violation of dignity or offensive environment

Related to a relevant protected characteristic

Sexual harassment

Less favourable treatment following harassment

Employer's liability

Relationship with other discrimination provisions

'Harassment' as a free-standing cause of action is a relatively recent statutory **18.1** creation, introduced by the Government in October 2005 to comply with the requirements of the EU Equal Treatment Directive (No.76/207), as amended by the EU Equal Treatment Directive (No.2002/73) (now consolidated into the recast EU Equal Treatment Directive (No.2006/54)), which obliged Member States to ensure that harassment was treated as unlawful discrimination. S.26 of the Equality Act 2010 (EqA) largely mirrors the protection from harassment found in the antecedent discrimination legislation, although in some respects it goes further by, for example, extending protection from harassment based on association or perception to all relevant protected characteristics (see 'Related to a relevant protected characteristic – harassment by association or perception' below).

Forms of harassment   18.2

The general definition of harassment is set out in S.26(1) and applies to all protected characteristics, except marriage and civil partnership and pregnancy and maternity. It states that a person (A) harasses another (B) if:

* A engages in unwanted conduct related to a relevant protected characteristic – S.26(1)(a); and

* the conduct has the purpose or effect of (i) violating B's dignity, or (ii) creating an intimidating, hostile, degrading, humiliating or offensive environment for B – S.26(1)(b).

Section 26(2) is designed to replicate the effect of S.4A(1)(b) of the Sex **18.3** Discrimination Act 1975 (SDA), which dealt specifically with sexual (as distinct

533

from sex-related) harassment. The definition of sexual harassment is similar to that of general harassment set out above, except that the unwanted conduct in question is 'of a sexual nature', as opposed to being 'related to a relevant protected characteristic' – S.26(2)(a).

Section 26(3) protects individuals who are treated less favourably by their employer because they either reject or submit to sexual harassment or harassment related to gender reassignment or sex. Such treatment is treated as a form of harassment and replicates the effect of similar provisions in S.4A(1)(c) SDA.

18.4 **Essential elements.** There are three essential elements of a harassment claim under S.26(1):

- unwanted conduct
- that has the proscribed purpose or effect, and
- which relates to a relevant protected characteristic.

In many cases, there will be considerable overlap between these elements – for example, the question of whether the conduct complained of was unwanted will overlap with the question of whether it created an adverse environment for the employee. This point was made by Mr Justice Underhill, then President of the EAT, in Richmond Pharmacology v Dhaliwal 2009 ICR 724, EAT (in the context of a claim for racial harassment brought under the Race Relations Act 1976 (RRA)). Nevertheless, he considered that it would be a 'healthy discipline' for a tribunal in any claim alleging unlawful harassment specifically to address in its reasons each of the three elements.

18.5 This chapter therefore deals with each element in turn. It also looks at what amounts to conduct 'of a sexual nature' for the purposes of sexual harassment, before turning to the third form of harassment proscribed by S.26(3), i.e. less favourable treatment for rejecting or submitting to sexual harassment or harassment related to gender reassignment or sex. We then briefly examine the extent of an employer's liability for harassment carried out by its employees or third parties before discussing the relevance of other discrimination provisions in the context of harassment.

18.6 **Departure from comparative approach.** Before the specific harassment provisions were introduced in October 2005, an employee who believed that he or she had been subjected to discriminatory 'harassment' at work had to bring a claim under the direct discrimination provisions of the relevant legislation. For example, a woman complaining of sexual harassment had to establish – in accordance with Ss.1(1)(a) and 6(2)(b) SDA – that, on the ground of her sex, she had suffered less favourable treatment than was or would have been meted out to a man and that she had been subjected to a detriment as a result. Fitting harassment within the direct discrimination provisions could, at times, be problematic and somewhat contrived. As noted by Underhill P in Richmond Pharmacology v Dhaliwal (above), 'the old law [relating to harassment] was constructed, somewhat uncomfortably, out of the general statutory definitions of discrimination'.

A standalone claim of harassment under S.26 EqA, by contrast, does not require a comparative approach. It is not necessary for the worker to show that another person was, or would have been, treated more favourably. Instead, he or she simply needs to establish a link between the harassment and a protected characteristic. This departure from the traditional 'comparative' approach to equality towards one based upon dignity recognises that an act which violates dignity or damages a person's working environment can create a barrier to equality in the workplace.

18.7 However, the introduction of a free-standing cause of action for harassment does not mean that we can simply ignore the old case law on harassment amounting to less favourable treatment on the basis that it is now irrelevant. Many of the cases on issues such as the admissibility and/or relevance of evidence, the definition of 'unwanted conduct' and the operation of the burden of proof remain relevant and the principles derived from precedent will need to be considered. Furthermore, the protected characteristics of marriage and civil partnership and pregnancy and maternity are *not* covered by S.26. Thus a complaint alleging harassment related to either of these protected characteristics could still be framed as a direct discrimination claim under S.13 EqA (see 'Related to a relevant protected characteristic' below). Furthermore, if an employee is subjected to a campaign of harassment at work, elements of that treatment may more readily be categorised as 'detriments' than acts of harassment – and thus fit more easily into a direct discrimination claim. This is discussed further under 'Relationship with other discrimination provisions' below.

For further details about admissible evidence, see Chapter 33, 'Proving discrimination', in particular under 'General principles – admissibility' and 'Relevant evidence in sexual harassment claims'. The burden of proof is dealt with in Chapter 32, 'Burden of proof'. As noted in that chapter under 'Other forms of discrimination – harassment', although a harassment claim does not depend on the claimant showing less favourable treatment compared to an actual or hypothetical comparator, such a comparison will still be a useful tool for tribunals in weighing up whether or not the treatment complained of was related to a protected characteristic.

Unwanted conduct **18.8**

The Equality and Human Rights Commission's Code of Practice on Employment ('the EHRC Employment Code') notes that unwanted conduct can include 'a wide range of behaviour, including spoken or written words or abuse, imagery, graffiti, physical gestures, facial expressions, mimicry, jokes, pranks, acts affecting a person's surroundings or other physical behaviour' – para 7.7. The conduct may be blatant – for example, overt bullying – or more subtle; for example, ignoring or marginalising an employee.

The following have all been held to constitute unwanted conduct:

- the failure to provide female toilet facilities on a building site for an employee who was the only woman in a team of skilled bricklayers – Marcella and anor v Herbert T Forrest Ltd and anor ET Case No.2408664/09. In reaching its decision that this constituted harassment under the SDA, the tribunal took into account the fact that the Factories Act 1961 and other health and safety provisions clearly envisage that it is preferable for sanitary facilities to be provided separately for men and women, as well as M's evidence that she felt it was degrading to have to share a toilet – which did not have a lock on the door – with a number of men. This case also demonstrates how an omission or failure to act can amount to 'conduct' for the purposes of unlawful harassment

- the unilateral removal of various adjustments that had evolved to accommodate an employee's disability – Williams v North Wales Police ET Case Nos.2902135/08 and another

- a written warning (later overturned) – Grace v Royal Bank Of Scotland Insurance Services Ltd ET Case Nos. 1102412/09 and another

- office gossip – Nixon v Ross Coates Solicitors and anor EAT 0108/10

- nicknaming a French employee 'Inspector Clouseau' – Basile v Royal College of General Practitioners and ors ET Case No.2204568/10 (discussed under 'Related to a relevant protected characteristic – "related to"' below).

18.9 Furthermore, it appears from the Court of Appeal's obiter comments in Land Registry v Grant (Equality and Human Rights Commission intervening) 2011 ICR 1390, CA, that 'outing' a gay employee – i.e. revealing his or her sexual orientation – against his or her wishes can amount to unwanted conduct for the purposes of unlawful harassment. Indeed, the Acas Guide on 'Sexual Orientation and the Workplace' states that outing someone without their clear permission is inappropriate and a breach of that person's privacy and may constitute harassment. Note, however, that on the facts of Land Registry v Grant, G's 'outing' was held not to be unwanted because he had already put information about his homosexuality into the public domain – see '"Unwanted" – "invited" conduct' below.

A single act can amount to unwanted conduct and found a complaint of harassment 'if sufficiently serious' – para 7.8 EHRC Employment Code. In order to constitute unlawful harassment it would, of course, have to have the purpose or effect proscribed by S.26(1)(a) EqA – see 'Violation of dignity or offensive environment' below. In Insitu Cleaning Co Ltd v Heads 1995 IRLR 4, EAT, a single comment made by a manager to a female employee twice his age – 'Hiya, big tits' – was held to be unwanted and to constitute sexual harassment (for the purposes of a direct sex discrimination claim under the SDA). The EAT noted that whether a single act of unwanted conduct is sufficiently serious to found a complaint of harassment is a question of fact and degree.

Alternatively, and perhaps more commonly, the unwanted conduct could arise **18.10** from a series of events. In Reed and anor v Stedman 1999 IRLR 299, EAT (decided before the statutory definition of harassment was introduced into the legislation), the EAT upheld a tribunal's decision that S had been subjected to a course of conduct which amounted to sexual harassment – see under 'Violation of dignity or offensive environment – effect' below.

'Unwanted' 18.11

In Reed and anor v Stedman (above) and Insitu Cleaning Co Ltd and anor v Heads (above) (both decided before the statutory harassment provisions came into force), the EAT held that the word 'unwanted' is essentially the same as 'unwelcome' or 'uninvited'. This is confirmed by the EHRC Employment Code at para 7.8. The EAT in English v Thomas Sanderson Blinds Ltd 2009 ICR 543, CA, pointed out, perhaps self-evidently, that 'unwanted conduct' means conduct that is unwanted *by the employee*. This suggests that deciding whether conduct is unwanted should largely be assessed subjectively, i.e. from the employee's point of view. This could possibly become an issue where employee B is alleging that he or she has suffered harassment by virtue of having witnessed harassment suffered by employee C. Depending upon the circumstances, the employer might be able to argue that, although the treatment was unwanted by C, it did not affect B and therefore was not unwanted conduct so far as B was concerned.

That said, the conduct does not have to be directed specifically at the complainant in order for it to be unwanted by him or her. The EHRC Employment Code gives the following example at para 7.10: during a training session attended by both male and female workers, a male trainer directs a number of remarks of a sexual nature to the group as a whole. A female worker finds the comments offensive and humiliating to her as a woman. She would be able to make a claim for harassment, even though the remarks were not specifically directed at her. Some further examples:

- **Nixon v Ross Coates Solicitors and anor** EAT 0108/10: office gossip about the paternity of the claimant's unborn child was held to constitute harassment

- **Morgan v Halls of Gloucester Ltd** ET Case No.1400498/09: a black employee who overheard a colleague use the term 'golliwog' to describe a black colleague succeeded in his tribunal claim for racial harassment

537

- **X v Y** ET Case No.1605251/09: a gay employee, X – who had only told one or two trusted co-workers about his sexuality – succeeded in his claim for sexual orientation harassment following a 'fancy-dress day' at work to raise funds for charity: a number of his male colleagues dressed up as women, speaking in high-pitched voices and generally acting in a very camp manner. The conduct continued all day and was very much 'in the faces' of employees who had to attend work but were not involved in the event. Those people, including X, had little option but to witness the conduct irrespective of their feelings

- **Moonsar v Fiveways Express Transport Ltd** 2005 IRLR 9, EAT: M succeeded in claiming that she suffered sexual harassment amounting to direct discrimination contrary to the SDA when on three occasions male members of staff working alongside her downloaded pornographic images onto computer screens. Although the images were not circulated to M, she was in close proximity and was aware of what was happening

- **Basile v Royal College of General Practitioners and ors** ET Case No.2204568/10: B, a male employee of the College, witnessed a male colleague, R, making masturbatory hand gestures, sometimes accompanied by a vulgar noise. R gave evidence that this was all part of the humorous culture which helped to relieve the tension in the highly pressured kitchen environment. He also denied that it was in any way directed at B but acknowledged that he may have witnessed it on occasion. The tribunal upheld B's claim for sexual harassment under the SDA – see further 'Sexual harassment – conduct "of a sexual nature"' below.

18.12 The EHRC Employment Code itself envisages that a white worker who is offended by a black colleague's being subjected to racially abusive language can bring a racial harassment claim – para 7.10. The Explanatory Notes accompanying the EqA further state that an employer who displays any material of a sexual nature, such as a topless calendar, may be harassing its employees where this makes the workplace an offensive place to work for any employee, female or male. Potentially, therefore, an employer could find itself exposed to several claims for harassment arising out of the same incident, even when the conduct itself was only directed at one employee or, indeed, was not directed at any employee in particular.

There is no requirement that the alleged harasser be of the same or different sex, race, etc to the victim in order for a claim to be well founded. It is perfectly possible, for example, for a woman to be guilty of sex-related harassment towards another woman, as the following tribunal case demonstrates:

- **Gashi v European Pensions Management Ltd** ET Case No. 3100490/10: EPM Ltd became increasingly exasperated by G's persistent requests to leave work early to care for her children. On one occasion the company's female

538

Chief Executive, M, said to her, 'I'm very disappointed. You are playing the childcare thing, fine, I'm a woman too... please just stick up for the sex and do the job.' Later in the conversation M said, 'I think you remain restricted by your kids; you need to bend a bit further, get half an hour more childcare; I want you to tell me you have found someone else, employ a nanny.' The conversation ended with M asking, 'How do we get around the baby?' The tribunal held that this amounted to harassment related to sex (although it found that the company's requirement that G remain in the office until after 5 pm in order to supervise her staff effectively was a proportionate means of achieving a legitimate aim and so did not amount to indirect discrimination).

Nevertheless, whether or not the relevant parties share the protected **18.13** characteristic in question could possibly have a bearing on whether the conduct was unwanted. This was the thrust of the EAT's decision in Driskel v Peninsula Business Services Ltd and ors 2000 IRLR 151, EAT. The female claimant in that case complained of remarks of a sexual nature made by the male head of the department in which she worked. The tribunal rejected her claim, finding that the nature of the remarks was not such as to amount to sexual harassment giving rise to a claim of direct sex discrimination. The EAT overturned that decision, holding that in the context of an allegation of sexual harassment, a tribunal should not lose sight of the significance of the sex of not just the complainant but also of the alleged harasser. In its view, sexual badinage between two heterosexual males cannot be completely equated with badinage between a heterosexual male and a woman. Prima facie, the treatment is not equal: in the latter circumstance it is the sex of the alleged discriminator that potentially adds a material element which is absent between two heterosexual men.

Although this claim pre-dated S.4A SDA (a precursor to S.26(1) EqA) and was brought under the direct discrimination provisions of the SDA, the EAT considered the effect of the respondent's conduct on the claimant in a way that would still be valid under the EqA. In particular, the EAT held that, although the assessment by the tribunal of the conduct at issue is ultimately objective, the complainant's subjective perception of the behaviour that is the subject of the complaint should be taken into account – an approach that fits neatly with the requirements of S.26(4) (see under 'Violation of dignity or offensive environment – effect' below). The case is therefore authority for the proposition that although the complainant and harasser need not be of a different sex for a complaint of harassment to be well founded, a difference of sex can add an unwanted element to remarks or banter that would not be present between two heterosexual people of the same sex. The same could apply where, for example, the complainant and harasser are of different races.

'Inherently' unwanted conduct. In Reed and anor v Stedman 1999 IRLR 299, **18.14** EAT, the EAT noted that certain conduct, if not expressly invited, can properly be described as unwelcome. Normally, conduct that is by any standards offensive will automatically be regarded as unwanted. It could be described as 'inherently' unwanted and the claimant would not need to expressly object to make it clear that it was not welcome. If, for instance, the conduct in question obviously violates a claimant's dignity (as to which see under 'Violation of dignity or offensive environment' below), a failure to complain at the time is unlikely to undermine his or her claim. For example, as noted by the EAT in Reed v Stedman, a woman does not have to make it clear in advance that she does not want to be touched in a sexual manner. The EHRC Employment Code gives the following example of what it terms 'self-evidently' unwanted conduct: in front of her male colleagues, a female electrician is told by her supervisor that her work is below standard and that, as a woman, she will never be competent to carry it out. The supervisor goes on to suggest that she should instead stay at home to cook and clean for her husband. The electrician would not have to object to this conduct before it was deemed to be unlawful harassment – para 7.8.

18.15 Three further examples of conduct that has been held to be inherently unwanted:

- **Driskel v Peninsula Business Services Ltd and ors** 2000 IRLR 151, EAT: the EAT held that given the nature of the remarks in question – which entailed a male manager telling D, a female employee, to attend an interview in a short skirt and see-through blouse showing plenty of cleavage to persuade him to promote her – D's failure to complain was not significant

- **Moonsar v Fiveways Express Transport Ltd** 2005 IRLR 9, EAT: M worked as a data entry clerk for a courier company. On three occasions male members of staff downloaded pornographic images onto computer screens in the room in which they were working alongside M. Although the images were not circulated to M, she was in close proximity and was aware of what was happening. She did not complain to her employer about the incidents because, as she later explained to an employment tribunal, she valued her job and decided to 'keep her head down'. Although M had considered the behaviour unacceptable, her failure to complain, coupled with the fact that she had not been shown the images by the men, led the tribunal to conclude that she had not suffered sexual harassment. The EAT overturned the tribunal's decision, holding that, viewed objectively, the behaviour complained of clearly had potential to cause affront to a female employee and was thus to be regarded as degrading or offensive to women. The fact that M did not complain at the time was irrelevant, given the obviously detrimental effect that the behaviour had in undermining her dignity at work

- **Insitu Cleaning Co Ltd v Heads** 1995 IRLR 4, EAT: a single comment made by a manager to a female employee twice his age – 'Hiya, big tits' – was held to be unwanted and to constitute sexual harassment (for the purposes of a direct sex discrimination claim under the SDA). The EAT noted that whether a single act of unwanted conduct is sufficiently serious to found a complaint of harassment is a question of fact and degree. The EAT considered that no one other than a person used to indulging in loutish behaviour could think that the remark made to a female employee in this case was other than obviously unwanted.

18.16 *Claimant clearly has no objection.* If the claimant has made it clear, through words or conduct, that he or she personally has no objection to the conduct – even if most people would find it unacceptable – that conduct will not be unwanted. In English v Thomas Sanderson Blinds Ltd 2009 ICR 543, CA, E, a heterosexual, worked for TSB Ltd under an agency agreement. Although E's colleagues knew that he was not gay, they called him 'faggot' and joked about his sexuality in the in-house magazine. For some years, E did not complain and remained friends with the perpetrators. However, on 15 August 2005, E made a written complaint and asked for the 'constant innuendo' to stop. E claimed harassment on the ground of sexual orientation under Reg 5 of the Employment Equality (Sexual Orientation) Regulations 2003 SI 2003/1661 (a precursor to S.26 EqA). The Court of Appeal held that a heterosexual targeted by homophobic banter could make a complaint under the Regulations. On remittal, the tribunal – having regard to the evidence that E had participated in banter and name-calling, and had written similarly offensive articles 'riddled with sexist and ageist innuendo' for the in-house magazine – concluded that he could not reasonably have considered that the conduct prior to August 2005 violated his dignity. If that were the case, E would have complained and would not have been so friendly with his alleged tormentors. The tribunal considered whether the old adage 'keep your friends close but your enemies closer' might apply here but decided it did not. E himself admitted that the friendships had been genuine. Indeed, he had been on holiday with one of the perpetrators and had visited another in hospital. For that reason, the tribunal also rejected E's contention that he had only engaged in the banter in retaliation for the harassment that he was suffering.

The tribunal did, however, accept that an article written in August 2005 was a 'tipping point' and exceeded what E considered to be an acceptable level of personal attack and insult. It had prompted E to complain and appeared to have been read by his family. To use E's own expression, it 'had overstepped the mark'. However, although the tribunal considered that the article could amount to harassment, it did not uphold E's claim because it had been brought out of time. The EAT upheld the tribunal's decision in all respects.

18.17 The fact that the conduct has been going on for a long time with no apparent objection does not necessarily mean that the claimant accepts or condones it. This is exemplified by the case of Munchkins Restaurant Ltd and anor v Karmazyn and ors EAT 0359/09. K and her three fellow female claimants, aged between 23 and 32, worked as waitresses at MR Ltd, a restaurant in London. They attracted the attention of M, the 73-year-old controlling shareholder of, and 'driving force' behind, MR Ltd. He would often make sexual comments to

541

the claimants and ask them questions about their sex lives. He would also show them 'dirty' photos he kept in the safe, and catalogues of sex toys and gadgets that he brought into work. Nevertheless, the claimants worked at the restaurant for periods of between one and five years. When the assistant manager, G, became too ill to work in the restaurant in 2007, matters came to a head. K, who had been acting as assistant manager in G's absence, resigned on 1 July 2007 as she found being first in M's firing line too much to bear. The other three claimants soon followed, all of them citing M's behaviour among the reasons for their departure. The claimants brought complaints of sex discrimination, harassment and constructive dismissal against M and MR Ltd.

Although the employer admitted that there had been a degree of sexualised talk in the restaurant, it contended that that talk had not been unwelcome, and had often been initiated by the claimants. However, the tribunal was not convinced, finding that, by questioning the claimants about sex and showing them explicit photographs and catalogues, M had, on the ground of their sex, engaged in unwanted conduct that had the effect of violating their dignity and creating an intimidating, degrading, humiliating or offensive environment for them. The tribunal therefore upheld the claims of discrimination and harassment, and also concluded that the claimants had been constructively dismissed. The EAT held that there was no contradiction in the tribunal's finding that the claimants had suffered intolerable behaviour yet remained in employment. The tribunal had specifically made the point that the claimants were migrant workers with no certainty of employment if they left their jobs, and that they were constrained by financial and, in some cases, parental pressures. Furthermore, the tribunal had concluded that, on occasion, the claimants had initiated sexual conversations as defensive moves aimed at deflecting more personal questions about their own sex lives. The EAT made the point that there are many situations where people will put up with conduct which violates their personal dignity because they are constrained by social circumstances; for example, a battered wife who puts up with violence for her children's sake. That does not make the violence right or welcome, or any less criminal. By the same token, a lack of outward objection to harassment does not mean that the conduct is welcome.

18.18 **Grey areas.** Some types of conduct fall into a grey area and it may not be immediately apparent whether or not it is unwanted. For example, teasing or flirting might cross the boundary between acceptable and unwanted conduct, without the alleged perpetrator being aware that it had done so. And an employee who appears to 'take in good part', or play along with, what might be regarded by others as harmless banter, could in fact be offended by it but unwilling to complain. Tribunals will therefore often need to consider the context when deciding whether or not the conduct in question was unwanted. Two examples:

* **English v Thomas Sanderson Blinds Ltd** (above): the EAT upheld a tribunal's decision that – having regard to the fact that E had participated in banter

and name-calling and had written offensive articles 'riddled with sexist and ageist innuendo' for the in-house magazine – he could not reasonably have considered that jokes about his sexuality had the effect of violating his dignity or creating an intimidating, hostile, degrading, humiliating or offensive environment for him. If that were the case, E would have complained and would not have been so friendly with his alleged tormentors

- **Coney v Ceva Logistics UK Ltd and anor** ET Case No.1306820/08: a tribunal found that a racist remark made to C during a 'heated conversation' with a fellow employee (M) constituted racial harassment. This was despite a finding that C clearly 'gave as good as he got' in terms of swapping offensive insults (although, crucially, he did not racially abuse M). C's involvement was, however, taken into account by the tribunal when assessing compensation. In awarding just £500 for injury to feelings, it also took account of the fact that, while C found the remark upsetting, it was by no means the source of the greatest offence and provocation to him. (Compensation is dealt with in Chapter 35 'Compensation: general principles of assessment', and Chapter 36, 'Compensation: heads of damage'.)

Even if an employee does freely participate in banter at first, that does not mean **18.19** that subsequent banter cannot cross the line and become unwanted. Indeed in the English v Thomas Sanderson Blinds case, a homophobic article written in August 2005 was held to have been a 'tipping point' for E, which 'overstepped the mark'. Two further examples:

- **Queenscourt Ltd v Nyateka** EAT 0182/06: N, a black woman, worked in a fast food restaurant as a team leader. The working conditions, as found by the employment tribunal, consisted of a friendly atmosphere in which all staff got along well and there was a lot of banter. In particular, the tribunal found that employees were robust in their remarks and that between black and ethnic minority staff, words like 'nigger' and 'Paki' were used in a jocular manner. N brought a claim of racial harassment based on a single incident in which a white male colleague had made a sarcastic reference to her skin colour. The tribunal upheld N's claim and the EAT dismissed Q Ltd's appeal. According to the EAT, the tribunal had been entitled to find that despite the prevailing atmosphere in which racial banter was acceptable, and in which N may previously have used words herself that might in another context be seen as racist, the manager had used racial language that was not spoken in jest and which had caused real upset to N

- **Taj v GBM Services Ltd** ET Case Nos.3301281/07 and another: T, a Muslim, was employed as a security controller by GBMS Ltd. He brought a religious harassment claim against his employer after being subjected to religious jokes by his colleagues. The tribunal found that there was a culture of banter, including 'inappropriate' banter, in the workplace and that T was a willing participant. Indeed, jokes against Muslims had previously been told and T had not taken offence. However, during Ramadan, one colleague offered T and his Muslim co-workers sausage sandwiches; made noises to show them that he was enjoying his food; and turned down the lights so that they might start eating because it was dark. Even though T did not challenge this behaviour at the time, the tribunal held that it did violate his dignity and create an offensive environment 'because of the essential religious nature of Ramadan to those practising the Muslim faith' and because it amounted to a step too far in the climate of banter. In terms of the degree of violation, however, it was at the lower end of the scale, given that T had previously fully participated in the culture of joking. (The employer unsuccessfully appealed to the EAT on a separate point.)

18.20 As we saw under '"Inherently" unwanted conduct' above, an employee does not need to expressly object to conduct before it is deemed to be unwanted, particularly when the conduct is clearly offensive. However, in certain circumstances, whether or not an employee has objected – by words or conduct – may become highly relevant. As noted by the EAT in Driskel v Peninsula Business Services Ltd and ors 2000 IRLR 151, EAT, 'that which in isolation may not amount to discriminatory detriment may become such if persisted in notwithstanding objection, vocal or apparent'. Although this comment was made in the context of a direct discrimination claim (where it is necessary to show 'detriment'), the same would obviously hold true for a harassment claim for the purposes of establishing that the conduct was 'unwanted'. Furthermore, in Reed and anor v Stedman 1999 IRLR 299, EAT, the EAT noted (also in the context of a direct discrimination claim) that 'at the lower end of the scale', an employee may appear, objectively, to be unduly sensitive to what might otherwise be regarded as unexceptional behaviour. In this situation, the question for the tribunal is whether by words or conduct he or she made it clear that he or she found the behaviour unwelcome. Three examples of cases that hinged upon whether or not the claimant had objected:

* **Ahmed v Aphel Ltd** ET Case No.1306384/06: A, a Muslim, worked for A Ltd as a design engineer until he was dismissed in August 2006. He presented a number of claims to an employment tribunal, including that his colleagues had used sexually offensive language in the workplace in a way that was offensive to him on religious grounds. The tribunal dismissed his claims. While male employees may be expected to know that some types of language are likely to be offensive to women, there was, in its judgement, no such general understanding that Muslims object to sexual language. Accordingly, unless and until he objected to it, a male Muslim employee could not say that the use of such language was discriminatory or amounted to harassment on the ground of his Muslim faith. (This case can be contrasted with Taj v GBM Services Ltd (above) where jokes about Ramadan were held to amount to religious harassment against a Muslim employee, 'because of the essential religious nature of Ramadan to those

practising the Muslim faith'. It therefore did not matter that the employee did not challenge this behaviour at the time)

- **Mann v BH Publishing Ltd and anor** ET Case No.2203272/04: M spoke with what he described as a 'gay South African accent'. His manager, H, mimicked his accent from the outset of his employment. M brought a claim of harassment on the ground of sexual orientation, which was upheld. The tribunal found that there was no harassment for the first two days – H was a natural and talented mimic and the tribunal did not accept that the mimicry had any connection with M's sexuality. However, from the time M put his concerns to H, the mimicry became unwanted conduct with the purpose and effect of violating his dignity

- **Basi v Snows Business Forms Ltd** ET Case No.3100944/09: B, who was of Indian ethnic origin, overheard his line manager, F, say the word 'monkey' as B walked past. B asked whether the word was directed at him and was told that it was not. B gave F the benefit of the doubt but let him know that he found the comment racially offensive. Later that month they played golf together. B played a particularly good shot, which prompted F to call him a 'cheeky monkey'. B was upset by this and F, recalling the earlier incident in the office, duly apologised. The tribunal upheld B's claim for racial harassment. F had been put on notice that B would consider it a racial insult to be called a 'monkey'. Therefore, the ill-considered comment could reasonably have caused B to feel degraded and humiliated on the ground of his race.

'Invited' conduct. As noted above, the word 'unwanted' has been held to mean **18.21** essentially the same as 'unwelcome' or 'uninvited' and this is confirmed in the EHRC Employment Code. According to the Oxford Dictionary, one definition of 'uninvited' is 'unwarranted', while 'to invite' is defined, inter alia, as 'to elicit' or 'to tempt'. 'Invitation' is defined as a 'situation or action that tempts someone to do something or makes a particular outcome likely'. Therefore, if a claimant acts in such a way as to make certain conduct probable – for example, by provoking the incident in question – he or she may struggle to establish that the conduct is unwanted (unless that conduct is, for example, particularly egregious and offensive and/or there is a malicious or discriminatory intent behind it). In Ali v Mitie Security (London) Ltd ET Case No.2317931/10, for example, A, a Muslim black African of Somali origin, claimed that a colleague (H) had made offensive and abusive remarks concerning race and religion. However, his claim was dismissed because the tribunal found that he had deliberately instigated a controversial discussion with H concerning matters of race and religion and had continued the conversation even though H was not inclined to join in. In a case where he had deliberately provoked the exchange, he had failed to prove that the conduct he complained of was unwanted.

This principle is particularly important in the context of workplace gossip. Certain gossip – for example, about an employee's private life – can constitute unlawful harassment. However, if the employee has chosen to put certain facts about his or her private life into the public domain, he or she may struggle to establish that subsequent gossip about those facts is unwanted. Thus in Land Registry v Grant (Equality and Human Rights Commission intervening) 2011 ICR 1390, CA, the fact that G had already revealed his homosexuality at the employer's office in Lytham undermined his claim to have been harassed when he was 'outed' by a manager (K) at the employer's office in Coventry, following his transfer there. In the Court of Appeal's view (Lord Justice Elias giving the leading judgment), the fact that G had come out in Lytham was a highly significant factor when assessing whether there had been discrimination or harassment, irrespective of whether K knew G had come out or not. At any time, any one of the 300 or more employees at Lytham could, in conversation with a colleague at Coventry, have revealed perfectly innocently the fact that G was gay. They would have been justified in assuming that G would have no objection to this. It was not suggested that he revealed his sexual orientation in Lytham in circumstances where those in receipt of that information were required to keep it a secret. If a Lytham employee had revealed to someone in Coventry that G was gay, it would be bizarre if that employee could, by the mere innocent disclosure of that information, be liable for either direct discrimination or harassment. It would make a mockery of discrimination law to impose liability in these circumstances. An employer would be liable for discrimination for doing something which G had reasonably led it to believe would not cause him concern. Having made his sexual orientation generally public, any grievance G had about the information being disseminated to others was unreasonable and unjustified.

18.22 Elias LJ went on to note that the implications of a finding of discrimination or harassment in these circumstances would have been far-reaching. An individual may choose to make generally known in the workplace certain aspects of his or her private life, such as the fact that he or she has contracted some debilitating illness, or is pregnant, or has become a Christian. However, by putting these facts into the public domain, a person takes the risk that he or she may become the focus of conversation and gossip. In Elias LJ's judgement, if such information is discussed, even in idle gossip, then provided there is no ill intent, the disclosure of that information would not be an act of discrimination. That is so even if the victim is upset at the thought that he or she will be the subject of such idle conversation.

The Grant case is authority for the proposition that where an employee has put his or her sexuality into the 'public domain' by revealing it at one of the employer's premises, he or she cannot then complain if he or she is 'outed' at another of the employer's premises. We would suggest, however, that if an employee goes to work for a *different* employer, he or she could argue that his or her sexuality had not been put into the public domain so far as the new employer was concerned (and that as a result he or she should not be prevented from alleging harassment if 'outed' in the new job). As far as we are aware, this point has yet to be tested in the courts or tribunals.

Of course, if an employee reveals his or her sexuality or a serious illness to his or her manager *in confidence*, he or she would not be putting it into the public domain and would not be precluded from claiming that the conduct is unwanted if the information is divulged further. An example: **18.23**

- **Dos Santos v Fitch Ratings Ltd** ET Case No.2203907/08: in September 2008 D received a provisional diagnosis that he was HIV positive. He informed his line managers of this fact, but stressed to them that the information should be kept confidential. In fact, one of his line managers disclosed the diagnosis to the Group MD. The tribunal found that D suffered unlawful harassment on the ground of his disability. FR Ltd's action in disclosing the information was unwanted by D and had the effect of violating his dignity or creating an intimidating, hostile, degrading, humiliating or offensive environment for him. Although it did not have that purpose, it did have that effect. The tribunal awarded D £5,000 for injury to feelings.

Furthermore, as noted by Elias LJ in Land Registry v Grant (Equality and Human Rights Commission intervening) (above), the fact that an employee has revealed certain private information does not mean that subsequent remarks or references to that information can never constitute harassment. Clearly they can, 'an obvious example being where they are vituperative or offensive'. He went on: '[E]verything depends upon the particular circumstances. So, for example, it will generally be relevant to know to whom the remark was made, in what terms and for what purpose.' In Nixon v Ross Coates Solicitors and anor EAT 0108/10 N was employed by RCS at its Ipswich office for over ten years to bring in clients and assist with corporate hospitality. She was in a relationship with one of the firm's solicitors. However, at the staff Christmas party on 22 December 2007 she ended up publicly kissing the IT manager. They spent the night together in a room charged to the firm's account. Following the party, N took annual leave and then sick leave, during which she informed the firm's managing director (MD) that she was eight weeks' pregnant but did not want this disclosed until she had crossed the 12-week threshold. However, the HR manager, O, found out and started gossiping about who the father of N's unborn child might be. A tribunal dismissed N's claim for harassment under S.4A SDA (the precursor to S.26(1) EqA). While conceding that O had been 'indiscreet', the tribunal did not consider that her behaviour could be regarded as 'intimidating, hostile, degrading or humiliating'. The EAT upheld N's appeal. The harassment claim under S.4A was based on the fact that O was spreading gossip about the paternity of N's child. This gossip was connected with N's pregnancy, which in turn related to her sex, and constituted a course of unwanted conduct meeting the definition of harassment. The fact that N's behaviour at the Christmas party was public and so would inevitably give rise **18.24** to comment did not mean that confidential information about her pregnancy could be disclosed and in a derogatory manner. This case can be contrasted with the Land Registry v Grant case (above), since N had expressly requested that her pregnancy be kept quiet and had not disseminated the information generally around the office. Furthermore, the gossip about her pregnancy was done in a derogatory manner.

18.25 Violation of dignity or offensive environment

The second limb of the statutory definition of harassment requires that the unwanted conduct in question has the *purpose or effect* of:

- violating B's dignity – S.26(1)(b)(i), or

- creating an intimidating, hostile, degrading, humiliating or offensive environment for him or her – S.26(1)(b)(ii).

Accordingly, conduct that is intended to have that effect will be unlawful even if it does not in fact have that effect; and conduct that in fact does have that effect will be unlawful even if that was not the intention. As noted in the introduction to this chapter, unlike direct discrimination, there is no requirement to make a comparison with the treatment afforded to others.

18.26 The forbidden purpose or effect can be brought about by a single act or a combination of events. The EAT in Reed and anor v Stedman 1999 IRLR 299, EAT, made some useful comments about how effect should be assessed when dealing with a combination of events, suggesting that tribunals should adopt a cumulative approach, as opposed to measuring the effect of each individual incident. This is discussed further under 'Effect – series of incidents' below.

So far as single acts are concerned, the question of whether an act is 'sufficiently serious' (to quote from the EHRC Employment Code at para 7.8) to support a harassment claim is essentially a question of fact and degree – see Insitu Cleaning Co Ltd v Heads 1995 IRLR 4, EAT. In that case, a single comment made by a manager to a female employee twice his age – 'Hiya, big tits' – was held to constitute sexual harassment for the purpose of a direct sex discrimination claim under the SDA. In Rowland v Cryo Store Ltd ET Case No.2302560/09, by contrast, a tribunal held that a one-off remark, while sexist and offensive, was not serious enough to be harassment. R, who was employed by CS Ltd as a Senior Storage Technician, saw an e-mail between two company directors (H and W), which discussed managing her out of the business. The e-mail reminded W that he was 'now travelling in hostile territory' and so should make 'no sexist jokes' and 'whatever you do don't get her pregnant'. R subsequently resigned and claimed constructive dismissal. She also claimed that the remarks in the e-mail constituted sexual harassment. A tribunal upheld her constructive dismissal claim but not her harassment claim. While, in accordance with Insitu

Cleaning Co Ltd v Heads (above), a one-off act could constitute harassment, in this particular instance it did not do so. The offending remark, while offensive and sexist, was seen by only two people, R and W. It was made by a non-executive director, i.e. not a person present in the workplace. By contrast, the one-off act in the Insitu case was done in public in the workplace. Furthermore, R did not complain about the remark until some six weeks after the event. Her complaint was, in the tribunal's view, something of an afterthought.

18.27 The purpose or effect that conduct must have if it is to constitute harassment is fairly broad. As can be seen, the two strands of the definition are disjunctive, i.e. a claimant only has to show that the conduct had the purpose or effect *either* of violating dignity, *or* of creating the proscribed environment – not both. This differs from the position under the EU Equal Treatment Framework Directive (No.2000/78) and the recast EU Equal Treatment Directive (No.2006/54), which define harassment as occurring where unwanted conduct related to a protected ground takes place 'with the purpose or effect of violating the dignity of a person *and* of creating an intimidating, hostile, degrading, humiliating or offensive environment' (our stress). By replacing the word 'and' with 'or', domestic discrimination legislation is designed to reflect the domestic case law that has developed over the years – in particular in the context of sex and race discrimination – and offers a higher level of protection than the Directives originally envisaged.

In many cases, however, this difference between EU and national law may be more theoretical than real. In Richmond Pharmacology v Dhaliwal 2009 ICR 724, EAT, Mr Justice Underhill (then President of the EAT) pointed out that many or most acts which are found to create an adverse environment for an employee will also violate his or her dignity. However, he did also note that the reverse may not always be true. It is possible, for example, that certain one-off acts could violate an employee's dignity but would not be sufficient by themselves to create a degrading *environment* for him or her. We would add that there may be situations where an employee who witnesses a fellow employee being harassed could argue that an offensive environment had been created for him or her, but fail to show that his or her personal dignity had been violated.

18.28 It is worth noting here that Article 2(d) of the recast Equal Treatment Directive defines *sexual harassment* slightly differently in terms of the proscribed purpose or effect, namely: 'unwanted... conduct of a sexual nature... with the purpose or effect of violating the dignity of a person, *in particular* when creating an intimidating, hostile, degrading, humiliating or offensive environment' (our stress). This appears to envisage that if a degrading environment has been created or intended, this will have the purpose or effect of violating dignity. However, it also suggests – so far as sexual harassment is concerned – that dignity may be violated without such an environment having been created.

549

The elements of the second strand of the definition under S.26(1)(b)(ii) – i.e. that the environment created or intended must be 'intimidating, hostile, degrading, humiliating *or* offensive' (our stress) – are also likely to overlap, although they too are disjunctive (under both EU and national law). For convenience, we use the words interchangeably throughout the course of this chapter when describing the proscribed environment.

18.29 Purpose

A claim brought on the basis that the unwanted conduct had the purpose of violating the employee's dignity or creating an intimidating, hostile, degrading, humiliating or offensive environment obviously involves an examination of the perpetrator's intentions. As the perpetrator is unlikely to admit to having had the necessary purpose, the tribunal hearing the claim will need to draw inferences from the surrounding circumstances. Depending on the particular facts, a tribunal might be prepared to infer such a purpose where it had been made clear to the perpetrator on previous occasions that the conduct in question was unwanted and offensive. This is because it would be difficult for the perpetrator to argue that he or she did not have that purpose if he or she repeats the conduct, notwithstanding clear objection. An example:

- **Mann v BH Publishing Ltd and anor** ET Case No.2203272/04: M, who was South African, began working for BHP Ltd on 24 May 2004. He spoke with what he described as a gay South African accent, which his manager, H, mimicked from the outset. After two days, M told H that he objected to the mimicry and told him that he thought it was harassment on the ground of his sexual orientation. Despite this conversation, H continued to mimic M's accent, and from this time on M's colleagues began to tease and taunt him about his sexual orientation. M brought a claim of harassment on the ground of sexual orientation, which was upheld. The tribunal found that there was no harassment for the first two days – H was a natural and talented mimic and the tribunal did not accept that the mimicry had any connection with M's sexuality. However, from the time M put his concerns to H, the mimicry became unwanted conduct and had the purpose (and effect) of violating his dignity. The harassment was on the ground of M's sexual orientation, given the link that M himself had drawn and brought to H's attention.

18.30 Unlike a claim brought on the basis of effect (as to which see 'Effect' below), it is not necessary to examine the employee's perception of the conduct or whether it was reasonable for that conduct to have the intended purpose. Thus an employee who is hypersensitive can still bring a harassment claim if he or she can prove the proscribed purpose. For example, he or she might object to certain conduct that most people would regard as inoffensive. If that conduct is then repeated, notwithstanding his or her objection, that may assist in establishing a malign intention for the purpose of a harassment claim, even though objectively speaking the conduct in question would appear to be fairly inoffensive.

If the conduct is found to have had the purpose of violating dignity, it does not matter that it did not actually have that effect. However, as noted by Underhill P in Richmond Pharmacology v Dhaliwal 2009 ICR 724, EAT, it will be rare for a tribunal to find that conduct has the purpose but not the effect of violating dignity. It will be much more common for conduct to have the effect and not the purpose – for example, a comment supposedly said in jest. Nevertheless, the 'purpose route' could play an important part where the claimant is particularly robust and minimises his or her upset, even though the perpetrator intended his or her dignity to be violated. And as noted above, a hypersensitive employee would also need to take the 'purpose route' in order to establish harassment.

Effect
18.31

In practice, harassment claims are usually brought on the basis of 'effect', as it is generally considered easier to prove that conduct has a particular effect than to prove the purpose behind it. That said, the intent with which something is said or done can be relevant when assessing its effect – see 'Relevance of intent' below.

In deciding whether the conduct has the effect referred to in S.26(1)(b) (i.e. of violating a person (B)'s dignity or creating an intimidating, hostile, degrading, humiliating or offensive environment for B), each of the following must be taken into account:

- the perception of B

- the other circumstances of the case; and

- whether it is reasonable for the conduct to have that effect – S.26(4).

The test therefore has both subjective and objective elements to it. The subjective 18.32 part involves the tribunal looking at the effect that the conduct of the alleged harasser (A) has on the complainant (B) (see 'Subjective element' below). The objective part requires the tribunal to ask itself whether it was reasonable for B to claim that A's conduct had that effect (see 'Objective element' below). We suggest that the 'other circumstances' of the case should be used to shed light both upon the complainant's perception and upon whether it was reasonable for the conduct to have the effect. The EHRC Employment Code notes that relevant circumstances can include those of the complainant, such as his or her health, including mental health; mental capacity; cultural norms; and previous experience of harassment. It can also include the environment in which the conduct takes place – para 7.18. Where the employer is a public authority, the Code suggests that it may also be relevant whether the alleged perpetrator was exercising any of his or her rights under the Human Rights Act 1998, e.g. the right to freedom of expression (para 7.19).

551

Under the antecedent legislation, there was a slightly different emphasis. Conduct was regarded as having the proscribed effect if, 'having regard to all the circumstances, including *in particular the perception of that other person* [i.e. the alleged victim], it should reasonably be considered as having that effect' (our stress) – see, for example, S.3A(2) RRA. Therefore, the old law arguably placed greater emphasis upon the claimant's perception for the purposes of assessing effect. That said, there is likely to be little practical difference in the way the test is applied by tribunals.

The EAT in Richmond Pharmacology v Dhaliwal 2009 ICR 724, EAT, gave some guidance as to how the 'effect' test should be applied. It noted that the claimant must actually have felt, or perceived, his or her dignity to have been violated or an adverse environment to have been created. If the claimant has experienced those feelings or perceptions, the tribunal should then consider whether it was reasonable for him or her to do so.

18.33 **Caused by employer's conduct.** The proscribed effect must have been brought about *by the employer's conduct*. This is illustrated by the following case where the tribunal held that the source of the claimant's humiliation was his own conduct and that the employer's response (which the claimant alleged caused him humiliation) was a 'natural reaction' to that conduct:

- **Jones v Logica CMG Ltd and ors** ET Case No.1600659/07: J claimed that he was harassed on the ground of his age when he was questioned during a job interview about the fact that he had obtained his degree at the age of 39. J gave evidence that he felt humiliated by the interviewer's 'disapproving' and 'scornful' reaction, together with the persistent questioning about why he had been out of full-time employment for so long. The tribunal rejected his claim. It accepted the employer's evidence that it viewed the gaining of a degree at that age as a plus factor but that this was neutralised by the discovery that J had devoted most of his time between May 2003 and December 2005 to degree studies. The employer's expressions of surprise were an 'inevitable reaction' upon discovering that J had put misleading information on his application form in order to secure an interview (such as grossly exaggerating the amount of work experience he had). The tribunal accepted that J felt humiliated. However, it considered that the source of that humiliation was the 'far from complete' information he had chosen to give in his CV. It had nothing to do with the age at which he had taken his degree.

18.34 **Relevance of intent.** In Richmond Pharmacology v Dhaliwal (above) Mr Justice Underhill (then President of the EAT) held that in assessing effect, 'one question that may be material is whether it should reasonably have been apparent whether the conduct was, or was not, intended to cause offence (or, more precisely, to produce the proscribed consequences): the same remark may have a very different weight if it was evidently innocently intended than if it was evidently intended to hurt'. And in Land Registry v Grant (Equality and Human Rights Commission intervening) 2011 ICR 1390, CA, Lord Justice Elias confirmed that 'when assessing the effect of a remark, the context in which it is given is always highly material. Everyday experience tells us that a humorous remark between friends may have a very different effect than exactly the same words spoken vindictively by a hostile speaker. It is not importing intent into the concept of effect to say that intent will generally be relevant to assessing effect. It will also be relevant to deciding whether the response of the alleged victim is reasonable.'

However, it is important to keep in mind that a flippant or light-hearted comment *can* constitute harassment, just as much as one made aggressively. For example, in Driskel v Peninsula Business Services Ltd and ors 2000 IRLR 151, EAT, the EAT held that the tribunal had rather missed the point when concluding that a manager's remark that D should attend her interview wearing a short skirt and a see-through blouse to increase her chances of promotion was flippant and not intended to be taken seriously. What was relevant was that the remark (whether flippant or not) undermined the complainant's dignity as a woman. Of course, the difference in tone and intent will be an important factor when assessing compensation for injury to feelings. In Basi v Snows Business Forms Ltd ET Case No.3100944/09 (the facts of which are set out under 'Unwanted conduct – "unwanted"' above), for example, the tribunal awarded the relatively low amount of £1,500, on the basis that the remark at issue was not intentionally hurtful and was uttered in the heat of the moment.

Series of incidents. Although, as noted under 'Violation of dignity or offensive **18.35** environment' above, it is possible for an employee's dignity to be violated by a single incident (if sufficiently serious), it is more common for an individual to claim harassment on the back of a number of separate incidents. The EAT in Reed and anor v Stedman 1999 IRLR 299, EAT, gave some guidance as to how tribunals should approach such cases for the purposes of assessing effect. It counselled against carving up a case into a series of specific incidents and then trying to measure the harm or detriment in relation to each. Instead, it endorsed a cumulative approach and quoted the following passage from a USA Federal Appeal Court decision: '[T]he trier of fact must keep in mind that each successive episode has its predecessors, that the impact of the separate incidents may accumulate, and that the work environment created may exceed the sum of the individual episodes' (see USA v Gail Knapp (1992) 955 Federal Reporter, 2nd series). This approach was approved by the EAT in Driskel v Peninsula Business Services Ltd and ors (above), and although both cases were decided before the specific statutory provisions on harassment were introduced, there is no reason why the same approach should not apply under the EqA.

Subjective element. The first part of the statutory test set out in S.26(4) **18.36** involves examining the act from the complainant's perspective. In doing so, tribunals should bear in mind that different people have different tolerance levels. In Stuckey v Daido Industrial Bearings Europe Ltd and anor ET Case No.1700301/08, for example, S suffered from severe dyslexia and had a reading age of 9.5. He complained that throughout his employment he was called 'numpty' and was the butt of practical jokes. He claimed that this amounted to disability harassment. The tribunal upheld S's claim – the conduct related to S's disability and he was only treated that way because of his disability. Furthermore, his disability made him more susceptible to banter and teasing because he was less able to process it, laugh it off and give as good as he got. This meant he reacted badly, which provided further encouragement for those bullying him.

18.37   Although it is the objective element of the test (discussed below) which generally ensures that not every little incident will attract liability for harassment, the subjective element can also play an important role in this regard. The EAT in Richmond Pharmacology v Dhaliwal (above) made the point that the claimant must actually have felt or perceived his or her dignity to have been violated or an offensive environment to have been created. The fact that a claimant is slightly upset or mildly offended by the conduct in question may not be enough to bring about a violation of dignity or an offensive environment. In Land Registry v Grant (Equality and Human Rights Commission intervening) 2011 ICR 1390, CA, G's sexuality was revealed by his manager, K, at the employer's office in Lytham after he had 'come out' at its Coventry office. The Court of Appeal held that this disclosure was not unwanted conduct and this aspect of the decision is discussed under 'Unwanted conduct – "unwanted"' above. However, it went on to hold that even if in fact the disclosure was unwanted, the effect upon G could not amount to a violation of his dignity, nor could it properly be described as creating an intimidating, hostile, degrading, humiliating or offensive environment for him. The Court commented that tribunals must not cheapen the significance of these words since they are an important control to prevent trivial acts causing minor upsets being caught by the concept of harassment. G was no doubt upset that he could not release the information in his own way, but that was far from attracting the epithets required to constitute harassment. To describe this incident – as the tribunal did – as subjecting G to a 'humiliating environment' when he heard of it some months later was 'a distortion of language which brings discrimination law into disrepute'. Furthermore, the fact that G was made to feel uncomfortable for a short period at a dinner party attended by work colleagues where attention was drawn to the fact that he was gay did not mean that his dignity had been violated or an offensive environment created. Given that it was not the purpose of K to humiliate or embarrass him, the tribunal was not entitled to equate an uncomfortable reaction to humiliation.

Even if, viewed objectively, the conduct could reasonably be considered to violate a claimant's dignity, it will not do so if the claimant's subsequent actions demonstrate that he or she, personally, did not consider it to do so. Thus in

English v Thomas Sanderson Blinds Ltd 2009 ICR 543, CA, the EAT upheld a tribunal's decision to reject a claim for harassment arising out of certain homophobic language directed at E, because from E's perspective the conduct in question did not have the effect of either violating his dignity or creating an offensive environment for him: E by his own conduct had demonstrated that he did not consider it so. It rejected E's (rather unusual) argument that the tribunal had erred in law by applying a purely subjective test and not considering the conduct from an objective perspective, holding that the tribunal was right to ask about E's own perceptions and feelings in order to determine whether the effect of the unwanted conduct was to violate his dignity or create an adverse environment. There was, in its judgement, 'no general rule applicable to answer the question whether when fellow workers use homophobic or sexist language to each other (or language relating to any other protected characteristic), both commit unlawful harassment, one commits unlawful harassment or neither does'. It went on to comment that in many cases both employees will have committed unlawful harassment, having both the purpose and effect of violating the other's dignity or creating an adverse environment for him or her. However, in the instant case, where the fellow workers engaged in similar conduct towards each other, while remaining genuinely good friends, the tribunal was entitled to reach the conclusion it did. (Note that this case had been remitted by the Court of Appeal, which had held that a heterosexual targeted by homophobic banter could make a complaint under the Employment Equality (Sexual Orientation) Regulations 2003 SI 2003/1661 (a precursor to S.26 EqA).)

18.38 A claimant's assertion that certain conduct has violated his or her dignity should not necessarily be taken at face value if the facts demonstrate otherwise. After all, not everyone who claims to be 'offended' by something genuinely feels offended. Some may, for example, simply relish an argument or have a grudge against the alleged perpetrator and therefore will view anything he or she says in a negative light. In Daragheh v Staffordshire University and anor ET Case No.1315696/09, for example, D, an Iranian Muslim, was employed in the University's technical support team. P, the team leader, had instigated disciplinary proceedings against certain members of the team (not D) because he considered that they were being obstructive. D subsequently brought a tribunal claim alleging that P had racially harassed him. He complained that when he came back from a trip to Iran to observe Ramadan, P had asked him whether Ramadan was a big thing in his village. D said the reference to Ramadan as a 'thing' was somewhat offensive but he was particularly offended by P's assumption that he lived in a village, when he in fact came from Tehran. He believed that this demonstrated a perception that foreigners lived in mud huts or villages. On another occasion, when D was having a conversation with a fellow employee, B, about the cost of accommodation in Lithuania, P had joined by saying, 'they're all in tents over there'. Finally, in August 2009 P found a toy plastic gun in a drawer, tossed it to D and asked him whether it was 'any good to him'.

18.39 The tribunal was satisfied that on no occasion had P intended to cause offence. It accepted that the conduct was unwanted so far as D was concerned. It did, however, make the point that to a great extent any attempt at friendly interaction by P was likely to be unwanted given the technical support team's general hostility to him. The tribunal considered that the 'village/Ramadan' comment could properly be categorised as trivial and it should have been clear that no offence was intended. Nor did the tribunal consider that it could reasonably be taken to be offensive. P did not know where D came from in Iran and had simply wanted to find out what he had been doing on his trip there. The tribunal considered that P was making a rather clumsy attempt at friendliness and was trying to improve the relationship. Furthermore, although the comment about Lithuanians living in tents was an ill-advised one, looked at objectively it could not reasonably be said to have created an adverse environment for D. The comment was relatively trivial, was not directed at D or his ethnic origins, and only an over-sensitive individual would consider it to have violated his or her dignity or created a hostile environment. It was particularly significant, in the tribunal's view, that B, whose fiancée was Lithuanian, was not offended and thought it was a joke. It was an unguarded comment, probably made in the context of P having had a conversation about camping shortly before.

In the tribunal's view, the 'plastic gun' incident was the most serious. The tribunal thought this an insensitive comment and could see how it could be interpreted as being related to D's country of origin or his religion, bearing in mind the possible implication of terrorism. Nevertheless, although the comment was capable of amounting to racial harassment, the tribunal did not consider it did so in the particular circumstances of the case. It was satisfied that the comment was not racially motivated and accepted P's explanation that it was simply a misguided attempt to bond with D. Furthermore, D claimed that it seriously offended him and violated his dignity and yet he made no complaint at the time. It was significant that he had delayed so long in making a formal complaint. He was well aware of the grievance procedure as he had used it before and it seemed surprising that if the comment had seriously offended him he did not complain more quickly. The tribunal was therefore not satisfied that the comment genuinely had the effect of creating an adverse environment or violating D's dignity.

18.40 The tribunal concluded that when D did eventually raise his grievance alleging racial harassment, he was to a considerable degree motivated by his desire to retaliate against the disciplinary action that was being taken against some of his colleagues. His actions were part of the team's collective resistance to P. Although the tribunal had no doubt from his evidence that D now had a genuine sense of grievance, it considered this a case where D had gone back over events that had happened some time ago and had imbued them with more sinister motivations. Even viewed together, the acts in question did not suggest a campaign of harassment. They were isolated incidents picked upon by D in order to strengthen the team's complaint against P.

Note that it is possible for an employee who witnesses another employee's dignity being violated to bring a claim for harassment – see 'Unwanted conduct – "unwanted"' above. However, if he or she is offended on behalf of that person, as opposed to being offended in his or her own right, it is arguable that he or she has not personally experienced the proscribed effect.

Objective element. The objective aspect of the test is primarily intended to exclude liability where B is hypersensitive and unreasonably takes offence. As noted by the EAT in Richmond Pharmacology v Dhaliwal 2009 ICR 724, EAT, 'while it is very important that employers, and tribunals, are sensitive to the hurt that can be caused by racially offensive comments or conduct (or indeed comments or conduct on other grounds covered by the... legislation...) it is also important not to encourage a culture of hypersensitivity or the imposition of legal liability in respect of every unfortunate phrase'. It commented that 'if, for example, the tribunal believes that the claimant was unreasonably prone to take offence, then, even if she did genuinely feel her dignity to have been violated, there will have been no harassment within the meaning of the section. Whether it was reasonable for a claimant to have felt her dignity to have been violated is quintessentially a matter for the factual assessment of the tribunal. It will be important for it to have regard to all the relevant circumstances, including the context of the conduct in question.' **18.41**

Importantly, the tribunal must consider whether it was reasonable for the conduct to have the effect *on that particular claimant*. The EAT in Reed and anor v Stedman 1999 IRLR 299, EAT, made the point that since 'it is for each individual to determine what they find unwelcome or offensive, there may be cases where there is a gap between what the tribunal would regard as acceptable and what the individual in question was prepared to tolerate. It does not follow that because the tribunal would not have regarded the acts complained of as unacceptable, the complaint must be dismissed.'

Four cases where the claimant was reasonable in taking offence: **18.42**

- **Punch v Maldon Carers Centre** ET Case No.3202677/06: P's manager, L, suggested to her that her crutch was a trip hazard. The tribunal noted that this would not generally be reasonably considered as creating a hostile environment: employers need to give consideration to the health and safety of the workforce and the crutch could have been a trip hazard. However, in the instant case it was reasonable for it to have this effect, given the manager's generally unsympathetic attitude towards P and her failure to consider P's needs as a disabled person. It caused P to feel that bringing a crutch into the office was an issue with L. The tribunal therefore found unlawful disability harassment

- **Vaio v John Guest Engineering Ltd** ET Case No.3302165/09: V's colleagues placed screensavers displaying the English flag on department computers during the 2008 European Football Championships. V, who was of Italian origin, did the same with the Italian flag. If an employee posted an English flag, V would change it to an Italian one, and vice versa. The tribunal took the view that the posting of the St George's cross screensavers was not unwanted conduct. It formed part of normal football banter at the time of a major football championship. However, the inscription of the word 'shitaly' on a screensaver displaying the Italian flag and anti-Italian messages on the notice board, such as 'we hate Italians' and 'Italians go home', crossed the line into harassment since they went beyond what could be regarded as normal banter. The tribunal took into account the fact that V appeared to place great importance on his Italian national origin and the existence of a notice board at the back of his desk displaying pictures of the Italian team's world cup victory in 2006 evidenced his pride in that country's achievements. Having regard to his particular circumstances and perception, the tribunal considered that these matters had the potential to cause V to feel humiliated. (Note that, on appeal, the EAT overturned the harassment decision on the basis that the complaint was brought out of time and should not have been considered by the tribunal)

- **Acheampong v National Car Parks Ltd** ET Case No.2202209/07: A, aged 42, was employed by NCP Ltd as a mobile support officer. The company operated a number of unmanned car parks, and A's duties included visiting them to remove rubbish, collecting cash from payment machines and responding to specific problems such as machines jamming. In May 2007, A's line manager, H, suggested that A was not at that time being assigned to collect cash from the car parks because he could not fight off an attacker trying to steal the money. He then asked A his age. When A told him, H said: 'Life begins at 40, what you say about that?' A thought that H was suggesting that A's life had not begun at 40, and that he was a failure since his job involved collecting rubbish from car parks. In another conversation a few days later, A – who worked night shifts – discussed with H the possibility of transferring to day shifts because he was having trouble sleeping and finding it difficult to combine night work with taking his children to school. H responded that it was not good for A 'at his age' and with children to be doing night work. A resented the inference that his problems with night shifts were related to his age. The employment tribunal found that H's comments amounted to harassment on the ground of age

- **Lambert v British American Tobacco (Investments) Ltd** ET Case No.3100897/08: L, aged 56, worked as an administrator. In January 2007, a fellow employee circulated an e-mail to a number of colleagues (including L) entitled 'Perks of being over 50', which included: 'kidnappers are not very interested in you', 'you can live without sex but not your glasses', and 'things you buy now won't wear out'. Although L's harassment claim was dismissed for being out of time, the employment tribunal accepted that the e-mail 'amounted to unwanted conduct which had the effect of violating his dignity'.

And some examples of cases where the claimant unreasonably took offence: **18.43**

- **Guenther v One Stop Stores Ltd** ET Case No.2100521/06: G, who worked for OSS Ltd as a sales assistant, claimed that a body search carried out on him by one of OSS Ltd's female employees amounted to harassment on the ground of his sex. However, the tribunal held that the search did not have the purpose or effect of violating his dignity as it was conducted in the presence of another man, and nor was it excessive in its thoroughness

- **Smith v Vodafone UK Ltd** ET Case No 2302770/00: S worked as a customer service adviser. One day the team coach, C, noticed she had a punnet of melon slices on her desk and remarked, 'You've got some lovely melons there.' He then became embarrassed, laughed and apologised, commenting 'that did not sound right did it?' S said nothing further at the time but she complained later that C had been drawing attention to her breasts. Following an investigation the company concluded that C had made the remark quite innocently but apologised when he realised that the comment could be misconstrued. S did not accept the explanation and resigned, saying she had been humiliated by the incident. Her tribunal claim for harassment was dismissed. As a matter of fact and degree the comment did not amount to sexual harassment. The facts disclosed hypersensitivity on the part of S. There had been no previous history of innuendo or any inappropriate behaviour by C towards S. C meant the comment innocently, yet S took it to be a deliberate innuendo. In any event the double meaning was not a specific comment about S's chest. It was a corny joke 'in the tradition of seaside postcards and "Carry on" film puns' and did not affect S's dignity at work. The case could be 'easily distinguished' from Insitu Cleaning Co Ltd v Heads 1995 IRLR 4, EAT, where the comment 'Hiya, big tits' – said by a manager to a woman nearly twice his age – was a direct sexual remark which bore no innocent explanation. It was clearly and obviously offensive, patronising and highly demeaning and a direct reference to H's breasts

- **Davies v Abergavenny Mind Association** ET Case No.1606142/08: D, who was gay, worked as a support housing project worker for AMA. During preparations for an office Christmas party, one of his colleagues brought in some festive headwear and gave D a headband with two furry, flashing stars on springs. He put it on and everyone laughed, whereupon J – another colleague, with whom D had a difficult relationship – commented that he 'looked like a frigging fairy'. In subsequent proceedings D claimed, among other things, that this comment amounted to harassment. Although the tribunal was troubled by J's use of the word 'fairy', it accepted her evidence

559

that she was referring to a Christmas fairy and had not intended to offend. D's subjective perception was that J had made an offensive homophobic remark, but had it been made by anyone else D would in all probability have accepted it as a reference to Christmas and not to his sexuality. Because of the animosity that existed between J and D, he had assumed a homophobic motivation when none was present. Looked at objectively, J's remark could not have been considered to have the forbidden statutory effect

- **Vallely v Whitbread Group plc t/a Brewers Fayre** ET Case No.2500249/07: V, aged 54, worked for the employer behind a bar. She claimed that on one occasion a fellow employee, O, who was 61, said to her: 'It is easy to forget things at our age.' In dismissing V's claim, the tribunal held that O was making a 'common-or-garden comment' in which she appeared to be referring to her own shortcomings rather than criticising V. Looked at objectively, it could not amount to a humiliating or degrading situation

- **Omar v London United Busways Ltd** ET Case No.3301535/10: O, a practising Muslim, was employed by LUB Ltd as a bus driver. W was employed as a bus controller. O claimed that W's actions in allowing passengers onto a bus that he was due to drive, while he was upstairs praying, amounted to harassment on the ground of his Islamic faith. He had asked W to wait to board passengers until he had completed his prayers and although she waited for a brief period, she did not allow him to finish. His tribunal claim was not upheld. W had agreed that O could delay the departure of the bus until he had prayed but it was a cold day, there were penalties attached to not adhering to bus timetables, and it was entirely credible that W wanted to board the passengers to ensure the bus could depart as soon as possible after O had finished his prayers.

18.44 Related to a relevant protected characteristic

In order to constitute unlawful harassment under S.26(1) EqA, the unwanted and offensive conduct must be 'related to a relevant protected characteristic'. These relevant protected characteristics are listed in S.26(5). They are age, disability, gender reassignment, race, religion or belief, sex and sexual orientation. So far as race is concerned, it is now clear that protection from harassment extends to colour and nationality, as well as ethnic or national origins – S.9(1) EqA. Previously, colour and nationality were not explicitly covered by the provisions on harassment set out in the RRA, so anyone alleging harassment on one of those grounds had to present the claim as one of direct discrimination under S.1(1). For further details, see Chapter 10, 'Race', under 'Protection under antecedent legislation'.

The list in S.25(5) omits the protected characteristics of marriage and civil partnership, and pregnancy and maternity. While this may appear to be a somewhat curious omission, these characteristics are not covered by European law provisions on harassment, and it seems that no respondent to the Government's consultation exercise pressed for change on this point. The Government for its part saw no need to extend the protection afforded by the antecedent legislation. A complaint alleging harassment related to either of these protected characteristics could be framed as a direct discrimination claim under S.13 EqA (see Chapter 15, 'Direct discrimination'). Furthermore, any harassment related to civil partnership status would almost always amount to harassment related to sexual orientation, while any harassment related to pregnancy or maternity would almost inevitably amount to harassment related to sex, as the following cases demonstrate:

- **Hildreth v Collingwood Street Ltd and ors** ET Case No.2504768/06: the employer, upon being notified of the employee's pregnancy, suspended her with immediate effect; informed her that, if she continued with the pregnancy, she would be dismissed; and refused to allow her to return to work until she had decided whether she would be having a termination. An employment tribunal found that comments to the effect of 'keep the baby or the job' were offensive and upsetting to H and amounted to harassment on the ground of sex

- **Gardner v BBT Thermotechnology UK Ltd** ET Case No.1307647/07: during her maternity leave, G's manager had repeatedly sent her letters enquiring as to whether she was going to return from maternity leave and, if so, when. The letters threatened disciplinary action if she failed to respond. An employment tribunal found that the letters amounted to harassment on the ground of her sex

- **Nixon v Ross Coates Solicitors and anor** EAT 0108/10: office gossip about the paternity of the claimant's unborn child was held to constitute harassment. This gossip was connected with N's pregnancy, which in turn related to her sex, and constituted a course of unwanted conduct

- **Gashi v European Pensions Management Ltd** ET Case No. 3100490/10: EPM Ltd became increasingly exasperated by G's persistent requests to leave work early to care for her children, aged between 15 months and 11 years. The tribunal held that hostile comments made about her childcare commitments were sufficient to qualify as 'related to her sex' for the purposes of the SDA.

'Related to'
18.45

Section 26(1)(a) EqA requires that the conduct in question be *related to* a relevant protected characteristic. Under the antecedent statutory harassment provisions the conduct generally had to be *on grounds of* a particular characteristic. This departure from the previous statutory wording is largely due to the High Court's decision in R (Equal Opportunities Commission) v

561

Secretary of State for Trade and Industry 2007 ICR 1234, QBD. The EOC (now subsumed into the EHRC) sought judicial review of S.4A SDA – which at the time prohibited harassment 'on the grounds of [a woman's] sex' – contending that it failed properly to implement the Equal Treatment Directive, since this referred to harassment 'related to' sex. The EOC's main argument was that the definition of 'harassment' in S.4A(1)(a) was fundamentally different from that in the Directive. Defining harassment as offensive conduct 'on the ground of [the complainant's] sex' was too restrictive, as it required a causative link between the treatment and the gender of the complainant, whereas the Directive only requires a connection or association with gender. The EOC submitted that S.4A(1)(a) made it more difficult for claimants to bring a successful harassment claim as the complainant had to show that the unwanted conduct was directed towards her because she was a woman.

Mr Justice Burton, giving judgment in the High Court, agreed with the EOC that the Government had wrongly imported a causation element into sex-based harassment claims. He noted that causation is a concept that is relevant to direct discrimination only. It was therefore wrong to use identical wording for both Ss.1(1)(a) and 4A(1)(a) SDA where there was a clear distinction between a complaint of direct discrimination and a complaint of harassment. Burton J then considered whether the words 'on the ground of her sex' in S.4A(1)(a) could be construed in line with the Directive to mean 'related to'. In his view, however, it was impossible to 'read down' S.4A(1)(a) without the causation requirement so as to render it compliant with the Directive, while ensuring that the interpretation of the section was clear and comprehensible for employers and employees alike. As a result, he concluded that S.4A(1)(a) should be recast without the causation element.

18.46 Following this judgment S.4A SDA was duly amended to cover harassment 'related to [a woman's] sex or that of another person'. However, the remaining discrimination legislation covering strands such as race and sexual orientation continued to prohibit harassment 'on the grounds' of the relevant characteristic – see, for example, S.3A RRA. The only exception was the DDA, which prohibited harassment 'for a reason which relates to' the disability – see S.3B(1) DDA. This discrepancy has now been resolved: S.26(1)(a) EqA confirms that harassment occurs when it 'relates to' any of the relevant protected characteristics. Conduct will therefore be covered regardless of the reason for it, provided it has some connection with a protected characteristic. Of course, conduct that has previously been held to be 'on grounds of' a particular characteristic will fall under the umbrella of conduct 'related to' the characteristic for the purposes of the EqA. But other conduct that might not previously have been caught by the 'on grounds of' formulation will now be covered. For example, under the old legislation, even where the conduct complained of was specific to a protected characteristic, it did not automatically follow that the conduct was done on the ground of the characteristic: it remained open to the respondent to argue that the harassment of the claimant was not carried out because of the protected characteristic in question but because the claimant was disliked for other reasons, or for no particular reason at all.

In Loosley v Moulton and anor EAT 0468/04 L, a probation officer, complained to her employer about the behaviour of her male line manager, M. He had made remarks about her being 'on the game', and teased her by playing with her scarf and pulling her hair. Following what she perceived to be an inadequate investigation into her allegations, L resigned and brought a claim of direct discrimination under S.1(1)(a) SDA (the specific harassment provision had not yet been enacted). The tribunal noted that banter, with some sexual innuendo, was part of the office culture where L and M worked. L herself had participated in that culture, joking that, in a perfect world, she would be a madam in a high-class brothel. The tribunal rejected her claim on the basis that the reason for M's actions had not been that L was a woman, but that she was a member of a group of people in the office who engaged in banter. Thus no less favourable treatment 'on the ground of her sex', for the purpose of S.1(1)(a) SDA, had been established. In any event, the tribunal was not convinced that M's conduct had been unwanted or that L had objected to it.

L's appeal to the EAT, on the basis that M's conduct was so manifestly gender-specific that the tribunal's conclusion that the treatment was not on the ground of her sex was perverse, was dismissed. The EAT noted that Lord Nicholls in Macdonald v Ministry of Defence and another case 2003 ICR 937, HL, had made it clear that conduct familiarly known as 'sexual harassment' would only be actionable under the direct discrimination provisions of the SDA if the reason for the harassment is the victim's sex. Furthermore, it does not inevitably follow that where treatment is of a gender-specific nature, the reason for it is the victim's sex. The tribunal had asked itself the right question – namely, why was L treated by M in such a way? – and had been entitled to conclude that L had not received the treatment complained of by reason of her being a woman. **18.47**

The EAT's conclusion in the above case was understandable given L's contribution to the banter and the context of the office culture in which M's conduct took place. However, the conduct in question would probably now be 'related to sex' for the purposes of S.26(1) EqA, as well as conduct 'of a sexual nature' under S.26(2) – see 'Sexual harassment – conduct "of a sexual nature"' below. Therefore L's failure to show that the treatment she received was because she was a woman would not now be fatal to her claim. However, the tribunal's finding on the 'unwanted conduct' point would still pose a significant obstacle.

Although the 'related to' formula is wider than the old 'on the grounds of' formula, it has its limits, as the following tribunal case demonstrates: **18.48**

- **Omar v London United Busways Ltd** ET Case No.3301535/10: O, a practising Muslim, was employed by LUB Ltd as a bus driver. His

563

colleague, W, was employed as a bus controller. O claimed that W's actions in allowing passengers onto a bus that he was due to drive while he was upstairs praying amounted to harassment on the ground of his Islamic faith. He had asked W to wait to board passengers until he had completed his prayers. However, although she waited for a brief period, she did not allow him to finish. The tribunal dismissed his claim on the basis that it did not have the purpose or effect of violating his dignity or creating an offensive environment (as to which see 'Violation of dignity – effect' above). And in any event, the tribunal was satisfied that 'in no sense whatsoever' was W's conduct on the ground of O's religion under the Employment Equality (Religion or Belief) Regulations 2003 SI 2003/1660, and nor indeed was it 'related to' his religion for the purpose of Article 2(3) of the EU Race Equality Directive (No.97/80). W's focus was on the needs of the service. The bus was delayed. She wanted to board passengers so that the bus could be ready to depart as soon as O had finished. The tribunal rejected O's contention that when considering the concept of 'related', it should have regard to the claimant's motivation. While a claimant's motivation may shed some light on whether or not the respondent's conduct is related to religion, it does not necessarily do so.

18.49 **Disability-related harassment.** As noted above, S.3B(1) DDA prohibited harassment 'for a reason which relates to' the claimant's disability, a wider formulation than 'on the grounds of', which applied to most of the other discrimination strands at the time (other than sex discrimination). In order to satisfy the DDA definition, a disabled person did not therefore have to show that his or her disability was the *direct reason* why he or she was subjected to harassment. So, for example, an AIDS sufferer who was subjected to abuse because he or she was regularly absent to attend hospital appointments related to his or her illness would have a potential claim, as would a dyslexic person who was mocked for taking a long time to produce written reports. Similarly, a person with a mental or physical impairment that caused him or her to act in a particular way was protected – Buck v Bernard Mathews Foods Ltd (see below). The new 'related to' formulation under S.26 EqA is arguably slightly wider, given that there is no causative link whatsoever. Nevertheless, cases concerning disability-related harassment under the DDA will obviously be instructive. Some examples:

- **Buck v Bernard Mathews Foods Ltd** ET Case No.5400152/01: B, an insulin-dependent diabetic, was dismissed after he became angry and violent, used abusive language and walked out. Although his employer was aware of his condition, it did not know that his diabetes was not under control. A tribunal found that B was dismissed for a reason related to his disability, since his behaviour was a symptom of his condition

- **Dean v Abercrombie and Fitch** ET Case No.2203221/08: the employer had agreed to an adjustment to its 'look policy' for staff working on the shop floor, whereby D would be allowed to wear a cardigan so that she could cover the join of her prosthetic left arm. On her fifth day at work B, a manager, stated that D could not remain on the shop floor because she was breaking the policy, and ordered her to work in the stock room. The tribunal accepted that B had not intended to violate D's dignity or create a hostile and intimidating environment for her, but considered that B's conduct did have that effect. Given that B knew that D wore a prosthetic arm and that she was wearing a cardigan to cover it, B's conduct was related to D's disability and amounted to harassment

- **Punch v Maldon Carers Centre** ET Case No.3202677/06: P's manager, L, suggested to her that her crutch was a trip hazard. The tribunal recognised that employers need to give consideration to the health and safety of the workforce, and that the crutch could have been a trip hazard, but found that the manager's conduct could reasonably be considered as having the effect of creating a hostile environment – it was part of the manager's generally unsympathetic attitude towards P and her failure to consider P's needs as a disabled person. It caused P to feel that bringing a crutch into the office was an issue with L. The tribunal therefore found that L had been unlawfully harassed for a reason relating to her disability

- **MacDonald v Fylde Motor Company Ltd** ET Case No.2403390/10: M told the directors of FMC Ltd that he would no longer be able to work overtime in the evenings because he had to care for his stepfather, who was disabled. Notwithstanding this, the tribunal found that there was more than one example of the company putting pressure on M to work after 5.30 pm. Since these incidents were related to his caring responsibilities, they fell within the definition of disability harassment by association, as laid down in Coleman v Attridge Law and anor 2008 ICR 1128, ECJ (discussed under 'Harassment by association or perception' below).

Establishing the necessary link. Where direct reference is made to an **18.50** employee's protected characteristic or he or she has been subjected to overtly racist/sexist/homophobic, etc conduct, the necessary link will clearly be established. Some examples:

- **Jorsling v Clinton Cards plc** ET Case No.3201181/07: a manager continually referred to black people as 'coloured', despite being told by J, a black Caribbean employee, that she found this insulting. The manager's excuse that he was not familiar with the word's negative connotations did not wash with the employment tribunal, especially in view of J's clear objections. In the tribunal's judgement, his continued use of the word could be seen as designed to humiliate and insult J

565

- **Duran de Roque v Fortress Service Group plc** ET Case Nos.2500372/09 and another: D suffered from an inguinal hernia repair, causing scrotal swelling and nerve entrapment. The tribunal was satisfied that this amounted to a disability. It held that comments made referring to his 'dodgy bollocks' constituted harassment under the DDA

- **Evans v Peak Travel Services Ltd and ors** ET Case No.1701033/07: E began working for PTS Ltd, a taxi business, in June 2006. At that time her name was Dale Andrew Evans, and she was married with a daughter. The marriage broke up during the summer and in November she told her employer that she was a transsexual and would be undergoing a programme of gender reassignment. She planned to start dressing as a woman in January 2007 and let her hair grow into a feminine style. In mid-February E turned up for work to find a cartoon strip about transsexuals with her name on it. In March she arrived to find two employees discussing her clothing, and saying she looked like a tart. By the end of February she was living as a woman and had taken the name 'Lucy'. She was told by a manager that she could not use that name on work sheets until she had her gender reassignment certificate, but he also told her that even with the certificate, the company would still not recognise the change in name. A tribunal upheld her claim for harassment on the ground of gender reassignment contrary to S.4A(3) SDA. (Note that S.4A(3) outlawed harassment 'on the ground that B *intends to undergo, is undergoing or has undergone* gender reassignment' (our stress). Under S.26(1) EqA the harassment simply needs to be *related to gender reassignment*)

- **Taj v GBM Services Ltd** ET Case Nos.3301281/07 and another: T, a Muslim, was employed as a security controller by GBMS Ltd. During Ramadan, one colleague offered T and his Muslim co-workers sausage sandwiches; made noises to show them that he was enjoying his food; and turned down the lights so that they might start eating because it was dark. The tribunal held that this constituted harassment under the Employment Equality (Religion or Belief) Regulations 2003 SI 2003/1660 'because of the essential religious nature of Ramadan to those practising the Muslim faith'

- **Bould v Acme Jewellery Ltd** ET Case No.1302983/09: Following his 65th birthday, B's colleagues began to call him 'Ouldy Bouldy', made pejorative remarks about his supposed 'pensioner' status, suggested that he should have retired, and generally made derogatory comments about his age. This was held to constitute harassment under the Employment Equality (Age) Regulations 2006 SI 2006/1031.

18.51 Where the link between the conduct and the protected characteristic is less obvious, tribunals may need to analyse the precise words used, together with the context, in order to establish whether there is any (negative) association between the two. Some examples:

- **Coney v Ceva Logistics UK Ltd and anor** ET Case No.1306820/08: C was called a 'pikey wanker' during what the tribunal described as a 'heated conversation' with a fellow employee at CLUK Ltd. He complained of harassment under the RRA. The tribunal understood from dictionary research that the term 'pikey' is a derogatory term referring to a traveller, initially of Romany origin but expanded in recent use to include those previously seen as Irish 'tinkers' or, indeed, any traveller. It is a word that is synonymous with 'gypsy' but carries a deeper derogatory implication, denoting those perceived to be of a low social class, often associated with petty theft and similar crimes. The tribunal considered that the 'pikey' comment almost certainly arose out of a desire to insult C by reference to a perception that he was either of a travelling family or had family connections in the travelling community. Moving on to consider whether the comment was made on racial grounds, the tribunal admitted to being initially concerned that the term 'pikey' has today taken on wider connotations than its original use and might include travellers of any race. However, it concluded that the pejorative nature of the remark remains inextricably linked to its origin, which was undoubtedly racial. Furthermore, it had no doubt that in the context of how and when it was said to C, it had racial implications. It implied an assertion that because C was related to travellers, he shared the supposedly inferior characteristics of a different race from which travellers come. The comment, in that sense, was made 'on racial grounds'

- **Black v Royal Mail Group Ltd** ET Case No.1101668/08: B, an openly gay man, was employed as a postman by RMG Ltd. He became very friendly with a female colleague, H, but their friendship broke down. In 2008, H raised a grievance about B's mother, who also worked for the employer, under RMG Ltd's bullying and harassment policy. As part of the investigation T, a manager, was interviewed. He said that B was very 'effeminate and immature' and that H and B had a 'girly' relationship, and when they fell out it 'got quite bitchy'. The tribunal upheld B's claim that these comments amounted to harassment. Each of the terms 'effeminate', 'girly' and 'bitchy' were – when used in respect of a man – a direct reference to that man having female characteristics. Where the words were used to describe a man known to be gay, they were clearly derogatory. Although the tribunal accepted that T was not homophobic, his choice of words was clearly influenced, subconsciously, by his knowledge that B was gay

- **Davies v Abergavenny Mind Association** ET Case No.1606142/08: D, who was gay, worked as a supported housing project worker for AMA. During preparations for an office Christmas party, one of his colleagues brought in some festive headwear and gave D a headband with two furry, flashing stars on springs. He put it on and everyone laughed, whereupon J – another colleague, with whom D had a difficult relationship – commented that he 'looked like a frigging fairy'. In subsequent proceedings D claimed, among other things, that this comment amounted to harassment under the Employment Equality (Sexual Orientation) Regulations 2003 SI 2003/1661. Although the tribunal was troubled by J's use of the word 'fairy', it accepted her evidence that she was referring to a Christmas fairy and had not intended to offend. Because of the animosity that existed between J and D, he had assumed a homophobic motivation when none was present

- **Lewis v Millennium and Copthorne Hotels plc** ET Case No.2200464/07: L, a gay man, worked in HR. He claimed that his manager, B, mocked the way he wore his jacket with all three buttons done up, saying that it was funny and that he resembled the television character Mr Bean. The tribunal accepted that B's remarks were unwanted, derogatory comments which violated L's dignity. However, in its view, they were not made on the ground of L's sexual orientation. Mr Bean was not a gay character and B had not made any comments targeting gay people in particular

- **Basile v Royal College of General Practitioners and ors** ET Case No.2204568/10: B, who was French, was employed by the College as a porter. Over a period of four years, he was habitually referred to as 'Inspector Clouseau', 'Basil Brush' or 'Basil Fawlty'. Nicknames were also given to other members of staff. For example, an Irish employee was nicknamed 'Paddy'. The tribunal noted that the fact that B was given a nickname may have been related to things other than race. However, the choice of the nickname 'Inspector Clouseau', being that of a British comic creation of a stereotypically bumbling French character who speaks English with a heavy accent, was materially influenced by the claimant himself being French. The tribunal had no doubt from the evidence that this conduct created a humiliating environment for B and it was reasonable for it to do so. References to Basil Fawlty and Basil Brush did not, however, have any overt connection to being French. The tribunal considered the possibility that B was nevertheless picked on for that name-calling in part because he was French. However, the more obvious explanation was his name ('Basile') and the tribunal could not say that this would not have been done to a non-French person also called Basil. Therefore, those nicknames did not involve unlawful harassment

- **Ahmed v Aphel Ltd** ET Case No.1306384/06: A, a Muslim, worked for A Ltd as a design engineer until he was dismissed in August 2006. He presented a number of claims in the employment tribunal including that his colleagues used sexually offensive language in the workplace in a way that was offensive to him on religious grounds. The tribunal dismissed his claims. While male employees may be expected to know that some types of language are likely to be offensive to women, there was, in its judgement, no such general understanding that Muslims object to sexual language. Accordingly, unless and until he objected to it, a male Muslim employee could not say that the use of such language was discriminatory or amounted to harassment on the ground of his Muslim faith. This case can be contrasted with Taj v GBM Services Ltd (above), where jokes about Ramadan were held to amount to religious harassment against T, a Muslim employee, 'because of the essential religious nature of Ramadan to those practising the Muslim faith'.

If the employee makes it clear that he or she finds particular conduct offensive, **18.52** the repetition of that conduct is likely to ground a claim of harassment (provided, of course, that there is a link with a protected characteristic). Two examples:

- **Basi v Snows Business Ltd** ET Case No.3100944/09: B, who was of Indian ethnic origin, overheard his line manager, F, say the word 'monkey' as B walked past. B asked whether the word was directed at him and was told that it was not. B gave F the benefit of the doubt but let him know that he found the comment racially offensive. Later that month they played golf together. B played a particularly good shot, which prompted F to call him a 'cheeky monkey'. B was upset by this and F, recalling the earlier incident in the office, duly apologised. The tribunal upheld B's claim for racial harassment. F had been put on notice that B would consider it a racial insult to be called a 'monkey'. Therefore, the ill-considered comment could reasonably have caused B to feel degraded and humiliated on the ground of his race

- **Mann v BH Publishing Ltd and anor** ET Case No.2203272/04: M, who was South African, began working for BHP Ltd on 24 May 2004. He spoke with what he described as a gay South African accent and his manager, H, mimicked his accent from the outset of his employment. After two days, M told H that he objected to the mimicry and told him that he thought it was harassment on the ground of his sexual orientation. Despite this conversation, H continued to mimic his accent, and from this time on M's colleagues began to tease and taunt him about his sexual orientation. M brought a claim of harassment on the ground of sexual orientation, which was upheld. The tribunal found that there was no harassment for the first two days – H was a natural and talented mimic and the tribunal did not accept that the mimicry had any connection with M's sexuality. However, from the time M put his concerns to H, the mimicry became unwanted conduct and had the purpose (and effect) of violating his dignity. It was also on the ground of his sexual orientation, given the link that M himself had drawn and brought to H's attention.

Note that there is no requirement for the alleged harasser and victim to be of **18.53** the same or different sex, race, etc. However, this can have a bearing upon the effect of the conduct and whether or not it is unwanted – see under 'Unwanted conduct – "unwanted"' above. For example, an English man from London who mocks the accent of an English man from Liverpool is perhaps less likely to be guilty of racial harassment. However, if he mocked the accent of a

569

Welshman or of someone from overseas, this is more likely to be racial harassment (if the other elements of the test are satisfied).

18.54 *Drawing inferences.* As we have seen, an alleged harasser does not need to have used ageist, sexist, racist, etc language or engaged in behaviour that is overtly age-, sex- or race-specific before a harassment claim can be made under S.26 EqA, although it will obviously be easier to establish the necessary link if that is the case. Practical jokes, ignoring or marginalising an employee, and other forms of unpleasantness that are ostensibly 'neutral' are equally capable of constituting unlawful harassment. In most cases of this sort the issue will be whether the surrounding circumstances (including the treatment of other people) yield evidence from which a tribunal could draw an *inference* that the conduct in question is related to a relevant protected characteristic. In this regard, it would be useful for the claimant to establish that he or she has been less favourably treated than someone who does not share his or her protected characteristic. Once such evidence is present, it would then be for the respondent to prove otherwise. For further details, see Chapter 32, 'Burden of proof', in particular the section 'Other forms of discrimination – harassment', where harassment claims are specifically discussed.

18.55 Harassment by association or perception

In respect of disability and gender reassignment (but not the other protected characteristics), harassment was previously defined in such a way as to require that the complainant must him or herself possess the protected characteristic relied upon. This meant that a claim would not generally succeed where the treatment was based on the disability or gender reassignment of a third party or on the claimant's perceived disability or gender reassignment. For example, S.3B DDA referred to conduct 'for a reason which relates to *the disabled person's* disability' (our stress).

However, in EBR Attridge LLP (formerly Attridge Law) and anor v Coleman 2010 ICR 242, EAT, the EAT held that the DDA, despite its apparent limitations, was capable of being interpreted so as to protect those who suffered direct discrimination or harassment as a result of their association with a disabled person. This followed the ECJ's ruling in Coleman v Attridge Law and anor 2008 ICR 1128, ECJ, that the EU Equal Treatment Framework Directive (No.2000/78) protects those who, although not themselves disabled, nevertheless suffer direct discrimination or harassment owing to their association with a disabled person. (Note that the definition of 'harassment' under the SDA was altered by the Sex Discrimination Act 1975 (Amendment) Regulations 2008 SI 2008/656 to substitute the phrase 'on the ground of her sex' with the phrase 'related to her sex or that of another person', which meant that a person complaining of harassment under the SDA was no longer required to show that the alleged treatment took place because the complainant was a woman (or a man) – for further details see Chapter 12, 'Sex', under 'Protection under antecedent legislation'.)

As things stand now, it is clear from the wording of S.26(1)(a) EqA – which **18.56** makes no reference to the protected characteristic of any particular person – that victims of harassment (including disability- and gender reassignment-related harassment) do not have to possess the protected characteristic themselves in order for a claim to succeed. The EHRC Employment Code confirms that conduct will fall within S.26(1)(a) EqA where it is related to the worker's own protected characteristic, or where there is any connection with a protected characteristic, *whether or not the worker has that characteristic him or herself* – see paras 7.9–7.10. It gives a number of examples, including where 'a worker has a son with a severe disfigurement. His work colleagues make offensive remarks to him about his son's disability. The worker could have a claim for harassment related to disability' – para 7.10.

Two further examples of harassment by association:

- **MacDonald v Fylde Motor Company Ltd** ET Case No.2403390/10: M told the directors of FMC Ltd that he would no longer be able to work overtime in the evenings because he had to care for his stepfather, who was disabled. Notwithstanding this, the tribunal found that there was more than one example of the company putting pressure on M to work after 5.30 pm. Since these incidents were related to his caring responsibilities they fell within the definition of harassment by association, as laid down in Coleman v Attridge Law and anor (above)

- **Saini v All Saints Haque Centre and ors** 2009 IRLR 74, EAT: S's employer pressured him into providing incriminating information about a manager, C, who the employer wanted to dismiss because of his Hindu faith. The tribunal found that there was no unlawful harassment, since the harassment was not motivated by S's religion. The EAT held that the tribunal had wrongly focused on whether S had suffered harassment because of his own religion, when harassment 'on grounds of religion or belief' under the Employment Equality (Religion or Belief) Regulations 2003 SI 2003/1660 covered conduct on the ground of another person's religion or belief. Given the tribunal's finding that the employer's conduct towards S resulted from its desire to dismiss C on the ground of C's religion (which just happened to be the same as that of S), the EAT concluded that S's claim should have succeeded. In effect, the tribunal had concluded that the employer operated an anti-Hindu policy and S suffered harassment because of that policy.

Note that since neither pregnancy and maternity nor marital status and **18.57** civil partnership are relevant protected characteristics for the purpose of S.26 (see 'Related to a relevant protected characteristic' above), if a man were to be harassed on the basis of his association with a pregnant woman or a

571

married woman, he would need to claim harassment related to the protected characteristic of sex, or alternatively to claim direct discrimination under S.13 EqA.

The wide definition of harassment in S.26 covers harassment by perception as well as harassment by association. Harassment by perception occurs where the employee is wrongly perceived as having a particular protected characteristic and suffers unwanted conduct as a result. The EHRC Employment Code gives the example of a Sikh worker who wears a turban to work. His manager wrongly assumes he is Muslim and subjects him to Islamaphobic abuse. In these circumstances, the worker could have a claim for harassment related to religion or belief because of his manager's perception of his religion – see para 7.10.

18.58 In order to found a claim of harassment under S.26, the conduct in question does not even need to be directed at the employee. The EHRC Employment Code gives the example of a white worker who is offended by a black colleague being subjected to racially abusive language – see para 7.10. The white worker would not, it seems, necessarily need to establish that he or she has any particular association with the black colleague in question, or indeed any black person. We would suggest, however, that the conduct would have to be particularly serious for the white employee to establish that he or she has been personally affected to such a degree that his or her own dignity has been violated or that the working environment is offensive to him or her.

That said, subject to the proviso that the conduct must have the proscribed purpose or effect, it is clear that the protection from harassment has a wide remit. In Moxam v Visible Changes Ltd and anor EAT 0267/11, for example, the EAT overturned a tribunal's decision that the employer's foul-mouthed references to 'immigrants' in M's presence could not amount to harassment. The tribunal thought that M, who regarded herself as Afro-Caribbean, could not establish harassment on the ground of race under the RRA because she herself was not an immigrant. The EAT held that to be an error of law. The employer had conceded that 'immigrant' is a reference to a racial group, and it did not matter that it was not the claimant's racial group. The employer's strongly worded suggestion that the group was inferior could clearly amount to racial conduct capable of having the relevant effect on M. According to the EAT, 'it does not matter what racial group the claimant comes from, for she is entitled to be offended and to bring claims where she suffers as a result of any discriminatory language and conduct'.

18.59 ### 'Characteristic-themed' harassment
The EHRC Employment Code suggests at para 7.10 that a person is protected from harassment related to a relevant protected characteristic even where it is known that he or she does not have that characteristic – in other words, where

a protected characteristic is the *theme* of the harassment but there is no suggestion that the victim, or indeed anyone associated with him or her, possesses that characteristic. The Code gives the example of an employee who is known not to be gay being subjected to homophobic banter and name-calling. This situation arose in English v Thomas Sanderson Blinds Ltd 2009 ICR 543, CA, where the Court of Appeal held (by a majority) that such conduct was covered by the definition of harassment in the EU Equal Treatment Framework Directive (No.2000/78) and should therefore be covered by the Employment Equality (Sexual Orientation) Regulations 2003 SI 2003/1661 (a precursor to S.26 EqA). It seems that someone who witnesses such harassment could also have a claim under S.26 EqA and they too would not need to possess the protected characteristic in question – as noted above, the conduct in question *does not need to be directed at the worker* in order for him or her to claim harassment.

Sexual harassment 18.60

Section 26(2) EqA is designed to replicate the effect of S.4A(1)(b) SDA, which dealt specifically with sexual (as distinct from sex-related) harassment. S.26(2) provides that a person (A) harasses another (B) if:

- A engages in unwanted conduct of a sexual nature, and

- the conduct has the purpose or effect of violating B's dignity, or creating an intimidating, hostile, degrading, humiliating or offensive environment for B.

The equivalent provision in the SDA defined the prohibited conduct as 'unwanted *verbal, non-verbal or physical* conduct of a sexual nature' (our stress). Although the new provision omits the italicised words, it is clear that these types of conduct are all potentially covered. As can be seen, the definition is very similar to the definition of general harassment under S.26(1), except that the conduct must be 'of a sexual nature', as opposed to being 'related to a protected characteristic', e.g. sex. The 'unwanted conduct' requirement and the 'purpose or effect' requirement are dealt with in detail under 'Unwanted conduct' and 'Violation of dignity or offensive environment' respectively above and there is little that needs to be added here.

Conduct 'of a sexual nature' 18.61

In most cases, whether or not the conduct in question can be categorised as sexual in nature will be self-evident. The EAT in Driskel v Peninsula Business Services Ltd and ors 2000 IRLR 151, EAT, considered that sexual harassment should be defined on a commonsense basis by reference to the facts of each particular case. The following examples of sexual harassment are given in the EHRC's Employment Code: unwelcome sexual advances, touching, sexual assault, sexual jokes, displaying pornographic photographs or drawings, or sending e-mails containing material of a sexual nature (para 7.13).

Some case examples of sexual harassment:

- **Munchkins Restaurant Ltd and anor v Karmazyn and ors** EAT 0359/09: the restaurant's controlling shareholder, M, persistently attempted to have conversations with the claimants about sex and to show them photographs and catalogues of sex toys and gadgets. The claimants were also required to wear short skirts, which made them feel uncomfortable because they believed that M liked to look at their legs

- **M v N and anor** ET Case No.2400324/10: M's manager, O, told her to wear a low-cut top when going out to see a customer, lifted her coat when standing behind her to see a split in her skirt, slapped her bottom on a couple of occasions when she walked past his office, and suggested that they spend the night together in a hotel

- **McLean v Redecs Ltd** ET Case No.2349992/11: the owner of the company made continual unwelcome advances of a sexual nature to M, a female employee: he briefly locked her in a room in his flat, persistently invited her out for lunch or dinner, requested that she give a relationship with him 'a go', insisted that work conversations took place in his car, and told her that he was in love with her despite her assertion that she was not interested

- **Insitu Cleaning Co Ltd v Heads** 1995 IRLR 4, EAT: a manager greeted a female employee with the words 'Hiya, big tits'. The EAT commented that a remark by a man about a woman's breasts cannot sensibly be equated with a remark by a woman about a bald head or a beard. One is sexual, the other is not. (Nevertheless, we suggest that a derogatory remark about a man's bald head could potentially amount to harassment related to sex under S.26(1).)

18.62 In Reed and anor v Stedman 1999 IRLR 299, EAT, a tribunal found that sexual connotations were present in several incidents occurring between a male manager and the female claimant, such as his suggestion that sex was a beneficial form of exercise; his 'jokey' attempt to look up the claimant's skirt; his saying 'You're going to love me so much for my presentation that when I finish you will be screaming out for more and you will want to rip my clothes off'; his showing the claimant, and others, a newspaper cartoon depicting an affair in a marketing department; and his frequently standing behind the claimant when telling dirty jokes. Although the tribunal decided that no single incident was serious enough to be capable of founding a less favourable treatment claim (this case preceded the specific harassment provisions), it nonetheless found that there had been a series of sexual inferences with a pervading sexual innuendo and sexist stance. The EAT upheld the tribunal on appeal, noting that blatant acts of a sexual nature, such as deliberately looking up the victim's skirt, were likely to have given a different colour and significance to other incidents, such as asking to be shown personal photographs which the victim was perusing at work. Once a man has shown unwelcome sexual interest in a female employee, she may well feel bothered about attentions of his which, in a different context, would appear quite unobjectionable. Although the facts of the case were examined in the context of a direct discrimination claim, the EAT's pronouncements on what can amount to sexual harassment are still highly relevant.

Claimants and tribunals must be careful, however, not to read a sexual element **18.63** into conduct when none exists. Two examples:

- **Dos Santos v Preview Services Ltd** ET Case No.2700170/10: DS approached her supervisor with the words, 'Can I ask you a favour'. He replied, 'As long as it's not a sexual favour.' She said that this comment caused her offence and amounted to harassment. The tribunal dismissed her claim. The claimant's reaction to what was a passing remark in an ordinary interaction was disproportionate. If the supervisor had expressed the hope that the favour was to be sexual, or if it had been accompanied by inappropriate gestures, that could have fallen within the definition of harassment. However, the only way the remark could be received, given their long-term work relationship (over two years), was as a joke

- **British Telecommunications plc v Williams** 1997 IRLR 668, EAT: W, a female employee working in the accounts department of BT, was given a poor appraisal by her male manager, M, for 1993/4. In March 1994 she had a counselling meeting with M to discuss the appraisal. W presented a complaint of sex discrimination to a tribunal, alleging that M became sexually aroused during the interview, that he stared at her legs, and that he trapped her in the room. The tribunal accepted M's denial of these allegations, finding that he was nervous, and may well have perspired and shifted his eyes to the floor. It nevertheless held that he had conducted the interview in a sexually intimidating manner by reference, inter alia, to the fact that no one else was present, the proximity of the seating arrangements, the excessive length of the meeting, and the failure to provide more than one copy of the appraisal at the meeting. This, it said, indicated 'unimaginative and insensitive management'. In reading the report together a physical proximity was inevitably involved, which in these circumstances could appear threatening or distasteful. The EAT considered that the tribunal had correctly assessed that the substance of M's complaint of sex discrimination was sexual harassment. However, having accepted M's evidence that he was not sexually aroused during the interview, it should have dismissed the claim. Instead, it had concluded that the way in which M had conducted the meeting was 'sexually intimidating'. If, as would appear, this conclusion was reached on the basis that there was no woman present and the interview took place in a confined space, that conclusion had to be rejected. It was neither required by law nor desirable in practice that employers should have female supervisors for female staff or to ensure that male managers are chaperoned when dealing with female staff. The tribunal's suggestion was wholly misplaced and could be regarded as an unjustified generalised assumption based on sex of the type which the SDA was designed to make unlawful.

18.64 The EAT in the above case made the point that, particularly in cases involving allegations of sexual harassment, it is likely that the parties will have strongly held conflicting views as to what took place. To make suggestions of improper conduct without specific findings is unfair to both parties. Euphemisms should be avoided. For example, the tribunal's statement that this was not the occasion to 'cosy up' was without substance, unless it was making a finding that the manager did 'cosy up' to W and clarified precisely what it meant by the term.

Note that men can equally be victims of sexual harassment. Furthermore, there is no need for the victim to be of the opposite sex to the alleged perpetrator. Nor does the perpetrator have to be motivated by sexual desire for the complainant. Indeed, it is perfectly possible for the complainant and perpetrator to both be, for example, heterosexual males. Two examples:

- **Basile v Royal College of General Practitioners and ors** ET Case No.2204568/10: B, a male employee, witnessed a male colleague making masturbatory hand gestures, sometimes accompanied by a vulgar noise. On occasion he greeted B with the words 'How's it hanging?' The tribunal did not agree with the suggestion that, as a man, he would not have found the gestures troubling. It accepted that B in fact found them offensive and considered that, objectively viewed, being exposed to them created an offensive environment for him. Furthermore, the greeting was directed at the claimant and was intended to tease or mock him in a manner laced with sexual innuendo, which amounted to sexual harassment

- **Craddock v Fontoura t/a Countyclean** ET Case No.1402999/09: C, a single man, was employed as the sales manager of a cleaning company. The business manager, F, decided that he would 'play cupid' between C and the staff manager, G. He told C that it was time for him to settle down. C said he was happy being single and that he considered that a relationship between himself and G would be inappropriate, not only because they were colleagues but because of the significant age gap between them. Notwithstanding this, F continued to make comments, telling C that G fancied him and stating that he would send them on a course together so they could get to know each other better. C became increasingly self-conscious about his relationship with G. Their working relationship deteriorated and C resigned in June 2009. C succeeded before a tribunal in his claim for sexual harassment. Given that he had made it clear to F on a number of occasions that he did not wish him to make the comments, the tribunal concluded that the comments had the purpose of violating his dignity or creating an offensive environment for him. The fact that C himself referred on occasion to relationships with other women did not, in the tribunal's judgement, mean that he was acquiescing in the sexualisation of his relationship with G. The reference to relationships with other women was largely aimed at deflecting F's attempts to get him interested in G.

18.65 Nevertheless, in some instances the gender (and possibly also the age and/or status) of the respective parties may be relevant when assessing effect. In Driskel v Peninsula Business Services Ltd and ors 2000 IRLR 151, EAT, for example, the EAT considered that sexual badinage between two heterosexual males could not be completely equated with badinage between a heterosexual male and a woman. In the latter circumstance it is the sex of the alleged discriminator that potentially adds a material element which is absent between two heterosexual men.

Of course, even if the conduct is of a sexual nature, it will not be unlawful harassment unless it is unwanted conduct having the forbidden purpose or effect – see under 'Unwanted conduct' and 'Violation of dignity or offensive environment' above.

18.66 **Physical contact.** Obviously not all physical contact between two individuals amounts to sexual harassment. Whether or not it does so depends on a number of factors. These include: the nature of the physical contact and the part of the anatomy that is touched; the circumstances or the context in which the contact takes place; the relationship between the two individuals; whether the conduct is unwanted and the recipient has made clear that it is unwanted (see 'Unwanted conduct' above); the intentions of the person making the contact; the perception of the recipient of the conduct; and how a reasonable person would view or perceive the conduct (see 'Violation of dignity or offensive environment – effect' above) – Kalomoiris v John Lewis plc ET Case No.2202486/10. In that case, K was employed as a sales assistant at JL plc. A fellow shop assistant, R, approached him on the shop floor. He alleged that she slapped his bottom. However, a tribunal found that she touched or patted his lower back in the hip area when talking to him. It rejected his claim of sexual harassment, holding that K was over-sensitive and found unacceptable a level of physical contact with which most people would have no problem. R was an older colleague who was trying to be supportive. It noted that she was a small, 67-year-old Italian woman who had worked in the department for 40 years. She was perceived by all her colleagues as a kind, caring and motherly figure. She was a tactile person who in the course of communicating with others, men and women alike, touched them without consciously thinking about it. There was nothing sexual in the contact and nor was it for sexual gratification. It was not in any way related to K's gender.

In Sela v Ainsworths (London) Ltd ET Case No.2305575/06 a tribunal considered that if a man intentionally touches the front of a woman's body, that

577

would invariably be conduct 'of a sexual nature'. The facts were that S, an employee of AL Ltd, asked the IT Manager, K, for the password to her computer, which she had forgotten. He gave it to her written on a heart-shaped 'Post-it' note, which he placed on her right breast. S was shocked and upset by this and complained about it to her line manager. She received a letter of apology from K, who denied that the incident had been intentional. She lodged a grievance and K was given a severe reprimand, but the line manager dismissed S's allegation that the incident was sexually motivated. S resigned and brought a claim of sexual harassment, which the tribunal upheld. The tribunal thought that, wherever on the front of S's upper body K had put his hand, it was physical contact that was unwanted by S and it could not seriously be said that a man intentionally laying his hand on the front of a woman's body did not amount to conduct of a sexual nature.

18.67 ### Relevance of claimant's sexual behaviour

A particular bone of contention, so far as sexual harassment is concerned, is the extent to which a claimant's own sexual behaviour can be taken into account when assessing whether the conduct was unwanted and whether it violated his or her dignity. In Snowball v Gardner Merchant Ltd 1987 ICR 719, EAT, evidence as to the complainant's sexual behaviour was held to be relevant when deciding on the credibility of her allegations of sexual harassment, as well as the degree of detriment (if any) she had suffered and the extent of the injury to her feelings. In that case, S was cross-examined about her sexual attitudes and behaviour with a view to showing that she had not suffered any substantial detriment or injury to feelings by comments of a sexual nature and innuendo made by her manager. The employer alleged that S spoke candidly about sex to her male colleagues and sought to call witnesses in support of this. S challenged the employer's right to adduce evidence of this kind, but the EAT held that evidence about a woman's private and consensual sexual behaviour was admissible and relevant in assessing the degree of detriment and injury to her feelings caused by sexual harassment. It said that 'whether the complainant is either unduly sensitive or... is unlikely to be very upset by a degree of familiarity with a sexual connotation' was relevant, although the EAT added that tribunals had a discretion to disregard evidence creating an 'atmosphere of prejudice'.

A rather more progressive approach was taken in Wileman v Minilec Engineering Ltd 1988 ICR 318, EAT. There, the EAT accepted that a woman who wears 'scanty and provocative' clothes may nevertheless be offended by unwanted advances. The EAT also rejected the employer's argument that evidence that the complainant had posed, scantily clad, for a national newspaper could show that she had suffered little or no detriment because of sexual harassment. The fact that she was upset by the harassment was not in any way vitiated by the fact that she was perfectly willing to pose for the newspaper. This decision is significant because the EAT in effect recognised a woman's right to express her sexuality without prejudice to her right to decide what she finds offensive. The EAT also held that the tribunal had not erred in refusing to allow the complainant to call evidence of how the harasser was alleged to have harassed other women. Such evidence was not probative of any issue relevant to the complainant's own complaint. Sexual remarks made to a number of people have to be looked at in the context of their effect on each individual person. Each individual had the right, if he or she personally regarded the remarks as offensive, to treat them as such and to bring a complaint of sex discrimination under the SDA.

The EAT's assertion in Snowball that the tribunal ought to be able to consider **18.68** whether the claimant was unduly sensitive accords with the mixed objective and subjective approach to statutory harassment set down by S.26(4) – see 'Violation of dignity or offensive environment – effect' above. It is therefore arguable that the evidence as to the claimant's sexual behaviour and attitudes admitted in that case would still be relevant under S.26 when assessing whether treatment alleged to amount to statutory harassment should reasonably be considered to have had the proscribed effect. Furthermore, evidence of the claimant's sexual attitudes and behaviour may also have some bearing on the extent of any injury to feelings the claimant has suffered for the purpose of awarding compensation.

By the same token, it is arguable that the EAT's decision in Wileman – that evidence of how the harasser was alleged to have harassed other women was not relevant to the complaint at issue – may no longer hold good, given that under S.26(4), where a claimant is arguing that the alleged conduct had the effect – as opposed to the purpose – of violating her dignity or creating an intimidating, hostile, degrading, humiliating, or offensive environment, a tribunal will be required to examine that claim with a degree of objectivity that may not have been permissible before. The EAT there reasoned that sexual remarks made to a number of people have to be looked at in the context of their effect on each individual person. This is no longer strictly true – if the employer can show that no one else complained of the behaviour that is alleged to have so offended the claimant, that might support an argument that the claimant is unduly sensitive, which in turn may lead the tribunal to find that the conduct complained of could not *reasonably* have had the effect alleged – see S.26(4)(c). And if a claimant can show that other people did complain, that would surely support his or her case. However, the other part of the EAT's decision in Wileman – that a woman who had posed for a newspaper in a state of undress could still be upset by sexual harassment – must still be good law. S.26(4)(a) directs the tribunal to have regard to the claimant's perception in assessing the effect on him or her of behaviour said to amount to harassment, and there is nothing to stop a tribunal finding that a person is upset or offended by one form of sexual conduct and not another.

Sex-related harassment or sexual harassment? 18.69
It is arguable that many instances of sexual harassment could also amount to sex-related harassment under S.26(1) EqA. Therefore, it would be advisable for

579

a claimant to plead both in the alternative, thereby ensuring a fall-back position if, for example, the tribunal finds that the conduct in question was not of a sexual nature. Of course, if the conduct is clearly non-sexual – for example, *sexist*, as opposed to *sexual* comments or behaviour – the claim would be for sex-related harassment only.

18.70

Less favourable treatment following harassment

The EqA also protects individuals who are treated less favourably by their employer because they either *reject or submit to* certain forms of harassment; namely, sexual harassment or harassment related to gender reassignment or sex. S.26(3) EqA – which largely replicates S.4A(1)(c) SDA – provides that A harasses B if:

- A or another person engages in sexual harassment or harassment related to gender reassignment or sex; and

- because of B's rejection of or submission to the harassment, A treats B less favourably than A would treat B if B had not rejected or submitted to the harassment.

18.71 A claim under S.26(3) is similar, but not identical, to a victimisation claim (see Chapter 19, 'Victimisation'), in that it gives a remedy to a person who is treated unfavourably because of his or her refusal to tolerate unlawful conduct. One difference is that, in a victimisation claim, a person is protected only once he or she has done a protected act, such as bringing employment tribunal proceedings or raising a grievance about his or her treatment, whereas a claim under S.26(3) can be brought even if the claimant has done nothing about the unlawful treatment. A further difference is that for the purposes of S.26(3) the claimant must show *less favourable treatment*. So far as victimisation is concerned, S.27(1) has replaced the concept of 'less favourable treatment' (which appeared in the previous legislation) with that of 'detriment'. The less favourable treatment under S.26(3) may be perpetrated by the person who carried out the original harassment or – and this goes beyond the protection provided under S.4A(1)(c) SDA – *by a different person*. The antecedent provision only provided protection from less favourable treatment against the person who carried out the original harassment.

A complainant bringing a S.26(3) claim has several hurdles to clear, as the claim depends on sex or gender reassignment-related harassment (or sexual harassment) having occurred. Therefore, in order for a claim under this provision to succeed, all the elements of either S.26(1) (in so far as the conduct relates to gender reassignment or sex) or S.26(2) must be made out. *In addition*, less favourable treatment must be shown and a causal link between the two established.

Given the evidential problems inherent in bringing a claim under S.26(3), we **18.72** think it unlikely that the provision will be relied on all that often, especially as, provided all the elements of either S.26(1) or (2) are made out, the complainant already has a valid tribunal claim under one of those provisions without going any further. Indeed, so far as we are aware, there were no appellate decisions under S.4A SDA (the predecessor to S.26(3)). S.26(3) is most likely to be used where there has been a long interval between the act of harassment and the less favourable treatment, such that any claim relating to the harassment would be out of time. For example, suppose a woman is subjected to a campaign of sexual harassment, which she either tolerates without complaint or complains about and resolves informally. If a year later she is turned down for promotion and believes that she was overlooked because of her earlier submission to or rejection of the sexual harassment, she will potentially be able to bring a claim under S.26(3). However, her claim of sexual harassment under S.26(2) would be out of time.

Employer's liability

18.73

Employers are liable for acts of harassment carried out by employees in the course of their employment, but employers have a defence if they can show that they took all reasonable steps to prevent the employee from carrying out the act or acts – S.109 EqA. This replicates the position under the previous anti-discrimination legislation – see, for example, S.41 SDA and S.32 RRA. For further details, see Chapter 28, 'Liability of employers, employees and agents', under 'Employer's liability for acts of employees'.

Employers will also be liable for persistent harassment of their employees by third parties, provided certain conditions are satisfied – see S.40(2)–(4) EqA. This liability previously only applied in respect of sexual and sex-related harassment under the SDA but is now extended to all the protected characteristics covered by the harassment provisions. Liability only arises if the employee has been subjected to third-party harassment on at least two previous occasions and the employer is aware that it has taken place and has failed to take reasonably practicable steps to prevent it – S.40(2) and (3). Subsection (3) goes on to state that 'it does not matter whether the third party is the same or a different person on each occasion'. It does appear to matter, however, that the harassed employee is the same person each time. So where, for example, several different employees are subjected to harassment because of their race by a single customer, the employer will not be liable under S.40 until a single employee has been harassed for a third time. A third party is a person other than the employer or an employee of the employer – S.40(4) EqA.

Even if the conditions in S.40(2) and (3) are not made out, an employee may **18.74** have a claim for direct discrimination under S.13(1) if he or she can show that, in failing to prevent harassment, the employer has treated him or her less

581

favourably because of a characteristic protected by the EqA. Furthermore, case law under the RRA suggested that an employer could, in certain circumstances, be directly liable for third-party harassment under S.3A RRA (the equivalent of S.26 EqA) if it let the harassment go on unchallenged – see, for example, Gravell v London Borough of Bexley EAT 0587/06. Therefore, even where S.40(2) and (3) is not satisfied, an employee may be able to argue that the employer's inaction in the face of third-party harassment itself amounts to harassment under S.26 EqA. Note, however, that in Conteh v Parking Partners Ltd 2011 ICR 341, EAT, the EAT held that an employer could only be liable under S.3A for harassment carried out by a third party if the employer's failure to take action to safeguard the employee itself violated his or her dignity, or led to the creation of an intimidating, hostile, degrading, humiliating or offensive environment. In the case of third parties, it is likely to be difficult to establish that it was the employer's inaction that 'created' the relevant environment.

18.75 The way in which an employer deals with harassment (whether by a third party or otherwise) once it has occurred can itself amount to harassment if the employer's actions are responsible for creating a hostile environment. An example:

• **Rose-Brown v Home Office (UKBA)** ET Case No.2313044/10: RB, a black British woman of Afro-Caribbean origin, was employed as a chief immigration officer. On 14 October 2009 two black contractors came into the office to deal with excessive heat. One of RB's junior colleagues, R, a white woman, stated that it was only black and Asian people who did not feel hot in the office; that they were selfish in complaining that it was cold when the heat was turned down but refusing to wear extra layers of clothing; and if they did not like the weather they should go back to their own countries. RB complained immediately and R was suspended, given a written warning and required to attend diversity training. She was then allowed to return to her old job, where she sat some 15 feet from RB. RB was appalled at this and complained immediately. She felt distressed and undermined as a manager in that an individual who reported to her and had made highly offensive racist comments to her in public was being reinstated to the same office with no outward display of discipline. She also complained that R was taunting her because she blamed RB for what had happened. RB subsequently went off work sick, suffering from stress and anxiety. She was referred to occupational health, which recommended a transfer to a different office. RB brought a claim for harassment under S.3A RRA. The tribunal held that the claim in respect of R's initial behaviour was out of time. However, in allowing R to return to work in the same office as RB, the Home Office was itself guilty of harassment, in breach of S.3A RRA. RB had made it perfectly clear that R's return to the office was unwanted and although it did not have the purpose of creating an intimidating and hostile atmosphere, it had that effect

For further discussion on third-party harassment, see Chapter 28, 'Liability of employers, employees and agents', under 'Employer's liability for acts of third parties'.

Relationship with other discrimination provisions 18.76

As noted above, the introduction of a specific cause of action for harassment means that claimants no longer have to show that the offensive conduct was a 'detriment' that amounted to 'less favourable treatment' for the purpose of meeting the definition of direct discrimination. But this does not mean that direct discrimination is no longer relevant to incidents of harassment. If an employee is subjected to a campaign of harassment, elements of that treatment may more readily be categorised as detriments than as acts of harassment. For example, it is commonly accepted that bullying can take the form of severe or inappropriate management, such as removing responsibility from a person without consultation or continually overlooking someone for promotion. Where this happens because of a person's protected characteristic, the treatment falls more comfortably within the category of detriment amounting to less favourable treatment for the purpose of the direct discrimination provisions than the category of offensive conduct for the purpose of the harassment provisions.

A less favourable treatment claim might also usefully be added to a claim of harassment where the employer has failed to deal properly with the claimant's internal complaint of harassment. Such a failure may of itself amount to direct discrimination if it can be established that it constitutes less favourable treatment because of a protected characteristic. However, as the Court of Appeal's decision in Coyne v Home Office 2000 ICR 1443, CA, makes clear, the employer will not be guilty of discrimination if its inadequate response was demonstrably unrelated to the relevant protected characteristic of the claimant (in that case, sex).

Some examples where an employer's failure to deal properly with a complaint 18.77 of harassment was held to constitute direct discrimination:

- **Richards v Menzies Aviation (UK) Ltd** ET Case No.1402185/10: R was one of only two black people employed at Bristol airport by MA(UK) Ltd. He found a poster at work on which someone had written his name and decorated the letter 'O' with eyes, small ears, a large nose and mouth, and curly hair. R considered that this resembled a monkey and found it racially offensive. He was so upset that he was allowed to go home for the rest of the day. Later that week he wrote to the company setting out his concerns. There followed a meeting with a manager, who told R that he was overreacting. She did, however, speak to people in R's team and drew their attention to the dignity at work policy. She gave evidence that 'no one admitted drawing the picture and no one thought it was a drawing of a monkey. It started to get a bit silly. People found it unbelievable that a doodle could cause so much disruption.' She subsequently wrote to R telling him there was no evidence of race discrimination. The tribunal held that the drawing constituted harassment under S.3A RRA, but that the company was not liable for it because it had systems and codes of practice in place to prevent such conduct and had therefore established the statutory defence under S.32(3) RRA (now S.109(4) EqA) – see Chapter 28 under 'Liability of employers, employees and agents', under 'Employer's liability for acts of employees – "reasonable steps" defence'. However, it concluded that the way in which the company had dealt with R's complaint amounted to direct discrimination. It had failed to take the matter seriously because the manager who investigated the complaint was not of the same racial group as R and did not understand the offence the drawing caused him. The tribunal found that the manager did not take the complaint as seriously as she would have taken a complaint by a white person

- **Braithwaite v Terex Compact Equipment** ET Case No.1309586/08: B, a British black man, heard a colleague saying: 'If one of them jigaboos in the gatehouse wants to clamp my car I will sort it out.' He lodged a grievance and was subsequently told that this had been upheld. However, when B brought a race discrimination claim against TCE, the tribunal ruled that the grievance had not been upheld because TCE had taken no action to deal with it. TCE had conducted a cursory interview with some of the people named by B but had not instituted any disciplinary proceedings. TCE was, in the tribunal's view, telling B that his grievance was upheld as a way of placating him and postponing further trouble. This deliberate attempt to mislead B in order to avoid dealing with the issue constituted direct discrimination, since a complaint that did not involve race would have been dealt with properly

- **Faithful v AXA PPP Healthcare plc** ET Case No.1100218/09: F, a Brazilian woman, was employed as a personal assistant by AXA plc. F's accent was mimicked by a number of colleagues, including her line manager, and she was called nicknames relating to her nationality. They also made negative comments to F based on stereotypical assumptions about people from Brazil – for example, suggesting that she used cocaine. Her complaints were dismissed on the basis that she was overreacting and led to her being viewed as 'high maintenance' and becoming further isolated in the department, which she described as feeling like an 'apartheid regime'. When F raised a grievance the company rejected it, having initially attempted to steer her down an informal route. The tribunal held that the way in which AXA plc responded to the harassment, including the way it dealt with F's grievance, constituted direct discrimination. It did not, for example, consider the evidence fairly or consistently, finding anecdotal evidence given by F's white colleagues as proven while rejecting corroborated evidence produced by F.

Over a period of 18 months there was a manifest failure to protect F or to take action to prevent further acts of discrimination

• **Price v Presbyterian Church of Wales** ET Case No.1603021/07 and others: P, a gay man, worked for the Church as an assistant manager at one of its conference centres. From the outset of his employment his manager, J, allegedly swore and shouted at him on a daily basis, calling him a 'vain poof' among other things. She also kept angling for P to discuss his sexual orientation with her by repeatedly initiating conversations about homosexuals. In 2007 P complained to the Church's general secretary, but his grievance was dismissed as being uncorroborated and no action was taken. An employment tribunal upheld P's claim that he had suffered direct discrimination. It stated that the entire grievance process was inadequate and unreasonable. Moreover, it was unfair and unbalanced. Among other things, at no time did the Church address the issue of P being called a 'poof'; he was not given an opportunity to call witnesses; and the evidence of those witnesses who might have assisted his case was disregarded. In conclusion, the employer failed to carry out the in-depth investigation that would have taken place had a heterosexual employee raised such a grievance. Accordingly, P had been treated less favourably on the ground of sexual orientation.

18.78 It is important to note that harassment and direct discrimination claims are mutually exclusive, as are harassment and victimisation claims: a complainant cannot claim that both definitions are satisfied simultaneously *by the same course of conduct*. This is because S.212(1) EqA – echoing the antecedent discrimination legislation – provides that the concept of 'detriment' (which is the basis on which a direct discrimination claim could be brought in respect of conduct that could amount to harassment) does not include conduct that amounts to harassment. The Explanatory Notes explain that this is to clarify that where the Act provides explicit harassment protection, it is not possible to bring a claim for direct discrimination by way of detriment on the same facts. Interestingly the Explanatory Notes do not refer to victimisation claims. However, given that S.27 EqA now specifically refers to detriment as part of the definition of victimisation, it is clear that victimisation and harassment claims are also mutually exclusive.

It is conceivable that, on a strict reading of S.212(1) EqA, a claimant who has 'mis-labelled' his or her claim could be deprived of a remedy. For example, if a woman complains that her male line manager has been constantly interfering with her work and belittling and undermining her, she could bring a claim on the basis of a detriment amounting to less favourable treatment. The tribunal might be entitled to find that, although the treatment was indeed detrimental, and did amount to less favourable treatment because of the claimant's sex, it was more properly defined as harassment. Relying on a strict reading of S.212(1) EqA, the tribunal might then feel obliged to reject the detriment claim, reasoning that conduct amounting to harassment cannot be a detriment.

585

18.79 However, we would suggest that this is not the purpose of S.212(1) EqA, and that tribunals should not reject otherwise valid claims for this reason. The purpose of S.212(1), presumably, is to prevent double recovery – i.e. to prevent a claimant being compensated twice, under two different causes of action, for the same conduct. Where conduct could feasibly fall under both 'detriment' and 'harassment', then just because a tribunal finds that the conduct is more readily defined by one label should not mean that a claim brought under the other label should be rejected. Rather, the claimant should have a choice between the two causes of action. What's more, there would seem to be no reason why a claimant should be prevented from bringing both claims in the alternative, on the understanding that both cannot succeed. A claimant bringing a complaint of harassment should be able to argue less favourable treatment or victimisation in the alternative, giving him or her a second bite at the cherry if the harassment claim fails, and vice versa.

As noted under 'Related to a relevant protected characteristic' above, a complaint alleging harassment in respect of marriage and civil partnership or pregnancy and maternity must be framed as a direct discrimination claim under S.13, since these protected characteristics are not covered by S.26 (and therefore conduct in relation to them does not amount to 'harassment' for the purposes of the Act). S.212(5) EqA expressly provides that, where the EqA disapplies a prohibition on harassment in relation to a specified protected characteristic, this does not prevent conduct relating to that characteristic from amounting to a detriment for the purposes of a direct discrimination claim under S.13. The implication is that a person in these circumstances is not left without a remedy but can bring a complaint of direct discrimination based on the relevant protected characteristic. Arguably, however, the omission of marriage and civil partnership and pregnancy and maternity from the list of relevant protected characteristics in S.26(5) does not amount to a 'disapplication' of a prohibition on harassment for these purposes – the prohibition simply never arose in the first place. If that is correct, an individual who experiences harassment because of either of these characteristics would not need to rely on S.212(5) in order to bring a claim under S.13 or S.27.

18.80 In practice, the EqA hardly ever disapplies the prohibition of harassment, though one notable instance is discrimination in the context of schools, where, by virtue of S.85(10), the prohibition is disapplied in respect of harassment by responsible bodies of a school in relation to three of the protected characteristics: gender reassignment, religion or belief, and sexual orientation. Furthermore, the prohibition is disapplied in relation to religion or belief and sexual orientation in respect of harassment by:

- service providers – S.29(8). The Explanatory Notes provide that public functions which involve the provision of a service (for example, medical treatment on the NHS) are covered by this provision

- those who have the right to dispose of premises (for example, by selling, letting or subletting a property) – S.33(6)

- those whose permission is required for the disposal of premises (for example, to sell, let or sub-let a property) – S.34(4)

- those who manage premises – S.35(4); and

- associations – S.103(2).

19 Victimisation

Individuals wishing to bring a discrimination or harassment claim may be **19.1** deterred from doing so by fear of reprisals. To address this concern, equality legislation pre-dating October 2010 included specific provisions outlawing victimisation. This protection is now found in the Equality Act 2010 (EqA), albeit with some changes to the statutory language.

Previously, in order to prove victimisation, the claimant had to show that the employer had treated him or her less favourably than it had treated or would have treated other persons in the same circumstances, and did so by reason that the claimant had done or intended to do a protected act, such as making an allegation of discrimination or bringing a discrimination claim. The EqA takes a slightly different approach. S.27(1) provides: 'A person (A) victimises another person (B) if A subjects B to a detriment because (a) B does a protected act, or (b) A believes that B has done, or may do, a protected act.' By virtue of S.27(4), the victimisation provisions apply only where the person subjected to a detriment is an individual.

It follows from S.27(1) that a claimant seeking to establish that he or she has **19.2** been victimised must show two things: first, that he or she has been subjected to a *detriment*; and secondly, that he or she was subjected to that detriment *because of* a protected act. There is no longer any need, as there was under the previous equality legislation, for the claimant to show that his or her treatment was less favourable than that which would have been afforded to a comparator who had not done a protected act. The significance of this change is considered in detail under 'Detriment' below.

The following are 'protected acts' for the purpose of S.27(1):

- bringing proceedings under the EqA

- giving evidence or information in connection with proceedings under the EqA

589

- doing any other thing for the purposes of or in connection with the EqA, and

- making an allegation (whether or not express) that A or another person has contravened the EqA – S.27(2).

19.3 In addition, S.77 treats as protected acts certain things done in relation to pay secrecy clauses in employment contracts. This provision, first introduced in the EqA, is designed to stop employers covering up unlawful pay inequality by means of confidentiality clauses. In short, any attempt by an employee to discover whether there is pay discrimination at work will be protected, even if the employee thereby breaches or solicits a breach of a pay secrecy clause. We briefly consider this provision under 'Protected acts – pay disclosure protected acts' below. For a detailed discussion of pay secrecy clauses, see IDS Employment Law Handbook, 'Equal Pay' (2011), Chapter 9, 'Enforcement', under 'Pay secrecy clauses'.

In this chapter we examine the scope of the victimisation provisions in the EqA, before looking at the relevant circumstances in which victimisation by an employer can arise. We then consider the acts protected by the victimisation provisions, before discussing the meaning of 'detriment' and how this differs from the previous requirement to establish 'less favourable treatment'. Finally, we address the burden of proof in victimisation claims.

References to the 'EHRC Employment Code' are references to the Equality and Human Rights Commission's Code of Practice on Employment.

19.4 **Equal pay.** Note that, while the law on equal pay falls outside the scope of this Handbook, victimisation claims based on a previous equal pay claim or an alleged contravention of equal pay law are covered in the same way as discrimination and harassment claims. For a full discussion of equal pay law, see IDS Employment Law Handbook, 'Equal Pay' (2011).

19.5 Scope of provisions

The victimisation provisions give wide protection to employees who have been penalised for bringing, or involving themselves in almost any way with, a discrimination, harassment or equal pay complaint. It is not necessary for a tribunal claim to have been brought – the victimisation provisions cover a wide range of conduct related to the EqA, such as alleging a breach of the Act or doing anything 'in connection with' the Act – see 'Protected acts' below. Nor is it necessary for the employee to have a protected characteristic him or herself in order to claim protection from victimisation under the EqA. This is because, in a victimisation claim, the focus is not on the protected characteristic of the complainant but on his or her *actions* in alleging a breach or bringing a claim or in assisting in someone else's claim. Anyone whose conduct amounts to a 'protected act' can seek to rely on the statutory protection from victimisation – Cornelius v University College of Swansea 1987 IRLR 141, CA.

In Veitch v Red Sky Group Ltd 2010 NICA 39, NICA, the Northern Ireland Court of Appeal criticised an industrial tribunal in Northern Ireland for misunderstanding the fundamental nature of a victimisation complaint. The tribunal had decided that an employee's claims of disability discrimination and victimisation failed in their entirety because he was unable to satisfy the statutory definition of 'disability' under the Disability Discrimination Act 1995 (DDA) (see Chapter 6, 'Disability', for the definition under the EqA). The Court held that this was the wrong approach to the claim of victimisation. Regardless of whether a person is disabled, he or she is entitled to the statutory protection from victimisation. Accordingly, if the claimant is able to show less favourable treatment as a result of doing a protected act – in this case, bringing proceedings under the Act – the tribunal must make findings on the victimisation claim.

While S.27 EqA is broad enough to cover a myriad of employee activities, in **19.6** most cases the issue of victimisation is linked to a previous or concurrent tribunal claim by the claimant. Success or otherwise of the main claim is *not* a relevant factor in the success or otherwise of the victimisation claim. All depends on whether the employee is able to establish a link between any detriment suffered and the doing of the 'protected act', i.e. the bringing of the main claim. Accordingly, it may be that the claimant's original claim fails but a subsequent victimisation action leads to a large award of compensation. Some examples:

- **Braines v M Novakovic and Co** ET Case Nos.1201513/97 and another: B lost a claim for sex discrimination after her employer stopped her sick pay while she was pregnant, but won a claim of victimisation because, after the first day of the hearing, the employer had threatened to publicise a sexual relationship she had allegedly had in the past if she continued with the claim

- **Brown v Department for Education and Skills** ET Case Nos.2304579/00 and another: B failed in his equal pay claim, based on comparison with F, a female employee, because the DES was able to make out the 'genuine material factor' defence under S.1(3) of the Equal Pay Act 1970 (now S.69 EqA) – F had not been prepared to accept a lower salary and the DES had only paid what was necessary to secure her services. Some time after B had brought his claim, the men's toilets in the premises where he worked were deliberately flooded. CCTV footage showed B leaving the toilets shortly before the flood was discovered, and he was suspended from duty. He was later exonerated. B brought a victimisation claim under S.4 of the Sex Discrimination Act 1975 (SDA) (now S.27 EqA). The tribunal held that he had been unlawfully victimised. Consciously or subconsciously, the person who had investigated the flooding incident formed the view that B was a troublemaker and, as such, a likely culprit. Had the investigator been unaware of the fact that B had brought an equal pay claim, he would not have taken this view

- **Brown v Hidden Hearing Ltd** ET Case No.1101177/07: a tribunal dismissed B's discrimination and harassment claims, but upheld her victimisation complaint. It found that B was suspended on full pay, and told not to enter work premises without permission, because she had lodged a grievance alleging race discrimination against her supervisor. There was no evidence of any other employee who lodged a grievance being suspended

- **Bello v University of Greenwich** ET Case No.2318714/07: the tribunal found that B was discriminated against by being victimised unlawfully because he had made accusations of race discrimination. Once B had issued a race discrimination questionnaire and started proceedings a high level of distrust in him was evident, and this was one of the reasons why the employer had decided that the working relationship between B and his colleagues had broken down and he was dismissed. There was no suggestion that B had made the allegations of discrimination in bad faith, even though his complaints of discriminatory treatment, other than victimisation, were not upheld. He was awarded £10,000 for injury to feelings

- **Francis v Ocean Contract Cleaning London Ltd** ET Case Nos.2203348/10 and another: F, who was originally from Jamaica, was asked to prove her eligibility to work in the United Kingdom when her contract transferred to OCC Ltd. A copy was taken of her passport and sent to head office, which decided that it was unsatisfactory. She was told that she could not work until she had provided another form of identification – which she did not have – or left her passport with the company – which she refused to do. F lodged a grievance, claiming race discrimination. OCC Ltd rejected the grievance and sent her a P45, specifying her leaving date. She wrote to the company, asking whether she had been dismissed, but received no reply. Her subsequent claim of race discrimination was dismissed but her victimisation claim was upheld: sending F's P45 and refusing to explain why it had been sent were acts of victimisation. F was awarded £6,000 for injury to feelings.

19.7 The protection from victimisation provisions can even come into play in respect of the employer's conduct during the main proceedings. For example, in Lorde v Eden Brown Ltd ET Case No.2201996/09 the employer's defence of L's sex discrimination claim gave rise to victimisation. The employer had approached witnesses who were due to give evidence for L and frightened them off by telling them that, if they did so, compromise agreements they had concluded with the employer would not be honoured. The tribunal found that this caused stress and anxiety to L, since it meant she had to apply for witness orders to ensure the attendance of her witnesses. The tribunal awarded £8,000 for injury to feelings and £6,000 aggravated damages, noting that the employer had tried to subvert the course of justice, undermine L's right to a fair trial and damage her credibility.

The Court of Appeal has also indicated that failure to pay the compensation awarded by a tribunal in respect of the main claim may amount to unlawful victimisation, so long as the failure to pay was itself motivated by the fact of the employee having brought tribunal proceedings. In Coutinho v Rank Nemo (DMS) Ltd 2009 ICR 1296, CA, C won a claim of race discrimination and was awarded over £70,000 in compensation. He did not receive any money from RN Ltd, despite obtaining a county court order for payment, and he then claimed that the failure to pay was itself an act of victimisation under the Race Relations Act 1976 (RRA). The Court allowed the claim to proceed, rejecting RN Ltd's argument that it was an illegitimate attempt to enforce the award in the tribunal. The Court held that, even if RN Ltd paid the award immediately, the victimisation claim could still continue, with C seeking to recover damages for any loss of benefit or detriment suffered in consequence of RN Ltd's reluctance to pay. The Court added, however, that a victimisation claim cannot be brought in respect of an employer's failure to comply with a tribunal order for reinstatement or re-engagement because unfair dismissal law provided for an express statutory remedy (namely, an order for compensation) in these circumstances.

19.8 It should be pointed out here that the way in which the EqA operates has cast doubt on whether a former employee can bring a post-employment victimisation complaint under the Act – the type of complaint brought in the Coutinho case under the RRA. This apparent change in the law is discussed under 'Prohibited circumstances – post-employment victimisation' below.

In some cases, the complaint of victimisation will hang on a tribunal claim brought by *another* person in which the person victimised is or has been involved. The EHRC Employment Code gives the following example of an employee relying on the victimisation provisions in these circumstances: 'A non-disabled worker gives evidence on behalf of a disabled colleague at an Employment Tribunal hearing where disability discrimination is claimed. If the non-disabled worker is subsequently refused a promotion because of that action, they would have suffered victimisation in contravention of the Act' – para 9.3. Two cases:

- **Osborne v Sparva Furnishings Ltd** ET Case No.29292/86: O intended to give evidence for his wife when she brought a sex discrimination claim against the company that employed them both. When this became known to the company, hints were dropped that O's job was on the line owing to a downturn in business. After commissioning a consultant's report the company dismissed O for redundancy. Although a redundancy situation did exist, the tribunal found that the consultant had been fed misinformation and that O should not have been selected. The tribunal held that O had been

593

'set up' because of the support he was giving his wife in her complaint of discrimination. His victimisation claim was upheld

- **Laidlaw v South Durham Social Club** ET Case No.2500971/04: L was due to give evidence for his girlfriend in a sex discrimination claim against his employer. After taking two weeks' holiday, he did not turn up to work the next day because he was attending the tribunal as a witness. The employer knew this, as witness statements had been exchanged. L was disciplined for unauthorised absence and subjected to other less favourable treatment in his working arrangements. The tribunal held that he was victimised contrary to S.4 SDA (now S.27 EqA) because the employer knew he would be attending the tribunal and must have known he would not be attending work. He was subjected to a detriment for carrying out a protected act.

19.9 For the sake of completeness, it is worth adding that the protection under S.27 EqA is confined to those who have themselves done, or were intending to do, a protected act. The section's wording is not wide enough to cover an individual who claims to have suffered a detriment because of his or her association with someone who has done, or may have intended to do, a protected act. 'Victimisation by association' is therefore not covered.

19.10 Belief and suspicion

Protection under S.27(1) clearly applies where the discriminator *believes* that the person victimised has done or may do a protected act. For example, in France v Chief Constable of Hertfordshire Constabulary ET Case No.1200783/98 the claimant succeeded with a victimisation claim when, following his internal complaints of sex discrimination, the employer transferred him to a different unit in the knowledge that he intended to bring sex discrimination claims.

Under the pre-EqA legislation, protection against victimisation extended to situations where the employer *suspected* that the person victimised *intended* to do a protected act. This was emphasised in Miller v Crime Concern Trust Ltd EAT 0758/04 where the EAT held that a tribunal had erred in failing to consider whether the alleged discriminator had suspected that the claimant was going to make an allegation of race or sex discrimination. S.27(1) imposes a slightly different test: it applies where the employee does a protected act or where the employer '*believes* that [the employee] has done, or *may do*, a protected act' (our stress). It is unclear whether a *suspicion* that a person *intends* to do a protected act (under the old test) is the same as a *belief* that a person *may do* such an act (under S.27(1)). Strictly speaking, 'belief' suggests a higher level of credence than 'suspicion', but the fact that a person 'may do' an act suggests something less than that he or she 'intends' to do it. The new terms may, therefore, achieve the same balance as the previous legislation. The Explanatory Notes to the EqA actually use the old test to explain the scope of the victimisation provisions (see para 100). We would suggest that this implies that the change in wording was not intended to signal a substantive change in the law. In any event, it seems unlikely that tribunals will adopt a construction of the EqA that amounts to a regression in protection for employees so, since suspicions were covered by the old law, they are likely to be covered by the new provisions.

Three-stage victimisation test   19.11
Baroness Hale in Derbyshire and ors v St Helens Metropolitan Borough Council and ors 2007 ICR 841, HL, and Lord Nicholls in Chief Constable of West Yorkshire Police v Khan 2001 ICR 1065, HL, endorsed a three-stage test for establishing victimisation under the pre-EqA discrimination legislation. Their approach called for answers to the following questions:

- did the employer discriminate against the claimant in any of the circumstances covered by discrimination legislation?

- in doing so, did the employer treat him or her less favourably than others in those circumstances?

- was the reason for the less favourable treatment the fact that the claimant had done a protected act; or that the employer knew that he or she intended to do a protected act, or suspected that he or she had done, or intended to do, a protected act?

As previously mentioned, the definition of victimisation in S.27 EqA uses **19.12** somewhat different wording to that used in the antecedent equality legislation. It provides that: 'A person (A) victimises another person (B) if A subjects B to a detriment because (a) B does a protected act, or (b) A believes that B has done, or may do, a protected act.'

In light of the new wording, we would submit that the above three-stage test can be adapted as follows:

- did the alleged victimisation arise in any of the prohibited circumstances covered by the EqA? (See 'Prohibited circumstances' below)

- if so, did the employer subject the claimant to a detriment? (See 'Detriment' below)

- if so, was the claimant subjected to that detriment because he or she had done a protected act, or because the employer believed that he or she had done, or might do, a protected act? (See 'Protected acts' and 'Detriment "because of" protected act' below).

The explanation for the change of wording given in the Explanatory Notes is **19.13** that victimisation is no longer treated as a form of discrimination (para 103). Under equality legislation in force until 1 October 2010, one provision would make it unlawful for an employer to discriminate in employment, while other

595

sections would define 'discrimination' for that purpose. One of these sections would define victimisation as a form of discrimination. So, for example, S.4 SDA set out the definition of victimisation and stated that it amounted to discrimination, while S.6 stated that discrimination in employment was unlawful. In the EqA, by contrast, S.27 sets out the definition of victimisation and S.39(3) and (4) states that victimisation in employment is unlawful. Thus, there is no need to treat victimisation as a form of discrimination – it is unlawful *per se* – and so the need to define it in the same way as discrimination falls away.

In the next section we set out the circumstances in which victimisation is prohibited under the EqA. We then examine the nature of the protected acts covered by the victimisation provisions and discuss the meaning of 'detriment', before considering the relationship between the two; i.e. what it means for a detriment to be 'because of' a protected act. It should be borne in mind, however, that the stages of analysis overlap to some extent.

19.14 Prohibited circumstances

The circumstances in which discrimination by way of victimisation is prohibited in the employment field are set out in S.39(3) and (4) EqA. S.39(3) provides that an employer (A) must not victimise a person (B):

- in the arrangements A makes for deciding to whom to offer employment – S.39(3)(a)

- as to the terms on which A offers B employment – S.39(3)(b), or

- by not offering B employment – S.39(3)(c).

Section 39(4) provides that an employer (A) must not victimise an employee of A's (B):

- as to B's terms of employment – S.39(4)(a)

- in the way A affords B access, or by not affording B access, to opportunities for promotion, transfer or training, or for any other benefit, facility or service – S.39(4)(b)

- by dismissing B – S.39(4)(c), or

- by subjecting B to any other detriment – S.39(4)(d).

19.15 Section 39(7) provides that the reference to 'dismissing' B in S.39(4)(c) (above) 'includes a reference to the termination of B's employment… (a) by the expiry of a period (including a period expiring by reference to an event or circumstance); (b) by an act of B's (including giving notice) in circumstances such that B is entitled, because of A's conduct, to terminate the employment without notice' (i.e. constructive dismissal). However, S.39(7)(a) does not apply 'if, immediately after the termination, the employment is renewed on the same terms' – S.39(8). Accordingly, the expiry of a fixed-term contract without renewal or the employee's constructive dismissal may form the basis of a victimisation complaint.

Similar protection from victimisation is afforded to contract workers, office holders, partners in firms, and trainee or qualified barristers (or advocates in Scotland), etc – see Ss.41–58 EqA. For more information on who is covered by the Act, see Chapter 28, 'Liability of employers, employees and agents', and Chapter 29, 'Liability of other bodies'.

In practice it is the catch-all 'detriment' provision in S.39(4)(d) that is most frequently cited in victimisation claims. For the meaning of 'detriment' in the context of both S.27 and S.39(4)(d) EqA, see 'Detriment' below.

Post-employment victimisation   19.16
The wording of S.27(1) is capable of covering the situation where a former employee is subjected to a detriment by his or her former employer because of a protected act. However, victimisation by employers is not actually prohibited by S.27, which is simply a definition provision. As noted above, it is S.39(3) and (4) that specifically prohibits victimisation in employment, but this does not expressly apply to post-employment victimisation. S.108 prohibits discrimination and harassment that arises out of, and is closely connected to, a relationship which has ended (such as an employment relationship) – see Chapter 27, 'Post-employment discrimination'. However, as victimisation is no longer treated as a form of discrimination, it does not automatically fall within S.108. In fact, S.108(7) expressly states that the section does *not* apply to victimisation.

Thus, on the face of it, the EqA would appear *not* to cover victimisation of former employees by their former employers (unless it arises in the context of recruitment, which is covered by S.39(3)). However, such a literal interpretation of the statutory provisions would amount to a serious degradation of the protection previously afforded to employees. In Coote v Granada Hospitality Ltd 1999 ICR 100, ECJ, the European Court of Justice held that European law – specifically, in that case, what is now the recast Equal Treatment Directive (No.2006/54), which ensures equal treatment of men and women in employment – requires protection to be given to employees after the employment relationship has ended. Subsequently, in Rhys-Harper v Relaxion Group plc 2003 ICR 867, HL, the House of Lords ruled that the wording of the SDA, RRA and DDA, which referred to employment relationships in the present tense, had to be given an interpretation that extended protection to conduct following termination of employment, provided the discrimination (including victimisation) arose out of the employment relationship. The discrimination legislation was subsequently amended to include a specific provision to that effect (the predecessors to S.108).

19.17 When the Government Equalities Office (GEO) was alerted to this apparent drafting error in the EqA by the Discrimination Law Association, a network organisation of discrimination law practitioners, it stated that the Act was intended to cover claims for post-employment victimisation. In its view, this was achieved by the Act, read together with the relevant case law, as underpinned by EU Directives. That said, it acknowledged that 'the reliance on the case law means that this protection is not as clear as it could be on the face of the Act'.

This lack of clarity led a tribunal to reject a claim of post-employment victimisation in Jessemey v Rowstock Ltd and anor ET Case Nos.2700838/11 and another. In that case J was dismissed just before his 66th birthday. He contended that this was because of his age and that accordingly the dismissal was both unfair under the ERA and discriminatory under the EqA. While he was looking for alternative work he discovered that the employer had provided an unfavourable reference to an employment agency and he claimed that this amounted to an act of victimisation by reason of his bringing the tribunal proceedings in relation to his dismissal. The tribunal had no trouble finding that the provision of the 'particularly poor' reference was an act of victimisation. However, it rejected the claim on the ground that post-employment victimisation was excluded by virtue of S.108(7) EqA.

19.18 Despite the tribunal's conclusion in the Jessemey case, we contend that, for the reasons given above, S.39(4)(d) (which prohibits victimisation by subjecting a person to any detriment) should be interpreted as applying not only to current but also to former employees. This view is supported by the EHRC Employment Code, albeit without any authority being cited. Para 9.4 simply states that: 'Former workers are also protected from victimisation', while para 10.62 explains that: 'If the conduct or treatment which an individual receives after a relationship has ended amounts to victimisation, this will be covered by the victimisation provisions.'

19.19 ## Protected acts

The acts that are protected by the victimisation provisions are set out in S.27(2). They are:

- bringing proceedings under the EqA – S.27(2)(a)

- giving evidence or information in connection with proceedings under the EqA – S.27(2)(b)

- doing any other thing for the purposes of or in connection with the EqA – S.27(2)(c)

- making an allegation (whether or not express) that A or another person has contravened the EqA – S.27(2)(d).

These are substantially the same as those listed in the antecedent discrimination **19.20** legislation. There is also a new category of protected act introduced by S.77 EqA, which bans certain forms of pay secrecy clauses in employment contracts. S.77(4) states that seeking, making, seeking to make, or receiving a 'relevant pay disclosure' are all to be treated as protected acts. A 'relevant pay disclosure' for these purposes is a disclosure 'made for the purpose of enabling the person who makes it, or the person to whom it is made, to find out whether or to what extent there is, in relation to the work in question, a connection between pay and having (or not having) a particular protected characteristic' – S.77(3). In other words, an attempt to uncover the existence of pay inequality is also a protected act. Pay secrecy clauses are discussed in detail in IDS Employment Law Handbook, 'Equal Pay' (2011), Chapter 9, 'Enforcement', under 'Pay secrecy clauses'.

Transitional provisions
19.21
In the period between the EqA receiving Royal Assent on 8 April 2010 and coming into force on 1 October 2010, it became apparent that there was a loophole in the wording of S.27(2). Subsections (a) to (d) of that provision all refer to something done in respect of 'this Act', i.e. the EqA. Since the EqA repealed the previous discrimination legislation, this would have meant that a claimant bringing a claim of victimisation that was alleged to have occurred after 1 October 2010, but which arose from protected acts that occurred when the antecedent legislation was still in force, would have been left without legal redress. Article 8 of the Equality Act 2010 (Commencement No.4, Savings, Consequential, Transitional, Transitory and Incidental Provisions and Revocation) Order 2010 SI 2010/2317 closed this loophole by making it clear that references in S.27(2) to 'this Act' are to be read as also applying to the previous discrimination and equality enactments.

Bringing proceedings
19.22
Bringing any legal proceedings under the EqA will fall within S.27(2)(a) and therefore be protected. Most victimisation claims relate to reprisals suffered because of earlier proceedings brought by the claimant against the alleged victimiser, although concurrent proceedings are also covered (including the initial act of presenting a claim form to an employment tribunal – Northamptonshire County Council v Dattani EAT 314/91 and others). An example:

- **Green v Surrey and Sussex Health Care NHS Trust Ltd** ET Case Nos.2318487/07 and others: the tribunal dismissed G's claims of race discrimination, but upheld one complaint of victimisation. It found that he suffered a detriment when another employee said loudly that the Trust had 'got rid of one and there is still one here giving trouble and management still haven't done anything about him yet'. The fact that G had lodged a tribunal

599

claim was an essential element causing the comment to be made. G was awarded £3,500 for injury to feelings.

19.23 Subsection (a) is wide enough to cover any kind of proceedings under the EqA against *any* person. Suppose, for example, that an employee brings proceedings in an employment tribunal claiming equal pay with a male colleague. Some time later, she applies for a job with another company, which refuses to offer her employment because it knows that she brought an equal pay claim against her old employer. She could claim victimisation under S.39(3)(c) EqA (victimisation by not offering employment) against that company. In addition, S.27(2)(a) expressly covers *any kind* of proceedings under the EqA. Thus, if a person brings a claim under any of the non-employment provisions in the EqA – e.g. the services provisions – a victimisation claim may arise under S.27(2)(a) if that person's employer penalises him or her for bringing such an action.

19.24 **Giving evidence or information in connection with proceedings**
Subsection 27(2)(b) clearly protects giving evidence at a tribunal hearing. In Sowter v D and J Ingham t/a Branded Sportswear ET Case No.1805595/98, for example, a tribunal held that S had been selected for redundancy because she was due to give evidence against her employer in a sex discrimination claim brought by a colleague. Giving evidence prior to a hearing will also be covered, but only if proceedings have already been instigated. In Kirby v Manpower Services Commission 1980 ICR 420, EAT, K was demoted after he gave information to his local Community Relations Council that eventually led to race discrimination proceedings against his employer. The EAT held that K's claim that his demotion amounted to victimisation could not be brought under S.2(1)(b) RRA (equivalent to S.27(2)(b) EqA) because the incidents that gave rise to the demotion occurred three months before the proceedings were actually commenced. However, his claim did succeed under S.2(1)(c) RRA – see 'Acts done for the purposes of or in connection with the EqA' below.

19.25 **False evidence or information.** Giving false evidence or information is not a protected act if it is done in bad faith – S.27(3). This is not, however, the same as saying that the evidence or information must be true. If a claimant provides evidence or information in good faith that turns out to be inaccurate, he or she will still enjoy protection under S.27(2)(b) in respect of the provision of that evidence or information. For more detail on the meaning of 'bad faith' in a victimisation context, see under 'Allegations of a contravention of the EqA' below.

19.26 **Acts done 'for the purposes of or in connection with' the EqA**
Subsection (c) is generally seen as a sweep-up clause for actions not specifically covered by S.27(2)(a) and (b). The statutory wording has been simplified somewhat from that found in the original discrimination statutes. Previously, discrimination legislation referred to acts done 'under or by reference to' the

relevant equality enactment. Now, all acts done 'for the purposes of or in connection with' the EqA are covered. The ambit of the original wording came in for scrutiny by the EAT in Kirby v Manpower Services Commission 1980 ICR 420, EAT, which took a restrictive view of what constitutes action 'under' an Act. The EAT held that such action must be done under a specific statutory provision. On the facts, a report to the local Community Relations Council was not made under any specific provision. The phrase 'by reference to' was given a much wider interpretation, however. The EAT was prepared to assume that it was wide enough to cover the report to the Community Relations Council because the purpose of the report was to inform the Council that facts were available which ought to be investigated and which indicated a possible breach of the RRA. The Court of Appeal confirmed this interpretation in Aziz v Trinity Street Taxis Ltd and ors 1988 ICR 534, CA, where it stated that an act could properly be said to be done 'by reference to' the RRA if it were done by reference to the legislation 'in the broad sense, even though the doer does not focus his mind specifically on any provision of the Act'.

If an identical case were to be heard today under S.27(2)(c), the report would almost certainly be taken to have been made 'in connection with' the EqA. Indeed, it is arguable that it might also be viewed as having been made 'for the purposes of' the Act, a test that would appear to be wider than the previous 'under' test.

Allegations of a contravention of the EqA   19.27

Subsection (d) covers allegations, whether or not express, made by the claimant that the employer or another person has contravened the EqA. S.27(5) states that this includes a contravention by way of breach of an equality clause or rule relating to sex or maternity (see IDS Employment Law Handbook, 'Equal Pay' (2011), Chapter 2, 'Right to equal pay', under 'The sex equality clause', 'Occupational pension schemes' and 'Maternity'.) It is not necessary that the EqA actually be mentioned in the allegation or even be envisaged as coming into play. However, the asserted facts must, if verified, be *capable* of amounting to a breach of the EqA. Two examples:

- **Waters v Commissioner of Police of the Metropolis** 1997 ICR 1073, CA: a woman police officer accused a male colleague of sexually assaulting her. Following this accusation, she was subjected to various forms of harassment and other unfair treatment at work. The Court of Appeal held that, on the officer's own version of events, her colleague had not committed the assault 'in the course of his employment', and so the Commissioner of Police could not be held liable. It followed that she was not entitled to rely on her allegation of assault for the purpose of a victimisation claim as she had not alleged that her employer had committed an act which would amount to a contravention of the SDA

601

- **Beneviste v Kingston University** EAT 0393/05: B claimed that she had been victimised because she had raised various grievances. She admitted that she had not at the time complained that her treatment was on the grounds of sex or race but thought this did not matter. The EAT upheld the tribunal's decision that the grievances could not amount to protected acts, saying that a claim does not identify a protected act in the true legal sense 'merely by making a reference to a criticism, grievance or complaint without suggesting that the criticism, grievance or complaint was in some sense an allegation of discrimination or otherwise a contravention of the legislation'.

19.28 The result of the Waters case seems somewhat harsh, as claimants are unlikely to know, without the benefit of legal advice, whether the facts they are alleging could theoretically give rise to a successful claim in law. However, the effect of the narrow interpretation of subsection (d) may be less of a problem than might first appear: in many cases where subsection (d) is inapplicable, it may be possible to argue that the case falls within subsection (c) if the allegation can be said to have been made in connection with the EqA 'in the broad sense' – see Aziz v Trinity Street Taxis Ltd and ors 1988 ICR 534, CA.

Subsection (d) imposes no restrictions as to whom the allegations must relate to or to whom they must be made. In Davey v Aldam t/a John Charles Associates ET Case No.3101781/98 D complained to her employer's son about her employer's treatment of her. He said that he would speak to his father. The next day she was dismissed. A tribunal found that her dismissal amounted to victimisation. The allegations do not even have to be against the same person in respect of whom the claimant subsequently alleges victimisation – although it may arguably be harder for a claimant to demonstrate that an employer subjected him or her to a detriment because of a protected act where that act did not directly concern the employer.

Note that S.27(2)(d) covers allegations made about A (the alleged victimiser) or 'another person', so it is quite possible for an employer to victimise an employee because the employee has made allegations about an entirely unrelated person.

19.29 **False allegations.** Protection from victimisation under S.27(2)(d) is still available if the allegation turns out to be untrue. However, S.27(3) EqA provides that making a false allegation will not be protected if it is done in 'bad faith'. In HM Prison Service and ors v Ibimidun 2008 IRLR 940, EAT, a case which considered S.2(2) RRA (now S.27(3) EqA), the EAT confirmed that the victimisation provisions are designed to protect bona fide claims only. Accordingly, the EAT held that dismissing an employee for making numerous claims of race discrimination against his employer and his colleagues in order to harass the employer into offering him a settlement did not amount to victimisation.

602

The antecedent discrimination legislation used slightly different wording to that used in S.27(3), stating that an allegation would not amount to a protected act if it was 'false and not made in good faith' (see, for example, S.2(2) RRA and S.4(2) SDA). This test, which is essentially the same as that under S.27(3), which states that 'making a false allegation... is not a protected act if... the allegation is made... in bad faith', was considered by the EAT in GMB Union v Fenton EAT 0798/02 and others. In that case, F, an educational assistant at the GMB National College, was frustrated at being excluded from a GMB pension scheme and brought a claim under the Equal Pay Act 1970 against the union. However, as he admitted, his exclusion was in fact on the ground of his employment status, not gender, so his claim was held to be misconceived. He made a further claim of victimisation and the union claimed that there was no protected act because F's first claim, on which he relied, was false and made in bad faith. The EAT said that the test in S.4(2) had two limbs: first, whether an allegation was false, and secondly, whether the person making the allegation knew it was false at the time it was made. The EAT said that if a claimant 'has a belief that he has a good claim, but perhaps one that is not terribly likely to succeed, and he brings that claim with some collateral purpose, it appears to us that that does not necessarily make the bringing of that claim in bad faith. The issue is not the purpose, but the belief in the claim.' So the fact that a person is being opportunistic in making an allegation does not necessarily mean that the allegation is not made in good faith. However, according to the EAT, an allegation made in bad faith does not necessarily have to be 'treacherous'.

19.30 A strong belief in the claim was certainly evident in Martin v Devonshires Solicitors 2011 ICR 352, EAT. There, M made serious allegations against two partners in a solicitors' firm; she alleged that one had said that she was 'after the partner's money' (sic) and that another had called her a prostitute. DS investigated and found the allegations unproven. M continued to repeat them and was eventually dismissed. The EAT, hearing her victimisation claim, recognised that M could not be dismissed for the falseness of the allegations alone – which resulted from mental illness – without violating the discrimination provisions, unless those allegations were made in bad faith, which was not the case here. However, the EAT went on to hold that the victimisation claim failed because she had not been dismissed by reason of having made the allegations – see under 'Detriment "because of" protected act' below.

Bad faith was found in Bartusek v Northern Leisure Group Ltd ET Case No.1801849/07. There, B, a naturalised Briton, had come to this country from his native Serbia as a child. He had no particular religious belief but was from time to time addressed by his colleagues and others as 'Paki', 'Muslim' and 'Turk'. In turn, he called his colleagues by nicknames – 'Scottish Jew' and 'German Nazi bastard', for instance. He was disciplined for making false claims of racial harassment, and claimed he had thereby suffered unlawful victimisation. However, an employment tribunal dismissed his claim, noting that B was on

603

friendly or very friendly terms with his alleged antagonists to an extent wholly inconsistent with his claims. The tribunal concluded that B regarded bringing tribunal proceedings as a way of making money out of the sort of things that went on and were said in the workplace but which he embraced and participated in as 'one of the lads'. It followed that the allegations were not made in good faith.

19.31 **Pay disclosure protected acts**
As mentioned in the introduction to this chapter, S.77 EqA is a new provision designed to protect employees who discuss their pay with colleagues with a view to finding out whether there is a connection between pay and any of the protected characteristics covered by the Act. S.77(1) and (2) provides that terms in employment contracts that purport to restrict or prevent a person from seeking disclosure of, or disclosing or seeking to disclose, information about pay will be unenforceable to the extent that they prevent or restrict a disclosure made for the purpose of discovering whether there is such a connection.

Section 77(4) supports these provisions by providing that the following are protected acts for the purpose of S.27 EqA:

- seeking a disclosure that would be a relevant pay disclosure – S.77(4)(a)

- making or seeking to make a relevant pay disclosure – S.77(4)(b)

- receiving information disclosed in a relevant pay disclosure – S.77(4)(c).

19.32 A pay disclosure is 'relevant' for these purposes if it is 'made for the purpose of enabling the person who makes it, or the person to whom it is made, to find out whether or to what extent there is, in relation to the work in question, a connection between pay and having (or not having) a particular protected characteristic' – S.77(3). In other words, the exchange of information must be motivated by a desire to uncover pay discrimination, rather than simple curiosity. Pay secrecy clauses are discussed in IDS Employment Law Handbook, 'Equal Pay' (2011), Chapter 9, 'Enforcement', under 'Pay secrecy clauses'.

19.33 # Detriment

Under the previous equality legislation, in order to make out a complaint of victimisation, it was not enough for the claimant to show that he or she had suffered a disadvantage. Victimisation occurred only where the employee, having done a protected act, was treated less favourably by the employer than another person was or would have been treated. Indeed, many of the difficulties that arose in victimisation cases under the old legislation concerned the appropriate comparison that needed to be made to establish less favourable treatment.

604

It is apparent from the wording of S.27(1) EqA, which refers to detriment 'because of' a protected act, that the EqA has removed the absolute need for a tribunal to construct an appropriate comparator in victimisation claims. As the EHRC Employment Code states: 'The worker need only show that they have experienced a detriment because they have done a protected act or because the employer believes (rightly or wrongly) that they have done or intend to do a protected act' – para 9.11. In this respect the victimisation provisions in the EqA are similar to the provisions in Part V of the Employment Rights Act 1996 (ERA), which afford protection from detriment on specified grounds covered by that Act. For example, S.47B ERA makes it unlawful for an employer to subject a worker to a detriment 'on the ground that the worker has made a protected disclosure'. Assuming that 'because of' and 'on the ground of' are equivalent formulations of causation (which case law suggests they are), it can be said that victimisation under the EqA and protection from detriment under the ERA are now very similar in scope.

In its response to the Consultation on the Equality Bill, the Government stated **19.34** that the removal of the requirement for a comparator 'offers a more effective, workable system – not one in which it would necessarily be easier to win a case, but one where attention [is] rightly focused on considering whether the "victim" suffered an absolute harm, irrespective of how others were being treated in the same circumstances' (para 7.35 of the 'The Equality Bill – Government response to the Consultation', July 2008 (Cm 7454)). In practice, however, a comparison of the claimant's treatment with that of an appropriate comparator will often be an effective way of establishing whether the treatment was 'because of' the protected act. In Shrimpton v Liverpool Primary Care Trust ET Case No.2101183/08, for example, S was absent from work from April 2003 because of bullying. She brought a tribunal claim, alleging that she was disabled by reason of post-traumatic stress caused by the bullying and that the Trust had failed to make reasonable adjustments. The proceedings were stayed in December 2004 and a lengthy period of negotiation began. For much of that time both the Trust and S were seeking her return to work, but this could not be achieved because the person S accused of bullying her refused to enter into mediation. Finally, the parties agreed to settle S's tribunal claim for £35,000 and to terminate her employment. In November 2007 she applied for another post with the Trust. Although her qualifications and experience qualified her to be shortlisted, the Trust decided not to shortlist her on the ground that she had been paid a substantial amount of public money because she could no longer work for it. S's subsequent claim that this amounted to unlawful victimisation failed. The tribunal found that the appropriate comparator would be a person who had entered into a settlement that brought about the termination of her employment, but who had not brought a claim for disability discrimination. Such a person would have been treated in the same way as S.

605

Below we consider, by reference to case law under the previous equality legislation, what can amount to a 'detriment' for the purposes of S.27 EqA.

19.35 What amounts to 'detriment'?

Section 27(1) EqA replaces the concept of 'less favourable treatment', which appeared in the previous legislation, with that of 'detriment', which is not defined by the Act but is a familiar concept in discrimination law. Courts and tribunals have generally taken the view that it covers a wide range of conduct and treatment, and there is no reason to suggest that it will not be treated likewise under the EqA. That said, S.212(1) EqA expressly states that 'detriment' does not include conduct that amounts to harassment. A claim alleging conduct of that nature should generally be pursued by way of a claim under S.26 EqA (see Chapter 18, 'Harassment').

The victimisation provisions in the previous discrimination legislation established that 'less favourable treatment' could take many forms, ranging from general hostility to dismissal. The same is undoubtedly true of 'detriment' and so even the more subtle forms of victimisation will not necessarily escape the law. As Lord Hope observed in Derbyshire and ors v St Helens Metropolitan Borough Council and ors 2007 ICR 841, HL, 'fear of public odium or the reproaches of colleagues is just as likely to deter an employee from enforcing her claim as a direct threat'. His Lordship made those comments with regard to a local authority that had written to a group of school canteen employees, warning of the potential consequences for the school meals service if employees who were bringing equal pay claims were to win.

19.36 A similar conclusion was reached in GMB v Allen and ors 2007 IRLR 752, EAT. There, the respondent union had persuaded several female members to settle their equal pay claims for about 25 per cent of their potential value while negotiating the implementation of a new single pay structure with the local authority. The tribunal found that the union had victimised the women when it reminded the local authority of its agreement that all members should be treated the same whether or not they had brought litigation, as this meant that the payments which might otherwise be made to the claimants would have to be reduced in order to accommodate the other union members who had not lodged claims. On appeal, the EAT disagreed, holding that there was no less favourable treatment and the union was simply seeking to ensure that all were treated equally favourably by the local authority. However, it noted that the tribunal's finding that the union portrayed the claimants to other union members and to the local authority as 'self-centred money grabbers' was in principle capable of constituting detrimental treatment in the context of victimisation discrimination, but that this allegation had not been put to the tribunal. (Although the case subsequently went to the Court of Appeal – see GMB v Allen and ors 2008 ICR 1407, CA – the victimisation finding was not appealed.)

606

It is clear, then, that indirect pressure on employees to abandon their discrimination complaints can amount to a detriment. In Parker v Chancery (UK) Ltd ET Case No.1201764/07, for example, P was victimised when the employer tried to dissuade her from raising a grievance about unequal pay. When P had queried her pay relative to a male colleague whom she asserted was employed on equal work, she was told that if she raised a grievance it would create a difficult work environment and that she would be better off leaving and seeking alternative employment. The tribunal awarded £3,000 for injury to feelings, among other heads of compensation, having regard to the fact that the incident was one among several factors that led her to leave C Ltd's employment.

Furthermore, 'detriment' does not necessarily require financial loss, loss of an **19.37** opportunity, or even a very specific form of disadvantage. In Kashmiri v Metropolitan Police Authority and ors ET Case Nos.2202363/09 and another, for example, a tribunal upheld K's complaint that she had been victimised by a false allegation that she had eaten cake during Ramadan. K was upset about the allegation – it questioned her honesty and integrity and suggested she had lied to gain an advantage, i.e. a change in working hours while she was fasting. The tribunal found that the person made the false allegation as a way of getting back at K for naming her as a respondent in a race discrimination claim. K was awarded £2,000 for injury to feelings.

The House of Lords in Chief Constable of West Yorkshire Police v Khan 2001 ICR 1065, HL, established that an *omission* to act – such as a refusal to provide a reference – may constitute detrimental treatment. The House of Lords also stated that, although less favourable treatment involved some kind of disadvantage, it did not have to have damaging consequences. In that case, West Yorkshire Police refused to supply a reference for a serving police officer (who had applied to another force for a post) while that officer's race discrimination claim against West Yorkshire Police was pending. West Yorkshire Police argued that K had not been treated less favourably because he would have been worse off had the reference been supplied – he would not even have reached the interview stage, as he had done without having the reference. The House of Lords decided that K had clearly been treated less favourably because he had been refused a reference, whereas any other officer who did not have a race discrimination complaint pending before a tribunal would have been given one. However, it is not enough merely to show that the employee has been treated differently to others. Lord Scott made it clear that 'there must also be a quality in the treatment that enables the complainant reasonably to complain about it. I do not think, however, that it is appropriate to pursue the treatment and its consequences down to an end result in order to try and demonstrate that the complainant is, in the end, better off, or at least no worse off, than he would have been if he had not been treated differently. I think it suffices if the complainant can reasonably say that he would have preferred not to have been treated differently.'

19.38 Lord Scott's final point – looking at the treatment from the employee's point of view – encapsulates the concept of 'detriment' rather neatly, and later cases have taken a similar approach. Shamoon v Chief Constable of the Royal Ulster Constabulary 2003 ICR 337, HL, which concerned the meaning of 'detriment' in Article 8(2)(b) of the Sex Discrimination (Northern Ireland) Order 1976 SR 1976/1042, established that a detriment exists if a *reasonable* worker would or might take the view that the treatment was in all the circumstances to his or her disadvantage. The House of Lords felt that an unjustified sense of grievance could not amount to a detriment, but did emphasise that whether or not a claimant has been disadvantaged is to be viewed subjectively.

This 'detriment' test was subsequently confirmed by the House of Lords in Derbyshire and ors v St Helens Metropolitan Borough Council and ors (above). But there, Lord Neuberger went on to stress that the test is not satisfied merely by the claimant showing that he or she has suffered mental distress: it would have to be *objectively reasonable* in all the circumstances. For example, the bringing of an equal pay claim, to take the facts of the case, no matter how strong the claim may be, carries with it, like any other litigation, inevitable stress and worry. That, on its own, is not sufficient to amount to a 'detriment' for the purposes of the victimisation provisions.

19.39 Thus, the employee's own perception of having suffered a 'detriment' may not always be sufficient to found a victimisation claim. For instance, in Bayode v Chief Constable of Derbyshire EAT 0499/07 the Appeal Tribunal held that B, who had previously brought a race discrimination claim against his employer, was not victimised when his colleagues recorded incidents involving him in their notebooks as part of the employer's attempt to protect itself against any further claims by him. The EAT accepted that, depending on the circumstances, the use of the notebook entries might have provoked a legitimate and reasonable sense of grievance in B. However, there had been no inappropriate action by the employer in relation to any of the incidents recorded (indeed, it had been reasonable for the employer to follow up on the reports brought to its attention). Accordingly, the mere act of making a written record was not a 'detriment' under the RRA and B's victimisation claim was dismissed.

The EHRC Employment Code, drawing on the case law under the previous discrimination legislation, contains a useful summary of treatment that may amount to a 'detriment': 'Generally, a detriment is anything which the individual concerned might reasonably consider changed their position for the worse or put them at a disadvantage. This could include being rejected for promotion, denied an opportunity to represent the organisation at external events, excluded from opportunities to train, or overlooked in the allocation of discretionary bonuses or performance-related awards... A detriment might also include a threat made to the complainant which they take seriously and it is reasonable for them to take it seriously. There is no need to demonstrate physical or economic consequences. However, an unjustified sense of grievance alone would not be enough to establish detriment' – paras 9.8 and 9.9.

Some examples of the kind of treatment that has been found to constitute a **19.40** 'detriment' for the purposes of a victimisation claim:

- **Buhler v IPS Actuarial Services Ltd and ors** ET Case No.2200497/05: B raised a grievance of sex discrimination. At around the same time he was under investigation in connection with his management of his division of the company. He was dismissed. Following his dismissal, the company's solicitors wrote to him demanding compensation for some £3 million the company had allegedly lost as a result of his actions. The tribunal held that the company's failure to consider any course of action short of dismissal arose from the fact that B had made a complaint of sex discrimination, and its threat to take civil proceedings against B for recovery of damages was an act of retaliation. Both the failure to consider alternatives to dismissal and the threat of civil proceedings amounted to less favourable treatment for the purpose of the victimisation provisions of the SDA

- **Brown v Hidden Hearing Ltd** ET Case No.1101177/07: B had a difficult working relationship with her supervisor, P, and she lodged a grievance against him alleging race discrimination. HH Ltd considered that their working relationship had broken down and thought it best to remove one of them from the workplace pending the resolution of the grievance. B was told to stay at home on full pay pending the resolution of the grievance, expected to take about ten days. In a letter it then informed her that she was suspended, and not allowed to attend work without permission or contact any member of staff. B brought claims of race discrimination and victimisation. The tribunal found that there had been no race discrimination but upheld her victimisation complaint. In its view, the term 'suspension', viewed objectively, had disciplinary overtones for most employees. Furthermore, there was no evidence showing that this was normal procedure or that this course of action had been taken in similar circumstances. In actual fact, the Staff Handbook provided that no individual would be penalised for raising a grievance. On these facts, B had been subjected to detrimental treatment

- **Green v Surrey and Sussex Health Care NHS Trust Ltd** ET Case Nos.2318487/07 and others: the tribunal dismissed G's claims of race discrimination, but upheld a complaint of victimisation. It found that he suffered a detriment when another employee said loudly that the Trust had 'got rid of one and there is still one here giving trouble and management still haven't done anything about him yet'. The fact that G had lodged a tribunal

609

claim was an essential element causing the comment to be made. G was awarded £3,500 for injury to feelings

- **Hudson v Home Office and anor** ET Case No.2301061/09: H began working as an immigration officer in 1993. He had a heart condition that affected his mobility and caused him to bruise easily. In May 2004 he was informed that his job was to end as the terminal from where he worked was to close. There were difficulties in securing alternative work due to the need to accommodate his disability. The employer decided that a vacancy in Gatwick would be suitable but H refused, maintaining that the journey was too far. Eventually, the employer insisted that he return to work at an office in Croydon and specified a date on which he was to do so, saying that any reasonable adjustments necessary would be discussed with him then. He maintained his refusal to return and was ultimately dismissed. H's various claims of disability discrimination were mostly rejected, the tribunal finding that he had no intention of ever returning to work and was seeking a termination settlement. However, it found that H had suffered unlawful victimisation – at one stage, the employer had told H that a grievance he had lodged could be regarded as vexatious and/or malicious, which the tribunal took to be a threat made in retaliation for the grievance.

19.41 Detriment 'because of' protected act

To succeed in a claim of victimisation, the claimant must show that he or she was subjected to the detriment *because* he or she did a protected act or *because* the employer believed he or she had done or might do a protected act. Where there has been a detriment and a protected act, but the detrimental treatment was due to another reason, e.g. absenteeism or misconduct, a claim of victimisation will not succeed.

The previous equality enactments required the less favourable treatment to be 'by reason that' the person complaining of victimisation had carried out a protected act (or, in the case of S.55 DDA, 'for a reason' mentioned in the relevant subsection). The change in statutory wording to 'because' under S.27 EqA is unlikely to herald a substantive change to the test of causation. In Amnesty International v Ahmed 2009 ICR 1450, EAT (a race discrimination case), Mr Justice Underhill, then President of the EAT, noted that authorities interpreting the statutory language 'on grounds of' equated that phrase with 'by reason of'. He went on: 'Some of the authorities use a third phrase, asking whether the treatment in question was "because of" the proscribed factor. There can be no objection to this as a synonym for the statutory language.' Thus it seems safe to assume that 'on grounds of', 'by reason that' and 'because of' all mean much the same thing.

The meaning of 'because of' is discussed in detail in the context of direct **19.42** discrimination in Chapter 15, 'Direct discrimination', under '"Because of" protected characteristic', and there is no reason to assume that the same principles will not apply to claims of victimisation. The essential question in determining the reason for the claimant's treatment is always the same: what consciously or subconsciously motivated the employer to subject the claimant to the detriment? In the majority of cases, this will require an inquiry into the mental processes of the employer. If the necessary link between the detriment suffered and the protected act can be established, the claim of victimisation will succeed.

It is not always easy to determine whether detriment was meted out 'because of' a protected act. In Chief Constable of West Yorkshire Police v Khan 2001 ICR 1065, HL, the Chief Constable maintained that he had refused to give a reference to the police force to which K had applied for a post because he did not want to prejudice his position in K's pending race discrimination claim against West Yorkshire Police. The Court of Appeal held that the refusal was by reason of the fact that K had brought proceedings in the sense that, had K not brought the proceedings, he would have been provided with a reference. However, the House of Lords rejected this 'but for' approach to victimisation. While it was true that the reference was withheld by reason that K had brought the race discrimination claim in the strict causative sense, Lord Scott said that the language used in S.2(1) RRA was not the language of strict causation. Rather, it required the tribunal to identify 'the *real reason*, the core reason, the *causa causans*, the motive' (our emphasis) for the treatment complained of. Lord Scott concluded that the real reason for the refusal to provide the reference was that the provision of a reference might compromise the Chief Constable's handling of the case being brought against the West Yorkshire Police, which was a legitimate reason for refusing to accede to the request. Their Lordships were unanimous in their conclusion that K had not been refused a reference because he had done a protected act: employers who act 'honestly and reasonably' ought to be able to take steps to preserve their position in pending discrimination proceedings without laying themselves open to a charge of victimisation.

In Derbyshire and ors v St Helens Metropolitan Borough Council and ors **19.43** 2007 ICR 841, HL, the House of Lords revisited the correct interpretation of the phrase 'by reason that' for the purposes of a victimisation claim under S.4(1) SDA. The case also concerned allegations of victimisation that had arisen in the context of ongoing legal proceedings against the employer. Some 500 school catering staff had brought equal pay claims against the Council, most of which were settled. However, D and 38 of her colleagues did not accept the settlement terms and continued with their claims. Two months before the hearing of those claims, the Council wrote to the 39 claimants stating that it could not afford any immediate increase in pay. The Council also sent letters to all catering staff, warning of dire consequences, including potential redundancies and the withdrawal of school meal provision, if the claims were successful. D and her co-claimants argued that these actions amounted to victimisation contrary to the SDA.

A tribunal upheld the victimisation claims, finding that the letter sent to all staff was effectively a threat that the claimants might deprive their colleagues of their jobs. This was a detriment amounting to less favourable treatment, as the staff who had settled their claims were not affected by the letters in the same way as the claimants, who were made to feel distressed and under pressure to abandon their claims through fear of reproach from their colleagues. The EAT dismissed the Council's appeal against that decision, but the Council's further appeal was allowed by the Court of Appeal, which held, by a majority, that the letter was an 'honest and reasonable attempt' (within the meaning of Khan) to preserve the Council's position.

19.44 The employees appealed to the House of Lords, which unanimously allowed the appeal. Lord Hope noted that while the test adopted by their Lordships in Khan of whether the employer's conduct was 'honest and reasonable' could be 'a convenient way of determining whether the statutory test is satisfied', it was no substitute for the statutory test then contained in S.4(1) SDA – whether the employer's conduct was 'by reason that' the employee was insisting on her equal pay claim. Lord Neuberger of Abbotsbury, who gave the leading judgment, observed that a difficulty with the Lords' reasoning in Khan is that it suggested that whether or not a particular act can be said to amount to victimisation must be judged from the point of view of the alleged *discriminator*. According to his Lordship, it was true that the words 'by reason that' required consideration of why the employer had performed the particular act (in this case, the sending of the two letters), and to that extent it was necessary to assess the alleged act of victimisation from the employer's point of view. However, Lord Neuberger suggested that a more satisfactory approach involved focusing on the concept of 'detriment' – the basis upon which discrimination in St Helens was claimed – rather than on the words 'by reason that'. If, in the course of equal pay proceedings, the employer's solicitor were to write to the employee's solicitor setting out, in appropriately measured and accurate terms, the financial or employment consequences of the claim succeeding, or the risks to the employee if the claim fails, or terms of settlement which are unattractive to the employee, any distress thereby induced in the employee could not possibly be said to constitute 'detriment' under the test formulated by Lord Justice Brightman in Ministry of Defence v Jeremiah 1980 ICR 13, CA (and subsequently approved by the House of Lords in Shamoon v Chief Constable of the Royal Ulster Constabulary 2003 ICR 337, HL – see 'What amounts to "detriment"?' above). An alleged victim cannot establish 'detriment' merely by exhibiting mental distress: before he or she could succeed, it would have to be objectively reasonable in all the circumstances. Distress and worry induced by the employer's honest and reasonable conduct in the course of its defence or in the conduct of any settlement negotiations cannot (save in the most unusual circumstances) constitute 'detriment' for the purposes of the SDA (or, by analogy, the EqA).

In support of his argument for adopting the detriment test, Lord Neuberger pointed to Coote v Granada Hospitality Ltd 1999 ICR 100, ECJ – not cited in Khan – where the European Court of Justice focused on the effect of the relevant act on the alleged victim, rather than on the purpose of the alleged discriminator in carrying out the act. If Coote had been before the Lords in Khan, they might, in Lord Neuberger's opinion, have adopted a different juridical basis for their conclusion. Nevertheless, Lord Neuberger considered that his preferred approach would in practice produce the same result to that achieved following the reasoning adopted in Khan. It was hard to imagine circumstances where an 'honest and reasonable' action by an employer, in the context of an employee's equal pay claim, could lead to 'detriment' to the employee.

On the facts, their Lordships concluded, the tribunal had made no error of law **19.45** as it had correctly considered whether the two letters had given rise to detriment. The Council went further than was reasonable to protect its interests in the litigation and the reason for its doing so was that the claimants had brought the equal pay claims and were pursuing them. On the meaning of the words 'by reason that' a person has 'brought proceedings' in S.4(1)(a) SDA, Baroness Hale held that the tribunal had correctly pointed out that the reason for the adverse treatment could be the continuation as well as the commencement of proceedings. It would make no sense to prevent an employer from treating an employee badly because he or she had brought proceedings but not to prevent him from treating the employee badly if he or she refused to abandon them.

It is worth noting here that there were important differences between the facts in the Khan case and those in the St Helens case which may go some way to explaining the different outcomes. In both cases, the claimants' bringing of proceedings was the context (to put it neutrally) for the employer's actions. However, the degree to which those actions were linked to the proceedings was different. The bringing (and the continuance) of equal pay proceedings in St Helens was unarguably the motive for the Council's letters to the claimants – the tribunal found that the claimants' equal pay case 'was not simply the setting for the detriment: its continuance was the efficient cause'. The Council wanted to stop the equal pay claims, and so the claims were the core reason for the Council's actions. By contrast, the employer in Khan refused to do something (provide a reference) for fear of prejudicing its position in litigation. Had there been a finding in Khan that the employer had refused to provide the reference in order to persuade the claimant to give up his claim, the result would undoubtedly have been different. Both cases are discussed further under 'Conduct during legal proceedings' below.

613

19.46 An inquiry into the reason for the claimant's treatment also threw up interesting issues in Martin v Devonshires Solicitors 2011 ICR 352, EAT. There, M, who was employed as a legal secretary by DS, alleged that one of the firm's partners had said that she was 'after the partner's money' (sic) and another had called her a prostitute. Her grievance was investigated and dismissed. DS then started disciplinary proceedings against M for making false allegations. M lodged more grievances, followed by a tribunal claim based on the allegations against the two partners.

Meanwhile, a consultant psychiatrist expressed the opinion that M suffered from a recurrent depressive illness, with psychotic episodes during which she experienced paranoid delusions, and that she was at risk of spontaneous relapse. DS dropped the disciplinary procedure on the basis that M's allegations appeared to be the result of mental ill health. However, it subsequently dismissed her on the basis of a breakdown in the relationship of trust and confidence between them. M insisted that her allegations against the partners were true, and brought a further tribunal claim alleging, among other things, victimisation. In the meantime, the tribunal rejected her first claim, finding that the incidents allegedly involving the partners never took place. The tribunal hearing her second claim also dismissed the case. M appealed against the tribunal's finding in relation to her victimisation claim only.

19.47 The crucial issue before the EAT was the reason for M's treatment – i.e. what motivated the employer to act as it did. If the reason DS dismissed M was, wholly or in substantial part, because she had done a protected act, then it was liable for victimisation. If that was not the reason, DS was not liable. That said, the EAT took the view that there could in principle be cases where an employer has dismissed an employee (or subjected him or her to some other detriment) in *response* to the doing of a protected act, but where the employer could say that the *reason* for the dismissal was not the complaint as such but some feature of it which could properly be treated as *separable* – such as the manner in which the complaint was made. The EAT recognised that such a line of argument was capable of abuse, but this did not mean it was wrong in principle.

Returning to the facts of the case, the EAT noted that the tribunal had not found that the reason for M's dismissal was the manner in which her complaints were presented (except in so far as DS referred to the fact that some of her grievances were repeated). Instead, it identified as the reason a combination of inter-related features: the falseness of the allegations; the fact that M was unable to accept that they were false; the fact that both those features were the result of mental illness; and the risk of further disruptive and unmanageable conduct as a result of that illness. The EAT considered that this series of features, or consequences, of the complaint was properly and genuinely separable from the making of the complaint itself. The falseness of the complaint was the result of mental illness and the reason for M's dismissal was the perceived risk of future disruptive behaviour on account of that illness. The appeal was accordingly dismissed. (Note that cases where the manner of the employee's conduct accounted for the employer's treatment of him or her are discussed under 'Manner of carrying out protected act' below.)

The cases discussed above illustrate some of the more complex issues that can **19.48** arise when determining the reason for the claimant's treatment. Many cases, however, do not require such level of analysis as there will be little or no doubt as to the genuine reason for the employer's treatment. Some examples:

- **Briscoe v The Organic Pharmacy Ltd** ET Case No.2330124/08: B, a black woman, complained about her manager when he criticised her work volume by remarking, 'what banana boat do you think I came off?' The matter was investigated and the manager was given an oral warning. B was not informed of this and her performance declined. After a number of performance review meetings, she was called to a disciplinary hearing. B believed that she was being victimised and resigned. A tribunal upheld her claims for unlawful racial harassment and victimisation. It found that the first performance review was a reasonable response given B's decline in performance. However, the disciplinary proceedings were commenced within two-and-a-half days of a performance review meeting and the tribunal concluded that this was an act of victimisation. B was awarded £4,000 for injury to feelings

- **Marshall v Veolia ES (UK) Ltd** ET Case No.2801214/09: on 23 September 2008 M and her manager had an argument. She gave evidence that he had launched into a tirade of abuse, including sexist language. She was signed off work suffering from stress and depression and did not return. She lodged a grievance, as a result of which her manager was given a written warning. M said she could no longer work with the manager, since she feared a repetition of the incident. On 12 December she was informed that she was at risk of redundancy. M was scored lowest of the people in the pool, and she was dismissed. However, a tribunal found that M's selection for redundancy was an act of unlawful victimisation. M had done a protected act by complaining about her line manager and he was substantially involved in the redundancy process. She established a prima facie case that the decision to put her in a pool with two administrators even though she was a sales coordinator (and thus did not have the same skills) could have been made by reason of her protected act and her employer failed to prove the contrary

- **Stirrup v Obahor t/a Summers Dry Cleaners** IT Case No.593/10: S had brought an age discrimination claim over SDC's decision to reduce her hours, but had remained in its employment. Subsequently, she was suspended on full pay as a result of two incidents: one involving the loss of a customer's jacket, and the other concerning an insurance receipt. SDC invited her to a disciplinary hearing, but she responded explaining that she was suffering from work-related stress and would not be able to attend a hearing in the

615

workplace. The employer dismissed her for gross misconduct and rejected her appeal. An industrial tribunal (the case took place in Northern Ireland) considered that the grounds for dismissal were 'flimsy to say the least' and found the dismissal to be unfair. On the question of victimisation, the tribunal was satisfied that S had done a protected act (she had brought a claim of age discrimination) and that she had been subjected to less favourable treatment (a colleague who lost a customer's jacket was neither suspended nor dismissed). On the question of whether that treatment was meted out because of the protected act, the tribunal considered the timeline of events to be 'instructive': S had been suspended on 8 April 2010 while her age discrimination claim was to be heard on 19 April. Adding that to its finding that the allegations against S were ill-founded and the conduct and outcome of the disciplinary process were flawed, the tribunal concluded that the core reason for S's dismissal was the fact that she brought the discrimination claim against SDC

- **Diawara v Cook t/a Paul Cook Distribution, Catering and anor** ET Case No.1402843/10: following her dismissal, D's solicitor wrote to C, setting out her discrimination complaints against him. Shortly afterwards, C reported D to the police for fraud. The police questioned her for two hours at the police station in the presence of a solicitor. After two weeks, she was informed that no charges would be brought against her. The tribunal upheld her claims of discrimination and victimisation. It found that C had involved the police in retaliation for receiving D's solicitor's letter. The experience left D very shaken and she was awarded £4,000 for injury to feelings

- **McNicoll v Welsh Estates Ltd and ors** ET Case No.1602637/10: M applied for the position of manager at a Welsh country house hotel and was interviewed by B, the hotel's owner. M's application was unsuccessful: B believed that the hotel's older clientele would not take well to a younger manager (M was 29 at the time). However, B intimated that he might have a job for M at a pub in Cardiff. Following the rejection, M sent B a statutory questionnaire and B withdrew the potential job offer. M then submitted a tribunal claim for age discrimination and B e-mailed him, saying: 'I will make sure that you never work in this industry again in Wales.' The tribunal upheld M's age discrimination claim and found that the withdrawal of the job offer and the threat amounted to unlawful acts of victimisation contrary to Reg 4(1) of the Employment Equality (Age) Regulations 2006 SI 2006/1031 (now S.27(1) EqA). M was awarded £6,000 for injury to feelings.

19.49 **Significant influence**

It was clear under the pre-EqA discrimination provisions that a person claiming victimisation need not show that less favourable treatment was meted out *solely* by reason of the protected act. As Lord Nicholls indicated in Nagarajan v London Regional Transport 1999 ICR 877, HL (a race discrimination claim), if protected acts have a 'significant influence' on the employer's decision-making, discrimination will be made out. Nagarajan was considered by the Court of Appeal in Igen Ltd (formerly Leeds Careers Guidance) and ors v Wong and other cases 2005 ICR 931, CA, a sex discrimination case. In that case Lord Justice Peter Gibson clarified that for an influence to be 'significant' it does not have to be of great importance. A significant influence is rather 'an influence which is more than trivial. We find it hard to believe that the principle of equal treatment would be breached by the merely trivial.'

This test was applied by the EAT in Villalba v Merrill Lynch and Co Inc and ors 2007 ICR 469, EAT. In that case V, a market executive for ML, a global investment bank, was not performing well and her relationship with her manager was strained. She made a complaint of sex discrimination to the human resources department in November 2002. In January V received a bonus which was lower than she had hoped for. Shortly after this, she was told that it was not sustainable for her to continue in her role and she was offered an alternative position. V's employment was eventually terminated in July 2003. She brought tribunal proceedings claiming, among other things, that she had been victimised because of her discrimination complaint. The tribunal upheld some aspects of her victimisation claim, but found that her complaint was 'only a very small factor, not a significant influence' in the decision to remove her from her role, so this did not amount to an act of victimisation under the SDA. On appeal, the EAT confirmed that the tribunal had applied the correct test, saying 'we recognise that the concept of "significant" can have different shades of meaning, but we do not think that it could be said here that the tribunal thought that any relevant influence had to be important... If in relation to any particular decision a discriminatory influence is not a material influence or factor, then in our view it is trivial.'

19.50 In Garrett v Lidl Ltd EAT 0541/08, however, the tribunal failed to apply the correct test. In that case, G was employed as a store manager by L Ltd. In 2003 G was diagnosed with fibromyalgia syndrome, which causes pain, fatigue and muscle stiffness. In 2007 she lodged grievances alleging harassment from two of her colleagues and failures to make reasonable adjustments. Following a number of risk assessments, L Ltd decided that her disability could be best accommodated at a different store and decided to move her from Woolwich to Welling – G's contract contained a mobility clause and she had previously moved around between stores. G, however, wanted to stay at Woolwich and asked for adjustments to be made at that store. The move went ahead and she presented various claims of disability discrimination before an employment tribunal. In addition, she argued that requiring her to move to the Welling store against her express wishes – a decision, she alleged, that had been taken because she had lodged the grievances – amounted to unlawful victimisation. The tribunal dismissed her disability discrimination claims, finding that it was reasonable for L Ltd to take the view that her disability could be better

617

accommodated at the other store. Moreover, it was entitled to move her to Welling under the provisions of the mobility clause. As her discrimination claim failed, the tribunal concluded that the victimisation claim also had to fail.

On appeal, the EAT upheld the tribunal's decision that the reasonable adjustments to G's working conditions were best achieved at the Welling store. However, it held that the tribunal's decision on victimisation could not stand. To begin with, it had not been appropriate for the tribunal to dismiss the victimisation claim simply because it had rejected the discrimination claims. As far as discrimination was concerned, the move to Welling was the result of a failure to make reasonable adjustments at Woolwich. As far as victimisation was concerned, however, the move to Welling was said to have been caused, certainly in part, by the bad feeling engendered at Woolwich following the lodging of G's grievances. The EAT continued that, even if the main reason for the move was, as the tribunal had found, the legitimate business and operational reason – i.e. the implementation of a reasonable adjustment – the tribunal failed to apply the correct test for victimisation and determine whether the lodging of the grievances (that is, the protected act) had had a significant influence on the decision to move G to the Welling store. The issue was remitted to the tribunal for reconsideration.

19.51 These decisions are capable of applying equally to S.27(1) – the requirement that the detriment be 'because of' the protected act would seem to allow for multiple causes. This view is supported by the EHRC Employment Code, which notes at para 9.10 that the protected act need not be the only reason for detrimental treatment for victimisation to be established.

19.52 Length of time between protected act and detriment

A considerable length of time may elapse between the protected act being done and the detriment being suffered. In Chambers v Abbey National plc ET Case No.2200567/98, for example, C presented claims of unfair dismissal and sex discrimination in October 1994 (the protected act). However, it was not until August 1997 that her ex-employer gave her a bad reference (the less favourable treatment). This was nevertheless held to be treatment on the ground of her protected act.

The EHRC Employment Code confirms at para 9.12 that there is no time limit within which victimisation must occur after a person has done a protected act. A victimisation claim may still be successful years after the protected act, provided the person complaining is able to show a link between the detriment suffered now and the protected act from years gone by. As a general rule, however, the longer the period between the protected act and the detriment, the harder it is likely to be to show a nexus between the two, particularly where the employment relationship is ongoing.

Subconscious motivation

For many years the rule was that not only must there be a causal link between the protected act and the unfavourable treatment (now detriment), but it must also be shown that the discriminator acted from a motive which was consciously connected with the discrimination legislation – see Aziz v Trinity Street Taxis Ltd and ors 1988 ICR 534, CA. This was in direct contrast to the test in direct discrimination claims, where conscious motivation is not required. However, the need for conscious motivation as a prerequisite for a finding of victimisation was rejected by the House of Lords in Nagarajan v London Regional Transport 1999 ICR 877, HL. It is not necessary, therefore, for a tribunal to distinguish between 'conscious' and 'subconscious' motivation when determining whether a complainant has been victimised. The House of Lords ruled that victimisation may be 'by reason of' an earlier protected act if the discriminator subconsciously permitted that act to determine or influence his or her treatment of the complainant.

Their Lordships held that in this respect there is no reason why a victimisation complaint under S.2 RRA (now S.27 EqA) should be approached any differently than a direct discrimination complaint under S.1 RRA (now S.13 EqA). The key question is the same, namely: why did the complainant receive less favourable treatment? If the answer is that the discriminator treated the complainant less favourably by reason of his or her having done one of the protected acts, then the complaint of victimisation will be made out. This will be so even if the discriminator did not consciously realise that he or she was prejudiced against the complainant because the latter had done a protected act. 'Racial discrimination,' in the words of Lord Nicholls, 'is not negatived by the discriminator's motive or intention or reason or purpose'.

This means that an employer can be liable for discrimination or victimisation **19.54** even if its motives for the detrimental treatment are benign. As Lord Nicholls put it: 'Although victimisation has a ring of conscious targeting, this is an insufficient basis for excluding cases of unrecognised prejudice... Such an exclusion would partially undermine the protection S.2 [RRA] seeks to give.'

An example of subconscious motivation:

- **RS v GC** ET Case No.1402735/99: R worked for a police force. She made a complaint against her manager, M, alleging bullying and sexual harassment. The eventual outcome of the ensuing investigation was that M was allowed to retire. R received little support from her employer, was transferred to menial work, and was eventually dismissed. The tribunal concluded that she had been unlawfully victimised. There was no conscious victimisation, but because of her complaint she was treated as a vulnerable woman who was unable to withstand the rough and tumble of police life. Her employer concluded at an early stage that she could not be restored to her original post and 'she was ushered onto a path which led inexorably to her dismissal'.

19.55 That said, a discriminator cannot be even subconsciously influenced by a protected act of which he or she was not, directly or indirectly, aware. In Chief Constable of Cumbria v McGlennon 2002 ICR 1156, EAT, M claimed that he had been victimised for submitting a sex discrimination questionnaire. The EAT criticised the tribunal's decision for failing to properly address the question of whether M's superiors had been aware of the fact that M had submitted the questionnaire or, if they had not been so aware, whether their decision had been induced in some way by a person who was so aware.

Lack of knowledge of the protected act on the part of the alleged victimiser also proved fatal to the claimant's victimisation complaint in Deer v Walford and anor EAT 0283/10. There, D submitted that her former supervisor on a doctoral course, W, refused to give her a reference because she had previously brought a sex discrimination claim against the university. The tribunal rejected this submission, finding that W had limited knowledge of her earlier claim – he was only aware that she had 'some sort of legal case with someone or something linked to the university, and that it was linked to football'. In the tribunal's view, this was insufficient to establish a case of victimisation based on her earlier sex discrimination claim. The EAT upheld the decision, holding that the reason for W's refusal to give D a reference was not her earlier complaint but his view that her application for the post was 'hopeless'.

19.56 In South London Healthcare NHS Trust v Al-Rubeyi EAT 0269/09 A-R, a consultant paediatrician, raised a grievance alleging race and religious discrimination against a colleague, I. When I discovered that A-R had complained about her, she threatened to resign if A-R, who was on sick leave, was allowed to return to work. An investigation into the grievance, concluded some ten months after it was first raised, recommended that A-R should leave the paediatrics department. A-R left and brought claims of discrimination and victimisation. The tribunal dismissed her discrimination claims but found that, in refusing her a return to work, the Trust had victimised her. The EAT overturned the decision. It held that the tribunal was wrong to pin liability on the Trust solely via I's knowledge that A-R had brought a discrimination claim against her. On the evidence, I had no knowledge of the discrimination allegation until some time after she had made the threat. Nor was there any reason for her to suspect this type of complaint; A-R had made numerous complaints of bullying and harassment over the years, none of which had ever been accompanied by an allegation of discrimination. In any event, in determining whether there is the necessary link between the protected act and the detriment suffered, the statutory focus is on the employer. Thus, if the employer's decision not to allow A-R to return to work was significantly influenced by I's 'tainted reaction' to the grievance, then there would be scope for finding victimisation. However, there was no such evidence in this case – in fact, all the evidence showed that the employer's decision not to allow A-R to return to work was not connected to her grievance.

620

Manner of carrying out protected act 19.57

Employees may lose the protection of the anti-victimisation provisions because of the *manner* in which they carry out the protected act. In In re York Truck Equipment Ltd EAT 109/88, for example, X, a cleaner, alleged that she had been the victim of an attempted rape by one of her employer's tenants. She became dissatisfied at what she perceived as her employer's failure to investigate the incident adequately or to take appropriate measures against the alleged culprit. Eventually her persistence, and the manner in which she pursued her grievance, led to X being dismissed. She claimed sex discrimination because of the failure to act on her allegations and victimisation because of her dismissal in relation to those allegations. Both claims failed. The victimisation claim failed because the EAT upheld the tribunal's conclusion that X's dismissal was not by reason of the allegation which constituted a protected act but was due entirely to the manner in which she had made the allegation.

Similarly, in London Borough of Hackney and anor v Odedra EAT 253/96 O had brought a discrimination claim against the Council but then withdrawn it when the tribunal told her that her case had little prospect of success. The employer thought that this put an end to the matter and when, some time later, O resurrected the same issues, she was told to stop complaining. The tribunal hearing the ensuing victimisation claim found that O had been treated less favourably on account of the earlier proceedings, but the EAT overturned this decision because the tribunal had made no finding as to causation. In particular, it had not considered whether the Council's view that the manner in which O pursued her old complaints was unreasonable and vexatious was correct and whether this, and not the earlier proceedings, was the reason for it not dealing with those complaints. The case was remitted to a different tribunal.

An approach that distinguishes between a protected act and the manner of doing 19.58 that act has recently been endorsed by Mr Justice Underhill, then President of the EAT, in Martin v Devonshires Solicitors 2011 ICR 352, EAT. In his view, there were cases where the reason for the dismissal (or any other detriment) was not the protected act as such but some feature of it which could properly be treated as *separable* – such as the manner in which the protected act was carried out. He recognised that the distinction made is subtle, but maintained that such fine lines have to be drawn 'if the anti-victimisation provisions, important as they are, are to be confined to their proper effect and not to become an instrument of oppression'. Furthermore, he trusted tribunals to distinguish between features which should and should not be treated as properly separable from the protected act. The facts of the case are discussed under 'Detriment "because of" protected act' above.

Two cases where the tribunals were not persuaded that the employees' behaviour in pursuing their claims vitiated their claims of victimisation:

- **Obikwu and Ukwaju v British Refugee Council** ET Case Nos.1502553/06 and another: U, while working out her notice period after being dismissed

621

for redundancy (which amounted to an act of race discrimination), was overheard in an open-plan office talking on the telephone about taking legal action against BRC. She was called to an off-site meeting, told that the redundancy process was confidential, and threatened with disciplinary action if she continued to discuss such matters openly within the office. The tribunal was satisfied that being called to the meeting and questioned amounted to less favourable treatment. The reason for that interrogation was not that U had discussed confidential matters in an open-plan environment, but that she had vocalised her dissatisfaction at the way her dismissal was handled, which in essence was a complaint of race discrimination. Making such an allegation was a protected act and so the tribunal concluded that U had been victimised

- **Jimale and ors v Post Office Ltd** ET Case Nos.1400225–8/08: A was one of a group of four Somali agency workers, all of whom were practising Muslims. A dispute arose over their taking unofficial breaks to pray, following which they walked out and were not engaged by the Post Office for some six weeks. When they returned, A described a manager, H, who had been involved in the dispute, as 'racist about our faith'. The next day another manager, D, resolved the issue of prayer breaks with A. However, he took him to task over describing H as racist, stating that such conduct was unacceptable. A repeated the allegation, following which D informed the employment agency that he no longer required A's services due to the 'confrontational' and aggressive manner in which he had raised his complaint. A and the three other Somali workers all failed in claims of religious discrimination. However, A also claimed victimisation under the RRA. In respect of that claim, the tribunal found that the reason the Post Office determined that it no longer required his services was that he had continued his criticism, and it did not find any evidence of his having done so in an overly confrontational manner. Since the nature of his complaint was that H's actions were racist, A had done a protected act under S.2(1)(c) RRA. Furthermore, the company suspected he would bring a claim, protected by S.2(1)(a). The tribunal therefore upheld the complaint of victimisation.

19.59 The Jimale case can be contrasted with Pasab Ltd t/a Jhoots Pharmacy and anor v Woods EAT 0454/11 where W, a Muslim, was employed by JP Ltd as a trainee pharmacist. She was supervised by P, a Sikh, and worked with a trainee dispenser, S, also a Sikh. After W had complained about P and S speaking Punjabi in the workplace and discussing religious matters, a dispute arose as to her timekeeping and P informed her that she would have to reduce her lunch break to take account of the time she took off during the working day for prayers. W's response was to describe the employer as 'a little Sikh club that only looked after Sikhs'. She was suspended on the ground that she had made a racist comment and, after a disciplinary hearing, she was dismissed. An employment tribunal found that implicit in the 'Sikh club' comment was an allegation that people who were not Sikhs were treated less favourably – i.e. that direct religious discrimination was taking place. The tribunal did not accept the employer's contention that the comment was racist or discriminatory and therefore made in bad faith, since W had not made a generalisation that all Sikhs behave in a given way, but had made a specific allegation based on her own perception and experience as a Muslim working alongside Sikhs. It followed that the comment was a protected act, and since the tribunal was satisfied that disciplinary action and dismissal would not have come about if W had not made the comment, her dismissal amounted to victimisation. This decision was overturned by the EAT on appeal. It held that even if the remark were capable of amounting to a protected act, if it were viewed not as a protected act but as an offensive racist comment by the employer, then the reason for dismissal was not that W had done a protected act, but some other feature genuinely separable from the implicit complaint of discrimination.

Conduct during legal proceedings 19.60

Particular problems can arise with regard to establishing the reason for treatment where legal proceedings are ongoing. The courts have recognised that an employer may need to protect its position in legal proceedings and may legitimately seek to settle extant claims. In Chief Constable of West Yorkshire Police v Khan 2001 ICR 1065, HL, the Chief Constable of West Yorkshire Police maintained that he had refused to supply a reference to the police force to which K had applied for a post because he did not want to prejudice his position in K's pending race discrimination claim against him. The House of Lords accepted this argument. Lord Hoffmann observed that employers who act 'honestly and reasonably' ought to be able to take steps to preserve their position in pending discrimination proceedings without laying themselves open to a charge of victimisation. Their Lordships characterised the Chief Constable's refusal of a reference as a reasonable act done to protect his position in litigation, rather than retaliation for K having brought the proceedings in the first place, and decided that this was the real reason for the refusal. Accordingly, K had not been victimised because he had done a protected act.

Unfortunately, this approach is not without difficulties. For example, the House of Lords seemed to be advocating a test of reasonableness to decide whether or not there has been victimisation, whereas no such test exists (or existed) in the legislation. Furthermore, employees could find themselves in a situation where they were unable to obtain a reference until outstanding proceedings were concluded, making it potentially very difficult to obtain another job.

The approach in Khan was reconsidered by the House of Lords in the context **19.61** of equal pay claims in Derbyshire and ors v St Helens Metropolitan Borough Council and ors 2007 ICR 841, HL. In that case, some 500 school catering staff brought equal pay claims against the Council, most of which were settled. However, D and 38 of her colleagues did not accept the settlement terms and

623

continued with their claims. Two months before the hearing of those claims, the Council wrote to the 39 claimants stating that it could not afford any immediate increase in pay. The Council also sent letters to all catering staff, warning of dire consequences, including potential redundancies and the withdrawal of school meal provision, if the claims were successful. D and her co-claimants argued that these actions amounted to victimisation contrary to the SDA.

A tribunal upheld their claims and the EAT dismissed the Council's appeal. However, the majority of the Court of Appeal (Lord Justice Mummery dissenting) held that, although the Council's motive in sending the letters was to persuade the claimants to settle their claims, it did not follow that the Council had discriminated against them. The crucial question was whether the employer's conduct had been part of an honest and reasonable attempt to compromise the proceedings. The appeal was allowed and the case remitted to the tribunal for determination of that question. The employees appealed to the House of Lords.

19.62 The House of Lords approached the issue on the basis of whether the employer's actions were likely to jeopardise the claimants' right to pursue their claims, not on the basis of whether the letters were honest and reasonable efforts by the employer to protect its position. In Lord Hope's opinion, an employer ought to avoid doing anything that might make a reasonable employee feel that he or she is being unduly pressured to concede his or her claim. So, the focus ought to be on the detriment caused to the claimant by the employer's actions, rather than on the employer's purpose in so acting. In this case, the Council had gone further than was reasonable to protect its interests in the existing legislation. The tribunal had therefore come to the correct conclusion on the facts of the case.

On the face of it, the House of Lords' decision in St Helens allows employers considerably less scope than Khan for defending discrimination claims without risking allegations of victimisation. That said, the two cases are capable of being reconciled. In Khan, the employer's actions genuinely arose out of a desire to protect itself in litigation. In St Helens, by contrast, the Council did not merely seek to avoid prejudicing its position in the litigation – it wanted the claimants to abandon their claims. Furthermore, while the House of Lords in St Helens was critical of certain aspects of their Lordships' reasoning in Khan, it stressed that it was in agreement with its overall conclusion in the case. In fact, Lord Neuberger suggested that, even if the approach he advocated had been adopted in Khan, the result would have been the same.

19.63 Following the St Helens case, 'honest and reasonable' attempts by an employer to protect its position in litigation are not *automatically* protected from a charge of victimisation, but employers still retain some room for manoeuvre in this regard. In British Medical Association v Chaudhary 2007 IRLR 800, CA, the Court of Appeal held that the BMA did not victimise C when it refused to reconsider its decision not to offer him support in his complaint of race discrimination against the Royal College of Surgeons. C had warned the BMA that its refusal to assist him could also be viewed as race discrimination, and he asserted that the BMA's refusal to reconsider its earlier decision was a response to that allegation. However, the Court noted that, when deciding not to reconsider the decision not to offer support, the BMA was in the position of a potential respondent to a discrimination claim by C. That claim would have been out of time (the original refusal having taken place eight months previously), and the only way to give rise to a fresh claim would have been for the BMA to reconsider and once more to refuse. In those circumstances, by refusing to reconsider, the BMA was seeking to protect its position in respect of potential litigation, which was a legitimate response. The Court of Appeal acknowledged that the House of Lords in Derbyshire and ors v St Helens Metropolitan Borough Council and ors (above) had criticised the basis on which Chief Constable of West Yorkshire Police v Khan (above) had been decided. However, according to Lord Justice Mummery, giving the judgment of all the members of the Court, St Helens 'reaffirmed the essential statement of law that a person does not discriminate if he takes the impugned decision in order to protect himself in litigation'. (It is worth noting that Mummery LJ's dissenting judgment in the Court of Appeal in St Helens was expressly approved by the House of Lords in that case, so his opinion in Chaudhary carries substantial weight.)

Accordingly, employers are still entitled to take reasonable steps to defend themselves in litigation, but they must give thought to the effect of their actions on the employee concerned. If those actions, from the employee's point of view, could be regarded as undue pressure to give up his or her claim, then, on the basis of the analysis in the St Helens case, they may be viewed as amounting to detrimental treatment of the employee 'because' he or she brought a claim, and therefore potentially amount to victimisation.

Some examples: **19.64**

- **Commissioners of Inland Revenue and anor v Morgan** 2002 IRLR 776, EAT: the Appeal Tribunal upheld a tribunal's decision that the employer had victimised M when a memorandum had been circulated to M's colleagues, informing them that M had brought a race discrimination claim and warning them that some of their personal details might be revealed as a result of the disclosure process. This had an adverse effect on the attitude of M's colleagues towards her. The EAT considered that the sending of the memorandum was not a reasonable step taken to protect the employer's position. The circulation of the memorandum did not materially advance the employer's position in the proceedings and the employer's interests would not have been harmed had it not been done. It might have been different if the memorandum had simply been asking for witnesses to come forward, for example. The tribunal had not erred in concluding that the

625

memorandum had been sent 'by reason that' M had brought a race claim, within the language of the RRA. (Although this case was decided before St Helens, its rationale seems to accord with the current understanding of victimisation in the context of litigation)

- **Bayode v Chief Constable of Derbyshire** EAT 0499/07: the Appeal Tribunal held that B, who had previously brought a race discrimination claim against his employer, was not victimised when his colleagues recorded incidents involving B in their notebooks as part of the employer's attempt to protect itself against any further claims by him. (This case is discussed further under 'What amounts to "detriment"?' above)

- **Aziz v First Division Association** ET Case No.2330314/10: a tribunal struck out a claim of victimisation based on FDA's response to A's claim of race discrimination against it for failing to support her in litigation against her employer. FDA had denied A's claim by letter and had gone on to state that if A did not withdraw her claim, it reserved the right to seek costs against her. The tribunal found that the letter was written in a measured tone and was not intimidatory in any way – there was nothing improper in warning A that a costs application would be made if her claim failed.

19.65 Judicial proceedings immunity. A discussion of this area of the law would not be complete without mentioning, at least briefly, the principle of judicial proceedings immunity and its application to victimisation claims. Under the common law principle of judicial proceedings immunity, a witness enjoys absolute immunity from any action brought on the ground that his or her evidence is false, malicious or careless. In Heath v Commissioner of Police of the Metropolis 2005 ICR 329, CA, the Court of Appeal confirmed that judicial proceedings immunity applies to discrimination claims in the employment tribunal.

The principle of judicial proceedings immunity extends not only to the witness's actual evidence in the witness box but also to the preparation of witness statements, even if the trial never takes place – Darker v Chief Constable of West Midlands Police 2001 1 AC 435, HL. This is designed to protect people from being sued for statements made in evidence in judicial proceedings. In Parmer v East Leicester Medical Practice 2011 IRLR 641, EAT, the Appeal Tribunal considered a victimisation claim based on the content of witness statements served on the claimant by a respondent in an earlier failed race discrimination claim: the claimant argued that the statements contained untruths, and that the reason for that was that he had done a protected act (i.e. brought the discrimination claim). The tribunal found that the witness statements attracted judicial proceedings immunity and dismissed the victimisation claim. The EAT upheld the decision. Mr Justice Underhill, then President of the EAT, held that it was in the public interest that the immunity not only applied to claims of primary discrimination but also to claims of victimisation. Were it otherwise, it would be 'all too easy' for a claimant whose primary discrimination claim had failed to resurrect the allegations by way of 'collateral proceedings', complaining that the evidence given for the respondent constituted discrimination or victimisation. Accordingly, the witness statements at issue were subject to judicial proceedings immunity.

In South London and Maudsley NHS Trust v Dathi 2008 IRLR 350, EAT, the **19.66** Appeal Tribunal further held that letters from the respondent's advisers to the claimant's advisers written in the context of ongoing legal proceedings – one refusing disclosure of certain documents and another resisting a costs application – enjoyed absolute immunity from legal proceedings. However, the EAT went on to note that the policy of absolute immunity does not mean that a person who is discriminated against during the course of proceedings is left without a remedy. For example, the conduct of a party to proceedings is relevant to the issue of costs, which may be awarded for unreasonable conduct of those proceedings. Furthermore, an employment tribunal may make an award of injury to feelings and may increase it by an award of aggravated damages.

Proving victimisation   19.67

Victimisation claims under the EqA are subject to the 'shifting burden of proof', which is set out in S.136 of the Act. This section provides that the initial burden is on the claimant to prove facts from which the tribunal could decide, in the absence of any other explanation, that the respondent has contravened a provision of the Act (a 'prima facie case'). The burden then passes or 'shifts' to the respondent to prove that discrimination did not occur. If the respondent is unable to do so, the tribunal is *obliged* to uphold the discrimination claim.

The shifting burden of proof is designed to help claimants get the claim off the ground, since discrimination is notoriously hard to prove. However, the claimant is still required to show some prima facie evidence before there will be a case for the respondent to answer and tribunals will be alert to weed out baseless claims. For example, in Hill v Arriva Southern Counties Ltd ET Case No.1101308/10 the employer had referred to H's complaints of discrimination in the letter it sent dismissing her for gross misconduct. It noted, 'you are not a victim of harassment, victimisation or discrimination as you claim and these accusations are raised by you whenever the management team have a need to speak to you over work-related issues'. The tribunal concluded that this did not indicate victimisation. H had genuinely been dismissed for her unreasonable refusal to comply with management instructions. The reference to her allegations of discrimination arose only because H raised them orally and in writing before and during the disciplinary hearing.

One of the essential elements of the prima facie case that a claimant must make **19.68** out is that the employer actually knew about the protected act on which the

627

claimant bases his or her claim. In Scott v London Borough of Hillingdon 2001 EWCA Civ 2005, CA, the Court of Appeal upheld the EAT's decision that an unsuccessful job applicant had not been victimised for bringing a race discrimination complaint against a former employer. The Court ruled that knowledge of a protected act is a precondition of a finding of victimisation and that, as there was no positive evidence that the respondent knew of the claimant's previous complaint, there had been no proper basis for the tribunal to infer that the claimant had been victimised.

Section 136 is discussed in detail in Chapter 32, 'Burden of proof', and Chapter 33, 'Proving discrimination'.

20 Discrimination arising from disability

On coming into force on 1 October 2010, the Equality Act 2010 (EqA) **20.1** introduced an entirely new form of disability discrimination protection – protection against 'discrimination arising from disability'. This replaced the protection against 'disability-related' discrimination previously contained in S.3A(1) of the Disability Discrimination Act 1995 (DDA). The rationale for this change is outlined under 'Previous protection under the DDA' below. Suffice it to say here that, as a result of unexpected case law developments, the scope of the protection afforded by S.3A(1) DDA became so restricted as to render the provision virtually useless. The Equality Bill presented the then Labour Government with the opportunity to do something about this and, contrary to its original intention of simply reversing the restrictive case law and reinstating the *status quo ante*, it chose to not only extend the scope of indirect discrimination to cover disability but also to enact an entirely new ground of protection, one that made it unlawful to unjustifiably discriminate for a reason arising from disability. For all the superficial similarity in wording between 'disability-related discrimination' and 'discrimination arising from disability', there are crucial differences of substance between the old and new provisions. The new form of protection – set out in S.15 EqA – now sits alongside and complements the other key protections accorded to disabled persons (namely, protection from direct and indirect discrimination, harassment and victimisation; and the duty on employers to make reasonable adjustments).

Each of the elements that make up the right under S.15 EqA are discussed in detail under 'Elements of S.15 claim' below. In essence, the section provides that it will be unlawful for an employer or other person to treat a disabled person unfavourably not because of that person's disability itself (which would amount to direct discrimination within the terms of S.13 EqA) but because of something arising from, or in consequence of, the person's disability. So, for example, a worker who is treated unfavourably as a result of having to take a period of disability-related absence would have a claim under S.15 unless the employer can justify the unfavourable treatment on the basis that it is a proportionate means of achieving a legitimate aim. However, in order to be

629

liable, the employer must know or be reasonably expected to know that the disabled person has a disability. Thus, knowledge (or constructive knowledge) of the claimant's disability is crucial, and without it a discrimination claim under S.15 is bound to fail.

20.2 Previous protection under the DDA

In addition to providing protection from less favourable treatment on the ground of a person's disability (i.e. direct discrimination) under S.3A(5), the DDA also prohibited discrimination for disability-related reasons. S.3A(1) provided that 'a person discriminates against a disabled person if (a) for a reason which relates to the disabled person's disability, he treats him less favourably than he treats or would treat others to whom that reason does not or would not apply, and (b) he cannot show that the treatment in question is justified'.

However, the defence of justification was not available if the alleged discriminator was under a duty to make reasonable adjustments in relation to the disabled claimant and failed to do so, unless it could be shown that the less favourable treatment would have been justified even if the reasonable adjustments duty had been complied with – S.3A(6) DDA.

20.3   Initially, the protection offered by S.3A(1) was construed widely. For many years the leading case was Clark v TDG Ltd t/a Novacold 1999 ICR 951, CA, where the Court of Appeal held that, for the purpose of making the necessary comparison, there was no requirement that the 'others' mentioned in S.3A(1) be in the same, or not materially different, circumstances as those that apply to the complainant. It held that an employee who complained that he or she had been dismissed for absence resulting from a disability, making him or her unable to fulfil the requirements of his or her job, should be compared with someone who was not absent at all and therefore able to fulfil the requirements of his or her job. The Court rejected the argument that the comparison should be with someone who was also absent from work for the same length of time but for a reason other than disability. In effect, the Clark case established that disability-related discrimination as defined by S.3A(1) was directed at a different problem to that of direct disability discrimination under S.3A(5), in that the former afforded a remedy where a disabled person was adversely treated for a reason that was related to his or her disability unless the employer could justify the less favourable treatment. This would be so even if a non-disabled person would have been treated in exactly the same way had the reason for the employer's treatment been applied equally to him or her.

20.4   **The Malcolm decision.** The approach adopted by the Court of Appeal in Clark v TDG Ltd t/a Novacold (above) made it very easy for disabled claimants to clear the first hurdle imposed by S.3A(1). That approach survived for almost ten years until it was overturned by the House of Lords' decision in Mayor and Burgesses of the London Borough of Lewisham v Malcolm 2008 IRLR 700, HL. In Malcolm – a housing case brought under Part III of the DDA but in relation to which the same definitions of discrimination applied – their Lordships held that the appropriate comparator in a case of disability-related discrimination is a non-disabled person who is otherwise in the same circumstances as the disabled claimant. So, whereas under Clark v Novacold an employee dismissed for sickness absence arising from a disability would be compared to a person who had not been absent from work at all, the Malcolm comparator would be a non-disabled person who had also been absent, for a reason other than disability. In the vast majority of cases, there would be no doubt that the Malcolm comparator would have been treated the same as the disabled claimant, and so no less favourable treatment would occur.

After some initial doubt the Court of Appeal confirmed in Stockton on Tees Borough Council v Aylott 2010 ICR 1278, CA, that the narrower Malcolm approach applied in the employment field. Thus it went from being very easy to establish less favourable treatment under S.3A(1) DDA to being almost impossible. Indeed, cases decided after Malcolm, such as Aylott, acknowledged that the comparator for disability-related discrimination and the comparator for direct disability discrimination were the same. As Mr Justice Underhill (then President of the EAT) expressed it in Tameside Hospital NHS Foundation Trust v Mylott EAT 0352/09: 'The effect of Malcolm is to render the scope of S.3A(1) for all practical purposes no wider than that of S.3A(5), since a finding that the employer would have treated more favourably a comparator whose only difference from the claimant was that he was not disabled is necessarily a finding of direct discrimination.'

20.5 Thus, the effect of the Malcolm decision was to drive a coach and horses through the concept of disability-related discrimination as a form of discrimination distinct from direct disability discrimination. As an identical comparator test applied to both, the Malcolm approach more or less reduced disability-related discrimination to a form of justifiable direct discrimination, rendering S.3A(1) virtually moribund.

20.6 **The comparator test, post-Malcolm.** In Eagle Place Services Ltd and ors v Rudd 2010 IRLR 486, EAT, a bold attempt was made by the EAT to salvage something of substance from what was left of S.3A(1). In that case R – who had detached retinas in both eyes – worked as a lawyer for a major firm of solicitors (the client) but was actually employed by the service company of that firm. A number of adjustments were agreed and put in place on a trial basis, including enabling R to work from home two days a week. Everyone (including the client) agreed that the adjustments had proved a success. However, out of the blue, R was called to a meeting and summarily dismissed by the employer's head of Human Resources. In respect of his claims of unfair dismissal and disability discrimination, an employment tribunal found that the reasons given by the employer for dismissal were fallacious and that the real reason was that the client firm was being put at a commercial disadvantage by having to accommodate R's disability. It upheld R's claim of direct discrimination under S.3A(5) DDA on the basis that the appropriate hypothetical comparator – i.e. a lawyer of the same grade and skills as R who needed to work two days a week from home but not because of a disability – would not have suffered the same treatment, i.e. been dismissed. However, the tribunal rejected R's claim of disability-related discrimination on the basis that, as R was clearly able to perform his job to the complete satisfaction of the client once the adjustments were factored in, there was no 'reason which relate[d] to' his disability within the terms of S.3A(1) to explain the less favourable treatment he suffered.

On appeal, the employer sought to argue that the tribunal had erred by, among other things, adopting the wrong comparator when upholding R's claim of direct disability discrimination. R also cross-appealed, contending that the tribunal should have upheld his claim of disability-related discrimination. The EAT (Judge Serota QC presiding) ruled that the form of discrimination suffered by R in this case was probably both direct discrimination and disability-related discrimination, but that it was certainly the latter if a choice had to be made between the two. Upholding the cross-appeal, the EAT noted that the reason for R's dismissal had been found by the employment tribunal to be the wrong-headed opinion of the employer's head of HR that R's disability made him an inconvenient liability that would damage the client firm's commercial objectives. The fact that that view was both wrong and unreasonable did not mean that it was not held and that R's dismissal was for a reason related to his disability. On the contrary, the reason for his unfavourable treatment was clearly related to his disability – namely, the supposed effect of his disability on the client firm's commercial objectives.

20.7 Turning to the employer's appeal regarding the choice of comparator, the EAT observed that the appropriate comparator was likely to be the same in respect of claims of direct discrimination and disability-discrimination. In this case, the tribunal had been correct to construct the hypothetical comparator as being a lawyer at the same grade and with the same skills as the claimant who shared a similarly good relationship with the client and who needed for reasons other than disability to work at home for two days each week. And it had clearly been open to the tribunal to conclude that such a comparator would not have been dismissed. In so concluding, the EAT specifically rejected the employer's contentions (i) that the correct comparator, in view of the decision in Mayor and Burgesses of the London Borough of Lewisham v Malcolm (above), should have been someone who would inhibit or damage the client firm's commercial objectives but not by reason of disability, and (ii) that such a comparator would have been treated in exactly the same way as R. Serota J remarked: 'A decision to dismiss the comparator on those grounds would have been wholly unreasonable. It is simply not open to the respondent to say that it has not discriminated against the claimant because it would have behaved unreasonably in dismissing the comparator. It is unreasonable to suppose that it in fact would have dismissed the comparator for what amounts to an irrational reason. It is one thing to find, as in Bahl v Law Society 2004 IRLR 799, CA, that a named individual has behaved unreasonably to both the claimant and named comparators; it is quite another to find that a corporate entity such as [the client law firm] or its service company would behave unreasonably to a hypothetical comparator when it had no good reason to do so... We do not consider that Malcolm requires us to make an absurd comparison between a ·disabled claimant being treated unreasonably by reason of his being perceived to be a commercial liability and an employee who is not disabled similarly unreasonably believed to be a commercial liability.'

However, despite the EAT's attempt in the Rudd case (above) to breathe some life back into disability-related discrimination as a discrete ground of discrimination from direct discrimination, other cases appeared to establish that the two types of discrimination had, in the light of Mayor and Burgesses of the London Borough of Lewisham v Malcolm (above), become virtually synonymous. In City of Edinburgh Council v Dickson EAT 0038/09, for example, the Appeal Tribunal held that it had not been open to an employment tribunal to find that a claimant had been discriminated against primarily on the basis of direct discrimination, but in the alternative to uphold his claim on the basis of disability-related discrimination. In the EAT's view, the two ways of putting the case stood or fell together. What had to be established in any case of direct discrimination was what was influencing the mind of the decision-taker. In the instant case, there was no reason to suppose that the claimant's disability had influenced the employer's thinking when dismissing him for viewing pornography at work. The tribunal had found that the employer had unreasonably rejected the claimant's explanation that his untreated diabetic condition had contributed to his actions and that the rejection was therefore on the ground of that disability. However, the EAT ruled that the fact that the tribunal rejected an explanation related to the claimant's disability did not mean that the rejection was on the ground of that disability within the meaning of S.3A(5). Regarding the question of disability-related discrimination, the EAT held that it had not been open to the tribunal to find discrimination contrary to S.3A(1) in circumstances where direct disability contrary to S.3A(5) had not been established. As a consequence of the judgment in Malcolm, it was practically impossible for a claim for one to succeed where the other would not.

20.8 The EAT's reasoning in the Dickson case is to all intents and purposes identical to the Court of Appeal's in the subsequent case of JP Morgan Europe Ltd v Chweidan 2011 IRLR 673, CA. In that case the Court held that an employment tribunal had erred in upholding a claim of direct discrimination having rejected one of disability-related discrimination on the same facts. Given that, for both

633

types of claim, the comparator had to be in the same material circumstances as the claimant, a failure to show relevant less favourable treatment under S.3A(1) would make it difficult to show relevant less favourable treatment under S.3A(5). Although neither the EAT nor the Court of Appeal spelled this out in the JP Morgan case, it seemed clear that the reverse was also true, i.e. that a failure to establish relevant less favourable treatment under S.3A(5) would make it difficult to establish relevant less favourable treatment under S.3A(1). For either claim to succeed, the employee was in effect required to show that the disability itself, rather than its effects on his or her ability to fulfil a particular role, was the reason for the employer's treatment. Accordingly, S.3A(1) came to offer no greater protection from disability discrimination than that provided for by S.3A(5).

Although, following the enactment of the EqA in October 2010, disability-related discrimination has now been replaced with a different form of discrimination altogether (discrimination arising from disability), it may be that the EAT's decision in Eagle Place Services Ltd and ors v Rudd (above) will continue to have some influence on the way in which the EqA is interpreted. This proposition relates to the issue of whether, for the purposes of direct discrimination as defined in S.13 EqA, it is open to an employer to run the so-called 'bastard employer defence'; i.e. that a hypothetical comparator would have been treated in exactly the same unreasonable and unfair manner as the complainant. As we have seen, the EAT in Rudd had no truck with this defence, even though it was fully aware of the decision of the Court of Appeal in Bahl v Law Society (above) that unreasonable treatment does not necessarily give rise to an inference of less favourable treatment on unlawful discriminatory grounds. The EAT's assertion that 'it is simply not open to the respondent to say that it has not discriminated against the claimant because it would have behaved unreasonably in dismissing the comparator' provides an important qualification to the Bahl line of reasoning and has a potential impact on the proper approach to establishing direct discrimination that now applies in like manner to all protected characteristics, including disability. This issue is further explored in Chapter 15, 'Direct discrimination', under 'Comparator – no materially different circumstances'.

20.9 **New form of discrimination introduced by the EqA.** Returning to the effect of the House of Lords' decision in Mayor and Burgesses of the London Borough of Lewisham v Malcolm (above), in view of the significant restrictions placed by that case on disability-related discrimination, the Government decided to remedy the situation when enacting the EqA. In its consultation document, 'Improving Protection from Disability Discrimination', issued in November 2008, it proposed to restore the balance by extending protection from indirect discrimination to disability. However, as a consequence of the responses received, the Government reconsidered this proposal and decided to go further by introducing not only indirect disability discrimination, but also an entirely

634

new provision – S.15 – to replace disability-related discrimination. Accordingly, only claims relating to discrimination occurring before 1 October 2010 (the date of the coming into force of the EqA) continue to be governed by the provisions of the DDA, including S.3A(1).

Elements of S.15 claim 20.10

Section 15 EqA is headed 'Discrimination arising from disability'. By virtue of S.15(1), 'a person (A) discriminates against a disabled person (B) if:

- A treats B unfavourably because of something arising in consequence of B's disability, and

- A cannot show that the treatment is a proportionate means of achieving a legitimate aim'.

Section 15(2) goes on to state that '[S.15(1)] does not apply if A shows that A did not know, and could not reasonably have been expected to know, that B had the disability'. In other words, if the employer can establish that it was unaware that the claimant was disabled, it cannot be held liable for discrimination arising from disability.

The most obvious difference between the new protection under S.15 and the 20.11 previous protection against disability-related discrimination under S.3A(1) DDA – see 'Previous protection under the DDA' above – is that S.15(1) does not require the disabled person to show that his or her treatment was less favourable than that experienced by a comparator. The need for a comparator is entirely abandoned – see under 'Unfavourable treatment' below for further analysis of this point – and, as a consequence, the main issue that arose in respect of the application of S.3A(1) DDA – namely, who the comparator should be – is entirely side-stepped.

The Explanatory Notes to the EqA state that S.15 is 'aimed at re-establishing an appropriate balance between enabling a disabled person to make out a case of experiencing a detriment which arises because of his or her disability, and providing an opportunity for an employer or other person to defend the treatment' (para 70). The Notes give the example of an employee with a visual impairment who is dismissed because he cannot do as much work as a non-disabled colleague. This would potentially amount to discrimination arising from a disability, and if the employer sought to justify the dismissal, it would need to show that the dismissal was a proportionate means of achieving a legitimate aim.

It will be clear from the wording of S.15 (see above) that, to succeed with a 20.12 claim of discrimination arising from disability, the claimant must establish the following:

- that he or she has suffered *unfavourable treatment*

635

- that that treatment is *because of something arising in consequence of his or her disability*.

If the claimant establishes the above, the employer will be liable unless it can show:

- that the unfavourable treatment is *a proportionate means of achieving a legitimate aim*, and/or
- that it had no *knowledge* of the claimant's disability.

Each of these elements is examined below.

20.13 Unfavourable treatment
The first element of S.15(1) EqA is that the disabled employee must have been treated 'unfavourably'. This term is not defined in the EqA, although the Equality and Human Rights Commission's Code of Practice on Employment ('the EHRC Employment Code') states that it means that the disabled person 'must have been put at a disadvantage' – para 5.7. If S.15(1) is truly to reflect the position under S.3A(1) DDA that existed prior to the House of Lords' decision in Mayor and Burgesses of the London Borough of Lewisham v Malcolm 2008 IRLR 700, HL (see 'Previous protection under the DDA'), then unfavourable treatment will have to be construed widely in the same way as the concept of 'detriment' has been for other purposes relevant to anti-discrimination protection. For example, in one of the leading cases on disability-related discrimination pre-Malcolm – O'Hanlon v HM Revenue and Customs Commissioners 2007 ICR 1359, CA – the Court of Appeal held that the disabled claimant was less favourably treated by virtue of the way the employer had applied its standard sick pay policy to her. The policy provided for full pay for the first 26 weeks of sickness absence, followed by half pay for a further 26 weeks. Although an employment tribunal initially decided that there was no less favourable treatment when the claimant, who was on long-term sick leave related to her disability, had her pay reduced accordingly, the EAT (with whom the Court of Appeal agreed) overturned that decision. Compared to a non-disabled person who hadn't been on sick leave for a similar period, as S.3A(1) DDA then required, there was clearly less favourable treatment (although the EAT went on to hold that it was justified in the circumstances).

For those same facts to be covered by S.15(1), a tribunal would have to find that the employee had been treated 'unfavourably' by the application of the sick pay policy to her. At first glance, this appears to be a distortion of the natural language of the statute – how can it be unfavourable to carry through the effect of a policy that applies to everyone? The key is that the unfavourable treatment is 'because of something arising in consequence of [the employee's] disability'. So, it is not the application of the general policy to the disabled employee that is unfavourable, but that policy's specific effect on the employee.

636

Analogies with concepts of 'disadvantage' and 'detriment'. As noted above, the 20.14 EHRC Employment Code indicates that unfavourable treatment should be construed synonymously with 'disadvantage'. It states: 'Often, the disadvantage will be obvious and it will be clear that the treatment has been unfavourable; for example, a person may have been refused a job, denied a work opportunity or dismissed from their employment. But sometimes unfavourable treatment may be less obvious. Even if an employer thinks that they are acting in the best interests of a disabled person, they may still treat that person unfavourably' – para 5.7.

The concept of 'disadvantage' is also relevant to indirect discrimination – see Chapter 16, 'Indirect discrimination: proving disadvantage' under 'Particular disadvantage' – and so the same kinds of unfavourable treatment should be capable of founding either type of claim. Applying indirect discrimination principles, unfavourable treatment should not be restricted to refusal of a job, work opportunity or dismissal. Any instance in which the individual reasonably feels that he or she has suffered a detriment should be covered – Shamoon v Chief Constable of the Royal Ulster Constabulary 2003 ICR 337, HL. Furthermore, the fact that a disabled person complies with an employer's instructions does not necessarily mean that he or she does not thereby suffer disadvantage – Eweida v British Airways plc 2009 ICR 303, EAT.

It is clear from the examples given in the EHRC Employment Code that 20.15 unfavourable treatment need not be directed specifically at the disabled person. It may arise in consequence of a policy that applies to everyone – for example, a shift to night working or a team move to an open-plan office. Or it may arise in consequence of the employer's response to conduct that would have met with the same response had the person not been disabled – for example, disciplining an employee who uncharacteristically loses her temper because of severe pain caused by a disability. In this way, S.15 is similar to indirect discrimination, in that it covers treatment that, although not directed specifically at a disabled person, nonetheless has specific adverse effects on him or her. We consider the overlap between the two kinds of claim under 'Overlap with indirect discrimination' below.

No need for comparator. There is no need for a comparator in order to show 20.16 unfavourable treatment under S.15. This contrasts with the position under the DDA where, even pre-Malcolm, a comparator of some kind was necessary to establish that a disabled person has been treated less favourably for a reason related to his or her disability within the meaning of S.3A(1). Such a comparison was implied by the very words 'less favourable' – which raised the question 'less favourable than whom?' And even though, until the House of Lords' decision in Mayor and Burgesses of the London Borough of Lewisham v Malcolm (above), the Courts had interpreted the comparator requirement in the way that was least onerous to disabled claimants, the technical requirement to draw some kind of comparison between the claimant and another person remained.

637

The requirement for a comparator has now been dispensed with completely. It is possible to show 'unfavourable' treatment – just as it is possible in other contexts to show 'disadvantage' or 'detriment' – without needing to resort to a 'compare and contrast' exercise. A claimant bringing a claim of discrimination arising from disability under S.15 EqA is entitled to point to treatment that he or she alleges is unfavourable in its own terms.

Support for the proposition that a comparator is not needed in a S.15 claim can be found in S.23(1), which stipulates that: 'On a comparison of cases for the purposes of section 13, 14, or 19 there must be no material difference between the circumstances relating to each case.' The sections referred to deal with direct, combined and indirect discrimination respectively. Mention of S.15 is conspicuous by its absence. The obvious reason for this is that, since no comparison has to be made for the purposes of that section, there is no need for the legislature to direct the nature of the relevant comparison or comparator.

20.17 The effect of not having to make a comparison with the treatment of someone else is well illustrated by an example given in the EHRC Employment Code where a disabled worker with multiple sclerosis is dismissed on account of having taken three months' sick leave. The Code states: 'In considering whether... [this] amounts to discrimination arising from disability, it is irrelevant whether or not other workers would have been dismissed for having the same or similar length of absence. It is not necessary to compare the treatment of the disabled worker with that of her colleagues or any hypothetical comparator. The decision to dismiss her will be discrimination arising from disability if the employer cannot objectively justify it' – para 5.6.

The only other protected characteristic under the EqA that attracts protection in respect of 'unfavourable treatment' is pregnancy and maternity. Ss.17(2) and 18(2) afford protection in work and non-work contexts to women who are pregnant or on maternity leave in respect of any unfavourable treatment because of pregnancy or pregnancy-related illness, or because they are exercising their right to maternity leave. Prior to the introduction of the EqA, it was well established under both European and domestic law that pregnant women and women on maternity leave were not required to show that they were treated less favourably than a man in order to make out a claim of direct discrimination – see, for example, Webb v EMO Air Cargo (UK) Ltd 1994 ICR 770, ECJ, and Equal Opportunities Commission v Secretary of State for Trade and Industry 2007 ICR 1234, QBD. By recasting protection in terms of 'unfavourable treatment', the EqA makes it clear that this position has not changed and that there is no question of having to compare the treatment of a woman who is pregnant or on maternity leave with that of an actual or hypothetical male comparator in order to establish liability for pregnancy and maternity discrimination under the Act.

'Because of something arising in consequence of... disability' 20.18
For a claim under S.15(1) EqA to succeed, the unfavourable treatment must be shown by the claimant to be 'because of something arising in consequence of [his or her] disability'. In other words, the discriminatory treatment must be as a result of something arising in consequence of the claimant's disability, not the claimant's disability itself. A worker who is treated less favourably because he or she has severe colitis would be discriminated against because of his or her disability. Such treatment would comprise direct discrimination contrary to S.13 EqA (unless it could be shown that a non-disabled comparator in materially similar circumstances would have been treated in the same way). By contrast, a worker who is treated unfavourably because of his or her frequent need to visit the lavatory on account of suffering from colitis would be a person who was so treated 'because of something arising in consequence of [his or her] disability', contrary to S.15(1).

Establishing the reason for the unfavourable treatment. The significance of 20.19
the words 'because of' in S.15(1) should be noted. In earlier drafts of the EHRC Employment Code, examples used suggested that the reason for the unfavourable treatment at issue was entirely irrelevant. But this was erroneous – as was implicitly acknowledged by the EHRC when it dropped those examples from the approved version of the Code.

It is well established that, in the context of direct discrimination, the question of whether a person has been treated less favourably 'on the ground of' (under the antecedent legislation) or 'because of' (under S.13 EqA) a protected characteristic requires a tribunal to ask 'what was the alleged discriminator's reason for the treatment in question?' If the answer to this is not immediately apparent, then the tribunal must inquire into the mental processes – conscious or subconscious – of the alleged discriminator: see R (on the application of E) v Governing Body of JFS and the Admissions Appeal Panel of JFS and ors 2010 IRLR 136, SC. Under S.15(1) unfavourable treatment has to be shown to have been 'because of' something arising in consequence of the claimant's disability. Given the identical wording, it is highly likely that the same 'reason why' enquiry is relevant in this context as well, in which case it will not be sufficient for a claimant simply to establish that as a disabled person he or she has been treated unfavourably. Liability under S.15 will only arise if he or she shows – and the burden of proof is on the claimant – that the unfavourable treatment is 'because of' (i.e. consciously or subconsciously motivated by) something arising in consequence of his or her disability.

Types of 'consequences arising'. The EHRC Employment Code states that the 20.20
consequences of a disability 'include anything which is the result, effect or outcome of a disabled person's disability' – para 5.9. Examples given include the inability to walk unaided or to use certain work equipment and having to follow a restricted diet.

639

A further example from the Code:

> 'A woman is disciplined for losing her temper with a colleague. However, this behaviour was out of character and is a result of severe pain caused by her cancer, of which her employer is unaware. This disciplinary action is unfavourable treatment. The treatment is because of something which arises in consequence of the worker's disability' – para 5.9.

20.21 **Discrimination by association and perception not covered.** It should be noted that, in contrast to direct discrimination, the unfavourable treatment under S.15 has to arise because of a consequence of the disabled person's own disability and not because of disability in general. The alleged discriminator (A) must have treated the complainant (B) 'unfavourably because of something arising in consequence of *B's disability*' (our stress) – S.15(1). The effect of this is to preclude claims being brought in respect of a misperception that the claimant is disabled or because of the claimant's association with another person who is disabled. These avenues of complaint are open to those bringing claims of direct discrimination under S.13 given that the relevant statutory wording simply requires that the less favourable treatment be 'because of a protected characteristic' without stipulating that it has to be the complainant who has the relevant protected characteristic. For further details, see Chapter 15, 'Direct discrimination', under 'Discrimination by association' and 'Discrimination by perception'.

20.22 **Objective justification**

In practice, many claims based on S.15 EqA will turn on the issue of justification. Unlike direct discrimination under S.13 (which can only be justified if the protected characteristic is age), any allegation of discrimination arising from disability will only succeed if the employer (or other person against whom the allegation is made) is unable to justify the unfavourable treatment by pointing to a valid (i.e. non-discriminatory) reason for it.

The same was true under S.3A(1) DDA in respect of the now defunct 'disability-related discrimination' ground of discrimination. However, under that provision an employer had to show that the reason for the less favourable treatment was 'both material to the circumstances of the particular case and substantial' – S.3A(3) DDA. In Post Office v Jones 2001 ICR 805, CA, the Court of Appeal held that this was similar to the 'band of reasonable responses' test that applies in unfair dismissal cases. In other words, tribunals would not interfere with an employer's decision unless it was manifestly unreasonable. By contrast, S.15(1) EqA requires the employer to justify the unfavourable treatment as a 'proportionate means of achieving a legitimate aim'. On its face, this formulation sets a higher hurdle for employers than the old test and reflects the Government's decision to adopt the same test of objective justification – wherever it applies – across all the discrimination strands.

However, the apparent difference between the justification test under S.3A(3) **20.23** DDA and that under the EqA may not, in practice, be as great as first appears. This is because, with regard to the former, employers were precluded from running the justification defence where they had been under the duty to make reasonable adjustments but failed to comply with that duty. In those circumstances, a defence to disability-related discrimination could only be made out if the employer showed that the less favourable treatment would have been justifiable even if the reasonable adjustments duty had been complied with – S.3A(6). The EqA contains no equivalent to S.3A(6). This is almost certainly because the more exacting 'proportionality' test that now applies renders such a provision otiose: it is difficult to conceive of a case where it would be open to a tribunal to find that an employer's unfavourable treatment of the claimant because of something arising in consequence of his or her disability is justifiable as a proportionate means of achieving a legitimate aim if, at the same time, it is established that the employer could and should have made a reasonable adjustment to deal with the substantial disadvantage caused by the claimant's disability. This view is supported by the EHRC's Employment Code, which states: 'If an employer has failed to make a reasonable adjustment which would have prevented or minimised the unfavourable treatment, it will be very difficult for them to show that the treatment was objectively justified' – para 5.21.

In Williams v Ystrad Mynach College ET Case No.1600019/11 – one of the first cases to be decided under the relevant provisions of the EqA – an employment tribunal referred to para 5.21 of the Employment Code (quoted above) when specifically rejecting the employer's defence of justification to a claim of discrimination arising from disability. In that case the claimant, who suffered from hydrocephalus ('water on the brain'), was employed as a college lecturer under a 'professional academic contract'. Following a substantial period of absence for medical treatment, discussions between the claimant and the college took place regarding the terms for his return to work, including the option of transferring onto a short-term contract. This was resisted by the claimant, who wished to remain on his existing permanent contract but with a 50 per cent reduction in hours. In the event, the college unilaterally imposed the new contract, at which point the claimant brought claims of disability discrimination based on unfavourable treatment arising from his disability contrary to S.15 EqA and breach of the duty to make reasonable adjustments contrary to S.20. The tribunal upheld both claims.

With regard to the S.15 claim, the college conceded that the termination of the **20.24** claimant's existing contract and imposition of the inferior contract comprised 'unfavourable treatment' and that this arose in consequence of the claimant's disability. However, it contended that the unfavourable treatment was justified as a proportionate means of achieving a legitimate aim, namely that of ensuring continuity of services to its students. Rejecting this contention, the tribunal stated that it was 'not open to the respondent, retrospectively, to proffer a legitimate aim that was not in its mind at the time'. In this case, the college had imposed the new contract on the basis of an assumption about the claimant's prognosis for which there was no warrant according to the available medical evidence. It had not previously explained its actions in terms of the need to provide an unbroken service to students. Additionally, and in any event, the tribunal said that even if such a legitimate aim could be retrospectively relied upon, the college had implemented it in a disproportionate manner. In the tribunal's view, the unfavourable treatment in this case was incapable of justification because there was, at hand, a less discriminatory means of achieving the same legitimate aim: namely, the retention of the claimant on his existing contract but with reduced hours – which was the very adjustment he had sought.

Although a failure to make a reasonable adjustment will make it very difficult for the employer to argue that the unfavourable treatment was nonetheless justified, the converse is not necessarily true. Just because an employer has implemented reasonable adjustments does not guarantee that unfavourable treatment of the claimant will be justified. It may be that the particular adjustment is unrelated to the unfavourable treatment complained of, or only goes part way to dealing with the matter. The Employment Code gives the example of an employer who, at an employee's request, agrees to reduce her working hours to accommodate the debilitating effects of her multiple sclerosis but then dismisses her following a period of three months' absence. In that case, the 'adjustment is not relevant to the unfavourable treatment – namely, her dismissal for disability-related sickness absence – which her claim concerns. And so, despite the fact that reasonable adjustments were made, there will still be discrimination arising from disability unless the treatment is justified' – para 5.6. Having said that, an employer who has put in place a reasonable adjustment aimed at dealing with the matter will presumably be able to pray in aid of that adjustment when seeking to justify any residual unfavourable treatment.

20.25 **Guidance on objective justification.** The EHRC's Employment Code sets out guidance on objective justification that largely reflects existing case law in this area. In short, the aim pursued should be legal, should not be discriminatory in itself, and must represent a real, objective consideration. Although business needs and economic efficiency may be legitimate aims, the Code states that an employer simply trying to reduce costs cannot expect to satisfy the test – para 4.29. As to proportionality, the Code notes that the measure adopted by the employer does not have to be the only possible way of achieving the legitimate aim but the treatment will not be proportionate if less discriminatory measures could have been taken to achieve the same objective – para 4.31.

Since the standard of objective justification required to defend a claim of discrimination arising from a disability under S.15 is the same as that required to defend an indirect discrimination claim under S.19, it is reasonable to assume that the same principles apply to both tests. Certainly, the guidance set out in the

Code does not suggest otherwise. For a more detailed examination of objective justification see Chapter 17, 'Indirect discrimination: objective justification'.

Costs as a basis for justifying discrimination. According to the EHRC **20.26** Employment Code: 'The greater financial cost of using a less discriminatory approach cannot, by itself, provide a justification for applying a particular provision, criterion or practice. Cost can only be taken into account as part of the employer's justification for the provision, criterion or practice if there are other good reasons for adopting it' – para 4.32. This reflects the orthodox view derived from an interpretation of European case law concerning justification in the contexts of equal pay and indirect gender discrimination.

However, in Woodcock v Cumbria Primary Care Trust 2011 ICR 143, EAT – an age discrimination case – Mr Justice Underhill, then President of the EAT, observed that there was no principled basis for a rule that cost considerations can never by themselves constitute sufficient justification. However, when the case progressed to the Court of Appeal – Woodcock v Cumbria Primary Care Trust 2012 EWCA Civ 330, CA – Lord Justice Rimer stressed that an employer cannot justify discriminatory treatment 'solely' because the elimination of such treatment would involve increased costs.

Employer's knowledge of disability   20.27

An employer has a defence to a claim under S.15 EqA if it did not know (and could not reasonably have been expected to know) that the complainant had a disability – S.15(2). This is a key difference between discrimination arising from a disability under S.15 EqA and disability-related discrimination under S.3A(1) DDA as it applied prior to the decision in Mayor and Burgesses of the London Borough of Lewisham v Malcolm 2008 IRLR 700, HL. Under the DDA pre-Malcolm, an employer's knowledge of disability was irrelevant to whether disability-related discrimination had occurred. S.3A(1) provided that 'a person discriminates against a disabled person if (a) for a reason which relates to the disabled person's disability, he treats him less favourably than he treats or would treat others to whom that reason does not or would not apply, and (b) he cannot show that the treatment in question is justified'. Thus, the fact that the less favourable treatment arose for a disability-related reason was enough to engage the section – there was no need for any enquiry into the employer's motives or knowledge – see HJ Heinz Co Ltd v Kenrick 2000 ICR 491, EAT, where the EAT disapproved of the notion that an employer does not discriminate against a person for a reason related to that person's disability if the employer is not aware of the person's disability.

The Malcolm decision overruled Kenrick. Their Lordships considered that disability-related discrimination under S.3A(1) DDA did require the alleged discriminator to have actual or at least imputed knowledge of the disability,

643

unless the act complained of was inherently discriminatory. Moreover, that knowledge would need to inform and motivate the decision-making process in order to satisfy the 'reason why' test.

20.28 Although the Government intended S.15 EqA to recreate the pre-Malcolm protection offered by S.3A DDA, it has preserved the requirement for knowledge in S.15(2), which states that subsection (1) does not apply if the employer shows that it 'did not know, and could not reasonably have been expected to know' of the employee's disability. It is clear from this, however, that the employer cannot simply turn a blind eye to evidence of disability. While the EqA stops short of imposing an explicit duty to enquire about a person's possible or suspected disability, the EHRC Employment Code states that an employer must do all it can reasonably be expected to do to find out if a person has a disability – para 5.15. It suggests that 'employers should consider whether a worker has a disability even where one has not been formally disclosed, as, for example, not all workers who meet the definition of disability may think of themselves as a "disabled person"' – para 5.14.

The following example is provided in the Code at para 5.15:

> 'A disabled man who has depression has been at a particular workplace for two years. He has a good attendance and performance record. In recent weeks, however, he has become emotional and upset at work for no apparent reason. He has also been repeatedly late for work and has made some mistakes in his work. The worker is disciplined without being given any opportunity to explain that his difficulties at work arise from a disability and that recently the effects of his depression have worsened. The sudden deterioration in the worker's time-keeping and performance and the change in his behaviour at work should have alerted the employer to the possibility that these were connected to a disability. It is likely to be reasonable to expect the employer to explore with the worker the reason for these changes and whether the difficulties are because of something arising in consequence of a disability.'

20.29 The Code also makes the important point that knowledge of a disability held by an employer's agent or employee – such as an occupational health adviser, personnel officer or recruitment agent – will usually be imputed to the employer – para 5.17.

It is worth noting that the phrase 'could not reasonably have been expected to know' in S.15(2) EqA is worded in the same way as the employer's defence to a claim of failure to make reasonable adjustments under para 20 of Schedule 8 to the EqA (see Chapter 21, 'Failure to make reasonable adjustments', under 'Employer's knowledge of disability'). That defence states that the duty to make reasonable adjustments does not arise if the employer 'does not know, and could not reasonably be expected to know' that an individual has a disability and is likely to be placed at a substantial disadvantage by one of the employer's practices or a physical feature of its premises. Case law on reasonable knowledge under S.4A DDA (the precursor to para 20) is therefore likely to be relevant to the question of reasonable knowledge under S.15(2) EqA. For example, in Department for Work and Pensions v Hall EAT 0012/05 the EAT upheld a tribunal's finding of constructive knowledge based on the employee's refusal to answer questions about ill health and disability before starting the job; the fact that the employer was aware of the employee's very unusual behaviour once she started work; and the fact that her manager and the human resources department were aware of her claim for a disability tax credit.

Overlap with indirect discrimination

20.30

The examples of discrimination arising from a disability given in the EHRC's Employment Code make it clear that there will be a large area of overlap with indirect discrimination under S.19 EqA. Indeed, many of the examples could equally be characterised as indirect discrimination.

Consider O'Hanlon v HM Revenue and Customs Commissioners 2007 ICR 1359, CA, a disability-related discrimination case under old S.3A(1) DDA. In that case, the claimant was on long-term sick leave because of her depression. HMRC's sick pay policy provided for full pay for the first 26 weeks of sickness absence, followed by half pay for a further 26 weeks. The claimant complained of disability-related discrimination when her pay was reduced and then stopped in line with this policy. These facts fit very neatly into the definition of discrimination arising from a disability in S.15(1), as described under 'Unfavourable treatment' above: the reduction in pay can be described as unfavourable treatment because of something arising in consequence of O's disability. Equally, had S.19 EqA been in force at the relevant time, O could have argued that:

- HMRC had applied a provision, criterion or practice (PCP) to the effect that sick pay is halved after six months, and reduced to nothing after a year – S.19(2)

- the PCP applies, or would apply, to non-disabled people – S.19(2)(a)

- those who share O's disability, with its attendant impact on sickness absence, are put at a particular disadvantage compared with those who do not share O's disability – S.19(2)(b)

- it put O at that disadvantage – S.19(2)(c).

In both cases, the question of whether the treatment was justified would then arise. The employer would have to show that the treatment was a 'proportionate means of achieving a legitimate aim' under S.15(1)(b) or S.19(2)(d).

645

20.31 There are, however, key differences between discrimination arising from a disability and indirect discrimination. The EHRC Employment Code points out that 'indirect discrimination occurs when a disabled person is (or would be) disadvantaged by an unjustifiable provision, criterion or practice applied to everyone, which puts (or would put) people sharing the disabled person's disability at a particular disadvantage compared to others, and puts (or would put) the disabled person at that disadvantage... In contrast, discrimination arising from disability only requires the disabled person to show they have experienced unfavourable treatment because of something connected with their disability. If the employer can show that they did not know and could not reasonably have been expected to know that the disabled person had the disability, it will not be discrimination arising from disability' – paras 5.4 and 5.5.

The Code arguably makes more of the PCP point than is strictly justified. In most cases both the PCP and its effects will be clear. In the O'Hanlon example, the PCP, for the purposes of S.19, would have been the application of the sick pay policy to the employee, which also had the effects that engage S.15. The same applies to the examples of discrimination arising from a disability given by the Code – a disciplinary policy that results in action taken against an employee who uncharacteristically loses her temper because of severe pain caused by a disability is a PCP (see para 5.9). Indeed, it is hard to imagine a case of discrimination arising from a disability that could not also be characterised as the application of a PCP.

20.32 By contrast, the absence of a need to show group disadvantage under S.15 is potentially a key differentiating point between the two forms of discrimination. As noted in Chapter 16, 'Indirect discrimination: proving disadvantage', under 'Indirect discrimination in context – indirect disability discrimination', it may be difficult for a disabled person to show group disadvantage where the symptoms he or she experiences are not experienced, or not experienced in the same way, by everyone with the same disability. This limitation derives from the particular way the protected characteristic of disability is defined for the purposes of the EqA. In this regard, S.6(3)(b) states that: 'In relation to the protected characteristic of disability... a reference to persons who share a protected characteristic is a reference to persons who have the *same* disability' (our stress). It may therefore be significantly easier for a claimant to show unfavourable treatment because of something arising in consequence of the disability than it will be to show particular disadvantage likely to affect a whole group in the context of an indirect discrimination claim.

The other key difference is the relevance of the employer's knowledge of the complainant's disability. As noted under 'Employer's knowledge of disability' above, an employer who can show that it did not know, and could not reasonably have been expected to have known, that an individual had a disability will not be liable for discrimination arising from a disability – S.15(2) EqA. By contrast, generally speaking, the employer's knowledge of discriminatory effect is irrelevant to the question of whether indirect discrimination has occurred – see, for example, Redcar and Cleveland Borough Council v Bainbridge and ors and another case 2009 ICR 133, CA. The employer's knowledge of indirect discrimination will, however, be relevant to the question of objective justification. That said, the irrelevancy of the employer's knowledge in determining whether indirect discrimination has occurred was called into question by the EAT in Eweida v British Airways plc 2009 ICR 303, EAT, a religious discrimination case. There, Mr Justice Elias, then President of the EAT, pointed out that an employer cannot be expected to consider the potential discriminatory impact of its policies on beliefs it knows nothing about. Thus, where a religious belief is highly subjective and personal, it cannot give rise to a claim of indirect discrimination. (Note that the Eweida case was unsuccessfully appealed to the Court of Appeal – see Eweida v British Airways plc 2010 ICR 890, CA – but the issue of employer's knowledge was not considered.) In view of Elias P's observations, it may be that the two causes of action under Ss.15 and 19 are not that dissimilar in this regard.

21 Failure to make reasonable adjustments

Duty to make reasonable adjustments

The three statutory requirements

'Substantial disadvantage'

Employer's knowledge of disability

Reasonableness of adjustments

Common types of adjustment

Altering physical features – obtaining consent

Special cases

A pivotal feature of disability discrimination law is the duty on employers to **21.1** make reasonable adjustments, a failure to comply with which amounts to discrimination under the Equality Act 2010 (EqA). As recognised by Baroness Hale in the seminal case of Archibald v Fife Council 2004 ICR 954, HL, the duty is unique because it requires a degree of 'positive action' from employers to alleviate the effects of provisions, criteria or practices (PCPs), as well as the non-provision of auxiliary aids or the physical features of the workplace, on disabled employees and job applicants. In contrast to other areas of discrimination law, the duty to make reasonable adjustments can require an employer to treat a disabled person *more* favourably than it would treat others.

Originally contained in S.6 of the Disability Discrimination Act 1995 (DDA), the duty is now found in S.20 EqA. In relation to employment, S.20(13) EqA provides that S.20 is supplemented by Schedules 8 and 21 to the EqA, which have effect by virtue of Ss.83(10) and 189 respectively. The EqA introduced some relatively minor changes to the duty but the most far-reaching changes were made in 2004 by the Disability Discrimination Act 1995 (Amendment) Regulations 2003 SI 2003/1673, which came into force on 1 October 2004. These changes – which were necessary to bring the DDA into line with the EU Equal Treatment Framework Directive (No.2000/78) – saw the duty recast in S.4A DDA and involved the removal of the defence of justification to a failure to make reasonable adjustments.

Section 20 EqA sets out the general scope of the duty to make adjustments. **21.2** However, to understand the effect of the duty in the workplace, it is necessary to refer to other provisions of the Act, most notably S.39(5) EqA, which states

649

that the duty applies to an employer, and Schedule 8, which sets out specific provisions regarding the duty in the context of employment and occupation. As very few cases have yet to be dealt with under the EqA, the case law referred to in this chapter was all decided under the DDA. However, while the new statute contains some notable changes to the structure of the duty to make reasonable adjustments, along with some subtle changes in the statutory language, it is expected that the principles decided in relation to S.4A DDA hold true in relation to S.20 EqA.

The duty to make reasonable adjustments is dealt with in the Equality and Human Rights Commission's Statutory Code of Practice on Employment ('the EHRC Employment Code'), which was laid before Parliament on 12 October 2010. Reference to that Code is made throughout this chapter. The Code can be relied on as evidence in tribunal proceedings.

21.3 Duty to make reasonable adjustments

Under the DDA, separate provision was made in respect of the duty to make reasonable adjustments for each context in which that duty applied. So, for example, specific provisions in Part II dealt with the duty as it applied in the context of the employment field, and other discrete provisions contained within Part III dealt with the duty as it applied to goods, facilities and services, and public authorities. Under the EqA, by contrast, the core duty is set out in Ss.20 and 21, and these sections are then supplemented by additional context-specific detail in the Schedules to the EqA.

Section 20 EqA states that the duty to make adjustments comprises three requirements:

- a requirement, where a provision, criterion or practice (PCP) puts a disabled person at a substantial disadvantage in relation to a relevant matter in comparison with persons who are not disabled, to take such steps as it is reasonable to have to take to avoid the disadvantage – S.20(3)

- a requirement, where a physical feature puts a disabled person at a substantial disadvantage in relation to a relevant matter in comparison with persons who are not disabled, to take such steps as it is reasonable to have to take to avoid the disadvantage – S.20(4)

- a requirement, where a disabled person would, but for the provision of an auxiliary aid, be put at a substantial disadvantage in relation to a relevant matter in comparison with persons who are not disabled, to take such steps as it is reasonable to have to take to provide the auxiliary aid – S.20(5).

21.4 In relation to Part 5 of the EqA, which covers work and employment, S.39(5) states that 'a duty to make reasonable adjustments applies to an employer'. In other words, the three requirements outlined above apply in the context of employment.

Prior to the coming into force of the EqA, there was no explicit requirement for employers to provide auxiliary aids (though the requirement did appear in S.21(4) DDA in relation to premises and the provision of goods and services). However, the change is not as significant as it might at first seem – the provision of auxiliary aids, such as voice recognition computer software for an employee unable to type, has frequently been considered in the past as a possible adjustment in respect of the first two requirements listed above. Including it explicitly and independently is merely a reflection of the way in which the statutory duty to make reasonable adjustments has, in practice, been interpreted by courts and tribunals.

A failure to comply with the first, second or third requirement amounts to a failure to comply with the duty to make reasonable adjustments, and an employer will have discriminated against a disabled person if it fails to comply with the duty in relation to that person – S.21(1) and (2).

Requirement for information to be in an accessible format 21.5

Section 20(6) EqA provides that where the first or third requirement mentioned above (i.e. taking steps to avoid disadvantage caused by the application of a PCP or the lack of an auxiliary aid) relates to the provision of information, the steps that it is reasonable to have to take include steps for ensuring that the information is provided in an accessible format. 'Accessible format' is not defined in the Act but can include large print, Braille, electronic text, audio tape and accessible images. What is reasonable in any given case will obviously depend on the individual circumstances of the disabled person.

Scope of the duty 21.6

The current duty to make reasonable adjustments is of considerably wider scope than the original duty enacted in the DDA back in 1995. The most significant change came in 2004, when the Disability Discrimination Act 1995 (Amendment) Regulations 2003 SI 2003/1673 came into force, principally to give effect to the disability strand of the EU Equal Treatment Framework Directive (No.2000/78). Prior to that point, the duty in S.6 DDA had applied in respect of an employer's 'arrangements' and the physical features of the workplace. To give effect to EU law, the duty was recast in S.4A, and the word 'arrangements' was replaced by the now-familiar term 'provision, criterion or practice' (PCP). The recast S.4A also did away with the express limitation whereby the duty in respect of arrangements applied only to those arrangements made for determining to whom employment should be offered; or to any term, condition or arrangements on which employment, promotion, a transfer, training or any other benefit was offered or afforded.

21.7 **When does the duty begin and end?** The duty to make reasonable adjustments can arise even before an employment relationship exists – for example, by requiring an employer to make adjustments to its premises to accommodate a disabled candidate at interview. However, as explained below, it is not an anticipatory duty and is reliant on there being an 'interested disabled person' whom the employer knows or ought to know is placed at a substantial disadvantage by its PCPs, the physical features of its premises, or the failure to provide an auxiliary aid. The term 'interested disabled person' is used for the first time in the EqA, but does not herald any significant change from the DDA. Para 5 of Schedule 8 to the EqA explains that where the duty arises in respect of deciding to whom to offer employment, an interested disabled person is someone who is, or has notified the employer that he may be, an applicant for the employment in question. Where the duty arises in respect of employment itself, an interested disabled person is either an applicant for employment or an employee of the employer in question.

In general terms, the statutory duty to make reasonable adjustments arises when a disabled person is placed at a substantial disadvantage by the application of a PCP, by a physical feature, or by the non-provision of an auxiliary aid. In NCH Scotland v McHugh EAT 0010/06 the EAT was required to identify the time at which a disabled claimant might be in a position to contend that he or she has been placed at such a substantial disadvantage in the context of seeking a phased return to work following a substantial period of absence caused by the disability in question. In that case, the EAT ruled that the duty is not 'triggered' – to use the EAT's own word – unless and until the claimant indicated that he or she was intending or wishing to return to work. His Honour Judge McMullen observed: 'We agree that a managed programme of rehabilitation depends on all the circumstances of the case, but it does include a return to work date. And certainly, if additional management and supervision is to be required, they must be arranged in advance and not in a vacuum. Similarly, if additional costs were to be incurred by (not this case) the purchase of new equipment to counteract the effect of the environment on the disabled person, there would be no need to spend that money in advance of a clear indication that the claimant was returning. In our judgment, applying the trigger approach... it was not reasonable for the respondent to pursue the possibilities which the tribunal noted until there was some sign on the horizon that the claimant would be returning.'

21.8 Interestingly, another division of the EAT has suggested that there is no general proposition of law that the employer's duty to make reasonable adjustments does not arise until the disabled employee indicates when he or she will be able to return to work – see London Underground Ltd v Vuoto EAT 0123/09. In that case, the employer cited the Court of Appeal's decision in Home Office v Collins 2005 EWCA Civ 598, CA, as authority for that proposition. But as Mrs Justice Cox pointed out, the Collins case turned very much on its own facts. In any event, it is apparent on a close reading of Lord Justice Pill's judgment in Collins (with which the other members of the Court agreed) that the outcome of that case was determined not on the basis of whether the duty to make reasonable adjustments was triggered – the Court assumed that it was – but on whether the particular adjustment sought by the claimant (a phased return to work) was reasonable. The Court concluded that the adjustment was not reasonable in the circumstances.

Returning to the case before it, the EAT in Vuoto ruled that the medical evidence showed that the employee's absence was, in part, caused by stress arising from the employer's treatment of him; and that on that basis, the employment tribunal had been entitled to find that the employer had come under a duty to consider any reasonable adjustment that would have alleviated that stress and thus eased the path of the employee towards his return to work.

In Brown v Commissioners for Her Majesty's Revenue and Customs and ors **21.9** ET Case Nos.2510511/09 and another an employment tribunal adopted the line of reasoning in NCH Scotland v McHugh (above) when concluding that the statutory duty had not been triggered. In that case the claimant was absent from work for a period of three years until the termination of his employment. His absence was initially due to a physical impairment but was later extended by reason of the claimant developing a psychological illness. During this period the claimant's sick pay was reduced to half pay under the terms of the employer's sickness policy. In April 2009, the claimant asserted that he might be in a position to return to work provided a number of major adjustments were made and discussions between him and the employer took place regarding these. In August 2009, a medical report intimated that, owing to his current mental state, it was unlikely that the claimant would be able to return to his most recent job and set out a projected timeframe for his recovery of up to five years and possibly even longer. In consequence, the employer terminated the claimant's employment on capability grounds. Regarding the claim for breach of the duty to make reasonable adjustments, the tribunal pointed out that, apart from the claimant's bald statement that he might be able to return to work, there was no supportive medical evidence that he was realistically in a position to do so. On this basis, the statutory duty was not triggered and the employer had not waived the right to contend that this was the case by virtue of having entered into discussions about the possibility of returning to work and about the adjustments that would be necessary to accommodate this.

At the other end of the time spectrum, the question may arise as to when the employer's duty, once triggered, ceases. In one sense, there is an obvious answer: once any adjustments that were reasonable to make as a means of eliminating or reducing the substantial disadvantage to which the claimant would otherwise be put by the application of the PCP, etc have been fully implemented. In some cases, however, the duty on the employer does not end simply because certain

653

adjustments have been implemented. It may be reasonable (and therefore necessary) to make further adjustments somewhere down the line. In this sense, the employer can remain subject to an ongoing duty. In Bynon v Wilf Gilbert (Staffordshire) Ltd ET Case No.1301482/08, for example, a trainee manager sought and was granted an adjustment to enable her to return to less onerous cashier work following a period of absence owing to a mental health disorder. However, she went off sick once again, and although she contacted the employer about returning to work, no further adjustments were made and she was eventually dismissed without the employer having sought an up-to-date medical prognosis. Upholding the employee's claim of breach of the duty to make treasonable adjustments, an employment tribunal ruled that, although certain reasonable adjustments had been implemented at an earlier date, the employer should have made the further reasonable adjustment of holding off dismissal until it had established whether the claimant was fit to return to work in the cashier role – with or without adjustments – and, if not, whether she was fit to return in any other role.

21.10 In the somewhat unusual case of Kittle v Future Cleaning Services Ltd ET Case No.1809097/09 a number of adjustments had already been made by the employer aimed at reducing the workload of the claimant, who had skin cancer. However, after some time working under these arrangements, the claimant became dissatisfied with her reduced workload and started to press the employer for more work. Being dissatisfied with the employer's response, she brought disability discrimination claims, including a claim for breach of S.4A DDA (now S.20 EqA). An employment tribunal rejected that particular claim on the basis that, once the claimant had pressed for more work, the duty on the employer to make reasonable adjustments was extinguished.

21.11 **Post-employment.** The EHRC Employment Code states at para 6.8 that the duty to make reasonable adjustments may apply after employment has ended. S.108(1) EqA provides that an employer must not discriminate against a former employee if the discrimination arises out of, and is closely connected to, a relationship which used to exist between them and the conduct would, if it occurred during the relationship, contravene the EqA. Given that a failure to make reasonable adjustments amounts to discrimination by virtue of S.21, S.108(1) would appear to cover a failure that takes place once employment has ended without more. However, for the avoidance of doubt, S.108(4) explicitly states that the duty to make reasonable adjustments applies in respect of a former employee if he or she is placed at a substantial disadvantage in one of the three ways outlined in S.20. One scenario in which the duty might continue to apply would be in respect of an appeal hearing against dismissal – the employer would be obliged to make the same adjustments for a disabled person that it would need to make for a pre-dismissal disciplinary hearing.

A duty to consult on adjustments? The extent to which the duty to make **21.12** reasonable adjustments entails an obligation to consult an employee or job applicant over what adjustments might be suitable and/or reasonable has been the subject of contrasting EAT decisions. In Mid Staffordshire General Hospitals NHS Trust v Cambridge 2003 IRLR 566, EAT, C suffered from tracheitis and bowing of the vocal cords, which had led to a lengthy absence from work and a return for only two hours a day. When she was dismissed, C brought claims of disability discrimination, including one of a failure to make reasonable adjustments. The tribunal found that the Trust had breached the duty, since it had failed to seek, obtain or act on a full and proper assessment of C's position at any relevant time. The Trust appealed to the EAT, arguing that the tribunal had added a 'preliminary duty', which was an unwarranted gloss on the legislation.

Dismissing the appeal, Mr Justice Keith held that there must be many cases in which the disabled person has been placed at a substantial disadvantage in the workplace, but in which the employer does not know what it ought to do to ameliorate that disadvantage without making enquiries. To say that a failure to make those enquiries would not amount to a breach of the duty to make reasonable adjustments would in many cases render that duty practicably unworkable. A proper assessment of what is required to eliminate the disabled person's disadvantage is a necessary part of the duty, and cannot be separated from it, since the duty cannot be complied with unless the employer makes a proper assessment of what needs to be done.

However, a notably different tack was taken by Mr Justice Elias (then President **21.13** of the EAT) in Tarbuck v Sainsbury's Supermarkets Ltd 2006 IRLR 664, EAT. In that case, the tribunal, relying on the Mid Staffordshire decision, upheld T's claim of a failure to make reasonable adjustments, citing, among other things, the employer's failure to consult with her over the steps that might be taken to ameliorate the disadvantage she experienced when competing with other staff for jobs. On appeal, Elias P held that while it will always be good practice for the employer to consult, and it will potentially jeopardise the employer's legal position if it does not do so, there is no separate and distinct duty on an employer to consult with a disabled worker. The only question is, objectively, whether or not the employer has complied with its obligations to make reasonable adjustments. If the employer does what is required of it, then the fact that it failed to consult about the duty or did not know that the obligation existed is irrelevant. It may be an entirely fortuitous and unconsidered compliance, but that is enough. Conversely, if the employer fails to do what is reasonably required, it avails the employer nothing that it has consulted the employee. If there were a preliminary obligation to consult, it would have been spelt out in the legislation. It followed, in Elias P's view, that the Mid Staffordshire case was wrongly decided.

In subsequent cases, the EAT has followed Tarbuck – see, for example, Spence v Intype Libra Ltd EAT 0617/06 and Salford NHS Primary Care Trust v Smith

655

EAT 0507/10 (discussed under 'Common types of adjustment – rehabilitation following substantial absence' below).

21.14 Although the concept of a distinct duty to consult was rejected in Tarbuck v Sainsbury's Supermarkets Ltd (above), Elias P did state in that case that 'any employer would be wise to consult with a disabled employee in order to be better informed and fully acquainted of all the factors which may be relevant to a determination of what adjustment should reasonably be made in the circumstances. If the employer fails to do that, then he is placing himself seriously at risk of not taking appropriate steps because of his own ignorance. He cannot then pray that ignorance in aid if it is alleged that he ought to have taken certain steps and he has failed to do so.'

21.15 **Trial periods.** In obiter (i.e. non-binding) comments in Environment Agency v Rowan 2008 ICR 218, EAT, the EAT expressed its 'considerable difficulty' in seeing how an investigation or trial period can, of itself, amount to a reasonable adjustment. R worked part time as a clerk/typist for the Environment Agency in Cardiff. In 1993 she injured her back at work and, despite surgery in 1997, her condition deteriorated. In September 2003 she went on long-term sickness absence. She subsequently expressed the wish to be rehabilitated on a homeworking basis, which the Agency considered inappropriate. By 2004 R was unable to sit for long periods and her symptoms could only adequately be controlled by bed rest. She eventually resigned and claimed – among other things – that the Agency had failed to comply with its duty to make reasonable adjustments.

The tribunal accepted that R was disabled within the meaning of the DDA and that the Agency owed her a duty to make reasonable adjustments. It also found that in not offering her a period of home working on a trial basis, the Agency had failed to comply with the duty to make reasonable adjustments. However, the EAT overturned that decision on the basis that the tribunal had failed clearly to identify the nature and extent of the substantial disadvantage suffered by R. Judge Serota QC, presiding, also noted that there was no explanation as to how the proposed adjustment – i.e. the trial period of home working – would have overcome the adverse effects said to have been suffered by R. For instance, if she needed occasional bed rest during the day, this might have been accommodated in an office environment. The Appeal Tribunal stated: 'A trial period is akin to a consultation, or the obtaining of medical and other specialist reports; these do not of themselves mitigate or prevent or shield the employee from anything. They serve to better inform the employer as to what steps, if any, will have that effect, but of themselves they achieve nothing.' Serota J also cited these comments with approval in Salford NHS Primary Care Trust v Smith EAT 0507/10 – see under 'Common types of adjustment – rehabilitation' below for further details of this case.

656

It should be noted, however, that neither of these EAT decisions made any **21.16** reference to the earlier case of Smith v Churchills Stairlifts plc 2006 ICR 524, CA, in which the Court of Appeal upheld an employment tribunal's decision that an employer had failed to make a reasonable adjustment to allow a disabled employee a trial period in circumstances where his job offer was withdrawn out of concern that he would be unable to undertake a key task. Furthermore, trial periods have been regarded as reasonable adjustments by employment tribunals in a number of cases. For example, in Lamb v Chief Constable of Hampshire Constabulary ET Case No.3105684/09 the tribunal held that a disabled employee had been denied the reasonable adjustment of being given a three-month trial period to help determine whether a revised shift pattern would lead to an improvement in the employee's levels of absence.

Duty on employer, not employee. Although it is good practice to consult with **21.17** a disabled person over what adjustments might be suitable, the duty to make reasonable adjustments is on the employer, and the fact that a disabled employee and his or her medical advisers cannot postulate a potential adjustment will not, without more, discharge that duty. In Cosgrove v Caesar and Howie 2001 IRLR 653, EAT, C, a legal secretary, was dismissed after she had been off sick for a year suffering from depression and it was not known when she would be able to return. The tribunal held that she had not been discriminated against. It had considered whether the employer had been under a duty to make adjustments but placed great emphasis on the fact that neither C nor her general practitioner could think of a reasonable adjustment that would have enabled her to return to work.

On appeal, the EAT emphasised that the duty to make adjustments is on the employer. The EAT had no doubt that there would be cases where the claimant's evidence alone would establish a total unavailability of reasonable and effective adjustments. But it did not follow that just because the claimant and her GP were unable to come up with any useful adjustments the duty could be taken, without more, to have been complied with. If the employer had turned its mind to adjustments, there were possibilities, such as a transfer to another office or a change in working hours, that might have facilitated a return. In these circumstances, the EAT held that the tribunal had made an error of law in treating C's views and those of her GP as decisive on the issue of adjustments when the employer had given no thought to the matter itself.

There is a limit, however, to the lengths an employer will be expected to go to **21.18** comply with the statutory duty. In Bishun v Hertfordshire Probation Service EAT 0123/11 the EAT rejected the contention that the employer had not taken sufficient steps to determine what kind of technical equipment might help deal with the adverse effects of the employee's impairment (sleep apnoea). The employer had, in fact, referred the employee to the Access to Work service run through Jobcentre Plus, which would have helped in identifying and

657

implementing reasonable adjustments. The employee, however, had failed to engage with the service despite the employer's promptings. He unsuccessfully contended before the employment tribunal that the employer should not simply have put the onus on him to seek out the advice and assistance. On appeal, the EAT upheld the tribunal's conclusion that the employer had not been in breach of the duty to make reasonable adjustments. It rejected the employee's argument that the employer had an obligation to monitor progress with the application in respect of the Access to Work programme and should have been aware that, 12 months on, the matter was no further forward.

21.19 *Costs fall on employer.* So far as the costs of complying with the duty are concerned, S.20(7) EqA provides that a person subject to the duty to make reasonable adjustments may not, subject to express provision to the contrary, require a disabled person to pay to any extent the costs of compliance. There are currently no express provisions in the Act that would allow an employer to impose the cost of an adjustment on an employee. Note, however, that the cost of an adjustment may be a relevant factor in determining whether or not it is reasonable (see further below under 'Reasonableness of adjustments – financial and other costs of adjustment').

21.20 **No exemption for small employers.** Section 7 DDA used to provide that employers with fewer than 20 employees were exempt from the Act. This threshold was reduced to 15 employees in 1998 and subsequently removed in 2004. There is no exemption for small employers from any of the disability discrimination provisions in the EqA, although the size of the employer's undertaking can be a relevant factor for the tribunal to consider in respect of what would be a reasonable adjustment – see under 'Reasonableness of adjustments – employer's financial and other resources' below.

21.21 **Parallel duties.** If two or more persons are subject to a duty to make reasonable adjustments in relation to the same disabled employee, each of them must comply with the duty so far as it is reasonable for them to do so – para 2(5), Sch 8 EqA.

21.22 **Relationship with other discrimination provisions.** In many ways, the duty to make reasonable adjustments represents the most significant difference between disability discrimination and the other discrimination strands covered in the EqA. There is no duty to make adjustments for people of a particular race, gender, age, sexual orientation, or religion or belief. However, the S.20 duty is closely linked to the concept of indirect discrimination – both the duty to make reasonable adjustments under S.20 and the indirect discrimination provisions in S.19 EqA use the phrase 'provision, criterion or practice' (PCP) and focus on the disadvantage experienced by an individual. Despite the inclusion of disability among the protected characteristics to which indirect discrimination now applies (see Chapter 16, 'Indirect discrimination: proving disadvantage'), we expect that the vast majority of disabled claimants wishing to challenge a PCP that puts them at a disadvantage will pursue a claim under the reasonable adjustment provisions rather than claim indirect discrimination, owing to the greater focus in S.20 on the circumstances of the individual than on the PCP being applied.

Note that although it is a duty prescribed by statute, breach of the duty to make adjustments under S.20 does not support an action in tort for breach of statutory duty. Instead, S.21(2) provides that a failure to comply with the duty amounts to discrimination.

Cooperation of other employees

21.23

The effectiveness of a reasonable adjustment will often depend on the cooperation of other employees – for example, in helping to ensure that an autistic employee has a structured working day, or accompanying a visually impaired employee on off-site visits. The EHRC Employment Code suggests that, subject to concerns about confidentiality (see 'Issues of confidentiality' below), employers must ensure such cooperation (para 6.35), and further states that it is unlikely to be a valid defence to a claim that staff were obstructive or unhelpful when the employer tried to make reasonable adjustments. Indeed, an employer that fails to demonstrate that it has taken the issue of cooperation seriously and dealt with it appropriately could find itself facing claims of direct and indirect disability discrimination, discrimination arising from disability, victimisation and/or harassment in addition to any claim under S.21 (see Chapters 15–19).

Issues of confidentiality

21.24

Issues concerning confidentiality may arise in the context of making a reasonable adjustment, particularly where the disability is not obvious. This may be because the employer has to tell a supervisor about an adjustment and the reason for it, or because the employer needs to involve the disabled employee's colleagues. For example, where a person with epilepsy works in a factory, the employer may advise his or her colleagues about the effects of the condition and explain the methods for assisting with those effects to ensure the safety of the disabled employee.

However, it may be that the supervisor or manager responsible for implementing an adjustment does not need to know the exact reason why the adjustment is being made. An employer could be discriminating against (or harassing) a disabled employee by revealing information about him or her in circumstances where it would not reveal similar information about another employee for an equally legitimate management purpose. Discrimination (or harassment) could also arise if the employer did not consult the disabled person before revealing the information if this conflicts with its usual practice.

659

21.25 **Transfer of undertakings**

The question may arise on a transfer of an undertaking whether the transferee has to continue to make adjustments put in place by the transferor. Generally speaking, under Reg 4 of the Transfer of Undertakings (Protection of Employment) Regulations 2006 SI 2006/246 the employment contracts of transferred employees have effect as if they had been made between the employee and the transferee and all contractual rights therefore continue. However, as the right to an adjustment is not derived from contract but from statute, it would not automatically transfer under this provision unless the right to the adjustment has been incorporated into the employee's contract of employment. If, as is more usual, the adjustment has not acquired contractual status, the duty to make reasonable adjustments will nevertheless apply to the transferee as employer once the transfer has taken place. There is, however, the possibility that an adjustment considered reasonable in respect of the transferor would, owing to the different circumstances of the transferee, no longer be considered reasonable – see 'Reasonableness of adjustments' below.

21.26 The three statutory requirements

As previously discussed, the duty to make reasonable adjustments entails three separate 'requirements' (this being the word used in S.20 EqA) that apply where a disabled person is placed at a substantial disadvantage in comparison to non-disabled people. These requirements apply to any person upon whom the duty to make reasonable adjustments is imposed under the provisions of the EqA. Essentially, each requirement is couched in terms of a situation or circumstance in which a disabled person may be placed at a 'substantial disadvantage... in comparison with persons who are not disabled' unless an adjustment is made or provision is made for an auxiliary aid. The meaning of 'substantial disadvantage' and the required comparison are explored under '"Substantial disadvantage"' below.

21.27 The three requirements under S.20 are:

- to take such steps as are reasonable to avoid substantial disadvantage caused by the application of a PCP – S.20(3). This requirement might involve, for example, the modification of the terms of a general workplace policy or practice

- to take such steps as are reasonable to avoid substantial disadvantage caused by a physical feature – S.20(4). This requirement covers modifications that may have to be made to the built (i.e. physical) environment – such as the installation of an entrance ramp to aid access by wheelchair users

- where a disabled person would but for the provision of an auxiliary aid be put at a substantial disadvantage, to take reasonable steps to provide the auxiliary aid – S.20(5). (Note that 'auxiliary aid' includes a reference to an auxiliary service – S.20(11).) This requirement might involve, for example, the provision of special computer software or the services of an interpreter.

Each of these three requirements is discussed in detail below. First, however, we need to consider guidance derived from the case law that has general application across all three requirements.

General guidance on reasonable adjustment claims

21.28

Guidance on the approach to be taken in reasonable adjustment claims was given by the EAT in Environment Agency v Rowan 2008 ICR 218, EAT (see under 'Scope of the duty – trial periods' above). Judge Serota QC stated that a tribunal must consider:

- the PCP applied by or on behalf of the employer, or the relevant physical feature of the premises occupied by the employer

- the identity of non-disabled comparators (where appropriate), and

- the nature and extent of the substantial disadvantage suffered by the claimant.

The EAT went on to state that, in order to identify the substantial disadvantage suffered by the claimant, it may be necessary for the tribunal to look at the overall picture and consider the cumulative effect of both a PCP and a physical feature of the premises.

As the above case was decided under S.4A DDA, there was no mention of 21.29 auxiliary aids – the third component of the duty to make reasonable adjustments introduced by S.20 EqA. However, it seems clear that any potential auxiliary aids should also be considered before the tribunal goes on to determine the identity of any appropriate comparators. Auxiliary aids are also likely to come into play when the tribunal looks at the nature and extent of the substantial disadvantage.

Another case in which the EAT considered the general approach to reasonable adjustments claims was HM Prison Service v Johnson 2007 IRLR 951, EAT. J commenced employment with HM Prison Service as a prison psychologist at HMP Frankland in October 2002. From the beginning, she was subjected to hostile treatment from some of her colleagues. An investigation found that she had suffered harassment but concluded that there were 'insufficient grounds for action' against the employees concerned. J had two substantial periods of sickness absence in 2003, which were at least in part anxiety-related. In February 2004 she went off sick again with an adjustment disorder, which developed into a more severe psychiatric illness. She never returned to work and was dismissed in January 2005. J brought tribunal claims for, among other things, disability discrimination under the DDA.

The tribunal found that, from 19 September 2003, J suffered from a mental 21.30 illness that amounted to a disability within the meaning of the DDA. It decided

661

that the employer had discriminated against her in a number of respects, including by failing to comply with its duty to make reasonable adjustments. The employer appealed to the EAT. With regard to reasonable adjustments, Mr Justice Underhill stated that a tribunal must identify with some particularity what 'step' it is that the employer is said to have failed to take in relation to the disabled employee. The degree of specificity required in identifying that step depends on the facts of each case. In some cases it may be sufficient for the tribunal to state, for example, that there were plenty of other suitable jobs the employee could have been moved to; in others, a more detailed finding will be necessary. In J's case, the tribunal had failed to set out the specific step the employer had been required to take: merely suggesting that she should have been moved to a 'non-hostile environment' or offered 'other employment' in a non-prison environment, without finding that suitable jobs were available, was insufficient. As a result, the appeal on this point was allowed and the matter remitted to a different tribunal.

21.31 **Burden of proof.** The EAT has also made it clear that it is insufficient for a claimant simply to point to a substantial disadvantage caused by a PCP or physical feature (or presumably, in view of the additional requirement introduced by the EqA, lack of auxiliary aid) and then place the onus on the employer to think of what possible adjustments could be put in place to ameliorate the disadvantage. In Project Management Institute v Latif 2007 IRLR 579, EAT, Mr Justice Elias (then President of the EAT) expressly approved guidance on the application of the burden of proof in reasonable adjustment cases contained in para 4.41 of the Code of Practice issued by the former Disability Rights Commission (the 'Code of Practice for the elimination of discrimination in the field of employment against disabled persons or persons who have had a disability'). Elias P observed that: 'In our opinion, the Code is correct. The key point identified therein is that the claimant must not only establish that the duty has arisen, but that there are facts from which it could reasonably be inferred, absent an explanation, that it has been breached. Demonstrating that there is an arrangement causing a substantial disadvantage engages the duty, but it provides no basis on which it could properly be inferred that there is a breach of that duty. There must be evidence of some apparently reasonable adjustment which could be made. We do not suggest that in every case the claimant would have had to provide the detailed adjustment that would need to be made before the burden would shift. However, we do think that it would be necessary for the respondent to understand the broad nature of the adjustment proposed and to be given sufficient detail to enable him to engage with the question of whether it could reasonably be achieved or not.'

Elias P made it clear that in some cases the proposed adjustment may not be identified until *after* the alleged failure to implement it or, in exceptional cases, not until the tribunal hearing. In some circumstances, it may be appropriate for the tribunal itself to raise the matter of which particular adjustments might have been made – particularly where the claimant is unrepresented. In Noor v Foreign and Commonwealth Office 2011 ICR 695, EAT, the Appeal Tribunal quoted with approval the Latif decision regarding the burden of proof. It also observed, when allowing an appeal against a tribunal's decision to strike out a reasonable adjustments claim as having no reasonable prospect of success, that: 'An employment judge considering whether to strike out a claim where the disabled person establishes that an arrangement has caused substantial disadvantage ought to keep this guidance firmly in mind. In such circumstances the focus will, of course, be on any specific reasonable adjustment which the employee has put forward; but an employment judge should carefully consider whether there is any other potential reasonable adjustment and should strike the claim out only if it is plain and obvious that there is none.'

Summary of guidance. To summarise the position in the light of the above **21.32** case law: tribunals will be expected to identify the nature of the substantial disadvantage suffered by the claimant and to analyse which steps would have been reasonable for the respondent to take in order to prevent the claimant suffering from the disadvantage in question. The onus is firmly on the claimant and not the respondent to identify, in broad terms at least, the nature of the adjustment that would ameliorate the substantial disadvantage. Having done so, the burden then shifts to the employer to seek to show that the disadvantage would not have been eliminated or reduced by the proposed adjustment and/or that the adjustment was not a reasonable one to make.

In Secretary of State for Work and Pensions v Wakefield EAT 0435/09 the EAT remitted the case to the employment tribunal in circumstances where it found that the tribunal had not applied this approach correctly on two counts: (i) it failed to make sufficient detailed findings about the requirements of the claimant's particular role and how these placed her at a substantial disadvantage because of her disability; and (ii) it failed to identify, in the light of this, how and whether the proposed adjustments would have prevented the substantial disadvantage, together with an assessment, if appropriate, of the timescale within which such adjustments should have been provided. In the course of the EAT's judgment, Judge Ansell warned tribunals against blindly accepting the recommendations contained within occupational health reports and the like as to what adjustments could and should be made: it was the duty of the tribunal to analyse such recommendations in the light of the statutory requirements.

Requirement 1: application of a PCP causing substantial 21.33 disadvantage

The first situation in which the duty to make reasonable adjustments arises is where a 'provision, criterion or practice' (PCP) of the employer's puts a disabled person at a substantial disadvantage in relation to a relevant matter in comparison with persons who are not disabled – S.20(3) EqA. A PCP is one 'applied by or on behalf of' the employer – para 2(2)(a), Sch 8 EqA.

663

As mentioned earlier, the change from the term 'arrangements' to the EU-inspired 'provision, criterion or practice' had the effect of widening the scope of the duty to make reasonable adjustments and rendered obsolete some of the case law focusing on the meaning of 'arrangements'. The phrase 'provision, criterion or practice' was not defined in the DDA, and nor is it defined in the EqA. However, it is clear that everything that was held to amount to an arrangement under the original wording would amount to a PCP under the current test. The House of Lords in Archibald v Fife Council 2004 ICR 954, HL, confirmed that the terms, conditions and arrangements relating to the essential functions of the disabled person's employment are 'arrangements' (and thereby also a PCP). Thus, where an employee becomes incapable of performing the duties of the job he or she previously carried out, an employer will be under a duty to make adjustments, such as transferring the employee to another job, where it is reasonable to do so.

Although it is not defined in the statute, some assistance as to the meaning of 'PCP' is afforded by the EHRC's Employment Code, which states that the term 'should be construed widely so as to include, for example, any formal or informal policies, rules, practices, arrangements, criteria, conditions, prerequisites, qualifications or provisions. A [PCP] may also include decisions to do something in the future – such as a policy or criterion that has not yet been applied – as well as a "one-off" or discretionary decision' – para 4.5.

21.34 In practice, tribunals will often articulate the relevant PCP in terms that derive from their detailed findings as to the nature of the substantial disadvantage suffered by the claimant. Two examples (both concerning claimants who were diabetic):

- **Mason v Royal Mail Group Ltd** ET Case No.3202963/08: M, who was a diabetic and required insulin injections four times a day, was employed as a postman. In 2006 he was disciplined for failing to deliver several items of mail. The issue of his diabetes, and the effect on him of low blood sugar, was not raised during the disciplinary process, which resulted in a suspended dismissal. The same penalty was imposed in 2007 when, during a work to rule, M left a large number of items without seeking permission from his manager. That warning was still in force when he was called to another hearing in 2008 charged with inexcusable delay in delivering mail. During the hearing, M's representative referred to the impact on M of his diabetes in the 2006 incident, and also pointed out that he had suffered an attack of hypoglycaemia on the day before the latest incident. Nevertheless, M was dismissed and his internal appeal was unsuccessful. He brought claims of disability discrimination, including a complaint that the employer had failed to make reasonable adjustments. In upholding this claim, an employment tribunal found that there was a PCP that a postman or woman must have sufficient powers of concentration and/or memory to ensure that postbags have been checked and cleared before he or she goes out on a round. This put M at a disadvantage because there was a real risk that changes in his blood sugar level could cause loss of concentration and memory, exposing him to the risk of charges of carelessness or deliberate neglect of duty. The employer had failed to make reasonable adjustments by not undertaking an occupational health assessment of the impact of M's disability on his conduct

- **Clark v Newsquest Media (Southern) Ltd** ET Case No.3100102/10: C was a diabetic who had to self-test and self-inject with insulin four times a day. This required her to lift her top and inject herself, which took a matter of a few seconds. In October 2009 she attended an internal training course during which she injected herself. C was told by the trainer in front of the group that she should have disclosed the fact that she was diabetic. The following day, a manager told C that she thought it was inappropriate to inject herself in public and that she should have used the lavatory or a hallway instead. C brought a grievance in respect of these remarks, but this was rejected by the employer on the ground that the injecting had to be done in a designated and private area in accordance with arrangements agreed with HR. C resigned and claimed disability discrimination. Upholding her claim, an employment tribunal found that a PCP had been applied requiring the claimant to self-test and self-inject in private, and that this placed C at a substantial disadvantage in comparison with non-disabled persons. In the tribunal's view, the PCP was unnecessary as it was based on a number of unjustifiable assumptions, including that other employees might be embarrassed or offended or even caused harm if they had needle-phobia. The tribunal concluded that it would have been reasonable for the employer not to apply the PCP and its failure to do so was a breach of the reasonable adjustments duty.

21.35 In most cases where an employee contends that an employer failed to make reasonable adjustments to a PCP, the employee will be referring to a PCP that has been applied to him or her. However, in Roberts v North West Ambulance Service EAT 0085/11 the EAT held that nothing in the DDA actually required that the PCP be applied to the disabled employee. Instead, an employer is subject to a duty to make reasonable adjustments whenever it applies a PCP that places the disabled employee at a substantial disadvantage when compared with persons who are not disabled. This is capable of covering the scenario where a disabled employee is personally exempt from a PCP, but the effect of that PCP on other employees or the public places the disabled employee at a substantial disadvantage. (Given the similarity in wording, the same reasoning would almost certainly apply under the EqA.)

Where the disadvantage experienced by a disabled person arises from something other than a PCP (or, for that matter, a physical feature or the lack of an

665

auxiliary aid) then the employer will not be subject to a duty to make reasonable adjustments. An example:

- **Todd v HM Prison Service** ET Case Nos.1500052/07 and another: T, who worked in the Prison Service, suffered from clinical depression. In 1998 he joined HMP Whitemoor in Cambridgeshire as a physical education officer. However, he did not move from his home in West Yorkshire and had an arrangement with the Prison Service whereby it would pay his travelling and lodging costs. After a number of absences, T requested a transfer to a prison near his home as he believed that being closer to the family and friends who supported him would aid his recovery. A suitable vacancy was not found, and T was eventually dismissed on the ground of capability. As part of his subsequent employment tribunal claim, T argued that a reasonable adjustment would have been for the Prison Service to transfer him directly into a role at a Yorkshire prison without a competitive interview. The tribunal held that the duty to make adjustments did not arise because it was T's personal choice not to move near Whitemoor. The employer was not under a duty to make adjustments simply for the, albeit laudable, purpose of helping to improve the claimant's medical condition. The duty only arose if there was a PCP relating to the claimant's substantive job which needed to be alleviated because of his disability. None of the job-related requirements at Whitemoor placed T at a substantial disadvantage. The disadvantages he suffered arose from personal choices as to his living arrangements, medical practitioners and, from time to time, partners.

21.36 Note that PCPs are also relevant in the context of indirect discrimination claims. For an examination of the meaning of the term in the context of such claims, see Chapter 16, 'Indirect discrimination: proving disadvantage', under 'Provision, criterion or practice'.

21.37 Requirement 2: 'physical features' causing substantial disadvantage

The second situation in which the duty to make reasonable adjustments arises is where a physical feature puts a disabled person at a substantial disadvantage – S.20(4) EqA. A 'physical feature' is defined as a reference to:

- a feature arising from the design or construction of a building

- a feature of an approach to, exit from or access to a building

- a fixture or fitting, or furniture, furnishings, materials, equipment or other chattels (or moveable property in Scotland), in or on premises, or

- any other physical element or quality – S.20(10).

Note also that S.20(9) states that, in respect of physical features, a reference to avoiding a substantial disadvantage includes a reference to (a) removing the physical feature in question; (b) altering it; or (c) providing a reasonable means of avoiding it.

The EHRC Employment Code states that physical features can be temporary or **21.38** permanent (para 6.11). According to the Code, they include (but are not restricted to) steps, stairways, kerbs, exterior surfaces and paving, parking areas, building entrances and exits (including emergency escape routes), internal and external doors, gates, toilet and washing facilities, lighting and ventilation, lifts and escalators, floor coverings, signs, furniture and temporary or moveable items (para 6.12).

Premises occupied by the employer. In the context of work, the reference to a **21.39** 'physical feature' in S.20(4) is a reference to a physical feature of premises occupied by the employer – para 2(2)(b), Sch 8 EqA. This suggests that there would be no duty to make adjustments to a disabled employee's home if the employee worked from home or to the premises of, for example, customers of a disabled sales representative. However, there may be scope to argue, for example, that an adjustment to the premises of a home worker might be covered by the first requirement of S.20, which operates where a PCP puts a disabled person at a substantial disadvantage (see 'Requirement 1: application of a PCP causing substantial disadvantage'). Similarly, a disabled sales representative could argue that the employer should consider allocating him or her customers whose premises are accessible, or providing an auxiliary aid to enable him or her to access customers' premises.

Where it is not possible for an employer to make an adjustment to its physical premises, the employer may be able to make an adjustment to its working practices to minimise the disadvantage to a disabled employee.

Note that special rules apply where the employer occupies the premises under a lease – see under 'Altering physical features – obtaining consent' below.

Requirement 3: lack of 'auxiliary aid' causing substantial **21.40** disadvantage

The third and final situation in which the duty to make reasonable adjustments arises is where, but for the provision of an auxiliary aid, a disabled person would be put at a substantial disadvantage – S.20(5) EqA. In its ordinary meaning, an auxiliary aid is a piece of technology or equipment that is intended to assist a disabled person. Two common examples are an induction loop for people with hearing impairments and voice recognition software for people unable to type. In the context of the EqA, the term 'auxiliary aid' is drawn quite widely. As well as encompassing technological aids such as the examples above, the term also includes an 'auxiliary service' – S.20(11). In the employment field, providing an auxiliary service could mean, for example, providing a sign language interpreter or a support worker for a disabled employee (see para 6.13 of the EHRC Employment Code).

667

21.41 'Substantial disadvantage'

It is crucial to note that the duty to make reasonable adjustments arises only where the disabled person in question is put at a 'substantial disadvantage' in relation to a relevant matter in comparison with persons who are not disabled. S.212(1) EqA states that 'substantial' means more than minor or trivial. In Feld v NCP Services Ltd ET Case No.3103115/08 an employment tribunal rejected a claim brought by an employee who was deemed to be disabled by reason of cancer on the basis that the disadvantage from which she suffered was not substantial. On being made redundant, the claimant had expressed an interest in an alternative position but failed to turn up for the interview to discuss this with her employer. She contended that, as her cancer medication made her tired and the alternative job was located further away from her home, she had decided not to pursue the alternative job option. The tribunal concluded that the claimant's tiredness was not a substantial disadvantage and that the employer was not, therefore, under any duty to consider reasonable adjustments in relation to its decision to dismiss.

A similar conclusion was reached in Schular v Home Office ET Case No.2330695/10, where an employment tribunal rejected the claimant's contention that there had been a breach of the duty to make reasonable adjustments because, as a wheelchair user, she was placed at a substantial disadvantage by the employer's failure to install expensive electronic doors. As a result, she had to ask for assistance in opening doors when going to the lavatory, etc. She was also concerned that her colleague 'buddies' had not been trained in the use of evacuation equipment in the event of a fire or other emergency. The tribunal held that even if the electronic doors had been fitted, the claimant would still have needed someone to push her wheelchair as she did not have the upper body strength to manoeuvre it. And the fact that the claimant's 'buddies' had not been trained in the use of evacuation equipment did not mean that they would not have used their best endeavours to get the claimant out of the building in the event of an emergency. Therefore, C had not been placed at a substantial disadvantage by the employer's refusal to alter its premises or by application of the emergency exit policy.

21.42 Need to identify the nature of the disadvantage

Although substantial disadvantage represents a relatively low threshold, an employment tribunal should not assume that, simply because an employee is disabled, the employer is obliged to make reasonable adjustments. As the guidance set out in Environment Agency v Rowan 2008 ICR 218, EAT (see under 'The three statutory requirements – general guidance on reasonable adjustment claims' above) stipulates, a tribunal must consider the nature and extent of the disadvantage in order to ascertain whether the duty applies and what adjustments would be reasonable. In the Rowan case, one of the reasons for allowing the appeal was that the tribunal had failed to state how the adjustment that it thought reasonable – a trial period of home working – would actually have alleviated the claimant's substantial disadvantage.

A failure to focus clearly upon the alleged substantial disadvantage suffered by **21.43** the claimant in the context of the role he or she performs has caught out many a tribunal, as the following decisions of the EAT illustrate. In both cases, tribunals fell into error by making generalised assumptions about the nature of the disadvantage and failing to correlate the alleged disadvantage with the claimants' particular circumstances:

- **Royal Bank of Scotland v Ashton** 2011 ICR 632, EAT: A was disabled by reason of frequent migraines, as a result of which she incurred a considerable amount of time off work. RBS's sickness policy provided for 'trigger points' in cases of frequent absence which, when exceeded, could lead to disciplinary warnings and the suspension of contractual sick pay. In cases of disability or chronic sickness, the policy permitted the employer to 'relax' the strict application of the trigger points to permit an increase in the number of days' absence that could be taken into account before sick pay was stopped and disciplinary action was taken. An employment tribunal upheld A's reasonable adjustments claim on the basis that RBS should have – but did not – disapplied its sickness policy and thus deferred imposing a disciplinary sanction. The tribunal found that A had been placed at a substantial disadvantage by the application of the policy. On appeal, the EAT overturned that decision on the ground that the tribunal had failed to identify the specific disadvantage suffered by A. It observed: 'Unless that was identified, then logically one simply could not know whether any adjustment was reasonable because it would have to have a practical effect on the disadvantage. For that, one needs to know what the disadvantage is.' In the instant case, the policy was applied to everyone who worked for RBS, whether disabled or not. To the extent that someone who was disabled might suffer greater periods of sickness than the non-disabled, the discretion contained within the policy was applied so that A continued to receive full pay after the usual trigger points. On the face of it, therefore, as a disabled person she was treated advantageously rather than disadvantageously in terms of the way the policy was applied

- **Chief Constable of West Midlands Police v Gardner** EAT 0174/11: G, a part-time police officer, sustained a knee injury as a result of which he was found by a police medical appeal board to be permanently disabled from carrying out his normal duties. However, the board recommended that, with appropriate adjustments, he could carry out an office-based role. One particular adjustment G sought was to be permitted to carry out some of his new duties from home as part of a managed return to his contracted part-time hours. When this was refused, G brought a claim for breach of the duty

669

to make reasonable adjustments. Upholding that claim, an employment tribunal identified the substantial disadvantage suffered by G as his inability to consistently work at a police site even in a temporary role, which placed him at a disadvantage as he was at risk of having his contractual pay reduced and ultimately removed. On appeal, however, the EAT held that the tribunal had failed to set out what it was about G's disability that gave rise to the problems that put him at the substantial disadvantage identified. The EAT acknowledged that there would be many cases in which the nature of the substantial disadvantage was obvious, but there were also cases in which simply to identify a disability as a general condition (such as a knee condition) did not enable any party, and more particularly a court or tribunal, to identify the process of reasoning that led from that to the identification of a substantial disadvantage and an adjustment which was reasonable to have to make to avoid the disadvantage. The tribunal's conclusion remained unexplained by any description of what it was that G could and could not do in consequence of his disability, and there was therefore no information as to the nature of any step that might be taken in order to prevent that particular disadvantage. The tribunal's error was a failure to set out why the adjustment of remote working would or might have had the effect of preventing the PCP – namely, the requirement to work at a police site – having the effect of putting G at a substantial disadvantage in comparison with those who were not disabled. The matter was remitted to the tribunal for reconsideration.

21.44 The assessment of the alleged substantial advantage has to be based upon the facts pertaining to the claimant's actual disability rather than those based on (mis)assumptions. In Copal Castings Ltd v Hinton EAT 0903/04 both the claimant and his employer believed that he had type 1 diabetes, a condition that requires regular insulin injections and monitoring of blood sugar levels. As a result, the claimant asked for his working hours to be reduced, but the request was refused. It later transpired that he actually had type 2 diabetes, a less serious condition. However, when he lodged a tribunal claim arguing that the refusal of the part-time working request was a failure to make reasonable adjustments, the tribunal determined that it was appropriate to assess whether the claimant suffered a substantial disadvantage on the basis of the information that was known at the time he made the request, and went on to find that the employer had failed to meet the duty. On appeal, the EAT held that where both parties at the relevant time believed that there was a serious condition giving rise to the duty to make reasonable adjustments, but it later turns out that there was no such condition, the position must be judged on the true facts rather than on what the parties believed. Despite the parties' belief to the contrary, the claimant had not experienced a substantial disadvantage and the employer had not therefore been subject to the duty to make reasonable adjustments.

Comparators

21.45

The duty to make reasonable adjustments arises where a disabled person is placed at a substantial disadvantage 'in comparison with persons who are not disabled' – S.20(3)–(5) EqA. This makes it clear that a comparative exercise is required to ascertain whether a disabled person is put at a substantial disadvantage. Although the statutory wording might suggest that the comparison is to be made with the population at large, case law has established otherwise. In Smith v Churchills Stairlifts plc 2006 ICR 524, CA, for example, the employer had withdrawn the offer it made to S of a place on a training course after discovering that his disability would leave him unable to carry a full-sized radiator cabinet when visiting customers. The tribunal did not consider that a requirement that employees carry a cabinet put S at a substantial disadvantage compared with persons who are not disabled, since a majority of the population would find it difficult to carry the cabinets. On appeal, the Court of Appeal considered that the comparison undertaken by the tribunal was flawed. In its view, the correct comparators were not the population at large but the six successful candidates who were accepted onto the training course.

The EAT in Fareham College Corporation v Walters 2009 IRLR 991, EAT, emphasised that the comparative exercise in a reasonable adjustments claim, involving a class or group of non-disabled comparators, differs from that which is understood and applied in the individual, like-for-like comparison required in cases of direct sex or race discrimination. In that case, W had been on long-term sick leave as a result of her disability. The college was advised that W might be able to consider a phased return to work, but that it would be some months before she could fulfil her full role and hours. The college instead opted to hold a series of meetings with W in accordance with its absence management policy and eventually dismissed her. In upholding W's claim of discrimination by way of a failure to make reasonable adjustments, the tribunal rejected the college's contentions that W would not accept redeployment and that it could not accommodate her limited availability. Nor was the tribunal convinced that adjustments would have a detrimental effect on other staff.

On appeal, the college argued that the tribunal had failed to construct a non- **21.46** disabled comparator by which to test the disadvantage suffered by W in consequence of the refusal to permit a phased return to work. It argued that such a comparison should have taken account of evidence that other employees had previously been dismissed after a long sickness absence, which might indicate no less favourable treatment. Dismissing the appeal, the EAT held that it may not always be necessary to identify the non-disabled comparators. In many cases the facts will speak for themselves and the identity of the non-disabled comparators will be clearly discernible from the PCP found to be in play. In the instant case, the PCP was the employer's refusal to permit the claimant to have a phased return to work. It was entirely clear from this that the comparator group consisted of other employees who were not disabled and who were able to attend work and carry out the essential tasks required of them in their post. Members of that group were not liable to be dismissed on the ground of disability whereas the claimant, because of her disability, could not do her job, could not comply with the criterion, and was therefore liable to dismissal. She was thereby placed at a substantial disadvantage in comparison with non-disabled employees. It was not necessary for the claimant to satisfy the tribunal that someone who did not have a disability but whose circumstances were otherwise the same as hers would have been treated differently, and the employer's evidence as to another employee dismissed after a nine-month absence was misplaced. Such a like-for-like comparison has no place in a reasonable adjustments complaint.

The EAT's decision in Walters is reflected in para 6.16 of the EHRC Employment Code, which states: 'The purpose of the comparison with people who are not disabled is to establish whether it is because of disability that a particular [PCP] or physical feature or the absence of an auxiliary aid disadvantages the disabled person in question. Accordingly – and unlike direct or indirect discrimination – under the duty to make adjustments there is no requirement to identify a comparator or comparator group whose circumstances are the same or nearly the same as the disabled person's.'

21.47 Employer's knowledge of disability

The duty to make reasonable adjustments only arises where the employer knows, or ought to know, that the employee is disabled. Thus there is, in effect, an 'ignorance defence'. Para 20(1) of Schedule 8 to the EqA, which replicates the effect of S.4A(3) DDA, provides that a person is not subject to the duty if he does not know, and could not reasonably be expected to know:

- in the case of an applicant or potential applicant for work, that an interested disabled person is or may be an applicant for the work in question – para 20(1)(a)

- in any other case referred to in Part 2 of the Schedule, that an interested disabled person has a disability and is likely to be placed at a disadvantage by the employer's PCP, the physical features of the workplace, or a failure to provide an auxiliary aid – para 20(1)(b).

An 'interested disabled person' in this context is defined by reference to tables set out in Part 2 of the Schedule. These list who is an interested disabled person in relation to different categories of 'relevant matters' and the circumstances in which the duty applies in each case. The tables capture how the duty applies in a number of areas related to work; for example, to employers, qualifications bodies and trade organisations. In the context of employment, where the respondent is an employer, and the relevant matter is deciding to whom to offer employment, the interested disabled person is a person who is, or has notified the employer that the person may be, an applicant for the employment; and if the relevant matter is employment by the employer, the relevant interested person is either an applicant for employment by the employer or an employee of the employer – para 5, Sch 8.

As originally enacted, there was a curiosity of drafting in para 20 of Schedule 8. **21.48** This stated that the ignorance defence was available with regard to an applicant or potential applicant under para 20(1)(a), and 'in any other case referred to in this Part of this Schedule' under para 20(1)(b). 'This Part of this Schedule' is Part 3 of Schedule 8, which consists of para 20 alone. Para 20(2) sets out who is to be considered 'an applicant' for the purpose of para 20(1)(a) but nothing in para 20 indicates what the 'other cases' originally referred to in para 20(1)(b) were. Clearly, the intention behind para 20(1)(b) is to cover all other instances in which the duty applies – so the 'other cases' should be those relating to persons other than applicants for work, such as existing employees, office holders, barristers, etc, to whom the reasonable adjustments duty is owed. But this was not the literal effect of the wording. Existing employees, office holders, barristers, etc, are all referred to in Part 2 of Schedule 8, which means they would not be covered by the reference to 'any other case referred to in this Part of this Schedule' in Part 3 of Schedule 8.

At the time the EqA came into force – 1 October 2010 – our view was that tribunals would need to apply a purposive interpretation – excluding the words 'this Part of this Schedule' and relying on the definitions of 'interested disabled person' in Part 2 – to achieve the intended effect of the ignorance defence. Subsequently, the Government rectified the drafting curiosity by way of Article 6(2) of the Equality Act 2010 (Public Authorities and Consequential and Supplementary Amendments) Order 2011 SI 2011/1060, which came into force on 6 April 2011. This Article amended para 20(1)(b) of Schedule 8 so that the words 'any other case referred to in this Part of this Schedule' were replaced by 'in any case referred to in Part 2 of this Schedule'. Note, however, that for cases where the relevant events occured between 1 October 2010 and 5 April 2011, the purposive interpretation outlined above will still be necessary for the knowledge defence to have its intended effect.

Constructive knowledge   21.49

The words 'could not reasonably be expected to know' in para 20 of Schedule 8 leave scope for a tribunal to find that the employer had 'constructive' knowledge of the disability. In Department of Work and Pensions v Hall EAT 0012/05 the employment tribunal found that the DWP had constructive knowledge of an administrative assistant's psychiatric condition. It reached that finding on the basis of the claimant's refusal to answer questions about ill health and disability before starting her job with the DWP; the fact that the DWP was aware of her unusual behaviour, including verbal altercations with

673

colleagues, once she started work; and the fact that her manager and the Human Resources department had been aware of her claim for disabled person's tax credit. Upholding that decision on appeal, the EAT emphasised that the question of whether the employer had, or ought to have had, knowledge of the disability is a question of fact for the tribunal, and will only be interfered with when unsupported by the evidence.

Tribunals are likely to scrutinise an employer's claim of ignorance about an employee's disability to determine whether the employer's claim is rationally based. In Saunders v El Vino Co Ltd ET Case No.2200317/10, for example, an employment tribunal concluded that, judged objectively, there was no valid basis for the employer to contend that it remained in genuine ignorance of the employee's disability. In that case the claimant had had a knee operation that resulted in three weeks' absence from work. The operation was unsuccessful and, following her return to work, she informed the employer that another operation would be needed. A specialist report stated that the claimant would be likely to be absent for six to eight weeks after the second operation and would be close to fully recovered after two to three months. The employer considered that the cost of paying the claimant during her absence would be too great and dismissed her. With regard to her disability discrimination claim, the employer contended that it was not aware that the claimant was a disabled person at the time of dismissal. Rejecting that contention, the tribunal found that any actual lack of knowledge, when considered objectively, was not rational. This was based, among other things, on the fact that the claimant had expressly alleged that she was being discriminated against by reason of her disability in a letter by which she had sought to appeal against the decision to dismiss.

21.50 Enquiring about disability

Early case law under the DDA suggested that an employer was unlikely to be expected to make enquiries to ascertain whether an employee or job applicant had a disability. So, for example, in O'Neill v Symm and Co Ltd 1998 ICR 481, EAT, O'N was dismissed for sickness absence three months after starting a job. During that period she was diagnosed as having ME (myalgic encephalomyelitis) – or chronic fatigue syndrome – but did not inform her employer of that diagnosis. Among her claims against the employer was that it had failed in its duty to make reasonable adjustments by not altering her working hours to accommodate her illness. After noting that the tribunal had found that O'N had been regarded by her employer as an efficient employee and had displayed no symptoms that ought to have put it on enquiry, the EAT concluded that the phrase 'could not reasonably be expected to know' did not impose an obligation on the employer to make wider enquiries; for example, by seeking a medical opinion. In reaching this conclusion, the EAT took account of a passage in the then extant Disability Rights Commission's 'Code of Practice for the elimination of discrimination in the field of employment against disabled persons or persons who have had a disability', which stated: 'The Act does not prevent a disabled person keeping a disability confidential from an employer. But this is likely to mean that unless the employer could reasonably be expected to know about the person's disability anyway, the employer will not be under a duty to make a reasonable adjustment. If a disabled person expects an employer to make a reasonable adjustment, he will need to provide the employer – or, as the case may be, someone acting on the employer's behalf – with sufficient information to carry out that adjustment.'

However, the current EHRC Employment Code takes a notably different view from that expressed in the DRC Code and the O'Neill decision, stating that employers must 'do all they can reasonably be expected to do' to find out whether a claimant has a disability, which would seem to indicate that reasonable enquiries should be made. The Code posits the following example: 'A worker who deals with customers by phone at a call centre has depression which sometimes causes her to cry at work. She has difficulty dealing with customer enquiries when the symptoms of her depression are severe. It is likely to be reasonable for the employer to discuss with the worker whether her crying is connected to a disability and whether a reasonable adjustment could be made to her working arrangements' – para 6.19.

21.51 While knowledge of the disability places a burden on employers to make reasonable enquiries based on the information given to them, it does not require them to make every possible enquiry, particularly where there is little or no basis for doing so. In Ridout v TC Group 1998 IRLR 628, EAT – a case cited with approval by the EAT in Secretary of State for Work and Pensions v Alam 2010 ICR 665, EAT – R applied for a position with TCG and in her responses to the employer's medical questionnaire stated that she had a disability: she had had photosensitive epilepsy, which was controlled by medication, for 20 years. The interview took place on a dark winter evening in a room lit only by fluorescent lighting, which R realised could trigger an epileptic attack. R had a pair of sunglasses attached to a cord around her neck and on entering the room she expressed some disquiet about the lighting. The employer took her remarks as an explanation of the fact that she had sunglasses and might need to use them and proceeded with the interview. In the event, R did not use the sunglasses, nor did she exhibit any symptoms of illness or tell the employer that she felt disadvantaged. When she was not offered the job, however, she claimed that the company had discriminated against her by putting her at a disadvantage by its failure to make a reasonable adjustment to the premises. The employer told the employment tribunal that it had not realised that there was any need for it to make any adjustments to the premises. The tribunal was satisfied that it would not have been reasonable to expect the employer to have made any further enquiry into R's needs in advance of the interview once it had received

675

the completed application forms. It specifically rejected R's suggestion that the company should have obtained a specialist's report.

The tribunal went on to find that the employer could have done more if it had known that the lighting arrangements could trigger an epileptic attack. But the employer did not realise that steps needed to be taken until R made her comment about the lighting. And, even at that point, the tribunal did not think that the employer had been unreasonable in assuming that the presence of sunglasses meant that R could use them if the need arose and that it did not need to take any action. The tribunal also rejected R's suggestion that once she had mentioned the word 'epilepsy' the burden passed to the employer to do everything that needed to be done, under the DDA or otherwise. The DDA required employers to react appropriately to that which they know or could reasonably be expected to know. That placed a burden on the employer to make reasonable enquiries based on the information given to it. But it did not require it to make every possible enquiry even where there was little or no basis for doing so. In the tribunal's view, the employer could not reasonably have known of the possible detriment to R unless she had mentioned it. The tribunal then went on to say that even if it had been satisfied that the employer had failed to make reasonable enquiries, R had not in any case been subjected to a substantial disadvantage.

21.52 R complained to the EAT that the tribunal had erred in placing a burden on her to inform the prospective employer of the seriousness of her condition and that the decision that she had not been substantially disadvantaged was perverse. In the Appeal Tribunal's view, the tribunal had adopted the correct approach. It seemed to the EAT that the tribunal was entitled to conclude that no reasonable employer would be expected to know that the arrangements made for the interview procedure might disadvantage a particular applicant without being told so, especially, as in R's case, where the applicant was suffering from a rare condition. The EAT also agreed with the tribunal that R had not been placed at a substantial disadvantage.

With regard to R's complaint that the tribunal had erred in placing a burden on her to inform a prospective employer of her special needs, the Appeal Tribunal accepted that an applicant for a job cannot be expected to 'harp on' about his or her disability or go into great detail about the effects of the disability merely to cause the employer to make adjustments that it probably should have made in the first place. On the other hand, a balance must be struck and it would be equally undesirable if an employer, in order to protect itself from legal liability, were required to ask a number of questions about whether or not a person feels disadvantaged when the need to do so does not arise and which it would not ask of an able-bodied person. The EAT added that 'people must be taken very much on the basis of how they present themselves'. In the instant case the question of whether the prospective employer should have taken any other steps as a result of what was said at the interview depended almost entirely on the perception of both parties of what was happening during the interview process. It was for the tribunal to determine what had occurred on the basis of the evidence before it and the tribunal had not fallen into error in having required R to be more specific about her needs.

Asking for evidence of disability. If an existing employee asks for an adjustment **21.53** to be made because of a physical or mental impairment the effects of which are not obvious, the employer is entitled to ask for evidence that the impairment gives rise to a disability within the meaning of the 2010 Act. Take the example of an employee who says she has a mental illness whose effects require her to take time off work on a frequent, but irregular, basis. In this situation, an employer who is not satisfied that the woman is telling the truth could ask for evidence – such as a doctor's note – that the woman has an illness with the effects claimed.

The position is more complicated, however, in the context of recruitment. In many cases, it will not be permissible for an employer to request evidence of a job candidate's disability (or, indeed, to enquire about that individual's disability at all) before making a conditional or unconditional job offer. Pre-employment enquiries about health issues are thought to be one of the main reasons why disabled job applicants often fail to reach the interview stage. S.60 EqA is designed to address this problem, providing that an employer must not ask about a job applicant's health (including any disability) before offering him or her work or, where the employer is not in a position to offer work immediately, before including the applicant in a pool of persons to whom it intends to offer work in the future. One of the exceptions is where the question is necessary to establish whether the candidate will be able to undergo an assessment or whether the duty to make reasonable adjustments will apply in relation to that assessment – S.60(6)(a). Note that a contravention of S.60 is enforceable only by the EHRC. However, where an employer asks a question that is prohibited by S.60 and then rejects the job applicant, and the applicant brings a tribunal claim alleging direct disability discrimination, the burden of proof will shift to the employer to show that the reason for rejection was not discriminatory (see further Chapter 24, 'Recruitment', under 'Pre-employment health questions').

Knowledge of disadvantage
21.54
On a literal reading of the 'ignorance defence' contained in para 20 of Schedule 8, even where an employer knows that an employee has a disability, it will not be liable for a failure to make adjustments if it 'does not know, and could not reasonably be expected to know' that a PCP, physical feature of the workplace or failure to provide an auxiliary aid would be likely to place that employee at a substantial disadvantage. However, while such a view seems both sensible and consistent with the Explanatory Notes to the EqA, it should be noted that

677

S.4A(3)(b) DDA, which was substantively identical in scope to para 20, was the subject of apparently conflicting decisions at EAT level.

In Eastern and Coastal Kent Primary Care Trust v Grey 2009 IRLR 429, EAT, the Appeal Tribunal took the view that the requirements of S.4A(3)(b) were cumulative – i.e. to avoid the duty to make adjustments, the employer must show that it did not know of the disability; *and* that it did not know the disabled employee was likely to be at a substantial disadvantage compared with persons who are not disabled; *and* that it could not reasonably have been expected to know those things. However, in the subsequent case of Secretary of State for Work and Pensions v Alam 2010 ICR 665, EAT, a different division of the EAT, after noting that the passage in the Grey judgment in which the EAT suggested that the requirements of S.4A(3)(b) were cumulative was inconsistent with its decision to remit the case to the tribunal, took a different view. The EAT in Alam thought that two questions arise. First, did the employer know both that the employee was disabled and that his or her disability was liable to put him or her at a substantial disadvantage? If the answer to that question is 'no', a second question arises: namely, whether the employer ought to have known both those things. If the answer to that question is also 'no', the statutory duty to make reasonable adjustments is not triggered.

21.55 More recently, in Wilcox v Birmingham CAB Services Ltd EAT 0293/10, the then President of the EAT, Mr Justice Underhill, took the view that there was no conflict between the Grey and Alam decisions, properly understood. In his view, the effect of the knowledge defence in S.4A(4) DDA was that an employer will not be liable for a failure to make reasonable adjustments unless it had actual or constructive knowledge both (i) that the employee was disabled, and (ii) that he or she was disadvantaged by the disability in the way set out in S.4A(1) (i.e. by a PCP or physical feature of the workplace). As the EAT correctly pointed out in Alam, the second element of this test will not come into play if the employer does not know the first element.

It seems likely that the EAT's decision in the Wilcox case has laid to rest concerns about the scope of the knowledge defence in S.4A(3)(b) DDA. Moreover, Underhill P's decision is consistent with the slightly different wording of para 20 of Schedule 8 to the EqA, which does a better job than the predecessor provision of making clear that an employer must have knowledge of both the disability and the disadvantage in order for the adjustment duty to be triggered (see para 20(1)(b)).

21.56 The employment tribunal's decision in Thomson v Newsquest (Herald and Times) Ltd t/a The Herald and Times Group ET Case No.S/121509/09 (a case decided under the DDA) illustrates well how the separate requirement that the employer must have actual or constructive knowledge of the substantial disadvantage works in practice. T was employed as an advertising executive. Following the death of her mother in December 2007, she began to experience psychiatric problems for which she received treatment, but her condition deteriorated and, from February 2009, she was absent from work. In July 2009, the employer started disciplinary proceedings because T had failed to follow the company's attendance and leave policy by not keeping the company informed of her progress, failed to respond to messages, and failed to meet with managers or attend an occupational health appointment. On failing to attend the scheduled disciplinary hearing she was dismissed. Regarding her subsequent claim of disability discrimination, the employer conceded that it had applied a PCP that T should respond to mail. One of the claimed effects of her psychiatric condition was that she categorised things as 'safe' or 'unsafe' and that, as her condition deteriorated, she had developed a general fear of opening mail, answering calls and opening the door, as a result of which she did not respond to the letters from the employer. The employment tribunal accepted that requiring T to respond to mail had placed her at a substantial disadvantage compared with those who did not have her disability. It further found that the employer had actual knowledge of T's mental impairment. However, it found that nobody within the organisation knew or should reasonably have been expected to know of the disadvantage to which she was put by continuing to correspond with her by post. As no letters had been returned, the employer was entitled to believe that these had been delivered to T and read. In the tribunal's view, there was 'a significant difference between being aware that the claimant was ill, even suffering from a mental illness that would constitute a disability under the DDA, and being aware of the specific effect that that had on her in relation to mail opening and therefore the disadvantage that she was placed at as a result of the PCP being applied'. Accordingly, the statutory duty to make reasonable adjustments was not triggered.

Imputing knowledge of other employees to the employer   21.57

An employer cannot claim that it did not know about a person's disability if the employer's agent or employee (for example, an occupational health adviser, HR officer or line manager) knows in that capacity of the disability. The EHRC Employment Code makes it clear that such knowledge is imputed to the employer – see para 6.21. The duty to make reasonable adjustments would still apply even if the disabled person asked the agent or employee to keep the information confidential. This means that employers must have a confidential means of collating information about employees to ensure that they adhere to their duty to make reasonable adjustments.

However, the Code confirms at para 6.22 that information will not be imputed to the employer if it is gained by a person providing services to employees independently of the employer, even if the employer arranged for those services to be provided.

679

21.58 Reasonableness of adjustments

The duty to make adjustments arises only in respect of those steps that it is reasonable for the employer to take to avoid the disadvantage experienced by the disabled person or to provide an auxiliary aid. For employers, this limitation on the duty has undoubtedly grown in significance since the 2004 amendments to the DDA removed the defence of justification to a claim of discrimination by way of a failure to make reasonable adjustments. It means that where an interested disabled person is put at a substantial disadvantage by the employer's PCP, by a physical feature of the employer's premises or by the non-provision of an auxiliary aid, and the employer knows or ought to know of the disability and disadvantage, the employer can lawfully avoid making a proposed adjustment if it would not be a reasonable step to take.

In Smith v Churchills Stairlifts plc 2006 ICR 524, CA, the Court of Appeal confirmed that the test of reasonableness in this context is an objective one, and it is ultimately the employment tribunal's view of what is reasonable that matters. A claim of a failure to make reasonable adjustments may, therefore, require a tribunal to take the unusual step of substituting its own view for that of the employer, in marked contrast to the approach taken in respect of unfair dismissal, where such an approach amounts to an error of law. The contrast between the two jurisdictions was highlighted by the EAT in Royal Bank of Scotland v Ashton 2011 ICR 632, EAT. There the Appeal Tribunal held that an employment tribunal had erred by focusing, as would be appropriate in an unfair dismissal claim, on the reasonableness of the process by which the employer reached the decision not to make a proposed adjustment. The EAT emphasised that, since the reasonable adjustment provisions are concerned with practical outcomes rather than procedures, a tribunal's focus must be on whether the adjustment itself can be considered reasonable.

21.59 A significant change brought about by the EqA is the omission of specific factors to be considered when determining reasonableness. S.18B(1) DDA stipulated that, in determining whether it was reasonable for an employer to have to take a particular step in order to comply with the duty, regard should be had, in particular, to:

- the extent to which taking the step would prevent the effect in relation to which the duty was imposed (i.e. the effectiveness of the step)

- the extent to which it was practicable for the employer to take the step

- the financial and other costs that would be incurred by the employer in taking the step and the extent to which taking it would disrupt any of its activities

- the extent of the employer's financial and other resources

680

- the availability to the employer of financial or other assistance with respect to taking the step

- the nature of the employer's activities and the size of its undertaking

- where the step would be taken in relation to a private household, the extent to which taking it would (i) disrupt that household, or (ii) disturb any person residing there.

These factors are not mentioned in the EqA, although they are well known by **21.60** tribunals and will surely continue to be relevant in many cases. Indeed, all but the last factor are listed in para 6.28 of the EHRC Employment Code as examples of matters that a tribunal might take into account. The key difference under the EqA is that it is no longer an error of law for a tribunal to fail to consider one of these factors, so long as it has adequately considered whether the proposed adjustment would be reasonable. The Code reflects this when it states: 'What is a reasonable step for an employer to take will depend on all the circumstances of each individual case' (para 6.23).

Note that while the EqA does not contain a list of factors that must be taken into account by a tribunal in considering whether an adjustment would be a reasonable step to take, it does contain a power enabling Ministers to make regulations specifying such factors – S.22(1)(a). This power has not yet been exercised.

Effectiveness of the proposed adjustment
21.61

It is unlikely to be reasonable for an employer to have to make an adjustment that involves little benefit to the disabled person. In order to gauge the effectiveness of a proposed adjustment, the employer will almost certainly need to consult the disabled person concerned, who is likely to be best placed to assess whether the adjustment would make a difference. For example, employers should not assume that a visually impaired person will be able to read Braille. The appropriate adjustment may involve the use of taped information, which is preferred by some people with visual impairments.

Alternatively, or additionally, the employer may wish to consider obtaining an expert opinion on the likely effect of any proposed step. This could involve seeking medical evidence on the extent of an employee's disability and its effect on his or her ability to carry out the job that he or she is employed to do, or the opinion of an occupational health or workplace specialist – see further 'Workplace assessments' below. In many cases, the need for independent expert advice may not be necessary; although in cases involving medical conditions that are unusual or whose effects are less predictable, medical evidence may be vital.

In Romec Ltd v Rudham EAT 0069/07 the claimant suffered from chronic **21.62** fatigue syndrome and had been on a phased return-to-work programme. He

---
681

relapsed and was eventually dismissed on capability grounds. The employment tribunal, noting that prior to his dismissal the claimant had expressed a desire to continue with the rehabilitation programme, found that its extension would have been a reasonable adjustment as it would have provided the claimant with the opportunity to 'prove himself'. On appeal, the EAT held that the tribunal had failed to consider the essential question – whether the adjustment would have removed the disadvantage experienced by the claimant. The EAT accordingly allowed the appeal and remitted the issue to the same tribunal for reconsideration. The Appeal Tribunal instructed that if, based on the medical evidence and the failure of the first programme, the tribunal concluded that there was no prospect of a further programme succeeding in returning the claimant to his full duties, it would not be a reasonable adjustment. If, however, the tribunal found a real prospect of an extended programme resulting in a full return to work, it might be reasonable to expect the employer to take that course of action.

However, the EAT has also made it clear in Leeds Teaching Hospital NHS Trust v Foster EAT 0552/10 that there does not necessarily have to be a good or real prospect of an adjustment removing a disadvantage for that adjustment to be a reasonable one. It is sufficient for a tribunal to find simply that there would have been a prospect of it being alleviated. The same point was forcefully reiterated by another division of the EAT in Noor v Foreign and Commonwealth Office 2011 ICR 695, EAT, where His Honour Judge Richardson observed: 'Although the purpose of a reasonable adjustment is to prevent a disabled person from being at a substantial disadvantage, it is certainly not the law that an adjustment will only be reasonable if it is completely effective.'

21.63 The focus of a tribunal must be on whether the adjustment would be effective by removing or reducing the disadvantage the claimant is experiencing at work as a result of his or her disability, not whether it would advantage the claimant generally. In Tameside Hospital NHS Foundation Trust v Mylott EAT 0352/09 the employment tribunal had found that the Trust failed to make a reasonable adjustment when it declined to assist M in an application for ill-health retirement. On appeal, the EAT held that the duty to make reasonable adjustments does not extend 'to enabling a disabled employee who is no longer able to do the work (or any available alternative) to leave the employment on favourable terms'. In the EAT's view, the concept of an adjustment involves a step or steps that make it possible for the employee to remain in employment, and does not incorporate compensation for being unable to do so. A similar view was taken by the EAT in Salford NHS Primary Care Trust v Smith EAT 0507/10 in respect of the particular adjustments that the claimant in that case alleged should have been made by the employer. The Appeal Tribunal overturned the employment tribunal's decision that the employer should have put in place a rehabilitation programme and granted the claimant a career break. Neither of these adjustments would have had the effect of preventing the PCP in that case – which comprised the expectation that the claimant would perform her full-time role within the contracted hours – from placing her at a substantial disadvantage in comparison with persons who were not disabled.

By way of contrast, in Noor v Foreign and Commonwealth Office (above), the EAT ruled that an employment tribunal had fallen into error when it struck out the reasonable adjustments claim of an employee who, owing to his dyslexia/dyspraxia, contended that he should have been given a second interview after having been required to answer questions at the first interview about a competency that was not specified in the job advertisement. It was accepted that the claimant's impairment had put him at a substantial disadvantage, but the tribunal struck out his claim on the ground that it had no reasonable prospect of success because, in its view, even if he had been given a second interview he would not have been successful in securing the job. On appeal, the EAT ruled that the tribunal had erred. Judge Richardson observed: 'If the substantial disadvantage arises from arrangements for interview… and relates to the ability of the disabled person (compared to persons who are not disabled) to perform in interview for a job, then the purpose of the reasonable adjustment is to remove that disadvantage – in other words, to eliminate the practical difficulty and embarrassment which the provision, criterion or practice has caused and create a level playing field for the disabled person in interview. If a reasonable adjustment should have been made for this purpose it is not fatal to the disabled person's case that he or she would still not have obtained the job.'

Workplace assessments. One way in which employers can assess whether a **21.64** proposed type of adjustment might have the necessary effect of eliminating the substantial disadvantage suffered by a disabled employee is to conduct a workplace or occupational health assessment. Indeed, in appropriate circumstances, a failure to take this step may, of itself, comprise a breach of the statutory duty under S.20 EqA. Two examples:

- **Nikola-Erotokritou v Hertfordshire County Council** ET Case No.3302508/10: N-E was employed as a chef manager in a school from January 2008 until her dismissal in April 2010. She suffered from repetitive strain injury as a result, allegedly, of heavy lifting she had to do as part of her job. In consequence, she suffered a number of sickness absences. Her request for assistance was ignored by the employer. In view of the length of her sickness absences, the employer made enquiries about her health through its occupational health service. In August 2009 a consultant reported that she should be able to return to work so long as she had help with heavy lifting. The employer decided not to make adjustments to the lifting because N-E had made it clear that she would have difficulty with a number of other aspects of her work as well. Eventually, N-E was dismissed on capability grounds. An employment tribunal upheld her claim that the employer was in breach of its duty to make reasonable adjustments. The tribunal found that there was medical evidence to the effect that N-E was fit to return to her duties provided she had assistance with heavy lifting. The employer should have offered to make specific adjustments based on a workplace assessment. Had this been done, N-K would have been in a position to resume her job duties

- **Morgan v Northamptonshire Teaching Primary Care Trust** ET Case No.1201412/09: M was engaged as an agency worker from April 2008 to January 2009. During this period, he was diagnosed with Asperger's syndrome, which impaired his emotional understanding and caused difficulties with social interaction. In January 2009 he applied for a permanent post with the employer, which he made aware of his disability. He did well at interview and was made a conditional offer of employment, subject to receipt of two satisfactory references and clearance from occupational health. However, a reference from his former employer stated that it would not take him back, primarily because of his sickness and lateness. The reference acknowledged that the sickness and lateness were due to his recently diagnosed condition and that this was now being treated. A second reference was also poor, remarking on the deterioration in M's emotional health and performance. The employer decided to withdraw the job offer prior to receiving the outcome of the occupational health report. An employment tribunal upheld M's claim on the ground that, rather than simply withdrawing the job offer, the employer should have obtained a more detailed occupational health assessment and discussed in the light of this ways in which reasonable adjustments in the workplace could help M.

21.65 **Cumulative beneficial effect of different adjustments.** A measure that on its own may be ineffective could nevertheless be one of several adjustments which, when taken together, could remove or reduce the disadvantage experienced by the disabled person. For example, in Shaw and Co Solicitors v Atkins EAT 0224/08 the EAT held that the effectiveness of a change to A's working hours had to be assessed as a part of a package, along with proposals for her to work from home and use a chairlift to gain access to the employer's offices.

21.66 **Practicability**

Closely linked to the effectiveness of any proposed step is that step's practicability. A step that is relatively easy for the employer to take is more likely to be reasonable than one that is difficult. The former Disability Rights Commission's 'Code of Practice for the elimination of discrimination in the field of employment against disabled persons or persons who have had a disability' recognised that it might be impracticable for an employer who needs to appoint an employee urgently to have to wait for an adjustment, such as a change to an entrance, to be made. How long it might be reasonable for an employer to have to wait would depend on the circumstances. However, it might be possible to make a temporary adjustment in the meantime, such as

684

using another, less convenient entrance. Although this guidance is not replicated in the EHRC's Employment Code, there is no apparent reason why it would not hold true of the duty to make reasonable adjustments under the EqA.

In Secretary of State for Work and Pensions (Job Centre Plus) and ors v Wilson EAT 0289/09 W suffered from agoraphobia and panic and anxiety attacks in new situations. She had been working on a scheme in offices near to her home, but when it finished she was to be redeployed, and she proposed that she should work from home. The employer made various alternative proposals, such as providing a taxi, colleague or support worker to take her to and from the new offices, but W declined them all. In upholding W's claim of discrimination on account of a failure to make reasonable adjustments, an employment tribunal found that the employer had not dealt promptly and properly with W's request to work at home and its proposals were aimed more at defending likely proceedings than finding a just solution. On appeal, the EAT held that the tribunal had erred by not considering whether it would be practicable for the employer to permit W to work from home. On the evidence, it was clear that there were no suitable home working vacancies, that the work W was employed to do involved face-to-face contact with customers, and that workers needed access to confidential materials that were stored centrally and required supervision. On the basis of those factual findings, the only possible conclusion was that home working was not a practicable step and therefore was not a reasonable adjustment.

Financial and other costs of adjustment   21.67

Employers and tribunals are likely to take both the cost of making an adjustment and any disruption it would cause into account when assessing whether it would be a reasonable step to take. The EqA does not specify any upper cost limit above which all adjustments would be unreasonable, so cost implications are to be considered on a case-by-case basis. In Cordell v Foreign and Commonwealth Office 2012 ICR 280, EAT, the EAT noted that a tribunal is required to make a judgment based on what it considers right and just in its capacity as an industrial jury. This may include a number of considerations, such as the size of any budget dedicated to reasonable adjustments, what the employer has spent in comparable situations, what other employers are prepared to spend, and any policies set out in collective agreements. However, the EAT made the point that such considerations, even where they have been identified, can be of no more than suggestive or supportive value – there is no objective measure for assessing one kind of expenditure against another. (The facts of this case are considered in more detail below.)

The significance of the cost of a step may partly depend on what the employer might otherwise have to spend. For example, it is likely that it would be reasonable for an employer to have to spend at least as much on an adjustment to enable the retention of a disabled person – including any retraining – as

685

might be spent on recruiting and training a replacement. Conversely, an employer might successfully argue that an adjustment that would cost well in excess of the annual salary for the job in question would not be reasonable.

21.68 Two examples:

- **Pervez v Royal Bank of Scotland plc** ET Case No.112677/08: P, who was registered as partly blind, was offered a job as a customer services adviser, subject to the employer being able to make the necessary adjustments to enable him to do the job. The RNIB carried out an assessment, but found that the adjustments would cost between £35,000 and £60,000 and that even with those adjustments there was little likelihood that P would be able to carry out the full range of duties. The job offer was subsequently withdrawn. Dismissing P's claim of discrimination by way of a failure to make reasonable adjustments, the tribunal considered that it clearly made little sense to pay up to £60,000 to make adjustments for a role that attracted an annual salary of only £14,000. Although the employer was a bank with huge resources, the tribunal did not consider it reasonable for an employer to pay the sort of costs proposed where the adjustments would offer limited benefit. It should be noted, however, that cost was only one factor in this case: the employer's major concern was whether the technology would work, combined with the disruption that would be caused to other employees

- **Cordell v Foreign and Commonwealth Office** 2012 ICR 280, EAT: C, who was profoundly deaf, had worked for the FCO since 2001. In order to carry out her job, she used professionally qualified 'lipspeakers', who were trained to repeat spoken communications from a third party, reproducing the rhythm and phrasing of the speaker, and to use appropriate gestures and facial expressions as well as British Sign Language and finger spelling. In 2009, C successfully applied for promotion to the post of deputy head of mission at the British Embassy in Kazakhstan. Under the FCO's reasonable adjustments policy, which had come into force after consultation earlier that year, adjustments costing over £10,000 were subject to a detailed assessment procedure. After carrying out such an assessment, the FCO decided that it would be too expensive to provide a team of lipspeakers in Kazakhstan and withdrew the conditional job offer. The employment tribunal found that the likely annual cost of the proposed adjustments was at least £249,500. This amounted to five times C's salary, nearly the cost of running the entire embassy, and was a large proportion of the FCO's budget for reasonable adjustments. In these circumstances, it held that the proposed adjustments were not reasonable and the FCO had not failed in its duty. The EAT upheld the tribunal's decision, noting that its earlier decision in Pulham and ors v Barking and Dagenham London Borough Council 2010 ICR 333, EAT (an age discrimination case), showed that while the size of a relevant budget is not decisive, this does not mean it is not relevant. The tribunal was therefore perfectly entitled to take into account the FCO's budget for reasonable adjustments as part of the context. Furthermore, the fact that the tribunal considered that the cost would have to be met from existing resources was also legitimate. No one's resources, not even the Government's, are infinite. The EAT also rejected the argument that in light of the fact that the FCO would pay substantial school fees for the children of staff posted overseas, it was unreasonable not to make a commensurate payment on C's behalf. The tribunal had clearly considered this factor and its decision on this point was not perverse.

21.69 The cost of an adjustment will not necessarily be assessed in financial terms alone: the effect of an adjustment on the employer's workforce is clearly relevant to what is reasonable, and employers may be hesitant to agree to an adjustment that seems unfair to other employees. However, it should be remembered that the statutory duty entails a degree of positive action. An example:

- **Smith v HM Prison Service** ET Case No.2326450/09: since suffering injuries in a road accident in 2000, S had been unable to undertake the control and restraint duties of a prison officer and had been assigned lighter duties as an instructor, but continued to be paid as a prison officer. In 2006, the Prison Service undertook a review of all prison officers on restricted duties, concluded that S could not continue to be employed as a prison officer, and offered him the choice of medical retirement or employment as a civilian instructor on a lower rate of pay. The Prison Service argued that it would not have been a reasonable adjustment to continue the arrangement whereby S was paid as an officer for the work of an instructor as it would be unfair to the lower-paid civilian instructors who were performing the same work and could give rise to grievances and possibly an equal pay claim. The tribunal found that such an adjustment was reasonable, noting that the arrangement had existed for over six years without any objection from civilian instructors. The tribunal added that the Prison Service would surely have a defence to any equal pay claim – that the difference in pay was attributable to a genuine material factor other than sex.

It is clear, however, that the extent to which adjustments would have a detrimental effect on other employees is a consideration in determining whether they are reasonable or not. For example, an adjustment might cause a significant change in the temperature in a workplace, although in such circumstances it might be reasonable to provide a small office for the disabled employee, thus allowing him or her to reduce or increase the temperature without this having a detrimental effect on other staff.

21.70 In some circumstances, swapping the disabled person's role with that of another employee could amount to a reasonable adjustment. The effect on the other employee is obviously a relevant consideration, as are the size and nature of the employer's undertaking. In Chief Constable of South Yorkshire Police v Jelic

687

2010 IRLR 744, EAT, the employment tribunal had found that it would have been a reasonable adjustment to swap J's role with that of F, a police officer performing a role with minimal face-to-face contact with the public, in order to alleviate the disadvantage suffered by J as a result of his chronic anxiety syndrome. Upholding that decision on appeal, the EAT recognised that it will not always be reasonable to enforce a job swap. For example, it may not be reasonable for an employer to require a woman who works flexible hours owing to childcare responsibilities to swap her job with that of a disabled person working longer hours. However, the Appeal Tribunal emphasised that each case will turn upon its own facts and, on the present facts, the tribunal was entitled to decide as it did.

21.71 Employer's financial and other resources
Closely linked to the question of cost are the financial and other resources of the employer. It goes without saying that it is more likely to be reasonable for an employer with substantial financial resources to have to make an adjustment with a significant cost than for an employer with fewer resources. Similarly, what is reasonable for an employer with thousands of staff may not be reasonable for a small employer, as there will be less leeway to reallocate duties. In Parker v Oak Cash And Carry Ltd ET Case No.2700974/07, for example, P, a shop assistant, suffered from problems with her back and neck and had to go into hospital for an operation. She wanted to return to work on light duties and requested that she work only on the tills. The employer refused because till operators were expected to do other work and it did not believe it was realistic for P to return only as a till operator. P resigned, claiming that the employer had failed to make the reasonable adjustment of allowing her to return to work on light duties. Dismissing the claim, the tribunal noted that the employer was a small business with a small number of staff and that it was necessary for the employees who worked on the tills to undertake other duties during slack periods. Allowing P to return only on the tills would have added to the employer's costs and would have caused problems with other employees, whose duties would have been less varied as a result.

Tribunals have been known to take the relatively large resources of public sector organisations into account when assessing what would be a reasonable adjustment. More recently, however, tribunals appear to have had regard to the current restraints on public finances. In Gibbons v Dartford and Gravesham NHS Trust ET Case No.1101264/09, for example, G had a number of absences owing to her frequent migraines, a condition that the Trust accepted amounted to a disability. The level of absences led the Trust to engage its sickness absence policy and G was eventually dismissed. She argued that it would have been a reasonable adjustment for the Trust to ignore the level of her sickness absence, but the tribunal disagreed. It noted that the Trust had already made a number of adjustments – relaxing the conditions of the sickness absence policy and entering into discussions about a phased return to work – and concluded that, in light of the fact that the Trust as a public organisation must have regard to the public purse and budgetary constraints, it would not be reasonable completely to ignore a significant level of sickness absence.

Availability of financial and other assistance 21.72

A costly adjustment may be reasonable even for a small employer if assistance from an outside body is available. Furthermore, expert advice could help to identify an adjustment that the employer may not otherwise have considered. There are a number of sources of information and/or financial assistance available, including the Employment Service's Placing, Assessment and Counselling Teams (PACTs), the Access to Work scheme and charitable bodies.

While there is no express obligation on an employer to seek expert advice when considering reasonable adjustments, it may be reasonable for an employer to do this. For examples, see under 'Common types of adjustment – involving third parties' below.

Contributions from the disabled person. Section 20(7) EqA makes it clear **21.73** that a disabled person is not required to contribute to the cost of an adjustment. A disabled person may, however, be prepared to use a special piece of equipment belonging to him or her for work purposes. In these circumstances, it may be reasonable for the employer to allow the person to use the equipment and to make any other adjustments that are reasonable.

Nature and size of the employer 21.74

Closely linked to the employer's financial and other resources is the question of its size. This can be a particularly important factor when an employment tribunal is considering whether an adjustment involving redeployment is reasonable. For example, in Rixon v EDF Energy Consulting Ltd ET Case No.2305531/06 the tribunal, in finding that it would have been a reasonable adjustment to redeploy an employee who had been absent with stress caused by workplace bullying, considered that it was 'inconceivable' that an employer the size of EDF did not have another role that could be offered to the employee.

The nature of the employer's undertaking can also be an important factor in the tribunal's consideration of what is reasonable. A good example of this is Chief Constable of South Yorkshire Police v Jelic 2010 IRLR 744, EAT (discussed under 'Financial and other costs of adjustment' above), in which the EAT held that it would have been a reasonable adjustment to swap a disabled employee's role with that of a colleague. In reaching this decision, the EAT was influenced by the 'disciplined' nature of employment in the police force, where there is a clearly defined chain of command and orders are usually followed unquestioningly. A similar adjustment in a typical private sector office environment might not be considered reasonable, particularly if it could result

689

in an employment tribunal claim by the non-disabled employee (an employee forced to move into a role that is outside the terms of his or her contract may be able to claim unfair constructive dismissal).

21.75 In Todd v HM Prison Service ET Case Nos.1500052/07 and another (considered under 'The three requirements – requirement 1: application of a PCP causing substantial disadvantage' above) an employment tribunal determined that the employer did not need to make the adjustment of transferring a disabled employee closer to his home because the disadvantage suffered by the employee did not arise from the Prison Service's PCP. However, on the question of whether transferring the employee would have been reasonable, the tribunal noted that while each prison operates as a separate unit, the Prison Service is a national employer, and it would have been reasonable for such a national employer to ensure that the employee was transferred to a vacancy. Furthermore, the proposed adjustment would not have been rendered unreasonable simply because it involved passing the problem of the claimant's substantial absence record on to a different institution within the same employer organisation.

In cases concerning employers who provide a public service – such as NHS Trusts or Government departments – tribunals have occasionally taken account of the needs of the service users. For example, in Gibbons v Dartford and Gravesham NHS Trust ET Case No.1101264/09 the employment tribunal took account of the Trust's need 'to address matters affecting patient care' in deciding that it would not have been a reasonable adjustment to ignore the claimant's sickness absences. And in Chief Constable of Lincolnshire Police v Weaver EAT 0622/07 the EAT held that, in deciding whether placing a disabled employee on a scheme designed to retain the skills of retired police officers was a reasonable adjustment, the employment tribunal had erred by looking at the case only from the employee's perspective. It should have examined all the circumstances, which included the wider operational objectives of the police force – in particular, its desire to free up suitable positions for officers on 'restricted duties' who were still in active service.

21.76 **Other factors**

The EqA places no limits on the factors that an employment tribunal can take into account when assessing reasonableness, reflecting case law under the DDA which clearly stated that the examples provided in that statute were non-exhaustive. Other factors that may be relevant include:

- *health and safety* – if making a particular adjustment would increase the risk to health and safety of any person (including the disabled worker in question) then this is a relevant consideration in deciding whether it is reasonable to make that adjustment. Suitable and sufficient risk assessments should be used to help determine whether such risk is likely to arise – para 6.27 EHRC Employment Code

- *expenditure on other employees* – a tribunal may consider the expenditure on adjustments that has already been made for another disabled employee to be a relevant factor when determining reasonableness. The fact that an employer chooses to give one or more disabled employees an adjustment that goes beyond the strict requirements of the duty does not necessarily mean that similar adjustments have to be made for other people with a similar disability

- *cooperation of employee* – another factor that may be taken into account is the willingness of the employee to cooperate with attempts to identify reasonable adjustments. If the employee refuses to cooperate, it may not be reasonable for the employer to have to make any adjustment whatsoever. But whether this would be the case where the refusal to cooperate is itself a manifestation of the disability is questionable – the decision in Cosgrove v Caesar and Howie 2001 IRLR 653, EAT, indicates that an employer should, independently of the employee, turn its mind to the question of what adjustments may be appropriate (see the section on 'Duty to make reasonable adjustments' above, under 'Scope of the duty – duty on employer, not employee').

Common types of adjustment

21.77

The EqA does not place any limitations on the type of adjustment that might be considered reasonable, reflecting the fact that an employer's duty to make adjustments arises on a case-by-case basis, and that whether an employer has complied with the duty depends on what is reasonable in the circumstances.

One feature of the DDA that has not survived the transition to the EqA is the non-exhaustive list of possible adjustments previously set out in S.18B(2) DDA. However, a similar list appears in the EHRC Employment Code at para 6.33 and is set out below, along with examples (also taken from the Code):

- making adjustments to premises – this could include structural or physical changes such as widening a doorway, providing a ramp or moving furniture for a wheelchair user

- providing information in accessible formats – the format of instructions and manuals might need to be modified for some disabled workers (for example, produced in Braille or on audio tape) and instructions for people with learning disabilities might need to be conveyed orally with individual demonstration or in Easy Read. Employers may also need to arrange for recruitment materials to be provided in alternative formats

- allocating some of the disabled person's duties to another person – an employer may allocate minor or subsidiary duties to another worker if a disabled worker has difficulty doing them because of his or her disability.

691

For example, if a job occasionally involves going onto the open roof of a building, an employer might have to transfer this work away from someone with severe vertigo

- transferring the disabled person to fill an existing vacancy – if a worker becomes disabled, or has a disability that worsens, so he or she cannot carry on with the current job, and there is no reasonable adjustment that would enable him or her to do so, then the disabled person might have to be considered for any suitable alternative posts that are available. The employer may also need to consider retraining and other adjustments, such as equipment for the new post or a transfer to a position on a higher grade

- altering hours of working or training – for example, allowing the disabled person to work flexible hours to enable him or her to have additional breaks to overcome fatigue. This could also include permitting part-time working, or different working hours to avoid the need to travel in the rush hour. A phased return to work with a gradual build-up of hours may be appropriate in some circumstances

- assigning the disabled person to a different place of work or training – for example, moving a worker who uses a wheelchair to a ground-floor office, or to other premises of the same employer if the first building is inaccessible. Allowing the worker to work from home may also be a reasonable adjustment

- allowing the disabled person to be absent during working or training hours for rehabilitation, assessment or treatment – for example, allowing a worker who has become disabled more time off than would be afforded to non-disabled workers, in order that the disabled worker can undertake employment rehabilitation. A similar adjustment may be appropriate if a disability worsens or if a disabled person needs occasional treatment

- giving, or arranging for, training or mentoring (whether for the disabled person or any other worker) – this could be training in the use of particular equipment used by the disabled person, or an alteration to the standard workplace training to reflect the worker's particular disability

- acquiring or modifying equipment – for example, providing a specially adapted keyboard for someone with arthritis, a large screen for a visually impaired worker, an adapted telephone for someone with a hearing impairment, or other modified equipment. However, there is no requirement to provide or modify equipment for personal purposes unconnected with work, such as providing a wheelchair if a person needs one in any event but does not have one: the disadvantage in such a case does not flow from the employer's PCP or premises

- modifying procedures for testing or assessment – for example, a person with restricted manual dexterity might be disadvantaged by a written test, so an employer might have to give that person an oral test

- providing a reader or interpreter – for example, arranging for a colleague to read mail to a worker with a visual impairment, or hiring a reader

- providing supervision or other support – this could involve providing a support worker or arranging help from a colleague, in appropriate circumstances, for someone whose disability leads to uncertainty or lack of confidence in unfamiliar situations

- allowing a disabled employee to take a period of disability leave – for example, allowing a worker with cancer a period of leave to undergo treatment and rehabilitation, at the end of which he or she is permitted to return to his or her job

- participating in supported employment schemes, such as Workstep – such schemes exist to help disabled workers back into work. It may be a reasonable adjustment to allow a worker to make private phone calls during the working day to a support worker at the scheme

- employing a support worker to assist a disabled employee – for example, where an adviser with a visual impairment is required to make home visits, the employer could employ a support worker to assist the adviser

- modifying disciplinary or grievance procedures – for example, by allowing a worker with a learning disability to bring a friend (as opposed to a trade union representative or colleague) to a meeting about a grievance, and ensuring that the meeting is conducted in a way that does not disadvantage or patronise the disabled worker

- adjusting redundancy selection criteria – where the selection is based partly on sickness absence records, it may be a reasonable adjustment to ignore any periods of disability-related absence

- modifying performance-related pay arrangements – where a worker's pay is determined by output, but the worker needs frequent short breaks which the employer has agreed to as a reasonable adjustment, it may also be reasonable for the employer to pay an agreed rate (for example, the average hourly rate) for those breaks.

On occasion, it may be necessary for an employer to take a number of steps in **21.78** conjunction with one another. The example cited at para 6.34 of the EHRC Employment Code is of a blind woman who is given a new job with her employer in an unfamiliar part of the building. The following are given as reasonable adjustments an employer may have to make in these circumstances: (i) arrange facilities for the employee's guide dog in the new area; (ii) arrange

693

for her new instructions to be in Braille; and (iii) provide disability equality training for all staff.

Experience and research has shown that the majority of potentially reasonable adjustments will broadly fit into one of 11 categories:

- avoiding or delaying dismissal
- rehabilitation following substantial absence
- redeployment
- altering or reallocating duties
- altering hours of work
- altering place of work
- adjusting workplace practices, procedures or policies
- pay preservation and changes to pay/bonuses
- providing supervision or support
- acquiring or modifying equipment
- involving third parties.

These are examined in detail in the following sections.

21.79 Avoiding or delaying dismissal

In the early years of the DDA, case law suggested that the duty to make reasonable adjustments did not apply to the act of dismissing an employee. So, for example, in Clark v TDG Ltd (t/a Novacold Ltd) 1999 ICR 951, CA, the Court of Appeal held that a dismissed employee could not claim that it would have been a reasonable adjustment to take some action other than dismissing him. Subsequently, however, the EAT in Fareham College Corporation v Walters 2009 IRLR 991, EAT, took the view that amendments made to the DDA in 2004 removed any limitation on the duty, noting that para 5.5 of the then extant Disability Rights Commission's 'Code of Practice for the elimination of discrimination in the field of employment against disabled persons or persons who have had a disability' stated: 'The duty to make reasonable adjustments applies in recruitment and during all stages of employment, including dismissal. It may also apply after employment has ended.'

The view that the duty now applies to dismissals was also given support in Stockton on Tees Borough Council v Aylott 2010 ICR 1278, CA. There, Lord Justice Mummery (who also gave the leading judgment in the Clark case) made obiter (i.e. non-binding) comments supporting the view that, since Article 3(1)(c) of the EU Equal Treatment Framework Directive (No.2000/78) expressly includes within its scope 'employment and working conditions,

694

including dismissals and pay', the UK provisions implementing that Directive must also be interpreted as applying to dismissals. Furthermore, the EHRC Employment Code states that the duty in S.20 EqA applies to all stages of employment, including the act of dismissing an employee – para 6.8.

In practice, tribunals have for some considerable time assumed that the duty to **21.80** make reasonable adjustments applies to dismissal. In a number of cases, it has been held that a reasonable adjustment would have been to delay dismissal at least until a medical or workplace report could have been obtained to help determine whether the claimant had any prospect of returning to work after a period of disability-related absence and, if so, what further reasonable adjustments might be necessary to facilitate this. For example, in Bynon v Wilf Gilbert (Staffordshire) Ltd ET Case No.1301482/08 an employment tribunal ruled that there had been a breach of the statutory duty when an employer, which had become impatient with the length of time the claimant remained off sick, proceeded to dismissal without obtaining a proper medical prognosis. In the tribunal's view, it would have been a reasonable adjustment to hold off dismissal until the employer had established whether the claimant was fit to return to work (with or without adjustments) in the role to which she had been transferred by way an earlier reasonable adjustment and, if not, whether she was fit to return in any other role.

Previous reasonable adjustments had also been made in London Underground Ltd v Vuoto EAT 0123/09. In that case, certain adjustments to shift patterns had been made to accommodate the effects of the claimant's multiple sclerosis. When these were suddenly withdrawn after two years, the claimant went on sick leave suffering from stress. Subsequently, his attendance at work became patchy and the relationship between him and the employer deteriorated, which ultimately led to his dismissal. An employment tribunal upheld his claims of both unfair dismissal and disability discrimination. With regard to his reasonable adjustments claim, the claimant successfully contended that it would have been reasonable, among other things, to have allowed him to maintain his original agreed hours and for the employer to have adjusted its sickness policy to permit a greater level of sickness in his case than in that of someone without MS. On appeal, the EAT characterised these adjustments as a means of seeking to avoid dismissal, reasoning that had they been put in place they would probably have permitted the claimant to return to work and revert to a sustainable pattern of absence. The EAT rejected the employer's contention that the employment tribunal had wrongly taken into account the historical adjustments as these had no relevance to the substantial disadvantage that was the subject of the claimant's reasonable adjustments claim – namely, dismissal. In the EAT's view, the tribunal had not simply considered the adjustments from an historical perspective. Nor was it the case that the earlier adjustments had arisen entirely independently of the claimant's dismissal. Rather, they were inextricably linked with the dismissal: the attempt by the employer to separate the proposed adjustments from the decision to dismiss was wholly artificial on the facts of the case.

695

21.81 But not every adjustment aimed at preserving the employment of a disabled person will necessarily be regarded as being reasonable. In the first place, an employee who has been absent from work for a substantial period will have to show that there is at least some prospect of his or her returning to work so long as the required adjustments are made: if that prospect does not exist, the duty to make reasonable adjustments is not triggered – see under 'Duty to make reasonable adjustments – scope of the duty' above for further details. As a result, the employer may be entitled to proceed to dismiss on the ground of capability. In Purdy v East Midlands Motor Services Ltd ET Case No.2802562/08 an employment tribunal held that where a disabled employee gave evidence that he would not be fit to return to work as a driver for a substantial period, it was not a reasonable adjustment to expect the employer to hold off dismissal and wait for the claimant's return to health. (For fuller details of the issues to be considered when an employer contemplates dismissal for health-related reasons, see IDS Employment Law Handbook, 'Unfair Dismissal' (2010), Chapter 5, 'Ill health'.)

Secondly, there is the question of the reason for dismissal. If that reason is misconduct, then it may be a step too far for a claimant to contend that a modification of the workplace disciplinary policy would be a reasonable adjustment to make even in a case where there is a causal link between the employee's disability and the act of misconduct. In Gomez v GlaxoSmithKline Services Unlimited ET Case No.2352401/09 an employment tribunal rejected the reasonable adjustment claim of a claimant who alleged that his misconduct – taking the form of accessing internet pornography while at work – was explicable because of his particular impairment (severe depression). In that case, the tribunal assumed (without specifically deciding the point) that there was the necessary causal link, and asked itself whether downgrading the disciplinary sanction from dismissal to a lesser penalty (e.g. a warning) would have been a reasonable adjustment. It concluded, on the facts as found, that it would not. Among its reasons for so holding, the tribunal observed that not to have dismissed the claimant would have been seen as condoning serious breaches of a reasonable and sensible workplace policy. The tribunal was also satisfied that the claimant had been manipulative, self-pitying, and had failed to own up to responsibility for his own actions.

21.82 **Rehabilitation following substantial absence**

Closely aligned to the question of whether and how the employer's duty to make reasonable adjustments may be triggered in the context of dismissal is the issue of how the duty might apply in the context of the rehabilitation of a disabled employee who has been absent from work for a long time. In Home Office v Collins 2005 EWCA Civ 598, CA, Lord Justice Pill observed of the particular adjustment being proposed by the claimant in that case – namely, a phased return to work – that: 'Such a proposal does not fit easily into [a legislative provision] which contemplates adjustments to manage disability *while at work*' (our stress). However, as his Lordship was content to proceed on the basis that a phased return to work could potentially amount to a reasonable adjustment, the quoted remarks were merely obiter (i.e. non-binding).

In any event, it is fair to say that there has not been any broad support for the view that rehabilitation (in the sense of steps designed to ease the employee's path back to work) is incapable of constituting a reasonable adjustment. On the contrary, the courts and tribunals have fully recognised that it is often impractical for an employee with a disability to return immediately to full duties on a full-time basis after a period of sickness absence – see, for example, London Borough of Hillingdon v Morgan (discussed below) and London Underground Ltd v Vuoto EAT 0123/09 (discussed under 'Duty to make reasonable adjustments – scope of the duty' above). Furthermore, the EHRC Employment Code recognises that a phased return to work, involving a gradual build-up of hours, can be a reasonable adjustment – see para 6.33. The one qualification to this is that there must be at least some prospect of the employee being able to return to work for the statutory duty to be triggered – see under 'Duty to make reasonable adjustments – scope of the duty' above.

21.83 In London Borough of Hillingdon v Morgan EAT 1493/98 the EAT upheld an employment tribunal's decision that the employer had failed to comply with the duty to make reasonable adjustments by not allowing an employee who had become disabled to work from home temporarily to assist her transition back into full-time employment. M, a service information officer, developed ME (myalgic encephalomyelitis), or chronic fatigue syndrome (CFS). After eight months' sick leave M's doctors, including the employer's occupational health doctor, suggested that she ease herself gradually back into the work routine as her symptoms improved, preferably by starting off on a part-time basis. However, M's request to be given part-time work to do at home on a temporary basis until she had readjusted to work was refused. Instead, she was put onto the employer's redeployment scheme under which she was considered for job vacancies before they were advertised. M returned to work, could not cope and resigned. The tribunal decided that M had been placed at a substantial disadvantage by the employer's working arrangements compared with those who were not disabled. The tribunal also took the view that a local authority of the size of the employer could have provided M with the gradual reintroduction to work over a couple of months that she needed without undue expense or inconvenience. It held that the employer had been in breach of the duty to make reasonable adjustments, and the EAT upheld that decision on appeal.

The Morgan case is not, however, authority for the proposition that rehabilitation or a phased return to work is always a reasonable adjustment. This was made clear by the EAT in Salford NHS Primary Care Trust v Smith EAT 507/10, where S also suffered from CFS and was signed off work by her

GP. She accepted that she could not return to her post as a specialist occupational therapist. Instead, she wanted a very gradual phased return to work, involving reduced hours in a non-clinical role. S subsequently resigned on the basis that the Trust was refusing to consider this option. An employment tribunal held that the Trust had breached its duty to make reasonable adjustments. It noted that medical advice indicated that S was fit for rehabilitation, although not necessarily substantive work. Given the size and resources of the Trust, the tribunal took the view that attempts should have been made to give S something to do by way of rehabilitation, even if it was not productive work – for example, light duties two or three hours a day. The EAT overturned that decision on appeal. Any proposed reasonable adjustment has to be judged against the statutory requirement that it must prevent the PCP applied by the employer from placing the claimant at a substantial disadvantage when compared with persons who are not disabled – see '"Substantial disadvantage"' above. As was made clear by Mr Justice Elias in Tarbuck v Sainsbury's Supermarkets Ltd 2006 IRLR 664, EAT, adjustments that do not have the effect of alleviating the disabled person's disadvantage are not reasonable. The tribunal in the instant case had found that the PCP causing S substantial disadvantage was the Trust's expectation that she would perform her full role within the contracted hours. The nature and extent of the disadvantage was that she was unable to multi-task, deal with clients or work in a noisy or busy environment. Non-productive rehabilitation of the type proposed by the claimant would not prevent the PCP having a disadvantageous effect on S, because she would still be unable to perform a full day's work within the contracted hours.

21.84 Even where adjustments have been made to facilitate rehabilitation and the employee accordingly returns to work, the employer's statutory duty will not necessarily end there. Depending on the circumstances, further adjustments might be necessary to ensure the efficacy of the rehabilitation programme. In Cutler v HSBC Bank plc ET Case No.1601648/10 the employer, acting on the advice of its own occupational health specialist, allowed an employee who had been off sick with post-traumatic stress (and who had failed in her attempt to commit suicide) to follow a graded return to work on reduced hours. It was an aspect of the agreed adjustment that monitoring would take place alongside regular reviews. However, when the claimant did return, nobody within the organisation was given responsibility for overseeing and supporting the claimant. Indeed, the HR manager believed she was still off work and her new line manager remained in ignorance as to why she had been off work over the previous three months. In consequence, she found herself expected to work longer hours than envisaged by the return-to-work schedule and was placed under considerable pressure in her new role. In consequence, she again attempted suicide. An employment tribunal, upholding her claim of disability discrimination, found that the claimant had been placed at a substantial disadvantage by the application of a PCP, which it defined as 'permitting her to return to work prematurely without a coordinated or concerted effort between the line manager, occupational health and the HR department, and without a structured and informed phased return'. In the event she was disadvantaged by the PCP because her return to work was a chaotic and unsupervised process, rendering her liable to relapse. The duty to implement reasonable adjustments was thus triggered, and the employer breached that duty by failing to implement the phased return in accordance with its own occupational health consultant's advice, failing to hold a return-to-work meeting, and failing to give consideration to further adjustments to the claimant's working hours and job role.

Similar decisions have been made by employment tribunals in other cases. For example, in Sampford v Royal Mail Group ET Case No.1403691/09 the tribunal held that a claimant had been placed at a substantial disadvantage by the employer's failure to allow him to return to work without any rehabilitation programme or phased return to work. Owing to the claimant's feelings of vulnerability arising from his disability – chronic myeloid leukaemia – and the fact that a non-disabled person would not have suffered such feelings on returning to work, the employer should have implemented such reasonable adjustments. And in Lamb v Chief Constable of Hampshire Constabulary ET Case No.3105684/09 the employment tribunal held that the employer failed to make the reasonable adjustment of holding a formal review at the end of a three-month trial period during which the claimant worked under new shift arrangements. Owing to her disability – a mental impairment – she had a deteriorating absence record. The tribunal reasoned that had the review been conducted, and the claimant's own flexible working proposal been accepted, it was likely that her absence levels would have improved significantly.

21.85 If a rehabilitation programme has been implemented but has not proved a success, it will not necessarily be a reasonable adjustment for the programme to be extended. In Romec Ltd v Rudham EAT 0069/07 the claimant, who suffered from chronic fatigue syndrome, was permitted to ease himself back to work. However, he relapsed and was eventually dismissed on capability grounds. An employment tribunal found that, as the claimant had expressed a desire that the rehabilitation programme be extended, the extension would have been a reasonable adjustment since it would have given the claimant the opportunity to 'prove himself'. However, on appeal, the EAT held that the tribunal had failed to consider the essential question – whether the adjustment would have removed the disadvantage experienced by the claimant. If the conclusion was reached, based on the medical evidence and the failure of the first programme, that there was no prospect of a further programme succeeding in restoring the claimant to his full duties, an extension would not be a reasonable adjustment. If, however, there was a real prospect of an extended

699

programme resulting in a full return to work, it might be reasonable to expect the employer to take that course of action. The case was remitted for determination of this issue.

21.86 ### Redeployment

Where an employee is unable to continue in his or her current job as a result of a disability, the duty to make reasonable adjustments will often extend to taking positive steps to facilitate the employee's redeployment. An example:

- **Jewell v Stoke Mandeville Hospital NHS Trust** ET Case No.2700986/98: J worked in a coronary care unit but took sick leave when she had an epileptic seizure at work. An occupational health doctor expressed the view that the long-term solution was to find her work that did not involve direct clinical care or varying shift patterns, but in the short term J should not work alone on the ward or work night shifts. The employer decided that these requirements could not be met and refused to let her return. J remained on sick leave and was advised to apply for other posts internally. She was unsuccessful and was dismissed on the ground of ill health. The tribunal held that the employer had failed in its duty to make reasonable adjustments. The organisation was a large one and there were significant numbers of vacancies for other suitable posts. It would have been a perfectly reasonable adjustment for the personnel department to seek out an appropriate post and redeploy J. The duty was not satisfied by leaving J to apply for existing vacancies.

21.87 The duty is, of course, only to make such adjustments as are reasonable. However, in the context of redeployment, what is reasonable can include treating the disabled person *more* favourably than other, non-disabled employees who are vying for the post. Although it was decided under the pre-2004 version of the duty to make reasonable adjustments that was found in S.6(1) DDA, the leading case in this area remains the House of Lords' decision in Archibald v Fife Council 2004 ICR 954, HL. There, A had suffered complications from surgery that severely impeded her mobility and left her unable to continue in her job as a road sweeper. She applied for over 100 'desk jobs' with the Council, but as these posts were at a higher grade she was required to undergo a competitive interview process. A was unsuccessful in all her applications and was eventually dismissed. She brought a claim of discrimination by way of a failure to make reasonable adjustments, arguing that the Council should have transferred her to one of the posts without an interview. The tribunal took the view that the DDA did not require that a disabled person be treated more favourably than others, and that, since the employer's policy required that an employee applying for a job at a higher grade undergo competitive interviews, there was nothing else the employer could have done in relation to the applicant and the duty to make reasonable adjustments had not been breached. Neither the EAT nor the Court of Session considered that the duty extended to circumstances where an employee becomes incapable of performing his or her duties and there is nothing an employer can do to enable him or her to continue in the job.

The House of Lords took a different view, holding that the duty is triggered in circumstances where an employee becomes so disabled that she can no longer meet the requirements of her job description. Although other forms of disability discrimination do not require that a disabled person be treated more favourably than others, the duty to make reasonable adjustments is different, and necessarily entails a degree of positive discrimination, in that employers are required to take positive steps that they would not have to take for others. Moreover, depending on the circumstances, the duty could require an employer to transfer a disabled employee to a vacant post at a slightly higher grade, if the employee is qualified and suitable for the job, without requiring him or her to undergo a competitive interview.

It is worth pointing out that the Archibald case does not mean that an employer **21.88** must always redeploy rather than dismiss employees who become disabled. And it certainly does not mean that such employees should be given favourable treatment in the sense of promoting them to jobs beyond their qualifications or experience. Everything will depend on the circumstances and the question of reasonableness. As the House of Lords pointed out, it might be less appropriate to make an adjustment to a redeployment policy for high positions where it is important to make fine judgements about who will be best for the job.

In some cases, the employer may be expected to give priority to disabled employees requiring a transfer. In Kent County Council v Mingo 2000 IRLR 90, EAT, the Council's senior occupational health adviser recommended that M be redeployed when it seemed unlikely that he could return to his job as an assistant cook after a back injury. The Council operated a procedure that was designed to match internal job vacancies with redeployees. Category A redeployees were those at risk of, or under notice of, redundancy. Category B redeployees consisted of staff to be redeployed on grounds of incapability or ill health. The Council classified M as a category B redeployee. The significance of that was that category A redeployees were given priority consideration for suitable alternative employment. Over a six-month period M expressed an interest in various posts but was told on more than one occasion that they were reserved for category A redeployees. M was eventually dismissed on the ground of incapacity. The EAT held that the tribunal had been entitled to find that the Council had unlawfully discriminated by failing to make reasonable adjustments. A redeployment policy of giving preferential treatment to redundant or potentially redundant employees does not adequately reflect the statutory duty on employers, since it means that those with disabilities are placed at a disadvantage in the redeployment system. A reasonable adjustment would have been for the Council to treat M as a category A redeployee. This would have put him on a level playing field with those at risk of, or under notice of, redundancy. If the employer had allowed this to happen, M would have been redeployed and not dismissed.

21.89 Although an employer might be expected to seek cooperation from other employees to accommodate a disabled employee, the duty will rarely require it to compel another employee to move in order to create a vacancy. In Garipis v VAW Motorcast Ltd ET Case No.1803194/99 G had vibration white finger and tenosynovitis and was unable to carry out his job. An employment tribunal found that the employer had not failed in its duty to make reasonable adjustments where it had made every effort to redeploy him. There was one department in which G could have worked but there were no vacancies there and none of the staff in that department had been willing to transfer in order to create a vacancy for him. The tribunal rejected G's argument that the employer should have compelled an employee from that department to transfer. It did not consider compulsory transfer to be a practical option because of the extent to which this would have disrupted the employer's relations with other staff. That case can be contrasted with Chief Constable of South Yorkshire Police v Jelic 2010 IRLR 744, EAT, where the EAT held that it would have been a reasonable adjustment for a police force to swap the role of a disabled constable with that of a non-disabled colleague (see under 'Reasonableness of adjustments – nature and size of employer' above). However, in reaching this decision the Appeal Tribunal recognised that the employment tribunal's finding that such an adjustment would be reasonable was heavily influenced by the nature of employment in the police force.

An unnecessary delay in redeploying a disabled employee can amount to a failure to make reasonable adjustments. In Barqueiro v University College London Hospitals NHS Foundation Trust ET Case No.2201844/09, for example, the employee was placed on a redeployment register in May, but very little progress was made until October, when a new manager became proactive in seeking redeployment. A new role was eventually offered and accepted the following February. The employment tribunal held that the employer had been in breach of the duty in the period between May and October by unreasonably delaying in making the necessary adjustments.

21.90 **Creating a new post.** In some circumstances, the duty to make reasonable adjustments can even extend to creating a new post that takes account of an employee's disability. In Southampton City College v Randall 2006 IRLR 18, EAT, R, a teacher, was diagnosed with functional dysphonia – a condition that rendered him unable to speak normally. His duties were initially adjusted so that he taught mature students in small classrooms, but the next academic year he was allocated a full teaching timetable, which included teaching teenagers in a noisy environment. After a month, R was no longer able to continue working and he went on sick leave. The college refused to allow him to return to the adjusted duties, and then embarked on a restructuring process. A position of coordinating lecturer – a role similar to that performed by R prior to his sick leave – was advertised, and R applied. He was rejected after receiving the lowest grading of all the applicants. The interviewing panel did not take into account R's teaching record or performance over 26 years and refused to discuss his problems with his voice. He was then given the choice between accepting redundancy and retiring on the ground of ill health. He chose retirement, but subsequently claimed that the college had failed to make reasonable adjustments.

In upholding R's claim, the employment tribunal pointed out that the restructuring exercise had given the college 'a blank sheet of paper' in respect of job specification. Thus it was possible, said the tribunal, 'to devise a job which would take account of the effects of his disability (but harness the benefits of his long career and successful record)'. On appeal, the EAT held that the legislation does not preclude the creation of a new post in substitution for an existing one being a reasonable adjustment. As ever, it depends on the facts of the case, and in R's circumstances the college had done nothing, failing even to consider the adjustments that might be appropriate, despite the opportunity presented by the reorganisation. The tribunal had therefore been entitled to find that there had been a failure to make reasonable adjustments.

Altering or reallocating duties   21.91

Depending on the circumstances, it may be reasonable for an employer to excuse an employee from certain duties, or to reallocate duties to other employees. For example, in Nicklin v Vicky Martin Concessions Ltd ET Case No.2406032/08 a dyslexic shop assistant found it difficult to carry out a full stock count. An employment tribunal held that it would have been reasonable for the employer to provide assistance to the employee in relation to the stock count, or to arrange for another employee to carry out the task.

By way of contrast, in Needham v Silverlink Train Service Ltd ET Case No.1202119/07 the employment tribunal held that the reallocation of hours and duties was not a reasonable adjustment given that the claimant worked single-handedly as a station manager and the adjustment would have required the employer to hire someone else to take on those duties no longer performed by the claimant. The tribunal reasoned: 'Where there are a range of duties to be performed placing an individual on light duties or short hours requires someone else to carry out the remainder of the work. Given that the claimant's work required her to work alone, the point can only be addressed when considered with the next of her specified adjustments, namely a colleague to work alongside her. We accept the respondent's evidence that they have no need for two people to man the Wolverton Station and that it would be uneconomic for them to staff it with two and/or give her shorter hours. The stark reality is that if they provided someone else to work then they would not need the claimant.'

703

This case illustrates that, when considering whether an alteration or reallocation of duties would be reasonable, a tribunal is likely to pay particular attention to the employer's financial and staff resources – see under 'Reasonableness of adjustments – employer's financial and other resources' above.

21.92 **Altering hours of work**

A common adjustment sought by disabled employees is an alteration to working hours. There are many reasons why disabled people may find it difficult to comply with an employer's normal working hours. For example, a person with impaired mobility may experience extra difficulties with travelling to work, or have to fit in around the timetable of a carer. However, sometimes it is the nature of the disability itself that necessitates shorter or more regular hours. Two examples:

- **Caen v RBS Insurance Services Ltd** ET Case No.1801133/09: C was employed as a claims handler. In 2002, she suffered a nervous breakdown and it later transpired that she was also suffering from agoraphobia. As a result of this condition, C found it increasingly difficult to work a standard working day because – owing to her various anxieties – she did not want to travel to work when there were other cars on the road. Consequently, the employer permitted C to work from 6.30 am to 2 pm. This arrangement worked well until the Ministry of Justice proposed changes to the way in which claims would be administered by insurance companies such as the employer. This led to changes in the way C's office worked and she was told that she would have to work more normal hours, starting no earlier than 7.30 am. This caused C to become paranoid and she suffered anxiety attacks each morning before going to work. Eventually, C was dismissed and she pursued a number of claims, including that the employer had failed in its duty to make reasonable adjustments. Upholding the claim, the employment tribunal considered that once the concept of flexibility was agreed, there was no logical basis for saying that 6.30 am was inappropriate, but 7.30 am was appropriate. The employer had not demonstrated why starting at 6.30 am would not work and had thus failed in its duty to make reasonable adjustments

- **Mansoor v Secretary of State for Education and Employment** ET Case No.1803409/97: M worked as a clerical officer in a job centre. Until 1994 he worked flexitime. Thereafter, because of his poor timekeeping, he was required to work fixed hours. M had colitis and informed the employer that it was impossible for him to get to work at the scheduled start time because of his condition. He gave the employer permission to contact his GP and his consultant for confirmation. Notwithstanding that, the employer decided disciplinary action was warranted. At no time was M required to see the employer's medical adviser. Eventually, M was dismissed on account of his poor timekeeping and attendance. An employment tribunal found that the employer had failed to comply with the duty to make reasonable adjustments to accommodate M's disability. Adjustments could easily have been made by shortening M's hours or by removing the requirement to work fixed hours. Indeed, there was evidence to support the view that M would have been willing to work shorter hours and take a pay cut. However, none of these possibilities was acted upon by the employer.

Altering place of work

21.93

Moving an employee to an alternative office is a commonly sought adjustment and tribunals are likely to closely scrutinise an employer's reasons for rejecting such a request. For example, in Jasper v Commissioners for HM Revenue and Customs ET Case No.1700448/06 the claimant suffered from a hearing difficulty that was exacerbated by background noise. Her workstation was in a busy area near the main entrance to the office, and an occupational health report recommended that she be moved to a quieter area. When a quiet office became available on another floor, a proposal to move the claimant into it was vetoed by a senior manager because he claimed there had been serious disputes between the claimant and colleagues working on that floor. In finding that the move would have been a reasonable adjustment, the employment tribunal noted that the senior manager had provided no details of the alleged disputes, and concluded that they could not have been serious as neither the claimant's manager nor his manager was aware of them.

Home/remote working. The question of whether allowing an employee to **21.94** work from home would be a reasonable adjustment is highly dependent on the individual circumstances of the case and tribunals will need to examine the nature of the work being undertaken. For example, in Secretary of State for Work and Pensions (Job Centre Plus) and ors v Wilson EAT 0289/09 (considered under 'Reasonableness of adjustments – practicability' above) the EAT, in holding that home working was not a reasonable adjustment, considered it highly relevant that the work W undertook involved face-to-face contact with customers and required access to confidential information that was centrally held.

As always, when considering any reasonable adjustment, it is necessary for the employment tribunal to be satisfied that the adjustment sought by the claimant would have the effect of eliminating or reducing the substantial disadvantage caused by the application of the PCP in question or, as the case may, the disadvantageous physical feature or failure to provide an auxiliary aid. In Chief Constable of West Midlands Police v Gardner EAT 0174/11 the EAT held that a tribunal had fallen into error by simply concluding that home or remote working was a reasonable adjustment in the case of a police officer who had sustained a serious injury to his knee. The tribunal had failed to explain why the adjustment sought would or might have had the effect of preventing the PCP – i.e. the requirement to work at a police site – having the effect of putting

705

the claimant at a substantial disadvantage in comparison with those who are not disabled. The case was remitted for determination of that issue.

21.95 Adjusting workplace practices, procedures or policies

One very common type of adjustment that is often judged reasonable by employment tribunals is an adjustment to an employer's workplace practices, procedures or policies. These can run the whole gamut from recruitment policies (including the qualifications or competencies deemed necessary for particular jobs), through policies and work rules that apply during the currency of employment, to provisions dealing with the ending of employment (such as early retirement). Below, we look at some of the more typical policies and practices that are frequently the subject of reasonable adjustment requests.

21.96 Qualifications, examinations and competency standards.
Employers may need to consider adjusting the procedures surrounding recruitment, or the tests relevant to promotion or advancement. The following are three examples of where disabled claimants have succeeded in claims in this context:

- **Irvine v Chief Constable of Nottinghamshire Police** ET Case No.2602970/08: I applied for the position of Learning and Development Officer (LDO). In her application form she stated that she was diagnosed as having mild bipolar affective disorder, but did not consider herself to be disabled. She scored highest in the selection process and was provisionally offered the post, subject to attendance and medical checks. The checks were delayed by the employer's need to check I's medical history, as a result of which the head of the project became anxious about the impact this would have on the ability to meet delivery targets to secure funding. On the basis of I's attendance records, but before receiving a report from the employer's occupational health service, the provisional offer to I was withdrawn. She appealed and her appeal was upheld, but by that time occupational health had reported that if I was placed in a demanding role with significant work pressures and tight timescales, her medical problems could well resurface. The provisional offer was therefore withdrawn on health grounds. An employment tribunal upheld I's claim that she had been directly discriminated against by reason of disability and that the employer had failed to make reasonable adjustments. With regard to the latter, the PCP that had been applied to I was that applicants for the LDO role should be likely to comply throughout the period of appointment with the employer's Attendance Management Policy. This put I at a substantial disadvantage because of her disability. The tribunal found that the adjustments that had been proposed by the OH service – including altering performance timescales and granting sickness absence if I needed it – were reasonable and would have enabled I to have been appointed

- **Bid v KPMG LLP** ET Case No.1300313/09: B was employed as a graduate accountant trainee. Although she was dyslexic, she was not aware of this at the time she began her employment. As part of her training, B was required to take regular exams and the employer had a strict policy – which was also a contractual term – that trainees were only allowed two attempts at a paper. In October 2008, B failed her first attempt at a knowledge paper and her course tutor alerted the employer to the possibility that she might be dyslexic. B failed her second attempt at the paper and was dismissed. She claimed that the employer had failed in its duty to make reasonable adjustments. An employment tribunal agreed – it would have been a reasonable adjustment for the employer to have avoided applying its exam policy until such time as it was established whether B was disabled and, if so, whether that had affected her performance

- **Campbell v Commissioner of Police of the Metropolis** ET Case No.2318832/10: C, a detective constable specialising in the investigation of crimes of a serious sexual nature, had received commendations for work of exceptional quality. From 2007, he began to experience significant sleep problems, which in turn led to anxiety and depression. Ultimately, he was signed off sick for 74 consecutive days, returning to work in July 2009, after having been prescribed an anti-depressant/anti-anxiety drug. Upon his return, he was allocated less stressful duties. In November 2009, he applied to become a detective sergeant and also for a position of detective constable in SCD2, a unit established to investigate serious sexual offences. However, the Detective Superintendent who considered C's application assumed that C's episode of depression/anxiety was caused by work and decided that his application to join SCD2 should not be considered on its merits. Following two further unsuccessful applications to join SCD2, C brought claims of direct disability discrimination and breach of the duty to make reasonable adjustments. An employment tribunal upheld both claims. With specific regard to reasonable adjustments, the tribunal found that a failure by the employer to modify its assessment procedure so as to consider C's application on its merits amounted to a failure to make a reasonable adjustment: that adjustment was reasonable because C's past sickness absences were not an indicator of his future absences or unsuitability for the post. Such a step was entirely practicable for the employer to take and would have cost nothing.

21.97 It will not, however, be a reasonable adjustment to require matters such as competency requirements to be so modified as to undermine the objective of ensuring professional standards. In Burke v The College of Law and anor 2012 EWCA Civ 87, CA, the Court of Appeal upheld an employment tribunal's decision that adjustments made to solicitor's exams as part of the Legal Practice Course (LPC) were sufficient and that further adjustments were not reasonable. The claimant in that case was a student who had multiple sclerosis – a condition that caused him to suffer stress, fatigue and tiredness. In view of the claimant's

707

disability, adjustments were made to the LPC examination procedure, which included the provision of accommodation, the splitting of exams to allow breaks, and the extension of the exam timetable. However, the claimant contended that further allowance should have been made regarding the amount of time he was given to sit each exam. His claim was rejected by both the employment tribunal and, on appeal, by the EAT. On further appeal, the Court of Appeal held that the employment tribunal had sufficiently engaged with the issue of the reasonableness of the adjustments regarding the time requirement. The Court also reiterated observations made by the EAT that, beyond a certain point, provision of extra time would deprive examinations of the kind in issue of any value. In the instant case, the evidence was that such a point would be reached if time were to be extended by more than 100 per cent of that allocated to non-disabled candidates. In these circumstances, both the EAT and the Court of Appeal thought a finding that reasonable adjustments had been sufficiently made was inevitable.

A similar conclusion was reached by an employment tribunal in Lowe v Cabinet Office ET Case No.2203187/10 regarding the selection procedure for the Civil Service Fast Stream. The competition for this is very stiff, entailing as it does appointment on merit following a rigorous appraisal process. The claimant suffered from Asperger's syndrome, as a result of which she was prone to make people mistakenly assume that she was bored or uninterested in what they had to say, and made it difficult for her to read people's emotions and reliably interpret their comments and actions. Although she had been exempted from the online test stages of the Fast Stream process, she, along with all other candidates, was tested by an assessed group activity and practical activities at interview. Certain adjustments were made relating to the interview process, but the respondent declined to make any adjustment in respect of the competencies it regarded as key (such as building productive relationships and high level communication skills), or the level required in respect of these competencies. While accepting that this had put the claimant at a substantial disadvantage in comparison with non-disabled persons, the tribunal held that there had been no breach of the duty to make reasonable adjustments by the respondent's failure to weight her scores so as to downgrade the requisite competencies. The tribunal concluded: 'The recruitment exercise was a challenging one and was designed to find high quality candidates for the fast stream. Removing the disadvantage that the claimant's condition led her to suffer in the process would destroy the essence of this exercise. Given, in particular, the nature of the fast stream posts, that would not be a reasonable adjustment to have to make.'

21.98 *'Competence standard' applied by a qualifications body.* It should be noted that S.53(7) EqA stipulates that 'the application by a qualifications body of a competence standard to a disabled person is not disability discrimination unless it is discrimination by virtue of S.19 [indirect discrimination]'. A 'competence standard' for this purpose is defined by S.54(6) EqA as 'an academic, medical or other standard applied for the purpose of determining whether or not a person has a particular level of competence or ability'. The effect of S.53(7) is that the application to a disabled person of a competence standard so defined cannot trigger a claim for breach of the statutory duty to make reasonable adjustments. Only if indirect discrimination is made out will the disabled person have a valid claim, and only then if the discrimination cannot be objectively justified. For further details, see Chapter 29, 'Liability of other bodies', under 'Qualifications bodies – competence standard'.

In Burke v The College of Law and anor (above) the Court of Appeal found it unnecessary to consider the argument that the time constraint imposed on the LPC vocational course for those seeking to qualify as solicitors amounted to the application of a 'competence standard' for the purposes of S.14A(5) DDA (the precursor to S.53(7) EqA). That was because the Court took the view that consideration of that issue was rendered otiose in the light of its decision regarding the claimant's reasonable adjustments claim. However, at EAT level (Burke v The College of Law and anor EAT 0301/10), the Appeal Tribunal had upheld an employment tribunal's conclusion that the time constraint was indeed a competence standard based on the evidence that the exams were designed to assess the ability of each candidate to work at speed and under pressure, which was an important requirement for practice as a solicitor. Given that the Court of Appeal in the event passed no judgment on this matter, the EAT's decision remains binding as the only judicial consideration of the point.

Health and safety. Not surprisingly, given the crucial importance of health and **21.99** safety considerations and the fact that employers owe a duty of care both to members of their workforce and to the wider public, tribunals often conclude that adjustments that might have the effect of lowering standards of health and safety protection are not reasonable. Two examples:

- **Binks v London and South Eastern Railway Ltd** ET Case No.1502155/09: B, who suffered from melanoma in the region of his right eye, began working for LSER in 2000 as a train valet. In March 2007 he applied for a post as a train dispatcher. Initially, he failed the applicable eyesight test but two weeks later, after obtaining new glasses, he passed the test. He was recommended for a further review in six months but due to an oversight that review did not take place until October 2008, when he failed to meet the vision standard. Following an internal appeal, the employer's occupational health consultant concluded that B did not, and never would, meet railway visual standards and advised that he should not be required to undertake any safety critical activities. However, in December 2008 B passed an eyesight risk assessment and the health and safety adviser confirmed that he would authorise him to continue his full dispatch duties for six months. LSER interviewed B in January 2009 and asked about the possibility of his condition deteriorating, to which B replied that the position was uncertain: he could remain as he was or he could go blind. The following month B was informed by his employer that it would not allow him to carry out safety critical duties but would support him to find alternative employment. B's subsequent claim of disability discrimination was dismissed by an employment tribunal. The medical standard imposed by LSER had put B at a substantial disadvantage, but as trains are inherently dangerous the tribunal rejected the contention that the employer should have alleviated the strict requirements of the vision standard. Although B had been able to pass the vision test, that was only by using his good eye to compensate for the weaker one. LSER took account of the view expressed by occupational health that B should not carry out safety critical work, and in the circumstances it was reasonable to remove him from train dispatch duties, regardless of the risk assessment

- **Elston v Stockton on Tees Borough Council** ET Case No.2509590/10: E, who suffered from severe asthma, was employed as a passenger assistant. Her job functions included accompanying three children suffering from autism to school in the mornings and back home in the afternoon in a taxi driven by a self-employed taxi driver. In 2009 she had nine days' sickness absence, which triggered the sickness review procedure in November. On 1 December she was admitted to hospital as an emergency, and was off work for a week. She was referred to occupational health and, following a further admission to hospital, the employer carried out a workplace assessment, as a result of which recommendations were made that robust measures should be put in place to ensure the safety of E and the children she accompanied. The employer decided to withdraw E from her duties pending a risk assessment and a further occupational health referral, and she was subsequently dismissed in May 2010 after the employer had decided that there were no duties on which E could safely be employed. An employment tribunal dismissed her claim of breach of the duty to make reasonable adjustments. It concluded that there was a risk that E could have had an asthma attack while at work whatever adjustments were made, and furthermore that there was a clear risk that her condition would impair her capacity to care for vulnerable children. The employer had reasonably concluded that it could not fulfil its duty of care both to E herself and to service users if it allowed her to remain in her job. And it was satisfied that there were no suitable vacancies into which E could have been transferred.

21.100 However, it is not necessarily the case that a disabled employee who is put to substantial disadvantage by the application of a workplace health and safety policy can never succeed in a reasonable adjustments claim. The following cases show that if reasonable adjustments could be made that would have the effect of mitigating an employer's genuine health and safety concerns, or if there is no rational basis for the concerns in the first place, then the employer may be found to have failed to comply with its S.20 EqA duty:

- **Bakali v Transport for London** ET Case No.3303769/09: B worked for TFL as a station assistant. In 2003 he was involved in a serious road traffic accident as a result of which he suffered brain damage and serious damage to his left arm. This led to a prolonged period of hospitalisation during which his employment was terminated. In March 2007 B applied to return to his old job but by that time he was suffering from secondary epilepsy. TFL took considerable time in obtaining the necessary medical information, but in June 2009 B's application was finally rejected on the ground that, should it be necessary for a station to be evacuated, B's sudden disablement or collapse might affect his safety or the safety of others. An employment tribunal upheld his reasonable adjustments claim. Although the tribunal accepted that it had been objectively reasonable for TFL to adopt stringent health standards for safety and public confidence reasons, it had failed to make the necessary and reasonable adjustment of appointing B to a post where he would not be required to assist in evacuation. A limited number of such posts were available and the adjustment would have entailed no additional cost to the employer

- **Preston v Bedford Borough Council** ET Case No.1200380/10: P worked for the respondent Council as an environmental health officer. In October 2007, following a seizure, she was diagnosed with a brain tumour and commenced a period of sickness absence. Three months later, an occupational health adviser advised that she would be fit to return to work in the 'near future' provided some adjustments were made. In March 2008, after a return-to-work meeting, the council decided that it was not possible to make reasonable adjustments to enable P to return as it believed 'public safety' issues were involved. Instead, she was placed on medical suspension. After a further meeting in March 2010, P obtained an updated medical report from a specialist neurologist that concluded that there were no difficulties in her returning to full-time employment. Despite this, the Council proceeded to dismiss P by reason of lack of capability. An employment tribunal upheld her claim that the Council had failed to comply with its duty to make reasonable adjustments. In its view, it had not been reasonable to suspend P in 2008. Instead, the tribunal found that she should have been given the opportunity to return to work and to have an assessment of what adjustments were necessary. The Council's contention that P was a risk to the public was unreasonable, as there was no evidence she was a risk to anyone.

Absence and sickness policies. It is axiomatic that disabled workers are more **21.101** likely than others to have high levels of sickness or other types of absence associated with medical treatment. In consequence, they may well fall foul of workplace policies and rules dealing with ill health and absence. Not surprisingly, therefore, one of the most common types of adjustment sought by disabled workers is an adjustment to the terms of such policies or rules to take

711

account of their special situation. The question invariably arises whether such adjustments are reasonable in the circumstances.

In Bray v Camden London Borough EAT 1162/01 the EAT approved an employment tribunal's conclusion that, as a matter of principle, it is not a reasonable adjustment to ignore disability-related absences entirely when calculating sickness levels and the like. The EAT observed that, if the contrary were the case, the logical consequences would be that a disabled employee could be absent throughout the working year without the employer being in a position to take any action in relation to that absence. Applying this rationale, an employment tribunal in Robertson v Quarriers ET Case No.S/104674/10 ruled that an adjustment to the employer's 'Management Attendance Standards', by which the claimant sought to have all disability-related absence discounted, was not a reasonable adjustment. In that case the claimant – who was diabetic – had had 62 days' ill-health absence in the year from September 2008 to September 2009. Under the employer's policy, a review of the contractual position of any employee was triggered if he or she sustained a specified level of absence. The tribunal's reason for rejecting the claimant's proposed adjustment was that the employer would otherwise 'be forced to disapply its own standards with regard to any disabled employee and thereby be unable to operate the mechanism it had set in place to review and manage the contractual relations between the employer and the employee to maintain a reasonable level of attendance. If, as the claimant appeared to suggest, any absence due to disability should be disregarded or discounted, the result would be that an employer would have no control over the degree of absences to be tolerated from disabled employees.'

21.102 It is important to note what the above cases did and did not decide. They did *not* rule out the possibility of an employer coming under the statutory duty to adjust aspects of sickness or absence management policies in order to eliminate or reduce the substantial disadvantage that the application of such policies might cause to disabled workers. What these cases do show, however, is that it will rarely – if ever – be a reasonable adjustment to require an employer to disapply the terms of such policies to disabled employees by discounting *all* sickness-related absence. An employer is entitled to manage the issue of ill health and absence within the workplace, and a disabled employee cannot expect that he or she is removed entirely from the scope of a policy that is put in place as a management tool for this purpose.

The following cases illustrate that, once a review of a disabled employee's absence record is under way, it may well be a reasonable adjustment for the employer to take into account the substantial disadvantage caused to the employee by the strict application of the terms of the relevant policy:

- **Brennan and anor v Denne Joinery Ltd and anor** ET Case No.1100934/10 and another: B, an epileptic employee, was selected for redundancy by DJ

Ltd ostensibly on account of her sickness record. An employment tribunal found that one of the true reasons for her dismissal was, in fact, her sexual orientation and that her dismissal was therefore both discriminatory on that ground and unfair. In addition, B contended that DJ Ltd, when carrying out the redundancy exercise, should have discounted disability-related absences since, by using these as the principal criterion for selection, she had been put at a substantial disadvantage in comparison with non-disabled persons. Upholding B's claim, the tribunal found that one of two alternative reasonable adjustments should have been made: either DJ Ltd should have accorded attendance a lower weighting generally, given the importance to the company's continued existence of having members of staff who performed well and were adaptable; or it should have discounted to some extent a limited number of absences related to disability. It was no answer for the employer to point out that B's attendance record was no worse than that of the two candidates within the redundancy pool. Had B's record been adjusted, her scoring would have improved, and this might have led to one of the non-disabled candidates being selected for redundancy instead

- **Ware v British Gas Trading Ltd** ET Case No.1606202/10: W suffered from a back injury, which deteriorated throughout his employment with BGT Ltd. Despite various adjustments being made, his absence record was affected, which led to BGT Ltd holding a meeting under its attendance management procedure in September 2009 at which it was agreed that W would have a target of no more than 15 days' absence in a year. However, by April 2010 he had already reached that limit, and, in consequence, the final stage of the attendance management procedure was triggered, which ultimately led to a decision that he should be dismissed on capability grounds. When considering W's claim of discrimination by reason of a failure to make reasonable adjustments, an employment tribunal accepted that none of the adjustments specifically proposed by him – such as a reduction in hours of work – would have been likely to affect his attendance and that the medical evidence did not support any conclusion that there was likely to be an increased level of attendance in the future. However, the tribunal concluded that BGT Ltd should have used its discretion to discount W's disability-related absences: no evidence had been produced by the employer to indicate that the 15-day threshold was of any particular significance, and if there was no magic in the 15-day period in itself it was perfectly possible that a higher number of days was also reasonable or that a discount in its entirety was also reasonable. BGT Ltd had therefore failed to show that the adjustments that were made to the attendance management policy were all those that could reasonably have been made.

Of course, even if adjustments are made, the level of a disabled employee's **21.103** absence may reach the point where dismissal on the ground of capability is a reasonable course for the employer to take. This is particularly so if there are

713

no further adjustments that can reasonably be made that would be likely to have a beneficial effect on the employee's absence record in the future. Dismissal will also be an option if the employee in question has failed to make use of available medical treatment that would advantageously impact on the level of his or her absence. In Baldwin v Royal Mail Group Ltd ET Case No.3502171/10, for example, B had been an insulin dependent diabetic since 1975, and had worked for RMG Ltd since 1997. He had a total of 411 days' absence, of which 254 related to an eye problem linked to his diabetes. In 2009 B was referred to occupational health, which reported that he had issues with the management of his condition. A second report later that year indicated that B would continue to require a higher than average level of sickness absence and suggested that RMG Ltd should consider tolerating this. However, by this time B was already on a stage-2 warning. Although RMG Ltd chose to discount some of B's absences, by the end of the year he had had further absences and was eventually dismissed in February 2010 because his management of his condition was poor and some of his absences could have been avoided had he taken proper action. On one occasion, for example, despite knowing insulin was date-sensitive, he had failed to check its date and had used out-of-date insulin, which had led to another period of sickness absence. An employment tribunal dismissed his claim of breach of the duty to make reasonable adjustments. In its view, it was not reasonable for RMG Ltd to have discounted the later absences because B was by then able to control his condition and so avoid being absent but had failed to do this.

21.104 *Sick pay.* The EHRC Employment Code states that although there is no automatic obligation to extend contractual sick pay beyond the usual entitlement when a worker is absent as a result of disability-related sickness, an employer should consider whether it would be reasonable to do so – para 17.21. This matter has been addressed by the Court of Appeal in two important cases. The first was Meikle v Nottinghamshire County Council 2005 ICR 1, CA, where the claimant had been absent on sick leave for a prolonged period owing to her employer's failure to make reasonable adjustments. The Court of Appeal held that there was no reason to exclude the direct payment of sick pay by the employer to the employee from the scope of the duty. It followed that a tribunal had erred in finding that the duty did not apply to an employer who had halved the sick pay of a disabled employee in accordance with the company sick pay policy.

The Meikle decision led many to assume that where an employee is absent from work for a disability-related reason, it is necessary to make adjustments to the sick pay policy in order to continue to pay him or her full pay despite the fact that his or her contractual entitlement to sick pay has run out. However, the matter was revisited in O'Hanlon v HM Revenue and Customs Commissioners 2007 ICR 1359, CA, where the employer operated a sickness policy that entitled employees to full pay for the first 26 weeks and half pay for the next

26 weeks in any four-year period. The claimant, who suffered from clinical depression, had 365 days of sickness absence in the relevant four-year period, 320 of which were on account of her disability. She brought a tribunal claim contending that she should be paid full pay for all disability-related sickness absence because the stress caused by her lack of income was exacerbating her condition. The employment tribunal concluded that the sick pay scheme placed the claimant at a substantial disadvantage compared to non-disabled employees, and the duty to make reasonable adjustments was therefore engaged. It went on, however, to find that the employer had discharged that duty, in that the claimant had been allowed to return to work part time between her periods of disability-related absence. Furthermore, paying the claimant full pay indefinitely would act as a disincentive for her to return to work, which was not a desirable outcome.

The EAT upheld the tribunal's decision that the employer had discharged its **21.105** duty to make reasonable adjustments. When the case reached the Court of Appeal, the question had narrowed to whether the employer should have considered whether to increase sick pay by assessing the financial hardship and resulting stress suffered by the employee. Upholding the decisions of both the tribunal and the EAT, the Court concluded that there were no special circumstances that rendered it reasonable to expect the employer to pay the employee's salary in full when, having exhausted her entitlement to sick pay under the rules of the sick pay scheme, she was absent from work for a disability-related reason.

Although the Court of Appeal's decision was based on a fairly narrow ground, the judgment clearly endorsed the broader approach to the issues taken by the EAT. In particular, Lord Justice Hooper, who gave the leading judgment, could see considerable force in the EAT's view that it will only be in highly exceptional circumstances that it could be considered a reasonable adjustment to give a disabled person higher sick pay than would be payable to a non-disabled person who in general does not suffer the same disability-related absences. That would not be an appropriate adjustment, in the EAT's view, because it would require tribunals to usurp the management function of the employer by deciding whether employers were financially able to meet the costs of modifying their policies in order to make these enhanced payments. Although tribunals are required to have regard to financial factors and the financial standing of the employer, there is a very significant difference between a tribunal doing that in respect of a single claim where the cost is relatively limited and doing that in respect of a claim that if successful would inevitably apply to many others and would have very significant financial as well as policy implications for the employer. Moreover, stated the EAT, the purpose of the legislation is to assist disabled workers to obtain employment and to integrate them into the workforce rather than simply put more money in their wage packets, which may in some circumstances act as a disincentive to return to work.

715

21.106 The Court of Appeal in O'Hanlon did not, however, take the view that Meikle v Nottinghamshire County Council (above) was wrongly decided. On the contrary, it endorsed the distinction drawn by the EAT – that Meikle was a different category of case because the employee's sickness absence had itself been caused by a failure to make reasonable adjustments. Consistent with this distinction, the EHRC Employment Code states that 'if the reason for absence is due to an employer's delay in implementing a reasonable adjustment that would enable the worker to return to the workplace, maintaining full pay would be a further reasonable adjustment for the employer to make'– para 17.22.

21.107 **Redundancy selection.** As the duty to make reasonable adjustments can extend to treating a disabled employee *more* favourably than his or her colleagues, it may be reasonable for an employer to make adjustments to its criteria for selecting employees for redundancy. For example, many employers use levels of sickness absence as one of the selection criteria. Where an employee has experienced a high level of disability-related sickness absence, the use of such a criterion will place him or her at a substantial disadvantage compared with non-disabled candidates for redundancy. It may therefore be a reasonable adjustment for the employer to ignore all the disabled person's disability-related absences or increase a disabled person's score for the absence criterion. In Robson v Domino Ltd ET Case No.1400506/09 R, who was diabetic and suffered from chronic fatigue syndrome, returned to work in January 2008 after a long sickness absence. He came back on a phased return and was not given any sales targets for five months. However, in October 2008 the employer began consulting its employees about redundancy and R was eventually selected and dismissed. His scores were adversely affected by his absence: the employer had restricted its considerations to the previous 12 months, during much of which R had either been absent or doing reduced work and his drive and energy had been affected. In upholding R's claim of disability discrimination, the employment tribunal found that it would have been a reasonable adjustment to increase R's scores in order to remove the disadvantage caused by his disability.

Another case where the employer failed to make the reasonable adjustment of adapting redundancy scoring was Brennan and anor v Denne Joinery Ltd and anor ET Case No.1100934/10 and another, discussed under 'Absence and sickness policies' above.

21.108 Note, however, that if an adjustment to the scores and/or the redundancy criteria would still not prevent the disabled employee from being made redundant, then it will not be a reasonable adjustment for the employer to make and the employee will not be able to bring a complaint under S.20 EqA – Lancaster v TBWA Manchester EAT 0460/10. Also, an employer who embarks on a substantial redundancy selection process in ignorance of the fact that one of the employees within the selection pool is disabled may not be expected to rerun the entire scoring process in the event that the employee

716

discloses his or her disability a late stage. In Cox v Bath and North East Somerset District Council ET Case No.1402226/10 the employment tribunal held that it was not a reasonable adjustment to review the entire selection process after the claimant had disclosed that he was dyslexic only at the point of being selected for redundancy. The tribunal concluded that it was not practicable for the employer to rescore the claimant fairly and accurately on the basis of the assessment of his dyslexia. This would inevitably have entailed a hypothetical and highly speculative process requiring assumptions to be made about the impact of dyslexia on different aspects of the claimant's work and would have required the employer to apply scoring figures that were fully capable of objective justification in the event that the revised scorings were challenged by others within the selection pool. The rescoring would have been largely reliant on guesswork and as such was not a reasonable adjustment in the circumstances.

Redundancy dismissals are considered further in Chapter 26, 'Dismissal', under 'Redundancy'.

Disciplinary and grievance procedures. An employer may have to consider **21.109** altering aspects of its disciplinary and grievance procedures if these put a disabled employee at a substantial disadvantage. For example, it would generally be considered a reasonable adjustment for an employer to provide an interpreter for a deaf employee charged with misconduct – see OCS Group Ltd v Taylor EAT 0803/04 and Osborne-Clarke v Commissioners of Inland Revenue ET Case No.1400656/04. Similarly, it may be reasonable to allow an employee with dyslexia or learning difficulties to be accompanied to a grievance or disciplinary hearing by a friend or relative, as opposed to the trade union representative or colleague permitted by statute – Robertson v Otis Ltd ET Case No.3302817/10; and Scalfe v EWGA Ltd ET Case No.1403182/10.

In Williams v Bannatyne Fitness Ltd ET Case No.1311340/09 an employment tribunal found that it would have been a reasonable adjustment to have permitted a disabled employee who was unable to take notes to record an absence review hearing.

Early retirement. A disabled employee may reach a point where, owing to **21.110** disability-related ill health, there is no realistic prospect of his or her returning to work. The question may arise in those circumstances whether a reasonable adjustment should be made to an employer's capability (or equivalent) policy to enable the employee to take early retirement. In Hatcliffe v British Telecommunications plc ET Case No.2802774/08 an employment tribunal rejected such a claim on the basis that the reasonable adjustments duty is never triggered in circumstances where the adjustment is directed at leaving employment rather than preserving it. In that case, the claimant – who suffered from severe depression and who was judged by the employer's occupational health service to be unlikely to be able to return to work – was precluded from accessing a redeployment assistance programme that held out the prospect of retirement on ill-health grounds because the eligibility criteria required employees to demonstrate that they could potentially make a sustained return to work. Citing the Court of Appeal's decision in O'Hanlon v HM Revenue and Customs Commissioners 2007 ICR 1359, CA (discussed under 'Absence and sickness policies' above), the tribunal concluded that there was no breach by the employer of the duty to make reasonable adjustments in this case. The purpose of adjustments was to help employees to obtain or remain in employment, whereas the claimant's proposed adjustment would have had the opposite effect.

21.111 **Other workplace practices and policies.** A rigid adherence to HR policies can put disabled people at a substantial disadvantage, and employers may need to consider modifying such policies to accommodate a disabled person's needs. For example, in Cumbria Probation Board v Collingwood EAT 0079/08 C was employed as a probation officer. From September 2004, he suffered from depression and his symptoms got progressively worse over the following months. In November 2005 he attempted to have a conversation with his HR manager but she applied the employer's policy that she could not discuss matters in confidence with employees. The following January, C wanted to discuss with M personnel matters going back 18 months, and this request was also refused because the employer's policy prevented consideration of matters that went back further than six months. C presented a claim for disability discrimination on the basis that, inter alia, these policies constituted a failure to make reasonable adjustments. The employment tribunal upheld the claim – by applying the policy of not having confidential conversations with employees, the employer had failed in its duty to make reasonable adjustments because the depression from which C suffered meant that he had a need to speak in confidence. The six-month rule was also a breach of the duty – an aspect of C's illness was the need to have issues properly addressed in order to move forward, and it would have been reasonable for the employer to allow C properly to verbalise his concerns and discuss matters that had occurred over the previous 18 months. The EAT upheld this decision on appeal.

In Titchener v Technique Training Ltd ET Case No.2801808/09 the workplace practice policy under scrutiny was a ban on communicating through mobile phone text messaging. As a result of this policy, staff were often given instructions verbally. The claimant – who was profoundly deaf – asked to be permitted to use his mobile phone so he could communicate by text messages but the employer R refused to allow this. In the employment tribunal's view, this amounted to a failure to make a reasonable adjustment, as was the employer's failure to maintain and monitor a system of using a book in which instructions for the claimant could be written.

718

In Hinsley v Chief Constable of West Mercia EAT 0200/10 the workplace rule **21.112** under scrutiny related to the claimant's resignation from her position as a probationary police officer. H had handed in her resignation despite concerted attempts by her managers to dissuade her from resigning. Shortly afterwards, she was diagnosed with depression and indicated that she wished to withdraw her resignation as she had made a hasty decision in a distressed state brought on by her mental impairment. The Chief Constable considered her request, but rejected it in the belief that there was no provision under the Police Regulations 2003 for reinstatement or re-engagement once a police officer had left the force. An employment tribunal, rejecting H's claim of breach of the duty to make reasonable adjustments, found that the duty to make reasonable adjustments had been engaged but that her reinstatement as a probationer was not a reasonable adjustment in the circumstances. Allowing H's appeal against that decision, the EAT held that there was in fact no statutory bar under the 2003 Regulations against H's reinstatement or re-engagement. It was plain that, but for that perceived bar, taking H back into service without the need for her to reapply from scratch would have been a reasonable adjustment in view of the fact that the quality of H's performance was not in issue and, prior to accepting her resignation, her managers had sought to persuade her to retract it.

Pay preservation and changes to pay/bonuses
21.113

Although the duty to make reasonable adjustments requires a degree of positive discrimination, it is unlikely to be considered a reasonable adjustment simply to pay a disabled employee more than an equivalent non-disabled employee on account of his or her disability. Such a step does not address a substantial disadvantage, and therefore falls outside the duty – see Goodger v Secretary of State for Justice (discussed below).

Where, however, an employee's disability restricts his or her ability to earn remuneration compared to non-disabled employees, he or she is likely to be placed at a substantial disadvantage and in some circumstances adjustments may be required. The EHRC Employment Code gives the following example: 'A disabled man with arthritis works in telephone sales and is paid commission on the value of his sales. His impairment gets worse and he is advised to change his computer equipment. He takes some time to get used to the new equipment and, as a consequence, his sales fall. It is likely to be a reasonable adjustment for his employer to pay him a certain amount of additional commission for the period he needs to get used to the new equipment' – para 14.8.

The cases below illustrate the issues that can arise when considering whether it **21.114** is a reasonable adjustment to preserve the pay of disabled employees whose hours have been reduced or job functions altered on a temporary basis to accommodate their disability:

719

- **Newcastle-Upon-Tyne Hospital NHS Foundation Trust v Bagley** EAT 0417/11: following a serious injury sustained at work, B was paid by the respondent Trust at 85 per cent of her wages while she remained on sick leave. When she started to contemplate a return to work, she discussed the possibility of a phased return, but the Trust would only offer to pay her for the time she actually worked during the return-to-work period. This made it impossible for her to return as she could only work one day off and one day on and could not afford in the long term to sacrifice 40 per cent of her salary. An employment tribunal upheld her claim of breach of the duty to make reasonable adjustments. It accepted that B had been placed at a substantial disadvantage because of her disability and considered that the cost saving to the Trust of not making the adjustment of keeping her pay at 85 per cent of full salary during a phased return was an insufficient reason not to make the adjustment. The EAT overturned the tribunal decision on appeal. It identified the PCP in question as the Trust's policy 'of paying people for the work they do'. This, according to the EAT, did not breach the duty to make reasonable adjustments as it did not place B at a disadvantage in comparison to someone who was not disabled. It simply placed her in the same situation as anyone else returning to work on a part-time basis for whatever reason. Furthermore, paying B 85 per cent pay for 60 per cent work would not have been a reasonable adjustment because of the implications this might have for the Trust generally in respect of employees working part time (whether because of disability or because of other personal circumstances).

- **Goodger v Secretary of State for Justice** ET Case No.2351349/10: G worked in the prison service and was placed for salary purposes on the operational support grade (OSG). He was diagnosed with osteoarthritis in his foot and by February 2010 the employer's occupational health consultant had confirmed that he was not fit for his duties on the OSG, but did not qualify for medical retirement since he could give good service in a sedentary role. He accepted a regrading to an administrative role, but this resulted in a significant reduction in pay. He claimed that in reducing his pay, the employer had failed to make the reasonable adjustment of protecting his original salary. An employment tribunal dismissed his claim. G had not been put at a substantial disadvantage in comparison with people who were not disabled: the policy of transferring staff from OSG to administrative roles and salaries was applied not only to disabled people but also to employees as a result of a redundancy situation or an application for flexible work. The tribunal also accepted that the duty to make reasonable adjustments did not oblige the employer to pay G more than was required. Protection under the DDA (now the EqA) was designed to enable disabled people to remain in work at the salary that is appropriate for the work being done.

Providing supervision or support   21.115

The duty to make reasonable adjustments can include the provision of someone to help or support the disabled employee. In Abbott v Governors of St Mary's Catholic Primary School ET Case No.3204241/97, for example, A, who was registered blind, was employed as a teacher. As a result of her disability, she needed a classroom assistant. T was appointed to assist A using discretionary funding provided by the local education authority. When T resigned, the school told A that the funding for the assistant's post had ceased. A was subsequently absent from work because of a stress-related illness. The school made no further enquiries as to funding for the assistant's post and A took early retirement. The tribunal held that it would have been reasonable for the school to have ensured that a classroom assistant was available to A. The funding had not ceased. Rather, the school had decided that it did not want to continue providing the assistant unless the funding was guaranteed rather than discretionary. The school could have tried to find a parent to act as A's assistant pending recruitment of a permanent replacement. In the meantime, the school should have reassured A that it remained committed to ensuring her return to work. This would have relieved the stress and anxiety that A was feeling. The tribunal found that the costs of recruiting an assistant could have been covered by the school's budget and so the school's failure to take these simple steps constituted a failure to make reasonable adjustments.

Acquiring or modifying equipment   21.116

As we saw under 'The three statutory requirements – requirement 3: lack of auxiliary aid causing substantial disadvantage' above, one of the requirements of the duty to make reasonable adjustments is to take reasonable steps to provide an auxiliary aid where that aid would address a substantial disadvantage experienced by a disabled person – S.20(5) EqA. This reflects both good practice and case law, which has shown that modifying equipment or providing new equipment that is tailored to a disabled person's needs can be a reasonable means of removing a substantial disadvantage. The availability, cost and likely effectiveness of any equipment will obviously be relevant considerations in determining what is reasonable. For example, it will usually be reasonable for an employer to provide an adapted keyboard to an employee, but it is less likely to be reasonable to have to provide an adapted vehicle, owing to the much higher cost.

Involving third parties   21.117

A number of disability charities and organisations offer support and consultancy services to employers to help them better integrate disabled job applicants and employees into the workforce. In some cases, the engagement of such organisations has been considered a reasonable adjustment by employment tribunals:

- **Marchant v FC Brown (Steel Equipment) Ltd t/a Bisley Office Equipment** ET Case No.2300633/09: M was dyslexic and dyspraxic. Following a

721

problem in 2006 to do with the application of labels to units, the employer formed the view that M was anxious about his role and engaged an organisation called Employment Solutions. It came and spent a week with M in the factory and produced a learning and development plan for him. As part of the plan it was agreed that any poor performance or disciplinary issues should be notified to Employment Solutions so that a monitoring visit could be carried out. In August 2008, M was allocated the task of placing file bars into the drawers of cabinets. After a while M became frustrated with the task as he believed he was holding up the production line. He was then heard throwing a file bar at a cabinet before leaving work early as he was getting flustered. Following a disciplinary hearing, M was given a final written warning and he eventually resigned. The employment tribunal upheld M's disability discrimination claim – the failure to notify Employment Solutions of the problem was a failure to make a prearranged reasonable adjustment

- **Newsome v Williams t/a CW Accounting Services** ET Case No.2508895/08: N suffered from paranoid schizophrenia. In August 2008, a colleague complained that N had approached him and began shouting and swearing at him as he was trying to eat his lunch. A disciplinary investigation ensued which led to N being summarily dismissed for threatening, violent and intimidating behaviour. N subsequently lodged proceedings in the employment tribunal alleging, among other things, that his employer had failed in its duty to make reasonable adjustments. The employment tribunal upheld the claim, stating that one of the possible adjustments the employer could have made was to involve an independent third party, like the mental health charity Rethink, in the disciplinary process. The conduct of the investigation served to exacerbate N's feelings that he was being bullied and ostracised by his colleagues, and a third party could have diffused the situation and investigated the causes of the dispute. This might even have obviated the need for disciplinary action.

21.118 ## Altering physical features – obtaining consent

Altering the physical features of premises in order to comply with the duty to make reasonable adjustments may require the employer to seek consent from other individuals, organisations or bodies. Guidance on this potentially tricky subject is provided in Appendix 3 to the EHRC Employment Code.

Note that under the DDA, provisions existed to the effect that it would never be reasonable for an employer to have to make an adjustment to premises that met design standards provided for in the relevant building regulations. While these provisions have been partially replicated in the EqA, they do not apply to employment.

722

Listed buildings and other statutory consents

There are a number of situations in which an employer may have to obtain a statutory consent before a change can be made to a building. These include planning permission, listed building consent, scheduled monument consent and fire regulations approval. By virtue of para 1 of Schedule 22 to the EqA, an employer does not commit an act of disability discrimination if its actions are required to comply with an enactment. This means that an employer can, and should, obtain all the necessary consents before making any alteration to a building. If the statutory consent is not forthcoming, the employer does not have to make the change.

This has implications for the practicability of making reasonable adjustments. For example, the delay caused in obtaining consent may mean that an immediate adjustment is not reasonable. In these circumstances it may be that there is a reasonable temporary measure, which does not require consent, that could be adopted in the meantime. Employers may need to look at ways of making reasonable adjustments that either do not require consent or are likely to receive it. It may be useful for an employer to consult the local planning authority in advance to ensure that planning consent will be granted.

Alterations to leasehold premises

There can be additional complications in relation to reasonable adjustments to premises if the employer occupies premises under a lease. If the employer is a tenant or sub-tenant, the lease may prohibit it from making alterations or may only allow alterations to be made with the consent of the landlord. This situation is dealt with by Schedule 21 to the EqA and Regs 10–14 of the Equality Act 2010 (Disability) Regulations 2010 SI 2010/2128 (the Disability Regulations), which essentially replicate the equivalent provisions in the DDA.

Paragraph 3 of Schedule 21 provides that where an employer occupies premises under a tenancy, is proposing to make an alteration to the premises so as to comply with the duty to make reasonable adjustments, and would not otherwise be entitled to make the alteration, the tenancy has effect as if it provided for:

- the employer to be entitled to make the alteration with the written consent of the landlord

- the employer to have to make a written application for that consent

- the landlord not to withhold that consent unreasonably, and

- the landlord to be able to give the consent subject to reasonable conditions.

An employer is to be treated as not otherwise entitled to make an alteration if **21.121** the tenancy imposes conditions that apply if the employer makes alterations, or if the landlord is entitled under the tenancy to attach conditions to a consent to the alteration – para 3(5).

723

If a question arises as to whether the employer has made the alteration (and, accordingly, complied with a duty to make reasonable adjustments), any constraint attributable to the tenancy must be ignored unless the employer has applied to the landlord in writing for consent to the alteration – para 3(4). In other words, the employer cannot simply rely on a restriction in the tenancy as a reason for not making a reasonable adjustment; it must apply for consent.

A 'tenancy' is defined in S.38 EqA as a tenancy created (whether before or after the passing of the Act) by a lease or sub-lease, by an agreement for a lease or sub-lease, by a tenancy agreement, or in pursuance of an enactment.

21.122 **Landlord withholding consent.** In addition to the situation where the landlord expressly turns down the request for consent to an alteration, Reg 10 of the Disability Regulations provides that the landlord is taken to have withheld consent if, within 42 days of receiving the application, it:

- fails to reply in writing either consenting to or refusing the application, or

- replies in writing consenting to the alteration subject to obtaining the consent of another person required under a superior lease or pursuant to a binding obligation, but fails to seek that consent – Reg 10(2).

The landlord is not to be taken to have withheld consent where the employer fails to provide such plans and specifications as it is reasonable for the landlord to require before consenting to the alteration; and within 21 days of receiving the application, the landlord replies requesting such plans and specifications – Reg 10(3). If, however, the employer provides those plans and specifications on request, then the date of their receipt causes a new 42-day period to start running in line with Reg 10(2) – Reg 10(4).

21.123 **When is consent withheld unreasonably?** Whether or not consent has been withheld unreasonably will depend on the circumstances of the case. The EHRC Employment Code states that: 'A trivial or arbitrary reason would almost certainly be unreasonable. Many reasonable adjustments to premises will not harm the landlord's interests and so it would generally be unreasonable to withhold consent for them' – para 9, Appendix 3.

Regulation 11 of the Disability Regulations also provides that a landlord will be taken to have unreasonably withheld consent where the lease provides that the landlord shall give consent to an alteration of the kind in question and the landlord has withheld consent to that alteration.

21.124 **When is consent withheld reasonably?** As with the question of what is unreasonable, what is reasonable will largely depend on the circumstances of the case. It will probably be reasonable for a landlord to withhold consent where the adjustment would result in either a permanent reduction in the value of the landlord's interest in the premises or significant disruption or inconvenience to other tenants – para 8, Appendix 3 EHRC Employment Code.

In addition, Reg 12 of the Disability Regulations provides that the landlord will be taken to have acted reasonably where:

- there is a binding obligation requiring the consent of another person to an alteration; the landlord has taken steps to obtain that consent; and consent has not been given, or has been given subject to conditions that make it reasonable for the landlord to withhold consent, or

- the landlord does not know, and could not reasonably be expected to know, that the alteration is one that the employer proposes to make to comply with the duty to make reasonable adjustments.

What if the consent is subject to conditions? Regulation 13 of the Disability **21.125** Regulations provides that the following conditions are to be taken to be reasonable for the purposes of Schedule 21:

- the employer must obtain any necessary planning permission and any other consent or permission required by or under any enactment

- the work must be carried out in accordance with any plans or specifications approved by the landlord

- the landlord must be permitted a reasonable opportunity to inspect the work (whether before or after it is completed)

- the consent of another person required under a superior lease or a binding agreement must be obtained

- the occupier must repay to the landlord the costs reasonably incurred in connection with the giving of the consent.

What if the landlord has a superior landlord? Regulation 14 of the Disability **21.126** Regulations modifies the provisions in Schedule 21 where the employer occupies premises under a sub-tenancy. In effect, the same modifications that apply to a tenancy agreement between the employer and the landlord will apply to the agreement between the landlord and the superior landlord. The provisions above relating to the reasonable and unreasonable withholding of consent would also apply to the superior landlord.

Joining landlords in proceedings. In employment tribunal proceedings **21.127** concerning a claim of a failure to make a reasonable adjustment to the employer's premises, either the employer or claimant may apply to the tribunal to join the employer's landlord or a superior landlord to the proceedings – para 5(1) and (2) Sch 21. If the request is made before the hearing of the complaint begins, the tribunal must join the landlord – para 5(3)(a). If the request is not made until after the hearing of the complaint has begun, the tribunal has a discretion as to whether to grant the request – para 5(3)(b). If the request is not made until after the tribunal has determined the complaint, the tribunal must refuse the request – para 5(3)(c).

725

If the landlord is joined as a party, the tribunal may determine whether the landlord has refused consent to the alteration, has consented subject to a condition, and whether the refusal or condition is unreasonable – para 5(4). Where a tribunal finds a consent or condition to be unreasonable, para 5(5) provides that it may:

- make such a declaration as it thinks appropriate

- make an order authorising the employer to make a specific alteration to the premises (and requiring the employer to comply with any specified conditions)

- order the landlord to pay compensation to the claimant.

21.128 The EHRC Employment Code states: 'If the tribunal orders the landlord to pay compensation, it cannot also order the employer to do so' – para 13, Appendix 3. However, while that was expressly stated to be the case under the DDA, it is questionable whether it is a correct interpretation of the EqA. It appears that an employment tribunal now has the power to award compensation against both the employer (under S.124(2) EqA) and the landlord (under para 5 of Schedule 21). The tribunal may award compensation against the landlord under para 5(5) instead of, or in addition to, awarding compensation against the employer under S.124(2) EqA, but if it orders the landlord to pay compensation it must not do so in reliance on S.124(2) – para 5(6).

21.129 **Other consents required**
Paragraph 2 of Schedule 21 to the EqA provides that where an employer is subject to a binding obligation in respect of premises that requires it to obtain consent to a physical alteration, it is always reasonable for the employer to have to take steps to obtain that consent, but it will never be reasonable for the employer to have to make the alteration before the consent is obtained. Binding obligations in this context are legal obligations in relation to premises, however arising, but exclude any obligations under a tenancy. Common examples would be mortgages, charges or restrictive covenants.

21.130 # Special cases

While the bulk of this chapter has dealt with the duty to make reasonable adjustments as it applies to employers, it should be noted that Part 5 of the EqA also applies the duty to a number of other bodies, organisations and individuals that have a connection to employment. These are:

- principals offering work to contract workers (see 'Contract workers' below) – S.41(4)

- partnerships – S.44(7)

- limited liability partnerships (LLPs) – S.45(7)

- barristers and their clerks – S.47(7)

- advocates and their clerks – S.48(7)

- a person with the power of appointment to a personal office, or the power to set or terminate the term of appointment – S.49(9)

- a person with the power of appointment to a public office, or the power to set or terminate the term of appointment – S.50(11)

- a person who can make a recommendation for or give approval to an appointment to a public office – S.51(4)

- qualifications bodies – S.53(6)

- employment service-providers (other than in the provision of a vocational service) – S.55(6)

- trade organisations – S.57(6)

- local authorities, in relation to their members – S.58(6)

- occupational pension schemes – S.61(11).

21.131 The principles discussed earlier in this chapter in relation to employment also apply, with appropriate modifications, to the duty to make reasonable adjustments in all the circumstances listed above. The modifications are set out in Schedule 8 to the EqA and largely relate to the identity of the persons to whom the duty relates (referred to as 'interested disabled persons').

For details of liability for discrimination by the organisations and individuals listed above, see Chapter 28, 'Liability of employers, employees and agents', and Chapter 29, 'Liability of other bodies'. There are a few additional points regarding contract workers and reasonable adjustments, which are addressed below.

Contract workers

21.132 In the context of a tripartite relationship where a contract worker is employed by one company or organisation (the employer) and supplied to another (the principal) to perform work, the duty to make reasonable adjustments applies to the principal as well as the employer – S.41(4).

21.133 **Duty on employer of contract worker.** Paragraph 5 of Schedule 8 to the EqA provides that the employer of a disabled contract worker is obliged to make reasonable adjustments on each occasion that it supplies the worker to a principal to perform work. The duty arises if the worker is likely to be placed at a substantial disadvantage that is the same or similar in the case of each of the principals to whom he or she is or might be supplied by:

- a PCP applied by or on behalf of all or most of those principals

727

- a physical feature of the premises occupied by each of those principals, or
- the non-provision of or failure to provide an auxiliary aid.

21.134 The steps that it is reasonable for the employer to take in this context are those that would be reasonable for it to take if the contract worker were being supplied to, rather than by, the employer.

The EHRC Employment Code gives the following example of how the duty to make reasonable adjustments can arise in respect of the employer of a contract worker: 'A blind secretary is employed by a temping agency which supplies her to other organisations for secretarial work. Her inability to access standard computer equipment places her at a substantial disadvantage at the offices of all or most of the principals to whom she might be supplied. The agency provides her with an adapted portable computer and Braille keyboard, by way of reasonable adjustments' – para 11.11.

21.135 **Duty on principal.** The duty owed by a principal is substantially the same as that owed by the employer of a contract worker, but para 6(2) of Schedule 8 provides that the principal is not required to do anything that the employer is required to do by virtue of para 5. The EHRC Employment Code explains that this means that the principal is responsible for any *additional* adjustments that are necessary solely because of its own PCPs, the features of its own premises, or to avoid the non-provision of or failure to provide an auxiliary aid – para 11.12. Returning to the example cited above, the Code suggests that 'a bank which hired the blind secretary may have to make reasonable adjustments which are necessary to ensure that the computer provided by the employment business is compatible with the system which the bank is already using'.

The Code further suggests that in deciding whether any and, if so, what adjustments should be made by a principal, the length of the assignment is an important factor – para 11.13. In determining what would be a reasonable step for a principal to take in order to remove a substantial disadvantage experienced by a contract worker, a tribunal should take into account the duration for which the worker will be engaged by the principal. It may not be reasonable for a principal to have to make substantial adjustments for a worker who will be with the principal for only a short time. The Code gives the example of an accountant supplied by an employment business to cover a short-term, unexpected absence. If such a worker were to request a modification to his or her working hours, it might not be reasonable for the accountancy firm (the principal) to have to agree, given the limited time in which to negotiate and implement the changes.

22 Other forms of prohibited conduct

Gender reassignment discrimination due to absence
Pregnancy and maternity discrimination

So far, we have considered the four main forms of unlawful conduct under the **22.1** Equality Act 2010 (EqA) that apply to most, if not all, of the protected characteristics – direct and indirect discrimination, harassment and victimisation, as well as the two types of prohibited conduct specific to disability – discrimination arising from a disability and failure to make reasonable adjustments. In this chapter, we turn our attention to the two remaining forms of conduct made unlawful by the Act: gender reassignment discrimination relating to a period of absence from work, and pregnancy and maternity discrimination.

It has been unlawful to discriminate against a transsexual person because he or she is proposing to undergo, is undergoing or has undergone a process of gender reassignment since 1999, when specific provision to that effect was introduced into the Sex Discrimination Act 1975 (SDA) – see S.2A SDA. S.2A(2) and (3) explicitly extended that protection to the arrangements made by an employer in relation to any period of absence from work due to gender reassignment and this protection is now contained in S.16 EqA. However, as before, there will only be discrimination in these circumstances where the employer would have treated an employee away from work on medical or other grounds more favourably: there is no automatic protection from discrimination where a transsexual person is absent from work while undergoing gender reassignment.

Women who are pregnant or on statutory maternity leave are afforded special **22.2** protection from discrimination in the workplace by virtue of S.18 EqA, which makes it unlawful for an employer to treat a woman unfavourably because of her pregnancy or a pregnancy-related illness, or because she is exercising, has exercised or is seeking to, or has sought to, exercise the right to maternity leave. The main elements of the protection against pregnancy and maternity discrimination, previously found in S.3A SDA, are summarised below. For more details, see IDS Employment Law Handbook, 'Maternity and Parental Rights' (2009), Chapter 13, 'Discrimination and equal pay', under 'Direct discrimination'.

729

22.3 Gender reassignment discrimination due to absence

There are nine protected characteristics covered by the EqA, one of which is 'gender reassignment' – see S.4. The definition of gender reassignment, which is contained in S.7 of the Act, is discussed in detail in Chapter 7, 'Gender reassignment'. A person who is discriminated against on the ground that he or she is proposing to undergo, is undergoing or has undergone a process of gender reassignment can bring a claim of direct or indirect discrimination or harassment in the normal way (see Chapters 15–18). In addition, S.16 EqA provides special protection for employees who are absent from work because of gender reassignment (and any references to gender reassignment discrimination in the Act include discrimination within S.16 – S.25(3)(b).)

A transsexual person undergoing gender reassignment is likely to have to take time off work to attend medical appointments and undergo surgical procedures. Furthermore, where complications arise as a result of the gender reassignment treatment, he or she may be too ill to attend work. To protect the employee in these circumstances, S.16(2) states that 'a person (A) discriminates against a transsexual person (B) if, in relation to an absence of B's that is because of gender reassignment, A treats B less favourably than A would treat B if:

- B's absence was because of sickness or injury; or

- B's absence was for some other reason and it is not reasonable for B to be treated less favourably'.

22.4 An absence is 'because of gender reassignment' if it is because the person is proposing to undergo, is undergoing or has undergone a process (or part of a process) for the purpose of reassigning his or her sex by changing physiological or other attributes of sex – Ss.7(1) and 16(3) (see further Chapter 7, 'Gender reassignment').

The effect of S.16 is that if a transsexual person who is dismissed after, say, six months' absence while undergoing gender reassignment would not have been dismissed if he or she had been absent for the same amount of time because of sickness or injury, he or she will have a claim of less favourable treatment under S.16. Where the comparison is between absence because of gender reassignment and absence for a reason other than sickness or injury, there is an added requirement: for a claim under S.16 to succeed, not only must there have been less favourable treatment as between the two different types of absence, but that less favourable treatment must have been *unreasonable*. It is therefore open to an employer to argue that, for example, it was reasonable to treat an employee absent on compassionate leave to care for a sick partner more favourably than a transsexual employee absent from work because of gender reassignment.

The Equality and Human Rights Commission's Code of Practice on Employment **22.5** ('the EHRC Employment Code') gives the following examples of when S.16(2) would come into play:

- a transsexual worker takes time off to attend a Gender Identity Clinic as part of the gender reassignment process. His employer cannot treat him less favourably than she would treat him for absence due to illness or injury; for example, by paying him less than he would have received if he were off sick (para 9.31)

- a worker undergoing gender reassignment has to take some time off for medical appointments and also for surgery. The employer records all these absences for the purposes of its attendance management policy. However, when another worker breaks his leg skiing the employer disregards his absences because 'it wasn't really sickness and won't happen again'. This indicates that the treatment of the transsexual worker may amount to discrimination because the employer would have treated him more favourably if he had broken his leg than it treated him because of gender reassignment absences (para 17.27).

As we have seen in Chapter 7, gender reassignment is a slow process that can **22.6** take many months or even years. Protection under S.16 starts even before the transsexual person has received any medical treatment: it is available from the time he or she *proposes* to undergo gender reassignment. Once the employer is aware of the employee's intention, any request for time off relating to the transition process must therefore be handled sensitively. An example from the EHRC Employment Code: 'A transsexual worker tells her boss that she intends to undergo gender reassignment and asks him if she can take an afternoon off as annual leave to attend counselling. The request is brusquely refused although there are sufficient staff members on duty that day to cover for her absence. This could amount to gender reassignment discrimination' (para 9.32).

The Code points out, at para 9.33, that the EqA does not define a minimum or maximum time that must be allowed for absence because of gender reassignment. As a matter of good practice, it suggests that employers should discuss with transsexual staff how much time they will need in relation to the gender reassignment process and accommodate those needs in accordance with their normal practice and procedures.

Relevance of disability discrimination law   **22.7**
Transsexualism is generally understood to be a mental disorder, known as 'gender dysphoria' or 'gender identity disorder', rather than a mental illness. It is therefore unlikely that an individual suffering from gender dysphoria will,

731

without more, be able to satisfy the definition of a disabled person under the EqA – i.e. someone suffering from a mental impairment that has a substantial and long-term adverse effect on his or her ability to carry out normal day-to-day activities (see Chapter 6, 'Disability', under 'Meaning of "disability"'). That said, there are circumstances in which the disability provisions in the EqA may become relevant. Those who are, or are considering, transitioning may suffer from depression, which, in its most serious form, has the potential to adversely affect any aspect of the individual's day-to-day life. Moreover, gender reassignment surgery, like any surgery, carries with it risks. Any complications may not only take the employee away from work for a considerable period of time, but also affect the employee's long-term health. In these circumstances, employers should consider whether a transsexual employee would qualify as a disabled person under the EqA.

22.8 # Pregnancy and maternity discrimination

'Pregnancy and maternity' is one of nine protected characteristics covered by the EqA – see S.4. The scope of the protected characteristic is discussed in Chapter 9, 'Pregnancy and maternity'. S.18 EqA outlaws pregnancy and maternity discrimination in the employment field. It is designed to replicate the effect of S.3A SDA, which was inserted by the Employment Equality (Sex Discrimination) Regulations 2005 SI 2005/2467 and subsequently amended by the Sex Discrimination Act 1975 (Amendment) Regulations 2008 SI 2008/656 (see 'Unfavourable treatment' below). S.25(5) EqA makes it clear that any references in the EqA to pregnancy and maternity discrimination are to discrimination falling within the scope of S.18.

Under S.18, an employer discriminates against a woman if it treats her unfavourably because:

- of pregnancy or an illness resulting from it, where the treatment takes place 'in the protected period in relation to a pregnancy of hers' – S.18(2) (see 'Protected period' and '"Pregnancy of hers"' below)

- she is on compulsory maternity leave – S.18(3), or

- she is exercising or seeking to exercise, or has exercised or sought to exercise, the right to ordinary or additional maternity leave – S.18(4).

22.9 Paragraph 8.22 of the EHRC Employment Code gives examples of treatment that is likely to contravene S.18(2). They include treating a woman unfavourably during the protected period because of the costs to the business of covering her work or because of performance issues arising as a result of morning sickness or other pregnancy-related conditions. It sets out the following two scenarios:

- a pregnant employee has booked time off to attend a medical appointment related to her pregnancy. Her employer insists this time must be made up through flexitime arrangements or her pay will be reduced to reflect the time off. This is unlawful: a pregnant employee is under no obligation to make up time taken off for antenatal appointments and an employer cannot refuse paid time off to attend such classes (para 17.26)

- a worker has been off work because of pregnancy complications since early in her pregnancy. Her employer has now dismissed her in accordance with the sickness policy which allows no more than 20 weeks' continuous absence. This policy is applied regardless of sex. The dismissal is unfavourable treatment because of her pregnancy and would be unlawful even if a man would be dismissed for a similar period of sickness absence, because the employer took into account the worker's pregnancy-related sickness absence in deciding to dismiss (para 17.25).

Below, we highlight the most important aspects of a claim under S.18. A more **22.10** detailed discussion of this type of claim can be found in IDS Employment Law Handbook, 'Maternity and Parental Rights' (2009), Chapter 13, 'Discrimination and equal pay', under 'Direct discrimination'.

Scope of protection 22.11
Section 18 outlaws pregnancy and maternity discrimination in the employment context. The EqA, like the SDA before it, takes a broad view of what constitutes 'employment' for this purpose, covering those employed 'under a contract of employment, a contract of apprenticeship or a contract personally to do work' – S.83(2)(a). Given this wide definition, most workers (i.e. those employed under a contract of personal service as well as under a contract of employment) are covered. However, S.213 EqA provides that references to maternity leave in the Act should be defined by reference to the Employment Rights Act 1996 (ERA). The right to ordinary and additional maternity leave is confined to 'employees' only – S.230(1) ERA – with the result that non-employees (i.e. those who are not employed under a contract of employment) are only entitled to special protection under S.18 EqA during their pregnancy and for the two weeks of compulsory maternity leave immediately following the end of the pregnancy.

Protected period 22.12
The 'protected period' during which S.18(2) (pregnancy discrimination) applies begins at the start of the woman's pregnancy – S.18(6). If she has the right to ordinary and additional maternity leave, it ends on the expiry of the additional maternity leave period or when she returns to work after the pregnancy, if that is earlier – S.18(6)(a). If the woman does not have the right to ordinary and additional maternity leave (typically, because she is not an employee), the protected period ends two weeks after the end of her pregnancy, i.e. at the end of the period of compulsory maternity leave referred to in S.72 ERA – S.18(6)(b) EqA. Ordinary and additional maternity leave are dealt with in Ss.71

733

and 73 ERA respectively (see S.213 EqA, which defines references to maternity leave in the Act by reference to the ERA), and in the Maternity and Paternity Leave etc Regulations 1999 SI 1999/3312.

Where a woman is treated unfavourably because of pregnancy or a pregnancy-related illness, and the decision to treat her in that way was taken during the protected period but not implemented until after the end of that period, the treatment is nevertheless to be regarded as occurring during the protected period – S.18(5).

22.13 **'Pregnancy of hers'**
The requirement in S.18(2) that the unfavourable treatment of the claimant must relate to a 'pregnancy of hers' means that the treatment must be related to the claimant's *own* pregnancy. Discrimination by association is not covered by this provision. In Kulikaoskas v MacDuff Shellfish 2011 ICR 48, EAT, the Appeal Tribunal in Scotland held that an employee allegedly dismissed because of his partner's pregnancy could not bring a pregnancy discrimination by association claim under S.3A SDA (now S.18 EqA). The employee sought to rely on Coleman v Attridge Law and anor 2008 ICR 1128, ECJ (see Chapter 15, 'Direct discrimination', under 'Discrimination by association'), in which the European Court of Justice held that the EU Equal Treatment Framework Directive (No.2000/78) protects those who, although not themselves disabled, nevertheless suffer direct discrimination or harassment owing to their association with a disabled person. However, the EAT held that Coleman could be distinguished as it did not relate to the EU Pregnant Workers Directive (No.92/85) or the recast EU Equal Treatment Directive (No.2006/54). In the EAT's view, neither of those Directives affords protection against pregnancy discrimination by association. Thus, the EAT was not required to interpret the SDA so as to allow such a claim and a reference to the ECJ was unnecessary.

On a further appeal, the Court of Session took a different view and decided to make a reference to the ECJ for a preliminary ruling, asking whether the recast EU Equal Treatment Directive (No.2006/54) prohibits less favourable treatment of a person on the grounds of a woman's pregnancy generally, or on the ground of his partner's pregnancy or that of a woman otherwise associated with him. The reference was made on 11 January 2012 so judgment is unlikely to be given until early 2013.

22.14 When the Kulikaoskas case was before the EAT, the Appeal Tribunal also considered the claimant's situation under the EqA (which was not in force at the relevant time). It expressed the view that it was 'not entirely clear' whether the EqA would protect an employee who was dismissed because of his partner's pregnancy. For the reasons outlined above, it is not possible for a person in that position to bring a pregnancy discrimination by association claim under S.18 EqA. It appears, however, that an employee may be able to claim direct *sex* discrimination under S.13 because of his or her association with a pregnant woman. The EHRC Employment Code states that 'a worker treated less favourably because of association with a pregnant woman, or a woman who has recently given birth, may have a claim for sex discrimination' (para 8.16). Arguably, then, if a man is dismissed or treated less favourably at work because of his partner's pregnancy, he could claim direct sex discrimination by association under S.13. It is also possible that he could claim direct discrimination by association under S.13 because of the protected characteristic of *pregnancy or maternity* – see further 'Relationship with direct discrimination under S.13' below.

The reference in S.18(2) to a 'pregnancy of hers' also appears to exclude claims of unfavourable treatment arising from an incorrect perception that the claimant is pregnant. In any event, and more significantly, the protection afforded by S.18 only applies during the protected period of a woman's pregnancy and statutory maternity leave, so it is clear that a woman who was not actually pregnant could not rely on this provision. Again, she would have to fall back on a direct discrimination claim – see 'Relationship with direct discrimination under S.13' below.

Unfavourable treatment

22.15

Section 3A SDA, the predecessor to S.18, was amended in 2008 to comply with the High Court's ruling in R (Equal Opportunities Commission) v Secretary of State for Trade and Industry 2007 ICR 1234, QBD. In that case the High Court held that the original version of S.3A did not correctly implement EU law because it introduced an impermissible requirement for a woman's treatment to be compared with the treatment that she would have received had she not become pregnant or taken maternity leave. In light of this ruling, the requirement for a comparator was removed from 6 April 2008 by the Sex Discrimination Act 1975 (Amendment) Regulations 2008 SI 2008/656. Thenceforth, women were protected under S.3A SDA if their employer simply treated them 'less favourably' on any of the prohibited grounds.

As originally drafted, S.18 EqA provided that discrimination would occur where the woman was treated 'less favourably than is reasonable'. In Committee, the Solicitor General explained the reason for the additional test of reasonableness. She stated: 'It is unclear, on one view, with whom or what treatment is to be compared, so we have tried to make the position clearer. It is settled law that a woman claiming discrimination because of pregnancy or maternity is not required to compare her treatment with that of an actual or hypothetical male or female comparator, and the Bill does not change that. [S.18] will clarify the current position by introducing an objective standard by reference to which it can be tested whether discrimination has taken place.' However, the TUC argued that the effect of the new wording was to 'open the way for a reasonableness defence to a pregnancy or maternity claim when there

735

was previously no defence and no such defence is permissible in EU law'. The Government accepted that the effect of the provision would be to weaken protection against pregnancy and maternity discrimination. Accordingly, it abandoned the proposed wording, replacing it with the concept of 'unfavourable treatment'. While this is not defined in the Act, it is likely to be interpreted in line with the familiar concept of 'detriment' that applies in discrimination cases.

22.16 Although S.18 does not require the claimant to show that she has been unfavourably treated by reference to the treatment that would have been afforded to a male comparator or a non-pregnant female comparator, the EHRC Employment Code suggests that evidence of the treatment afforded to others may be useful to help determine if the treatment is in fact related to pregnancy or maternity leave. It gives the following example: 'A company producing office furniture decides to exhibit at a trade fair. A pregnant member of the company's sales team, who had expected to be asked to attend the trade fair to staff the company's stall and talk to potential customers, is not invited. In demonstrating that, but for her pregnancy, she would have been invited, it would help her to show that other members of the company's sales team, either male or female but not pregnant, were invited to the trade fair' – para 8.19.

22.17 **Relationship with direct discrimination under S.13**
It has long been established that less favourable treatment of a woman during the protected period on the grounds of her pregnancy or the consequences of that pregnancy amounts to direct *sex* discrimination without the need for a comparison with a man in similar circumstances – Webb v EMO Air Cargo (UK) Ltd 1994 ICR 770, ECJ. Thus there is potential for overlap between pregnancy and maternity discrimination on the one hand and sex discrimination on the other. To avoid this problem, S.18(7) EqA stipulates that '[S.]13, so far as relating to sex discrimination, does not apply to treatment of a woman in so far as... (a) it is in the protected period in relation to her and is for a reason mentioned in [S.18(2)], or (b) it is for a reason mentioned in [S.18(3) or (4)]' (see above).

The effect of S.18(7) is to ensure that S.18 is used for pregnancy and maternity discrimination claims during the protected period and that such claims are not brought under the direct sex discrimination provisions under S.13. That is not to say, however, that the latter section will never be relevant. Where unfavourable treatment because of pregnancy or maternity is not covered by S.18 (for example, because it falls outside the protected period), the woman can bring a sex discrimination claim under S.13. In this situation, it is arguable that she would also be able to claim direct discrimination under S.13 because of the protected characteristic of pregnancy and maternity. This is because S.13(1) refers to less favourable treatment 'because of a protected characteristic', and pregnancy and maternity appears in the list of protected characteristics in S.4 EqA – see our discussion of the application of S.13 to the protected characteristic of pregnancy and maternity in Chapter 15, 'Direct discrimination', under 'Preliminary matters – protected characteristics covered by S.13'.

If S.13 does indeed cover direct pregnancy and maternity discrimination, this **22.18** would also permit claims based on association and perception, which cannot be brought under S.18 (see under '"Pregnancy of hers"' above). Furthermore, there would be nothing to prevent a woman whose claim fell within S.18 from pursuing a claim of direct pregnancy and maternity discrimination under S.13 in relation to an act occurring during the protected period (either instead of, or in addition to, a S.18 claim). This is because S.18(7) (above) only disapplies S.13 'so far as relating to sex discrimination' (our stress) – it does not preclude claims of *pregnancy and maternity* discrimination under S.13. That said, there is no obvious reason why a woman whose claim fell within S.18 would choose instead (or additionally) to pursue a S.13 claim, given the additional requirement for a comparator under S.13.

Part 4

Discrimination in the workplace

23 Workplace discrimination: general principles

> **How the Equality Act applies to 'work'**
>
> **Scope of 'employment'**
>
> **EHRC Code of Practice on Employment**
>
> **Acas guidance**

In Chapters 1–22 of this Handbook, we discuss the sources of discrimination **23.1** law, the characteristics that attract protection under the Equality Act 2010 (EqA), and the types of conduct that are prohibited under the Act. In Chapters 24–27, we consider how the legal principles discussed in those chapters apply in the field of work. These chapters broadly align with the various stages of the employment relationship: Chapter 24 covers recruitment, Chapter 25 deals with discrimination during employment, Chapter 26 is concerned with dismissal, and Chapter 27 looks at post-employment discrimination. In this short introductory chapter, we consider some points of general relevance to all stages of the employment relationship.

How the Equality Act applies to 'work'   23.2

In Chapter 1, 'UK discrimination law', we explain that the intention behind the EqA was to harmonise discrimination law by consolidating the different strands of discrimination (such as age, sex, race, disability, etc) and the different fields to which the law applies (such as employment, education, the provision of services to the public) into a single Act. One effect of this harmonisation is that the definitions of prohibited conduct (direct and indirect discrimination, harassment, victimisation, failure to make a reasonable adjustment, etc) contained in Part 2 of the Act are silent as to the circumstances in which that conduct is prohibited.

Instead, each field to which the EqA applies is covered by its own separate Part, and in the case of work and employment, this is Part 5 (Ss.39–83). Chapters 1 and 2 of Part 5 (Ss.39–63) deal with the situations in which prohibited conduct is unlawful in a work-related context. Chapter 3 (Ss.64–80) covers equal pay (which is dealt with in IDS Employment Law Handbook, 'Equal Pay' (2011), and Chapter 4 addresses a number of supplementary matters, such as offshore work and statutory interpretation.

741

The main work-related provisions are Ss.39 and 40 EqA, which cover discrimination against employees and applicants (the broad definition of 'employment' for these purposes is considered under 'Scope of "employment"' below). However, there are also provisions covering contract workers (S.41); police officers (Ss.42–43); partnerships (Ss.44–46); barristers, advocates and their clerks (Ss.47–48); office-holders (Ss.49–52); qualifications bodies (Ss.53–54); employment service providers (Ss.55–56); trade organisations (S.57); and local authority members (Ss.58–59). S.60 EqA introduces new restrictions on pre-employment health questions (considered in Chapter 24, 'Recruitment', under 'Pre-employment health questions'), while Ss.61–63 provide for a non-discrimination rule in occupational pension schemes (which fall outside the scope of this Handbook).

23.3 Scope of 'employment'

The provisions covering discrimination in the workplace refer to 'employment', 'employers' and 'employees' but it is important to understand that the scope of employment in this context is defined by S.83 EqA, not by the law of contract.

Section 83(2) provides that, for the purposes of Part 5 of the Act, employment means:

- employment under a contract of employment, a contract of apprenticeship or a contract personally to do work

- Crown employment

- employment as a relevant member of the House of Commons staff

- employment as a relevant member of the House of Lords staff.

23.4 Although not strictly falling within this definition, other provisions stipulate that police officers (S.42) and members of the armed forces (S.83(3)) are also to be treated as employees. References to 'an employer' or 'an employee', or to 'employing' or 'being employed', are to be read with S.83(2), and a reference to an employer also includes a reference to a person who has no employees but is seeking to employ one or more other persons – S.83(4).

For a detailed consideration of the categories of worker which are protected from discrimination under the EqA, see Chapter 28, 'Liability of employers, employees and agents', and Chapter 29, 'Liability of other bodies'.

23.5 EHRC Code of Practice on Employment

Under S.14 of the Equality Act 2006 (EqA 2006), the Equality and Human Rights Commission (EHRC) has the power to issue statutory Codes of Practice in connection with any matter addressed by the EqA 2010. Such Codes should

742

contain provisions designed to facilitate compliance with the 2010 Act and promote equality of opportunity – S.14(2) EqA 2006. A Code made under S.14 is not actionable in and of itself, but its provisions are admissible as evidence in criminal or civil proceedings and must be taken into account where a court or tribunal considers them to be relevant – S.15(4) EqA 2006.

The EHRC's Code of Practice on Employment ('the EHRC Employment Code') was brought into force on 6 April 2011 by the Equality Act 2010 Codes of Practice (Services, Public Functions and Associations, Employment, and Equal Pay) Order 2011 SI 2011/857. Running to over 300 pages, the Code is split into two parts: the first explains the protected characteristics, forms of prohibited conduct, exceptions and enforcement; the second offers guidance on avoiding discrimination at all stages of the employment relationship. Both parts of the Code include numerous examples, many of which draw on case law under the discrimination enactments that preceded the EqA 2010.

23.6 We make frequent reference to the EHRC Employment Code throughout the next four chapters. It should be noted, however, that in some respects the Code is already out of date: it makes no reference to the repeal on 1 October 2011 of the default retirement age and associated age discrimination exceptions (both of which are considered in Chapter 26, 'Dismissal', under 'Retirement'). Moreover, while the Code does a useful job of explaining all the key concepts, many employers will be frustrated that while it frequently explains that the employer might need to provide objective justification for a potentially discriminatory measure, rarely does it offer any enlightenment on the circumstances in which such justification might be established. To some extent this is a reflection of discrimination law, as it is rarely possible to say with certainty whether justification would be established in any given case. To plug the gap we have endeavoured to provide case examples wherever possible.

Acas guidance

23.7

The EHRC is not the only Government-funded body providing employers and employees with advice on the provisions of the EqA. Acas offers a range of guidance booklets and leaflets, both in paper form and on its website (www.acas.org.uk).

In contrast to the EHRC Employment Code, Acas guidance is non-statutory in nature. Accordingly, a tribunal is not obliged to take it into account when interpreting the EqA, although there is nothing to prevent a tribunal from doing so if it considers it appropriate. One Acas guidance that is particularly relevant at the moment is the booklet, 'Age and the workplace: putting the Equality Act 2010 and the removal of the default retirement age (DRA) into

743

practice'. As we saw above, the EHRC Employment Code has yet to be updated to take account of the removal of the DRA, meaning the Acas guidance is more up to date in this area.

We consider the implications of the removal of the DRA in Chapter 26, 'Dismissal', under 'Retirement'.

24 Recruitment

Knowledge of disability

Pre-employment health questions

Arrangements for deciding to whom to offer employment

Terms on which employment is offered

Discrimination by not offering employment

In the context of employment, it is at the recruitment stage that discrimination **24.1** is often likely to occur. Employers who are consciously or unconsciously prejudiced against individuals possessing a particular protected characteristic are likely to demonstrate that prejudice when faced with job applications from such individuals. There is also a danger of indirect discrimination occurring during recruitment. This will happen where one or more of the recruitment criteria applied by the employer puts, or would put, persons possessing a protected characteristic at a particular disadvantage, and there is no objective justification for the employer's actions. Victimisation can also occur – particularly if the employer knows or suspects that a job applicant has brought a discrimination claim against a previous employer and is therefore seen (consciously or unconsciously) as a potential troublemaker.

Discrimination in the recruitment process is prohibited by S.39(1) of the Equality Act 2010 (EqA), which provides that an employer (A) must not discriminate against a person (B):

- in the *arrangements* A makes for deciding to whom to offer employment – S.39(1)(a)

- as to the *terms* on which A offers B employment – S.39(1)(b)

- by *not offering* B employment – S.39(1)(c).

Victimisation against job applicants is dealt with separately in S.39(3), which **24.2** provides that an employer (A) must not victimise a person (B):

- in the arrangements A makes for deciding to whom to offer employment – S.39(3)(a)

- as to the terms on which A offers B employment – S.39(3)(b)

- by not offering B employment – S.39(3)(c).

Thus, victimisation will be unlawful in the same circumstances as discrimination under S.39(1).

745

24.3   Harassment in the recruitment process is dealt with by S.40(1)(b), which provides that: 'An employer (A) must not, in relation to employment by A, harass a person (B)... who has applied to A for employment.' In certain circumstances, employers are also liable under S.40(2)–(4) for repeated harassment of employees and job applicants by third parties: for further details, see Chapter 28, 'Liability of employers, employees and agents', under 'Employer's liability for acts of third parties'.

The duty to make reasonable adjustments – considered at length in Chapter 21, 'Failure to make reasonable adjustments' – applies throughout the recruitment process: S.39(5) simply states, without further qualification, that the duty applies to an employer. Note, though, that the employer must have actual or constructive knowledge that the person applying for the job is disabled – see 'Knowledge of disability' below.

24.4   'Employment' is defined in S.83(2) and covers 'employment under a contract of employment, a contract of apprenticeship or a contract personally to do work', as well as crown employment and employment in the Houses of Parliament – see Chapter 28, 'Liability of employers, employees and agents', under 'Who is protected? – job applicants'. 'Employer' for the purposes of these provisions includes 'a person who has no employees but is seeking to employ one or more other persons' – S.83(4). So, a start-up business would be covered by the above provisions from the moment it decides to recruit staff, not from the day it actually takes on its first employee.

In addition to the provisions in S.39 covering discrimination in the recruitment of *employees*, Part 5 of the EqA also includes provisions covering the recruitment of certain categories of individual who do not satisfy the definition of employment in S.83 EqA. These provide that partnerships (S.44), LLPs (S.45), barristers (S.47), advocates (S.48) and those with the power of appointment to a public or private office (Ss.49–52) are prohibited from discriminating against applicants or candidates in the same three circumstances provided for in S.39(1) and (3). It follows that case law under S.39 (and its predecessor provisions) will be equally relevant to a claim of discrimination in recruitment brought under one of these other sections. For further details see Chapter 29, 'Liability of other bodies'.

24.5   In this chapter we begin by looking at two disability-specific issues – how an employer's knowledge of a candidate's disability can affect its obligations during the recruitment process, and how the EqA curtails employers' ability to ask health-related questions. We then consider the three forms of discrimination in recruitment that are outlawed by S.39(1) and (3): namely, discrimination in the arrangements for deciding to whom to offer employment; discrimination in the terms on which employment is offered; and discrimination by way of a failure to make an offer of employment.

Knowledge of disability 24.6

One particular difficulty faced by employers during recruitment is knowing whether an applicant has a disability in order to determine whether reasonable adjustments need to be made to the recruitment process. Recognising this, para 20(1) of Schedule 8 to the EqA provides that: 'A [i.e. the person on whom the S.20 duty to make reasonable adjustments is imposed] is not subject to a duty to make reasonable adjustments if A does not know, and could not reasonably be expected to know... (a) in the case of an applicant or potential applicant, that an interested disabled person is or may be an applicant for the work in question.' This provision makes it clear that the duty to make adjustments does not arise until the employer knows, or ought reasonably to know, that a specific individual is disabled.

In addition, S.15 EqA – discrimination arising from disability – does not apply 'if A [the alleged discriminator] shows that A did not know, and could not reasonably have been expected to know, that B [the person alleging unfavourable treatment] had the disability' – S.15(2).

So, while it is important for employers to establish at an early stage if any job 24.7 applicants are disabled and what can be done to alleviate any disadvantage they may experience in the recruitment process as a result of that disability, an employer who cannot reasonably be expected to know of the disability will not be required to make reasonable adjustments and will not be liable for discrimination arising from the disability. In considering the question of reasonable knowledge, it is important to bear in mind the statutory limitations placed on the types of question an employer can legitimately ask job applicants about health and disability. These limitations are discussed in the next section.

Pre-employment health questions 24.8

Pre-employment enquiries about health issues are thought to be one of the main reasons why disabled job applicants often fail to reach the interview stage. Evidence also suggests that they have a powerful deterrent effect on potential applicants who are disabled. In view of this, the entirely new provision in S.60 EqA is highly significant. This provides that, other than in specified circumstances, an employer must not ask a job applicant a question about his or her health before:

- offering work to the applicant – S.60(1)(a), or

- where the employer is not in a position to offer work, including the applicant in a pool from which the employer intends, when in a position to do so, to select a person to whom to offer work – S.60(1)(b).

24.9 For these purposes, whether or not a person has a disability is to be regarded as an aspect of that person's health – S.60(13). 'Work' is defined in S.60(9) to include employment, contract work, a position as a partner or a member of an LLP, a pupillage or tenancy, an appointment to a personal or public office, or the provision of an employment service – S.60(9). A reference to offering work is a reference to making a conditional or unconditional offer of work, and in relation to contract work is a reference to allowing a person to do the work subject to fulfilment of one or more conditions – S.60(10).

The effect of S.60 is that, except in certain specified situations, an employer must not ask about a job applicant's health until that person has either been offered a job (on a conditional or unconditional basis) or been included in a pool of successful candidates to be offered a job when a suitable position arises (see para 201 of the Explanatory Notes that accompany the EqA). The Explanatory Notes state: 'This provision will limit the making of enquiries and therefore help to tackle the disincentive effect that an employer making such enquiries can have on some disabled people making applications for work' – para 206.

24.10 **Exceptions.** There are a limited range of circumstances in which an employer is entitled to ask questions about health before offering an applicant employment or entering him or her into a pool for selection at a later date. The exceptions are where the question is necessary for the purpose of:

- establishing whether the applicant will be able to comply with a requirement to undergo an assessment, or establishing whether the duty to make reasonable adjustments is or will be imposed on the employer in connection with a requirement to undergo an assessment – S.60(6)(a)

- establishing whether the applicant will be able to carry out a function which is intrinsic to the work concerned – S.60(6)(b). Where the employer believes that the duty to make reasonable adjustments will apply in connection with the work, a function is only to be treated as intrinsic to the work if it would remain intrinsic to that work once that duty has been complied with – S.60(7). (For further discussion of when job functions may be regarded as being 'intrinsic' in this context, see under 'Arrangements for deciding to whom to offer employment – application forms' below)

- monitoring diversity in the range of persons applying to the employer for work – S.60(6)(c)

- supporting positive action in respect of disabled people – S.60(6)(d)

- if there is a requirement for the person performing the work in question to have a particular disability, establishing whether the applicant has that disability – S.60(6)(e).

748

In addition, S.60(14) EqA provides that S.60 does not apply to anything done for the purpose of vetting applicants for work for reasons of national security.

It is significant that pre-employment health questions are permitted under **24.11** S.60(6)(a)–(e) only if they are *necessary* for any of the prescribed purposes. This appears to set a high threshold for employers, but there is no guidance in the EqA as to when the test of necessity will be satisfied. However, the Explanatory Notes give two examples at para 206 of situations in which an exception would apply:

- applicants are asked on an application form whether they have a disability that requires the employer to make a reasonable adjustment to the recruitment process. This is to allow, for example, people with a speech impairment more time for interview. This enquiry would be permitted

- an applicant applies for a job in a warehouse, which requires the manual lifting and handling of heavy items. As manual handling is a function which is intrinsic to the job, the employer is permitted to ask the applicant questions about his or her health to establish whether he or she is able to do the job (with reasonable adjustments for a disabled applicant, if required). The employer would not be permitted to ask the applicant other health questions until offering the candidate a job.

Further examples are provided in the Equality and Human Rights Commission's **24.12** Code of Practice on Employment (2010) ('the EHRC Employment Code'):

- an application form states: 'Please contact us if you are disabled and need any adjustments for the interview.' This would be lawful under the Act

- an employer is recruiting play workers for an outdoor activity centre and wants to hold a practical test for applicants as part of the recruitment process. It asks a question about health in order to ensure that applicants who are not able to undertake the test (for example, because they have a particular mobility impairment or have an injury) are not required to take the test. This would be lawful under the Act

- an employer wants to recruit a deafblind project worker who has personal experience of deafblindness. This is an occupational requirement of the job and the job advert states that this is the case. It would be lawful under the Act for the employer to ask on the application form or at interview about the applicant's disability

- a construction company is recruiting scaffolders. It would be lawful under the Act to ask about disability or health on the application form or at interview if the questions related specifically to an applicant's ability to climb ladders and scaffolding to a significant height. The ability to climb ladders and scaffolding is intrinsic to the job.

749

24.13 **Enforcement of S.60.** Strictly speaking, S.60 does not create any rights for job applicants, as a contravention of S.60(1) is enforceable as an unlawful act only by the EHRC – S.60(2). This means that a job applicant cannot seek compensation in an employment tribunal simply for having been asked a question about health. However, as S.60(3) makes clear, while an employer does not contravene any of the disability discrimination provisions in the Act merely by asking about an applicant's health, its conduct in reliance on information given in response may be a contravention of a 'relevant disability discrimination' provision. If an employee makes a complaint that he or she has been discriminated against after providing information in response to a question about health which falls outside the permitted exceptions in S.60(6) (see 'Exceptions' above), the tribunal must draw an inference of discrimination from the particulars of the complaint and require the employer to provide a non-discriminatory explanation – S.60(5).

A 'relevant disability provision' for the purposes of S.60(5) is defined in S.60(11). It includes a complaint of direct disability discrimination under S.39(1)(a) or (b) – i.e. in the arrangements for deciding to whom to offer employment or by not offering employment. It also covers the equivalent provisions applying to contract workers, partnerships, limited liability partnerships, barristers, advocates, personal and public offices, and employment services.

24.14 Arrangements for deciding to whom to offer employment

Section 39(1)(a) EqA stipulates that 'an employer (A) must not discriminate against a person (B) in the arrangements A makes for deciding to whom to offer employment'. The term 'arrangements' in this context has been carried through to the EqA from the antecedent discrimination legislation, and, while it is not defined in the statute, case law under the previous legislation established that it is to be construed widely. The EHRC Employment Code states that arrangements for the purposes of the EqA 'are not confined to those which an employer makes in deciding who should be offered a specific job. They also include arrangements for deciding who should be offered employment more generally. Arrangements include such things as advertisements for jobs, the application process and the interview stage' – para 10.8.

It should be noted that S.39(1)(a) and (3)(a) make it unlawful for A (the employer) to discriminate 'in the arrangements A makes', not 'in making the arrangements'. Thus, discrimination that occurs in the operation of those arrangements, once made, will also be covered. It does not matter that the person who originally made the arrangements is not the person actually operating them – Nagarajan v London Regional Transport 1999 ICR 877, HL.

Lord Nicholls in that case upheld the EAT's view in the earlier case of Brennan v JH Dewhurst Ltd 1984 ICR 52, EAT, that S.4(1)(a) RRA (a precursor to S.39(1)(a) EqA) 'encompasses more than setting up the arrangements, for instance, for interviewing applicants for a job. The phrase also includes the manner in which the arrangements are operated; for instance, the way the interviewing arrangements are in fact conducted.' A key point to bear in mind, in his Lordship's view, is that it is the employer, not the individual employee, who is deemed to be doing the discriminating, by virtue of what is now S.32(1) EqA. Therefore 'it matters not that different employees were involved at different stages, one employee acting in a racially discriminatory or victimising fashion and the other not. The acts of both are treated as done by the respondent employer.' Thus, in that case, the fact that the interviewers were consciously or unconsciously influenced by the fact that the interviewee had previously brought discrimination proceedings against the company rendered the 'arrangements' discriminatory.

24.15 Conversely, evidence of discriminatory intent on the part of the employer is not enough to establish discrimination unless the arrangements themselves operate in a discriminatory way. In Impey v Hertfordshire County Council EAT 245/78 the complainant applied for a school caretaker's job. The headmistress wrote a letter to the head of the education department which stated that 'Mrs Impey will be called for interview, but, in confidence, may I say that I would prefer to appoint a man'. The EAT held that the tribunal had been entitled to find that there was no discrimination in practice; the letter itself did not form part of the arrangements for selection.

There are a number of different aspects to an employer's recruitment 'arrangements' that may fall foul of the discrimination legislation – either through a claim under S.39(1)(a) or as evidence of a discriminatory attitude when rejecting an application for employment, which would fall under S.39(1)(c). We examine these below.

Method of recruitment

24.16 The first 'arrangement' for recruitment an employer is likely to make is the selection of a recruitment method. Some methods may unjustifiably exclude or cut down on applications from people with a particular characteristic, or from people who do not have a particular characteristic. A classic example of this is word of mouth recruitment – a cheap, yet potentially hazardous approach for employers. If the only method by which an employer seeks applications is by spreading the word among the existing workforce, indirect discrimination could arise if that workforce is dominated by, or significantly lacking in, persons possessing a particular protected characteristic. For example, in Locke v Lancashire County Council ET Case No.5179/79 the complainant applied for a job as a Fire Control Operator (FCO). Such jobs were rarely advertised, recruitment usually being via a list of firemen's wives available to fill the vacancies. Hence, no man had ever been employed as an FCO. This was held to be a clear policy of single-sex recruiting and amounted to unlawful discrimination.

24.17 **Personal acquaintance.** The Court of Appeal has held that where one particular individual is identified as the only suitable candidate and hand-picked for a particular high-level post because of his or her unique experience, abilities and profile, there will be no indirect discrimination – Lord Chancellor and anor v Coker and anor 2002 ICR 321, CA. The 'pool of comparison' in such cases will consist only of that candidate, and it will therefore be impossible to establish that the requirement to be personally known to the recruiter has a disparate impact upon any particular protected group.

In the Coker case, the then Lord Chancellor, Lord Irvine of Lairg, sought to appoint a new Special Adviser. The post was never advertised, and it was admitted that the Lord Chancellor did not look outside his circle of personal acquaintances for potential candidates. A female solicitor brought proceedings alleging that she had been directly and indirectly discriminated against on the ground of sex in respect of the arrangements made for the appointment of a Special Adviser.

24.18 The Court held that the 'pool of one' consisting of the personal acquaintance hand-picked or 'headhunted' by the Lord Chancellor prevented any disparate impact occurring and thus prevented any finding of indirect discrimination. Lord Phillips MR further observed that: 'Making an appointment from within a circle of family, friends and personal acquaintances is seldom likely to constitute indirect discrimination. Those known to the employer are likely to represent a minute proportion of those who would otherwise be qualified to fill the post. The requirement of personal knowledge will exclude the vast proportion of the pool, be they men, women, white or another racial group. If the above proposition will be true in most cases of appointments made on the basis of personal acquaintanceship, it was certainly true of the appointment of Mr Hart by the Lord Chancellor. This was because those members of the elite pool who were personally known to the Lord Chancellor were, on the unchallenged evidence, reduced to a single man. However many other persons there may have been who were potential candidates, whatever the proportions of men and women or racial groups in the pool, the requirement excluded the lot of them, except Mr Hart. Plainly it can have had no disproportionate effect on the different groupings within the pool.'

This decision clearly raises the prospect that headhunting a particular individual on a discriminatory basis will not be susceptible to challenge. However, it should be noted that although the Court's statements are ostensibly of a broad and general application, it was careful to qualify them, and it may be that the decision is limited to very senior appointments. As a virtually contradictory 'postscript', the Court emphasised that its judgment was not concerned with the practice of recruiting by word of mouth, and added: 'It does not follow, however, that this practice [of recruiting from family, friends and acquaintances] is unobjectionable. It will often be open to objection for a number of reasons. It may not produce the best candidate for the post. It may be likely to result in the appointee being of a particular gender or racial group. It may infringe the principle of equal opportunities... It is possible that a recruitment exercise conducted by word of mouth, by personal recommendation or by other informal recruitment method will constitute indirect discrimination... If the arrangements made for the purpose of determining who should be offered employment or promotion involve the application of a requirement or condition to an applicant that he or she should be personally recommended by a member of the existing workforce that may, *depending of course on all the facts*, have the specified disproportionately adverse impact on one sex or on a particular ethnic group' (our stress).

Use of employment agencies. Many employers now outsource the recruitment **24.19** process to employment agencies and employment businesses. Others will choose to recruit through job centres, careers services or educational establishments, all of which will be acting in the capacity of an agent. It is important to note in this respect that, under S.109(2) EqA: 'Anything done by an agent for a principal, with the authority of the principal, must be treated as also done by the principal.' It does not matter whether that thing is done with the principal's knowledge or approval – S.109(3). Accordingly, where an employer chooses to recruit via an agency, it is important that the agency knows that it must act in accordance with the employer's equal opportunities policies – any discrimination on the part of the agency could lead to liability for the employer.

Furthermore, employers should be careful when deciding which employment agency or agencies they use. If, for example, an agency specialises in finding work for the over-50s, an employer's use of that agency alone might limit the opportunities for younger people to apply. Moreover, if an employer chooses to recruit through agencies, job centres or schools where certain groups tend not to be fully represented – e.g. recruiting only from public schools or from a racially unbalanced area of a city – this may also constitute indirect discrimination where the practice cannot be justified. Hussein v Saints Complete House Furnishers 1979 IRLR 337, ET, illustrates the point. Here an employer told a careers officer that the company did not want anyone from a central area of Liverpool. Since 50 per cent of the population in that area was black compared to a black population of 2 per cent for Merseyside as a whole, the employer's condition excluded a larger proportion of black people than white people. The condition was therefore indirectly discriminatory.

Generally speaking, an employer's use of a range of employment agencies, job **24.20** centres, etc will help to avoid discrimination. Moreover, most reputable employment agencies will have detailed equal opportunities policies of their own which aim to eliminate both direct and indirect discrimination in recruitment.

An employment agency itself can be liable for discrimination in one of two capacities: as an employer (provided the relationship between the claimant and the agency satisfies the test of employment in S.83 EqA – see Chapter 28, 'Liability of employers, employees and agents' under 'Who is protected?'); or as an employment service provider, the definition of which incorporates the provision of services 'for finding employment for persons' and 'supplying employers with persons to do work' – see S.56(2) EqA. Under S.55(1)(a), an employment service provider must not discriminate against a person in the arrangements it makes for selecting persons to whom to provide, or to whom to offer to provide, the service. An example:

- **Chappell v Vital Resources Ltd** ET Case No.1301251/07: C, aged 61, responded to VR Ltd's advertisement for electric meter installers. He had over 30 years' relevant experience. Although his application initially received very positive feedback, after he was asked his age, the agency told him that the job was no longer available. It later transpired that jobs were offered to two other applicants who were younger and far less experienced than C. He lodged an employment tribunal claim alleging direct age discrimination. The tribunal held that C had suffered direct discrimination. Material to its conclusion was the fact that the agency could not offer a plausible explanation for why it had offered a formal interview to the two less experienced candidates but not to C.

24.21 Advertisements

As stated above under 'Arrangements for deciding to whom to offer employment', the EHRC Employment Code takes the view that the term 'arrangements' in S.39(1)(a) and (3)(a) includes job advertisements. Although this makes absolute sense, it does represent a departure from the position that applied under the Sex Discrimination Act 1975 (SDA), the Race Relations Act 1976 (RRA) and the Disability Discrimination Act 1995 (DDA). Those statutes included specific provisions prohibiting discriminatory advertisements (S.38 SDA, S.29 RRA and S.16B DDA), which were enforceable in employment tribunals by the EHRC (and before that, by its predecessor bodies). Case law under those statutes – in particular Cardiff Women's Aid v Hartup 1994 IRLR 390, EAT – indicated that the existence of the specific provisions meant that job advertisements were excluded from an employer's 'arrangements' for deciding to whom to offer employment: this meant that only the EHRC could bring action as a result of the content of an advertisement, although an employee who had an application for employment refused could use an advertisement as evidence of a discriminatory attitude on the part of the employer.

Crucially, the specific provisions covering discriminatory advertisements were not re-enacted in the EqA: instead, the Equality Act 2006 was amended, so that new S.24A allows the EHRC to take enforcement action via the county courts in respect of, among other things, any act which would be unlawful under Part 5 of the EqA. So, assuming Parliament had no intention of removing the EHRC's power to deal with discriminatory job adverts, it must follow that such adverts are now to be treated as part of an employer's arrangements under S.39(1)(a) and (3)(a), just as the Code maintains.

Claimant must have genuine interest in job. Although S.39 EqA is entitled **24.22** 'Job applicants and employees', the wording of S.39(1)(a) and (3)(a) is such that, theoretically, a person who has not even applied for a job, but has been put off applying by the terms of the advertisement, could bring a claim on the basis that the job advert is discriminatory (though not a claim of harassment, as S.40 only applies to employees and job applicants). However, two recent decisions of the EAT on age discrimination suggest that the claimant must have been genuinely interested in the job to be able to rely on S.39.

The first case, Keane v Investigo and ors EAT 0389/09, was brought by a job applicant in her late forties, who had unsuccessfully applied for a number of junior accountancy roles for which she was overqualified. She conceded that she had not been genuinely interested in the jobs, but nonetheless argued that she had suffered discrimination. The Appeal Tribunal, presided over by its President, Mr Justice Underhill, noted that the definition of direct discrimination requires some kind of 'less favourable' treatment of the complainant, and the definition of indirect discrimination requires the claimant to have been treated to his or her 'disadvantage'. Those elements are commonly and usefully referred to together as 'detriment'. An applicant, such as the claimant, who is not considered for a job which he or she is not interested in cannot in any ordinary sense of the word be said to have suffered a detriment – or, to be more precise, to have been (comparatively) unfavourably treated or put at a disadvantage.

Underhill P was also presiding over the EAT in the second case, Berry v **24.23** Recruitment Revolution and ors EAT 0190/10 and others. There B, a man in his fifties, had brought a number of age discrimination claims against employers and employment agencies, even though he had not applied for the jobs, which he claimed were advertised in a discriminatory manner. The EAT held that since B had no intention of applying for the jobs in question, the terms of the advertisements could not be said to have deterred him from doing so, with the result that he suffered no detriment. Interestingly, Underhill P noted that B had apparently contacted numerous employers about alleged age-discriminatory job advertisements, reaching out-of-court settlements with some of them. While not expressing a view on B's motivation, he emphasised that discrimination legislation is not intended to provide a source of income to people who complain about discriminatory job advertisements but who have no desire to fill the

755

vacancies in question. Underhill P added that those who try to exploit the legislation for financial gain were liable to have costs awarded against them, as indeed had happened to the claimant in Keane v Investigo and ors (above). For details on the award of costs in tribunal claims, see IDS Employment Law Handbook, 'Practice and Procedure' (2006), Chapter 18.

24.24 **Placing of advertisements.** One recruitment 'arrangement' will be the decision whether to advertise a vacancy internally or externally. The Employment Code advises that: 'Before deciding only to advertise a vacancy internally, an employer should consider whether there is any good reason for doing so. If the workforce is made up of people with a particular protected characteristic, advertising internally will not help diversify the workforce. If there is internal advertising alone, this should be done openly so that everyone in the organisation is given the opportunity to apply' – para 16.21.

If an employer opts to advertise a vacancy externally, it should give some thought as to where best to place the advertisement, since the choice of publication, website or location could restrict the potential readership and amount to indirect discrimination. For example, by choosing to advertise a vacancy only in a magazine aimed at the under-40s, an employer would place people over 40 at a disadvantage, as they would be much less likely to purchase the magazine and therefore learn about the vacancy. An employer may, therefore, be required to show that the decision to place the advert in that magazine alone was a proportionate means of achieving a legitimate aim.

24.25 **Wording of advertisements.** An employer's choice of words in a job advertisement can potentially give rise to discrimination. For example, advertising for 'a waitress' or 'a fireman' would amount to direct sex discrimination and should be avoided. Furthermore, the use of terms that are loaded with age-related connotations can lead to an inference of discrimination, as happened in McCoy v James McGregor and Sons Ltd and ors IT Case No.237/07, when the employer advertised for a candidate with 'youthful enthusiasm'.

Employers should also be wary of using words which, although not discriminatory on their face, imply a preference for a certain type of person. For example, the use of words such as 'fit', 'strong' or 'energetic' could discriminate against disabled people or older people. Similarly, wording that suggests the recruiter is looking for candidates at a certain stage in their careers can be discriminatory. An example:

- **Rainbow v Milton Keynes Council** ET Case No.1200104/07: the Council advertised for a teacher 'in the first five years of their career' at the school where R, who had 34 years' teaching experience, worked as a supply teacher. The Council rejected R's application for the post, contending that her application letter did not address certain key areas – such as why she was the right person for the job – in enough depth. An employment tribunal found that the Council had not proved that there was a good reason for failing to shortlist R, her application having made a clear case as to why she should be awarded the post. The decision to reject R's application was not direct discrimination as it was clear that the reason she was rejected was the cost of employing her – she would have been entitled to a substantially larger salary than less experienced teachers – rather than her age. However, the tribunal went on to find that she had suffered indirect discrimination – R and others of her age group were likely to have more than five years' experience and were therefore put at a disadvantage, and the Council had neither provided evidence to back up its assertion that appointing R would be unaffordable, nor demonstrated that it had considered other, less discriminatory alternatives.

That said, an injudicious choice of words in a job advertisement will not lead **24.26** to an automatic finding of discrimination: it will all depend on the surrounding factual circumstances. In Montgomery v Sellar Property Group and anor ET Case No.2201918/08, for example, the employer had placed a job advert for a 'dynamic young accountant'. The 53-year-old claimant applied for the post and was unsuccessful. However, in rejecting his claim of age discrimination, an employment tribunal found that, despite the wording of the advert, age had not played a part in the recruitment process: a 58-year-old man had been shortlisted, but the employer had eventually decided against recruiting anyone due to financial pressures.

Advertising for someone with a particular protected characteristic. **24.27** Ordinarily, an advertisement that states that applicants must possess a particular protected characteristic will amount to direct discrimination. However, the EqA provides an exception where the 'occupational requirement' for a person with a particular protected characteristic meets the test set out in paras 1–3 of Schedule 9 to the Act (see Chapter 30, 'General exceptions' under 'Occupational requirements'). The EHRC Employment Code advises that, if an employer is relying on an occupational requirement exception, this should be clearly stated in the job advert. The following example is provided by the Code:

> 'An employer advertises for a female care worker. It is an occupational requirement for the worker to be female, because the job involves intimate care tasks, such as bathing and toileting women. The advert states: "Permitted under Schedule 9, part 1 of the Equality Act 2010" – para 16.27.'

Disability. Special considerations apply in respect of disability discrimination. **24.28** Even where disability is not an occupational requirement for a post, an employer can still advertise a job as only open to disabled candidates, due to the asymmetrical nature of direct disability discrimination: a non-disabled candidate cannot complain of being less favourably treated, because of disability, than a disabled candidate – S.13(3) EqA. Some employers display the

757

Employment Service's two-tick disability symbol, which incorporates the slogan 'Positive about disabled people', on their advertisements.

24.29 **Graphics, images and illustrations within advertisements.** It is not only the words that need to be carefully chosen: the overall impact of an advertisement should also be borne in mind. For this reason, care must be taken with graphics, photographs and illustrations to ensure that, for example, the advertisement does not show only men doing a particular job. In Equal Opportunities Commission v Rodney Day Associates Ltd ET Case No.7937/88 (a case brought by the EOC under old S.38 SDA, which outlawed discriminatory adverts) a job agency put an advertisement headed 'Genuine Opportunities for Rugby Players' in various local newspapers. The agency wanted to recruit staff to improve the standard of rugby union in their area but the EOC argued that the advertisements indicated an intention to discriminate. The advertisement featured a sketch of a male player and was worded to appeal to players of a reasonable level. The tribunal held that, although women could play rugby, the advertisement would be understood by a reasonable person as appealing to male players, who would then get preferential treatment. The advertisement indicated an intention to discriminate either directly or indirectly and so was in breach of S.38 SDA.

However, the mere fact that an advertisement, or recruitment material on an employer's website, does not feature images of a mix of people with different protected characteristics is, without more, unlikely to give rise to a prima facie case of discrimination. Again, a tribunal will consider all the circumstances. An example:

- **Odi v Intellectual Property Office** ET Case No.1601948/10: O, a black African, claimed that IPO had directly racially discriminated against her by its refusal to select her for interview for the position of procurement manager. In support of her claim O referred to IPO's website, which, on a page entitled 'About Us', included a photograph of people who were, with the exception of an Asian man with very pale skin, white. The tribunal declined to draw an inference of discrimination from this. It recognised that publicity material for organisations will often seek to identify a visibly diverse range of people drawn from all walks of life (not just in terms of ethnicity) as both employees and customers. This could operate as an important form of permissible positive action, thereby encouraging applications and custom from traditionally under-represented groups. However, the tribunal commented that failure to show a particular person from a particular group – such as a black person – does not mean that there is prima facie evidence of discrimination against members of that group. Indeed, as the industrial jury, it ought to be wary of making pronouncements that might lead employers to engage in a kind of visual tokenism, an approach that others might consider patronising.

Job and person specifications
24.30

A clear and accurate job description provides an objective basis from which to draft a bias-free person specification and devise relevant selection criteria for applicants, thereby helping to eliminate discrimination from the recruitment process. However, the use of unnecessary requirements in a job or person specification is prone to give rise to indirect discrimination. The EHRC Employment Code cautions against relying on an existing job or person specification, instead advising that such specifications should be reviewed each time a job vacancy arises. The following example is used: 'An employer uses a person specification for an accountant's post that states "employees must be confident in dealing with external clients" when in fact the job in question does not involve liaising directly with external clients. This requirement is unnecessary and could lead to discrimination against disabled people who have difficulty interacting with others, such as some people with autism' – para 16.4.

Some employers operate a policy of interviewing all disabled candidates who meet the minimum criteria for appointment to a post. Such a policy is lawful – a non-disabled person cannot complain of being treated less favourably due to S.13(3) EqA – but it is important that the minimum criteria are clearly spelt out in the job and person specification.

Occupational requirements. A significant exception to the principle of non-**24.31** discrimination is contained in Schedule 9 to the Act. Under para 1 of Schedule 9, an employer will not contravene S.39(1)(a) or (c) by applying a requirement to have a particular protected characteristic, if the employer shows that, having regard to the nature or context of the work:

- it is an occupational requirement
- the application of the requirement is a proportionate means of achieving a legitimate aim, and
- the person to whom the employer applies the requirement does not meet it (or the employer has reasonable grounds for not being satisfied that the person meets it).

The term 'occupational requirement' (OR) is not defined in the EqA and, given **24.32** that para 1 of Schedule 9 adopts different wording to that used in the antecedent legislation, there is a degree of uncertainty as to its scope. Such uncertainty is compounded by an apparent conflict between the Explanatory Notes to the EqA, which state that an occupational requirement must be 'crucial to the post, and not merely one of several important factors', and the EHRC Employment Code, which states that 'the requirement must not be a sham or pretext and there must be a link between the requirement and the job' (para 13.7). The wording of the Code represents a significantly lower hurdle for employers than

759

the guidance in the draft version of the Code that was previously put out for consultation, which, reflecting the Explanatory Notes, stated that an OR must be 'crucial' to the post.

Examples of circumstances in which the occupational requirement exception might apply could include a black actor being required for a theatrical role to ensure that the performance is authentic; and where considerations of privacy or decency require a public changing room or lavatory attendant to be of the same sex as those using the facilities. A full consideration of the OR exception can be found in Chapter 30, 'General exceptions', under 'Occupational requirements'.

24.33 **Days and hours of work.** A job specification which stipulates that the post can only be filled on a full-time basis could give rise to indirect discrimination against women, since more women than men have primary childcare responsibilities and are likely to work part time as a result. It could also give rise to indirect disability discrimination – since fewer disabled people will be able to work full time – and discrimination arising from disability (if a job applicant is unable to meet the requirement due to his or her disability). Similarly, stipulating that work must be done on a Friday, Saturday or Sunday could give rise to indirect religious discrimination against Muslims, Jews and Christians respectively. In all these instances, employers should be prepared to objectively justify the days and hours of work stated in a job specification by reference to the operational needs of the business. For further details, see below under 'Terms and conditions on which employment is offered – days and hours of work'.

24.34 **Disability.** Job and person specifications present particular issues where disability discrimination is concerned and need to be scrutinised to ensure that they do not include unnecessary or marginal requirements that might exclude a disabled person who could do the job, either with or without a reasonable adjustment. The EHRC Employment Code provides the following example: 'A requirement that the applicant must be "active and energetic" when the job is a sedentary one is an irrelevant criterion. This requirement could be discriminatory against some disabled people who may be less mobile' – para 16.13.

It is preferable for a job description or person specification to focus on what needs to be achieved by the task or tasks in question, rather than on how the task should be done. For example, stating that a person must be 'willing to travel' where a job requires travel is less problematic than stating that the person 'must have a driving licence', as the former requirement will not exclude people who cannot drive because of their disability. That said, there will be circumstances where the job explicitly requires that the person appointed be able to drive, and in such circumstances two issues arise for consideration: (1) whether the requirement, which could amount to unfavourable treatment for the purpose of discrimination arising from disability, or to a provision, criterion or practice that puts people with the disability in question at a particular disadvantage, can be justified as a proportionate means of achieving a legitimate aim; and (2) whether there are any reasonable adjustments which the employer could make to the requirement. In Chadwick v Twin Valley Homes Ltd ET Case No.2403430/09 the claimant was rejected for a post on the basis that she did not have a driving licence or a car, both of which were considered essential for the role. The employment tribunal considered that the application of the requirement was a sound, reasonable and justifiable commercial decision, and noted that the adjustments proposed by the claimant would either have required other employees to be transferred to different jobs or the employer to spend up to £16,000 per year on taxis.

Age limits. The provisions covering age discrimination in the EqA do not **24.35** prevent an employer including a minimum or maximum age for job applicants. However, as such a requirement is prima facie directly discriminatory on the ground of age, it will need to be objectively justified as a proportionate means of achieving a legitimate aim. At European level, the European Court of Justice (ECJ) has been relatively sympathetic towards laws setting a maximum age for entry into, or continuance in, a given profession. In Wolf v Stadt Frankfurt am Main 2010 IRLR 244, ECJ, the Court held that a maximum recruitment age of 30 imposed on applicants for the Frankfurt fire service was justified as a 'genuine and determining occupational requirement' (GOR) under Article 4(1) of the EU Equal Treatment Framework Directive (No.2000/78). Interestingly, the GOR found by the Court was the possession of 'high physical capacities', but the fact that this was linked to age was considered sufficient to engage Article 4(1). In the Wolf case, the German government produced expert evidence to support its case that natural physical decline would be a serious concern for those working in the fire service. In Petersen v Berufungsausschuss für Zahnärzte für den Bezirk Westfalen-Lippe 2010 IRLR 254, ECJ, by contrast, the Court appeared to accept age-related decline as a valid *assumption* on which an objective justification may be based, but rejected it because the age bar did not apply uniformly across the public and private sectors. See also Prigge and ors v Deutsche Lufthansa AG 2011 IRLR 1052, ECJ.

At domestic level, tribunals have tended to demand evidence of a decline with age, rather than simply relying on assumptions. An example:

- **Baker v National Air Traffic Services Ltd** ET Case No. 2203501/07: NATS Ltd was responsible for training and providing air traffic controllers (ATCOs) for UK airports and airspace. B satisfied all the criteria for recruitment as an ATCO except one: NATS Ltd operated an absolute bar on considering applications from anyone aged 36 or over. When his application was rejected, B claimed direct age discrimination. An employment tribunal accepted that the age bar pursued four legitimate aims: achieving a high success rate in training; providing a reasonable period of post-qualification service, so as to justify the £600,000 that NATS Ltd asserted it cost to train

761

an ATCO; providing an adequate supply of ATCOs for the United Kingdom; and ensuring that safety processes and systems were not compromised. However, the tribunal considered that there was a lack of clear evidence that the age bar was reasonably necessary to achieve any of the stated aims, and some evidence to show that it contributed to an under-supply of ATCOs. NATS Ltd had relied on speculation and assumption to apply an absolute age bar, which excluded a number of suitably qualified candidates. As a result, the age bar was not a proportionate means of achieving any of NATS Ltd's aims.

24.36 Note that, until 6 April 2011, an employer enjoyed an exemption from the age discrimination provisions if it refused to entertain applications from people who were within six months of the age of 65 or of the employer's normal retirement age, whichever was the greater – para 9, Sch 9 EqA. However, that provision was repealed by the Employment Equality (Repeal of Retirement Age Provisions) Regulations 2011 SI 2011/1069. Accordingly, all age limits on recruitment to a post must be objectively justified.

24.37 **Appearance.** Although employers have a relatively free rein when determining standards of appearance in the workplace, caution should be exercised before including in a person specification requirements that might conflict with religious dress such as turbans and headscarves. For example, in Noah v Desrosiers (trading as Wedge) ET Case No.2201867/07 a female applicant for a job at a hair salon was told that stylists would be expected to wear their hair in a style representative of the salon's image. Since the claimant, a Muslim, wore the traditional hijab headscarf, which covers the wearer's hair entirely, she did not pursue the application further and brought a claim of religious discrimination. Upholding that claim, the tribunal accepted that the desire to have all employees display their hair in order to promote the salon's business was a legitimate aim, but concluded that the treatment afforded to the applicant was not a proportionate means of achieving that aim: not wearing a headscarf in a salon was not an intrinsic part of the role of a stylist, and there was no evidence that the employer had turned its mind to other, less discriminatory alternatives.

Similarly, appearance requirements and dress codes may need to be adjusted if they place a disabled job applicant at a substantial disadvantage. In Dean v Abercrombie and Fitch ET Case No.2203221/08 – a case concerning discrimination in employment rather than recruitment – an employment tribunal considered that it would be a reasonable adjustment to the employer's 'look policy' (a series of requirements relating to make-up and the wearing of the employer's clothing) for a disabled employee to be allowed to cover up her prosthetic forearm with a cardigan.

24.38 **Experience.** Employers sometimes require job applicants to have a minimum number of years' relevant experience. This is potentially indirectly discriminatory against young workers who have not had the opportunity to obtain the necessary experience. Such a requirement must therefore be objectively justified. It is clearly legitimate for an employer to appoint someone suitable to fill a vacancy. However, a time-based experience requirement is unlikely to be justifiable unless the employer can show that the applicant genuinely needs to have the minimum period of experience stipulated in order to carry out the work properly.

A requirement specifying a relatively small number of years' experience is more likely to be justifiable than one specifying many years of experience. This is because length of experience is much more likely to be a genuine indicator of skills and competencies during the first few years of employment than it is over a longer period. To illustrate: it is highly likely that a solicitor with two years' post-qualification experience (PQE) will be more competent than a colleague with only one year's PQE, and his or her charge-out rate will probably reflect this. However, there is much less reason to assume that a solicitor with ten years' PQE will be more competent than someone with, say, seven or eight.

24.39 That is not to say, however, that employers have to disregard candidates' experience altogether. Clearly the question of what applicants have done in the past is closely linked to the question of what skills and competencies they can demonstrate. Rather than requiring a minimum number of years' experience at a certain level, employers might instead be able to set requirements, or at least guidelines, as to the type or breadth of experience needed for the particular job.

Rejecting a candidate as 'over-qualified' on the basis that he or she has too much experience could amount to indirect discrimination against older workers, who are obviously more likely to be experienced than their younger counterparts. While an employer may have legitimate concerns that a worker with extensive experience might lack motivation for the job, or will find it difficult to take instructions from a less experienced colleague, these concerns are unlikely to justify a blanket requirement that an applicant be inexperienced.

24.40 **Health requirements.** If an employer states that people with a particular illness or disability are ineligible for a post, this will generally amount to direct disability discrimination. Similarly, it is not open to an employer to stipulate that applicants for a post must not be pregnant, since this would amount to direct pregnancy discrimination – Dekker v Stichting Vormingscentrum voor Jong Volwassenen (VJV-Centrum) Plus 1992 ICR 325, ECJ. That remains the case even where the employer is recruiting a replacement for a member of staff absent on maternity leave – Webb v EMO Air Cargo (UK) Ltd 1994 ICR 770, ECJ.

Employers should also avoid apparently neutral health requirements that are not relevant to the job in question. A general rule that all applicants must be 'in good health' is particularly problematic as, although health and disability are

763

not necessarily synonymous, such a requirement could be viewed as direct disability discrimination. Furthermore, as such a requirement could dissuade disabled people from applying because of something arising in consequence of their disability, it could also amount to discrimination arising from disability. The same rule could also give rise to indirect age discrimination as health generally declines with age. In both cases – indeed, with any health requirement that places disabled people or older job applicants at a disadvantage – the employer would need to show justification, i.e. that the rule is a proportionate means of achieving a legitimate aim. The existence of other, less discriminatory alternatives such as more specific health or fitness requirements would be likely to lead to the conclusion that the rule is disproportionate.

24.41 Of course, an employer's ability to enquire about a job applicant's state of health is now circumscribed by the new rules on pre-employment health questions contained in S.60 EqA. Details of this provision can be found under 'Pre-employment health questions' above, but for present purposes it should be noted that an employer is not prevented from asking questions in relation to a function that is 'intrinsic' to the job in question. Accordingly, it would seem prudent for employers to include in any job or person specification, or in recruitment literature, those functions which it considers 'intrinsic'.

24.42 Qualifications

The qualifications required should match the needs of the job since the imposition of inappropriate or unnecessarily high standards that discriminate against certain groups is likely to be unlawful. Further, educational achievements or career patterns which are different from the norm should not be automatically dismissed as inferior but analysed individually. For example, a requirement that the successful applicant must have at least 5 GCSEs would discriminate against applicants educated abroad if other equivalent overseas qualifications were not taken into account.

24.43 **Requirement to have a degree.** The requirement that candidates have a degree-level qualification has been the subject of a number of age discrimination claims, one of which – Homer v Chief Constable of West Yorkshire Police 2012 UKSC 15, SC – went up to the Supreme Court. In that case H was ineligible for promotion to a senior grade of legal adviser to the police because he did not hold a law degree, which was an 'essential' requirement for the post. He argued that this requirement amounted to indirect age discrimination because his age – 61 – prevented him from completing a law degree before retirement. He succeeded in his claim before an employment tribunal, which took the view that the requirement disadvantaged H and others of his age group (i.e. those aged 60–65) and was not proportionate. This decision was initially overturned on appeal, the Court of Appeal holding that any disadvantage suffered by H resulted not from age discrimination in respect of his age group but from his impending withdrawal from the workplace. As the same disadvantage would have been suffered by persons from the comparator group (i.e. those aged between 30–59) who also stopped working before obtaining a degree qualification (e.g. for family reasons or because of early retirement), the disadvantage suffered could be said to have been caused by age.

On further appeal, the Supreme Court disagreed with this reasoning. In the judgment of Baroness Hale (with whom the other Supreme Court Justices agreed), it was not right to equate leaving work because of impending compulsory retirement (which at the time was perfectly lawful) with other reasons for leaving (such as family reasons). In the latter case a person would generally have some choice in the matter, whereas a person faced with compulsory retirement would have no choice. Nor was it realistic to differentiate between age and compulsory retirement. As Baroness Hale expressed it: 'Put simply, the reason for the disadvantage was that people in [H's] age group did not have time to acquire a law degree. And the reason why they did not have time to acquire a law degree was that they were soon to reach the age of retirement.' The upshot was that the case was remitted to the tribunal to determine whether the indirect discrimination caused by the application of the law degree requirement could be objectively justified by the employer.

24.44 The Homer case shows how a requirement to hold a degree as a prerequisite for career advancement can disproportionately affect those who are approaching compulsory retirement. But now that there is no longer a statutory default retirement age of 65 (as to which see Chapter 5, 'Age', under 'Protection under the Equality Act – abolition of the statutory retirement age'), the particular circumstances that gave rise to the disadvantage suffered by the claimant in Homer are less likely to recur. However, a question of potentially greater significance is whether older workers (e.g. those in the 55–65 age group) can argue that it is indirectly discriminatory to require a degree as a condition for accessing a workplace benefit on the basis that it is harder for people of that age to satisfy such a condition. This question was not tackled in Homer as the claimant had not specifically raised it as an alternative basis of his indirect age discrimination claim.

It is certainly true that the incidence of people going to college or university and obtaining degrees has exponentially increased over the last 20 or so years as successive Governments have promoted tertiary education as a key plank of their general education policy. This has meant that, generally speaking, people under the age of about 40 are more likely to have a degree than those over that age. Does this mean that the requirement to hold a degree indirectly discriminates against older workers? It is a question that was tackled by the employment tribunal in McCluskey v Edge Hill University ET Case No.2405206/07. In that case, the tribunal accepted M's contention that people in their late fifties were less likely to have a degree and, therefore, that the requirement to have a degree put people of M's age group – as well as M herself – at a particular disadvantage.

765

However, the tribunal went on to accept that it was a legitimate aim for a university operating in a highly competitive market to have a mix of academic staff who in all instances possessed a degree. Furthermore, such a measure was proportionate to ensure the maintenance of high academic standards. Although the justification defence thwarted the claim in this case, it is important to remember that the employer was a university, and it is open to question whether the defence would be as successful if the argument were deployed in a different employment context.

24.45 Application forms

Pro forma application forms should be carefully worded to ensure that they ask only questions that are relevant to the job. The EHRC Employment Code advises that information identifying a candidate's protected characteristics – gender, ethnic origin, marital status, religion, sexual orientation, age or disability – should be withheld from those who are shortlisting or interviewing – para 16.39. If this information is required for diversity monitoring purposes, requesting it on the main application form is not the only option: the Code advises sending a monitoring form by e-mail once an application form has been received – para 16.40. However, a less time-consuming method that many employers have adopted is to include questions about protected characteristics on a detachable part of the application form, which can be retained by HR while the substantive information on the form – such as the applicant's qualifications and previous experience – can be forwarded to those tasked with selection.

If the information about a protected characteristic is required for a reason other than diversity monitoring, the Code advises that employers 'should include a clear explanation as to why this information is needed, and an assurance that the information will be treated in strictest confidence' – 16.41. The Code suggests that the only reason other than monitoring for which such questions can be asked is assessing whether a candidate meets an occupational requirement for the post (see Chapter 30, 'General exceptions', under 'Occupational requirements'). For most of the protected characteristics this is certainly true, but disability is an exception: an employer can also ask limited questions about a candidate's disability for the purposes of complying with the duty to make reasonable adjustments, or to determine whether the candidate will be able to carry out a function intrinsic to the job.

24.46 Asking about disability on application form. An employer is not required to make changes in anticipation of applications from disabled people generally. It is only if the employer knows or could reasonably be expected to know that a particular disabled person is, or may be, applying and is likely to be substantially disadvantaged by the employer's provisions, criteria and practices; the physical features of the employer's premises; or the failure to provide an auxiliary aid, that the duty arises. If the employer does not ask about disability prior to selecting or rejecting a candidate for interview, it may find itself liable for a failure to make reasonable adjustments on the basis that it *ought* to have known about the disability and taken steps to alleviate the disadvantage. An example:

- **Williams v Channel 5 Engineering Services Ltd** ET Case No.2302136/97: W, who is deaf, applied for the job of a television re-tuner. He was interviewed and filled in an application form. There was no space on the form to note any disability but the interviewer knew that W was deaf. W was accepted on the three-day training programme at the end of which deployment was envisaged. On the third day, the course involved a video with voice-over but no subtitles. W's request for assistance with that part of the session was refused and he left the course because he knew he would not be able to complete that part of the training. After intervention by W's mother, arrangements were made for W to complete the course, by which time the requirement for re-tuners had fallen off. In finding that the employer had failed to make reasonable adjustments, the employment tribunal commented that if the employer had made provision for applicants to state that they are disabled and, if so, the way in which they are disabled, it would have been in a position to ensure that W was supplied with the necessary equipment the first time round to complete his training course.

24.47 Where employers do ask job applicants about disabilities, this can give rise to a potential conflict for disabled applicants. On the one hand, they may fear that they will be discriminated against if they reveal their disability. On the other hand, they may be putting themselves at a disadvantage if they fail to reveal the disability as an employer is only under a duty to make reasonable adjustments when it knows or ought reasonably to know about the disability. Assistance is provided here by S.60 EqA, which limits the questions an employer can ask a candidate about health prior to deciding to make an offer of employment. As noted under 'Pre-employment health questions' above, an employer runs a significant risk of a direct disability discrimination claim if it asks questions about health for a reason other than one of those prescribed in S.60(6) EqA.

24.48 *Adjustments to the form.* Where an employer requires job applicants to fill out an application form, it is likely to be a reasonable adjustment to provide forms and accept applications in an accessible format where necessary – see para 16.35 of the EHRC Employment Code. The same would be true of any recruitment literature that accompanies, or takes the place of, an application form. If an employer does not allow an applicant to submit an application in an alternative form and the candidate is not shortlisted for interview as a result, this could amount to both discrimination arising from disability and a failure to make reasonable adjustments. An example:

- **Oldham v The Leonard Cheshire Foundation t/a Leonard Cheshire** ET Case No.2300971/99: O, who had a serious visual impairment caused by multiple sclerosis, telephoned the employer to ask if she could submit an application for the post of deputy director of services by audio-tape. The employer, which provided living accommodation for disabled persons and had a high profile in disability matters, told O that she had to complete an application form. O's husband was not available to write out the application for her so she used a mechanical aid that enabled her to write in her own hand. This was a laborious process and O did not feel that she had done herself justice on the application. She was not shortlisted for interview. At the subsequent tribunal hearing the employer conceded it had unlawfully discriminated against O by failing to make reasonable adjustments.

24.49 **Age-related information.** Asking a job applicant to provide his or her age or date of birth on a job application form is not in itself discriminatory. However, by asking such questions an employer risks the allegation that age has played a part in the recruitment decisions. For this reason, employers should consider putting any age-related questions, along with any questions relating to ethnic origin, marital status, etc, on a separate sheet or tear-off section, giving adequate assurances that the information will be confidential, that access to it will be restricted, and that it will be used only for the effective implementation of equal opportunities policies.

There are other, less direct, questions – for example, questions relating to the dates on which the applicant attended university or the dates of their previous employment – which can give an indication of how old the applicant is. So, although asking for dates of study or previous employment is not discriminatory in itself, doing so could add weight to an applicant's claim that he or she was rejected for age reasons. The Employers Forum on Age states that 'creating a truly age-neutral application form means that the people actually recruiting the candidate won't know anything about their age or chronological career history'.

24.50 However, there may well be very cogent reasons why an employer needs to know the dates relating to an applicant's employment history. For example, if the applicant has had ten jobs in the previous two years, this could raise questions as to his or her loyalty and commitment; and if the applicant has relevant experience for the job but has not actually worked at all in the last 15 years, this could raise questions as to whether his or her skills have lapsed. Similarly, grade boundaries for public exams have changed over time and an understanding of when those exams were taken may help the employer assess the applicant's skills and competencies vis-à-vis other applicants. And in any event, even if the dates when the applicant achieved certain qualifications are not requested, the types of qualifications earned (for example, GCSEs as opposed to O-levels) will give clues as to the applicant's age.

Employers should certainly consider carefully the purpose behind each question on an application form. Information useful in one recruitment process may well be practically irrelevant in another, so the form should be tailored accordingly. Employers should also ensure that those involved in the recruitment exercise receive proper diversity training to ensure that they do not allow age discrimination to creep into their decision-making. If an employer can show a logical reason why particular age-related information was requested, and can show that the recruitment process was carried out in an appropriate manner, it is unlikely to attract age discrimination liability.

Language. Where an employer uses an applicant's application form to test his **24.51** or her abilities or standard of English, this is can lead to indirect race discrimination. In Isa and anor v BL Cars Ltd ET Case Nos.27083/80 and another two Pakistani applicants were required to complete application forms in their own handwriting. Since neither could read or write English, they were unable to do so and were consequently refused employment. BL admitted that this was discriminatory and unjustifiable because their jobs as labourers did not require an ability to write.

Processing applications   **24.52**
It is important that employers process employment applications fairly and consistently. To this end, it has become common practice for questions about any of the protected characteristics covered by the EqA to appear in a removable section of the application form, so that those responsible for the HR function can use them for monitoring purposes and for complying with the duty to make reasonable adjustments. This practice is endorsed by para 16.39 of the EHRC Employment Code, which suggests that those persons responsible for selecting who to interview and who ultimately to appoint should only be provided with those sections of completed application forms relevant to the selection process.

When processing applications, employers should be aware that refusing to consider a candidate on the basis that he or she has previously brought, or given evidence in, a discrimination claim would amount to victimisation – see Chapter 19, 'Victimisation'.

Retention of information. There are many reasons why it is important for **24.53** employers to retain information about every application for employment they receive: documentary evidence will be required to defend any allegation of discrimination in the recruitment process; unsuccessful applicants often request feedback; and employers need to understand the positives and negatives arising from each round of recruitment. The Code warns that employers should 'keep records that will allow them to justify each decision and the process by which it was reached and to respond to any complaints of discrimination. If the employer does not keep records of their decisions, in some circumstances, it could result in an employment tribunal drawing an adverse inference of discrimination' – para 16.44.

The Code identifies the type of information an employer should retain as:

• any job advertisement, job description or person specification used in the recruitment process

769

- the application forms or CVs, and any supporting documentation from every candidate applying for the job

- records of discussions and decisions by an interviewer or members of the selection panel; for example, on marking standards or interview questions

- notes taken by the interviewer or by each member of the panel during the interviews

- each interview panel member's marks at each stage of the process; for example, on the application form, any selection tests and each interview question (where a formal marking system is used)

- all correspondence with the candidates.

24.54 An employer retaining the above information should, however, be aware of its obligations under the Data Protection Act 1998; in particular, the obligation to hold on to personal data no longer than is reasonably necessary. For further details of employers' duties under the 1998 Act, see the 'Employment Practices Code' produced by the Information Commissioner's Office.

24.55 **Shortlisting.** The task of reducing the number of applications to a shortlist of potentially suitable candidates is an important part of the recruitment process, but is also a point at which discrimination can creep in. Para 16.50 of the EHRC Employment Code provides the following guidelines for good practice:

- wherever possible, more than one person should be involved in shortlisting applicants, to reduce the chance of one individual's bias prejudicing an applicant's chances of being selected

- the marking system, including the cut-off score for selection, should be agreed before the applications are assessed, and applied consistently to all applications

- where more than one person is involved in the selection, applications should be marked separately before a final mark is agreed between the people involved

- selection should be based only on information provided in the application form, CV or, in the case of internal applicants, any formal performance assessment reports

- the weight given to each criterion in the person specification should not be changed during shortlisting; for example, in order to include someone who would otherwise not be shortlisted.

24.56 If an employer knows (or has reasonable grounds for knowing) that an applicant has a disability and is likely to be put at a substantial disadvantage by the employer's provisions, criteria or practices, the physical features of the employer's premises, or the failure to provide an auxiliary aid, the employer should consider whether there is any reasonable adjustment that would bring the disabled person within the field of applicants to be considered even though he or she would not otherwise fall to be considered because of that disadvantage. If the employer could only make this judgement on the basis of more information than is currently available, it may amount to a failure to make a reasonable adjustment for the employer not to put the disabled person on the shortlist for interview. Indeed, it is fairly common practice to shortlist *all* disabled applicants who meet the *minimum* criteria for the job – sometimes referred to as a guaranteed interview scheme. While nothing in the EqA could strictly compel an employer to adopt such a practice, it might be considered a reasonable adjustment in some circumstances. Moreover, automatically shortlisting disabled applicants will not result in claims of direct disability discrimination from non-disabled applicants who were not shortlisted as a non-disabled person cannot rely on the disability discrimination provisions to bring a claim on the basis of being treated less favourably than a disabled person – S.13(3) EqA (see further Chapter 6, 'Disability').

If an employer is inconsistent in applying the job and person specifications to the applications before it, an inference of discrimination can arise. It is important to note, however, that not every instance of sub-standard recruitment practices will lead to such an inference – often the failings will be unrelated to a protected characteristic. Two examples: **24.57**

- **Bojarowska-Mayhew v The Phoenix Surgery** ET Case No.3103468/09: BM qualified as a GP in her homeland of Poland but all her post-graduate experience was in the United Kingdom. She applied for a post as a GP with the surgery and when she was not shortlisted she brought a claim for direct discrimination contrary to S.1(1) RRA. She maintained that there was little possibility that the shortlisted candidates could be better qualified or experienced than she was. She claimed the reason she was not shortlisted was that local GP practices did not like Eastern European GPs as it was possible for them to work in the United Kingdom despite having little experience of the UK healthcare system. The tribunal dismissed her claim. It noted that the application process was neither fair nor transparent. Indeed, the tribunal considered that it might have been one of the worst recruitment processes it had seen in that there was no verifiable contemporaneous evidence to justify what was done and how it was done. However, that did not mean it was discriminatory. It was not sufficient for BM to say 'because I was the best qualified and because I did not make the shortlist there must have been an actionable discriminatory basis'. The tribunal was satisfied that the surgery applied criteria that it thought reasonable and fit and which bore on the particular aspects of their practice, even though those criteria could be open to criticism. It may well have been unfair to mark BM down because her application did not contain mission statements, as she suggested. However, that had nothing to do with her race. Put quite simply, BM did not get the job she applied for because of the application of criteria that had nothing to do with race

- **Young v Luton Borough Council** ET Case No. 1202170/06: Y, who suffered from complex post-traumatic stress disorder, applied for a part-time role with the Council. The Council operated a guaranteed interview scheme for disabled applicants who met the minimum essential criteria, and Y stated on her application form that she considered herself disabled. When she was not shortlisted for the post, Y claimed disability-related discrimination and direct disability discrimination, arguing that she met all the essential criteria for shortlisting, meaning that the reason she was not shortlisted must have been her disability. An employment tribunal, noting that at least one other disabled applicant had progressed to the interview stage, concluded that the failure to shortlist had nothing to do with disability and was instead attributable to the Council's failure to apply the selection criteria properly.

24.58 Immigration issues

Employers face potentially conflicting obligations where immigration is concerned, since they must balance their statutory responsibility for checking a person's eligibility to work in the United Kingdom with the need to avoid race discrimination. Although there are a number of restrictions on the right of nationals of countries outside the European Economic Area to work in the United Kingdom, a blanket refusal to consider applications from people requiring a work permit is likely to amount to indirect race discrimination. An example:

- **Osborne Clarke Services v Purohit** 2009 IRLR 341, EAT: the employer's online application system for solicitors' training contracts informed P, an Indian national without a work permit, that it was 'unable to accept applications from candidates who require a work permit to take up employment in the United Kingdom'. An employment tribunal found this policy to be indirect discrimination on the ground of nationality, and rejected the employer's argument that, since Government guidance indicated that work permits were unlikely to be granted for trainee solicitors, the policy was justified. Upholding that decision on appeal, the EAT held that since there was no evidence of a dialogue between the employer and the immigration authorities, the employer could not begin to establish the level of evidence required to prove justification on an objective basis.

24.59 However, tribunals are not unsympathetic to the situation employers find themselves in and appear to be adopting a relatively lenient approach where a genuine mistake has been made. Two examples:

- **Unegbu v Dimension Data Network Services Ltd** ET Case No.2701761/07: U, a Nigerian, came to the United Kingdom in 2006 on a Highly Skilled Migrant Permit Visa. In 2007, he applied to DDNS Ltd, an agency that supplies specialist IT staff, for a post working as an IT analyst for Airbus. The agency informed U that all applicants for the post would require a British passport in order to gain security clearance, as the work concerned a project Airbus was undertaking for the Ministry of Defence. This was incorrect; although security clearance was needed, there was no requirement for a British passport. U claimed that the agency's refusal to consider his application amounted to race discrimination. The tribunal did not accept that U had experienced direct discrimination, but did find that the erroneous application of a bar on non-British passport holders was an act of indirect discrimination. However, given that it was unintentional and the error resulted from a breakdown in communication, the tribunal did not consider it just and equitable to award compensation

- **Kazombiaze v Kalyx Ltd** ET Case No.1900170/08: K applied to K Ltd for a job as a prison custody officer and was invited to a pre-selection event. He was told he had to bring with him photographic identification such as a passport in order to gain entrance to the prison. K took his driving licence, but was also asked to produce his passport, which contained his residence permit showing that he had 'limited leave to remain' in the United Kingdom. On the basis of an erroneous belief that security clearance would not be granted to someone who had only a limited right to remain, K Ltd refused to allow K's application to proceed any further. It then checked the situation with the Home Office, discovered its error, and invited K to the next selection event, which he refused to attend because he was unhappy with the way he had been treated. An employment tribunal dismissed K's claim of race discrimination, holding that K Ltd had made a mistake which was understandable in the light of the difficult regime of regulation and security requirements applying to staff in prisons.

Checks on right to work in the United Kingdom. Under S.15 of the **24.60** Immigration, Asylum and Nationality Act 2006 employers are liable to civil penalties of up to £10,000 per employee if they employ someone who is subject to immigration control who has not been granted leave to enter or remain in the United Kingdom; or whose leave is invalid, has ceased to have effect (whether by reason of curtailment, revocation, cancellation, passage of time or otherwise) or is subject to a condition preventing that person from accepting the employment. A person subject to immigration control is a person who requires leave to enter or remain in the United Kingdom under the Immigration Act 1971. In short, British citizens and Commonwealth citizens with the right of abode in the United Kingdom are not subject to immigration control. Nationals of the European Economic Area and Switzerland are also free to live and work in the United Kingdom. In order to avoid a fine in the event that it inadvertently employs someone who is ineligible to work in the United Kingdom, an employer should obtain documentary evidence from that person, before employment commences, indicating that they are entitled to work in the

773

United Kingdom (a 'statutory excuse'). The employer must be satisfied that the documents are not forgeries and must retain copies. If the documents indicate that the applicant's leave to remain is limited, the employer must make annual checks during the course of employment to ensure that the right to work still applies.

Under the 2006 Act an employer is not strictly obliged to check the documentation of *every* potential employee: the documentary checks only become relevant where enforcement action is being taken against an employer because it has employed a person who is not entitled to work in the United Kingdom. As a result, an employer pressed for time might be inclined to forgo checks on any potential employees who it considers are obviously from the United Kingdom. However, as such an assumption is likely to be based on skin colour or accent, it gives rise to the possibility of race discrimination. To avoid this, a safer course of action would be for employers to ask *all* job applicants to prove their entitlement to work in the United Kingdom. This is certainly the view of the UK Border Agency, which recommends in its Code of Practice, 'Guidance for Employers on the Avoidance of Unlawful Discrimination in Employment Practice While Seeking to Prevent Illegal Working' (2008), that employers obtain a statutory excuse for all potential employees. The Code also states that employers should be careful not to treat job applicants who produce a document giving them only limited leave to remain less favourably than applicants who have unlimited leave to remain, by reason that their status will have to be checked periodically. Similarly, where applicants are unable to produce the relevant documentation straight away, the employer should not automatically assume that they are working in the United Kingdom illegally. A breach of the Code will not make a person liable to civil or criminal proceedings, but may be taken into account by a tribunal – S.23(4).

24.61 Interviews

Interviewing candidates gives employers the opportunity to obtain all the necessary information upon which to make an informed decision as to the most suitable applicant for a job. However, a failure to conduct interviews in a fair, unbiased and structured way may lead to claims of discrimination. The EHRC Employment Code recommends that 'employers take steps to make sure all job interviews are conducted strictly on the basis of the application form, the job description, the person specification, the agreed weight given to each criterion, and the results of any selection tests, so that all applicants are assessed objectively, and solely on their ability to do the job satisfactorily' – para 16.57. Wherever possible, staff conducting interviews should be given training to help them avoid stereotyped assumptions, apply a scoring method objectively, and prepare and ask only questions that are relevant.

Thought may need to be given to the timing of the interview: arranging interviews towards the beginning or end of the working day could disadvantage women, for example, as they are more likely than men to have childcare commitments. Similarly, dates that coincide with major religious festivals could give rise to indirect religious discrimination. In both instances, the employer may need to provide objective justification for the timing of the interview – in this respect it is likely to assist the employer if the timing of the interview accords with the expected time that the successful applicant would be working.

Questions related to age and experience. Although interviews exist primarily **24.62** so that an employer can assess a candidate's aptitude and interest in a job, restricting questions about matters such as 'drive and motivation' to older job applicants can amount to discrimination:

- **McCoy v James McGregor and Sons Ltd and ors** IT Case No.237/07: M, who was 58 years old, saw an advert for a sales representative post with JMS Ltd that called for 'at least five years' experience' and 'youthful enthusiasm'. Having over 20 years' experience in the relevant trade, he applied for the job and initially spoke to a director, D, who, on being told M's age, asked whether he thought he had the 'drive and motivation to be successful in this trade'. This line of questioning was pursued in the two subsequent interviews M had with JMS Ltd. In the first, for example, D stated: 'Terry, you're 58. How can you convince me that you still have the drive and motivation to be successful in this position? Are you still hungry enough to succeed?' Shortly after the second interview, M was informed that his application had been unsuccessful. The two successful applicants were aged 42 and 43 – one had given his date of birth on his CV, while the other had omitted it but at some time during the course of the selection process, it had been written on his CV by D. Neither was asked whether they still had the drive and motivation for the role. An employment tribunal attached great significance to the use of the phrase 'youthful enthusiasm' and drew from it an inference that age played a part in the selection process. Moreover, the tribunal took the view that there was a clear link in D's mind between the concepts of 'age' and 'energy', 'enthusiasm' and 'motivation'. The tribunal also attached weight to the line of questioning pursued with M at both interviews, since this was clearly age-related. The combined effect of these inferences was that M had proved facts from which the tribunal could conclude that JMS Ltd had discriminated against him on the ground of his age. Although JMS Ltd argued that the decision not to appoint M was due not to his age but rather to the greater 'enthusiasm' and 'dynamism' of the successful applicants, the tribunal did not accept this explanation, instead concluding that age was taken into account at every stage of the recruitment process.

It is commonplace for interviewers to ask candidates to give examples from **24.63** personal experience of how he or she has dealt with various situations. Although younger applicants are likely to have less experience, the adoption of such a line of questioning is unlikely to amount to age discrimination. For example, in

775

Keen v Greater Manchester Fire and Rescue Service ET Case No.2405911/10 K had applied to be a retained firefighter. During the interviews, the employer looked for specific examples of what interviewees had personally done in various situations, such as work, home, hobbies and voluntary work. K was not successful and claimed that he had suffered indirect age discrimination: he was aged 21 and had spent the last 5 years as a student, and so had no work experience that he could use in his interview answers. The employment tribunal dismissed his claim. The requirement imposed by the employer was that interviewees demonstrate compliance against certain competencies by reference to evidence from personal experience drawn from the workplace, home, hobbies or voluntary work. The tribunal took judicial note of the fact that people in their early twenties may have attained considerable experience in school, at college or university and in pursuit of hobbies in their spare time. There was no evidence that people in this age group were placed at a disadvantage by application of the requirement.

24.64 **Questions about childcare and family matters.** In rare cases, gender-related questions may be entirely appropriate because they relate to the capacity of a candidate to do the job in question. According to the EAT in Saunders v Richmond-upon-Thames London Borough Council 1978 ICR 75, EAT, such questions are not, of themselves, discriminatory: the issue is whether they are evidence of a discriminatory attitude. (Note, however, that that case pre-dates the introduction of specific rules relating to harassment, which could possibly apply to questions about whether a job applicant plans to start a family – see 'Harassment at interview' below.) In Twilley v Tomkins ET Case No.27506/92 a woman candidate for a pools collection vacancy was, according to a tribunal, legitimately questioned about her childminding arrangements and the attitude of her husband to her working evenings as such questions had been asked of both male and female candidates and were pertinent because regular evening work depended upon the cooperation of employees' partners. And in Woodhead v Chief Constable of West Yorkshire Police EAT 285/89 the complainant, a married mother of two, applied to join the police force but was rejected after attending a three-day assessment course, which included practical exercises and an interview by a panel. At least half of her 25-minute interview was devoted to questions about her domestic arrangements, ranging over family finances, her ability to continue with a course of study, childcare arrangements and whether she would be able to juggle a demanding job with family life. She complained that this line of questioning was based on gender stereotypes and assumptions about the general suitability of women as police officers. The EAT, however, said that the questions relating to the complainant's domestic life had to be put into the context of the special nature and demands of police work. It was not discriminatory for an employer to ensure that a woman had thought through the implications of undertaking a stressful and demanding occupation.

Ordinarily, however, childcare, family life and domestic plans will have no specific relevance to the job in question, and in these circumstances tribunals are likely to perceive questioning on such matters as having a discriminatory undertone. In one case where a woman was asked questions at a job interview about whether she intended to have any more children, the tribunal concluded that the purpose of such enquiry was to filter out those female candidates who were of childbearing age and whose families were not complete or perceived to be complete – Johnston v Fultons Fine Furnishing Ltd ET Case No.02087/94. The tribunal noted in that case that the candidates shortlisted for a second interview were of an age where it was uncommon for women to have children. The complainant was awarded £3,000 for injury to feelings.

Asking questions about compatibility with colleagues of the opposite sex **24.65** should also be avoided. In Makiya v London Borough of Haringey ET Case No.03023/89 a woman who was known to be very committed to equal opportunities applied for a post as design and technology adviser. During her interview she was asked how she would deal with reactionary male teachers. None of the other interviewees, who were all male, were asked the equivalent question. The tribunal upheld her complaint of sex discrimination because the question indicated that in the mind of the questioner she, as a woman, would encounter a problem in coping with reactionary male teachers and was therefore less suitable for the job.

Reasonable adjustments. It is generally wise for employers to enquire whether **24.66** any adjustments would be needed for the interview either on the application form or in the letter inviting the applicant for interview. This gives the employer time to put any necessary adjustments in place. If an applicant has put an employer on notice of his or her disability, a failure to take action may mean the employer has breached the duty to make reasonable adjustments. An example:

- **Gailey v Haes Systems Ltd** ET Case No.6002720/99: G applied for a job with HS Ltd, clearly stating on his CV that he was blind. When he arrived for an interview there was no one to greet him. He got lost and then had to find his own way round the building to the right stairway. At the top of the stairs he called out and was met by a secretary, who asked him to fill out a form, not realising that he was blind. An employment tribunal found that the employer, knowing G was blind, should have arranged for someone in the office to have looked out for him on his arrival so that assistance could be offered.

However, some disabled job applicants are reluctant to inform a potential employer of their disability in advance of interview, for fear that their application will not be given serious consideration. In such circumstances, the extent of the duty to make adjustments is less than if the employer had known (or ought to have known) in advance of the disability and its effects: any consideration of

777

whether an adjustment is reasonable will take into account the practicability of implementing the necessary change at short notice.

24.67 **Harassment at interview.** Harassment during the recruitment process is most likely to occur at the interview stage so it is important that any employees tasked with interviewing job applicants have undergone equal opportunities training. Without proper training, an interviewer could unwittingly ask a question that amounted to harassment under S.26(1) EqA: namely, a question that is (a) unwanted and related to a protected characteristic; and (b) has the purpose or effect of either violating B's (i.e. the job applicant's) dignity or creating an intimidating, hostile, degrading, humiliating or offensive environment for B.

It is important to note here the conduct need only be *related to*, rather than *because of* or *on the ground of*, the protected characteristic: this is undoubtedly an easier test of causation for a claimant to meet. Indeed, it could potentially cover unwanted questions asked of a female job applicant about childcare or her plans to start a family, since such questions are related to her sex; or a line of questioning that focused on the effects of a job applicant's disability.

24.68 A further point to note is that there need not be any intention to harass on the part of the interviewer, since S.26 applies where the conduct complained of has the purpose *or effect* outlined above. However, this is unlikely to lead to a flood of successful claims from over-sensitive job applicants, because when deciding whether conduct had such an effect, a tribunal should take into account the perception of the claimant, the other circumstances of the case, and whether it is reasonable for the conduct to have that effect – S.26(4).

24.69 *Sexual harassment.* In addition to harassment 'related to a protected characteristic' under S.26(1), the EqA also prohibits two forms of sexual harassment in S.26(2) and (3). The first arises where a person, A, engages in unwanted conduct of a sexual nature that has the purpose or effect referred to in S.26(1)(b) (i.e. of either violating B's dignity or creating an intimidating, hostile, degrading, humiliating or offensive environment for B) – S.26(2). The second occurs where (a) A or another person engages in unwanted conduct of a sexual nature or that is related to gender reassignment or sex, (b) the conduct has the purpose or effect referred to in S.26(1)(b) (i.e. of either violating B's dignity or creating an intimidating, hostile, degrading, humiliating or offensive environment for B), and (c) because of B's rejection of or submission to the conduct, A treats B less favourably than A would treat B if B had not rejected or submitted to the conduct – S.26(3).

In order to avoid these forms of sexual harassment arising during an interview employers should ensure that anyone carrying out the interview has undergone sufficient training. Many employers go a step further by ensuring that interviews are conducted by a panel rather than on a one-to-one basis.

However, a failure to adopt such a practice is unlikely, without more, to amount to sex discrimination. In British Telecommunications plc v Williams 1997 IRLR 668, EAT, the question arose whether it was necessary for an employer to ensure that male managers responsible for carrying out interviews were 'chaperoned'. In overturning a tribunal's finding of sex discrimination, the EAT held that there was no such obligation on employers. The EAT ruled that, inasmuch as the tribunal's conclusion that an interview between a female candidate and male interviewer had been sexually intimidating was based on the fact that there was no other woman present and the interview took place in a confined space, the tribunal had erred in law. In the EAT's view, it was neither required by law nor desirable in practice that employers should arrange for male managers to be chaperoned when dealing with female staff. That particular case arose in the context of an appraisal interview but we are of the view that the EAT's reasoning would apply equally to an employer's recruitment arrangements.

Selection criteria and tests 24.70

The criteria used to select candidates for interview or appointment, and the tests used to measure candidates against those criteria, are particularly susceptible to inadvertent discrimination. Clear, relevant and objective selection criteria may enable employers to avoid claims of discrimination, and will certainly help in defending any claim. Where selectors fail to adopt such terms of reference but rely instead on 'gut feelings' or hunches, their subjectivity and the dangers of unconscious discriminatory assumptions may sway a tribunal towards the view that discrimination has occurred.

Wherever possible, the relevant selection criteria should be agreed *in advance* of any applications being received, as this will insulate the employer from any suggestion that the criteria were devised with a particular applicant in mind. In Bishop v The Cooper Group plc t/a Coopers Thames Ditton ET Case No.60910/92 the tribunal was not impressed by the employer's contentions when seeking to justify the selection criteria that had been applied. The tribunal called them a 'post-hoc rationalisation' of why the two male candidates were successful in their applications for apprenticeships as car technicians while a highly qualified female was rejected.

An example of poor selection criteria leading to a finding of discrimination:

- **Lyons v The Leeds Teaching Hospitals NHS Trust** ET Case No.1803471/07: L – aged 40 – sought a full-time position as a customer services team leader. Following an interview, he was rejected for, among other things, being 'over-experienced'. When he requested feedback on his application, L was told that, although he had strong managerial experience, he did not have recent experience of working at a 'very junior level'. The successful candidate was 21 years old and did not fulfil the essential criteria for the post. The

779

employment tribunal upheld L's claim, finding that the interview panel had applied a number of subjective behavioural criteria which were potentially age discriminatory. The panel's assessment fell broadly within the heading of 'team-fit', and took account of criteria such as 'adaptability', 'flexibility', 'keenness' and 'informal style'. The claimant, who had scored poorly on 'team fit', had been 'subjected to discrimination on grounds of age because of subjective generalisations that older candidates are less likely to possess those characteristics than younger ones'. In respect of 'over-experience' as a reason for not recruiting L, the tribunal had no hesitation in determining 'that an older candidate for employment is more likely to be over-experienced than one younger'.

As this case shows, the use of 'experience' as a selection criterion can be problematic. While on the one hand employers often rely on past experience as an indicator that a candidate will be up to the job; on the other hand, experience and age often go together, thereby opening up the potential for age discrimination to creep in. To avoid this, employers will need to demonstrate that their experience requirements have nothing to do with age. An example:

- **Rains v Commission for Racial Equality** ET Case No.2306496/06: R, aged 50, applied for an HR role that primarily involved employee relations case work. Impressed by R's CV, the recruitment consultant recommended him to the employer. However, the employer decided not to shortlist R as it believed he did not demonstrate the relevant experience it was looking for – R's recent experience had been at policy and strategic level. In feedback communicated to the consultant, R was considered 'over-qualified' for the role. The tribunal rejected R's claim that failure to shortlist him constituted both direct and indirect age discrimination. With regard to the latter, R argued that two shortlisting criteria – 'the ability to hit the ground running' and 'recent operational employer relations experience' – put people in his age bracket of 50 plus at a substantial disadvantage compared to younger people. The tribunal disagreed, holding that there was no evidence that persons in R's age group could not satisfy the selection criteria. In its view, recent hands-on case-work experience was not necessarily more prevalent in any particular age group, and it did not accept R's argument that individuals employed in HR necessarily worked their way through case-working and onto higher level work involving strategy- and policy-making.

24.71 **Selection and aptitude tests.** The use of selection tests to measure the attitudes, abilities and interests of job applicants has grown steadily in the last few years. The types of test used range from aptitude tests, covering matters such as verbal aptitude and numeracy, to personality tests. If tests are carefully selected, professionally designed and properly managed, they can minimise bias in the selection process and be a valuable tool for employers when making recruitment decisions. Conversely, poor selection and interpretation of tests can have an adverse effect on the opportunities for particular groups in the workforce.

Much of what was above under 'Application forms' also applies to literacy tests, general knowledge questions and written essays or studies. In particular, written tests that require a good knowledge of the English language should only be used where relevant to the job at hand:

- **Sunner and ors v Air Canada and anor** ET Case Nos.2303121/97 and others: AC decided to contract out its catering services in which the claimants were employed. Many of the employees did not wish to transfer to a new employer, so AC identified a number of vacancies within the organisation and invited the employees to apply for these posts. The posts included that of commissary attendant, aircraft cleaner, baggage attendant and customer sales person. The claimants were required to do a written test. The tribunal held that AC had indirectly discriminated against three of the applicants in requiring them to take the written test. English was not their first language and they had difficulty in understanding the questions. Having regard to the nature of the available jobs, AC had not shown that the requirement for the test was justifiable.

Physical tests. In certain jobs, physical fitness is an important requirement and **24.72** applying a fitness test to applicants may be considered a less discriminatory route to ensuring applicants have the necessary physical attributes than applying an age limit. However, where selection tests are designed to measure fitness, employers must ensure that they are conducted on a gender-neutral basis. In Allcock v Chief Constable, Hampshire Constabulary ET Case No.3101524/97 a male police constable applied for a vacancy in his force's dog-handling section. As part of the pre-interview selection process, all male candidates were required to complete a two-mile multi-terrain course within 16 minutes, while female candidates had to do the same within 17 minutes. The more generous timing for women was accounted for by the fact that, according to the employer, men have greater aerobic and anaerobic potential. The complainant completed the course in 16 minutes and 16 seconds and accordingly failed. Had he been a woman, his timing would have been sufficient to make him eligible to proceed to the next stage of the recruitment procedure. A tribunal upheld his claim of discrimination. Its reasoning was that if a female police officer who completed the course within 17 minutes is considered to be fit to carry out the duties of a dog handler, a man who completes the course in the same time must surely also qualify.

If a job applicant is unable to complete a physical fitness test due to his or her disability, the provisions on discrimination arising from disability (S.15) and reasonable adjustments (S.20) may come into play. Since the former provision does not require a comparator, employers cannot rely on the fact that the same test applies to all applicants and should instead be prepared to show that use of the test is justified. Where the work requires a high level of fitness, the test is likely to pursue a legitimate aim – the health and safety of employees and the public – so the focus will be on whether the method of testing adopted by the employer was proportionate. This is likely to dovetail with the duty under S.20, since an employer must consider whether there are any adjustments it could make to the tests or the pass mark to alleviate substantial disadvantage experienced by a disabled applicant.

24.73 Medical examinations

Offers of employment may be subject to the applicant undergoing a satisfactory medical examination or assessment, often taking the form of answering questions on a health questionnaire, but sometimes involving a more detailed examination by an occupational health specialist. However, as explained under 'Pre-employment health questions' above, an employer must not ask about an applicant's health until such time as the employer has either decided to offer the applicant employment or entered the applicant into a pool from which to select an employee once work becomes available – S.60(1). This rule is subject to five exceptions set out in S.60(6). These include questions asked for the purpose of establishing whether the employer needs to make a reasonable adjustment to the recruitment process or whether the applicant will be able to carry out an intrinsic function of the job (with reasonable adjustments if necessary).

An employer's medical examinations and assessments would constitute 'arrangements' within the meaning of S.39 EqA and, as a result, employers should consider the purpose of the medical examination and ensure that all employees/applicants are treated in the same way. For example, asking only older applicants to undergo an examination would amount to direct age discrimination. In such circumstances an employer would need to show objective justification, which is unlikely when there is the less discriminatory alternative of examining all candidates. If an employer insists on medical checks only for disabled candidates, an inference of discrimination is likely to arise. Even if all applicants are examined, an employer may still be discriminating if, for example, the information in a medical report is used to exclude a disabled person from consideration without taking into account, first, the ability of that individual to do the job and, secondly, whether there is any reasonable adjustment that could be made.

24.74 Consequences of failing to disclose medical history. The new rules on pre-employment health questions in S.60 (outlined under 'Pre-employment health questions' above) present a dilemma for employers who discover that a job-applicant has lied about his or her medical history at some stage in the recruitment process. Ordinarily, an employer discovering deceit on the part of a job applicant would be well within its rights to pursue the application no further. However, where the non-disclosure of medical history is related to a disability, the employer taking such a course of action could be exposed to the full panoply of disability discrimination provisions. If, for example, the questions posed to the applicant fell outside the categories of 'permitted' questions about health outlined in S.60(6), the employer would need to provide a non-discriminatory explanation for the decision not to continue with the application. Even if the question was legitimate, the treatment of the disabled applicant could be regarded as 'unfavourable' and arising in consequence of the applicant's disability, with the result that the employer would need to show objective justification. Moreover, it may need to consider whether a reasonable adjustment could be made to the policy that an applicant who does not fully disclose his or her medical history will not be appointed. That said, where a job demands a high degree of honesty and integrity, such an adjustment may not be seen as reasonable and therefore would not need to be made. An example:

- **Arnold v Royal Bank of Scotland plc** ET Case No. 2410581/07: A applied for a job with RBS in September 2007. During 2005, in his previous employment, he had suffered from mental illness and had taken medical retirement, but in his application for the job with RBS he edited out this illness and said he had left his previous job because it was a short-term assignment that had ended. He also stated that he was in receipt of jobseekers' allowance, whereas he was in fact receiving incapacity benefit. He was offered the job by RBS, but when it discovered he had not been honest in his application the offer was withdrawn. A claimed that he was reluctant to disclose the full details of his illness on the form for fear of prejudicing his application, but would have done so face to face. Dismissing his claim of disability discrimination, an employment tribunal held that A's lies, or lack of candour, were related to his disability but no distinction could be drawn between the fact of a lie and its subject matter. RBS was offering a job in which the risk of fraud was high and the strongest precautions had to be taken by ensuring the integrity of employees. Requiring RBS to lower its standards of honesty and integrity could not be a reasonable adjustment.

If a disabled person deliberately conceals a disability prior to being given a job, **24.75** there is an argument to suggest that he or she could be dismissed for deceit if the employer later finds out about it. However, in the vast majority of cases such an argument seems doomed for a number of reasons. First, the EHRC Employment Code recognises that people with disabilities may be reluctant to disclose them, and there is nothing in the EqA which could compel an employee or job applicant to disclose his or her disability to an employer – para 17.52. Secondly, as we have seen above, it could amount to discrimination arising from disability. Thirdly, in Fitzpatrick v British Railways Board 1992 ICR 221, CA, the Court of Appeal held that the dismissal of an employee allegedly for failure to disclose relevant information on an application form was automatically unfair under S.152(1)(b) of the Trade Union and Labour Relations (Consolidation) Act 1992 (dismissal on grounds related to union activities), since the real reason for the dismissal was the employee's past union activities (which she had not mentioned on the form). By analogy, in the case of disability an applicant could argue that the real reason for dismissal was the disability – not the failure to disclose it.

The action an employer takes on discovering an employee's disability may be influenced by the risk caused to the disabled person and his or her colleagues by the failure to disclose. Under S.7 of the Health and Safety at Work etc Act 1974 employees are under a duty to have regard for their own safety and that of others. An employee who conceals a disability might be in breach of this provision and this could be a factor in any case brought against the employer for unfair dismissal and/or discrimination.

24.76 Stepping away from employment legislation for a moment, it is worth noting the High Court's decision in Cheltenham Borough Council v Laird 2009 IRLR 621, QBD. In that case the employer failed in its claim for damages against a former employee whom it alleged had misrepresented her medical history in a pre-employment questionnaire. Although the employment had been conditional on the employee completing the health questionnaire and being passed fit for employment, the Court found that, due to the poor drafting and subjective nature of many of the questions, she had not made any misrepresentation in failing to disclose her history of depressive illness when filling in the questionnaire.

24.77 ## Terms on which employment is offered

By virtue of S.39(1)(b) EqA, 'an employer (A) must not discriminate against a person (B)... as to the terms on which A offers B employment'. The EHRC Employment Code provides a single example of discrimination in the terms on which employment is offered: 'An employer offers a job but extends their usual probation period from three months to six months because the preferred candidate is a woman returning from maternity leave or a person with a disability. This would be discrimination in the terms on which the person is offered employment' – para 16.69. However, avoiding discrimination in the terms on which employment is offered is more complicated than merely offering the same terms to all successful applicants, irrespective of any protected characteristic the potential employee may have: while such an approach is a good starting point, it overlooks the subtleties of indirect discrimination, not to mention the complications presented by the duty to make reasonable adjustments.

While S.39(1)(b) covers all the terms offered to *new employees*, case law under the predecessor provision in the Sex Discrimination Act 1975 (SDA) strongly suggests that it does not extend to the terms on which an *existing employee* is offered promotion. In Clymo v Wandsworth London Borough Council 1989 ICR 250, EAT, the Appeal Tribunal held that S.6(1) SDA was concerned with situations arising *before* a contract of employment is entered into. In that case, the claimant librarian asked to be able to work part time following her return from maternity leave, and to be able to share her job with her husband (also a librarian). Her requests were refused and C claimed that the refusal was an act of indirect discrimination under S.6(1)(b) (in that it imposed a term of her employment that she must work full time) and a detriment under S.6(2)(b). Her claims were dismissed by the tribunal, a decision upheld by the EAT.

For present purposes, it is sufficient to note that the EAT held that since the **24.78** claimant was at all material times employed by the local authority, S.6(1) did not apply. It stated: 'From a plain reading of these subsections it seems to us that S.6(1) is dealing with situations arising before a contract of employment is entered into, where an employer has a job or an opportunity to offer... By way of contrast S.6(2) applies to situations where a woman is already in employment with a respondent employer.'

It is reasonably clear, therefore, that a claim in respect of an offer of promotion on discriminatory terms would have to be brought under S.39(2)(a) EqA – which prohibits discrimination as to an employee's terms of employment, rather than S.39(1)(b) EqA. S.39(2) EqA is discussed in Chapter 25, 'Discrimination during employment'.

Sex and pregnancy and maternity limitation. The scope of S.39(1)(b) is **24.79** limited by S.39(6) in respect of the protected characteristics of sex and pregnancy and maternity. S.39(6) provides that S.39(1)(b) 'does not apply to a term that relates to pay – (a) unless were B to accept the offer, an equality clause or rule would have effect in relation to the term, or (b) if paragraph (a) does not apply, except in so far as making an offer on terms including that term amounts to a contravention of subsection (1)(b) by virtue of section 13... or 18'. So, what is the practical effect of this limitation? There are three circumstances in which a claim of sex or pregnancy and maternity discrimination can be brought under S.39(1)(b):

- the first is where the term in question does not relate to pay. Here the exception in S.39(6) is not engaged so S.39(1)(b) applies as normal

- the second is where the term in question relates to pay and an equality clause or rule would apply in relation to that term if the applicant were to accept the job offer. An equality clause would apply where an employer pays a person less than it pays a comparator of the opposite sex for equal work, and there is no material factor explaining the differential in pay. In such circumstances, the clause operates to modify the claimant's contract to include the more favourable term enjoyed by the comparator. An equality rule operates in the same way, but applies to the terms of an occupational pension scheme rather than a contract of employment. In general, the jurisdictions of equal pay and sex discrimination are mutually exclusive (see IDS Employment Law Handbook, 'Equal Pay' (2011), Chapter 1,

'Law in Context' under 'EqPA v SDA: which Act applies?' for a thorough consideration of the distinction). However, an equal pay claim, operating as it does through the medium of the contractual equality clause, can only be brought once employment has commenced: S.39(6)(a) therefore allows a discrimination claim to be pursued under S.39(1)(b) by the applicant who does not want to take up the offer of employment on unequal terms

- the third and final circumstance is where the term in question relates to pay but an equality clause or rule would *not* apply in relation to that term if the applicant were to accept the job offer, and the term amounts to direct sex discrimination under S.13 or direct pregnancy or maternity discrimination under S.18. Para 161 of the Explanatory Notes to the EqA provide the following example: 'An employer offers a woman a job on lower pay than the set rate because she is pregnant when she applies. She cannot bring an equality clause case as there is no comparator. However, she will be able to claim direct discrimination.'

24.80 Rate of pay determined by experience

Although it is a widespread practice for the rate of starting pay, at least in part, to be determined by the job applicant's previous experience, such a pay practice could give rise to indirect age discrimination, since younger applicants may be disadvantaged due to having had less time in which to accumulate the necessary experience. Age is not the only ground on which indirect discrimination could occur: women may also have had less chance to gain experience due to childcare commitments, and disabled applicants may have been prevented from gaining experience due to their disabilities. In all these circumstances, the employer may need to show justification for the pay practice. Many of the considerations outlined in the section on 'Arrangements for deciding to whom to offer employment' under 'Job and person specifications – experience' above will apply here.

24.81 Days, hours and location of work

The terms on which an employer offers a successful job applicant employment will often stipulate the days on which, the hours during which and the place at which the work should be done. Direct discrimination could occur here if the employer offers a less favourable working pattern to the applicant because of his or her protected characteristic: for example, in Dunlop v Royal Scottish Academy ET Case No.S/3696/76 the employer was found to have discriminated against the claimant, a female security guard, by refusing to allow her to work night shifts. However, indirect discrimination is more likely to occur in these circumstances, since an apparently neutral requirement that would apply to all employees can place certain groups – such as women with childcare commitments, adherents of particular religions and disabled people – at a disadvantage.

Women with childcare commitments. It is generally recognised that **24.82** substantially more women than men in the United Kingdom have primary childcare commitments. For this reason, a working pattern that clashes with these commitments is likely to place women at a disadvantage and, if a female job applicant is so disadvantaged, the employer may need to objectively justify the working pattern. For a lengthy consideration of the circumstances in which tribunals have found such requirements to be, or not to be, justified, see Chapter 25, 'Discrimination in employment' under 'Terms of employment – working hours'.

Religious worship. A number of major religions specify a holy day on which **24.83** adherents worship, and in some cases it is a facet of that religion that followers will not work on the holy day. If an employer offers employment on the condition that the applicant works on a day which is for him or her a holy day, objective justification may be necessary. An example:

- **James v MSC Cruises Ltd** ET Case No.2203173/05: J was a practising member of the Seventh-day Adventist Church. In September 2005 she applied for a position with an employer which sold and marketed cruise holidays. Although she was successful, when she received the offer letter J explained that she could not work on Saturday as this was the Sabbath. Practising Seventh-day Adventists abstain during their Sabbath from secular work in order to worship, teach, learn and celebrate. The employer responded that if J could not work on Saturdays then she would be unable to take up the offer of employment. J subsequently brought an indirect religious discrimination claim. The tribunal found the relevant disadvantage caused by the requirement of Saturday working but decided that it was justified. It accepted the employer's evidence that trading on Saturdays was an essential feature of the tourism industry, since this was when couples were more likely to be available jointly to explore holiday opportunities and make immediate decisions. It also had regard to the fact that Saturday working was not popular among existing staff; that a rota had been put in place to share the burden equally; and that the employer reasonably believed that any exceptions would create tension among colleagues.

Disabled applicants. A job offer made on a 'full time only' basis could **24.84** potentially discriminate against a disabled job applicant. While such a requirement would not amount to direct disability discrimination, it could amount to indirect discrimination (on the basis that fewer disabled people are able to comply with the requirement) or discrimination arising from disability (if an applicant's disability leaves him or her unable to work a full-time schedule). In either case, the employer could seek to rely on the defence of objective justification: to do so it would have to show that the requirement for full-time working pursued a legitimate aim, and that it was a proportionate means of achieving that aim. In respect of proportionality, the employer may

787

need to show that it considered alternatives – the existence of a less discriminatory alternative that would achieve the same aim would act as a bar to proportionality. However, it is not just in respect of objective justification that an employer should consider the alternatives to requiring a disabled applicant to work full time: consideration of the alternatives is also pivotal to establishing that the duty to make reasonable adjustments has been complied with – see 'Adjustments to terms of employment' below.

24.85 **Adjustments to terms of employment**
If the terms on which an employer makes an offer of employment place a disabled person at a substantial disadvantage, it may need to consider whether those terms could be subject to a reasonable adjustment. What is reasonable will depend on the individual circumstances of the case, but a common example of an adjustment to terms and conditions is a modification or reduction of working hours – a disabled person may, for example, need to avoid the rush hour, or may need to work part time due to tiredness caused by his or her disability.

The requirement to make reasonable adjustments only applies to provisions, criteria and practices of the employer in relation to what might be called 'job-related' matters and not in relation to personal care facilities for the employee – Kenny v Hampshire Constabulary 1999 ICR 27, EAT. In that case, the EAT held that the employer was not under a duty to provide a carer to assist K, who had cerebral palsy, in using the lavatory. The EAT thought that an employer should be required to consider making physical adjustments to accommodate the presence of a personal carer provided by the disabled person but it would be going too far to suggest that it actually had to provide the carer.

If a disabled job applicant has difficulty reading or understanding the written terms of employment that he or she is offered, the employer may have to make a reasonable adjustment by providing them in an accessible format or providing a member of staff to explain the terms.

24.86 ## Discrimination by not offering employment

By virtue of S.39(1)(c) EqA, 'an employer (A) must not discriminate against a person (B)... by not offering B employment'. This subsection and its predecessors have probably accounted for the largest number of complaints of discrimination in recruitment – and is the most difficult to prove in practice because it depends on a complainant showing that, but for the discrimination, he or she would have been offered the job. All of the factors dealt with above in respect of arrangements for determining whom to offer employment and the terms on which employment is offered can come into play here. Each aspect of the recruitment process will be scrutinised by the tribunal to see if the outcome of the recruitment decision was tainted by discrimination.

The EHRC Employment Code recommends giving feedback to unsuccessful shortlisted candidates if this is requested – para 16.72. As the Code rightly points out, demonstrating objective reasons for why the candidate was not appointed can minimise the risk of discrimination claims. Unsuccessful candidates can also use the statutory discrimination questionnaire procedure provided for in S.138 EqA to ascertain the reason they were not appointed – see Chapter 33, 'Proving discrimination' under 'Requesting information and disclosure of evidence – statutory questionnaires'. Where an employer fails to provide reasons for rejecting a candidate, the tribunal may conclude that discrimination lay behind the decision. An example:

- **Bouzir v Country Style Foods Ltd** ET Case No.1809300/09: B, a practising Muslim, applied for a job with CSF Ltd and attended an interview wearing a headscarf. During the interview she was asked if she would take it off while at work because of the hygiene requirement to wear a hairnet. She explained that she was a Muslim but that she would be willing to remove the scarf while at work and said she had done so previously when working in food manufacturing environments. When she was not appointed, B served a statutory questionnaire on CSF Ltd but did not receive a reply. In her subsequent religious discrimination claim, an employment tribunal found that CSF Ltd was unable to provide any convincing explanation as to why B was not offered a post – she had more relevant experience than some of the successful candidates. Taken with CSF Ltd's failure to reply to the questionnaire, the tribunal concluded that CSF Ltd was concealing or not admitting the true reason for not appointing her, and that reason was her Muslim religion, which was clearly evidenced by her attendance at the interview wearing a headscarf.

24.87 Discrimination can also arise in the feedback an employer provides to unsuccessful candidates. In Khan v Kent Country Nurseries Ltd ET Case No.11996/82 a letter which said: 'Regrettably I must decline your application since a young mum with three kiddies would be failing in her domestic duties to take up the opportunity that I offer' was held to be clear and unequivocal sex discrimination. Not all examples will be as obvious as this – but it illustrates that the motives behind a letter are irrelevant if its content amounts to direct discrimination. In Dwyer v Ciro Pearls Ltd ET Case No.12243/82 a branch manager was made responsible for hiring a new sales assistant. She received little assistance from her head office in this task but nevertheless advertised, interviewed and selected one of two applicants. The unsuccessful male applicant received a letter which said, 'it was a terrible job for me to decide between you and a young woman but due to company policy I had to favour a woman'. There was no such policy and the tribunal held that the complainant had been discriminated against.

24.88 There are three circumstances in which an employer can expressly refuse to offer a candidate employment because of a protected characteristic. These are:

- where possessing a particular protected characteristic is an 'occupational requirement' within the meaning of paras 1–3 of Schedule 9 to the EqA – see Chapter 30, 'General exceptions', under 'Occupational requirements'

- where there is an objectively justified age limit for the post in question (see the section on 'Arrangements for deciding to whom to offer employment' under 'Job and person specifications – age limits' above)

- where the candidate's disability renders him or her unsuitable for the post, and there are no reasonable adjustments that can be made to the job or to the employer's premises.

We discuss this last ground below, before turning to the possible discriminatory consequences of some common grounds for refusing to offer, or withdrawing an offer of, employment.

24.89 Rejection related to disability

One practical effect of the new rules on pre-employment health enquiries contained in S.60 EqA (see 'Pre-employment health questions' above) is that employers are likely to make only minimal enquiries into a claimant's disability at the early stages of the recruitment process (i.e. only enough to establish if any adjustments need to be made for interview, etc). This means that any more detailed examination of how a disability could impact on the applicant's ability to perform the job will generally be left until *after* he or she has been identified as the preferred candidate. As a result, there will inevitably be some disabled applicants who have an offer of employment withdrawn after the employer fully comprehends the nature and effect of the candidate's disability and concludes that there are no adjustments that could be made that would enable the candidate to assume the post. An example:

- **Gates v East Of England Ambulance Service NHS Trust** ET Case No.3202611/09: G was diagnosed with multiple sclerosis (MS) in September 2008. In January 2009 she applied for a post with R as an emergency dispatcher. She stated on the application form that she had no disabilities and she was offered a post conditional on satisfactory references and health clearance. She stated on the health questionnaire that she had MS. The employer's occupational health service advised that G should be employed only if she could be given day work, since irregular hours could worsen her symptoms. However, her GP and consultant believed that her condition was mild and that she would be able to undertake the post, which involved shift work. The employer had no posts that required only day-time working and the offer was withdrawn. Rejecting G's claims of disability discrimination, an employment tribunal found that a hypothetical comparator who could not do shift work would not have been appointed, and the employer had proved that the offer was withdrawn not because of G's disability but because of the effect that shift work would have had on her health. Appointing her to the post would have put her at an unjustified risk. There were no reasonable adjustments that could be made given the financial constraints under which the employer had to operate.

However, employers should be wary of making assumptions about either the **24.90** disability or the adjustments that might be possible, as such assumptions can give rise to a failure to make reasonable adjustments. Three examples:

- **Chilcott v Newcross Healthcare Solutions** ET Case No.1700206/10: C, who had hearing difficulties, applied for a post as a healthcare assistant. At his initial interview NH Ltd believed he was a good candidate, but NH Ltd's HR department expressed concern that employees must be able to hear nurse call bells, fire alarms and clients' calls for assistance. NH Ltd sought references, and asked referees if any adaptations had had to be made to his working environment. One referee said that C had been provided with a vibrating pager. NH Ltd invited C to an induction day, during which a 3-hour DVD on health and safety and working practices was shown. C was not able to hear it and asked if subtitles could be provided. NH Ltd decided that C's application should be declined since he could not be employed without a pager and it was impracticable to install such devices in its 100 client locations. C claimed that NH Ltd failed to make reasonable adjustments and directly discriminated against him. Upholding that claim, an employment tribunal determined that NH Ltd had failed to take sufficient steps to ascertain the specific impact of C's disability on his ability to undertake the work and failed to investigate sufficiently before deciding that adjustments would not be feasible. C was awarded £6,000 for injury to feelings

- **Waite v Government Communications Bureau** ET Case No.2306479/00: W suffered from repetitive strain injury (RSI). When she applied for a post with GCB she told them that it did not affect her ability to work provided she could use a special keyboard and voice recognition software (VRS). The employer had been advised that people with RSI should not use a keyboard for more than three hours a day and that its network could not accommodate VRS. W was therefore informed that she could not be appointed. W then said that VRS was not necessary. She had the software in her current post in a different government department but did not use it to any great extent. She also made it clear that with the special keyboard and the properly set-up workstation in her current post there had been no recurrence of the RSI. GCB spoke to its medical adviser but he advised against her employment without VRS. The employer confirmed the decision not to employ her. W's discrimination claim was successful. GCB had treated her less favourably by not offering her employment because it thought that it could not accommodate her disorder, even though she was performing similar work at another government department without any difficulty. It had also failed to make reasonable adjustments to its recruitment process, which would have enabled it to make a fair and informed decision regarding her suitability to work. When W explained that she did not need VRS, the employer should have made further enquiries of W, her current employer and GCB's occupational health adviser to find out how important VRS was and whether W could do the job without that adjustment. GCB was not justified in failing to make those further enquiries

- **Weston v Webbs Country Foods Ltd** ET Case No.1402186/98: W suffered from cerebral palsy. He attended a job interview with WCF Ltd and was regarded as suitable by the interviewer. Between the date of the interview and his planned start date, the employer's personnel manager decided that, because W appeared to have difficulty walking, it would be too dangerous for him to be employed. The personnel manager had no proper understanding of W's disability and had not seen him walking. She made her decision on the basis of a discussion with a colleague who knew W. When W turned up for work, he was told he could not have the job because he would be a liability – he would not be able to work fast enough and would have difficulty standing for long periods. An employment tribunal held that W had been treated less favourably. The employer had made its decision because of an assumption based on incomplete knowledge.

24.91 To be unlawful, the refusal to employ a disabled job applicant must either be because of, or arising in consequence of, the applicant's disability. In Reid v Premier Monitoring Services Ltd ET Case No.1502245/00 R had impaired mobility following the removal of a kneecap. PMS Ltd provided him with a special chair and made a report to the Board recommending that his hours be altered and his pay subsidised through Remploy. However, before the report could be approved, R resigned to go to another job. He had in fact resigned earlier that year but his manager had persuaded him to stay on. The new job did not work out and R applied to PMS Ltd to have his old job back, but it declined. R's disability discrimination claim failed. His former employer had shown that it was more than willing to do whatever was reasonably practicable to accommodate R's condition. It did not refuse to employ him because he was disabled: the refusal was because it had no confidence that he wanted to make a long-term commitment to the job.

24.92 **Health and safety grounds.** In certain circumstances, an employer may have to withdraw a job offer or decline to offer employment to a candidate on health and safety grounds. If the health and safety concern is centred on a candidate's disability, an employer will need to show that it has carefully assessed the risk posed by (or to) the disabled applicant, and that the refusal, arising as it does in consequence of the disability, is objectively justified. Ensuring the health and safety of others is certain to be considered a legitimate aim, so such cases will hinge on whether the employment tribunal considers the refusal to employ the disabled employee to be proportionate. If there is a reasonable adjustment that could be made to the role to remove the health and safety risk, this would be a less discriminatory means of achieving the legitimate aim, with the result that the refusal to offer employment would not be a proportionate means of achieving the same aim. Two contrasting examples:

- **Wynn v Multipulse Electronics Ltd** ET Case No.2301416/07: W, who was profoundly deaf, applied for a job with the employer and was invited to an interview. However, his interview was cancelled because the employer had not arranged a British Sign Language (BSL) interpreter. W was eventually told that the employer could not, on health and safety grounds, employ a person who required a BSL interpreter to communicate. In upholding W's discrimination claim, the employment tribunal observed that the employer's actions were 'predicated on ignorant, erroneous, stereotypical assumptions of the claimant's abilities'. In reality, W was likely to have required a colleague to work alongside him on occasions, the services of a BSL interpreter very infrequently, and a pager for communication in case of emergency

- **Tyrell v British Airways plc** ET Case No.2300931/99: T applied for a job as a baggage handler at Heathrow Airport and indicated on his application form that he had epilepsy and was deaf in one ear. He was successful at the interview and was invited to undergo a medical examination by the employer's occupational physician. In her medical report, the physician noted that the job of baggage handler involved driving 'airside', i.e. within the area of aircraft operations. Medical standards that had been set by the DVLA and adopted by airport authorities specifically stated that a person should not drive airside unless he or she had remained free of epileptic attacks for at least ten years without taking anticonvulsant medication. T did not meet this criterion. The report also stated that T did not meet the medical requirements for work at unguarded heights, in fuel tanks or in confined spaces, or on moving machinery. The employer's recruitment adviser considered those elements of the job that T would be incapable of carrying out and concluded that, if she allocated those elements to someone else, it would mean reallocating virtually the whole job as baggage handler. In her view, there was no reasonable adjustment that would enable T to perform the job and he was informed that he had not been successful in his application. Rejecting T's claim of disability discrimination, the employment tribunal noted that safety was of critical importance in airside operations at airports, that baggage handling was a standard routine in the employer's operations, and that the employer operated flexible rotas that made it impracticable for T to be allocated certain tasks but not others. It concluded that the employer had not failed to comply with the duty to

793

make reasonable adjustments because none of the steps that it could have taken would have alleviated the problem. In the tribunal's view, the refusal to appoint T as a baggage handler was fully justified.

24.93 Rejection due to pregnancy

A refusal to employ a job applicant on the ground that she is pregnant will amount to unfavourable treatment because of the pregnancy contrary to S.18(2)(a) EqA. There are no exceptions to this rule: employers cannot rely on health and safety grounds to refuse to employ a pregnant woman, even if they consider that the job poses a risk to her health or that of her baby, as this would still amount to unfavourable treatment because of the pregnancy. Instead, where a pregnant women is identified as the most suitable candidate, she should be appointed as normal, and a risk assessment should be carried out in line with Regs 3 and 16 of the Management of Health and Safety at Work Regulations 1999 SI 1999/3242. If the assessment reveals a risk to the mother or baby, the employer is obliged to take any reasonable steps to mitigate that risk, including altering working hours or conditions. If the risk would persist in spite of such alterations, the employer should provide suitable alternative work or, where that does not exist, suspend the employee on maternity grounds (with pay). The health and safety provisions governing pregnant workers are examined in detail in IDS Employment Law Handbook, 'Maternity and Parental Rights' (2009), Chapter 2.

24.94 References

Many employers make offers of employment subject to the receipt of satisfactory references. Where such a policy is applied even-handedly, it is unlikely to amount to direct or unjustified indirect discrimination. However, particular care should be taken in respect of references for disabled job applicants, especially where the content of a negative reference relates to that candidate's disability. An example:

- **Morgan v Northamptonshire Teaching Primary Care Trust** ET Case No.1201412/09: M, who had been diagnosed with Asperger's Syndrome while working for the Trust as an agency worker, applied for a permanent position. He did well at interview and was offered employment subject to references and clearance from occupational health and the Criminal Records Bureau. A reference from his former employer stated that they would not take M back, primarily because of his sickness and lateness. The reference acknowledged that the sickness and lateness were due to his recently diagnosed condition that was now being treated. The second reference was also poor, remarking on the deterioration in M's emotional health and performance. The Trust decided to withdraw the job offer prior to receiving the outcome of the occupational health report. An employment tribunal found that, by sticking to its policy of requiring two satisfactory references, the Trust had failed to make the reasonable adjustment of obtaining a more detailed occupational health assessment and discussing with M ways in which reasonable adjustments in the workplace could help him.

Care should also be taken whenever a reference mentions a previous **24.95** discrimination claim brought by the job applicant. Not only is such a reference likely to amount to victimisation on the part of the referee, it can also give rise to discrimination on the part of the employer if it acts on the contents of the reference and rejects the applicant. An example:

- **Lucas v Bettercare Keys Ltd and anor** ET Case No.3501266/10: L suffered from a disability affecting her sleep pattern, with the result that she was not always fully awake during the day. She resigned from her previous employment because she said her employer had discriminated against her and she lodged a tribunal claim. She applied to BK Ltd for a post as a mobile manager and was offered the job. BK Ltd required references before she could begin work, and she provided two glowing examples, but her previous employer gave a very damning reference. It stated that her attendance was not good, she did not like authority, and she had taken the employer to a tribunal. L was informed that the job offer was withdrawn. An employment tribunal found that the reference from L's former employer, which was inextricably bound up with her disability, was the primary reason for the withdrawal of the offer and upheld her claim of disability discrimination.

25 Discrimination during employment

In Chapter 24, 'Recruitment', we focus on discrimination in the recruitment **25.1** process. In this chapter we consider discrimination arising during the currency of the employment relationship. Such discrimination can take many forms. It can occur where the employer treats an employee less favourably because he or she has a protected characteristic; where the impact of an apparently neutral workplace practice or policy disadvantages a group sharing a protected characteristic and that practice or policy cannot be objectively justified; or where an employer fails in its duty to make a reasonable adjustment for a disabled employee.

Section 39(2) of the Equality Act 2010 (EqA) provides that an employer (A) must not discriminate against an employee of A's (B):

- as to B's terms of employment – S.39(2)(a)

- in the way A affords B access, or by not affording B access, to opportunities for promotion, transfer or training or for receiving any other benefit, facility or service – S.39(2)(b)

- by dismissing B – S.39(2)(c)

- by subjecting B to any other detriment – S.39(2)(d).

Victimisation against employees is dealt with separately in S.39(4) EqA, which **25.2** provides that an employer (A) must not victimise an employee of A's (B):

- as to B's terms of employment – S.39(4)(a)

- in the way A affords B access, or by not affording B access, to opportunities for promotion, transfer or training or for any other benefit, facility or service – S.39(4)(b)

- by dismissing B – S.39(4)(c)

- by subjecting B to any other detriment – S.39(4)(d).

797

25.3 Thus, victimisation will be unlawful in the same circumstances as direct and indirect discrimination under S.39(2).

In this chapter we cover three of the four circumstances set out in S.39(2) and (4) – discriminatory dismissals under S.39(2)(c) and (4)(c) are addressed in Chapter 26, 'Dismissal'. In the final section of this chapter, we consider the effect of S.40(1)(a) EqA, which provides that an employer (A) must not, in relation to employment by A, harass a person (B) who is an employee of A's.

25.4 Terms of employment

Section 39(2)(a) and (b) EqA stipulates that 'an employer (A) must not discriminate against an employee of A's (B) as to B's terms of employment', or 'in the way A affords B access, or by not affording B access, to opportunities for promotion, transfer or training or for any other benefit, facility or service'. S.39(4)(a) and (b) similarly stipulates that an employer must not victimise an employee in respect of the same matters. Broadly speaking, 'terms of employment' and 'opportunities for receiving any other benefit' cover all contractual terms and conditions of employment, whether express or implied. This includes a wide range of matters such as pay, hours of work, holiday entitlement, holiday pay, job mobility and fringe benefits. Benefits that are not considered terms of the contract will fall into the category of 'any other benefit'. (Note that the terms on which a prospective employee is *offered* employment would not fall under S.39(2)(a) or (b) but under S.39(1)(b) – see Chapter 24, 'Recruitment', under 'Terms on which employment is offered'.)

The terms of employment under which an employee works will also be treated as provisions, criteria and practices for the purposes of the employer's duty to make reasonable adjustments under S.20 EqA. Thus, where those terms place a disabled employee at a substantial disadvantage, the employer will be under a duty to take such steps as are reasonable to remove that disadvantage.

25.5 **Void and unenforceable terms.** In addition to providing the means for an employee to seek compensation for the discriminatory effect of a contractual term, the EqA also includes provisions rendering discriminatory terms unenforceable. A contractual term is unenforceable against a person in so far as it constitutes, promotes or provides for treatment of that or another person that is of a description prohibited by the EqA – S.142. A county court or sheriff court (but not an employment tribunal) may on application by an interested party make an order that a term which is unenforceable as a result of S.142 be removed or modified – S.143.

Collective agreements rarely have contractual force in their own right (though some of the terms of the agreement may be incorporated into the contracts of individual employees). This means that Ss.142 and 143 could not be used to void or modify a discriminatory term within such an agreement. However,

S.145(1) provides that such a term will be void in so far as it constitutes, promotes or provides for treatment of a description prohibited by the EqA. In addition, a 'rule of an undertaking' – i.e. a condition of employment, rather than a contractual term – will be unenforceable against a person in so far as it constitutes, promotes or provides for treatment of the person that is of a description prohibited by the EqA – S.145(2).

Exclusion of equal pay claims   25.6

The scope of S.39(2)(a) in respect of *sex* discrimination is extremely limited, due to the fact that the EqA has retained the demarcation between 'sex discrimination' and 'equal pay' that applied under the Sex Discrimination Act 1975 (SDA) and the Equal Pay Act 1970 (EqA). This division between the two regimes is enforced by Ss.70 and 71 EqA, the broad effect of which is that sex discrimination in contractual terms founds an equal pay, rather than a discrimination, claim. (Equal pay claims are covered by Chapter 3 of Part 5 of the EqA and are discussed in detail in IDS Employment Law Handbook, 'Equal Pay' (2011).)

Section 70(1) and (3) provides that S.39(2) has no effect in relation to a term that is modified or included by virtue of a sex equality clause, or would be so modified were it not for a successful 'material factor' defence under S.69 EqA. (A similar exclusion applies in relation to Ss.49(6) and 50(6), which cover discrimination against office holders.) Furthermore, neither the inclusion of a less favourable term (compared with that of an actual comparator doing equal work) in the employee's terms, or the failure to include in the employee's terms a term equal to that enjoyed by such a comparator, is to be treated as sex discrimination – S.70(2). This replicates what used to be S.8(5) SDA and means that if all the elements for an equal pay claim are present (equal work, actual comparator, etc), then the claimant cannot choose to bring a sex discrimination claim instead – it is the 'equal pay' route or nothing. If the claim is defeated by the employer's 'material factor' defence, there will be no prospect of a sex discrimination claim in the alternative.

Section 6(6) SDA specifically excluded contractual pay claims from the scope   25.7
of the Act, and this provision is replicated by S.71 EqA. This states that S.39(2) does not apply to a term of a person's work that relates to pay but in relation to which a sex equality clause has 'no effect'. Thus, the default position – as previously – is that pay claims are excluded from the sex discrimination provisions, *regardless* of whether the elements of an equal pay claim are present. However, S.71(2) goes on to state that this exclusion applies 'except in so far as treatment of the person amounts to a contravention of [S.39(2)] by virtue of S.13 [direct discrimination] or 14 [dual discrimination – a provision that has not been brought into force]'. This represents a key difference between the position set out in S.71 EqA and the position under the old law as set out in S.6(6) SDA as it specifically allows for a claim of sex discrimination in pay to

799

be brought under the sex discrimination provisions in limited circumstances. The significance of this is that sex discrimination in pay may, for the first time, be established on the basis of a hypothetical comparison.

So, what circumstances will be covered by S.71(2)? The Explanatory Notes to the EqA emphasise that the provision can only apply where the sex equality clause provided for in S.66 EqA does not operate. This is most likely to be the case where the claimant is unable to point to a flesh-and-blood comparator doing equal work, but has some other evidence that direct sex discrimination is influencing her pay. The Notes provide the following example: 'An employer tells a female employee "I would pay you more if you were a man". In the absence of any male comparator the woman cannot bring a claim for breach of an equality clause but she can bring a claim of direct sex discrimination... against the employer.'

25.8 But based on the actual wording of S.71, we take the view that its potential may be far wider than the limited example given in the Explanatory Notes suggests. Provided that direct sex discrimination can be established to explain a pay differential, it is possible to conceive of S.71 being used to found a remedy under S.39(2) in respect of a number of claims for which there was previously no remedy simply because they did not fit within the equal pay framework. Four examples spring to mind:

- where the size of the pay differential between a man and woman (who are not employed on equal work) is out of all proportion to the differences between their jobs

- where an employee is paid the same as a colleague whose job is rated as being of lower value

- where a successor of the opposite sex is paid more for the same role

- where the claimant can identify a comparator being paid more for equal work, but the location at which the comparator works is sufficiently autonomous that the claimant cannot bring an equal pay claim based on a cross-workplace comparison.

25.9 An identical exclusion applies in respect of sex equality rules. A sex equality rule applies to occupational pension schemes and has the effect that if a relevant term of the scheme is less favourable to the employee than it is to a comparator of the opposite sex doing equal work, the offending term is modified so as not to be less favourable – S.67(2)(a). Similarly, any term that confers a discretion capable of being exercised in a way that would be less favourable to the employee than to the comparator is modified so as to prevent the exercise of the discretion in this way – S.67(2)(b).

Sex equality clauses and rules are discussed in greater depth in IDS Employment Law Handbook, 'Equal Pay' (2011), Chapter 2, under 'The sex equality clause' and 'Occupational pension schemes'.

Maternity discrimination exclusion

25.10

In the same way that Ss.70 and 71 make the equal pay provisions of the EqA the proper avenue of redress for complaints of sex discrimination in relation to contractual terms, so S.76 makes the maternity equality clause the proper avenue for complaints of maternity discrimination in relation to contractual terms. S.76(1) and (1A) provides that S.39(2) has no effect in relation to a term of the woman's work that is modified by a maternity equality clause, or that relates to pay but in relation to which a maternity equality clause has no effect. A maternity equality clause is implied into a woman's contract by virtue of S.73(1). Its effect is that any pay rise a woman receives during maternity leave (or would have received if she had not been on maternity leave) is taken into account when calculating maternity pay. In addition, it provides that a woman who takes maternity leave is entitled to a number of contractual payments (including bonuses) that would have been made to her had she not been on leave – S.74. Furthermore, by virtue of S.76(2), the modification of a woman's contractual terms as a result of a maternity equality clause will not count as pregnancy and maternity discrimination.

An identical exclusion applies in respect of maternity equality rules. A maternity equality rule applies to occupational pension schemes and has the effect that time spent on maternity leave is treated as time working for the purposes of the scheme – S.75 EqA.

Maternity equality clauses and rules are discussed in greater depth in IDS Employment Law Handbook, 'Equal Pay' (2011), Chapter 2, under 'Maternity'.

Pay and remuneration

25.11

Among the main terms of any employment contract are those setting out what remuneration an employee will receive in exchange for his or her services. Terms relating to basic pay (in the form of wages or salary), commission, enhanced redundancy pay and bonuses are covered by S.39(2)(a), while non-contractual enhanced redundancy pay or bonus arrangements will amount to a benefit and therefore fall under S.39(2)(b).

Paying an employee more or less than an actual or hypothetical comparator because of the protected characteristic of disability, gender reassignment, marital or civil partnership status, race, religion or belief, or sexual orientation will amount to direct discrimination. The situation is somewhat different in respect of the protected characteristic of age, as an employer can defend a direct pay discrimination claim by showing that the pay practice was justified as a proportionate means of achieving a legitimate aim (see 'Age and

801

remuneration' below). (Pay discrimination because of sex or maternity is covered by the equal pay provisions in Ss.64–80 EqA, not S.39(2) – see 'Exclusion of equal pay claims' above).

25.12 Establishing a disparity in pay – i.e. less favourable treatment – may require the claimant to break down the pay package he or she receives, and that of his or her comparator, into its constituent elements and argue that the less favourable treatment in respect of one of those elements is because of a protected characteristic (e.g. race). This is, in effect, the same as the term-by-term comparison that takes place in equal pay cases (see IDS Employment Law Handbook, 'Equal Pay' (2011), Chapter 2, under 'Sex equality clause – term-by-term comparison'). However, such a comparison will not always be necessary. In Wakeman and ors v Quick Corporation and anor 1999 IRLR 424, CA, the Court of Appeal held that a tribunal had been entitled to look at the pay package as a whole in determining that the less favourable treatment of the claimants – British employees of a Japanese company who were paid substantially less than colleagues seconded from Japan – was not due to their race, but to the fact of the comparators' secondment. The Wakeman case merits further mention, as the Court of Appeal rejected an argument that the difference in treatment, coupled with the lack of transparency in the employer's pay system, meant that the tribunal should have drawn an inference of discrimination and required the employer to prove that the reason for the less favourable treatment was not the employees' race. Wakeman was, however, decided before the introduction of statutory rules providing for a limited reversal of the burden of proof in discrimination cases (see Chapter 32, 'Burden of proof'). It is surely arguable that a difference in treatment between persons possessing a protected characteristic and persons not possessing that characteristic, coupled with an opaque pay system, are precisely the type of factual circumstances that could now lead a tribunal to conclude that an employer must provide a non-discriminatory explanation for the pay practice.

25.13 **Pay secrecy.** A major obstacle for claimants seeking to claim pay discrimination can be the absence of pay data on which to base a comparison. While there have been moves towards pay transparency in the public sector, it remains the case that many employees do not know what their colleagues are paid. If an employee suspects that he or she is being paid less than a colleague because of a protected characteristic, one course of action would be to seek information from the employer by way of the statutory discrimination questionnaire (see Chapter 33, 'Proving discrimination'). Another option would be to make direct enquiries of colleagues.

Some employers impose contractual restrictions on employees' ability to discuss pay with colleagues, breach of which could lead to disciplinary action. However, a degree of protection is afforded by S.77 EqA. This renders void any contractual term in so far as it prevents a person from making or seeking a 'relevant pay disclosure' and provides protection against victimisation for any person involved in making or seeking such a disclosure. A 'relevant pay disclosure' is one made for the purpose of enabling the person who makes it, or the person to whom it is made, to find out whether or to what extent there is, in relation to the work in question, a connection between pay and having (or not having) a protected characteristic – S.77(3). Protection in respect of 'relevant pay disclosures' was included in the Act to address concerns that pay secrecy clauses, which make workplace discussions of pay an actionable breach of contract, hinder progress towards eliminating the gender pay gap. However, the provision was intentionally drafted to cover all protected characteristics. So, a disabled man who suspects that disabled people are being paid less than non-disabled people would be protected from repercussions if he engaged in discussions with colleagues to confirm or deny those suspicions, even if he did so in breach of a pay confidentiality clause in his contract.

Employers should note, however, that S.77 is relatively limited in scope: it does **25.14** not compel any transparency on the part of the employer; and it does not render void a contractual provision preventing general enquiries about pay, only one which prohibits making or seeking a 'relevant pay disclosure'.

Age and remuneration. The introduction of the Employment Equality (Age) **25.15** Regulations 2006 SI 2006/1031 ('the Age Regulations') presented a number of problems where pay and benefits were concerned, as so many of the established practices in British workplaces were influenced, at least in part, by the age of the worker in question. In order to lessen the financial impact of the introduction of the Regulations, the Government included three exemptions relevant to remuneration, all of which have been re-enacted in the EqA:

- redundancy age bands – by virtue of para 13 of Schedule 9 to the EqA, an enhanced redundancy scheme that applies the same age multipliers as those used in the statutory redundancy scheme will not contravene the prohibition on age discrimination (see under 'Benefits, facilities and services – enhanced redundancy schemes' below for a consideration of when schemes that do not meet the exemption can be justified)

- service-related pay and benefits – para 10 of Schedule 9 provides an absolute exception for 'benefits' awarded with reference to a length-of-service criterion of up to five years, and allows a length-of-service criterion of over five years where the employer reasonably believes that it 'fulfils a business need' (a lesser standard than objective justification). In practical terms, this makes it unlikely that a claimant could successfully claim that pay and benefits determined by length of service are unjustified indirect age discrimination

- national minimum wage – para 11 of Schedule 9 makes it clear that an employer who pays all workers the appropriate rate of the NMW will not

803

be in breach of the age discrimination rules, even though young workers will be paid less than adult workers as a result.

25.16 All three exemptions are considered in greater detail in Chapter 31, 'Specific exceptions', under 'Age exceptions'. But even where an age-related exemption does not apply, the employer may still argue that any direct or indirect age discrimination in its pay practices is objectively justified as a proportionate means of achieving a legitimate aim. However, expressly paying an employee less because of his or her age (direct discrimination) is likely to be harder to justify than a pay practice that has a disparate impact on certain age groups (indirect discrimination), as the former has a greater discriminatory effect and is therefore less likely to be considered proportionate.

25.17 **Pay protection.** A number of initiatives in recent years aimed at implementing equal pay and reducing expenditure in the public sector have seen negotiated 'pay protection' arrangements put in place for certain employees. While most cases concerning pay protection have been about gender equality (see IDS Employment Law Handbook, 'Equal Pay' (2011), Chapter 8, under 'Examples of specific material factors – pay protection'), there have been some instances of pay protection arrangements being put in place for employees over a certain age. This has generally come about as a result of the introduction of the Age Regulations, with employers attempting to reduce the financial hardship that would otherwise occur as a result of the immediate withdrawal or equalisation of pay or benefits.

Employers must be aware, however, that a pay protection arrangement that prolongs age discrimination will require objective justification. For example, in Pulham and ors v Barking and Dagenham London Borough Council 2010 ICR 333, EAT, the employer determined that its scheme aimed at recognising long service among staff, which paid a monthly increment on top of salary to employees who had 25 years' continuous service and had reached the age of 55, needed to be phased out following the introduction of the Age Regulations in 2006. Agreement was reached with trade unions to close the scheme to new entrants from 1 April 2007. At that point, those benefiting from the scheme had payments frozen at the prevailing rate by way of a pay protection arrangement. P, who met the length of service requirement but not the age requirement, brought a claim of age discrimination when she was denied access to the scheme. An employment tribunal determined that the pay protection arrangement, although involving direct age discrimination, was justified. It accepted that pay protection pursued a legitimate aim, since there was a need to cushion the blow for employees already in the scheme, and went on to find the arrangements to be proportionate, noting that the cost of extending the scheme to all employees with the requisite service was at least £47,000; that the Council's £5.5m reserve for dealing with historic equal pay claims had been expended; and that the pay protection arrangements had been agreed with unions.

804

On appeal, the EAT was of the view that, although equal pay cases such as **25.18** Redcar and Cleveland Borough Council v Bainbridge and ors 2009 ICR 133, CA, demonstrated that the elimination of recognised discrimination must be immediate and full, there was an obvious and fundamental distinction between those cases and the instant case in that those cases were concerned with sex discrimination, which had been unlawful for 30 years. While there were clear policy reasons why an employer who has failed to correct unlawful discrimination over many years should not be given further time to do so, the age discriminatory features of the employer's scheme in the instant case were perfectly lawful until shortly before the pay protection arrangements were put in place. There was no reason why an employer faced with the introduction of the Age Regulations should be absolutely disentitled to incorporate an element of pay protection into the adjustments necessary to conform with the new law, notwithstanding that this will of its nature involve a degree of continuing discrimination.

However, in concluding that the pay protection arrangements were justified, the tribunal had erred in treating as decisive the fact that they had been negotiated with the trade union. While a tribunal is certainly entitled to have regard to the fact that a discriminatory measure has been negotiated with the representatives of the workforce, it cannot abdicate the responsibility of itself carrying out the necessary proportionality exercise. The tribunal had further erred in its reliance on the fact that the budget which the employer had allocated to meeting historic equal pay claims was exhausted. Any such allocation was the employer's own choice, as was the size of the budget, and plainly an employer cannot be permitted definitively to limit the extent of its own obligations by the choices that it makes. The tribunal's reliance on this factor was particularly questionable in view of the fact that the budget in question was intended for the wholly different purpose of settling equal pay claims.

Reasonable adjustments to pay. While it would never be considered a **25.19** reasonable adjustment to simply pay a disabled employee more than he or she would otherwise receive as a means of ameliorating a substantial disadvantage, there may be situations where an adjustment to the employer's method of calculating pay or bonuses is considered reasonable. This is most likely to occur where the pay is linked to performance, and the disability is inhibiting performance. The Equality and Human Rights Commission's Code of Practice on Employment ('the EHRC Employment Code') uses the following example: 'A disabled man with arthritis works in telephone sales and is paid commission on the value of his sales. His impairment gets worse and he is advised to change his computer equipment. He takes some time to get used to the new equipment and as a consequence his sales fall. It is likely to be a reasonable adjustment for his employer to pay him his previous level of commission for the period he needs to get used to the new equipment' – para 14.8. (Note that S.13(4) EqA states that, in the context of the definition of direct discrimination, where the

805

protected characteristic at issue is disability, an employer does not discriminate against a non-disabled person solely because he treats or would treat disabled persons more favourably.)

25.20 Working hours

Contractual terms stipulating an employee's working hours can give rise to direct discrimination if an employee is given less favourable hours because of a protected characteristic. For example, in Armstrong v DB Regio Tyne and Wear Ltd ET Case No.2500602/11 the employer undertook a review of working practices that led to A being removed from a 'support roster' that had enabled him to meet his childcare commitments. When A's subsequent request for flexible working was turned down he brought a claim of sex discrimination. The tribunal, finding in favour of A, noted that two women with childcare commitments had been allowed to stay on the support roster, and determined that a hypothetical female comparator in A's position would have been treated more favourably than him, since the assertions of women as to their difficulties in meeting childcare needs were accepted more readily than those of their male counterparts. It followed that the employer had directly discriminated against A because of his sex.

Cases of *direct* discrimination in relation to working hours are quite rare, however. The more common form of discrimination in these circumstances is indirect – where an apparently neutral approach to working hours places certain groups at a disadvantage and cannot be shown to be objectively justified. The EHRC Employment Code identifies three potential pitfalls for employers:

- a requirement to work full-time hours may indirectly discriminate against women because they are more likely to have childcare responsibilities

- a requirement to work full-time hours could indirectly discriminate against disabled people with certain conditions (such as ME). It could also amount to a failure to make reasonable adjustments

- a requirement to work on certain days may indirectly discriminate against those with particular religious beliefs – para 17.10.

We now consider these three matters in turn.

25.21 Childcare responsibilities.
Parents of children aged up to 17, or disabled children aged up to 18, enjoy a statutory right to request flexible working arrangements – see IDS Employment Law Handbook, 'Maternity and Parental Rights' (2009), Chapter 11, 'Flexible working', for full details. While an employer is not obliged to concede to such a request and need not give detailed reasons for refusal, the decision to reject a request can give rise to claims of indirect sex discrimination. The EHRC Employment Code gives the following example at para 17.11:

'An employee's contractual hours are 9 am – 3 pm. Under the flexible working procedures, she has formally requested to work from 10 am – 4 pm because of childcare needs. Her employer refuses, saying that to provide staff cover in the mornings would involve extra costs. This refusal would be compatible with the flexible working procedures, which do not require a refusal to be objectively justified. However, in some circumstances, this could amount to indirect sex discrimination. Where a refusal to permit certain working patterns would detrimentally affect a larger proportion of women than men, the employer must show that it is based on a legitimate aim, such as providing sufficient staff cover before 10 am, and that refusing the request is a proportionate means of achieving that aim.'

25.22 The rationale behind such a claim is that, since women are more likely than men to bear the primary childcare burden, a refusal to allow flexible working – or for that matter, the imposition of working arrangements that are incompatible with school or nursery hours – amounts to the application of a provision, criterion or practice (PCP) that puts women at a particular disadvantage. In London Underground Ltd v Edwards (No.2) 1999 ICR 494, CA, the Court of Appeal held that, in determining whether a shift system was indirectly discriminatory, it was legitimate for a tribunal to take into account the fact that women were far more likely than men to be lone parents with childcare responsibilities. And more recently, in Chief Constable of West Midlands Police v Blackburn and anor 2008 ICR 505, EAT (an equal pay case), Mr Justice Elias, then President of the EAT, suggested that an employment tribunal was entitled, in considering the disparate impact of a measure, to rely on the 'common knowledge' that women have greater childcare responsibilities than men. This suggests that a claimant will not necessarily be expected to provide statistical evidence to show that the PCP places women at a particular disadvantage.

However, there have been cases where the EAT has been less willing to endorse the assumption that, without more, full-time working or certain shift patterns place women at a disadvantage. In Sinclair Roche and Temperley and ors v Heard and anor 2004 IRLR 763, EAT, for example, the Appeal Tribunal held that an employment tribunal had not been entitled to conclude that women have the greater responsibility for childcare in our society and that as a consequence a considerably larger proportion of women than men are unable to commit themselves to full-time working. The EAT suggested that it was not appropriate to make such a generalisation in relation to men and women solicitors, or men and women working in high-powered and highly paid jobs in the City.

25.23 More recently, a decision of the EAT in Scotland has suggested that, where the employer operates an absolute bar on flexible working arrangements, establishing that the bar puts women at a disadvantage may be difficult. In Hacking and Paterson and anor v Wilson EATS 0054/09 the Appeal Tribunal held that, in circumstances where the employer operated a policy whereby all requests by property managers for flexible working were to be refused, the correct pool for comparison in determining disparate impact was not all property managers, but instead such of the employer's property managers as, at the relevant time, wanted flexible working to be available. The EAT went on to state that the fact that all property managers would have received a negative response to a request for flexible working did not mean that all would have suffered what could properly be characterised as a disadvantage or that the disadvantage to them would necessarily have been the same. Rather, it is necessary for a tribunal to look at the negative consequences of the refusal. It is not, in the EAT's view, 'inevitable' that women will be disproportionately adversely affected by a refusal to grant flexible working. It noted that society has changed dramatically and that many women now return to full-time work after childbirth and more men take on childcare responsibilities. Moreover, while the childcare arrangements available to some women are such that they cannot work full time, other choose not to work full time. A negative response to the request for flexible working may, accordingly, give rise to differing effects. Where the effect is on an employee who is able to work full time but does not wish to do so, it is difficult to see that it would be correct to talk in terms of that employee being disadvantaged. Where the effect does amount to a disadvantage, the question of whether it amounts to a particular disadvantage that is liable to be experienced by women as opposed to men arises.

In our view, the EAT has somewhat exaggerated the effect of changes to childcare arrangements in recent years. Although more men do now take on childcare responsibilities, the distribution of those responsibilities is still skewed heavily towards women. While a tribunal is not obliged to take into account 'common knowledge' and would be entitled to demand evidence from a claimant that she, and others of her sex, are put at a particular disadvantage by an employer's approach to flexible working, that evidence should not be particularly hard to come by in the majority of cases. The greater area of dispute is surely whether the PCP in relation to working hours can be objectively justified. In contrast to a claim under the flexible working rules, this will involve an examination of the legitimacy of the employer's reasons for refusing flexible working.

25.24 Two examples:

- **Giles v Geach and anor t/a Cornelia Care Homes** ET Case No.3100720/06: in January 2005 G, who worked part time, was told that she must switch to full-time work in the office from April. G's suggestions of jobsharing or working the additional hours from home were refused. The tribunal had no doubt that the defence of justification was not made out. Rejecting the employer's argument that the cost implications of G working at home would be enormous, the tribunal noted that the employer had taken no steps to assess those costs or the health and safety implications of such an adjustment. Furthermore, its argument that G was at risk of making errors through lack of concentration arising from childcare responsibilities if she worked at home was based on 'wholly outdated stereotypical attitudes'

- **Chandler v American Airlines Inc** ET Case No.2329478/10: C, who had worked for AA since 1998, was employed as a lead agent at the time she made an application for flexible working following the birth of her second child. Her application was refused, but AA agreed to a further reduction in her working hours, to 81.25 a month, on her return in April 2009. AA carried out a review of its passenger services in July 2009 and as a result the posts of lead agents were abolished and post-holders were invited to apply for posts of operational coordinator or team leader. C applied for a post as team leader and was successful, but AA informed her that the post was full time, and although it would honour her hours and roster pattern for a trial period of four months, it would expect her to increase her hours to full time at the end of that period. She told AA that she was not in a position to work full time, and at the end of the trial period she was given a choice: she could work full time, consider a job share as an operational coordinator, consider suitable alternative employment or accept a redundancy package. She accepted redundancy under duress and brought a claim of sex discrimination. On the basis of its recognition that significantly more women than men have primary responsibility for childcare, the employment tribunal held that a requirement to work full time was to the detriment of women and was not a proportionate means of achieving AA's legitimate aim of improving management. AA had accepted before the tribunal that the post could have been undertaken other than on a full-time basis, although not on the hours that C had been working. It followed that there was a less discriminatory alternative to the requirement to work full time, which could not therefore be justified.

Disability. Employers must give serious consideration to requests from disabled employees to alter or reduce working hours where it would help to alleviate a substantial disadvantage. Two examples: **25.25**

- **Caen v RBS Insurance Services Ltd** ET Case No.1801133/09: C was employed as a claims handler. In 2002, she suffered a nervous breakdown and it later transpired that she was also suffering from agoraphobia. As a result of this condition, C found it increasingly difficult to work a standard working day because – owing to her anxieties – she did not want to travel to work when there were a lot of other cars on the road. Consequently, the employer permitted C to work from 6.30 am to 2 pm. This arrangement worked well until the Ministry of Justice proposed changes to the way in which claims would be administered by insurance companies such as the employer. This led to changes in the way C's office was run and she was told

809

that she would have to work more normal hours, starting no earlier than 7.30 am. This caused C to become paranoid and she suffered anxiety attacks each morning before going to work. Eventually, C was dismissed and she pursued a number of claims, including that the employer had failed in its duty to make reasonable adjustments. Upholding the claim, the tribunal considered that once the concept of flexibility was agreed, there was no logical basis for saying that 6.30 am was inappropriate, but 7.30 am was appropriate. The employer had not demonstrated why starting at 6.30 am would not work and had thus failed in its duty to make reasonable adjustments

- **Mansoor v Secretary of State for Education and Employment** ET Case No.1803409/97: M worked as a clerical officer in a job centre. Until 1994 he worked on flexitime. Thereafter, because of his poor timekeeping record, he was required to work fixed hours. M had colitis and informed the employer that it was impossible for him to get to work at the scheduled start time because of his condition. He gave the employer permission to contact his GP and his consultant for confirmation. Notwithstanding that, the employer decided disciplinary action was warranted. At no time was M required to see the employer's medical adviser. Eventually, M was dismissed on account of his poor timekeeping and attendance. A tribunal found that the employer had failed to comply with the duty to make reasonable adjustments to accommodate M's disability. Adjustments could easily have been made by shortening M's hours or by removing the requirement to work fixed hours. Indeed, there was evidence to support the view that M would have been willing to work shorter hours and take a pay cut. However none of these possibilities was acted upon by the employer.

25.26 While shorter working hours may amount to a reasonable adjustment in some cases, employers should avoid making stereotypical assumptions about the abilities and capabilities of disabled people and should not simply reduce working hours without consulting the employee. For example, in Coombes v The Bradford Exchange ET Case No.2303160/06 the employee had a chronic condition involving bone deformity, which meant that he walked with a stick and led to high levels of disability-related absence. The employer suggested reducing the employee's working hours, but he rejected the suggestion. A reduction was then imposed on him. An employment tribunal found that the change was not a reasonable adjustment, and it was made because of the employee's disability, with the result that it amounted to disability discrimination.

It is not only the times at which an employee begins and finishes work and the total number of hours worked that may need to change – an employer may also need to amend shift patterns and rotas if their effect is to cause a substantial disadvantage to a disabled employee. An example:

- **Stevenson v Severn River Crossing plc** ET Case No.1402306/10: S was employed as a toll collector, a job that required a lot of stretching and bending down, particularly for low vehicles. She began to suffer from osteoarthritis in 2007 and in December 2009 she was diagnosed with fibromyalgia. An occupational health report in June 2008 recommended that S be allocated to work at those toll booths that largely dealt with heavy goods vehicles (HGVs), because the height of the vehicles reduced the amount of bending required. Subsequent reports recommended that S be allowed to start working no earlier than 8 am to enable the effect of her medication to wear off, and that heating should be provided in the toll booth. S maintained that the heating provided was inefficient, and that her shift patterns meant a large amount of bending was still necessary. An employment tribunal determined that the employer failed to make the reasonable adjustments of having a systematic approach to the rotas in order to ensure that S was placed in the lanes having a high degree of HGV traffic and of providing adequate heating.

25.27 As the provisions of the Working Time Regulations 1998 SI 1998/1833 demonstrate, working hours do not simply constitute the time at which an employee starts and finishes work: they also include the rest breaks to which an employee is entitled. The Regulations provide for a break of 20 minutes in any shift of over six hours, but an employer may need to consider providing additional or longer breaks to a disabled employee if his or her disability causes a greater degree of fatigue than generally experienced by people who do not have that disability. The EHRC Employment Code provides the following example: 'A worker has recently been diagnosed with diabetes. As a consequence of her medication and her new dietary requirements, she finds that she gets extremely tired at certain times during the working day. It is likely to be a reasonable adjustment to allow her to take additional rest breaks to control the effects of her impairment' – para 17.15.

25.28 **Religious observance.** An employee whose working hours prevent him or her from meeting a religious commitment – such as attending a session of worship or observing a day of rest – may argue that the working hours are indirectly discriminatory. In such circumstances the employer will have to show that its arrangements as to working hours are objectively justified. For example, in Cherfi v G4S Security Services Ltd EAT 0379/10 C, a Muslim, worked for G4S as a security guard in Highgate, where the client required all security officers to remain on site throughout their shifts. Consequently, he was refused permission to travel to Friday prayers at a mosque in Finsbury Park. However, there was a prayer room on site and C had the option of working on Saturday or Sunday rather than Friday. C claimed that the PCP of requiring him to remain at work during Friday lunchtimes constituted indirect religious discrimination. An employment tribunal held that, although the PCP did place C at a disadvantage as a practising Muslim by not allowing him to attend prayers in congregation, G4S would be in danger of financial penalties or even losing its contract with its client if a full complement of security staff was not on site throughout the

811

day. C had refused a variety of arrangements offered to accommodate his requirements. Thus, the tribunal found that the PCP was a proportionate means of achieving a legitimate aim – i.e. meeting the operational needs of the business. On appeal, the EAT upheld this decision. In its view, the tribunal had carried out the necessary balancing act, having considered both the reason why G4S refused to allow C to leave the site on Friday lunchtimes and the impact of this on C. The discriminatory effect of the PCP was limited to preventing C from attending congregational prayers during working hours. C was not prevented from praying at the Highgate site, and nor was he prevented from working on a Friday or pressured to accept work on a Saturday or Sunday. In view of this, and also having regard to the alternatives that had been open to C, the conclusion as to justification was one that the tribunal was entitled to reach.

25.29 Holiday entitlement

All employees are entitled to a minimum of 5.4 weeks' paid annual leave (including bank holidays) by virtue of Regs 13 and 13A of the Working Time Regulations 1998 SI 1998/1833. In addition, many employees are entitled to further contractual leave. In respect of both types of leave, the contract is likely to contain terms governing the taking of leave, stipulating, for example, when notice must be given and times at which leave may not be taken. Any discrimination in respect of an employee's holiday entitlement will therefore fall within S.39(2)(a), as discrimination as to the terms of his or her contract. Alternatively, such discrimination could fall within S.39(2)(b) or (4)(b), on the basis that holiday is a 'benefit', or S.39(2)(d) where the employee claims to have been subjected to a detriment in relation to holiday entitlement. Similarly, any victimisation in relation to an employee's holiday entitlement is likely to be caught by S.39(4)(a), (b) or (d).

One relatively common practice is to award employees additional holiday entitlement once they have completed a given period of service with the employer. Although such a practice could potentially represent indirect age discrimination, it is covered by para 10 of Schedule 9 to the EqA. This provides an absolute exception for 'benefits' awarded with reference to a length-of-service criterion of up to five years, and allows a length-of-service criterion of over five years where the employer reasonably believes that providing the benefit 'fulfils a business need' – for further details see Chapter 31, 'Specific exceptions', under 'Age exceptions'. It seems fairly clear that awarding additional holiday in recognition of long service fulfils the business needs of encouraging loyalty and minimising staff turnover, so it is unlikely that an employee would be successful in challenging this practice.

25.30 Occupational pensions

Discrimination in the rules and operation of an occupational pension scheme would not fall within the scope of S.39(2)(a) because such schemes retain a legal entity distinct from that of the employer. Thus, the terms of the scheme are not terms of employment. Instead, specific provisions contained in Ss.61–63 EqA cover discrimination in occupational pension schemes (considered briefly under 'Non-discrimination rule' below).

Note, however, that any discrimination in respect of the way in which an employer affords staff *access* to an occupational pension scheme would be covered by either S.39(2)(a) or (b), in addition to coming within the specific provisions set out below.

Non-discrimination rule. Under S.61(1) and (2) EqA, a non-discrimination **25.31** rule is to be read into every occupational scheme. Such a rule requires that a 'responsible person' (A) must not discriminate against another person (B) in carrying out any of A's functions in relation to the scheme; and he or she must not, in relation to the scheme, harass or victimise B. A responsible person for these purposes is a trustee or manager of the scheme, an employer whose employees are, or may be, members of the scheme, or a person exercising an appointing function in relation to an office the holder of which is, or may be, a member of the scheme – S.61(4).

The rules of an occupational pension scheme are subject to the non-discrimination rule. So if, for example, the rules of a scheme provide for a benefit which is less favourable for one member than another because of race, they must be read as though the less favourable provision did not apply. S.62 EqA provides trustees and managers of the scheme with powers to amend discriminatory aspects of the scheme.

A responsible person is also under a duty to make reasonable adjustments when **25.32** the provisions, criteria and practices of the scheme place a disabled member at a substantial disadvantage – S.61(10). The EHRC Employment Code provides the following example at para 14.44:

'The rules of an employer's final salary scheme provide that the maximum pension is based on the member's salary in the last year of work. Having worked full time for 20 years, a worker becomes disabled and has to reduce her working hours two years before her pension age. The scheme's rules put her at a disadvantage as a result of her disability, because her pension will only be calculated on her part-time salary. The trustees decide to convert her part-time salary to its full-time equivalent and make a corresponding reduction in the period of her part-time employment which counts as pensionable. In this way, her full-time earnings will be taken into account. This is likely to be a reasonable adjustment to make.'

Probation   **25.33**
Many employment contracts include a term providing for a probationary period at the beginning of the employment relationship. During this probationary

period, the contractual period of notice required on either side is usually very short, and employees are often measured against a series of goals to assess whether they are settling into the role. Failure to successfully complete the probationary period will tend to lead to performance management procedures being put in place or the employee being dismissed, so it is important that an employer acts fairly and consistently in applying probationary arrangements.

Where a change is made to an employee's probationary arrangements in the aftermath of that employee making, or giving information in connection with, a claim or allegation of discrimination, that change may amount to victimisation under S.39(4)(a). An example:

- **Hunt v Dorking** ET Case No.2301874/07: H was promoted in September 2006 and was told that she would be given a further salary increase of £2,000 per annum on completion of a training course in January 2007. In November 2006 two employees who were junior to H altered an e-mail message sent to various members of staff so that H's name became synonymous with a sexually offensive word. She complained and the employer dealt with the matter firmly, but it was clear that H's manager believed she had acted unacceptably in making a complaint and that she should simply have got on with her job. H was not given the pay increase and was subjected to a further period of probation, as a result of which she resigned. An employment tribunal held that she had been constructively dismissed, and went on to find that the decision to extend her probation period was reached because she had done the protected act of complaining about the harassment contained in the e-mail. It therefore followed that the employer had victimised H and she was awarded £11,000 for injury to feelings.

25.34 Some learning disabilities could prevent a disabled employee from satisfactorily completing an induction period. Similarly, a disability that restricts the number of hours a week an employee can work, or one that reduces the employee's rate of productivity, could impact on that employee's ability to complete a probation period. Where disability presents an employee with a substantial disadvantage in respect of a probation period, reasonable adjustments will be required. However, while an extension of the period might well be considered reasonable, an employer is unlikely to be expected to completely set aside the need for probationary employees to demonstrate the necessary level of competence in the post:

- **Peckett v Ministry of Justice** ET Case No.1810129/09: P had an HIV infection and a spastic paraparesis, which impacted on his mobility. He was offered a job as a court usher in May 2008, subject to a six-month probationary period. He began work on 8 September 2008. He had two weeks off work suffering from an eye infection shortly after he began work, and at a return-to-work meeting he was told that his probation was to be extended by a further two months and further absences could result in a formal warning. He found the job more physically demanding than he had expected and had a discussion with his supervisor about adjustments to reduce the time he spent on his feet. He was referred to occupational health in respect of his mobility issues. As a result of that referral he was scheduled to work only in the quieter courts. On 26 December he had a heart attack, which he maintained was related to HIV, and began a further period of sickness absence. He was issued with a formal warning relating to his absence on 3 March 2009 and his probationary period was extended by a further six weeks. At a meeting on 11 June, when P was still off work following his heart attack, he was dismissed for failing to meet the standards expected of a probationary member of staff. He claimed the dismissal was discriminatory, but an employment tribunal dismissed the claim. It noted that the MoJ had already made the reasonable adjustment of extending the probationary period in order to help P meet the required standard, and while the tribunal was not convinced that his heart attack was related to his HIV, it considered in any event that the MoJ's practice of only confirming in employment people who could demonstrate that they were likely to give satisfactory attendance was justified. An employee cannot demonstrate that he or she meets the performance requirements of a role unless he or she attends to do so. Ten months was an adequate period in which to allow an employee to demonstrate performance and competence.

Absence and sickness
25.35

An employer's approach to absence and sickness is usually dictated by a combination of contractual terms and workplace rules and policies. As a result, discrimination arising in this context will generally be covered by a combination of S.39(2)(a) and (b). Where an absence management procedure is put in place, any negative action taken under that procedure is likely to amount to a detriment, and so be caught by S.39(2)(d).

Generally speaking, provided an employer makes clear its policies relating to sickness absence and operates those policies in a consistent manner, the chance of discrimination arising is small. However, there are two areas in which particular care must be taken: disability and pregnancy.

Disability-related absences. The law governing disability-related absences has undergone substantial upheaval in recent years. For many years, claimants subjected to detrimental treatment as a result of disability-related absences from work routinely brought claims of disability-related discrimination under S.3A(1) of the Disability Discrimination Act 1995 (DDA). However, in Mayor and Burgesses of the London Borough of Lewisham v Malcolm 2008 IRLR 700, HL, the House of Lords held that the comparator for the purposes of disability-related discrimination under S.3A(1) was a non-disabled person who was otherwise in the same circumstances as the disabled claimant. So, in a case 25.36

815

involving disability-related absence, the Malcolm comparator would be a non-disabled person who had also been absent but for a reason other than disability. In the vast majority of cases, there would be no doubt that the Malcolm comparator would have been treated in the same way as the disabled claimant, and so no less favourable treatment would occur.

As a result of the Malcolm decision, the protection afforded by S.3A(1) DDA became extremely limited and provided no greater protection than that offered by S.3A(5), which covered direct discrimination and required a similar comparison. The Government therefore decided to use the opportunity presented by the enactment of the EqA to remedy the situation by introducing a new claim of 'discrimination arising from a disability' under S.15, in addition to claims of direct and indirect disability discrimination under Ss.13 and 19, harassment under S.26 and victimisation under S.27.

25.37 It is clear that, if an employee is subjected to disciplinary action or dismissal for absences that are caused by a disability, there will be no direct discrimination under S.13 if the employer treats, or would treat, a non-disabled employee having the same number of absences in the same way. Direct discrimination is only likely to arise where there is a difference in treatment between a disabled employee and a non-disabled employee. An example:

- **Law v New College Swindon** ET Case No.1402504/04: the employer's sickness policy stated that a period of absence due to injury sustained during the performance of an employee's duties would not count against his or her entitlement to paid sick leave. When L went off sick with work-related stress, however, the employer counted the absence against his entitlement to sick pay, which L argued amounted to disability discrimination. The employment tribunal agreed, finding that a proper construction of the contractual clause was that it applied to *any* harm sustained through work. By being excluded from the provisions of the clause, L was treated less favourably than people who sustained a physical injury.

25.38 In contrast to direct discrimination, discrimination arising from disability under S.15 does not require a comparator. Such discrimination occurs where a person is treated unfavourably because of something arising in consequence of his or her disability, and that treatment is not justified as a proportionate means of achieving a legitimate aim. This definition almost certainly covers the situation of an employee subject to disciplinary action for disability-related absences, meaning that the key issue in most cases will be whether the unfavourable treatment – such as a disciplinary warning or denial of a benefit – can be justified.

Case law has demonstrated that it will often be considered a reasonable adjustment to vary or waive aspects of sickness absence policies where absence is disability-related, although there is no automatic requirement to do so –

what is reasonable will always depend on the individual circumstances of the case. In practice, there is likely to be considerable overlap between the test of reasonableness under S.20 EqA (which governs the duty to make reasonable adjustments) and the objective justification test under S.15. However, given the difference in statutory wording, claimants might find it advantageous to claim under both heads.

Three cases involving absence and sickness policies: **25.39**

- **Holden v Commissioners for HM Revenue and Customs** ET Case No.2404292/06: H was disabled by reason of asthma and had a number of other medical conditions causing her to take time off work. She was made subject to HMRC's formal attendance procedure because of the number of days' absence she had taken. She claimed that HMRC was in breach of its duty to make reasonable adjustments by not excluding her disability-related absences and refusing to move her to a new manager. In dismissing her claim, the employment tribunal found that a policy that permits disabled people to remain at home on full pay indefinitely, or allows them regularly to fail to attend work for considerable periods, even with a medical certificate, is not in the interest of disabled employees since it removes the incentive to return to work. Furthermore, employers cannot be expected indefinitely to accommodate employees whose attendance is regularly unreliable

- **Patval v London Borough of Camden** ET Case No.2203464/07: P was disabled as a result of a road accident, which caused him to be absent for over four months. Additional long-term absences due to his disability led to his absence being monitored under the employer's sickness policy and a subsequent referral to its occupational health service. In 2007 his pattern of absence changed from long-term absences to short-term ones. Between January and May he was absent on six occasions for 18 days in total, and was eventually dismissed. In dismissing P's claim of discrimination by way of a failure to make reasonable adjustments, the employment tribunal noted that the employer had considered reasonable adjustments; some of which had been made and some of which had been offered to P but rejected. But the tribunal did not accept that simply removing P from the operation of the employer's sickness policy altogether was a reasonable adjustment. P's position was important to the employer's operation and his absences had an adverse effect both on his colleagues and on the running of the business. The employer was entitled to reach the conclusion that further absences, whether long- or short-term, would occur, and to say that enough was enough

- **Herbert v Department for Work and Pensions** ET Case No.2406254/04: H suffered a depressive illness that led to long periods of sickness absence. The employer instigated its sickness absence procedure and sought a medical report on H's condition. The report was positive, but within weeks

817

H had suffered a relapse and had further absences from work. The employer did not have confidence in the report due to the relapse and dismissed H. The employment tribunal noted that there was evidence to show that H's absences had not caused significant disruption, and it would have been reasonable in the circumstances for the employer to have allowed a higher threshold for disability-related absences before action was triggered under its sickness absence policy.

25.40 **Pregnancy-related absences.** The fact that no comparator is needed in cases of pregnancy and maternity discrimination under S.18 EqA – it outlaws *unfavourable* rather than *less favourable* treatment – means that treating pregnancy-related absences that occur during the 'protected period' (the period between the inception of pregnancy to the end of the woman's statutory maternity leave) as equivalent to 'normal' sickness absence is likely to amount to discrimination. Note, however, that where a woman is absent from work after the end of her statutory maternity leave, and that absence is related to the pregnancy, S.18 is not engaged and her treatment instead falls, for the purposes of direct sex discrimination, to be compared with that of a man absent from work. For further details, see IDS Employment Law Handbook, 'Maternity and Parental Rights' (2009), Chapter 13, 'Discrimination and equal pay', under 'Direct sex discrimination – pregnancy-related illness'.

25.41 **Place of work**

Any discrimination relating to the place (or places) at which an employee is contractually required to work is likely to fall within S.39(2)(a), while the decision to transfer, or not to transfer, an employee to another workplace would fall under S.39(2)(b) (see 'Promotion, training and transfer' below). Matters concerning places of work that do not fit into either category would fall under the 'any other detriment' provision in S.39(2)(d).

It is important to note here that one of the three 'triggers' for the S.20 duty to make reasonable adjustments is the situation where the physical features of the employer's premises place a disabled employee at a substantial disadvantage when compared with people who are not disabled. Accordingly, it might be a reasonable adjustment in such circumstances to move the employee to a place of work where he or she does not experience that disadvantage. That could entail a move to another floor or office, another site (where the employer has multiple workplaces) or allowing the employee to work from home. What is a reasonable step to take in the circumstances will depend on the disability in question, and also on factors such as the effectiveness of the step, practicality, the employer's financial and staff resources and the effect on other employees.

25.42 One particular adjustment that is regularly requested is the right to work from home. To succeed in a claim of breach of the duty to make reasonable adjustments in circumstances where a request for home-working has been refused, an employee will need to show why his or her disability means the employer's requirement to work at a place other than home places him or her at a disadvantage. In Environment Agency v Rowan 2008 ICR 218, EAT, R had injured her back at work and been on long-term sick leave. She wished to be rehabilitated on a home-working basis, but her employer did not think this appropriate. An employment tribunal determined that, by not offering R home-working on a trial basis, the employer had failed in its duty to make reasonable adjustments. On appeal, however, the EAT held that the tribunal failed to clearly identify the nature and extent of the substantial disadvantage suffered by R. As the EAT pointed out, this finding is crucial to the subsequent consideration of what adjustments might be reasonable in order to prevent that disadvantage. It is impossible for a tribunal to say that home-working is a reasonable adjustment without first considering why a requirement to work in an office is disadvantageous to the claimant.

Particular care should be taken when exercising 'mobility clauses' included in the contract of employment (these provide an employer with contractual authority to move an employee to another workplace), as the effect on disabled employees may be more severe than for their non-disabled colleagues. As a result, reasonable adjustments to such contractual terms may be necessary.

Promotion, transfer and training 25.43

Section 39(2)(b) EqA stipulates that 'an employer (A) must not discriminate against an employee of A's (B) in the way A affords B access, or by not affording B access, to opportunities for promotion, transfer or training or for any other benefit, facility or service'. And S.39(4)(b) states that an employer must not victimise an employee in any of these ways. In the following sections, we are concerned with discrimination in opportunities for promotion, transfer and training. Benefits, facilities and services are addressed later in this chapter under 'Benefits, facilities and services'.

Promotion 25.44
As with recruitment from outside the organisation, which is considered in Chapter 24, the risk of discrimination in internal promotion is always present. Although an employer should have more information on which to make an objective and unbiased assessment of suitability for promotion and transfer than when taking a decision to recruit, there is still a risk of discrimination arising. This could occur in the operation of an appraisal, in the selection and promotion or transfer process or in the practical arrangements necessary to enable the promotion or transfer to take place. An employer could run into trouble if it cannot explain why an apparently less well qualified individual of a different age, race, sex, etc from the complainant has achieved promotion while the complainant has not. This is particularly so if an internal recruitment

819

procedure or equal opportunities policy has not been followed, or if the selection process involved irrelevant criteria, subjective criteria, or criteria that were indirectly discriminatory. Difficulties can also arise if promotion decisions are influenced by employees' performance appraisals where the performance management process has itself been affected by bias.

Section 39(2)(b) is concerned with affording or denying access to *opportunities for promotion*. This covers a wider range of situations than simple promotion or non-promotion, extending to the training, experience and guidance that is necessary to achieve promotion in a given organisation. An example:

- **Dinar v Burger King Ltd** ET Case No.15555/95: D, a Sudanese man, worked for a fast-food chain. He complained that he was given more menial tasks to do than his white colleagues and that, as a result, he failed to qualify for promotion. A tribunal found that the system for allocating menial tasks and the system for promotion were both in the absolute discretion of the manager and that both systems were abused. As a result, D's duties were restricted in such a way that he lacked the experience in different areas necessary to achieve promotion and so was denied the opportunity of promotion. As the tribunal found that D's less favourable treatment was on racial grounds, his claim of race discrimination succeeded.

25.45 It will be a rare case when an employer openly admits that an employee was denied access to an opportunity for promotion because of a protected characteristic. More commonly, a claimant will seek to prove facts from which a tribunal can infer that the reason he or she was not promoted is a protected characteristic, as this will shift the burden on to the employer to provide a non-discriminatory explanation for the treatment. In Aderemi v Transport for London and anor ET Case No.2222629/09 A, who was the only black African in his team, had received consistently excellent appraisals and been described by his line manager, M, as one of his most efficient managers. A took on significant extra responsibilities in the hope of securing career advancement, but M did not consider that they warranted an increase in A's salary band. Eventually, and against M's advice, the employer determined that A's role should be re-evaluated, but these plans were put on hold, with A eventually being notified four months later that that re-evaluation had been scrapped. When A subsequently brought a claim of race discrimination, an employment tribunal noted that although he was an outstanding performer, the pay of his comparators had increased proportionally to a far greater extent than A's. This, coupled with the lack of a stern reaction to an e-mail in which M had expressed the view that A wanted promotion 'because he has so many mouths to feed', was sufficient to shift the burden onto the employer to provide a non-discriminatory reason why A was not promoted. In the tribunal's view, the employer could not do so, since its corporate culture was permissive of unconscious race discrimination.

820

The lack of a defence of justification to direct discrimination (except where the protected characteristic is age) means that even a well-intentioned denial of an opportunity for promotion can lead to liability for discrimination, if that denial was 'because of' a protected characteristic. This is clearly demonstrated by Amnesty International v Ahmed 2009 ICR 1450, EAT. In that case A, a UK national of northern Sudanese origin, worked for AI as a campaigner on issues relating to Sudan, particularly the crisis in Darfur. In 2007 she applied for promotion to the post of Sudan researcher, but, after she was selected as the preferred candidate by the promotion panel, senior management became concerned that her ethnicity would be a problem in the role and decided not to appoint her. She resigned and brought a claim of, among other things, race discrimination. The employment tribunal noted that, given the background of ethnic tension between North and South Sudanese, AI had concluded that employing someone of the claimant's ethnic origin in the post of Sudan researcher would compromise its perceived impartiality in the ongoing conflict in Sudan, and expose both the researcher and those with her to increased risks when working in the region. Although the tribunal accepted that these concerns were genuine, it upheld A's claim of direct race discrimination. The tribunal pointed out that, although AI had decided not to promote A because of its concerns about safety and impartiality, the reason for both those concerns was her ethnic identity. In the tribunal's view, 'but for the claimant's ethnic origin she would undoubtedly have been appointed'. On appeal the EAT, while noting that AI had approached the matter with 'great conscientiousness' and had shown its 'continued faith' in the employee by encouraging her to apply for other jobs within its organisation, upheld the tribunal's decision that AI had directly discriminated against A.

Communicating opportunities. There is potential for discrimination in the **25.46** way in which promotion opportunities are made known to employees. For example, in El Gamal v Dynamiq Cleaning Ltd ET Case No.1610077/09 E, an Egyptian by birth, complained of race discrimination when he was not informed of a supervisory vacancy. Upholding his claim, an employment tribunal noted that the employer's recruitment guidelines had not been followed, that a less experienced colleague of E's had been appointed to the role, and that this colleague, like the manager tasked with selecting someone for promotion, was Sudanese. It considered that race was the reason the successful candidate was promoted, which meant E had suffered direct discrimination. To avoid such discrimination, employers should ensure that opportunities are advertised to the entire workforce, and that any formal recruitment and promotion procedures are applied.

Where a disabled employee is prevented by his or her disability from finding out about promotion opportunities because of the way in which these opportunities are made known to employees, it is likely to be considered a

821

reasonable adjustment to provide the necessary information directly to the employee in an accessible format.

25.47 **Victimisation in promotion.** Section 39(4)(b) EqA provides that 'an employer (A) must not victimise an employee of A's (B) in the way A affords B access, or by not affording B access, to opportunities for promotion, transfer or training'. As a result, it is not open to an employer to operate a policy of excluding from opportunities for promotion an employee who has done a protected act. 'Protected acts' are discussed in detail in Chapter 19, 'Victimisation', under 'Protected acts'. They include:

- bringing proceedings under the EqA

- giving evidence or information in connection with proceedings under the EqA

- doing any other thing for the purposes of or in connection with the EqA

- making an allegation (whether or not express) that the employer or another person has contravened this Act – S.27(2).

25.48 An example of victimisation in promotion:

- **Ellis v Buzzacott LLP** ET Case No.2202976/09: E lodged an internal grievance claiming of harassment by a male colleague. During the informal grievance meeting she was warned that if her grievance progressed to the formal stage and no further evidence was found, her complaint could be deemed to be malicious, leading to disciplinary action being taken against her. The employer also determined that, while the grievance was ongoing, a planned promotion for E should be put on hold. E resigned and claimed constructive dismissal and unlawful victimisation contrary to the Sex Discrimination Act 1975. Upholding her claim, an employment tribunal found that the employer had acted in breach of contract in mismanaging the grievance process, warning E she could be subject to the disciplinary procedure and putting her promotion on hold. E was subjected to those actions because she had made a complaint of harassment against a male colleague, which was a protected act, and so it followed that she had been victimised.

25.49 **Qualifications needed for promotion.** There is a possibility of indirect discrimination arising when an employer sets out a criterion that candidates for promotion must have a particular qualification in order to be successful, and a group sharing a protected characteristic is placed at a particular disadvantage by that criterion. This has been highlighted as a issue where age and degree-level qualifications are concerned, as older employees are statistically less likely to hold degrees.

In Homer v Chief Constable of West Yorkshire Police 2012 UKSC 15, SC, H had worked for a number of years as a legal adviser for the Police National Legal Database (PNLD). At the time he was recruited, a law degree was one route into the job but H was recruited because he had 30 years' experience as a serving police constable and a lesser legal qualification. Subsequently, a law degree became 'essential' for recruitment as a legal adviser. However, this did not affect H because his experience still qualified him for the post. He declined his employer's offer to pay for him to do a law degree part time because – as he would not finish before his proposed retirement date at the age of 65 – he saw no purpose in this. When, a year later, the employer undertook a regrading exercise, H, by then 61, had his application to be regraded at the top of the three new grades rejected as he did not have a law degree, one of the nine qualifying conditions. H lodged an employment tribunal claim, arguing that the requirement to have a law degree amounted to indirect age discrimination because his age prevented him from completing the degree before his retirement.

25.50 The tribunal found that the criterion that those at the top grade of the legal adviser post must have a law degree put people in H's age group – those aged 60–65 – at a particular disadvantage as they could not achieve the qualification before PNLD's normal retirement age of 65 (the case preceded the abolition of the default retirement age). On the other hand, those in the comparator group, aged 30–59, could complete a law degree – and so achieve the top pay grade – before retirement. On appeal, that decision was initially overturned. The Court of Appeal considered that any disadvantage H suffered resulted not from age discrimination in respect of his age group but from his impending withdrawal from the workplace. Exactly the same disadvantage would have been suffered by persons from the comparator group who also stopped working before obtaining a degree qualification (e.g. for family reasons or because of early retirement). Therefore, the degree qualification requirement had not put H or members of his age group at a particular disadvantage. However, on further appeal, the Supreme Court overturned the Court of Appeal's decision. It held unanimously that it was incorrect to equate leaving work because of impending compulsory retirement with other reasons for leaving (such as family reasons). In the latter case a person would generally have some choice in the matter, whereas a person faced with compulsory retirement would not. Nor was it realistic to differentiate between age and compulsory retirement, since the two things were interlinked. The Supreme Court remitted the case to the tribunal to determine whether the indirect age discrimination suffered by H was objectively justified.

It should be noted that the statutory default retirement age of 65 – which was a crucial factor in the Supreme Court's decision that the degree qualification requirement put older workers at a disadvantage – has now been abolished: see Chapter 5, 'Age', under 'Protection under the Equality Act – abolition of the statutory retirement age' for details. This makes it less likely that employers will inadvertently discriminate against older workers by applying PCPs that

823

disproportionately affect workers simply on account of their impending enforced retirement. However, a wider question that was not specifically tackled in Homer is whether older workers, faced with the need to satisfy qualification requirements to secure career advancement, can claim to be indirectly discriminated against because they are statistically less likely than younger workers to hold the necessary qualifications. It is, for example, almost certainly the case that more people under the age of 40 are likely to have a degree than those over that age given the huge increase in the numbers entering tertiary education over the last 25 years. The argument that a degree qualification requirement does indeed indirectly discriminate against older workers was run in McCluskey v Edge Hill University ET Case No.2405206/07 (a case concerning discrimination in recruitment rather than in promotion). There, the employment tribunal accepted M's contention that people in their late fifties were less likely to have a degree and, therefore, that the requirement to have a degree put people of M's age group – as well as M herself – at a particular disadvantage. However, in that particular case the tribunal also found that it was a legitimate aim for a university operating in a highly competitive market to have a mix of academic staff who in all instances possessed a degree. Furthermore, such a measure was proportionate to ensure the maintenance of high academic standards. Although the justification defence thwarted the claimant's argument in the McCluskey case, it is important to remember that the employer here was a university, so it is open to question whether the defence would be as successful if the argument were deployed in a different employment context.

25.51 **Reasonable adjustments to promotion arrangements.** As with recruitment, an employer may need to consider adjusting the provisions, criteria and practices it applies in respect of promotion if they place a disabled employee at a substantial disadvantage when compared with non-disabled colleagues.

One common adjustment sought by disabled employees in these circumstances is that of disregarding disability-related absences when considering whether an employee is suitable for promotion. As seen above under 'Terms of employment – absence and sickness policies', employers who choose to treat disability-related absences in the same way as sickness absences that are not related to disability will need to show both objective justification and that it would not have been a reasonable adjustment to discount the absences. However, an employer will not necessarily face liability for taking account of disability-related absence where it has already made all the adjustments that would be reasonable. In Whitham v Npower Ltd ET Case No.2513436/09 W, who suffered from Crohn's disease, had a poor attendance record as a result of his disability. The employer made adjustments, including varying W's expected attendance rate. He was called to a formal capability hearing at which a revised attendance target was set and he was given a first written capability warning. On the same day W applied for a promotion. His manager completed a reference form for him, which stated explicitly that no absences and no written capability warnings should be included in the reference if they related to matters covered by the DDA. Despite this, the manager included details of W's attendance record and the written notification of capability, with the result that the application for promotion was unsuccessful. Dismissing W's claim of discrimination, the tribunal found that the employer had reviewed the issue when W complained about the inclusion of exempt material in the reference but had concluded that although the manager had completed the form incorrectly, in all the circumstances – including the history of W's absences and the adjustments that had been made over a four-year period – it was appropriate to take into account the fact that W was subject to a formal capability process. The tribunal considered that it is not a reasonable adjustment to require an employer to exclude the formal notification of capability if it can be shown that all reasonable adjustments had already been made.

Employees with learning difficulties such as dyslexia, impaired vision, hearing **25.52** difficulties or mobility issues that affect their ability to write may be placed at a substantial disadvantage by the arrangements for assessing who is a suitable candidate for promotion. The extent of the adjustment necessary will depend on the circumstances of both the employer and the disabled employee. Two examples:

- **Pritchard v Foreign and Commonwealth Office** ET Case No.2202354/09: P had been profoundly deaf from birth and, as with most people with profound life-long deafness, she experienced considerable difficulty in understanding and communicating in written and spoken English. She was employed by P as an administrative officer and she applied for promotion to the next grade. This required her to pass a written test and she asked the FCO to provide a BSL/English interpreter to translate the questions. It refused but said it would provide an interpreter to convey instructions given orally. P sat the test but was not successful and she claimed that the FCO had failed to make the reasonable adjustment of providing the interpreter she had requested. An employment tribunal dismissed her claim, finding that the test ensured that candidates would have a sufficient command of written English to cope with the work at the higher level. It would be neither reasonable nor practicable to promote a candidate to the next level if the work could only be done with full-time professional support

- **Haynes v Chief Constable of Gloucestershire Constabulary** ET Case No.1400859/08: an occupational health assessment by the Constabulary established that H had dyslexia, which impaired his ability to read, write, assimilate and integrate new information under time constraints. When H was preparing to go before a promotion board, the Constabulary determined that it would be appropriate to delay the interview so that H could receive proper support, give him the questions he was to be asked 90 minutes

825

before the interview, and provide him with coaching sessions. Despite these adjustments, H did not pass the promotion board. He applied for promotion the next year, but sought as an adjustment an assessment made solely on workplace assessments and reports. However, the Constabulary refused and required that H complete an application form, setting out in 250 words evidence as to why he should be promoted. He was rejected on the initial sift of applications and claimed discrimination by way of a failure to make reasonable adjustments. The employment tribunal did not consider that the Constabulary had failed in respect of the first promotion board, since it had made all the necessary adjustments to remove the disadvantage. However, it did consider that, on the second application for promotion, the requirement for H to set out in no more than 250 words his competences and abilities did put him at a disadvantage; a reasonable adjustment would have been to call him to an interview to explore this point. The tribunal rejected the argument that it would have been a reasonable adjustment to dispense with the promotion board altogether, since there would still have been a need for an interview which carried with it the same adjustments as were reasonable for the promotion board.

25.53 As with recruitment, the means of assessing candidates for promotion should reflect skills the successful candidate will actually need to apply in the role. In Wakefield v HM Land Registry ET Case No.2613066/06 W suffered from a stammer, although he had successfully been able to communicate with people as part of his job. He believed that his speech impediment, which worsened in stressful situations, damaged him at interviews that were essential for him to gain further promotion. He asked for an adjustment whereby he would be assessed on his merits, but without any oral examination. The employer refused, and claimed that to judge W only on written work would be to put him at a disadvantage. Having found that the employer had to make reasonable adjustments, an employment tribunal recommended that in future interviews W should be given pre-agreed questions in advance to enable him to provide written answers and held that if the job in question required specific oral communication skills, any testing should be related specifically to the skills required, rather than using an interview as a test of his general oral skills.

It may be the case that, having provisionally offered promotion to a disabled employee, the employer has to withdraw the offer because there are no reasonable adjustments that would enable the employee to fulfil the new role. In such circumstances, the question for an employment tribunal is whether the employer's conclusion on the adjustments was correct. For example, in Cordell v Foreign and Commonwealth Office 2012 ICR 280, EAT,who was deaf, worked for the FCO in Warsaw supported by professional lipspeakers. In 2009 she was offered promotion to a role in Kazakhstan, subject to an assessment of whether, and at what cost, her disability could be accommodated there. The FCO concluded that even if support could be found, which was uncertain, it would be prohibitively expensive – a yearly cost in the region of five times C's annual salary – and so it withdrew the offer. C claimed direct discrimination – on the basis that the FCO could potentially pay out a similar sum in a school fees allowance for the children of staff posted overseas – and a failure to make reasonable adjustments. The tribunal did not consider staff with children to be an appropriate comparator, and further took the view that the reason C was not appointed was the prohibitive cost, rather than her disability. The adjustments C proposed would be of disproportionate expense, amounting to almost the entire staff budget of the embassy, so it followed that they were not reasonable.

On appeal, the EAT upheld both findings. On direct discrimination, it agreed **25.54** that the school fees allowance was not an appropriate point of comparison, noting that C would be eligible for that allowance herself if she had children of school age. Turning to reasonable adjustments, the EAT noted that tribunals are required to make a judgement on how much it is reasonable to expect employers to spend based on what the tribunal considers right and just in its capacity as an industrial jury. This may include a number of considerations, such as the size of any budget for reasonable adjustments, what the employer has spent in comparable situations, what other employers are prepared to spend and the policy set out in any applicable collective agreement. However, such considerations, even where they have been identified, can be of no more than suggestive or supportive value – there is no objective measure for assessing one kind of expenditure against another. It was clear to the EAT that the tribunal had not been distracted by the cost of the adjustments relative to the embassy staff budget and C's annual salary, but had instead been putting the amounts into context as part of the consideration of reasonableness.

Transfer
25.55

Discrimination claims turning on a denial of access to opportunities for transfer are less common than claims about promotion or training. If a person brings a claim based on his or her failure to get a better job in another part of the employer's organisation, it will probably be on the basis of a denial of access to promotion. Transfer cases will generally relate to situations in which someone has failed to secure an equivalent job in another part of the organisation. This is most likely to occur in redundancy and reorganisation situations.

In cases where the employee is forced to transfer against his or her wishes (allegedly because of a protected characteristic), the claim is likely to fall within the 'any other detriment' provisions in S.39(2)(d) (see under 'Any other detriment' below) rather than the 'transfer' provisions of S.39(2)(b). However, this is not universally so. In Bradford Health Authority v Ramtohul EAT 250/88 (a race discrimination case), for example, a Mauritian charge nurse succeeded in a complaint under a provision equivalent to S.39(2)(b) when he was required to transfer against his wishes to a different hospital after failing to be promoted.

25.56 As with recruitment and promotion, an employer's ability to defend a claim of discrimination arising out of the way it affords opportunities for transfer will be greatly enhanced if it adheres to an equal opportunities policy and ensures that the selection process is objective and transparent. A lack of transparency and a failure to adhere to pre-defined standards are both factors which, coupled with a difference in treatment between a person having a protected characteristic and a person who does not have that protected characteristic, are likely to contribute to a tribunal inferring discrimination. Two cases in which tribunals have inferred discriminatory reasons for a transfer:

- **Backer v Chief Constable of Greater Manchester Police** ET Case No.2402981/07: B, a Sikh of Indian origin, made a number of applications to transfer from his role with West Yorkshire Police to Greater Manchester Police, but all his requests were denied. He submitted a race relations questionnaire and, dissatisfied with the response, brought a race discrimination claim. The tribunal considered that the answers to the questionnaire were evasive and, coupled with the fact that the Greater Manchester force was nowhere near its stated target for recruitment of ethnic minority officers, this was enough to shift the burden on to the employer to explain its conduct. The tribunal was 'unconvinced' by the employer's explanation, with the result that it upheld the claim

- **Harper v Moulton College** ET Case No.1200970/09: H, who was 58 years old, was employed in a role overseeing training advisers. L, who was 34 years old, held the same role. H was called to a meeting where she was told that she was to be relocated, and would be required to undertake different duties. Her working hours would also change. She was unhappy about the attempt to impose such a unilateral change and lodged a grievance. She subsequently went on sick leave, suffering from stress. When her grievance was dismissed, she resigned and claimed unfair dismissal and age discrimination. In respect of the discrimination complaint, an employment tribunal noted that L had not been required to transfer. The employer argued that H had a lower case-load than L and so was more suitable for transfer. However, the tribunal found this reason to be disingenuous, as H's case-load was actually higher. Accordingly, it inferred that the real reason H was being transferred was that she was approaching the end of her working life (in conventional terms), whereas L had considerably more years' work ahead of her.

25.57 If, as in the case above, an employer decides to transfer an employee because of the employee's age, the employer will have an opportunity to show that that decision was justified as a proportionate means of achieving a legitimate aim (provided that the employer has pleaded justification – which the employer failed to do in Harper). However, such an argument will have to be highly convincing if it is to succeed. In one high profile case, O'Reilly v British Broadcasting Corporation and anor ET Case No.2200423/10, the BBC contended that its decision to transfer a 51-year-old female presenter from a television programme when it moved to a primetime slot, and replace her with younger presenters, was justified as a means of achieving its aim of appealing to primetime audiences, including younger viewers. However, an employment tribunal found that, although the aim was legitimate, choosing younger presenters was not necessary to appeal to such an audience and, even if it were, it would not be proportionate to do away with older presenters simply to pander to the assumed prejudice of younger viewers.

In some circumstances an employer may need to consider transferring a disabled employee to another post or another workplace if the employer's provisions, criteria and practices, the physical features of the workplace, or the non-provision of an auxiliary aid place that employee at a substantial disadvantage when compared to a non-disabled person. In Chief Constable of South Yorkshire v Jelic 2010 IRLR 744, EAT, the Appeal Tribunal upheld the finding of an employment tribunal that it would be a reasonable adjustment for the police force to swap J's role with another job which was occupied by F. The EAT stressed that a tribunal is not precluded from holding that it would be a reasonable adjustment to create a new job for a disabled employee if the particular facts of the case support such a finding. A significant factor in this decision was that the police force was a disciplined environment and F could simply have been ordered to move out of his job. This suggests that such an adjustment would rarely be considered reasonable in civilian workplaces where more account would have to be taken of the views of those affected by the adjustment.

25.58 Note that employers should take care when making arrangements to transfer disabled employees who have reasonable adjustments already in place. It is not safe to assume that adjustments which are appropriate in one workplace will be appropriate for all workplaces, and a fresh assessment and consultation with the employee would be a prudent course of action.

Training
25.59

The majority of employers provide job-related training of some sort. Aside from initial training and continuing development of core job skills offered to, or imposed on, all workers as a matter of course, many employers offer training aimed at progressing employees' careers. This type of training can range from basic courses in areas such as IT or health and safety to preparation for professional qualifications. Training of this sort can confer a sizeable benefit on the worker, not only in terms of his or her continued progression through the ranks in his or her current employment but also in developing skills that make him or her more attractive to employers generally. It is necessary, therefore, that the provision of training be open to all workers on a non-discriminatory basis.

829

In order to prove discrimination, it is sufficient for an individual to show that the employer *failed to consider* him or her for training because of a protected characteristic. There is no requirement to show that he or she actually applied for training and was rejected. In one sex discrimination case, McDonald v Fife Health Board ET Case No.S/1423/84, a female employee was not considered for training on a new machine despite having longer service than, and comparable qualifications to, the man selected. M claimed that she had been denied access to training because she had rejected the sexual advances of a male senior colleague who recommended employees for training. The tribunal held that M could not base her claim on her failure to be selected because the final decision on who should be trained did not rest with her alleged harasser. However, they did hold that there was an act of discrimination in not considering M for selection because, given her experience, she should have been in the running. They concluded that the principal reason M was not considered was that she had rebuffed her colleague's advances. He had then treated her less favourably on the ground of sex by not recommending her, and this denied her access to the opportunity for training.

25.60 Employers should be very wary of basing decisions about who should be offered training on assumptions about the value of offering training to different age groups of worker. For example, some businesses may have an age-related cut-off point for access to training, based on the assumption that older workers are soon to leave the world of work and are therefore less in need of training. A refusal of a training opportunity because of age will have to be objectively justified if the employer is to avoid direct age discrimination liability. In Baker v National Air Traffic Services Ltd ET Case No.2203501/07 (a case concerning an age bar in recruitment) an employment tribunal accepted that seeking to provide a reasonable period of post-qualification service, so as to justify the cost of training, was a potentially legitimate aim. However, an absolute bar on employees over a certain age receiving training is unlikely to be considered a proportionate means of achieving such an aim, given the existence of less discriminatory alternatives: an employer seeking to ensure a return on expensive training can make decisions on a case-by-case basis, and where necessary protect its position by entering into an agreement that the employee will refund some or all of the cost of training if he or she leaves before the end of a specified period.

25.61 **Reasonable adjustments and training.** If aspects of an employer's training arrangements place a disabled employee at a substantial disadvantage when compared with a non-disabled employee, the employer will need to consider what adjustments might remove that disadvantage. The EHRC Employment Code recommends that: '[I]f a worker with a mobility impairment is expected to be attending a course, it is likely to be a reasonable adjustment for the employer to select a training venue with adequate disabled access. An employer may need to make training manuals, slides or other visual media accessible to a visually impaired worker (perhaps by providing Braille versions or having materials read out), or ensure that an induction loop is available for someone with a hearing impairment' – para 17.72.

The type of adjustment needed will depend on the individual requirements of the disabled person. In Huskisson v Abbey National plc ET Case No.5000954/00 H, who was dyslexic, undertook initial training to be a financial adviser. He encountered difficulties in conducting interviews and in tailoring his product knowledge to suit customers' needs. He wrote to the employer suggesting that his problems were caused by his dyslexia. The employer concluded that H's lack of progress meant that further training would be of no use and it dismissed him. The employment tribunal found that the problems H experienced during his training were precisely the type described and predicted by H's expert witness, a psychologist specialising in dyslexia. At no stage did the employer consider obtaining expert advice about whether H's problems were linked to his dyslexia. The tribunal found that dismissal was not justified and that the employer had also failed to make reasonable adjustments, such as providing an adequate level of supervision and an electronic organiser and allowing him more time.

25.62 Where an employee develops a disability that prevents him or her from continuing in the existing job, the employer should consider redeploying the employee as an alternative to dismissal as part of the duty to make reasonable adjustments. This may involve providing training for the employee to prepare him or her for the new post. In Lee v Norfolk Mental Healthcare NHS Trust ET Case No.1502125/00, for example, L was a qualified carpenter and joiner who began to suffer from back pain in 1994. The employer made some arrangements to help him carry out his work. In 1995 and 1996 L applied for three internal vacancies which would have resulted in him doing jobs that would not have affected his back. He was not successful but was put on lighter duties. In 1997 he began to suffer problems with his sinuses, aggravated by dust and fumes in the workshop. The employer carried out a risk assessment and it showed a clear risk to L in respect of his back and sinus problems. L applied for two further posts but was again unsuccessful. In March 2001 he applied for and was granted ill-health retirement. An employment tribunal held that while the employer had made some adjustments, it had not taken sufficient steps to help L find a new post where his disability would not place him at a substantial disadvantage. He could have undertaken one of the posts for which he applied had he been given training, and the tribunal considered that the provision of that training would have been a reasonable adjustment.

However, a refusal to allow a disabled person to undergo training may be justified on health and safety grounds. In Forbes v Department of Social Security ET Case No.2101506/00 the employer refused to allow F to attend a visiting officer training course because of his epilepsy and the fact that he did not have a driving licence. A report from F's GP and the employer's occupational health

831

department concluded that there was a risk of him having an epileptic fit while on a home visit. He had grand mal epilepsy and had a fit about every three months. This possibility posed a health and safety risk to both F and the person he was visiting. The decision not to allow him to attend the course was confirmed. An employment tribunal held that the employer was justified in refusing to allow him to attend the course because of health and safety concerns. There was no cost-effective adjustment that could be made.

25.63 Benefits, facilities and services

It is unlawful by virtue of S.39(2)(b) for an employer to discriminate when providing employees with access to opportunities for receiving benefits, facilities or services. A similar prohibition applies to victimisation – S.39(4)(b). While there is no statutory definition of what amounts to a benefit, facility or service, para 14.14 of the EHRC Employment Code advises that benefits can be contractual or discretionary and can include: 'canteens, meal vouchers, social clubs and other recreational activities, dedicated car parking spaces, discounts on products, bonuses, share options, hairdressing, clothes allowances, financial services, healthcare, medical assistance/insurance, transport to work, company car, education assistance, workplace nurseries, and rights to special leave'. This list is non-exhaustive. (Note that as benefits, facilities and services can be contractual, there is considerable overlap with S.39(2)(a), which is considered under 'Terms of employment' above.)

Discrimination by organisations contracted by an employer to provide facilities, benefits or services to its employees is not covered by the employment provisions in Part 5 of the EqA, but is instead dealt with in Part 3 of the Act, which covers discrimination by service providers. Those provisions fall outside the scope of this Handbook.

25.64 Section 39(2)(b) should not be interpreted as requiring employers to provide the same benefits, facilities and services to all employees. In essence, employers can discriminate in respect of these matters on grounds such as seniority, the nature of the job, and the employee's performance; what employers cannot do is discriminate on any of the grounds prescribed by the EqA. (Note, however, that there is an exemption from the age discrimination provisions in respect of 'benefits' awarded with reference to a length-of-service criterion of up to five years, and of over five years where the employer reasonably believes that providing the benefit 'fulfils a business need' – para 10, Sch 9 EqA. This exemption is discussed in Chapter 31, 'Specific exceptions', under 'Age exceptions'.)

If an employer assumes that, because of an employee's protected characteristic, he or she would have no interest in a benefit, facility or service – say, for example, free gym membership – and the employer fails to offer it as a result,

832

this will amount to direct discrimination if the failure amounts to less favourable treatment. In this respect, a tribunal is likely to consider whether the employee actually had an interest in the benefit, facility or service concerned, or whether the employer's assumption is correct. It may, however, be the case that a failure to offer a benefit, facility or service to a disabled employee who could not or would not want to take up the offer could nevertheless amount to less favourable treatment due to the sense of exclusion it creates.

Where conditions are attached to the provision of a benefit, facility or service, **25.65** these could amount to indirect discrimination under S.18 EqA if they place a protected group at a particular disadvantage and cannot be objectively justified. The same conditions could also amount to discrimination arising from disability contrary to S.15 if they are harder to satisfy for a disabled employee because of something arising as a consequence of his or her disability. As with indirect discrimination, the employer would have to show that the conditions were objectively justified as a proportionate means of achieving a legitimate aim. For example, many employers run absence management schemes which reward employees for not having taken a day's sickness absence during a set period. An employee who has to take a number of disability-related sickness absences would suffer unfavourable treatment for the purposes of S.15 as a result and the employer would need to show that the application of the scheme was a proportionate means of minimising sickness absence. The employee could also argue that the terms for accessing the scheme placed people sharing his or her disability at a particular disadvantage and therefore amounted to indirect discrimination, requiring the employer to show that the conditions applied were a proportionate means of achieving a legitimate aim. However, given that establishing discrimination arising from disability does not require evidence that the provision, criterion or practice applied by the employer affected people with the employee's disability generally, rather than just the employee, most claims challenging the conditions on which benefits, facilities or services are afforded are likely to be brought under S.15, rather than S.18.

Where the conditions attached to the provision of a benefit, facility or service put disabled employees at a substantial disadvantage in relation to non-disabled employees, the employer will also need to consider amending any qualification criteria as a reasonable adjustment under S.20 EqA.

In some circumstances, it would be considered a reasonable adjustment to **25.66** extend to a disabled employee a benefit, facility or service that he or she would not normally receive in order to remove a substantial disadvantage the employee experiences as a result of the employer's provisions, criteria and practices, the physical features of the workplace, or the lack of an auxiliary aid. The EHRC Employment Code provides two examples in this respect:

'An employer arranges for a colleague to read mail to a worker with a visual impairment at particular times during the working day. Alternatively, the employer might hire a reader' – para 6.33.

'An employer has a policy that designated car parking spaces are only offered to senior managers. A worker who is not a manager, but has a mobility impairment and needs to park very close to the office, is given a designated car-parking space. This is likely to be a reasonable adjustment to the employer's car-parking policy' – para 6.10.

25.67 Insurance

One type of benefit that causes particular problems when it comes to anti-discrimination law is insurance. The key problem here is that the insurance industry is in the business of discriminating – it uses characteristics such as age, sex, race, religion, sexual orientation and disability to profile risk and arrive at an insurance premium for a given policy. So, for example, whereas an employer is under an obligation not to discriminate in the way that it affords employees access to medical insurance, the price quoted for that insurance, and indeed the availability of the insurance, may vary substantially from employee to employee.

Employers are afforded some assistance in this regard by para 20 of Schedule 9 to the EqA. This states that 'it is not a contravention of this Part of this Act, so far as relating to relevant discrimination, to do anything in relation to an annuity, life insurance policy, accident insurance policy or similar matter involving the assessment of risk if (a) that thing is done by reference to actuarial or other data from a source on which it is reasonable to rely, and (b) it is reasonable to do it'. 'Relevant discrimination', for this purpose, is defined by para 20(2) as gender reassignment discrimination, marriage and civil partnership discrimination, pregnancy and maternity discrimination and sex discrimination. The effect of these provisions, as noted by the Explanatory Notes, is that the employer may, for example, legitimately provide for payments of premiums that differ for men and women, so long as this is reasonable in the light of actuarial or other reliable data. See further Chapter 30, 'General exceptions', under 'Insurance contracts'.

25.68 One way in which employers have sought to deal with the discriminatory nature of the insurance market is to provide flexible benefits packages. These usually provide a set amount to be spent on a menu of benefits such as medical and dental insurance, health club membership, etc. From an employer's perspective, the advantage of such a scheme is that any discrimination in the provision of insurance is on the part of the insurer, not the employer. This much was demonstrated in Swann v GHL Insurance Services UK Ltd Case No.2306281/07, where the employer's flexible benefits scheme included private medical insurance (PMI) where premiums were payable by the employees, although certain eligible employees were awarded a limited 'flex fund' with which to purchase benefits under the scheme. When that fund was exhausted, those employees could purchase extra benefits by way of a salary sacrifice. The cost of premiums under the PMI was age-related. S, aged 51, purchased PMI under the flexible benefits scheme. She qualified for the flex fund but, because of the amount of PMI that she wanted to purchase, she also bought extra by way of salary sacrifice. She alleged direct age discrimination in the employment tribunal because the premiums under the PMI were more costly for her than they would be for a younger employee. The tribunal dismissed the claim, holding that, for the purpose of determining whether S was subjected to less favourable treatment on the ground of age, the relevant treatment was the provision of an amount of money for an employee to purchase one or more benefits from within the flexible benefits package; such treatment was 'not related to the age of an employee'.

A key concern expressed by employers responding to the consultations on the abolition of the default retirement age (DRA) was that they would be exposed to age discrimination claims due to their inability to provide benefits such as life assurance, health insurance and medical insurance to employees aged over 65, as those employees would fall outside the terms of the company insurance policy. This concern is now addressed by para 14(1) of Schedule 9 to the EqA, which provides that it will not be an act of age discrimination for an employer 'to make arrangements for, or afford access to, the provision of insurance or a related financial service to or in respect of an employee for a period ending when the employee attains whichever is the greater of (a) the age of 65 and, (b) the state pensionable age'. In very similar terms, para 14(2) provides that it will not be an act of age discrimination to provide such services only to employees who have not attained the greater of those two ages. Note, however, that these exemptions only apply where the insurance or related financial service is, or is to be, provided to the employer's employees or a class of those employees in pursuance of an arrangement between the employer and another person; or where the employer's business includes the provision of insurance or financial services of the description in question, by the employer – para 14(3).

Enhanced redundancy schemes

25.69

Many employers operate enhanced redundancy schemes, which provide for an employee to receive a sum above and beyond the statutory redundancy payment should he or she be dismissed by reason of redundancy. Although discrimination in such schemes is considered here on the basis that such payments represent a benefit and therefore fall within S.39(2)(b), claims may also be brought under S.39(2)(a) if the entitlement to an enhanced redundancy payment is contractual.

Much like the statutory redundancy payments scheme provided for in the Employment Rights Act 1996 (ERA), enhanced redundancy schemes have, historically at least, used age as a differentiating factor when determining the sum an employee will receive upon redundancy. Under para 13 of Schedule 9

835

to the EqA, there is a specific exemption from the age discrimination rules for any enhanced redundancy scheme modelled on the statutory scheme that applies multipliers based on the statutory redundancy payment multipliers (considered in detail in Chapter 31, 'Specific exceptions', under 'Age exceptions'). The statutory multipliers, prescribed under S.162 ERA, provide that a redundant employee is entitled to half a week's pay in respect of every year of employment under the age of 22; a week's pay for every year between the ages of 22 and 40; and one and a half weeks' pay for every year aged 41 and over, subject to an overall maximum of 20 years.

25.70 Where an enhanced scheme is not modelled on the statutory scheme, any discrimination because of age will fall to be objectively justified. Three decisions of the EAT have considered the justification question in this context. In the first, MacCulloch v Imperial Chemical Industries plc 2008 ICR 1334, EAT, M, who was aged 36, received a severance payment based on a combination of age and length of service. Her payment amounted to 55 per cent of gross annual salary. By contrast, an employee with ten years' service who had reached the age of 50 would have received 175 per cent of gross salary. An employment tribunal found that the redundancy scheme directly and indirectly discriminated against M but that the discrimination was justified. ICI plc's aim of encouraging and rewarding loyalty was legitimate, as was its objective of protecting older employees by giving them a larger financial payment. The tribunal also accepted that the scheme, being generous, was extremely popular, and that as a result compulsory redundancies were avoided and it was easier to manage change. The scheme was therefore a proportionate means of achieving a legitimate aim. M appealed to the EAT.

Upholding the appeal, the EAT held that while the tribunal had identified certain legitimate aims of the scheme, it had not properly determined if the measures adopted were proportionate ways of achieving those aims. The principal features that the tribunal appeared to consider were the generosity and general acceptance of the scheme. In the EAT's view, while these features may well be relevant in helping to achieve the aims of the scheme, they did not deal at all with the issue of whether the difference in treatment was justified. Nor was there any recognition of the degree of difference in payment made to M and the chosen comparator, and an assessment as to whether this was reasonably necessary to achieve the scheme's objective. While refusing to rule out the possibility that a scheme such as ICI plc's may be justified, the EAT concluded that the analysis needed to reach that conclusion was lacking from the tribunal's decision.

25.71 Although that was enough to deal with the MacCulloch appeal, Mr Justice Elias, then President of the EAT, went on to offer views on legitimate aims in this context. He rejected M's argument that the tribunal had simply taken what ICI plc had asserted to be the scheme's aims at face value rather than determining

836

whether these were in fact the true aims of the scheme. In Elias P's view, the tribunal had been entitled to accept the employer's objective of rewarding loyalty as the reason for linking payments to length of service. He also approved the tribunal's finding that encouraging turnover and facilitating career progression for other staff are, in principle, capable of being legitimate aims that might be furthered by increasing payments for older workers. In addition, he considered that, as regards ICI plc's aim of helping older employees who are particularly vulnerable in the job market, it was not necessary for ICI plc to produce evidence that older workers find it harder to obtain work than younger workers, since the tribunal had been fully entitled to draw on its own experience in this respect. (That last point is of particular interest because, on the basis of the most recent ONS figures on the UK labour market, it actually appears that it is *younger* employees who have more difficulty finding work in the current environment. It should also be noted that the MacCulloch appeal was heard three years before the repeal of the default retirement age of 65.)

The second case, Loxley v BAE Systems Land Systems (Munitions and Ordnance) Ltd 2008 ICR 1348, EAT, concerned a scheme which gave an entitlement to a redundancy payment based mainly on length of service. However, only those under 60 were so entitled, and those aged between 57 and 60 had their payments reduced according to tapering provisions. L was 61 at the time he agreed to take redundancy and was not entitled to the contractual redundancy payment. The rationale for excluding those over 60 was that, until 1996, employees were required to retire at 60 and could do so on a full pension. The tapering requirements and the exclusion of the over-60s were designed to prevent those close to retirement from receiving a windfall in the event that they were made redundant. In 1996 the retirement age was raised to 65, although until 1 April 2006 employees could still take their pension at 60 without incurring a penalty to their accrued benefits. An employment tribunal rejected L's claim, finding the scheme justified by the need to prevent employees close to retirement receiving a windfall. The tribunal also thought that the fact that the scheme had been agreed in consultation with trade unions went some way to support the contention that it was justified.

On appeal the EAT – also presided over by Elias P – considered that the **25.72** tribunal's decision could not stand. As in MacCulloch v Imperial Chemical Industries (above), the tribunal had not fully engaged with the question of proportionality. Nor could it be said that the tribunal had undertaken the necessary analysis of financial information to determine whether L's exclusion from the scheme achieved a legitimate aim. Elias P went on to state that the fact that an employee is entitled to immediate benefits under a pension scheme will always be a highly relevant factor that an employer can properly consider when determining what redundancy rights, if any, the employee ought to receive. No doubt in some, perhaps many, cases it will justify excluding such an employee from the redundancy scheme altogether. However, this is not inevitably the case. Ultimately, it must depend upon the nature of both schemes. The fact that an agreement is made with the trade unions is potentially a relevant consideration when determining whether treatment is proportionate. Plainly, the imprimatur of the trade union does not render an otherwise unlawful scheme lawful, but any tribunal will rightly attach some significance to the fact that the collective parties have agreed a scheme which they consider to be fair. There is, however, always the risk that the parties will have been influenced, consciously or unconsciously, by traditional assumptions relating to age. Hence the reason why any justification relied upon by the employer, even when the treatment under consideration is supported by the union, must be subject to critical appraisal.

The final case is Kraft Foods UK Ltd v Hastie 2010 ICR 1355, EAT. There, after almost 40 years' employment with KF Ltd, H took voluntary redundancy in 2008. Under the company's redundancy scheme, employees were entitled to three-and-a-half weeks' pay for each year of service, which, in H's case, translated into £90,100. However, the scheme provided that the maximum amount payable on redundancy should not exceed the amount the employee would have earned, at his or her current rate of pay, if he or she had remained in employment until the normal retirement age of 65. As a result, H's redundancy payment – given that he was just over two years away from his 65th birthday – was capped at £76,560. H complained to an employment tribunal, alleging that the application of the cap – resulting in a reduction of almost £14,000 to his redundancy payment – amounted to indirect age discrimination. An employment tribunal found that although the redundancy scheme itself pursued a number of legitimate aims – such as the need to reward long service and manage change effectively – the imposition of a cap did not pursue a legitimate aim. Moreover, even if it had accepted the company's submission that preventing an employee from receiving a windfall shortly before his or her 65th birthday amounted to a legitimate aim, it would have decided that the company had failed to strike a proportionate balance between its needs and the PCP's discriminatory effect on H. Accordingly, the tribunal found that the cap was not justified.

25.73 On appeal, the case was heard by Mr Justice Underhill – Elias P's successor as President of the EAT. Having examined the scheme in question, he considered that its purpose was to compensate employees who took voluntary redundancy for the loss of the earnings which they had a legitimate expectation of receiving if their employment had continued. Although redundancy schemes, whether contractual or statutory, do not directly link the payments to the loss, Underhill P considered that this anomaly is long-established and rooted in industrial practice. Given the scheme's purpose, unless a cap was incorporated into the scheme, payments to employees who were close to retirement would exceed what was necessary to cover the amount of their future loss of earnings. By way of illustration, an employee with H's earnings and length of service, who was made redundant at the age of 64 years and 11 months, would receive £90,000

838

compensation for the loss of the chance to earn some £3,000 in the remaining month of his or her employment. It necessarily followed that it was a legitimate aim to prevent such excess compensation. In Underhill P's view, the tribunal had lost sight of this aim by wrongly taking into account the fact that employees who were affected by the cap and those who were not would equally be entitled to receive full pensions (at least if they were aged over 60). Entitlement to a pension was an issue entirely independent and separate of the windfall argument.

On the question of whether the cap was a proportionate means of achieving the aim of preventing a windfall, H argued that the cap essentially performed the same role as a taper, such as had existed in the statutory redundancy scheme prior to the introduction of the Employment Equality (Age) Regulations 2006 SI 2006/1031. Since the taper had been removed at the time unjustified age discrimination in employment was outlawed, H contended that the Government had recognised that a practice of this kind could not be justified. Underhill P acknowledged that there were similarities between the cap and a taper. However, he did not accept H's argument for two reasons. First, looking at the consultation papers that preceded the Age Regulations, it was not safe to infer that the Government had considered the practice of tapering to be unjustifiable. Secondly, Underhill P thought that the cap was a more accurate means of preventing a windfall than a taper. Since a cap and a taper were the two common means of achieving this aim, it followed that the more accurate means – the cap – was proportionate. The imposition of the cap was therefore justified and the appeal would be allowed.

25.74 The jurisprudence on age discrimination in enhanced redundancy schemes is still in its infancy, and its future development will no doubt be heavily influenced by the fact that, as of 1 October 2011, the default retirement age of 65 has been abolished. This development could prove particularly important to questions of proportionality.

'Any other detriment' **25.75**

By virtue of S.39(2)(d) EqA, an employer must not discriminate against an employee 'by subjecting him or her to any other detriment'. A similar provision applies to victimisation – S.39(4)(d). These are 'catch-all' provisions designed to cover anything not caught by S.39(2)(a)–(c) and (4)(a)–(c) (considered in the sections above).

Meaning of detriment **25.76**
The term 'detriment' is widely used in the EqA but, in common with the discrimination legislation that preceded it, the Act offers no statutory definition of the term. However, that is not to say that courts and tribunals lack guidance in this respect: the right not to be subjected to a detriment on prohibited grounds is an important aspect of modern employment law, with provisions

839

being found in a number of legislative enactments in addition to the EqA. As a result, the appeal courts have frequently been called upon to consider the boundaries of this familiar term and we consider some of this jurisprudence below. In addition, the EHRC Employment Code advises that 'generally, a detriment is anything which the individual concerned might reasonably consider changed their position for the worse or put them at a disadvantage' – para 9.8.

In Ministry of Defence v Jeremiah 1980 ICR 13, CA, the Court of Appeal took a wide view of the words 'any other detriment'. Lord Justice Brandon said it meant simply 'putting under a disadvantage', while Lord Justice Brightman stated that a detriment 'exists if a reasonable worker would or might take the view that [the action of the employer] was in all the circumstances to his detriment'. Subsequent judgments of the Court of Appeal have concurred with this broad approach. For example, in De Souza v Automobile Association 1986 ICR 514, CA, the Court said the term meant 'disadvantaged in the circumstances and conditions' of work. According to Lord Justice May, the question is to be considered 'from the point of view of the victim. If the victim's opinion that the treatment was to his or her detriment is a reasonable one to hold, that ought, in my opinion, to suffice.'

25.77 This view was approved by the House of Lords in Shamoon v Chief Constable of the Royal Ulster Constabulary 2003 ICR 337, HL, where their Lordships emphasised that a sense of grievance which is not justified will not be sufficient to constitute a detriment. However, the Court of Appeal had erred in finding that S had not suffered a detriment when she had been barred from carrying out appraisals of more junior officers on the basis that, in order to constitute a detriment, the claimant had to demonstrate that she had suffered some physical or economic consequence that was materially to her detriment. The House of Lords held that the Court of Appeal had erred in law in this respect, in that there is no requirement for the claimant to show that he or she has suffered some physical or economic consequence. This echoed the Court of Session's decision in Porcelli v Strathclyde Regional Council 1986 ICR 564, Ct Sess (Inner House), where it was said that 'detriment' simply meant 'disadvantage'. A more restrictive approach was firmly rejected. Accordingly, there is no need to establish that the employer's actions had consequences in terms of the employee's contract of employment – for example, demotion – in order to show detriment.

In Moyhing v Barts and London NHS Trust 2006 IRLR 860, EAT, a male nurse, M, was required, pursuant to hospital policy, not to carry out certain intimate duties involving women without being chaperoned by a female member of staff. M brought a claim of sex discrimination before an employment tribunal. It was common ground that M had been treated less favourably on the ground of his sex, in that female trainee nurses were not required to be chaperoned when performing intimate procedures on male patients. The tribunal held that the hospital's policy was logical and there were good and sound reasons for adopting it. Therefore, M's objection was unjustifiable and the policy could not be regarded as having given rise to a detriment. The EAT, however, held that the tribunal had erred in finding that M's claim that he had suffered a detriment was undermined by his 'unjustified objection' to the Trust's policy on chaperoning. Direct discrimination, it reiterated, could not be justified, and the fact that there may be good and sound reasons for distinguishing between men and women was no defence. The tribunal's assumption that, where the reason for a discriminatory policy is cogent and rational, that policy cannot lead to a detriment, was clearly wrong, and would have the effect of allowing justification for direct discrimination in through the back door.

Finally, in Rhys-Harper v Relaxion Group plc (and other consolidated cases) **25.78** 2003 ICR 867, HL, the House of Lords held that a failure to provide a non-contractual benefit will not normally constitute a detriment, unless it is a benefit which is normally provided or would be provided to others in comparable circumstances. So, a former employee who was refused a reference in circumstances in which other former employees were not might be able to claim to have suffered an unlawful detriment under the EqA, if a protected characteristic were proved to be the reason for the difference in treatment.

Examples of 'any other detriment'. It would be impossible to list every type of **25.79** detriment an employee could suffer. It may be useful, however, to give a few examples of the sort of treatment that has been found to amount to a detriment:

- a failure to investigate an employee's complaints that her work colleagues were harassing her – Race v University of York ET Case No.1806953/00

- a failure to tell a diabetic employee that he was only being removed from his job temporarily pending medical investigation and leading him to believe that he was being removed permanently – Garrett v Brotherwood Automobility Ltd ET Case No.3101189/00

- inconsistent treatment by not automatically slotting a disabled employee into a new post when his job disappeared following a restructuring exercise – Ludgate v London Borough of Brent ET Case No.3300069/00

- moving an employee onto another machine in order to separate him from a racist colleague – Deson v BL Cars Ltd EAT 173/80

- applying the sick pay scheme (half-pay) to an employee who became ill while he was suspended on full pay – Owen v Isle of Anglesey County Council ET Case No.2901076/00

- accepting work colleagues' taunting of a partially sighted employee as 'only a joke' – Smith v Trustees of St Andrews Hospital ET Case No.1201904/00

841

- insisting that an employee attend work five days a week when she was only fit to attend three days a week and sought to work at home the remaining two days – Brown v South Bank University ET Case No.2305234/97

- alleging that the employee was 'playing the race card' when making a complaint about his manager – Royal Bank of Scotland plc v Morris EAT 0436/10

- leaving a note in some client paperwork making a derogatory reference to the employee's sexual orientation. Although the note was intended to be private and the employee was never meant to see it, it clearly amounted to a detriment – Bivonas LLP and ors v Bennett EAT 1254/11.

25.80 By way of contrast, the following have been held not to amount to a detriment:

- monitoring incidents involving an employee who had previously brought a discrimination claim – Bayode v Chief Constable of Derbyshire EAT 0499/07

- arranging a seminar at an out-of-office venue which an employee could not attend because of his agoraphobia. Although he was not required to attend, it made him feel excluded and depressed – Ellis v Suffolk County Council ET Case No.1500019/01

- not allowing a blind employee to tape-record a disciplinary hearing to discuss his sickness record where part of the employees' job was to minute meetings, which he did without using a tape recorder – Jelly v South London Dial-a-Ride Ltd ET Case No.2302376/01

- putting a disabled employee on a trial period in relation to his attendance following a prolonged absence when the employer's contractual procedures for doing so were applied equally to all employees – Morrison v Secretary of State for Education and Employment ET Case No.6404862/00

- taking state benefits into account when deciding on the appropriate level of pay during suspension pending a disciplinary investigation – Mills v Ministry of Defence ET Case No.1701178/97.

Two aspects of the employment relationship that can give rise to allegations of discrimination and which generally fall under the category of 'any other detriment' require further consideration: disciplinary and grievance procedures, and standards of dress and appearance in the workplace.

25.81 Disciplinary and grievance procedures

Any disciplinary action taken by an employer against an employee is likely to amount to a detriment for the purposes of S.39(2)(d) and (4)(d) EqA. Similarly, the outcome of a grievance procedure could be a detriment, as could a failure to take disciplinary action against an employee accused of workplace discrimination or harassment.

842

As discrimination can often arise during the disciplinary and grievance process, it is important for employers to put in place clear policies on both equal opportunities and disciplinary procedures, and ensure that these are applied consistently. By having an equal opportunities policy and providing equal opportunities training, an employer has the legal basis for taking disciplinary action against an employee, for example a manager, who breaches the policy by committing an act of discrimination, victimisation or harassment. Moreover, should an employer seek to argue that it is not liable for discrimination carried out by its employees because it took all reasonable steps to prevent the discrimination taking place (see Chapter 28, 'Liability of employers, employees and agents', under 'Employer's liability for acts of employees'), the existence and implementation of an equal opportunities policy is likely to play a significant role in evidence.

Having a disciplinary procedure in place is similarly important, not least **25.82** because it makes the task of investigating allegations of discrimination in the workplace that much more straightforward. More importantly, however, by putting in place a defined process that provides for an objective assessment of where fault lies, employers can reduce the possibility of subjectivity creeping in, thereby reducing the likelihood of discrimination influencing the process.

Subjecting an individual to disciplinary measures that would not have been pursued, or would have been pursued differently, against individuals of a different race can amount to discrimination. In Rasab and ors v John Haggas plc ET Case No.64867/92 and others, for example, complaints of race discrimination arose from the employer's attempt to introduce new working practices. The problem was that the factory at which the employees worked operated a shift system which, for historical reasons, was racially segregated. All day-shift workers were white and all night-shift workers were Asian. The night-shift workers received letters telling them that if they did not comply with new working practices, they would be warned and then dismissed and the night shift would be closed. In the event, 33 of the claimants were not asked to make changes to their working practices and the remaining 49, though they received several warnings, were not dismissed and not required to adopt the new practices. The tribunal had no difficulty, however, in holding that all the claims succeeded. When the white workers had been informed of the coming changes, they had been approached with much more tact and courtesy. There was a history of treating the Asian workers differently from the white workers and this had been reflected in the way in which management had tried to introduce the new practices.

Ensuring consistency, both in the pursuit of disciplinary charges and in the action taken if those charges are proved, is of paramount importance in avoiding claims of direct discrimination. Where inconsistency does arise between employees possessing different protected characteristics, this may be

843

sufficient to shift the burden of proof to the employer to provide a non-discriminatory explanation for the inconsistency.

25.83 An example:

- **Hawkins v Royal Mail Group Ltd and anor** ET Case No.3201304/08: H was employed by RM Ltd as a delivery manager. She moved to a new office in April 2005 and discovered that the previous manager had already told staff that she was a lesbian. Another member of staff at that workplace, B, was also a lesbian. H was unpopular with some of the workforce – feedback forms included comments about her sexual orientation, complaints that she did not know how to talk to men, and allegations of favouritism to B. In 2006 H was transferred to a different office. Shortly afterwards B lodged a grievance that she was being bullied and discriminated against on the ground of her sexual orientation. During the course of the ensuing investigation, allegations were made against H. These were investigated and H was called to a disciplinary hearing where she was dismissed for acting in an inappropriate sexual way with another colleague in front of other employees, failing to tackle verbal harassment and giving out confidential information. She brought claims including sexual orientation discrimination to an employment tribunal, which noted that there were differences in the way complaints against H were dealt with compared to how the complaints made by B against heterosexual employees were managed. In the tribunal's view, RM Ltd had operated to double standards: not investigating serious allegations of homophobic bullying and pursuing charges against H without examining evidence from both sides. Moreover, RM Ltd described it as inappropriate for H to be in a sexual relationship with B when she was her manager, yet another manager had entered into a heterosexual relationship with a woman he managed, and with whom he was publicly affectionate at work, and no action whatsoever was taken against them. The tribunal considered that these inconsistencies, and the generally unreasonable approach RM Ltd took to investigating the allegations against H, required it to seek a high level of proof from the employer that the treatment was not discriminatory. Although RM Ltd pleaded that the investigating officer lacked experience, this was not considered a sufficient explanation, with the result that H had suffered direct sexual orientation discrimination.

25.84 Claims of discrimination often arise where inconsistent disciplinary sanctions are imposed on different employees, where the employees are not of the same gender, race, etc. Employers should therefore be prepared to offer reasons as to why the employee subjected to the harsher sanction was more culpable than his or her colleague. Where no such explanation is forthcoming, this may indicate a degree of bias in the disciplinary process. For example, in Silva v Post Office ET Case No.28686/95 there was an altercation between S, a Sri Lankan, and a white colleague. S was at first dismissed and then, when his appeal was upheld,

844

he was transferred to another site where both his earnings and his opportunities for overtime decreased. More serious allegations had been made against S's white colleague, but a lesser penalty had been imposed on him. There was no logical explanation for the difference in treatment and a tribunal attributed the heavier penalty imposed on S to race discrimination.

Victimisation. It is not unknown for employers to use the disciplinary process **25.85** as a means of 'getting back' at troublesome employees. Where, however, the employer instigates disciplinary action against an employee following his or her involvement, as complainant or witness, in an allegation or claim of workplace discrimination, the action is likely to amount to victimisation. Two examples:

- **Stirrup v Obahor t/a Summers Dry Cleaners** IT Case No.593/10: S had brought an age discrimination claim over SDC's decision to reduce her hours, but had remained in its employment. Subsequently, she was suspended on full pay as a result of two incidents: one involving the loss of a customer's jacket, and the other concerning an insurance receipt. SDC invited her to a disciplinary hearing, but she responded explaining that she was suffering from work-related stress and would not be able to attend a hearing in the workplace. The employer dismissed her for gross misconduct and rejected her appeal. An industrial tribunal (the case took place in Northern Ireland) considered that the grounds for dismissal were 'flimsy to say the least' and found the dismissal to be unfair. On the question of victimisation, the tribunal was satisfied that S had done a protected act (she had brought a claim of age discrimination) and had been subjected to less favourable treatment (a colleague who lost a customer's jacket was neither suspended nor dismissed). On the question of whether that treatment was meted out because of the protected act, the tribunal considered the timeline of events to be 'instructive': S had been suspended on 8 April 2010 while her age discrimination claim was to be heard on 19 April. Adding that to its finding that the allegations against S were ill-founded and the conduct and outcome of the disciplinary process flawed, the tribunal concluded that the core reason for S's dismissal was that she brought the discrimination claim against SDC

- **Taj v GBM Services Ltd** ET Case No.3301281/07: T had lodged a series of grievances after colleagues entered into a campaign of teasing Muslim workers with food during Ramadan. His grievances were not dealt with promptly – and in some cases not at all – and he was subjected to disciplinary action for excessive use of the work telephone system. In addition to finding that the failure to deal adequately with his complaints was in itself discrimination, an employment tribunal found that the disciplinary action was an act of victimisation. The evidence showed that the cost of the phone calls was trivial, inviting no more than informal action. If, contrary to that view, more serious action was warranted, it should have been taken across

845

the workforce after a thorough investigation. No employee other than T had been investigated, which led the tribunal to conclude that he was singled out because of his grievances.

25.86 In seeking to discourage frivolous complaints in the workplace, some disciplinary procedures and policies warn that action will be taken against any employee found to have made a false allegation. However, this can be problematic, as it takes no account of whether the allegation was made in good faith. Under S.27(3) EqA, giving false evidence or information, or making a false allegation, is not a protected act if the evidence or information is given, or the allegation made, in bad faith. But this is not the same as saying that the evidence, information or allegation must be true and if a claimant provides evidence or information, or makes an allegation, in good faith which turns out to be inaccurate, he or she will be regarded as having done a protected act under S.27(2). Thus, employers seeking to avoid liability for victimisation should only take disciplinary action against employees who have made false allegations in bad faith. An example:

- **Bartusek v Northern Leisure Group Ltd** ET Case No.1801849/07: B was a naturalised Briton who came to this country from his native Serbia as a child. He had no particular religious belief but was addressed by his colleagues and others as 'Paki', 'Muslim' and 'Turk' from time to time. In turn, he called his colleagues by nicknames such as 'Scottish Jew' and 'German Nazi bastard'. He was disciplined for making false claims of racial harassment, and claimed he had thereby suffered unlawful victimisation. However, an employment tribunal dismissed his claim, noting that B was on friendly or very friendly terms with his alleged antagonists to an extent wholly inconsistent with his claims. The tribunal concluded that B regarded bringing tribunal proceedings as way of making money out of the sort of things that went on and were said in the workplace but which he embraced and participated in as 'one of the lads'. It followed that the allegations were not made in good faith.

25.87 **Disciplining staff for religious expression at work.** Under S.10 EqA employees have a right not to be discriminated against because of their religious or philosophical beliefs. This does not, however, mean that an employee is free to manifest his or her beliefs in the workplace in whatever way he or she chooses. Case law has established that employers can place restrictions on employees, particularly where manifestation of their beliefs would clash with other anti-discrimination provisions.

The leading case is Ladele v London Borough of Islington and anor 2010 ICR 532, CA, in which L, a registrar, refused to conduct civil partnership services because of her Christian belief that same-sex unions were contrary to God's law. The Court of Appeal agreed with the EAT that the Council did not directly discriminate against L on the ground of religion when it threatened her with dismissal for refusing to carry out the services. The reason for its treatment of her was not her religious belief but her refusal to carry out her duties – the Council required all registrars to carry out marriages and civil partnerships, and L was treated no differently to anyone else. Nor was there indirect discrimination, since the Council had a legitimate aim, which was to provide its services in a non-discriminatory way in accordance with its 'Dignity for All' policy. Requiring L to perform civil partnerships was a proportionate means of achieving that aim. The effect on L of implementing the policy was held not to impinge on her religious beliefs since she remained free to hold those beliefs and to worship as she wished. (For more detailed consideration of this case, and the reference that has been made to the European Court of Human Rights, see Chapter 11, 'Religion or belief', under 'Manifestation of religion or belief – is UK approach compliant with Article 9?'.)

25.88 The distinction between holding religious beliefs and manifesting such beliefs also arose for consideration in Chondol v Liverpool City Council EAT 0298/08. In that case C, a committed Christian, was employed as a social worker on secondment to Mersey Care NHS Trust. The Trust became concerned by what it perceived as C's failure to recognise professional boundaries. For example, he gave a copy of the Bible to a service user, who subsequently complained. Following his eventual dismissal, C brought proceedings claiming, among other things, that his dismissal constituted an act of direct discrimination. The tribunal dismissed the claim. The actual reason for the Trust's treatment of C – namely, the disciplinary action that contributed to his dismissal – was its belief that he had been inappropriately promoting his religion to service users, not his religion itself. The tribunal was satisfied that the Trust would have acted in precisely the same way towards another member of staff regardless of what religion or view (religious or otherwise) it believed was being promoted.

Before the EAT, C's main argument was that the tribunal's decision on direct discrimination was unsustainable as it had constructed the wrong comparator. The correct comparator was someone known to have been either of no belief or of an unrelated belief, which is not similarly protected, and who had behaved in the same manner as C was alleged to have done. The EAT rejected this argument: the tribunal had made it clear that the Trust had not acted on the ground of C's religion, but rather on the ground that he was improperly foisting it on service users. Consequently, the whole question of how to define the correct comparator was academic.

25.89 Two further cases that involved the expression of religious views at work:

- **Maitland v Wilmott and anor** ET Case No.1301020/07: M was a supply teacher who taught religious education (RE). She allegedly referred to some of her pupils as 'devils' and told one girl that she was not good enough to be a Christian, and that if she ever got married it would end in divorce. M's assignment was eventually terminated because she was seen as too 'evangelical'. The tribunal rejected her direct discrimination claim. M's assignment was

847

terminated because, among other things, she was attempting to impose her own religious views rather than teach RE in a factual and objective way

- **Rao v University Hospitals of Leicester NHS Trust** ET Case No.1901029/09: R, who had a strong Christian faith, began working for the Trust as a nurse in 2005. He enrolled for a course in palliative care in May 2008. During one session, students were asked to participate in a simulation where they were expected to discuss the effect of advanced illness on sexual relations with other students acting as patients. R declined to do this because he did not believe that it was appropriate. Instead, he suggested to the 'patient' that she might find visiting a church for an hour helpful, even when she told him that she did not go to church. R also told her that the doctor could not say when she would die as only God could do that. R resigned midway through a disciplinary process for breaching the Nursing and Midwifery Council's Code of Conduct. R's direct discrimination claim was rejected by the employment tribunal. The treatment that he had been subjected to was not on the ground of his religion but on the ground of the inappropriate manifestation of his religion and the reasonable expectation that this would reoccur in the future.

25.90 **Disciplining staff for expression of non-religious beliefs.** There is no overarching right to freedom of expression in the workplace: employers can, and frequently do, discipline employees for expressing views that are offensive, contrary to company policy or liable to damage business. However, disciplining an employee for expressing a philosophical belief that falls within the scope of S.10 EqA could amount to direct discrimination. As explained in Chapter 11, 'Religion or belief', under 'Protection under the Equality Act – "philosophical belief"', the term 'philosophical belief' has been given a fairly broad meaning by the EAT – see Grainger plc and ors v Nicholson 2010 ICR 360, EAT. Thus, not only would disciplining an employee for expressing views consistent with atheism and humanism be covered by the statutory provisions, but disciplinary action because of beliefs based on political philosophies or doctrines, such as socialism, Marxism, communism and free-market capitalism, would also be caught. However, as with the religion cases discussed immediately above, an employee is unlikely to succeed in a claim of belief discrimination if the manner in which he or she expressed those beliefs was offensive. But what of the situation where the belief itself is offensive, at least to some? In Grainger, the EAT suggested that 'a political philosophy which could be characterised as objectionable' – such as concerted racism or homophobia – was unlikely to be protected because it would fall foul of the criterion that a protected belief must be worthy of respect in a democratic society and not incompatible with human dignity. And in Kelly and ors v Unison ET Case No.2203854–7/08 the tribunal held that the claimants did not enjoy protection in respect of their belief in an extreme version of socialism that was dedicated to revolution and the overthrow of the state.

Disciplinary procedures and disability. Employers should check that **25.91** disciplinary procedures are free of any bias against disabled employees, but should also consider whether the way such procedures are applied could give rise to discrimination arising from disability. This could be the case, for example, where the disciplinary procedure stipulates that an employee may only be accompanied to a hearing by a colleague or trade union representative. If the employee is deaf or suffers from learning difficulties, such a provision could amount to unfavourable treatment and would require justification. The employer would also need to turn its mind to reasonable adjustments, such as allowing the employee to be accompanied by a friend, adviser or British Sign Language interpreter. Two examples:

- **Bid v KPMG LLP** ET Case No.1300313/09: B was employed as a graduate accountant trainee, and although she was dyslexic she was not aware of this at the time. As part of her training, B was required to take regular exams and KPMG had a strict policy – which was also a contractual term – that trainees only be allowed two attempts at a paper. In October 2008, B failed her first attempt at a knowledge paper and her course tutor alerted KPMG to the possibility that she might be dyslexic. B failed her second attempt at the paper and was dismissed. In subsequent proceedings, B claimed that KPMG failed in its duty to make reasonable adjustments. The employment tribunal agreed – it would have been a reasonable adjustment for KPMG to have avoided applying its exam policy until such time as it was established whether B was disabled and, if so, whether that had affected her performance

- **Cumbria Probation Board v Collingwood** EAT 0079/08: C was employed as a probation officer. From September 2004, he suffered from depression and his symptoms got progressively worse over the following months. In November 2005, C attempted to have a conversation with his HR manager, M, but she applied the employer's policy that she could not discuss matters in confidence with employees. The following January, C wanted to discuss with M matters in his history going back 18 months, and this request was also refused because M could not consider matters that went back further than six months. C presented a claim for disability discrimination on the basis that, inter alia, these policies constituted a failure to make reasonable adjustments. The tribunal upheld the claim – by applying the policy of not having confidential conversations with employees, CPB had failed in its duty to make reasonable adjustments because C's depression meant that he had a need to speak in confidence. The six-month rule was also a breach of the duty – one aspect of C's illness was the need to have issues properly addressed in order to move forward, and it would have been reasonable for the employer to allow C to properly verbalise his concerns and discuss matters over the previous 18 months. This decision was approved by the EAT on appeal.

849

25.92 **Failure to investigate employees' complaints.** A process for handling grievances – be it formal or informal – goes hand in hand with a disciplinary procedure and is similarly vulnerable to allegations of discrimination. If an employer fails to treat a grievance seriously because of a protected characteristic, this will amount to a detriment and direct discrimination.

Furthermore, an employee who fails to establish discrimination (or harassment) in relation to his or her original complaint may nevertheless be able to show that the employer failed to investigate the complaint adequately and that this in itself amounted to a detriment. In Sandhu and anor v The Leicester Foundry Co Ltd ET Case Nos.32180/83 and another, for example, S and M complained persistently to management of racial abuse and unfair allocation of holidays. The tribunal held that the management's habit of ignoring the two Asian workers' justified complaints, and its failure to investigate those complaints, amounted to a detriment on the ground of race.

25.93 Note, however, that a failure to deal adequately with complaints does not constitute discrimination merely because the initial complaint concerned discrimination (or harassment). Such a failure will only give rise to a claim if the employer would have behaved differently in response to a similar complaint from an appropriate comparator – see Eke v Commissioners of Customs and Excise 1981 IRLR 334, EAT. So, where an employee's complaint of racial harassment at the hands of a client was dealt with inadequately by a manager because of his fear of 'rocking the boat' and scaring that client away, the employee did not suffer direct race discrimination, as the reason for the manager's inaction was nothing to do with race – Conteh v Parking Partners Ltd, 2011 ICR 341, EAT.

Cases involving a failure to pursue an employee's grievance may alternatively be brought under S.39(2)(b) and (4)(b) (as opposed to S.39(2)(d) and (4)(d)), which covers access to 'other benefits, facilities and services' – see 'Benefits, facilities or services' above. Failure to address a grievance may also amount to a breach of contract, even if it is not discriminatory – see IDS Employment Law Handbook, 'Contracts of Employment' (2009).

25.94 **Dress codes and appearance**

Many employers require employees to meet certain standards of dress or appearance at work. If the dress or appearance code forms part of the terms of the worker's contract, claims of discrimination in the application of the code could be brought under S.39(2)(a) or (4)(a). However, given the wide definition of 'detriment' (outlined under 'Meaning of detriment' above) it may be more suitable to bring the claim under S.39(2)(d) and (4)(d), since the application of a dress or appearance code could amount to 'any other detriment', irrespective of the contractual status of the code.

Sex discrimination and dress codes. As the EHRC Employment Code **25.95** recognises, it is not necessarily direct sex discrimination for a dress code to stipulate different standards of dress for men and women, provided an equivalent standard is required of both sexes. For example, a dress code might legitimately stipulate that men must wear a collar and tie and women must wear a blouse. However, the Code goes on to warn that 'it may be direct discrimination if a dress code requires a different overall standard of dress for men and for women; for example, requiring men to dress in a professional and business-like way but allowing women to wear more casual clothes. It could also be direct discrimination if the dress code is similar for both sexes but applied more strictly to men than women – or the other way round' – para 17.41.

The argument that a dress code subjects an employee to a detriment will not succeed if the tribunal takes the view that the restrictions imposed by the employer are so slight as not to be actionable (i.e. if they are *de minimis*). Two examples:

- **Murphy and Davidson v Stakis Leisure Ltd** ET Case No.S/0534/89 and S/0590/89: a tribunal held that company rules requiring female employees at a casino to wear nail varnish did not amount to a detriment but, even if they did, the tribunal would have regarded them as de minimis

- **Wilson v Royal Bank of Scotland plc** ET Case No.27869/86: the bank introduced a requirement that men had to wear a suit instead of a uniform. W refused because his suit was not suitable for summer wear and he could not afford a new one. He claimed sex discrimination on the ground that women could wear what they liked, provided they were smartly dressed. His claim failed because the tribunal thought that W had suffered no detriment; both sexes were required to dress smartly and there was no greater burden on men to comply.

These cases should be compared with Hutcheson v Graham and Morton Ltd **25.96** ET Case No.S/626/83, where the complainant, a senior female employee, was required to wear a nylon overall while men could wear lounge suits. The tribunal held that she had suffered a detriment because the uniform was uncomfortable and indicated a lower status than that of male employees of lower rank. Similarly in Jarman v The Link Stores Ltd ET Case No.2505091/03 J, a man, was repeatedly sent home without pay for wearing earrings and was given a written warning for this. TLS Ltd operated a dress code whereby men were not allowed to wear earrings and had to keep any chains covered. Women, on the other hand, only had to ensure that their jewellery was kept to a minimum and was discreet and appropriate for company work. Eventually, at a meeting with the staff body, it was agreed that men would be allowed to wear one small earring in each ear. The tribunal found that J had been treated less favourably than a woman would have been by being subjected to the detriment

851

of being sent home without pay for wearing jewellery that would have been considered acceptable for a woman. It awarded him £750 for injury to feelings.

Comparing the treatment of women and men in respect of clothing or appearance can prove problematic because conventional ideas about dress tend to distinguish between the sexes. This means that, for example, while earrings and long hair may be acceptable for women, they may be seen as unacceptable for men. Conventional ideas, of course, evolve with time, but even now a man would find it almost impossible to prove that he has been treated less favourably because he is not allowed to wear a skirt to work – see, for example, Ryder-Barratt v Alpha Training Ltd ET Case No.43377/91.

25.97 A 'swings and roundabouts' approach to assessing an employer's dress code was sanctioned by the EAT in Schmidt v Austicks Bookshops Ltd 1978 ICR 85, EAT. In that case the EAT stated that a tribunal should consider the employer's clothing rules as a whole rather than garment by garment, and assess whether the general effect of the rules is more restrictive for one sex than the other. The EAT concluded that the 'realistic and better way of formulating' the comparison was to say that 'there were in force rules restricting wearing apparel and governing appearance which applied to men and also applied to women although, obviously, women and men being different, the rules in the two cases are not the same'. Thus, if the employer enforces rules even-handedly, so far as comparison is possible, it will have treated men and women alike. In the instant case, although female shop assistants were not allowed to wear trousers, men were also subject to certain restrictions, such as a ban on wearing tee shirts. As a result, a female employee could not show that she had received less favourable treatment.

The Court of Appeal adopted the same approach in Smith v Safeway plc 1996 ICR 868, CA. That case concerned the dismissal of a male delicatessen assistant in a supermarket for breach of the employer's appearance rules. Those rules required both male and female food handlers to wear hats and both sexes were prohibited from having 'unconventional hair styles or colouring'. However, the details of the rules on hair length were different for men and women in that women were allowed to have long hair if they wore it clipped back, but men could not let their hair grow below shirt-collar length. The complainant had a ponytail, which was tolerated while it could be kept under his hat, but he was dismissed once it had grown too long for that and after he refused to cut it to an acceptable length. His complaint of discrimination was rejected by a tribunal. The EAT, however, took the view that it was self-evident that the restriction on hair length for male employees amounted to less favourable treatment and that hair length is not a function of any physiological difference between men and women but merely a question of custom and fashion.

25.98 The Court of Appeal sided with the tribunal and the employer. In its view, the tribunal had been entitled to find on the facts that the prohibition of ponytails

852

for male employees did not constitute less favourable treatment because the same standard was rigorously applied to both male and female employees in respect of the requirement that they maintain a conventional appearance while at work. Wholeheartedly endorsing the Schmidt approach, the Court ruled that a code that applies a conventional standard of appearance is not of itself discriminatory: while one of the aims of the sex discrimination legislation is to prevent unequal treatment of the sexes arising from conventional attitudes, this does not render discriminatory an appearance code that applies a common standard as to what is conventional. The Schmidt approach requires that, looking at the dress code as a whole, neither sex must be treated less favourably as a result of its enforcement. It could not be accepted that changes in society had rendered the above reasoning unsound in law, or that it was not applicable in the instant case. The Schmidt approach was not confined to matters of dress but could be extended to questions of hairstyle. The fact that restrictions on hair length affect an employee's appearance outside working hours may be a relevant consideration when applying the appropriate test, but does not itself affect the test.

In applying the Schmidt approach to the facts of the case, the Court of Appeal pointed out that the tribunal had had to consider two interrelated questions. The first was whether the prohibition on long hair being worn by men could properly be justified on the ground that it represented a requirement of conventional appearance. On this, the tribunal had clearly come to the conclusion that the prohibition was justified. Secondly, the tribunal asked whether, in the context of the dress code as a whole, the restriction on the freedom to govern one's own appearance resulted in men being treated less favourably than women. The tribunal decided that it did not, and, in reaching that conclusion, had applied the correct approach. This did not mean that as a rule of law a restriction on hair length for male employees can never be discriminatory, but simply that on the facts of the instant case the tribunal was entitled to reach the conclusion that it did.

25.99 The Schmidt and Smith approach was subsequently confirmed in Department for Work and Pensions v Thompson 2004 IRLR 348, EAT. In that case, T, a man, worked for the DWP in a Jobcentre Plus branch, but was not 'customer-facing'. The DWP introduced a dress code whereby all male staff were required to wear a collar and tie, and female staff to dress 'appropriately and to a similar standard'. T refused to wear the collar and tie, which resulted in a written warning. Following the warning, T complied under protest and brought a sex discrimination claim. Almost 7,000 similar claims depended upon its outcome. The tribunal found that T was required to wear a collar and tie because he was a man. It further found that he had been subjected to two detriments. The first related to his being forced to change his style of dress in circumstances where he felt this to be unnecessary – this constituted less favourable treatment since no particular item of clothing was mandatory for women, who continued to

853

dress as before. The second was the disciplinary action brought against him. On appeal, however, the EAT considered that the tribunal had asked the wrong question. It should have had regard to the overarching requirement imposed by the respondent for all employees to dress smartly and to an appropriate standard. The issue was not resolved by asking whether the requirement that men wear a collar and tie demanded a higher level of smartness than was required of women. The EAT concluded that the question the tribunal should have addressed was whether the required level of smartness could only be achieved by requiring men to wear a collar and tie. If, for example, a level of smartness for men appropriate to an undertaking such as Jobcentre Plus could be achieved by their dressing other than in a collar and tie, then the lack of flexibility in the dress code would suggest that male members of staff were being treated less favourably than female members. The EAT therefore allowed the appeal and remitted the case to a different tribunal to consider the point afresh.

The conclusion must be that, so long as restrictions on choice of dress or appearance are imposed to an equal degree on men and women, an employer will not be in breach of the EqA, even where those restrictions are not identical for both sexes: indeed, this conclusion accords with the EHRC Employment Code. However, where a dress code is imposed for one sex but not for comparable employees of the other, then that code is likely to give rise to less favourable treatment and thus liability for direct discrimination. This was the outcome in Stoke-on-Trent Community Transport v Cresswell EAT 359/93, where the EAT upheld a tribunal's conclusion that a woman dismissed for wearing trousers was directly discriminated against in circumstances where the employer imposed no equivalent dress or appearance rule on male employees.

25.100　It should be noted that if an employer applies a particularly demeaning dress code to women, this could amount to unlawful harassment (see 'Workplace harassment' below). For example, in Lemes v Spring and Greene Ltd ET Case No.2201943/08 the dress code for female bar staff at the employer's premises changed from a loose fitting black shirt and black trousers or skirt to a short red dress with a low neckline. L refused to accept the new uniform and her employment came to an end. An employment tribunal found that the change to the dress code was unwanted, related to sex and had the effect of violating L's dignity.

25.101　**Dress codes, cross-dressing and gender reassignment.** Particular considerations arise where transvestite and transsexual employees are concerned. The Court of Appeal's decision in Smith v Safeway plc (above) was followed by the EAT in Kara v London Borough of Hackney EAT 325/95 where the Appeal Tribunal held that the complainant, a male transvestite, was not discriminated against when his employer prohibited him from wearing women's clothing to work. The EAT pointed out that both male and female employees were required to attend work looking 'clean, neat and appropriately dressed'. The EAT concluded that the employer was acting lawfully in requiring the complainant to attend work dressed as a man.

However, the Kara case was decided in 1995 before there was any protection under discrimination law for a person who 'is proposing to undergo, is undergoing or has undergone a process (or part of a process) for the purpose of reassigning the person's sex by changing physiological or other attributes of sex' – the definition of gender reassignment found in S.7 EqA. As explained in Chapter 7, 'Gender reassignment', the EqA provides express protection from direct and indirect discrimination because of gender reassignment and in many cases presenting as a member of the opposite gender will be a preliminary step in the process of gender reassignment and therefore covered by the Act. So where an employee who cross-dresses as a necessary precursor to gender reassignment is required by his or her employer to dress and present as a member of his or her birth gender, this is likely to amount to a detriment, giving rise to a direct discrimination claim under S.13 and possibly an indirect discrimination claim under S.19. Furthermore, requiring a pre-operative transsexual employee to present as a member of his or her birth gender may also constitute harassment related to gender reassignment or sex contrary to S.26 EqA. But where the employee does not intend to undergo gender reassignment (i.e. is a transvestite rather than a transsexual), the Kara decision is likely to be followed.

Dress codes and religious attire. In addition to giving rise to direct 25.102 discrimination, dress codes may also result in indirect discrimination if they put groups sharing a protected characteristic at a disadvantage, and that disadvantage cannot be objectively justified. Such discrimination can potentially arise where a dress code prevents an employee from wearing an item that is a manifestation of his or her religious beliefs. An extensive account of the jurisprudence in this area can be found in Chapter 11, 'Religion or belief', under 'Manifestation of religion or belief – is a right to manifest protected by S.10 EqA?'. For present purposes, we will focus on points likely to be of practical importance to employers and employees alike.

The first point to note is that the courts, in determining whether a provision, criterion or practice of the employer's places the claimant and others sharing his or her religious beliefs at a particular disadvantage, have drawn a distinction between clothing and jewellery that is a doctrinal requirement – such as the hijab, the turban and the skull cap, which some Muslims, Sikhs and Jews respectively believe they are obliged to wear – and clothing and jewellery that is worn as a *personal* manifestation of faith. It was held in Eweida v British Airways plc 2010 ICR 890, CA, that the Christian employee's silver cross belonged in the latter category and for that reason – evidenced by the fact that no other employee among a workforce of 30,000 had sought to wear a cross

855

over his or her uniform – the Court of Appeal considered that she was unable to show that the employer's uniform policy placed persons sharing her religious beliefs at a particular disadvantage. By way of contrast, the EAT in Azmi v Kirklees Metropolitan Borough Council 2007 ICR 1154, EAT, accepted that the employer's policy of requiring classroom assistants not to wear clothing that covered the face or which interfered unduly with the employee's ability to communicate properly with pupils was clearly a provision, criterion or practice that put persons of the claimant's belief – she was a devout Muslim – at a particular disadvantage when compared with others.

25.103 The second point is that, even where group disadvantage has been established, tribunals have tended to find employers' dress codes to be objectively justified. In the Azmi case (above), for example, the EAT held that the requirement was justified as a proportionate means of achieving the legitimate aim of raising the educational achievements of the school children. Similarly, in Dhinsa v Serco and anor ET Case No.1315002/09 a tribunal held that the Prison Service's policy of restricting all staff except Sikh chaplains from wearing the kirpan – a ceremonial sword worn by Amritdhari Sikhs – at work was a proportionate means of achieving the aim of preventing attacks on staff or prisoners.

Finally, it should be remembered that the protection afforded by S.10 EqA covers philosophical as well as religious beliefs. In Lisk v Shield Guardian Co Ltd and ors ET Case No.3300873/11 the claimant alleged that he had been discriminated against by his employer when it refused him permission to wear a poppy at work. However, that claim foundered on the test for a philosophical belief that was set out by Mr Justice Burton in Grainger plc and ors v Nicholson 2010 ICR 360, EAT (examined in Chapter 11, 'Religion or belief', under 'Protection under the Equality Act – "philosophical" belief'). The tribunal was not satisfied that a belief that people should wear a poppy as a mark of respect attained the necessary level of cogency, seriousness, cohesion and importance; nor did it concern a weighty and substantial aspect of human life and behaviour.

25.104 **Reasonable adjustments to dress codes.** Where an employer's dress code places a disabled employee at a substantial disadvantage compared to non-disabled employees, it is likely to be considered a reasonable adjustment to amend the code for that employee. In Dean v Abercrombie and Fitch ET Case No.2203221/08 the employer – a clothing retailer – operated a 'look policy' with which all customer-facing employees were expected to comply. It required staff to wear the employer's garments and stipulated that women's make-up should have a 'fresh and natural' appearance. D, who was born without a left forearm and used a prosthetic arm, spoke with management at her induction and it was agreed that, because she felt uncomfortable exposing the join of her prosthetic, she would be allowed to wear a cardigan covering the join while working on the shop floor. An employment tribunal found that when a manager, unaware of the adjustment, ordered the employee to leave the shop floor and work in the warehouse, D had been subjected to disability discrimination.

Workplace harassment 25.105

Section 40(1)(a) EqA stipulates that an employer (A) must not, in relation to employment by A, harass a person (B) who is an employee of A's. This reflects the fact that, while harassment was once considered a facet of discrimination, it is now a distinct form of prohibited conduct under S.26. S.26(1) states that a person (A) harasses another (B) if:

- A engages in unwanted conduct related to a relevant protected characteristic, and

- the conduct has the purpose or effect of violating B's dignity or creating an intimidating, hostile, degrading, humiliating or offensive environment for B.

For the purposes of S.26, the 'relevant protected characteristics' are age, **25.106** disability, gender reassignment, race, religion or belief, sex and sexual orientation – S.27(5). This means that an individual cannot bring a claim of harassment related to the characteristics of marriage and civil partnership or pregnancy and maternity. That said, harassment on either of those grounds might well be related to sex (or, in some circumstances, sexual orientation) in any event. There is also the possibility that the 'harassing' conduct could give rise to a direct discrimination claim under S.13 (in the case of marriage and civil partnership) or a claim of pregnancy and maternity discrimination under S.18.

In addition to harassment 'related to a... protected characteristic' under S.26(1), the EqA prohibits two forms of *sexual harassment* in S.26(2) and (3). The first arises where a person, A, engages in unwanted conduct of a sexual nature that has the purpose or effect referred to in S.26(1)(b) (i.e. of either violating B's dignity or creating an intimidating, hostile, degrading, humiliating or offensive environment for B) – S.26(2). The second occurs where (a) A or another person engages in unwanted conduct of a sexual nature or that is related to gender reassignment or sex, (b) the conduct has the purpose or effect referred to in S.26(1)(b) (i.e. of either violating B's dignity or creating an intimidating, hostile, degrading, humiliating or offensive environment for B) and (c) because of B's rejection of or submission to the conduct, A treats B less favourably than A would treat B if B had not rejected or submitted to the conduct – S.26(3).

Unwanted conduct 25.107
The definitions of harassment and sexual harassment in S.26 EqA all stipulate that the conduct in question must be *unwanted*. This means essentially the same as 'unwelcome' or 'uninvited' (para 7.8 of the EHRC Employment Code)

857

and is to be viewed subjectively from the standpoint of the complainant. For conduct to be unwanted it is not a prerequisite that the complainant had made a prior express objection to the conduct – a one-off incident can amount to harassment, provided it satisfies all the limbs of the statutory test.

The fact that a complainant does not complain about conduct over a sustained period, while relevant to the question of whether that conduct was unwanted, is not determinative of it. In Munchkins Restaurant Ltd and anor v Karmazyn and ors EAT 0359/09 and another the EAT held that an employment tribunal had not erred in upholding the sex discrimination and harassment claims made by some waitresses against a restaurant proprietor who had for a number of years engaged them in unwanted conversation about sex and shown them explicit photographs and catalogues of sexual material. It was not perverse of the tribunal to find that the claimants had been subjected to intolerable conduct while continuing to work at the restaurant. It was not at all extraordinary that the claimants, who were migrant workers constrained by financial pressure and the fear that they might not obtain other work, would have soldiered on in the circumstances. As the EAT observed, there are many situations in life where people will put up with unwanted conduct which violates their personal dignity because they are constrained by social circumstances to do so. Nor was it perverse of the tribunal to find that the conversations of a sexual nature were unwelcome to the claimants, even though they had sometimes been the initiators of such conversations. It was clear on the tribunal's findings that the claimants' initiation of such conversations was a defensive move which enabled them to divert much of the intrusive personal questioning which otherwise would have taken place as to their own sexual preferences, habits and contacts.

25.108 Although a claimant does not have to show that he or she objected to the conduct in order to establish that it was unwanted, the fact that he or she did *not* object to it can be strong evidence that it was not unwanted, and was in fact welcome. This is all the more so where the complainant has previously been an active and willing participant in the potentially offensive behaviour of which he or she later complains. For example, in Burke v Secure Options Ltd ET Case No.2400138/06 the tribunal found that the claimant was not subjected to unwanted conduct by the circulation of pornographic e-mails around the office. The claimant did not complain to her employer until some time after she had received the e-mails, and the evidence at the time was that she had been a party to and had enjoyed them. On occasions, if she was excluded from the circulation of sexually explicit e-mails, she would want to know why. She had shown no reluctance whatsoever to complain about other matters and the tribunal was satisfied that if she had been at all upset by the e-mails she would have complained at the time.

That said, it should be remembered that context is crucial in claims of harassment. An employee's participation in edgy or risqué banter does not mean that he or she automatically waives any possibility of claiming harassment. This is made clear in Munchkins Restaurant Ltd and anor v Karmazyn and ors (above) and also in Queenscourt Ltd v Nyateka EAT 0182/06, where the claimant, N, was a black woman who worked in a fast food restaurant as a team leader. The tribunal found that there was a friendly atmosphere in the restaurant in which all staff got along well and there was a lot of banter. In particular, the tribunal found that the employees were robust in their remarks and that between black and ethnic minority staff words like 'nigger' and 'Paki' were used in a jocular manner. N brought a claim of racial harassment based on a single incident in which a white male colleague had made a sarcastic reference to her skin colour. The tribunal upheld N's claim, and the EAT dismissed Q Ltd's appeal against that decision. According to the EAT, the tribunal had been entitled to find that despite the prevailing atmosphere in which racial banter was acceptable, and in which N may previously have used words herself that might in another context be seen as racist, the manager had used racial language that was not spoken in jest, and which had caused real upset to N.

25.109 The statutory definitions refer to unwanted *conduct*, a term that potentially encompasses a wide range of behaviour. Physical acts would almost certainly be covered, so any form of physical bullying or violence related to a protected characteristic would amount to unwanted conduct. Oral abuse is also covered, so offensive language, taunts, insults, name-calling and swearing might all, if related to a protected characteristic, give rise to a claim of harassment. Similarly, spreading rumours about a person, undermining or belittling him or her or interfering with his or her work would also give rise to a claim if the requisite connection is established. However, conduct need not be physical or oral in order to be offensive. In Richards v Menzies Aviation (UK) Ltd ET Case No.14025/10 the claimant, a black British man of Jamaican origin, found a drawing of a monkey with his name on it at his workplace. The tribunal held this to be an act of harassment related to his race. The employer's response when the claimant complained about the drawing – a white manager had insisted that he was overreacting and that the drawing was not a racial slur – was also held to be direct race discrimination.

The widespread use of e-mail at work presents a risk of harassment occurring at the press of a button, because offensive messages sent by e-mail or posted on a company's intranet would certainly be covered. In Elahi v Lanz Ltd ET Case No.2201425/10, for example, the employer forwarded to all staff an e-mail which the tribunal found to be 'undoubtedly offensive and derogatory of the Muslim faith'. This was found to amount to harassment of E, a Muslim employee.

25.110 Adopting an uncompromising and inflexible stance in the face of difficulties presented by an employee's disability could also give rise to harassment. For example, in Clark v Newsquest Media (Southern) Ltd ET Case No.3100102/10

859

C had type 1 diabetes, which meant she had to inject herself with insulin throughout the day and take blood tests before and after each injection. On an induction training course in her new job, the employer objected to her injecting herself in the training room in front of others, and told her she should leave the room to do this. She was upset, and wrote to the employer setting out her concerns. The employer treated her letter as a grievance, but rejected it, instructing C that she had to perform her injections in private according to an agreed system, except in cases of emergency. She resigned, and brought disability discrimination claims to an employment tribunal. The tribunal noted that the employer appeared to believe that other employees would be embarrassed or offended or even be caused harm if they suffered from a needle phobia or if C carelessly discarded a needle. There was no basis for these assumptions – no employee had expressed concern and C had not been consulted about the disposal of needles. The employer's insistence on C injecting herself privately was humiliating and disruptive to her work, and amounted to harassment. In subjecting C to this condition the employer also failed to make reasonable adjustments.

In certain circumstances, unwanted conduct could take the form of disclosure of personal information related to a protected characteristic. For example, in Dos Santos v Fitch Ratings Ltd ET Case No.2203907/08 one of D's line managers, in direct violation of D's express wishes, revealed the fact that D was HIV positive to the group managing director. An employment tribunal found that this was unwanted conduct that related to disability and, given the sensitivity of the information disclosed, had the effect of violating D's dignity and creating an intimidating, hostile, degrading, humiliating or offensive environment for him. By way of contrast, the Court of Appeal in HM Land Registry v Grant 2011 ICR 1390, CA, overturned a tribunal's finding that a gay employee had been subjected to harassment when, following a transfer to a different office, he was 'outed' by his new line manager's conversations with colleagues. The Court considered that the tribunal had overlooked the importance of the fact that G had been open about his sexuality at the previous office. In such circumstances, it was questionable whether the conduct was unwanted, and it could not be said that it either violated G's dignity or created an intimidating, hostile, degrading, humiliating or offensive environment.

25.111

Conduct 'related to' a protected characteristic

As we saw in Chapter 18, 'Harassment', the use of the words 'related to a protected characteristic' in S.26(1) EqA gives the provision a broader reach than that of its predecessors in the now-repealed anti-discrimination legislation. For example, old S.3A(1) of the Race Relations Act 1976 (RRA) required the offending conduct to be *on the grounds of* race. Such a formulation is now considered to be too close to that of direct discrimination, in that it poses the question of why the alleged harasser acted as he or she did, and has been eschewed in favour of 'related to', a phrase that encompasses everything formerly covered by 'on grounds of' – that is, conduct meted out *by reason of* a protected characteristic – but also extends to any circumstance where there is simply *a connection* between the conduct and the protected characteristic. As the EHRC Employment Code points out, this means that protection against unwanted conduct is provided even where the worker does not have the relevant protected characteristic, including where the employer knows that the worker does not have the relevant characteristic. It gives the example of homophobic banter and name-calling aimed at a colleague who is known to be heterosexual (see para 7.10).

Conduct having the proscribed purpose or effect   25.112

In a case brought under any of the three forms of harassment provided for under S.26 EqA, it is necessary for the tribunal to consider whether the conduct in question had the purpose or effect of:

- violating the complainant's dignity, or

- creating an intimidating, hostile, degrading, humiliating or offensive environment for the complainant – S.(1)(b).

As observed by Mr Justice Elias in Richmond Pharmacology Ltd v Dhaliwal 2009 ICR 724, EAT, the test for harassment which is now found in S.26 EqA imposes liability on employers on two alternative bases. An employer can be held liable where the *effect* of the conduct was to create an intimidating, hostile, degrading, humiliating or offensive environment or violating the complainant's dignity, even if that was not the intended purpose. Conversely, the employer may be liable where the intention was to create the proscribed circumstances, but did not in fact do so. However, the latter case will be rare, as it would be surprising if the conduct had not resulted in the proscribed consequences where the employee has subsequently brought a harassment claim. In most cases the primary focus is likely to be on the effect of the unwanted conduct rather than on the employer's purpose, although this does not necessarily exclude consideration of the harasser's mental processes.

Where a case is pleaded on the basis that the purpose of the unwanted conduct **25.113** was to bring about the proscribed circumstances, the tribunal hearing the claim must determine the intentions of A, the alleged harasser. As A is unlikely to admit to having intended to harass B, the tribunal will be required to draw inferences as to whether A had the necessary purpose from the surrounding circumstances. In our view, a tribunal might be prepared to infer that A had such a purpose where the victim had made it clear on previous occasions that the conduct in question was unwanted and offensive. An example:

861

- **Mann v BH Publishing Ltd and anor** ET Case No.2203272/04: M, who was South African, began working for BHP Ltd on 24 May 2004. M spoke with what he described as a gay South African accent. His manager, H, mimicked his accent from the outset of his employment. After two days, M told H that he objected to the mimicry and thought it was harassment on the ground of his sexual orientation. Despite this, H continued to mimic his accent, and from this time on his colleagues began to tease and taunt M about his sexual orientation. M brought a claim of harassment on the ground of sexual orientation, which was upheld. The tribunal found that there was no harassment for the first two days – H was a natural and talented mimic, and the tribunal did not accept that the mimicry had any connection with M's sexuality. However, from the time that M put his concerns to H, the mimicry violated his dignity and amounted to harassment on the ground of M's sexual orientation. The behaviour of his colleagues also amounted to unlawful discrimination.

25.114 Given the likely dearth of evidence as to the purpose of unwanted conduct, we anticipate – in line with Elias J's view in Richmond Pharmacology Ltd v Dhaliwal (above) – that the bulk of claims will be made on the basis that A's conduct had the *effect* of violating B's dignity or creating an intimidating, hostile, degrading, humiliating or offensive environment for B. This brings into play a further subsection, S.26(4), which states that, in determining whether conduct has that effect, a tribunal must take into account:

- the perception of B

- the other circumstances of the case

- whether it is reasonable for the conduct to have that effect.

25.115 Although it doesn't expressly state as much, S.26(4) requires that tribunals consider the claimant's subjective view of the alleged harassing conduct, but ultimately approach the question of whether the conduct had the prescribed effect from an objective viewpoint. The reasonableness aspect of the test is intended to exclude liability in cases of inadvertent harassment where B is 'hypersensitive' and unreasonably takes offence, reflecting the position that has developed through case law on harassment within the context of direct discrimination under the Sex Discrimination Act 1975 and the RRA – see, for example, Driskel v Peninsula Business Services Ltd and ors 2000 IRLR 151, EAT. An example of a harassment case involving a 'hypersensitive' claimant:

- **Kalomoiris v John Lewis plc** ET Case No.2202486/10: K was employed as a sales assistant by JL plc. He had a tendency to react badly to physical contact and claimed to have been harassed as a result of two instances of unwanted contact from a female colleague: one involving his bottom being slapped, the other involving a hand placed on his lower back. The tribunal noted that the colleague in question was a 67-year-old Italian woman, described by colleagues as a kind and caring person, a motherly figure, who was tactile and touched people in the course of communicating with them without consciously thinking about it. The tribunal concluded that the conduct had nothing to do with K's gender, and went on to find that although K considered that it violated his dignity, he was oversensitive and found unacceptable a level of personal contact with which most people would not have a problem. Accordingly, JL plc had not harassed K.

A tribunal's findings of fact can only be disturbed on appeal on the ground of **25.116** perversity, so the question of whether a claimant has reacted in an oversensitive way to unwanted conduct is something that will nearly always be determined at first instance. In Richmond Pharmacology Ltd v Dhaliwal 2009 ICR 724, EAT, the Appeal Tribunal held that an employment tribunal had been entitled to find that a remark to a female employee of Indian ethnic origin referring to the possibility of her being 'married off in India' violated her dignity and constituted harassment within the meaning of the RRA. The EAT accepted that a person's dignity is not necessarily violated by things said or done which are trivial or transitory, particularly if it should have been clear that any offence was unintended. Although tribunals, as well as employers, had to be careful not to encourage a culture of hypersensitivity, in this case, the remark – which evoked the stereotype of forced marriage – could reasonably have been perceived to violate D's dignity.

As we have seen under 'Conduct "related" to protected characteristic' above, the harassment provisions do not require that the alleged victim of harassment actually possesses the protected characteristic to which the unwanted conduct relates. Thus, a heterosexual employee can bring a claim of harassment on the basis that he was subjected to homophobic abuse at work – English v Thomas Sanderson Blinds Ltd 2009 ICR 543, CA. However, where an employee does not possess the characteristic in question, he or she is likely to face a greater challenge in convincing the tribunal that the conduct had the effect of violating his or her dignity or of creating an intimidating, hostile, degrading, humiliating or offensive environment. The English case went up to the Court of Appeal on a point of law – whether the harassment provisions then in force covered homophobic harassment of a heterosexual employee – but returned to the tribunal for a consideration of whether the homophobic remarks in question had the required effect. In Thomas Sanderson Blinds Ltd v English EAT 0316–7/10 the tribunal found that although E had been called names such as 'faggot' and been the subject of innuendo in the company magazine, the evidence showed that he had participated in banter and name-calling and had written similarly offensive articles 'riddled with sexist and ageist innuendo' for the magazine. Accordingly, the tribunal concluded that he could not reasonably have considered that the conduct had the effect of violating his dignity or creating an intimidating, hostile, degrading, humiliating or offensive environment for him. If that were the case, E would have complained and

863

would not have been so friendly with his alleged tormentors. On appeal, the EAT upheld the tribunal's decision.

25.117 Third party harassment

The EqA specifically extends an employer's liability to harassment of employees by a third party – for example, a customer, client, supplier or other member of the public who has access to the workplace. S.40(2) renders employers liable if they fail to take 'such steps as would have been reasonably practicable' to prevent the third party from harassing the employee. The EHRC Employment Code suggests that, depending on the employer's size and resources, reasonably practicable steps might include having a harassment policy in place and notifying third parties that harassment of employees is unlawful and will not be tolerated by, for example, displaying a public notice – para 10.24.

However, such liability only arises if the employee has been subjected to third-party harassment on at least two previous occasions, and the employer is aware that it has taken place – S.40(3). This subsection goes on to state that 'it does not matter whether the third party is the same or a different person on each occasion'. It does appear to matter, though, that the harassed employee is the same person each time. So where, for example, several different employees are subjected to harassment because of their race by a single customer, the employer will not be liable under S.40 until a single employee has been harassed for a third time.

25.118 Even if the conditions in S.40(2) and (3) are not made out, an employee might have a claim for direct discrimination under S.13(1) if he or she can show that the employer has treated him or her less favourably because of a protected characteristic by failing to prevent third-party harassment (such a claim would most likely proceed on the basis that the failure amounted to a detriment – see above under 'Any other detriment – disciplinary and grievance procedures'). Furthermore, case law under the RRA suggested that an employer could, in certain circumstances, be directly liable for third-party harassment under S.3A RRA (the equivalent of S.26 EqA) if it let the conduct go unchallenged – see, for example, Gravell v London Borough of Bexley EAT 0587/06. Therefore, even where S.40(2) and (3) is not satisfied, an employee may be able to argue that an employer's inaction in the face of third-party harassment itself amounts to harassment under S.26 EqA. Note, however, that in Conteh v Parking Partners Ltd 2011 ICR 341, EAT, the Appeal Tribunal held that an employer could only be liable under S.3A RRA for harassment carried out by a third party if the employer's failure to take action to safeguard the employee itself violated his or her dignity, or led to the creation of an intimidating, hostile, degrading, humiliating or offensive environment.

Reasonable steps defence

25.119

There is no defence of objective justification to a claim of harassment. This remains the case even where the harassment is related to the protected characteristic of age (unlike direct age discrimination, which can be justified). However, while an employer cannot argue that harassment was justified, it may be able to argue that it should not be held liable for harassment carried out by employees.

Section 109(1) and (3) EqA provides that anything done by an employee 'in the course of employment' is to be treated as being done by the employer, irrespective of whether that thing was done with the employer's knowledge and approval. The term 'in the course of employment' is to be given a broad interpretation, reflecting the fact that it appears in legislation designed to eliminate discrimination and harassment – Jones v Tower Boot Co Ltd 1997 ICR 254, CA. Accordingly, an employer is potentially liable for any act of harassment that takes place at work. S.109 does, however, contain a defence for employers. S.109(4) provides 'in proceedings against A's employer (B) in respect of anything alleged to have been done by A in the course of A's employment it is a defence for B to show that B took all reasonable steps to prevent A from doing that thing, or from doing anything of that description'.

The old statutory defence referred to 'such steps as were reasonably practicable' **25.120** (see, for example, S.41(3) SDA and S.32(3) RRA), but the change in wording is not thought to be too significant. That said, it is just possible that employment tribunals may interpret the addition of the word 'all' in S.109(4) EqA as setting down a stricter test, although we are not aware of any case where a tribunal has done so. It is worth pointing out that it is no defence for an employer to argue that, even if he had taken all reasonable steps, that would not have prevented the harassment in question. If an employer has not taken such steps, and an employee has committed an act of harassment in the course of his or her employment, then that is the end of the matter as far as liability is concerned.

What are reasonable steps? The question of what amounts to 'all reasonable **25.121** steps' will depend on the circumstances. For instance, more will be expected of an employer who has had problems in the past with harassment. The EHRC Employment Code suggests that the following are likely to include reasonable steps:

- implementing an equality policy

- ensuring workers are aware of the policy

- providing equal opportunities training

- reviewing the policy as appropriate, and

- dealing effectively with employee complaints – para 10.52.

865

The defence is, however, limited to preventative steps that have been taken *before* the act complained of. So the way in which an employer responds to an allegation will not allow it to evade liability. This is not to say that the way in which an employer deals with complaints is not of crucial importance. Failing to respond adequately, by whatever means, can amount to a further instance of discrimination, and if the employer does not take steps to ensure that such acts do not happen again, then it will be unable to establish a defence in future cases. The liability of employers for the discriminatory acts of its employees and third parties is discussed in greater detail in Chapter 28, 'Liability of employers, employees and agents'.

25.122 Harassment outside the workplace

As we saw above under 'Reasonable steps defence', S.109(1) EqA imposes on an employer liability for anything done by its employees 'in the course of employment' – S.109(1). Furthermore, it does not matter if the thing complained of is done with the employer's knowledge and approval – S.109(3). One consequence of this provision is that an employer can be liable for harassment of an employee by his or her colleague(s) which takes place away from the workplace.

The question of whether discrimination or harassment that took place outside the workplace was nevertheless done 'in the course of employment' depends on the connection the tribunal sees between the employment relationship and the event or location at which the offending conduct took place. This is a question of fact, not law, so it will be difficult to interfere with a tribunal's findings on this point on appeal. This was demonstrated in Sidhu v Aerospace Composite Technology Ltd 2001 ICR 167, CA, where S and his family were subjected to racial abuse by a colleague, KS, at a family day out organised by their mutual employer, ACT Ltd. In considering whether ACT Ltd was vicariously liable for the acts of race discrimination that took place on the family day out, an employment tribunal noted that the day out had neither been at the workplace nor during working hours, and that most participants had been friends and family and not employees. It therefore concluded that the events in question took place outside S and KS's employment and, consequently, the employer was not liable for KS's acts. The Court of Appeal confirmed the tribunal's decision and rejected S's argument that the tribunal should have concluded that ACT Ltd's supervision of the event brought it within the course of employment as it was far from clear that there had been any meaningful supervision. It was possible that another tribunal could have reached a different conclusion, but on the facts the tribunal had been entitled to conclude that the day out had not been in the course of employment.

25.123 However, the mere fact that alleged discriminatory acts occurred outside the workplace or outside working hours does not inevitably lead to the conclusion that what happened was not in the course of employment. A tribunal will decide every case on its own particular facts. For example, it may decide that discriminatory conduct occurring at a social event had taken place 'in the course of employment' as the event had, effectively, been an extension of the workplace. This was the conclusion of the EAT in Chief Constable of Lincolnshire Police v Stubbs and ors 1999 ICR 547, EAT, where a police officer complained of two incidents of sexual harassment by a colleague: one at a pub after work and a second at another officer's leaving party outside of work. The EAT held that the acts of sex discrimination had been committed in the course of employment. Although neither incident occurred at the police station, the EAT thought that they were 'social gatherings involving officers from work either immediately after work or for an organised leaving party'.

The liability of employers for discriminatory acts that take place outside the workplace is discussed in greater detail in Chapter 28, 'Liability of employers, employees and agents'.

26 Dismissal

In Chapter 25, 'Discrimination during employment', we discuss discrimination **26.1** that occurs during the currency of the employment relationship. In this chapter, we turn to how discrimination can occur when the employment relationship is ended. The main provisions of interest here are S.39(2)(c) and 39(4)(c) of the Equality Act 2010 (EqA), which provide that an employer (A) must not discriminate against or victimise an employee of A's (B) by dismissing B. For the purposes of S.39, 'dismissal' includes not only express termination of employment, but also termination through the expiry of a fixed-term contract (including expiry by reference to an event or circumstance) unless the contract is immediately renewed on the same terms – S.39(7)(a) and (8). It also includes constructive dismissal, which occurs where the employee, owing to the repudiatory conduct of the employer, is entitled to resign and regard him or herself as dismissed – S.39(7)(b).

In certain circumstances, a dismissal may also contravene S.40(1)(a) EqA, which provides that an employer (A) must not, in relation to employment by A, harass a person (B) who is an employee of A's. Furthermore, an employer's provisions, criteria and practices in respect of dismissal will be subject to the duty to make reasonable adjustments if they place a disabled employee at a substantial disadvantage when compared with non-disabled people. The EAT confirmed in Fareham College Corporation v Walters 2009 IRLR 991, EAT, that the duty to make reasonable adjustments applies to the act of dismissal as well as the events leading up to it. Consequently, a dismissal that occurs because the employer is unwilling to make reasonable adjustments to prevent it is an act of disability discrimination on the basis of the failure to make such adjustments.

Given the numerous ways in which discrimination can arise when employment **26.2** is terminated, it is generally considered prudent for employers to have in place procedures or policies relating to disciplinary matters, redundancy, and, where relevant, retirement. Those responsible for implementing such procedures and

869

policies will require equal opportunities training to ensure that they are applied in a non-discriminatory fashion. As we will see below, taking such steps is not only good practice; they can, to a certain extent, insulate an employer from the inference that conscious or unconscious bias has infected the dismissal process.

In this chapter we consider the circumstances in which a tribunal might find that an employee has been dismissed because of a protected characteristic, or that an employer's procedures in relation to dismissal were tainted by unjustified indirect discrimination or discrimination arising from disability. We also look at the issues surrounding redundancy and retirement before turning to examine how discrimination can give rise to a repudiatory breach of contract entitling an employee to resign and claim constructive dismissal. First, however, we consider the relationship between discrimination claims arising from a dismissal and claims of unfair dismissal under the Employment Rights Act 1996 (ERA).

26.3 Relationship between discriminatory and unfair dismissals

A claim that a dismissal is discriminatory under S.39(2)(c) EqA, or an act of victimisation under S.39(4)(c), may overlap with a claim of unfair dismissal under the ERA (considered at length in IDS Employment Law Handbook, 'Unfair Dismissal' (2010)) and in many cases claims will be simultaneously advanced under both heads. There are, however, a number of differences between the two jurisdictions of which employers and claimants should be aware. The key differences, which we consider in more detail below, are:

- the qualifying period of continuous employment that applies to unfair dismissal claims

- the role of reasonableness in an unfair dismissal claim

- the approach to compensation and remedies

- the separate definitions of employment under the EqA and the ERA

- procedural matters such as time limits and the burden of proof.

26.4 No qualifying period for discrimination claims
As we explain in Chapter 28, 'Liability of employers, employees and agents', under 'Who is protected?', there is no period of continuous employment which an employee must serve in order to be entitled to bring a claim under the EqA. Thus, for example, an employee dismissed on his or her first day of employment in circumstances that amount to discrimination or victimisation would be able to bring tribunal proceedings and recover compensation for loss of earnings and injury to feelings.

870

This contrasts with the position under the ERA, where the right not to be unfairly dismissed contained in S.94 only comes into effect once the employee has at least two years' continuous employment (see IDS Employment Law Handbook, 'Unfair Dismissal' (2010), Chapter 2, 'Exclusions from right to claim', under 'Continuous service threshold'), unless the reason for dismissal falls within the category of 'inadmissible reasons' for dismissal for which there is no qualifying period and in respect of which any dismissal is regarded as automatically unfair (see IDS Employment Law Handbook, 'Unfair Dismissal' (2010), Chapter 10, 'Automatically unfair dismissals', under 'List of automatically unfair reasons') – S.108 ERA. There is a small degree of overlap between the automatically unfair reasons for dismissal under the ERA and the discrimination provisions in the EqA – such as a dismissal 'for family leave reasons', which is an automatically unfair reason for dismissal under S.99 ERA and could also amount to pregnancy and maternity discrimination under S.18 EqA – but in the majority of cases a discrimination claim will be the only option for a dismissed employee who lacks the requisite period of qualifying service to claim unfair dismissal.

Note that until 6 April 2012 an employee only needed to show one year's continuous employment to bring a claim under the ERA. Some commentators have speculated that the increase in the qualifying period for unfair dismissal claims to two years will lead to an increase in claims of discriminatory dismissals.

Reasonableness 26.5

In any unfair dismissal claim it is for the respondent employer to prove that dismissal is for one of the 'potentially fair' reasons listed in S.98(1) and (2) ERA: capability/qualifications, conduct, redundancy, the existence of a statutory restriction on that person's employment, or 'some other substantial reason'. If the employer does so, the tribunal must consider whether the decision to dismiss was reasonable in all the circumstances of the case – see S.98(4). This exercise is markedly different from that which must be undertaken in a discrimination case: i.e. determining whether an employee was dismissed because of a protected characteristic, or if the employer's dismissal procedures and practices are unjustifiably disadvantageous to a particular group.

Can a discriminatory dismissal ever be fair? Tribunals have often found that 26.6 there was discrimination in the lead up to a dismissal, but that the dismissal itself was not discriminatory or unfair. However, it will be a very rare scenario indeed in which a dismissal could be held to be an act of discrimination, but reasonable in all the circumstances. This is because, if the dismissal is found by the tribunal to have occurred because of a protected characteristic, then the respondent will not have made out a fair reason for dismissal, and the unfair dismissal claim will succeed without the need to examine whether or not the dismissal was reasonable in all the circumstances. In other words, it is virtually impossible to conceive of circumstances in which a dismissal on discriminatory grounds will be capable of constituting a fair dismissal under the ERA. The only circumstances we can think of where such a situation might arise is where the reason for the dismissal is unintentionally indirectly discriminatory or where the claimant is claiming unfair constructive dismissal but it is found that the act of discrimination did not amount to a fundamental breach of contract (a prerequisite for a constructive dismissal claim).

26.7 *Indirectly discriminatory dismissals.* The EAT confirmed in Clarke and anor v Eley (IMI) Kynoch Ltd 1983 ICR 165, EAT, that a dismissal that is unlawful under a discrimination enactment is not necessarily unfair. In that case, female claimants were ostensibly dismissed on the ground of redundancy, in circumstances where the employer's selection criteria required part-time staff to be dismissed before full-time staff would be considered for redundancy (a 'last in, first out' policy would then be applied to full-time staff). The female claimants, who worked part time, were dismissed pursuant to these criteria. The tribunal found that the dismissals were indirectly discriminatory, and that the indirect discrimination could not be objectively justified on the facts of the case. It went on to find that, because the dismissals were unlawfully discriminatory, they were also unfair under (what is now) the ERA. The EAT overturned this finding that a discriminatory dismissal must always be unfair. It qualified its rejection of this proposition, however, by saying that 'it would in our view need very special circumstances to justify a holding that an unlawfully discriminatory dismissal was a fair dismissal'.

In our view, such 'special circumstances' would have to involve an indirectly discriminatory redundancy policy or a provision, criterion or practice relating to the application of another potentially fair reason for dismissal, which cannot be justified, but where the reason for the dismissal for the purposes of the ERA claim is found to be the redundancy (or other potentially fair reason) rather than the employee's protected characteristic. The tribunal would then have to consider whether the employer had acted reasonably in all the circumstances in deciding to dismiss under S.98(4) ERA. The answer might be that it did and that the dismissal was therefore fair, despite the simultaneous finding that there had been unlawful indirect discrimination.

26.8 *Constructive dismissal.* In Shaw v CCL Ltd 2008 IRLR 284, EAT, S claimed direct and indirect sex discrimination and constructive unfair dismissal when she resigned following the rejection of her request for flexible working. A tribunal upheld the discrimination claim and also found that the rejection of her request was a detriment related to pregnancy or childbirth contrary to S.47C ERA. However, it dismissed the constructive dismissal claim on the ground that the rejection of the request was not a fundamental breach of S's contract. Allowing the appeal, the EAT held that, by rejecting the request because she was a woman, or by applying a condition which adversely impacted on women, CCL Ltd had fundamentally breached the implied term of trust and confidence in S's contract. However, it declined to rule on the submission that every act of direct or indirect discrimination will amount to a fundamental breach of this term and entitle an employee to treat him or herself as unfairly dismissed.

Unfairness does not equate to discrimination. Neither employers nor **26.9** claimants should fall into the trap of assuming that because an employer has acted unreasonably and unfairly in dismissing an employee, it follows that the dismissal was discriminatory. It is well established that just because an employer behaves unreasonably it does not mean that there has been discrimination, but it may be evidence supporting that inference if there is nothing else to explain the behaviour – Anya v University of Oxford and anor 2001 ICR 847, CA. Thus, while an employer's unreasonable behaviour might *contribute* to the factual circumstances which would lead a tribunal to infer discriminatory reasons for a dismissal, *on its own* it is unlikely to be enough to shift the burden of proof to the employer to provide a non-discriminatory explanation for the dismissal (see further 'Dismissal "because of" protected characteristic' below and Chapter 32, 'Burden of proof').

As it is quite conceivable that a dismissal which is found not to have been discriminatory under the EqA may nevertheless be held to be unfair under the ERA, any claimant who potentially has simultaneous discrimination and unfair dismissal claims should bring both. If the discrimination claim fails the unfair dismissal claim may still succeed, as the claimant may be able to show that the dismissal was not for the reason stated by the employer (even if discrimination is not proved) or that the dismissal, while for a potentially fair reason, was nevertheless unreasonable in all the circumstances. For example:

- **Jones v Express Newspapers plc and anor** ET Case No.10839/96: J alleged that he was discriminated against when dismissed as Assistant Editor of the *Sunday Express* on the ground that the Editor was operating a feminist agenda by wanting more female employees. The tribunal accepted that the dismissal was unfair in that there was no reason for it other than the personal preference of the Editor, which as a basis for dismissal was both irrational and whimsical. However, it rejected J's sex discrimination complaint since there was no evidence that there was any agenda on the Editor's part relating to sex.

Compensation and remedies
26.10

In many cases, a successful claimant will receive a larger award of compensation for a discriminatory dismissal under the EqA than for an unfair dismissal under the ERA. A detailed consideration of compensation under the EqA can be found in Chapter 35, 'Compensation: general principles of assessment', and Chapter 36, 'Compensation: heads of damage'. The two things we should point out at this stage are that no ceiling exists on the amount of losses a claimant can recover as compensation for discrimination, and that a tribunal may make an

873

award for injury to feelings. This contrasts with unfair dismissal, where a claimant can receive a basic award based on length of service of up to £12,900, and a compensatory award covering past and future loss up to a maximum of £72,300 (from 1 February 2012), but no award for injury to feelings. (Of course, if both complaints succeed, the employee will not be entitled to recover double compensation in respect of the same head of loss.)

Furthermore, awards of compensation in unfair dismissal may be the subject of two significant forms of deduction: 'Polkey reductions', where the tribunal takes into account the chance that the dismissal would have occurred in any event even if a fair procedure had been followed; and reductions for contributory fault on the part of the employee. Neither form of deduction is applicable in a discrimination claim. For a detailed examination of deductions from awards of compensation for unfair dismissal, see IDS Employment Law Handbook, 'Unfair Dismissal' (2010), Chapter 18.

26.11 **Reinstatement/re-engagement.** As an alternative to a compensatory award for unfair dismissal, the successful claimant can ask to be reinstated (i.e. given his or her old job back) or re-engaged (i.e. taken on by the same employer in a comparable role) – S.112 ERA. These remedies are only available in respect of unfair dismissal claims under the ERA. However, an employer's refusal to comply with a reinstatement or re-engagement order could, depending on the circumstances, amount to discrimination or victimisation.

26.12 **Definition of 'employee'**
Although both the right not to be subjected to discrimination in employment under the EqA and the right not to be unfairly dismissed under the ERA are stated to apply to 'employees', the statutory definitions of that term are different in the two Acts. The right to claim unfair dismissal under the ERA applies only to those who work pursuant to a contract of employment or apprenticeship (i.e. a contract of service rather than a contract for services). However, the scope of the EqA is wider, in that it applies to 'employment under a contract of service, a contract of apprenticeship, or a contract personally to do work' – S.82(2) (see further Chapter 28, 'Liability of employers, employees and agents' under 'Who is protected?'). The EqA also prohibits discrimination against job applicants, agency workers and trainees. With regard to trainees, the practical importance of the Act's wider scope is illustrated by Lana v Positive Action Training in Housing (London) Ltd 2001 IRLR 501, EAT – a case brought under the predecessor provisions in the Sex Discrimination Act 1975 (SDA). L was a trainee quantity surveyor placed by PAT Ltd with a third party which agreed by a contract with PAT Ltd to provide work experience to L. When L became pregnant, the third party terminated the work experience contract with PAT Ltd. In turn, PAT Ltd terminated L's training contract on the ground that, due to circumstances beyond its control, there was no longer any funding for it. L was not able to bring a claim of automatically unfair dismissal under S.99

ERA, because she was not an employee. However, she was able to bring a claim of direct sex discrimination under S.14 SDA, because PAT Ltd was a provider of training.

Procedural matters

26.13

There are three important procedural differences between unfair dismissal and unlawful discrimination claims.

Questionnaires. Under S.138 EqA, an employee who believes that he or she 26.14 has been subjected to discrimination can submit a prescribed questionnaire to the employer to elicit information relating to the circumstances of the alleged discriminatory act, such as a dismissal. The employer's answers are admissible in tribunal proceedings, and the tribunal may draw an adverse inference if those answers are evasive or equivocal, or the employer fails to reply. No comparable procedure exists in respect of unfair dismissal claims. Questionnaires are covered in Chapter 33, 'Proving discrimination' under 'Requesting information and evidence – questionnaires'.

Burden of proof. The EqA will generally be more favourable to the claimant 26.15 than the ERA when it comes to the burden of proof. Once the claimant has made out a prima facie case of discrimination, it will be for the respondent to provide a non-discriminatory explanation – S.136(2) and (3) EqA. By contrast, the ERA requires the claimant to prove that he or she has been dismissed. The burden then shifts to the employer to prove the reason for the dismissal. If the employer succeeds in showing a potentially fair reason for dismissal, there is a neutral burden for the purposes of determining whether or not the dismissal was fair. The burden of proof in discrimination claims is discussed in Chapter 32, 'Burden of proof'.

Time limits. The provisions for extending the time limit for submitting a claim 26.16 under the EqA are more favourable than under the ERA: the latter requires the late claimant to show that it was 'not reasonably practicable' to submit the claim within the three-month limitation period, whereas under the EqA the tribunal can extend time if it considers it 'just and equitable' to do so – S.123(1)(b) EqA. The issue of time limits is considered further in Chapter 34, 'Enforcing individual rights', under 'Time limits'.

Dismissal 'because of' protected characteristic

26.17

As we have seen above, S.39(2)(c) provides that an employer must not discriminate against an employee by dismissing him or her. An employer will directly discriminate against an employee if, in dismissing him or her, it treats that employee less favourably than it would treat others, and that treatment is 'because of' a protected characteristic – S.13(1) EqA.

875

In some, albeit rare, circumstances an employer may, unwisely, directly cite a protected characteristic as the reason for dismissal. It is more likely, however, that the employer will contend that the dismissal was for one of the potentially fair reasons provided for in the ERA – e.g. misconduct, ill-health or capability (see above under 'Relationship between discriminatory and unfair dismissals'), and the tribunal will be left to determine whether that reason holds true, or whether in fact a protected characteristic was the conscious or unconscious reason behind the dismissal. For a dismissal to be directly discriminatory, it is not necessary for the claimant to show that a protected characteristic was the *sole* reason for dismissal: if the characteristic 'had a significant influence on the outcome, discrimination is made out' – Nagarajan v London Regional Transport 1999 ICR 877, HL.

26.18 The partial reversal of the burden of proof provided for in S.136(2) and (3) EqA plays an important role in dismissal cases. If there are facts from which the court or tribunal could decide, in the absence of any other explanation, that the employer dismissed the employee because of a protected characteristic, the tribunal must hold that the dismissal was discriminatory unless the employer can show that it did not contravene the provision (see further Chapter 32, 'Burden of proof').

The factual circumstances from which a tribunal could infer discriminatory reasons for a dismissal are numerous, but common examples would include the employer's approach to equal opportunities, including any policies it may have in place; the way in which similar incidents were dealt with in the past; the employee's relationship with his or her managers and colleagues; any history of grievances or disciplinary charges; and how thoroughly the employer investigated the matter before deciding to dismiss. We must stress, however, that a mere difference in treatment between the claimant and a comparator who does not share the same protected characteristic will not be sufficient to shift the burden on to the employer to provide a non-discriminatory explanation – there must be some further indication that the protected characteristic was the reason that lay behind the dismissal.

26.19 Given the abundance of case law concerning discriminatory dismissals, and the unique issues presented by the different protected characteristics, we examine dismissals relating to each of those characteristics in turn below. There is one exception: cases concerning pregnancy and maternity dismissals are dealt with in IDS Employment Law Handbook, 'Maternity and Parental Rights' (2009), Chapter 12, 'Detriment and unfair dismissal', and Chapter 13, 'Discrimination and equal pay'.

26.20 ## Age
A person who is dismissed on the ground of his or her age will be able to bring a claim of direct age discrimination under S.13 EqA. It is fairly unusual, outside

the sphere of retirement (see below), for an employer to admit that it dismissed an employee simply because of his or her age. A direct discrimination claim can arise, however, where an employer dismisses an employee ostensibly for, say, poor performance or redundancy, but the employee believes that his or her age was a factor in the employer's decision to dismiss.

One form of dismissal in which age inevitably plays a major role is retirement. As readers will be aware, this area underwent substantial change in 2011 when the default retirement age of 65, together with the associated statutory retirement procedure, was repealed. Given the particular issues that arise in retirement cases, this subject is dealt with separately under 'Retirement' below. In this section, we consider how age discrimination can arise in non-retirement cases.

26.21 Note that a unique feature of direct age discrimination is that, in common with all indirect discrimination claims, the employer has a defence if it can show that the treatment was a proportionate means of achieving a legitimate aim – see Chapter 5, 'Age', under 'Protection under the Equality Act – justifying direct discrimination' for further details.

26.22 **Ageist attitude and remarks.** One circumstance that might lead a tribunal to conclude that age played a part in a dismissal is where there is an 'ageist' culture in the workplace. Such a culture was found to exist in Court v Dennis Publishing Ltd ET Case No.2200327/07 where the tribunal, in finding that a 55-year-old director's dismissal for redundancy was an act of direct discrimination, considered it relevant that the owner of the company had published a book in which he said that 'by the time talent is in its mid to late forties or early fifties, it will have become very expensive. Young talent can be found and underpaid for a short while providing the work is challenging enough.' The tribunal held that this philosophy had affected the attitude of the employer's managers, each of whom had read the book.

In Kessell v Passion for Perfume ET Case No.1700345/07 the claimant's age was perceived as a threat. K, aged 41, worked as a part-time fragrance consultant and was the oldest member of her team. Her manager, S, was 36. S often made disparaging remarks relating to K's age, such as suggesting that she was deaf and should be wearing glasses. Eventually, K was dismissed for gross misconduct because she refused to work on a Saturday as it conflicted with her weekend job. The tribunal accepted that S had a negative attitude about K's age and perceived the experience that came with it as a threat. It concluded that S would not have dismissed a younger member of staff whose external commitments had clashed with their work schedule.

26.23 That case can be contrasted with Uppal v Anuyu Hair and Beauty Ltd ET Case No.2300762/07 where U, aged 50, worked as an assistant in the employer's beauty salon. U and other witnesses claimed that U's line manager, R, often

877

made uncomplimentary remarks about U's age. For example, R would allegedly ask the salon's clients to guess U's age, and was quoted as saying that U would be replaced by 'someone younger, prettier and slimmer'. U was eventually dismissed for indulging in 'malicious gossip' about R. The employment tribunal rejected U's evidence, holding that R – who struck the tribunal as a 'serious and business-like proprietor' – was 'highly unlikely to have engaged in potentially offensive remarks about anyone's age which would inevitably carry with it the risk of offending older clients'.

In Live Nation (Venues) UK Ltd v Hussain and other cases EAT 0234–6/08 the EAT overturned a tribunal's finding that a dismissal amounted to direct age discrimination. The managers making the decision to dismiss believed the employee to be ageist – in that they thought he disliked being managed by younger members of staff – but this did not support the tribunal's finding that they had dismissed him on the ground of his age. Furthermore, the finding that management believed the employee to be 'too old to change', while capable of giving rise to an inference of age discrimination, was unsupported by evidence.

26.24 **Capability.** In the absence of a statutory retirement procedure and default retirement age, both of which were repealed in 2011 (see 'Retirement' below), it is expected that employers will make greater use of capability and performance management procedures as a means of dealing with an age-related decline in productivity and performance. Capability, as a potentially fair reason for dismissal under S.98(2)(a) ERA, is assessed by reference to skill, aptitude, health, or any other physical or mental quality. Although it is an undisputed fact that age can have a bearing on a person's capability, tribunals have thus far been slow to endorse employers' assumptions that a person above or below a given age is incapable of adequate performance in a job. Where an employer dismisses an employee for reasons of capability without undergoing any formal assessment of his or her abilities, the tribunal may infer that the dismissal was motivated by age discrimination.

Employers should avoid the mistake made in Martin v SS Photay and Associates ET Case No.1100242/07, which was to assume that the claimant's age represented a health and safety risk. M, aged 70, worked as a cleaner in the employer's surgery. In November 2006, the employer left a note in M's locker saying: 'I'm sorry for having to break some bad news to you, due to your age and health problems you have fallen into the high risk category for health and safety. We cannot allow you to continue cleaning the practice.' The employment tribunal upheld M's direct discrimination claim. M's dismissal letter had specifically referred to her age, and the employer had not obtained any medical evidence to prove that M's age and state of health constituted a health and safety risk. (We would suggest that there will be very few circumstances in which an employee's age per se represents such a health and safety risk that dismissal is justified. Such circumstances are likely to be confined to jobs involving a high degree of danger and/or physical fitness.)

Note that we consider indirect discrimination in capability dismissals below under 'Indirectly discriminatory dismissals – capability'.

Dismissed for being too young. Although most age discrimination cases have **26.25** been brought by older employees who claim to have been treated less favourably than their younger counterparts, the statutory provisions provide equal protection to those discriminated against because they are considered too young. In Thomas v Eight Members Club and anor ET Case No.2202603/07, for example, T, aged 19, worked as a membership secretary for the employer's private members club. In August 2007 she was dismissed after being told by her manager that she was too young to do the job, and that if he had met her a few years later she would have been able to do it. The employment tribunal upheld T's direct discrimination claim.

Almost identical facts occurred in Wilkinson v Springwell Engineering Ltd ET Case No.2507420/07. W was a teenager when she began working as an office administrator in the employer's engineering business. In March 2007 she was dismissed, allegedly on the ground of incapability – she was told that she only performed 90 per cent of her duties – but the employment tribunal accepted that W had been told that she was being dismissed for being too young. Accordingly, it upheld her direct discrimination claim.

Disability
26.26

If an employer dismisses an employee because of his or her disability, when it would not dismiss a comparable non-disabled employee, this will amount to direct discrimination under S.13 EqA. Where an employee is dismissed not because of his or her disability per se, but because of something arising in consequence of his or her disability (such as persistent absences), the dismissal will amount to 'discrimination arising from disability' under S.15, unless, that is, the employer can show that dismissal was justified as a proportionate means of achieving a legitimate aim. The third form of disability discrimination that can arise in the dismissal process is a failure to make reasonable adjustments under S.21. The duty to make such adjustments will arise whenever a provision, criterion or practice (PCP) that the employer applies has the effect of placing a disabled employee at a substantial disadvantage when compared with people who are not disabled – S.20.

From a dismissed claimant's perspective, it is obviously preferable to frame the claim as one of direct discrimination rather than one of discrimination arising from disability or failure to make reasonable adjustments, since direct discrimination cannot be justified and is not subject to any test of reasonableness. In practice, however, many claimants are likely to plead all three heads simultaneously, since the distinction between a dismissal because of disability

879

and a dismissal because of something arising in consequence of disability will not always be clear. Moreover, the fact that no actual or hypothetical comparator is required for a claim under S.15 and that the comparison in a reasonable adjustment case under S.20 is with a group – people who are not disabled – rather than an individual, mean that those two forms of discrimination cover a potentially much wider range of circumstances than direct discrimination.

26.27 The difference in comparative exercises was highlighted in this context in Fareham College Corporation v Walters 2009 IRLR 991, EAT. In that case the College dismissed W after a lengthy sickness absence rather than offer her a phased return to work. In upholding the decision of an employment tribunal that the College had breached the duty to make reasonable adjustments, the EAT stressed that the tribunal had not erred in failing to consider evidence that a non-disabled employee had been dismissed after a similar period of absence. The more general comparative exercise required in a reasonable adjustments claim, involving a class or group of non-disabled comparators, differs from that which is understood and applied in the individual, like-for-like comparison required in cases of direct discrimination claims: indeed, in many cases the facts will speak for themselves and the identity of the non-disabled comparators will be clearly discernible from the PCP found to be in play. In W's case, the PCP was the College's refusal to permit W to have a phased return to work. It was entirely clear from this that the comparator group was other employees who were not disabled and who were able forthwith to attend work and carry out the essential tasks required of them in their post. Members of that group were not liable to be dismissed on the ground of disability whereas the claimant, because of her disability, could not do her job, could not comply with the criterion, and was liable to dismissal. She was thereby placed at a substantial disadvantage in comparison with other, non-disabled employees.

While the circumstances in which an employer would expressly dismiss an employee solely because of his or her disability are relatively rare, direct discrimination can also occur where an employer makes assumptions about the disability and, as a result, treats the disabled employee less favourably than it would treat a comparator. For example, in Tudor v Spen Corner Veterinary Centre Ltd and anor ET Case No.2404211/05 the employer dismissed T after she lost her sight following a stroke. In upholding T's direct disability discrimination claim, the employment tribunal found that the employer had made generalised and stereotypical assumptions about the employee and rushed to a decision without a proper consideration of the circumstances and any adjustments it could make. In the tribunal's view, the employer would not have acted in that way in respect of a hypothetical comparator with a broken leg.

26.28 The question of the correct comparator arose in High Quality Lifestyles Ltd v Watts 2006 IRLR 850, EAT, where the EAT held that an employment tribunal had erred in ruling that the dismissal of an HIV positive employee amounted to direct disability discrimination. Although the tribunal had found that the reason for dismissal was the risk of transmission of HIV, it had wrongly compared his treatment to that which would have been received by a person in the same position as the claimant, but without HIV. The EAT noted that for the purposes of direct disability discrimination the comparator is a person whose 'relevant circumstances including his abilities' are the same as 'or not materially different' to those of the claimant. In its view, the word 'including' meant that the 'relevant circumstances' imputed to a comparator are wider than just his or her abilities. It followed that in the instant case the tribunal should have imputed to the comparator an equally infectious disease, before going on to consider whether the comparator would also have been dismissed. Accordingly, the tribunal's finding of direct discrimination was set aside. (Note, however, that the tribunal's finding of disability-related discrimination – the precursor to discrimination arising from disability – was not set aside and we would strongly argue that an employer that dismisses an employee because of the risk of transmission of HIV will need to provide objective justification to avoid liability for 'discrimination arising from disability' under S.15 EqA. The legitimate aim in such cases is surely minimising the risk of transmission, so the question for the tribunal would be one of proportionality – i.e. were there less discriminatory ways of minimising the risk?)

26.29 The Court of Appeal adopted a less rigid approach to the comparator question in Stockton on Tees Borough Council v Aylott 2010 ICR 1278, CA. There A, who suffered from bipolar affective disorder, brought grievances against various colleagues alleging bullying and harassment. Those complaints were not upheld, and the report that rejected them recommended that A not return to work until his bipolar disorder had stabilised. After a lengthy period of sick leave, A returned to work in a different department where his line manager monitored his performance closely and set work-related deadlines. Following further absences and a heated discussion with his line manager, he once again went off sick. The employer decided to suspend him and conduct a disciplinary investigation, but withdrew that decision on learning that A had been admitted to hospital on account of his mental illness. A did not return to work, and the employer eventually dismissed him on the ground of ill health. A brought a tribunal claim alleging unfair dismissal and disability discrimination.

With regard to direct discrimination, the tribunal thought that the appropriate comparator was someone who had been off work for a similar number of days to A, but who did not have bipolar disorder. A comparator with a similar sickness record in respect of, for example, a complicated broken bone or other surgical problem would not have been subjected to the same treatment – namely, the imposition of deadlines and performance monitoring, culminating in dismissal for ill health. The tribunal added that the decision to suspend A and conduct a disciplinary investigation – although subsequently withdrawn – and the subsequent dismissal amounted to direct discrimination 'based on a stereotypical view of mental illness'.

26.30 On appeal, the EAT considered that the tribunal had erred in upholding the claim on the basis of the employer's 'stereotypical view of mental illness'. Instead, it should have assessed the treatment that would have been afforded to an employee who did not have bipolar disorder, but who, like A, had recently been moved to a different post and whose past behaviour and performance had caused concern. In the EAT's view, the tribunal should have established whether A had been less favourably treated than an appropriate comparator before determining the grounds for that difference in treatment. When the case reached the Court of Appeal, Lord Justice Mummery applied the guidance of the House of Lords in Shamoon v Chief Constable of the Royal Ulster Constabulary 2003 ICR 337, HL (a sex discrimination case), that the question of less favourable treatment than an appropriate comparator and the question of whether that treatment was on the relevant prohibited ground may be so intertwined that one cannot be resolved without the other being determined at the same time. There is essentially a single question: did the claimant, on the proscribed ground, receive less favourable treatment than others? Applying that approach to the present case, the answer to whether or not A suffered less favourable treatment on the ground of his disability lay in the reason for his dismissal. The tribunal had found that A's mental disability was the ground of his dismissal. Its reasons for that finding included the employer's stereotypical view of, and reactions to, mental illness.

In light of the tribunal's findings, the Court considered that the EAT had been wrong to find an error of law in the tribunal's decision on direct discrimination. The tribunal could not be criticised for leaving out of the circumstances of its comparator a move to a new post and past behaviour and performance causing concern, since those circumstances clearly arose from A's disability. Moreover, the reference to the employer's stereotypical view of mental illness was not too vague to support a finding of direct discrimination, since the tribunal was not relying on an unproven assertion of stereotyping: it had made detailed findings of fact about the employer's reaction to A's mental illness, and had been entitled to draw inferences from those findings.

26.31 **Consultation and investigation.** It is widely considered good practice to consult with an employee prior to any dismissal, but consultation takes on added importance where disabled employees are concerned. It may not be immediately apparent that an employee's ill health, poor work performance or misconduct is related to a disability. However, in the context of discrimination arising from a disability under S.15 EqA and the duty to make reasonable adjustments under S.20, an employer must do all it can reasonably be expected to do to find out whether an employee has a disability. It is therefore essential that the employer's disciplinary procedure provides scope for talking to the employee to find out what the problems are. Where an employer assumes that disability is not an issue, or makes stereotypical assumptions about the effects of a disability, a finding of discrimination is likely.

Gender reassignment   26.32

If a person is dismissed because he or she is proposing to undergo, is undergoing or has undergone a process of gender reassignment, the dismissal will amount to direct discrimination under S.13 EqA. If an employee is dismissed because of absences arising from the gender reassignment process, an additional provision – S.16 EqA – may also be relevant. The effect of this provision is twofold. First, it is discriminatory to treat transsexual people less favourably for being absent from work because of gender reassignment than they would be treated if they were absent because of sickness or injury – S.16(2)(a). Secondly, it is discriminatory to treat gender reassignment absences less favourably than dismissals for reasons other than sickness or injury, unless it is reasonable for the absences to be treated less favourably – S.16(2)(b).

Marriage and civil partnership   26.33

A person who is dismissed because he or she is married or in a civil partnership will be able to claim direct discrimination under S.13. However, a person who is dismissed because he or she is *not* married or in a civil partnership cannot rely on S.13 to found a claim – S.13(4) EqA.

Cases involving dismissal on the ground of marriage or civil partnership status are few and far between, but in North East Midlands Co-operative Society Ltd v Allen 1977 IRLR 212, EAT, the Appeal Tribunal held that a tribunal had correctly concluded that a newly married employee had been both unfairly dismissed and discriminated against contrary to the Sex Discrimination Act 1975 (the precursor to the EqA). In that case the employer operated a rule whereby, when a female employee married, her original contract was deemed to have been terminated by reason of her marriage and a fresh contract negotiated. This was a case of straightforward direct discrimination on the ground of marital status.

Race   26.34

A person who is dismissed because of his or her race will be able to bring a claim of direct race discrimination under S.13. An employer must never be influenced by race when deciding to dismiss – even if the employee's conduct is such as to justify dismissal. Although an inconsistency in treatment between two employees of different races is not on its own sufficient to raise a prima facie case of race discrimination, it can be a strong indicator, particularly when combined with other factors.

An inference of discrimination was drawn by the tribunal in Guppy v Walton Civil Engineering and Surface Contractors Ltd and anor ET Case

883

No.3102391/06, in which G, WCESC Ltd's only black employee, was dismissed after an altercation with a white colleague, C. During the course of the altercation, C became aggressive, called G a 'black bastard' and a 'nigger', and then picked up a broom and hit him on the arm and leg. To prevent further assault, G held C in a headlock and punched him twice, only releasing him after receiving a reassurance that C would not attack him again. C suffered cuts to his face, resulting in his having to attend hospital and take time off work. G suffered minor injury but was able to continue working that day. After an investigation by the operations director, D, a disciplinary hearing was held at which G gave his account of events, including pointing out that C had been racially abusive. However, D did not ask what racially abusive words had been used, and nor did he put the allegation of racist abuse to C. Instead, having relied on two witness statements – one in the name of C, and another, unsigned, in the name of a colleague, H – that were at odds with the original account, D determined that G was to blame for the incident and that he had attacked C, causing him significant injury. G was dismissed for gross misconduct and brought a claim of race discrimination.

26.35 An employment tribunal concluded that the disciplinary process was 'seriously flawed'. The employer had ignored the fact that the original statements were largely consistent with one another and were more likely to be reliable. It had not acted consistently when photographing the injuries to C and G, and had raised an unsubstantiated allegation that G's was an old injury. In addition, the tribunal found it troubling that reliance was placed on an unsigned, contradictory statement in the name of H. From the moment the investigation began, the focus had been on C's injuries and not on the injury and racial abuse experienced by G. Given that C was white and G was black, this raised a prima facie case of race discrimination, in respect of which the employer had totally failed to provide an adequate, non-discriminatory explanation. The dismissal therefore amounted to race discrimination.

Of course, not every dismissal that follows a racial incident in the workplace will be discriminatory, and employees would be foolish to assume that having been the victim of racial discrimination or harassment provides immunity from censure for misconduct. In Sidhu v Aerospace Composite Technology Ltd 2001 ICR 167, CA, for example, the employer's disciplinary policy stated that in cases of violence provocation would not be taken into account. S was involved in a fight following a racially motivated attack on him by other employees. The employer dismissed S and the other employees involved. The Court of Appeal held that the employer was not guilty of discrimination against S because there was no suggestion that the policy itself would be applied any differently to someone who was of a different race to S.

26.36 When comparing the treatment received by a dismissed employee to that which was or would have been received by a comparator of a different race, it is necessary to take account of all the surrounding circumstances. In Ahmad v Morse Chain Division of Borg Warner Ltd ET Case No.25005/78 a black employee was dismissed for fighting while his white antagonist was not. However, although potentially discriminatory, the dismissal did not amount to either unfair dismissal or race discrimination in the circumstances because the disparate treatment could be justified on non-racial grounds: the black worker, but not the white worker, was already under warning for a previous fighting incident.

The mere fact that an employer has behaved unreasonably in dismissing an employee does not mean that it acted in a discriminatory fashion. However, where that unreasonableness is extreme in its nature, the tribunal may conclude that the claimant has shown a prima facie case of discrimination and require the employer to provide a non-discriminatory explanation.

An example: **26.37**

- **Gayle v Works 4 Ltd** ET Case No.2300786/07: G, who was of Afro-Caribbean descent, was required by his employer, W4 Ltd, to periodically submit to random drugs tests. It was known that employees who failed a test, or who deliberately failed to attend for a drugs test, were usually dismissed. The result of one test, which had been rearranged due to a conflicting medical appointment, was negative, but the information supplied to W4 Ltd indicated trace elements of cannabis and cocaine. Although the information supplied by the testing company also made clear that this did not equate to a positive test, W4 Ltd took the view that it indicated drug use, and required G to attend another test. Before the second test, G was admitted to hospital and signed off work for two weeks. On his return, he was called to a disciplinary meeting for having failed to attend the second test. In a break from usual practice, R, W4 Ltd's managing director, dealt with the disciplinary hearing. Despite G producing an e-mail from the testing company confirming that the results of the first test were negative, a sick certificate, and a letter from his GP explaining the condition that had caused his visit to hospital, R stated that he believed G was trying to avoid having the test because he had drugs in his system and that G would have to be dismissed. R presented no evidence to back up his assertion, other than saying he had heard it through 'word of mouth'. Nor did he respond to the suggestion that his actions were influenced by G's race. The letter of dismissal G eventually received not only referred to the missed test, but relied on the traces found in the original drugs test. After his internal appeal failed, G brought claims of unfair dismissal and race discrimination. The tribunal, rather unsurprisingly, found the dismissal to be both procedurally and substantively unfair. Turning to the second issue, it accepted that mere unreasonableness cannot lead to an inference of race discrimination. However, it considered that the extreme unreasonableness and the 'sham'

885

disciplinary process were enough to shift the burden of proof to W4 Ltd to provide a non-discriminatory explanation. There had been no acceptance from W4 Ltd that the disciplinary procedure had been flawed, and nor did it recognise that the approach to the initial test results was unduly cynical. No explanation for G's treatment was put forward by W4 Ltd, nor was there evidence from which the tribunal could infer a non-discriminatory reason. His claim of race discrimination was therefore upheld.

26.38 **Nationality.** As explained in Chapter 10, 'Race', under 'Grounds of "race"', the protected characteristic of race in S.9 EqA covers much more than skin colour and ethnicity. Nationality is an element of race for these purposes, so a dismissal that was significantly influenced by the claimant's nationality would be discriminatory. In Wardle v Crédit Agricole Corporate and Investment Bank 2011 ICR 1290, CA, a tribunal found that a French bank directly discriminated against W when it overlooked him for promotion in favour of a French colleague. Some months later he was summarily dismissed. The tribunal held that this dismissal was both unfair and an act of victimisation. (Note that the case was subsequently appealed to the Court of Appeal on the question of compensation but the tribunal's findings on liability were not challenged.)

26.39 **Language.** Language is not an element of race under S.9, so if an employer dismisses an employee because of poor language skills, or breaching an instruction as to which language to use in the workplace, this is unlikely to amount to direct race discrimination. In Salmi v European Wellcare Homes Ltd ET Case No.2105043/07 the employer ran a number of residential care homes for the elderly, which were subject to regulation by the Commission for Social Care Inspection (CSCI). One of CSCI's requirements was that only English be spoken in care homes, so that residents are not confused by a variety of languages. S, who was originally from Morocco, was employed as a chef in one of the care homes. An argument erupted between S and two colleagues in September 2007, during the course of which he shouted and swore in a foreign language (the tribunal transcript does not identify which). A disciplinary meeting then took place, at which EWH Ltd determined that S was guilty of misconduct. As S already had a warning on his file, he was dismissed. In his claim for unfair dismissal and race discrimination, S argued that, since he had sworn and shouted in his native tongue, the treatment he received should be compared with that which would have been accorded to a white British person speaking English. The tribunal disagreed and accepted instead the comparator advanced by EWH Ltd – a white British person speaking a foreign language, either in anger or to practise their language skills. Such a comparator, the tribunal explained, would have been disciplined for misconduct, since he or she too would have broken the rule that only English be spoken in the care home.

It should be noted, however, that although the race discrimination provisions do not prevent an employer setting language standards in the workplace, and taking action up to and including dismissal to enforce those standards, such standards are likely to amount to a PCP for the purposes of an indirect discrimination claim (see 'Indirectly discriminatory dismissals' below), and may therefore require objective justification if they place a protected racial group at a particular disadvantage.

Religion or belief

26.40

A person who is dismissed because of his or her religion or belief will be entitled to bring a claim of direct discrimination under S.13 EqA. However, although religion or belief discrimination frequently makes headlines, the fact remains that, as with sexual orientation, there is a comparatively small body of case law concerning dismissal because of religion or belief – a reflection both of the fact that this strand of discrimination law is relatively new, and that many employers and staff adopt the mantra of 'never discuss religion in the workplace'.

One of the most challenging situations an employer can face is where an employee's religious or other beliefs come into conflict with the employer's obligations in respect of one of the other protected characteristics under the EqA; in particular, sexual orientation. Thus far, the jurisprudence in this area has drawn a distinction between an employee's right to hold religious beliefs – which is absolutely protected – and his or her right to manifest those beliefs, which does not attract the same level of protection where it clashes with the employer's obligations under the anti-discrimination law and with the rights of others.

Three examples in the context of dismissal:

26.41

- **Chondol v Liverpool City Council** EAT 0298/08: C, a committed Christian, was employed as a social worker on secondment to Mersey Care NHS Trust. The Trust became concerned by what it perceived as C's failure to recognise professional boundaries. For example, he gave a copy of the Bible to a service user, who subsequently complained. Following his eventual dismissal, C claimed his dismissal constituted an act of direct discrimination. The tribunal dismissed the claim. The actual reason for the Trust's treatment of C – namely, the disciplinary action which contributed to his dismissal – was its belief that he had been inappropriately promoting his religion to service users, and not his religion itself. The tribunal was satisfied that the Trust would have acted in precisely the same way towards another member of staff regardless of what religion or view (religious or otherwise) it believed was being promoted. Before the EAT, C's main argument was that the tribunal's decision on direct discrimination was unsustainable as it had constructed the wrong comparator. The correct comparator was someone known to have been either of no belief or of an unrelated belief, which is not similarly protected, and who had behaved in the same manner as C was alleged to have done. The EAT rejected this argument: the tribunal had made it clear that the Trust had not acted on the ground of C's religion, but rather on the ground that he was improperly foisting it on service users. Consequently, the whole question of how to define the correct comparator was academic

- **McFarlane v Relate Avon Ltd** 2010 ICR 507, EAT: M, a committed Christian and a former elder of a large multicultural church, worked as a counsellor for RA Ltd, which provides confidential sex therapy and relationship counselling services to couples, irrespective of sexual orientation. It is part of M's Christian belief that marriage is the union of one man and one woman, for life, and that same-sex sexual activity is contrary to God's law. RA Ltd and its counsellors are members of the British Association for Sexual and Relationship Therapy, and are governed by its code of ethics. This requires members to 'work in ways that respect the value and dignity of clients... with due regard to issues such as... sexual orientation'. It stipulates that each therapist must be aware of his or her own prejudices and avoid discrimination. RA Ltd has an equal opportunities policy couched in similar terms. M refused to provide psycho-sexual therapy counselling services to same-sex couples, and was eventually dismissed as a result. An employment tribunal rejected his complaint of direct discrimination, as the dismissal was based on the employee's refusal to comply with the employer's equal opportunities policy rather than on his Christian beliefs. Dealing with the additional complaint of indirect discrimination, the tribunal held that RA Ltd's requirement for all counsellors to adhere to its equal opportunities and ethical practice policies put counsellors with the same religious beliefs as M at a particular disadvantage when compared to others. However, that requirement was a legitimate aim and the disadvantage to M was justified as a proportionate means of achieving this aim. Both decisions were upheld by the EAT on appeal, where it was stressed that an employer can legitimately refuse to accommodate views which contradict its fundamental principles

- **Maitland v Wilmott and anor** ET Case No.1301020/07: M was a supply teacher who taught religious education (RE). She allegedly referred to some of her pupils as 'devils' and told one girl that she was not good enough to be a Christian, and that if she ever got married it would end in divorce. M's assignment was eventually terminated because she was seen as too 'evangelical'. The tribunal rejected her direct discrimination claim. M's assignment was terminated because, among other things, she was attempting to impose her own religious views rather than teach RE in a factual and objective way.

26.42 The right not to be discriminated against on the grounds of religion or belief also covers non-religious beliefs, as well as a lack of religion or belief. The conditions for a belief to attract statutory protection were set out by the EAT in Grainger plc v Nicholson 2010 ICR 360, EAT – see Chapter 11, 'Religion or belief', under 'Protection under the Equality Act'. As two of these conditions are that the belief must attain a certain level of 'cogency, seriousness, cohesion and importance' and 'be worthy of respect in civilised society', an employer is unlikely to fall foul of the law if it dismisses an employee for belonging to an extremist group or for expressing racist beliefs. An example:

- **Marsden l'Anson v Chief Constable of West Yorkshire Police** ET Case No.1804854/09: M, a civilian staff member, was employed as an imaging officer. He was also a singer and songwriter. In March 2007, M was suspended for devoting an excessive amount of work time to using the employer's equipment for his personal material. The employer also believed that some of the material was racist and that M had links with the BNP. Following his eventual dismissal, M brought discrimination proceedings. He described his philosophical belief as 'a belief in my cultural identity and ancestry, including the promotion and celebration of English culture and history'. The employment tribunal dismissed the claim. M's belief only manifested itself in the songs that he wrote and performed – it did not impact upon any other aspect of his life. Therefore, in accordance with Grainger, M's belief had not attained a certain level of 'cogency, seriousness, cohesion and importance'.

Sex   26.43

Dismissal on the ground of sex will amount to direct discrimination under S.13 EqA. However, it is now practically unheard of for an employee to be told that he or she is being dismissed simply because of his or her gender. Most disputes concerning sex discrimination and dismissal relate instead to treatment that has a close connection with gender and tend to fall into one of four categories: pregnancy and maternity (which is now a protected characteristic in its own right and is dealt with in IDS Employment Law Handbook, 'Maternity and Parental Rights' (2009), Chapters 12 and 13); flexible working and childcare; redundancy policies (see 'Redundancy' below); and constructive dismissal (see 'Constructive dismissal' below). Cases falling within the last three categories generally involve allegations of indirect discrimination, but there continue to be some cases where direct sex discrimination is argued.

Employers should avoid making assumptions about the respective roles of men and women. In Skyrail Oceanic Ltd v Coleman 1981 ICR 864, CA, the employer dismissed C two days after her marriage to an employee of a rival travel agency. The employer had discussed with its rival the potential for leaks of confidential information, and had agreed that it would be better to dismiss C than her husband as he was likely to be the main breadwinner in the household. The Court of Appeal held that since the assumption was based on sex, and the dismissal was a direct result of that assumption, it followed that the dismissal was discriminatory.

26.44 To a large extent, direct sex discrimination claims now depend on a tribunal drawing inferences from surrounding circumstances and determining that gender was the reason why the employer acted as it did. However, such inferences must have an evidential basis. In B and anor v A 2010 IRLR 400, EAT, the employer summarily dismissed A, without any proper investigation or disciplinary procedure, following an allegation of rape from a colleague. An employment tribunal noted that the employer considered that A posed a risk of further violence against members of staff and held that this, coupled with the failure to follow procedures, was sufficient to draw an inference that the employer had been motivated by a stereotypical view of male aggression. Overturning that decision on appeal, the EAT stressed that while the employer's behaviour was sufficiently surprising to call for some explanation, and that its explanation for the failure to follow correct procedures was irrational in that the risk of violence could have been dealt with by suspension, this was not enough to establish sex discrimination.

The EAT emphasised that any conclusions as to an employer's motivation must be based on the evidence and, while 'tribunals must of course be alive to the fact that stereotypical views of male and female behaviour remain common, there must still in any given case be sufficient reason to find that the putative discriminator was motivated by such a view (or, in cases which turn on the burden of proof, that there is sufficient reason to believe that he could have been so motivated)'. There was no such reason in the instant case, where the evidence disclosed a complete and obvious reason why the employer believed that the claimant posed a continuing threat of violence – namely, that the employer believed that the claimant had acted violently towards a colleague and that he had threatened to 'get her' if she told anyone what had happened. If the hypothetical female alleged aggressor had acted with comparable violence towards her victim, and had made the same threats, there was no reason whatever to suppose that the employer would not have had the same fears.

26.45 As we saw above under 'Age', a tribunal determining whether age discrimination has occurred may draw inferences from an ageist attitude on the part of an employer. Similar inferences can be drawn where an employer displays a sexist attitude and subsequently dismisses a female employee. For example, in Rojas v Market One Europe LLP ET Case No.3300120/10 R was made redundant shortly after she refused to end a flexible working arrangement due to childcare commitments. An employment tribunal found the redundancy to be a sham, as there was work available for R. In considering whether her employment was terminated because of her sex, the tribunal was influenced by an e-mail circulated by her manager headed 'how to speak womanese'. The fact that he gave in to the temptation to circulate the e-mail at work told the tribunal that he was able to allow his prejudices to overcome his professionalism. That suggested that he could allow his prejudices about women with children working at home to overcome his professionalism, and supported the tribunal's conclusion that R was dismissed because of her sex.

Allegations of sex discrimination are prone to arise where an employee is dismissed because of his or her relationship with, or marriage to, a colleague or someone who works for a rival company. The question for a tribunal in such circumstances is not whether there was a connection between the relationship and the dismissal, but whether a person of the opposite sex would have been treated any differently in the same circumstances. An example:

- **Dunphy v Plane Station Group plc and anor** ET Case No. 2204311/04: D had worked for her employer for ten years, and from the beginning of her employment had formed a close relationship with the chief executive officer, I. They moved in together in 1996, but took steps to conceal their relationship from the employer. I's contract was terminated acrimoniously in March 2004. The employer knew that D and I had a close working relationship, and after I's departure asked D if she was still in contact with him as the company was extremely concerned about the possibility of confidential information being divulged to him. She said she was not. The employer found out about the relationship in August 2004 and D was suspended. Following an investigation into her deception over her continuing relationship with I, and because of the potential conflict of interest, she was dismissed. Among other things, D claimed that the dismissal was direct sex discrimination on the basis of gender stereotyping. The tribunal dismissed her claims. A male senior manager in a long-standing relationship with a female director or chief executive officer would have been treated in the same way as D in similar circumstances.

Sexual orientation

26.46

A person who is dismissed because of his or her sexual orientation will be entitled to bring a claim of direct discrimination under S.13 EqA. There have been relatively few cases where the claimant has complained that his or her dismissal was due to sexual orientation. However, inferences might be drawn against an employer who tolerates or promotes homophobia in the workplace, or deals with complaints about sexual orientation discrimination in a different way to other discrimination complaints. Another matter likely to draw the tribunal's scrutiny is any correlation between the claimant revealing his or her sexual orientation to the employer and the date of dismissal.

In Lisboa v Realpubs Ltd and ors EAT 0224/10 the workplace in question had a reputation as London's first gay pub. L, who was gay, was employed in the pub shortly after it was taken over by R Ltd, whose business model was to take financially struggling pubs and turn them into 'gastropubs' offering both food and drink. As part of this 'repositioning' R Ltd instructed L to put up a sign stating that 'this is not a gay pub' (although this plan was abandoned at L's

891

request). He was also instructed to seat families and mixed-sex groups in prominent positions, so that they could be seen from outside the pub. A number of male staff were dismissed and replaced by women, and the pub manager, H, made homophobic remarks in L's presence. L resigned and claimed sexual orientation discrimination. An employment tribunal held that while H's comments were directly discriminatory, the other matters L complained of were not. They were simply part of a lawful repositioning of R Ltd's business. L appealed.

26.47 On appeal, the EAT rejected the tribunal's analysis, noting that it had stopped at the point where it found that the pub's repositioning strategy was lawful. The correct question was to ask whether R Ltd had gone too far in embracing a policy of taking negative steps to make the venue less welcoming to gay customers, and whether gay customers might reasonably take the view that as a result of the measures adopted they were disadvantaged compared with other customers. Based on the factual evidence found by the tribunal, it was clear that gay customers were treated less favourably, and it followed that in being asked to treat gay customers in this way, L was also discriminated against on the ground of sexual orientation.

Pub rebranding was also at issue in Etheridge and anor v Gamebirds Inn Ltd ET Case Nos.1401997/05 and others. E and his male partner, M, ran a pub called the Rummer. In 2005, the pub was transferred to GI Ltd in accordance with the Transfer of Undertakings (Protection of Employment) Regulations 1981 SI 1981/1794. Two of the employer's directors met with E and M to discuss refurbishment plans for the pub. During this conversation, the couple were told that they would no longer fit in and were offered compromise agreements. Shortly after the pub reopened with a new manager, E and M learned that GI Ltd did not want a gay couple managing the Rummer because it would encourage more gay people to frequent the premises. An employment tribunal held that E and M were unfairly dismissed and had suffered direct discrimination on the ground of sexual orientation.

26.48 Where an employee receives a frosty or hostile reception to his or her 'coming out' at work, he or she may feel that there is no alternative but to resign and claim constructive dismissal (see 'Constructive dismissal – failure to deal with complaints' below). For example, in M&L Sheet Metals Ltd v Willis EAT 0474/09 M complained of a campaign of bullying and harassment following his disclosure that he was gay at a company-sponsored boxing match. When his grievance and subsequent appeal were rejected, he resigned and claimed both harassment on the ground of sexual orientation and constructive dismissal. Of the 13 incidents of harassment that M relied on, an employment tribunal found that four were proved as there was corroborating evidence. It was satisfied that M resigned in response to the effect of those incidents and to M&L Ltd's failure to uphold his grievance, and upheld his claims for harassment and constructive unfair dismissal. The EAT refused to interfere with the finding that he was constructively dismissed. It found no error of law and dismissed M&L Ltd's appeal.

A failure to deal with sexual orientation discrimination in the workplace may lead to a finding of direct discrimination (and unfair dismissal) where the employee concerned is dismissed for retaliating. An example:

- **Yahiaoui v Aramark Ltd** ET Case No.3200198/08: Y was employed as a Chef de Partie. In 2007, he was dismissed for gross misconduct for assaulting G, the male Executive Chef of A Ltd. Throughout his disciplinary hearing, Y maintained that he had finally reacted to a prolonged campaign of sexual harassment by G, who had, among other things, slapped Y's bottom and put his arms around him. Although Y had made numerous complaints about this, nothing was ever done. A tribunal upheld Y's claims of unfair dismissal as well as harassment on the ground of sexual orientation. Furthermore, A Ltd's failure to investigate Y's complaints also constituted an act of direct discrimination. It had consistently failed to explore Y's allegations and had even suggested that G's conduct was 'playful'. A hypothetical comparator in the same relevant circumstances as Y, but who was not gay or perceived to be gay, would have had their complaints of harassment taken more seriously.

26.49 However, the statutory provisions do not provide blanket immunity for employees who retaliate against colleagues who act in a discriminatory manner – if a tribunal is satisfied that the employer would have treated employees of a different sexual orientation in the same way, the disciplinary response will not amount to discrimination.

While it is possible for an employer to discriminate against an employee on the ground of sexual orientation without actually knowing what the employee's sexual orientation is, ignorance may amount to a defence where such knowledge is a central feature of the case. For example, in Crouch v Mills Group Ltd and anor ET Case No.1804817/06 C worked in one of the employer's convenience stores. He was assumed to be heterosexual. Indeed, he regularly made comments to his manager, R, about wanting to have sex with her, and claimed to others that he could 'pull her' and other women. C contended that, during a conversation with R, he revealed the fact that he was gay and that, in response, she refused to talk to him. She also allegedly shortened his lunch break entitlement from one hour to half an hour. C was eventually dismissed for incapability and brought a number of complaints in an employment tribunal, including one for direct discrimination. The tribunal dismissed the claim. It rejected C's contention that he had told R of his homosexuality, and found that MG Ltd was not aware of his sexual orientation. Furthermore, C was not unreasonably ostracised, and nor did he have his lunch break shortened. C had not proved any facts or raised any inferences from which the tribunal could conclude that MG Ltd had committed an act of discrimination.

26.50 Indirectly discriminatory dismissals

Claims that a dismissal is indirectly discriminatory are quite different to direct discrimination claims, since it is not necessary for the claimant to show that his or her protected characteristic was the reason for dismissal. Nor, for that matter, is there any need to establish an individual comparator. Instead, a claimant must seek to establish that the *consequences* of being treated in the *same way* as everyone else are unjustifiably disadvantageous to those with his or her protected characteristic.

Section 19(1) EqA provides that an employer indirectly discriminates against an employee if it applies a provision, criterion or practice (PCP) which is discriminatory in relation to a protected characteristic of the employee's. A PCP is discriminatory in relation to a protected characteristic if:

- the employer applies, or would apply, it to persons with whom the employee does not share the characteristic

- it puts, or would put, persons with whom the employee shares the characteristic at a particular disadvantage when compared with persons with whom the employee does not share it

- it puts, or would put, the employee at that disadvantage, and

- the employer cannot show it to be a proportionate means of achieving a legitimate aim – S.19(2).

26.51 Applying this definition to dismissal, it is apparent that a dismissal will be indirectly discriminatory if it involved the application of a PCP which entailed the necessary disadvantage (see Chapter 16, 'Indirect discrimination: proving disadvantage'), and cannot be objectively justified (see Chapter 17, 'Indirect discrimination: objective justification').

Where the disadvantage is inadvertent, a tribunal may hold that the dismissal was fair under the ERA but discriminatory under the EqA – see above under 'Relationship between discriminatory and unfair dismissals – reasonableness'. It is also feasible that a tribunal could find that a PCP which arose during the dismissal process was indirectly discriminatory, but that it did not affect the dismissal itself. In such circumstances, the claim would properly fall under S.39(2)(d) – discrimination by subjecting the employee to 'any other detriment' (see Chapter 25, 'Discrimination during employment') – and the employee would be restricted to recovering those losses that flowed from the discriminatory PCP and an award for injury to feelings, rather than compensation for all losses flowing from the dismissal.

26.52 Since a prerequisite of an indirect discrimination claim is that the employer must have applied to the employee a PCP, claims of indirectly discriminatory dismissals are most likely to arise where the dismissal follows an assessment of either the needs of the business, or the skills, performance or capability of the employee. An obvious example is redundancy, where the employer will apply selection criteria based on the needs of the business and the skills of the employee, but may additionally have provisions and practices relating to consultation and the identification of suitable alternative employment. (Redundancy dismissals are discussed in greater depth under 'Redundancy' below.)

Capability   26.53
Where an employer seeks to dismiss an employee on capability grounds, there is, generally speaking, a need for the employer to apply a set of criteria against which capability is measured. Indirect discrimination can arise, however, if these criteria are such that a protected group of employees are prone to score lower than those not of that group, and the employer cannot show that the criteria are justified as a proportionate means of achieving a legitimate aim.

One example that springs to mind is where an employer requires employees to undergo regular health checks, and dismisses those who cannot meet the required standard of health. Such a requirement is potentially indirectly discriminatory against older workers, as they are likely to be disadvantaged by the requirement to a greater degree than younger workers. It may also disadvantage disabled employees and would, in all probability, be subject to the duty to make reasonable adjustments.

As we have seen above under 'Dismissal because of protected characteristic – **26.54** race', language is not synonymous with race for the purposes of the EqA. However, laying down language requirements can amount to indirect discrimination, as such requirements are a PCP applied by the employer which place people who do not speak the language in question at a particular disadvantage. Accordingly, employers seeking to dismiss an employee because of his or her poor language skills may need to consider whether the language requirement is actually necessary to the job. If it serves no purpose, then a tribunal is unlikely to consider it a proportionate means of achieving a legitimate aim.

Showing justification for indirectly discriminatory dismissal   26.55
If a claimant succeeds in establishing that his or her dismissal flowed from the application of a PCP that placed him or her and those who share the same protected characteristic at a particular disadvantage, the employer will need to show that the application of the PCP was justified as 'a proportionate means of achieving a legitimate aim' if it is to avoid a finding of indirect discrimination. The justification defence is discussed in considerable detail in Chapter 17, 'Indirect discrimination: objective justification'. In the specific context of dismissal, it is worth noting that tribunals will balance the employer's needs – the

895

legitimate aim – against the discriminatory effect of the measure the employer is applying. The greater the discriminatory effect of a measure, the higher the hurdle of justification becomes.

26.56 Redundancy

Redundancy is a type of dismissal, and therefore any discrimination or victimisation in the redundancy process will be caught by S.39(2)(c) and (4)(c) EqA. While the EqA does not contain any provisions that relate specifically to redundancy, an employee may seek to rely on the Act where:

- the redundancy was a 'sham', in that the dismissal was not by reason of redundancy, but instead came about because of the employee's age, disability, gender reassignment, marital or civil partnership status, pregnancy or maternity, race, religion or belief, sex, or sexual orientation and thus constituted direct discrimination – see above under 'Dismissal "because of" protected characteristic'

- the employee's selection for redundancy constituted victimisation for having brought a discrimination claim or taking other action protected under the Act – see 'Victimisation dismissals' below

- the application of the selection criteria, the failure to offer alternative employment, or any other aspect of the redundancy process, was influenced by a protected characteristic and thereby amounted to direct or indirect discrimination

- the redundancy involved treating a disabled employee unfavourably because of something arising in consequence of his or her disability, and/or there was a reasonable adjustment which the employer could have made in order to avoid the redundancy of a disabled employee.

26.57 In unfair redundancy selection cases (i.e. where the employee is claiming unfair dismissal under the ERA), provided the employment tribunal has found that the selection criteria applied were objective, it should not subject those criteria or their application to over-minute scrutiny – British Aerospace plc v Green and ors 1995 ICR 1006, CA. Where, however, an employee is made redundant and claims discrimination, the tribunal will need to examine the selection criteria in some detail for any signs of discrimination and will also need to consider whether the criteria were applied in a discriminatory manner.

In this section we briefly discuss the circumstances that can give rise to discrimination in the redundancy process. For a more detailed consideration of this area, reference should be made to IDS Employment Law Handbook, 'Redundancy' (2011), Chapter 9, 'Discriminatory redundancy'. Note that particular issues can arise with regard to age discrimination and enhanced redundancy schemes, many of which continue to use age as a factor to determine the payout to which an employee is entitled. As such discrimination is in the terms of the employment, rather than in the act of dismissal, it is considered in Chapter 25, 'Discrimination during employment', under 'Benefits, facilities and services – enhanced redundancy schemes'.

Sham redundancies   26.58

If an employee ostensibly dismissed for redundancy claims that the actual reason for dismissal was a protected characteristic, an employment tribunal is likely to take as a starting point the question of whether there existed a 'redundancy situation' within the meaning of the ERA. The definition of 'redundancy' for these purposes is found in S.139(1) of that Act and is explored in detail in IDS Employment Law Handbook, 'Redundancy' (2011), Chapter 2. For present purposes, it is only necessary to know that the definition covers three scenarios: closure of a business or business unit; closure of the employee's workplace; and diminishing need for employees to do the available work. If none of these scenarios apply, then a dismissal cannot be by reason of redundancy for the purposes of the ERA – and, if the employer has argued that it is, the dismissal will be unfair. Of course, the fact that the dismissal is unfair does not mean that the reason which lay behind that unfairness was discriminatory. However, the fact that an employer has used 'redundancy' as a cloak to disguise its true reason for dismissal may be enough for a tribunal to conclude that it must seek a non-discriminatory explanation from the employer.

One telling indicator that an alleged redundancy might not be all that it seems 26.59
is where another person is recruited to fill the role, or a very similar role, to that vacated by the 'redundant' employee. This could support the inference that it was the characteristics of the claimant, rather than a reduction in the need for employees to do his or her type of job, that brought about the dismissal. An example:

- **Green v Woodcote Golf Club** ET Case No.2301619/07: G, 52, was a head greenkeeper at a golf club. In September 2006, his employer informed him that his role was being replaced by a new position of 'course manager', and that he was to be made redundant. The new job was subsequently given to a substantially younger person. Upon receiving the job description for the new role, G observed that – apart from the requirement for a Higher National Diploma-level qualification – it was identical to his redundant position. Furthermore, during an earlier discussion about his plans to retire, the employer told G that he was an 'old-fashioned type of greenkeeper'. The employment tribunal upheld G's direct discrimination claim. The employer's comments about his being 'old-fashioned' – in addition to other factors such as its belief that G could not be trained in the new role – all pointed towards an inference of discrimination which the employer could not rebut.

897

26.60 Suspicion may also be aroused where an employer selects for redundancy an employee who has previously made a discrimination complaint, particularly if there is a close temporal connection between the complaint and the selection. In Netherwood v RVB Westbury Ltd ET Case No.1401092/08 N lodged a grievance claiming that she was being discriminated against and bullied as part of a strategy to force her resignation so that a man without her childcare responsibilities could be employed in her place. Less than two months later, she was made redundant. An employment tribunal held that N was unfairly dismissed because there was no redundancy situation – it was a contrivance to effect her dismissal. That contrivance had come about because the employer believed N's grievance was based on lies and that it could not work with someone who told lies: this was a clear case of unlawful victimisation.

Of course, not every redundancy that follows soon after a discrimination complaint has been made will be an act of victimisation. Provided an employer can show that the reason the employee was selected was neither the complaint nor the protected characteristic in question, it will avoid a finding of discrimination, even if the redundancy dismissal itself is unfair. An example:

- **O'Connor v Able Piling and Construction Ltd** ET Case No.3100428/10: O was Australian. He claimed that on his return to work from Australia in October 2009 the words 'Fuck off u immigrant' were written on the inside of the van used primarily by him. He was offended by the words and reported the matter to the employer, who did not take the complaint seriously and took no action on it. O's manager forwarded two racist e-mails to O in January 2010, but the employer regarded them as jokes in poor taste and took no action. O was subsequently made redundant, with the employer stating that he was selected because of his poor attitude. An employment tribunal found that a racist culture existed at the employer's workplace and that O had been subjected to racial harassment for which he was awarded compensation of £4,500. Furthermore, his dismissal was unfair because the employer had failed to adopt a redundancy procedure of any kind. However, the tribunal did not accept that O's selection had had anything to do with his race or national origins – the evidence showed that O had been disgruntled since a demotion following his return from Australia, and that was the reason the employer dismissed him. His claim of discriminatory dismissal was therefore rejected.

26.61 **Preferential treatment**

An employer who positively discriminates in favour of an employee because he or she has a protected characteristic will leave itself open to discrimination claims from other employees who do not share that characteristic and are thereby disadvantaged (except in the case of disability discrimination, which does not 'work both ways' – i.e. an employee cannot claim protection under the EqA on the ground that he or she is *not* disabled).

898

Nowhere is this more aptly demonstrated than in Eversheds Legal Services Ltd v De Belin 2011 ICR 1137, EAT, where the EAT upheld a claim of direct sex discrimination brought by a man selected for redundancy from a pool of two. The other employee was a woman on maternity leave, who had been awarded a notional score for 'lock up', a measure of how quickly employees secured payment from clients for work completed. He received an actual score of 0.5 points for lock up, and 27 points overall, while she was given the maximum two points for lock up, and scored 27.5 points overall. The EAT upheld the tribunal's finding that the claimant had suffered less favourable treatment on the ground of his sex. The Appeal Tribunal rejected ELS Ltd's argument that it had a defence under S.2(2) of the Sex Discrimination Act 1975 (now S.13(6)(b) EqA), which provides that no discrimination arises out of 'special treatment afforded to women in connection with pregnancy or childbirth'. According to the EAT, S.2(2) did not create a blanket exemption and the special treatment afforded must not favour such employees beyond what is reasonably necessary to compensate them for the disadvantages occasioned by their condition. Decisions of the European Court of Justice (ECJ) such as Johnston v Chief Constable of the Royal Ulster Constabulary 1987 ICR 83, ECJ, indicated that the principle of proportionality applied to the right to 'special treatment'. Consequently, S.2(2) should be construed so as only to refer to treatment which is 'a proportionate means of achieving the legitimate aim of compensating [a woman] for the disadvantages occasioned by her pregnancy' or maternity leave. The EAT noted that where a maternity or pregnancy benefit is disproportionate, a disadvantaged colleague should be able to claim sex discrimination. In its view, giving legislation protecting pregnant women and those on maternity leave an excessively wide interpretation would bring it into disrepute. In the claimant's case, it was apparent that there were less discriminatory ways of achieving a fair result, such as scoring both candidates as at an earlier date when they were both at work. Awarding a notional maximum score was disproportionate.

(Note, however, that preferential treatment is possible, in limited respects, **26.62** when offering suitable alternative employment as employers have a statutory responsibility to offer suitable alternative employment first to any employees made redundant while on maternity, additional paternity or adoption leave – even if this means that a person of the opposite sex is thereby denied it. Essentially, once a woman on maternity leave has been selected for redundancy, she moves to the front of the queue for redeployment (for full details, see IDS Employment Law Handbook, 'Maternity and Parental Rights' (2009), Chapter 4, 'Returning to work after maternity leave', under 'Redundancy during maternity leave'). As this amounts to 'special treatment' and is afforded to women in connection with pregnancy or childbirth, it is covered by S.13(6)(b) EqA and excluded from the scope of the sex discrimination provisions.

899

Similarly, given that a non-disabled person cannot benefit from the provisions of the EqA, moving a disabled employee to the head of the queue for redeployment in a redundancy situation (but behind any employees on maternity leave, etc) will not incur liability in discrimination law, whereas moving people of a particular race or sex would. A tribunal might, in fact, consider it a reasonable adjustment to offer a disabled employee preferential treatment. In Kent County Council v Mingo 2000 IRLR 90, EAT, the Appeal Tribunal held that a policy which gave preferential treatment to redundant or potentially redundant employees by prioritising them for redeployment over employees who suffered incapability or ill health was discriminatory. In the EAT's view, the Council could have made a reasonable adjustment to the policy to ensure that disabled employees received the benefit of priority consideration for deployment along with employees liable to be made redundant.

26.63 Selection criteria

It is generally considered good practice for an employer engaging in a programme of redundancies to identify in advance the criteria on which employees will be selected for redundancy. By doing so, the employer minimises the potential for subjective and discriminatory factors to influence the selection process. However, injudicious selection criteria can themselves be discriminatory. Occasionally, such discrimination will take the direct form – for example, where an employee is selected for redundancy because of his or her age. More likely, however, the discrimination will be indirect, i.e. where one or more of the selection criteria put an employee who has a particular protected characteristic at a particular disadvantage when compared with persons who do not share that characteristic and the use of that criterion cannot be justified as a proportionate means of achieving a legitimate aim.

Employers will need to consider reasonable adjustments where selection criteria place a disabled employee at a substantial disadvantage when compared with non-disabled colleagues. The type of adjustment that will be appropriate will depend on the nature of the criterion and the circumstances and resources of the employer. Note, however, that if an adjustment to the scores and/or the redundancy criteria would still not prevent the disabled employee from being made redundant, then it would not be a reasonable adjustment for the employer to make and the employee would not be able to bring a complaint under S.21 EqA (failure to comply with duty to make reasonable adjustments) – Lancaster v TBWA Manchester EAT 0460/10. That said, in order to comply with the duty to make reasonable adjustments, the employer can treat the disabled employee *more favourably* in the selection exercise, since non-disabled employees are not entitled to bring claims of disability discrimination – S.13(3) EqA.

26.64 Employers should be aware of the possibility of discrimination claims being brought by employees who are *not* selected for redundancy. Depending on the circumstances, the terms on which redundancy is offered may be very favourable and the employer may be inundated with requests for voluntary redundancy. A claim by an employee who considers that the basis on which he or she was retained was discriminatory would properly be brought under S.39(2)(b) – on the basis that the redundancy package was a benefit, facility or service – or S.39(2)(d), on the basis that the denial of redundancy was a detriment. Although such claims are brought under a different subsection, there is no difference in the way in which a tribunal would approach the question of whether the selection criteria were discriminatory.

Below, we consider those selection criteria that are particularly prone to give rise to allegations of indirect discrimination.

Last in, first out. Traditionally, one of the most common methods of selecting **26.65** employees for redundancy has been the 'last in, first out' (LIFO) method. What this means is that the employees with the shortest length of service are selected for redundancy first. From an employer's perspective, LIFO carries the benefit of minimising the level of redundancy payments which are, of course, determined by length of service (see IDS Employment Law Handbook, 'Redundancy', Chapter 6, 'Redundancy payments'). It also means that more experience is retained within the business.

However, while LIFO does not directly discriminate on the ground of age – it does not automatically follow that an employee with ten years' service will be older than an employee with three years' service – it clearly constitutes a provision, criterion or practice which will, generally speaking, adversely impact on younger workers. It follows, therefore, that an employer seeking to use LIFO as part of a redundancy selection exercise must be prepared to demonstrate that its use is objectively justified. If it cannot do so, the use of LIFO will be unlawful indirect age discrimination.

The objective justification of a length of service criterion in a collective **26.66** redundancy agreement came before the Court of Appeal in Rolls Royce plc v Unite the Union 2010 ICR 1, CA. Unusually, the claim was not on appeal from the EAT but from the High Court, as Unite had sought a declaration that relevant provisions in the collective agreement it had reached with the employer could not lawfully be relied upon. The action was brought under Part 8 of the Civil Procedure Rules, under which the Court can determine a question where there is unlikely to be a substantial dispute of fact. Mr Justice Morison, sitting in the High Court, was of the view that the use of the criterion was justified by the legitimate aim of bringing about redundancies peaceably. The Court of Appeal accepted that Morison J had not directly addressed the question of proportionality but held that, viewed objectively, the inclusion of the length of service criterion was a proportionate means of achieving a legitimate aim. That aim was the reward of loyalty and the overall desirability of achieving a stable workforce in the context of a fair process of redundancy selection. The proportionate means were amply demonstrated by the fact that the length of

901

service criterion was only one of a substantial number of criteria for measuring employee suitability for redundancy and that it was by no means determinative. Equally, the length of service criterion was entirely consistent with the overarching concept of fairness.

Given the Court's ruling, it would seem that where LIFO is adopted as part of a selection matrix, rather than as the sole means of determining selection, its use is likely to be justified. Use of LIFO alone is unlikely to be considered proportionate, however. Tribunals may well be inclined to take a similar approach with other indirectly discriminatory selection criteria.

26.67 **Experience.** Many employers would regard an 'experience' criterion as being synonymous with LIFO. However, it is not unheard of for employers to also take into account past experience with other employers when selecting employees for redundancy. In this respect, many of the same considerations would arise in respect of age discrimination – while it is not necessarily the case that older employees will have more relevant experience than their younger colleagues, generally speaking, an experience criterion will disadvantage younger employees. In addition, requiring experience in an industry or job that is dominated by people possessing a particular protected characteristic could perpetuate past discrimination. Where an employer is called upon to justify the use of experience as a selection criterion, establishing why the experience is called for and how much experience is necessary are likely to play a key role.

26.68 **Health and attendance records.** Using levels of sickness absence as part of a redundancy selection matrix is relatively commonplace: it is an objective criterion and appeals to employers as it weeds out those employees with the worst attendance records. However, employers should be cautious about including disability-related absences in their calculations. Relying on such absences will amount to unfavourable treatment arising as a consequence of the employee's disability under S.15 EqA and the employer will be required to objectively justify their inclusion if it is to avoid a finding of discrimination.

Furthermore, tribunals have frequently held it to be a reasonable adjustment under S.20 to discount disability-related absences. The Equality and Human Rights Commission's Code of Practice on Employment ('the EHRC Employment Code') provides the following example: 'A call centre retenders for a large contract and has to reduce its price to secure the work in the face of low-cost competition from overseas. The employer therefore decides that attendance records are a particularly important selection criterion for redundancy. This has the potential to disadvantage disabled employees who require additional time off for medical treatment. It is likely to be a reasonable adjustment to discount some disability-related sickness absence when assessing attendance as part of the redundancy selection exercise' – para 19.17. The period over which attendance is measured should also be considered. This is particularly relevant to a newly disabled person who may have had an excellent attendance record for many years of service but who has had to have substantial time off in the recent past following the onset of the disability.

Pregnancy-related absences must be ignored completely when selecting **26.69** employees for redundancy. Failure to do so will result in a finding of pregnancy and maternity discrimination under S.18 EqA, which states that an employer will discriminate against a woman if it treats her unfavourably because of her pregnancy or maternity leave. There is no justification defence.

Productivity. In respect of roles where it can be measured, productivity is often **26.70** a preferred selection criterion owing to its objectivity. However, such a criterion can apply to the disadvantage of disabled employees whose disability has a negative impact on productivity. As a result, an employer may need to consider making adjustments to the scoring for such employees to compensate for their disability. While this may seem unfair to other employees caught up in the redundancy exercise, and indeed the impact on such employees of changing the scores is a factor to be considered in determining whether such an adjustment is reasonable, it should be remembered that the duty to make reasonable adjustments can entail a degree of positive discrimination in favour of disabled employees.

Using productivity as a selection criterion may also indirectly discriminate against older employees where their job is physically demanding, as their productivity is likely to decline with age. However, since assessing productivity is one of the least discriminatory means of selecting candidates for redundancy, the use of this criterion may well be justified in an age discrimination claim.

Cost of employment. As redundancies are often part of a cost-cutting exercise, **26.71** an employer may well want to include in the selection criteria the cost of making a particular employee redundant. However, such a criterion is potentially indirectly discriminatory on the ground of age, since in many cases the more costly employees are also the older employees. Accordingly, an employer may need to justify its reliance on cost factors.

The prevailing jurisprudence is that, in justifying discrimination, cost cannot itself be a legitimate aim, but can combine with other factors to provide justification – Cross v British Airways plc 2005 IRLR 423, EAT (see below under 'Retirement – justifying retirement' for a more detailed consideration of this point). The EAT recently considered an employer's use of cost in redundancy selection in HM Land Registry v Benson and ors 2012 IRLR 373, EAT. There the employer needed to reduce headcount and offered a voluntary redundancy/ early retirement scheme. Having more applicants than could be accommodated within the £12 million budget allocated to the project, the employer decided to select those employees who would cost least to dismiss, so as to maximise the number of redundancies achievable within the budget. This had the effect of excluding from consideration those employees aged between 50 and 54 who would have been entitled to early retirement on an unreduced pension if selected. An employment tribunal upheld indirect age discrimination claims from five of the affected employees, finding that the employer could have afforded to select them, albeit that that would have cost an extra £19.7 million.

26.72 Overturning that decision on appeal, the EAT held that the budget of £12 million was an intrinsic part of the employer s legitimate aim, which was to achieve the maximum number of redundancies possible within the budget. The tribunal had erroneously treated the limit on the budget as an aspect of the 'means' adopted by the employer to achieve more broadly defined aims. The tribunal's finding that the extra £19.7 million was not 'unaffordable' implied that it thought the employer could find the funds without becoming insolvent. That was to treat the language of 'real need', in the context of objective justification, as connoting a requirement of absolute necessity. This was the wrong approach. The task of the employment tribunal is to accept the employer's legitimate decision as to the allocation of its resources as representing a genuine 'need', but to balance it against the impact complained of. Had the tribunal done that here, it would have found the employer's means proportionate, since it was evident that there was no other available means of achieving the aim.

In so holding, the EAT distinguished the facts of the case from those in Pulham and ors v London Borough of Barking and Dagenham 2010 ICR 333, EAT. In that case the EAT had stated that an employer 'cannot automatically justify a failure to eliminate discrimination by allocating the costs of doing so to a particular budget and then declaring that budget to be exhausted'. That was a case of a directly discriminatory pay practice, which the employer wished to continue on the basis that it would cost too much to eliminate. Here, by contrast, the budget was for a particular project (the redundancy programme) that was not directly discriminatory, but which, as it turned out, required a selection exercise that could only practicably be done on an indirectly age discriminatory basis.

26.73 The employer's selection on the ground of cost in HM Land Registry v Benson and anor (above) was also challenged by a female employee who was not allowed to take voluntary redundancy because she was on a career break at the relevant time and so would represent no cost saving. She was not notified that employees in her position would be excluded; if she had been, she would have given notice to return to work within the relevant period. The EAT rejected the employer's appeal against the tribunal's decision that this amounted to indirect sex discrimination. While the exclusion of employees on long-term absence was in principle capable of being justified by reference to the same legitimate aim that justified indirect age discrimination in selection, the tribunal found that the failure to notify this employee was unfair, which meant that the application of the criterion to her could not be relied on as proportionate.

Flexibility. Selection criteria based on 'flexibility' or 'adaptability' can be open   26.74
to abuse, as they leave considerable room for subjective assessment of the
candidates for redundancy. Where employers wish to identify the most flexible
employees in the selection pool, it is best to be specific about what that flexibility
entails. If it is simply a euphemism for full-time working and availability for
overtime, a tribunal might determine that the employer was in fact seeking to
dispense with those employees who had caring commitments and therefore had
less flexibility over their working hours. Even where the employer has no such
conscious motive, the fact that the childcare burden continues to fall
disproportionately on women means a tribunal might be satisfied that the
flexibility criterion put women at a particular disadvantage, meaning that the
employer would need to show objective justification.

Objective justification is likely to be established where flexibility is intrinsic to
the job. For example, in Holness v After Build Ltd ET Case No. 2303407/09 H
was employed part time, in a job-sharing role, as a customer care coordinator.
It became apparent to the employer that the role was not really suitable for job-
sharing and needed to be done full time in order to avoid frequent delays and
communication breakdowns. H was given the choice of redundancy or taking
the job on a full-time basis, and was dismissed as redundant after the employer
rejected her compromise of working an additional day a week. She claimed that
the requirement to work full time was to her detriment, since she could not
comply due to childcare responsibilities, and so amounted to indirect sex
discrimination. Dismissing her claim, an employment tribunal accepted that
the requirement placed H at a disadvantage, but considered that in applying the
criterion, the employer was trying to ensure that in times of recession it was
providing its services to clients in the most efficient manner. That was a
legitimate aim and the means of achieving it were proportionate.

The use of a flexibility criterion can also disadvantage disabled employees. Para   26.75
19.16 of the EHRC Employment Code warns that the use of flexibility as a
selection criterion runs the risk of a finding of direct disability discrimination
or discrimination arising from disability, as disabled people may have more
difficulty adapting to a new workplace, different hours or new tasks. Where the
nature of the employee's disability is such that he or she would score lower on
the flexibility criterion than if he or she were not disabled, the employee will be
placed at a substantial disadvantage and the employer will need to consider
reasonable adjustments, such as adjusting the score upwards or assessing the
employee only on criteria that are not affected by the disability.

Discriminatory application of redundancy policy   26.76
Even where a redundancy situation is genuine and the selection criteria are free
of any inherent direct or indirect discrimination (or discrimination arising from
disability), there remains the potential for discrimination to arise in the way in
which the employer's redundancy policy, including the selection criteria, is

905

applied. For example, in Obikwu and anor v British Refugee Council ET Case No.1502553/06 and another the employer abandoned aspects of its own policies when selecting people for redundancy and the redundancy interviews were scored in a manner that was 'eccentric and lacking in transparency'. An employment tribunal considered that these factors, coupled with the fact that after the redundancy selection had taken place no black workers remained and two white females were retained without undergoing a selection process, was sufficient to establish a prima facie case of discrimination. While the tribunal was satisfied that there was no conscious discrimination, it held that the employer had failed to show that unconscious discrimination had played no role in the selection of the claimants for redundancy, with the result that their dismissals were discriminatory.

As redundancy selection involves weighing the respective merits of employees against one another, there is a danger for subjective assumptions to creep in, and this can give rise to discrimination. In particular, employers should beware selecting an employee on the basis of assumptions about his or her disability. In British Sugar plc v Kirker 1998 IRLR 624, EAT, K, who worked as a shift chemist, had had very poor eyesight since birth. He was registered as partially sighted and was entitled to be registered blind. K was selected for redundancy and brought a successful discrimination claim against his employer. The tribunal found that the employer had failed to mark him objectively when applying the selection criteria and that his disability had clouded its judgement. He was viewed as somehow different from his work colleagues and as someone with no future with the company. The EAT upheld the tribunal's decision on appeal.

26.77 **Demographics of remaining workforce.** Tribunals may be inclined to infer discrimination if a redundancy exercise results in a significant change in the demographics of the workforce. For example, in Obikwu and anor v British Refugee Council (above) the tribunal was influenced by the fact that the redundancy exercise resulted in no black employees being retained. Another example is Court v Dennis Publishing Ltd ET Case No.2200327/07, where the tribunal inferred that C was selected for redundancy because of his age. Crucial to this finding was the fact that, following C's redundancy, all members of his former team were at least 20 years younger than him. In this regard, the tribunal pointed out that a prima facie case is unlikely to be made out simply because of a difference in age and a difference in treatment. However, this was a situation where there was an imbalance of numbers. Taking by way of analogy a claim of sex discrimination, if there is one male and one female applicant for a post, the failure of one of them to be appointed cannot create a prima facie case. But if there are five female candidates and only one male, and the male is appointed, then a tribunal could draw an inference of sex discrimination. In the tribunal's view, the same reasoning applied to C.

Changes to selection criteria. As explained above, it is considered good **26.78** practice to identify a series of objective selection criteria in advance of undertaking the selection exercise. Where such criteria are changed during the course of the exercise, this could give rise to an inference that the employer is seeking to engineer the dismissal or retention of a particular employee for discriminatory reasons. An example:

- **Walker and ors v DCE Consultants Ltd and anor** ET Case Nos.2301417/09 and others: W was a 38-year-old managing director. In a meeting he referred to the company as being top heavy with 'older, grey-haired consultants'. A redundancy exercise was started in August 2008. The employer applied a matrix to determine who should be selected for redundancy, which went through seven versions before finally being used to select the claimants, who were all in their 50s. Another consultant, who was in his 40s, had scored much lower in relation to performance indicators, but was retained. The claimants were dismissed as redundant. A tribunal drew the inference that the employer had changed the matrix to get the result it wanted and held that, on the basis of the comments made by W, the claimants were targeted for redundancy because of their age.

Failure to offer alternative employment. For the purposes of unfair dismissal **26.79** law, a failure on the part of the employer to offer suitable alternative employment (where it is available) to an employee selected for redundancy can render the redundancy dismissal unfair (see IDS Employment Law Handbook, 'Redundancy' (2011), Chapter 8, 'Unfair redundancy', under 'Unreasonable redundancy – alternative employment'). For the purposes of the EqA, such a failure can give rise to discrimination if was influenced by a protected characteristic.

In Tower Hamlets v Wooster 2009 IRLR 980, EAT, for example, the employee, W, was on secondment when a reorganisation took place, with the result that his post became redundant. Under the terms of the Council's pension scheme, W was entitled to an early retirement pension if he remained in the Council's employment until his 50th birthday on 11 July 2007. The Council, concerned about the increased cost this represented, made only token efforts at redeployment and accelerated W's dismissal so that he was made redundant at 49. An employment tribunal found that, in the absence of any plea of objective justification, this amounted to direct age discrimination. Upholding that decision on appeal, the EAT noted that there was clear evidence that the desire to save the cost of W's early retirement pension had a significant influence on the Council's decision to dismiss W when it did. (For a case where a plea of objective justification was successfully made, see Woodcock v Cumbria Primary Care Trust (below).)

Timing of dismissal. Age discrimination can arise where an employer **26.80** moves to make an employee redundant by a certain date in order to avoid an

907

age-related entitlement to a benefit. In a case with similar facts to Tower Hamlets v Wooster (above), Woodcock v Cumbria Primary Care Trust 2012 EWCA Civ 330, CA, the employer departed from its usual procedure and issued W with a notice of dismissal prior to a redundancy consultation meeting. Its motivation, given W's contractual notice period, was that he would become entitled to enhanced pension rights if his dismissal was held back until after the meeting. An employment tribunal held that avoiding this entitlement was a legitimate aim, and that dismissing W – who had been on a redeployment register for over a year since his job had effectively disappeared – was a proportionate means of achieving it. Upholding that decision on appeal, the Court of Appeal held that the discrimination was justified in the circumstances by the employer's legitimate aim of giving effect to its genuine decision to terminate W's employment by reason of redundancy. Where an employer has allowed an employee, as a matter of pure discretion exercised in the employee's interests, to remain in employment until close to an 'age-critical' date, it would be wrong in the Court of Appeal's view if the employer were then held to have unlawfully discriminated against the employee by taking into account the imminence of that date in deciding when to bring the employment to an end.

As a general rule, an employer is not entitled to cut procedural corners, at least where the procedures are designed to protect the employee, in order to achieve dismissal before the employee attains an age-related milestone. However, consultation is concerned with substance and the Court of Appeal considered that the tribunal was entitled to find in the very particular circumstances of the case that it was justifiable for the employer to accelerate the giving of notice in order to prevent it incurring a disproportionate liability in pension costs. The employer had only become vulnerable to that potential liability because the redundancy process had been extended, to the claimant's benefit, for far longer than he had been entitled to expect, and the detriment to the employee of being given notice before, rather than shortly after, a consultation meeting could in the circumstances reasonably be judged by the tribunal to be insignificant. (Note, however, that this case should now be read in light of Seldon v Clarkson Wright and Jakes (A Partnership) 2012 UKSC 16, SC – see 'Retirement' below.)

26.81 Retirement

Following substantial changes to the law in 2011, there is no longer an exception from the age discrimination provisions in respect of retirement. Accordingly, the compulsory retirement of any employee on reaching a given age will amount to direct age discrimination under S.13(1) EqA, and the employer will be required to show that the retirement was justified as a proportionate means of achieving a legitimate aim if it is to avoid liability under S.39(2)(c) – S.13(2). Many employers have abandoned fixed retirement ages in the light of the

908

change in the law, but others have opted to retain their retirement age and argue that it is objectively justified.

Justifying retirement
26.82

As the default retirement age (DRA) was only abolished in 2011, there is as yet very little case law giving guidance on the circumstances in which retirement of employees will be objectively justified. However, a law firm's policy of retiring partners – to whom the DRA did not apply – at 65 was subjected to scrutiny by the Supreme Court in Seldon v Clarkson Wright and Jakes (A Partnership) 2012 UKSC, SC. This case is discussed in some detail below.

Focus is on justification of the retirement age, not its application. One thing 26.83 that is reasonably clear from Seldon v Clarkson Wright and Jakes (A Partnership) (above) is that the focus should be on the justification of the retirement age itself rather than its application to the claimant. Before the Supreme Court, S argued that CWJ had to show that its particular less favourable treatment of *him* was justified. However, in keeping with the decisions of the EAT and the Court of Appeal, Baroness Hale accepted that 'where it is justified to have a general rule, then the existence of that rule will usually justify the treatment which results from it'. She drew a distinction between justifying the application of the rule to a particular individual, which in many cases would negate the purpose of having a rule, and justifying the rule in the particular circumstances of the business. So, while CWJ would not need to show justification for the decision to exercise the retirement clause in its partnership deed, it would need to establish that having a retirement clause was justified by the circumstances of the firm as they happened to be on the date S was retired.

Legitimate aims. For an employer-specified retirement age to be justified, it 26.84 must be applied in pursuit of a legitimate aim. Essentially, this part of the justification test prompts an employer to provide the 'reason why' it wants to enforce a retirement age. The EHRC Employment Code states that for an aim to be legitimate it must be 'legal, should not be discriminatory in itself, and it must represent a real, objective consideration' – para 4.28. In Seldon v Clarkson Wright and Jakes (A Partnership) (above) the tribunal had accepted that the following three aims of the respondent firm's retirement policy were potentially legitimate:

- giving senior solicitors the opportunity of partnership, thereby ensuring that they do not leave the firm

- facilitating partnership and workforce planning; and

- limiting the need to expel partners by way of performance management, thus contributing to the congenial and supportive culture in the firm.

S appealed, arguing that direct age discrimination could only be justified by 26.85 reference to broad *social policy and economic policy objectives of the state*,

909

such as those relating to employment policy, the labour market or vocational training, and not the individual business needs of particular employers or partnerships, and that since the aims of giving senior solicitors a path to partnership and maintaining a congenial culture were individual to the firm and did not pursue such an objective, they could not justify age discrimination. In dismissing his appeal and confirming the decision of the EAT to remit the case to the tribunal, Baroness Hale – with whom Lords Hope, Brown, Mance and Kerr were all in agreement – acknowledged that, contrary to the tribunal's view, the justification test for direct discrimination is narrower than that for indirect discrimination: direct discrimination can only be justified by reference to legitimate objectives of a public interest nature, rather than purely individual reasons particular to the employer's situation, such as cost reduction or improving competitiveness. In this respect, the ECJ (in cases such as Incorporated Trustees of the National Council on Ageing (Age Concern England) v Secretary of State for Business, Enterprise and Regulatory Reform 2009 ICR 1080, ECJ, and Fuchs and anor v Land Hessen 2012 ICR 93, ECJ) had identified two broad categories of legitimate social policy objective: 'inter-generational fairness' and 'dignity'.

Applying the ECJ jurisprudence to the instant case, Baroness Hale held that the staff retention and workforce planning aims were not, as S contended, simply individual aims of the business, but instead fell within the category of 'inter-generational fairness'. Furthermore, the aim of limiting the need to use performance management to expel partners clearly fell within the 'dignity' category of legitimate aim. As a result, all three aims had the requisite 'social policy/public interest' dimension and were thus legitimate.

26.86 Simply establishing an aim that falls within one of the above categories will not be sufficient, however. The employer must then go on to show that it is legitimate in the particular circumstances of the employment concerned. Baroness Hale gave two examples. First, the aim of improving the recruitment of young people in order to achieve a balanced and diverse workforce. 'This is in principle a legitimate aim. But if there is in fact no problem in recruiting the young and the problem is in retaining the older and more experienced workers then it may not be a legitimate aim for the business concerned.' Her second example was the aim of avoiding the need for performance management. This may be a legitimate aim, but if in fact the business already has sophisticated performance management measures in place, it may not be legitimate to avoid them for only one section of the workforce.

An employer seeking to justify a retirement age should not simply parrot the three aims cited in Seldon v Clarkson Wright and Jakes (A Partnership) (above), since they are to some extent specific to the atypical situation of a partnership. However, the general themes relied upon are instructive – the case has given a clear indication that both workforce planning and facilitating career advancement for younger workers can *potentially* justify the retirement of older colleagues, and, perhaps more surprisingly, has given a degree of endorsement to the idea that a fixed retirement age could be justified by the need to avoid the 'unpleasantness' of applying a capability and performance management procedure to an older employee.

There is further support for the argument that providing access to employment **26.87** for young people can potentially justify a fixed retirement age in Petersen v Berufungsausschuss für Zahnärzte für den Bezirk Westfalen-Lippe 2010 IRLR 254, ECJ, which concerned a German law that set a maximum age limit of 68 for doctors and dentists in the public sector. And in Rosenbladt v Oellerking Gebäudereinigungsgesellschaft mbH 2011 IRLR 51, ECJ, the European Court held that a German law providing for compulsory retirement of employees able to claim a pension pursued the legitimate aim of sharing employment between the generations. The Rosenbladt case also provides support for the 'dignity' aim relied on in Seldon v Clarkson Wright and Jakes (A Partnership) (above), as the ECJ held that the same German law could be justified by reference to the need to avoid the potentially humiliating requirement of dismissing employees who are no longer capable of working.

In addition to legislation providing for compulsory retirement, the Court in Rosenbladt also considered a retirement provision contained in a collective agreement. This had the aims of facilitating employment for young people, planning recruitment and allowing for good management of an age-balanced staff, all of which the ECJ considered legitimate.

Health and safety. In Prigge and ors v Deutsche Lufthansa AG 2011 IRLR **26.88** 1052, ECJ, the ECJ held that the objective of air traffic safety could not be considered a legitimate aim for the purposes of Article 6(1) of the Framework Directive. By excluding air traffic safety from the 'social policy' objectives identified within that Article, the ECJ confined itself to the strict wording of that provision. In order to justify direct age discrimination, the legitimate aims must be social policy objectives, such as those related to employment policy, the labour market or vocational training.

Can cost be a legitimate aim? One question that remains is whether cost can **26.89** ever be a legitimate aim. In Woodcock v Cumbria Primary Care Trust 2011 ICR 143, EAT, Mr Justice Underhill, then President of the EAT, was of the view that an employer should be entitled to justify discriminatory treatment simply on the basis that the cost of avoidance would be 'disproportionately high'. However, when the case progressed to the Court of Appeal – Woodcock v Cumbria Primary Care Trust 2012 EWCA Civ 330, CA – Lord Justice Rimer stressed that an employer cannot justify discriminatory treatment 'solely' because the elimination of such treatment would involve increased costs. This approach was endorsed in Seldon v Clarkson Wright and Jakes (A Partnership) (above), where the Supreme Court emphasised that cost reduction (or improving

911

competitiveness) are not social policy objectives capable of amounting to legitimate aims for the purpose of justifying direct age discrimination.

However, it should be pointed out that in reaching this conclusion, the Court relied on the direct age discrimination case of Fuchs and anor v Land Hessen 2012 ICR 93, ECJ, where the European Court held that a German law stipulating a retirement age of 65 for civil servants was potentially justified under the Framework Directive. In so holding, the ECJ held that *Member States* can take budgetary considerations into account and that cost could underpin a social policy and influence the nature or extent of the measures adopted, although such considerations cannot in themselves constitute a legitimate aim. Thus, it appears that while a desire to save costs cannot, of itself, amount to a legitimate aim, it may possibly be relied upon to support a legitimate social objective.

26.90 **Proportionality.** If a legitimate aim has been established, the tribunal must then consider whether the means deployed to achieve it were proportionate, i.e. that the retirement age was a proportionate means of achieving the aim. This is a balancing exercise, which weighs the aim against the discriminatory effect the retirement has on employees who reach the retirement age. Among the issues for consideration are why the employer has chosen the particular retirement age, the alternatives (be they a higher retirement age or a completely different approach), and how the retirement age has been applied in practice. Where a retirement age is deployed as a means of guarding against an age-related drop in performance, tribunals are likely to demand clear evidence that the age set by the employer correlates with a decline in performance.

Unfortunately, there is a lack of judicial guidance at domestic level on the issue of proportionality in the context of retirement. In Seldon v Clarkson Wright and Jakes (A Partnership) (above) the Supreme Court said little about proportionality as the case had already been remitted to the tribunal as a result of the EAT's finding that it had not been shown that the choice of 65 was an appropriate means of achieving the third aim relied upon by CWJ – limiting the need to expel partners by way of performance management. The question for the tribunal was therefore whether the other two aims – giving senior solicitors the opportunity of partnership, and facilitating partnership and workforce planning – were sufficient to establish justification in the absence of the third aim. However, Baroness Hale did stress that to be proportionate, a measure must be *both* an appropriate means of achieving the legitimate aim *and* (reasonably) necessary in order to do so. She also warned that 'businesses will now have to give careful consideration to what, if any, mandatory retirement rules can be justified'. This is particularly so now that the DRA of 65 has been abolished.

26.91 At European level, the ECJ in Rosenbladt v Oellerking Gebäuderei-nigungsgesellschaft mbH 2011 IRLR 51, ECJ, held that the means of achieving the two aims behind a German retirement law (see 'Legitimate aims' above) were proportionate since the law took account of the fact that the people concerned were entitled to a pension and allowed for employees and employers to collectively agree the retirement mechanism in relation to particular jobs. This decision might support the setting of a retirement age in line with state pension age, although the low level of the state pension in the United Kingdom, coupled with the substantial fall in occupational pension provision over the last two decades, could undermine the proportionality argument. The ECJ's finding also seems to suggest that collectively agreed retirement ages are more likely to be proportionate than those imposed by the employer. However, there are numerous examples of collectively agreed measures being held to be unjustifiably discriminatory, so employers should be wary of simply relying on the fact that a retirement age was agreed with a trade union to justify its use.

In the Rosenbladt case, a collective agreement reached under the German retirement legislation was held to be proportionate since the employees, once retired, were not barred by law from seeking alternative work. A similar argument could be run in the United Kingdom, since an employee who is forced to retire is able to seek alternative work (as there is no longer a statutory exemption allowing an employer to refuse to employ someone who has reached the DRA). However, it is hard to imagine proportionality being established on this ground alone – the fact that an employee can seek work elsewhere is a poor justification for denying him or her the work he or she already has, particularly in an economic climate where those who lose their jobs are statistically likely to be unemployed for some time.

In Prigge and ors v Deutsche Lufthansa AG 2011 IRLR 1052, ECJ, another reference from Germany, the ECJ had to consider whether a collectively agreed prohibition on commercial airline pilots flying at the age of 60, for reasons of air safety, was compatible with the Framework Directive. The ECJ held that the collective agreement for Lufthansa pilots, which provided for automatic retirement at 60, was at odds with both national and international law, which allows pilots aged between 60 and 64 to fly a commercial aircraft provided they do so as part of a multi-pilot crew and are the only pilot in that crew who has reached the age of 60. As such, the age limit was not necessary to secure public safety, and nor was it justified on this ground as a genuine and determining occupational requirement. It therefore constituted a disproportionate requirement.

26.92 So far as we are aware, the most thorough consideration given to the proportionality question by a domestic tribunal was in Martin and ors v Professional Game Match Officials Ltd ET Case No.2802438/09. There, an employment tribunal considered whether the employer could justify a retirement age of 48 that applied to assistant referees at professional football matches in England. Having found that the retirement age pursued a legitimate aim of

913

creating a career route for match officials, the tribunal went on to find that it was a disproportionate means of achieving that aim, because the aim could have been achieved in a less discriminatory fashion. Rather than fix a retirement age, the employer could have subjected officials to fitness and competence tests, and demoted those who performed poorly to a lower level of match. Moreover, given that retirement ages for football match officials varied across Europe, with no retirement age whatsoever in the Netherlands, it was incumbent on the employer to explain why the retirement age of 48 would achieve its aim, something the employer had failed to do.

A retirement age of 65 for the judicial office of recorder was found to be disproportionate in Hampton v Lord Chancellor and anor 2008 IRLR 258, ET. The retirement age had been lowered from its statutory level of 70 in 1998 in order to secure a greater pool of candidates for appointment to the senior judiciary. An employment tribunal found that the aim behind the retirement age was legitimate, but that the means deployed to achieve it went further than was reasonably necessary. The evidence showed that not all recorders over the age of 65 would continue to 70; that 3 per cent of recorders were appointed judges each year; and that a retirement age of 70 would still leave a large pool of candidates for appointment.

26.93 Fairness of retirement dismissals
Even where a retirement age is found to be objectively justified (and therefore not discriminatory on the ground of age), the employer may need to show that the dismissal was fair under the ERA. 'Retirement' was removed from the list of potentially fair reasons for dismissal found in S.98 ERA in 2011 at the same time as the DRA was abolished – see Reg 3 Employment Equality (Repeal of Retirement Age Provisions) Regulations 2011 SI 2011/1069. In the absence of retirement as a potentially fair reason, we assume that employers will seek to argue that retirement dismissals fall under 'some other substantial reason of a kind such as to justify the dismissal of an employee holding the position which the employee held' under S.98(1)(b) ERA. If this argument is successful, the tribunal will then need to determine whether the employer acted reasonably or unreasonably in treating retirement as a sufficient reason for dismissal under S.98(4). The justification question is likely to be influential here as it is hard to imagine many circumstances in which a tribunal would find an employer's retirement age objectively justified but then go on to hold that dismissing an employee in line with that retirement age fell outside the range of responses of a reasonable employer (and vice versa). However, as we explain under 'Relationship between discriminatory and unfair dismissals – reasonableness' above, the two are not synonymous and tribunals must consider each claim separately, applying the different test that applies to each.

914

Constructive dismissal

As mentioned at the outset of this chapter, dismissal for the purposes of S.39 EqA includes constructive dismissal, which occurs where the employee, owing to the repudiatory conduct of the employer, is entitled to resign and regard him or herself as dismissed – see S.39(7)(b). In many instances, discriminatory conduct on the part of the employer will breach the term of mutual trust and confidence implied into every contract of employment, repudiate the contract and entitle the employee to resign and claim dismissal. However, this is not a foregone conclusion – the relevant legal test for constructive dismissal is one of contract, not discrimination, law.

It is important to understand that not every breach of contract will be repudiatory – i.e. of a nature that entitles the wronged party to treat the contract as being at an end. So, even if a tribunal finds that an employee who resigns in response to an incident of discrimination has suffered discrimination, it is not inevitable that the tribunal will find that a dismissal occurred as a result. The following case demonstrates this point:

- **Amnesty International v Ahmed** 2009 ICR 1450, EAT: A, who was of northern Sudanese origin, applied for promotion to the post of Sudan researcher, a position that she was filling on a temporary basis. However, AI felt that her ethnicity would compromise its perceived impartiality and expose A and those with her to increased safety risks when travelling in Sudan or Eastern Chad. Consequently, A was notified that for these reasons she would not be appointed, but this did not mean that she should not apply for other similar posts. A resigned and claimed, among other things, race discrimination and unfair constructive dismissal. Although the EAT upheld the employment tribunal's decision that A had suffered direct race discrimination, it rejected the tribunal's finding that the employer had also breached the implied term of trust and confidence. The EAT emphasised that a finding of unlawful discrimination does not inevitably mean that the employer has breached the implied term. In the present case AI had not done so: it had reached its decision after a thorough and reasoned process, motivated by no racial prejudice.

Even where the employer's actions do amount to a repudiatory breach of **26.95** contract, the employee can only claim constructive dismissal if his or her resignation was caused by the breach. Thus, an employee who waits too long before resigning, or otherwise acts in such a way as to indicate that he or she would wish the contract to continue, will be taken to have waived the breach and affirmed the contract. For example, in Bunning v GT Bunning and Sons Ltd 2005 EWCA Civ 104, CA, the claimant, B, informed her employer that she was pregnant, at which point the employer became obliged to carry out a risk assessment in accordance with Reg 16 of the Management of Health and Safety at Work Regulations 1999 SI 1999/3242 (a failure to carry out such a risk assessment automatically amounts to pregnancy and maternity discrimination – see IDS Employment Law Handbook, 'Maternity and Parental Rights' (2009), Chapter 2, 'Health and safety protection'). After carrying out the assessment the employer concluded that there was no reason why B should not continue working in its workshop and informed her that it expected her to return to work as a welder. B disputed the adequacy of the risk assessment and refused to return to the workshop. The employer then offered her alternative work in the stores, which she accepted. Another risk assessment was carried out and B subsequently started work there. After two weeks, however, she had a miscarriage. She resigned, alleging that GTB Ltd's inadequate assessment of the safety risks at the workshop, as well as its failure to reply to her letter on time, amounted to a breach of the implied term of trust and confidence, thus entitling her to treat herself as constructively dismissed.

An employment tribunal was satisfied that the employer had failed to carry out adequate risk assessments in respect of the jobs in the workshop and in the stores. Accordingly, it upheld the claim that B had been subjected to a detriment because of her pregnancy. However, it rejected the claim that B had been constructively dismissed. The tribunal noted that the risk assessment relating to the workshop had been inadequate, and that the employer had been in fundamental breach of contract in instructing B to return to work as a welder. B, however, did not resign at that time, and by accepting the stores job had waived the employer's earlier breaches of contract. While she worked in the stores, she had made no safety complaints about her working conditions, and the second inadequate risk assessment had not influenced her decision to resign. The Court of Appeal upheld the tribunal's finding that B had not been constructively dismissed. The tribunal had correctly expressed the view that, had B resigned in response to the inadequate first risk assessment and the employer's initial insistence that she return to the workshop, a finding of unfair constructive dismissal would have been probable. Her acceptance of the stores job, however, waived the employer's breaches or affirmed the contract.

Below, we consider some of the more common discriminatory circumstances that might lead an employee to resign and claim constructive dismissal.

26.96 Harassment

When one considers the definition of harassment under S.27(1) EqA – that is, unwanted conduct which is related to a protected characteristic and has the purpose or effect of violating a person's dignity or creating an intimidating, hostile, degrading, humiliating or offensive environment for him or her – it is clear that an employee subjected to harassment in the workplace could well respond by handing in his or her resignation. Even if the employer was unaware of the harassment, it could nonetheless be held liable for a discriminatory constructive dismissal in these circumstances because anything done by an employee in the course of his or her employment is treated as being done by the employer – S.109(1) EqA.

Although it must be shown that the employee resigned in response to the repudiatory breach of contract, the fact that he or she put up with the harassing conduct for some time before resigning will not necessarily prevent a finding that there has been a discriminatory constructive dismissal. In Munchkins Restaurant Ltd and anor v Karmazyn and ors EAT 0359/09 the claimants were subjected to a campaign of sexual harassment by M, the proprietor of the respondent restaurant, who had for a number of years engaged them in unwanted conversation about sex and shown them explicit photographs and catalogues of sexual material. The claimants put up with this behaviour for a number of years but matters came to a head when the assistant manager, G, became too ill to work in the restaurant. K, who had been acting as assistant manager in G's absence, resigned when she found being first in M's firing line too much to bear. The other three claimants soon followed, all of them citing M's behaviour among the reasons for their departure. Upholding the decision of an employment tribunal that K and the other claimants had experienced sex discrimination, harassment and constructive dismissal, the EAT stressed that it was not perverse of the tribunal to find that the claimants had been subjected to intolerable conduct and yet had continued to work at the restaurant. Such a finding was supported by evidence which showed that the claimants were migrant workers with no certainty of continued employment; that they were constrained by financial pressure and the fear that they might not obtain other work; that they had originally had the comfort of a general manager who acted as a buffer between them and the owner; and that they had therefore managed to find a balance between conduct which was unwelcome and unlawful and the advantages which their jobs gave them. There are many situations in life where people will put up with unwanted conduct that violates their personal dignity because they are constrained by social circumstances to do so.

26.97 In Dos Santos v Fitch Ratings Ltd ET Case No.2203907/08 an employment tribunal found that D had been subjected to disability-related harassment when his line manager went against his express wishes and disclosed the fact of D's HIV status to the group managing director. The tribunal additionally found that the disclosure was a breach of the implied term of trust and confidence, and although S had remained in employment while a grievance over the disclosure was heard, he could not be taken to have waived the breach and affirmed the contract. It was clear that when S resigned it was in response to the disclosure of his HIV status and the rejection of the associated grievance, that the employer was in a repudiatory breach of contract, and accordingly that S had been constructively dismissed.

26.98 **Employer not dealing with complaints**

As we explained in Chapter 25, 'Discrimination during employment', an employer who fails to deal adequately with an employee's complaints or formal grievances about discrimination may be liable for a further act of discrimination if it can be shown that that failure came about because of a protected characteristic. Another possible consequence of such a failure is that the employee may resign and claim constructive dismissal. For the dismissal itself to be discriminatory, the tribunal must be satisfied that the reason the employee resigned was an act of discrimination, rather than the employer's failure to uphold the complaint.

In Nixon v Ross Coates Solicitors and anor EAT 0108/10 N had complained to management that a colleague, O, was spreading rumours about the possible paternity of her expected child, speculating that it might have been conceived as a result of a fling at the office Christmas party. When the employer rejected N's grievance and ordered her to return to work at the same office as O rather than allowing her to work at an alternative site, she resigned. An employment tribunal determined that the employer's actions breached the implied contractual term of trust and confidence and entitled N to resign, but held that there had been no discrimination or harassment on grounds of sex or pregnancy and maternity. On appeal, the EAT held that the tribunal had overlooked the fact that the rumours constituted a course of unwanted conduct that was connected with her pregnancy and met the statutory definition of harassment. Similarly, the refusal to allow her to work at the other office was pregnancy discrimination. However, the EAT did not find that these matters made the constructive dismissal itself discriminatory.

26.99 **Refusal to allow flexible working**

Under the statutory flexible working procedure (see IDS Employment Law Handbook, 'Maternity and Parental Rights' (2009), Chapter 11), an employee cannot legally force an employer to acquiesce to a flexible working request. The procedure merely affords the employee the right to make a request and have it considered seriously, and the penalty for breach is an award of compensation rather than an order enforcing the request. However, where the request is made by a woman it is to some extent backed up by indirect sex discrimination law, since in refusing a request the employer may be applying a provision, criterion or practice (PCP) which puts women at a particular disadvantage (see Chapter 25, 'Discrimination during employment', under 'Terms of employment – hours of work'). Thus, where a tribunal is not satisfied that the PCP is objectively justified, and determines that the claimant resigned in response to its application, the refusal to grant flexible working would give rise to a discriminatory constructive dismissal. Two examples:

- **Shaw v CCL Ltd** 2008 IRLR 284, EAT: S's request for part-time working upon her return from maternity leave was refused by the employer. She resigned following the rejection of an appeal against that decision, and while the tribunal upheld her claim that the refusal to allow her to return to work part time was direct and indirect sex discrimination, it held that she had not been unfairly dismissed, as her resignation had come in response to the refusal of the flexible working application. Since the employer had been contractually entitled to refuse that request, there had been no repudiatory breach of contract. Overturning that aspect of the decision on appeal, the EAT held that the tribunal had drawn a false distinction between S's request to work part time and her formal flexible working application: in reality, the former was embedded in the latter. S had resigned in response to her employer's outright rejection of a part-time working request, made for discriminatory reasons. This constituted a failure to maintain trust and confidence between the parties and thus amounted to a repudiatory breach of contract

- **Littlejohn v Transport for London** ET Case No.2200224/07: L, who held a managerial position at TfL, put in a flexible working request before her return to work from maternity leave, seeking a change from full-time work to working two days in the office and one day at home. TfL refused her request, taking the view that a job share would not work. L resigned and succeeded before the tribunal with her claims of indirect sex discrimination and unfair constructive dismissal. The tribunal found that TfL had not provided justification for refusing L's request. In reaching this conclusion, it took into account the following matters: TfL did not believe that a job share would work but had not actually considered whether it was workable in practice; it was concerned about its ability to recruit to a part-time position but the evidence showed that L's was a popular job and finding someone part time could have been explored; the tribunal did not accept that L's management function was incapable of being performed by two individuals; TfL had failed to look into alternatives that would have allowed L to remain in her job; and L was only asking for part-time work for one year and TfL could have allowed this for a trial period.

Failure to make reasonable adjustments   26.100

There is substantial scope for overlap between constructive dismissal and the duty to make reasonable adjustments, since, although not all adjustments are contractual in nature, an employer's actions and omissions in failing to comply with the duty may also be regarded as a breach of the implied contractual term of mutual trust and confidence. Although the EqA is clear that dismissal includes constructive dismissal, the Disability Discrimination Act 1995 (DDA) was silent on this point. However, the Court of Appeal in Meikle v Nottinghamshire County Council 2005 ICR 1, CA, made it clear that a failure to make reasonable adjustments could give rise to a discriminatory constructive dismissal under the DDA, so there is no change in the substance of the law. In the Meikle case the Court held that an employment tribunal had been entitled to find that the claimant was constructively dismissed when the school at which she worked failed to make adjustments following her losing her sight in one eye.

26.101 Two further examples:

- **Marchant v FC Brown (Steel Equipment) Ltd t/a Bisley Office Equipment** ET Case No.2300633/09: M was dyslexic and dyspraxic. Following a problem in 2006 to do with the task of applying labels to units, the employer formed the view that M was anxious about his role and engaged an organisation, ES, which spent a week with M in the factory and produced a learning and development plan for him. As part of the plan it was agreed that any poor performance or disciplinary issues should be notified to ES so that a monitoring visit could be carried out. In August 2008, M was allocated the task of placing file bars into the drawers of personal units. After a while M became frustrated with the task because he believed that his slowness was holding up the production line. He was then heard throwing a file bar at a cabinet before leaving work early as he was getting flustered. The employer convened a disciplinary hearing without contacting ES and M was given a final written warning. He eventually resigned and claimed unfair constructive dismissal and disability discrimination. The employment tribunal held that the failure to notify ES of the problem was a failure to make a prearranged reasonable adjustment and therefore amounted to discrimination. The tribunal went on to find that the same failure was a breach of the implied term of trust and confidence in response to which M had been entitled to regard himself as constructively dismissed

- **Powell v Marks and Spencer plc** ET Case No.1307573/09: P had been caught shoplifting from a Debenhams store in March 2008 and shortly thereafter she went on sick leave suffering from stress. She attended an absence review meeting, at which she informed the employer that she suffered from Tourette's syndrome and had an obsessive–compulsive disorder. The employer raised the issue of shoplifting and P said that she believed it resulted from her medical condition. She was told that on her return to work she would be subject to disciplinary proceedings. A further meeting was planned for 16 June but her GP wrote to the employer saying she was unfit to attend any meetings and would remain unfit until she had seen a psychologist. P made it clear to the employer in October that the likelihood of her early return to work would be boosted if she did not have the threat of disciplinary proceedings hanging over her. The employer did not respond to this, but instead in November invited her to a meeting that was to consider whether her employment should be terminated. She resigned in December, saying that the constant threats had left her with no other option.

An employment tribunal found that, rather than genuinely seeking to secure a long-term return to work by P, the employer was actually trying to get her back to work so she could be suspended while disciplinary proceedings were initiated. The employer should at least have offered P the opportunity to take part in the disciplinary proceedings while she was off work. By failing to make this reasonable adjustment, the employer had discriminated against P and was in fundamental breach of her contract, with the result that she was also constructively dismissed.

Victimisation dismissals

26.102

Section 39(4)(c) EqA provides that an employer (A) must not victimise an employee of A's (B) by dismissing B. As explained in Chapter 19, 'Victimisation', S.27(1) EqA provides that victimisation occurs where A subjects B to a detriment because B has done a protected act or because A believes that B has done, or may do, a protected act. There are seven categories of protected act under the EqA, four of which are set out in S.27(2):

- bringing proceedings under the EqA

- giving evidence or information in connection with proceedings under the EqA

- doing any other thing for the purposes of or in connection with the EqA, and

- making an allegation (whether or not express) that A or another person has contravened the EqA.

In addition, S.77 EqA treats as protected acts certain things done in relation to 26.103 pay secrecy clauses in employment contracts. S.77(4) provides that seeking, making or seeking to make, or receiving a 'relevant pay disclosure' – i.e. a disclosure which relates to whether there is a connection between pay and having (or not having) a particular protected characteristic – are to be treated as protected acts.

For discussion of the scope of the protected acts covered by the EqA, see Chapter 19, 'Victimisation', under 'Protected acts'.

While the protected acts listed in S.27(2) mimic those previously found in the 26.104 antecedent discrimination legislation, there is a major difference between the victimisation test in the EqA and that found in previous legislation. Unlike the old provisions, the test under S.27(1) does not require the claimant to show that the employer had treated him or her less favourably than it treated or would treat other persons in the same circumstances, and that the employer did so by reason that the claimant had done or intended to do a protected act. Instead, the claimant need only establish that he or she was subjected to a detriment because of the protected act. As far as dismissal is concerned, it is

921

self-evident that dismissing an individual is a detriment, with the result that the focus will be on whether the dismissal came about because of the protected act. And although the legislation no longer expressly requires a comparison of the claimant's treatment with that of an appropriate comparator, it will often be an effective way of establishing the reason for the dismissal.

As with a claim where an employee alleges he or she was dismissed because of a protected characteristic (see 'Dismissal "because of" protected characteristic' above), a claim that an employee was dismissed because of a protected act is likely to hinge on the inferences a tribunal draws from the evidence, as an evidential 'smoking gun' linking the dismissal to a protected act is unlikely to emerge.

26.105 Two cases where dismissal was held to have occurred because of a protected act:

- **Abdi v Royal Mail Group plc** ET Case No.1401724/06: A, a Somali Muslim, was employed by RM plc as a postman, initially on a six-month trial period. That trial period was extended because RM plc had concerns about his behaviour as a result of two incidents, one with a colleague and one with the shift manager. The trial period was further extended because A had not been doing the full range of duties as a result of a back injury. Before that extension had concluded, A was called to a meeting at which he was dismissed because of his poor relationships with colleagues, including his manager, and his alleged inability to accept being directed. He claimed that he was dismissed because he had carried out five protected acts – he had raised with RM plc the issue of prayer mats, had raised the issue of racist graffiti, had drafted a letter on behalf of himself and other employees complaining about the treatment of a Somali Muslim, and had raised concerns and made complaints about the treatment of Muslim employees. An employment tribunal accepted that these were protected acts, and noted a number of irregularities in RM plc's approach: the decision to dismiss was made by a person against whom A had made a complaint; A had appealed against the rejection of a grievance only two days before he was called to the meeting; there had been no conduct issues arising between the time his trial period was extended and the date he was dismissed; and he was dismissed well before the trial period ended. These factors all supported an inference that the reason for A's dismissal was the protected acts, thus requiring RM plc to provide a non-discriminatory explanation. In the tribunal's view, RM plc had utterly failed to provide such an explanation and had even resorted to fabrication by asserting that A's injury played a role in the dismissal

- **Browne v Central Manchester University Hospital NHS Foundation Trust** ET Case No.2407264/07: B was the only black divisional director of the Trust. When the Trust developed concerns about B's performance, it did not follow the capability procedure, but instead sent B a letter stating that he was putting his continued employment in jeopardy. B was subsequently told that his job was untenable and the situation not sustainable. These assertions were repeated a few days later. It was some weeks before the Trust invoked its formal capability procedure. B then lodged a grievance saying that he believed the outcome was already decided in the light of the earlier comments made to him, and he alleged race discrimination. The Trust wrote to him two days later saying there would be an investigation and a hearing to determine whether it retained the necessary trust and confidence in him. B was suspended and then dismissed. An employment tribunal upheld B's claim of victimisation, accepting that his allegation of race discrimination had been made in good faith, and not as a spurious and opportunistic move as the Trust seemed to have thought. The Trust reacted badly to the allegation, closing ranks around the senior employee involved and moving quickly to dismiss B. Moreover, the Trust seemed unconcerned at a pattern, year on year, of black employees being more likely to be subject to dismissal than white employees. Although there had been legitimate concerns about B's performance, the tribunal was satisfied that the protected act had a significant influence on the outcome.

Dismissal because of manner of complaint 26.106

Giving false evidence or information, or making a false allegation, is not a protected act if the evidence or information is given, or the allegation is made, in bad faith – S.27(3). This provision gives rise to two important points. The first is that giving false information or evidence, or making a false allegation, in *good faith* will be a protected act. Secondly, where an employee makes an allegation of discrimination in the hope of harassing the employer into making a financial settlement, rather than out of any genuine sense of grievance, the employer will not be committing an act of victimisation by dismissing the employee – HM Prison Service and ors v Ibimidun 2008 IRLR 940, EAT.

In the Ibimidun case the claimant, I, had made a claim of race discrimination against HMPS that was settled. During the remainder of his employment, he brought five further sets of race discrimination proceedings against his employer and various colleagues. These involved multiple claims, most of which were dismissed, although one claim for victimisation was upheld in 2003. He appealed or sought reviews of the claims that were dismissed. Four costs orders were made against him because he had insisted on pursuing claims that had no prospect of success. Making the last of these, an employment tribunal stated that the claimant himself did not believe that his claim had a reasonable prospect of success and that his motive in pursuing the case was not to seek compensation, but to harass his employer into offering a settlement. Referring to that finding, HMPS dismissed I, stating that he was harassing individual members of staff by making unreasonable allegations, causing stress to

923

colleagues and putting a strain on resources, and that trust had broken down between it and I.

26.107 An employment tribunal upheld I's claim of victimisation, holding that the claims were protected acts, that I had been dismissed because of the protected acts, and that S.2(2) of the Race Relations Act 1976 (RRA) (now S.27(3) EqA) – which excluded 'treatment of a person by reason of any allegation made by him if the allegation was false and not made in good faith' from the scope of the victimisation provisions – did not apply because although all the allegations were made in bad faith, one of them was not false. Overturning the tribunal's decision on appeal, the EAT held that the reason for I's dismissal was not simply the fact that he had brought a tribunal claim, but that he had brought it to harass his employer. In the Appeal Tribunal's view, the victimisation provisions do not exist to protect such an act. They are designed to protect bona fide claims, not claims brought with a view to harassing the respondents to them. On the question of good faith, the EAT endorsed the tribunal's interpretation of the legislation – that an allegation must be both false and not made in good faith to fall within S.2(2) RRA. However, it held that the tribunal's finding that one of the allegations was not false had not been supported by its other evidential findings. (Note that while the wording used in S.27(3) EqA is slightly different to that in the antecedent discrimination legislation, the test is essentially the same and we would argue that the EAT's conclusions in Ibimidun therefore remain valid.)

Closely allied to the question of whether an allegation or the provision of information or evidence was made in bad faith is the familiar argument that a dismissal came about, not because the employee concerned had done a protected act, but because of the manner in which the employee did that act. A similar argument arises in the context of unfair dismissal claims where the employee asserts that he or she has been automatically unfairly dismissed for asserting a statutory right (see IDS Employment Law Handbook, 'Unfair Dismissal' (2010), Chapter 12, 'Dismissal for asserting a statutory right', under 'Reason for dismissal – manner in which complaint made'). In Martin v Devonshires Solicitors 2011 ICR 352, EAT, the EAT described the underlying principle thus: 'In our view there will in principle be cases where an employer has dismissed an employee (or subjected him to some other detriment) in response to the doing of a protected act (say, a complaint of discrimination) but where he can, as a matter of common sense and common justice, say that the reason for the dismissal was not the complaint as such but some feature of it which can properly be treated as separable.'

26.108 In Pasab Ltd t/a Jhoots Pharmacy and anor v Woods EAT 0454/11 W, a Muslim, was employed by JP Ltd as a trainee pharmacist. She was supervised by P, a Sikh, and worked with a trainee dispenser, S, also a Sikh. After W had complained about P and S speaking Punjabi in the workplace and discussing religious matters, a dispute arose as to her timekeeping and P informed her that she would have to reduce her lunch break to take account of the time she took off during the working day for prayers. W's response was to describe the employer as 'a little Sikh club that only looked after Sikhs'. She was suspended on the ground that she had made a racist comment and after a disciplinary hearing, she was dismissed. An employment tribunal found that implicit in the 'Sikh club' comment was an allegation that people who were not Sikhs were treated less favourably – i.e. that direct religious discrimination was taking place. The tribunal did not accept the employer's contention that the comment was racist or discriminatory and therefore made in bad faith, since W had not made a generalisation that all Sikhs behave in a given way, but had made a specific allegation based on her own perception and experience as a Muslim working alongside Sikhs. It followed that the comment was a protected act, and since the tribunal was satisfied that disciplinary action and dismissal would not have come about if W had not made the comment, her dismissal amounted to victimisation. This decision was overturned by the EAT on appeal. It held that even if the remark was capable of amounting to a protected act, if the remark was viewed by the employer not as a protected act but an offensive racist comment, then the reason for dismissal was not that W had done a protected act, but some other feature genuinely separable from the implicit complaint of discrimination.

Although the EAT in Martin v Devonshires Solicitors 2011 ICR 352, EAT (above), recognised that the classic example of this principle in action is where the employer claims that the reason for the dismissal was the manner in which the complaint was made, the facts of the Martin case are actually quite different. M, a legal secretary employed by DS, had been dismissed after making a number of unproven allegations against various partners. An employment tribunal dismissed her claim of victimisation, accepting DS's argument that a number of related and separable features of the allegations, and not the allegations themselves, were the reason for dismissal, including the fact that the allegations were false; that they arose from the employee's mental illness, which she did not recognise; and that similar behaviour was likely to occur in the future with a risk of significant workplace disruption. On appeal, the EAT upheld the tribunal's finding that these features of the allegations were properly separable from the allegations themselves.

26.109 While HM Prison Service and ors v Ibimidun (above) and Martin v Devonshires Solicitors (above) demonstrate circumstances in which employers have lawfully dismissed employees who have made persistent allegations of discrimination, a note of caution should be struck. The EAT in Martin was particularly aware of the potential for the argument that an employee had raised a complaint in an unacceptable manner to be abused, stating: 'It would certainly be contrary to the policy of the anti-victimisation provisions if employers were able to take steps against employees simply because in making a complaint they had, say, used intemperate language or made inaccurate statements. An employer who purports to object to "ordinary" unreasonable behaviour of that kind should be treated as objecting to the complaint itself, and we would expect tribunals to be slow to recognise a distinction between the complaint and the way it is made save in clear cases. But the fact that the distinction may be illegitimately made in some cases does not mean that it is wrong in principle.'

27 Post-employment discrimination

Chapters 24–26 look at the ways in which discrimination can arise in the **27.1** recruitment process and during the course of, and ending of, the employment relationship. In this chapter, we are concerned with the circumstances in which unlawful discrimination can occur after the employment relationship has been ended. We first examine the case law that provides the background to the current legislative provisions in this area. We then consider the specific provision in the Equality Act 2010 (EqA) that covers post-employment discrimination – S.108 – and discuss other provisions of the Act that might extend beyond the end of the employment relationship. Finally, we consider how a claimant can establish that post-employment discrimination, victimisation or harassment has the necessary connection to the employment relationship to found a claim. The most common circumstances in which post-employment discrimination occurs are where the former employee requests a reference from his or her previous employer or where an employer is carrying out a post-dismissal appeal procedure.

Protection under antecedent legislation **27.2**

The question of whether the now-repealed Sex Discrimination Act 1975 (SDA), Race Relations Act 1976 (RRA) and Disability Discrimination Act 1995 (DDA) covered discriminatory acts that occurred after employment had terminated was one which vexed the courts and tribunals for a number of years prior to the House of Lords' decision in Rhys-Harper v Relaxion Group plc and other cases 2003 ICR 867, HL.

For some time, the leading judgment was the Court of Appeal's decision in Adekeye v Post Office (No.2) 1997 ICR 110, CA, where it was held that a summarily dismissed employee could not bring a complaint under the RRA about the way his internal appeal had been conducted because, at the time of the alleged act of discrimination, he was no longer 'employed'. On the face of it, all three Acts required the employment relationship to be ongoing at the time the alleged discrimination took place: S.6(2) SDA made it unlawful for an employer to discriminate against 'a woman employed by him'; S.4(2) RRA prohibited an employer from discriminating against 'a person employed by

927

him'; and under S.4(2) DDA an employer was prohibited from discriminating against 'a disabled person whom he employs'.

27.3 However, by the time the House of Lords came to hear the joined appeals in Rhys-Harper v Relaxion Group plc and other cases (above), the European Court of Justice had held in Coote v Granada Hospitality Ltd 1999 ICR 100, ECJ, that the EU Equal Treatment Directive (No.76/207) (now the recast EU Equal Treatment Directive (No.2006/54)) required Member States to introduce into their national legal systems such measures as were necessary to ensure judicial protection for workers whose employers, after the employment relationship had ended, refused to provide references as a reaction to legal proceedings brought to enforce compliance with the principle of equal treatment within the meaning of that Directive. The Coote decision resulted in courts and tribunals attempting to apply a purposive construction to the SDA so that it covered post-employment discrimination in the circumstances outlined by the ECJ. However, as neither the DDA nor the RRA at that time contained provisions that derived from an EU Directive, there was no obvious legal basis for a purposive construction of those Acts, with the result that tribunals continued to apply Adekeye v Post Office (No.2) (above) in respect of race and disability discrimination claims. This state of affairs meant that a schism began to develop in the protection afforded by the anti-discrimination legislation, and six cases – covering all three Acts – were heard together by the House of Lords in an attempt to provide some clarity. The facts of the cases were as follows:

- Rhys-Harper v Relaxion Group plc: this case involved a female employee, R, who had been dismissed and was pursuing an appeal against that dismissal. In the course of her appeal, she complained to her employer about sexual harassment to which she had allegedly been subjected by her manager during her employment. Although she was out of time for bringing a claim in relation to the harassment itself, she brought a claim that the employer's subsequent investigation into her complaint was carried out in a manner that was discriminatory

- D'Souza v Lambeth London Borough Council: D was unfairly dismissed and an employment tribunal ordered the Council to reinstate him. The Council refused and the tribunal subsequently ordered it to pay compensation. However, D brought a further complaint under the RRA that the failure to reinstate him was discriminatory, in that it was motivated by race, and was also an act of victimisation in retaliation for his previous claim, which had included a complaint of race discrimination

- Jones v 3M Healthcare Ltd: J complained of victimisation in that his former employer had failed to return property which J claimed belonged to him after he had successfully sued the employer for disability discrimination in relation to his dismissal

- Kirker v British Sugar plc and anor; Angel v New Possibilities NHS Trust; Bond v Hackney Citizens Advice Bureau: the employees, all of whom had previously brought claims of disability discrimination against their employers, claimed that their former employers had victimised them by refusing to provide a job reference or by writing a reference that was unfavourable.

Their Lordships unanimously disapproved of the Court of Appeal's approach **27.4** in Adekeye in restricting the application of the RRA to the duration of the contract itself. The Court of Appeal had interpreted the statute in a manner that was too literal, was insufficiently purposive, and paid insufficient heed to the context. Their Lordships considered that it was absurd to make a distinction between, for example, a reference given the day before employment ends and one given the day after.

There was unanimous support for the view that the same rule in respect of post-termination discrimination should apply across all discrimination statutes, even though the wording of the relevant provisions in the SDA, RRA and DDA differed slightly. Furthermore, their Lordships were of the view that it served no purpose to distinguish between discrimination and victimisation claims (this point has become very significant under the EqA – see 'Protection under the Equality Act – post-employment victimisation' below).

Turning to the rule itself, the majority of their Lordships were of the view that **27.5** where legislation outlaws discrimination by an employer against a person 'employed by him' or 'whom he employs', the natural and proper interpretation of such a provision is that once two persons enter into the relationship of employer and employee, the employee is intended to be protected against discrimination by the employer in respect of all the benefits arising from that relationship, whether those benefits arise as a matter of strict legal entitlement or not. This being the purpose, it would make no sense, so far as protecting employees from discrimination is concerned, to draw an arbitrary line at the precise moment the contract of employment ends. It cannot have been the intention of Parliament that the prohibition against discrimination should apply to discrimination in an internal appeal against dismissal where the appeal takes place before the dismissal takes effect, but not where it takes place after. Similarly, it cannot have been intended to permit an employer to victimise an employee for bringing discrimination claims against it, so long as the victimisation is postponed until after the employee has been dismissed. Nor can a sensible distinction be drawn between giving a reference the day before employment ends and giving a reference the day after. The preferable approach is to recognise that the employment relationship is the feature that triggers the employer's obligation not to discriminate. Once triggered, this obligation applies to all the incidents of the employment relationship, whenever they arise.

Following their Lordships' decision in Rhys-Harper, provisions were inserted into the SDA, RRA and DDA, making post-employment discrimination

929

unlawful where it arose 'out of and [was] closely connected to' the employment relationship. Similar provisions were included, from the outset, in the regulations outlawing discrimination on grounds of sexual orientation, religion or belief and age. When the predecessor discrimination enactments were repealed by the EqA on 1 October 2011, these provisions were consolidated into S.108 EqA.

27.6 Protection under the Equality Act

The Equality Act 2010 includes a specific provision covering discrimination and harassment in relationships that have ended – S.108. However, the scope of that provision is narrower than the prohibition on post-employment discrimination that was established by the House of Lords in Rhys-Harper v Relaxion Group plc and other cases 2003 ICR 867, HL, because S.108(7) expressly excludes victimisation. As a result, it is necessary to split discussion of post-employment discrimination under the EqA into two parts. First, we examine the terms of S.108, before turning to consider post-employment victimisation, and whether, despite S.108(7), it remains unlawful under the EqA.

27.7 Section 108

Section 108(1) and (2) EqA (which deal with discrimination and harassment respectively) provide that a person must not discriminate against or harass another if:

- the discrimination or harassment 'arises out of and is closely connected to a relationship which used to exist between them', and

- conduct of a description constituting the discrimination or harassment would, if it occurred during the relationship, contravene the EqA.

The protection afforded by these provisions applies even if the employment relationship ended before S.108 came into force (on 1 October 2010) – S.108(3). However, the Explanatory Notes to the EqA make it clear that, for S.108 to apply, the conduct complained of must take place after the commencement of S.108. Para 351 of the Notes states: 'S.108 applies to conduct which takes place after the Act is commenced, whether or not the relationship in question ended before that date. If the conduct occurred before [S.108] was commenced, it would be dealt with under the previous legislation.'

27.8 In addition to the protection from post-employment discrimination and harassment provided for in S.108(1) and (2), S.108(4) EqA provides that a duty to make reasonable adjustments applies to A after the employment relationship has ended in so far as B continues to be placed at a substantial disadvantage as mentioned in S.20 (as to which, see Chapter 21, 'Failure to make reasonable adjustments' under '"Substantial disadvantage"'). For these purposes, the statutory provisions on reasonable adjustments must be construed as if the relationship had not ended – S.108(5). The Equality and Human Rights Commission's Code of Practice on Employment ('the EHRC Employment Code') gives the example of a former worker with lifetime membership of the works social club who cannot get into the club because of a physical impairment. Once the former employer is made aware of the situation, it will need to consider making reasonable adjustments (para 10.60).

For the purposes of the enforcement provisions in Part 9 of the EqA (discussed in Chapter 34, 'Enforcing individual rights'), a contravention of S.108 relates to the Part of the EqA that would have been contravened if the relationship had not ended – S.108(6). In other words, a breach of S.108 triggers the same enforcement procedures as would have applied if the treatment had occurred during the employment relationship.

Post-employment victimisation   27.9

Section 27 EqA provides that victimisation occurs where an employer (A) subjects another person (B) to a detriment because (a) B does a protected act, or (b) A believes that B has done, or may do, a protected act. A 'protected act' includes bringing proceedings under the EqA or making an allegation that A or another has contravened the EqA (see Chapter 19, 'Victimisation'). Neither S.108(1) or (2) make any mention of victimisation. Under the previous discrimination enactments, this would have been of little significance, as victimisation was regarded as a form of discrimination. However, as discussed in Chapter 19, the situation under the EqA is different, because victimisation is now a distinct form of prohibited conduct. Thus, for it to be included within the scope of S.108, it would need to be expressly mentioned in that provision. But in fact the opposite is true, because S.108(7) clearly stipulates that 'conduct is not a contravention of this section in so far as it also amounts to victimisation of B by A'. Victimisation is thus specifically excluded from the scope of S.108.

It is not entirely clear what purpose Parliament had in mind when enacting S.108(7), since removing protection for post-employment victimisation runs contrary to the United Kingdom's obligations under EU law. At no stage during the passage of the EqA through Parliament did the Government indicate that it intended to do away with post-employment victimisation claims. Nevertheless, the employment tribunal in Jessemey v Rowstock Ltd and anor ET Case No.2700838/11 – to our knowledge, the first case considering post-employment victimisation under the EqA – determined that such claims are no longer possible. Having found that the claimant was given a negative reference because he had brought a tribunal claim against his former employer, the tribunal held that 'because of the drafting of the Equality Act the tribunal cannot consider any remedy for this victimisation… the claim for post-employment victimisation fails as it is not rendered unlawful by S.108'.

931

27.10 However, while the tribunal in Jessemey was certainly correct to state that post-employment victimisation is not rendered unlawful by S.108, its conclusion that there is no remedy in such circumstances is open to dispute. The tribunal did not consider whether such victimisation is rendered unlawful by any other provision in the EqA. Nor, for that matter, does it appear that the tribunal considered any pre-EqA case law, or the effect of EU law.

As discussed in Chapter 2, 'European discrimination law', courts and tribunals ruling on the provisions of the EqA must, so far as possible, interpret them consistently with EU law. Article 11 of the EU Equal Treatment Framework Directive (No.2000/78) states that: 'Member States shall introduce into their national legal systems such measures as are necessary to protect employees against dismissal or other adverse treatment by the employer as a reaction to a complaint within the undertaking or to any legal proceedings aimed at enforcing compliance with the principle of equal treatment.' A similarly worded provision is included in Article 24 of the recast Equal Treatment Directive (No.2006/54) and Article 9 of the Race Directive (No.2000/43). These provisions fall to be interpreted in light of Coote v Granada Hospitality Ltd 1999 ICR 100, ECJ (see 'Protection under antecedent legislation' above), the effect of which is that protection offered by the Directives extends to workers whose employers refuse to provide references after the employment relationship has ended as a reaction to legal proceedings brought to enforce compliance with the principle of equal treatment. Thus it is clear that EU law obliges Member States to put in place measures protecting employees from post-employment victimisation.

27.11 However, in order to give effect to EU law, tribunals should not attempt to twist the meaning of S.108 to include victimisation, as this is simply not possible given the clear wording of S.108(7). Instead, it is necessary to turn attention to those provisions that render victimisation unlawful when it occurs prior to the termination of the employment relationship. The definition of victimisation is set out in S.27 EqA (see above). But while this definition is capable of covering post-employment victimisation, it is simply that – a definition – and does not actually prohibit victimisation. This is done by S.39 EqA, which applies the S.27 definition of victimisation to the field of employment.

Section 39(3) covers victimisation in recruitment. This provides that 'an employer (A) must not victimise *a person* (B) in the arrangements A makes for deciding to whom to offer employment; as to the terms on which A offers B employment; or by not offering B employment' (our stress). Since S.39(3) applies to victimisation of a person by an employer, it can be read, without difficulty, as applying to the situation where an employee has done a protected act – such as bringing discrimination proceedings against his or her former employer – and on reapplying for employment with the same employer, is subjected to a detriment.

932

However, while S.39(3) would assist a claimant in the rare situation where he **27.12** or she is seeking work from a former employer, it would not cover the more typical post-employment victimisation scenarios – such as where a former employer refuses to provide a reference, or gives a malicious reference, or refuses to hear an appeal against dismissal, because the employee in question did a protected act. In these circumstances, the employee would need to rely on S.39(4), which covers victimisation in employment, and argue that it must be interpreted consistently with both EU law (see above) and the House of Lords' decision in Rhys-Harper v Relaxion Group plc and other cases 2003 ICR 867, HL (see below).

Section 39(4) EqA provides that an employer (A) must not victimise an employee of A's (B):

- as to B's terms of employment – S.39(4)(a)

- in the way A affords B access, or by not affording B access, to opportunities for promotion, transfer or training or for any other benefit, facility or service – S.39(4)(b)

- by dismissing B – S.39(4)(c)

- by subjecting B to any other detriment – S.39(4)(d).

Subsections (a) and (c) would appear to have no relevance to post-employment **27.13** victimisation. However, a failure to provide a reference could certainly amount to a detriment for the purposes of both S.27 and S.39(4)(d), and could also be viewed as 'not affording' the former employee access to a 'benefit, facility or service' contrary to S.39(4)(b). For these provisions to be engaged, however, it is necessary for the term 'an employee' to extend to former employees.

This brings us back to the decision in Rhys-Harper v Relaxion Group plc and other cases (above), where the House of Lords had to consider three provisions: S.6(2) SDA, which made it unlawful for an employer to discriminate against 'a woman employed by him'; S.4(2) RRA, which prohibited an employer from discriminating against 'a person employed by him'; and S.4(2) DDA, which prohibited an employer from discriminating against 'a disabled person whom he employs'. Their Lordships held that these provisions had to be interpreted as covering incidents of discrimination (including victimisation) that arise from the employment relationship, but which occur after its termination (see 'Protection under antecedent legislation' above). By analogy, the same logic would surely apply to S.39(4), with the result that an employer can be liable for the victimisation of a former employee, provided that the tribunal is satisfied that the victimisation had a sufficient connection with the terminated employment relationship. This test is very similar to that which applies under S.108, where the claimant must show that the discrimination or harassment

933

'arises out of and is closely connected to' the employment relationship – see 'Connection between prohibited conduct and employment'.

27.14 The view that post-employment discrimination is covered by S.39(4) is supported by the EHRC Employment Code, albeit without any authority being cited. Para 9.4 simply states that: 'Former workers are also protected from victimisation', while para 10.62 explains that: 'If the conduct or treatment which an individual receives after a relationship has ended amounts to victimisation, this will be covered by the victimisation provisions.' Furthermore, when the Government Equalities Office (GEO) was alerted to the apparent drafting error in the EqA by the Discrimination Law Association, an organisation of discrimination law practitioners, it stated that the Act was intended to cover claims for post-employment victimisation. In its view, this was achieved by the Act, read together with the relevant case law, as underpinned by EU Directives. That said, it acknowledged that 'the reliance on the case law means that this protection is not as clear as it could be on the face of the Act'.

27.15 Connection between prohibited conduct and employment

Irrespective of whether it is a claim of discrimination or harassment brought under S.108 EqA, or one of victimisation brought under S.39 EqA read with Rhys-Harper v Relaxion Group plc and other cases (above), a post-employment claim has two elements. The claimant must show that:

- he or she has been subjected to prohibited conduct, i.e. discrimination, harassment or victimisation. (The principles in this regard are no different to a claim of discrimination, etc during the course of the employment relationship and are dealt with in Chapter 15, 'Direct discrimination'; Chapter 16, 'Indirect discrimination: proving disadvantage'; Chapter 17, 'Indirect discrimination: objective justification'; Chapter 18, 'Harassment'; and Chapter 19, 'Victimisation'), and

- despite the termination of the employment relationship, there was still a sufficiently close connection between the prohibited conduct and that relationship.

27.16 For the purposes of post-employment discrimination and harassment, S.108(1)(a) and (2)(a) require that the prohibited conduct 'arises out of and is closely connected to' the employment relationship. This phrase is not defined in the EqA, and nor was it defined when it appeared in the predecessor discrimination enactments. However, tribunals have interpreted it in the light of the analysis set out by the House of Lords in Rhys-Harper v Relaxion Group plc and other cases (above).

934

In Rhys-Harper their Lordships stated that the obligation on an employer not to discriminate covers all 'incidents' of the employment relationship that occur after termination, and cited examples such as contractual obligations in relation to confidentiality, restrictive covenants, pensions or bonuses. 'Incidents' of the employment relationship will also include other, non-contractual benefits – such as the opportunity to obtain a reference or to have recourse to an internal appeal against dismissal. Though the House of Lords rejected an arbitrary temporal limitation on the reach of discrimination law, Lord Hobhouse accepted that the further removed the conduct is in time from the employment, the more difficult it may become to show that there was a sufficient connection between the two.

References 27.17

In many ways a malicious reference is the most obvious example of post-employment discrimination, and a number of cases have considered the circumstances in which an employer's reference for a former employee, or its refusal to provide a reference, can amount to discrimination, harassment or victimisation.

There is no doubt that a reference, or the decision to deny a former employee a reference, 'arises out of' the terminated employment relationship and nor could it be disputed that it is 'connected' to that relationship. Moreover, the courts have rejected the notion that there comes a point at which the connection between a reference and the employment relationship to which it relates is severed by the passage of time. In Rhys-Harper v Relaxion Group plc and other cases (above) the employers unsuccessfully argued that it was unfair that employers could potentially be exposed to claims years after employment has terminated. Their Lordships stressed that if it is not the employer's practice to give references after a certain amount of time has elapsed, then refusal of a reference after that time will not give rise to a discrimination claim. Subsequently, in Metropolitan Police Service v Shoebridge 2004 ICR 1690, EAT, the employer argued that there must be some cut-off point to a former employer's liability, which should be restricted to events occurring immediately after employment ended. The EAT rejected this argument. It was plain from their Lordships' speeches in Rhys-Harper that liability for discrimination was not limited to the first occasion on which a reference was requested. It was an inevitable consequence of that decision that a complaint of discrimination or victimisation arising from the giving of, or refusal to give, a reference will potentially lie against employers for years to come.

Given that the connection between a reference and the employment to which it **27.18** relates is fairly obvious, most cases will turn on the question of whether the content of the reference, or the decision not to provide one, amounted to discrimination, victimisation or harassment. In this regard, there are distinct advantages to adopting a formal policy on references, since it both provides guidance to employees who are asked to write references, and can go some way to insulating employers from the inference that a reference was given, or not given, for discriminatory reasons (or as an act of victimisation or harassment). That said, adopting a standardised approach to providing references can lead to negative inferences if that approach is not then followed.

In Pricewaterhousecoopers LLP v Popa EAT 0030/10 the employer operated a very rigid and prescriptive policy covering the provision of references. Under this policy, former employees were coded as to the type of reference that would be provided. The code for P's reference was changed after she brought proceedings against the employer, and a paragraph in the reference letter relating to honesty and integrity was omitted when the employer next provided her with a reference. An employment tribunal upheld P's claim of victimisation, finding that the factual circumstances of the change in code following the tribunal claim were sufficient to shift the burden of proof to the employer to provide an explanation other than victimisation, and that the employer could offer no coherent, rational explanation for the change. The suggestion that an administrator had simply exercised discretion in the light of the way that the request for a reference was framed was rejected by the tribunal due to the employer's prescriptive policy on references. On appeal, the EAT held that the tribunal had been entitled to reject the employer's explanation. However, the Appeal Tribunal was of the view that the tribunal had erred by failing to consider whether, in providing a reference without the paragraph relating to honesty and integrity, the employer had subjected P to a detriment (it being noted that the reference had not affected P's employment prospects). Accordingly, the EAT remitted that matter to the tribunal.

27.19 **Compromise agreements.** An agreed reference can form part of a compromise agreement under which an employer and former employee settle a dispute arising on termination of employment. Should an employer depart from the terms of an agreed reference, the employee will have a remedy in contract law under the terms of the compromise agreement. However, the decision to provide a different reference could also amount to a contravention of the EqA. An example:

• **Onwuchekwa v Chelmsford Borough Council** ET Case No.3200490/08: O lodged a grievance against the Council's Chief Executive, P, alleging that he had discriminated against her as a black woman. This dispute was settled, and a compromise agreement was reached when O left the Council's employment. When she applied to another local authority, SC, for a job, it contacted P to ask about O. He stated that O was very 'task-focused', and that she had left the Council in circumstances involving a compromise agreement and this limited what could be said about her. She was not appointed. An employment tribunal noted that what P said and implied in the telephone conversation was inferior to the terms of a reference agreed as part of the compromise package – it was less substantial and less balanced. Moreover, P had not considered O's original allegation of discrimination to have any foundation; it was the only one ever lodged against him and it was obviously capable of causing lasting resentment. Given this, the tribunal concluded that it was more probable than not that the decision to give a less favourable reference was significantly influenced by O's protected act (i.e. the allegation of discrimination).

References following gender reassignment. Employers should tread carefully **27.20** when responding to requests for references in respect of employees who have undergone or are undergoing gender reassignment as confidentiality issues may arise. In X v Morgan and anor ET Case No.3102873/04 X had undergone gender reassignment surgery to change her sex from male to female. Following the surgery, she returned to work for the employer as a supply teacher, but was dismissed after only two lessons. She brought, and settled, discrimination proceedings against the employer, and also issued a press release about the case, with the aim of raising the profile and cause of transsexuals, but it backfired and she became the victim of some vitriolic personal attacks. In October 2003 X registered with a teacher recruitment agency. She informed her former employer that she had put it down as a referee, giving details of the new name she had adopted and asking it to maintain her confidentiality. The employer sent a positive reference to the recruitment agency, but also faxed a side memo saying that when X had worked for it she had been a male teacher, and mentioned the possibility that the case had caused social problems which could make effective teaching a problem. X did not get any work through the agency and switched to a different one. She discovered the existence of the memo from her former employer when she made a Data Protection Access request. As a result, she lodged proceedings against the employer. When she approached the employer for a reference in February 2005, it replied that it was not willing to provide a reference; it would be prepared to confirm her employment details, but would feel bound to confirm the name under which she undertook the work, this being a basic element of employment identity. An employment tribunal found that the employer's disclosure of X's previous male identity and the reference to X in the side memo as 'he' and 'him', were both instances of less favourable treatment on the ground of gender reassignment. Additionally, the employer's reference to the previous proceedings brought by X amounted to unlawful victimisation, as did the refusal to provide the second reference.

Two important factors to note about the above case are that the employer was put on notice by its former employee that she wanted to maintain her confidentiality regarding gender reassignment, and that the employer was fully aware that X had undergone reassignment. It is doubtful that the same result would be reached where an employer unknowingly reveals that a former employee has undergone gender reassignment, since the employer's ignorance

937

would make it extremely difficult for the claimant to establish that there has been less favourable treatment because of gender reassignment.

27.21 **Unsolicited contact with current employer.** In Metropolitan Police Service v Shoebridge 2004 ICR 1690, EAT, the Met argued that tribunals do not have jurisdiction to hear discrimination and victimisation claims arising out of a former employer's unsolicited contact with a subsequent employer. However, the EAT rejected the idea that such unsolicited contact is not an incident or benefit arising out of the contract of employment or the employment relationship as referred to by Lord Nicholls in Rhys-Harper v Relaxion Group plc and other cases (see 'Connection between prohibited conduct and employment' above). The Appeal Tribunal could see no distinction between Lord Nicholls' analysis of the scope of the employment relationship and the presumed facts of the instant case. The examples he gave of the kind of non-contractual expectation an employee will have were not limited to an expectation that a requested reference will assist the employee in obtaining a new job. There was no difference between the act of an employer in spoiling a subsequent employment on an unsolicited basis and the act of an employer in giving or refusing a formal reference.

However, the EAT thought that the version of the test set out by Lords Hobhouse and Rodger in Rhys-Harper was one which tribunals would find easier to adopt. Their suggestion, as paraphrased by the EAT, was that tribunals should consider 'whether there is a substantial connection with the employment relationship, or a sufficiently close connection with the employment, or whether the employer was here discriminating *qua* employer, or whether the facts alleged are sufficiently proximate to, or not remote from, the employment or the employment relationship'. Although it is a matter for the tribunal whether this test is satisfied, the EAT thought that if an employer 'deliberately set out to spoil a subsequent employment, however long after its own employment had ceased, or so acted, knowing of the likely consequences of its actions', it would be acting in its role as former employer. There would be sufficient proximity and a sufficiently close connection with the employment to give rise to a cause of action.

27.22 Another case involving unsolicited contact with a new employer was MacDonald v Leeds Women's Aid and ors ET Case No.1805149/03. There M had brought, and settled, a sex discrimination claim against LWA. She had begun working for a new employer and, as part of her duties, she accompanied a person to LWA's premises, and met her there on another occasion. LWA claimed that M was aggressive to two of its workers, complained to her new employer, and banned her from entering the premises again. She claimed that the ban amounted to unlawful victimisation. Upholding her claim, an employment tribunal could see no rational reason for the complaint against M to be exaggerated in the way it had been, to be reported to M's employer and then result in her being banned from the premises. LWA failed to show that there was a good explanation for its actions and so the tribunal was obliged to conclude that M's earlier proceedings against LWA, which were a protected act, were part of the reason for the complaint.

Appeals   27.23

An employee's appeal against dismissal would certainly amount to an 'incident' of the employment relationship, and thereby satisfy the S.108 requirement that the conduct 'arises out of and is closely connected to' the employment relationship. Thus, claimants will be able to recover compensation for any discrimination, harassment or victimisation that takes place in the appeal process. For a detailed consideration of how such discrimination might arise, see Chapter 25, 'Discrimination during employment', under '"Any other detriment" – disciplinary and grievance procedures'.

The duty to make reasonable adjustments under S.20 EqA will apply to the appeal process if any of the provisions, criteria or practices adopted by the employer as part of that process place a disabled person at a substantial disadvantage when compared with people who are not disabled. The duty will also apply wherever the physical features of the employer's premises or the non-provision of an auxiliary aid place a disabled employee at a substantial disadvantage. The types of adjustment that would be considered reasonable will depend on the employer's circumstances and the nature of the disability, but examples would include moving the timing or location of the appeal hearing and providing a lip-reader, lipspeaker or British Sign Language interpreter. Moreover, since the duty to make reasonable adjustments extends to the decision to dismiss, it must also by extension apply to the decision of whether or not to uphold the dismissal on appeal.

In a case that is analogous to post-dismissal appeal cases, Hinsley v Chief **27.24** Constable of West Mercia EAT 0200/10, H sought to withdraw her resignation as a probationary police officer that she had submitted during a period when she was suffering from depression. West Mercia Police considered her request, but determined that there was no provision in the Police Regulations 2003 SI 2003/527 that would permit it to reinstate H. An employment tribunal found that the duty to make reasonable adjustments was engaged, but that reinstatement was not a reasonable adjustment. It found that there was no provision for an ex-office holder to be re-engaged or reinstated, other than through the qualifying process set out in the Regulations, and it would not be a reasonable adjustment to require West Mercia Police to go beyond its statutory and regulatory powers. Overturning that decision on appeal, the EAT held that, as a matter of construction, there was no bar to the reappointment of H, in the form of her reinstatement or re-engagement. While there was no express provision in the 2003 Regulations catering for that course, there was none

939

prohibiting it. Given the tribunal's other findings, it was apparent that, but for the perceived bar which the EAT found not to exist, it would have been a reasonable adjustment for H to be reinstated.

27.25 ## Conduct during tribunal proceedings

An employer's conduct during tribunal proceedings does not have as obvious a connection to the employment relationship as a reference or appeal against dismissal. Accordingly, where an employee claims that he or she has been discriminated against, victimised or harassed at any stage in proceedings, the initial focus is likely to be on the question of whether the conduct had a sufficient connection to the employment relationship.

The matter fell for consideration by the EAT in Nicholls v Corin Tech Ltd and ors EAT 0290/07. N had been pursuing a disability discrimination claim against CT Ltd, whose defence was being conducted by B, a director and ultimate owner of the company. N alleged that just after he left the tribunal hearing room, B had subjected him to abuse and threatened him with violence if he continued with his claims. N relied on that alleged conduct as the basis for a victimisation claim under the DDA, but an employment tribunal chairman determined that he had no jurisdiction to hear that claim, since the conduct of proceedings in an employment tribunal attracts judicial proceedings immunity. N appealed to the EAT, where CT Ltd and B argued that, even if the alleged conduct took place, it was not actionable under the DDA because it could not be found to arise out of, or be closely connected to, the previous employment relationship between CT Ltd and N, with the result that it could not be unlawful under S.16A(3) DDA (a predecessor provision of S.108 EqA).

27.26 The EAT – proceeding, for the purposes of the jurisdictional appeal, on the assumption that N's allegations were true – considered that if it was intended or calculated to deter an employee from continuing proceedings brought in the employment tribunal to vindicate his rights as an employee, conduct of the kind alleged by N would be sufficiently closely connected to the previous employment relationship to be caught by S.16A(3). In considering whether the connection is sufficiently close, it is legitimate, and indeed necessary, to take account of the purpose behind the provision. At least in part that purpose must be to secure compliance with the United Kingdom's obligations under EU law to ensure that employees, including ex-employees, are not inhibited in exercising their rights to seek judicial protection of their rights as employees. However, the EAT stressed that if an employer's conduct at a tribunal hearing is not intended or calculated to deter an ex-employee from exercising his or her rights, it will not have a sufficiently close connection to the terminated employment relationship. Turning to the tribunal chairman's finding that the alleged conduct would attract judicial proceedings immunity, the EAT noted that the principle behind such immunity is that parties and witnesses who take part in judicial proceedings should be able to express themselves freely, and not be inhibited by the thought that they might be sued for something they say. As the alleged threats took place in the corridor outside the hearing, they did not form part of the judicial process and were therefore not subject to immunity.

Tribunal orders and awards
27.27

Employees have no right to bring claims under the EqA arguing that their former employer has breached the Act by failing to comply with a tribunal's order of reinstatement or re-engagement. This much was made clear by the House of Lords in Rhys-Harper v Relaxion Group plc and other cases 2003 ICR 867, HL, where one of the cases on appeal – D'Souza v Lambeth London Borough Council – concerned an employee who claimed that his employer's refusal to comply with an order for reinstatement was an act of race discrimination and victimisation. Their Lordships were of the view that the refusal to comply with a tribunal's order is not conduct falling within the scope of the RRA (and now, by extension, the EqA), since the benefit acquired by an employee from the order does not arise from the employment relationship. Such an order is a discretionary statutory remedy for unfair dismissal, attracting its own sanctions in the event of non-compliance.

By way of contrast, the Court of Appeal in Coutinho v Rank Nemo (DMS) Ltd and ors 2009 ICR 1296, CA, held that a tribunal did have jurisdiction to hear the claim of victimisation based on the employer's failure to honour a tribunal's award of compensation for unfair dismissal and race discrimination. The action was not an illegitimate attempt to enforce a tribunal judgment or a county court order, but was brought on the basis that the employer's unexplained conduct in not complying with a judgment obtained by a former employee was unlawful because it was discriminatory. It was necessary to inquire into the reason why the employer had not paid the award and, if it was established by direct evidence or by inference that the reason was retaliation against the claimant for having brought proceedings for discrimination against the employer, then there could be a possible link to the previous employment relationship sufficient to support a claim for post-termination discrimination.

The Court thought that the instant case could be distinguished from Rhys- 27.28 Harper, since in that case the claimant could not claim further compensation under the RRA for the failure to reinstate him, since the unfair dismissal legislation itself provided an express and specific statutory remedy against an employer who failed to do what the tribunal ordered by way of reinstatement. That was the only statutory remedy available and there was therefore no room for a victimisation claim for failure to reinstate.

Part 5

Liability for discrimination

28 Liability of employers, employees and agents

Who is protected?

Employer's liability for acts of employees

Employer's liability for harassment by third parties

Liability of principals for agents

Personal liability of employees and agents

Instructing, causing and inducing discrimination

Aiding discrimination

In this chapter we consider the provisions in the Equality Act 2010 (EqA) that **28.1** govern the liability of employers, employees and agents for acts of discrimination at work. We begin by addressing the question of who is protected under the Act, before discussing the extent to which an employer, or a principal, can be held liable for the acts of others. We also look at the circumstances in which individual employees and third parties can themselves be held personally liable. Finally, we explain the law governing liability for instructions to discriminate, and for causing, inducing or aiding discrimination.

Reference is made throughout to the Equality and Human Rights Commission's Statutory Code of Practice on Employment ('the EHRC Employment Code'). Although not binding on tribunals, the provisions of the Code are highly influential and may be used as evidence in a tribunal claim.

Who is protected? 28.2

Part 5 of the EqA prohibits discrimination by employers against existing or prospective employees. The definition of 'employment' is broad, as it was under the previous equality legislation. It covers individuals working under a contract of employment, apprentices, and self-employed people working under a contract personally to do work. The EqA also gives former employees the right to bring a complaint in respect of discrimination or harassment that takes place after the employment relationship has ended. In addition, Part 5 of the EqA prohibits discrimination in relation to a broader category of individuals in the work context, including contract workers, police officers, Crown employees and office holders, partners in firms, and trainee or qualified barristers (or advocates in Scotland).

In this section we consider the various types of worker afforded protection under the EqA (e.g. job applicants, employees, former employees, contract workers, etc). For more detailed discussion of the circumstances in which discrimination (and victimisation, harassment and failure to make reasonable adjustments) can arise, see Chapter 24, 'Recruitment'; Chapter 25, 'Discrimination during employment'; Chapter 26, 'Dismissal'; and Chapter 27, 'Post-employment discrimination'.

Note that, unlike most claims for unfair dismissal under the Employment Rights Act 1996 (ERA), there is no period of continuous employment which an employee must serve in order to be entitled to bring a claim under the EqA. Thus, for example, an employee dismissed on his or her first day of employment in circumstances that amount to discrimination or victimisation would be able to bring tribunal proceedings and recover compensation for loss of earnings and injury to feelings.

28.3 Territorial limits

In contrast to the antecedent discrimination legislation, the EqA is silent as to its territorial scope. Previously, the scope of discrimination legislation was limited to employment at an establishment in Great Britain. By abandoning that proviso, Parliament has left it to employment tribunals to determine the territorial scope of the Act, guided no doubt by the approach taken in unfair dismissal cases, following the test laid down by the House of Lords in Lawson v Serco Ltd and other cases 2006 ICR 250, HL. For a full discussion, see Chapter 34, 'Enforcing individual rights', under 'Jurisdiction of tribunals – territorial jurisdiction'.

28.4 Definition of employment

The EqA protects applicants for 'employment' (see 'Job applicants' below) and those already in 'employment' (see 'Employees' below). Central to this protection is the definition of employment found in S.83(2) EqA. This defines 'employment' as:

- employment under a contract of employment, a contract of apprenticeship or a contract personally to do work – S.83(2)(a)

- Crown employment – S.83(2)(b)

- employment as a relevant member of House of Commons staff – S.83(2)(c)

- employment as a relevant member of House of Lords staff – S.83(2)(d).

Section 83(4) EqA clarifies that '[a] reference to an employer or an employee, or to employing or being employed, is... to be read with' S.83(2); and that 'a reference to an employer also includes a reference to a person who has no employees but is seeking to employ one or more other persons'. Thus, a prospective employer is subject to the discrimination provisions in the EqA.

The definition of employment under S.83(2) EqA is substantially wider than the corresponding definition in S.230(1) ERA – and wider even than the employer-worker relationship outlined in S.230(3) of that Act – since it encompasses situations where a genuinely self-employed person contracts personally to do work.

Job applicants 28.5

Section 39(1) and (3) EqA deals with discrimination against job applicants. Their combined effect is that an employer (A) must not discriminate against or victimise a person (B):

- in the arrangements A makes for deciding to whom to offer employment – S.39(1)(a) and (3)(a)

- as to the terms on which A offers B employment – S.39(1)(b) and (3)(b)

- by not offering B employment – S.39(1)(c) and (3)(c).

Furthermore, 'an employer (A) must not, in relation to employment by A, harass a person (B)… who has applied to A for employment' – S.40(1)(b). In certain circumstances, employers may also be liable for harassment of job applicants by third parties – see under 'Employer's liability for harassment by third parties' below.

Finally, employers are under a duty to make reasonable adjustments in respect **28.6** of disabled job applicants who are placed at a substantial disadvantage by the employer's provisions, criteria and practices; the physical features of the employer's premises; or the failure to provide an auxiliary aid – S.39(5). Employers are entitled to ask questions about disability for the purposes of complying with the duty to make reasonable adjustments, but otherwise the scope for an employer to ask a job applicant about his or her disability is limited by S.60 EqA, breach of which can lead to an inference of discrimination (see Chapter 24, 'Recruitment', under 'Pre-employment health questions' for details).

In Czikai v Freemantle Media Ltd and ors EAT 0606/10 the EAT upheld the decision of an employment tribunal that an unsuccessful contestant on a television talent show could not claim disability discrimination under the employment provisions in the Disability Discrimination Act 1995 (DDA) (which contained a definition of employment broadly in line with that in S.83(2) EqA). The claimant was not in the position of a job applicant, as the audition she attended was not held for the purposes of deciding who should be given employment, but instead to determine who would advance to the next round, and ultimately who would win the prize offered by the show.

As mentioned previously, the reference to 'an employer' in Ss.39(1) and (3) EqA **28.7** 'includes a reference to a person who has no employees but is seeking to employ

947

one or more other persons' – S.83(4) EqA. As a result, a potential employer cannot evade liability for discrimination in recruitment by citing the fact that it is not an employer.

Discrimination, victimisation and harassment against job applicants is covered in detail in Chapter 24, 'Recruitment'.

28.8 Employees

Discrimination and victimisation against employees are dealt with in S.39(2) and (4), the combined effect of which is that an employer (A) must not discriminate against or victimise an employee of A's (B):

- as to B's terms of employment – S.39(2)(a) and (4)(a)

- in the way A affords B access, or by not affording B access, to opportunities for promotion, transfer or training or for receiving any other benefit, facility or service – S.39(2)(b) and (4)(b)

- by dismissing B – S.39(2)(c) and (4)(c)

- by subjecting B to any other detriment – S.39(2)(d) and (4)(d).

Section 39(7)(a) provides that the reference to 'dismissing' B in S.39(2)(c) and (4)(c) 'includes a reference to the termination of B's employment... by the expiry of a period (including a period expiring by reference to an event or circumstance)'. However, S.39(7)(a) does not apply 'if, immediately after the termination, the employment is renewed on the same terms' – S.39(8). S.39(7)(b) provides that dismissal includes termination 'by an act of B's (including giving notice) in circumstances such that B is entitled, because of A's conduct, to terminate the employment without notice' (i.e. constructive dismissal).

28.9 Furthermore, 'an employer (A) must not, in relation to employment by A, harass a person (B)... who is an employee of A's' – S.40(1)(a). In certain circumstances, employers may also be liable for harassment of employees by third parties – see under 'Employer's liability for harassment by third parties' below.

Finally, employers are under a duty to make reasonable adjustments in respect of disabled employees who are placed at a substantial disadvantage by the employer's provisions, criteria and practices; the physical features of the employer's premises; or the failure to provide an auxiliary aid – S.39(5).

The application of the above provisions is considered further in Chapter 25, 'Discrimination during employment', and Chapter 26, 'Dismissal'. For present purposes we are concerned with one question: who is an employee for the purposes of Ss.39 and 40?

28.10 **Need to show contractual relationship.** As we have seen under 'Definition of employment' above, S.83(2) defines employment as: employment under a contract of employment, a contract of apprenticeship or a contract personally to do work; Crown employment; employment as a relevant member of House of Commons staff and employment as a relevant member of House of Lords staff. S.83(4) goes on to provide that a reference to an 'employee' or an 'employer' is to be read with S.83(2). Thus, for a person to be an employee for the purposes of the EqA, he or she must fit into one of the six categories provided for in S.83(2). Putting aside the latter three categories for the moment (which are considered under 'Crown employees' and 'House of Commons and House of Lords staff' below), it is apparent that for a person to be employed there must be a contract in existence.

However, it is not always a straightforward matter to determine whether or not a contract exists. Below we consider some of the areas of dispute likely to arise in discrimination claims. For a more detailed analysis of employment contracts, reference should be made to IDS Employment Law Handbook, 'Contracts of Employment' (2009), Chapter 1, 'Basic requirements'.

Relationship governed by statute. Certain employment relationships have **28.11** been held to be governed by statute, rather than contract, with the result that they fall outside the scope of discrimination law (at least in the employment field). In Ealing, Hammersmith and Hounslow Family Health Services Authority v Shukla 1993 ICR 710, EAT, for example, S applied for a job as a general practitioner. He started proceedings for sex discrimination when the FHSA failed to appoint him. The tribunal made a preliminary ruling that it had jurisdiction to hear S's claim but was overturned by the EAT, which held that the relationship between a GP and an FHSA was based on statutory provisions rather than contract. However, that decision appeared to conflict with Roy v Kensington and Chelsea and Westminster Family Practitioner Committee 1992 IRLR 233, HL, where Lord Lowry, in giving the leading judgment, was prepared to state, obiter, that the relationship might be a contractual one. Nonetheless, in North Essex Health Authority v David-John 2004 ICR 112, EAT, a race discrimination case, the EAT relied upon the decision in the Shukla case, holding that while it was true that the arrangement with the Health Authority imposed a number of obligations on a GP in relation to the patients on his or her lists, it was satisfied that those obligations were statutory rather than contractual. (The EAT also found that if it was wrong and there was a contract between the GP and the Health Authority, the requirement that it be a contract for personal performance was not met because, in the EAT's view, the GP was not required to personally treat the patients on his or her list.)

Similarly, it has been held that a dentist had no contract of any sort with the Health Board with which she was registered – Tayside Health Board v Killick EAT 1291/98. The EAT pointed out that K offered services not to the board but to patients who, to a greater or lesser extent, paid for them. The Board had no freedom to select dentists, or even to control their decisions to delegate. It was

949

merely a regulatory licensing authority in respect of any person with appropriate qualifications. It followed that there was no need to consider whether K was in an 'employment' within the meaning of S.82(1) of the Sex Discrimination Act 1975 (SDA) (the equivalent provision to S.83(2) EqA).

28.12 **Volunteers.** Another relationship where it can be difficult to establish the existence of a contract is that involving volunteer posts. On the fact of it, the word 'volunteer' would seem to rule out a contractual relationship, since it suggests that there is no obligation. However, employment tribunals must look behind the labels ascribed to a relationship to determine whether it in fact falls within S.83(2) EqA. In Murray v Newham Citizens Advice Bureau 2001 ICR 708, EAT, M had applied to the CAB to become a trainee voluntary adviser. The EAT overturned the tribunal's decision that the position for which M had applied did not amount to 'employment' for the purposes of the DDA. In the EAT's view, the tribunal had erred in concluding that the documentation relating to the volunteer adviser post and training programme – which required the applicant to agree to a number of matters, including a commitment to volunteer on a particular two days a week – placed no obligation on either party. It had also erred in putting too great an emphasis on the absence of pay (under the agreement, M was entitled only to be reimbursed for travel expenses) to support its conclusion that there was no contractual arrangement with mutually binding obligations. In the EAT's view, the absence of pay was just one of a number of factors to be weighed in the balance. The EAT remitted the matter to a tribunal to make the necessary findings of fact from which it could conclude whether M's application to become a trainee voluntary adviser was an application for 'employment' for the purposes of the DDA.

In South East Sheffield Citizens Advice Bureau v Grayson 2004 ICR 1138, EAT, however, the EAT cast considerable doubt on whether unpaid volunteers could be said to be in 'employment' for the purposes of the discrimination legislation, holding that the tribunal had erred in concluding that volunteers at a CAB who worked under an agreement that stipulated a 'usual minimum weekly commitment' of six hours, were 'employees' for the purposes of the DDA. The EAT began by stating that, in order for a volunteer worker to be found to be an employee under either a contract of service or a contract personally to do work, there must be an arrangement under which, in exchange for valuable consideration, the volunteer is contractually obliged to render services to, or work personally for, the employer. The crucial question, said the EAT, was whether the volunteer agreement imposed a contractual obligation upon the CAB to provide work for the volunteer, and upon the volunteer personally to do any work so provided. In the EAT's view, the phrase 'usual minimum commitment' in the volunteer agreement simply indicated what the CAB reasonably expected of its volunteers and did not create a legal obligation that they must work those hours. The work expected of them was unpaid and expressed to be voluntary. (The EAT did not think that the provision of training, supervision, experience and an indemnity against expenses and negligence liability could be viewed as consideration by the CAB for a minimum work commitment on the part of the volunteer.) Furthermore, it was open to a volunteer at any point, either with or without notice, to withdraw his or her services from the CAB, in which event it would have no contractual remedy against him or her – something the EAT regarded as being a crucial element of a contractual obligation. On that basis, the EAT concluded that there was no contractual obligation on the volunteers to do any work and therefore they were not in 'employment' within the meaning of the DDA.

The matter was subsequently considered by the Court of Appeal in X v Mid **28.13** Sussex Citizens Advice Bureau 2011 ICR 460, CA, where the claimant, who had a disability, had signed a volunteer agreement which was stated to be 'binding in honour only... and not a contract of employment or legally binding'. X frequently failed to turn up on the days when she was expected, and when the CAB asked her not to attend any more, she brought a claim of disability discrimination. The tribunal found that she was not an employee under the DDA, and that it therefore had no jurisdiction to hear the case. X appealed against this decision to the EAT, arguing that her role at the CAB constituted an 'occupation' for the purposes of the EU Equal Treatment Framework Directive (No.2000/78) ('the Framework Directive'), and that the tribunal should accordingly have construed the DDA so as to allow her claim to proceed. X argued that the effect of Mangold v Helm 2006 IRLR 143, ECJ (an age discrimination case), as modified by Bartsch v Bosch und Siemens Hausgeräte Altersfürsorge GmbH 2009 1 CMLR 5, ECJ, required the national court to set aside the definition of 'employer' and 'employee' in the DDA, and instead to construe those words in accordance with the general principle of equality in the Framework Directive, which in turn required protection for voluntary workers engaged in an 'occupation'.

The EAT rejected this argument in its entirety, holding that the Framework Directive does not require the UK Government to provide for voluntary workers, with no contractual relationship, to be protected under the DDA. Furthermore, even if there were such a requirement, it would not be appropriate for tribunals to rewrite domestic legislation in this way, as this was a matter for Parliament. The Appeal Tribunal also rejected a further argument advanced by X, that the arrangements for voluntary workers at the CAB were made 'for the purpose of determining to whom [the bureau] should offer employment'. The EAT considered that, although many paid advisers had previously worked as unpaid volunteers, this was not the purpose of the arrangements, but rather a possible consequence.

X subsequently appealed to the Court of Appeal, which dismissed her claim **28.14** on largely the same grounds as the tribunal and the EAT. Lord Justice Elias, who gave the only reasoned judgment, considered that it was not possible to

951

accept the claimant's argument that, even if she could not bring her claim under the domestic legislation, she nevertheless came within the scope of the Framework Directive. It did not follow that, because the principle of non-discrimination is so important in EU law, the only reasonable inference is that the Directive was intended to apply to volunteers. The Directive is plainly limited in its field of operation and the only question is whether CAB volunteers fall within its scope. Even adopting the broad and generous interpretation that is consistent with a purposive approach, it was clear that the claimant fell outside the Directive's scope. First, it was far from obvious that it would be thought desirable to include volunteers within the scope of the discrimination legislation relating to employment. Secondly, it was inconceivable that the draftsman of the Directive would not have dealt specifically with the position of volunteers if the intention had been to include them. Volunteers are extensively employed throughout Europe, and it is unrealistic to believe that they were intended to be covered by concepts of employment and occupation which would not naturally embrace them. The concept of worker has been restricted to persons who are remunerated for what they do. The concept of occupation is essentially an overlapping one, and there was no reason to suppose that it was intended to cover non-remunerated work. Moreover, the fact that there had been proposals to amend the Directive so as to include volunteers made it plain that in the view of the EU institutions the voluntary sector is not covered by the Directive as currently drafted.

28.15 Elias LJ considered it likely that the concept of 'occupation' under the Directive was intended to refer to a class or category of jobs, and that the concept of 'employed' and 'self-employed' was intended to refer to particular jobs. That would explain why the Directive in terms forbids discrimination with respect to access to an occupation but does not, for example, provide that there should be no discrimination with respect to the terms of the occupation. In other words, it is concerned with rules or practices imposed by professional or other collective bodies which can, by granting qualifications or licences of some sort, restrict the right of someone to enter into a particular job, be it described as a profession or an occupation. It is concerned with access to a particular sector of the job market rather than with the particular job someone seeks or holds. This analysis was consistent with the fact that the concept of 'worker' under EU law is not defined by reference to those with a contract; it is capable of embracing all those who perform work for another for remuneration, whether pursuant to a contract or some other relationship. There is no need for a concept of occupation to capture those employed in a particular job. But even if that analysis were wrong and the concept of occupation were capable of identifying a particular post falling outside the definition of employment or self-employment, the concept would still not include a volunteer such as the claimant in the instant case.

Not all 'volunteer' workers are necessarily without employment rights as a result of this decision, however. As Elias LJ pointed out in the course of his judgment, volunteers come 'in many shapes and sizes' and it cannot be assumed that all will have the same status in law as the claimant in the instant case. Volunteers who have a contract 'personally to do work' will be covered by the definition of 'employment' contained in S.83(2) (see 'Definition of employment' above and 'Personal service' below). Others may be covered because they are engaged in a work experience or vocational training placement (see 'Trainees' below).

Agency workers. The requirement of a contractual relationship can cause **28.16** problems when it comes to agency workers supplied by employment agencies and businesses to carry out work for third parties, since it is not always clear whether such workers are employed by the agency, by the third party for whom they actually carry out the work, or by neither. In the absence of much-needed legislation on the subject, it has been largely left to the courts to determine the status of agency workers – more often than not, in the context of establishing whether there is a contract of employment in existence for the purpose of claiming unfair dismissal under the ERA.

The traditional view has been that, in the absence of an unambiguous provision to the contrary, agency workers are not employees of either the employment business or the end-user for the purposes of the ERA, meaning that they do not qualify for any of the key statutory employment rights conditional upon being an employee under that Act. More recently, however, the courts have began to show an increased willingness to imply a contract of employment between the agency worker and the end-user in certain circumstances. In Dacas v Brook Street Bureau (UK) Ltd 2004 ICR 1437, CA, the Court of Appeal advised that when determining the employment status of a worker who was part of a triangular relationship with an employment business and an end-user, tribunals should consider the possibility of there being an implied contract of employment between the worker and the end-user. Although the Dacas guidance was obiter (i.e. incidental to the decision and non-binding), it was later approved and applied by the Court of Appeal in Cable and Wireless plc v Muscat 2006 ICR 975, CA.

Subsequently, in James v Greenwich London Borough Council 2007 ICR 577, **28.17** EAT, the EAT set out guidance that tightly defined the circumstances in which a tribunal may infer an implied contract. This guidance included the following points:

- the issue in agency cases is whether the way in which the contract is in fact performed is consistent with the agency arrangements or whether it is only consistent with an implied contract between the worker and the end-user

- the key feature is not just the fact that the end-user is not paying the wages, but that it cannot insist on the agency providing the particular worker at all.

953

Provided the arrangements are genuine and the actual relationship is consistent with them, it is not then necessary to explain the provision of the worker's services or the fact of payment to the worker by some contract between the end-user and the worker, even if such a contract would also not be inconsistent with the relationship. The express contracts themselves both explain and are consistent with the nature of the relationship and no implied contract is justified

- when agency arrangements are genuine and, when implemented accurately, represent the actual relationship between the parties – as is likely to be the case where there was no pre-existing contract between the worker and the end-user – it will be rare that there will be evidence entitling the tribunal to imply a contract between the worker and the end-user. If any such contract is to be inferred, there must, subsequent to the relationship commencing, be some words or conduct entitling the tribunal to conclude that the agency arrangements no longer dictate or adequately reflect how the work is actually being performed and that the reality of the relationship is only consistent with the implication of the contract. It will be necessary to show that the worker is working pursuant to mutual obligations binding him or her to the end-user

- the mere passage of time (i.e. the fact that a temporary agency worker has worked for a particular client for a considerable period) does not justify the implication of a contract between the worker and the end-user on the ground of necessity

- it will be more readily open to a tribunal to infer a contract in a case such as Cable and Wireless plc v Muscat (above), where the agency arrangements are superimposed on an existing contractual relationship between the worker and the end-user. In such cases, the tribunal is not strictly implying a contract as such, but rather is concluding that the agency arrangements did not bring the original contract to an end.

28.18 This guidance was subsequently approved by the Court of Appeal in James v Greenwich London Borough Council 2008 ICR 545, CA. In rejecting the agency worker's appeal, the Court played down what many considered to be a conflict of authorities in this area – with the Court of Appeal in cases such as Dacas v Brook Street Bureau (UK) Ltd (above) seemingly in favour of implying employment contracts in agency situations, and the EAT appearing dead-set against the idea. In the view of Lord Justice Mummery, who gave the lead judgment in James (as well as that in Dacas), there was simply no conflict at all. His synthesis was thus: just as it is wrong (as the Court in Dacas pointed out) to regard all agency workers as falling outside the protection of the ERA, it is also wrong (as the EAT has been aware) to suggest that such workers 'should all be treated as employees in disguise'. In each case, the question 'must be decided in accordance with common law principles of implied contract and, in some very extreme cases, by exposing sham arrangements'.

While this line of cases has been concerned with the narrower definition of employment found in the ERA, the question of whether it is possible to imply a contract of employment between an agency worker and an end-user is no less relevant for the purposes of the wider definition found in the EqA. However, the situation is complicated somewhat by S.41 EqA, which provides specific protection for 'contract workers' where they are discriminated against by the end-user or 'principal' – see 'Contract workers' below. In BP Chemicals Ltd v Gillick and anor 1995 IRLR 128, EAT (a sex discrimination case decided before the line of cases referred to above), the EAT rejected an agency worker's submission that she was employed by BP (the end-user) even though there was no direct contractual relationship between them. The EAT considered that this was an unacceptable extension of the scope of the SDA. In its view, the wide definition of employment found in S.82 SDA (the precursor to S.83 EqA) – 'employment under a contract of service or of apprenticeship or a contract personally to execute any work or labour' – must be taken to refer to a contract between the party doing the work and the party for whom the work is done. Moreover, the EAT thought that this view was reinforced by the presence of S.9 SDA (the equivalent provision to S.41 EqA) – in other words, it was unnecessary to find that there was a contract of employment between the agency worker and the end-user in the light of the protection already provided to contract workers under S.9.

While it is unclear from the EAT's decision whether it was ruling out the **28.19** possibility of an implied contract of employment between the agency worker and the end-user altogether, it should be noted that the tribunal in that case had already found that there was an employment relationship between the agency worker and the *agency*. Knowing that a cause of action under the SDA already existed for the agency worker in respect of the agency, the EAT went on to hold that the presence of S.9, which provided the applicant with an additional claim against the end-user, made it unnecessary to give a broad interpretation to the definition of employment in S.82 in order to find a contract between the agency worker and the end-user.

So where does this leave us, post-James, with regard to implying contracts between agency workers and end-users for the purposes of claims under the discrimination legislation? It is worth reiterating that the James guidance makes it quite clear that it will be rare for a contract of employment to be implied between a contract worker and an end-user. For claimants in discrimination cases where a contract of employment (whether express or implied) exists between the agency worker and the agency, the claimant will potentially be able to claim both under the employment provisions of the EqA against the agency, and under S.41 against the end-user. And while the Dacas decision requires

955

courts and tribunals to consider the possibility of an implied contract of employment between end-user and agency worker when considering such tripartite agreements, it is not unreasonable to assume that they will be less likely to imply a contract where causes of action against both the agency and the end-user already exist. Indeed, in Cairns v Visteon UK Ltd 2007 ICR 616, EAT (an unfair dismissal case), the EAT upheld the decision of an employment tribunal that it was not necessary to imply a contract of employment between an agency worker and an end-user in circumstances where the worker already had a contract of employment with the agency. In the EAT's view, the existence of the contract with the agency was clearly a relevant factor that the tribunal had been entitled to take into account when determining whether it was necessary to imply a second contract. The EAT added that, while not entirely ruling out the possibility of dual contracts, it found it difficult to envisage circumstances in which it would be necessary to imply a second contract. The additional existence of the protection afforded by S.41 will arguably make the implication of a second contract even less likely in discrimination cases.

28.20 Note, however, that S.41(1) only provides protection from discrimination by the end-user (the 'principal') to a worker 'who is (a) employed by another person, and (b) supplied by that other person in furtherance of a contract to which the principal is a party (whether or not that other person is a party to it)'. This seems to suggest that in order for an agency worker to be able to claim against the end-user under S.41, he or she must be 'employed' by the agency within the meaning of S.83(2) EqA. Where there is no contract of employment (express or implied) within the meaning of S.83(2) between the agency and the agency worker, and therefore no cause of action against either the agency under the employment provisions or the end-user under S.41, the courts and tribunals may be more willing to imply a contract between the agency worker and the end-user.

28.21 **Personal service.** An employee for the purposes of the EqA can be someone who is in fact self-employed, provided that they contract to personally perform work – S.83(2)(a). In this respect the scope of discrimination law is substantially wider than the right not to be unfairly dismissed under the ERA, which is restricted to those working under a contract of employment.

The requirement of personal service is not new – it was present in the definition of employment in all antecedent discrimination legislation and has been the subject of a considerable amount of case law. In Mirror Group Newspapers Ltd v Gunning 1986 ICR 145, CA (a case brought under similarly worded provisions of the SDA), G applied to MGN Ltd to take over her father's 'agency' contract for the wholesale distribution of Sunday newspapers. When her application was rejected, she complained to a tribunal that MGN Ltd's refusal was on account of her being a mother with family commitments and therefore amounted to unlawful sex discrimination. In holding that G's work did not come within the definition of employment in the SDA, the Court of Appeal emphasised that, in order to fall within the scope of 'a contract personally to execute any work or labour', the execution of such personal work or labour must be the *dominant purpose* of the contract. Personal responsibility for the carrying out and efficiency of the work was not itself sufficient. Since the dominant purpose of the contract between MGN Ltd and G's father was simply the regular and efficient distribution of newspapers, it fell outside the scope of the Act. Furthermore, there was no evidence that under the contract G's father was obliged personally to engage in the operation of the distribution agreement.

The concept of the 'dominant purpose' of a contract has been applied in the **28.22** subsequent case law. In Patterson v Legal Services Commission 2004 ICR 312, CA, the Court of Appeal held that a solicitor was not seeking 'employment' with the Legal Services Commission when she applied for a legal aid franchise because, although she was a sole practitioner, she was not obliged to carry out the work under the contract personally. In reaching this decision, the Court stated that, in accordance with the principles set out in the Mirror Group case, the two questions that must be posed are: was the applicant obliged under the contract to personally carry out work or labour? And, if so, was that obligation the dominant purpose of the contract? Similarly, in Inland Revenue Commissioners and ors v Post Office Ltd 2003 ICR 546, EAT – a case concerned, among other things, with the definition of 'employee' in the ERA and the definition of 'worker' in the National Minimum Wage Act 1998 and the Working Time Regulations 1998 SI 1998/1833 – the EAT held that an option to carry out work personally did not make the personal carrying out of the work the dominant purpose of the contract, even though the parties might have expected the person concerned to perform the work personally. And in Sheehan v Post Office Counters Ltd 1999 ICR 734, EAT, S, a sub-postmaster, was held not to be employed for the purposes of the DDA because the dominant purpose of the sub-postmaster's contract did not require personal performance. The EAT decided that the parts of the contract which did require personal performance by S – namely, the parts relating to the management of the business – were minor and ancillary to the contract's main purpose. In the EAT's view, the dominant purpose of the contract was the regular and efficient carrying out of the Post Office services which, under the terms of the contract, S was not required to carry out himself and could instead delegate to his staff.

However, the well-established dominant purpose test was called into question by the Court of Appeal in Mingeley v Pennock and anor t/a Amber Cars 2004 ICR 727 CA – a race discrimination case – where it stated that 'the search for dominant purpose can be elusive'. The Court further questioned whether it was Parliament's intention to exclude arrangements such as those in the case before it from the scope of the RRA. Nevertheless, as Lord Justice Buxton put it, this 'may not have been what Parliament intended, but it is undoubtedly what Parliament said, and it is undoubtedly what this Court has on a number of

957

occasions interpreted Parliament as saying'. With that in mind, the Court upheld a tribunal's decision that a taxi driver who had an arrangement with a firm which supplied him with customers in return for £75 per week was not in 'employment' with the firm, and thus could not bring his claim of race discrimination. This was based on the tribunal's findings that the driver was under no obligation personally to execute any work or labour and that, even if he was under such an obligation, that obligation could not rightly be described as the dominant purpose of the contract.

28.23 The applicability of the dominant purpose test was considered by the Supreme Court in Jivraj v Hashwani 2011 ICR 1004, SC, where it held that the appointment of an arbitrator in a commercial dispute was not concerned with 'employment' under the Employment Equality (Religion or Belief) Regulations 2003 SI 2003/1660. (The Regulations contained substantially the same definition of 'employment' as is now found in S.83 EqA.) The Supreme Court overturned the Court of Appeal, which had relied on the fact that the Framework Directive, which the Regulations had implemented, applies to 'employment' in the broadest sense. The Supreme Court referred to ECJ case law, such as Allonby v Accrington and Rossendale College and ors 2004 ICR 1328, ECJ (an equal pay case), which draws a clear distinction between 'workers' on the one hand, and independent suppliers of services who are not in a relationship of subordination with the person who receives the services on the other. While the Supreme Court accepted that the dominant purpose of the contract is relevant, it is not the sole test for determining employment – the relationship between the parties should also be considered. Applying that approach, the Court held that while arbitrators render personal services and receive fees, they do not perform those services under the direction of the parties. They are independent of the parties and therefore fall within the latter category of an independent provider of services.

28.24 *Delegation.* The fact that an individual does not actually perform all of the work personally will not necessarily mean that the dominant purpose test will not be met. So long as the contracting party performs the essential part of the work, he or she is free to assign or delegate other aspects to another person. For example, a solicitor may delegate some of the legal work on a case to an assistant and rely on a secretary to carry out ancillary tasks, like typing and posting letters and other documents – Kelly and anor v Northern Ireland Housing Executive 1998 ICR 828, HL. (Note that in Patterson v Legal Services Commission (above) the Court's conclusion that the solicitor applying for a legal aid franchise was not obliged to carry out the work personally was not arrived at on the basis that she could delegate some of the work, but on the ground that the contract would not have imposed obligations on her to do the legal aid work in question personally in the first place, and would have provided that she was entitled to instruct 'approved representatives' to carry out the work.)

A 'contract personally to do work' may be an implied one. In Mankoo v British School of Motoring Ltd EAT 657/82 the EAT held that a self-employed driving instructor operating under a franchise agreement would be covered by the statutory definition of employment in the RRA. The agreement contained no express obligation for the personal execution of work but the EAT, looking at the substance of the transaction and not its form, held that such an obligation could be implied. And in Dawes v Raleigh Industries Ltd ET Case No.15582/95 a tribunal inferred the existence of a similar term in a sports sponsorship contract. Raleigh had agreed to sponsor D, an international cyclist, in return for her wearing its logo in races. According to the tribunal, the company was only interested in D because of her skill and expertise as a cyclist. The sponsorship contract entitled it to cancel its sponsorship if she failed to qualify for the 1996 Olympics – thus making it necessary for her to participate in certain races in order to win a place in the British team. These facts were enough, in the tribunal's view, to establish the existence of an implied obligation on D to perform work personally.

Substitution clauses. The question of whether the fact that an individual can **28.25** provide a replacement will prevent a finding that the contract's dominant purpose is to carry out the work personally has generated a good deal of case law. For example, in Robinson v Highswan Associates t/a Republic Nightclub and ors EAT 1020/01 the EAT held that a self-employed DJ who worked at a nightclub every Monday but could, if he was unable to appear, send a suitable replacement to do the work was in employment for the purposes of the materially identical provision in the Race Relations Act 1976 (RRA). Referring to Byrne Brothers (Formwork) Ltd v Baird and ors 2002 ICR 667, EAT, in which the EAT held that a term in a contract giving a limited power to provide a substitute did not prevent four self-employed carpenters who normally carried out the work themselves from falling within the definition of 'worker' found in the Working Time Regulations 1998 SI 1998/1833, the EAT held that, notwithstanding the DJ's limited ability to provide a substitute, the dominant purpose of the arrangement was for him to provide his music services.

It appears from these cases that the right to provide a replacement must be limited in some way if it is not to prevent the worker claiming protection under the discrimination legislation. For example, it may be limited to where the individual is unable to perform the work personally for some reason (e.g. ill health); or it may be that the replacement must be suitable or that the approval of the other party to the proposed replacement must be sought. A blanket right to provide a substitute is unlikely to meet the requirement of 'personal service'. This was the situation in Hawkins v Darken t/a Sawbridgeworth Motorcycles 2004 EWCA Civ 1755, CA, where the Court of Appeal reinstated the decision of an employment tribunal, overturned by the EAT, that a self-employed van driver who could employ somebody else to undertake his deliveries had failed to show that the dominant purpose of the contract was the personal performance of the work, meaning that he was not employed by the company for the purposes of the DDA.

28.26 However, the realisation that a substitution clause in a contract could allow employers to escape liability for unfair dismissal, discrimination, etc, has led to a suspicion that in some cases a clause was inserted simply in order to achieve that result and did not reflect the true nature of the contract; in other words, that the substitution clause was a 'sham'. There have been a number of cases where the courts have considered whether such clauses can be set aside, culminating in Autoclenz Ltd v Belcher and ors 2011 ICR 1157, SC, a case in which the employer argued that the claimants – car valeters – were subcontractors and not 'workers' under S.230(3) ERA because they worked neither under a contract of employment nor under a contract whereby they undertook 'to do or perform personally any work' (the ERA equivalent of the requirement 'personally to do work' in S.83(2)(a) EqA). Their contracts contained clauses allowing them to supply a substitute to carry out the work on their behalf and stating that there was no obligation on A Ltd to offer work or on the valets to accept work.

When the case reached the Supreme Court, their Lordships endorsed a line of case law to the effect that the standard for proving a 'sham' clause in the employment context is not as stringent as it is in ordinary contract law. Cases such as Protectacoat Firthglow Ltd v Szilagyi 2009 ICR 835, CA, indicated that, whereas in the context of commercial contracts a clause will only be disregarded as a sham if it is the product of the contracting parties' common intention to deceive others, no such intention to deceive is required in employment contracts. The Court held that a clause may be disregarded if it simply does not represent the true intentions of the parties. The employment tribunal should discern the true intentions or expectations of the parties (and therefore their implied agreement and contractual obligations), not only at the inception of the contract but at any later stage where the evidence shows that the parties have expressly or impliedly varied the agreement between them. The Court noted that while employment is a matter of contract, the factual matrix in which the contract is cast is not ordinarily the same as that of an arm's length commercial contract, and it recognised that it is often the case that organisations offering work or requiring services are in a position to dictate the terms on which such work or services are done. Thus, the relative bargaining power of the parties must be taken into account in deciding whether the terms of any written agreement in fact represent what was agreed. The true agreement will often have to be gleaned from all the circumstances of the case, of which the written agreement is only a part.

28.27 When the Autoclenz case was before the Court of Appeal, Lady Justice Smith (whose judgment was endorsed by the Supreme Court) indicated that an employment tribunal will have to examine all the relevant evidence, including the written term itself, read in the context of the whole agreement, to determine whether a substitution clause accurately reflects the working relationship. It should consider evidence of how the parties conducted themselves in practice and what their expectations of each other were. The latter may be so persuasive that the tribunal can draw an inference that the practice reflects the true obligations of the parties. But the mere fact that the parties conducted themselves in a particular way does not of itself mean that that conduct accurately reflects the legal rights and obligations. For example, Smith LJ noted that there could well be a legal right to provide a substitute worker, and the fact that that right was never exercised in practice would not necessarily mean that it was not a genuine right. Applying Smith LJ's analysis to the facts of the actual case before it, the Supreme Court held that the tribunal had been entitled to conclude that car valets, whose contracts specified that they were self-employed subcontractors, were in reality workers. Although their contracts contained clauses allowing them to supply a substitute to carry out the work on their behalf and stating that there was no obligation on A Ltd to offer work or on the valets to accept work, the tribunal's view was that these clauses did not reflect the true legal obligations of the parties. The valets were expected to turn up and to do the work provided, were fully integrated into A Ltd's business, and were subject to a considerable degree of control by A Ltd. The Supreme Court, agreeing with the Court of Appeal, held that the tribunal had been entitled to come to that conclusion.

The Supreme Court's decision suggests that attempts to evade the application of discrimination and employment law by inserting 'substitution' or 'obligations' clauses into contracts are unlikely to succeed where those clauses do not reflect the reality of the working relationship. For a more detailed consideration of the issues arising in Autoclenz Ltd v Belcher and ors (above), see IDS Employment Law Handbook, 'Contracts of Employment' (2009), Chapter 1, 'Basic requirements', in the section 'Who is an employee?', under 'Multiple test – sham contracts'.

Illegal contracts. The fact that an employment contract is tainted with illegality **28.28** will not of itself prevent a discrimination claim. After a line of conflicting EAT decisions on the matter, the Court of Appeal addressed the subject of illegality and discrimination in Hall v Woolston Hall Leisure Ltd 2001 ICR 99, CA. In that case H was employed by WHL Ltd as a chef in a golf club from July 1994 until her dismissal in March 1995 after her employer learned that she was pregnant. She complained to a tribunal that she had been dismissed by reason of her pregnancy and that this amounted to sex discrimination. The tribunal found that H had been unlawfully discriminated against on the ground of her sex contrary to S.6(2)(b) SDA. However, at the remedies hearing, WHL Ltd submitted that H could not recover anything because her contract of employment was tainted with illegality as the company had not been paying proper tax on her earnings. Both the tribunal and the EAT held that, since H had continued to work in the knowledge that her employer was defrauding the Inland Revenue, she had no legal rights under the contract at the time she was dismissed and therefore suffered no loss and was not entitled to compensation under the SDA. H appealed.

The Court of Appeal upheld the appeal, holding that H was entitled to compensation for her financial loss following her dismissal for pregnancy, which was unlawful under the SDA despite the fact that she knew that her employer had been defrauding the Inland Revenue. The Court reviewed the authorities on illegality in English law and considered how it operated as a defence to a claim in tort (discrimination is a statutory tort). It found that while the underlying test remains one of public policy, in order for an employer successfully to plead the defence of illegality there must be a causal link between the employee's claim and the illegality. On this basis, the Court stated that: 'The correct approach of a tribunal in a sex discrimination case should be to consider whether the applicant's claim arises out of or is so clearly connected or inextricably bound up or linked with the illegal conduct of the applicant that the court could not permit the applicant to recover compensation without appearing to condone that conduct.'

28.29   In the Court's view, there was no such causal link between H's acquiescence in the unlawful failure by the employer to deduct tax and national insurance and her sex discrimination claim. The illegality consisted only of the employer's manner of paying wages, and the duty to pay tax and national insurance rested on the employer. H had not actively participated in the illegality and the Court could see nothing that showed her guilty of any unlawful conduct. Nor had she received any benefit from the employer's failure to account for tax and national insurance contributions to the Revenue. Lord Justice Peter Gibson stated that '[H's] acquiescence in the employer's conduct, which is the highest her involvement in the illegality can be put, no doubt reflects the reality that she could not compel the employer to change its conduct. That acquiescence is in no way causally linked with her sex discrimination claim.'

The principle established in the Woolston Hall decision is confirmed by the EHRC Employment Code, which states that: 'The fact that a contract of employment is illegal or performed in an illegal manner will not exclude an Employment Tribunal having jurisdiction to hear an employment-related discrimination claim. This will be so provided that the discrimination is not inextricably linked to illegal conduct (so as to make an award of compensation appear to condone that conduct)' – para 10.5.

28.30   An example of a case where the discrimination was inextricably linked to illegal conduct is Vakante v Addey and Stanhope School (No.2) 2005 ICR 231, CA, where V, a Croatian national, sought asylum in the United Kingdom. He obtained a post as a trainee teacher at a school, having stated that his asylum claim was pending but falsely indicating that he did not need a work permit. At no point did he apply for permission to work. He was subsequently dismissed from his post and brought a claim of race discrimination. Applying the Woolston Hall formula, the Court of Appeal held that V was solely responsible for his illegal conduct in working for the school and creating an unlawful situation, on which he then had to rely in order to establish that there was a duty not to discriminate against him. V's complaints of discriminatory treatment were so inextricably bound up with his illegal conduct in obtaining and continuing employment with the school that, if the tribunal were to permit him to recover compensation, it would appear to condone his illegal conduct. He had therefore disqualified himself from pursuing his claim. The Court declined to comment on whether the EC Race Equality Directive (No.2000/43) applied since it was not in force at the time that V's case arose for consideration. However, it noted that it raised a number of interesting points, including whether the Directive has any impact on the defence of illegality under domestic law.

The Vakante case was distinguished by the EAT in Hounga v Allen and anor 2012 EWCA Civ 609, CA, where H had illegally entered the United Kingdom from Nigeria to work as a domestic servant. When H was dismissed, she claimed race discrimination. The EAT held that, on the facts of this case, the employer was not able to successfully plead the defence of illegality because the discrimination claim was not inextricably linked or connected with H's illegal conduct. Unlike the Vakante case, the claimant's involvement in the illegality was much less than that of the employer. However, the EAT's decision was overturned by the Court of Appeal, which held that there was no escaping the tribunal's findings that H knew what she was doing and knew it was wrong.

28.31 Similarly, in Zarkasi v Anindita and anor EAT 0400/11 Z illegally entered the United Kingdom from Indonesia in order to undertake domestic work. After her employment ended, she sought to claim unfair dismissal, unlawful deductions from wages and race discrimination. A tribunal dismissed Z's employment protection claims on the ground that her contract of employment was illegal from the outset. However, in accordance with Hall v Woolston Hall Leisure Ltd 2001 ICR 99, CA, it allowed Z's discrimination claim to proceed, but rejected it on the merits. The tribunal found that A's 'exploitation' at the hands of the employer resulted from her immigration status, but that this was not a racial ground within the meaning of the RRA. On appeal, the EAT accepted that this analysis was correct. It rejected Z's argument that the correct comparator was someone who was British and who had rights to reside and work in Great Britain, who would not have been exploited in this way. The EAT noted that, if this were correct, there would be discrimination in any situation where a person in this jurisdiction (whether legally or not) was precluded from taking up employment and sought to enforce his or her rights in respect of work that had actually been obtained. That could not be right.

One question that remains unanswered by Hall v Woolston Hall Leisure Ltd (above) (and the EHRC Employment Code) relates to statutory illegality. Contracts of employment that are directly prohibited by statute – for example, those that infringe restrictions on the employment of children or of pregnant women in certain types of work – are generally held to be not only unenforceable but also void. Therefore, there would appear to be no employment relationship upon which a discrimination claim could bite. In such circumstances, a tribunal might be forced to hold that the applicant is not 'employed' within the meaning of the EqA and is therefore not entitled to bring a claim.

28.32 **Ministers of religion.** Until fairly recently it was generally assumed that ministers of religion were not covered by discrimination law, on the basis that the relationship between a minister of religion and his or her church was not a contractual one. However, in Percy v Board of National Mission of the Church of Scotland 2006 ICR 134, HL, the House of Lords held, by a four-to-one majority (Lord Hoffmann dissenting), that notwithstanding the religious nature of the services P, an ordained Church of Scotland minister, was engaged to provide, there was a contract in existence between her and the Church of a kind falling within the definition of employment contained in the SDA, meaning that she could proceed with her claim of sex discrimination against the Church. P was appointed to the position of associate minister in a parish. Her terms and conditions for the post stated, among other things, that her appointment was for five years and her salary was at the level of the minimum stipend. There was also provision for travelling expenses and holiday entitlement. Following an investigation into allegations of misconduct against her, she resigned as an ordained minister, and thus from her post as an associate minister, and brought a claim before an employment tribunal under the SDA. Rejecting her claim on the ground that it had no jurisdiction to hear it, the tribunal held that although there was a contract in existence between the two parties, given the essentially religious nature of her duties P was not employed by the Church within the meaning of S.82(1) SDA. It further held that the complaint comprised 'matters spiritual' within the meaning of S.3 of the Church of Scotland Act 1921, with the result that it fell within the exclusive jurisdiction of the courts of the Church of Scotland.

P's appeal against that decision – rejected by both the EAT and the Court of Session – was eventually allowed by the majority of the House of Lords. Lord Nicholls stated that, on their face, the documents relating to P's appointment showed that she had entered into a contract with the Church to provide services to it on agreed terms and conditions. Notwithstanding the religious nature of those services, the contract was a contract 'personally to execute work' within the definition of S.82(1) SDA. Taking a fairly broad and purposive approach to the question of who falls within the definition of 'employment' for the purposes of the discrimination legislation, the House of Lords made it clear that courts should be wary of denying jurisdiction without good reason, with Lord Nicholls stating that 'it is time to recognise that employment arrangements between a church and its ministers should not lightly be taken as intended to have no legal effect and, in consequence, its ministers denied this [statutory] protection'. Delivering a concurring judgment, Lord Hope also considered the provisions of the EU Equal Treatment Directive (No.76/207) (now consolidated into the recast Equal Treatment Directive (No.2006/54)) and concluded that the determinative factor was 'the fact that she undertook to perform services for another in return for remuneration'. That brought her within the definition of 'worker', with the result that the conditions under which she agreed to perform the services were 'working conditions' within the scope of the Directive. On the question of whether the civil courts' jurisdiction was excluded by the Church of Scotland Act 1921, which reserves to the Church exclusive jurisdiction 'in matters spiritual', Lord Nicholls was of the view that if the Church authorities enter into a contract of employment with one of their ministers, the exercise of statutory rights attached to the contract would not be regarded as a spiritual matter. Accordingly, the matter came within the jurisdiction of the tribunal.

Another significant aspect of this decision is their Lordships' views on the **28.33** relationship between office holders and employment, with Lord Nicholls insisting that a person may be both an office holder and an employee. Lord Hoffmann, giving the dissenting judgment, appeared to disagree with the notion that the fact that an individual is an officer holder does not necessarily mean that he or she cannot also be an employee, stating that it was an established proposition 'that a minister of a church has no employer but holds an office'. In Lord Hoffmann's view, there was no employment contract in the instant case because the claimant's duties 'were not contractual at all. They were duties of her office.' He did, however, concede that, as a result of changes to the SDA introduced in October 2005 making it unlawful to discriminate against various office holders (which are replicated in Ss.49–52 EqA – see 'Office holders' below), it was arguable that the claimant would have been able to bring her claim as an office holder.

Whether or not a minister of religion can claim to be employed under a contract of employment, a contract to perform work personally, or to be an office holder will depend upon the facts in the particular case: in MacDonald v Free Presbyterian Church of Scotland EATS 0034/09, for example, the EAT found a Presbyterian Minister to be an office holder, and not engaged under any contractual arrangement, with the result that he could not bring a claim for unfair dismissal. However, an office holder would be entitled to bring a claim for discrimination – see 'Office holders' below.

Firms and companies as 'employees'. Commentators have generally assumed **28.34** that only individuals are capable of entering into 'employment', as defined, given that firms and companies cannot be said to perform work 'personally', because they necessarily rely on individuals – directors, partners, employees,

965

agents or contractors, etc – to act on their behalf. However, the House of Lords challenged this assumption in a limited way in Kelly and anor v Northern Ireland Housing Executive 1998 ICR 828, HL. The Northern Ireland Housing Executive is a public body that maintains a panel of solicitors to act on its behalf in public liability claims brought against it. Solicitors' firms that wish to apply to join this panel have to designate a partner or principal who will accept overall responsibility for the relevant work and a solicitor who will be mainly involved in carrying it out. The partner/principal and the solicitor named on the application may be the same person, as was the situation in the instant case.

K was a partner in a two-partner firm; L was a sole practitioner. Both were Roman Catholics who alleged unlawful discrimination under the Northern Ireland Fair Employment Acts when the Housing Executive declined to shortlist them for panel membership. At a preliminary hearing the Fair Employment Tribunal concluded that neither K nor L had been an applicant for 'employment' (the Fair Employment Acts contain the same definition of 'employment' as the discrimination legislation). The Northern Ireland Court of Appeal disagreed so far as L was concerned and held that, as a single practitioner, he should be treated the same as any other individual who sought a contract to provide services personally. It distinguished K's situation on the ground that she was a partner in a firm. Unlike L, K had not been the potential contracting party – the firm had. Because a firm was incapable of performing work personally, there had been no application for 'employment' within the meaning of the Act.

28.35 The case went on appeal to the House of Lords, which was faced with a number of options. Their Lordships could uphold the Northern Ireland Court of Appeal's decision – but this would require them to approve the unsatisfactory distinction between a single practitioner and a member of a partnership; they could restore the Fair Employment Tribunal's decision – but this would be credible only if they could identify some feature that genuinely distinguished a solicitor in sole practice from any other self-employed individual offering to provide a service; or they could try to find some basis on which K too might be said to have been an applicant for 'employment' – but in so doing they would need to avoid extending the definition of 'employment' too far. In the end, by a bare majority (Lords Slynn, Griffiths and Steyn), their Lordships chose the final option; the minority (Lords Lloyd and Clyde) favoured the second option.

The majority rejected the artificiality of drawing any significant distinction between L and K on the basis of the difference in the internal structure of their respective businesses. They preferred instead to interpret the concept of 'employment' broadly to encompass the special circumstances of K's case. It is important to understand the following points about the majority's decision:

- although agreed on the final outcome, their Lordships differed in their reasons for reaching it. Lord Slynn (with whom Lord Steyn agreed) held that K's firm, not K, should be treated as the potential contractor, and that a firm could contract personally to perform work. In doing so, he relied on the fact that the Interpretation Act 1978 defines 'person' as including a body of unincorporated persons unless the contrary intention appears. Lord Griffiths expressly rejected this approach. Instead, he pointed out that if the Housing Executive had appointed K's firm to its solicitors' panel, K would have been a contracting party as well – the rights and obligations of partnerships being both joint and several between the partners. Accordingly, the House of Lords' decision should not be seen as authority for the proposition that a firm may be treated as an 'employee' for the purposes of the EqA. Only Lords Slynn and Steyn favoured that approach

- the Northern Ireland Housing Executive's application procedure laid great emphasis on the identity and experience of the solicitor who was to do the work. Both Lord Slynn and Lord Griffiths explained that this was an important factor in their decision to recognise the existence of a potential contract by K or K's firm to do work 'personally'. In other circumstances, the identity of the person who does the work may not be so important, and the case may be distinguishable from the present case on that account

- the majority decision in K's favour was dependent on the fact that she was a partner in the firm and not merely an employee. The importance of this distinction was an integral part of the reasoning in Lord Griffiths' judgment (see above), and Lord Slynn also made much of it. He explained that the circumstances in which a firm could be said to contract to perform work personally were limited to where 'one or more of the partners is intended to and does execute the work'. If, therefore, K's firm had designated an employed lawyer rather than a partner to take the lead role in its work for the Executive, the application probably would not have qualified as an application to enter a contract to perform work personally.

28.36 One can infer from the House of Lords' decision that it will never be permissible to treat a *company* as an 'employee' for the purposes of the EqA, because, unlike a firm, a corporate body is treated in law as a legal entity separate from all the individuals – directors, employees, etc – who work for it.

Note that a firm's liability for discrimination against its partners or potential partners is considered under 'Partners and members of limited liability partnerships' below.

Apprentices and trainees

28.37 The definition of employment in S.83(2)(a) EqA includes 'employment under a contract of apprenticeship'. Thus, it will be unlawful for an employer to discriminate against an apprentice just as it is unlawful to discriminate against an employee (see 'Employees' above). In the context of discrimination law, little is likely to turn on the distinction between a contract of employment and a contract of apprenticeship. The distinction is much more important in the

967

context of unfair dismissal and redundancy, as it is a feature of apprenticeships that they are for a fixed period and cannot be terminated by the employer giving notice – see Wallace v CA Roofing Services Ltd 1996 IRLR 435, QBD (a redundancy case).

The EqA does not contain a general provision covering discrimination against trainees in the workplace. Thus, for a trainee to be covered, he or she will need to fit into one of the other categories of protection. The definition of employment in S.83(2) means that, apprenticeships apart, the scope for a trainee to be treated as an 'employee' for the purposes of Ss.39 and 40 will be limited: many trainees, especially those in Government-sponsored training schemes, have no legal contract of any sort with their 'trainer'. Moreover, where a contract does exist, it will not amount to a contract of employment or a contract personally to do work if the primary purpose of the contract is training. So, in Daley v Allied Suppliers Ltd 1983 ICR 90, EAT, the Appeal Tribunal held that a trainee engaged in work experience under the MSC Youth Opportunities Programme was employed neither by the company providing the work experience nor by the MSC itself. The object of the contract was not the execution of work or labour but the acquisition of work experience.

28.38 Trainees may be able to claim protection under Ss.55–56 EqA, however. These provisions make it unlawful to discriminate against, harass or victimise a person when providing an employment service, and place a duty on providers of employment services (referred to as 'employment service-providers') to make reasonable adjustments for disabled people. These sections replace separate provisions in the old legislation covering vocational training, employment agencies and assisting persons to obtain employment: a single provision now covers all these aspects. For details, see Chapter 29, 'Liability of other bodies', under 'Employment service-providers'.

28.39 Crown employees

As mentioned above, the definition of 'employment' for the purposes of the EqA extends to Crown employment – S.83(2)(b). Thus, the Act applies to the Crown and to Crown employment in the same way as it applies to private employers – see 'Employees' above. S.83(9) provides that 'Crown employment' has the meaning given in S.191 ERA, which states that 'Crown employment' is 'employment under or for the purposes of a government department or any officer or body exercising on behalf of the Crown functions conferred by a statutory provision' – S.191(3).

Section 83(7) EqA provides that in the case of a person in Crown employment, a reference to that person's dismissal is a reference to the termination of that person's employment. This provision reflects the special status of Crown servants, who are said to be 'appointed' rather than 'employed', with their appointment being 'at will' and terminable by the Crown without notice.

House of Commons and House of Lords staff   28.40

The definition of 'employment' in S.83(2) EqA also covers 'employment as a relevant member of the House of Commons staff' and 'employment as a relevant member of the House of Lords staff' – S.83(2)(d)–(c).

Section 83(5) EqA states that a 'relevant member of the House of Commons staff' has the meaning given in S.195 ERA, i.e. any person 'who was appointed by the House of Commons Commission or is employed in the refreshment department, or… who is a member of the Speaker's personal staff' – S.195(5). Normally, the House of Commons Commission is the employer of staff appointed by the Commission, and the Speaker is the employer of his or her personal staff and of any person employed in the refreshment department and not appointed by the Commission – S.83(5)(a) EqA and S.195(6) ERA. However, the House of Commons Commission or the Speaker may designate a person to be treated as the employer of any description of staff (other than the Speaker's personal staff) – S.83(5)(b) EqA and S.195(7) ERA.

As with Crown employees, S.83(7) EqA provides that in the case of a person   28.41
employed as a relevant member of the House of Commons staff, a reference to the person's dismissal is a reference to the termination of the person's employment.

Section 83(6) EqA provides that a 'relevant member of the House of Lords staff' has the meaning given in S.194 ERA, i.e. 'any person who is employed under a contract of employment with the Corporate Officer of the House of Lords' – S.194(6) ERA.

Former employees   28.42

Former employees (and other individuals who are protected under Part 5 of the EqA, e.g. contract workers, partners, etc) have the right under S.108 to bring a complaint in respect of any discrimination or harassment that takes place after the employment relationship has ended. The most common circumstances in which post-employment discrimination occurs are where the former employer requests a reference from his or her previous employer or where an employer is carrying out a post-dismissal appeal procedure. S.108 derives from similar provisions in the previous equality Acts.

Section 108(1) and (2) EqA state that a person (A) must not discriminate against or harass another (B) if:

- the discrimination or harassment 'arises out of and is closely connected to a relationship which used to exist between them', and

- conduct of a description constituting the discrimination or harassment would, if it occurred during the relationship, contravene the EqA.

969

The protection afforded by the provisions outlined above applies even if the employment relationship ended before S.108 came into force – S.108(3). However, the Explanatory Notes to the EqA make it clear that, for S.108 to apply, the *conduct* complained of must take place after the commencement of S.108 (which was 1 October 2010). Para 351 of the Notes states: 'S.108 applies to conduct which takes place after the Act is commenced, whether or not the relationship in question ended before that date. If the conduct occurred before [S.108] was commenced, it would be dealt with under the previous legislation.'

28.43 In addition, S.108(4) EqA provides that a duty to make reasonable adjustments applies to A if B is placed at a substantial disadvantage by the employer's provisions, criteria and practices; the physical features of the employer's premises; or the failure to provide an auxiliary aid. For these purposes, the statutory provisions on reasonable adjustments must be construed as if the relationship had not ended – S.108(5). The EHRC Employment Code gives the example of a former employee with life-time membership of the works social club who is no longer able to access the club because of a mobility impairment. Once the employer becomes aware of the situation, it will need to consider making reasonable adjustments – para 10.60. Another example of a situation in which the duty can arise after an employment relationship has ended is where the employer is hearing an appeal against dismissal.

For the purposes of the enforcement provisions in Part 9 of the EqA (discussed in Chapter 34, 'Enforcing individual rights'), a contravention of S.108 relates to the Part of the EqA that would have been contravened if the relationship had not ended – S.108(6). In other words, a breach of S.108 triggers the same enforcement procedures as if the treatment had occurred during the employment relationship (see para 353 of the Explanatory Notes).

28.44 If the treatment complained of constitutes victimisation, it will not be dealt with under S.108 but under 'the victimisation provisions' – S.108(7). Although the victimisation provisions do not explicitly mention post-employment conduct, our view is that the demands of EU law are such that tribunals are obliged to apply S.39(4) EqA – the provision which outlaws victimisation of an employee – in such a way that it also covers victimisation of a former employee (see Chapter 27, 'Post-employment discrimination', under 'Protection under the Equality Act – post-employment victimisation' for details).

28.45 **Contract workers**

As mentioned above under 'Employees', the EqA contains specific provisions prohibiting discrimination against contract workers (such as agency workers) by the end-user of their services (known in the Act as a 'principal'). S.41 EqA provides that a principal must not discriminate against or victimise a contract worker:

- as to the terms on which the principal allows the worker to do the work – S.41(1)(a) and (3)(a)

- by not allowing the worker to do, or to continue to do, the work – S.41(1)(b) and (3)(b)

- in the way the principal affords the worker access, or by not affording the worker access, to opportunities for receiving a benefit, facility or service – S.41(1)(c) and (3)(c)

- by subjecting the worker to any other detriment – S.41(1)(d) and (3)(d).

Section 41(2) further provides that a principal must not, in relation to contract work, harass a contract worker, while S.41(4) states that a duty to make reasonable adjustments applies to a principal (as well as to the employer of a contract worker).

28.46 It should be noted that contract workers enjoy separate protection from discrimination by their employer (typically, the agency for which they work and which places them with the principal) under S.39 EqA – see 'Employees – agency workers' above.

In Leeds City Council v Woodhouse 2010 IRLR 625, CA (the facts of which are considered below under 'Meaning of "principal" and "contract worker"'), the Court of Appeal made obiter, but no doubt influential, comments, advising tribunals that the question of whether a contract worker falls within the discrimination legislation should not be dealt with as a preliminary issue unless the case is very straightforward. The scope of evidence relevant to the applicability of S.41 EqA might not be immediately obvious to a tribunal, and as the issue is largely one of fact, it should ideally be determined by a full tribunal rather than by an employment judge sitting alone.

28.47 **Meaning of 'principal' and 'contract worker'.** Section 41(5) defines a 'principal' as a person who makes work available for an individual who is (a) employed by another person and (b) supplied by that other person in furtherance of a contract to which the principal is a party (whether or not that other person is a party to it). S.41(6) defines 'contract work' as work of the type mentioned in S.41(5), i.e. work made available by a principal. S.41(7) goes on to define a 'contract worker' as an individual supplied to a principal in furtherance of a contract to which the principal is a party.

According to para 148 of the Explanatory Notes, S.41 is designed to replicate the effect of previous legislation, while codifying case law (which we set out below) to make it clear that there does not need to be a direct contractual relationship between the employer and the principal for the protection to apply. This point is further emphasised in the EHRC Employment Code, which states: 'There is usually a contract directly between the end-user and the supplier, but this is not always the case. Provided there is an unbroken chain of contracts

971

between the individual and the end-user of their services, that end-user is a principal and the individual is therefore a contract worker' – para 11.8.

28.48 An unbroken chain of contracts was found to exist in MHC Consulting Services Ltd v Tansell and anor 2000 ICR 789, CA, a case where T was not an employee of the agency that supplied his services to the end-user. He was a computer specialist who, in order to secure the benefits of limited liability, had chosen to provide his services through the establishment of his own company. He was employed by this company, which contracted with an employment agency, which in turn supplied his services to an insurance company. The Court of Appeal upheld the EAT's decision that T could bring a complaint of disability discrimination against the insurance company (the end-user, or – to use the language of the EqA – the principal). Lord Justice Mummery, delivering the judgment of the Court, thought it irrelevant that there was no direct contractual relationship between the limited company that employed the individual and the insurance company that made the work available. Taking into account the underlying purpose of the discrimination legislation, the Court considered it more probable than not that Parliament had intended to confer protection in these circumstances.

While S.41 is clearly designed to cover situations where an employment agency supplies workers, such as clerical staff or nurses, to an end-user (principal) under a contract of supply, it is by no means confined to this situation. In Harrods Ltd v Remick and ors 1998 ICR 156, CA, the question was whether women employed as saleswomen at concessions in Harrods could sue Harrods for race discrimination. Harrods frequently enters into concession agreements with businesses that wish to sell their goods to customers inside its store. Although concessionaires supply the goods on sale in the concession, the contract in the instant case provided that the goods were to be 'sold' to Harrods immediately before their sale to the public. Harrods then received the marked price, and accounted to the concessionaire for the sum, after deducting a percentage. The contract also required any person employed by a concessionaire within the store to comply with Harrods' dress code and with the store's rules concerning conduct. The penalty for breaching either of these conditions was withdrawal by Harrods of 'store approval' for the individual worker in question, with the result that that person would be banned from working in the store. Harrods argued that it was not the 'principal' of workers employed by concessionaires because it did not exercise managerial power or control over them and because the supply of workers was not the 'dominant purpose' of the contract between the concessionaires and Harrods. The Court of Appeal denied that either of these was a decisive factor. The real test was whether the employer is under a contractual obligation to supply individuals to do work that could properly be described as 'work for' the principal. On the facts of the case, the Court of Appeal held that workers in the concessions could indeed be said to 'work for' Harrods, which was therefore their principal.

The Harrods decision was considered by the Northern Ireland Court of Appeal **28.49** in Jones v Friends Provident Life Office 2004 IRLR 783, NICA, another case that fell outside the traditional employment agency scenario. J worked for her husband's estate agency business, WI. She became a 'company representative' (CR) for FP, a company that provides investment policies and pensions, so that as WI's employee, she was licensed to sell FP's financial products to WI's customers. When FP subsequently withdrew her status as a CR she brought a claim of sex discrimination against it. At a preliminary hearing, the tribunal decided that it had jurisdiction to hear J's complaint on the basis that she was a contract worker under Article 12 of the Sex Discrimination (Northern Ireland) Order 1976 (No.1042 (NI 15)) (an equivalent provision to S.41 EqA). FP appealed to the Northern Ireland Court of Appeal, arguing that the work carried out by J under her contract with WI as a CR was not work 'for' FP, the principal, for the purposes of Article 12. Although FP benefited from J's work in that its policies were sold, J was working for her husband in order to earn commissions for his business. It was not clear to the Court whether it was sufficient that claimants merely establish that the principal benefited from the work done by them. The EAT in CJ O'Shea Construction Ltd v Bassi 1998 ICR 1130, EAT, had taken the view that such a proposition was doubtful, and in the Harrods case the matter had been left as one of fact and degree. However, with that caveat in mind, it concluded that, while there were several factual distinctions between the Harrods case and the instant one, the tribunal had been entitled to reach the conclusion that J's work was done for FP as well as for her husband's company.

The second issue the Court had to decide was whether, on the proper construction of Article 12, J had been 'supplied' by WI under a contract made with FP. The Court had reservations about the correctness of the conclusion in O'Shea (above) that where a company had contracted with another to deliver concrete by vehicle, complete with a driver able to unload it, that driver had been 'supplied' to that company under a contract. While the Court thought it desirable for the contract workers provisions to be construed broadly so as to protect a wide range of workers employed to perform work for someone other than their nominal employers, this should be subject to two conditions. First, it was implicit in the philosophy underlying the provisions that the principal must be in a position to discriminate against the contract worker. The principal must therefore be able to influence or control the conditions under which the employee works. Secondly, it is also inherent in the concept of supplying workers under a contract that it is contemplated by the employer and the principal that the former will provide the services of employees in the course of performance of the contract. In the instant case, J's employer entered into a contract with the principal, FP, to sell FP's products. However, her employer was not allowed to sell those products and, in order to fulfil the contract, it had to employ a CR to make the sales. Accordingly, it was contemplated that WI

973

would employ J to do that work. J had been trained and authorised by FP, who had a large say in how she was to carry out the work, and FP was in a position to withdraw her authority to make the sales by ending her status as a CR. In these circumstances, the Court found that her case was covered by Article 12 and dismissed the appeal.

28.50 The view that a principal must have influence or control over a worker was revisited by the Court of Appeal in Leeds City Council v Woodhouse 2010 IRLR 625, CA. That case involved a complex contractual arrangement whereby Leeds City Council engaged an 'arm's length management organisation' (ALMO) to manage some of the Council's housing stock. The ALMO also contracted with other bodies to provide certain services in respect of the housing stock. One such contractor was the Council's property services division (PSD), which was engaged to provide a range of maintenance services under an agreement with the ALMO. W was employed by the ALMO and in his role of principal regeneration officer he would sometimes need to check the work of C, an employee of PSD, to ensure that it was done to the ALMO's satisfaction. W alleged that C made racist comments about him during work-related meetings and, as a result, brought race discrimination claims against the Council, C and the ALMO. However, the Council and C argued that the tribunal did not have jurisdiction to hear the claims against them because W was not a contract worker within the meaning of S.7 RRA. In holding that W was a contract worker for the purposes of S.7, the tribunal considered that that provision should be broadly construed and that all the work done by the ALMO's employees, including that done by W, was done for the benefit of the Council. That decision was upheld by the EAT, and the Council appealed to the Court of Appeal, arguing that, in light of the NICA's decision in Jones v Friends Provident Life Office (above), the tribunal had been wrong to find that, for S.7 to apply, it was sufficient that the work done by W was for the benefit of the Council. It contended that the Council had to have control or influence over W for him to be a contract worker.

The Court of Appeal accepted that in both Jones v Friends Provident Life Office (above) and Harrods Ltd v Remick and ors (above) the principals had control or influence over the contract workers, and that there was a lack of such control or influence in the instant case. However, the Court did not consider that this undermined the tribunal's reasoning. Each case is fact-sensitive and it will not always be necessary for control and influence to be demonstrated before a case can come within the remit of S.7 RRA (now S.41 EqA). The tribunal had considered that, due to the extreme closeness of the relationship between the contracting parties, it could properly be said that W's work was being done for the Council regardless of whether there was any control or influence. Given that the ALMO had only one customer – the Council – and that it only existed to provide services to the Council, the first question identified in the Harrods case, that of whether the work done by W was work done for the Council, had been answered in the affirmative.

The Council also argued that the circumstances in which W and C came into **28.51** contact were pursuant to the service agreement between the ALMO and the PSD, and not to the management agreement between the ALMO and the Council. Under the service contract it was the PSD and C who had been working for the ALMO: it was not a case of W being supplied to the Council, but rather one of C being supplied by it. In dismissing the submission that this alternative interpretation of the contractual arrangements between the Council and the ALMO invalidated the tribunal's reasoning, the Court of Appeal noted that it had not been suggested to the tribunal that the service agreement was the only contract that had brought W and C together, and that the management contract was therefore irrelevant. The fact was that, under the management agreement, the ALMO was obliged to employ staff to service the contract, and was therefore supplying workers pursuant to its contract with the Council. This view was not undermined by the suggestion that C had been supplied to the ALMO under the service agreement, nor by the fact that the ALMO could have, but did not, contract with another body to provide the same service. Accordingly, the second question as identified in the Harrods case – whether W was a person whom the ALMO had supplied to the Council under a contract – was also answered in the affirmative and the Council's appeal was dismissed.

Police   28.52
By virtue of S.42(1) a police constable is treated as being employed by his or her chief officer of police in respect of any acts done by the chief officer (or, in Scotland, the chief constable), and by the police authority in respect of any acts done by it. A similarly worded provision in S.42(2) extends identical protection to police cadets, defined in S.43(4) as persons appointed to undergo training with a view to becoming a constable.

According to the Explanatory Notes, S.42 'is designed to replicate the provisions in previous legislation and extends coverage to constables at [the Scottish Police Services Authority] and [the Scottish Crime and Drugs Enforcement Agency]. It also removes the requirement to pay out of police funds compensation and related costs arising from the personal liability of chief officers (or in Scotland, chief constables) for acts which are unlawful under the EqA. Payments of compensation and related costs arising from the personal liability of chief officers (or in Scotland, chief constables) will instead be dealt with by the Police Act 1996 and the Police (Scotland) Act 1967, as for all other police officers' – para 153.

'Holding the office of constable'. Section 42(1) states that 'holding the office **28.53** of constable is to be treated as employment', but the Act offers no further guidance on what amounts to holding such office. Some assistance is afforded

975

by the EHRC Employment Code, which states that those holding the office of constable include 'special constables and those in private constabularies such as the British Transport Police' – para 11.15. Note, though, that constables working for certain bodies are specifically excluded from S.42(1) – see 'Special cases' below.

28.54 **'Chief officer'.** In relation to an appointment under the Metropolitan Police Act 1829, the City of London Police Act 1839, the Police (Scotland) Act 1967 or the Police Act 1996, a 'chief officer' means the chief officer of police for the police force to which the appointment relates – S.43(2)(a) and (8) EqA. In relation to any other appointment, the 'chief officer' is the person under whose direction and control the body of constables or other persons to which the appointment relates is – S.43(2)(b). In the case of a constable or other person under the direction and control of a chief officer of police, the 'chief officer' is that chief officer of police – S.43(2)(c). In relation to any other constable or any other person, the 'chief officer' is the person under whose direction and control the constable or other person is – S.43(2)(d).

A reference in S.43(2) to a 'chief officer of police' includes, in relation to Scotland, a reference to a chief constable – S.43(9).

28.55 **'Responsible authority.'** In relation to an appointment under the Metropolitan Police Act 1829, the City of London Police Act 1839, the Police (Scotland) Act 1967 or the Police Act 1996, a 'responsible authority' means the police authority that maintains the police force to which the appointment relates – S.43(3)(a) and (8) EqA. In relation to any other appointment, the 'responsible authority' is the person by whom a person would (if appointed) be paid – S.43(3)(b). In the case of a constable or other person under the direction and control of a chief officer of police, the 'responsible authority' is the police authority that maintains the police force for which that chief officer is the chief officer of police – S.43(3)(c). In relation to any other constable or any other person, the 'responsible authority' is the person by whom the constable or other person is paid – S.43(3)(d).

A reference in S.43(3) to a 'chief officer of police' includes, in relation to Scotland, a reference to a chief constable – S.43(9).

28.56 **Special cases.** Section 42(1) EqA – which essentially provides that a police constable is treated as employed by his or her chief officer of police in respect of any acts done by the chief officer and by the police authority in respect of any acts done by it – does not apply to:

- service with the Civil Nuclear Constabulary – S.42(3)

- a constable at the Serious Organised Crime Agency (SOCA), including a constable seconded to SOCA to serve as a member of its staff – Ss.42(4) and 43(5)

976

- a constable at the Scottish Police Services Authority (SPSA), including a constable seconded to SPSA to serve as a member of its staff, and who is not a constable at, or seconded as a police member to, the Scottish Crime and Drugs Enforcement Agency (SCDEA) – Ss.42(4) and 43(6) and (7)

- a constable at, or seconded as a police member to, SCDEA – Ss.42(4) and 43(7).

Constables serving with the Civil Nuclear Constabulary are treated as employees of the Civil Nuclear Police Authority – S.42(3) EqA and S.55(2) Energy Act 2004. A constable at SOCA or SPSA is to be treated as employed by it in respect of any act done by it in relation to the constable – S.42(5) EqA, while a constable at SCDEA is to be treated as employed by the Director General of SCDEA in respect of any act done by the Director General in relation to the constable – S.42(6).

Armed forces

28.57

Section 83(3) EqA provides that Part 5 of the Act, which deals with employment, applies to service in the armed forces as it applies to employment by a private person. For these purposes, references in Part 5 to terms of employment, or to a contract of employment, are to be read as including references to terms of service, and references to associated employers are to be ignored.

However, given the need for the armed forces to maintain combat effectiveness, the EqA allows for exceptions in relation to disability, age and sex. Para 4(3) of Schedule 9 to the EqA states that 'this Part of this Act, so far as relating to age or disability, does not apply to service in the armed forces; and S.55, so far as relating to disability, does not apply to work experience in the armed forces'. Para 4(1), which is narrower in scope, provides that 'a person does not contravene S.39(1)(a) or (c) or (2)(b) by applying in relation to service in the armed forces a relevant requirement if the person shows that the application is a proportionate means of ensuring the combat effectiveness of the armed forces'. Para 4(2) goes on to provide that a 'relevant requirement' is 'a requirement to be a man, [or] a requirement not to be a transsexual person'. Both these exceptions are discussed further in Chapter 30, 'General exceptions', under 'National security – armed forces'.

Partners and members of limited liability partnerships

28.58

In so far as a partnership (referred to in the EqA as a 'firm') or a limited liability partnership (LLP) operates as an employer, it is liable under Ss.39 and 40 EqA in the normal way – see 'Job applicants' and 'Employees' above. However, partners (or prospective partners) in firms and members (or prospective members) of LLPs are not employees of the partnership or LLP and are therefore not covered by these provisions. Instead, protection from discrimination in the field of employment is provided by Ss.44 and 45, which provide broadly similar

977

rights to partners and members against the firm or LLP to those of an employee or job applicant against an employer.

28.59 **Definition of 'partnership', 'firm' and 'LLP'.** For the purposes of the provisions outlined in this section, 'partnership' and 'firm' have the same meaning as in the Partnership Act 1890 and a 'proposed firm' means 'persons proposing to form themselves into a partnership' – S.46(2) and (3) EqA. In the case of a limited partnership, only those partners who are involved in the operation of the firm ('general partners', as defined in S.3 of the Limited Partnerships Act 1907) are covered by the provisions on liability discussed below – S.44(8). An LLP has the same meaning as in the Limited Liability Partnerships Act 2000 and a proposed LLP means 'persons proposing to incorporate an LLP with themselves as members' – S.46(4) and (5).

28.60 **Liability.** Section 44 EqA deals with partnerships, while S.45 deals with LLPs. However, the relevant provisions are almost identical and both sections are intended to replicate the effect of the previous discrimination legislation. Accordingly, a firm or proposed firm, or an LLP or proposed LLP, must not discriminate against or victimise a person:

* in the arrangements it makes for deciding to whom to offer a position as a partner or member

* as to the terms on which it offers the person a position as a partner or member

* by not offering the person a position as a partner or member – Ss.44(1) and (5) and 45(1) and (5).

In relation to existing partners or members, a firm or an LLP (A) must not discriminate against or victimise a partner or member (B):

* as to the terms on which B is a partner or member

* in the way A affords B access, or by not affording B access, to opportunities for promotion, transfer or training or for receiving any other benefit, facility or service

* by expelling B

* by subjecting B to any other detriment – Ss.44(2) and (6) and 45(2) and (6) EqA.

28.61 The reference above to 'expelling' a partner of a firm or a member of an LLP includes a reference to the termination of the person's position as such by the expiry of any period (including a period expiring by reference to an event or circumstance); by the act of the person (including giving notice) in circumstances such that the person is entitled, because of the conduct of other partners or members, to terminate the position without notice (i.e. constructive termination);

and, in the case of a partner, as a result of the dissolution of the firm – S.46(6) EqA. Where the position is terminated by expiry of a period or by dissolution of the firm, however, there will be no expulsion if, immediately after the termination, the position is renewed on the same terms – S.46(7).

A firm or LLP must not harass a partner or member, or a person who has applied for the position; while a proposed firm or LLP must not harass a person who has applied for the position of partner or member – Ss.44(3) and (4) and 45(3) and (4) EqA.

Finally, a duty to make reasonable adjustments applies to a firm or LLP, or a **28.62** proposed firm or LLP – Ss.44(7) and 45(7) EqA. However, unlike the duty to make reasonable adjustments for employees, a disabled partner or member may have to make a contribution towards the cost of making reasonable adjustments. This is because the cost of making adjustments must be borne by the firm or LLP, and paras 7 and 8 of Schedule 8 to the EqA provide that where a disabled person is or becomes a partner or member, he or she may be required to make a reasonable contribution to the expense. According to the EHRC Employment Code: 'In assessing the reasonableness of any such contribution (or level of such contribution), particular regard should be had to the proportion in which the disabled partner or member is entitled to share in the firm's or LLP's profits, the cost of the reasonable contribution and the size and administrative resources of the firm or LLP' – para 11.23. The Code gives the example of an architect who uses a wheelchair joining a firm as partner, and receiving 20 per cent of the profits. The Code suggests it is likely to be reasonable to require the architect to pay 20 per cent of the cost of installing a lift.

Trainee and qualified barristers/advocates **28.63**
The EqA contains specific provisions in S.47 governing the liability of barristers and their clerks for discrimination against pupil barristers and tenants. Although pupils and tenants are not employees, the relevant provisions are similar to those that apply in the employment context. References below to a 'tenant' include references to a barrister who is permitted to work in chambers (including as a squatter or door tenant) – S.47(9).

The Explanatory Notes state that S.47 EqA 'replaces provisions in previous legislation providing similar protection for barristers, pupils, tenants and prospective pupils or tenants in barristers' chambers. However, it no longer protects clients and clerks from discrimination by barristers because they can respectively seek redress under the "services" provisions or under other work provisions (S.39 and S.41) of the Act' – para 164.

Section 47 EqA provides that a barrister (A) must not discriminate against or **28.64** victimise a person (B):

- in the arrangements A makes for deciding to whom to offer a pupillage or tenancy

- as to the terms on which A offers B a pupillage or tenancy

- by not offering B a pupillage or tenancy – S.47(1) and (4).

With regard to existing pupils and tenants, a barrister (A) must not discriminate against or victimise a person (B) who is a pupil or tenant:

- as to the terms on which B is a pupil or tenant

- in the way A affords B access, or by not affording B access, to opportunities for training or gaining experience or for receiving any other benefit, facility or service

- by terminating the pupillage

- by subjecting B to pressure to leave chambers

- by subjecting B to any other detriment – S.47(2) and (5).

28.65 A barrister must not harass a pupil or tenant, or a person who has applied for pupillage or tenancy – S.47(3). In addition, barristers are under a duty to make reasonable adjustments for disabled pupils and tenants by virtue of S.47(7). The Employment Code gives the following example: 'Barristers' clerks at a set of chambers routinely leave messages for barristers on scraps of paper. This practice is likely to disadvantage visually impaired members of chambers and may need to be altered for individual disabled tenants and pupils' – para 11.30.

It is also unlawful for a person instructing a barrister (for example, a client or instructing solicitor) to discriminate against, harass or victimise the barrister in relation to the giving of instructions – S.47(6).

28.66 The above provisions on liability (except S.47(6)) apply in relation to a barrister's clerk (or a person carrying out the functions of a barrister's clerk) as they apply in relation to a barrister – S.47(8).

Section 48 EqA contains almost identical provisions to those outlined above in relation to advocates in Scotland, taking into account the different terminology that applies to the Scottish legal profession: i.e. 'advocates' instead of barristers; 'a stable' instead of chambers; and a 'devil' instead of a pupil.

28.67 **Office holders**
People who hold, or seek appointment to, a personal or public office enjoy protection against discrimination, harassment and victimisation by virtue of Ss.49–52 EqA. S.49 applies to personal offices, while Ss.50–51 cover public offices. S.52 deals with interpretation and Schedule 6 to the Act sets out various exceptions.

The relevant provisions are, for the most part, designed to replicate the effect of provisions in the previous equality legislation. The main differences are that protection under the EqA now extends to those appointed on the recommendation or approval of law-making bodies such as the Scottish Parliament and the National Assembly for Wales, and to those appointed by a member of the executive on the recommendation or with the approval of a non-departmental public body.

Personal and public offices. A 'personal office' is defined in S.49 EqA as an **28.68** office or post:

- to which a person is appointed to discharge a function personally under the direction of another person – S.49(2)(a), and

- in respect of which an appointed person is entitled to remuneration – S.49(2)(b).

A person is regarded as discharging functions personally under the direction of another person 'if that other person is entitled to direct the person as to when and where to discharge the functions' – S.49(10). A person is not regarded as entitled to remuneration merely because he or she is entitled to expenses or compensation for lost income or benefits – S.49(11).

The definition of 'public office' is set out in S.50. It is an office or post, **28.69** appointment to which is made:

- by a member of the executive – S.50(2)(a)

- on the recommendation of, or subject to the approval of, a member of the executive – S.50(2)(b), or

- on the recommendation of, or subject to the approval of, the House of Commons, the House of Lords, the National Assembly for Wales or the Scottish Parliament – S.50(2)(c).

A 'member of the executive' is a Minister of the Crown; a government department; the Welsh Minister, the First Minister for Wales or the Counsel General to the Welsh Assembly Government; or any part of the Scottish Administration – S.212(7) EqA.

An office or post that is both a personal office and a public office is treated as **28.70** being a public office only – S.52(4) EqA.

According to the EHRC Employment Code, 'office holders include offices and posts such as directors, non-executive directors, company secretaries, positions on the board of non-departmental public bodies, some judicial positions and positions held by some ministers of religion' – para 11.32. This list is, however, non-exhaustive and as long as an office satisfies the requirements of S.49(2) or S.50(2), it will be covered by the Act.

981

28.71 **'Power to appoint'.** A person (A) who has the power to make an appointment to a personal office, or a public office falling within S.50(2)(a) or (b) (see 'Personal and public offices' above), must not discriminate against or victimise a person (B):

- in the arrangements A makes for deciding to whom to offer the appointment
- as to the terms on which A offers B the appointment
- by not offering B the appointment – Ss.49(3) and (5) and 50(3) and (5) EqA.

'Appointment' to an office or post does not include election to it, with the result that elected offices fall outside the scope of these provisions – S.52(5).

In addition, a person who has the power to make an appointment to a personal office or a public office falling within S.50(2)(a) or (b) must not harass a person seeking, or being considered for, the appointment – Ss.49(4) and 50(4).

28.72 Finally, a duty to make reasonable adjustments applies to a person who has the power to make an appointment to a personal office or a public office falling within S.50(2)(a) or (b) – Ss.49(9)(a) and 50(11)(b). The EHRC Employment Code gives the following example: 'A selection process is carried out to appoint a chair for a public health body. The best candidate for the appointment is a disabled person with a progressive condition who is not able to work full time because of her disability. The person who approves the appointment should consider whether it would be a reasonable adjustment to approve the appointment of the disabled person on a job-share or part-time basis' – para 11.47.

There is no provision prohibiting discrimination on the part of someone with the power to make an appointment to a public office falling within S.50(2)(c). Such a provision would be of limited, if any, application because the power to appoint is likely to rest with the legislative body rather than an individual. Note, however, that there are provisions prohibiting discrimination, victimisation, harassment and a failure to make reasonable adjustments by a 'relevant person' in relation to a public office falling within S.50(2)(c) – see below under 'Relevant persons'.

28.73 **Power to recommend or approve appointment to public office.** Whereas Ss.49 and 50 cover discrimination by a person with the power of appointment to an office, S.51 addresses discrimination by persons with the power to make a recommendation for or give approval to an appointment to a public office within S.50(2)(a) or (b). A person (A) who has such a power must not discriminate against or victimise a person (B):

- in the arrangements A makes for deciding who to recommend for appointment to the office or to whose appointment to give approval
- by not recommending B for appointment to the office

982

- by making a negative recommendation of B for appointment to the office

- by not giving approval to B's appointment to the office – S.51(1) and (3).

In addition, a person who has the power to recommend or approve an **28.74** appointment to a public office falling in either S.50(2)(a) or (b) must not harass a person seeking or being considered for recommendation or approval – S.51(2). The person with power to recommend or approve an appointment is also under a duty to make reasonable adjustments for disabled people who seek or are being considered for appointment – S.51(4).

In relation to a public office that falls within S.50(2)(a) (i.e. an office or post, appointment to which is made by a member of the executive), a reference in S.51 to a person who has the power to make a recommendation for or give approval to an appointment is a reference to a 'relevant body' that has that power – S.51(5). A 'relevant body' for these purposes is a body established by or in pursuance of an enactment or by a member of the executive (for example, a non-departmental public body).

Relevant persons. The EqA provisions on liability also apply to anyone who is **28.75** a 'relevant person' in relation to a personal or public office. This reflects the fact that an office holder can be appointed by one person and then an entirely different person can be responsible for other matters, such as providing facilities to the office holder or giving instructions about the performance of the office.

A 'relevant person' (A) in relation to a personal or public office (except a public office within S.50(2)(c) – see under 'Personal and public offices' above) must not discriminate against or victimise a person (B) appointed to the office:

- as to the terms of B's appointment

- in the way A affords B access, or by not affording B access, to opportunities for promotion, transfer or training or for receiving any other benefit, facility or service

- by terminating B's appointment

- by subjecting B to any other detriment – Ss.49(6) and (8) and 50(6) and (9) EqA.

Terminating an appointment includes termination by the expiry of a period **28.76** (including a period expiring by reference to an event or circumstance); and termination by the act of the person appointed (including giving notice) in circumstances such that the person is entitled, because of the relevant person's conduct, to terminate the appointment without notice (i.e. constructive termination) – S.52(7). However, it does not include termination by the expiry of a period if, immediately after the termination, the appointment is renewed on the same terms – S.52(8).

A 'relevant person' (A) in relation to a public office appointment which is made on the recommendation of, or subject to the approval of, the House of Commons, the House of Lords, the National Assembly for Wales or the Scottish Parliament (i.e. a public office falling within S.50(2)(c)) must not discriminate against or victimise a person (B) appointed to the office:

- as to the terms of B's appointment

- in the way A affords B access, or by not affording B access, to opportunities for promotion, transfer or training or for receiving any other benefit, facility or service

- by subjecting B to any other detriment (other than by terminating the appointment) – S.50(7) and (10) EqA.

28.77 In addition, a relevant person in relation to a personal or public office must not harass a person appointed to that office – Ss.49(7) and 50(8). The duty to make reasonable adjustments in the context of disability discrimination also applies – Ss.49(9)(b) and 50(11)(a).

28.78 *Who is a 'relevant person'?* S.52(6) sets out a table listing matters in the first column, and relevant persons in the second. For each of the matters specified in the table, the relevant person is as follows:

- a term of appointment: the person who has the power to set the term

- access to an opportunity: the person who has the power to afford access to the opportunity (or, if there is no such person, the person who has the power to make the appointment)

- terminating an appointment: the person who has the power to terminate the appointment

- subjecting an appointee to any other detriment: the person who has the power in relation to the matter to which the conduct in question relates (or, if there is no such person, the person who has the power to make the appointment)

- harassing an appointee: the person who has the power in relation to the matter to which the conduct in question relates.

A 'relevant person' does not include the House of Commons, the House of Lords, the National Assembly for Wales or the Scottish Parliament – S.52(6).

28.79 **Excluded offices.** Schedule 6 to the EqA sets out various circumstances in which the provisions concerning office holders in Ss.49–52 do not apply. Para 1 of Schedule 6 provides that an office or post is not a personal or public office in so far as it is covered (or would be covered, in the absence of another exception in the EqA) by one of the other forms of protection in Part 5 of the Act: employment (S.39); contract work (S.41); partnerships (S.44); LLPs (S.45);

barristers (S.47); advocates (S.48); or employment services (S.55, so far as it relates to work experience). The effect of para 1 is that Ss.49–52 will apply only in so far as other work provisions do not – so, for example, where an office holder is also an employee, he or she will be protected by the employment provisions in S.39 and cannot therefore bring a claim under Ss.49–52 against her employer. She could, however, rely on Ss.49–52 as against the person who appointed her and/or any relevant person.

Most political offices or posts are also excluded from protection. Those excluded are listed in para 2(2) of Schedule 6 and include members of the House of Commons and House of Lords, ministers, members of the Scottish Parliament and the National Assembly for Wales, and local councillors. Furthermore, a life peerage or any other dignity or honour conferred by the Crown is not a personal or public office – para 3, Sch 6. It should be noted, however, that the conferral of honours and dignities is treated as a public function for the purposes of the EqA, and that public bodies' activities in relation to honours and dignities are subject to the public sector equality duty under S.149 EqA (see Chapter 38, 'General public sector equality duty', and Chapter 39, 'Specific public sector equality duties').

Employer's liability for acts of employees

28.80

Section 109(1) EqA provides that an employer is liable for acts of discrimination, harassment and victimisation carried out by its employees in the course of employment. The section replaces similar provisions in the previous equality legislation, with the result that the substantial body of case law generated by the antecedent provisions will continue to be relevant.

Under S.109(1) 'anything done by a person (A) in the course of A's employment must be treated as also done by the employer'. It matters not whether that thing is done with the employer's knowledge or approval – S.109(3). However, the employer has a defence under S.109(4) where it can show that it took all reasonable steps to prevent A from doing that thing, or from doing anything of that description.

Thus, for an employer to be liable for the discriminatory conduct of one of its **28.81** employees, three things must be established:

- that there is, or was at the relevant time, an employment relationship between the employer and the alleged discriminator (see 'Who is protected? – definition of employment' above)

- that the conduct occurred 'in the course' of employment, and

- that the employer did not take all reasonable steps to prevent the conduct in question.

In many cases, showing that there is an employment relationship between the employer and the alleged discriminator is a straightforward exercise. However, one particular area of difficulty surrounds agency workers. As discussed under 'Who is protected? – employees', there is limited scope under the EqA for agency workers to be treated as employees of the end user. Where employment is established, the end-user employer will be liable for any discriminatory acts by the agency worker under S.109(1) in the normal way. Where, however, the employment test is not satisfied (which will generally be the case), S.109(1) will not apply. In these circumstances, there may be two alternative routes by which the end-user of an agency worker could be liable for his or her actions. First, the end-user could be liable under S.40 for failing to prevent harassment by a third party (see 'Employer's liability for harassment by third parties' below). Secondly, under S.109(2) a principal is liable for the acts of its agents while acting under the principal's authority (see 'Liability of principal for agents' below).

28.82 **'In the course of employment'**

The first question to be addressed in determining whether an employer is vicariously liable for the discriminatory acts of an employee is whether the employee was acting 'in the course of' his or her employment. According to the EHRC Employment Code, 'the phrase "in the course of employment" has a wide meaning: it includes acts in the workplace and may also extend to circumstances outside such as work-related social functions or business trips abroad. For example, an employer could be liable for an act of discrimination which took place during a social event organised by the employer, such as an after-work drinks party.' The wording of S.109 is not new: the equivalent provisions in the predecessor discrimination enactments all used the term 'in the course of employment', with the result that there is a substantial body of case law to fall back on.

Employment law originally adopted the approach of the common law in tort cases, whereby an employer is only liable for acts done by employees when those acts are connected with acts which the employer has authorised and which could rightly be regarded as modes, albeit improper modes, of doing the authorised acts – see, for example, Irving and anor v Post Office 1987 IRLR 289, CA. However, in Jones v Tower Boot Co Ltd 1997 ICR 254, CA, the Court of Appeal expressly rejected the proposition that the common law principles of vicarious liability are to be imported into anti-discrimination legislation. The case concerned J, a 16-year-old of mixed race, who resigned after a month in his job as a result of the physical and verbal assaults he had suffered from two of his colleagues. His arm had been burnt with a hot screwdriver, metal bolts had been thrown at his head, his legs had been whipped and he had been called names such as 'chimp', 'monkey' and 'baboon'. Relying on the Court of Appeal's decision in Irving, the EAT overturned a tribunal's decision that the employees had been acting in the course of their employment. It was impossible, the EAT said, 'by any stretch of the imagination', to regard what the employees had done as an improper mode of performing the tasks they were employed to do.

The Court of Appeal restored the tribunal's decision. It explained that the **28.83** Irving case was not, in fact, authority for the proposition that the common law principles should apply in statutory discrimination cases. Although its decision certainly proceeded on that basis, the Court in Irving never addressed its mind to the question. In the instant case, the Court of Appeal accepted that there is a broad conceptual similarity between the common law principles of vicarious liability and an employer's secondary liability under S.32(1) RRA (the equivalent of S.109(1) EqA), but insisted that the two contexts are not so similar as to require that the phrase 'course of employment' in the statute be read as subject to the gloss imposed upon it at common law. To do so would impose a far more restricted meaning than the natural everyday meaning of the words allowed and would result in the anomaly that the more heinous the act of discrimination, the less likely it would be that the employer would be found liable. That would cut across the underlying policy of the discrimination legislation, which is to deter harassment by making the employer liable for the unlawful acts of employees, while providing a defence for the conscientious employer that has done its best to prevent such harassment.

The Court of Appeal concluded that the words 'in the course of... employment' are to be construed in the sense in which every layperson would understand them. The question of whether an employee's discriminatory acts were done in the course of his or her employment, thereby rendering the employer liable for them, should be treated as a question of fact, which, the Court stated, an employment tribunal is well suited to resolve.

The decision in Waters v Commissioner of Police of the Metropolis 1997 ICR **28.84** 1073, CA, illustrates that, even adopting the broad approach set out in Jones v Tower Boot Co Ltd (above), there are limits to an employer's liability for harassment. In that case a police constable claimed that she had been victimised by her employer after complaining of a sexual assault by a male colleague. In order to succeed in her claim, she had to establish that her employer was liable under the SDA for the alleged assault. A tribunal found that the male officer was not acting 'in the course of his employment' when the alleged assault took place. It reached this decision by applying the common law test of vicarious liability, rejected subsequently in the Tower Boot case. When Waters reached the Court of Appeal, however, it was held that the tribunal would have arrived at the same conclusion on the issue of vicarious liability even if it had adopted the correct approach. The parties were off duty at the time of the alleged assault and the male officer was a visitor to the woman's room in the police section house. The parties were in the same position as would have applied if they had

987

been social acquaintances with no working connection. The Court held that, in those circumstances, it was inconceivable that any tribunal applying the correct test could have found that the alleged assault was committed in the course of the male officer's employment.

Similarly, in HM Prison Service and ors v Davis EAT 1294/98 D, a prison officer at Cardiff Prison, alleged that she had received an unexpected visit at home one evening from a colleague, R, who then made wholly unwanted sexual advances towards her. D brought a claim of sex discrimination against the employer and the tribunal found the employer vicariously liable because the sexual harassment was 'in relation to employment'. One of the reasons the tribunal gave for this decision was that the employer's disciplinary code stated that the conduct of employees 'on and off duty' must not bring discredit on the Prison Service. The code also provided for disciplinary action to be taken when an alleged criminal offence was committed 'away from the workplace'. Since the employees were subject to a contract of employment that governed their behaviour 24 hours a day, it followed that R's off-duty conduct towards the applicant occurred in the course of employment. The EAT found this argument unacceptable. In its view, the fact that an employer can legitimately complain about an employee's activities outside employment does not bring that activity within the course of employment. The EAT held that the incident of harassment had only the most slender of connections with work and had not occurred 'in the course of employment'. In reaching this decision, the EAT expressed the view that the instant case was indistinguishable from that of Waters v Commissioner of Police of the Metropolis (above). Indeed, the only real difference was that in the Waters case the incident occurred in accommodation owned by the employer – something that led the EAT to find even less reason in the instant case for holding that the harassment took place in the course of employment.

28.85　The dividing line between 'employment' and off-duty conduct can become even more blurred where social events involving colleagues are involved. In Chief Constable of Lincolnshire Police v Stubbs and ors 1999 ICR 547, EAT, S and W were police officers with the Lincolnshire Police who had both been seconded to the Regional Crime Squad (RCS). While they were working in the RCS, two incidents occurred which led S to complain that she was being sexually harassed by W. One of these happened when S went for a drink at a pub after work with several fellow officers. The second incident, which also took place in a pub, occurred at another officer's leaving party. The tribunal held that W's acts of sex discrimination had been committed in the course of his employment. The Chief Constable appealed, arguing that as the incidents had taken place in pubs and both were social occasions at which everyone was off duty, they had not occurred in the course of W's employment. The EAT rejected this argument, stating that the tribunal had to consider whether what had taken place between S and W occurred in circumstances that were 'an extension of their employment'. This was a question of the exercise of good judgement by the tribunal. The EAT thought that the borderline between those cases for which an employer is liable and those for which it has no liability may be difficult to pinpoint. While the tribunal would need to consider whether or not the person was on duty and whether or not the conduct occurred on the employer's premises, these were but two of the factors which needed to be looked at. In the instant case, although the two incidents did not occur at the police station, they were 'social gatherings involving officers from work either immediately after work or for an organised leaving party'. In the EAT's view, these incidents came within the definition of 'course of employment' as this phrase was explained by the Court of Appeal in Jones v Tower Boot Co Ltd (above). It would have been different if the discriminatory acts had occurred during a chance meeting between W and S at a supermarket.

Two further case examples that illustrate the difficulty of drawing the line **28.86** in practice:

- **Livesey v Parker Merchanting Ltd** EAT 0755/03: the EAT held that a tribunal had erred in deciding that, while acts of sexual harassment perpetrated by a male employee on a female colleague that took place in a hotel at a firm's Christmas party were carried out in the course of employment, similar acts that occurred during a car ride home afterwards did not. In the EAT's view, bearing in mind the comments made in Chief Constable of Lincolnshire Police v Stubbs and ors (above), there was no justification for the tribunal drawing a distinction between the two incidents, which it regarded as constituting part of a course of conduct. However, the EAT went on to uphold the tribunal's conclusion that the employer had made out the defence under S.41(3) SDA (now contained in S.109(4) – see '"Reasonable steps" defence' below)

- **Sidhu v Aerospace Composite Technology Ltd** 2001 ICR 167, CA: at a family day out organised by ACT Ltd, a member of staff, S, and his family were subjected to racial abuse by a colleague, KS. The incident escalated and both S and KS were subsequently dismissed for gross misconduct. In considering S's claim of race discrimination, the tribunal noted that the day out had neither been at the workplace nor during working hours, and that most participants had been friends and family and not employees. It therefore concluded that the events in question took place outside S and KS's employment and, consequently, ACT Ltd was not liable for KS's acts. The Court of Appeal confirmed the tribunal's decision and rejected S's argument that the tribunal should have concluded that ACT Ltd's supervision of the event brought it within the course of employment. It was far from clear that there had been any meaningful supervision. It was possible that another tribunal could have reached a different conclusion, but on the facts the tribunal had been entitled to conclude that the day out had not been in the course of employment.

28.87 Note that while the Court of Appeal's decision in Jones v Tower Boot Co Ltd (above) was a welcome departure from the common law principles of vicarious liability, it did create an anomaly in that it became easier to establish vicarious liability under the discrimination legislation than under the common law, where the more serious the conduct, the less likely the employer was to be found liable. However, the House of Lords reassessed the common law test in Lister and ors v Hesley Hall Ltd 2001 ICR 665, HL, and decided to adopt a broader approach, holding that the correct test is whether the employee's wrongful acts were so closely connected with his or her employment that it would be fair and just to hold the employer vicariously liable. More recently, in the conjoined appeals of Weddall v Barchester Healthcare Ltd; Wallbank v Wallbank Fox Designs Ltd 2012 IRLR 307, CA, the Court of Appeal had to determine whether an employee's violent reaction to a lawful workplace instruction was sufficiently closely connected to his or her employment to render the employer vicariously liable for assault. The first case – Weddall – concerned an employee who, on being telephoned by a colleague to enquire whether he could cover a shift, got on his bicycle in a drunken state, rode to his workplace, and assaulted the colleague. The Court of Appeal upheld the county court judge's decision that the employer was not vicariously liable for the assault – the employee's conduct was separate and distinct from his employment, and he was acting for his own personal reasons. In the second case – Wallbank – the employee in question had reacted violently to an instruction from his manager, resulting in the manager suffering a fractured vertebrae. The Court considered that the violence was closely related to the employment in both time and space; it was a spontaneous and almost instantaneous, if irrational, response to an instruction. For that reason, it overturned the county court and held the employer vicariously liable. The Court was, however, at pains to stress that there is no general rule that every act of violence by a junior to a more senior employee, in response to an instruction at the workplace, would be an act for which the employer is vicariously liable.

The less restrictive approach to vicarious liability at common law outlined above has brought the common law test closer to the statutory test adopted in Jones v Tower Boot Co Ltd (above), although some important differences still remain, not least the fact that employers have a defence to secondary liability under the statutory test if they can show that they took reasonable steps to prevent the discrimination (see '"Reasonable steps" defence' below).

28.88 Two further points should be made here. First, it should be noted that an employer is potentially liable for the actions of *all* employees, not just managers. And, as noted under 'Who is protected?' above, the definition of 'employment' in S.83(2) EqA is very wide and can include many workers otherwise regarded as self-employed, as well as contract workers. Thus an employer can be liable for acts of discrimination committed by a wide range of individuals, not simply those working under a contract of employment.

990

'Reasonable steps' defence   28.89
Section 109(4) EqA provides employers with a defence to a claim under S.109. It states that: 'In proceedings against A's employer (B) in respect of anything alleged to have been done by A in the course of A's employment it is a defence for B to show that B took all reasonable steps to prevent A... (a) from doing that thing, or (b) from doing anything of that description.' Thus, it is a defence for the employer to show that it took all reasonable steps to prevent employees from *either* committing a particular discriminatory act *or* committing such acts in general. The EHRC Employment Code provides the following example:

'An employer ensures that all their workers are aware of their policy on harassment, and that harassment of workers related to any of the protected characteristics is unacceptable and will lead to disciplinary action. They also ensure that managers receive training in applying this policy. Following implementation of the policy, an employee makes anti-Semitic comments to a Jewish colleague, who is humiliated and offended by the comments. The employer then takes disciplinary action against the employee. In these circumstances the employer may avoid liability because their actions are likely to show that they took all reasonable steps to prevent the unlawful act' – para 10.50.

The old legislation referred to 'such steps as were reasonably practicable' (see, for example, S.58(5) DDA) but the change in wording is not thought to be significant. That said, it is just possible that employment tribunals may interpret the addition of the word 'all' in S.109(3) EqA as setting down a stricter test. If, for example, a tribunal were to conceive of a step that it thought would have been reasonable for the employer to take but which was not taken, the omission of that step would mean that not all reasonable steps were taken, with the consequence that the defence might fail.

The onus rests firmly on the employer to establish the defence. An employer   28.90
can do so by showing either that it attempted to prevent the particular act of discrimination or that it attempted to prevent that kind of act in general. The defence is limited to steps taken before the discriminatory act occurred; this much is apparent from the use of the word 'took' in the past tense, which 'requires the employer to prove what he had done in the past' – Mahood v Irish Centre Housing Ltd EAT 0228/10. It is not sufficient for an employer to show that the discrimination was promptly remedied – see, for example, Fox v Ocean City Recruitment Ltd EAT 0035/11.

What amounts to 'all reasonable steps' will depend on the circumstances but examples might include providing supervision or training and/or implementing an equal opportunities policy. The EHRC Employment Code suggests the following at para 10.52:

• implementing an equality policy

991

- ensuring workers are aware of the policy
- providing equal opportunities training
- reviewing the policy as appropriate, and
- dealing effectively with employee complaints.

28.91 The EAT has issued guidance as to the approach tribunals should adopt when determining whether an employer has satisfied the 'reasonable steps' defence. In Canniffe v East Riding of Yorkshire Council 2000 IRLR 555, EAT, it held that the proper test of whether the employer has established the defence is to identify:

- first, whether there were any preventive steps taken by the employer, and
- secondly, whether there were any further preventive steps that the employer could have taken that were reasonably practicable.

In the Canniffe case, C alleged that she had been subjected to a number of serious sexual assaults and threats of assault by K, a colleague. The tribunal dismissed the complaint on the ground that the employer had satisfied the requirements of the defence in S.41(3) SDA (the equivalent of S.109(4) EqA). In reaching this decision it focused on whether anything the employer did or could have done would have made any difference given the types of act about which C complained. C appealed to the EAT on the ground that the tribunal had asked itself the wrong question in relation to S.41(3). She submitted that the 'no difference' test that the tribunal had applied was a complete rewording of the statute. She further argued that the result of such a test was that the worse and more unusual the conduct, the easier it would be for an employer to take advantage of the defence. The EAT accepted her submissions. It held that the correct approach was, first, to identify whether the employer took any steps at all to prevent the employee from doing the act or acts complained of in the course of his or her employment and, secondly, having identified what steps, if any, the employer took, to consider whether there were any further steps that could have been taken that were reasonably practicable. The question as to whether such steps would in fact have been successful in preventing the act of discrimination in question was not determinative.

28.92 The EAT pointed out that the tribunal had not asked itself the 'missing question'; namely, whether there were any other steps that could reasonably have been taken that the respondent did not take. The EAT said that where employers or managers are not aware of any risk of inappropriate sexual behaviour or harassment by an employee, particularly towards another employee, it may be sufficient for the tribunal simply to ask whether there was a policy in place and whether it was disseminated. This is particularly relevant where there has been a one-off incident of serious sexual harassment. The EAT contrasted that situation with one where the management or other employees knew or suspected

992

that there was a risk that a particular employee might carry out inappropriate acts towards a certain employee or other employees. In the instant case, C had confided in her supervisor, and two other employees had also known about the way that K behaved, although it was not clear whether they knew that K was actually assaulting C. The EAT thought that, on the basis of that evidence, it might have been open to a tribunal to conclude that, because those employees had not taken any steps to prevent what was happening, the employer could not satisfy the defence in S.41(3). It postulated that perhaps C's supervisor could have taken steps to warn or to watch K, or that he could have reported K on a no-names basis. Conversely, it noted that a tribunal might conclude that there was nothing more that was reasonably practicable that the employer could have done in the circumstances. However, the EAT declined to make a judgment on the facts and it set aside the decision, directing that there should be a rehearing of the case by a different tribunal.

The Canniffe case indicates that if employees are aware that a fellow employee **28.93** has committed or has a propensity to commit an act of discrimination and they fail to take steps to inform the employer or otherwise attempt to prevent the discrimination, the employer may be vicariously liable for that failure to act. To avoid this, employers would have to take reasonable steps to encourage employees to report discrimination. One way to do this would be to make it clear in any harassment or equal opportunities policy that employees with knowledge or suspicion of possible discrimination should inform the employer – on an anonymous basis if necessary.

The employer succeeded in showing that all reasonable preventive steps had been taken in Al-Azzawi v Haringey Council (Haringey Design Partnership Directorate of Technical and Environmental Services) EAT 158/00. A, an architect of Iraqi Arabic ethnic origin, was a senior architect in the Design Partnership Department of the Council until his dismissal on 31 March 1999. On 8 September 1997, A was present at a discussion about the venue for an upcoming union quiz evening. During this discussion, a co-worker referred to 'bloody Arabs' who he claimed had disrupted the event the previous year. A complained about this statement and the co-worker was suspended from duty pending an investigation. After finding that the co-worker was guilty of misconduct, but not of gross misconduct, the Council gave him a written warning that remained live for two months and required him to write an apology to A. A brought a claim alleging, among other things, that the Council was vicariously liable for the remark made by his co-worker. A tribunal upheld this part of A's claim.

The EAT held that the tribunal's findings did not support this conclusion. In **28.94** considering whether the Council had taken such steps as were reasonably practicable to prevent the discriminatory comment, the tribunal misled itself by looking only at events after the incident and focusing on the disciplinary process and what it perceived to be a lenient penalty. However, the tribunal had found that the Council had put in place policies on racial awareness; that employees, including the wrongdoer in question, had received training on such policies; and that employees who violated the policies were disciplined. Moreover, the tribunal expressly rejected the suggestion that the Council only paid lip service to its policies. The EAT therefore held that the evidence accepted by the tribunal could only lead to the conclusion that the Council had taken all such steps as were reasonable to prevent race discrimination.

In reaching its conclusion, the EAT noted that the aim of the statutory provision is to prevent discrimination from occurring. It follows that when considering whether an employer has made out the defence, the employment tribunal must look at events that took place before the discriminatory incident(s). Subsequent events are relevant to the question of whether the statutory defence has been made out only in so far as they shed light on what occurred before the act complained of (for example, by demonstrating that an equal opportunities policy which exists on paper is not in fact operated in practice).

28.95 The EAT in Canniffe v East Riding of Yorkshire Council (above) stressed that, in considering whether there were any further steps an employer could have taken that were reasonably practicable, the question of whether those steps would in fact have successfully prevented the act of discrimination was not determinative. An employer who has not taken reasonable steps will not be exculpated simply because, if those steps had been taken, they would not have prevented the discriminatory conduct from occurring. However, this does not mean that a tribunal cannot take any account of the difference, if any, that taking those steps is likely to have had when considering whether the defence is made out. In Croft v Royal Mail Group plc (formerly Consignia plc) 2003 ICR 1425, CA, the employer refused to let an employee who was undergoing male-to-female gender reassignment use the female lavatories at work because of opposition by female employees. The employee brought claims under S.2A SDA alleging discrimination on the ground of gender reassignment by both the employer and by some of her colleagues. The Court of Appeal held, among other things, that the tribunal had been entitled to hold that, although the complainant had suffered acts of discrimination by fellow employees, the employer was not liable for those acts because it had taken such steps as were reasonably practicable to prevent the discrimination. It was not possible to accept the complainant's argument that the tribunal had concentrated on the potential effect of measures that the employer could have taken, rather than considering whether those measures were reasonably practicable. The Court of Appeal stated that in considering whether an action is reasonably practicable within the meaning of S.41(3) SDA (now S.109(4) EqA), it is permissible to take into account the extent of the difference, if any, which the action is likely to make. Steps which require time, trouble and expense may not be reasonable steps if, on assessment, they are likely to achieve nothing.

Criminal offences

28.96

Section 109(1) does not make an employer liable for any criminal offences under the Act that are committed by employees (other than offences under Part 12 relating to disabled persons and transport, which are outside the scope of this Handbook) – S.109(5).

Protection from Harassment Act 1997

28.97

It is worth noting that in Majrowski v Guy's and St Thomas's NHS Trust 2006 ICR 1199, HL, the House of Lords ruled that an employer can be vicariously liable under the Protection from Harassment Act 1997 for acts of harassment committed by employees in the course of their employment. Significantly, unlike liability for harassment under the EqA, the 1997 Act – which imposes both civil and criminal liability and was principally aimed at tackling the practice of stalking – provides no defence for the employer. It follows that claimants alleging that they have suffered workplace harassment who are unable to succeed under the EqA because the employer has a defence under S.109(4) may have an alternative cause of action for damages in the civil courts under the 1997 Act. Note, however, that the Act only applies where there has been a course of conduct amounting to harassment and where the acts complained of took place 'in the course of employment'.

Employer's liability for harassment by third parties

28.98

Under S.40(2) EqA employers are liable for persistent harassment of their employees (and job applicants) by third parties. Previously this liability only applied to sexual and sex-related harassment under the SDA. However, it has now been extended by the EqA to cover all the protected characteristics to which the harassment provisions apply (i.e. age, disability, gender reassignment, race, religion or belief, sex and sexual orientation) – see further Chapter 18, 'Harassment', under 'Related to a relevant protected characteristic'.

An employer (A) will be treated as harassing an employee or job applicant (B) for the purposes of S.40(2) EqA where:

- a third party harasses B in the course of B's employment – S.40(2)(a), and

- A failed to take such steps as would have been reasonably practicable to prevent the third party from doing so – S.40(2)(b).

A 'third party' is a person other than A or an employee of A's – S.40(4). It could be a customer, client, supplier or other member of the public who comes into contact with A's employees.

28.99

The provisions on third-party harassment do not apply 'unless A knows that B has been harassed in the course of B's employment on at least two other

995

occasions by a third party' – S.40(3). Thus, S.40 retains the controversial 'three strikes' provision that applied under the SDA: liability will arise only when harassment has occurred on at least two previous occasions and the employer is aware that it has taken place and has failed to take reasonable steps to prevent it happening again. However, 'it does not matter whether the third party is the same or a different person on each occasion' – S.40(3) (a provision that did not appear in the SDA). It does appear to matter, though, that the harassed employee (B) is the same person each time. So where, for example, several different employees were subjected to harassment by a single customer, the employer will not be liable until a single employee has been harassed for a third time. (Stop press: the Government is consulting on repealing S.40 – see Introduction to this Handbook.)

28.100 The EHRC Employment Code provides the following two examples:

'A Ghanaian shop assistant is upset because a customer has come into the shop on Monday and Tuesday and on each occasion has made racist comments to him. On each occasion the shop assistant complained to his manager about the remarks. If his manager does nothing to stop it happening again, the employer would be liable for any further racial harassment perpetrated against that shop assistant by any customer' – para 10.20.

'An employer is aware that a female employee working in her bar has been sexually harassed on two separate occasions by different customers. The employer fails to take any action and the employee experiences further harassment by yet another customer. The employer is likely to be liable for the further act of harassment' – para 10.21.

28.101 **'Reasonable steps' defence**
As with S.109 (see 'Employer's liability for acts of employees' above), employers have a defence under S.40(2)(b) where they can show that they have taken such steps as would have been reasonably practicable to prevent the third party from committing harassment. The EHRC Employment Code suggests the following steps that an employer might take:

- notifying third parties that harassment of employees is unlawful and will not be tolerated; for example, by displaying a public notice

- inclusion of a term in all contracts with third parties notifying them of the employer's policy on harassment and requiring them to adhere to it

- encouraging employees to report any acts of harassment by third parties to enable the employer to support the employee and take appropriate action

- taking action on every complaint of harassment by a third party – para 10.24.

Harassment claims under S.40(1)

28.102

It is arguable that, in certain circumstances, an employee harassed at work by a third party may be able to establish that his or her employer is liable for that harassment, without relying on S.40(2) EqA. This is because S.26 EqA defines harassment as unwanted conduct *related to* a protected characteristic, which has the purpose or effect of violating the complainant's dignity or creating an intimidating, hostile, degrading, humiliating or offensive environment for them. In contrast with the statutory language of the predecessor discrimination enactments (other than the SDA), there is no requirement that the conduct be 'on grounds of' the protected characteristic in question. Thus, an employee could potentially argue that, by failing to take adequate steps to prevent harassment by a third party, the employer has itself subjected the employee to harassment (because that failure is related to a protected characteristic and has the purpose or effect required by S.26), and is therefore in breach of S.40(1) EqA, which prohibits an employer subjecting job applicants or employees to harassment.

The possibility of an employer being liable under S.40(1) for failing to prevent harassment by a third party does, however, have to be assessed in light of the EAT's decision in Conteh v Parking Partners Ltd 2011 ICR 341, EAT. In that case the EAT upheld an employment tribunal's decision that an employer was not liable for harassment under the RRA when a client subjected its employee to racial abuse. The EAT considered that the employer's inaction could not be said to have 'created' the environment proscribed by the legislation. It accepted that more than one party could be responsible for such an environment: it could initially have been created by the acts of a third party and thereafter made worse by the employer's inaction, effectively leaving him or her without means to remedy it. However, this would be rare and it was certainly not the case here.

If liability for harassment by third parties can be established under S.40(1), it **28.103** will most likely be relied upon by claimants who cannot satisfy all the conditions of S.40(2) and (3). Take, for example, the situation where a single customer sexually harasses a number of employees, but does not harass any particular employee more than once. S.40(2) would not be engaged in these circumstances, but the employer could be potentially liable under S.40(1) for not taking steps to prevent the harassment.

Liability of principals for agents

28.104

Section 109(2) EqA makes a principal liable for discriminatory acts committed by an agent while acting under the principal's authority. It provides that: 'Anything done by an agent for a principal, with the authority of the principal, must be treated as also done by the principal.' It does not matter whether that thing is done with the principal's knowledge or approval – S.109(3). In Bungay v Saini EAT 0331/10 the EAT, considering the predecessor provisions

997

to S.109(2) EqA found in Reg 22(2) of the Employment Equality (Religion or Belief) Regulations 2003 SI 2003/1656, held that a tribunal had been entitled to find that two board members of an advice centre had been acting as its agents when they operated the centre in a discriminatory matter. The EAT emphasised that the test of authority is whether, when doing a discriminatory act, the discriminator was exercising authority conferred by the principal and not whether the principal had in fact authorised the discriminator to discriminate.

The previous equality enactments expressly stated that a principal's authority could be 'express or implied', and 'precedent or subsequent'. This is not spelled out in S.109 but it is likely that the same rules will continue to apply under the EqA.

28.105 **Criminal offences.** Section 109(2) EqA does not make a principal liable for any criminal offences under the Act that are committed by agents (other than offences under Part 12 relating to disabled persons and transport, which are outside the scope of this Handbook) – S.109(5).

28.106 **Agency workers**

In keeping with previous discrimination legislation, there is no express provision in the EqA dealing with an employer's vicarious liability for the acts of agency workers. In Mahood v Irish Centre Housing Ltd EAT 0228/10 – a case decided under the provisions of the RRA – the EAT stated that such liability can arise in two situations. First, where an employment contract can be implied between the end-user and the agency worker under the principles outlined in James v London Borough of Greenwich 2008 ICR 545, CA (see under 'Who is protected – employees' and 'Employer's liability for acts of employees' above). Secondly, where the agency worker was acting as the employer's agent within the meaning of what is now S.109(2) EqA.

We would add a third situation in which liability could arise. This is where the agency worker harasses an employee and the employee argues that the agency worker is a third party for the purposes of S.40(3) EqA – see above under 'Employer's liability for harassment by third parties'.

28.107 # Personal liability of employees and agents

Where an employer or principal is liable for the discriminatory acts of employees and agents under S.109 EqA (see 'Employer's liability for acts of employees' and 'Liability of principals for agents' above), the employees and agents may themselves be personally liable under S.110 EqA. While incorporating some aspects of the equivalent provisions in the previous discrimination enactments, S.110 makes it explicit that an employee or agent who commits an act of discrimination is personally liable: previously, the same result was achieved by the circuitous route of making the employee or agent liable for knowingly aiding the employer to do an unlawful act. One key difference is that under the new provisions it is not necessary to show that the employee or agent knew that the act was unlawful. However, it is still necessary that the employer or principal be vicariously liable under S.109 EqA (or would be so liable but for the fact that the 'all reasonable steps' defence has been made out).

A person (A) contravenes S.110 if:

- A is an employee or agent

- A does something that, by virtue of S.109(1) or (2) (see under 'Secondary liability' above), is treated as having been done by A's employer or principal (as the case may be), and

- the doing of that thing by A amounts to a contravention of the EqA by the employer or principal (as the case may be) – S.110(1) EqA.

28.108 A does not contravene S.110 if he or she relies on a statement by the employer or principal that the act in question does not contravene the EqA, and it is reasonable for A to do so – S.110(3). The EHRC Employment Code gives the following example of the application of S.110:

> 'A line manager fails to make reasonable adjustments for a machine operator with multiple sclerosis; even though the machine operator has made the line manager aware that he needs various adjustments. The line manager is not aware that she has acted unlawfully because she failed to attend equality and diversity training, provided by her employer. The line manager could be liable personally for her actions as her employer's action, in providing training, could be enough to meet the statutory defence' – para 10.55.

The Code goes on to state that if the line manager had asked the company director if she needed to make these adjustments, and the director had incorrectly informed her that the machine operator was not covered by the EqA because he was not a wheelchair user, then the line manager would not be liable, but the employer would – para 10.56.

28.109 If the employer or principal knowingly or recklessly makes a statement in this context that is 'false or misleading in a material respect', it commits a criminal offence and is liable on summary conviction to a fine not exceeding level 5 on the standard scale (currently £5,000) – S.110(4) and (5).

The provisions on enforcement in Part 9 of the EqA apply to a contravention of S.110 by the employee or agent as if it were a contravention by the employer or principal – S.110(6). The enforcement provisions are discussed in Chapter 34, 'Enforcing individual rights'; Chapter 35, 'Compensation: general principles of assessment'; and Chapter 36, 'Compensation: heads of damage'.

28.110 Instructing, causing and inducing discrimination

Section 111 EqA makes it unlawful for a person to instruct, cause or induce someone to discriminate, harass or victimise another person on any of the grounds covered by the Act, regardless of whether the person so instructed, etc, actually does so. It replaces equivalent provisions in the predecessor discrimination enactments, while also harmonising the inconsistencies that previously existed across the different strands of discrimination law.

Section 111(1)–(3) states that a person (A) must not instruct, cause or induce another person (B) to do in relation to a third person (C) anything which contravenes Parts 3–7, S.108(1) or (2), or S.112(1) of the EqA. This is referred to in the legislation as 'a basic contravention', and covers, among other things, all forms of discrimination, victimisation and harassment in employment.

28.111 Inducement in this context can be direct or indirect – S.111(4). The EHRC Employment Code echoes this, adding that inducement 'may amount to no more than persuasion, and need not necessarily involve a benefit or loss' – para 9.18. S.111(8) further provides that a reference to causing or inducing something includes a reference to *attempting* to cause or induce it.

The Code gives an example of a managing partner of an accountancy firm who, on becoming aware that the head of the administrative team plans to appoint a senior receptionist with a physical disability, does not issue a direct instruction, but instead suggests that this would reflect poorly on the administrative team leader's judgement, and thus affect his or her future with the firm. This would amount to causing or attempting to cause or induce the head of the administration team to commit an act of discrimination – para 9.18.

28.112 In order for S.111 to apply, the relationship between the person giving the instruction, etc (A) and the person so instructed, etc (B) must be 'such that A is in a position to commit a basic contravention in relation to B' – S.111(7). This means there must be a relationship in respect of which discrimination, harassment or victimisation is itself prohibited (for example, an employment relationship – see 'Who is protected?' above). So if, for example, a customer in a shop complains to the manager about being served by someone with a disability and threatens to withdraw his or her custom, the customer's conduct would not be caught by S.111 because the customer and the shop manager are not in a relationship where it is unlawful for the customer to discriminate, harass or victimise the manager.

Proceedings for a contravention of S.111(1)–(3) can be brought by B, C or the EHRC – S.111(5). But if either B or C wish to bring a claim, they must establish that they suffered a detriment as a result of A's conduct (for a discussion of the meaning of the term 'detriment', see Chapter 25, 'Discrimination during employment', under 'Any other detriment'). However, it does not matter whether the basic contravention actually occurred, or whether any other proceedings have been (or may be) brought as a result of A's conduct – S.111(6). In other words, it 'does not matter whether the person who is instructed, caused or induced to commit an unlawful act carries it out. This is because instructing, causing or inducing an unlawful act is in itself unlawful. However, if the person does commit the unlawful act, they may be liable. The person who instructed, caused or induced them to carry it out will also be liable for it' – para 9.21 EHRC Employment Code.

28.113 For the purposes of the enforcement provisions in Part 9 of the EqA, a contravention of S.111 is to be treated as relating to the provision of the Act which:

- where the claim is brought by B, A is in a position to contravene in relation to B because of the relationship between them, or

- where the claim is brought by C, B is in a position to contravene in relation to C because of the relationship between them – S.111(9).

The enforcement provisions of the Act are discussed in Chapter 34, 'Enforcing individual rights'; Chapter 35, 'Compensation: general principles'; and Chapter 36, 'Compensation: heads of damage'.

Aiding discrimination

28.114

In addition to prohibiting a person from instructing, causing or inducing discrimination, the EqA also includes a provision making it unlawful to aid acts of discrimination. S.112(1) EqA states that a person (A) must not knowingly help another (B) to do anything which contravenes Parts 3–7, S.108(1) or (2), or S.111 of the EqA. As with S.111, this is referred to in the legislation as 'a basic contravention', and covers, among other things, all forms of discrimination, victimisation and harassment in employment. The helper has to 'know' that discrimination, harassment or victimisation is a likely outcome, but such an outcome does not have to be the intention of the helper.

The EHRC Employment Code states that 'help' should be given its ordinary meaning, and that help given to someone to discriminate, harass or victimise will be unlawful 'even if it is not substantial or productive, so long as it is not negligible'. The example given is where a manager who wants to ensure a female candidate is appointed asks a junior employee in the HR department to find out the sex of candidates, where this information had been removed from application forms. The junior employee is likely to be liable under S.112, even though the manager is unsuccessful at excluding male candidates – para 9.27.

Section 112(2) provides that where the helper is relying on a statement by B that the act for which help is given is not unlawful, and it is reasonable for him or her to rely on that statement, he or she will escape liability. The Code states that, in the example given above, if the manager told the junior employee that he was under a duty to balance the sexes in the workplace, and it is reasonable for the junior employee to rely on this, then she will escape liability – para 9.29. According to the Code, 'reasonable' means 'having regard to all the circumstances, including the nature of the act and how obviously discriminatory it is, the authority of the person making the statement and the knowledge that the helper has or ought to have' – para 9.30.

28.115 It a criminal offence for B to knowingly or recklessly make a statement that the help sought is not discriminatory – S.112(3). So, in the example above, if the manager either knows the statement is not true or 'simply does not care whether it is true or not', then the manager will be liable at civil law, and will also have committed a criminal act. This is punishable by a fine not exceeding level 5 on the standard scale (currently £5,000).

For the purposes of the enforcement provisions in Part 9 of the EqA, a contravention of S.112 is to be treated as relating to the provision of the Act to which the basic contravention relates – S.112(5). The enforcement provisions of the Act are discussed in Chapter 34, 'Enforcing individual rights'; Chapter 35, 'Compensation: general principles'; and Chapter 36, 'Compensation: heads of damage'.

29 Liability of other bodies

In Chapter 28, 'Liability of employers, employees and agents', we outlined the **29.1** extent of liability for discrimination in relationships broadly analogous to that of employer-employee, including principal-contract worker, partnership-partner and chambers-barrister. The Equality Act 2010 (EqA) also identifies several organisations and bodies with employment connections that, while not analogous to the employment relationship, nonetheless have some impact on the world of work. In most instances, these organisations and the legislative provisions that apply to them are broadly the same under the EqA as under the previous discrimination enactments.

In this chapter, we consider the scope for liability imposed on these organisations and bodies. We consider first trade organisations, including trade unions and organisations representing employers, before going on to look at the position of bodies empowered to award certain qualifications. We then discuss the liabilities and obligations of trustees of occupational pension schemes, those providing employment services such as work experience and careers advice, and local authorities. Finally, we note briefly the duties that may be imposed on landlords who own premises occupied by employers, for whom the duty to make adjustments to physical features of the premises may be an issue.

This chapter deals largely with matters that fall outside the scope of the **29.2** Statutory Code of Practice on Employment produced by the Equality and Human Rights Commission ('the EHRC Employment Code') and laid before Parliament on 12 October 2010. The EHRC has the power to promulgate statutory Codes of Practice on all aspects of the EqA. However, at the time of going to press, no Code has been published covering discrimination by trade organisations and qualifications bodies. Moreover, given the budget cuts at the EHRC, it seems unlikely that a statutory Code of Practice in this area will be forthcoming in the foreseeable future. As a result, the EHRC's previous publication, 'Revised Code of Practice: Trade Organisations, Qualifications

Bodies and General Qualifications Bodies' (2008) ('the 2008 Code') remains relevant, at least in so far as it relates to provisions that have been re-enacted in substance in the EqA. We have therefore referred to this Code where relevant.

29.3 Trade organisations

A trade organisation – such as a trade union or employers' organisation – is liable for discrimination, harassment and victimisation *as an employer* in the normal way in so far as it acts as an employer. For example, such organisations typically employ officials, lawyers, administrative personnel and press officers to support their members and publicise issues on their behalf. These employment relationships are subject to employment law, including the EqA, just like any other. However, the EqA (like its predecessors) makes special provision to prohibit discrimination in the manner in which such organisations treat their members and prospective members.

The relevant provision is S.57 EqA. This makes it unlawful for a trade organisation (A) to discriminate against a person (B):

- in the arrangements A makes for deciding to whom to offer membership of the organisation – S.57(1)(a)

- as to the terms on which it is prepared to admit B as a member – S.57(1)(b)

- by not accepting B's application for membership – S.57(1)(c).

29.4 Section 57(2) goes on to prohibit discrimination by a trade organisation (A) against a member (B):

- in the way it affords B access, or by not affording B access, to opportunities for receiving a benefit, facility or service – S.57(2)(a)

- by depriving B of membership – S.57(2)(b)

- by varying the terms on which B is a member – S.57(2)(c)

- by subjecting B to any other detriment – S.57(2)(d).

Harassment is dealt with by S.57(3) EqA, which provides that 'a trade organisation must not, in relation to membership of it, harass (a) a member, or (b) an applicant for membership'. Victimisation is covered in similar form to the prohibition on discrimination in S.57(1) and (2). S.57(4) makes it unlawful for a trade organisation to victimise a person in the arrangements it makes for deciding to whom to offer membership of the organisation; as to the terms on which it is prepared to admit B as a member; or by not accepting B's application for membership. S.57(5), meanwhile, makes it unlawful for a trade organisation to victimise a member in the way it affords the member access, or by not affording the member access, to opportunities for receiving a benefit, facility or service; by depriving the member of membership; by varying the terms on which the member is a member; or by subjecting the member to any other detriment. Finally, S.57(6) places trade organisations under a duty to make reasonable adjustments in respect of disabled people, being much the same duty placed on employers – see 'Duty to make reasonable adjustments' below.

The 2008 Code gives an example of discriminatory treatment by a trade union: **29.5**

'A trade union member who has a mental health condition – which her branch secretary is aware of – is refused admission to a meeting because the branch secretary wrongly assumes that she would seriously disrupt the meeting with loud interjections. The branch secretary has treated her less favourably than other members by refusing her entry to the meeting. The treatment was on the ground of the woman's disability (because assumptions would not have been made about a non-disabled person)' – para 4.7.

Scope of S.57 EqA   29.6
The reach of S.57 EqA is governed by S.57(7), which defines 'a trade organisation' thus: 'A trade organisation is (a) an organisation of workers, (b) an organisation of employers, or (c) any other organisation whose members carry on a particular trade or profession for the purposes of which the organisation exists.' This is the same definition that used to apply under the previous discrimination legislation. Thus, the case law under that legislation will inform the scope of S.57 EqA.

The definition in S.57(7) makes it self-evident that trade unions are covered by S.57. So, for example, the British Medical Association, which is registered as a trade union, comes within its scope – British Medical Association v Chaudhary 2007 IRLR 800, CA. In less clear-cut cases, the EAT has held that courts and tribunals should take a broad look at the characteristics of the body in question in order to determine whether it is a 'trade organisation' – see National Federation of Self-Employed and Small Businesses Ltd v Philpott 1997 ICR 518, EAT. There, the Appeal Tribunal concluded that the National Federation of Self-Employed and Small Businesses was an organisation of employers, even though some of its members were not employers and the Federation argued that it represented its members' interests as businesses rather than as employers. In reaching this conclusion, the EAT relied on the fact that 90 per cent of the Federation's members were employers, that it concerned itself with employment matters through an employment affairs committee, and that the Federation had arranged to be included in the list of organisations to be consulted for selecting members representing the employer's side on employment tribunals.

In Medical Protection Society and ors v Sadek 2004 ICR 1263, CA, the Court **29.7** of Appeal held that the Medical Protection Society (MPS) – a body that supports doctors and other health care professionals facing legal problems arising from their clinical practice – was covered by S.11 of the Race Relations Act 1976 (RRA). The Court rejected the MPS's submission that those who

1005

practise a profession are not 'workers', holding that this was inconsistent with the RRA's definition of a 'profession' as including 'any vocation or occupation' (the same definition is now found in S.212(1) EqA.) On that basis, the Court held that the MPS fell within the first category of what is now S.57(7)(a), 'an organisation of workers'.

The Court went on to note that, since the third category of organisation under S.11 RRA (now S.57(7)(c) EqA) refers to 'any *other* organisation' (our stress), an organisation could not fall into the third category if it fell into the first or second category. It added that if the MPS had not fallen into the first category, the Court would have regarded it as falling within the scope of the third. On this point, it rejected the argument that the third category is limited to organisations that represent a single profession. The MPS had argued that since it represented medical practitioners, dental practitioners and various other professions, it did not represent 'a particular profession'. The Court of Appeal decided that it would be illogical to restrict S.11 RRA in this way. It also rejected the MPS's argument that it fell outside S.11 since it did not exist for the purposes of its members' professions but rather for the purposes of the members themselves. The Court held that the requirement that the organisation exist 'for the purposes of' the profession was only intended to exclude organisations whose purposes were unrelated to the members' profession(s), such as organisations whose members may come from a particular profession but whose purpose is, for example, sporting or cultural. The Court endorsed the approach of the EAT, which had decided that the focus of the statutory language was not so much on whether the organisation exists for the purpose of the profession of its members, but rather on whether the organisation exists for the purpose of enabling or assisting its members to carry on their profession.

29.8 The EAT referred to the Sadek case (above) in Wagunyanya v Medical Defence Union Services Ltd EAT 0270/06. There, it held that an employment judge had erred in striking out a claim of discrimination against the Medical Defence Union for lack of jurisdiction on the basis that the MDU did not come within S.11 RRA. The EAT noted that the judge was either unaware of, or had omitted to recall, the Sadek decision. Although the EAT could not decide the point itself, as it depended on findings of fact that the employment tribunal had yet to make, it gave the view that had the judge been aware of Sadek, he would not have reached the same decision on S.11.

In 1 Pump Court Chambers v Horton EAT 0775/03 the EAT had to consider whether, in order to fall within the third category as set out in what is now S.57(7) EqA, the body must have the primary purpose of promoting or protecting a profession 'as a whole'. The EAT rejected this argument, pursued by a barristers' chambers defending a disability discrimination claim brought by an applicant seeking pupillage, holding that it would be too narrow a construction of S.13 of the Disability Discrimination Act 1995 (DDA) (now

S.57 EqA) to find that it covered only organisations that exist for the purposes of a profession as a whole. The EAT went on to note two possible interpretations of S.13: first, that in order to fall within the third category, an organisation must exist for the 'carrying on' of the profession in question; alternatively, that it must exist 'for the purposes of' the profession itself. It concluded that a barristers' chambers can be said to exist for either reason. By the time the case reached the Court of Appeal (as Higham and ors v Horton 2005 ICR 292, CA) it was conceded that a barristers' chambers amounts to a trade organisation for the purposes of S.13. The Court went on to hold, however, that an application to a set of chambers for pupillage is not an application for membership of the chambers and therefore fell outside the scope of the section. (Note that discrimination by barristers' chambers against applicants for pupillage or tenancy is expressly covered by the EqA at S.47 – see Chapter 28, 'Liability of employers, employees and agents', under 'Who is protected? – trainee and qualified barristers/advocates'.)

29.9 It is important to distinguish between organisations that serve the interests of their members and those that serve the interests of the public since, it seems, the latter do not fall within S.57 EqA. In Cox v General Medical Council EAT 0076/01 the EAT decided that the GMC was not a trade organisation within S.13 DDA because its primary purpose was to protect the public, not to promote the medical profession. While the EAT did not disagree with the claimant's assertion that the activities of the GMC serve to maintain the status and reputation of the medical profession and are thus of a benefit to it, that consideration could not displace the predominant purpose of public protection. In the EAT's view, if the medical profession does indeed benefit from the GMC and its functioning, that is arguably because the GMC does not exist for the medical profession's 'purpose' but for the 'purpose' of the public, setting standards that are not compromised by self-interest.

Historically, it has been important to distinguish between trade organisations and qualifications bodies. In Kelly v Football Association EAT 0015/05 the EAT rejected a complaint of disability-related discrimination in relation to the FA's refusal to award a UEFA 'A' football coaching licence. The claim was based on facts occurring at a time when the DDA covered trade organisations but not qualifications bodies (see 'Qualifications bodies' below). An employment tribunal rejected the claim for lack of jurisdiction, holding that the award of a coaching licence was not the same as the granting of membership of a trade organisation. The EAT upheld that decision. It rejected the claimant's attempt to bring himself within the trade organisation provisions of the DDA via his membership of the Football Association Coaches Association, which is regulated by the FA. Although the award by the FA of the 'A' licence would have had a beneficial impact on the claimant's career, his membership status would have remained unchanged. Accordingly, there was no way in which the FA could be said to have discriminated in relation to membership.

29.10 Since the EAT's decisions in Kelly v Football Association and Cox v General Medical Council (above), the law has moved on and now prohibits discrimination by qualifications bodies across all strands of discrimination law – see 'Qualifications bodies' below. The EAT in Cox noted that the absence of such protection in the DDA as it then stood was clearly the result of a deliberate choice by Parliament, not wishing to risk compromising the academic and professional standards of such bodies. However, the DDA was amended in October 2004 by the Disability Discrimination Act 1995 (Amendment) Regulations 2003 SI 2003/1673, which, among other things, inserted a new S.14A, making qualifications bodies subject to a legal obligation not to discriminate or harass disabled people in the conferring of professional or trade qualifications. A new S.14B extended the duty to make reasonable adjustments to qualifications bodies.

29.11 **Duty to make reasonable adjustments**

As noted above, trade organisations are subject to the duty to make reasonable adjustments as set out in Ss.20–22 EqA – S.57(6). The extent and nature of this duty, which applies in respect of disabled people, are described in detail in Chapter 21, 'Failure to make reasonable adjustments'. However, it is worth noting here the duty's particular impact on trade organisations.

As in relation to employment, the extent of the duty to make reasonable adjustments depends on whether the disabled person is a potential applicant for membership, an applicant for membership, or a member of the trade organisation in question. In relation to a disabled person who is an applicant for membership, or who has notified the trade organisation that he or she may be an applicant, the organisation is obliged to make reasonable adjustments when deciding to whom to offer membership of the organisation – paras 2 and 17, Sch 8 EqA. However, that obligation only arises in relation to the first and third requirements of the reasonable adjustments duty set out in S.20(3) and (5); namely, provisions, criteria and practices that the organisation applies, and auxiliary aids that the organisation provides. The trade organisation is *not* obliged to make adjustments to physical features of premises within S.20(4). In contrast, in respect of membership of the organisation, all three elements of the duty in S.20(3)–(5) apply to applicants for membership and members of the organisation.

29.12 The 2008 Code gives some examples of reasonable adjustments that trade organisations might be called on to make:

- a disabled member wishes to attend a course, but the programme for the day does not allow him sufficient rest breaks. He would therefore be at a substantial disadvantage because of his disability. The trade organisation rearranges the programme for the day to include more breaks

- a trade organisation for carpenters has an application form with several paragraphs in small print. A partially sighted carpenter cannot read the whole form and is therefore at a substantial disadvantage because he cannot fill it in correctly. The trade organisation provides him with an application form in large print

- a disabled woman who is unable to use public transport wishes to attend a trade fair in central London, organised by a trade organisation of which she is a member. There is very little parking in the area and the information brochure suggests that 'visitors to the trade fair are advised to come by public transport'. The woman asks the trade organisation if it can arrange a parking space and it does so – para 5.2.

Qualifications bodies 29.13

Sections 53–54 EqA deal with discrimination by 'qualifications bodies', i.e. bodies that award qualifications specifically for a trade or profession. These sections replace similar provisions in the previous equality legislation and extend the protection to cover discrimination in the arrangements made for determining upon whom a relevant qualification should be conferred. Discrimination by qualifications bodies is dealt with in this Handbook because such bodies provide a gateway to employment. It should be noted that Ss.95–98 and Schedule 13 to the EqA contain similar provisions relating to bodies that award other types of prescribed qualifications. However, those provisions are outside the scope of this Handbook.

The EHRC Employment Code does not deal with the effect of the EqA in relation to qualifications bodies. Para 11.52 of the Code states that this will be addressed in a separate Code, but as we stated at the outset of this chapter, budget cuts at the EHRC place the publication of any new Codes of Practice in doubt. Reference is made to the 2008 Code where relevant.

Under S.53(1) EqA, it is unlawful for a qualifications body (A) to discriminate **29.14** against a person (B):

- in the arrangements it makes for deciding upon whom to confer a relevant qualification – S.53(1)(a)

- as to the terms on which it is prepared to confer a relevant qualification on B – S.53(1)(b)

- by not conferring a relevant qualification on B – S.53(1)(c).

In relation to a person on whom the qualifications body has already conferred a relevant qualification (B), the qualifications body must not discriminate:

- by withdrawing the qualification from B – S.53(2)(a)

- by varying the terms on which B holds the qualification – S.53(2)(b)

- by subjecting B to any other detriment – S.53(2)(c).

29.15 It is also unlawful to victimise B in relation to the conferment of a relevant qualification by doing any of the things listed at S.53(1) and (2) – S.53(4) and (5) EqA. Furthermore, holders of and applicants for qualifications are protected from harassment under S.53(3). The duty to make reasonable adjustments in respect of disabled people also applies to a qualifications body – S.53(6) (see 'Duty to make reasonable adjustments' below).

With regard to discrimination and victimisation, these provisions appear to cover a wider range of matters than the equivalent provisions under the previous equality enactments. The limit of the protection offered by the antecedent equality enactments was illustrated in Tariquez-Zaman v General Medical Council EAT 0292/06 and another. There, the EAT held that an employment tribunal had no jurisdiction to hear a complaint of race discrimination against the GMC under S.12 RRA. TZ, a registered medical practitioner, was subjected to a disciplinary procedure under the rules that applied to the GMC's registered members. Before that procedure concluded, TZ voluntarily relinquished his authorisation to practise medicine, removing his name from the medical register. He subsequently brought a tribunal complaint of race discrimination based on the GMC's conduct of the disciplinary procedure. He argued that this amounted to a variation of the terms of his authorisation to practise medicine, or a withdrawal of that authorisation, within S.12 RRA. An employment tribunal rejected that argument. Since TZ had voluntarily relinquished his authorisation to practise, GMC had not withdrawn it. Furthermore, it is not a variation of terms to activate professional disciplinary procedures and to pursue them. Therefore, the GMC had not done anything within S.12 RRA, meaning that the tribunal had no jurisdiction to hear the complaint. The EAT agreed with that conclusion on appeal.

29.16 At the time of the Tariquez-Zaman decision, S.12 RRA did not refer to discrimination by a qualifications body by way of 'any other detriment', as S.53(2)(c) EqA now does. It is possible that, had TZ been able to put his case on the basis of detriment, it might have succeeded, or at least not fallen at the first hurdle. While the EAT had a sound basis on which to hold that there was no withdrawal of authorisation or variation of terms within what is now S.53(2)(a) and (b) EqA, it is well established that the application of a disciplinary procedure to a person for discriminatory reasons may amount to a 'detriment'. In this respect, therefore, S.53 EqA is potentially wider than its predecessor provisions such as S.12 RRA.

Some other examples of discriminatory treatment taken from the 2008 Code:

- a general qualifications body has a practice of not allowing wheelchair users to undertake a GCSE qualification in dance, because it has assumed that all wheelchair users are incapable of undertaking this qualification, and it has operated this policy without considering the individual circumstances of each person

- a person with a severe visible disfigurement is not allowed to undertake a GNVQ in leisure and tourism because the body conferring this qualification believes this disability will prevent the person from gaining employment in this sector – paras 4.7–4.8.

Scope of S.53 EqA 29.17

A qualifications body is one that can confer a relevant qualification – S.54(2) EqA. A 'relevant qualification' for this purpose is 'an authorisation, qualification, recognition, registration, enrolment, approval or certification which is needed for, or facilitates engagement in, a particular trade or profession' – S.54(3) EqA. Note that the authorisation or qualification granted by a qualifications body need not be intended to facilitate employment in a profession or trade. What matters is that the qualification does in fact facilitate it. With regard to 'facilitating' employment, the Explanatory Notes accompanying the EqA state that this encompasses any qualification 'which better enables a person to [carry out a particular trade or profession] by, for example, determining whether the person has a particular level of competence or ability' – para 189.

The above definition of 'qualifications body' is substantially the same as that which applied under the antecedent equality enactments. Thus, the old case law still applies. For instance, as noted under 'Trade organisations – scope of S.57 EqA' above, the EAT in Cox v General Medical Council EAT 0076/01 accepted that the GMC would be a qualifications body under the relevant provisions of the RRA and Sex Discrimination Act 1975 (SDA) then in force. Later, in Tariquez-Zaman v General Medical Council EAT 0292/06 and another, the EAT did not question the claimant's entitlement in principle to bring a claim against the GMC (although it held that it lacked jurisdiction for other reasons). That same conclusion would apply under the EqA.

The Legal Services Commission – the body with power to grant legal aid 29.18 franchises to solicitors' firms – has also been held to be a qualifications body. In Patterson v Legal Services Commission 2004 ICR 312, CA, the Court of Appeal held that accreditation, in the form of the award of a legal aid franchise and the right to display the Commission's logo, amounted to an 'authorisation' within the meaning of S.12 RRA. It further held that the authorisation in question 'facilitates' the carrying on of the profession of solicitor, because it makes the carrying on of the profession easier for the franchisee. It followed that the employment tribunal did have jurisdiction to hear a race discrimination claim brought by a sole practitioner against the Commission in response to its having rejected his application for a legal aid franchise.

1011

Note that some bodies are potentially covered by both S.53 and S.57 EqA (see 'Trade organisations' above). For example, for many years the Law Society regulated entry to the solicitors' profession while also acting as a professional association for solicitors (the regulatory role has now been taken over by the Solicitors Regulation Authority). Furthermore, as the 2008 Code notes at para 7.4, 'membership of certain trade organisations (for example, the Institute of Linguists or the Chartered Institute of Personnel and Development) itself amounts to a professional or trade qualification... Where this is the case, decisions about granting, varying or withdrawing membership of the trade organisation will also be subject to the rules about conferring professional or trade qualifications.'

29.19 It has been established that there is no requirement that a discriminatory term (as opposed to the qualification itself) have any impact on the employment prospects of the person discriminated against or that he or she show actual proof of damage. A complainant must simply show that the qualification facilitates his or her job prospects and that attached to such qualification is a term that is discriminatory – British Judo Association v Petty 1981 ICR 660, EAT. In that case P, a judo coach, was granted a certificate by the BJA as a qualified referee. After she had acted as referee in the All England Men's Competition, the BJA instituted a policy of not allowing women to referee men's competitions. Upholding her complaint of sex discrimination under what was then S.13 SDA, the EAT held that:

- the referee's certificate did help P in her job as coach, so the motives of the BJA in issuing it were immaterial

- it was not necessary that the discrimination should harm P's job prospects, since the Act simply renders unlawful discrimination in the terms on which a qualifications body confers a qualification

- the BJA had either issued a discriminatory referee's certificate or had discriminated against P by varying the terms of her certificate – both were unlawful regardless of any actual loss suffered by P.

29.20 However, there must be some connection with employment for S.53 to be engaged. Registration as an amateur footballer with a local league was held not to fall within S.12 RRA. In Jeffrey-Shaw v Shropshire County Premier Football League and anor EAT 0320/04 the EAT decided that registration as a footballer entitled to compete in amateur leagues did not relate to the employment field even in the widest sense, since such registration could not be viewed as the granting of a qualification or authorisation to a person who has satisfied appropriate standards of competence to practise a profession, calling or trade.

Qualifications bodies need to be distinguished from other organisations that can confer professional or commercial advantages. In Kelly and anor v Northern Ireland Housing Executive 1998 ICR 828, HL, a religious discrimination case concerning equivalent provisions in the Fair Employment (Northern Ireland) Act 1976, the House of Lords held that the word 'qualification' conveys the idea of some sort of status conferred on a person in relation to his or her work, trade, profession or calling, which relates only to the lawful carrying on of that work, and which is either necessary or advantageous to the lawful carrying on of that work. It could not be said that the appointment of a successful candidate to the Executive's panel of solicitors for the carrying out of litigation on its behalf conferred any type of status on him or her. Even though the definition of 'qualification' includes 'authorisation', 'recognition' or 'approval' which facilitates employment, and the Executive was in a position to authorise a firm to engage in prestigious and much sought-after work, their Lordships were not satisfied that 'qualification' as defined covered the appointment of a duly qualified professional person to carry out remunerated work on behalf of a client, however prestigious that client might be. Similarly, in Tattari v Private Patients Plan Ltd 1998 ICR 106, CA, the Court of Appeal concluded that a medical insurance company choosing practitioners for inclusion on its list of approved specialists was not a qualifications body because it did not have the power or authority to confer on a person a professional qualification or other approval needed to practise a profession. It was merely stipulating that a particular qualification was required for the purpose of its commercial agreements.

Judicial offices. The question of whether the appointment of magistrates/ **29.21** justices of the peace (JPs) amounts to the conferment of a qualification was considered in Arthur v Attorney-General and anor 1999 ICR 631, EAT. In that case an employment tribunal declined jurisdiction in a claim brought under the RRA concerning the rejection of the claimant's application for nomination as a magistrate by the Middlesex Area Advisory Committee (AAC) on the basis that the AAC was not a qualifications body. The EAT, following the Court of Appeal in Tattari v Private Patients Plan Ltd (above), upheld that decision on appeal. It found, among other things, that being a JP was not an 'occupation' and that the AAC was simply a committee sifting applications, not a qualifications body conferring an 'approval'. (It should be noted, however, that all of the equality enactments were subsequently amended to extend coverage to 'office holders'. This category would almost certainly have caught nominations to the magistrature, as it was intended to apply to most judicial roles. And since the EqA has the same reach as the antecedent legislation as amended, it is likely that the provisions in Ss.49–52 EqA dealing with office holders and applicants for public office afford protection to those carrying out judicial roles – see Chapter 28, 'Liability of employers, employees and agents', under 'Who is protected? – office holders'.)

Political parties. Selection competitions for political office – and indeed for **29.22** party endorsements in 'primaries' – will not engage S.53 EqA. In Ali and anor v McDonagh 2002 ICR 1026, CA, the Court of Appeal held that two members of the Labour Party – one seeking selection as a party candidate for local government elections; the other seeking reselection as a candidate – could not proceed with claims of race discrimination under S.12 RRA after they were suspended from the party and thereby excluded from consideration. The Court held that, in selecting a candidate for local government elections or allowing a person to be nominated to the pool from which prospective candidates are to be selected, the Labour Party was not a body that could 'confer an authorisation or qualification' on a member seeking such selection, which is 'needed for, or facilitates, engagement in a particular profession'. It added that it had doubts as to whether being a local councillor amounts to being engaged in a profession or occupation within the meaning of that section since it was not salaried work; still more so if the profession or occupation is limited to being selected as a candidate for local elections.

This decision was subsequently affirmed by the House of Lords in Watt (formerly Carter) and ors v Ahsan 2008 ICR 82, HL, where Lord Hoffmann stated that 'the notion of an "authorisation or qualification" suggests some kind of objective standard which the qualifications body applies, an even-handed, not to say "transparent", test which people may pass or fail. The qualifications body vouches to the public for the qualifications of the candidate and the public rely upon the qualification in offering him employment or professional engagements. That is why S.12 falls under the general heading of discrimination "in the employment field". But that is far removed from the basis upon which a political party chooses its candidates. The main criterion is likely to be the popularity of the candidate with the voters, which is unlikely to be based on the most objective criteria.'

29.23 Note that appointment to political office is also excluded from the protection for office holders and applicants for office provided by Ss.49–52 EqA – see Chapter 28, 'Liability of employers, employees and agents', under 'Who is protected? – office holders'.

29.24 **Excluded bodies.** Various institutions are excluded from the scope of S.53 by S.54(4). Most significantly, the governing bodies of schools and institutions of further and higher education are not covered – S.54(4)(b) and (c). Furthermore, any body that awards 'general qualifications', such as Edexcel and AQA, is not covered – S.54(4)(a). Thus, no discrimination complaint can be made in respect of the award (or refusal) of GCSEs, A-levels and degrees, etc, under S.53. (Note, though, that educational institutions and general qualifications bodies are subject to separate liabilities and duties under Ss.85, 91 and 96 EqA. A consideration of these provisions is outside the scope of this Handbook.) Finally, S.54(4)(d) and (e) excludes any bodies, such as local authorities, that exercise functions under the Education Acts or the Education (Scotland) Act 1980 from the scope of S.53.

Enforcement   29.25

Complaints of discrimination by qualifications bodies are made to employment
tribunals – S.120(1) EqA. However, S.120(7) states that a tribunal does not
have jurisdiction 'in so far as the act complained of may, by virtue of an
enactment, be subject to an appeal or proceedings in the nature of an appeal'.
This means that where there is a statutory right of appeal against decisions of
the qualifications body, that statutory procedure must be used. Complaints
against the decision of a medical practices committee are referred to the
Secretary of State for Health; complaints against the Law Society to the Court
of Appeal; complaints against licensing justices to the Crown Court; and
complaints against the Driving Standards Agency to a magistrates' court.
Accordingly, although in all four of these instances the decision-makers would
otherwise be qualifications bodies within S.53 EqA, the existence of the
statutory appellate body deprives the tribunal of jurisdiction. That appellate
body will be the appropriate forum for any complaint that the qualifications
body's decision was tainted by disability discrimination.

It is not sufficient for these purposes that the qualifications body has an in-built
appeals process. S.120(7) applies where the appeal, or the proceedings 'in the
nature of an appeal', may be brought 'by virtue of an enactment'. The EAT has
previously held that this phrase in effect means that the appeal must be brought
under an Act of Parliament or subordinate legislation, such as a statutory
instrument or Order in Council – see Zaidi v Financial Intermediaries Managers
and Brokers Regulatory Association 1995 ICR 876, EAT. The definitions
section of the EqA – S.212 – bears this out, stating that an enactment means an
Act of Parliament, an Act of the Scottish Parliament, an Act or Measure of the
National Assembly for Wales, or subordinate legislation. Accordingly, S.120(7)
will not apply in respect of appeals that are merely approved or regulated by a
statutory body if the appeal itself is not governed by an enactment.

The Zaidi case concerned the Financial Intermediaries Managers and Brokers   29.26
Regulatory Association (FIMBRA), which is recognised by the Secretary of
State for Business, Innovation and Skills as a self-regulating organisation (SRO)
under the Financial Services Act 1986. That Act provides that a person may not
carry on an investment business unless he or she is an authorised or exempted
person and that membership of an SRO (such as FIMBRA) confers such
authorisation. Z brought a claim against FIMBRA alleging that she had been
refused membership on the ground of race. An employment tribunal held that
S.54(2) RRA – the equivalent of S.120(7) EqA – meant that it had no jurisdiction
to hear her claim because FIMBRA had an internal appeal process with
statutory authority. After examining the statutory provisions in some detail, the
EAT overturned this finding on the ground that the appeal process referred to
by the tribunal was not actually provided for by the Financial Services Act or
any of its subordinate legislation, but was instead derived from FIMBRA's
articles of association. The fact that FIMBRA was subject to scrutiny by the

1015

Secretary of State in accordance with the legislation did not have the effect of giving statutory force to rules issued under those articles of association.

29.27 **Absence of futher appeal.** In Chaudhary v Specialist Training Authority Appeal Panel and ors (No.2) 2005 ICR 1086, CA, the Court held that an appeal body's rejection of a doctor's appeal against a Specialist Training Authority (STA)'s refusal of his application for entry onto the Register of Specialists was covered by the old S.54(2) RRA exemption, with the result that an employment tribunal had no jurisdiction to hear his claim of race discrimination. In so holding, the Court dismissed the doctor's contention that the appeal panel's decision was not subject to the S.54(2) exclusion because there was no subsequent statutory right of appeal against it. Applying the decision in Khan v General Medical Council 1996 ICR 1032, CA, the Court of Appeal held that the relevant 'act' for the purposes of S.54(2) was the STA's act of refusing the doctor's application for entry onto the Register and not the panel's decision upholding the STA's conclusions. It noted that the exception in S.54(2) would not work if it could be defeated by the absence of a further appeal from the statutory appeal panel. The Court went on to reject the argument that reserving the redress procedure to the statutory appeal panel, instead of the employment tribunal, infringed the right to a fair trial under Article 6 of the European Convention on Human Rights, as effected in UK law by the Human Rights Act 1998. In the Court's view, the appeal procedure in the instant case, backed as it was by the right to seek judicial review, provided an effective remedy. Furthermore, it noted that it would be open to the court on a judicial review to consider whether the appeal panel had acted in a discriminatory manner.

29.28 **Effect on liability for aiding discrimination.** A person who helps another to commit an act that contravenes the EqA will be liable for aiding a discriminatory act. Such liability, the extent of which is discussed in Chapter 28, 'Liability of employers, employees and agents', under 'Aiding discrimination', applies to discrimination by the bodies and organisations noted in this chapter as it does to discrimination in employment and analogous contexts – see S.112 EqA. However, where there is no cause of action before an employment tribunal because a qualifications body has its own statutory appeal mechanism, another body cannot unlawfully aid the discriminatory act allegedly done by the qualifications body. This was the conclusion of the EAT in Igboaka v Royal College of Pathologists EAT 0036/09. There, the Royal College of Pathologists delayed investigating grievances made by I pending the outcome of an investigation by the GMC into his fitness to practise. The claimant's complaint that the GMC's investigation was discriminatory could not be brought in an employment tribunal, following the Court of Appeal's conclusion in Khan v General Medical Council (above) that the statutory right of appeal from decisions made by the GMC incurred the exemption under old S.54(2) RRA. The EAT in the present case held that this meant that the College could not be said to have aided the GMC in that alleged act of discrimination.

Duty to make reasonable adjustments   **29.29**
Qualifications bodies are subject to the duty to make reasonable adjustments as
set out in Ss.20–22 EqA and Schedule 8 – S.53(6) EqA. The extent and nature
of that duty, which applies in respect of disabled people, are explained in detail
in Chapter 21, 'Failure to make reasonable adjustments'. However, it is worth
noting here the duty's particular impact on qualifications bodies.

The scope of the duty to make reasonable adjustments as it applies to
qualifications bodies is the same as applies to trade organisations. By a
combination of paras 2 and 15 of Schedule 8 to the EqA, the qualifications
body is obliged to make reasonable adjustments when deciding upon whom to
confer a relevant qualification in relation to a disabled person who is an
applicant for the conferment of the qualification or who has notified the
qualifications body that he or she may be such an applicant. However, the
obligation only arises in relation to the first and third requirements of the
reasonable adjustments duty set out in S.20(3) and (5); namely, provisions,
criteria and practices that the qualifications body applies, and auxiliary aids
that the qualifications body provides. The qualifications body is *not* obliged to
make adjustments to physical features of premises within S.20(4). In contrast,
in respect of the conferment of a qualification, all three elements of the duty in
S.20(3)–(5) apply to applicants for the conferment of the qualification and
holders of the qualification.

The 2008 Code gives some examples of adjustments that it would be likely to   **29.30**
be reasonable for a qualifications body to make:

● a qualifications body holds an awards ceremony at its headquarters. A newly
  qualified woman who uses a wheelchair wants to attend the ceremony but
  is at a substantial disadvantage because the stage where the awards are
  presented is only accessible by stairs. The qualifications body provides a
  ramp up to the stage

● a general qualifications body allows a person with Chronic Fatigue Syndrome
  who, due to effects of her impairment, is unable to travel to an examination
  venue to take the examination (which is properly invigilated by a teacher
  from her college) at her home. She is also granted extra time to undertake
  the examination – para 5.2.

The only case of note concerning qualification bodies and the duty to make
reasonable adjustments is Project Management Institute v Latif 2007 IRLR
579, EAT. There, the EAT upheld an employment tribunal's decision that PMI
failed to make reasonable adjustments in relation to the blind claimant sitting
the Project Management professional examination. L asked that she be allowed
to take the exam on her own laptop computer in the examination centre or,
alternatively, that her screen-reading software be installed in the examination
centre computer. She also asked for a reader to support her by explaining

1017

diagrams. PMI allowed a reader/recorder and gave L twice the usual time to sit the examination but did not allow her to take in her own computer. Although she passed, she complained of failure to make reasonable adjustments under what was then S.14B DDA. The tribunal upheld her complaint and awarded £3,000 for injury to feelings. It found that PMI had refused properly to consider L's suggestions for adjustments that suited her way of working, assuming instead that arrangements that had been successfully put in place for other blind candidates would be acceptable to her. Although L was able to pass the exam using the adjustments imposed by PMI, she did suffer an understandable sense of anger and frustration, and deserved to be compensated for the discrimination she had suffered.

29.31 **Disability discrimination: competence standards**
The prohibition on discrimination by qualifications bodies under S.53 EqA applies to all the 'protected characteristics' – i.e. age, disability, gender reassignment, marriage and civil partnership, pregnancy and maternity, race, religion or belief, sex and sexual orientation. However, special provision is made in respect of disability discrimination in so far as competence standards are concerned. S.53(7) provides that 'the application by a qualifications body of a competence standard to a disabled person is not disability discrimination unless it is discrimination by virtue of S.19 [indirect discrimination]'. Accordingly, the application of a competence standard to a disabled person is never direct discrimination (S.13), discrimination arising from disability (S.15) or a failure to make reasonable adjustments (S.21). Only if indirect discrimination is made out will the disabled person have a valid claim, and only then if the discrimination cannot be objectively justified – see Chapter 17, 'Indirect discrimination: objective justification'.

A similar restriction applied under S.14A DDA, albeit that there it was expressed in more convoluted terms. Under S.14A(3), the application of a competence standard was deemed automatically justified as potential disability-related discrimination, under S.3A(1) DDA, so long as the standard was or would be applied equally to persons who did not have the particular individual's disability, and its application was a proportionate means of achieving a legitimate aim. This amounted, in effect, to a test of justifying indirect discrimination. S.14A(4) went on to state that S.3A(2) and (6) DDA – the duty to make reasonable adjustments – did not apply where S.14A(3) applied. This left direct disability discrimination, under S.3A(5) DDA, which could potentially give rise to a claim in respect of the application of a competence standard. However, so long as the same standard was applied to all, such a claim would never get off the ground. In sum, therefore, the S.53(7) EqA exception has almost identical scope to that which applied under the DDA.

29.32 A 'competence standard' is defined by S.54(6) EqA as 'an academic, medical or other standard applied for the purpose of determining whether or not a person has a particular level of competence or ability'. This definition is wide enough to apply to almost any qualification, since competence and ability are precisely what qualifications are intended to assess. The 2008 Code notes at para 8.27 that an eyesight test imposed as part of a pilot's qualification, and knowledge of the UK tax system for an accountancy qualification, would both be competence standards. However, it goes on to state that 'a certain length of experience of doing something will not be a competence standard if it does not determine a particular level of competence or ability' – para 8.29. In this regard, the Code suggests that a requirement for a certain number of years' continuous experience, that a candidate complete 12 qualifying sessions (for qualification as a barrister), or that a candidate be currently employed in a particular profession, would not be a competence standard. It also points out the difference between a standard itself and the arrangements made for testing that standard. So, for example, while requiring a particular standard of written English may be a competence standard, the way in which that standard is tested may be susceptible to the duty to make reasonable adjustments. However, para 8.31 cautions: 'Sometimes, of course, the process of assessing whether a competence standard has been achieved is inextricably linked to the standard itself. The conferment of some qualifications is conditional upon having a practical skill or ability which must be demonstrated by completing a practical test. The ability to take the test may itself amount to a competence standard.'

To our knowledge, the only case considering the meaning of competency standards under the DDA was Burke v The College of Law and anor EAT 0301/10, which concerned the examination element of the Legal Practice Course (LPC), a vocational course designed to prepare students for practice as a solicitor. The exams are supervised, timed, and required to be taken at the College's premises in Guildford. B, an LPC student who suffered from multiple sclerosis, brought a tribunal claim arguing that the College had failed to make reasonable adjustments to these exam conditions. Central to his complaint was the College's refusal – after it had already made a series of adjustments to B's exam conditions including the provision of 60 per cent more time, accommodation in Guildford and rest breaks during exams – to allow B further time to complete his exams or to allow him to complete them at home. The tribunal held that the time constraint for taking each exam was a competence standard, with the result that the duty to make reasonable adjustments did not apply. B appealed, arguing that the time constraints were not a competence standard because the College had already agreed to vary them.

The EAT upheld the tribunal's decision. The tribunal had been entitled to **29.33** conclude that the time constraint was a competence standard based on the evidence before it that the exams were designed to assess the ability of each candidate to work at speed and under pressure, which was an important requirement for practice as a solicitor. The fact that the College had granted B some additional time to complete his exams did not negate the tribunal's finding that the timing element was a competence standard, since the fact that an employer made an adjustment does not mean that it was compelled to do so by the legislation. There was, in any event, a clear distinction between giving a candidate some extra time, such that the nature of the exam (and competence standard) is maintained, and giving such an amount of extra time that the exam is no longer testing the required competency. The case was appealed to the Court of Appeal – Burke v The College of Law and anor 2012 EWCA Civ 37, CA – but, having held that the tribunal clearly found that the employer had made reasonable adjustments to the time requirement, the Court declined to rule on the question of whether that requirement was a competence standard. Accordingly, the EAT's decision remains the only consideration of this point.

29.34 Occupational pension schemes

The EqA requires all occupational pension schemes to include a non-discrimination rule. Under the previous equality legislation, a similar rule applied in respect of age, disability, religion or belief and sexual orientation, but not in respect of race, gender reassignment, marriage and civil partnership, and sex. The non-discrimination rule in the EqA applies to all protected characteristics.

29.35 The non-discrimination rule

Section 61(1) EqA provides that all occupational pension schemes (as defined by S.1 of the Pension Schemes Act 1993 – see S.212(1) EqA) 'must be taken to include a non-discrimination rule'. A non-discrimination rule is defined in S.61(2) as a provision by virtue of which a 'responsible person' (A) must not:

- discriminate against another person (B) in carrying out any of A's functions in relation to the scheme

- harass B in relation to the scheme

- victimise B in relation to the scheme.

Section 61(4) provides that the following people are 'responsible persons' for the purposes of S.61(2):

- the trustees or managers of the scheme (as defined by S.124 of the Pensions Act 1995 – see S.212(11) EqA)

- an employer whose employees are, or may be, members of the scheme (i.e. active, deferred or pensioner members as defined by S.124 of the Pensions Act 1995 – see S.212(10) EqA)

- a person exercising an 'appointing function' in relation to an office where the office holder is, or may be, a member of the scheme. An 'appointing function' is the function of appointing a person; terminating a person's appointment; recommending a person for appointment; or approving an appointment – S.61(6).

29.36 The provisions of an occupational pension scheme have effect subject to the non-discrimination rule – S.61(3). This means that where there is a conflict between the non-discrimination rule and a rule of the scheme that would otherwise require the trustees or managers to act in a discriminatory way, the non-discrimination rule prevails and the scheme must be read as if the discriminatory provision did not apply.

A breach of a non-discrimination rule is treated as a contravention of Part 5 of the Act (work) for the purposes of the enforcement provisions in Part 9 of the EqA – S.61(7) (discussed in Chapter 34, 'Enforcing individual rights'). The Explanatory Notes to the EqA clarify that the provisions in Part 9 do not prevent the investigation or determination of any matter in accordance with Part 10 of the Pension Schemes Act 1993 by the Pensions Ombudsman as the Ombudsman's investigations are not legal proceedings (see para 206).

29.37 Duty to make reasonable adjustments. The duty to make reasonable adjustments applies to responsible persons – S.61(11). The extent of the duty, which applies in respect of disabled people, is examined in detail in Chapter 21, 'Failure to make reasonable adjustments'. It applies to the carrying out of the responsible person's functions in relation to the scheme and is owed to any disabled person who is or may be a member of the scheme – para 19, Sch 8 EqA.

The EHRC Employment Code gives the following example:

'The rules of an employer's final salary scheme provide that the maximum pension is based on the member's salary in the last year of work. Having worked full time for 20 years, a worker becomes disabled and has to reduce her working hours two years before her pension age. The scheme's rules put her at a disadvantage as a result of her disability, because her pension will only be calculated on her part-time salary. The trustees decide to convert her part-time salary to its full-time equivalent and make a corresponding reduction in the period of her part-time employment which counts as pensionable. In this way, her full-time earnings will be taken into account. This is likely to be a reasonable adjustment to make' – para 14.44.

29.38 Exceptions. A non-discrimination rule does not apply in relation to a person who is a 'pension credit member' of a scheme, as defined by S.124 of the Pensions Act 1995 – Ss.61(5) and 212(11) EqA. Pension credit members are not protected against discrimination because their rights are derived from an order of the court, rather than directly from employment. Pension credit members are,

1021

however, entitled to some disability discrimination protection with regard to communications relating to the scheme – see under 'Communications' below.

In addition, a Minister of the Crown may make an order specifying 'rules, practices, actions or decisions relating to age' that the employer or the trustees or managers of a scheme can maintain or use without being in breach of a non-discrimination rule – S.61(8) EqA. Before making an order authorising the use of rules, practices, actions or decisions that are not in use before the order comes into force, the Minister must consult appropriate persons – S.61(9). The relevant order made under this provision is the Equality Act (Age Exceptions for Pension Schemes) Order 2010 SI 2010/2133. For further details, see Chapter 31, 'Specific exceptions', in the section 'Age exceptions', under 'Pension schemes – contributions to personal pension schemes'.

29.39 Section 61(10) EqA further provides that a non-discrimination rule does not have effect in relation to an occupational pension scheme in so far as an equality rule has effect in relation to it (or would have effect but for Part 2 of Schedule 7, which deals with exceptions to the equal pay provisions in so far as they apply to occupational pension schemes). An equality rule is a sex equality or maternity equality rule – S.212(1). For further details about equality rules, see IDS Employment Law Handbook, 'Equal Pay' (2011), Chapter 2, 'Right to equal pay', under 'Occupational pension schemes'.

Finally, para 205 of the Explanatory Notes states that a non-discrimination rule under S.61 'does not apply to pension rights built up or benefits payable for periods of service before the commencement of this section. Periods of service prior to this date will be subject to the previous discrimination legislation.'

29.40 **Non-discrimination alterations**

It is not always a simple matter to remedy unequal treatment in pension schemes. While an employer has absolute discretion over terms of employment, and so can be expected to put right any discrimination in those terms, pension scheme trustees and managers are limited by the deeds of the scheme and, in the absence of special provision, may be hampered by this in dealing with proven discrimination. S.62 EqA therefore provides for 'non-discrimination alterations' to be made to an occupational pension scheme. These are, according to S.62(5), 'such alterations to the scheme as may be required for the provisions of the scheme to have the effect that they have in consequence of S.61(3) [the non-discrimination rule]'. The power to make these alterations only applies if one of three conditions is made out:

- the trustees or managers do not have power to make non-discrimination alterations to the scheme – S.62(1)

- the trustees or managers do have such power, but the procedure for making alterations is liable to be unduly complex or protracted – S.62(2)(a)

- the trustees do have such power, but the procedure for making alterations involves obtaining consents which cannot be obtained or which can be obtained only with undue delay or difficulty – S.62(2)(b).

The Explanatory Notes give an example at para 218 of the latter two situations **29.41** (i.e. where the trustees or managers do have power to make changes but the procedure is unduly complex or long-winded). The example is of a large scheme requiring consultation with all members before an amendment to the rules can be made. If such consultation is impracticable because some deferred members cannot be traced, then the trustees may make the necessary alterations to scheme rules relying on the power in S.68. (Note that there is apparently no obligation to achieve such compliance with the complex or protracted rules as is practicable. So, in the example given in the Explanatory Notes, the trustees would presumably not be obliged to undertake consultation with those members who could be traced.)

Non-discrimination alterations must be made by resolution – S.62(3), and may have retroactive effect – S.62(4).

Communications
29.42

As previously noted, the non-discrimination rule in S.61 does not apply to 'pension credit members' of an occupational pension scheme. These are those members who have rights under the scheme by virtue of another person having shared their personal rights, such as by way of a divorce settlement. However, the non-discrimination rule does apply to a disabled person who is a pension credit member as it applies in relation to a disabled person who is a 'deferred member' or 'pensioner member' of the scheme in respect of *communications* about the scheme – S.63(1). 'Communications' for these purposes include the provision of information and the operation of a dispute resolution procedure – S.63(2). The same exception regarding communications to disabled pension credit members is made in respect of S.120 EqA (jurisdiction of employment tribunals in work cases); S.126 (remedies in relation to occupational pension schemes); and para 19 of Schedule 8 ('relevant matters' and 'interested disabled persons' in relation to occupational pension schemes).

Employment service-providers
29.43

Sections 55–56 EqA make it unlawful to discriminate against, harass or victimise a person when providing an employment service, and place a duty on providers of employment services (referred to as 'employment service-providers') to make reasonable adjustments for disabled people. These sections of the EqA replace separate provisions in the old legislation covering vocational training, employment agencies and assisting persons to obtain employment with a single provision covering all these matters.

An employment service-provider 'must not discriminate against a person in the arrangements the service-provider makes for selecting persons to whom to provide, or to whom to offer to provide, the service; as to the terms on which the service-provider offers to provide the service to the person; [or] by not offering to provide the service to the person' – S.55(1). It is also unlawful for a service-provider to discriminate in the terms on which it provides the service to a person, by not providing the service to a person, by terminating the provision of the service to a person, or by subjecting a person to any other detriment – S.55(2). Furthermore, a service-provider must not victimise a person in any of the ways noted under S.55(1) and (2) above – S.55(4) and (5). Harassment by employment service-providers is prohibited by S.55(3), which makes it unlawful to harass a person who asks it to provide the service, or a person for whom it provides the service.

29.44 The application of S.55 depends on the provision of 'employment services'. This is not exhaustively defined by the Act, but S.56(2) states that it includes all of the following:

- the provision of vocational training – S.56(2)(a)

- the provision of vocational guidance – S.56(2)(b)

- making arrangements for the provision of vocational training or vocational guidance – S.56(2)(c)

- the provision of a service for finding employment for persons (e.g. the services provided by recruitment agencies, headhunters and Jobcentre Plus) – S.56(2)(d)

- the provision of a service for supplying employers with persons to do work – S.56(2)(e)

- the provision of a service in pursuance of arrangements made under S.2 of the Employment and Training Act 1973 (which allows the Secretary of State to make arrangements for the purpose of assisting persons to select, train for, obtain and retain employment or to obtain suitable employees) – S.56(2)(f)

- the provision of a service in pursuance of arrangements made or a direction given under S.10 of the 1973 Act (which allows the Secretary of State to make arrangements relating to the provision of careers services) – S.56(2)(g)

- the exercise of a function in pursuance of arrangements made under S.2(3) of the Enterprise and New Towns (Scotland) Act 1990 (which allows Scottish Enterprise and Highlands and Islands Enterprise to make arrangements for the purpose of assisting persons to train for employment, assisting persons to establish themselves as self-employed, and providing temporary employment for unemployed people) – S.56(2)(h)

- an assessment related to the conferment of a relevant qualification within the meaning of S.53 EqA (see under 'Qualifications bodies' above), except in so far as the assessment is by the qualifications body which confers the qualification – S.56(2)(i).

The reference to 'vocational training' here covers training for employment and work experience – S.56(6) EqA. So work placements and internships are potentially covered. Para 194 of the Explanatory Notes elaborates on what is intended to be covered by S.55, stating that it includes 'providing CV writing classes, English or Maths classes to help adults into work; training in IT/keyboard skills; or providing work placements'.

However, various forms of training and guidance are expressly excluded by **29.45** S.56(3)–(5). These are any training and guidance in relation to which another provision of Part 5 of the EqA (discrimination in work) applies; training and guidance to which the responsible body of a school has power to provide access; and training and guidance to which a university or other higher or further education institution has power to provide access. Accordingly, no complaint of discrimination in relation to work experience, work placements and internships arranged by a school, college or university can be brought in the employment tribunal. Such complaints must be brought under the education provisions in Part 6 of the EqA (consideration of which falls outside the scope of this Handbook).

Taken together, the above provisions cover a wide variety of organisations involved in employment-related activities. Employment agencies, employment businesses, careers guidance services and headhunters are all potentially covered. In addition, the EHRC Employment Code indicates that 'Jobcentre Plus, the Sector Skills Council and intermediary agencies that provide basic training and work experience opportunities such as the Adult Advancement and Careers Service and other schemes that assist people to find employment' are also within the scope of Ss.55 and 56 – see para 11.59. Note, though, that such organisations are only liable for discrimination in relation to the matters specifically set out by S.55 (see above). An organisation that provides some services falling within Ss.55 and 56, but also exercises functions not within Ss.55 and 56, will not be liable for discrimination with regard to those other functions. The EAT made this point in Igboaka v Royal College of Pathologists EAT 0036/09. It accepted that the Royal College of Pathologists occasionally made arrangements for vocational training that potentially fell within what was then S.13 RRA (now subsumed into S.55 EqA). However, the claimant's complaint related to another part of the RCP's functions; namely, its investigation of grievances he had raised. Thus the RCP was not open to the allegation that it had discriminated in the provision of vocational training and so no valid claim under old S.13 RRA could be made.

29.46 Reasonable adjustments

Employment service-providers are subject to a duty to make reasonable adjustments in respect of disabled people. The extent of the duty depends on the nature of the employment service at issue. S.55(6) EqA lays down the general rule that the duty to make reasonable adjustments applies to an employment service-provider. However, it goes on to state that the duty does not apply in relation to the provision of a 'vocational service'. Instead, S.55(7) stipulates that the general reasonable adjustments duty that is imposed on non-employment service-providers by S.29(7)(a) EqA also applies to a person concerned with the provision of vocational services. The two kinds of duty are slightly different in scope. The duty imposed by S.55(6) is the duty that applies in relation to 'work' in Part 5 of the Act, the detail of which is set out in Schedule 8. The duty imposed by S.29(7) is the one that applies in relation to 'services' generally in Part 3 of the Act, which is fleshed out by Schedule 2. We consider the extent of each kind of duty separately below.

For the purpose of this distinction, S.56(7) defines 'vocational services' by reference to the kinds of employment services listed in S.56(2) (noted above). The first four categories of employment service – namely, provision of vocational training, provision of vocational guidance, making arrangements for the provision of vocational training or vocational guidance, and provision of a service for finding employment for persons or assisting persons to obtain employment – are deemed to be 'vocational services'. However, 'vocational training' for these purposes only refers to training for employment (S.56(6)(a)) and not work experience (S.56(6)(b)). Finally, employment and career services provided under S.2 or S.10 of the Employment and Training Act 1973 are also vocational services in so far as they also come within those four categories of employment service.

29.47 The combined effect of these rather tortuous provisons is that:

- those providing a service for supplying employers with persons to do work; those providing employment or career services under S.2 or S.10 of the Employment and Training Act 1973; those exercising functions of Scottish Enterprise relating to employment; and those (other than qualifications bodies) making assessments related to the conferment of a relevant qualification within S.53 EqA are all employment service-providers. They are subject to the duty to make reasonable adjustments imposed by S.55(6) – see 'Employment service-providers generally' below

- those providing work experience are also employment service-providers, and are subject to the S.55(6) duty, but that duty applies in a modified way, elaborated by Schedule 8 – see 'Employment service-providers providing work experience' below

- those providing training for employment or vocational guidance; those making arrangements for the provision of training for employment or vocational guidance; and those providing a service for finding employment for persons or assisting persons to obtain employment, are vocational service-providers. They are subject to the S.29(7) EqA duty, which applies in relation to 'services' generally, under Part 3 of the Act, which is elaborated by Schedule 2 – see 'Vocational services' below.

The EHRC Employment Code appears a little confused on the reach of the reasonable adjustments duty in relation to employment service-providers. It states at para 11.57 that 'an employment service provider has a duty to make reasonable adjustments, except when providing a vocational service'. This is not strictly true. As noted above, a person concerned with the provision of vocational services is by virtue of S.55(7) also subject to a duty to make reasonable adjustments, only the duty in question is slightly different.

Note that S.55(7) goes on to state that, while the reasonable adjustments duty **29.48** on providers of vocational services is imposed under S.29(7) (contained in Part 3 of the Act), 'a failure to comply with that duty in relation to the provision of a vocational service is a contravention of this Part for the purposes of Part 9 (enforcement)'. Thus, remedies for breach of either duty are to be sought in the same way – namely, in the employment tribunal.

Employment service-providers generally. The reasonable adjustments duty **29.49** that applies to employment service-providers (except providers of vocational services) under S.55(6) is much the same as that which applies to employers. The duty is as set out in Ss.20–22 and, as it is a duty imposed by Part 5 of the Act, Schedule 8 applies to define the limits of the duty. Accordingly, the general principles regarding the duty to make reasonable adjustments, as described in Chapter 21, 'Failure to make reasonable adjustments', apply.

The scope of the duty on employment service-providers is, it seems, much wider than that imposed on employers and other individuals and organisations identified in Part 5. Schedule 8 sets out the manner in which the duty applies to each organisation and individual. So, for example, para 5 specifies that when considering to whom to offer employment, an employer owes the duty to job applicants and to potential applicants of whose interest it has been notified. With regard to other employment matters, such as terms of employment and dismissal, by contrast, the employer owes the duty to employees and job applicants. Similar specification is made in relation to barristers, office holders, partners in law firms, etc, by paras 6–19 of Schedule 8. However, no similar provision is made in relation to employment service-providers. Para 3 of Schedule 8 provides that employment service-providers owe their duty to an 'interested disabled person' in relation to the employment services they provide. Para 4 states that an 'interested disabled person' is a person defined according to paras 5–19, noted above. But none of these paragraphs defines who an

1027

'interested disabled person' is in relation to employment services. While para 16 defines an 'interested disabled person' in relation to the provision of work experience, which is one kind of employment service, it does not say anything about who an 'interested disabled person' is with regard to the provision of other kinds of employment service.

29.50 The implication is that employment service-providers owe a duty to make reasonable adjustments to the world at large, i.e. any disabled person who might seek to use the service, not just to those who have indicated that they may be interested in the service. The Explanatory Notes and the EHRC Employment Code support this view. Both refer to the duty on employment service-providers as an 'anticipatory' duty (see paras 188 and 11.53 respectively). Although they do not spell out what is meant by 'anticipatory', the same term is defined by the separate Code of Practice that applies in relation to the general duty on service-providers imposed by Part 3, the EHRC 'Code of Practice on Services, Public Functions and Associations' (2010). That Code indicates that an anticipatory duty requires 'consideration of, and action in relation to, barriers that impede people with one or more kinds of disability *prior to an individual disabled person seeking to use the service*' (our stress) – para 7.20. The 2010 Code goes on to note that 'service providers should therefore not wait until a disabled person wants to use a service that they provide before they give consideration to their duty to make reasonable adjustments', and that 'failure to anticipate the need for an adjustment may create additional expense, or render it too late to comply with the duty to make the adjustment' – para 7.21.

It is unfortunate that the broad impact of the duty on employment service-providers is not made express by the legislation. Its anticipatory nature is not specified, and must be inferred from the lack of any restriction on its scope in Schedule 8. However, the EHRC Employment Code is clear that this is the intention behind these provisions of the EqA, and so this is how they will be applied by courts and tribunals.

29.51 As for what the duty means in practice, its most widespread impact is likely to be on employment agencies, which provide 'a service for supplying employers with persons to do work' under S.56(2)(e) EqA. The anticipatory nature of the duty means that agencies ought to consider how accessible their services and premises are to disabled people. The Explanatory Notes give the following example: 'An agency advertises job vacancies on its website. It will need to have the website checked for accessibility and make reasonable changes to enable disabled people using a variety of access software to use it' – para 193.

29.52 **Employment service-providers providing work experience.** Work experience is treated as an employment service by virtue of S.56(2)(a) EqA, which covers 'vocational training'. 'Vocational training' is defined by S.56(6) as '(a) training for employment, or (b) work experience (including work experience the duration of which is not agreed until after it begins)'. S.56(7) includes 'vocational training' within the definition of vocational services, in relation to which the Part 3 reasonable adjustments duty applies, rather than the Part 5 duty (which applies in the context of 'work'). However, S.56(7) goes on to state that the S.56(6)(b) limb of vocational training is *not* treated as a vocational service. This means that the provision of work experience, as defined by S.56(6)(b), is subject to the S.55(6) duty to make reasonable adjustments (as discussed under 'Employment service-providers generally').

However, the application of the S.55(6) duty in these circumstances is circumscribed by Schedule 8 to the EqA, which provides detail on how and when the duty applies. Para 16 sets down two broad situations in which the duty has effects in relation to work experience. First, the duty applies when the employment service-provider is deciding to whom to offer to provide the work experience. In this situation, the service-provider owes the duty to make reasonable adjustments to a disabled person 'who is, or has notified [the service-provider] that the person may be, an applicant for the provision of the service'. Secondly, in relation to the provision of the service generally, the service-provider owes the duty to a person who applies to it for the provision of the service, and to a person to whom it provides the service.

There is also a restriction on the extent of the duty that is not available to **29.53** employment service-providers generally. Para 20(1) and (3) of Schedule 8 together provide that the service-provider is not obliged to make reasonable adjustments if it 'does not know, and could not reasonably be expected to know –

* in the case of an applicant or potential applicant, that an interested disabled person is or may be an applicant for the work in question;

* in any other case referred to in this Part of this Schedule, that an interested disabled person has a disability and is likely to be placed at the disadvantage referred to in the first, second or third requirement [of S.20 EqA]'.

Thus, there is an 'ignorance defence' available to a service-provider of work experience. This is the same defence available to employers and other persons and organisations subject to the duty to make reasonable adjustments under Schedule 8. For more detail, see Chapter 21, 'Failure to make reasonable adjustments'.

Vocational services. The cumulative effect of S.55(6) and (7) is that while **29.54** providers of vocational services are not subject to the same reasonable adjustments duty that applies to employers and employment service-providers generally, they are subject to a broadly similar duty that otherwise applies mainly to non-employment service-providers. This duty, which applies by virtue of S.29(7) in Part 3 of the Act (which is concerned with 'services and public functions') is different in small but potentially significant ways to the duty that applies to employers and others under Part 5 (which is concerned with 'work'). For instance, para 2(3) of Schedule 2 provides that where a physical feature of premises puts a disabled person, compared with non-disabled people, at a substantial disadvantage in relation to the provision of a service, the service-provider must take such steps as it is reasonable to have to take to avoid the disadvantage, or to adopt a reasonable alternative method of providing the service or exercising the function. This alternative method of alleviating the disadvantage is not part of the reasonable adjustments duty imposed on employers. Schedule 2 also places a restriction on the extent of the reasonable adjustments duty. Para 2(7) states that nothing in the duty, as it applies to service-providers, requires the service-provider to take a step 'which would fundamentally alter (a) the nature of the service, or (b) the nature of [the service-provider's] trade or profession'.

29.55 Local authorities

Section 58 EqA deals with the liability of a local authority for discrimination against its 'members' in relation to the carrying out of their official business. It extends protection previously found in the DDA to all the protected characteristics covered by the EqA.

'Local authority' is defined in S.59(2) as including county councils, district councils and parish councils in England, London borough councils, the Greater London Authority, county councils, community councils and county borough councils in Wales, and Scottish community councils and area councils constituted under S.2 of the Local Government etc (Scotland) Act 1994. However, a 'member' of a local authority is not defined other than in relation to the Greater London Authority, in respect of which a 'member' means the Mayor of London and those elected to the London Assembly – S.59(5). The EHRC Employment Code indicates that a local authority 'member' will usually mean an elected member of a local authority, such as a councillor (see para 11.69).

29.56 Section 58 provides that a local authority must not, in relation to a member's carrying out of official business:

- discriminate against or victimise the member in the way the authority affords the member access to opportunities for training or for receiving any other facility, or by not affording the member access to such opportunities – S.58(1)(a) and (3)(a)

- discriminate against or victimise the member by subjecting him or her to any other detriment – S.58(1)(b) and (3)(b)

- harass the member – S.58(2).

Thus, liability is restricted to discrimination against members in relation to the *carrying out of their official business*. There is no general prohibition on discrimination in the arrangements made for determining who should become a member of a local authority, in the terms of that membership or in respect of removal from membership.

Certain actions are excluded from the concept of 'detriment' referred to in **29.57** S.58(1)(b) and (3)(b) above. S.58(4)(a) and (b) states that a member's not being appointed or elected to an office of the authority or to one of its committees or sub-committees (or an office of such a committee) is not to be considered a detriment for this purpose. Nor, under S.58(4)(c) and (5), is the member's not being appointed or nominated in exercise of a power of the authority to appoint or make nominations for appointment to a body.

In common with all other bodies covered by the EqA, local authorities are obliged to make reasonable adjustments in respect of disabled people. The duty applies only in relation to the member's carrying out of offical business – para 18(1) Sch 8. So, as with the prohibition on discrimination, victimisation and harassment towards members, the local authority is only liable with regard to those who are actually members, not those interested in seeking to become members.

The second sub-paragraph of para 18 creates a power for the Government to **29.58** restrict the extent of the duty to make reasonable adjustments by way of regulations. Under this power, regulations may provide for certain provisions, criteria or practices, or physical features, to be deemed not to place a disabled person at a substantial disadvantage compared to non-disabled people. Regulations may also set down specific steps that it will always or never be deemed reasonable for the local authority to take to alleviate a substantial disadvantage. As at the date of writing, no such regulations have been issued. A similar power was available under S.15C(4) DDA but never exercised.

Landlords of premises occupied by employers **29.59**

As discussed in Chapter 21, 'Failure to make reasonable adjustments', under 'Altering physical features – listed premises and leases', making reasonable adjustments to physical features of premises may require the employer to seek consent from other individuals. Commonly, the landlord of premises rented by an employer to whom a duty to make reasonable adjustments applies will, under the terms of the lease, retain ultimate authority over whether physical alterations may be made. The procedure employers must follow to acquire consent to adjustments they are obliged to make where such adjustments are not permitted under the terms of the lease are set out in Chapter 21. Briefly, para 3 of Schedule 21 to the EqA provides that an employer may secure authority to make the alterations by writing to the landlord to seek consent. The landlord must not withhold the consent unreasonably, and may give consent subject to reasonable conditions.

1031

From the landlord's point of view, the key issues are what amounts to withholding consent 'unreasonably' for the purposes of para 3, and what sanctions may apply if para 3 is breached. As to the reasonableness of withholding consent, para 6 permits regulations to be made to define the circumstances in which a landlord is taken, for the purpose of Schedule 21, to have withheld consent, to have withheld consent reasonably, to have withheld consent unreasonably, and to have imposed reasonable or unreasonable conditions on consent that it has given. The Equality Act 2010 (Disability) Regulations 2010 SI 2010/2128 have been made under this power, and Regs 10–14 make provision for the matters mentioned by para 6 of Schedule 21. These obligations are considered in detail in Chapter 21, 'Failure to make reasonable adjustments', under 'Altering physical features – listed premises and leases', along with the remedies for breach of the landlord's duties, prescribed by para 5 of Schedule 21.

Part 6
Exceptions

30 General exceptions

Occupational requirements

National security

Charities

Provision of services to the public

Employment services

Insurance contracts

Statutory authority

Positive action

State immunity

Judicial proceedings immunity

In this chapter and in Chapter 31, 'Specific exceptions', we consider the various **30.1** exceptions to the principle of non-discrimination contained in the Equality Act 2010 (EqA). Such exceptions can be split into two categories. In this chapter we look at those that have more or less general application across all the protected characteristics. These include perhaps the most significant exception, 'occupational requirements', as well as exceptions covering national security; charities; the provision of services to the public; employment services; and statutory authority. In Chapter 31, we discuss those exceptions that relate to specific characteristics, such as age, religion or belief and sex.

In this chapter we also consider the limited ways in which the EqA allows an employer to engage in 'positive action' and briefly discuss state and judicial proceedings immunities. References in this chapter to the EHRC Employment Code are to the statutory Code of Practice on Discrimination in Employment published by the Equality and Human Rights Commission. Although not binding on tribunals, the provisions of the Code are highly influential and may be used as evidence in a tribunal claim.

Occupational requirements

30.2

All but one of the equality enactments that preceded the EqA provided for a general defence to a claim of discrimination where an employer could show that having or not having a protected characteristic, or a related characteristic, was an unavoidable requirement for a particular job – an 'occupational requirement'. Such a requirement might apply if, for example, a black actor is required for a theatrical role to ensure that the performance is authentic. This defence is now contained in Schedule 9 to the EqA (which is given effect by S.83(11)) and covers all characteristics protected by the Act.

Under the previous equality enactments, the occupational requirement exception applied in different ways to different strands of discrimination. Discrimination on the ground of race, religion or belief, sexual orientation or age could be lawful if a general test of 'genuine and determining' occupational requirement (GOR) was satisfied. With regard to sex, gender reassignment, colour and nationality, instead of a general defence, specific differences of treatment were permitted as 'genuine occupational qualifications' (GOQ) – for example, where the authenticity of a dramatic performance called for a person of a particular race, or where a job involving intimate personal contact called for a person of a particular gender. There was no general or specific exception in respect of disability, because the Disability Discrimination Act 1995 (DDA) did not protect non-disabled people: if a disabled person were selected for employment specifically because of his or her disability, a non-disabled person would have no legal remedy for the less favourable treatment that that would involve.

30.3 Under the EqA a general occupational requirement defence applies to all protected characteristics, including disability. The specific GOQs that applied under the Sex Discrimination Act 1975 (SDA) and the Race Relations Act 1976 (RRA) no longer exist, as the new general exception contained in Schedule 9 to the EqA is intended to provide a defence in all circumstances that were previously covered by a GOQ – see below under 'Comparison of new ORs with old GOQs'.

30.4 New statutory wording

Paragraph 1(1) of Schedule 9 states that 'a person (A) does not contravene a provision mentioned in sub-paragraph (2) by applying in relation to work a requirement to have a particular protected characteristic, if A shows that, having regard to the nature or context of the work:

(a) it is an occupational requirement,

(b) the application of the requirement is a proportionate means of achieving a legitimate aim, and

(c) the person to whom A applies the requirement does not meet it (or A has reasonable grounds for not being satisfied that the person meets it)'.

Sub-paragraph (2) lists the sections that are in effect disapplied when an occupational requirement is established. We consider the forms of discrimination that this may permit under 'Discrimination permitted by occupational requirement' below.

General considerations. Several elements of the above definition need **30.5** considering. First, the occupational requirement (OR) must relate to the 'nature or context' of the work. This is no different to the requirement that applied under the separate equality enactments, albeit that there it was expressed rather more fully, e.g. 'having regard to the nature of the employment or the context in which it is carried out' (S.4A(1) RRA). The shorter form of words should import no practical difference – what is required is that a court or tribunal consider whether the nature of the work is such that having, or not having, a particular protected characteristic can be deemed an occupational requirement.

Secondly, whatever requirement is applied, it must be established that the person in question does not meet it, or that the employer has reasonable grounds for not being satisfied that the person meets it. This repeats a requirement common to the GOR defences in the separate equality enactments. No case law has turned on this criterion, and it is not dwelt on by the Explanatory Notes that accompanied the EqA or the EHRC Employment Code, so it must be thought to be a straightforward and uncontroversial test. Para 1(4) provides that the words in brackets in para 1(1)(c) are to be ignored in respect of ORs based on sex. This qualification has the common-sense effect that it is not for the employer to be 'satisfied' that a person is a man or a woman. The person either is or is not. In contrast, it is open to an employer who applies a religious OR, for example, to show that it has cause not to be satisfied that an applicant adheres to the religion or belief that he or she claims.

Dropping of 'genuine and determining' criteria. Probably the most important **30.6** elements of the defence are paras (a) and (b) – the requirement that an applicant or employee have a particular protected characteristic must be an 'occupational requirement', and the application of that requirement must be a proportionate means of achieving a legitimate aim. With regard to 'occupational requirement', as noted above, the corresponding phrase in the previous equality enactments was 'genuine and determining occupational requirement' (GOR) – see, for example, S.4A(2)(a) RRA and Reg 7(2)(a) of the Employment Equality (Religion or Belief) Regulations 2003 SI 2003/1660. This is also the wording of the relevant European legislation. Member States are permitted to legislate for 'genuine and determining occupational requirements' in respect of all the protected characteristics now covered by the EqA – see Article 4 of the EU Race Equality Directive (No.2000/43), Article 4 of the EU Equal Treatment Framework Directive (No.2000/78) and Article 14(2) of the recast EU Equal Treatment Directive (No.2006/54). The dropping of the words 'genuine and determining' in the EqA is therefore somewhat surprising. It might have been thought that, given that the stated purpose of the EqA was to consolidate and harmonise, unnecessary changes of wording were to be avoided wherever possible since they would inevitably lead to speculation that the law may have been substantively changed.

At first glance, having to show an 'occupational requirement' would appear to be less onerous than having to show a 'genuine and determining occupational requirement'. The loss of 'genuine' on its own would be unlikely to make any difference – tribunals do not need express direction from statute to reject sham reasons. But the criterion that a GOR be 'determinative' sets the bar emphatically high, at least as a matter of natural language. However, the Government has given assurances that the change in wording is not significant and that the exception is not out of step with EU law. Baroness Thornton, speaking on the Government's behalf at the Equality Bill's Report Stage in the House of Lords, noted that the words 'genuine and determining' did not add anything to the word 'requirement' and so were unnecessary. In other words, 'if a requirement is not genuine, the facts will show that. If it is not determining, by definition it cannot be a requirement.' She also noted that Member States are not required to copy the wording of Directives that they are obliged to implement: they only have to achieve the intended result. Significantly, the Explanatory Notes state that an OR must be 'crucial to the post, and not merely one of several important factors', suggesting that the 'determining' requirement still applies even without the statute saying so. (This is the same elaboration that was used to explain the 'determinative' requirement by the then Department of Trade and Industry in its guidance on the GOR defence as it applied in relation to religion or belief.)

30.7 Nevertheless, it is worth noting that the EHRC Employment Code simply states: 'The requirement must not be a sham or pretext and there must be a link between the requirement and the job' (para 13.7). Arguably, this represents a significantly lower hurdle for employers than the guidance in the draft version of the Code that was previously put out for consultation, which, reflecting the Explanatory Notes, stated that an OR must be 'crucial' to the post. It should, however, be remembered that tribunals are merely required to take the Code into account when interpreting the EqA, but are obliged to interpret the Act's provisions consistently with EU law. In our view, therefore, the narrower construction required by the EU Directives would trump the above extract from the Code.

30.8 **'Proportionate means of achieving a legitimate aim'.** Having established that an occupational requirement relates to the nature or context of the work in question, the employer must then show that 'the application of the requirement is a proportionate means of achieving a legitimate aim' – para 1(1)(b). Although the GOR defence that previously existed in relation to race, age, sexual orientation and religion or belief demanded that the application of the requirement be proportionate, it made no reference to a 'legitimate aim', which is a concept more readily identified in the realm of objectively justifying indirect discrimination. While the new wording of the OR defence reflects the language of the Directives in this regard, as previously stated it does so without explicitly adopting the 'genuine and determining' formulation attached to the requirement – although, as noted above, the Government's view appears to be that the 'determining' requirement still applies.

The Explanatory Notes support the interpretation of the OR exception along the same lines as the justification defence. The examples it gives of where an OR might apply include requiring a black man to play the part of Othello, and considerations of privacy or decency requiring a public changing room or lavatory attendant to be of the same sex as those using the facilities. These are both, conceivably, 'determining' or (adopting the test set out in the Explanatory Notes) 'crucial' requirements for the post in question. However, the Explanatory Notes also give the example of an organisation for deaf people, which might legitimately employ a deaf person who uses British Sign Language to work as a counsellor to other deaf people whose first or preferred language is BSL. If it is correct that an OR still needs to be determining despite the absence of any express requirement to that effect in the EqA, it is difficult to square that need with this example of permissible discrimination. It surely cannot be said that deafness is a determinative requirement for the role, when a non-deaf person trained in BSL might do the job just as well. Even the less stringent standard of objective justification would be difficult to satisfy here – the discriminatory effect of reserving a job to a deaf person seems disproportionate to the legitimate aim of providing effective counselling services to deaf people. This example suggests that where users would prefer to receive a service from someone with the same protected characteristic, then that will support an OR defence, but this is arguably a lower standard than 'crucial'.

The Explanatory Notes also give the example of unemployed Muslim women **30.9** who might not take advantage of the services of an outreach worker to help them find employment if they were provided by a man. If these examples are accepted, the principle could extend very far indeed – community cohesion jobs might be restricted to those with the same ethnicity as the community in which they will be working; marriage guidance posts might be reserved to married people; and so on.

The straight wording of the EqA and the examples given in the Explanatory Notes therefore suggest a broad interpretation of the OR exception, which the Government apparently did not intend. That said, the broad interpretation of the OR defence is reflected in the EHRC Employment Code. Although the Code sets out very few examples of ORs, it does state that 'a unisex gym could rely on an occupational requirement to employ a changing room attendant of the same sex as the users of that room. Similarly, a women's refuge which lawfully provides services to women only can apply a requirement for all members of its staff to be women' (para 13.8). That much would seem to reflect the position under the SDA, but at para 13.9 the Code provides a further example which again implies that the preference of service users for a person to have a protected characteristic could give rise to an occupational requirement:

'A local council decides to set up a health project which would encourage older people from the Somali community to make more use of health services. The council wants to recruit a person of Somali origin for the post because it involves visiting elderly people in their homes and it is necessary for the post-holder to have a good knowledge of the culture and language of the potential clients. The council does not have a Somali worker already in post who could take on the new duties. They could rely on the occupational requirement exception to recruit a health worker of Somali origin' – para 13.9.

30.10 As with the Explanatory Notes, the above example from the Code is open to criticism, because the requirement of the job is to 'have a good knowledge of the culture and language of elderly people in the Somali community' rather than to be 'a person of Somali origin'. While there will undoubtedly be a correlation between people having the requisite knowledge and being of Somali origin, the relationship between the two is not axiomatic: there could well be people with that knowledge who are not of Somali origin, and applying the OR exception to this scenario would exclude such people.

30.11 **Impact of EU law.** Employers will have to tread carefully when seeking to rely on the OR provisions. They would be well advised not to take the wording of the statute and the examples given in the Explanatory Notes and Code of Practice at face value, as together they give the impression that para 1 of Schedule 9 allows employers to discriminate on the basis of something much less than a 'determining' or 'crucial' requirement. Anything perceived as too broad will be susceptible to a challenge that it is in breach of the narrow exceptions permitted under the relevant EU Directives, and tribunals can be expected to construe Schedule 9 in the light of any relevant mandatory provisions of EU law.

However, although it was not noted in the Parliamentary debates, nor in the Explanatory Notes or EHRC Employment Code, EU law may itself be becoming less stringent on the question of what may be accepted as a GOR. In Wolf v Stadt Frankfurt am Main 2010 IRLR 244, ECJ, the European Court of Justice held that imposing an age limit on applications to join the fire service was defensible under Article 4(1) of the EU Equal Treatment Framework Directive (No.2000/78) ('the Framework Directive'). The requirement was justified on the basis that frontline work in the fire service requires a high level of physical capacity, which inevitably declines with age. The ECJ accepted that it was proportionate for the age limit to take into account not only the need for new recruits to be able to meet the physical demands of the job, but also the need for them to be able to offer a reasonable length of service in frontline jobs. In essence, the ECJ allowed the employer to rely on age as an indicator of physical fitness. This was a surprising result. Given that under the Framework Directive age discrimination can be objectively justified in the same way as indirect discrimination, there was really no need to resort to the GOR defence, which is clearly intended to be preserved for exceptional cases – recital 23 of the Preamble to the Directive notes that it should be used in 'very limited circumstances'. If the same reasoning were applied to other strands of discrimination, a GOR might permit the application of a lower age limit to women, or even the exclusion of women from the fire service altogether, on the ground that they are not as physically strong as men.

However, there are strong grounds for thinking that the Wolf decision is of no **30.12** application in the United Kingdom. Although it was decided by reference to Article 4(1), which provides the underlying basis for the GOR defence in the EqA, that Article simply provides that Member States *may*, not must, make provision allowing for an occupational requirement defence in respect of a characteristic which is *related to* one of the protected grounds (under the Framework Directive these are age, religion or belief, sexual orientation and disability). That is the furthest possible derogation from the principle of non-discrimination in Article 2(1). The UK Government, however, by enacting the GOR defence in the EqA, has stipulated that the defence can only apply where the characteristic *is* the protected ground. This, in effect, offers greater protection for employees than required by the Directive, something which is permitted by EU law.

Comparison of new ORs with old GOQs. If the new OR exception is to **30.13** adequately consolidate the old GOR and GOQ defences, as the Government maintains that it does, the across-the-board standard must be levelled down to the lowest that these separate defences permitted. It is therefore worth noting what the old GOQs were, as this will give some indication of what is intended to be permitted under the new OR defence.

In relation to sex discrimination, S.7 SDA made exceptions where:

- the essential nature of the job called for a man or woman for reasons of physiology, other than physical strength or stamina, or for reasons of authenticity in dramatic performances

- the preservation of decency or privacy was at issue, because the work involved physical contact, or was done in sanitary facilities or in the presence of persons in a state of undress

- the work was to be done in a private home with a degree of physical or social contact, or knowledge of intimate details of a person's life, where objection might reasonably be taken to the work being done by a person of the opposite sex

- the nature or location of the establishment at which the work was to be done required the worker to live on the premises, and there were no appropriately segregated sleeping and sanitary facilities

- the work was to be done at a men-only (or women-only) hospital, prison or other establishment for persons requiring special care, supervision or attention

- the work was the provision of personal services promoting welfare or education, which could most effectively be provided by a person of a particular sex

- the work was likely to involve the performance of duties outside the United Kingdom in a country whose law or customs were such that the duties could only effectively be performed by a man

- the job was one of two to be held by a couple who were married or in a civil partnership.

Section 7B SDA applied a similar but not quite so extensive list of GOQs to gender reassignment discrimination.

30.14 In relation to discrimination on the ground of colour or nationality, GOQs under S.5 RRA excused discrimination where a person of a particular racial group was required for the purpose of authenticity in a dramatic performance, an artistic work or in a public restaurant, or for the purpose of providing personal welfare services.

Given the Government's insistence that the old GOQs have been consolidated into the general OR defence, all these reasons should still be potentially valid grounds for an exemption under the EqA. Nonetheless, employers who relied on specific GOQs under the old statutes should review their reasons for doing so to ensure they are compliant with the new provisions. In particular, employers should consider whether the requirement for a person with a particular protected characteristic is a proportionate means of achieving a legitimate aim, in accordance with the new general test. Although the old GOQs are intended to be preserved under Schedule 9, tribunals will still expect employers to show that they have gone through the process of considering whether there is a legitimate aim behind any discriminatory practices, and whether the discriminatory effect is minimised so as to ensure that the means of achieving that aim are proportionate.

30.15 **Discrimination permitted by occupational requirement**
The employment provisions listed in para 1(2) of Schedule 9 that are disapplied when an OR is made out are:

- S.39(1)(a) – discrimination in the arrangements the employer makes for determining who shall be offered employment

- S.39(1)(c) – discrimination by not offering employment

1042

- S.39(2)(b) – discrimination in the way the employer affords access, or does not afford access, to opportunities for promotion, transfer or training or for receiving any other benefit, facility or service

- S.39(2)(c) – discrimination by dismissal.

However, by virtue of para 6(5) of Schedule 9, references to S.39(2)(b) are read as if the words 'or for receiving any other benefit, facility or service' are omitted. Therefore, only discrimination in relation to promotion, transfer or training is permitted under that subsection. The OR defence does not cover discrimination in respect of the way an employer affords or does not afford access to the receipt of other benefits, facilities or services.

The remaining forms of discrimination prohibited by S.39 – discrimination in **30.16** the terms on which employment is offered (S.39(1)(b)), in the terms on which the employment is conducted (S.39(2)(a)), or by way of any other detriment (S.39(2)(d)) – cannot be defended on the basis of an occupational requirement. Nor can any form of prohibited conduct in employment that does not fall within S.39 – namely, victimisation and harassment.

The scope of S.39 is discussed in detail in Chapter 24, 'Recruitment'; Chapter 25, 'Discrimination during employment'; Chapter 26, 'Dismissal'; and Chapter 27, 'Post-employment discrimination'.

Only direct discrimination covered by OR defence. Paragraph 6 of Schedule **30.17** 9 provides that any reference to a contravention of S.39 is a reference to a contravention by virtue of S.13, which defines direct discrimination (see Chapter 15, 'Direct discrimination'). So, other forms of employment-related discrimination – indirect discrimination and discrimination arising from disability – are not covered by the OR exception.

This marks a change from the position under the antecedent equality enactments in that indirect discrimination *was* previously covered by the GOR exceptions. An occupational requirement could, therefore, be used to defend a claim of indirect discrimination under the now-repealed legislation. However, indirect discrimination has always been capable of being objectively justified (see Chapter 17, 'Indirect discrimination: objective justification') and as objective justification has generally been construed more generously to the employer than the GOR defence, this meant that the GOR was effectively otiose in relation to indirect discrimination. Accordingly, the fact that the new OR exception cannot be relied upon to excuse indirect discrimination has had little impact, if any, on the ability of an employer to defend a claim of indirect discrimination.

Application to partnerships, personal and public offices, etc. Paragraph 1(2) **30.18** of Schedule 9 – see above – also covers the corresponding provisions that apply in relation to partnerships (S.44(1)(a) and (c) and (2)(b) and (c)); limited liability partnerships (S.45(1)(a) and (c) and (2)(b) and (c)); personal offices (S.49(3)(a) and (c) and (6)(b) and (c)); and public offices (S.50(3)(a) and (c) and (6)(b) and (c)). So, discriminatory decisions concerning to whom a partnership or personal or public office should be offered; the arrangements for making that decision; access to promotion, training or transfer in the context of a partnership or personal or public office; and expulsion from a partnership or termination of an appointment, will not be unlawful where an OR applies. The same qualifications noted above in relation to employment apply to these categories as well, so that discrimination in relation to 'any other benefit, facility or service' is not permissible under an OR, and nor is indirect discrimination, discrimination arising from disability, victimisation or harassment.

The OR exception is also available to individuals who have responsibility for making recommendations for, or giving approval to appointments to, public offices (S.51(1)) – para 1(2)(g), Sch 9. The OR may apply in the arrangements the person makes for deciding who to recommend or approve for appointment, in not recommending a person or making a negative recommendation, or in not approving a person's appointment.

30.19 **Contract workers.** With regard to contract workers, an OR may excuse discrimination that manifests itself in a principal 'not allowing the worker to do, or continue to do, the work' (S.41(1)(b)) – para 1(2)(b), Sch 9. So, a refusal to take on a proposed contract worker, or the termination of an existing worker's contract, may attract the OR defence. However, the OR defence will not apply to any of the other forms of discrimination from which contract workers are protected, such as discrimination in the terms of work, in access to opportunities for receiving a benefit, facility or service, or by way of any other detriment. This reflects the application of the OR defence in relation to employment (see above) and is consistent with the position under the antecedent equality enactments, which permitted discrimination that consisted of refusing to offer or terminating a contract to do work, but did not allow any such discrimination in the terms on which such work was done.

30.20 **Application to specific protected characteristics**
The OR defence covers all of the protected characteristics listed in S.4, including pregnancy and maternity discrimination and discrimination related to marriage or civil partnership status (neither of which were covered by the GOQ defence in the SDA) and disability discrimination. However, its application in respect of three characteristics – sex, age and disability – warrants special mention.

30.21 **Application to sex.** The new OR defence maintains one important difference between the old GOR and GOQ defences with regard to the protected characteristics of sex. The GOQ provisions that applied to sex, gender reassignment, colour and nationality did not cover dismissal, expulsion from a partnership, termination of appointment to an office or termination of a contract working arrangement. The status quo has been preserved in relation to sex – para 6(6) and (7) of Schedule 9 provides that an OR based on sex will not be valid to justify a discriminatory dismissal, termination, etc. However, discriminatory dismissals, terminations, etc, based on gender reassignment, colour and nationality are now subject to the OR exception.

Application to age. As explained in Chapter 5, 'Age', under 'Protection under the Equality Act – justifying direct discrimination', direct discrimination on the ground of age can be justified as a proportionate means of achieving a legitimate aim – see S.13(2) EqA. Given this, it is hard to imagine the circumstances in which an employer would be better served by relying on the OR defence than by seeking to justify the discrimination. In either instance, the employer would need to show that applying an age requirement was a proportionate means of achieving a legitimate aim, but the OR defence is more narrowly construed, in that an employer must also show that, having regard to the nature and context of the work, having the protected characteristic in question is an occupational requirement. **30.22**

Application to disability. A significant change introduced by the EqA was the extension of the OR exception to cover disability discrimination: previously, the DDA made no allowance for genuine occupational requirements or qualifications. This was because, under that Act, a non-disabled person could not claim discrimination if a disabled person were treated more favourably, as that Act only protected those who could establish that they had a disability. The same is true under the EqA, in that S.13(3) provides that an employer does not discriminate against a non-disabled person only because it treats or would treat disabled persons more favourably than it treats the non-disabled person. But the definition of direct discrimination itself is wide enough to allow anyone, disabled or not, to claim to have been treated less favourably 'because of' disability. This means that employers who discriminate in favour of disabled people, for whatever reason, may need to rely on an OR defence to avoid claims of direct discrimination. Of course, because of S.13(3), the OR defence is effectively otiose in relation to more favourable treatment of disabled people by comparison with non-disabled people. However, it might still have a role to play where an employer has good reasons for restricting employment to persons with a particular disability. The employer would then be able to rely on the defence in relation to a claim of discrimination brought by a person with a *different* disability. **30.23**

National security **30.24**

The exception for discriminatory acts done on the ground of national security is in very broad terms. S.192 EqA states simply: 'A person does not contravene this Act only by doing, for the purpose of safeguarding national security, anything it is proportionate to do for that purpose.' This looks, at first glance, like a very wide-ranging exception. However, it is not new, as the corresponding exceptions under the previous equality enactments were in similarly broad terms. For example, S.42 RRA, which was typical, exempted any act 'done for the purpose of safeguarding national security if the doing of the act was justified by that purpose'. Thus, except for a change of terminology, the national security exemption under the EqA is much the same as it was under the previous enactments.

With regard to the proportionality aspect of the test, we do not consider that the test of 'proportionate for that purpose' is any different from the previous test of 'justified by that purpose'. The notion of 'proportionality', discussed in detail in Chapter 17, 'Indirect discrimination: objective justification', carries the implication that the employer or other responsible person must strive to minimise the discrimination when discrimination is unavoidable – evidence that a less discriminatory measure could just as effectively have been adopted will undermine proportionality. Although there was no illuminating case law on the scope of the previous national security defence, there is no reason to think that the previous test of justification was any different – a measure that is more discriminatory than necessary can hardly be said to be justified.

30.25 **Armed forces**

As explained in Chapter 28, 'Liability of employers, employees and agents', under 'Who is protected? – armed forces', the protection from discrimination generally applies to those serving in the armed forces. However, given the need for the armed forces to maintain combat effectiveness, the EqA allows for various exceptions in relation to age, disability and sex.

With regard to age and disability, para 4(3) of Schedule 9 states that 'this Part of this Act, so far as relating to age or disability, does not apply to service in the armed forces; and section 55, so far as relating to disability, does not apply to work experience in the armed forces'. Thus, no complaint of age discrimination or disability discrimination may be brought in respect of service in the armed forces. This was equally the case under the DDA and the Employment Equality (Age) Regulations 2006 SI 2006/1031. (Note that on a literal interpretation of para 4(3), 'this Part of this Act' refers to the part of Schedule 9 in which those provisions appear. This would make no sense, as those paragraphs would then purport to exempt contraventions of the exceptions. Schedule 9 is given effect by S.83 EqA. S.83(1) states that the section applies 'for the purposes of this Part' and S.83(11) provides that 'Schedule 9 (exceptions) shall have effect'. It is therefore possible to read Schedule 9 as if it were within Part 5 of the Act, so that references to 'this Part' can be taken as references to Part 5, giving sense to the paragraphs noted above and achieving the same result as the exceptions under the DDA and the Age Regulations. However, we are not aware of any accepted rule of statutory interpretation to this effect.)

The armed forces exception in relation to sex discrimination is more narrowly **30.26** drawn than the exception in relation to age and disability. It is also more narrowly drawn than the exception previously laid down in the SDA. S.85(4) SDA stated that 'nothing in [the SDA] shall render unlawful an act done for the purpose of ensuring the combat effectiveness of the armed forces'. This exception allowed the armed forces a wide margin of discretion in designating practices that would otherwise be unlawful as being directed towards the purpose of ensuring combat effectiveness. The corresponding exception in the EqA, set out at para 4(1) and (2) of Schedule 9, is somewhat more restrictive. Para 4(1) states that 'a person does not contravene S.39(1)(a) or (c) or (2)(b) by applying in relation to service in the armed forces a relevant requirement if the person shows that the application is a proportionate means of ensuring the combat effectiveness of the armed forces'. Para 4(2) goes on to provide that a 'relevant requirement' is 'a requirement to be a man, [or] a requirement not to be a transsexual person'.

The restrictive nature of these provisions compared to S.85(4) SDA manifests itself in a number of ways. First, while the broad drafting of the previous provision would have permitted any sex-related requirement to be applied in the name of combat effectiveness, para 4 applies only to requirements that a person be a man or that a person not be a transsexual person. Secondly, instead of laying down a general exception from the principle of non-discrimination because of sex, para 4 only disapplies S.39(1)(a) or (c) or (2)(b) where combat effectiveness is at issue. These are the prohibitions on discrimination in the arrangements an employer makes for deciding to whom to offer employment, by not offering employment, and in the way the employer affords access, or does not afford access, to opportunities for promotion, transfer or training. So, discrimination in the terms on which employment is offered, the terms of employment or by way of dismissal or any other detriment under S.39(1)(b) and (2)(a), (c) and (d) are no longer covered by the armed forces exception. Finally, for the exception to apply, it must be shown that the relevant requirement at issue is 'a proportionate means of ensuring the combat effectiveness of the armed forces'. No such proportionality qualification applied under the equivalent provision in the SDA. Thus, the armed forces are afforded a much narrower margin of discretion in deciding what measure of discrimination is unavoidable.

Charities

30.27

Charities benefit from a general exemption under S.193 EqA, which permits them to restrict the benefits they provide to people sharing a certain protected characteristic, so long as the charitable instrument allows this and the provision of benefits in this way is either a proportionate means of achieving a legitimate aim, or aims to prevent or compensate for a disadvantage linked to the protected

1047

characteristic – S.193(1) and (2). This exemption does not extend to benefits consisting of employment, contract work or vocational training, except where the protected characteristic is disability – S.193(9) and (10).

The exemption in S.193(1) and (2) does not permit charities to discriminate on the ground of colour – S.193(4). Thus, where a charitable instrument enables the provision of benefits to a class defined by reference to colour, that instrument will have effect as if that limitation were not there. So, for example, if a charitable bequest was made to provide employment assistance to white deaf people, such assistance would have to be made available to all deaf people.

30.28 Section 193(3) makes specific exception for supported employment aimed at disabled people. It provides that 'it is not a contravention of this Act for a person who provides supported employment to treat persons who have the same disability or a disability of a prescribed description more favourably than those who do not have that disability or a disability of such a description in providing such employment'. It goes on to provide that a Minister of the Crown may lawfully agree to arrangements for the provision of supported employment which will, or may, have that effect. This is to allow, for example, a charity which supports people with a particular disability to give preference to people with that disability; otherwise it would be unlawfully discriminating against people with a different disability. The Explanatory Notes state, by way of example, that 'it is lawful for the RNIB to employ, or provide special facilities for, visually impaired people in preference to other disabled people' (para 611).

30.29 Provision of services to the public

The EqA covers more than just discrimination in employment. Among other things, it also applies, by virtue of Part 3, to discrimination in the provision of goods, facilities and services. The boundary between the two areas may be blurred when an employer who is in the business of providing services to the public discriminates in the way it makes those same services available to its employees. To ensure that any claim is brought under the correct provision of the Act, para 19 of Schedule 9 lays down an exception to the prohibition on discrimination in employment where the discrimination ought more properly to be dealt with under Part 3. Para 19(1) provides that 'A does not contravene a provision mentioned in sub-paragraph (2) in relation to the provision of a benefit, facility or service to B if A is concerned with the provision (for payment or not) of a benefit, facility or service of the same description to the public'. The provisions listed at para 19(2) are S.39(2) and (4) (discrimination and victimisation in employment); S.41(1) and (3) (discrimination and victimisation against a contract worker); Ss.44(2) and (6) and 45(2) and (6) (discrimination and victimisation against partners and limited liability partners); and Ss.49(6) and (8) and 50(6), (7), (9) and (10) (discrimination and victimisation against personal and public office holders).

There are, however, various circumstances in which a complaint of discrimination in access to benefits, facilities or services that the employer also provides to the public may still be brought under the 'work' provisions contained in Part 5 of the Act. A complaint of discrimination in employment (or contract work, partnership, etc) may be made if there is a material difference between the way in which the benefit, facility or service is offered to employees, contract workers, partners, etc, and the way it is offered to the public. Para 19(3)(a) states that the exception in para 19(1) will not apply if 'the provision by A to the public differs in a material respect from the provision by A to comparable persons'. 'Comparable persons' in this regard means, as appropriate, other employees, other contract workers supplied to the same principal, other partners of the same firm, other members of the limited liability partnership, or other persons holding offices or posts not materially different to that held by B – para 19(4). The Explanatory Notes illustrate the difference thus:

- 'if an employee of a car hire company is denied the hire of one of its cars (on the same terms available to the general public) because he is black, the employee must claim under the "services" section of the Act in the county court, rather than through an employment tribunal under the "work" provisions of the Act'

- 'if the same employee's employment contract provides that he is allowed to hire the company's cars at a discount (which members of the public would not get), but the employee is refused the discount when he goes to hire one of the firm's cars because he is a Muslim, then the employee would be able to make a discrimination claim under [Part 5]' – para 860.

30.30 There are two other situations where discrimination in access to benefits, facilities or services that are also provided to the public may give rise to a complaint of discrimination in employment, despite the exception in para 19(1) of Schedule 9. The first is where the provision of the benefit, facility or service to B (i.e. the employee, contract worker, etc) is 'regulated by B's terms' – para 19(3)(b). 'Terms', for this purpose, means terms of employment, terms on which B is allowed to do contract work, terms on which B has partnership or membership of an LLP, or terms of B's appointment to an office, as appropriate – para 19(5). Thus, where access to the benefit, facility or service is a contractual matter, complaints of discrimination may be made under the work provisions of the Act. The second is where 'the benefit, facility or service relates to training' – para 19(3)(c).

These provisions differ in two minor respects from those that applied under the antecedent discrimination enactments. First, the equivalent exceptions in those enactments did not extend to partnerships or limited liability partnerships. Previously, any complaint by a partner or member about the way in which the partnership or LLP afforded him or her benefits, which it also provided to the public, could always be brought in the employment tribunal. Now, such complaints may only be brought in an employment tribunal if one of the exceptions to the exemption noted above is made out. Secondly, with regard to contract workers, the equality enactments did not carve out benefits, facilities or services contained in the contract worker's terms, or those relating to training, for special treatment, as para 19(3)(b) and (c) now does.

30.31 Employment services

Section 55 of the Equality Act 2010 outlaws discrimination by 'employment service providers'. These are widely defined by S.56 to include, among others, those who provide vocational training or guidance (such as work experience), those who make arrangements for the same, and those who provide services for finding people employment, or for supplying employers with people to do work. Para 5 of Schedule 9 sets down a number of exceptions that make it lawful for such service providers to discriminate in the provision of their services in certain circumstances.

Paragraph 5(1) states that 'a person (A) does not does not contravene S.55(1) or (2) [discrimination in arrangements for selection, terms on which a service is offered, not providing a service, etc] if A shows that A's treatment of another person relates only to work the offer of which could be refused to that person in reliance on paragraph 1, 2, 3 or 4'. Para 5(2) goes on to provide that the same exception applies in relation to A's treatment of another person relating to training for work of a description mentioned in para 5(1). Paras 1–4 mentioned here cover four exceptions: the 'occupational requirements' exception (see 'Occupational requirements' above); the organised religion and religious ethos exceptions (see Chapter 31, 'Specific exceptions' under 'Religion or belief exceptions') and the armed forces exception (see 'National security – armed forces' above). Accordingly, a service provider has a defence to a charge of discrimination if one of the exceptions mentioned here applies to the work in relation to which the service was or would have been offered.

30.32 The service provider also has a defence if he or she relies on an assurance given by the person who has the power to offer the work in question that such an exception applies. In this regard, para 5(3)(a) of Schedule 9 provides that there is no contravention of S.55(1) or (2) where A acts in reliance on a statement made to him or her by a person with the power to offer the work in question to the effect that, by virtue of para 5(1) or (2), A's action would be lawful. However, it must have been reasonable for the service provider to rely on this statement – para 5(3)(b). It would therefore be open to a tribunal to refuse to apply the exception if the service provider wilfully ignored unlawful discrimination. Para 5(4) and (5) goes on to provide that knowingly or recklessly making a materially false or misleading statement to a service provider is a criminal offence, punishable on summary conviction by a fine of up to £5,000.

Insurance contracts

It is fairly uncontroversial to state that a certain amount of gender discrimination is acceptable where it is based on life expectancy and other factors that demonstrably differ as between the sexes. Accordingly, S.45 SDA made special provision in respect of insurance and other matters, which applied to employment as well as to the provision of goods and services. Para 20 of Schedule 9 to the EqA makes the same provision with the same effect. Para 20(1) states that 'it is not a contravention of this Part of this Act, so far as relating to relevant discrimination, to do anything in relation to an annuity, life insurance policy, accident insurance policy or similar matter involving the assessment of risk if (a) that thing is done by reference to actuarial or other data from a source on which it is reasonable to rely, and (b) it is reasonable to do it'. 'Relevant discrimination', for this purpose, is defined by para 20(2) as gender reassignment discrimination, marriage and civil partnership discrimination, pregnancy and maternity discrimination and sex discrimination. The effect of these provisions, as noted by the Explanatory Notes, is that the employer may, for example, legitimately provide for payments of premiums that differ for men and women, so long as this is reasonable in the light of actuarial or other reliable data.

Statutory authority

The statutory authority exceptions cover a multitude of what would otherwise be transgressions of the EqA. They apply wherever other legislation requires differences of treatment because of a protected characteristic. Broadly, such differences of treatment arise in relation to health and safety, the protection of pregnant women and new mothers, religious education, employment by the Crown in military and intelligence posts, and nationality and residence requirements. They are provided for in Schedules 22 and 23 to the Act, which are given effect by Ss.191 and 196 respectively.

Statutory requirement

The statutory requirement exception in para 1(1) of Schedule 22 to the EqA is available in respect of different forms of discrimination depending on the protected characteristic at issue. In relation to discrimination in work (including employment, partnerships, contract work, public offices, etc), which is covered by Part 5 of the Act, para 1(1) envisages that statutory requirements relating to age, disability or religion or belief may apply. It has the effect that:

- a person (P) does not breach any provision of Part 5 in relation to age if he or she does anything he or she must do pursuant to a requirement of an enactment

1051

- P does not breach any provision of Part 5 in relation to disability if he or she does anything he or she must do pursuant to a requirement of an enactment, or a relevant requirement or condition imposed by virtue of an enactment

- P does not breach any provision of Part 5 in relation to religion or belief if he or she does anything he or she must do pursuant to a requirement of an enactment, or a relevant requirement or condition imposed by virtue of an enactment.

30.36 An enactment for these purposes would include Acts of Parliament, legislation produced by the devolved administrations in Scotland and Wales, and secondary legislation such as statutory instruments and ministerial orders. Para 1(3) clarifies that 'enactment' includes Measures of the General Synod of the Church of England, and that enactments passed or made on or after the date on which the EqA was passed are included. Para 1(4) then defines 'relevant requirement or condition' as one imposed by a Minister of the Crown, a member of the Scottish Executive, the National Assembly for Wales, the Welsh Ministers, the First Minister for Wales or the Counsel General to the Welsh Assembly Government.

This general exception replaces the exceptions that previously applied to disability and age discrimination under S.59 DDA and Reg 27 of the Employment Equality (Age) Regulations 2006 SI 2006/1031. However, no such exception applied in respect of religion or belief under the Employment Equality (Religion or Belief) Regulations 2003 SI 2003/1660 and so Schedule 22 represents a widening of the exception in this regard.

30.37 In contrast, S.41(1) RRA did contain an exception for acts done under statutory authority that discriminated on the ground of colour or nationality (but not race or ethnic or national origins). There is no general 'statutory authority' exception for colour and nationality in Schedule 22 and so S.41(1) can be said to have been repealed without re-enactment. However, S.41(2) RRA, which made a specific exception for various legislative requirements related to nationality and residence, does reappear in Schedule 23. Para 1(1) of Schedule 23 applies to acts done in pursuance of an enactment, an instrument made under an enactment by a member of the executive, arrangements made with the approval of a Minister of the Crown, or done to comply with a requirement imposed under an enactment by a member of the executive or a condition imposed by a Minister of the Crown. Para 1(2) provides that there is no contravention of Part 5, among other things, when a person does anything within para 1(1) 'which discriminates against another because of the other's nationality'. Furthermore, para 1(3) provides that there is no contravention of Part 5, among other things, where A discriminates against B within the scope of para 1(1) 'by applying to B a provision, criterion or practice which relates to (a) B's place of ordinary residence [or] (b) the length of time B has been present or resident in or outside the United Kingdom or an area within it'. This exception covers, for example, the points-based system for assessing foreign nationals' eligibility for a work permit.

The Explanatory Notes make it clear that the exception set down by para 1 of Schedule 22 applies only where the employer has no choice under legislation but to discriminate. (Although the Notes do not refer in quite such terms to the nationality exception under Schedule 23, given the similarity of the drafting of these provisions, we would suggest that the same approach should be applied.) The Explanatory Notes indicate that the para 1, Schedule 22 exception might apply where an employer dismisses a disabled employee because health and safety regulations leave it with no other choice, or where an employer refuses to employ someone who is not old enough to hold an LGV licence to drive a large goods vehicle. Case law guidance decided under the antecedent provisions such as that laid down by the House of Lords in Hampson v Department of Education and Science 1990 ICR 511, HL, is also likely to be of relevance. Although that case considered S.41 RRA, which has not been fully re-enacted, the wording of that provision has clearly inspired para 1, in so far as both allow for an exception where the employer acts in pursuance of an enactment, requirement or condition. Their Lordships in Hampson restricted the S.41 RRA exception to acts done in necessary performance of an express obligation. Accordingly, they refused to allow the exception to excuse discrimination where the Crown, a local authority or another statutory body is given *discretion* to act under an enactment, and chooses to exercise that discretion in a way that has discriminatory effects.

Protection of women   30.38

The prohibition of sex and pregnancy and maternity discrimination is without prejudice to legislation that provides for special protection of women with regard to pregnancy or maternity, or any other circumstances giving rise to risks specifically affecting women. Para 2(1) of Schedule 22 to the EqA, which is in substantially the same form as S.51 SDA, provides that 'a person (P) does not contravene a specified provision only by doing in relation to a woman (W) anything P is required to do to comply with —

(a) a [pre-SDA] enactment concerning the protection of women

(b) a relevant statutory provision (within the meaning of Part 1 of the Health and Safety at Work etc Act 1974) if it is done for the purpose of the protection of W (or a description of women which includes W)

(c) a requirement of a provision specified in Schedule 1 to the Employment Act 1989 (provisions concerned with protection of women at work)'.

These provisions would cover, for example, the employer's duty under Reg 16   30.39
of the Management of Health and Safety at Work Regulations 1999 SI 1999/3242 to suspend a new or expectant mother from work if a risk assessment

shows up risks that cannot reasonably or adequately be minimised by altering the woman's working conditions or hours of work.

This exception applies only in relation to the 'specified provisions', being Part 5 (work) and Part 6 (education, but only so far as relating to vocational training) of the EqA – para 2(4). It also only applies to excuse discrimination related to sex or pregnancy and maternity – para 2(8).

30.40 **Exclusion of right to equal treatment.** The provisions listed above giving special protection to women in employment may not be the subject of a claim by men seeking equality of terms (i.e. an equal pay claim). Para 1 of Schedule 7 to the EqA (to which S.80(8) EqA gives effect) provides that 'neither a sex equality clause nor a maternity equality clause has effect in relation to terms of work affected by compliance with laws regulating (a) the employment of women; [or] (b) the appointment of women to personal or public offices'. Para 2 goes on to state that 'a sex equality clause does not have effect in relation to terms of work affording special treatment to women in connection with pregnancy or childbirth'. This prevents men bringing claims for special treatment to which only women are entitled, such as claims for paternity leave and pay comparable to that given in respect of maternity.

The effect of sex equality and maternity clauses in equal pay claims is discussed in IDS Employment Law Handbook, 'Equal Pay' (2011), Chapter 2. Briefly, a 'sex equality clause' is implied into every employee's contract of employment, enabling an employee to bring a tribunal claim where he or she is treated less favourably than a comparable employee of the opposite sex in relation to a contractual term – S.66 EqA. A 'maternity equality clause' is implied into the terms of a woman's work by virtue of S.73(1) and enshrine her right to benefit from pay rises in the calculation of her contractual maternity pay.

30.41 **Religious education**

Some of the exceptions to the prohibition on discrimination that existed before the EqA came into force were laid down in Acts of Parliament and statutory instruments other than the equality enactments. For example, the exceptions relating to religious education were contained in the Education Act 1989. The EqA repealed the relevant sections of the 1989 Act and re-enacted the exceptions in para 3(1) of Schedule 22. This provides that there is no breach of Part 5 of the EqA in doing a 'relevant act' in connection with the employment of another in a 'relevant position'. A 'relevant position' is 'the head teacher or principal of an educational establishment; the head, a fellow or other member of the academic staff of a college, or institution in the nature of a college, in a university; [or] a professorship of a university which is a canon professorship or one to which a canonry is annexed' – para 3(2). A 'relevant act' is 'a requirement of an instrument relating to the establishment that the head teacher or principal must be a member of a particular religious order; a requirement of an instrument relating to the college or institution that the holder of the position must be a woman; [or] an Act or instrument in accordance with which the professorship is a canon professorship or one to which a canonry is annexed' – para 3(3).

This exception has the same scope as that set out in S.5 of the 1989 Act. Its effect is that the governing instruments of schools, colleges, universities and other further education institutes may continue to specify that the head teacher or principal be of a certain religious order, that a particular academic position be held by a woman, or that the holder of a professorship be an ordained priest, without entailing acts of religious or sex discrimination. (Note, however, that the exception for instruments requiring that an academic post be held by a woman only applies to instruments that took effect before 16 January 1990, the day on which the 1989 Act exceptions came into force – para 3(4).)

In addition, para 4 of Schedule 22 accords special powers to religious schools **30.42** with regard to the appointment and dismissal of teachers for reasons related to religious education. Para 4 covers the same ground as Reg 39 of the Employment Equality (Religion or Belief) Regulations 2003 SI 2003/1660, by providing that there is no contravention of the EqA where a person does 'anything which is permitted for the purposes of:

- S.58(6) or (7) of the School Standards and Framework Act 1998 (dismissal of teachers because of failure to give religious education efficiently);

- S.60(4) and (5) of that Act (religious considerations relating to certain appointments); [or]

- S.124A of that Act (preference for certain teachers at independent schools of a religious character)'.

Crown employment   30.43

Certain posts in the civil, diplomatic, armed or security and intelligence services are reserved exclusively to British and/or Commonwealth citizens. For example, as the Explanatory Notes point out, security and intelligence service positions are automatically reserved to UK nationals, and service in the armed forces is generally open only to British, Commonwealth or Irish citizens and British protected persons. This, naturally, has a discriminatory effect but is specifically permitted by para 5 of Schedule 22 to the EqA. Para 5(1) provides that 'a person does not contravene this Act by making or continuing in force rules mentioned in sub-paragraph (2); by publishing, displaying or implementing such rules; [or] by publishing the gist of such rules'. The rules mentioned in sub-paragraph (2) are those restricting employment in the service of the Crown, employment by a prescribed public body, or the holding of a public office, to persons of particular birth, nationality, descent or residence.

30.44 **Positive action**

A degree of positive action has been permitted by the discrimination legislation for some time. Under the antecedent legislation, employers were entitled to direct training at, and encourage applications from, groups they reasonably considered to be under-represented in their particular sector. What was not permitted was any kind of positive action in selection – a person's protected characteristics could not form any part of the employer's decision-making in recruitment and promotion.

Although there is some evidence that a number of employers, primarily in the public sector, made use of the permitted positive action measures under the old legislation, there was 'widespread uncertainty about whether, and to what extent, such measures [were] lawful' (para 5.6, 'The Equality Bill – Government response to the Consultation', July 2008 (Cm 7454)). The Government was also concerned that the old positive action provisions were not wide enough to tackle the kinds of disadvantage suffered in today's society. Ethnic minority job applicants, for example, may be just as well qualified or more qualified than the majority population, yet under-representation still persists in certain sectors (see para 4.38, 'A Framework for Fairness: Proposals for a Single Equality Bill for Great Britain' (June 2007)).

30.45 To speed up progress in tackling disadvantage and persistent under-representation, the Government decided to broaden the scope of positive action to the extent permitted by EU law. The EqA largely maintains the old approach with regard to training and encouraging applications, which are now covered by a general power to take positive action set out in S.158 EqA. The new S.158 is, however, potentially broader in some respects than the equivalent provisions under the old legislation – for further details, see below. More controversially, the EqA introduced a new power under S.159 EqA entitling employers to take positive action when recruiting or selecting for promotion. This new provision is subject to a number of important conditions, including that it can be relied on only where the candidates are equally well qualified.

The general power to take positive action, set out in S.158 EqA, was brought into force in October 2010 along with the majority of the other substantive provisions in the Act. However, S.159 was not brought into force until 6 April 2011. This delay has meant that there is no statutory guidance on the scope of that provision: the EHRC Employment Code was issued in October 2010, and accordingly only covers the general power in S.158. The EHRC has indicated that a revised Code – covering both Ss.158 and 159 – will be issued in due course.

General power 30.46

Section 158 EqA allows the use of positive action measures to alleviate disadvantage experienced by people who share a protected characteristic, reduce their under-representation in relation to particular activities, and meet their particular needs. The Explanatory Notes state: 'It will, for example, allow measures to be targeted to particular groups, including training to enable them to gain employment... Any such measures must be a proportionate way of achieving the relevant aim' – para 511.

The new power in S.158 EqA harmonises the various provisions on positive discrimination that appeared in the previous equality enactments but goes beyond those provisions in certain respects. Generally, permissible measures under the antecedent provisions were limited to providing training to under-represented groups and encouraging members of those groups to apply for posts. Broadly speaking, such steps were permitted under the SDA and the RRA where there was, or had been in the previous 12 months, under-representation of a particular group in the national or regional workforce, or within the employer's organisation. There were similar positive action provisions in the Employment Equality (Religion or Belief) Regulations 2003 SI 2003/1660, the Employment Equality (Sexual Orientation) Regulations 2003 SI 2003/1661 and the Employment Equality (Age) Regulations 2006 SI 2006/1031. However, they did not explicitly refer to under-representation but applied where it reasonably appeared that the act in question prevented or compensated for disadvantages linked to the relevant protected characteristic. This less prescriptive approach was based on the wording of the relevant EU Directives.

In addition, S.47(3) SDA allowed training to be given to those who were in 30.47 special need of it because they had taken career breaks for domestic or family reasons, and S.35 RRA contained a wider provision that enabled measures to be taken to meet the special needs of a particular racial group in respect of education, training or welfare, or any ancillary benefits. This provision of the RRA, which was not subject to an explicit under-representation test, could be relied on to provide special measures such as English language training.

Section 158 EqA introduces a single test for positive action across all the protected characteristics that specifically allows measures designed to overcome disadvantage, meet specific needs or encourage participation in the relevant activity. S.158 is potentially wider than the old provisions in that it contains a more flexible test of under-representation than the RRA and SDA. In addition, it is not as prescriptive as to the measures that may be taken to achieve the stated aims and potentially allows an employer to provide measures that go beyond training and encouragement.

30.48 **Scope of S.158.** Section 158 applies if a person (P) reasonably thinks that:

- persons who share a protected characteristic suffer a disadvantage connected to the characteristic – S.158(1)(a)

- persons who share a protected characteristic have needs that are different from the needs of persons who do not share it – S.158(1)(b), or

- participation in an activity by persons who share a protected characteristic is disproportionately low – S.158(1)(c).

The protected characteristics to which S.158(1) applies are all those listed in S.4 EqA – see Chapter 4, 'Characteristics covered by the Equality Act'.

30.49 The EHRC Employment Code points out that sometimes the bases on which action can be taken will overlap. For example, people sharing a protected characteristic may be at a disadvantage, and that disadvantage may also give rise to a different need or be reflected in their low level of participation in particular activities (see para 12.13).

While some evidence will be required to show disadvantage, different needs or low participation, an employer is not required to produce sophisticated statistical data or research to back up its decision to take positive action. The Code states that obtaining evidence 'may simply involve an employer looking at the profiles of their workforce and/or making enquiries of other comparable employers in the area or sector' – para 12.14.

In a case where at least one of the three conditions in S.158(1) applies, S.158(2) provides that the EqA does not prohibit P from taking any action that is a proportionate means of achieving one of the following aims:

- enabling or encouraging persons who share the protected characteristic to overcome or minimise that disadvantage – S.158(2)(a)

- meeting those needs – S.158(2)(b), or

- enabling or encouraging persons who share the protected characteristic to participate in that activity – S.158(2)(c).

It should be noted that the three aims listed in S.158(2)(a)–(c) EqA directly correspond to each of the three situations described in S.158(1)(a)–(c) (see above).

30.50 **Disadvantage.** The first situation envisaged by S.158 EqA arises where the employer (or other relevant individual or organisation) 'reasonably thinks that... persons who share a protected characteristic suffer a disadvantage connected to the characteristic' – S.158(1)(a).

A 'disadvantage' for these purposes is not defined in the Act, but the EHRC Employment Code suggests that it may include 'exclusion, rejection, lack of opportunity, lack of choice and barriers to accessing employment opportunities. Disadvantage may be obvious in relation to some issues such as legal, social or economic barriers or obstacles which make it difficult for people of a particular protected group to enter into or make progress in an occupation, a trade, a sector or workplace' – para 12.16.

Where S.158(1)(a) applies, the employer may take 'any action which is a **30.51** proportionate means of achieving the aim of… enabling or encouraging persons who share the protected characteristic to overcome or minimise that disadvantage' – S.158(2)(a). According to the Code, such action might include:

- targeting advertising at specific disadvantaged groups; for example, advertising jobs in media outlets that are likely to be accessed by the target group

- making a statement in recruitment advertisements that the employer welcomes applications from the target group; for example, 'older people are welcome to apply'

- providing opportunities exclusively to the target group to learn more about particular types of work opportunities with the employer; for example, internships or open days

- providing training opportunities in work areas or sectors for the target group; for example, work placements (para 12.17).

Different needs. The second situation covered by S.158 arises where the **30.52** employer 'reasonably thinks that… persons who share a protected characteristic have needs that are different from the needs of persons who do not share it' – S.158(1)(b).

There is no statutory definition of 'different needs' for the purposes of S.158(1)(b), but the EHRC Employment Code offers the following guidance: 'A group of people who share a particular protected characteristic have "different needs" if, due to past or present discrimination or disadvantage or due to factors that especially apply to people who share that characteristic, they have needs that are different to those of other groups. This does not mean that the needs of a group have to be entirely unique from the needs of other groups to be considered "different". Needs may also be different because, disproportionately, compared to the needs of other groups, they are not being met or the need is of particular importance to that group' – para 12.18. The example is given of an employer whose monitoring data on training shows that its workers over the age of 60 are more likely to request training in advanced IT skills than workers outside this age group. The employer could provide training sessions primarily targeted at this group of workers.

30.53 Where S.158(1)(b) applies, the employer may take 'any action which is a proportionate means of achieving the aim of... meeting those needs' – S.158(2)(b). The EHRC Employment Code suggests that such action could include:

- providing exclusive training to the target group specifically aimed at meeting particular needs; for example, English language classes for staff for whom English is a second language

- the provision of support and mentoring; for example, to a member of staff who has undergone gender reassignment

- the creation of a work-based support group for members of staff who share a protected characteristic and who may have workplace experiences or needs that are different from those of staff who do not share that characteristic (para 12.19).

30.54 **Low participation.** The third and final situation in which S.158 applies is where the employer 'reasonably thinks that... participation in an activity by persons who share a protected characteristic is disproportionately low' – S.158(1)(c).

The EHRC Employment Code suggests that the employer 'will need to have some reliable indication or evidence that participation is low compared with that of other groups or compared with the level of participation that could reasonably be expected for people from that protected group... This might be by means of statistics or, where these are not available, by evidence based on monitoring, consultation or national surveys' – paras 12.21 and 12.23.

30.55 The Code gives the example of an employer with two factories, one in Cornwall and one in London. Each employs 150 workers. The Cornish factory employs two workers from an ethnic minority background and the London factory employs 20 workers from an ethnic minority background. The ethnic minority population is 1 per cent in Cornwall and 25 per cent in London. In the Cornish factory the employer would not be able to meet the test of 'disproportionately low', since the number of its ethnic minority workers is not low in comparison to the size of the ethnic minority population in Cornwall. However, the London factory, despite employing significantly more ethnic minority workers, could show that the number of ethnic minority workers employed there was still disproportionately low in comparison with their proportion in the population of London overall.

The Code goes on to state, giving examples, that it may be sufficient for the employer to show that participation is low compared with the proportion of people with that protected characteristic nationally, locally, or within the particular workforce (see para 12.22).

30.56 In the circumstances described in S.158(1)(c), the employer may take 'any action which is a proportionate means of achieving the aim of... enabling or encouraging persons who share the protected characteristic to participate in that activity' – S.158(2)(c). The Code suggests that such action could include:

- setting targets for increasing participation of the targeted group

- providing bursaries to obtain qualifications in a profession such as journalism for members of the group whose participation in that profession might be disproportionately low

- outreach work such as raising awareness of public appointments within the community

- reserving places on training courses for people with the protected characteristic; for example, in management

- targeted networking opportunities; for example, in banking

- working with local schools and FE colleges, inviting students from groups whose participation in the workplace is disproportionately low to spend a day at the company

- providing mentoring (para 12.24).

Proportionate means of achieving aim. Any action taken by an employer in **30.57** reliance on S.158 must be a 'proportionate means of achieving' one of the aims set out in S.158(2)(a)–(c), above. The requirement for positive action to be 'proportionate' reflects the case law of the European Court of Justice on positive action (see, for example, Marschall v Land Nordrhein-Westfalen 2001 ICR 45, ECJ) and corresponds to the test of justification set out elsewhere in the EqA – for example, in the context of indirect discrimination (see Chapter 17, 'Indirect discrimination: objective justification'). The Explanatory Notes state: 'The extent to which it is proportionate to take positive action measures which may result in people not having the relevant characteristic being treated less favourably will depend, among other things, on the seriousness of the relevant disadvantage, the extremity of need or under-representation and the availability of other means of countering them' – para 512.

Exceptions. There are various exceptions (or potential exceptions) to the **30.58** general power to take positive action under S.158. Regulations made by a Minister of the Crown may specify action, or descriptions of action, to which S.158(2) does not apply – S.158(3). According to para 513 of the Explanatory Notes, the underlying intention is to provide greater legal certainty about what action is proportionate in particular circumstances. At the time of writing, no regulations have been made under this provision.

In addition, S.158(4)(a) provides that S.158 does not apply to 'action within S.159(3)', i.e. treating a person (A) more favourably in connection with recruitment or promotion than another person (B) because A has the protected characteristic but B does not (see 'Recruitment and promotion' below). The effect of this is that an employer who wishes to take positive action in the context of recruitment and promotion must rely on S.159, and cannot invoke the general power in S.158.

30.59 It should also be noted that S.158 does not apply to a case covered by S.104, which allows registered political parties to make arrangements in relation to the selection of election candidates to address the under-representation of people with particular protected characteristics. As it does not concern employment, S.104 is outside the scope of this Handbook.

Finally, S.158(6) provides that S.158 'does not enable P to do anything that is prohibited by or under an enactment other than this Act'. Thus, S.158 does not allow any action to be taken that would be prohibited by another Act of Parliament or by subordinate legislation.

30.60 Recruitment and promotion

Section 159 EqA is a new provision that deals with positive action specifically in the context of recruitment and promotion. It permits (but does not require) an employer to take a protected characteristic into account when deciding who to recruit or promote where people having the protected characteristic are at a disadvantage or are under-represented. However, it contains a number of significant limitations. In particular, it operates only where the candidates are equally well qualified, and it does not permit employers to adopt a blanket policy of treating candidates who share a particular protected characteristic more favourably than others who do not. It follows that employers cannot apply quota systems or adopt a policy of automatically favouring disadvantaged groups. Instead, they must consider each case on its merits.

The Explanatory Notes give the example at para 521 of a police service that employs disproportionately low numbers of people from an ethnic minority background. It identifies a number of candidates who are as qualified as each other for recruitment to a post, including a candidate from an under-represented ethnic minority background. According to the Explanatory Notes, it would not be unlawful to give preferential treatment to that candidate, provided the comparative merits of other candidates were also taken into consideration.

30.61 Scope of S.159. Section 159 EqA applies when a person ('P') 'reasonably thinks' that:

- persons who share a protected characteristic suffer a disadvantage connected to the characteristic – S.159(1)(a), or

- participation in an activity by persons who share a protected characteristic is disproportionately low – S.159(1)(b).

These two conditions replicate those set out in S.158(1)(a) and (c) EqA (see **30.62** under 'General power' above). The protected characteristics to which S.159 applies are all those listed in S.4 EqA.

Where either of the two conditions referred to in S.159(1) (above) is satisfied, 'Part 5 [of the EqA] (work) does not prohibit P from taking action within [S.159(3)] with the aim of enabling or encouraging persons who share the protected characteristic to… (a) overcome or minimise that disadvantage, or (b) participate in that activity' – S.159(2). The permissible 'action' referred to in S.159(2) is 'treating a person (A) more favourably in connection with recruitment or promotion than another person (B) because A has the protected characteristic but B does not' – S.159(3).

Section 159 EqA is subject to three important qualifications that limit the **30.63** circumstances in which it will apply. Action is permitted under S.159(2) only if:

- A is as qualified as B to be recruited or promoted

- P does not have a policy of treating persons who share the protected characteristic more favourably in connection with recruitment or promotion than persons who do not share it, and

- taking the action in question is a proportionate means of achieving the aim referred to in S.159(2) – S.159(4).

Recruitment. As noted above, S.159 permits more favourable treatment 'in **30.64** connection with recruitment or promotion' – S.159(3). 'Recruitment' for these purposes is defined broadly in S.159(5) as a process for deciding whether to:

- offer employment to a person

- make contract work available to a contract worker

- offer a person a position as a partner in a firm or proposed firm

- offer a person a position as a member of an LLP or proposed LLP

- offer a person a pupillage or tenancy in barristers' chambers

- take a person as an advocate's devil or offer a person membership of an advocate's stable (in Scotland)

- offer a person an appointment to a personal office

- offer a person an appointment to a public office, recommend a person for such an appointment or approve a person's appointment to a public office, or

- offer a person a service for finding employment.

For further details of the scope of the EqA in the various scenarios mentioned above, see Chapter 28, 'Liability of employers, employees and agents', and Chapter 29, 'Liability of other bodies'.

30.65 **'As qualified as'.** As previously noted, S.159 applies only if 'A is as qualified as B to be recruited or promoted' – S.159(4)(a). This is a significant limitation on the scope of the provision. It means that an employer who, in an attempt to redress an imbalance in the composition of its workforce, recruits or promotes a person from a disadvantaged or under-represented group in preference to another, better qualified candidate will be guilty of unlawful discrimination against the unsuccessful applicant, irrespective of the benign motive.

The EqA does not elaborate on the meaning of 'as qualified as', and this is likely to give rise to uncertainty in practice. According to the Explanatory Notes: 'The question of whether one person is as qualified as another is not a matter only of academic qualification, but rather a judgement based on the criteria the employer uses to establish who is best for the job which could include matters such as suitability, competence and professional performance' – para 518. And at the Equality Bill's House of Lords Committee stage, Baroness Royall of Blaisdon, on behalf of the Government, stated: 'Any assessment of candidates' suitability will depend on a number of factors relevant to the job in question, such as experience, aptitude, physical ability, or performance during an interview or assessment. Formal qualifications are only one way in which a candidate's overall suitability may be assessed.'

30.66 The current version of the EHRC Employment Code that was laid before Parliament in October 2010 does not address positive action in recruitment and promotion (as S.159 was not then in force). However, the earlier draft version that was the subject of consultation counselled a broad approach to S.159 EqA. It stated: 'The phrase "as qualified as"… requires a full and objective assessment of each candidate's suitability, skills, qualifications (professional and academic), competence and professional performance. Although there are absolutely no fixed rules as to how this assessment should be undertaken, it will usually involve an employer preparing an objective set of criteria that relate to the job or post and then conducting an objective assessment or evaluation of each candidate against that set of criteria and against each other.' (Note that the EHRC has indicated that a revised Code – covering S.159 – will be issued in due course.)

It appears that there will be no need for the candidates to match each other identically on a point-by-point basis – an overall approach will suffice. Employers thus have some leeway to make a case that a candidate is as qualified as another according to their chosen criteria. In practice, however, it is difficult to eliminate all subjective elements from an employer's assessment and the outcome will rarely be clear-cut, meaning that employers are unlikely to feel confident going down this route.

Where an employer is faced with two or more candidates who are as qualified **30.67**
as each other in the broad sense referred to above, the consultative draft version
of the EHRC Employment Code suggested that it 'may use a candidate's
protected characteristic as the "tipping factor" in any recruitment decision'.
The draft Code went on to say, however, that it is not mandatory to prefer a
candidate from a disadvantaged or low participation group in this situation,
and that 'the employer still has the prerogative to choose one of the other
candidates, provided the reason for the employer doing so does not in itself
amount to direct or indirect discrimination'.

Given the uncertainty surrounding the breadth of S.159 EqA, the Conservatives
tabled an amendment to the Equality Bill to change 'as qualified as' to 'equally
qualified to'. The intention was to make it clear that S.159 does not allow an
employer to appoint someone with a protected characteristic who meets the
minimum criteria for a post over a better candidate who exceeds those criteria.
The amendment was rejected because the Government feared that employers
might interpret the change as requiring candidates to have equal academic
qualifications or other formal qualifications of a similar nature.

At the Equality Bill's House of Lords Committee stage, Baroness Royall of **30.68**
Blaisdon made it clear that a less qualified candidate who meets the minimum
criteria for a job cannot be preferred over a superior candidate, and expressed
the Government's view that the Act achieves that result without the need for a
change in wording. She stated: 'Where the assessment process, in whatever
form it takes, evaluates one candidate as having scored, say, 95 per cent and
another 61 per cent, those candidates cannot be considered as being as qualified
as each other to undertake the job. It is immaterial whether the pass mark was
set at 60 per cent, 50 per cent or 40 per cent; the clearly superior candidate
must always be offered the job. We are confident that the clause as drafted
achieves that effect.'

No automatic preferences. Another important limitation on the practical **30.69**
scope of S.159 EqA is that positive action is permitted 'only if... P does not
have a policy of treating persons who share the protected characteristic more
favourably in connection with recruitment or promotion than persons who do
not share it' – S.159(4)(b) EqA. In other words, there must be an objective
assessment of the candidates' qualifications. Thus an employer who, for
example, shortlists all job applicants who share a particular characteristic and
meet the minimum criteria, but applies a higher standard to other candidates,
would not be able to rely on S.159 EqA.

Proportionate means of achieving aim. The third limitation is that any action **30.70**
taken by an employer in reliance on S.159 EqA must be a 'proportionate means
of achieving' one of the aims set out in S.159(2). The requirement for the action
to be 'proportionate' reflects the case law of the European Court of Justice on
positive action, and corresponds to the test of justification set out elsewhere in

1065

the EqA – for example, in the context of indirect discrimination (see Chapter 17, 'Indirect discrimination: objective justification'). The Equality Bill as originally drafted did not contain a proportionality requirement in relation to S.159, but the Government agreed to this provision at the House of Lords Committee stage to make clear what it already considered to be implicit, and to reflect the terminology used in S.158 (see under 'General power' above).

In the context of the general power to take positive action under S.158, to which the proportionality test also applies, the Explanatory Notes state: 'The extent to which it is proportionate to take positive action measures which may result in people not having the relevant characteristic being treated less favourably will depend, among other things, on the seriousness of the relevant disadvantage, the extremity of need or under-representation and the availability of other means of countering them' – para 512. Similar considerations are likely to apply in relation to S.159.

30.71 **Exceptions.** Section 159 'does not enable P to do anything that is prohibited by or under an enactment other than this Act' – S.159(6). Thus, S.159 does not allow any action to be taken that would be prohibited by another Act of Parliament or by subordinate legislation.

30.72 **Likely impact of S.159.** Section 159 has generated a lot of negative media coverage – and there was for some time a prevailing view that it would never come into force – but the potential injustice that some commentators have claimed it capable of causing has, in our view, been overstated. As noted above, the provision does not allow for 'quotas' or selection regardless of merit; nor are employers obliged to use the power, as the measure is entirely voluntary. Accordingly, individuals cannot challenge an employer merely for not taking positive action. Although an unsuccessful minority candidate might argue that an employer's failure to avail itself of S.159 is evidence of a discriminatory approach to recruitment, we think this argument is unlikely to find much favour. It is likely that many employers will be wary of taking positive action even when the stringent conditions set out above are satisfied, fearing a challenge from the unsuccessful candidate, who might argue that he or she is better qualified than the preferred candidate. For these reasons we consider that the practical impact of the measure is likely to be limited.

30.73 **Application to disability**

Sections 158 and 159 apply to the protected characteristic of disability in the same way as they apply to the other protected characteristics. They are, however, of limited value in a disability context, as S.13(3) EqA provides that where the protected characteristic is disability, an employer will not be liable for direct discrimination against someone who is not disabled only because it treats a disabled person more favourably. This replicates the position that existed under the DDA. It follows that it is perfectly lawful for employers to engage in positive discrimination in order to increase opportunities for people with disabilities without recourse to S.158 or S.159.

Two examples from the EHRC Guidance for Employers:

- an employer has a policy of shortlisting and interviewing all disabled applicants who meet the minimum requirements for a job. The law would allow this. It would not be unlawful discrimination against a non-disabled applicant who also meets the minimum requirements but is not shortlisted

- each year, an employer allocates a certain amount of money per worker to pay for training. They decide to allocate an additional budget to provide two sessions of management training which is only available to disabled staff. This would not be unlawful discrimination against non-disabled workers.

There is, of course, no obligation on employers to treat a disabled person more **30.74** favourably than a non-disabled person. That said, employers are required to take such steps as are reasonable to remove any substantial disadvantage suffered by disabled persons, which may in practice have the effect of disabled applicants or employees being treated more favourably than other applicants or employees – see Chapter 21, 'Failure to make reasonable adjustments'.

The only time S.158 or S.159 might come into play would be where an employer seeks to favour a person with a particular disability over someone with a different disability. However, it is difficult to envisage many situations where the requirements of S.158 or S.159 would be satisfied in these circumstances.

State immunity   **30.75**

The general rule of international law is that foreign (including Commonwealth) states and all emanations of their governments are entitled to immunity in civil actions unless they are engaging in purely commercial transactions or they elect to waive that immunity. In UK law, this immunity is provided for in S.1(1) of the State Immunity Act 1978 (SIA). However, the SIA contains a number of deviations from the general rule, two of which are of relevance as far as discrimination is concerned.

Employment contracts   **30.76**
Section 4(1) SIA removes the general immunity in respect of proceedings relating to a contract of employment between a foreign state and an individual if:

- the contract was made in the United Kingdom, or

- the work is to be wholly or partly performed in the United Kingdom.

Taken on its own, S.4(1) SIA would seem to suggest that a foreign state cannot rely on state immunity as a defence to a claim of discrimination. There are, however, important exceptions to S.4(1) where immunity *will* still apply. For a start, under S.16 members of foreign missions within the meaning of the Vienna Convention on Diplomatic Relations 1961 and members of a consular post within the meaning of the Vienna Convention on Consular Relations 1963 are excluded from the scope of S.4(1). S.16 applies to members of the diplomatic staff if they are part of the administrative and technical staff of the embassy or consulate. This has been held to include fairly minor staff. In Arab Republic of Egypt v Gamal-Eldin and anor 1996 ICR 13, EAT, for example, S.16 was held to cover two drivers at the Embassy's medical office.

30.77 Further exceptions to the application of S.4(1) depend on whether or not a commercial activity is involved. If the employee was employed by the foreign state for non-commercial purposes – e.g. as a diplomat or other embassy employee – then S.4(1) does not apply if:

- the employee is a national of the foreign state at the time he or she starts proceedings, or

- at the time when the contract was made the employee was neither a national of the United Kingdom nor habitually resident there, or

- the parties to the contract have agreed in writing to bestow immunity on the employing state – S.4(2).

If, however, the work performed under the contract is for an office, agency or establishment maintained by the foreign state in the United Kingdom for commercial purposes, then the foreign state may not rely on S.4(2) unless the individual was habitually resident in the employing state at the time the contract was made – S.4(3).

30.78 Death and personal injury

There may be circumstances where a person who is excluded from the remit of S.4(1) can nevertheless pursue a discrimination claim against a foreign state. This is because S.5 SIA stipulates that a foreign state is not immune 'as respects proceedings in respect of death or personal injury, or damage to or loss of tangible property, caused by an act or omission in the United Kingdom'. Unlike S.4, S.5 is not subject to qualification in S.16 or any other provision: a foreign state enjoys no immunity in respect of these matters. The question that arises is whether a discrimination claim is 'proceedings in respect of... personal injury, or damage to, or loss of, tangible property' for the purposes of S.5 such as to allow a claimant to bring such a claim against a foreign state.

Two decisions of the EAT have explored this issue. The first, Military Affairs Office of the Embassy of the State of Kuwait v Caramba-Coker EAT 1054/02, established that a claim for compensation in respect of psychiatric or stress-based illness arising from discrimination is a claim for personal injury and therefore covered by S.5. In the second case, Federal Republic of Nigeria v

Ogbonna 2012 ICR 32, EAT, the Nigerian Government argued that the decision in Caramba-Coker was inconsistent with international law on state immunity and that 'personal injury' in this context should be restricted to physical injury. Rejecting those submissions, the Appeal Tribunal reaffirmed that there is no reason why the term 'personal injury' should not be given its normal meaning in domestic law, which is apt to incorporate both psychiatric and physical injury. That meaning does not, however, go as far as to incorporate injury to feelings or economic loss. Accordingly, the effect of S.5 is that applicability of state immunity to claims which are excluded by a combination of S.4(1) and S.16 will depend on the type of damage the claimant alleges that he or she has suffered as a result of discrimination. Only where the claim includes an allegation of psychiatric (or, less likely, physical) injury will it be allowed to proceed.

Waiver of immunity   30.79

A foreign state may be held to have waived its immunity if it has submitted to the jurisdiction of the courts – S.2(1). A state is deemed to have so submitted 'if it has intervened or taken any step in the proceedings' – S.2(3). In Arab Republic of Egypt v Gamal-Eldin and anor 1996 ICR 13, EAT, the medical counsellor at the Egyptian Embassy wrote to the tribunal explaining the situation. According to the EAT, the letter did not constitute the taking of steps in the proceedings or a submission to jurisdiction. Furthermore, the counsellor did not have authority to submit to jurisdiction.

International organisations   30.80

Note that the International Organisations Act 1968 permits Orders in Council to be made which confer similar immunities and privileges to those conferred by the SIA on certain international organisations and persons connected with such organisations.

Judicial proceedings immunity   30.81

The general exceptions identified up to this point have all been provided for by statute – be it the EqA or some other enactment. There is, however, one significant common law exception which provides that an act or omission that would otherwise be discriminatory cannot be relied upon to found a claim: judicial proceedings immunity. This is the name given to the well-established legal principle which provides that a witness enjoys absolute immunity from any action brought on the ground that his or her evidence is false, malicious or careless. In Darker v Chief Constable of West Midlands Police 2001 1 AC 435, HL, the House of Lords confirmed that immunity extends not only to the actual evidence of the witness in the witness box but to the preparation of witness statements, even if the trial never takes place. Immunity is extended as a matter of public policy to ensure that witnesses are able to give the evidence that they ought to give and to participate in the administration of justice without fear of subsequent legal liability.

In Heath v Commissioner of Police of the Metropolis 2005 ICR 329, CA, the Court of Appeal held that the immunity applied not only to common law claims such as defamation and negligence but also to the statutory torts created by discrimination legislation. In the view of Lord Justice Auld, the rationale for applying the immunity – that witnesses need to be able to give the evidence that they ought to give and thus to participate in the administration of justice without fear of being subjected to subsequent legal liability – applied equally to discrimination claims. Moreover, Auld LJ was satisfied that the immunity was contrary to neither Article 6 of the European Convention on Human Rights (which guarantees access to justice), nor the United Kingdom's obligations under the various EU equal treatment Directives.

30.82 As a result of Heath, it is clear that a witness's evidence in testimony, or in a witness statement, will not found a claim of discrimination or harassment, even if it is expressed in highly discriminatory terms. However, in Parmer v East Leicester Medical Practice 2011 IRLR 641, EAT, the claimant argued that victimisation claims represented an exception to judicial proceedings immunity. In support of this argument he cited the European Court of Justice's decision in Coote v Granada Hospitality Ltd 1999 ICR 100, ECJ, where it was held that European law required Member States to introduce into their national legal systems such measures as are necessary to ensure judicial protection for workers whose employers, after the employment relationship has ended, refuse to provide references as a reaction to legal proceedings brought to enforce compliance with the principle of equal treatment within the meaning of that Directive. Additional reliance was placed on the decision in Zaiwalla and Co and anor v Walia 2002 IRLR 697, EAT, where the Appeal Tribunal upheld an award of aggravated damages made because of the respondent's conduct in defending the proceedings.

The EAT rejected the submission that victimisation claims represent an exception, taking the view that the ratio in Heath v Commissioner of Police of the Metropolis (above) clearly extended to victimisation as it did to the other forms of discrimination claim. Moreover, Zaiwalla did not assist the claimant as it was decided before Heath and at a lower level, and in any event the question before the EAT in that case had related to the scope of the power to award aggravated damages, rather than the scope of judicial proceedings immunity.

30.83 However, while judicial proceedings immunity would extend to an employer's conduct of tribunal proceedings, it would seemingly not cover things done or said after the conclusion of a hearing. In Nicholls v Corin Tech Ltd and ors EAT 0290/07 the claimant brought a claim of post-employment victimisation, alleging that his former employer had threatened him, in the corridor of the tribunal building, shortly after he left the hearing. The EAT held that if the allegation proved to be true, it would not be caught by judicial proceedings immunity, because the principle that witnesses to judicial proceedings should be able to express themselves freely, and not be inhibited by the thought that they might be sued for something they say, does not extend to incidents that do not form any part of the judicial process.

31 Specific exceptions

31.1 The principle of non-discrimination is not absolute: both European and UK discrimination law accept that there are certain situations in which it is legitimate to discriminate. In Chapter 30, 'General exceptions', we consider those exceptions that apply across all, or most, of the protected characteristics covered by the Equality Act 2010 (EqA). In this chapter we discuss the specific exceptions to the principle of non-discrimination that apply only to particular characteristics.

References in this chapter to the EHRC Employment Code are to the statutory Code of Practice on Discrimination in Employment published by the Equality and Human Rights Commission. Although not binding on tribunals, the provisions of the Code are highly influential and may be used as evidence in a tribunal claim.

Age exceptions

31.2 The EqA provides for a number of exceptions relating to age discrimination, although one very significant exception – the default retirement age (DRA) – was removed in 2011 by the Employment Equality (Repeal of Retirement Age Provisions) Regulations 2011 SI 2011/1069. Those Regulations repealed para 8 of Schedule 9 to the EqA, which provided that it was not an act of discrimination to dismiss an employee on reaching the DRA of 65, or the employer's normal retirement age if lower, if the reason for dismissal was retirement. Also repealed was para 9 of Schedule 9, which stipulated that it was not an act of discrimination or victimisation to refuse to offer employment to a person who had reached the DRA or would reach it within six months of the application for employment.

The two exceptions above were repealed as from 6 April 2011. Accordingly, where an employee was retired on the basis of reaching the DRA prior to that date, or was denied employment having been within six months or less of the DRA, the exceptions continue to apply. There may also be a small number of transitional cases (i.e. where the notice of retirement was issued prior to 6 April 2011, but the dismissal for retirement took place after that date) in respect of which para 8, but not para 9, continues to apply.

Below, we consider those age exceptions which have survived the repeal of the DRA: these concern service-related benefits; the national minimum wage; enhanced redundancy payments; insurance and financial services; childcare benefits; and pensions.

31.3 Service-related benefits

The common practice of improving pay and benefits as employment continues – such as awarding extra holiday after a certain number of years – inevitably amounts to indirect age discrimination because older workers are more likely to have completed the requisite amount of service than younger workers. However, rather than require employers to show that such pay and benefits practices are objectively justified as a proportionate means of achieving a legitimate aim, the EqA instead provides for a two-pronged exception (found in para 10 of Schedule 9 to the EqA), the effect of which is identical to the predecessor provisions in Reg 32 of the Employment Equality (Age) Regulations 2006 SI 2006/1031 ('the Age Regulations').

31.4 Absolute exception for length of service up to five years. There is an absolute exemption from the age discrimination rules for benefits based on a length of service up to five years. This is provided for in para 10(1) of Schedule 9, which provides: 'It is not an age contravention for a person (A) to put a person (B) at a disadvantage when compared with another (C), in relation to the provision of a benefit, facility or service in so far as the disadvantage is because B has a shorter period of service than C.' Para 10(2) then goes on to restrict the exemption to benefits awarded in respect of length of service of up to five years, thus: 'If B's period of service exceeds 5 years, A may rely on sub-paragraph (1) only if A reasonably believes that doing so fulfils a business need.'

31.5 'Fulfils a business need'. Paragraph 10(2) is a streamlined version of its predecessor provision in Reg 32(2) of the Age Regulations, under which the award of benefits by reference to length of service of more than five years was permitted if the employer could show that it 'reasonably appears' that the way in which the criterion was used fulfilled 'a business need for [its] undertaking'. That provision went on to note that a business need might be encouraging the loyalty or motivation, or rewarding the experience, of some or all workers. By way of contrast, para 10(2) does not specify examples of what a 'business need' might be. However, we do not consider that the scope of the test has been affected, as the examples given in old Reg 32(2) were clearly not intended to be exhaustive.

In addition to the Employment Code, the EHRC has issued non-statutory guidance for employers on various aspects of the Equality Act 2010 (available at www.equalityhumanrights.com). Under the heading 'Situations where equality law is different', the EHRC notes that the same considerations – experience, loyalty and motivation – may validly lie behind the award of service-related benefits.

Calculating length of service. The method of calculating length of service is **31.6** set out in para 10(3)–(6) of Schedule 9. Under para 10(3), the employer may choose to calculate by reference to:

- the period for which the employee has been working for the employer at or above a level (assessed by reference to the demands made on the employee) that the employer reasonably regards as appropriate, or

- the period for which the employee has been working for the employer at any level.

The period for which the employee has been working for the employer must be **31.7** based on the number of weeks during the whole or part of which the employee worked for the employer – para 10(4). An employer is entitled, so far as is reasonable, to discount periods of absence and periods that the employer reasonably regards as related to absence – para 10(5). However, where the calculation is made by reference to the period for which the employee has been working for the employer at any level (i.e. under the second limb of para 10(3)), the employee is deemed to have been working for an employer during any period which:

- counts as a period of employment with that employer due to the continuity of employment provision in S.218 of the Employment Rights Act 1996 (ERA) (which governs continuity for the purposes of, inter alia, unfair dismissal and redundancy), or

- if S.218 does not apply, is treated as a period of employment by an enactment pursuant to which the employee's employment was transferred to the employer – para 10(6). This second limb would cover, for example, employment transferred as a result of the Transfer of Undertakings (Protection of Employment) Regulations 2006 SI 2006/246.

Paragraph 10(7) goes on to provide that the length of service exemption does **31.8** not extend to termination payments, replicating the effect of old Reg 32(7). Para 10(7) states that 'a benefit, facility or service which may be provided only by virtue of a person's ceasing to work' does not fall within the exemption. Thus, using length of service as a criterion in a redundancy scheme will need to

1075

be specifically justified under the standard test that applies to all forms of indirect discrimination.

Note that the exemption for service-related benefits applies to excuse all instances of discrimination under the EqA. Therefore it goes wider than benefits based on length of service in 'employment' by also covering contract workers, partnerships, public offices, etc.

31.9 National minimum wage

The rates of the national minimum wage (NMW) are inherently age discriminatory. As at 1 October 2011, workers aged 21 and over are entitled to a minimum rate of £6.08 per hour; those aged 18–20 to a minimum rate of £4.98 per hour; and those aged 16 or 17 to a minimum rate of £3.68 per hour – Regs 11 and 13 National Minimum Wage Regulations 1999 SI 1999/584. These rates are reviewed annually.

When the Age Regulations brought in the prohibition on age discrimination in employment in October 2006, the Government decided to maintain the NMW age bands on the basis that they are objectively justified as a means of making it easier for younger workers to find employment. Accordingly, Reg 31 of the Age Regulations made an exception for discrimination that involved paying discriminatory rates based on the NMW bands. This exception is now replicated in para 11(1) of Schedule 9 to the EqA, which states that 'it is not an age contravention for a person to pay a young worker (A) at a lower rate than that at which the person pays an older worker (B) if (a) the hourly rate for the national minimum wage for a person of A's age is lower than that for a person of B's age, and (b) the rate at which A is paid is below the single hourly rate'. For this purpose, 'a young worker is a person who qualifies for the national minimum wage at a lower rate than the single hourly rate; and an older worker is a person who qualifies for the national minimum wage at a higher rate than that at which the young worker qualifies for it'. The 'single hourly rate' for these purposes is the highest rate of NMW set down by Reg 11 of the NMW Regulations (currently £6.08).

31.10 Two points need to be made about this exception. First, it does not allow an employer, on age grounds, to pay different rates to those *within* the same NMW age band. So, for example, an employer cannot, on age grounds, pay an 18-year-old less than a 20-year-old unless doing so is objectively justified (which, in all likelihood, it will not be).

Secondly, para 11 does not allow an employer, on age grounds, to pay different rates to workers in different NMW age bands where it pays young workers *more than* the adult NMW rate. So, for example, if an employer were to pay a 23-year-old worker £10 per hour and a 20-year-old worker £8 per hour, it would not be protected by para 11(1) since both workers earn more than the adult NMW rate of £6.08. Thus, the younger worker could succeed with a claim for direct age discrimination if the pay differential is not objectively justified. Somewhat oddly, if the employer were instead to pay the 23-year-old worker £10 per hour and the 20-year-old worker £5 per hour – a much greater differential, and thus, on the face of it, a more severe example of direct age discrimination – it would be protected by para 11(1), as the 20-year-old would be earning less than the adult NMW rate.

Apprentices. Amendments to the NMW Regulations taking effect in October **31.11** 2010 introduced a minimum wage for apprentices for the first time, being a standard rate of, currently, £2.60 per hour. Para 12 of Schedule 9 provides that it is not an age contravention to pay an apprentice who does not qualify for the NMW at a lower rate than an apprentice who does.

Enhanced redundancy payments   **31.12**

The limited exemption from the age discrimination rules for benefits awarded by reference to length of service does not, as noted above, cover termination payments, such as redundancy payments. While it is normal practice for redundancy schemes to calculate awards by reference to length of service, the indirect discrimination inherent in such a practice must be justified according to the standard test. The same applies where redundancy schemes calculate payments by reference to an employee's age in service. This is not a common practice but it is by no means unheard of, and the direct discrimination that it entails must be objectively justified.

However, the EqA – like the Age Regulations before it – allows for a limited exception in respect of redundancy schemes based on the statutory redundancy payment framework. As set out by S.162 ERA, this framework grants:

- one and a half weeks' pay for each year in employment in which the employee was not below the age of 41

- one week's pay for each year in employment in which the employee was between the ages of 22 and 40, and

- half a week's pay for each other year of employment.

A maximum of 20 years' employment may be taken into account for the **31.13** purpose of this calculation; and a week's pay, for this purpose, is capped at an amount that is periodically reviewed in line with inflation – S.227 ERA. Furthermore, the employee must have two years' continuous employment to be eligible for any payment at all – S.155 ERA.

The exception in respect of enhanced redundancy payments is contained in para 13 of Schedule 9. Para 13(1) provides that 'it is not an age contravention for a person to give a qualifying employee an enhanced redundancy payment of an amount less than that of an enhanced redundancy payment which the person gives to another qualifying employee, if each amount is calculated on the same

1077

basis'. So, the employer may only rely on the exception in relation to 'qualifying employees'. A person is a qualifying employee 'if the person –

(a) is entitled to a redundancy payment as a result of S.135 ERA [i.e. one who has been dismissed as 'redundant', laid off or put on short-time working in circumstances defined in the ERA]

(b) agrees to the termination of the employment in circumstances where the person would, if dismissed, have been so entitled

(c) would have been so entitled but for S.155 ERA (requirement for two years' continuous employment), or

(d) agrees to the termination of the employment in circumstances where the person would, if dismissed, have been so entitled but for the requirement of two years' continuous employment'– para 13(3).

31.14 Para 13(2) then goes on to stipulate that nor is it an age contravention 'to give enhanced redundancy payments only to those who are qualifying employees by virtue of sub-paragraph (3)(a) or (b)', i.e. the first two categories listed above. Thus, an employer may lawfully restrict enhanced redundancy payments to those who have completed two years' continuous employment (in the same way as the statutory scheme), or it may choose to ignore the qualifying period.

Only enhanced redundancy payments that are calculated on the basis of the same age and service criteria that apply under the statutory scheme are permitted under the para 13 exception (para 13(4)), but the employer is allowed to make certain specified enhancements. Under para 13(5), it '(a) may treat a week's pay as not being subject to a maximum amount; (b) may treat a week's pay as being subject to a maximum amount above that for the time being specified in section 227(1) ERA; (c) may multiply the appropriate amount for each year of employment by a figure of more than one'. This wording does not make it clear whether the employer may do more than one of these things – the options (a), (b) and (c) are capable of a conjunctive or disjunctive interpretation. However, Reg 33(4), which made corresponding provision under the Age Regulations, was clear that the employer could do any combination of these things and there is no reason to think that the same freedom does not apply under the new rules. Para 13(6) goes on to state that, whether or not the employer makes an enhancement mentioned in para 13(5), it may also multiply the final total by a figure of more than one.

31.15 This exception for enhanced redundancy payments is very limited. Only schemes that apply a multiplier to the statutory bands will come within it. Accordingly, most contractual redundancy schemes based on age and/or length of service will be unlawful unless objectively justified as a proportionate means of achieving a legitimate aim – for a consideration of justification in this context, see Chapter 25, 'Discrimination during employment', under 'Benefits, facilities and services – enhanced redundancy schemes'.

Insurance and related financial services
31.16

When originally enacted, para 14 of Schedule 9 to the EqA included an exception relating to life assurance which applied when a person took early retirement because of ill health. Broadly speaking, its effect was that an employer would not commit an act of age discrimination by providing an employee with life assurance cover between the date of retirement and the employer's normal retirement age, or if there is no such age, 65. However, Reg 2(4) of the Employment Equality (Repeal of Retirement Age Provisions) Regulations 2011 SI 2011/1069 inserted an entirely new para 14 into Schedule 9. The new exception is broader than its predecessor, as it covers both insurance and 'related financial services'.

Paragraph 14(1) of Schedule 9 to the EqA now provides that 'it is not an age contravention for an employer to make arrangements for, or afford access to, the provision of insurance or a related financial service to or in respect of an employee for a period ending when the employee attains whichever is the greater of the age of 65 and the state pensionable age'. In similar terms, para 14(2) provides that 'it is not an age contravention for an employer to make arrangements for, or afford access to, the provision of insurance or a related financial service to or in respect of only such employees as have not attained whichever is the greater of the age of 65, and the state pensionable age'. The state pensionable age in this context is the pensionable age determined in accordance with the rules in para 1 of Schedule 4 to the Pensions Act 1995 – para 14(4).

By virtue of para 14(3), the above provisions only apply where 'the insurance **31.17** or related financial service is, or is to be, provided to the employer's employees or a class of those employees:

(a) in pursuance of an arrangement between the employer and another person, or

(b) where the employer's business includes the provision of insurance or financial services of the description in question, by the employer'.

As a result of para 14(3), the exceptions in para 14(1) and (2) do not extend to the situation where an employer provides employees with a cash payment to self-insure. It is debatable, however, whether it would cover a flexible benefits scheme under which an employer provides vouchers to employees which can be spent on a range of benefits, including insurance: the pivotal question is whether the service is being provided 'in pursuance of' an arrangement between the employer and the voucher provider.

31.18   Due to the way para 14(1) and (2) is drafted, the exceptions are only available to employers who cease to provide benefits on an employee reaching 65 (or the state pensionable age when that rises above 65). An employer who is more generous – by, for example, providing life insurance for employees up to age 70 – would not be covered. However, that does not mean that such an employer would be automatically liable to age discrimination – any age discrimination in the provision of benefits that is not caught by para 14 can still be objectively justified.

31.19   Childcare benefits
The age-related exceptions set out in Schedule 9 to the EqA are all re-enactments or revisions of exceptions originally provided for by the Age Regulations apart from one: the childcare benefits exception. The Government decided to create this new exception because of the effect of the European Court of Justice's decision in Coleman v Attridge Law and anor 2008 ICR 1128, ECJ. In that case the ECJ held that the protection from disability discrimination in the EU Equal Treatment Framework Directive (No.2000/78) ('the Framework Directive') is not limited to employees who are themselves disabled. Thus, where an employer treats an employee less favourably than another, and that less favourable treatment is based on the disability of that employee's child for whom the employee is the primary carer, the treatment in question will be in breach of the prohibition on disability discrimination. Although the ECJ did not expressly make the point, this principle is clearly capable of applying equally to the other protected characteristics covered by the Framework Directive; namely, age, religion or belief and sexual orientation. Thus, it might be unlawful to treat an employee less favourably because the employee cares for an elderly relative, at least if it can be shown that the treatment is related to the relative's age. The new definition of direct discrimination in S.13 EqA is wide enough to include such 'associative' discrimination related to all of the protected characteristics covered by the Act – for further details see Chapter 15, 'Direct discrimination', under 'Discrimination by association'.

The Government's view – explained by the Explanatory Notes at para 851 – was that the prohibition of associative discrimination could potentially render unlawful the provision of facilities, such as childcare, where access is limited by reference to the child's age. It therefore decided to introduce an exception so that employers could continue to provide such facilities without fear of age discrimination claims. Para 15(1) of Schedule 9 to the EqA therefore stipulates that 'a person does not contravene a relevant provision, so far as relating to age, only by providing, or making arrangements for or facilitating the provision of, care for children of a particular age group'. Para 15(3) elaborates on 'facilitating' the provision of childcare, stating that it includes paying for some or all of the cost of provision, helping the parent find a suitable carer, and enabling the parent to spend more time providing care for the child or otherwise assisting the parent with respect to the care of the child. A 'child', for this purpose, is any child under the age of 17 – para 15(4). This is the same age limit as that which currently applies in respect of the right to request flexible working arrangements under Part 8A of the ERA.

A 'relevant provision' for this purpose is defined by para 15(2) of Schedule 9. It **31.20** includes discrimination in employment under S.39(2)(b). In addition, the exemption can be relied on with regard to what would otherwise be discrimination against contract workers (S.41(1)(c)), partners (S.44(2)(b)), limited liability partners (S.45(2)(b)), barristers (S.47(2)(b)), advocates (S.48(2)(b)), personal office holders (S.49(6)(b)), public office holders (S.50(6)(b)), trade union members (S.57(2)(a)) and local authority members (S.58(3)(a)).

Pension schemes   31.21

The greatest number of exceptions to age discrimination protection applies in the context of occupational and personal pensions. A detailed analysis of the complex rules regarding the interface between pensions and age discrimination is beyond the scope of this Handbook, but an overview of the statutory position is provided below. Previously, Reg 11 of the Age Regulations laid down a general rule that there should be no discrimination on the ground of age against members or prospective members of occupational pension schemes by the employer or the trustees or managers of such schemes when carrying out their functions (including those relating to the admission to and treatment of members of the scheme) – 'the non-discrimination rule'. However, Schedule 2 to the Age Regulations then set out a large number of specific exceptions in this regard.

The broad equivalent of Reg 11 is now to be found in S.61 EqA, which applies the non-discrimination rule to all the protected characteristics covered by the Act, not just age. However, by virtue of S.61(8), a Minister of the Crown is authorised to specify by order the exceptions to the general rule in S.61. Pursuant to this, the Equality Act (Age Exceptions for Pension Schemes) Order 2010 SI 2010/2133 (as amended by the Equality Act 2010 (Age Exceptions for Pension Schemes) (Amendment) Order 2010 SI 2010/2285) re-enacts in large measure all the exceptions previously set out in the Age Regulations.

Outline of occupational pension scheme exceptions. Article 3 of the 2010 **31.22** Order (as amended) provides that it is not a breach of the non-discrimination rule in S.61 EqA for the employer, or trustees or managers of an occupational pension scheme to maintain or use in relation to the scheme rules, practices, actions or decisions (a) set out in Schedule 1 to the Order, or (b) as they relate to rights accrued or benefits payable in respect of periods of pensionable service prior to 1 December 2006. Regarding the first category of exceptions

1081

mentioned in (a), Schedule 1 sets out no fewer than 33 different types of exception. These include:

- setting minimum and maximum ages for admission to schemes, including different ages for different categories of worker – para 1

- using age criteria in actuarial calculations – para 2

- providing for differences in member or employer contributions attributable to differences in members' pensionable pay or actuarial rates – para 3

- providing under a money purchase (defined contribution) arrangement for different rates of member or employer contributions according to the ages of members, so long as the aim of this is to equalise or make more nearly equal the amount of benefit that members of different ages who are otherwise in a comparable situation will be entitled to under the scheme – para 4(a)

- providing under a money purchase arrangement for equal rates of member or employer contributions irrespective of the ages of members – para 4(b)

- providing under a final salary (defined benefit) arrangement for different rates of member or employer contributions according to the ages of members to the extent that each year of pensionable service entitles members in a comparable situation to accrue a right to defined benefits based on the same fraction of pensionable pay, so long as the aim in setting the different rates is to reflect the increasing cost of providing the defined benefits in respect of members as they get older – para 5

- closing schemes to new members from a particular date – para 26

- increasing pensions in payment which are made to members over the age of 55 but not to members below that age – para 28

- providing for differences in the rate of increase of pensions in payment for members of different ages where the objective is to maintain the relative value of members' pensions – para 29.

31.23 **Contributions to personal pension schemes.** Personal pension schemes (including group personal pension schemes) are not specifically covered by S.61 (which applies to occupational pension schemes only), but employers are nonetheless prevented by the general anti-discrimination provisions of the EqA from discriminating on age grounds when making contributions to employees' personal pensions. Accordingly, para 16 of Schedule 9 makes provision for exceptions relating to personal pension schemes.

Paragraph 16(1) permits a Minister of the Crown to make an order specifying that certain age-related practices, actions or decisions in the context of contributions to personal pension schemes will not be age contraventions. Pursuant to this, Schedule 2 to the Equality Act (Age Exceptions for Pension

Schemes) Order 2010 sets out various exceptions relating to employers' contributions to personal pension schemes, allowing employers to:

- make contributions of different rates according to workers' ages where the aim of doing so is to equalise or make more nearly equal the amount of benefit that workers of different ages in comparable situations will become entitled to

- make contributions of different rates attributable to differences in remuneration payable to those workers

- limit contributions by reference to a maximum level of remuneration

- apply a minimum age for commencing payments to the scheme

- apply different minimum ages for commencing payments in respect of different groups or categories of workers

- make equal rates of contributions irrespective of the age of workers in respect of whom contributions are made.

Disability exceptions 31.24

There are a number of ways in which disability is treated differently to the other protected characteristics in the EqA. Most obviously, direct disability discrimination only works in one direction: a non-disabled person cannot bring a claim of disability discrimination founded on the basis of a disabled person being treated more favourably – S.13(3) (see further Chapter 15, 'Direct discrimination', in the section 'Less favourable treatment', under 'Exceptions – disability'.

As a result of S.13(3), the need for specific exceptions relating to disability is extremely limited. However, a number of exceptions that have a more general application – and are therefore considered in Chapter 30, 'General exceptions' – specifically apply to disability). These are:

- employment in the armed forces – no complaint of disability discrimination may be brought in respect of service in the armed forces – para 4(3), Sch 9 (see Chapter 30, 'General exceptions', under 'National security – armed forces')

- charities – charities enjoy an exemption that allows them to provide benefits consisting of employment, contract work and vocational training to disabled people only – S.193(10) EqA. In addition, S.193(3) makes specific exception for supported employment aimed at disabled people (see Chapter 30, 'General exceptions', under 'Charities').

1083

31.25 ## Maternity exceptions

Chapter 3 of Part 5 of the EqA deals with a woman's entitlement to have her contractual terms preserved throughout her pregnancy and maternity leave. While there is no right to equal treatment with regard to contractual pay during maternity leave, the woman is entitled to benefit from pay increases occurring, and various bonuses awarded, during that time – for full details see IDS Employment Law Handbook, 'Equal Pay' (2011), Chapter 2, 'Right to equal pay', under 'Maternity – no entitlement to full pay during maternity leave'.

Paragraph 17 of Schedule 9 to the EqA makes corresponding provision with regard to non-contractual pay and benefits. It provides that a person 'does not contravene S.39(1)(b) or (2), so far as relating to pregnancy and maternity, by depriving a woman who is on maternity leave of any benefit from the terms of her employment relating to pay' – para 17(1). 'Terms', in this context, means terms other than those contained in the contract of employment (or apprenticeship, or to do work personally), and 'pay' means benefits that consist of the payment of money by way of wages or salary – para 17(4) and (5). So, the basic rule is that not awarding a discretionary bonus to a woman on maternity leave, for example, will not amount to sex discrimination.

31.26 However, para 17 goes on to make certain exceptions to this exception. Para 17(2) provides that 'the reference in [para 17(1)] to benefit from the terms of a woman's employment relating to pay does not include a reference to –

(a) maternity-related pay (including maternity-related pay that is increase-related)

(b) pay (including increase-related pay) in respect of times when she is not on maternity leave, or

(c) pay by way of bonus in respect of times when she is on compulsory maternity leave'.

'Maternity-related pay', for this purpose, means pay to which a woman is entitled '(a) as a result of being pregnant, or (b) in respect of times when she is on maternity leave' – para 17(6). So, while a woman on maternity leave need not be given a gratuitous discretionary bonus, if the bonus relates to company performance during a time when the woman was present at work, then it would have to be given under para 17(2)(b). Similarly, if the bonus relates to performance during a time when the woman was on maternity leave, she should be awarded a proportionate bonus in respect of the time during which she was on compulsory maternity leave. These provisions achieve the same effect as did S.6A of the Sex Discrimination Act 1975 (SDA).

Race exceptions

31.27

There are two exceptions that relate specifically to race discrimination. These concern the provision of training for non-European Economic Area (EEA) residents and the wearing of turbans by Sikhs.

Training for non-EEA residents

31.28

Most exceptions discussed in this chapter have entailed special dispensation for employers to treat particular groups *less* favourably. Para 4 of Schedule 23 to the EqA – which re-enacts S.36 of the Race Relations Act 1976 – is unusual in that it provides for *more* favourable treatment of foreign nationals. Its purpose is to enable people from developing countries to acquire skills that may not be available in their country of residence. Para 4(1) provides that 'a person (A) does not contravene this Act, so far as relating to nationality, only by providing a non-resident (B) with training, if A thinks that B does not intend to exercise in Great Britain skills B obtains as a result'. A 'non-resident', for this purpose, is a person not ordinarily resident in a state of the European Economic Area – para 4(2).

The kind of training covered by this exception, set out by para 4(3) and (4), is:

- if A employs B in employment whose sole or main purpose is the provision of training in skills, anything A does in or in connection with the employment

- if A as a principal allows B to do contract work whose sole or main purpose is the provision of training in skills, anything A does in or in connection with allowing B to do the work

- in the two above cases or any other, affording B access to facilities for education or training or ancillary benefits.

The scope of this exception is expanded when it relates to military training. 31.29 Under para 4(5), 'in the case of training provided by the armed forces or Secretary of State for purposes relating to defence', a 'non-resident' is anyone not ordinarily resident in Great Britain. Thus it will be lawful to provide European citizens with relevant training, to the exclusion of British nationals. Also, in the case of military training, the employment or contract work is covered if its purposes *include* the provision of training in skills – that does not have to be its 'sole or main purpose'.

Sikhs and turbans – construction sites

31.30

The Employment Act 1989 introduced important provisions relating to Sikhs who wish to wear turbans instead of safety helmets on construction sites. S.11 of that Act exempts a Sikh who is wearing a turban on a construction site from the application of any statutory provision that would otherwise require him to wear a safety helmet. If a Sikh who is not wearing a safety helmet is accidentally

1085

injured, any damages recoverable will be restricted to damages for the injury that would have occurred even if he had worn a safety helmet. This concession only applies to Sikhs and it only applies on construction sites.

Section 12 of the 1989 Act, which was amended upon the coming into force of the EqA, spells out the implications of these provisions for discrimination law. Basically, if an employer imposes a provision, criterion or practice (PCP) that a Sikh should wear a safety helmet on a construction site, then – unless the employer has reasonable grounds to believe that the Sikh would not wear a turban at all times on such a site – it will be taken to have discriminated indirectly as the PCP will be deemed not to be justifiable – S.12(1). So if, for example, the Sikh is refused a job or is dismissed or suffers any other detriment as a result, the employer will have no defence. If the employer does have reasonable grounds for believing that the Sikh would not wear a turban at all times, then the PCP will not be deemed to be unjustifiable (although it may be found to be so) and the question of indirect discrimination will be considered in the normal way (see Chapter 17, 'Indirect discrimination: objective justification').

Finally, S.12(2) is designed to prevent a non-Sikh complaining of special treatment afforded to Sikhs by enacting that such special treatment is neither directly nor indirectly discriminatory in relation to any other person.

31.31 **Sikhs and turbans in other workplaces.** A construction site is defined as 'any place where any building operations or works of engineering construction are being undertaken' – S.11(7) of the 1989 Act. If an employer requires hard hats to be worn in a workplace that does not fall within this definition and thereby indirectly discriminates against Sikhs, the issue of whether the requirement is justifiable will be a question of fact for the tribunal to decide.

In Dhanjal v British Steel General Steels ET Case No.50740/91 a tribunal held that safety requirements could amount to justification for an apparently discriminatory requirement to wear a helmet. D was a Sikh who wore a turban and worked for BSGS at a steel mill. At first D's employer did not require him to wear a safety helmet in hard hat areas – on the assumption that it would not be liable for any injury he incurred as a result. Following a review of safety procedures, however, the local inspector of factories advised the employer that the Health and Safety at Work etc Act 1974 (which requires employers to provide employees with a safe place and system of work) did not allow for any exemptions on religious grounds. The employer concluded that it would have to insist that all employees – including Sikhs – wore safety helmets in the designated areas. D made it clear that he could not comply with this requirement and, after attempts to relocate him failed, he was dismissed. The tribunal held that his dismissal was fair and that there had been no unlawful discrimination. It held that the employer had been entitled to take the view that, whenever considerations of safety conflicted with the religious needs of employees, safety should prevail. The first duty of the employer was to protect the workforce against risks to their safety and health. It was also essential for the company to protect itself against prosecution under the 1974 Act. In the absence of any specific exception to that duty along the lines of the one relating to construction sites, it was clear that safety requirements had to prevail over any requirement not to discriminate on the ground of race.

Religion or belief exceptions 31.32

In addition to the general occupational requirement defence in para 1 of Schedule 9 to the EqA (see Chapter 30, 'General exceptions', under 'Occupational requirements'), Schedule 9 contains two specific occupational requirement defences that relate to the protected characteristic of religion or belief: one concerning employment for the purposes of an organised religion; the other concerning work with organisations that have an 'ethos' based on religion or belief.

Organised religion exception 31.33

Employment for the purposes of an 'organised religion' qualifies for special treatment under the EqA, as it did under the previous equality enactments. Only those employers who can meet the strict conditions set out in para 2 of Schedule 9 can rely on an organised religion exception. The Explanatory Notes indicate that the exception is intended to cover 'a very narrow range of employment: ministers of religion and a small number of lay posts, including those that exist to promote and represent religion' (para 799). The key conditions are these:

- the employment to which the requirement is applied 'is for the purposes of an organised religion' – para 2(1)(a), and

- the person to whom the requirement is applied does not meet it (or, except in the case of sex, the employer has reasonable grounds for not being satisfied that the person meets it) – para 2(1)(c) and (8); and *either*

- the requirement is applied so as to comply with the doctrines of the religion (the compliance principle) – para 2(1)(b) and (5); *or*

- because of the nature or context of the employment, the requirement is applied so as to avoid conflicting with the strongly held religious convictions of a significant number of the religion's followers (the non-conflict principle) – para 2(1)(b) and (6).

There is no definition of 'organised religion' in the Act, and nor was there one 31.34 in the SDA or the Employment Equality (Sexual Orientation) Regulations 2003 SI 2003/1661 ('the Sexual Orientation Regulations'). The Equality Bill originally sought to define what was meant by employment 'for the purposes of an organised religion', restricting it to employment that wholly or mainly involved leading or assisting in the observation of liturgical or ritualistic practices of a religion, or promoting or explaining its doctrine. However, this wording came in for criticism on the ground that it narrowed the scope of the defence. Neither the SDA nor the Sexual Orientation Regulations sought to restrict the concept of employment *for the purposes of* organised religion, and some religious organisations feared that defining the posts potentially covered by the exception would unduly restrict their freedom to tailor their employment practices to the requirements of their doctrines. The Conservative peer Baroness O'Cathain channelled these criticisms into an amendment removing the definition from the Bill with the effect that the wording of the EqA in this regard is now substantially the same as the wording of the pre-existing exceptions under the SDA and the Sexual Orientation Regulations.

The Government's position was that the proposed new wording was not intended to introduce substantive change, but merely to clarify the scope of the law. Baroness Royall of Blaisdon, speaking on the Government's behalf in response to Baroness O'Cathain, noted that the Government had seen examples of where the exemption in the Sexual Orientation Regulations 'appeared to have been misused, such as in relation to the finance director of a church'. Now that the status quo has been preserved, such examples may come up again. However, employment tribunals must also apply the guidance of the High Court in R (on the application of Amicus and ors) v Secretary of State for Trade and Industry 2007 ICR 1176, QBD, on the scope of the exception. The High Court there pointed out that the organised religion exception must be construed narrowly and in a manner compatible with the EU Equal Treatment Framework Directive (No.2000/78) ('the Framework Directive'). In particular, the exception in respect of employment for the purposes of an 'organised religion' is narrower in scope than that covering employment in a 'religious organisation'. The Court accepted that, for example, employment of a teacher in a faith school was likely to fall within the latter category but not the former.

31.35 The requirements that an employer may apply for the purposes of an organised religion are set out in para 2(4) of Schedule 9. They are:

- a requirement to be of a particular sex
- a requirement not to be a transsexual person
- a requirement not to be married or a civil partner
- a requirement not to be married to, or the civil partner of, a person who has a living former spouse or civil partner
- a requirement relating to circumstances in which a marriage or civil partnership came to an end
- a requirement related to sexual orientation.

Clearly, all the circumstances to which these requirements relate – marriage, divorce, gender and sexuality – are likely to conflict with the strictures of organised religions.

The scope of the requirements that may be applied under para 2(4) is much the **31.36** same as that permitted by the Sexual Orientation Regulations and the SDA, the changes in wording being mostly cosmetic. For instance, while the SDA permitted a requirement 'relating to not being married or to not being a civil partner', the equivalent in para 2(4) is a requirement 'not to be married or a civil partner'. Although the new wording appears slightly more restrictive, it is hard to envisage any practical difference. This also means that case law on the old legislation should apply equally to para 2. In particular, the High Court's judgment in R (on the application of Amicus and ors) v Secretary of State for Trade and Industry (above), regarding the meaning of a requirement 'related to' sexual orientation, should still be treated as good law. The Court there held that this encompasses more than just a requirement that a person be of a particular sexual orientation. It also covers the manifestation of sexual orientation through sexual behaviour.

The EHRC Employment Code provides the following example of how the organised religion exception might apply: 'The trustees of a Mosque want to employ two youth workers, one who will provide guidance on the teachings of the Koran and the other purely to organise sporting activities not involving promoting or representing the religion. The trustees apply an occupational requirement for both workers to be heterosexual. It might be lawful to apply the occupational requirement exception to the first post but not the second post because the second post does not engage the "compliance" or the "non-conflict" principle' – para 13.15.

Compatibility with European law. The amendment that Baroness O'Cathain **31.37** successfully introduced to remove the definition of 'for the purposes of an organised religion' in the Equality Bill also removed a proportionality test that was originally included. Para 2(5) and (6), as originally drafted, would have required the employer to show that any requirement sought to be relied upon was *a proportionate means* of complying with the doctrines of the religion, or avoiding conflict with the religious convictions of the religion's followers. The removal of this criterion meant that the status quo was maintained when the EqA came into force, i.e. the employer need show only that the requirement is directed at the compliance or non-conflict principle, not that it is a proportionate means of achieving it.

There has been some concern that this state of affairs is in breach of European law. In November 2009 the European Commission had sent a Reasoned Opinion to the UK Government, expressing concern that the prohibition on sexual orientation discrimination laid down in the Framework Directive had not been fully implemented in UK law. In particular, the Commission noted

1089

that the exception for religious organisations was too wide. At the time, the original version of the Equality Bill – containing the proposed changes to the law noted here – was progressing through the Houses of Parliament. Thus, it was assumed that the Bill would address the European Commission's concerns in this regard (although the Government denied that those concerns had motivated the original drafting of these provisions). Now that, following Baroness O'Cathain's intervention, the status quo has been maintained, the breach of European law, as the Commission saw it, persists. That said, it is not entirely clear that the Commission was correct to take this view. In 2007, the High Court in R (on the application of Amicus and ors) v Secretary of State for Trade and Industry (above) reviewed the exception as it applied under the Sexual Orientation Regulations and held that it was, in fact, compliant with the Framework Directive, as it enshrined a requirement of proportionality despite the absence of an express provision to that effect. It remains to be seen whether the Commission will be satisfied with the state of UK law on this point. It is entitled to refer the matter to the ECJ if it is satisfied that domestic legislation is in breach of a Directive. However, at the time of going to press, the Commission had given no indication of its intentions in this regard.

31.38 **Discrimination permitted by the organised religion exception.** Where an organised religion exception is established, it is lawful to discriminate in a similar range of contexts to those covered by the general occupational requirements (OR) defence (explained in Chapter 30, 'General exceptions', under 'Occupational requirements'). As with the general exception, the organised religion exception applies only to direct discrimination. Para 2(2) of Schedule 9 permits discrimination in employment with regard to the arrangements for determining who should be offered employment, refusals to offer employment, access to opportunities for promotion, transfer or training, and dismissal. Appointments to personal and public offices are also covered to the same extent as they are covered by the general OR defence, but partnerships and contract work are not. Under para 2(3), the organised religion OR may also apply to permit discrimination by a qualifications body in its arrangements in conferring, not conferring or withdrawing a qualification, among other things, so long as the qualification is for the purposes of employment covered by the organised religion exception and the compliance or non-conflict principle is engaged.

31.39 **Ethos based on religion or belief**

While the organised religion exception considered above will only apply in an extremely limited range of circumstances, para 3 of Schedule 9 to the EqA provides for a further, and wider, exception centred on an employer's 'ethos'. Para 3 states that 'a person (A) with an ethos based on religion or belief does not contravene a provision mentioned in paragraph 1(2) [prohibition on discrimination in employment, contract work, etc] by applying in relation to work a requirement to be of a particular religion or belief if A shows that, having regard to that ethos and to the nature or context of the work –

(a) it is an occupational requirement,

(b) the application of the requirement is a proportionate means of achieving a legitimate aim, and

(c) the person to whom A applies the requirement does not meet it (or A has reasonable grounds for not being satisfied that the person meets it)'.

References to an 'ethos' aside, this defence is in identical terms to the general OR exception provided for in para 1(1) of Schedule 9 – see Chapter 30, 'General exceptions', under 'Occupational requirements'.

The specific defence for organisations with a religious ethos was previously **31.40** contained in Reg 7 of the Employment Equality (Religion or Belief) Regulations 2003 SI 2003/1660 ('the Religion or Belief Regulations'). That provision laid down two separate (but not mutually exclusive) defences for applying a requirement that job applicants be of a particular religion or belief. Reg 7(2) was the 'genuine occupational requirement' (GOR) defence that has now been reformulated as the 'occupational requirement' defence in para 1 of Schedule 9 (and discussed in Chapter 30). Like all the previous GOR defences, Reg 7(2) required that the GOR be 'genuine and determining' – a requirement that has been dropped in the new OR defence with which it has been replaced by para 1. The specific 'religious ethos' defence was then contained separately in Reg 7(3). It applied only where the employer had an ethos based on religion or belief and was in almost identical terms to the general defence under Reg 7(2), except that there was no need to show that the GOR was 'determining'. Although the defences were rarely tested in the courts in the six years that they were in force under the Religion or Belief Regulations, it was generally assumed that the absence of the 'determining' criterion under Reg 7(3) meant that the standard was lower than under Reg 7(2). It made logical sense to apply a less stringent test only if the employer could clear the additional hurdle of showing a religious ethos.

Two points arise from this analysis of legislative history. First, it re-emphasises the queries and doubts about the Government's insistence that dropping the 'determinative' requirement in the reformulated OR defence makes no difference of substance. The word clearly made – or at least was intended to make – a difference of substance between Reg 7(2) and Reg 7(3) of the Religion or Belief Regulations. Secondly, it raises the question of why there is a separate defence under the EqA for organisations with a religious ethos, when its scope is now exactly the same as that of the general OR defence under para 1. In fact, the religious ethos defence is, if anything, harder to make out than the general defence – under para 3, the employer has the additional burden of establishing the existence of the ethos and that the OR relates to it.

31.41 There was relatively little case law considering the religious ethos exception under the Religion or Belief Regulations. However, in Sheridan v Prospects For People With Learning Disabilities ET Case No.2901366/06 and Hender v Prospects For People With Learning Disabilities ET Case No.2902090/06 an employment tribunal held that a Christian charity providing support services for people with learning disabilities could not rely on the Reg 7(3) exemption to operate a blanket 'Christians-only' employment policy. The tribunal approached the issue in three stages. First it considered the charity's ethos, the nature of the employment and the context in which it was carried out. Then it asked whether a particular religion or belief was a GOR for the support worker posts in question. Finally, it asked whether the GOR was proportionate in the circumstances.

On the first point, the tribunal accepted that the charity had a Christian ethos, but rejected the assertion that it primarily existed to serve Christ, and so required Christian staff to fulfil this 'mission': the charity's primary objective was to provide support services to people with learning difficulties. The tribunal found that the overwhelming support given was secular in nature; the majority of people supported were not Christians; and a significant number of the charity's support workers were not practising Christians. As to whether being a practising Christian was essential to performing the functions of a support worker, the tribunal found that the fact that the charity had, for some years, run its services with a significant number of non-practising Christians in these roles, coupled with its decision not to dismiss them after reasserting its 'Christians-only' employment policy in 2005, pointed away from there being a GOR for these roles. On the question of proportionality, the tribunal found that a few functions of the support worker posts had a Christian element, but the concept of proportionality required the charity to consider whether these functions could be carried out by other members of staff, or whether it was sufficient to apply a lesser requirement than being a practising Christian – such as requiring staff to be ethos-sympathetic. The charity had not done so.

31.42 Another case that illustrates the narrow confines of the religious ethos exception is Glasgow City Council v McNab 2007 IRLR 476, EAT. There, a local authority unsuccessfully sought to rely on Reg 7(2) to excuse its refusal to interview an atheist teacher for promotion to a role involving pastoral care at a Catholic school. It also argued in the alternative that Reg 7(3) was engaged, but an employment tribunal determined that a local authority cannot possess a religious ethos. Confirming that decision on appeal, the EAT stressed that a local authority has no business seeking to follow or further any particular religious ethos. If the intention had been that an employer could qualify for the protection afforded by Reg 7(3) if only part of its organisation had an ethos based on religion or belief, one would have expected such a right to have been expressly stated by the legislature. In any event, the fact that an education authority operates a statutory system under which it enables religious denominations to advance their ethos through schools maintained by it does not mean that it espouses the same ethos as the school. An education authority could be maintaining schools for various denominations at the same time, with each denomination holding a different ethos that could contradict that of another denomination for which a school is maintained.

Discrimination permitted by the religious ethos exception. Where the **31.43** religious ethos exception applies, the employer is permitted to discriminate in the matters set down in para 1(2) of Schedule 9. These are the same areas in which discrimination is permitted by the general OR defence – see Chapter 30, 'General exceptions', under 'Occupational requirements – discrimination permitted by occupational requirement'.

Article 9 of the European Convention on Human Rights 31.44
In Bull and anor v Hall and anor 2012 EWCA Civ 83, CA – a claim of sexual orientation discrimination in the provision of goods and services – the devout Christian owners of a bed and breakfast argued that to find them liable for discrimination for having refused to rent a double room to a homosexual couple would be an unjustified interference with their right to manifest religious beliefs under Article 9 of the European Convention on Human Rights. The Court of Appeal rejected this argument, holding that, to the extent that the discrimination provisions limited the owners' manifestation of their religious beliefs, the limitations were necessary in a democratic society for the protection of the rights and freedoms of others, and therefore fell within the derogation permitted by Article 9(2).

Although the Bull case was concerned with the provision of goods and services, there is no reason why an employer could not seek to defend a discrimination at work claim on the same basis. However, such a defence is unlikely to get very far given the Court of Appeal's decision in Bull and the fact that the EqA already provides for organised religion and religious ethos exceptions (as discussed under 'Organised religion exception' and 'Ethos based on religion or belief' above).

In the Bull case, it was the respondents who sought to rely on their right to **31.45** manifest their religion under Article 9 to *defend* a claim of sexual orientation discrimination. However, in employment cases, it is normally the applicant who seeks to rely on Article 9 to bolster his or her claim of religion or belief discrimination against the employer. Such claims are discussed in detail in Chapter 11, 'Religion or belief', under 'Manifestation of religion or belief'.

Sex exceptions 31.46

As explained in Chapter 30, 'General exceptions', under 'Occupational requirements – new statutory wording', the genuine occupational qualification (GOQ) provisions in the SDA have been consolidated into the general

1093

occupational requirement (OR) defence under para 1 of Schedule 9 to the EqA. There are, however, two further categories of exception which are relevant to the protected characteristic of sex: communal accommodation and sport.

31.47 Communal accommodation

We note in Chapter 30, 'General exceptions', under 'Occupational requirements', that the SDA used to provide an exception from the prohibition on sex discrimination where there was a need to use single-sex accommodation for the effective performance of the job in question. One example would be work on an oil-rig where it is impracticable for the employer to provide separate accommodation for female workers. As explained in Chapter 30, the Government's view is that this exception is now incorporated into the occupational requirement defence in para 1 of Schedule 9 to the EqA.

The SDA also made an exception for discrimination in employment related to the provision of communal accommodation where the accommodation arrangements did not render it impossible or unfeasible for members of one sex to do a particular job, but nonetheless put them at a disadvantage – S.46 SDA. That exception has now been re-enacted in para 3 of Schedule 23 to the EqA. 'Communal accommodation' for this purpose is defined as residential accommodation that includes dormitories or other shared sleeping accommodation, which for reasons of privacy, or because of the nature of sanitary facilities serving the accommodation, should only be used by persons of the same sex – para 3(5) and (6). Para 3(1) provides that with regard to sex and gender reassignment, nothing in the EqA renders unlawful anything done 'in relation to (a) the admission of persons to communal accommodation; [or] (b) the provision of a benefit, facility or service linked to the accommodation'. In relation to (a), para 3(2) provides that the exception only applies if the accommodation is 'managed in a way which is as fair as possible to both men and women'; and in relation to gender reassignment, para 3(4) requires that account be taken of whether and how far the conduct in question is a proportionate means of achieving a legitimate aim.

31.48 This exception allows employers who provide residential accommodation to provide it to one sex only provided it is done as fairly as possible. So, for example, an employer whose workforce is 90 per cent male may offer the accommodation only to male employees. However, there is a catch for the employer. Under para 3(8), it must make such arrangements as are reasonably practicable to compensate for the refusal of use of the accommodation or the refusal to provide the benefit, facility or service. So, in our example, female employees could expect a payment in lieu to compensate for not being provided with accommodation.

Sport 31.49

Section 44 SDA rendered discrimination lawful in relation to sports, games or other competitive activities where the physical strength, stamina or physique of the average woman put her at a disadvantage compared to the average man. Accordingly, nothing required male soccer, rugby or athletics teams to be opened up to women. This exception has been recreated in S.195(1) EqA, which provides that 'a person does not contravene this Act, so far as relating to sex, only by doing anything in relation to the participation of another as a competitor in a gender-affected activity'. A 'gender-affected activity', for this purpose, is defined by S.195(3) as 'a sport, game or other activity of a competitive nature in circumstances in which the physical strength, stamina or physique of average persons of one sex would put them at a disadvantage compared to average persons of the other sex as competitors in events involving the activity'. Thus, as under the SDA, the sport exception related to gender applies where there are physical reasons for separating the sexes – such as in football, rugby or athletics – but not in non-physical sports and games such as chess or bridge.

Section 195(4) EqA goes on to provide that, 'in considering whether a sport, game or other activity is gender-affected in relation to children, it is appropriate to take account of the age and stage of development of children who are likely to be competitors'. This is a new provision, there being no equivalent in the SDA. It suggests that natural physical differences between the sexes might not be so pronounced or relevant in children, with the effect that there may be no gender-related disadvantage that would justify separating the sexes in children's sporting competitions.

Sexual orientation exception 31.50

The EqA preserves the exemption from sexual orientation discrimination that Reg 25 of the Sexual Orientation Regulations introduced in relation to the provision of employment benefits dependent on marital or civil partnership status. Reg 25 is re-enacted at para 18 of Schedule 9 to the EqA with no change of scope. It provides that 'a person does not contravene this Part of this Act, so far as relating to sexual orientation, by providing married persons and civil partners (to the exclusion of all other persons) with access to a benefit, facility or service' – Reg 18(2). Therefore, so long as employers accord the same benefits, etc, to civil partners and married couples, they will not incur liability for discrimination because of sexual orientation in respect of those who are neither married nor in a civil partnership.

The Civil Partnership Act 2004 came into force on 5 December 2005. Prior to that date, the exception only applied in respect of married people. This position is maintained by para 18(1), which provides that 'a person does not contravene this Part of this Act, so far as relating to sexual orientation, by doing anything which prevents or restricts a person who is not married from having access to a benefit, facility or service –

(a) the right to which accrued before 5 December 2005... or

(b) which is payable in respect of periods of service before that date' – para 18(1).

31.51 The effect of this provision is that employers will not incur liability for sexual orientation discrimination on the basis that they used to offer benefits – such as survivor pensions – to married couples but not to unmarried couples.

Part 7

Proving discrimination

32 Burden of proof

Legal framework

Applicability of shifting burden of proof rule

Stage one: establishing a 'prima facie case'

Stage two: proving absence of discrimination

Can first stage be bypassed?

Standard of proof

Other forms of discrimination

Where crucial facts are in dispute, the law imposes a burden of proof to **32.1** determine which side has the ultimate responsibility of proving his or her case to the court or tribunal. As a general rule in civil proceedings, the onus of proving the case is placed on the claimant – he or she must show that the court or tribunal has jurisdiction to hear the claim, that he or she is entitled to bring the claim, and that he or she is entitled to the remedy sought. The civil law standard of proof is 'on the balance of probabilities' – see 'Standard of proof' below. This means that if the claimant satisfies a tribunal that his or her version of events in support of the claim is at least 51 per cent 'more likely than not', the claim will succeed – provided, of course, that the employer does not go on to establish a valid defence.

In discrimination claims claimants benefit from a slightly more favourable burden of proof rule in recognition of the fact that discrimination is frequently covert and therefore can present special problems of proof. Broadly speaking, the rule provides that, once the claimant has proved facts from which an employment tribunal could decide that an unlawful act of discrimination has taken place, the burden of proof 'shifts' to the respondent to prove a non-discriminatory explanation. Unfortunately, the operation of this provision – which was initially codified in a specific EU Directive dealing with burden of proof in discrimination matters and subsequently in UK anti-discrimination law – has been the subject of some confusion and hence much litigation. This chapter aims to clarify when and how the burden of proof rule applies. Chapter 33, 'Proving discrimination', examines the ability of employment tribunals to draw inferences of discrimination from the surrounding facts, which is an important factor in the application of the burden of proof rule to discrimination claims.

It should be noted that the shifting burden of proof has the greatest impact in **32.2** complaints of *direct discrimination*, where it is necessary to establish that the

1099

claimant has been treated less favourably than another because of a protected characteristic – see Chapter 15, 'Direct discrimination', for a full consideration of this type of claim. In such cases the primary facts from which inferences may potentially be drawn are likely to be highly contentious. This is therefore the area in which the burden of proof tends to be the most hotly contested and, incidentally, where the most confusion reigns about what is needed to establish a 'prima facie case of discrimination' – see 'Stage one: establishing a "prima facie case"' below.

Nevertheless, it is worth emphasising that the two-stage shifting burden of proof also applies, where appropriate, to the other forms of discrimination under the EqA, i.e. harassment under S.26, victimisation under S.27, indirect discrimination under S.19 and the failure to make reasonable adjustments under S.20. Although similar principles apply, what needs to be proved obviously depends, to a certain extent, on the nature of the legal test set out in the respective statutory sections. We therefore give some separate consideration to these claims under 'Other forms of discrimination' below.

Generally speaking, and unless indicated otherwise, the term 'discrimination' in this and the following chapter is used in its broadest sense to encompass all forms of discriminatory behaviour covered by the EqA, including direct and indirect discrimination, harassment and victimisation.

32.3 Legal framework

The procedural rule known as the 'shifting burden of proof' in the context of anti-discrimination law is an EU law concept that derives from the EU Burden of Proof Directive (No.97/80) ('the Burden of Proof Directive'). It was implemented into domestic law under the antecedent discrimination legislation, and can now be found in S.136 EqA. Below we examine the position under EU law and how it has been implemented domestically.

32.4 EU law

Following a number of decisions of the European Court of Justice (ECJ) recognising the particular difficulty faced by complainants in proving acts of discrimination, the Burden of Proof Directive came into force on 1 January 2001. That Directive was subsequently superseded by the recast Equal Treatment Directive (No.2006/54) ('the recast Directive'), which – like the Burden of Proof Directive – relates to sex discrimination and equal pay. Recital 30 to the preamble of the recast Directive states that 'provision should... be made to ensure that the burden of proof shifts to the respondent when there is a prima facie case of discrimination'. Article 19(1) requires EU Member States to take 'such measures as are necessary' to ensure that once a complainant of discrimination establishes 'facts from which it may be presumed that there has been direct or indirect discrimination' – i.e. a prima facie case of discrimination – 'it shall be for the respondent to prove that there has been no breach of the principle of equal treatment'. Article 19(2) goes on to state that 'this shall not prevent Member States from introducing rules of evidence which are more favourable to plaintiffs'.

The wording of Article 19 is mirrored in Article 8 of the EU Race Equality Directive (No.2000/43) – which relates to race – and Article 10 of the EU Equal Treatment Framework Directive (No.2000/78) – which relates to religion, belief, disability, age and sexual orientation. The Preambles to all three of these current equality Directives confirm – in almost identical terms – that 'the appreciation of the facts from which it may be presumed that there has been direct or indirect discrimination remains a matter for the relevant national body in accordance with national law or practice'. In other words, there would appear to be a considerable amount of latitude accorded to national law and practice regarding what amounts to a prima facie case of discrimination. As noted by the ECJ in Kelly v National University of Ireland 2012 ICR 322, ECJ, that latitude is, however, mitigated by the EU principle of effectiveness, in that Member States cannot implement – or indeed apply – EU-derived rules in such a way as to render their exercise virtually impossible or excessively difficult, and thus deprive them of any effectiveness. In that regard, the ECJ observed that the shifting burden of proof 'seeks to ensure that the measures taken by the Member States to implement the principle of equal treatment are made more effective, in order to enable all persons who consider themselves wronged because the principle of equal treatment has not been applied to them to have their rights asserted by judicial process after possible recourse to other judicial bodies'.

A useful analysis of the shifting burden of proof can be found in a recent **32.5** Opinion given to the ECJ by Advocate General Mengozzi in the case of Meister v Speech Design Carrier Systems GmbH (Case C-415/10). He noted that the three equality Directives mentioned above have opted for a mechanism making it possible to lighten the burden of proof on the claimant, though not remove it completely. Citing the decision in Kelly v National University of Ireland (above), he observed that the mechanism consists of two stages: first, the claimant must sufficiently establish the facts from which it may be presumed that there has been discrimination – in other words, he or she must establish a prima facie case of discrimination; and secondly, if that presumption is established, the burden of proof thereafter lies on the respondent. According to the Advocate General, a measure of balance is thus maintained, enabling the alleged victim of discrimination to claim his or her right to equal treatment but preventing proceedings from being brought against the respondent solely on the basis of his or her assertions. He acknowledged that the relevant Directives provide that the balance may be upset should a Member State choose to do so – *but only in favour of the claimant*. Nevertheless, upsetting that balance is a matter of the Member State's own volition.

The ECJ's decision in this case, which has now been handed down, expressly refers to the Advocate General's Opinion and – albeit adopting a less in-depth analysis of the shifting burden of proof – does not contradict the logic of his reasoning: see under 'Stage one: establishing a "prima facie case" – flexible approach preferable' below.

32.6 The 'shifting' burden of proof is sometimes referred to as the 'reverse' burden of proof by lawyers, practitioners and judges. However, as the Advocate General pointed out in his Opinion in Meister, this description is not strictly speaking accurate. The claimant still has the initial burden of proving on the balance of probabilities facts from which discrimination could be presumed. Only if that presumption is established does the burden of proof thereafter lie on the respondent. Therefore the burden of proof, although somewhat reduced, nevertheless falls on the claimant. The difference with the normal burden of proof is that ordinarily the claimant would have to provide sufficient evidence to persuade a tribunal that discrimination has actually taken place, as opposed to sufficient evidence from which discrimination can be presumed. This, however, can be a subtle distinction and it is, perhaps, not surprising that there is some confusion – particularly in cases involving complex issues of fact – as to precisely what has to be proved in order for the burden of proof to be shifted to the respondent employer. This is a point revisited below under 'Stage one: establishing a "prima facie case"'.

32.7 Domestic law

In order to comply with the EU Equality Directives (see above), the procedural 'shifting burden of proof' rule was introduced into domestic law under the antecedent discrimination legislation. The relevant statutory provisions provided that, where a claimant proves facts from which an employment tribunal could conclude in the absence of an adequate explanation that the respondent has committed an act of discrimination against the claimant, it must uphold the complaint *unless* the respondent proves that it did not commit (or is not to be treated as having committed) such an act – see, for example, S.63A(2) of the Sex Discrimination Act 1975 (SDA), S.54A of the Race Relations Act 1976 (RRA) and S.17(A)(1C) of the Disability Discrimination Act 1995 (DDA). These provisions strengthened the common law position established by prior case law whereby the tribunal *could* infer discrimination, in the absence of an adequate explanation by the respondent, but was *not obliged* to do so – King v Great Britain-China Centre 1992 ICR 516, CA.

The statutory basis for the shifting burden of proof rule can now be found in S.136 EqA, which harmonises the burden of proof across all of the equality strands (i.e. protected characteristics). S.136(2) provides that if there are facts from which the court or tribunal could decide, in the absence of any other explanation, that a person (A) contravened a provision of the EqA, the court *must* hold that the contravention occurred; and S.136(3) provides that S.136(2) does not apply if A shows that he or she did not contravene the relevant provision. The slight change in wording compared with that used in the antecedent legislation is not intended substantively to alter the way in which the burden of proof rule applies, Accordingly, the case law under the antecedent statutory provisions remains relevant. As before, if the claimant establishes a prima facie case of unlawful discrimination, his or her claim will succeed unless the employer can prove that there was a non-discriminatory reason for the treatment in question.

Statutory remit. The shifting burden of proof rule in S.136 applies to all claims **32.8** of direct and indirect discrimination, victimisation and harassment under the EqA (although, as we shall see under 'Stage one: establishing a "prima facie case"' below, it has the greatest impact in direct discrimination claims). S.136(5), however, provides that the rule 'does not apply to proceedings for an offence under this Act'. Although 'offence' is not defined, the Explanatory Notes accompanying the 2010 Act state that the exception to the shifting burden of proof rule applies to *criminal* offences. On this basis, if the alleged discrimination gives rise to a criminal offence, the usual criminal burden of proof applies – i.e. the complainant must prove the case beyond reasonable doubt. This exception is permitted by the EU Equality Directives, all of which provide that the shifting burden of proof 'shall not apply to criminal procedures' – see, for example, Article 19(5) of the recast Directive.

The EqA specifically provides that the shifting burden of proof provisions also apply to breaches of an equality clause or rule – S.136(4). Previously, there was no burden of proof provision in equal pay claims. In practice, however, the Equal Pay Act 1970 worked along the same principles, whereby the claimant was required to establish a difference in pay between her or himself and a worker of the opposite sex, and it was for the employer to then prove that the difference in pay was genuinely due to a material factor which was not the difference of sex. The burden of proof in respect of equal pay claims is dealt with in IDS Employment Law Handbook, 'Equal Pay' (2008) – see, in particular, Chapter 8, 'Material factor defence', under 'Preliminary issues – burden of proof'.

Under the antecedent discrimination legislation relating to race, the shifting **32.9** burden of proof only applied to complaints alleging that the respondent had 'committed an act of discrimination, on grounds of race or ethnic or national origins... or... an act of harassment' – S.54A RRA. This meant that it did not apply to claims of victimisation under the RRA – Oyarce v Cheshire County Council 2008 ICR 1179, CA. Nor, according to the EAT in Okonu v G4S Security Services (UK) Ltd 2008 ICR 598, EAT, did it apply to claims of race discrimination on the grounds of colour or nationality. However, the EAT subsequently held in both Abbey National plc and anor v Chagger 2009 ICR 624, EAT, and Edozie v Group 4 Securicor plc and anor EAT 0124/09 that the

1103

normal shifting burden of proof rule *did* apply to discrimination on the ground of colour. S.136 EqA has now fully addressed the inconsistency and resolved the confusion: it is clear that the shifting burden of proof applies to all discrimination and victimisation claims, including those pertaining to race, colour and nationality.

32.10 **The Barton/Igen guidelines.** Detailed guidance on the application of the shifting burden of proof was given by the EAT in Barton v Investec Henderson Crosthwaite Securities Ltd 2003 ICR 1205, EAT (in the context of direct discrimination under the SDA). This subsequently became known as the Barton guidelines. The Court of Appeal in Igen Ltd (formerly Leeds Careers Guidance) and ors v Wong and other cases 2005 ICR 931, CA, had the opportunity to consider this guidance in three conjoined appeals involving claims of direct sex and race discrimination. The Court confirmed that the correct approach for an employment tribunal involves two stages. At the first stage, the claimant has to prove facts from which the tribunal could infer that discrimination has taken place. Only if such facts have been made out to the tribunal's satisfaction (i.e. on the balance of probabilities) is the second stage engaged, whereby the burden then 'shifts' to the respondent to prove – again on the balance of probabilities – that the treatment in question was 'in no sense whatsoever' on the protected ground.

32.11 The Court explicitly endorsed the Barton guidelines, albeit with some adjustments, and confirmed that they apply across all strands of discrimination. The guidelines, as modified by the Court of Appeal, can be summarised as follows:

- it is for the claimant to prove, on the balance of probabilities, facts from which the employment tribunal could conclude, in the absence of an adequate explanation, that the respondent has committed an act of discrimination. If the claimant does not prove such facts the claim will fail

- in deciding whether the claimant has proved such facts it is important to bear in mind that it is unusual to find direct evidence of discrimination. Few employers would be prepared to admit such discrimination, even to themselves. In many cases the discrimination will not be intentional but merely based on the assumption that 'he or she would not have fitted in'

- the outcome at this stage will usually depend on what inferences it is proper to draw from the primary facts found by the tribunal (see further Chapter 33, 'Proving discrimination', under 'Inferring discrimination')

- the tribunal does not have to reach a definitive determination that such facts would lead it to conclude that there was discrimination – it merely has to decide what inferences could be drawn

- in considering what inferences or conclusions can be drawn from the primary facts, the tribunal must assume that there is no adequate explanation for those facts

- these inferences could include any that it is just and equitable to draw from an evasive or equivocal reply to a questionnaire (see Chapter 33, 'Proving discrimination', under 'Requesting information and disclosure of evidence – statutory questionnaires')

- inferences may also be drawn from any failure to comply with a relevant Code of Practice (see Chapter 33, 'Proving discrimination', under 'Inferring discrimination – breach of EHRC Codes of Practice')

- when the claimant has proved facts from which inferences could be drawn that the respondent has treated the claimant less favourably on a protected ground, the burden of proof moves to the respondent

- it is then for the respondent to prove that he did not commit or, as the case may be, is not to be treated as having committed, that act

- to discharge that burden it is necessary for the respondent to prove on the balance of probabilities that his treatment of the claimant was in no sense whatsoever on the protected ground

- the respondent must not only provide an explanation for the facts proved by the claimant, from which the inferences could be drawn, but that explanation must be adequate to prove on the balance of probabilities that the protected characteristic was no part of the reason for the treatment

- since the respondent would generally be in possession of the facts necessary to provide an explanation, the tribunal would normally expect cogent evidence to discharge that burden – in particular, the tribunal will need to examine carefully explanations for failure to deal with the questionnaire procedure and/or any Code of Practice.

Unfortunately, these guidelines have not laid to rest the issue of how the **32.12** burden of proof works in practice in the context of discrimination claims. In particular, there remains a fair amount of confusion about what constitutes a prima facie case of discrimination for the purpose of shifting the burden of proof onto the respondent. We examine this issue under 'Stage one: establishing a "prima facie case"' below. However, before going on to look in more detail at the workings of the shifting burden of proof rule, we deal first with a common misconception that is perhaps responsible for some of the confusion in this area – that the burden of proof rule must be applied, as a matter of course, in all discrimination claims.

1105

32.13 Applicability of shifting burden of proof rule

The shifting burden of proof rule is intended to assist claimants to establish discrimination, and to help employment tribunals to establish whether or not discrimination has actually taken place. The policy reason behind it is that discrimination can often be covert and therefore notoriously difficult to substantiate. However, as a number of EAT decisions have recently emphasised, it is not the case that the rule need always be applied – in fact, to do so could be counterproductive. The circumstances in which the rule may not be applicable are outlined in the following sections.

32.14 Facts not contested

Perhaps self-evidently, the rule is not relevant if there are no disputed facts needing to be proved. In Hartlepool Borough Council v Llewellyn and ors and other cases 2009 ICR 1426, EAT (an equal pay claim), the EAT observed that the employment tribunal had needlessly paid 'ritual obeisance' to the burden of proof rule given that the issue to be addressed was one of pure law and there were no disputed facts requiring proof. It was, said the EAT, 'a sign of the unhelpfully talismanic status that Igen v Wong [see the section 'Legal framework' under 'Domestic law – the Barton/Igen guidelines' above] has acquired that employment tribunals feel obliged to refer to it in virtually every discrimination case'.

32.15 Discriminatory element

The shifting burden of proof rule only applies to the discriminatory element of any claim. Thus, as pointed out by recital 31 of the Preamble to the Framework Directive, it is not for the respondent to prove that, for example, the claimant adheres to a particular religion or belief, has a particular disability, is of a particular age or has a particular sexual orientation.

Furthermore, the burden remains upon the claimant to prove that the alleged discriminatory treatment actually happened and that the respondent was responsible. This is illustrated by Brunel University v Webster and ors – one of the conjoined appeals heard by the Court of Appeal in Igen Ltd (formerly Leeds Careers Guidance) and ors v Wong and other cases 2005 ICR 931, CA. An employment tribunal found that the word 'Paki' was said in the vicinity of W while she was on the telephone at work. However, it dismissed her claim against the University for direct race discrimination because the accommodation office in which she worked was a busy public place through which numerous visitors passed during the day and 'Paki' could have been said by anyone, not just the accommodation staff. It concluded that there were no facts from which an inference of discrimination could be drawn. The EAT allowed W's appeal, holding that she had satisfied the first stage of the burden of proof by proving that the discriminatory act could have been committed by one of the respondent's employees. The Court of Appeal overturned this decision, holding that under S.54A RRA (now S.136 EqA), the claimant must show a probability, rather than a mere possibility, that the respondent *had committed* the unlawful act. Furthermore, the Court considered that the wording of S.54A RRA pointed to the legislative intention that 'the respondent should explain why he has done what he has been proved by the complainant to have done, rather than to the respondent having to prove the fact that it was not he who did it at all'.

In Laing v Manchester City Council 2006 ICR 1519, EAT (a race discrimination **32.16** claim), Mr Justice Elias, then President of the EAT, confirmed that 'it is for the employee to prove that he suffered the treatment, not merely to assert it, and this must be done to the satisfaction of the tribunal after all the evidence has been considered '. Similarly in Transport for London and anor v Aderemi EAT 0006/11 the EAT overturned the tribunal's finding of race discrimination based upon facts from which it 'could conclude' that TfL had treated A less favourably than it would have treated a hypothetical comparator. A had to establish, on the balance of probabilities, that TfL was actually responsible for delaying or obstructing A's promotion from Band 3 to Band 4 (the alleged less favourable treatment), not just that it could have been.

In Project Management Institute v Latif 2007 IRLR 579, EAT – a claim brought under S.4A DDA (now S.20 EqA) for failure to make reasonable adjustments to a provision, criterion or practice (PCP) in order to avoid a substantial disadvantage – the EAT 'very much doubt[ed]' whether the burden shifts at all in respect of establishing the PCP, or demonstrating the substantial disadvantage. These are simply questions of fact for the employment tribunal to decide after hearing all the evidence, with the onus of proof resting throughout on the claimant. In particular, the EAT observed that these are not issues about which the employer has information or beliefs within its own knowledge and which the claimant cannot be expected to prove. To talk of the burden shifting in such cases was, in the EAT's view, confusing and inaccurate. This case is considered further under 'Other areas of discrimination – failure to make reasonable adjustments' below.

Clear positive findings   32.17

In Martin v Devonshires Solicitors 2011 ICR 352, EAT, the EAT stressed that while 'the burden of proof provisions in discrimination cases... are important in circumstances where there is room for doubt as to the facts necessary to establish discrimination – generally, that is, facts about the respondent's motivation... they have no bearing where the tribunal is in a position to make positive findings on the evidence one way or the other, and still less where there is no real dispute about the respondent's motivation and what is in issue is its correct characterisation in law'. The EAT accordingly upheld an employment tribunal's finding that a firm of solicitors did not victimise an employee under either the SDA or the DDA by dismissing her because she had made allegations of discrimination against various partners. A number of related and separable features of the allegations, and not the allegations themselves, were the reason for dismissal, including the fact that the allegations were false, that they arose from the employee's mental illness, and that similar behaviour was likely to occur in the future with a risk of significant workplace disruption. The EAT further held that once the tribunal had found that the non-discriminatory reasons given by the employer reflected its genuine motivation, the burden of proof did not come into the equation and the tribunal had not erred by failing to refer to the shifting burden of proof rule.

The above ties in with the comment of Mr Justice Elias, then President of the EAT, in Laing v Manchester City Council 2006 ICR 1519, EAT, that, 'if [the tribunal] is satisfied that the reason given by the employer is a genuine one and does not disclose either conscious or unconscious racial discrimination, then that is the end of the matter. It is not improper for a tribunal to say, in effect, "there is a nice question as to whether or not the burden has shifted, but we are satisfied here that even if it has, the employer has given a fully adequate explanation as to why he behaved as he did and it has nothing to do with race".' By the same token, Elias P considered that 'the tribunal cannot ignore damning evidence from the employer as to the explanation for his conduct simply because the employee has not raised a sufficiently strong case at the first stage. That would be to let form rule over substance.'

32.18 In Gay v Sophos plc EAT 0452/10 the EAT concluded that the employment tribunal had, when rejecting G's age discrimination claim, made positive findings that age was not a factor in S plc's treatment of G. It therefore dismissed the grounds of G's appeal, which had been based upon the tribunal's failure to apply the shifting burden of proof. G, aged 55, was Vice-President of S plc's Europe, Middle East and Africa division. Following a company restructuring, she was given notice of dismissal for redundancy and placed on garden leave. She was not considered for possible alternative roles, whereas her younger colleagues – also under notice of redundancy – were offered alternative employment. G complained to her employer that this amounted to age discrimination. Her dismissal nevertheless took effect without any alternative employment being considered. G subsequently brought claims for direct age discrimination and victimisation. The tribunal dismissed these, finding that G's treatment was due to factors other than age – in particular that the company did not believe that she would accept a more junior position, which would entail a substantial cut in salary (since otherwise the cost of employing her would be disproportionate to the value of the role).

G appealed, arguing that the tribunal had not applied, nor indeed made any reference to, the shifting burden of proof in circumstances in which it ought to have done so. The EAT observed that the allegation of discrimination depended on the unexpressed, and quite possibly unconscious, motivation of the relevant decision-makers. It was thus a 'classic case' in which a claimant may be assisted by the shifting burden of proof. Nevertheless, the EAT dismissed G's appeal, noting that since Laing v Manchester City Council (above) it is now very well-established that a tribunal is not obliged to follow the two-stage approach – see further 'Can first stage be bypassed?' below. If it makes a positive finding that the acts complained of were motivated by non-discriminatory considerations, that necessarily means that the burden of proof – even if it had transferred to the respondent – has been discharged.

The EAT further observed that at times the tribunal in the instant case had **32.19** stated that it was 'not satisfied' that the difference in treatment between G and her comparators regarding alternative employment was related to G's age. If that was an indication that the tribunal regarded the burden of proof as being on the claimant, the EAT remarked that that could be viewed as undermining the positive findings as to the real (and non-discriminatory) reasons for the difference in treatment. However, in the EAT's view, these phrases could not be read in isolation. The tribunal had proceeded to make positive findings as to the reasons why the decision-makers in question believed that G could not be accommodated within another role. Although the tribunal's language was not as watertight as it could have been, it was adequately clear that the tribunal did indeed intend to make a positive finding that G's age was not a factor in her treatment. Furthermore, that finding was not perverse and therefore G's challenge on that basis also failed.

Of course, for a tribunal to make a positive finding of fact, it must have a clear evidential basis and provide clear reasons for doing so, otherwise its decision could be successfully challenged for perversity. If the evidence overwhelmingly points one way or the other, the tribunal will obviously be in a position to make positive findings. It is worth bearing in mind that a tribunal is, in theory at least, entitled to make a positive finding if it considers that the evidence in support indicates that it is 51 per cent (i.e. on a balance of probabilities) more likely than not. Clearly, however, the more finely balanced the evidence, the less the tribunal will be in a position to make a positive finding of fact and the more it will be required to apply the shifting burden of proof rule to assist in reaching a conclusion as to whether the allegation of discrimination has been made out.

It should also be stressed that if a tribunal cannot make a positive finding of **32.20** fact as to whether or not discrimination has taken place, it *must* apply the shifting burden of proof. In Country Style Foods Ltd v Bouzir 2011 EWCA Civ 1519, CA, the Court of Appeal held that an employment tribunal had erred in law when it rejected B's race discrimination claim – arising out of CSF Ltd's rejection of his job application – because there was 'no evidence' to show that his race was the reason why he was not offered the position. It had wrongly proceeded directly to a conclusion that B had *not* proved his case of race discrimination without applying the burden of proof provisions. Therefore, the

1109

EAT had been right to allow B's appeal and order the matter to be remitted to a different tribunal for a rehearing. The facts of this case are discussed in more detail under 'Stage one: establishing a "prima facie case" – flexible approach preferable' below.

32.21 Inherent or subjective discrimination?

It is well established that direct discrimination can arise either from an act that is inherently discriminatory or from an act which, because of the employer's motivation, is subjectively discriminatory – for further details see Chapter 15, 'Direct discrimination', under '"Because of" protected characteristic'. The category of direct discrimination at issue will be an important factor governing the applicability of the burden of proof rules, as explained below.

32.22 **Inherent discrimination.** Where it is alleged that the treatment – or more accurately the reason for the treatment – is inherently discriminatory, an employment tribunal is simply required to identify the factual criterion applied by the respondent and there is no need to inquire into the employer's mental processes. Therefore, if the reason is clear or the tribunal is able to identify the criteria or reason on the evidence before it, there will be no question of inferring discrimination and thus no need to apply the burden of proof rule: either the reason/criterion is discriminatory or it is not. An example of this kind of inherent direct discrimination can be found in James v Eastleigh Borough Council 1990 ICR 554, HL. There, the Council was guilty of direct sex discrimination when it operated a policy allowing pensioners free entry to its swimming pools. The criterion was inherently discriminatory because men and women had different state pensionable ages, with the result that men had to wait five years longer than women before they could benefit from the policy.

Similarly, in Amnesty International v Ahmed 2009 ICR 1450, EAT, the EAT upheld an employment tribunal's decision that the claimant had suffered direct race discrimination when she was denied promotion on the basis that her ethnic origin exposed her – and others with her – to increased safety risks while travelling, and potentially compromised the employer's impartiality. The EAT noted that although the tribunal had referred to the shifting burden of proof provisions, its conclusion did not depend on their application. It had made an explicit finding as to the reason for the claimant's treatment, which 'render[ed] the elaborations of the "Barton/Igen guidelines" otiose'. The EAT went on to comment that 'there would be fewer appeals to [the EAT] in discrimination cases if more tribunals took this straightforward course and only resorted to [the statutory burden of proof provisions] where they felt unable to make positive findings on the evidence without [their] assistance'.

32.23 Another example of inherent discrimination can be found in R (E) v Governing Body of JFS and anor 2010 IRLR 136, SC, in which the majority of the Supreme Court held that it was clear that the claimant's son was refused admittance to a Jewish orthodox school because of his inability to satisfy the conditions recognised by the Office of the Chief Rabbi as conferring the status of a Jew. Since those conditions were based upon a child's ethnic origins, the act of refusal was inherently discriminatory. Accordingly, there was no need to inquire into the Chief Rabbi's conscious or unconscious motivation for applying the conditions; nor did it matter whether he was motivated by a sincerely held religious belief (since there is no justification for direct race discrimination).

Finally, in Dziedziak v Future Electronics Ltd EAT 0270/11 the EAT held that an instruction by the claimant's line manager not to speak in her own language (Polish) was inherently discriminatory on the ground of nationality and therefore race. In so concluding, Mr Justice Langstaff (President of the EAT) observed: 'We are satisfied that the [employment] tribunal here were finding... that the claimant was discriminated against by something that was intrinsically part of her nationality... Given a difference in treatment linked to race to the detriment of an individual, the burden [of proof] is capable of passing, and we see nothing wrong in law in the tribunal concluding therefore that the respondent was required to provide an explanation which, because [it] did not do so, the respondent was found to have discriminated against on this basis.' It is interesting to note that in this case the EAT did apply the shifting burden of proof rule to a case in which it had apparently been found that the reason for the treatment was inherently discriminatory. Arguably, however, in light of the case law discussed above, there was strictly speaking no need to do so.

Subjective discrimination. Where the act complained of is not in itself **32.24** discriminatory and the reason for the less favourable treatment is not immediately apparent, it is necessary to explore the employer's mental processes (conscious or unconscious) to discover the ground or reason behind the act. In this type of case, the tribunal may well need to have recourse to the shifting burden of proof rules to establish an employer's motivation. As noted by Baroness Hale in the JFS case (above), 'there are other cases in which the ostensible criterion is [not inherently discriminatory] – usually, in job applications, that elusive quality known as "merit". But nevertheless the discriminator may consciously or unconsciously be making his selections on the basis of race or sex.' To illustrate her point, she referred to the following famous passage from Lord Nicholl's judgment in Nagarajan v London Regional Transport 1999 ICR 877, HL: 'All human beings have preconceptions, beliefs, attitudes and prejudices on many subjects. It is part of our make-up. Moreover, we do not always recognise our own prejudices. Many people are unable, or unwilling, to admit even to themselves that actions of theirs may be racially motivated. An employer may genuinely believe that the reason why he rejected an applicant had nothing to do with the applicant's race. After careful and thorough investigation of a claim, members of an employment tribunal may decide that the proper inference to be drawn from the evidence is that, whether the employer realised it at the time or not, race was the reason why he acted as he did.'

32.25 **Danger in mechanically applying the rule**

If employment tribunals were to apply the burden of proof rule in a strict and mechanical way to every case of discrimination, they could risk getting bogged down in technicalities, when – as noted by Mr Justice Elias in Laing v Manchester City Council 2006 ICR 1519, EAT – their focus 'must at all times be the question whether or not they can properly and fairly infer… discrimination.' Given the somewhat artificial way in which the shifting burden of proof rule works, a tribunal might find itself reaching a perverse decision that is contrary to the facts when all the evidence demonstrates that discrimination has or, as the case may be, has not taken place. It is undoubtedly for this reason that many appellate cases have emphasised that there is no need to take too strict an approach to the burden of proof rule – for example, the Court of Appeal in Khan and anor v Home Office 2008 EWCA Civ 578, CA, held that the rule 'need not be applied in an overly mechanistic or schematic way'.

Taking this one step further, in cases such as Martin v Devonshires Solicitors 2011 ICR 352, EAT (discussed under 'Clear positive findings' above), the EAT appears to be increasingly recognising that if, for example, a tribunal can make positive findings as to an employer's motivation, it need not revert to the burden of proof rules at all. Nevertheless, as observed by the EAT in Gay v Sophos plc EAT 0452/10 (also discussed under 'Clear positive findings' above) it is good practice, particularly where either or both parties have put the burden of proof at the centre of their submissions, for a tribunal to address the issue, and, if it is not going to follow the approach urged upon it, to explain why.

32.26

To assist tribunals, claimants should think carefully about how they plead their case and whether they need the tribunal to apply the shifting burden of proof rule. Are they, for example, dissatisfied with the explanation given by the employer and think there is a discriminatory motive behind it? If so, they should direct the tribunal to apply the shifting burden of proof and explain why a prima facie inference of discrimination should be drawn. Or do they consider that the evidence clearly (or at least on the balance of probabilities) establishes discrimination? If so, their claim should be successful without needing to resort to the shifting burden of proof. However, in the event that the tribunal disagrees, the claimant would be advised in the alternative to plead the case based upon the shifting burden of proof. The employer, for its part, should consider whether it can establish a clear non-discriminatory reason for the treatment, in which case it should direct the tribunal to dismiss the discrimination claim without recourse to the complicated burden of proof provision set out in S.136 EqA.

32.27 Stage one: establishing a 'prima facie case'

If the claimant is unable to establish a clear case of discrimination he or she can attempt to shift the burden of proof onto the respondent by establishing what is commonly known as a 'prima facie case of discrimination'. This phrase has long been used as the judicial shorthand for satisfying stage one of the two-stage shifting burden of proof described under 'Legal framework' above. Indeed, the Preambles to all three EU Equality Directives specifically use the term in that context. For example, recital 30 to the Preamble of the recast Directive states that 'provision should... be made to ensure that the burden of proof shifts to the respondent when there is a *prima facie case of discrimination*' (our stress). Although the EqA does not use the term (and nor did the previous discrimination legislation), it is clear from S.136(2) that a prima facie case of discrimination is established if there are 'facts from which the court could decide, in the absence of any other explanation, that [the respondent] contravened the provision concerned' (i.e. unlawfully discriminated against the claimant). Note that the antecedent burden of proof provisions used the phrase 'in the absence of an *adequate* explanation' (our stress), as opposed to 'in the absence of any other explanation'. The significance (if any) of this slight change in wording is considered under 'Employer's explanation' below.

32.28 It is perhaps no exaggeration to say that the issue of what amounts to a 'prima·facie case of discrimination' lies at the heart of the shifting burden of proof and can in some cases be pivotal to the success or failure of discrimination claims. Of course, it is difficult to determine with absolute precision the point at which such a prima facie case will come about, since it depends upon what inferences can be drawn from the surrounding facts, which inevitably differ from case to case. However, even allowing for this, there appears to be a disproportionate amount of confusion on the subject, as the copious amount of domestic case law attests. In contrast, there has been little significant ECJ guidance on the issue, which is, perhaps, surprising given that the concept derives from EU law. One reason for the comparative lack of ECJ input thus far is, no doubt, that the recitals to all three Equality Directives provide that 'the appreciation of the facts from which it may be presumed that there has been direct or indirect discrimination remains a matter for the relevant national body in accordance with national law or practice'. Indeed, this national autonomy to decide the 'prima facie' issue was emphasised by the ECJ in Kelly v National University of Ireland 2012 ICR 322, ECJ. Nevertheless, it is important to bear in mind that the degree of national autonomy is not unlimited: the EU principle of effectiveness means that Member States cannot apply the shifting burden of proof in such a way as to compromise the achievement of its intended objectives – a point that was also made by the ECJ in Kelly. In this regard, the ECJ stated that, although the Burden of Proof Directive (now incorporated into the recast Equal Treatment Directive (No.2006/54)) does not specifically entitle claimants in discrimination cases to information from the employer in order that they may establish a prima facie case of discrimination, it could 'not be ruled out' in that particular case that the university's refusal to disclose documents that might assist the claimant to do so could risk compromising the achievement of the objective pursued by the Directive and thus depriving it of effectiveness. Furthermore in Meister v Speech Design Carrier Systems GmbH Case C-415/10, ECJ (another recent case in which the ECJ has had the opportunity to examine the shifting burden of proof), the ECJ held that in the context of establishing a prima facie case of discrimination, 'it must be ensured that a refusal of disclosure by the defendant is not liable to compromise the achievement of the objectives pursued by the [relevant EU Directives]'. For further details see Chapter 33, 'Proving discrimination', under 'Requesting information and disclosure of evidence'.

32.29 Less favourable treatment

In Laing v Manchester City Council 2006 ICR 1519, EAT, Mr Justice Elias (then President of the EAT) suggested that a claimant can establish a prima facie case of discrimination by showing that he or she has been less favourably treated than an appropriate comparator. He considered that at the first stage 'the onus lies on the employee to show potentially less favourable treatment from which an inference of discrimination could properly be drawn'. Typically, this will involve identifying an actual comparator treated differently or, in the absence of such a comparator, a hypothetical one who would have been treated more favourably. That would entail a consideration of 'all material facts as opposed to any explanation' (see 'Employer's explanation – "material facts" versus "explanation"' below). He then went on to say that 'it is only if the claimant succeeds in establishing that less favourable treatment that the onus switches to the employer to show an adequate, in the sense of non-discriminatory, reason for the difference in treatment'.

In Network Rail Infrastructure Ltd v Griffiths-Henry 2006 IRLR 865, EAT (handed down two months prior to Laing), Elias P – again presiding – commented that, provided employment tribunals adopt a realistic and fair analysis of the employer's explanation at the second stage, there could be no justification for requiring positive evidence of discrimination at the first stage, bearing in mind the real difficulties in establishing discrimination.

32.30

Establishing potentially less favourable treatment requires a nuanced approach. The claimant must, of course, establish that the comparator is, aside from the relevant protected characteristic, in the same, or not materially different, circumstances (see further Chapter 15, 'Direct discrimination', under 'Comparator – no materially different circumstances'). In the Network Rail case (above), Elias P considered that there would be a prima facie case of discrimination if a black employee was at least as well qualified as a white employee and only the white employee was promoted if they were the only two candidates for promotion. However, he pointed out that the case becomes weaker where there are a number of candidates and the unsuccessful black candidate is rejected along with a number of equally well-qualified white candidates, since there is then no distinction between all the unsuccessful candidates.

For further details about what constitutes less favourable treatment, see Chapter 15, 'Direct discrimination', under 'Less favourable treatment'.

Hypothetical comparator. Where the claimant's situation is completely unique **32.31** or there is a material difference in circumstance, the position becomes slightly more complicated. The claimant must then rely upon a hypothetical comparator and establish that the comparator *would* have been more favourably treated, which, in itself, will involve the tribunal having to draw inferences as to likely treatment from the surrounding facts. In Shamoon v Chief Constable of the Royal Ulster Constabulary 2003 ICR 337, HL (which involved direct sex discrimination), Lord Rodger noted that in many 'hypothetical comparator' cases 'the [claimant] leads more general evidence and invites the tribunal to find facts from which it can infer that her employer treated her less favourably than he would have treated a male employee in the same circumstances'. Lord Scott also commented that the fact that there is a material difference does not prevent the 'comparator' having some evidential value for the claimant, capable of supporting the requisite inference of discrimination. He did, however, make the point that the evidential value will be variable and will inevitably be weakened by material differences in circumstances. This approach was endorsed by Lord Hoffmann in Watt (formerly Carter) and ors v Ahsan 2008 ICR 82, HL, when he observed that the question of whether the differences between the circumstances of the complainant and those of the putative statutory comparator are 'materially different' is often likely to be disputed. He considered, however, that in most cases, 'it will be unnecessary for the tribunal to resolve this dispute because it should be able, by treating the putative comparator as an evidential comparator, and having due regard to the alleged differences in circumstances and other evidence, to form a view on how the employer would have treated a hypothetical person who was a true statutory comparator'.

In Ferri v Key Languages Ltd ET Case No.2302172/04 F failed to establish less favourable treatment, as against a hypothetical comparator, and thus did not succeed in establishing a prima facie case of discrimination. F claimed that she had been subjected to aggressive behaviour, belittling treatment and emotional pressure on the ground of her religious belief, and cited in support of her claim the fact that she had been told not to wear a large ruby cross – which she wore as a Catholic to signify her faith – because it was 'loud' and overtly religious. An employment tribunal dismissed her claim, finding that F responded badly to criticism, and concluded that the employer would have treated anybody with the same work performance, temperament and approach to criticism in the same way. The background evidence regarding the cross was highly relevant and exactly the type of evidence from which it might have been appropriate to draw an adverse inference, but the employer's evidence was powerful and cogent, there was contemporaneous evidence of F's shortcomings, and she had been wearing the cross when she was interviewed and offered the job. The tribunal therefore concluded that F had not been less favourably treated and the burden of proof had not shifted to KL Ltd. This case arguably provides an example of material facts being used to explain, or at least clarify, why an employer acted as it did at the first stage – see 'Employer's explanation – "material facts" versus "explanation"' below.

32.32 **Something more?** Although Elias P in both Laing v Manchester City Council 2006 ICR 1519, EAT, and Network Rail Infrastructure Ltd v Griffiths-Henry 2006 IRLR 865, EAT, appeared to accept that less favourable treatment (discounting the employer's explanation) can establish a prima facie case of discrimination, most case law concerning the statutory burden of proof rule suggests that something *more* than less favourable treatment is required. This is discussed under 'Is something more than less favourable treatment required?' below.

32.33 Employer's explanation

It seems tolerably clear that the employer's explanation (if any) for the treatment should be left out of the equation at the first stage (although as we explain under 'Is something more than less favourable treatment required?' below, Lord Justice Mummery's judgment in Madarassy v Nomura International plc 2007 ICR 867, CA, appears to have muddied the waters somewhat in this regard). The Court of Appeal in Igen Ltd (formerly Leeds Careers Guidance) and ors v Wong and other cases 2005 ICR 931, CA, stated that the tribunal must assume that there is no adequate explanation, observing that 'the tribunal is required to make an assumption at the first stage which may be contrary to reality'. The Court of Appeal took the word 'adequate' from the antecedent legislation, which, as noted above, used the phrase 'in the absence of an *adequate* explanation' (our stress), as opposed to the current wording, 'in the absence of any other explanation'. By removing the word 'adequate', S.136(2) EqA appears to clarify that the tribunal must assume there is no explanation for the treatment at the first stage (adequate or otherwise).

32.34 **'Material facts' versus 'explanation'.** In Laing v Manchester City Council 2006 ICR 1519, EAT, the claimant submitted that the stage-one assumption that there is no explanation for the treatment complained of means that tribunals must ignore any evidence from the respondent tending to undermine the claimant's case. Mr Justice Elias rejected that argument. In his view, the Court of Appeal in Igen v Wong (above) had made it clear that the tribunal is entitled to have regard to all material facts at stage one, including facts adduced by the employer. The EqA now implicitly endorses this view: whereas the previous legislation stated that a prima facie case was established 'if *the complainant* proves facts' (our stress), S.136(2) states that a prima facie case is made out 'if there are facts' from which a tribunal could decide that an act of unlawful discrimination has taken place.

Mr Justice Elias emphasised in Laing that there is a distinction between an employer's explanation for allegedly discriminatory treatment (which should be left to the second stage) and facts adduced by the employer to counter or put into context the claimant's evidence (which it is permissible for the tribunal to consider at the first stage). He used the example of a group of male workers, one of whom is black, whose pay is withheld by their employer because they are working to rule. The black worker would be able to point to white colleagues who are not working to rule and whose pay is not being withheld. Taking his evidence in isolation, Elias P thought that the tribunal would have to conclude that he had been treated differently in circumstances that could point to race discrimination. However, Elias P considered that it would then be open to the employer to rebut this prima facie case by, for example, adducing evidence that white workers had been treated in the same way. In his view, such evidence could not properly be described as an 'explanation' for the black employee's treatment. Rather, it was merely factual evidence giving a fuller picture and thereby demonstrating that there was nothing about the circumstances to justify an inference of race discrimination, whatever the reason for withholding the money may be. The explanation for the treatment, if that were to become material – i.e. if a prima facie case were established and the case therefore proceeded to the second stage – would be that the money was withheld because the claimant was working to rule.

32.35 Drawing a line between 'material facts' and 'explanation' can be tricky. Elias P recognised that the two are not 'hermetically sealed compartments' and that 'there is plainly a relationship between them'. He noted that 'facts will frequently explain, at least in part, why someone has acted as they have. The fact that an employee has committed misconduct will also provide the reason why the employer disciplines him. So facts are not unrelated to the explanation, although they are not to be confused with it.'

32.36 **Refusal to provide information.** Just as the employer can adduce evidence at the first stage to rebut the employee's prima facie case, the ECJ's decision in Meister v Speech Design Carrier Systems GmbH Case C-415/10, ECJ, suggested that, depending upon the circumstances, an employer's refusal to provide information capable of constituting facts from which it may be presumed that there has been discrimination could, itself, assist the claimant to establish a prima facie case of discrimination. In this particular case, the claimant – a rejected job applicant who was not called to interview – sought information concerning the identities of those who were called for interview and the criteria used by the employer to determine who to appoint. The ECJ took the view that 'a [respondent's] refusal to grant any access to information may be one of the factors to be taken into account in the context of establishing [a prima facie case of discrimination]' if the national court decides – taking into account all the circumstances of the case – that that refusal risks compromising the achievement of the objectives pursed by EU law (as outlined under 'Legal framework – EU law' above). For further details, see Chapter 33, 'Proving discrimination', under 'Requesting information and disclosure of evidence'.

32.37 Is something more than less favourable treatment required?
As we have seen, Mr Justice Elias appeared to accept in both Laing v Manchester City Council 2006 ICR 1519, EAT, and Network Rail Infrastructure Ltd v Griffiths-Henry 2006 IRLR 865, EAT, that less favourable treatment (discounting the employer's explanation) can establish a prima facie case of discrimination for the purposes of direct discrimination. Support for this approach can arguably be found in Shamoon v Chief Constable of the Royal Ulster Constabulary 2003 ICR 337, HL, albeit that that case was decided under the previous common law burden of proof rules whereby tribunals could infer discrimination in the absence of an adequate explanation but were not obliged to do so. Lord Hope in Shamoon stated, in the context of a sex discrimination claim brought by a female chief inspector against her employer, that 'the question is whether the way in which the [claimant] was in fact treated was different from the way the other chief inspectors would have been treated. If the answer to that question is yes, and there is no other explanation, it can be inferred that she was treated less favourably than they would have been on the ground of her sex.'

However, most case law concerning the statutory burden of proof provisions suggests that something *more* than less favourable treatment is required. To a certain extent, this stems from a sometimes overlooked passage in Igen Ltd (formerly Leeds Careers Guidance) and ors v Wong and other cases 2005 ICR 931, CA. It is worth quoting the relevant passage in full: Lord Justice Peter Gibson (giving the judgment of the Court) stated: '[T]he [statutory] language… seems to us plain. It is for the complainant to prove the facts from which… the tribunal could conclude, in the absence of an adequate explanation, that the respondent committed an unlawful act of discrimination. It does not say that the facts to be proved are those from which the [tribunal] could conclude that the respondent "could have committed" such [an] act.' He continued, 'the relevant act [for the purposes of direct race discrimination] is… that… the alleged discriminator treats another person less favourably and… does so on racial grounds. All those facts are facts which the complainant, in our judgment, needs to prove on the balance of probabilities.'

32.38 This passage is perhaps slightly ambiguous. However, what it appears to be emphasising is that the claimant must prove *on the balance of probabilities* facts from which the tribunal could infer that the respondent has committed an act of discrimination (i.e. has committed less favourable treatment because of a protected characteristic). It is not being prescriptive as to what type of facts could lead to such an inference. Indeed the Barton/Igen guidelines appear to leave a considerable amount of discretion to the tribunal in this regard, stating that the outcome at the first stage will usually depend on what inferences it is proper to draw from the primary facts found by the tribunal – see Chapter 33, 'Proving discrimination', under 'Inferring discrimination', for details of the kinds of facts and evidence from which discrimination can be inferred. Nor is the passage, of course, saying that the claimant has to prove *all aspects* of the discrimination claim at the first stage (i.e. adduce facts to establish less favourable treatment *and* the discriminatory motivation), since this would self-evidently contradict EU law, which, as we have seen, enshrines in all the current equality Directives the concept of a shifting burden of proof once the claimant has raised a prima facie case – see under 'Legislative framework – EU law' above. In the context of the Court of Appeal's judgment in Igen, the real point being made by Peter Gibson LJ is presumably that the claimant must prove that the respondent actually *committed* the alleged discriminatory act (as to which see under 'Applicability of shifting burden of proof rule – discriminatory element' above).

Relevant evidence at the first stage. The passage from Igen v Wong quoted **32.39** above was cited with approval by Lord Justice Mummery in Madarassy v Nomura International plc 2007 ICR 867, CA. However, his Lordship appears to have drawn from it a proposition that was arguably not intended by the Court of Appeal in Igen. Mummery LJ thought it significant that Peter Gibson LJ had expressly rejected the argument that it was sufficient for the complainant simply to prove facts from which the tribunal could conclude that the respondent *could have* committed an unlawful act of discrimination. On this basis, Mummery LJ proceeded to emphasise that the burden of proof does not shift to the employer merely by virtue of the fact that there is a difference in 'status' between the claimant and his or her comparator (in that case sex) alongside the fact that there has been a difference in treatment between them.

Mummery LJ pointed out (quite rightly) that the employer should be able to adduce at stage one evidence to show 'that the acts which are alleged to be discriminatory never happened; or that, if they did, they were not less favourable treatment of the complainant; or that the comparators chosen by the complainant or the situations with which comparisons are made are not truly like the complainant or the situation of the complainant'. This is not contentious and accords with Elias P's approach in Laing v Manchester City Council, which incidentally was heavily relied upon and, indeed, expressly approved by Mummery LJ in Madarassy.

His Lordship then went on to say that the employer can also adduce evidence **32.40** at the first stage to show 'that even if there has been less favourable treatment of the complainant, it was not on the ground of her sex'; and he included in his list of the types of evidence an employer may adduce, 'available evidence of the reasons for the differential treatment'. This would appear to blur the distinction drawn in Laing between evidence as to material facts that rebuts the employee's prima facie case (which the tribunal should consider at the first stage) and

1119

evidence that seeks to explain the prima facie discriminatory treatment (which should be left to the second stage). The difficulty with this blurring is that if a tribunal considers the employer's evidence of a non-discriminatory reason for the less favourable treatment before even prima facie evidence of such discrimination has been established, the whole purpose of the two-stage test begins to collapse. And it could effectively require the claimant to establish that the less favourable treatment was because of the relevant protected characteristic (sex/race/disability, etc), whereas the burden should be on the employer to show that it was not.

Mummery LJ also appeared to suggest that while the respondent's explanation may result in the rejection of a prima facie case of discrimination – and so cause the claim not to progress beyond the first stage – the absence of an explanation may not be relied upon to establish such a prima facie case. Note, however, that the Court of Appeal in Igen v Wong held that it was not an error of law for a tribunal to draw an inference of discrimination simply from *unexplained unreasonable conduct* at the first stage of the two-stage burden of proof test – see Chapter 33, 'Proving discrimination', in the section 'Inferring discrimination', under 'Hostile or unreasonable behaviour – unexplained unreasonable conduct'. Equally, the ECJ's decisions in both Kelly v National University of Ireland 2012 ICR 322, ECJ, and Meister v Speech Design Carrier Systems GmbH Case C-415/10, ECJ, suggest that the refusal of an employer to provide information that would assist in explaining its treatment could be relevant in establishing a prima facie case of discrimination if the national court decides – taking into account all the circumstances of the case – that that refusal risks compromising the achievement of the objectives pursued by the relevant EU Directives in the context of the shifting burden of proof. For further details, see Chapter 33, 'Proving discrimination', under 'Requesting information and disclosure of evidence'.

32.41 **Application of the 'Madarassy approach'.** Subsequent case law has relied heavily upon the 'Madarassy approach', while the 'Laing approach' has to a certain extent been relegated to the sidelines (even though it was expressly approved by Mummery LJ). In Hammonds LLP and ors v Mwitta EAT 0026/10, for example, the EAT overturned an employment tribunal's finding that the claimant, a solicitor of mixed race, had established a prima facie case of race discrimination on the basis that significantly less work had been given to her than to her white comparators, thus showing a pattern of marginalisation. The EAT held that this was an insufficient basis from which to draw an inference of discrimination. Those facts indicated a difference in race and a difference in treatment, which at most showed a possibility that the claimant's law firm *could have* discriminated on the ground of race in allocating work but not that it *had* done so. Furthermore, in the EAT's view, if the tribunal had inferred race discrimination from the lack of explanation for such treatment, that was, in light of Mummery LJ's judgment in Madarassy, also an error.

In addition, the EAT in Transport for London and anor v Aderemi EAT 0006/11 (discussed under 'Applicability of shifting burden of proof rule – discriminatory element' above) also relied upon Madarassy, as well as on Peter Gibson LJ's judgment in Igen Ltd (formerly Leeds Careers Guidance) and ors v Wong and other cases (above), when holding that something more than less favourable treatment is required in order to establish a prima facie case (although less favourable treatment is a necessary prerequisite). It overturned an employment tribunal's decision of race discrimination that had been based upon facts from which the tribunal 'could conclude' that the employer had treated the claimant less favourably than it would have treated a hypothetical comparator, stating that this was 'redolent of precisely the same error identified by [Peter Gibson LJ] in Igen v Wong' – i.e. when he stated 'it is for the complainant to prove the facts from which... the tribunal could conclude, in the absence of an adequate explanation, that the respondent committed an unlawful act of discrimination. It does not say that the facts to be proved are those from which the [tribunal] could conclude that the respondent "could have committed" such [an] act'. The EAT went on to agree with the employer that the tribunal had wrongly conflated less favourable treatment, which had to be proved on the balance of probabilities, and the issue of whether there was a prima facie case that such treatment was meted out on the ground of race.

Not a rule of law. In Hussain v Vision Security Ltd EAT 0439/10 Mr Justice **32.42** Underhill (then President of the EAT) made the point that Mummery LJ's statement in Madarassy v Nomura International plc (above) that something more than a difference in treatment and status is required to shift the burden of proof should not be treated as a rule of law to be applied in every case. He noted that Mummery LJ was rejecting a submission that the burden of proof is, automatically and in all cases, reversed merely by proof of difference in the relevant status and difference in treatment. Mummery LJ himself emphasised in Madarassy that judicial guidance is not a substitute for the statutory wording (reiterating the view expressed by Peter Gibson LJ in Igen v Wong). And in any event, it is worth noting that the fact that an employee has been treated *differently* does not necessarily mean that he or she has been treated *less favourably* – see Chapter 15, 'Direct discrimination', under 'Less favourable treatment – what amounts to less favourable treatment?'.

Furthermore, a strict interpretation and application of Madarassy may arguably depart too far from the position advocated by Mr Justice Elias in Laing v Manchester City Council 2006 ICR 1519, EAT – which of course followed the Court of Appeal's decision in Igen v Wong – that if an employee can adduce evidence to establish that he or she has genuinely been less favourably treated (taking into account all material facts), this could be a sufficient basis for inferring discrimination at the first stage if the employer cannot rebut that evidence (leaving aside the explanation). Elias P's approach has considerable force, not least because it maintains a clear distinction between what the claimant has to prove at stage one to establish a prima facie case of discrimination and what the respondent has to prove at stage two to rebut the prima facie case. There is therefore less danger of a claimant effectively being required at stage one to prove every element of the claim and of stage two becoming an opportunity for the employer to defend the claim, rather than being an opportunity for the claimant to shift the burden of proof. In this regard, it is relevant to note that Mummery LJ actually approved Elias P's approach in Laing, stating that it was 'sound in principle and workable in practice'.

32.43 Moreover, in many cases involving treatment that is not overtly race-, sex-, or age-, etc specific, the claimant may struggle to establish anything other than the fact that he or she has been treated differently to other employees who do not share the relevant protected characteristic (particularly where the employer is adept at covering up any discriminatory motivation). For example, a woman who is bullied in a gender-neutral way may suspect that the bullying is based on her sex, but have no proof other than that her male colleagues were not subjected to similar treatment. A strict interpretation of Madarassy could therefore make it prohibitively difficult for a claimant to shift the burden onto the respondent, precisely when he or she most needs to do so, i.e. when the discrimination is at its most covert. This perhaps risks jeopardising the intended objectives of the EU burden of proof provisions.

32.44 Flexible approach preferable

Although a strict application of Madarassy could risk upsetting the balance too far in the employer's favour, some might argue that a rule of law that simply allows the claimant to point to less favourable treatment in order to establish a prima facie case of discrimination, while having the merit of simplicity, may go too far in the opposite direction. Case law has stressed on a number of occasions that a flexible approach is required when applying the burden of proof. For example, in Khan and anor v Home Office 2008 EWCA Civ 578, CA, the Court of Appeal held that the burden of proof rules 'need not be applied in an overly mechanistic or schematic way'. And Elias P in Laing v Manchester City Council (above) emphasised that 'the process of drawing an inference of discrimination... is a matter for factual assessment and... [is] situation-specific'. He deprecated the development of 'sophisticated quasi-rules of law' to govern that assessment, emphasising that a tribunal's focus must at all times be on the question of whether or not it can properly and fairly infer discrimination. He also cautioned against letting 'form rule over substance'.

32.45 **Drawing logical inferences from the primary facts.** Simply put, the outcome at the first stage will usually depend on what inferences it is proper to draw from the primary facts found by the employment tribunal. Indeed, this is emphasised by the Barton/Igen guidelines (see the section 'Legal framework', under 'Domestic law – the Barton/Igen guidelines' above). However, as noted under 'Is something more than less favourable treatment required?' above, the guidelines are not prescriptive as to what type of facts could lead to such an inference and appear to leave a considerable amount of discretion to the tribunal in this regard. Therefore, provided a tribunal makes clear findings of facts, based upon the evidence, and draws logical and appropriate inferences from these findings, its decision as to whether or not a prima facie case of discrimination has been made out should be watertight and unchallengeable. Note that the principal types of fact and evidence from which discrimination can be inferred are discussed in Chapter 33, 'Proving discrimination', under 'Inferring discrimination'.

Striking the appropriate balance. When applying the shifting burden of proof, **32.46** tribunals should keep in mind the balance, which – as noted by Advocate General Mengozzi in his Opinion given in Meister v Speech Design Carrier Systems GmbH (Case C-415/10), ECJ) – is required by EU law to be struck between, on the one hand, enabling victims of discrimination to claim their right to equal treatment and, on the other, preventing proceedings from being pursued against employers solely on the basis of an employee's bare assertions – see 'Legal framework – EU law' above. In so doing, they should also bear in mind that, while a Member State may choose to upset the balance further in favour of the claimant, there is no indication that UK law intends to make the shifting burden of proof any more favourable to the claimant than the minimum standard required by EU law.

Clear less favourable treatment. Adopting a flexible approach based upon this **32.47** balance to be struck between employer and employee – together with the tribunal's discretion to draw logical inferences from the primary facts – should mean that, if clear less favourable treatment is established, very little more (if anything) will be needed to tip the balance in favour of a prima facie case and allow the tribunal to draw the requisite inference of discrimination. In keeping with the EU principle of effectiveness, tribunals may need to bear in mind that if discrimination is particularly covert, there will be little more than less favourable treatment to go on to raise the inference that discrimination is the motivating factor, consciously or subconsciously, for that treatment. In other instances, perhaps, the less favourable treatment will be less clear but the employee may be able to adduce stronger evidence of, for example, discriminatory motivation, which again allows him or her to establish a prima facie case. Furthermore, where the claimant is relying upon a hypothetical comparator, the evidence from which less favourable treatment can be inferred may overlap considerably with the evidence from which it may be inferred that it was done because of a protected characteristic.

In Hussain v Vision Security Ltd EAT 0439/10 (discussed under 'Is something more than less favourable treatment required? – not a rule of law' above) the fact that there was a clear case of less favourable treatment was highly significant in establishing a prima facie case of discrimination. H had been employed by

MSG Ltd as a security guard, working at a site along with two colleagues, C and E. When MSG Ltd's services were no longer required at the site, the three were told that they would be redeployed. Three vacancies arose at the site of another client, G Ltd. Two were given to C and E, who were in their thirties. The third was filled through external recruitment. It was never offered to H, who was 64. H claimed age discrimination. An employment tribunal dismissed his claim, accepting the evidence of R, the manager handling the redeployment, that H had refused employment at the second site. That decision was overturned on appeal and the matter was remitted to the same tribunal.

32.48 By the time of the second hearing, MSG Ltd's business had transferred to VSG Ltd, which was accordingly joined as second respondent to the proceedings. In light of further evidence adduced, which brought to light inconsistencies in R's evidence, the tribunal no longer accepted that H had been offered a job at G Ltd's site. Nevertheless, it went on to dismiss the claim, holding that H had not proved facts from which it could conclude that there had been unlawful discrimination. The fact that he had been treated less favourably than comparators who were about 30 years younger than him was not in the tribunal's view sufficient (and nor did the fact that R was an unreliable witness make any difference). The EAT overturned the tribunal's decision, holding that the matters relied upon by H were indeed sufficient to shift the burden of proof. There were three vacancies at G Ltd's site: two were offered to H's colleagues, who were in their thirties, but the third was not offered to H, who was on the brink of pensionable age. R had given an untruthful explanation for the difference in treatment. It could perhaps be added, although this was of less significance, that he had also failed to deal with correspondence from H expressly alleging age discrimination. In the particular circumstances of the case, which went beyond the mere fact that the claimant was older than his comparators, the EAT believed that a prima facie case of age discrimination was shown. The EAT observed that that would have been its view even had it accepted the respondents' submission that employees were not required to retire at a certain age. A general policy was one thing, but it did not negate, or indeed necessarily weigh very heavily against, an inference that an individual manager in particular circumstances was motivated by discriminatory considerations. Whatever MSG Ltd's policy generally may have been, it was a matter of common knowledge that assumptions about whether employees of the claimant's age should continue in employment, or enjoy equal opportunities in a particular employment situation, are still very common. That R should have been influenced, consciously or unconsciously, by H's age was not in any sense implausible, even without any specific evidence of prior manifestation of ageist attitudes.

The EAT added that it would not have shrunk from holding that the tribunal's decision was perverse: it was the view of all three panel members upon first reading the papers in this case that the differential treatment did indeed raise a prima facie case of age discrimination, and it was important to see what explanation the respondents could advance to rebut the inference of discrimination. However, the EAT considered that the tribunal probably went wrong not by a perverse application of the right test but by failing to understand what that test involved. Its reasoning was so shortly stated that it was frankly impossible to see what process the tribunal went through in saying that it was unable to conclude that MGS Ltd had been motivated by the claimant's age. The EAT inferred, partly from the very shortness of the reasoning and partly also from the repeated references to the Court of Appeal's decision in Madarassy v Nomura International plc 2007 ICR 867, CA, that the tribunal was proceeding on the basis of what it understood to be a rule of law rather than on an assessment of what inference was to be drawn from the primary facts.

The Northern Ireland Court of Appeal's decision in Rice v McEvoy 2011 NICA **32.49** 9, NICA, also suggests that the *extent* of the less favourable treatment in question could be relevant in establishing a prima facie case. The Court in that case stated that 'if an employer acts in a wholly unreasonable way, that may assist in drawing an inference that the employer's purported explanation for his actions was not in fact the true explanation and that he was covering up a discriminatory intent'. The extent to which discrimination can be inferred from unreasonable conduct is discussed in Chapter 33, 'Proving discrimination' under 'Inferring discrimination – hostile or unreasonable behaviour'.

Strong evidential comparator. Another useful illustration of a prima facie **32.50** case can be found in the Equality and Human Rights Commission's Code of Practice on Employment ('the EHRC Employment Code'). It gives the following example at para 4.32 in the section on 'Burden of proof': a worker of Jain faith applies for promotion but is unsuccessful. Her colleague, who is a Mormon, successfully gets the promotion. The unsuccessful candidate obtains information using the questions procedure in the EqA (see Chapter 33, 'Proving discrimination', under 'Requesting information and disclosure of evidence – statutory questionnaires') which shows that she was better qualified for the promotion than her Mormon colleague. The employer will have to explain to the tribunal why the Jain worker was not promoted and that religion or belief did not form any part of the decision. In this example, the claimant has not strictly speaking been less favourably treated than an actual comparator. An actual comparator would be similarly qualified, whereas the Mormon colleague is less well qualified. Nevertheless, this very difference in circumstance can be used to establish less favourable treatment from which discrimination may be inferred under the first stage when considering the application of the shifting burden of proof rule in S.136 EqA.

Refusal to provide information. The ECJ's decision in Meister v Speech Design **32.51** Carrier Systems GmbH (above) also suggests that a prima facie case of discrimination can, in certain circumstances, be established by apparent less favourable treatment in circumstances where the employer refuses to provide information capable of constituting facts from which it may be presumed that there has been discrimination. In this regard, and as noted in the Advocate General's Opinion, account could be taken of the fact that M's qualifications matched the post to be filled and yet the employer did not call her for a job interview (despite the fact that it called other applicants to such an interview). In the Advocate General's Opinion, it was also relevant that M responded to the publication of a job vacancy and did not submit a spontaneous application. The Advocate General went on to state that the refusal of disclosure by an employer must be assessed differently if the claimant clearly does not fit the required profile (and therefore will clearly be unable to establish less favourable treatment), has been called for an interview or has submitted a spontaneous application. For further details, see Chapter 33, 'Proving discrimination', under 'Requesting information and disclosure of evidence'.

32.52 Some examples of cases analysing whether the surrounding facts support a prima facie case of discrimination:

- **Court v Dennis Publishing Ltd** ET Case No.2200327/07: the employment tribunal was willing to infer age discrimination when C was selected for redundancy ahead of his much younger colleagues. The tribunal took into account the fact that the claimant was the oldest, by some distance, of a team of five. The tribunal also drew inferences from the fact that the owner of the respondent company had published a book, 'How To Get Rich', in which he advised that 'talent' gets more expensive as it gets older, and recommended replacing senior staff with younger, cheaper employees. Although the owner himself was not involved in the redundancy procedure, the tribunal noted that members of senior management had read the book, and was willing to infer that the owner's ageist philosophy had infected the company

- **Canadian Imperial Bank of Commerce v Beck** EAT 0141/10: the inclusion of 'younger' in the list of attributes given by the employer to the recruitment agency charged with replacing an employee purportedly dismissed for redundancy was sufficient to raise a prima facie case that he had been dismissed because of his age, which the employer had been unable to disprove

- **McCoy v James McGregor and Sons Ltd and ors** IT Case No.237/07: a Northern Ireland industrial tribunal held that JMS Ltd's decision not to offer employment to M, a 58-year-old job applicant, while offering employment to two applicants aged 42 and 43, amounted to direct age discrimination. The tribunal attached great significance to the job advertisement's use of the phrase 'youthful enthusiasm' and drew from it an inference that age played a part in the selection process. It also attached weight to questions raised during M's interviews about his age, drive and motivation. Neither of the successful candidates had been asked whether they still had the drive and motivation for the role. The combined effect of these findings was that M had proved facts from which the tribunal could conclude that JMS Ltd had discriminated against him on the ground of his age

- **Laing v Manchester City Council** 2006 ICR 1519, EAT: the EAT held that the employment tribunal was entitled to conclude that unreasonable conduct meted out by a supervisor to a black employee did not amount to a prima facie case of race discrimination since the supervisor dealt with all employees, black or white, in the same unreasonable way. Taking account of that fact and the supervisor's lack of managerial experience, the tribunal was not having regard to the explanation for her specific conduct towards L, and thus had not fallen into error. In other words, these were material facts that could be legitimately adduced by the employer at the first stage to rebut L's prima facie case. They clarified that L had not in fact been treated less favourably, rather than explaining any less favourable treatment that might have occurred

- **Madarassy v Nomura International plc** 2007 ICR 867, CA: the evidence indicated that M's colleague, B, shouted at members of staff whether they were male or female. According to the employment tribunal, 'there was equality of shouting regardless of gender'. The Court of Appeal noted that this was the culture of the workplace. It might be horrible, but it was not sexist. The tribunal had therefore not erred in dismissing M's complaint of discrimination against B at the first stage as there was no comparative less favourable treatment

- **Stockton on Tees Borough Council v Aylott** 2010 ICR 1278, CA: the Court of Appeal held the employment tribunal, having made detailed findings of fact about the Council's reaction to A's mental illness (bipolar affective disorder), had been entitled to draw inferences from those findings to the effect that his dismissal on the ground of ill health amounted to disability discrimination. For example, the tribunal found that there was some panic on the part of the Council with regard to the claimant's return to work following a lengthy period of sick leave. There was a 'total change' in the working relationship. Strict deadlines were set and his performance was closely monitored. The subsequent decision to carry out a disciplinary investigation and to suspend A – although subsequently withdrawn when he was admitted to hospital as a result of his illness – was 'extremely harsh'. Furthermore, a letter from the Human Resources manager to Occupational Health referred to A's behaviour as 'intimidating and scary' when that did not reflect the statements given by A's fellow employees. In the Court of Appeal's judgment, 'those findings were more than sufficient to take the case out of that kind of case in which there is only the fact of disability and the fact of dismissal, which could not alone properly support an inference of discrimination'

- **Network Rail Infrastructure Ltd v Griffiths-Henry** 2006 IRLR 865, EAT: the EAT agreed with the employment tribunal that G-H had established a prima facie case of race and sex discrimination by not being selected for one of five posts following a reorganisation of NRI Ltd. Out of eight other candidates (all white males), GH had been assessed as the second lowest by NRI Ltd. The EAT accepted that the mere fact that G-H was a black woman and the successful candidates were white men would not have been sufficient to justify an inference of discrimination. However, the tribunal had also identified the fact that five of her colleagues were appointed out of a total of eight. Another highly relevant factor was that G-H was, on the face of it, as equally qualified as the five successful candidates were for the relevant position. In addition, the tribunal had identified certain defects in the assessment carried out in respect of G-H, which called for some explanation. When all these factors were taken into account, there was a perfectly sound basis on which a tribunal could properly infer that there was a prima facie case of discrimination. (Note, however, that the EAT went on to hold that the tribunal had erred in actually inferring discrimination at the second stage)

32.53 In Country Style Foods Ltd v Bouzir 2011 EWCA Civ 1519, CA, B, an Algerian national, together with his Latvian wife – both of Muslim faith – applied for positions as production operatives with CSF Ltd, a food processing company. They were invited to interview on 7 July 2009 and brought with them their UK work permits and marriage certificate. The company questioned the validity of these documents and, before he could complete his interview, B went to the local police station to get them certified. When he returned with the certified documents, he was told that there was no time available for the rest of his interview but that he and his wife would be telephoned about induction training, which was taking place in two days' time. They received no such telephone call but nevertheless turned up on the induction day to discover that training was being given to two groups of white people, and to be told that they could not participate as their applications had been unsuccessful. B asked for a letter of explanation but was told that this was against company policy. He and his wife eventually received a letter on 13 August saying that the successful candidates had previous bakery experience. In fact, only 3 of the 30 candidates had such experience. CSF Ltd did not reply to statutory questionnaires asking detailed questions about the make-up of the applications for the vacancies and the candidates appointed. Its explanation for this was that the HR staff thought that the claims had been settled. Nor did the company reply to their request for copies of certain documents, including their application forms and interview notes. Indeed, the company was unable to produce these documents at all during the proceedings. An employment tribunal rejected claims for race discrimination brought by B and his wife (although it upheld her additional claim for religious discrimination). The case eventually reached the Court of Appeal, which held that the tribunal had erred in law in rejecting B's claim because it had failed to apply the burden of proof provisions to the facts of the case. In the Court's view, the tribunal had made a number of findings which, taken as a whole, could properly lead to the conclusion that B had been treated less favourably on the ground of his national origins. These findings were: the company's failure to complete B's interview after returning from the police station; its failure to inform B about the induction as promised; its failure to answer the questionnaires; its inaccurate letter of explanation for not offering B employment; and the non-disclosure of documents, such as application forms.

Stage two: proving absence of discrimination 32.54

If and when the claimant establishes a prima face case of discrimination, then the second stage of the burden of proof test is reached, with the consequence that the burden of proof shifts onto the respondent. According to the Court of Appeal in Igen Ltd (formerly Leeds Careers Guidance) and ors v Wong and other cases 2005 ICR 931, CA, the respondent must at this stage prove on the balance of probabilities that its treatment of the claimant was in no sense whatsoever based on the protected ground.

The guidance given by the EAT in Barton v Investec Henderson Crosthwaite Securities Ltd 2003 ICR 1205, EAT (as slightly modified subsequently by the Court of Appeal in Igen – see the section 'Legal framework', under 'Domestic law – the Barton/Igen guidelines' above) adopted the formulation of 'no discrimination whatsoever' from the Burden of Proof Directive, Article 2(1) of which stated that 'for the purposes of this Directive, the principle of equal treatment shall mean that there shall be no discrimination whatsoever based on sex, either directly or indirectly'. That Directive was incorporated into the recast Directive, which consolidated and repealed the seven separate Directives that up to that point dealt with gender equality with effect from 15 August 2009 – see under 'Legal framework – EU law' above. The relevant provisions of the Burden of Proof Directive appear in similar form in Article 19 of the recast Directive, except that the recast Directive does not adopt the formulation of 'no discrimination whatsoever', and instead stipulates that 'there shall be no direct or indirect discrimination on grounds of sex'. The same formulation appears in the other two current equality Directives – namely, the Framework Directive (relating to religion, belief, disability, age and sexual orientation) and the EU Race Equality Directive (No.2000/43), both of which stipulate that there shall be no direct or indirect discrimination on the relevant protected grounds. It is, however, highly unlikely that the recast Directive is intended to regress from the level of protection previously afforded by the seven separate Directives, including the Burden of Proof Directive, and it is uncontroversial that Directives Nos.2000/78 and 2000/43 are intended to offer the same level of protection as the recast Directive in respect of the particular discrimination

1129

fields they cover. Furthermore, the formulation 'no discrimination whatsoever' is still frequently used by the courts and tribunals. In any event, it is hard to see that the word 'whatsoever' adds anything of substance to the general prohibition set out in all three of the current equality Directives.

32.55 Of course, in order to establish exactly what the employer has to prove, regard will need to be had to the statutory language relating to the particular type of discrimination at issue. Thus, for the purposes of direct discrimination under S.13 EqA, the employer must prove that the treatment was not (or in no sense whatsoever) 'because of a protected characteristic'; and for the purposes of harassment under S.26 EqA, the employer must prove that the treatment in question was not (or in no sense whatsoever) 'related to a relevant protected characteristic'.

The EHRC Employment Code notes at para 3.11 in the section on 'Direct discrimination' that 'because of' is intended to have the same meaning as 'on grounds of', found in the earlier legislation. Accordingly, some distinct principles that can be distilled from the pre-EqA case law still have application. For instance, it is clear that the protected characteristic does not need to be the only reason for the treatment complained of. In Owen and Briggs v James 1982 ICR 618, CA, the Court of Appeal held that while the protected characteristic (in that case race) need not be the only reason for the treatment, it must have been a substantial reason. However, the EAT went one step further in O'Neill v Governors of St Thomas More Roman Catholic Voluntarily Aided Upper School and anor 1997 ICR 33, EAT, taking the view that the protected characteristic need not even be the main reason for the treatment, so long as it was an 'effective cause'. The Code of Practice confirms this, noting that 'the protected characteristic needs to be a cause of the less favourable treatment, but does not need to be the only or even the main cause'.

32.56 In Network Rail Infrastructure Ltd v Griffiths-Henry 2006 IRLR 865, EAT, Mr Justice Elias made the point that the burden imposed on the employer will depend on the strength of the prima facie case. He considered that a black candidate who is better qualified than the only other white candidate and does not get the job imposes a greater burden at the second stage than would a black candidate rejected along with some others who were equally qualified (assuming that the tribunal properly finds a prima facie case in such a situation). The standard of proof necessary to establish a proven case of discrimination is considered further under 'Standard of proof' below.

It is important that, at the second stage, the employment tribunal does in fact place the burden on the respondent to prove its case on the balance of probabilities. A striking example of the tribunal getting it wrong in this respect arose in EB v BA 2006 IRLR 471, CA. There, EB was employed by BA, a worldwide management consultancy firm. She alleged that, following her male-to-female gender reassignment, BA selected her for redundancy, ostensibly on the ground of her low number of billable hours. EB claimed that BA had reduced the amount of billable project work allocated to her and thus her ability to reach billing targets as a result of her gender reassignment. Her claim was dismissed by the tribunal and the EAT and she appealed to the Court of Appeal, which accepted her argument that the tribunal had erred in its approach to the burden of proof under what was then S.63A SDA (now S.136 EqA). Although the tribunal had correctly found that EB had raised a prima facie case of discrimination and that the burden of proof had shifted to the employer, it had mistakenly gone on to find that the employer had discharged that burden, since all its explanations were 'inherently plausible' and had not been discredited by EB. In so doing, the tribunal had not in fact placed the burden of proof on the employer because it had wrongly looked to EB to disprove what were otherwise 'plausible' explanations. It was not for EB to identify projects to which she should have been assigned. Instead, the employer should have produced documents or schedules setting out all the projects taking place over the relevant period along with reasons why EB was not allocated to any of them. Although the tribunal had commented on the lack of documents or schedules from BA, it had failed to appreciate that the consequences of that absence could only be adverse to BA. The Court of Appeal held that the tribunal's approach amounted to requiring EB to prove her case when the burden of proof had shifted to the respondent.

In Canadian Imperial Bank of Commerce v Beck EAT 0141/10 (also discussed **32.57** under 'Stage one: establishing a "prima facie case" – flexible approach preferable' above) the EAT held that where a claimant has raised a prima facie case of age discrimination, it is sufficient for an employment tribunal to say that it was not persuaded that the employer's explanation was right, rather than reject it, and a tribunal may reasonably prefer to go no further than to say that the burden of proof has not been discharged. The EAT also rejected the contention that the tribunal had erroneously drawn an adverse inference from the fact that the head of the department – who was involved in the decision to make the claimant redundant – had not given evidence before it. The tribunal had simply noted that this had made it difficult for it to assess whether he was significantly influenced by the claimant's age. This highlights the importance of a party ensuring that its key witnesses give evidence at the tribunal hearing, especially in discrimination cases where the employer may find itself on the wrong end of the burden of proof provisions. Once the tribunal had decided there was a prima facie case that age was a factor in the claimant's dismissal, the employer's chances of rebutting the allegation were severely hampered by the absence of the one person best placed to provide a non-discriminatory explanation.

An employer who has transparent procedures in place and keeps contemporaneous records to explain its treatment of employees is less likely to fall foul of the stage-two shift in the burden of proof. Conversely, an employer who fails to adopt such measures may well encounter difficulties. In this regard, in Komeng v Sandwell Metropolitan Borough Council EAT 0592/10 the EAT made the point that employment tribunals should 'take care before accepting an explanation that the reason for less favourable treatment (if proven) lies merely in general poor administration. There is always the risk that poor administration masks real disadvantage to a particular group or a particular individual on prohibited grounds.'

32.58 Two examples:

- **Jaff v Royal Mail Group Ltd** ET Case No.1400760/09: J, an Iraqi Kurd by ethnicity and a naturalised British citizen, began working for RMG Ltd in June 2005. He did not have a good relationship with his line manager. In September 2008 he responded to an internal notice inviting applications for the post of acting manager. He was told that no decision would be made on his application until the New Year, but in the meantime two other British employees were invited to train as acting managers and their training was arranged. When J approached his manager about his application he was told that he had been unsuccessful because he was not suitable management material. An employment tribunal was satisfied that there were facts from which it could infer that, in the absence of an explanation by RMG Ltd, there had been direct race discrimination. The procedure for the selection of acting managers was unwritten and informal; no regular appraisals were carried out or training records kept and it was left to the discretion of line managers to select acting managers from their staff on an ad hoc basis. There were no criteria to assist the manager in his task, nor did he have access to the employees' personnel files, and nor had he received any equal opportunities training beyond a short video. There was no application form on which J could set out his qualifications and experience and no interviews were held. The employer's decision was thus wholly subjective. The tribunal noted that the risk of discrimination in internal promotions is always present and it was concerned that the lack of any formal procedure gave rise to a situation that must inevitably lead to a risk of discrimination, a risk that in the instant case had become a reality. The tribunal found that J was disadvantaged as a member of an ethnic minority who did not enjoy the same easy relationship with his line manager – in whose sole discretion the power of advancement was vested – as did his British comparators. These matters all contributed to the less favourable treatment. RMG Ltd's handling of the matter, albeit unintentionally, amounted to direct discrimination causing considerable injury to J's feelings (for which he was awarded £7,000)

- **Kissiedu v The Jewellery Collection LLP t/a Smooch** ET Case No.3300688/09: K, a black employee, was interviewed by JC LLP for the role of sub-adviser. Following the interview K was offered and accepted the position. She was then required to attend training, which was carried out by a director. JC LLP regarded the training as part of the recruitment process but this was not made known to K, who saw it as a mere formality. After the training, K was told via text that she was no longer to be appointed. She brought a claim for direct race discrimination. An employment tribunal held that two white women who had been present at the training session were the appropriate comparators. It was accepted that both these women had received more direct attention during the session and that both went on to become sub-advisers. The tribunal found that the criteria that JC LLP claimed to have applied in assessing K were highly subjective and the decision was based entirely upon the director's view of K and her abilities. If, as JC LLP claimed, it was seeking a black adviser to extend its market and K was seen to possess the necessary skills, it was difficult to understand why other measures were not taken at least to find out why the training had been unsatisfactory. Furthermore, the tribunal noted that JC LLP did not have an equal opportunities policy. It claimed the policy was in the director's head. That was not sufficient and was evidence of subjectivity. Such a policy needed to be objective and be seen to be implemented. Furthermore, despite JC LLP's submissions that it wanted a black person to extend the business, it was notable that there were no advisers from other ethnic backgrounds working for the company, except one Asian person, and that the person subsequently appointed to the role had been white. Therefore, K had established a series of facts demonstrating less favourable treatment from which the tribunal could infer race discrimination. Since the tribunal found JC LLP's explanations to be unsatisfactory, it drew the inference of race discrimination, while accepting that the discrimination in question may have been subconscious.

32.59 The above cases were fully reasoned and the respective tribunals were able to cite detailed facts or circumstances sufficient to conclude that the employers had not discharged the onus cast upon them at the second stage of the application of the burden of proof rule to explain away the prima face case of discrimination. However, the mere fact that an employer's recruitment process leaves something to be desired is not, without more, likely to be a sufficient basis for inferring race discrimination, as the following case demonstrates:

- **Bojarowska-Mayhew v The Phoenix Surgery** ET Case No.3103468/09: BM qualified as a GP in her homeland of Poland but all her post-graduate experience was in the United Kingdom. She applied for a post as a GP with the respondent surgery and when she was not shortlisted she brought a claim for direct race discrimination. She maintained that there was little possibility that the shortlisted candidates could be better qualified or experienced than she was. She claimed the reason she was not shortlisted was that local GP practices did not like Eastern European GPs as it was possible for them to work in the United Kingdom when they had little experience of the

UK healthcare system. An employment tribunal dismissed BM's claim. It noted that the application process was neither fair nor transparent. Indeed, the tribunal considered it might have been one of the worst recruitment processes it had seen in that there was no verifiable contemporaneous evidence to justify what was done and how it was done. But that did not mean it was race discriminatory. The tribunal was satisfied that the surgery applied criteria that it thought reasonable and fit and which bore on the particular aspects of its practice, even though that criteria could be open to criticism. It might well have been, as BM suggested, unfair to mark her down because her application did not contain mission statements. However, that had nothing to do with her race. Put quite simply, BM did not get the job she applied for because of the application of criteria that had nothing to do with race.

32.60 The employer's reason for the treatment of the claimant does not need to be laudable or reasonable in order to be non-discriminatory. Two examples:

- **B and anor v A** 2010 IRLR 400, EAT: the employer summarily dismissed a male employee without any proper investigation or disciplinary procedure on the ground that he posed a risk of further violence against members of staff. The EAT held that the employment tribunal had erred in holding that the employer had thereby directly discriminated against the employee on the ground of sex. Although the employer's behaviour was surprising, and its explanation for the failure to follow correct procedures was irrational in that the risk of violence could have been dealt with by suspension, that was not enough to establish sex discrimination and the tribunal's findings did not support its conclusion that the employer had been motivated by a stereotypical view of male aggression. In fact, the evidence disclosed an obvious (and non-discriminatory) reason why the employer believed that the claimant posed a continuing threat of violence – namely, that it believed that the claimant had acted violently towards a colleague and that he had threatened to 'get her' if she told anyone what had happened

- **B v A** 2007 IRLR 576, EAT: the EAT held that a solicitor who dismissed his assistant, with whom he was in a personal relationship, upon discovering her apparent infidelity, did not discriminate on the ground of sex. The tribunal's finding that the reason for dismissal was his jealous reaction to the claimant's apparent infidelity could not lead to the legal conclusion that the dismissal occurred because she was a woman.

32.61 Further discussion about the employer's reason for the treatment in question – in the context of direct discrimination, harassment and victimisation – can be found, respectively, in Chapter 15, 'Direct discrimination', under '"Because of" protected characteristic'; Chapter 18, 'Harassment', under 'Related to a relevant protected characteristic'; and Chapter 19, 'Victimisation', under 'Detriment "because of" protected act'.

Can first stage be bypassed?

Having said that the shifting burden of proof involves two stages, case law suggests that in some instances, particularly where the claimant is relying upon a hypothetical comparator, it may be appropriate to dispense with the first stage altogether and proceed straight to the second stage. To a large extent, this possibility can be put down to the House of Lords' decision in Shamoon v Chief Constable of the Royal Ulster Constabulary 2003 ICR 337, HL, which, in fact, predates the statutory burden of proof rules. Their Lordships in that case noted that when considering the question of whether an individual has been less favourably treated on the ground of sex, employment tribunals often apply a sequential approach, first determining whether the claimant received less favourable treatment than the appropriate comparator, and subsequently whether the less favourable treatment was on the ground of sex. Thus tribunals often consider the reason for the treatment only if the less favourable treatment issue is resolved in the claimant's favour. The less favourable treatment is thus treated as a threshold that the claimant must cross before the tribunal is called upon to decide why the claimant was accorded such treatment. However, Lord Nicholls considered that – especially where the identity of the relevant comparator is a matter of dispute – this sequential analysis may give rise to needless problems. In his words: 'Sometimes the less favourable treatment issue cannot be resolved without, at the same time, deciding the reason why issue. The two issues are intertwined.'

Lord Nicholls was not, of course, referring to the two-step burden of proof rules here since they were not in force at the time. However, in Laing v Manchester City Council 2006 ICR 1519, EAT, Mr Justice Elias relied upon his comments for the purposes of the statutory burden of proof rule to posit the theory that 'it might be sensible for a tribunal to go straight to the second stage... where the employee is seeking to compare his treatment with a hypothetical employee. In such cases the question whether there is such a comparator – whether there is a prima facie case – is in practice often inextricably linked to the issue of what is the explanation for the treatment.' In Brown v Croydon London Borough Council and anor 2007 ICR 909, CA, Elias P was given the opportunity to put this theory into practice. B, a black employee, made various complaints of direct race discrimination against the Council, including that his white line manager, J, had sought to extend B's six-month probationary period on the ground that he did not fit into the team. An employment tribunal rejected his claim of direct race discrimination, finding that J was seeking to manage his department properly and would have dealt with a hypothetical comparator in the same way irrespective of race. B appealed, arguing that the tribunal had impermissibly conflated the two-stage burden of proof test into one, having proceeded straight to an examination of the respondent's explanation for the treatment complained of. In the EAT, Elias P noted that in some 'hypothetical comparator' cases it may be relatively plain to a tribunal that the burden has switched to the employer – for example, where the employer acts in a way that would be quite atypical for other employers. Conversely, he considered that if the employer acts in a way that would appear perfectly sensible and does the kind of thing that most employers would do, then the burden of proof is unlikely to transfer. His Lordship gave the example of an employer who warns an employee for drunkenness at work, and it is not disputed that the employee was drunk. It was not likely, in the absence of particular evidence demonstrating otherwise, that that would create an inference of less favourable treatment so as to require some explanation from the employer. However, Elias P considered that in other cases the issue of 'less favourable treatment' is so intertwined with 'the reason why' that a sequential analysis can give rise to needless problems and should be dispensed with. As was made clear by Lord Nicholls in Shamoon, it is often both difficult and artificial to separate the two limbs of less favourable treatment and the reason why. On the facts of the particular case before it, that was the position here, and the tribunal had been fully entitled in the circumstances, given that the essential facts were not in dispute, to focus on the reason why – i.e. to proceed to the second stage of the burden of proof enquiry.

32.63 On further appeal, Lord Justice Mummery in the Brown case agreed with Elias P's reasoning that it was not necessary in this particular case for the tribunal expressly to address the two-stage test sequentially. He considered that although it would normally be good practice to apply the two-stage test, it was not an error of law for a tribunal to proceed straight to the second stage in cases such as the instant one, where this does not prejudice the claimant. The tribunal had therefore not erred in adopting this approach. Indeed, far from prejudicing B, the approach had relieved him of the obligation to establish a prima facie case.

The problem is, of course, that an employer might legitimately argue that *it* has been prejudiced by the first stage being bypassed should the tribunal go on to conclude that the employer has not discharged the burden of proof to explain the apparent discrimination at stage two. Elias P alluded to this in Laing v Manchester City Council (above), stating that if tribunals miss out the first stage, they will have to 'bear in mind' the risk to an employer of being 'found not to have discharged a burden which the tribunal ought not to have placed on him in the first place'. It is this concern that the EAT presumably had in mind in Milton Keynes General Hospital NHS Trust and anor v Maruziva EAT 0003/09 when it observed that an employment tribunal should be less willing to dispense with the two-stage test if it *rejects* the employer's explanation for the treatment in question – and thus upholds the discrimination claim. In this regard, it is notable that in both the Brown and Laing cases, where the courts sanctioned the decision of the respective tribunals to proceed straight to the issue of the employer's explanation for apparent discrimination, the employer's explanation was accepted and the claimants' claims of direct discrimination were dismissed.

The correct approach would therefore appear to be as follows: **32.64**

- the employment tribunal should examine whether or not the issue of less favourable treatment is inextricably linked with the reason why such treatment has been meted out to the claimant. If such a link is apparent, the tribunal might first consider whether or not it can make a positive finding as to the reason, in which case it will not need to apply the shifting burden of proof rule – see under 'Applicability of shifting burden of proof rule – clear positive findings' above

- if the tribunal is unable to make a positive finding and finds itself in the 'catch-22' situation of being genuinely unable to decide the issue of less favourable treatment without examining the reason, it must in our view examine the reason (i.e. conduct the stage two enquiry), and it should be for the employer to prove that the reason is not discriminatory, failing which the claimant must succeed in his or her discrimination claim.

It is perhaps slightly misleading to say that this involves bypassing the first stage altogether. Before the burden 'shifts' to the respondent, the claimant would still need to establish:

- that the treatment is to his or her detriment in some way

- that his or her objections to the treatment are justifiable (this should be fairly easy to establish, since the employer has thus far been unable to clearly establish a valid reason for the treatment in question), and

- (possibly) some additional evidence from which it can be inferred that the treatment in question could have been done on a protected ground (the types of facts and evidence from which discrimination can be inferred is dealt with in Chapter 33, 'Proving discrimination', under 'Inferring discrimination').

Furthermore, the employer may be able to rebut the employer's prima facie **32.65** case by, for example, establishing that other employees have been treated in the same way.

The above approach would appear to maintain the balance, which – as noted by Advocate General Mengozzi in his Opinion given in Meister v Speech Design Carrier Systems GmbH Case C-415/10, ECJ) – is required by EU law between, on the one hand, enabling victims of discrimination to claim their right to equal treatment and, on the other, preventing proceedings from being pursued and succeeding against employers solely on the basis of an employee's bald assertions of discrimination – see 'Legal framework – EU law' above. It also takes into account the fact that a flexible approach is required when applying the burden of proof – see under 'Stage one: establishing a "prima facie case" – flexible approach preferable' above.

1137

32.66 The case of Stockton on Tees Borough Council v Aylott 2010 ICR 1278, CA, provides an example of less favourable treatment (in that case dismissal) being inextricably linked with the reason for that treatment (thus requiring the adoption of the approach outlined above for the purposes of applying the burden of proof). The employment tribunal made detailed findings of fact about the Council's reaction to A's mental illness (bipolar affective disorder) and drew inferences from those findings to the effect that his dismissal on the ground of ill health amounted to disability discrimination. The Court of Appeal considered that if A's dismissal was on the ground of his disability, it was likely that he was treated less favourably than a hypothetical comparator not having the particular disability would have been treated in the same relevant circumstances. The finding of the reason for his dismissal supplied the answer to the question whether he received less favourable treatment: the real question was not so much about the hypothetical comparator as whether the employment tribunal's finding on the reason for dismissal was supported by evidence. In this case the issue of less favourable treatment of the claimant (as compared with the treatment of the hypothetical comparator) added little to the process of determining the direct discrimination issue. The Court made the point that it was not saying that a hypothetical comparator can be dispensed with altogether in a case such as this: it is part of the process of identifying the ground of the treatment and it is good practice to cross-check by constructing a hypothetical comparator. But it said that there are dangers in attaching too much importance to the construct and to less favourable treatment as a separate issue if the tribunal is satisfied by all the evidence that the treatment (in this case the dismissal) was on a prohibited ground. This case is also considered under 'Stage one: establishing a "prima facie case" – flexible approach preferable' above.

32.67 Standard of proof

In the majority of cases, an employment tribunal will determine the outcome of the case not by resting its decision on a failure by the party upon whom the burden of proof lies to discharge that burden, but on conclusions reached about the quality and sufficiency of the evidence presented by both sides. In this respect, both parties must adduce evidence sufficient to prove those facts necessary to determine the case in their favour. Lawyers speak of the 'standard of proof' – that is, the degree of cogency that evidence must reach to discharge the legal burden of proof. What this boils down to is a consideration by the tribunal of the strength of all the evidence of the respective parties, after which the tribunal decides which side has made out its case 'on the balance of probabilities'.

In Miller v Minister of Pensions 1947 2 All ER 372, Div Ct, Mr Justice Denning explained the civil standard of proof in the following terms: '[The degree of cogency] is well settled. It must carry a reasonable degree of probability, but not so high as is required in a criminal case. If the evidence is such that the tribunal can say: "we think it more probable than not", the burden is discharged, but if the probabilities are equal, it is not.' In other words, if the party upon whom the legal burden of proof lies is able to convince the tribunal that the evidence that he or she has adduced makes it more likely than not that his or her version of the facts is correct, then the tribunal should decide in his or her favour. Anything less and the party will have failed to make out his or her case. It should be noted that the standards of proof applicable in civil and criminal proceedings are different. Whereas civil proceedings are decided on the 'balance of probabilities', the criminal standard of proof is that a charge must be proved 'beyond reasonable doubt'. The latter is a much higher and more exacting standard and the prosecution in any criminal trial has the duty to discharge the burden of proving the defendant's guilt by providing evidence that is sufficiently cogent to allay any reasonable doubts that the jury might have over the question of guilt.

Although the standard of proof in all civil proceedings is the same, courts have **32.68** recognised that certain facts are more difficult to prove than others. This has long been recognised in the ordinary civil courts, particularly in cases brought under family and child-care law jurisdictions that involve allegations of sexual abuse. In one such case – Re H (minors) 1996 AC 563, HL – Lord Nicholls commented that 'the inherent probability or improbability of an event is itself a matter to be taken into account when weighing the probabilities and deciding whether, on balance, the event occurred. The more improbable the event, the stronger must be the evidence that it did occur before, on the balance of probability, its occurrence will be established.' His Lordship went on to make it clear that he was not proposing a general principle that serious cases, such as those concerning allegations of sexual assault or harassment, require a higher standard of proof than other less serious matters. Rather, the more serious the allegation, the less likely it is to be true and therefore the more cogent will the evidence need to be for the tribunal to be satisfied that the event was more likely than not to have occurred.

The Barton/Igen guidance (see the section 'Legal framework', under 'Domestic law – the Barton/Igen guidelines' above) contains several reminders of the standard of proof in civil cases and notes that it is for the claimant to prove, on the balance of probabilities, the facts that might lead to an inference of discrimination. If the claimant succeeds in shifting the burden of proof, it then falls to the respondent to prove, again on the balance of probabilities, that his treatment of the claimant involved no discrimination whatsoever. The guidance goes on to state that 'the tribunal would normally expect cogent evidence [from the respondent] to discharge that burden'. This is because the relevant evidence in most discrimination cases will normally be in the hands of the respondent rather than the claimant – for example, where discrimination is alleged in a recruitment exercise, the respondent will be in possession of material such as assessment scores and interview notes and should be able to demonstrate convincingly that no discriminatory considerations were involved. So, although the standard of proof is the same on both parties –

both have to make out their case on the balance of probabilities – tribunals will have regard to the respective positions of employee and employer, and will expect the cogency of the evidence they present to be commensurate with the availability to them of relevant evidence.

32.69 In his Opinion in Meister v Speech Design Carrier Systems GmbH Case C-415/10, ECJ, Advocate General Mengozzi stated that the same consideration concerning the relative cogency of evidence is also applicable at the first stage to the benefit of the claimant: he intimated that where the employer is withholding essential information that could assist the claimant to establish a prima facie case of discrimination, this can, in certain circumstances, itself be used by the claimant to support a prima facie case of discrimination. The Advocate General expressed the view that where a job applicant appears to be entirely dependent on the goodwill of the employer with regard to obtaining information capable of constituting facts from which it may be presumed that there has been discrimination, the balance required by EU law between the freedom of employers to recruit the people of their choice and the rights of job applicants to enforce the principle of equal treatment would seem to have been upset.

Faced with such circumstances, in order to restore that balance, Advocate General Mengozzi considered that national courts must, in general, adopt a *lower level of requirement* than that which would normally apply, in relation to the characterisation of those facts that make possible a presumption of discrimination, in particular so that the rights conferred on individuals by EU law may be efficaciously guaranteed and given effective judicial protection. In the Advocate General's view, for the purpose of the assessment to be carried out the following important evidence adduced in the particular case under consideration should not be overlooked: the fact that M's qualifications matched the post to be filled and yet the employer did not wish to call her for a job interview, despite calling other applicants to such an interview; and the fact that M responded to the publication of a job vacancy and did not submit a spontaneous application. For further details, see Chapter 33, 'Proving discrimination', under 'Requesting information and disclosure of evidence'.

32.70 The ECJ's decision, which has now been handed down in the Meister case, expressly refers to the Advocate General's Opinion and – albeit adopting a much less in-depth analysis of the shifting burden of proof – does not contradict the logic of his reasoning (see under 'Stage one: establishing a "prima facie case" – flexible approach preferable' above).

32.71 ## Other forms of discrimination

It is worth emphasising that the two-stage shifting burden of proof applies not only to direct discrimination but also, where appropriate, to the other forms of discrimination outlawed by the EqA, i.e. harassment under S.26, victimisation under S.27, indirect discrimination under S.19 and failure to make reasonable adjustments under S.20. Although similar principles apply, what needs to be proved obviously depends, to a certain extent, on the nature of the legal test set out in the respective sections.

Harassment   32.72

Under the general definition of harassment in S.26 EqA, a person (A) harasses another person (B) if:

- A engages in unwanted conduct related to a relevant protected characteristic – S.26(1)(a); and

- the conduct has the purpose or effect of violating B's dignity or creating an intimidating, hostile, degrading, humiliating or offensive environment – S.26(1)(b).

Although claims of harassment under S.26 EqA do not depend on the claimant establishing less favourable treatment, the shifting burden of proof rule set out in S.136 will still be of use in establishing that the unwanted conduct in question was 'related to a relevant protected characteristic' for the purpose of S.26(1)(a). Of course, where the conduct complained of is clearly related to a protected characteristic – for example, where a claimant has been subjected to verbal abuse in race-specific terms – then the employment tribunal will not need to revert to the shifting burden of proof rules at all. By contrast, where the conduct complained of is ostensibly indiscriminate – for example, where the claimant has been subjected to teasing and bullying for no apparent reason – the shifting burden of proof may be applicable to establish whether or not the reason for the treatment was his or her race.

Before the burden can shift to the respondent, the claimant will need to establish **32.73** on the balance of probabilities that he or she has been subjected to 'unwanted conduct' having the 'purpose or effect of violating his or her dignity or creating an intimidating, hostile, degrading, humiliating or offensive environment' for him or her. However, this, in our view, will not be enough to establish a prima facie case of harassment under S.26 EqA. The claimant clearly does not need to prove that the conduct is related to a protected characteristic because that would be no different to the normal burden of proof. Nevertheless, in our view, he or she needs to adduce some evidence to suggest that the conduct *could* be so related. Evidence that he or she is being treated differently to other employees who do not share his or her protected characteristic may be useful in this regard. There was no such evidence in Commissioner of Police of the Metropolis and anor v Osinaike EAT 0373/09 and the claimant's racial harassment claim thus failed. In that case the EAT overturned a tribunal's finding that an employee whose employer had told her that it intended to refer her for a psychiatric assessment in response to her continued difficulties at work had suffered racial harassment under the RRA. Although her situation had been ineptly handled by the employer, there was no evidence that matters would have been handled differently had O been white rather than black. This case is discussed further in Chapter 33, 'Proving discrimination', under 'Inferring discrimination – hostile or unreasonable behaviour'.

Therefore, although a harassment claim does not depend on the claimant showing less favourable treatment compared to an actual or hypothetical comparator, such a comparison will still be a useful tool for tribunals in weighing up whether or not the treatment complained of is related to a protected characteristic. In Bell v Scorpion Engineering Ltd ET Case No.1401065/07, for instance, the fact that the claimant was unable to establish less favourable treatment was fatal to her harassment claim. B, aged 26, worked as an assistant to the office manager for the employer, a small company providing garage services. She claimed that she was harassed because she was the youngest person in the company and cited the fact that a workshop foreman in the company was 'bossy and overbearing' towards her as an example of such conduct. An employment tribunal rejected her claim, holding that the foreman in question was no more bossy and overbearing than he was to other employees. Accordingly, there was no evidence to suggest that the treatment B had received was on account of her age.

32.74 It should, however, be emphasised that a claimant does not necessarily have to establish less favourable treatment in order to establish a prima facie case of unlawful harassment. In Ridge v Land Registry ET Case No.1700563/08 R suffered from depression. He had four periods of absence in 2007 and returned to work after the last absence in January 2008. Over the next few months he lodged five grievances, all of which were investigated and ultimately rejected. An employment tribunal upheld his claim that the delay in responding to his grievances amounted to harassment. The tribunal was satisfied that it could draw an inference that the harassment was for a reason relating to R's disability, in that the employer perceived that R was becoming a nuisance.

Harassment is dealt with in detail in Chapter 18, 'Harassment'.

32.75 **Victimisation**
Previously, in order for a claimant to prove victimisation, he or she had to show that the employer had treated him or her less favourably than it treated or would treat other persons in the same circumstances by reason that the claimant had done or intended to do a 'protected act', such as bringing proceedings under discrimination law or making an allegation of discrimination. The EqA takes a slightly different approach. S.27(1) provides: 'A person (A) victimises another person (B) if A subjects B to a detriment because (a) B does a protected act, or (b) A believes that B has done, or may do, a protected act.' The EqA thereby removes the absolute need for the employment tribunal to construct an appropriate comparator and for the claimant to establish less favourable treatment.

If the claimant establishes that he or she has done a protected act and that he or she has then suffered a detriment at the hands of the employer, a prima facie case of discrimination will be established if there is evidence from which a tribunal can infer a causal link. For example, if the detriment is suffered shortly after the protected act occurred, this might raise an inference of victimisation, requiring the employer to prove that the protected act was *not* the reason for the treatment in question. Note that one of the essential elements of the prima facie case that the claimant must make out appears to be that the employer actually knew about the protected act on which the claimant bases his or her claim. In this regard, the Court of Appeal, in Scott v London Borough of Hillingdon 2001 EWCA Civ 2005, CA, upheld the EAT's decision that an unsuccessful job applicant had not been victimised for bringing a race discrimination complaint against a former employer. The Court ruled that knowledge of a protected act is a precondition of a finding of victimisation and that as there was no positive evidence that the respondent knew of the claimant's previous complaint, there had been no proper basis for the tribunal to infer that the claimant had been victimised.

32.76 The position is slightly more complicated when the complainant is relying upon limb (b) of S.27(1), i.e. attempting to establish that he or she has been subjected to a detriment because the employer *believes* that B has done, or may do, a protected act. Here, aside from detriment, the claimant will presumably need to establish that he or she has done something of which the employer is aware, that could be construed by the employer as a protected act or that could lead the employer to believe that he or she will commit a protected act.

Victimisation is dealt with in detail in Chapter 19, 'Victimisation'.

Indirect discrimination
32.77 The two-stage process in S.136 is virtually built into the definition of indirect discrimination under S.19(2) EqA, with the result that there is much less scope – or need – for a separate consideration of the burden of proof. The claimant in an indirect discrimination claim must first show that a provision, criterion or practice (PCP) has been applied that puts (or would put) him or her – as well as persons who share his or her protected characteristic – at a particular disadvantage (S.19(2)(a)–(c)). Effectively, this is the equivalent of the first stage of the burden of proof test in that it requires a prima facie case of discrimination to be established on the basis of the evidence.

Only if this hurdle is surmounted does the focus shift to the employer, who must prove objective justification – i.e. that the PCP was imposed in furtherance of a legitimate aim and was a proportionate means of achieving that aim (S.19(2)(d)). This is the equivalent of the second stage of the burden of proof test. This is not to say, however, that the employer has no part to play at the first stage of an indirect discrimination claim. The employer will still be able

1143

to contest the claimant's evidence of a disparate impact caused by the PCP at issue by, for example, challenging the basis on which any statistical analysis has been undertaken.

32.78 In Dziedziak v Future Electronics Ltd EAT 0270/11 the EAT dealt with a contention that an employment tribunal had erred when it failed to apply S.63A SDA (now S.136 EqA) in order to effect the shift in the burden of proof onto the employer in the context of an indirect sex discrimination complaint. The claimant alleged that she had been discriminated against by being marked down during a redundancy selection exercise by the use of attendance criteria that took into account instances where she had been late for work owing to the need, as a single parent, to care for a sick child. In fact, as the EAT held, the employment tribunal had been unable to find any clear-cut evidence that lateness to work was used as a factor in the redundancy assessment. Even so, the claimant contended that it was sufficient to raise a prima facie case of indirect discrimination simply to show that a PCP has been applied that may put women generally at a disadvantage. In the claimant's view, the requirement to show that the PCP actually put the claimant at a disadvantage operated only once the burden had shifted when, as part of the respondent's case, it would be open to it to show that there had been no discrimination or that the discrimination was objectively justified. In rejecting this contention outright, Mr Justice Langstaff, President of the EAT, summarised the matters that had to be established in a claim of indirect sex discrimination in order for the burden of proof to shift:

- that there was a PCP

- that the relevant PCP disadvantaged women generally

- that what was a disadvantage generally created a particular disadvantage to the individual claimant.

Only once all the above had been firmly established would the burden formally shift to the employer to provide both an explanation of, and justification for, the discrimination. On the facts of the particular case, the EAT remarked that it was plain that the employment tribunal had not got to (nor could ever have got to) the stage of reversing the burden of proof: it had not been shown on the balance of probabilities that lateness was used by the employer as a factor in the redundancy selection process – i.e. there was, on balance, no sufficient evidence that the claimant had suffered the disadvantage that she would have had to be shown to have suffered in order to meet the definition of indirect discrimination under what is now S.19 EqA.

32.79 In effect, the EAT's decision in the Dziedziak case eloquently bears out the point already made that the very way in which indirect discrimination is defined incorporates the shifting burden of proof rule. As such there is little scope for that rule to apply in a decisive manner or independently from the various elements of proof that are part and parcel of an indirect discrimination claim.

Indirect discrimination is dealt with in full in Chapter 16, 'Indirect discrimination: proving disadvantage', and Chapter 17, 'Indirect discrimination: objective justification'.

Failure to make reasonable adjustments   32.80

The duty to make reasonable adjustments under S.20 EqA requires employers to take 'such steps as it is reasonable to have to take' to remove certain disadvantages to disabled people posed by working practices and the physical features of the premises. In Project Management Institute v Latif 2007 IRLR 579, EAT (also mentioned under 'Applicability of shifting burden of proof rule – discriminatory element' above), the EAT gave guidance as to how employment tribunals should approach the burden of proof in such cases. L was registered blind and wanted certain adjustments made to be enabled to sit an exam. Some adjustments were made, but some were not, and L alleged that the respondent had breached its duty to make reasonable adjustments under what is now S.20. The EAT held that where it is alleged that the employer has failed to make reasonable adjustments, the burden of proof only shifts once the claimant has established, not only that the duty to make reasonable adjustments had arisen, but also that there are facts from which it could reasonably be inferred – absent an explanation – that it has been breached. Demonstrating that there is an arrangement causing a substantial disadvantage engages the duty, but it provides no basis on which it could properly be inferred that there is a breach of that duty. Rather, there must be evidence of some apparently reasonable adjustment that could have been made. The EAT noted that the respondent is in the best position to say whether any apparently reasonable amendment is in fact reasonable given its own particular circumstances. Therefore, the burden is reversed only once a potentially reasonable amendment has been identified.

The level of detail a claimant will have to provide as to the type of adjustment will vary from case to case: the EAT stated in the Latif case (above) that it would not be in every case that the claimant would have to provide the detailed adjustment that would have to be made before the burden shifted, but 'it would be necessary for the respondent to understand the broad nature of the adjustment proposed and to be given sufficient detail to enable him to engage with the question of whether it could reasonably be achieved or not'. The EAT accepted that the proposed adjustment might well not be identified until after the alleged failure to implement it, and in exceptional cases, not even until the tribunal hearing. Indeed, in certain circumstances, the EAT thought it would be appropriate for the matter to be raised by the tribunal itself, particularly if the employee is not represented. For example, where a Code of Practice provides an example of an adjustment which on the face of it appears appropriate, that is something the tribunal should take into account. The EAT considered that it would be perfectly proper for a tribunal to expect an employer to show why it would not have been reasonable to make that adjustment in the particular case, although of course the employer must have a proper opportunity of dealing with the matter.

Failure to make reasonable adjustments is dealt with in detail in Chapter 21, 'Failure to make reasonable adjustments'.

33 Proving discrimination

In Chapter 32 we examine the workings of the so-called 'shifting burden of **33.1** proof' rule in discrimination claims as set out in S.136 of the Equality Act 2010 (EqA). Formally, the burden of proof shifts onto the employer only if the claimant satisfies an employment tribunal that there is a 'prima facie' case of discrimination. This will usually be based upon *inferences* of discrimination drawn from the primary facts and circumstances found by the tribunal to have been proved on the balance of probabilities. Such inferences are crucial in discrimination cases given the unlikelihood of there being direct, overt and decisive evidence that a claimant has been treated less favourably because of a protected characteristic (or, as the case may be, harassed by being subjected to unwanted conduct related to a protected characteristic or victimised by reason of having done a protected act). The first part of this chapter explores the range of circumstances and evidence from which inferences of discrimination can typically be drawn.

We then move on from the specifics of inferring discrimination to more general issues regarding the admissibility of evidence in discrimination cases and the quality of such evidence. Finally, we look at how a claimant might go about obtaining information and evidence to support his or her claim of discrimination. The key matters here are the use that can be made of a statutory questionnaire procedure by which a potential claimant can seek an explanation for and relevant information concerning suspected discriminatory treatment even before commencing tribunal proceedings, and the power of tribunals to order disclosure of relevant evidence once proceedings have started.

Inferring discrimination   33.2

As explained in Chapter 32, 'Burden of proof', under 'Legal Framework – domestic law', S.136 EqA applies a shifting burden of proof rule to the determination of liability for discrimination. This entails a two-stage test. At the first stage, the claimant has to prove facts from which the court or tribunal could decide that discrimination has taken place, which is commonly described as a 'prima facie case of discrimination'. At the second stage – which is only engaged if such facts have been made out to the tribunal's satisfaction (i.e. on the balance of probabilities) – the burden 'shifts' to the respondent, who must

1147

prove (again on the balance of probabilities) a non-discriminatory reason for the treatment in question. The case law guidance on the application of this statutory rule – derived from the EAT's decision in Barton v Investec Henderson Crosthwaite Securities Ltd 2003 ICR 1205, EAT, as approved and slightly modified by the Court of Appeal in Igen Ltd (formerly Leeds Careers Guidance) and ors v Wong and other cases 2005 ICR 931, CA – makes it clear that the outcome at the first stage will usually depend upon what inferences it is proper to draw from the primary facts found by the court or tribunal – see Chapter 32, 'Burden of proof', in the section 'Legal framework', under 'Domestic law – the Barton/Igen guidelines'. Whenever an employment tribunal has decided to draw an inference that has enabled the claimant to show a prima facie case of discrimination, it *must* uphold the complaint of discrimination *unless* the respondent can prove a non-discriminatory explanation – see S.136(2) EqA. Given this, it is appropriate to consider the general principles that govern the drawing of inferences of discrimination and then outline some of the factual scenarios or evidential findings that commonly lead to inferences being made.

33.3 General principles

Employment tribunals have a wide discretion to draw inferences of discrimination where appropriate. However, they must do so based on clear findings of fact. It is well established that inferences may be drawn not only from the specific incidents and acts detailed in the claimant's claim taken in isolation, but also from the full factual background of the claim, including evidence about the conduct of the respondent before and after the act about which the complaint is made. For example, in Rihal v London Borough of Ealing 2004 IRLR 642, CA (a race discrimination case), the Court of Appeal held that an employment tribunal had been entitled to take into account its finding that a glass ceiling operated within the respondent Council when upholding the claimant's claim that he had been passed over for promotion for a discriminatory reason. The Council's own figures showed that no non-whites held senior management positions within the claimant's department, and the tribunal was entitled to draw an inference of a culture of racial stereotyping that influenced, albeit unconsciously, management decisions.

There is a danger, however, if a tribunal relies simply upon generalised assumptions or a mere impression of a discriminatory culture as the basis for drawing an inference in a particular case. As Lord Justice Peter Gibson put it in Chapman v Simon 1994 IRLR 124, CA, 'a mere intuitive hunch… that there has been unlawful discrimination is insufficient without facts being found to support that conclusion'. The Court of Appeal again stressed this point in Anya v University of Oxford and anor 2001 ICR 847, CA, where it held that the employment tribunal in that case had failed to make specific findings of fact in relation to various circumstantial allegations raised by the employee, and so had no material from which it could properly draw an inference of discrimination.

In Stockton on Tees Borough Council v Aylott 2010 ICR 1278, CA, the Court **33.4** of Appeal fully acknowledged that direct discrimination can occur when, for example, assumptions are made by the respondent that a claimant, as an individual, has characteristics associated with the protected group to which the claimant belongs, irrespective of whether the claimant or most members of the group have those characteristics. However, Lord Justice Mummery cautioned tribunals against concluding that liability for discrimination has been established simply by relying on an *unproven* assertion of stereotyping persons who share the same particular protected characteristic as the claimant. His Lordship emphasised that direct discrimination claims must be decided in accordance with the evidence, not by making use, without requiring evidence, of a verbal formula such as 'institutional discrimination' or 'stereotyping' on the basis of assumed characteristics. There must be evidence from which the tribunal could properly infer that wrong assumptions were being made about that person's characteristics and that those assumptions were operative as part of the conscious or subconscious motivation for the respondent's detrimental treatment, such as a decision to dismiss – see further 'Stereotypical assumptions' below.

Inferences to be drawn from actual, not assumed, findings of fact. In British **33.5** Medical Association v Chaudhary 2007 IRLR 800, CA, an employment tribunal made the mistake of inferring discrimination from *assumed* facts, as opposed to clear findings of fact based upon the evidence. C was employed as a registrar in urology at a hospital in Manchester. In 1997 the Royal College of Surgeons (RCS) declined to approve C's hospital post as suitable for training purposes, with the result that he could not be promoted to the grade of 'specialist registrar'. C opted to bring race discrimination claims against the RCS in respect of this decision and wrote to the BMA seeking legal assistance. The BMA declined to provide him with support. C subsequently brought employment tribunal claims against the BMA under the Race Relations Act 1976 (RRA), arguing that it had discriminated against him (both directly and indirectly) and victimised him when declining to provide him with legal assistance. The tribunal upheld C's victimisation and indirect discrimination claims. After an unsuccessful appeal to the EAT, the BMA appealed to the Court of Appeal, which overturned the tribunal's decision. Among other things, it held that the tribunal's inference that led to its conclusion that indirect discrimination had occurred was without foundation, and thus perverse. The tribunal had found that the BMA had refused to consider the strength of C's claims against the RCS, simply brushing the matter aside. The Court of Appeal also noted that the tribunal had appeared to *assume* that C had a good case against the RCS and that the BMA was blind to this (although it never said what evidence there was to support this or what evidence there would have been to support it if the BMA had investigated matters as it should have done). The tribunal went on to draw an inference that the BMA had applied a criterion or condition that it would not support *race* discrimination claims against

1149

certain regulatory bodies. When the evidence was analysed, however, it became apparent that the BMA had sound reasons for believing that the RSC had considered C's case in accordance with its rules, and that there was no basis for suspecting that its decision not to approve C's post as suitable for training had been tainted by discrimination. Therefore, the Court of Appeal set aside the record award of £814,877 made by the tribunal.

33.6 **Employer's rebuttal evidence.** As noted in Chapter 32, 'Burden of proof', under 'Stage one: establishing a "prima facie case" – employer's explanation', when deciding what inferences can be drawn when considering whether a prima facie case has been made out for the purposes of applying the shifting burden of proof rule, the respondent's *explanation* for the alleged discriminatory treatment should generally be discounted, this being a matter for the second stage (i.e. consideration of whether the respondent can prove that discrimination has not occurred based on the evidence presented). However, the respondent is permitted at the first stage to rebut any evidence adduced by the claimant to establish a prima facie case – for example, in relation to evidence of any past conduct that has been prayed in aid by the claimant to suggest that the respondent had a discriminatory motivation for the treatment in question. The respondent could seek to rebut this evidence by, for example, arguing that the prior conduct has no link with the treatment complained of and therefore it cannot be used to establish an inference of discrimination. Or it could argue that its past behaviour was justified and not discriminatory. The respondent is not here adducing evidence to explain the alleged discriminatory treatment: rather, it is explaining its past conduct with a view to demonstrating that no inference of discrimination can be drawn from it for the purposes of the present claim.

33.7 **Inferences should be drawn from the totality of the evidence.** Although, as noted above, tribunals are obliged to make findings of fact in relation to the circumstantial matters raised by the claimant, it is not necessary for a tribunal to make a specific finding as to whether any of those matters would of itself amount in law to a discrete act of discrimination – Qureshi v Victoria University of Manchester and anor 2001 ICR 863, EAT. The tribunal must look at the totality of its findings of fact and decide whether they add up to a sufficient basis from which to draw an inference that the respondent has treated the complainant less favourably on the protected ground.

33.8 **Stereotypical assumptions**

If an employment tribunal finds that an employer has acted upon stereotypical assumptions about a claimant's protected characteristic, it will almost certainly uphold the claimant's discrimination claim. However, it must be careful not to rely upon an unproven assertion of stereotyping as this will amount to an error of law. In Stockton on Tees Borough Council v Aylott 2010 ICR 1278, CA, the Court of Appeal stated that discrimination claims must be decided in accordance with the evidence, not by making use, without requiring evidence, of a verbal formula such as 'institutional discrimination' or 'stereotyping' on the basis of assumed characteristics. There must be evidence from which the tribunal could properly infer that wrong assumptions were being made about that person's characteristics and that those assumptions were operative in the detrimental treatment, such as a decision to dismiss. The Court went on to hold that there was evidence from which the tribunal in the instant case could, and did, make detailed findings of primary fact about the employer's reactions to the claimant's mental illness (bipolar affective disorder) and thus could properly make inferences from those facts to support the conclusion that the employer dismissed the claimant on the ground of his mental disability. The employer's decision to dismiss was based, in part at least, upon assumptions it made about the claimant's particular mental illness rather than on the basis of up-to-date medical evidence about the effect of his illness on his ability to continue in employment.

In Aitken v Commissioner of Police of the Metropolis 2012 ICR 78, CA, by contrast, the Court of Appeal upheld an employment tribunal's decision that the claimant in that case, a police constable who was recommended for medical retirement following an incident of aggressive behaviour linked to his mental illness, did not suffer direct or disability-related discrimination under the Disability Discrimination Act 1995 (DDA). The Court rejected the argument – raised for the first time on appeal, and unsupported by evidence – that his behaviour was a 'necessary facet' of his disability and therefore the employer's action must be regarded as discriminatory. On the facts found by the tribunal, this was not a case like Aylott (above) where the employer acted on the basis of stereotypical assumptions about mental disability. Here, the tribunal had expressly rejected that allegation, finding instead that the employer acted on the basis of how the claimant appeared to others. The police force would have treated a non-disabled person whose behaviour also appeared to be threatening and aggressive in an identical way.

33.9 Three further examples of cases in which an employee's allegation that the employer had acted on a stereotypical assumption about a protected characteristic was rejected:

- **Johnson v Coopers Lane Primary School Governors** EAT 0248/09: J, a black employee, alleged that letters sent to her by her managers, which suggested that she had mental health problems, and her subsequent suspension on medical grounds, amounted to less favourable treatment based upon a stereotypical view held by the majority of employers that black or African-Caribbean people are more likely to have mental health problems than their white comparators. The letters had been sent following a marked deterioration in J's attitude towards her colleagues and had a detrimental impact upon her work. An employment tribunal found that the employer had behaved unreasonably in suggesting that J had mental health problems given that she had not raised any such issue as an explanation for her conduct. However, it concluded (by a majority) that she had failed to show that she had been treated less favourably than a hypothetical white employee. The EAT dismissed J's appeal. It held that, while tribunals have to be alert to subconscious discrimination and analyse employers' actions and statements with care, a case of discrimination cannot simply be founded upon an alleged stereotypical view that white employers might have about black people's mental health issues. The minority were wrong to accept such a view as a basis for finding that a prima facie case of discrimination had been established, so causing the burden of proof to shift. It was also wrong to find that there was no material upon which the employer could conclude that J was unwell. The majority had been right to find that although there had been unreasonable treatment, the burden of proof did not pass because of the considerable volume of material that explained the non-discriminatory actions of J's managers

- **B and anor v A** 2010 IRLR 400, EAT: the employer summarily dismissed a male employee without any proper investigation or disciplinary procedure on the ground that he posed a risk of further violence against members of staff. The EAT held that the employment tribunal's findings did not support its conclusion that the employer had been motivated by a stereotypical view of male aggression. In order to find that the employer's genuine fear of further violence was at least to some extent influenced by the fact that the claimant was a man, it was not sufficient for the tribunal to point to the existence of gender stereotypes about male violence. There had to be some evidence that the employer had been motivated by such stereotypes, and there was no such evidence in the instant case. On the contrary, it was clear on the tribunal's own findings that the reason the employer feared that the claimant posed a risk of future violence was that it believed that the claimant had raped his colleague. It would have been a different story if the tribunal had accepted the claimant's main contention – namely, that the reason why the employer was so quick to believe the alleged victim's allegation, even to the extent of not being prepared to listen to the claimant's side of the story, was that the employer was subconsciously assuming that women making accusations of rape are always to be believed. If that had been shown to be the case, the employer's conduct would, in the EAT's view, have been discriminatory. As Mr Justice Underhill (then President of the EAT), observed: 'To act on an automatic assumption, conscious or unconscious, that an accusation of rape by a woman against a man must be well founded is itself a stereotype based on gender, and to act on such an assumption would be to act on the ground of the man's sex'

- **Odi v Intellectual Property Office** ET Case No.1601948/10: O, a black African, claimed that the IPO had directly racially discriminated against her by its refusal to select her for interview for the position of procurement manager. In support of her claim O referred to the IPO's website, which, on a page entitled 'About Us', included a photograph of people who were, with the exception of an Asian man with very pale skin, white. The employment tribunal declined to draw an inference of discrimination from this. It recognised that publicity material for organisations will often seek to identify a visibly diverse range of people drawn from all walks of life (not just in terms of ethnicity) as both employees and customers. This could operate as an important form of permissible positive action, thereby encouraging applications and custom from traditionally under-represented groups. However, the failure to show a particular person from a particular group – such as a black person – did not mean that there is prima facie evidence of discrimination against members of that group. Indeed, as the industrial jury, the tribunal observed that it had to be wary of making pronouncements that might lead employers to engage in a kind of visual tokenism, an approach that others might consider patronising.

Hostile or unreasonable behaviour   33.10
Courts and tribunals have emphasised on a number of occasions that discrimination cannot be inferred from unreasonable conduct alone. In Commissioner of Police of the Metropolis and anor v Osinaike EAT 0373/09, for example, the EAT overturned an employment tribunal's finding that a black employee whose employer had told her that it intended to refer her for a psychiatric assessment in response to her continued difficulties at work had suffered racial harassment under the RRA. Although her situation had been ineptly handled by the employer, there was no evidence before the tribunal that the decision to refer had been made on racial grounds. Simply showing that the employer's conduct was unreasonable or unfair was not, by itself, enough to raise an inference of discrimination and trigger the shifting of the burden of proof. The EAT acknowledged that, if unreasonable conduct occurred alongside other indications that there might be discrimination on racial grounds, that would alter the position, but those indications must relate to the prohibited ground.

'I'm a bastard to everyone.' If the evidence indicates that an employer treats all   33.11
employees equally unreasonably – often colloquially referred to as the 'bastard employer' defence – it is not appropriate to infer discrimination. As noted in Commissioner of Police of the Metropolis v Virdi EAT 0598/07 by Mr Justice Underhill – whose decision to dismiss the claimant's claim of victimisation under the RRA was upheld by the Court of Appeal (2009 EWCA Civ 477) – 'inferences are not drawn as a sanction for bad behaviour'. Some examples:

- **British Medical Association v Chaudhary** 2007 IRLR 800, CA: the Court of Appeal commented that 'it is fair to say that the fact that Dr Chaudhary, an Asian doctor, appeared to have been treated unfairly

1153

might well, we accept, give rise to a duty to investigate the possibility that he has been discriminated against; but if enquiries reveal that he has been treated according to the rules which apply equally to everyone and have been applied equally to everyone, there would be no case on direct discrimination'. It went on to overturn the tribunal's finding of victimisation on the basis that the BMA had acted honestly and reasonably to protect its position with regard to litigation

- **Laing v Manchester City Council** 2006 ICR 1519, EAT: the EAT held that an employment tribunal was entitled to conclude that unreasonable conduct meted out by a supervisor to L, a black employee, did not amount to a prima facie case of race discrimination since the supervisor dealt with all employees, black or white, in the same unreasonable way. Taking account of that fact and the supervisor's lack of managerial experience, the tribunal had failed to have regard to the explanation for her specific conduct towards L, and thus had not fallen into error. The EAT added that even if, contrary to its view, it was appropriate to find that a prima facie case of discrimination had been made out, it was evident from the tribunal's decision that it had considered the employer's explanation for the treatment of L and had concluded that it had nothing to do with race. L was a difficult employee, whose performance was unsatisfactory. Some criticism of his conduct was plainly justified notwithstanding that the supervisor's manner of dealing with the issue patently left a lot to be desired

- **Madarassy v Nomura International plc** 2007 ICR 867, CA: the evidence indicated that M's colleague, B, shouted at members of staff whether they were male or female. According to the employment tribunal, 'there was equality of shouting regardless of gender'. The Court of Appeal noted that this was the culture of the particular workplace. It might be horrible, but it was not sexist. The tribunal had therefore not erred in dismissing M's complaint of discrimination against B at the first stage when considering the shifting burden of proof rule as there was no comparative less favourable treatment.

33.12 The extent to which an employer can rely upon the 'bastard employer' defence to argue that it would have treated a hypothetical comparator in the same unreasonable way is open to debate. In Glasgow City Council v Zafar 1998 ICR 120, HL, Lord Browne Wilkinson considered that 'the conduct of a hypothetical reasonable employer is irrelevant. The alleged discriminator may or may not be a reasonable employer. If he is not a reasonable employer he might well have treated another employee in just the same unsatisfactory way as he treated the complainant, in which case he would not have treated the complainant "less favourably".' His Lordship also approved the words of Lord Morison, who delivered the judgment of the Court of Session that 'it cannot be inferred, let alone presumed, only from the fact that an employer has acted

1154

unreasonably towards one employee, that he would have acted reasonably if he had been dealing with another in the same circumstances'.

Conversely, the Court of Appeal in Anya v University of Oxford and anor 2001 ICR 847, CA, considered that an employer who wishes to rely upon the 'bastard employer' defence will need to produce actual evidence that the hostility or unreasonable behaviour was not directed at the claimant alone. In its view, a 'theoretical possibility' that the employer behaves equally badly to all employees will not suffice. However, the Court of Appeal in Bahl v Law Society 2004 IRLR 799, CA, took the view that this part of the judgment in Anya was merely obiter (i.e. not strictly necessary to the decision and therefore non-binding) and reiterated the House of Lords' judgment in Zafar. It did, however, consider that discrimination may be inferred if there is no explanation for unreasonable treatment, stating, 'this is not an inference from unreasonable treatment itself but from the absence of any explanation for it' – see further 'Unexplained unreasonable conduct' below.

Notwithstanding the above, strong support for the 'Anya approach' can be **33.13** found in Eagle Place Services Ltd v Rudd 2010 IRLR 486, EAT (albeit that the Anya decision was not expressly cited). In that case, the employer accepted that it had acted unreasonably in dismissing the claimant but denied that this constituted less favourable treatment and sought to show this by reference to a hypothetical comparator. The EAT rejected this, holding that 'it is simply not open to the respondent to say that it has not discriminated against the claimant because it would have behaved unreasonably in dismissing the comparator. It is unreasonable to suppose that it would in fact have dismissed the comparator for what amounts to an irrational reason. It is one thing to find as in Bahl that a named individual has behaved unreasonably to both the claimant and named comparators; it is quite another to find that a corporate entity... would behave unreasonably to a hypothetical comparator when it had no good reason to do so.' This decision is explored in greater depth in Chapter 20, 'Discrimination arising from disability', under 'Previous protection under the DDA'.

Unexplained unreasonable conduct. In Igen Ltd (formerly Leeds Careers **33.14** Guidance) and ors v Wong and other cases 2005 ICR 931, CA, the Court of Appeal cautioned against too readily inferring unlawful discrimination merely from unreasonable conduct. However, it held that it was not an error of law for an employment tribunal to draw an inference of discrimination from unexplained unreasonable conduct at the first stage of the two-stage burden of proof test.

In Milton Keynes General Hospital NHS Trust and anor v Maruziva EAT 0003/09 the fact that no explanation was given for the claimant's treatment was held to be a relevant factor to the question of whether it was appropriate for the tribunal to draw an inference of race discrimination in that case. The EAT held that a tribunal was 'bound to conclude' that M, a black senior staff nurse, had been directly discriminated against on the ground of colour when: (a) the ward sister spoke harshly to her on more than one occasion; (b) white staff were not treated in that way; and (c) no explanation was given for M's treatment other than a denial that it happened (which was not accepted by the tribunal).

33.15 Furthermore, in Rice v McEvoy 2011 NICA 9, NICA, the Northern Ireland Court of Appeal considered that if an employer acts in a wholly unreasonable way, this may assist in drawing an inference that the employer's purported explanation for its actions was not in fact the true explanation and that it was covering up a discriminatory intent. The Court, however, did go on to say that this is not in itself determinative of the issue as to whether or not the employer has discriminated. The tribunal must make it clear whether and why it rejects the explanation offered by the employer, and must be careful not to apply the 'band of reasonable responses' approach applicable in unfair dismissal cases whereby the employer is judged to have discriminated simply because, in the tribunal's view, no reasonable employer would have behaved in the same way. Something more is needed.

A similar approach is reflected in the EAT's decision in B and anor v A 2010 IRLR 400, EAT (the facts of which are set out under 'Stereotypical assumptions' above). In that case, the Appeal Tribunal stated that if there had been no explanation for the employer's surprising behaviour, then the employment tribunal might well have been entitled to draw an inference of discrimination, but there was, in fact, a non-discriminatory explanation. This emerged from two key findings that the tribunal itself had made based on the evidence presented to it, namely: (i) that the reason that the Chief Executive believed the alleged rape victim was telling the truth was not, as alleged by the claimant, simply that she was a woman, but that he had a close working relationship with her and it was natural for him to believe what she was telling him; and (ii), that the reason the claimant was dismissed without due process was the employer's genuine fear that he posed a risk of further violence to colleagues.

33.16 Although in Madarassy v Nomura International plc 2007 ICR 867, CA, Lord Justice Mummery observed that the absence of an adequate explanation for differential treatment is not relevant to whether there is a prima facie case of discrimination, we would respectfully suggest that there is little difference between an employer putting forward no explanation and putting forward an explanation that appears to be inadequate (in the sense of not being credible). Indeed, in Eagle Place Services Ltd v Rudd (above), the fact that the employer had 'no good reason' for its unreasonable treatment of R was crucial to the EAT's decision in favour of the claimant. Accordingly, we suggest that a tribunal may, in certain circumstances, be able to infer discrimination from unreasonable conduct alone, at least where there is no (or no adequate) explanation for such conduct.

Genuine non-discriminatory reason. In Bahl v Law Society 2004 IRLR **33.17**
799, CA, the Court of Appeal noted that proof of equally unfair treatment is
one way of avoiding an inference of unlawful discrimination but is not the
only way. The Court agreed with Mr Justice Elias – who decided the case at
EAT level – that 'the inference may also be rebutted… by the employer
leading evidence of a genuine reason which is not discriminatory and which
was the ground of his conduct. Employers will often have unjustified albeit
genuine reasons for acting as they have.' If the employer wishes to rely upon
such a reason, this would be taken into account at the second stage under the
two-stage burden of proof test – see Chapter 32, 'Burden of proof', under
'Stage two: proving absence of discrimination' for details. Alternatively, a
tribunal may be able to make a clear finding as to the employer's reason, in
which case it will not need to revert to the two-stage burden of proof at all
– see Chapter 32 under 'Applicability of burden of proof rules – clear
positive findings'.

In Teva (UK) Ltd v Goubatchev EAT 0490/08 the EAT noted that, 'at the
second stage, the employer does not need to justify the treatment of the
complainant or establish that he acted reasonably or fairly because all he needs
to do is to show that the true reason for the less favourable treatment was not
discriminatory'. That said, the *credibility* of the employer's purported reason
will be relevant in establishing whether or not it is genuine and thus whether or
not a tribunal should infer discrimination. Furthermore, if an employer can
justify the treatment, it will more easily be able to defeat the claim – see under
'Is the treatment unreasonable?' below. It is important also for tribunals to bear
in mind that it is for the employer to prove a non-discriminatory reason at the
second stage and if the evidence as to this is inconclusive, the discrimination
claim should be upheld.

Is the treatment unreasonable? Of course, whether or not the treatment really **33.18**
is unreasonable, as alleged by the claimant, will be a relevant factor. As stated
by the House of Lords in Shamoon v Chief Constable of the Royal Ulster
Constabulary 2003 ICR 337, HL, an unjustified sense of grievance cannot
amount to a detriment for the purpose of less favourable treatment. Sometimes,
it may be obvious from the material facts at the prima facie stage whether or
not the grievance is unjustified. In other instances, this may only become
apparent from a closer scrutiny of the employer's explanation at the second
stage. For a discussion of the distinction between 'material facts' and
'explanation', see Chapter 32, 'Burden of proof', under 'Stage one: establishing
a "prima facie case" – employer's explanation'.

If the treatment is justified, this should, in most cases, enable the employer to
defeat the discrimination claim. For example, in Ferri v Key Languages Ltd
ET Case No.2302172/04, F claimed that she had been subjected to aggressive
behaviour, belittling treatment and emotional pressure on the ground of her

religious belief. K Ltd defeated her direct discrimination claim because it provided powerful and cogent evidence of F's shortcomings which explained its treatment of her. Of course, with the notable exception of age discrimination, direct discrimination itself cannot be justified. However, in this instance the employer's justification was being used to explain why no inference of direct discrimination should be drawn in the first place. This case is discussed in more detail in Chapter 32 under 'Stage one: establishing a "prima facie case" – less favourable treatment'.

33.19 Conversely, the more unreasonable the treatment, the more likely a tribunal will be to decide that the employer's explanation is not credible and thus infer discrimination. As noted by the Northern Ireland Court of Appeal in Rice v McEvoy 2011 NICA 9, NICA, if an employer acts in a wholly unreasonable way, this may assist in drawing an inference that the employer's purported explanation for his actions was not in fact the true explanation and that he was covering up a discriminatory intent.

33.20 **Unfair dismissal.** A classic example of unreasonable treatment is an employee being found to have been unfairly dismissed contrary to S.94 of the Employment Rights Act 1996. However, discrimination cannot be inferred from unreasonableness alone, from which it follows that an unfair dismissal will not necessarily be discriminatory. In Isaaq v AMS Security (Northern) Ltd ET Case No.2802396/08 an employment tribunal refused to draw an inference that a dismissal of a black employee for misconduct, albeit unfair, was race discriminatory, even though the incident in question also involved some racial abuse against him. I, a Somalian, was employed as a security guard by AMS Ltd. The workforce was a mixture of nationalities, including white British, Somalian, Pakistani and Liberian. On 12 May 2008 I was involved in a confrontation with a fellow employee, C, which ended up with the two men having to be separated. There were two witnesses, both of whom claimed that I had been the instigator, although he denied this. He also alleged that C had called him a 'fucking black bastard'. I was summarily dismissed following a disciplinary hearing, AMS Ltd believing that I had been the aggressor and had caused physical injury to C.

So far as I's claim for race discrimination was concerned, the tribunal noted that there was no evidence to suggest that AMS Ltd, which had a mixed and diverse workforce, had taken disciplinary action in relation to its Somali workers which would not be taken in relation to non-Somali workers. Since the tribunal had made a finding that the dismissal was honestly by reason of I's aggressive conduct, it followed that it was not for any reason connected with I's race or nationality. The tribunal considered that AMS Ltd would have made the same finding in relation to a worker of any nationality or race who it honestly believed had been involved in aggressive conduct, such as had been attributed to I. (The tribunal did, however, uphold I's claim of race discrimination in respect of the racist comment, awarding £1,000 for injury to feelings.)

To a certain extent, the more unreasonable the circumstances of the dismissal **33.21** and/or the more marked the disparity in treatment with other employees (who do not share the claimant's protected characteristic), the more likely a tribunal is to conclude that the dismissal requires an explanation, failing which it will infer race discrimination. Two examples:

- **Curniffe v Aldwyck Housing Association Ltd** ET Case No.1200846/09: C, who was black, had worked for AHA Ltd as an Area Housing Officer for six years and had an unblemished record. In 2007 C's 'patch' was increased, meaning that he had to look after more properties – 572 in total. This was 60% higher than average. He had a number of discussions with AHA Ltd about his excessive workload but in February 2008 the company threatened him with disciplinary action if his performance did not improve. He became very upset, broke down in tears, and complained of chest pains. Following a period of sickness absence, a risk assessment was carried out and he was again warned that disciplinary action would be taken against him if his performance did not improve. In April he was sent on a time management course and in July he was given a final written warning for unsatisfactory conduct and performance. He was subsequently summoned to a disciplinary hearing in respect of an alleged error he had made. AHA Ltd upheld the allegations, at least in part, and because he was on a final warning he was dismissed. The tribunal was satisfied that a comparable employee of a different race would not have been treated as C had been treated and would not have been dismissed. AHA Ltd's own records indicated that a disproportionate number of black employees had been dismissed. The fact that three other black staff brought grievances alleging disproportionate disciplinary action, while well short of being conclusive, was an indication that other people felt that race was sometimes an issue in disciplinary action. Furthermore, when AHA Ltd's deputy chairman investigated previous allegations of race discrimination, he had done so on the basis of false and misleading statistics. These factors were 'more than enough' for the tribunal to conclude that C's race could have been a factor in AHA Ltd's treatment of him. Therefore, the onus was on the company to satisfy the tribunal that the treatment was in no sense whatever on the ground of his race, which it had wholly failed to do

- **Atiase v Direct Health Group Ltd** ET Case No.2801106/09: A, a black African, began working for DHG Ltd on 15 June 2005 as a care worker, caring for service users in their own homes. During the Christmas holiday period, A provided additional cover to four service users, including F, whose regular carer was on annual leave. When A visited F on the morning of 27 December he found that the medication pack was empty and so F could not be given his medication. A reported this in F's service user log. A paid F two more visits that day and reported on both occasions that F's medication had still not arrived. A discussed the lack of medication with F, who replied that he was fine. The following day A again attended F three times. On each occasion he reported in the log that the medication was not available. In the evening, he noted 'supply to arrive – client okay and set for bed later'. On 29 December F was visited by another care worker, G, a white British woman. She stayed for five minutes and made no mention of the lack of medication. G visited again on the morning of 30 December. Her log stated, '[F] wanted to stay in bed a bit longer... all okay on leaving.' When A visited at lunchtime that day he discovered that F had fallen and cut his face. As a result F was admitted to hospital. A was subsequently suspended and then dismissed for gross misconduct. G received a final written warning and at no stage was she suspended from work. A brought a claim for direct race discrimination and unfair dismissal against DHG Ltd. The tribunal considered that G was an actual comparator for the purposes of A's race discrimination claim because her circumstances were the same as or not materially different from A's. It went on to conclude that A had been treated less favourably: G was not suspended pending investigation and only received a final written warning; she had visited F nearer to his fall; she failed to note in the service log that medication had not been provided and it was apparent that she had not even read the previous entries in the log; her visits to F were never more than five minutes in duration (whereas A's were considerably longer); and on her second visit F remained in bed, which might have alerted a more perceptive care worker to a problem. On balance, the tribunal said it was satisfied that the less favourable treatment could have been on racial grounds. It went on to uphold A's race discrimination claim because DHG Ltd had failed to prove, on the balance of probabilities, that its treatment of A was in no sense whatsoever on racial grounds. A's unfair dismissal claim was also upheld due to the disparity in treatment between him and G.

33.22 Note that in Community Law Clinic Solicitors Ltd and ors v Methuen EAT 0024/11, the EAT held that discrimination claims should not be permitted to proceed to trial where an employee who has been dismissed simply asserts that his or her replacement is of a different race, sex, etc. In the Appeal Tribunal's view, this could not give rise to a prima facie case of discrimination sufficient to shift the burden of proof onto the employer. Accordingly, an employment tribunal judge erred by not striking out such a claim as having no reasonable prospect of success. This case is unusual since case law is clear that only in exceptional cases should a tribunal strike out a discrimination claim as having no reasonable prospect of success before hearing full evidence where the central facts are in dispute – Ezsias v North Glamorgan NHS Trust 2007 ICR 1126, CA; A v B 2011 ICR D9, CA. In the Methuen case, the crucial facts were not in dispute and it was therefore much easier for the EAT to decide that the claim had no reasonable prospect of success.

Breach of policies and procedures   33.23

The importance to an employer of having a well-communicated and well-enforced equal opportunities policy can hardly be overstated. Elsewhere in this Handbook, we consider the scope of employers' liability under S.109 EqA, and note that for an employer to be able to disclaim liability for the discriminatory acts of his employees, he will need to show that he has taken 'reasonable steps' to prevent employees doing such acts – see Chapter 28, 'Liability of employers, employees and agents', under 'Employer's liability for acts of employees – "reasonable steps" defence'. Some form of equal opportunities policy is generally required if an employer is to benefit from this defence and rebut any charge of secondary liability for its employees' actions.

Case law has shown that an employer's failure to follow procedures set down by such a policy can support an inference of discrimination. In Anya v University of Oxford and anor 2001 ICR 847, CA, the Court of Appeal criticised an employment tribunal for not setting out what, if any, conclusions it drew from the respondent university's failure to abide by its own equal opportunities policy. The claimant, who was black, had complained of direct race discrimination in the university's award of a research assistant post to the only other shortlisted candidate, a white man. No 'person specification' had been drawn up to outline the skills that were necessary for the post and no references had been taken up in respect of the candidates, in clear breach of the university's policy. However, the tribunal was impressed by the honesty of the university's witnesses at the hearing and accepted the university's explanation that the rejection of the claimant was purely down to his scientific capabilities. The EAT upheld that decision on appeal, but the Court of Appeal held that the tribunal had erred by, among other things, not making findings about the departures from policy and considering what inference could be drawn from them. The case was remitted to a new tribunal to be heard afresh.

An equal opportunities policy, if followed, may also be a useful tool in rebutting   33.24
allegations of discriminatory conduct. However, in Hussain v Vision Security Ltd EAT 0439/10 the EAT expressed the view in an age discrimination case that 'a general policy is one thing, but it does not negative, or indeed necessarily weigh very heavily against, an inference that an individual manager in particular circumstances was motivated by discriminatory considerations. Whatever [the employer's] policy generally may have been, it is a matter of common knowledge that assumptions about whether employees of the appellant's age should continue in employment, or enjoy equal opportunities in a particular employment situation, are still very common.' This case is discussed in more detail in Chapter 32, 'Burden of proof', under 'Stage one: establishing a "prima facie case" – flexible approach preferable'.

1161

33.25 Breach of EHRC Code of Practice

Inferences may also be drawn from an employer's failure to follow a statutory Code of Practice. For present purposes, the relevant Code is the Equality and Human Rights Commission's Code of Practice on Employment ('the EHRC Employment Code'), which came into force on 6 April 2011. This covers all aspects of discrimination in employment, replacing the previous Codes on different strands of discrimination law and, where necessary, harmonising their content. Failure to observe any provision of a Code of Practice does not of itself render the person liable, but in any proceedings before a tribunal under the EqA the Code will be admissible in evidence and if the tribunal is satisfied that any provision of the Code is relevant, it must take that provision into account when making its determination – S.15(4) EqA.

In Bell and anor v City of Newcastle-upon-Tyne ET Case No.4510/95 a school cleaner complained that she had been sexually harassed by a male colleague and sued the City Council, which employed them both. The Council argued that it was not liable for the colleague's conduct because it had implemented an equal opportunities policy and had, therefore, done everything reasonably practicable to prevent sex discrimination in the workplace (a defence then available to employers under S.41(3) of the Sex Discrimination Act 1975). However, Article 35 of the Code of Practice then in force relating to sex discrimination recommended that employers not only formulate equal opportunities policies, but also ensure that their employees knew about them (see now Articles 18.13–18.16 of the EHRC Employment Code). When it transpired that the claimant had not been told about the Council's equal opportunities policy or the redress it offered to victims of sexual harassment, the tribunal took this fact into account and held the Council liable to the claimant for her colleague's discriminatory conduct.

33.26 When deciding whether it is possible to draw an inference from a breach of a Code of Practice, the tribunal must not forget that there might be many reasons for a failure to comply and many of those reasons, although unjustified, may preclude an inference being drawn that the failure was for a prohibited discriminatory ground. This was emphasised by the EAT in Teva (UK) Ltd v Goubatchev EAT 0490/08. In the EAT's view, if the reason for the breach was a genuinely held incorrect interpretation of the Code, that would in many circumstances preclude an inference of discrimination. In the instant case the employment tribunal had drawn an adverse inference of race discrimination from the employer's failure to comply with the Code of Practice then in force relating to racial equality in employment. The EAT held that in doing so, the tribunal had erred in law because it had failed to explain how it reached the conclusion that the employer's reasons for failing to comply with the Code were connected with racial matters.

In Odi v Intellectual Property Office ET Case No.1601948/10 O, a black African, claimed that IPO had directly racially discriminated against her by its refusal to select her for interview for the position of procurement manager. An employment tribunal noted that IPO had – contrary to the Code of Practice then in force on racial equality in employment – required job applicants to disclose nationality and national origin and failed to emphasise the acceptability of equivalent foreign qualifications. The tribunal suspected that O, a black African who had not been selected for interview, would not have brought a race discrimination claim against the IPO if the first question had never been asked – it aroused her suspicion. In the final analysis, however, the tribunal did not consider it relevant because the evidence showed that the sifting panel paid no regard, consciously or otherwise, to the information she disclosed.

Statistical evidence 33.27

The use of statistical evidence to establish a presumption of discrimination is clearly of most use in claims of indirect discrimination under S.19 EqA, where the claimant must establish that a provision, criterion or practice (PCP) has been applied which, although of general application, has a disparate adverse impact on persons who share the same protected characteristic as the claimant and thereby places him or her at a disadvantage. One method of establishing disparate impact can involve a statistical comparison of the advantaged and disadvantaged groups with regard to the application of the PCP at issue – see Chapter 16, 'Indirect discrimination: proving disadvantage', under '"Particular disadvantage" – the statistical approach: relative proportions'.

Statistical evidence can, however, also be useful outside the scope of indirect discrimination. Its relevance in relation to claims of direct discrimination was established in West Midlands Passenger Transport Executive v Singh 1988 ICR 614, CA (a race discrimination case). There, the complainant sought and obtained disclosure of data showing the numbers of white and non-white applicants for, and appointees to, posts that were broadly comparable to that for which he had unsuccessfully applied. The Court recognised that this data might be something from which the employment tribunal could infer discrimination if it revealed a pattern of treatment towards persons of S's racial group, and might also be used to rebut the respondent's contention that it operated an effective equal opportunities policy. The Court recognised the difficulties that complainants face when attempting to prove direct discrimination and noted that in many cases the only way for them to do so is by the tribunal drawing appropriate inferences from all the evidence. It accepted that the kind of statistics available in the instant case could potentially justify an inference of discriminatory behaviour, which may or may not be rebutted by a satisfactory explanation from the employer.

Just as in indirect discrimination cases, where statistics are in danger of being 33.28 over-analysed so that their significance is exaggerated or misunderstood, tribunals hearing complaints of direct discrimination must be wary of drawing inferences from minor statistical variations. This point was demonstrated by the Court of Appeal in Appiah and anor v Governing Body of Bishop Douglass Roman Catholic High School 2007 ICR 897, CA, in which judgment was given at the same time as Madarassy v Nomura International plc 2007 ICR 867, CA, the two cases (plus one other) raising an overlapping point on the burden of proof. Appiah involved a student's claim that her exclusion from school was discriminatory on the ground of race. The statistics showed that black Caribbean students made up 15 per cent of the school roll but accounted for 27 per cent of exclusions; black African students accounted for 20 per cent of the roll and 26 per cent of exclusions; and for white students the figures were 26 and 17 per cent respectively. The Court of Appeal held that the county court judge, who had rejected the claim, had been right to conclude that there was little, if any, probative value in the statistics. Although there was a stark imbalance in the figures in respect of black Caribbean students, this was not true of the figures in respect of black African students, the claimant's racial group. The figures being reasonably close, the statistics could only gain probative force if it could be shown that a significant number of the previous exclusions of students in the racial group in question were or might have been discriminatory.

In Odi v Intellectual Property Office ET Case No.1601948/10 – discussed under 'Breach of EHRC Code of Practice' above – an employment tribunal refused to draw adverse inferences from statistical evidence that between 1 April 2007 and 31 March 2010 the IPO received 53 job applications from people whose ethnicity was described as 'black', yet selected only two for interview and appointed just one. By contrast, of 903 white candidates, 260 had been selected for interview and 102 were appointed. The tribunal commented that these statistics ought to prompt the IPO to ask whether it was doing enough to encourage applications from members of ethnic minority groups. Nevertheless, it accepted the IPO's unchallenged evidence that about 5 per cent of its workforce was drawn from members of ethnic minorities. The tribunal also bore in mind that O's evidence, taken as a whole, did not support her claim of race discrimination.

33.29 **Failure to provide information**

As detailed under 'Requesting information and disclosure of evidence' below, claimants are entitled to use a statutory questionnaire procedure by which they can seek answers to, or information about, an employer's decisions or practices in advance of bringing discrimination claims in a tribunal. In D'Silva v NATFHE (now known as University and College Union) and ors 2008 IRLR 412, EAT, the EAT held that, although inferences can be drawn from a failure to provide information or an evasive or equivocal response to a statutory questionnaire, this is so only in appropriate cases: in the words of Mr Justice

Underhill, the drawing of inferences is not a 'tick-box exercise'. The EAT observed that there was a tendency in discrimination cases for respondents' failures in answering a questionnaire, or in providing information or documents, to be relied on by claimants, and even sometimes tribunals, as automatically raising a presumption of discrimination. In its view, this was not the correct approach. In deciding whether it was appropriate to draw an inference, the tribunals should first consider whether, in the particular circumstances of a case, the failure in question is capable of constituting evidence supporting the inference that the respondent acted discriminatorily in the manner alleged. In other words, any alleged failure on the respondent's part, however reprehensible, is only of relevance if it potentially sheds light on the actual discrimination complained of and thus, necessarily, on the 'mental processes' of the decision-maker. If it does, the tribunal must then consider the respondent's explanation for any alleged failure and whether, in light of that explanation, it is justified in drawing the inference.

The extent to which an employer's failure to provide information, which could assist the claimant to establish a prima facie case of discrimination, can itself be used to establish a presumption of discrimination has recently come under the spotlight at EU level. In Kelly v National University of Ireland 2012 ICR 322, ECJ, K unsuccessfully applied to the University for a place on a Master's degree course in social science. He subsequently brought a sex discrimination claim to an Irish Equality Tribunal, claiming that he was better qualified to be offered a place on the course than the least qualified female candidate. The tribunal concluded that K had failed to establish a prima facie case of discrimination. He appealed to the Circuit Court and applied for disclosure from the University of the following documents: the retained applications, their attachments and the 'scoring sheets' of the relevant candidates. The Circuit Court refused the disclosure application and K appealed against that decision to the High Court, which concluded that national law did not require the University to disclose the documents in unredacted form. However, it sought a preliminary ruling from the European Court of Justice as to whether the Burden of Proof Directive (No.97/80) (now incorporated into the recast Equal Treatment Directive (No.2006/54)) entitled K to this information. In answer, the ECJ stated that, although the Burden of Proof Directive does not specifically entitle claimants in discrimination cases to information from the employer in order that they may adduce facts establishing a prima facie case of discrimination, it could 'not be ruled out' in the instant case that the University's refusal to disclose documents, in the context of establishing such facts, could risk compromising the achievement of the objective pursued by the Directive and thus depriving it of effectiveness. It was for the national court to ascertain whether or not that was the case.

An Opinion provided by Advocate General Mengozzi in Meister v Speech **33.30** Design Carrier Systems GmbH Case C-415/10, ECJ, endorses the ECJ's

---

1165

decision in Kelly and provides further useful analysis in this regard. The ECJ, which has now handed down judgment in this matter, reached a similar conclusion as the Advocate General, albeit adopting a less in-depth analysis of the shifting burden of proof. The case involved another unsuccessful application – this time for the position of software developer with SDCS GmbH in Germany. M was not called to an interview and was not provided with any information as to why she had been unsuccessful. She brought sex, age and discrimination claims against the company in Germany and requested that it provide the file of the successful applicant. The company failed to do so. Both the court at first instance and the German Court of Appeal dismissed M's claims on the basis that she had not submitted sufficient evidence to support a presumption of discrimination.

M brought an application for a review of the Court of Appeal's decision before the Bundesarbeitsgericht, Germany's Federal Labour Court. That Court noted that German law requires the claimant to establish the facts and to produce evidence – and not just mere allegations – to support a presumption of discrimination. This meant that it was not sufficient for M to show that she had applied for the job, that her application had been unsuccessful and that she fit the required profile set out in the advertisement, and then simply assert her sex, age and racial origin. The Bundesarbeitsgericht acknowledged that M had clearly suffered less favourable treatment than other persons in a comparable situation, since she was not called for a job interview, unlike other persons who also submitted an application to the respondent company. However, M had not been able to establish that this was on the grounds of her sex, age or ethnic origin. The Court went on to note that the failure of the respondent to provide information when rejecting the application was precisely the reason why M was unable to fulfil the obligation to adduce evidence to support a presumption of discrimination. It was in the light of this that it made a referral to the ECJ regarding the extent to which an employer's failure to disclose information can be used to establish a presumption of discrimination.

33.31 Advocate General Mengozzi noted in his Opinion that the case presents a thorny question: how can a job applicant enforce observance of the principle of equal treatment when his or her application for a job was rejected by the putative employer, which failed to provide any information whatsoever as to why the application was unsuccessful or in respect of the recruitment procedure and its outcome? He observed that an employer who refuses to disclose such information could 'make his decisions virtually unchallengeable', thereby jeopardising the attainment of the objective pursued by the EU rule regarding the shifting burden of proof – which is principally intended to ensure the effective implementation of the principle of equal treatment – see Chapter 32, 'Burden of proof', under 'Legal framework – EU law'. The Advocate General considered that it should also be borne in mind that it is harder for an external job applicant to obtain evidence or facts from which it may be presumed that there has been discrimination than it is for an existing employee who seeks to prove, for example, that the employer applies discriminatory measures in respect of conditions of employees' pay. The job applicant is entirely dependent on the goodwill of the potential employer with regard to obtaining information capable of constituting facts from which it may be presumed that there has been discrimination, and he or she may experience genuine difficulty in obtaining such information which is, nevertheless, essential in order to trigger the shift in the burden of proof in order to lighten the applicant's evidential load.

Turning to the decision of the European Court in Kelly, the Advocate General considered that the ECJ was 'unequivocally stating' that in assessing whether an employer's failure to provide information has the effect of compromising the achievement of the objective pursued by the shifting burden of proof rule, it is necessary, in order to assess the attitude of the putative employer, to consider not only its failure to respond but also to take account of the wider factual context in which that failure occurred. In that regard, he considered the following to be important evidence in the instant case that should not be overlooked: (i) the fact that M's qualifications clearly matched the post to be filled, and yet she was not called for an interview; and (ii) the fact that the employer persisted in refusing to call her for an interview following the publication of a new advertisement on the internet with the same content. The Advocate General did, however, emphasise that the refusal of disclosure by an employer must be assessed differently in circumstances where the applicant clearly does not fit the required profile, has been called for an interview or has submitted a spontaneous application.

As noted above, the ECJ's decision in this case does not adopt the same in— **33.32** depth analysis of the shifting burden of proof. Nevertheless, it expressly refers to the Advocate General's Opinion and reaches a similar conclusion. In a judgment which can perhaps be said to implicitly follow the logic of the Advocate General's reasoning (or at least does not contradict it), the ECJ concluded that 'a [respondent's] refusal to grant any access to information may be one of the factors to be taken into account' in the context of establishing a prima facie case of discrimination, if the national court decides – taking into account all the circumstances of the case – that that refusal risks compromising the achievement of the objectives pursed by EU law (discussed under 'Legal framework – EU law' above). This decision has potentially far-reaching significance. It could apply to all types of claimants, not just job applicants, who are having difficulty acquiring crucial information from the employer. Indeed, unlike the Advocate General, the ECJ does not attach any special significance to job applicants in the context of acquiring such information. Note, however, that the ECJ is not saying that a respondent's refusal to provide information will *automatically* lead to a presumption of discrimination. It states that all the circumstances of the case (including, in particular, the refusal to provide information) must be taken into account when deciding whether such a presumption arises. Thus, for example, where a job applicant clearly does not fit the required profile, any refusal by the potential employer to provide information, 'however reprehensible' – to quote from the EAT's decision in D'Silva v NATFHE (above) – will be of little significance. Furthermore, if, for example, there is an innocent explanation for the respondent's failure to provide the information, that is likely to preclude an inference of discrimination, as indeed was the case in D'Silva (this aspect of the EAT's decision is discussed further under 'Requesting information and disclosure of evidence – statutory questionnaires' below).

33.33 Admissibility and quality of evidence

It is worth noting that the overriding consideration in determining the kind of evidence that may be put before an employment tribunal is that the evidence must be *relevant*. As Lord Simon of Glaisdale observed in Director of Public Prosecutions Appellant v Kilbourne 1973 AC 729, HL (a criminal law case), 'evidence is relevant if it is logically probative or disprobative of some matter which requires proof'. According to Lord Justice Hoffmann in Vernon v Bosley 1994 PIQR P37, CA, 'the degree of relevance needed for admissibility is not some fixed point on a scale, but will vary according to the nature of the evidence and in particular the inconvenience, expense, delay or oppression which would attend its reception... although a judge [in a civil case] has no discretion to exclude admissible evidence, his ruling on admissibility may involve a balancing of the degree of relevance of the evidence against other considerations which is in practice indistinguishable from the exercise of a discretion'. In HSBC Asia Holdings BV and anor v Gillespie 2011 ICR 192, EAT, the EAT made the point that 'relevance is not an absolute concept'. Evidence might be 'logically' or 'theoretically' relevant but nevertheless too marginal, or otherwise unlikely to assist the court, for its admission to be justified.

In discrimination cases, where a tribunal has a wide discretion to draw inferences from the surrounding facts, it is perhaps more likely that evidence relating to peripheral and background matters will be relevant. However, this can only be taken so far. In the Gillespie case (above) the EAT held that evidence of alleged acts involving people in other departments many years previously was inadmissible, stating that it was 'fanciful' to suppose that this evidence would assist the tribunal in deciding whether the claimant had been discriminated against on the ground of sex. This case is considered further under 'Previous and subsequent events' below.

33.34 In ALM Medical Services Ltd v Bladon 2002 ICR 1444, CA, the Court of Appeal stated that 'it is for the tribunal, with the assistance of the parties and their representatives, to identify the relevant issues for decision and to exercise its discretionary case management powers to decide whether the evidence adduced or the questions put to the witnesses in cross-examination are relevant'.

1168

However, while the Court placed strong emphasis on the discretion of the tribunal, and suggested that an appeal court should be reluctant to interfere with the exercise of that discretion, it remains true to say that a tribunal has no power to refuse to admit evidence that is relevant to one or more of the issues in the case, and to do so will amount to an error of law.

In practice, arguably the most common basis used by tribunals for properly excluding relevant evidence is where a ground of 'privilege' is made out. The various grounds on which privilege can be claimed in respect of documentary evidence are outside the scope of this Handbook. For a comprehensive treatment of the issue, see IDS Employment Law Handbook, 'Employment Tribunal Practice and Procedure' (2006), Chapter 6, 'Responding to opponent's case', under 'Disclosure and inspection of documents – privilege'.

Hearsay
33.35

The Civil Evidence Act 1995 defines hearsay as 'a statement made otherwise than by a person while giving oral evidence in the proceedings which is tendered as evidence of the matters stated' – S.1(2)(a). Hearsay evidence can be of particular use in supporting the credibility of a claimant or a witness in a complaint of harassment under S.26 EqA, where the claimant is likely to have trouble establishing, without witnesses, cogent evidence that an incident of harassment took place. For example, the claimant might call a witness to give evidence that the claimant complained to him or her of the incident at the time. This kind of evidence can be relevant under the common law doctrine of 'recent complaint', which acknowledges that it may be relevant to the assessment of the credibility of a person making an allegation that he or she complained about it to a third party at or close to the time of the incident – see, for example, Peart v Dixons Store Group Retail Ltd EAT 0630/04. Similarly, a tribunal might properly draw an inference from the fact that a claimant who complains of discrimination or harassment made no such complaint to anyone at the time. For example, in Atabo v Kings College London and ors 2007 EWCA Civ 324, CA, an employment tribunal, in dismissing a claim, took into account the fact that the claimant had made no contemporaneous mention to a mentor with whom she could discuss matters confidentially of the discrimination and harassment she later claimed to have suffered. Leave to appeal against the tribunal's decision was subsequently refused by both the EAT and the Court of Appeal.

Hearsay evidence is commonly but incorrectly described as being evidence of something a third party has said or written. The crucial omission in this definition is that it is hearsay only if the evidence is adduced in order to prove the truth of what was said or written. It is not hearsay if it is adduced in order merely to prove, for example, that the words were spoken, or that the person making the statement must have been in a certain place at a certain time to have spoken those words. Hearsay is generally divided into two forms, or 'degrees'. First-degree hearsay comprises an oral or written statement previously made by a person, which is proved by the production of the document in which he or she made it, or by the direct oral evidence of a witness who heard him or her make it, or by that person's own direct oral evidence that he made the statement. Second-degree hearsay (or 'double-hearsay') comprises the situation where, for example, witness A swears that B told him that C had said something. In this case, A's testimony as to the facts stated by C is second-hand hearsay. The same applies if a document asserts that the author of the document was told something by another.

33.36 The complex rules relating to the admissibility of hearsay evidence in civil proceedings were abolished by the Civil Evidence Act 1995, which states in S.1 that 'in civil proceedings evidence shall not be excluded on the ground that it is hearsay'. Even prior to this, employment tribunals – by virtue of what is now rule 14(2) of the Tribunal Rules 2004 (contained in Schedule 1 to the Employment Tribunals (Constitution and Rules of Procedure) Regulations 2004 SI 2004/1861) – were not subject to the rule against hearsay and, in practice, tribunals often have to admit first-hand hearsay statements in order to determine the facts and the areas of contention that lie behind those facts. For example, confidential allegations by an informant about an employee's conduct may be made to a personnel officer. The employee may as a result be dismissed and the personnel officer called to give evidence in the ensuing tribunal proceedings. Although such evidence would be hearsay, it would nevertheless be vital in order to enable the tribunal to assess whether the employer had reasonable grounds for dismissing. Indeed, the refusal to admit hearsay evidence in dismissal cases may even amount to an error of law. In Coral Squash Clubs Ltd v Matthews and anor 1979 ICR 607, EAT, the company sought to adduce information about an employee that was given to it by a colleague. The tribunal refused to admit the information into evidence, but on appeal the EAT held that it had been wrong to do so. It was information that had influenced the company in its decision to dismiss and was therefore relevant. The fact that the person who gave the information to the employer was not called to give evidence (even though this would have been possible) was a matter that went to the weight of the evidence and not to its admissibility. However, a tribunal will not act unlawfully in excluding hearsay if its admission 'could in some way adversely affect the reaching of a proper decision in the case'.

Whenever tribunals admit hearsay evidence it is important that they do not lose sight of the problems associated with such evidence. The drawback is essentially that the maker of the statement that is being reported second-hand is rarely called to give evidence him or herself and so the veracity of that statement cannot be tested by cross-examination of the person who made it. Tribunals should therefore pay careful regard to assessing the quality of the hearsay and should determine the extent to which (i) the evidence is credible, and (ii) the statement of the person is being accurately and authentically reported.

Credibility and collateral issues

33.37

Collateral evidence is evidence that is not probative of any of the issues which a party must prove (or disprove), but which is sought to be introduced to cast doubt on either the character or credibility of a witness for the other side – for example, to show that the witness has done wrong on a previous occasion and so is likely to have done wrong on the occasion in question. There are times when such evidence will be permitted – for example, in Burford v Servispak Ltd and anor ET Case No.1300511/05 an employment tribunal allowed the claimant in a sexual harassment case to call witnesses to give evidence that the alleged harasser had also sexually harassed them – but as a general rule it is excluded. The rule serves the two-fold purpose of limiting extraneous issues (which can lead to proceedings becoming unfocused and lengthy) and limiting the scope for the tribunal to be swayed by evidence that is prejudicial rather than probative. The tribunal in Burford admitted the evidence on the basis that the tribunal members were experienced in dealing with material of that nature and would be capable of distinguishing between matters of primary importance and peripheral considerations.

Although collateral matters can be pursued in cross-examination, the party cross-examining will usually be bound by the answers given and cannot bring evidence to contradict them – Snowball v Gardner Merchant Ltd 1987 ICR 719, EAT. Case law in the Appeal Tribunal is divided on the question of whether the rule applies equally where *credibility* is in issue. In Aberdeen Steak Houses Group plc v Ibrahim 1988 ICR 550, EAT, the EAT held that when questions put in cross-examination are relevant only to the credibility of the witness, the party cross-examining will not be allowed to introduce evidence to rebut the answers given. However, in the Snowball case (above) the EAT held that anything that goes to the credibility of a witness is relevant to the issue before the tribunal and is not to be disregarded as a side issue. Although in neither case was a ruling on that issue essential to the disposal of the appeal (and so both opinions are obiter dicta), most learned commentary seems to favour the view expressed in the Ibrahim case on this point.

Previous and subsequent events

33.38

A claimant in a discrimination case is entitled to lead evidence as to matters alleged to have occurred before or after the act complained of in support of the allegation that that act was motivated by discriminatory considerations – see, for example, Anya v University of Oxford and anor 2001 ICR 847, CA. Evidence of events subsequent to the alleged act of discrimination is admissible where it is logically probative of a relevant fact – Chattopadhyay v Headmaster of Holloway School and ors 1982 ICR 132, EAT. A subsequent event was held to be highly relevant to the claimant's age discrimination claim in Canadian Imperial Bank of Commerce v Beck EAT 0141/10. The claimant, aged 41, was purportedly dismissed for redundancy. The EAT upheld an employment tribunal's decision that the inclusion of 'younger' in the list of attributes given to the recruitment agency charged with replacing him was sufficient to raise a prima facie case that he had been dismissed because of his age, which the employer had been unable to disprove.

Similarly, evidence is admissible of previous acts of discrimination as tending to show that the employer was motivated by discriminatory considerations in treating the claimant as it did – Din v Carrington Viyella Ltd (Jersey Kapwood Ltd) 1982 ICR 256, EAT. However, the fact that there has been a previous act of discrimination does not necessarily mean that the act complained of is also discriminatory. An example:

- **Khan and anor v Home Office** 2008 EWCA Civ 578, CA: the claimants appealed against an employment tribunal's finding that their redundancy dismissals had not been discriminatory. They argued that, having found the employer's earlier handling of their grievances to be discriminatory, the tribunal should not have been satisfied that there was a non-discriminatory reason for the employer failing to comply with its own redundancy policy and procedures. The EAT rejected their appeal, as did the Court of Appeal. Notwithstanding the discrimination that had tainted the grievance procedure, the employer had clearly convinced the tribunal that it thought that it had no choice but to dismiss the claimants because of their refusal to accept what it believed to be suitable alternative posts. At that stage, they were treated no less favourably than any hypothetical comparator would have been.

33.39 In the Chattopadhyay case (above) the EAT made it clear that the test of admissibility is not whether the evidence of a previous or subsequent event – if admitted – would be decisive, but whether it might *tend to prove* the case. So where, for example, a woman claims not to have been promoted because of her sex, evidence that she had been treated in a hostile way subsequent to the decision not to promote may be of probative value in establishing that the person taking the promotion decision was motivated by discriminatory considerations. If the complainant could establish (i) that the alleged discriminator had behaved in a hostile way and (ii) that such hostility was gender-based, then both (i) and (ii) would be relevant facts in making out the complaint. Moreover, it would not be right to exclude evidence showing fact (i), where it is a fact that calls for an explanation, in the absence of proof of fact (ii) – i.e. gender-based motive – if fact (i) is such that an inference of sexist intent could reasonably be drawn from it.

The fact that the claimant is out of time to bring proceedings in respect of a prior incident does not prevent an employment tribunal from using that incident to infer that the subsequent act complained of is discriminatory. An example:

- **Cartamundi UK Ltd v Worboyes** EAT 0096/09: W alleged that a colleague, F, had directed a racist and derogatory comment towards her. There followed a lengthy sequence of events during which her relationship with F deteriorated and she raised various allegations of racism against F, by way of grievances, none of which were upheld. Ultimately, both W and F were demoted and had their rates of pay reduced identically. W presented an ET1, making 15 separate complaints of discrimination and victimisation. An employment tribunal ruled that nine of them – including the alleged racist comment and CUK Ltd's failure to take disciplinary action against F – were out of time but found that the six live complaints were made out. It went on to hold that both the racist comment and the failure to take action were facts from which the tribunal could infer less favourable treatment against W on the ground of her race. CUK Ltd appealed, submitting that the tribunal had impermissibly made findings of unlawful discrimination in relation to two complaints which had been ruled to be out of time. The EAT dismissed the appeal. It was clear from the tribunal's reasoning that it appreciated that acts which were out of time constituted background evidence only but that they might inform its decision on the live complaints.

33.40 However, the further back the incident goes, the more likely it is to be excluded. In HSBC Asia Holdings BV and anor v Gillespie 2011 ICR 192, EAT, G had been employed by HSBC in a senior management role in various different departments over a period of 17 years prior to her dismissal in 2006. She subsequently brought tribunal claims for unfair dismissal and sex discrimination. The bulk of her discrimination claims concerned acts alleged to have occurred in the two years preceding her dismissal. However, she also sought to rely on numerous other incidents by way of background to support her claim that HSBC had allowed a culture of discrimination to flourish. Those incidents had allegedly taken place between 1991 and 2001, many years before her dismissal. At a pre-hearing review, the employment judge found that he did not have the power to restrict G's evidence as it could potentially shed light upon the culture that she alleged existed. However, this ruling was overturned on appeal. The EAT stressed that the basic rule was that if evidence was relevant then it was admissible. However, relevance was not an absolute concept. Evidence could be logically or theoretically relevant but nonetheless too marginal, or otherwise unlikely to assist the court, for its admission to be justified. The Appeal Tribunal noted that prior incidents that were not complained of in their own right, typically because they were out of time, could still be important in so far as they shed light on whether the actual acts complained of occurred or constituted discrimination. Nevertheless, if a judge was satisfied on the facts of a particular case that the evidence in question would be of no material assistance in deciding the issues in that case, and that its admission would cause inconvenience, expense, delay or oppression, so that justice would be best served by its exclusion, he or she should be prepared to rule accordingly.

In the instant case, the evidence that the employment judge was asked to exclude did not directly relate to any of the pleaded acts. On the contrary, it was clearly background material. In those circumstances, he had the power to make a judgement as to whether the evidence of those matters was sufficiently relevant to the pleaded issues to be admissible. He had declined to exercise that power and his decision therefore had to be overturned. The EAT concluded that the 1991–2001 allegations were not sufficiently relevant to be admissible. They involved virtually none of the same individuals. Evidence showing a discriminatory culture in the department in which G worked would plainly be relevant, but the 1991–2001 allegations did not relate to that department. The tribunal's task was to decide whether the pleaded events after 2006 occurred and if so whether they were discriminatory. It was fanciful to suppose that the tribunal would be assisted in reaching its decision about those matters by considering evidence of other alleged acts involving people in other departments many years previously.

33.41 **'Evidential' comparators**

For the purpose of direct discrimination, there may often be no actual comparator for the claimant to rely upon owing to material differences in circumstances. However, as noted by Lord Scott of Foscote in Shamoon v Chief Constable of the Royal Ulster Constabulary 2003 ICR 337, HL, the fact that there is a material difference does not prevent the 'comparator' having some evidential value for the claimant capable of supporting the requisite inference of discrimination. He did, however, also make the point that the evidential value will be variable and will inevitably be weakened by material differences in circumstances. This approach was endorsed by Lord Hoffmann in Watt (formerly Carter) and ors v Ahsan 2008 ICR 82, HL, who observed that the question of whether the differences between the circumstances of the complainant and those of the putative statutory comparator are 'materially different' is often likely to be disputed. His Lordship considered, however, that in most cases, 'it will be unnecessary for the tribunal to resolve this dispute because it should be able, by treating the putative comparator as an evidential comparator, and having due regard to the alleged differences in circumstances and other evidence, to form a view on how the employer would have treated a hypothetical person who was a true statutory comparator'.

In Odediran v ROC UK Ltd ET Case No.2331640/08 an employment tribunal relied upon an evidential comparator in the way suggested by Lord Hoffmann when inferring race discrimination. O, a black employee of Nigerian origin, worked for ROC UK Ltd as assistant store manager of a petrol service station. ROC UK Ltd discovered that, in breach of company procedures, for a week in August 2008 neither O nor his white manager, S, had completed daily safety checks. S was responsible for failing to complete the checks on two days, and O was responsible for the same failure for four days. ROC UK Ltd

1174

investigated and decided that as S had been under pressure covering shifts and normally performed well no further action would be taken against him, but that O should be subject to further disciplinary action. He was called to a disciplinary hearing where he was dismissed. O brought a claim for direct race discrimination.

The tribunal accepted that S was not a true comparator for direct discrimination **33.42** purposes because there were substantial differences between them: they had different levels of seniority and different disciplinary records (O had a final written warning on his file for failure to follow company policies and procedures, whereas S had nothing on his file). However, that did not mean that what occurred to S was totally irrelevant. It was quite proper to consider what occurred to him as part of the evidence in relation to determining why O was treated in the way he was. The tribunal rejected the allegation that the dismissal itself was an act of discrimination, taking into account his final written warning and the disciplinary hearing's findings that he had not carried out the safety checks. The real issue in this case related to what occurred after the initial investigation, when the company decided to subject O to a formal disciplinary hearing but decided to take no action against S. The tribunal wholly failed to understand why two individuals, each of whom had failed to carry out checks when they were in charge of the site, were not both subject to disciplinary hearings. It was quite proper to draw the inference that the reason for the difference in treatment could be race. The tribunal was not satisfied by the explanation put forward by ROC UK Ltd; namely, that S had been under pressure covering shifts and normally performed well. It therefore upheld O's race discrimination claim.

In some instances, an evidential comparator may be of more assistance than an actual comparator. The very material difference in circumstance may itself point towards an inference of discrimination. This is illustrated by the following example provided in the EHRC Employment Code at para 4.32: a worker of Jain faith applies for promotion but is unsuccessful. Her colleague, who is a Mormon, successfully gets the promotion. The unsuccessful candidate obtains information using the questionnaire procedure (see under 'Requesting information and disclosure of evidence – statutory questionnaires' below) which shows that she was better qualified for the promotion than her Mormon colleague. The employer will have to explain to the tribunal why the Jain worker was not promoted and that religion or belief did not form any part of the decision. In this example, the claimant has not strictly speaking been less favourably treated than an actual comparator. An actual comparator would be similarly qualified, whereas the Mormon colleague is *less well qualified*. Nevertheless, this very difference in circumstance is effectively being used to establish less favourable treatment from which discrimination can be inferred.

1175

33.43 **Relevant evidence in sexual harassment claims**
One area of controversy that has arisen specifically in respect of sexual harassment claims brought by women centres on the evidential question of whether a woman's character and sexual attitudes have any relevance in assessing the effect on her of the alleged harassment. Sexual harassment (i.e. unwanted conduct of a sexual nature) has been a free-standing cause of action since 1 October 2005 – first under S.4A(1)(b) SDA, and now under S.26(2) EqA. The same applies to sex- (i.e. gender-) based harassment under S.4A(1)(a), which now falls under the EqA's general definition of harassment in S.26(1) and which applies to all of the protected characteristics, including sex. Prior to 1 October 2005, a woman who believed she had been subjected to sexual harassment or harassment on the ground of her sex had to show that she had been subjected to a detriment amounting to less favourable treatment on the ground of her sex under S.1(2)(a) SDA (direct discrimination). Case law on the relevance of evidence relating to a woman's character and sexual attitudes has therefore built up around those provisions.

In Snowball v Gardner Merchant Ltd 1987 ICR 719, EAT, evidence as to the complainant's sexual behaviour was held to be relevant when deciding on the credibility of her allegations of sexual harassment, as well as the degree of detriment (if any) she had suffered and the extent of the injury to her feelings. In that case, S was cross-examined about her sexual attitudes and behaviour with a view to showing that she had not suffered any substantial detriment or injury to feelings by comments of a sexual nature and innuendo made by her manager. The employer alleged that S spoke candidly about sex to her male colleagues and sought to call witnesses in support of this. S challenged the employer's right to adduce evidence of this kind, but the EAT held that evidence about a woman's private and consensual sexual behaviour was admissible and relevant in assessing the degree of detriment and injury to her feelings caused by sexual harassment. It said that 'whether the complainant is either unduly sensitive or... is unlikely to be very upset by a degree of familiarity with a sexual connotation' was relevant, although the EAT added that tribunals had a discretion to disregard evidence creating an 'atmosphere of prejudice'.

33.44 A rather more progressive approach was taken in Wileman v Minilec Engineering Ltd 1988 ICR 318, EAT. There, the EAT accepted that a woman who wears 'scanty and provocative' clothes may nevertheless be offended by unwanted advances. The EAT also rejected the employer's argument that evidence that the complainant had posed scantily clad for a national newspaper could show that she had suffered little or no detriment because of sexual harassment. The fact that she was upset by the harassment was not in any way vitiated by the fact that she was perfectly willing to pose for the newspaper. This decision is significant because the EAT in effect recognised a woman's right to express her sexuality without prejudice to her right to decide what she finds offensive. The EAT also held that the employment tribunal had not erred in refusing to allow the complainant to call evidence of how the harasser was alleged to have harassed other women. Such evidence was not probative of any issue relevant to the complainant's own complaint. Sexual remarks made to a number of people have to be looked at in the context of their effect on each individual person. Each individual had the right, if he or she personally regarded the remarks as offensive, to treat them as such and to bring a complaint of sex discrimination under what was then the SDA.

Now that harassment is a separate cause of action, there is a specific test that must be satisfied for the complaint to be well founded. Under S.26(1) EqA a person (A) harasses another (B) if:

- A engages in unwanted conduct related to a relevant protected characteristic – S.26(1)(a); and

- the conduct has the purpose or effect of violating B's dignity, or creating an intimidating, hostile, degrading, humiliating or offensive environment for B – S.26(1)(b).

The specific sexual harassment definition set out in S.26(2) is similar, except that the unwanted conduct in question is 'of a sexual nature', as opposed to being 'related to a relevant protected characteristic' – S.26(2)(a).

33.45 In either case, in deciding whether the conduct has the proscribed effect, the following factors must be taken into account: the perception of B; the other circumstances of the case; and whether it is reasonable for the conduct to have that effect – S.26(4). This means that where a complainant is arguing that the alleged conduct had the effect – as opposed to the purpose – of violating his or her dignity or creating an intimidating, hostile, degrading, humiliating or offensive environment, a tribunal will be required to examine that claim with a degree of objectivity that may not have been permissible before, albeit that the personal characteristics of the complainant must still be taken into account. If, on the other hand, it is shown that the conduct complained of had the purpose of violating the complainant's dignity or creating a harassing environment, then the tribunal is not required to make any further enquiry.

So where does this leave the case law on what amounts to relevant evidence in sexual harassment claims? The EAT's assertion in Snowball v Gardner Merchant Ltd (above) that the tribunal ought to be able to consider whether the claimant was unduly sensitive accords with the mixed objective and subjective approach to statutory harassment set down by S.26(4). It is therefore arguable that the evidence as to the claimant's sexual behaviour and attitudes admitted in that case would still be relevant under S.26 when assessing whether treatment alleged to amount to statutory harassment should reasonably be considered to have had the proscribed effect. Furthermore, evidence of the claimant's sexual attitudes and behaviour may also have some bearing on the extent of any injury to feelings the claimant has suffered for the purpose of awarding compensation. Such evidence may therefore still be relevant and admissible under the new rules.

33.46 By the same token, it is arguable that the EAT's decision in Wileman v Minilec Engineering Ltd (above) – that evidence of how the harasser was alleged to have harassed other women was not relevant to the complaint at issue – may no longer hold good under the statutory regime. The EAT there reasoned that sexual remarks made to a number of people have to be looked at in the context of their effect on each individual person. This is no longer strictly true – if the employer can show that no one else complained of the behaviour that is alleged to have so offended the claimant, that might support an argument that the claimant is unduly sensitive, which in turn may lead the tribunal to find that the conduct complained of could not reasonably have had the effect alleged. However, the other part of the EAT's decision in Wileman – that a woman who had posed for a newspaper in a state of undress could still be upset by sexual harassment – must surely still be good law. S.26(4) directs the tribunal to have regard to the claimant's perception in assessing the effect on him or her of behaviour said to amount to harassment, and there is nothing to stop a tribunal finding that a person is upset or offended by one form of sexual conduct and not another.

Harassment is fully discussed in Chapter 18, 'Harassment'.

33.47 # Requesting information and disclosure of evidence

In practice, the task of establishing facts from which an employment tribunal can draw an inference of discrimination can be a difficult task, as the crucial evidence will usually be in the possession of the employer. There are three important means of helping complainants obtain information from an employer prior to the tribunal hearing:

- discrimination questionnaires
- requests for additional information; and
- disclosure and inspection of documents.

Each of these is discussed below. Any information given by the employer will obviously be valuable to the claimant in seeking to establish the facts sufficient to raise a prima facie case of discrimination. Furthermore, the tribunal may be entitled to draw an inference from a failure by the employer to provide the information requested or from an evasive or equivocal response.

33.48 ## Statutory questionnaires

Section 138 EqA replicates the statutory questionnaire procedure that existed under the previous discrimination legislation by providing a mechanism by which a person who believes he or she has been discriminated against can question the alleged discriminator. This questionnaire – or 'question and answer' – procedure is specific to discrimination cases and is there to help a claimant obtain information from an employer prior to the tribunal hearing. It may assist the claimant to establish facts from which the tribunal can draw a conclusion of discrimination. Use of the questionnaire procedure is not mandatory. (Stop press: the Government is consulting on repealing S.138 – see Introduction to this Handbook.)

Section 138(2) requires a Minister to prescribe questionnaire and response forms for this purpose, although the questions and answers do not have to be in a prescribed form to be admissible as evidence in proceedings – S.138(3). Pursuant to this requirement, the Equality Act 2010 (Obtaining Information) Order 2010 SI 2010/2194 ('the Order') prescribes the relevant forms by which persons who believe they have been subject to contraventions of the EqA can obtain information from the putative respondent. Separate forms are prescribed in respect of breaches of the equality of terms (i.e. equal pay) provisions of the Act and contraventions of all other provisions of the Act. The Schedules to the Order set out the suggested formats for the questions and answers in each case.

33.49 The questionnaire procedure is normally used before tribunal proceedings are started, but it can also be used once they have begun. Article 4 of the Order specifies that questions must be served on the respondent either:

- before proceedings under the EqA have been commenced; or

- where proceedings under the Act relating to the contravention have been commenced, before (i) the end of the period of 28 days beginning on the day on which proceedings were commenced, or (ii) such later time as the court or tribunal specifies.

In Williams v Greater London Citizens Advice Bureaux Service 1989 ICR 545, EAT, the EAT held that the terms of the Race Relations (Questions and Replies) Order 1977 SI 1977/842 (a precursor to S.138 EqA and the 2010 Order) clearly contemplated that tribunals should be given control over matters relating to discrimination questionnaires after a certain stage and it was not for the EAT to interfere when a tribunal refused to extend time where there had been no satisfactory explanation for the delay. For full details of the time limits that apply with regard to the questionnaire procedure, see IDS Employment Law Handbook, 'Employment Tribunal Practice and Procedure' (2006), Chapter 6, 'Responding to opponent's case', under 'Written answers and statutory questionnaires'.

33.50 An employer is not obliged to answer a questionnaire and there is no provision for ordering further information on any of the matters stated in the reply. However, provided the questionnaire is properly served, it is admissible in evidence before an employment tribunal, together with any replies supplied by the employer – S.138(3) EqA. Any replies given will obviously provide the claimant with a valuable source of information in seeking to establish the facts sufficient to raise a prima facie case of discrimination. Furthermore, the tribunal is entitled to draw an inference from a failure by the employer to answer the questions posed within eight weeks or from an evasive or equivocal answer – S.138(4). There are, however, certain specified circumstances in which a tribunal is not entitled to draw any inferences. These are where the respondent's answers would otherwise prejudice a criminal matter or the commencement or withdrawal of criminal proceedings – S.138(5), or where the refusal to answer a question or the provision of an unhelpful answer is for the purpose of safeguarding national security – Article 6 of the Order.

The drawing of inferences from an unanswered questionnaire or late or evasive replies is otherwise a matter for the tribunal's discretion – a respondent's failures in answering a questionnaire do not *automatically* give rise to a presumption of discrimination. In D'Silva v NATFHE (now known as University and College Union) and ors 2008 IRLR 412, EAT, a trade union's reasons for not recording acceptances and refusals under the legal assistance scheme along ethnic lines was held not to give rise to an inference of racial discrimination. There was no link between, on the one hand, the decision that led to the design of the union's computer systems which recorded and stored the information regarding the grant and refusal of legal assistance and, on the other, the actual decision regarding the provision of legal assistance to the claimant. Those two matters were wholly distinct. The union disclosed that it did not record acceptances or refusals under the legal assistance scheme according to members' ethnicity. This was because its computer systems did not permit this information to be recorded routinely, and the exercise of going through the files of every person who had applied for legal assistance and matching them with files that showed their ethnic origin would have been disproportionately burdensome.

33.51 Some further examples involving a respondent's failure to answer a statutory questionnaire:

- **Purser v Environmental Cleansing Ltd** ET Case No.1303362/03: an employment tribunal drew an inference from an unanswered questionnaire. P was the only female employed as a lorry driver in a male-dominated environment. She was absent from work one day when her car was unavailable. A colleague had agreed to collect her but did not show up and she was unable to contact the colleague or her employer by telephone. She was dismissed at the end of the next working day and subsequently learned that she had been replaced by a male driver. She was given no reason for dismissal but was told that it was 'not personal'. P served a questionnaire on EC Ltd, to which it failed to reply. Her claim of sex discrimination was eventually upheld. The tribunal found that in the circumstances, and having particular regard to EC Ltd's failure to reply without giving a reason for that failure, it was appropriate to draw the inference that P's dismissal was on the ground of her sex

- **Pallett and ors v Lenon and ors** ET Case No.3301212/04: an employment tribunal dismissed the claimant's complaint of victimisation after her application for employment was rejected following her previous employer's refusal to give a full reference. Although the prospective employer had been slow and evasive in responding to the SDA questionnaire served on it by P, it was not appropriate to draw inferences in the context of this case given that the employer had been able adequately to explain P's rejection for non-discriminatory reasons

- **Steel v Chief Constable of Thames Valley Police** EAT 0793/03: the EAT refused to interfere with an employment tribunal's finding that it was not proper to draw an inference from the respondent's reply to a statutory questionnaire. Although the response was delivered 21 months late, and the tribunal accepted that some of the answers in it were evasive or equivocal, the reply dealt fully with the most significant issue in the allegation of discrimination, namely, the question of comparators. In the light of other corroborative evidence put forward by the respondent, there was no call to draw an inference of discrimination.

Supplementary and other questions. In addition to the specific questions set **33.52** out in the statutory questionnaire, claimants can include their own supplementary questions. The same rules regarding admissibility and the drawing of inferences apply to these. In Dattani v Chief Constable of West Mercia Police 2005 IRLR 327, EAT, the EAT extended the principles that apply in the context of statutory questionnaires to questions raised by a claimant outside of the questionnaire procedure. It held that the provisions dealing with admissibility and the drawing of adverse inferences contained in the comparable provisions under the RRA applied to questions posed by an aggrieved person, whether in accordance with the statutory questionnaire procedure or otherwise. The policy informing these provisions was that an employer who is asked a direct question in writing by an aggrieved person and who fails to respond or does so evasively ought to be treated in the same way irrespective of whether the question has been asked under the statutory procedure. Accordingly, an employment tribunal was entitled to draw any inference it saw fit from incorrect or misleading information provided by an employer in a letter to the employee, in its notice of appearance and in further and better particulars.

Requests for additional information
33.53

If a tribunal claim form (ET1) or a response (ET3) is not specific enough, either party can apply to the employment tribunal for additional information to be given by the other side, or the tribunal may ask of its own volition for additional information from either party – rule 10(2)(b) of the Rules of Procedure contained in Schedule 1 to the Employment Tribunals (Constitution and Rules of Procedure) Regulations 2004 SI 2004/1861. Where a party is seeking an order for additional information, he or she must comply with certain requirements set out in rule 11, such as explaining to the employment judge how an order for additional information would assist him or her in dealing with the proceedings efficiently and fairly.

Orders for additional information, including the penalties for non-compliance, are explained in detail in IDS Employment Law Handbook, 'Employment Tribunal Practice and Procedure' (2006), Chapter 6, 'Responding to opponent's case', under 'Obtaining additional information'.

33.54 Disclosure and inspection of documents

Under rule 10(2)(d) of the Rules of Procedure contained in Schedule 1 to the Employment Tribunals (Constitution and Rules of Procedure) Regulations 2004 SI 2004/1861, an employment judge has the power, either on the application of a party or on his or her own initiative, to order 'any person in Great Britain to disclose documents or information to a party or to allow a party to inspect such material as might be ordered by a county court (or in Scotland, by a sheriff)'. The tribunal may order standard disclosure – generally encompassing all documents a party wishes to rely on, as well as documents that may adversely affect a party's case – and/or specific disclosure, ordering a particular document to be disclosed. Since it is now the practice of tribunals to hold case management discussions as a matter of course in discrimination claims, tribunal judges will usually order standard disclosure or inspection within the context of such discussions. Where, however, a party seeks specific disclosure or inspection, a tribunal will normally expect the application to have been preceded by a written request to the other side.

Unlike High Court or county court proceedings, there is no general duty on parties to tribunal proceedings to exchange lists of the documents in their possession or allow inspection. Only if the tribunal makes an order does the other side come under any specific duty to begin a process of disclosure and inspection.

33.55 Note that, unlike the statutory questionnaire procedure, an order for disclosure of documents is available only after proceedings have been instituted. Claimants and respondents should also note that disclosure cannot take place unless the documents are already in existence. In Carrington v Helix Lighting Ltd 1990 ICR 125, EAT (a race discrimination case), the EAT upheld an employment tribunal's refusal to order an employer to compile a schedule of statistics identifying ethnic minority employees. There was no existing documentation covering the ethnic origins of the workforce and producing a schedule of statistics would have meant creating the evidence from scratch. The EAT held that there was no power to order the employer to do this.

Claimants may apply for disclosure of any documents in the employer's possession that they think will help them prove their case. An application for a disclosure order must include an explanation of how the order would assist the tribunal or employment judge in dealing with the proceedings efficiently and fairly – rule 11(3). So, for example, parties claiming disclosure should show that the document(s) may contain information that will advance their own case or damage their opponent's case. Where disclosure is requested from a person who is not a party to the proceedings, the tribunal must also be satisfied that an order is necessary, either for disposing fairly of the proceedings or for saving expense – rule 10(5).

A tribunal will not allow disclosure to be used as part of a 'fishing expedition', **33.56** i.e. to search for documents to back up a so-far unsubstantiated claim – Ministry of Defence v Meredith 1995 IRLR 539, EAT. In that case M, an ex-servicewoman, applied for disclosure of documents to support her claim for aggravated damages against the MoD. The EAT supported a tribunal's decision to deny M's request. The basis of her claim for aggravated damages was certain hurtful remarks that she alleged a medical officer had made to her. It was impossible to see how the disclosure of documents that might have shown a discriminatory attitude within the MoD generally would help. The application, the EAT concluded, was clearly a fishing expedition.

Parties to a claim may object to disclosure on a number of grounds. Reference should be made to IDS Employment Law Handbook, 'Employment Tribunal Practice and Procedure' (2006), Chapter 6, 'Responding to opponent's case', under 'Disclosure and inspection of documents – privilege', for full details. Briefly, in discrimination cases employers tend to object to disclosure on one of three grounds: that the documents sought are subject to 'privilege'; that the information sought is irrelevant; or that the order would be oppressive as the information requested would be too burdensome to produce. In disability discrimination cases, confidentiality can also be a relevant issue, particularly in relation to medical records. However, medical reports and records can be of considerable importance in such claims and a refusal by a claimant to disclose such information where an order has been made can lead to the claim being struck out. In Hanlon v Kirklees Metropolitan Council EAT 0119/04, for example, the EAT upheld a striking-out order where the claimant refused to disclose his medical records on the ground that it was an invasion of his privacy, contrary to Article 8 of the European Convention on Human Rights. Such a right had to be balanced against the right of the employer to a fair hearing.

Part 8

Enforcement and remedies

34 Enforcing individual rights

Extent of the Equality Act

Jurisdiction of tribunals

Time limits

Restricted reporting and anonymity orders

Void and unenforceable terms

Settling claims

Remedies

Costs

Judicial review

Striking-out claims

In this chapter we outline the main procedural aspects of bringing a discrimination **34.1** claim before an employment tribunal. This includes the extent of the Equality Act 2010 (EqA), the provisions which afford tribunals with jurisdiction to hear claims, the territorial reach of the EqA, and the time limits that apply to claims. We also consider the principal remedies for discrimination, with the exception of compensation, which is dealt with in Chapter 35, 'Compensation: general principles', and Chapter 36, 'Compensation: heads of damage'. Note that many of the statutory references in this chapter are to the Employment Tribunals Act 1996 (ETA). References to the 'Rules of Procedure' are to the Rules of Procedure contained in Schedule 1 to the Employment Tribunals (Constitution and Rules of Procedure) Regulations 2004 SI 2004/1861. These came into force on 1 October 2004.

For a full discussion of the procedural requirements involved in bringing a discrimination or any other employment claim, see IDS Employment Law Handbook, 'Employment Tribunal Practice and Procedure' (2006).

Extent of the Equality Act
34.2

The EqA applies in the main to Great Britain (i.e. England, Scotland and Wales) but not to Northern Ireland, which will continue to have its own separate equality legislation. However, the socio-economic duty set out in Part 1 of the EqA would, if ever brought into effect, apply only to England and Wales. The

1187

Coalition Government has announced, however, that it has no intention of implementing this provision.

In a number of areas the 2010 Act also confers powers on the Scottish and Welsh Ministers to make regulations governing the operation of those areas within their territorial jurisdiction. One of these is the power for Scottish Ministers to impose specific public sector equality duties on Scottish bodies and for Welsh Ministers to do likewise for Welsh bodies – see S.155(1) EqA. Obviously, if utilised, the resulting legislation will only apply to Scotland or Wales as appropriate.

34.3 Jurisdiction of tribunals

The Equality Act 2010 (EqA) governs the enforcement of individual rights for all heads of discrimination. S.120 EqA stipulates that employment tribunals have exclusive jurisdiction to hear complaints from individuals about the following matters:

- an act of alleged discrimination, harassment or victimisation against the complainant in the employment field under Part 5 of the Act – S.120(1)(a) (see Chapter 28, 'Liability of employers, employees and agents', under 'Who is protected?')

- an act of discrimination that occurs once the employment relationship has ended contrary to S.108 – S.120(1)(b) (see Chapter 27, 'Post-employment discrimination', under 'Coverage under the Equality Act')

- an act of instructing, causing or inducing discrimination (S.111), or aiding discrimination (S.112) – S.120(1)(b) (see Chapter 28, 'Liability of employers, employees and agents', under 'Instructing, causing and inducing discrimination' and 'Aiding discrimination')

- an application by a 'responsible person' for a declaration as to rights in relation to a 'non-discrimination rule' regarding an occupational pension scheme – S.120(2). A non-discrimination rule is a rule that is implied into all pension schemes to modify terms that give rise to unequal treatment that cannot be justified. Thus, if a term is less favourable on the ground of a protected characteristic, it is modified so as to be not less favourable. A 'responsible person' means a trustee or manager of the scheme; an employer whose employees are or may be members of the scheme; or a person who appoints an office holder who is or may be a member of the scheme – S.61(4) (see Chapter 29, 'Liability of other bodies', under 'Trustees and managers of occupational pension schemes')

- an application by the trustees or managers of an occupational pension scheme for a declaration as to their rights and those of a member in relation to a dispute about the effect of a non-discrimination rule – S.120(3)

(see Chapter 29, 'Liability of other bodies', under 'Trustees and managers of occupational pension schemes')

- a complaint by an employee or prospective employee that a term of a collective agreement is void, or a rule of an undertaking is unenforceable under Ss.145 and 146 (see 'Void and unenforceable terms' below)

- questions about a non-discrimination rule that have arisen in a claim or counterclaim in court proceedings and which have been referred by the court under S.122 EqA – S.120(4). S.122 provides for court proceedings relating to a non-discrimination rule to be transferred to an employment tribunal. Where proceedings in a court are pending and it appears to the court that a claim or counterclaim relating to a non-discrimination rule could more conveniently be determined by an employment tribunal, the court may strike out the claim or counterclaim – S.122(1). If a question about a non-discrimination rule arises during court proceedings, the court may refer the question to an employment tribunal for determination and stay or sist the proceedings in the meantime – S.122(2). An employer is treated as a party to any such proceedings relating to a breach of a non-discrimination rule and is entitled to appear at the tribunal and be heard – S.120(5).

34.4 The jurisdiction of employment tribunals is exclusive in the sense that it is not open to an employee who has been discriminated against to choose to bring his or her claim in the civil courts rather than to a tribunal – S.113(1). There is an exception in respect of the High Court's powers of judicial review of decisions of public authorities – S.113(3)(1). This means that a general challenge to the policies of a public authority may still be mounted by way of judicial review – see 'Judicial review' below.

Complaints about discrimination outside the employment field – e.g. in the provision of goods, facilities and services to the public – are brought in the county court (or sheriff court in Scotland) – S.114 EqA. In London Borough of Waltham Forest v Martin EAT 0069/11 (a case decided under the similar jurisdiction provisions in the Race Relations Act 1976) the claimant presented a race discrimination claim to an employment tribunal alleging that his employer – the local authority – had (a) discriminated against him in its capacity as a prosecuting authority when it brought a prosecution over fraudulent claims for benefits, and (b) had also discriminated against him when it gave him a final written warning for the same offence in its capacity as an employer. The EAT held that the employment tribunal had no jurisdiction to entertain the complaint relating to the decision to prosecute, as this fell outside the employment field. That left only the matter concerning the issuing of a written warning over which the tribunal did have jurisdiction. We can deduce from the EAT's decision that where a claimant considers that he or she has been discriminated against by the same body, acting in both an employment and a provision of services context, separate claims will need to be lodged in an employment tribunal and county court – there is no power for a court or tribunal to merge the two claims.

34.5 Employment tribunals do not have jurisdiction to deal with complaints against qualifications bodies in respect of the conferment of qualifications where there is statutory provision allowing the complainant to appeal – S.120(7) (see Chapter 29, 'Liability of other bodies', under 'Qualifications bodies'). Nor do they have jurisdiction to deal with complaints under S.60(1) concerning enquiries about disability and health in relation to recruitment – S.120(8). S.60 is only enforceable under Part 1 of the Equality Act 2006 by the Equality and Human Rights Commission (EHRC) – S.60(2). For more on pre-employment health questions generally, see Chapter 24, 'Recruitment'. For more on the EHRC's enforcement powers, see Chapter 37, 'Equality and Human Rights Commission', under 'Powers'.

Note that provisions in the Employment Act 2002 and the Employment Act 2002 (Dispute Resolution) Regulations 2004 SI 2004/752 (the statutory disciplinary, dismissal and grievance procedures) prevented employment tribunals from hearing a complaint where the employee had failed to follow the statutory grievance procedures. These procedures were abolished in April 2009, but transitional provisions mean that there may still be some cases (broadly, where the discriminatory act took place or began before 6 April 2009) where they still apply. For details of the transitional provisions, see IDS Employment Law Supplement, 'Disciplinary and Grievance Procedures' (2009), Chapter 1.

34.6 Members of the armed forces

An employment tribunal does not have jurisdiction to determine a claim relating to an act done when the claimant was serving as a member of the armed forces unless the person has made a 'service complaint' under the existing procedure or a complaint under the old service redress procedures, and the complaint has not been withdrawn – S.121 EqA. A complaint is treated as withdrawn if it has not been referred to the Defence Council – S.121(2) and (3). But the fact that a member of the armed forces subsequently makes a complaint to an employment tribunal does not affect the continuation of his or her service complaint or service redress procedure – S.121(5).

In Molaudi v Ministry of Defence 2011 ICR D19, EAT, the Appeal Tribunal held that the corresponding requirement in the Race Relations Act 1976 (S.75(9)(a)) that a member of the armed forces had to make a service complaint before he could make an employment tribunal claim on the same basis was not satisfied by a service complaint which had been rejected by the military authorities as being time-barred.

1190

Territorial jurisdiction

Contrary to the position under the antecedent discrimination legislation, the EqA is silent as to its territorial scope. The previous Acts applied to employment 'at an establishment in Great Britain' and provided protection to those who worked 'wholly or partly' in Great Britain, as well as to those who worked wholly outside Great Britain but fulfilled specific criteria (subject to exceptions for complaints of race discrimination on grounds of colour and nationality). Briefly, those criteria were that the employee must have worked for a business that had an establishment in Great Britain and been resident in Great Britain either when he or she applied for the job or at any time during the course of the employment.

According to the Explanatory Notes to the EqA, the decision to abandon territorial limits in the EqA follows the precedent of the Employment Rights Act 1996 (ERA) and leaves it to employment tribunals to determine whether or not the Act applies – para 15. (S.196 ERA, which excluded employees who 'ordinarily work[ed] outside Great Britain' from the right to claim unfair dismissal and other protections under that Act, was repealed by the Employment Relations Act 1999.)

Although not explained in the Explanatory Notes to the EqA, the fact that **34.8** there is no territorial limit set down in the Act means, in practice, that when determining whether they have jurisdiction to hear a discrimination claim, tribunals will be guided by the test laid down by the House of Lords in Lawson v Serco Ltd and two other cases 2006 ICR 250, HL – the leading case on territorial jurisdiction under the ERA. In Lawson their Lordships held that, as a general principle, the right not to be unfairly dismissed under S.94 ERA applies to employees who were working in Great Britain at the time of dismissal.

Lord Hoffmann, who delivered the leading judgment in the case, divided employees into three categories for the purpose of establishing whether a UK employment tribunal has territorial jurisdiction to hear a claim of unfair dismissal:

- in the standard case, the question will depend on whether the employee was working in Great Britain at the time of dismissal

- in the case of peripatetic employees (who include, for example, airline pilots and international management consultants and salesmen), the employee's base – the place at which he or she started and ended assignments – should be treated as his or her place of employment. The question then is whether the base was in Great Britain at the time of dismissal

- employees working and based abroad may in exceptional circumstances be entitled to claim unfair dismissal, even though they are not employed in Great Britain at the time of dismissal, provided their employment has sufficiently strong connections with Great Britain and British employment law. This would cover, for example, expatriate employees, such as foreign correspondents on British newspapers, who live and work in a foreign country but who nevertheless remain permanent employees of their British employer, and expatriate employees of a British employer who work within a British enclave in a foreign country; for example, at a British military base.

34.9 Lord Hoffmann emphasised that whether an employee was employed in Great Britain (or, in the case of a peripatetic employee, was based there) must be decided according to the factual position at the time of the dismissal, rather than according to where the employee could be employed under the terms of the contract of employment.

The territorial reach of the ERA under the Lawson v Serco test is narrower than that of the old discrimination statutes, since it excludes those recruited in Britain for a British business but who work outside Great Britain, unless they fall within the third category above (i.e. showing a sufficiently strong connection to Great Britain and its legal systems). Consequently, some employees who were previously covered by discrimination law could be excluded from the protection of the EqA. It should be noted, however, that in the context of unfair dismissal, the Supreme Court has held that Lord Hoffmann's categories do not set down a hard-and-fast rule: they are but examples of the general principle that a claim should have greater connections to Great Britain and British employment law than to any other country and jurisdiction – see Duncombe v Secretary of State for Children, Schools and Families (No.2) 2011 ICR 1312, SC, and Ravat v Halliburton Manufacturing and Services Ltd 2012 ICR 389, SC.

34.10 If the application of Lawson does indeed result in narrower protection under the EqA, affected claimants may seek to argue that the principle established in Bleuse v MBT Transport Ltd and anor 2008 ICR 488, EAT, applies. That case held that the Lawson test ought to be modified in its application to UK law where necessary to give effect to directly effective rights derived from EU law. Since most discrimination laws are so derived, it is strongly arguable that a wider test will apply to claims brought under the EqA. Furthermore, decisions of the European Court of Justice such as Mangold v Helm 2006 IRLR 143, ECJ, and Kücükdeveci v Swedex GmbH und Co KG 2010 IRLR 346, ECJ, suggest that non-discrimination is a general and fundamental principle of EU law, and, in so far as national law conflicts with the fundamental requirements of EU Directives implementing this principle, national courts and tribunals should be expected to disapply the conflicting provisions to give effect to the overriding EU provisions. Alternatively, courts or tribunals should interpret the provisions of domestic law so as to give effect to directly effective rights derived from EU law – which was the approach taken in Bleuse. Either way, the wider test of territorial jurisdiction would apply to workers in the private sector, as well as their public sector counterparts, who are entitled to rely upon the directly enforceable rights contained in the EU Directives.

Work on ships and hovercraft. While the silence on territorial scope was, **34.11** according to the Explanatory Notes which accompany the EqA, deemed 'acceptable for most workers' (para 289), the EqA gives scope for a Minister to say how and when the employment provisions of the Act will apply to those who work on ships, constantly moving between waters under the jurisdiction of different states. S.81(1) EqA contains a provision that requires a Minister to prescribe regulations specifying the extent to which Part 5 of the EqA applies to work on ships and hovercraft and to seafarers generally. The terms 'ship', 'hovercraft' and 'seafarer' are defined in other subsections of S.81 and, in particular, a seafarer is defined as 'a person employed or engaged in any capacity on board a ship or hovercraft' (S.81(5)). For the purposes of this section, it does not matter whether the employment arises or the work is carried out within or outside the United Kingdom – S.81(2) – meaning that the regulations may make provision for work on ships outside Great Britain.

The Equality Act 2010 (Work on Ships and Hovercraft) Regulations 2011 SI 2011/1771 came into force on 1 August 2011. Reg 3 covers seafarers working wholly or partly within Great Britain (including UK waters adjacent to Great Britain). Such seafarers are covered by Part 5 of the Act if they work on '(a) a United Kingdom ship and the ship's entry in the register maintained under section 8 of the Merchant Shipping Act 1995 specifies a port in Great Britain as the ship's port of choice, or (b) a hovercraft registered in the United Kingdom and operated by a person whose principal place of business, or ordinary residence, is in Great Britain' – Reg 3(1). In addition, seafarers are covered by all of Part 5 of the Act (except in relation to marriage and civil partnership) if working on '(a) a ship registered in or entitled to fly the flag of an EEA State other than the United Kingdom, or (b) a hovercraft registered in an EEA State other than the United Kingdom' – Reg 3(2). However, to be covered by Reg 3(2), the following conditions must be satisfied:

- the ship or hovercraft is in UK waters adjacent to Great Britain

- the seafarer is a British citizen, or a national of an EEA state other than the United Kingdom or of a designated state, and

- the legal relationship of the seafarer's employment is located within Great Britain or retains a sufficiently close link with Great Britain.

Regulation 4 covers seafarers working wholly outside British waters. This **34.12** provides that Part 5 of the Act will apply to a seafarer working wholly outside Great Britain and UK waters adjacent to Great Britain if the seafarer is on a ship or hovercraft registered in the ways outlined in Reg 3(1) (above) – Reg 4(1). There are two preconditions, however:

- the seafarer is a British citizen, or a national of an EEA state other than the United Kingdom or of a designated state, and

- the legal relationship of the seafarer's employment is located within Great Britain or retains a sufficiently close link with Great Britain.

34.13 Regulations 3 and 4 broadly re-enact the approach to ships and hovercraft that was taken under the antecedent discrimination legislation. The major omission in the EqA is that there is no longer a specific provision allowing the discrimination in employment provisions to be extended to work on board a British-registered aircraft.

The major departure from the old law is found in Reg 5. Previously, S.9(1) and (2) RRA contained an exception for seamen recruited abroad allowing them to be discriminated against on the ground of nationality in relation to pay. This led to a complaint from the European Commission, which considered that the provision was in breach of the obligation to treat EU migrant workers in the same way as national workers in employment-related aspects such as pay. In response to this complaint, Reg 5 now provides that it is not unlawful to differentiate in relation to pay where a person applied for work as a seafarer outside Great Britain or was recruited as a seafarer outside Great Britain and is not a British Citizen or a national of another EEA state or designated state.

34.14 Offshore work. The EqA also provides scope for an Order in Council to be made to extend specified provisions of Part 5 of the Act (covering discrimination at work) to individuals and corporate bodies working offshore – S.82. Such an Order was laid before Parliament on 28 July 2010, being the Equality Act 2010 (Offshore Work) Order 2010 SI 2010/1835. Article 2 of this Order provides that the entirety of Part 5 of the EqA applies to offshore work unless it takes place in the Northern Irish Area as defined by the Civil Jurisdiction (Offshore Activities) Order 1987 SI 1987/2197, or concerns a ship in the course of navigation or one that is dredging or fishing (which excludes the excavation of the sea-bed or its subsoil in the course of pipe laying).

Offshore work is defined by S.82(3) EqA as: activities in the territorial sea adjacent to the United Kingdom; activities such as are mentioned in S.11(2) of the Petroleum Act 1998 in waters within subsection (8)(b) or (c) of that section; or activities mentioned in S.87(1)(a) and (b) of the Energy Act 2004. The employment tribunals have jurisdiction to hear claims in relation to the first two – Article 3; claims relating to S.87(1) of the Energy Act must be brought in the High Court or Court of Session – Article 4.

34.15 Time limits

The general rule is that a complaint of work-related discrimination under Part 5 of the EqA (other than an equal pay claim) must be presented to the employment tribunal within the period of three months beginning with the date of the act complained of – S.123(1)(a) EqA. Thus, if an employee is dismissed because of a protected characteristic on, say, 10 March, the last day on which a complaint may be presented to a tribunal is 9 June, as the starting date is included in the computation. There is not, however, an absolute bar on claims being presented outside the three-month period, because S.123(1)(b) allows a claim to be brought within 'such other period as the employment tribunal thinks just and equitable' (see under 'Extension of time limits' below).

A claim is presented to an employment tribunal by sending the appropriate tribunal a 'claim form' – 'form ET1'. The claim is 'presented' when it arrives at the tribunal. Service can be in person, by post, or electronically. For further details, see IDS Employment Law Handbook, 'Employment Tribunal Practice and Procedure' (2006), Chapter 3, 'Time limits', under 'Calculating the time and "presenting" the claim'.

34.16 Although the statutory dispute procedures were abolished in April 2009, transitional arrangements mean that there may still be some cases (broadly, where the discriminatory act took place or began before 6 April 2009) where rules extending time limits to enable those procedures to be completed still apply. For details of the transitional arrangements, see IDS Employment Law Guide, 'Disciplinary and Grievance Procedures' (2009), Chapter 1.

Section 123 EqA is designed to replicate the equivalent provisions in the antecedent discrimination legislation, all of which provided that claims had to be brought within three months of the act complained of, or such other period as the tribunal considered just and equitable. Accordingly, the substantial body of case law concerning discrimination time limits will continue to apply to the provisions of the EqA.

Date of the act complained of

34.17 In presenting a complaint to an employment tribunal it is essential to pinpoint the date on which the act of discrimination complained of took place. Sometimes that identification will be a very straightforward matter. For example, dismissal is considered to be a single act which takes place on the date on which the employee's contract of employment is terminated. Where notice of dismissal is given, the EAT has held that the act of discrimination takes place when the notice expires, not when it is given – Lupetti v Wrens Old House Ltd 1984 ICR 348, EAT.

In Yaseen v Strathclyde Regional Council and anor EAT 6/90 the claimant was dismissed as a result of a series of reports made on him during his two years as a probationary teacher. An employment tribunal held that his claim was time-barred as the complaint alleged racial bias in the contents of the reports, the last of which had been completed some five months before he presented his claim. The EAT allowed his appeal, holding that he was entitled to wait for confirmation of his dismissal before deciding to act and the time limit began to run from the date of the termination of his contract.

34.18 In relation to unfair constructive dismissals, time begins to run from the date of termination of employment and not from the employer's repudiatory breach of contract – Meikle v Nottinghamshire County Council 2005 ICR 1, CA. It follows that time begins to run when the employee resigns or, if the resignation is with notice, from the date the notice expires.

Rejection for promotion is usually considered a single act – so that the date of promotion of the comparator is the date on which the alleged discrimination is said to have taken place (see, for example, Amies v Inner London Education Authority 1977 ICR 308, EAT). However, the outcome would be different if the employer concerned operated a discriminatory policy that continued in operation (see under 'Continuing acts of discrimination' below).

34.19 Where an employee who has been rejected for promotion appeals against that decision, the time limit runs from the date the appeal is rejected. In Virdi v Commissioner of Police of the Metropolis and anor 2007 IRLR 24, EAT, V's application for promotion was rejected and he lodged an internal appeal. This was heard on 2 June 2005, but he was only informed of the rejection of his appeal a day later. On 2 September 2005, V presented a race discrimination claim. The employment tribunal held that his claim was one day out of time. On appeal, the EAT upheld the tribunal's decision. The time limit began to run when the employer took the decision to reject his appeal – i.e. the date the 'act complained of was done' – and not when the decision was communicated to the employee. In the EAT's view, it may be desirable that time begins to run once the employee is made aware of the decision that confers the cause of action. However, such an interpretation was contrary to the specific wording of the legislation. Moreover, the detriment is suffered when the decision is taken and not once the employee knows about it. In fact, the employee may never know of the detriment. In so concluding, the EAT reached the same decision as did the Court of Appeal in Apelogun-Gabriels v London Borough of Lambeth and anor 2002 ICR 713, CA (another race discrimination case), although the Apelogun-Gabriels case was not referred to in its judgment.

Section 123(3) EqA makes special provision relating to the date of the act complained of in the following situations:

- conduct extending over a period is to be treated as done at the end of that period – S.123(3)(a)

- failure to do something is to be treated as done when the person in question decided on it – S.123(3)(b). In the absence of evidence to the contrary, a person is taken to decide on failure to do something either when the person does an act inconsistent with deciding to do something, or, if they do no inconsistent act, on the expiry of the period on which they might reasonably have been expected to do it – S.123(4).

Continuing acts of discrimination $\qquad$ 34.20

Much of the case law on time limits in discrimination cases has centred on whether there is continuing discrimination extending over a period of time, or a series of distinct acts. Where there is a series of distinct acts, the time limit begins to run when each act is completed, whereas if there is continuing discrimination, time only begins to run when the last act is completed. This can sometimes be a difficult distinction to make in practice.

The leading case is Barclays Bank plc v Kapur and ors 1991 ICR 208, HL, which involved a pension scheme that allegedly discriminated against a group of Asian employees. The argument on time limits centred on whether the operation of the pension scheme was a continuing act that subsisted for as long as the employees remained in the bank's employment (in which case their complaints were presented in time) or whether it was a single act that took place when the bank decided not to credit the employees' service in Africa for the purpose of calculating pension entitlement (in which case their complaints were time-barred). The House of Lords found in favour of the employees and ruled that the right to a pension formed part of their overall remuneration and if this could be shown to be less favourable than that of other employees it would be a disadvantage continuing throughout the period of employment. It would not be any answer to a complaint of race discrimination that the allegedly discriminatory pension arrangements had first occurred more than three months before the complaint was lodged.

Crucially, their Lordships drew a distinction between a continuing act and an **34.21** act that has continuing consequences. They held that where an employer operates a discriminatory regime, rule, practice or principle, then such a practice will amount to an act extending over a period. Where, however, there is no such regime, rule, practice or principle in operation, an act that affects an employee will not be treated as continuing even though that act has ramifications which extend over a period of time. Thus in Sougrin v Haringey Health Authority 1992 ICR 650, CA, the Court of Appeal held that a decision not to regrade an employee was a one-off decision or act even though it resulted in the continuing consequence of lower pay for the employee who was not regraded. There was no suggestion that the employer operated a policy whereby black nurses would not be employed on a certain grade; it was simply a question of whether a particular grading decision had been taken on racial grounds. That case can, however, be contrasted with the case of Owusu v London Fire and Civil Defence Authority 1995 IRLR 574, EAT, in which an employee complained that he was discriminated against by his employer's refusal to award him promotion. While the EAT agreed that a specific failure to promote or shortlist was a single act – despite its continuing consequences – it drew a distinction with the situation where the act (a failure to promote) took the form of 'some policy, rule or practice, in accordance with which decisions are taken from time

$\qquad$ **1197**

to time'. Accordingly, the tribunal did have jurisdiction to decide whether there was in fact such a discriminatory practice.

In Commissioner of Police of the Metropolis v Hendricks 2003 ICR 530, CA, the Court of Appeal made it clear that it is not appropriate for employment tribunals to take too literal an approach to the question of what amounts to 'continuing acts' by focusing on whether the concepts of 'policy, rule, scheme, regime or practice' fit the facts of the particular case. Those concepts are merely examples of when an act extends over a period and should not be treated as a complete and constricting statement of the indicia of 'an act extending over a period'. In that case the claimant, who was a female police officer, claimed, while on stress-related sick leave, that she had suffered sex and race discrimination throughout her 11 years' service with the police force. She made nearly 100 allegations of discrimination against some 50 colleagues. In determining whether she was out of time for bringing complaints in respect of these incidents, the EAT upheld an employment tribunal's ruling that no 'policy' of discrimination could be discerned and that there was accordingly no continuing act of discrimination. However, the Court of Appeal overturned the EAT's decision, holding that it had been sidetracked by the question of whether a 'policy' could be discerned in this case. Instead, the focus should have been on the substance of the claimant's allegations that the Police Commissioner was responsible for an ongoing situation or a continuing state of affairs in which female ethnic minority officers in the police force were treated less favourably. The question was whether that was an act extending over a period, as distinct from a succession of unconnected or isolated specific acts for which time would begin to run from the date when each specific act was committed.

34.22 Shortly after the promulgation of the decision in Hendricks, a differently constituted division of the Court of Appeal took a different view in Robertson v Bexley Community Centre t/a Leisure Link 2003 IRLR 434, CA, holding that the claimant's race discrimination claim failed because he had been unable to show that the employer operated a practice, policy, rule or regime that governed the acts he complained of. The conflict between these opposing decisions was finally resolved in favour of the test set out in Hendricks by the Court of Appeal in Lyfar v Brighton and Sussex University Hospitals Trust 2006 EWCA Civ 1548, CA. In that case, L brought 17 complaints of race discrimination against the employer concerning the way in which it had investigated complaints of bullying and harassment made against her by a colleague. At a pre-hearing review, the employment tribunal decided that L's complaints about the employer's internal investigation and the subsequent disciplinary hearing (although these were in themselves continuing acts of discrimination) were not linked to later complaints she had made about her manager's actions after the disciplinary hearing and the employer's handling of her grievance. As a result, the events giving rise to the 17 complaints were not part of one continuing act of discrimination, meaning that many of the earlier complaints were time-barred. The Court of Appeal upheld the tribunal's decision on the particular facts of the case. However, in reaching its decision, the Court clarified that the correct test in determining whether there is a continuing act of discrimination is that set out in Hendricks. Thus, tribunals should look at the substance of the complaints in question – as opposed to the existence of a policy or regime – and determine whether they can be said to be part of one continuing act by the employer.

Hendricks was also cited with approval by the Court of Appeal in Aziz v FDA 2010 EWCA Civ 304, CA – another race discrimination case – where the Court noted that in considering whether separate incidents form part of an act extending over a period, 'one relevant but not conclusive factor is whether the same or different individuals were involved in those incidents'. The judgment in Aziz also dealt with a procedural issue of 'considerable practical importance': on what basis should employment tribunals approach the question of whether a claim is time-barred at a pre-hearing review? The Court of Appeal approved the approach laid down in Lyfar (above), that the test to be applied at the pre-hearing review was to consider whether the claimant had established a prima facie case, or, to put it another way, 'the claimant must have a reasonably arguable basis for the contention that the various complaints are so linked as to be continuing acts or to constitute an ongoing state of affairs'.

Repeated discriminatory acts. In Rovenska v General Medical Council 1998 **34.23** ICR 85, CA, the Court of Appeal did not find it necessary to consider whether the maintenance of an allegedly discriminatory policy was a continuing act to determine that the ET1 in that case had been presented in time. It was sufficient, the Court said, that the employment tribunal application had been presented within three months of the last occasion on which the policy was applied. The case concerned R, a Czech doctor, who wished to obtain limited registration as a medical practitioner in the United Kingdom but whose applications for exemption from the language test imposed by the GMC on some (but not all) applicants with overseas qualifications were repeatedly rejected. After the fourth rejection on 2 December 1991, the Greenwich Council for Racial Equality wrote to the GMC on R's behalf, pointing out her qualifications and enclosing a reference from her tutor. On 10 January 1992 the GMC again refused her application for exemption and R presented a race discrimination claim on 31 March 1992. The GMC argued that time had started to run on 2 December 1991 and that the subsequent letter from the Greenwich Council for Racial Equality did not amount to a new application for exemption resulting in a further refusal, but was instead akin to a solicitor's letter of complaint. The Court of Appeal rejected the GMC's submission. The Council's letter advanced a new argument based on R's qualifications, attached a new reference and expressly asked for exemption. That was enough for it to amount to a new application, and so time only began to run on 10 January 1992.

The Court's decision in Rovenska illustrates that, where a discrimination complaint is based on the denial of a particular benefit, an employee can reactivate the time limit for presenting a tribunal claim by making another request for the benefit in question. The time limit will then begin to run from the date on which the later request is refused. In Cast v Croydon College 1998 ICR 500, CA, for example, the Court of Appeal was prepared to hold, as an alternative to its finding of a 'continuous act', that time had started to run on the last occasion that the employer had refused the employee's request for a part-time working or job-sharing arrangement.

34.24 Note that in certain circumstances, even where there has been a single act of discrimination, a cause of action might only crystallise at a later date. This is true in promotion cases – as noted above – where the date of promotion or appointment of a comparator (rather than the date the employee was rejected) sets time running. The situation may also arise where a comparator for the purposes of direct discrimination only comes into existence at a later date and the claimant, prior to this, had reasonably taken the view that he or she had no cause of action or that it was unlikely he or she would establish a prima facie case without a comparator – Clarke v Hampshire Electro-Plating Co Ltd 1992 ICR 312, EAT. When a second and distinct act of discrimination is the consequence of an earlier discriminatory act, the limitation period runs from the second act – see, for example, Record Production Chapel and ors v Turnbull and anor EAT 955/83.

34.25 **Post-termination conduct.** Discriminatory conduct that occurs after an employee has submitted a tribunal claim cannot be taken into account in considering whether there has been a continuing act of discrimination. However, the later incident may be relevant to the separate question of whether it is just and equitable for the tribunal to extend time in relation to the first incident – Robertson v Bexley Community Centre t/a Leisure Link 2003 IRLR 434, CA. Ideally, the claimant should have issued a fresh tribunal application after the second act of discrimination and asked the tribunal to hear both claims together (see 'Extension of time limit' below).

34.26 **Post-employment discrimination.** As we saw in Chapter 27, 'Post-employment discrimination', under 'Coverage under the Equality Act', an employee can bring discrimination, harassment and victimisation claims based on conduct occurring after the termination of the employment relationship, provided that he or she can show that the conduct had a sufficiently close connection to the employment relationship. There are no special rules regarding time limits in such cases and the matter is dealt with in the same way as discrimination that occurs during the employment relationship. It is possible, therefore, for a continuing act of discrimination to begin during the employment relationship and continue into post-termination conduct.

Job applicants. A job applicant cannot complain of an act of continuing **34.27** discrimination, even if the employer has a discriminatory policy or practice, because there is no continuing employment relationship between the applicant and the employer once the application process is completed. Discrimination in these circumstances is treated as a single act of discrimination and the complaint must be brought within three months. In Tyagi v BBC World Service 2001 IRLR 465, CA, T, who was of Indian origin, worked for the BBC World Service. He twice applied unsuccessfully for a particular post. Three months after his second application, his employment ended. One year later, he brought a tribunal claim alleging that he had been discriminated against on the ground of race in relation to his applications. He argued that his claim – made under S.4(1) RRA, which prohibited discrimination against applicants (now S.39(1) EqA) – was in time because the employer's recruitment policies were generally discriminatory towards him and other members of ethnic minorities in Britain, with the result that the act he complained of should be treated as being done at the end of the period during which those policies were in effect. In so contending, T relied on remarks made by the EAT in Amies v Inner London Education Authority 1977 ICR 308, EAT, to the effect that there is continuing discrimination so long as a discriminatory rule continues to operate.

The Court of Appeal rejected T's claim. In particular, it said that T had misunderstood the reasoning in Amies, which referred to a situation where an existing employee had brought a complaint of continuing discrimination for being denied access to opportunities for promotion under S.4(2) RRA (the equivalent to S.39(2)(b) EqA). In these circumstances, the time limit for bringing the claim would not begin to run against the employee until the discriminatory policy came to an end or the individual's employment was terminated. However, that situation was distinctly different to T's. T was no longer an employee but a job applicant. As a job applicant he had brought his claim under S.4(1) RRA (the equivalent to S.39(1) EqA), which only protected against discrimination in relation to the particular employment offered. Any such discrimination suffered would constitute a single act about which anybody – a job applicant or current employee – could complain to a tribunal so long as the complaint was brought within the three-month time limit.

Note that a complaint against a general discriminatory practice can be brought **34.28** by the EHRC, pursuant to its powers under the Equality Act 2006 – see Chapter 37, 'Equality and Human Rights Commission', under the sections on 'Powers' and 'Enforcement', for full details.

Discriminatory omissions **34.29**

As we have seen above, the notion of a continuing act is not always an easy one to grasp. The situation is confused further when what has to be pinpointed in time is not a continuing act but a continuing omission. Under S.123(3)(b) EqA, a failure to do something is to be 'treated as occurring when the person in

1201

question decided upon it'. Thus, a failure to confer a benefit on an employee is treated as being done when the employer decides that the employee should not receive that benefit. The time limit for bringing a claim begins to run from the date of the decision, rather than the date when the decision takes effect.

This puts the employee at a clear disadvantage, however, for if he or she does not know when the decision was actually reached, how can he or she be expected to know when the time limit for presenting a claim expires? S.123(4) EqA sheds some light on when the person in question will be treated as having decided upon a failure to do something: it provides that in the absence of evidence to the contrary, a person shall be taken to have decided upon a failure to do something when he or she does an act inconsistent with doing it (such as conferring the benefit on another employee) or, if he or she does no inconsistent act, when the period expires within which he or she might reasonably have been expected to have done that act.

34.30 The statutory requirement that a discriminatory omission 'shall be treated as done when the person in question decided upon it' has been interpreted in a manner favourable to employees. In Swithland Motors plc v Clarke and ors 1994 ICR 231, EAT, four car salesmen made complaints of sex discrimination when the company taking over the dealership for which they worked refused to keep them on, preferring instead to recruit female sales staff. The salesmen only learned of the company's decision on the day of the takeover, but it had in fact been made two to three weeks earlier, when the dealership was still in the hands of receivers. The four men presented employment tribunal applications within three months of the takeover, but more than three months after the date the decision was made. The EAT, however, chose to interpret the word 'decided' as meaning 'decided at a time and in circumstances when the employer is in a position to implement that decision'. Accordingly, time began to run from the day of the takeover, and not before. The EAT observed that the alternative interpretation would have led to an absurd result: any number of unsuccessful bidders could have become liable to claims for unlawful discrimination, having formed the discriminatory intention but without ever being in a position to give effect to it.

34.31 **Failure to make reasonable adjustments.** As seen in Chapter 21, 'Failure to make reasonable adjustments', under 'Duty to make reasonable adjustments', an employer is under a duty to make reasonable adjustments where its provisions, criteria or practices, the physical features of its premises or the failure to provide an auxiliary aid place a disabled employee or job applicant at a substantial disadvantage compared with non-disabled persons. This raises an important question in respect of time limits – is a failure to make adjustments a continuing act, or is it an omission?

In Humphries v Chevler Packaging Ltd EAT 0224/06 H was employed as a full-time machine operator. She began to experience pain in her arm and shoulder, and became unable to do her job. The employer offered her lower-paid alternative work as a cleaner, which she turned down. She went on sick leave, was absent for 18 months, and then resigned. She claimed that the employer had failed to make reasonable adjustments while she was on sick leave that would have enabled her to return to work. The issue arose as to whether her application was out of time. H argued that there was a continuing failure by the employer to make reasonable adjustments, so that this was a continuing 'act' and fell to be considered under para 3(1) of Schedule 3 to the DDA (now S.123(3)(a) EqA). However, the employment tribunal held that a failure to act is 'a non-act' or an omission and that time accordingly ran from the date H was offered the cleaning job. The EAT confirmed that a failure to act is an omission, and that time begins to run when an employer decides not to make the reasonable adjustment. In H's case, time began to run when the employer wrote to her saying that the only available job was the cleaning job (an act that was inconsistent with its duty to make reasonable adjustments), and as her claim was presented some seven months after this, she was out of time.

The Court of Appeal considered the question further in Kingston upon Hull **34.32** City Council v Matuszowicz 2009 ICR 1170, CA. In 2003, M commenced work for the Council as a teacher in Hull Prison. He was disabled, his right arm having been amputated above the elbow, and he had problems negotiating the heavy prison doors. In order to alleviate the problem, the Council moved him to a similar facility within the city but his difficulties persisted and in October 2005 he was given lighter duties. Two months later he was placed on gardening leave. In August 2006 the department in which he worked was transferred to Manchester City College.

On 31 January 2007, M lodged a claim of disability discrimination in the employment tribunal. He complained, among other things, that the employer had breached its duty to make reasonable adjustments. The basis of this claim was that, by August 2005, it had become clear that M was ill-suited for work in a prison environment and the Council had failed to address this problem. The Council sought to argue that the claim was out of time, since the duty to make reasonable adjustments had arisen as long ago as August 2005. The tribunal, however, found that the alleged breach was a continuous act which began in August 2005 and continued until the transfer to Manchester City College in August 2006. As the parties were agreed that a three-month extension of the time limit applied due to the then-extant statutory grievance procedures, the claim was in time. The EAT agreed with the Council that the tribunal's classification of the claim as continuous act was erroneous, holding that M's claim was of a 'one-off' act of discrimination in August 2005. M appealed to the Court of Appeal.

The Court of Appeal noted that for the purposes of claims where the employer was **34.33** not deliberately failing to comply with the duty, and the omission was due to lack of diligence or competence, or any reason other than conscious refusal, it is to be treated as having decided upon the omission at what is in one sense an artificial date. In the absence of evidence as to when the omission was decided upon, the legislation provides two alternatives for defining the point when the person is to be taken as having decided upon the omission (see S.123(4) EqA). The first of these, which is when the person does an act inconsistent with doing the omitted act, is fairly self-explanatory. The second option, however, requires an inquiry that is by no means straightforward. It presupposes that the person in question has carried on for a time without doing anything inconsistent with doing the omitted act, and it then requires consideration of the period within which he might reasonably have been expected do the omitted act if it was to be done. In terms of the duty to make reasonable adjustments, that seems to require an inquiry as to when, if the employer had been acting reasonably, it would have made the reasonable adjustments. That is not at all the same as inquiring whether the employer did in fact decide upon doing it at that time. Both Lord Justice Lloyd and Lord Justice Sedley acknowledged that imposing an artificial date from which time starts to run is not entirely satisfactory, but they pointed out that the uncertainty and even injustice that may be caused could be to a certain extent alleviated by the tribunal's discretion to extend the time limit where it is just and equitable to do so (see under 'Extension of time limits' below). Sedley LJ added that 'claimants and their advisers need to be prepared, once a potentially discriminatory omission has been brought to the employer's attention, to issue proceedings sooner rather than later unless an express agreement is obtained that no point will be taken on time for as long as it takes to address the alleged omission'.

In M's case, the claim as formulated asserted a case of continuing omission to comply with the duty to make reasonable adjustments. On the terms of the claim as put forward, that omission continued until 1 August 2006. The Court accepted that the Council could have asserted an intervening date from which time started to run on the basis of there being an inconsistent act or the expiry of the period in which, had the employer been acting reasonably, it would have made the adjustments. However, no case of that kind was advanced by the employer either in its ET3 or before the employment tribunal or the EAT. It followed that the appeal would be allowed. The claim was in time and would be remitted for consideration by the employment tribunal.

34.34 In the course of giving judgment, Lloyd and Sedley LJJ highlighted a distinct oddity about the statutory provisions now found in S.123 EqA: they create a situation where, on the question of whether a claim is in time or not, it may be in the interests of the employer to argue that it might reasonably have been expected to have dealt with the reasonable adjustment earlier, and in the interests of the employee to assert that the employer had not been unreasonably slow to act. 'Both contentions,' concluded Sedley LJ, 'will demand a measure of pokerfaced insincerity which only a lawyer could understand or a casuist forgive.'

Extension of time limits

34.35

The three-month time limit for bringing a discrimination claim is not absolute: employment tribunals have discretion to extend the time limit for presenting a complaint where they think it 'just and equitable' to do so – S.123(1)(b) EqA. Tribunals thus have a broader discretion under discrimination law than they do in unfair dismissal cases, as the Employment Rights Act 1996 provides that the time limit can only be extended if the applicant shows that it was 'not reasonably practicable' to present the claim in time.

In Robertson v Bexley Community Centre t/a Leisure Link 2003 IRLR 434, CA, the Court of Appeal stated that when employment tribunals consider exercising the discretion under what is now S.123(1)(b) EqA, 'there is no presumption that they should do so unless they can justify failure to exercise the discretion. Quite the reverse, a tribunal cannot hear a complaint unless the applicant convinces it that it is just and equitable to extend time so the exercise of the discretion is the exception rather than the rule.' However, the Court of Appeal also stressed that the EAT should be very reluctant to overturn the exercise of an employment tribunal's discretion in deciding what is 'just and equitable'. In order to succeed, it would have to be shown that the tribunal took into account facts which it ought not to have done, or that it took an approach to the issue which was very obviously wrong, or that the decision was so unreasonable that no tribunal properly directing itself could have reached it.

This approach was confirmed by the Court of Appeal in Chief Constable of Lincolnshire Police v Caston 2010 IRLR 327, CA. There a police officer presented a claim of disability discrimination outside the three-month time limit. The employment tribunal decided it was just and equitable to extend the time limit, taking into consideration the claimant's mental ill health, which had led her to mislead her solicitors as to the date of the 'trigger point' for time-limit purposes. However, in the course of his judgment, the employment judge quoted with approval a comment from a textbook that tribunals and appellate courts had adopted 'a liberal approach' to extension of time. The employer challenged the decision to extend time on the basis that this comment showed the tribunal had committed an error of law, and taken the wrong approach. Both the EAT and the Court of Appeal refused to overturn the tribunal's decision. Looked at objectively, there was ample material on which the tribunal could exercise the discretion, and whether the chairman thought he was being 'liberal' or not in his interpretation was irrelevant. 34.36

In exercising their discretion to allow out-of-time claims to proceed, tribunals may also have regard to the checklist contained in S.33 of the Limitation Act 1980 (as modified by the EAT in British Coal Corporation v Keeble and ors 1997 IRLR 336, EAT). S.33 deals with the exercise of discretion in civil courts in personal injury cases and requires the court to consider the prejudice that each party would suffer as a result of the decision reached, and to have regard to all the circumstances of the case, and in particular the length of, and reasons for, the delay; the extent to which the cogency of the evidence is likely to be affected by the delay; the extent to which the party sued has cooperated with any requests for information; the promptness with which the plaintiff acted once he or she knew of the facts giving rise to the cause of action; and the steps taken by the claimant to obtain appropriate advice once he or she knew of the possibility of taking action. In Department of Constitutional Affairs v Jones 2008 IRLR 128, CA, the Court of Appeal emphasised that these factors are a 'valuable reminder' of what may be taken into account, but their relevance depends on the facts of the individual cases, and tribunals do not need to consider all the factors in each and every case.

34.37 Some examples of how the discretion to extend time has been exercised:

- **Osajie v London Borough of Camden** EAT 317/96: O initially made an internal complaint of discrimination to the Council, which, in breach of its own equal opportunities policy, failed to provide a prompt response. As a result, O's subsequent tribunal application was presented out of time. In overturning the employment tribunal's decision not to exercise its discretion, the EAT held that it was just and equitable to allow the claim to proceed. O had been perfectly entitled to seek information from the Council before deciding whether or not to pursue a discrimination claim

- **McRoberts v Adams** EAT 499/92: A's claim was presented to an employment tribunal in time but named the wrong respondent. By the time she discovered her mistake, the application was time-barred. The EAT refused to interfere with the tribunal's decision to extend the time limit as there was clear evidence that A had made a genuine mistake as to the identity of her employer and there was no prejudice to the employer

- **Coxon v Xerox (UK) Ltd** ET Case No.6005609/99: C left her employment on 22 October 1997 and presented an application to the tribunal dated 16 December 1997, complaining of unfair dismissal, sex discrimination and breach of the Equal Pay Act 1970. The employment tribunal dismissed the complaints at a hearing in June 1999. She then presented three more applications to the tribunal, including a complaint of disability discrimination dated 30 September 1999. The tribunal reasoned that it was not just and equitable to exercise its discretion to extend the time limit for the disability claim. C had been aware of the possibility of bringing a claim under the DDA after seeking medical advice shortly after her employment ended, but had taken an informed decision at that time not to pursue the claim. The tribunal noted that while the first tribunal hearing might have given C a new perspective on the case, she made no attempt at that time to amend her claim and waited three months before taking any action on the matter

- **Barber v Bernard Matthews Foods Ltd** ET Case No.1501308/00: B, who suffered from carpal tunnel syndrome, was dismissed in September 1999 on capability grounds. However, his claim under the DDA was not presented until July 2000. A solicitor had told him that he had three years in which to bring a personal injury claim, but did not tell him that he had only three months in which to bring a claim under the DDA. The employment tribunal held that his claim could proceed. It was reasonable for B not to have known about the three-month time limit before he went to see the solicitor and it was reasonable to have thereafter relied on what the solicitor said. Furthermore, the company would suffer no prejudice, and if it did it was its own fault as notes should have been kept relating to B's dismissal.

As mentioned above, tribunals have a narrower discretion under the ERA to **34.38** allow out-of-time unfair dismissal claims where it was 'not reasonably practicable' for the claim to have been presented before the end of the three-month period – S.111(2) ERA. Therefore, whereas incorrect advice by a solicitor or even a wholly understandable misconception of the law cannot usually save a late tribunal application in an unfair dismissal case, the same is not necessarily true when the claim is one of discrimination – see Hawkins v Ball and anor 1996 IRLR 258, EAT, and British Coal Corporation v Keeble and ors 1997 IRLR 336, EAT.

Reasonable adjustment cases. In Department of Constitutional Affairs v Jones **34.39** 2008 IRLR 128, CA, the Court of Appeal highlighted the fact that in disability discrimination cases there is an additional factor to be taken into account when considering an application to extend the time limit, and that is the disability itself. In particular, in order to amount to a disability in law, the disability must last, or be expected to last, for at least 12 months, and this may involve the claimant having to predict whether he or she is likely to fall within the statutory definition of disability (for which, see Chapter 6, 'Disability', under 'Meaning of "disability"'). Further problems can arise with mental conditions. In Jones itself, the claimant was suffering from depression, but gave evidence that he was reluctant to acknowledge to himself that he had a mental illness amounting to a disability in law. The Court of Appeal refused to overturn the extension of time, though Lord Justice Pill stressed that he was not stating that there was 'any general principle that a person with mental health problems is entitled to delay as a matter of course in bringing a claim'.

Ongoing internal procedure. The fact that a complainant has awaited the **34.40** outcome of his or her employer's internal grievance procedures before making a claim is just one matter to be taken into account by an employment tribunal in considering whether to extend the time limit for making a claim – Apelogun-Gabriels v London Borough of Lambeth and anor 2002 ICR 713, CA. Two contrasting cases:

1207

- **Aniagwu v London Borough of Hackney and anor** 1999 IRLR 303, EAT: A's claim of race discrimination was presented one day out of time. The EAT found that he had delayed presenting his claim until after the relevant time limit had passed because he had hoped that an internal appeal would be resolved in his favour. The EAT held that A had been entitled to take the view that it would be sensible to redress his grievance internally before embarking on legal proceedings, and accordingly concluded that it would be just and equitable to allow A's claim to proceed

- **Robinson v Post Office** 2000 IRLR 804, EAT: R, who suffered from a chronic skin condition, was dismissed following a disciplinary hearing on 2 March 1999. He appealed under the internal disciplinary procedure. The appeal hearing was held on 20 April 1999 but was adjourned and the appeal process was still continuing when R presented a tribunal application on 23 June 1999. The employment tribunal refused to allow R's claim of disability discrimination to proceed out of time. The EAT upheld this decision, stating that the Aniagwu decision (see immediately above) did not mean that, whenever an internal procedure is ongoing, it will be just and equitable to extend the time limit. The correct approach is to consider the ongoing appeal as one factor to be balanced with all other relevant factors. The tribunal in this case had correctly weighed all the relevant factors, including the facts that R had been aware of the time limit, had ignored union advice, and had been capable of dealing with his affairs.

It is therefore advisable for an employee who hopes to resolve a grievance without resorting to an employment tribunal nevertheless to present a claim before the end of the time limit to safeguard his or her position.

34.41 **Omissions to make reasonable adjustments.** As previously mentioned (see 'Reasonable adjustment cases' above), there can be considerable problems for claimants in complying with the three-month time limit where the trigger is the employer's inadvertent failure to make reasonable adjustments. In Kingston upon Hull City Council v Matuszowicz 2009 ICR 1170, CA, the Court of Appeal stressed that the power to extend time should be considered in situations 'where the employee does not realise that the start date has occurred, or... the employer's decision has not been communicated to him' or if 'the employer were to seek to lull the employee into a false sense of security by professing to continue to consider what adjustments it ought reasonably to make, at a time long after the moment has arrived... when the employee is entitled to make a claim and time has started to run'. Lord Justice Sedley noted that in deciding whether to enlarge time under S.123(1)(b) employment tribunals 'can be expected to have sympathetic regard' to the difficulty created for some claimants.

Employer's time limit for submitting a response

34.42

Once a claimant's ET1 has been received and accepted, the employment tribunal will send a letter to the employer, together with a copy of the ET1 and a response form (ET3). The employer should then 'present a response' by completing and returning the ET3 to the tribunal within 28 days of the date on which it was sent a copy of the ET1. Where the employer fails to return the ET3 on time, it will be barred from taking any further part in the proceedings except for some very limited purposes – rule 9 Rules of Procedure. Furthermore, the employer's failure to file a response in time will lead the tribunal to issue a default judgment. Employment judges no longer have a discretion over this: they must issue a default judgment unless they are not satisfied that there is sufficient information to do so. In that case, the tribunal must issue an order giving a time limit for the employer to provide additional information. Failure to provide the additional information within the time limit will lead to the issuing of a default judgment – rule 8.

Restricted reporting and anonymity orders

34.43

The Employment Tribunals Act 1996 (ETA) allows employment tribunals to make 'restricted reporting orders' (RROs) in two circumstances that may be of relevance to claims under the EqA: (i) cases involving allegations of sexual misconduct (S.11 ETA), and (ii) disability discrimination cases where 'evidence of a personal nature' is likely to be heard (S.12 ETA). Below we consider a tribunal's jurisdiction to make RROs before going on to consider the procedure that must be adopted.

Jurisdiction to make RROs

34.44

An employment tribunal's jurisdiction to make an RRO is wider than might initially be thought upon reading the ETA and the Rules of Procedure. Although the need for such orders will primarily arise in the two circumstances addressed in Ss.11 and 12 ETA (allegations of sexual misconduct and disability cases involving 'evidence of a personal nature'), case law has established that human rights and EU law considerations can lead to RROs being an appropriate case management step in a wider range of circumstances.

Allegations of sexual misconduct. Section 11(2) ETA, when read with rule **34.45**
50(1)(a) of the Rules of Procedure, permits employment tribunals to make RROs in cases involving allegations of 'sexual misconduct'. This is defined by S.11(6) ETA to include the commission of a sexual offence, sexual harassment or other adverse conduct related to sex or sexual orientation.

An RRO made under S.11 prohibits the publication in Great Britain of any matter (written or broadcast) likely to lead members of the public to identify an individual as a person affected by or making the allegation of sexual misconduct – S.11(6) ETA. Only the person making, and any other person 'affected by', the

1209

allegation of sexual misconduct can have their identities so protected – S.11(6) ETA. The phrase 'person affected' must be interpreted narrowly, having regard to the principle of freedom of the press, and an employment judge should not impose a 'blanket' ban on naming any of the parties or witnesses to a case simply because it involves sexual misconduct – see R v London (North) Industrial Tribunal ex parte Associated Newspapers Ltd 1998 ICR 1212, QBD. In that case the High Court quashed an RRO. The case involved a number of allegations, including two of sexual misconduct. The Court said that where allegations of sexual misconduct form only a limited part of a much lengthier catalogue of complaints, the tribunal should try to limit the scope of the order to those directly involved in the alleged sexual misconduct. These would normally include the alleged perpetrator and victim, and in an appropriate case a witness of any sexual incident where the disclosure of that witness's identity might be capable of preventing the proper conduct of the hearing. Other witnesses might be included if appropriate but the tribunal should always consider the extent to which this is justified. Finally, note that the protection of an RRO can only be granted to an individual, there being no intention behind S.11 ETA to protect the reputation of a company or corporate body – Leicester University v A 1999 ICR 701, EAT.

34.46 **'Evidence of a personal nature' in disability cases.** Section 12(2) ETA, when read with rule 50(1)(b), gives employment tribunals the power to make RROs in disability discrimination cases where 'evidence of a personal nature' is likely to be heard. 'Evidence of a personal nature' is defined as 'any evidence of a medical, or other intimate nature, which might reasonably be assumed to be likely to cause significant embarrassment to the complainant if reported'. An RRO made under S.12 prohibits the publication in Great Britain, by means of print or broadcast or 'any other form', of any matter 'likely to lead members of the public to identify' the complainant or some other person named in the order – S.12(3) ETA.

34.47 **Other cases.** In limited circumstances, an employment tribunal or the EAT may make an RRO even if the case does not involve allegations of sexual misconduct or evidence of a personal nature. The common feature of these cases is that the right said to have been infringed was derived from either an EU Equality Directive or the European Convention on Human Rights.

In Chief Constable of West Yorkshire Police v A 2001 ICR 128, EAT, the Appeal Tribunal held that it had an inherent jurisdiction derived from European law to grant an RRO even in cases that do not fall squarely within the statutory provisions, provided that such an order is necessary to give a claimant an effective remedy under European law. The claimant was a male-to-female transsexual who claimed that she had been subjected to sex discrimination. There was no power under the then equivalent to the Rules of Procedure for the tribunal to make an RRO because there was no suggestion of any 'sexual misconduct'. The employment tribunal nevertheless made an RRO on the basis that it was required by Article 6 of the EU Equal Treatment Directive (No.76/207) to give the claimant an effective remedy, which would not be possible if she were deterred from pursuing the claim by the tribunal's refusal to protect her identity. No appeal was made against that part of the tribunal's decision. However, when the appeal on the substantive issues came before the EAT, it held that it could make an RRO covering the appeal proceedings based on the same requirement to give effect to European law, even though the facts did not fall within rule 23 of the EAT rules (which confers the power to make an RRO in sexual misconduct cases on the Appeal Tribunal – see 'Employment Appeal Tribunal' below). The EAT went on to note that rule 23 was defective in this respect. Despite that finding, rule 23 has not been subject to an amendment that would widen its scope to cover circumstances such as those in the West Yorkshire case.

A similar conclusion was reached in X v Commissioner of Police of the **34.48** Metropolis 2003 ICR 1031, EAT – another case involving a male-to-female transsexual, who brought a complaint of sex discrimination after she had been refused a post with the Metropolitan Police. She sought an RRO from the employment tribunal on the ground that she would be deterred from proceeding if forced to air in public details relating to her transgender status. The tribunal refused to make that order but the EAT allowed her appeal. It found that her case did involve allegations of sexual misconduct and therefore fell squarely within the then equivalent to rule 50(1), triggering the tribunal's discretion under the Rules to make an RRO. Nevertheless, the EAT went on to consider whether the employment tribunal had jurisdiction to make an RRO in circumstances where no question of sexual misconduct arises on the facts. It noted that there was a duty on the tribunal to enforce the terms of the then EU Equal Treatment Directive (No.76/207). A tribunal was therefore under a duty to interpret its procedural rules so as to ensure that a claimant was not hampered or deterred from seeking a remedy because of an inappropriately narrow reading of its powers to make orders. In the EAT's view, old rule 15(1) – the forerunner to current rules 10 and 60(1) – provided a tribunal with a wide power to regulate its own procedure. This empowered a tribunal to make orders analogous to, but wider than, RROs in circumstances where the facts of the case did not fall within the narrow definitions contained in what is now rule 50(1) so as to ensure anonymity where the claimant would otherwise be deterred from bringing a claim.

In A v B 2010 ICR 849, EAT, the Appeal Tribunal held that, despite the absence of any specific power in the ETA and Employment Appeal Tribunal rules, it was appropriate to issue both an RRO and an anonymity order to secure a party's right to a private and family life under Article 8 of the European Convention on Human Rights. The recognition in that case that an employment tribunal may have to step outside its specified powers in order to protect a party's privacy is potentially a very significant development in the law, as privacy concerns generally lie at the heart of any application to make an RRO.

34.49 Given that the above cases all confirm that there are circumstances in which an employment tribunal or the EAT may need to make an RRO or anonymity order to protect the EU- or ECHR-derived rights of transsexual employees, it is perhaps surprising that specific provision has not been made for such orders in either the Tribunal or the EAT Rules. As we explain under 'Cases not falling within S.11 or S.12 ETA' below, an employment tribunal can, in making such an order, rely on its general powers to manage proceedings in rules 10 and 60(1), but the EAT lacks an equivalent power, and must instead rely directly on the above jurisprudence when making an RRO or anonymity order that, strictly speaking, falls outside the powers afforded by the EAT Rules.

34.50 **Employment Appeal Tribunal.** The EAT also has the power to make an RRO, which is derived from S.31 ETA and rules 23 and 23A of the Employment Appeal Tribunal Rules 1993 SI 1993/2854. The EAT can make an RRO only in proceedings on an appeal against a tribunal's decision to make or not to make an RRO and in proceedings on an appeal against a tribunal's interlocutory decision in proceedings in which it has made an RRO which it has not revoked – S.31(2) ETA. Therefore it is not open to the EAT to grant an RRO on a substantive appeal against liability – A v B ex parte News Group Newspapers Ltd 1998 ICR 55, EAT. The provisions regulating the making of an RRO in the EAT are broadly equivalent to those operating in the employment tribunal, save that there is no provision in the EAT Rules allowing interested third parties to make representations at a hearing prior to a full RRO being made.

34.51 **Procedure for issuing an RRO**

An application for an RRO should be made at the earliest opportunity, and ideally at the same time as the tribunal claim form is submitted – X v Commissioner of Police of the Metropolis 2003 ICR 1031, EAT. An RRO can be made by an employment judge acting on his or her own initiative or upon the application of a party (either in writing or orally at the hearing) – rule 50(2). Since the introduction of the 2004 Rules of Procedure, a tribunal may now make either a 'full' order or a 'temporary' order, as discussed below.

34.52 **Temporary restricted reporting order.** A temporary RRO is designed to provide emergency protection to a party who fears extensive media interest in the case. A temporary RRO (unlike a full RRO) can be made at a case management discussion, and the employment judge does not have to hold a hearing or send a copy of the application to the other parties before making the order – rule 50(3). Once the temporary RRO has been made, the other parties are informed of it in writing as soon as possible and told of their right to revoke the temporary RRO or convert it into a full RRO within 14 days of the date on which it was made – rule 50(4). Where no such application is made, the temporary RRO lapses and ceases to have effect on the fifteenth day after it was made. If an application is made, the RRO continues until the hearing of that application takes place – rule 50(5).

Full restricted reporting order. Before the employment tribunal can make a **34.53** full RRO – at either a pre-hearing review or a substantive hearing – all parties must be given the opportunity to make oral submissions, irrespective of whether there was previously a temporary RRO in place – rule 50(6). Furthermore, rule 50(7) allows any person, provided he or she has a legitimate interest in whether the order is made, to make representations before a full RRO is made. This provision enables representatives of the press to apply to the tribunal to argue against the making of a full RRO in a particular case. However, it would appear that where proceedings are withdrawn, tribunals have no power to revoke an RRO, and as there has been no determination of liability and remedy, the effect is that the RRO remains in force in perpetuity.

The discretion to make an RRO (whether full or temporary) should not be exercised automatically at the request of one party, or even both parties. The Court of Appeal has stressed that a tribunal must still consider whether it is in the public interest that the press should be deprived of the right to communicate information to the public if it becomes available – X v Z Ltd 1998 ICR 43, CA. Having said that, an appellate court should be slow to interfere with a tribunal's exercise of its discretion – Donna Kay t/a Direct Sales Agency v Newcombe EAT 142/97.

Where a tribunal makes a full or temporary RRO, notice of the fact is to be **34.54** displayed on the notice board of the tribunal with any list of the proceedings taking place before the tribunal, and on the door of the room in which the proceedings affected by the order are taking place – rule 50(8)(c). This is principally so that journalists attending the hearing will understand the limits on what they are entitled to report. Tribunals have no power to exclude journalists or members of the public from their hearings, except on grounds of national security under rule 54 – R v Southampton Industrial Tribunal ex parte INS News Group Ltd and Express Newspapers plc 1995 IRLR 247, QBD.

Lapse of orders. A full RRO remains in force until both liability and remedy **34.55** are determined or until it is revoked, whichever is the sooner – rule 50(8)(b). This means that the RRO will only be lifted on the date the judgment is sent to the parties – rule 50(11). Although it is not expressly spelled out in the Rules of Procedure, the corollary of these provisions is that a full RRO, made in proceedings that are withdrawn and without the order being revoked, remains in force in perpetuity – Davidson v Dallas McMillan 2010 IRLR 439, Ct Sess (Inner House). The Court of Session in that case observed that it was not clear whether this result was due to an oversight in drafting the rules, or was deliberate.

Once an RRO has lapsed, all details related to a case may be reported, including information withheld from the tribunal's records (this might happen where a party repeats something that forms part of their own knowledge). If a party wishes to have further protection beyond the end of the proceedings, its best course of action would be to apply for an extended RRO – see the observations of Mr Justice Underhill in F v G (discussed immediately below).

34.56 **Cases not falling within S.11 or S.12 ETA.** As discussed under 'Jurisdiction to make RROs' above, the cases of X v Commissioner of Police of the Metropolis 2003 ICR 1031, EAT, and A v B 2010 ICR 849, EAT, have established that an RRO can be made in circumstances that do not exactly fit Ss.11 and 12 ETA and rule 50, but where EU-derived rights or human rights are engaged. In F v G 2012 ICR 246, EAT, the EAT held that an employment tribunal had correctly issued an 'anonymity order' permanently removing the names of the claimant, the college which employed her, and the college's students and staff from the employment tribunal's records. In approving the tribunal's decision, the Appeal Tribunal ruled that anonymity orders can be issued where persons affected by the case would otherwise suffer an infringement of their right to a private and family life under Article 8 ECHR – see under 'Anonymity orders and tribunal records' below for further discussion.

The EAT in F v G (above) also provided guidance for tribunals to follow in cases where anonymity orders and restricted reporting orders are required. Mr Justice Underhill advised that employment tribunals should begin by considering whether restrictions on reporting and/or anonymisation are required in order to protect the rights of a party or other affected person under Article 8, other Articles of the Convention, or EU law. In considering this, employment tribunals must pay full regard to the importance of open justice and consider the extent of any measures. It will be necessary to consider not only what restrictions are proportionate but for how long they need remain in place: permanent protection may or may not be appropriate.

34.57 Where protection is necessary and the measure can be taken pursuant to rule 50, that is the approach a tribunal should take. For cases falling outside the scope of rule 50 – because there is no allegation of the commission of a sexual offence or of sexual misconduct, nor any disability issue – the tribunal should issue the necessary measures pursuant to its general power to regulate proceedings under rule 10. Where the case falls within the scope of rule 50, but the powers afforded by that section are too narrow, a tribunal should make clear what action it is taking under rule 50, and what action is taken under the wider powers afforded by the decisions in X v Commissioner of Police of the Metropolis and A v B (above).

34.58 **Breach of a restricted reporting order.** Breach of an RRO will constitute a criminal offence, triable in the magistrates' court and punishable by a fine not exceeding level 5 on the standard scale (currently £5,000). In the case of publication of identifying matter in a newspaper or periodical, criminal liability attaches to the proprietor, editor and publisher – Ss.11(2)(a) and 12(3)(a) ETA. With other publications, liability attaches to the person publishing the matter – Ss.11(2)(b) and 12(3)(b). In the case of identifying matter being included in a radio or television programme, liability attaches to any body corporate engaged in providing the service in which the programme is included, and any person having functions in relation to the programme corresponding to those of an editor of a newspaper – Ss.11(2), 12(3)(c) and 31(3). Ignorance and lack of suspicion that the publication or programme included identifying matter is a defence – Ss.11(3), 12(4) and 31(4).

Anonymity orders and tribunal records   34.59
Note that prior to the introduction of the 2004 Rules of Procedure, employment tribunals had a separate power to make a 'register deletion order' in cases where allegations of a sexual offence were involved. This had the effect of requiring that the public register of judgments and any other public documents generated in the proceedings were modified to prevent identification of the persons making, or affected by, the allegation. Rule 49 in effect now provides that it is no longer necessary to have an order of the tribunal in such circumstances. Instead, there is simply a mandatory and automatic requirement on the employment judge or the Secretary of the Employment Tribunals to delete from the register of judgments or any public judgment, document or record of the proceedings any matter likely to identify persons making or affected by allegations of a sexual offence.

In addition, a tribunal may issue an order anonymising the tribunal records where a Convention right or EU-derived right is engaged, relying on its general power under rule 10 – see A v B 2010 ICR 849, EAT, and F v G 2012 ICR 246, EAT.

Void and unenforceable terms   34.60

As under the antecedent discrimination legislation, the Equality Act 2010 (EqA) contains provisions that render either void or unenforceable provisions in contracts, collective agreements, and the rules of undertakings (covering employers, trade unions and qualifying bodies) that constitute, promote or provide for discriminatory treatment that is prohibited by the Act.

Unenforceable terms in contracts   34.61
In common with preceding legislation, the EqA makes unenforceable a term of a contract 'if it constitutes, promotes or provides for treatment... [of a] person that is of a description prohibited by [the] Act' – S.142(1). The term is only unenforceable in so far as it constitutes a prohibited act. Thus, someone who

1215

would have been disadvantaged by any such term will still be able to rely on it to obtain any other benefit to which it entitles him or her.

In relation to *disability alone*, a non-contractual term that 'constitutes, promotes or provides for treatment of a person that is of a description prohibited by [the] Act' is also unenforceable if it is classed as a 'relevant non-contractual term' – S.142(2) EqA. A term meets this definition if: (a) it is a term of an agreement that is not a contract; and (b) it relates to the provision of an employment service within the terms of S.56(2)(a)–(e) (which include, for example, the provision of vocational training, an employment-finding service and careers services), or to the provision of insurance facilities under group insurance arrangements. So, for example, any discriminatory terms contained in private health insurance group policies would be particularly vulnerable to being rendered unenforceable under this provision. However, the phrase 'treatment of a description prohibited by [the] Act' referred to in S.142(1) and (2) does not include: (a) a less favourable term in a contract that should be modified by an implied sex equality or maternity equality clause, or (b) the failure to modify a term as a result of the operation of a sex equality clause – S.142(4). This exclusion clause is poorly drafted and its meaning is not abundantly clear. It would seem to mean that an individual cannot rely on the provisions of S.142 to remedy less favourable terms that should be remedied through the equality of terms provisions in Chapter 3 of Part 5 to the Act (these provisions are considered in IDS Employment Law Handbook, 'Equal Pay' (2011)). This accords with the Explanatory Notes, which state that S.142 does not apply to a term of a contract modified by an equality clause under Part 5, Chapter 3, because the term, once included or modified, is no longer discriminatory (para 467).

34.62 Furthermore, the provisions dealing with unenforceable terms in S.142 do not apply to contractual terms that may breach the public sector equality duty (see Chapter 38, 'General public sector equality duty'), to which different enforcement mechanisms apply – S.148(2).

Where a contract or other agreement contains an unenforceable term, a county court or sheriff may order that term to be removed or modified on the application of a person who has an interest in the contract or agreement – S.143(1) EqA. Such an order cannot be made unless every person who would be affected by it has been given notice of the application and been given an opportunity to make representations to the county court or sheriff – S.143(2). The order may include provision in respect of a period before it was made – S.143(3).

34.63 **Void terms in collective agreements**
Terms of a collective agreement or rules made by employers, qualifications bodies or trade organisations are rendered void or unenforceable to the extent

that they discriminate against a person or would otherwise lead to conduct prohibited by the EqA by S.145.

Section 145(1) makes void a term of a collective agreement 'in so far as it constitutes, promotes or provides for treatment' that is prohibited by the EqA. For these purposes, the definition of 'collective agreement' is exactly the same as that applicable in the context of trade union rights – see S.178 of the Trade Union and Labour Relations (Consolidation) Act 1992. The Explanatory Notes explain that the reason for making such terms void as opposed to unenforceable is that the terms of a collective agreement are in any case unenforceable unless incorporated into the contract of employment (para 476).

Unenforceable rules of undertakings

34.64

Section 145(2) EqA makes unenforceable rules of undertakings of employers, trade organisations and qualifications bodies in so far as they constitute, promote or provide for treatment prohibited by the Act. A rule made by a trade organisation or a qualifications body is one that applies to:

- its members or prospective members

- persons on whom it has conferred a relevant qualification, or

- persons seeking conferment by it of a relevant qualification – S.148(6).

A rule made by an employer is one that applies to:

- employees

- persons who apply for employment, or

- persons the employer considers for employment – S.148(7).

This section replaces similar provisions in previous discrimination legislation.

Declarations in respect of void term, etc

34.65

Section 146 EqA enables an employment tribunal to declare a term of a collective agreement void, or a rule of an undertaking unenforceable, when a person thinks that the agreement or rule might in the future have the effect of discriminating against him or her. This replaces similar provisions in previous legislation.

Section 146(1) states that the complaint must be made by a 'qualifying person'. This must be a person who is, or is seeking to be, an employee of an employer, whether the collective agreement was made by the employer itself or by an organisation or association of employers to which it belongs – S.146(5). To be eligible to bring a claim, the claimant must be potentially personally affected by the term or rule – S.146(2).

1217

If the tribunal finds the complaint to be well founded, it must make an order declaring that the term is void or the rule unenforceable – S.146(3). The order can include back-dated provisions – S.146(4).

34.66 Settling claims

Generally speaking, any term in an agreement that attempts to limit the operation of the employment provisions of the EqA or prevent a person from presenting a complaint to an employment tribunal under those provisions is unenforceable – S.144(1) EqA. There are two exceptions to this general rule that allow parties to reach a binding agreement to settle a dispute. The first is where a contractual settlement has been made with the assistance of an Acas conciliator (commonly known as a 'COT3 agreement' or 'conciliated settlement') – S.144(4)(a). The second exception is where the conditions for reaching a 'qualifying compromise agreement' have been fulfilled – S.144(4)(b). In this chapter we give a brief overview of the rules governing Acas-conciliated settlements and compromise agreements. For an in-depth analysis, see IDS Employment Law Handbook, 'Employment Tribunal Practice and Procedure' (2006), Chapter 9, 'Settlements, withdrawals and arbitration'.

34.67 Acas-conciliated settlements

The Employment Tribunals Act 1996 (ETA) seeks to encourage the use of the conciliation service provided by Acas in order to avoid litigation wherever possible. Whenever a complaint under S.120 EqA (tribunal jurisdiction) is presented to an employment tribunal, a copy is automatically sent to an Acas conciliator – S.19(1)(a) ETA and rule 21 Rules of Procedure. The conciliator is then under a duty to promote settlement of the dispute if he or she is requested to do so by both parties or, in the absence of such a request, if he or she thinks that there is a reasonable prospect of achieving a settlement – S.18(2) ETA. The conciliator may also be called in by either party before a complaint has been lodged with a tribunal. The same duty to promote a settlement then applies – S.18(3).

The conciliator can recommend the use of existing grievance procedures where appropriate – S.18(6) ETA. Anything said to a conciliator who is trying to bring about a settlement is privileged and may not be used in evidence before a tribunal without the consent of the person who said it – S.18(7).

34.68 Scope of settlement.
Where a COT3 agreement has been concluded, the complainant will lose his or her right to complain to a tribunal about the act in respect of which settlement has been reached. It is clear from the language of S.144(4) EqA that an agreement will only be effective if it settles a complaint under S.120. If no such complaint or potential complaint has been identified, the agreement will not be effective in this regard. This point is illustrated by Livingstone v Hepworth Refractories Ltd 1992 ICR 287, EAT, in which the

claimant, upon leaving the company after 38 years' service, did not raise any complaint of sex discrimination when a COT3 agreement was made. As a result, that agreement could not bar his subsequent claim under the SDA that the rules of the company pension scheme were discriminatory and should be altered so that he could receive higher benefits.

Settling future claims. It is perfectly possible for the terms of an Acas-conciliated settlement to purport to bar not only present but also future claims. However, in order for the claimant to effectively release claims or rights that he or she has not even contemplated, it is necessary that the COT3 agreement expressly state that this is the employee's intention. This point is illustrated in Royal National Orthopaedic Hospital Trust v Howard 2002 IRLR 849, EAT, where the EAT considered whether a COT3 barred a claim that arose from an employer's future act not contemplated by the parties at the time of the agreement. In that case, H brought claims of sex discrimination, marital discrimination and constructive dismissal, each of which was settled after Acas conciliation. The COT3 stated that the employer's payment was made 'in full and final settlement of these proceedings and of all claims which the claimant has or may have against the respondent' under a number of listed statutory provisions, including the SDA. Subsequently, the hospital prevented H from carrying out a day's work at the hospital in a private capacity. H complained of victimisation contrary to the SDA – a claim, the hospital argued, that was barred by the compromise agreement. The EAT held that 'the law does not decline to allow parties to contract that all and any claims, whether known or not, shall be released'. The question was whether, looking objectively at the settlement agreement, this was the intention of the parties, or whether some limitation has to be placed on the agreement's scope. Looking at the COT3 in H's case, the EAT concluded that the COT3's reference to claims which the claimant 'has or may have' could cover claims existing at the time of the agreement (whether or not they were known to the employee), but it was not sufficient to cover possible future claims. H's victimisation claim could therefore proceed. **34.69**

Compromise agreement **34.70**

The second method by which a discrimination claim can be lawfully settled is by means of a compromise agreement. In order to be effective in excluding tribunal jurisdiction in a discrimination claim, a compromise agreement must meet the strict conditions set out in S.147 EqA, as follows:

- the agreement must be in writing and relate to the particular complaint – S.147(3)(a) and (b)

- the complainant must, before entering into the contract, have received advice from a 'relevant independent adviser' covering the terms and effect of the proposed compromise agreement and, in particular, its effect on the employee's ability to pursue complaints before an employment tribunal – S.147(3)(c)

- when the adviser gives the advice, he or she must be covered by a contract of insurance or a professional indemnity covering the risk of a claim by the employee in respect of loss arising in consequence of the advice – S.147(3)(d)

- the agreement must identify the adviser and state that the conditions in subsections (c) and (d) above have been met – S.147(e) and (f).

Section 147(4) defines an independent adviser as one of the following:

- a qualified lawyer – i.e. a barrister (advocate in Scotland) in private practice or employed to give legal advice, a solicitor who holds a practising certificate or a person other than a barrister or solicitor who is an authorised advocate or litigator within the meaning of the Courts and Legal Services Act 1990 – S.147(4)(a)

- an officer, official, employee or member of an independent trade union who has been certified in writing by the trade union as competent to give legal advice and as authorised to do so on behalf of the trade union – S.147(4)(b)

- an advice centre worker (whether an employee or a volunteer) who has been certified in writing by the centre as competent to give advice and as authorised to do so on behalf of the centre – S.147(4)(c)

- a person so specified in an order made by the Secretary of State – S.147(4)(d).

34.71 The Equality Act 2010 (Qualifying Compromise Contract Specified Person) Order 2010 SI 2010/2192 provides that Fellows of the Institute of Legal Executives practising in a solicitor's practice also qualify as independent advisers for these purposes.

A person is not a relevant independent adviser in relation to a compromise agreement if he or she is a party to, or connected to a party to, the contract or the complaint – S.147(5)(a) and (b) EqA. A person is also not an independent adviser if he or she is employed by or is acting in the matter for a party to the contract or the complaint or a person connected with a party to the contract or the complaint – S.147(5)(c) and (d); or if the trade union or advice centre referred to in S.147(4)(c) (see above) is the other party or a person connected with the other party – S.147(5)(e); or if, in the case of an advice centre worker, the employee pays for the advice – S.147(5)(f). Note that S.147(5) was amended on 6 April 2012 by the Equality Act 2010 (Amendment) Order 2012 SI 2012/334, following concerns that, on a literal interpretation of the provisions, a complainant's solicitor was excluded from the category of 'independent adviser'. We consider this change in more detail under 'Drafting error' below.

34.72 Any two persons are treated as connected if one is a company of which the other (directly or indirectly) has control, or both are companies of which a third person (directly or indirectly) has control – S.147(8) EqA. Furthermore, two persons are also connected for the purposes of S.147(5) in so far as a connection between them gives rise to a conflict of interest, in relation to either the contract or the complaint – S.147(9).

The exclusions are broadly the same (though worded slightly differently) as those that applied under the antecedent discrimination legislation, except that the SDA and RRA also expressly excluded someone who was to be regarded as an independent adviser by virtue of a Ministerial order but did not meet the qualifying conditions contained in that order.

Drafting error. As originally enacted, S.147(5) EqA contained a serious **34.73** drafting error that could affect the legitimacy of compromise agreements signed prior to 6 April 2012 (that being the date on which S.147(5) was amended). The drafting error concerned S.147(5)(d), which stipulates that 'a person who is acting for a person within paragraph (a) or (b) in relation to the contract or the complaint' is not an independent adviser for the purposes of drawing up compromise agreements. Prior to amendment, S.147(5)(a) and (b) referred to 'a person who is a party to the contract or the complaint' and 'a person who is connected to' such a person. On a literal interpretation, this had the bizarre effect of seemingly precluding a solicitor instructed by the complainant from advising on the effect of the compromise agreement or from signing off the agreement. Such an interpretation would have driven a coach and horses through the compromise agreements provisions in the EqA and was clearly never Parliament's intention – a claimant's solicitor is the ideal candidate to advise on such matters.

The Government's initial view was that S.147(5) did not need amending. Indeed, the 'FAQs on commencement of the Equality Act', published on the website of the Government Equalities Office, specifically stated that S.147(5)(d) would not prevent a complainant's legal representative from acting as the qualified adviser for the purpose of a compromise agreement. This result could be achieved by the somewhat tortuous route of reading S.147(4) and (5) – which are concerned with who can and cannot be an independent adviser – as not referring to the complainant at all, since it is clear from the scheme of S.147 that the complainant and the independent adviser are separate people. The result, according to the GEO, is that S.147(5)(d) cannot be referring to a person acting for the complainant. However, after belatedly realising that the utility of compromise agreements hinges on their providing certainty that a claim has been settled, the Government issued the Equality Act 2010 (Amendment) Order 2012 SI 2012/334, which came into force on 6 April 2012. It amended S.147(5)(a) so that it reads 'a person, other than the claimant, who is a party to the contract or the complaint'. It follows that the complainant's legal adviser cannot fall within S.147(5)(d), as the person 'who is acting for a person within paragraph (a)'. Accordingly, the complainant's legal adviser is not precluded from being an independent adviser to the complainant.

34.74 It is important to note that the new S.147(5) EqA does not have retrospective effect. This means that where a compromise agreement was reached before the amendment came into force (i.e. on or before 5 April 2012), and the claimant received advice on its terms from his or her solicitor, the validity of that agreement depends on a court or tribunal adopting the GEO's interpretation of the old S.147(5).

34.75 **Statement that conditions have been met.** Under the antecedent discrimination legislation a compromise agreement had to contain a statement that all the conditions under the statute had been met. For example, in the DDA the conditions regulating compromise agreements were dealt with in para 2(2) of Schedule 3A to the Act, and para 2(2)(f) stated 'the contract must state that the conditions regulating compromise contracts under this Schedule are satisfied'. However, the EqA simply requires a statement that two specific conditions have been met – the fact that the complainant has received independent advice and that, on the date when that advice was given, an insurance contract or insurance indemnity was in force covering the risk should the complainant seek to recover loss arising from the advice – see S.147(3)(f).

No doubt this change addresses the quirks that would otherwise be thrown up as a result of all the discrimination strands being housed under a single Act. Previously, a claimant who sought to compromise different claims brought under one or more statutes – for example, where he or she alleged that his or her dismissal was both unfair and discriminatory on grounds of sex and race – would have to include a declaration that the requirements of a valid compromise agreement had been fulfilled under each Act. However, since the EqA envisages that claimants can bring claims of combined discrimination (though these provisions will not be implemented before April 2011), it is not surprising that they no longer have specifically to compromise claims under each of the protected characteristics. Furthermore, it is arguable that a compromise agreement that meets the validity requirements of, say, the ERA may also serve to compromise claims made under the EqA without a further statement of compliance or specific reference to the EqA, so long as the compromise agreement makes mention of the discrimination claim. This is necessary because one of the conditions that must be complied with in order to effect a valid compromise agreement is that the agreement 'relates to the particular complaint' – S.147(3)(b). In Palihakkara v British Telecommunications plc EAT 0185–6/06 the claimant was allowed to continue with claims of race and sex discrimination despite having signed a compromise agreement settling 'all claims'. This was because the agreement stated that the conditions of S.203 ERA had been satisfied but there was no similar statement in respect of the SDA or the RRA. Arguably, the position is now different, and a similarly worded agreement would be held to have effectively compromised all the complainant's claims.

Scope of settlement. Like a COT3 agreement, a properly constituted **34.76** compromise agreement will bar the employee from taking a claim any further. However, unlike COT3 agreements, there is a requirement that compromise agreements 'relate to the particular complaint' – S.147(3)(b). This does not mean that each claim or potential claim must be settled by a separate agreement. As with COT3 agreements, a single compromise agreement is capable of settling all the matters in dispute between the parties – Lunt v Merseyside TEC Ltd 1999 ICR 17, EAT.

In Hinton v University of East London 2005 ICR 1260, CA, the Court of Appeal considered what is required for an agreement to 'relate to the particular proceedings' for the purposes of S.203(3)(b) ERA. This provision relates to contracting out of the rights conferred by the ERA, but the principles established in that case apply equally to claims compromised under discrimination law. There, H, a lecturer, took voluntary redundancy. In June 2003 he signed a compromise agreement expressed to be 'in full and final settlement of all claims in all jurisdictions', attached to which was a lengthy list of possible claims to be compromised (although H had not, in fact, raised most of them). The list did not include claims under S.47B ERA, which protects employees from being subjected to a detriment because they have made a protected disclosure. This was despite the fact that H had in the past complained to his employer that he had suffered such detriments. In October 2003 H brought tribunal proceedings on the basis of these alleged detriments. The employment tribunal held that the compromise agreement did not prevent H from bringing the proceedings, because it did not specifically cover his complaint. The EAT, however, allowed the employer's appeal. In its view, H's S.47B allegations did not have to be particularised in the agreement to be compromised. The list of claims expressly excluded by the agreement was not intended to be exhaustive, but was merely illustrative of the type of claims covered, and the claim under S.47B was compromised by the general 'full and final settlement of all claims' wording. H appealed to the Court of Appeal.

The Court of Appeal held that, contractually, the compromise agreement was **34.77** wide enough to cover H's S.47B claim. However, it did not comply with the S.203 requirement that it relate to 'particular proceedings'. The 'particular proceedings' intended to be compromised had to be clearly identified, either by a generic description such as 'unfair dismissal' or by reference to the section of the statute giving rise to the claim. It was not sufficient for a compromise agreement to use 'a rolled-up expression such as "all statutory rights"', nor even to identify the proceedings only by reference to the statute under which they arose. In H's case, although from a contractual point of view the wording of the agreement was wide enough to cover his potential S.47B claim, the

1223

agreement had not specifically referred to S.47B, and thus did not 'relate to the particular proceedings' within the meaning of S.203(3)(b). H could therefore proceed with his claim.

34.78 **Compromising future claims.** In Lunt v Merseyside TEC Ltd (above) the EAT stated that Parliament did not intend to permit a blanket compromise agreement compromising claims which had never been raised. Accordingly, a compromise agreement cannot exclude complaints that have not yet arisen – unlike a negotiated settlement arising by way of Acas conciliation in the form of a COT3 (see 'Acas-conciliated settlements' above), a compromise agreement cannot be used to sign away all the employee's rights to bring tribunal claims. It would seem, then, that compromise agreements will be valid only in so far as they settle those complaints that have been raised – as a potential tribunal claim, if not in actual proceedings – by the date of the agreement.

In Hilton UK Hotels Ltd v McNaughton EAT 0059/04 the EAT stated that the Lunt case did not determine that a party cannot contractually compromise a future claim of which he or she has no knowledge. It went on to refer to the case of Royal National Orthopaedic Hospital Trust v Howard 2002 IRLR 849, EAT, which suggested that future claims can be compromised but must be so 'in language which is absolutely clear and leaves no room for doubt as to what it is [the parties] are contracting for'. However, whether the EAT's interpretation of the Lunt case is correct is open to debate, particularly as the Howard case to which the EAT referred was concerned with the scope of COT3 agreements and not with compromise agreements.

34.79 ## Remedies

The general provisions governing remedies for claims under the Equality Act 2010 (EqA) are contained in S.124 EqA. This gives employment tribunals three options (which are not mutually exclusive) when deciding on an appropriate remedy: (i) to make a declaration as to the rights of the complainant and the respondent; (ii) to order the respondent to pay compensation to the complainant; and/or (iii) to make an appropriate recommendation – S.124(2). In this chapter we cover declarations and recommendations. Compensation is dealt with in Chapter 35, 'Compensation: general principles' and Chapter 36, 'Compensation: heads of damage'.

34.80 ### Declarations

By virtue of S.124(2)(a) EqA, an employment tribunal upholding a claim under the Act may make 'a declaration as to the rights of the complainant and the respondent in relation to the matters to which the proceedings relate'. A declaration is simply a statement that the employer has violated the employee's rights – although just how simple a statement it is will depend on how complex the discrimination claim was. It does not require the employer to take any particular action.

A declaration is the appropriate remedy where an employee or job applicant has suffered no loss – although tribunals often make some award for injury to feelings (see Chapter 36, 'Compensation: heads of damage', under 'Injury to feelings') even if there is no direct financial loss as a result of the discrimination.

Three examples:

34.81

- **Berry v GB Electronics Ltd** EAT 0882/00: B, who was profoundly deaf, was made redundant after almost 40 years' service. The EAT held that the method by which he was selected for redundancy and the manner in which he was dismissed amounted to disability discrimination. However, the EAT agreed with the employment tribunal's finding that B would have been selected for redundancy in any event. It was also of the view that it was not the manner of dismissal but the fact that he was greatly hurt and distressed by being dismissed from a job which he had held for almost 40 years at about 20 minutes' notice that most upset B. As a result, the appropriate remedy was to make a declaration that the employer had discriminated against B on the basis of his disability and that the manner of his dismissal was discriminatory 'and to leave it at that'. In reaching its conclusion, the EAT stated that: 'It would be hoped that [the] declaration will make other employers aware of the need for appropriate and sympathetic treatment of other persons suffering from similar types of disability to Mr Berry at the time of their dismissal'

- **Marshall v Governing Body of Langtree Community School and anor** ET Case No.1701005/00: M, the head teacher of a primary school, wanted to reduce her working days from five to three a week following her return to work from maternity leave. She informed her employer that she was unable to return full time due to childcare responsibilities and suggested a job share for her post. The employer rejected the job-share proposal and told her that, due to a recent fall in the school's standards, the position of head teacher could only be performed by one person on a full-time basis. M brought a tribunal claim under the SDA. The employment tribunal found that the employer had indirectly discriminated against M in that it had required the post of head teacher to be undertaken full time, as the proportion of women who could comply with this requirement was considerably smaller than the proportion of men. Furthermore, the employer had not considered whether the post could be undertaken part time and had therefore failed to show that the full-time requirement was justified. Accordingly, the tribunal made a declaration that the condition of five-day working for the post of head teacher was discriminatory and not justifiable

- **Eggington v Jones Dooly (Air Freight) Ltd** ET Case No.516924/95: E brought a claim under the Equal Pay Act 1970 that the employer had unlawfully denied her access to its pension scheme on the ground that she was employed on a part-time basis. The employment tribunal upheld her claim and made a declaration (under the equivalent provision in the Equal Pay Act 1970) that she was entitled to retrospective membership of the employer's occupational pension scheme as from 1 February 1982 to 31 December 1994.

34.82 A declaration is also appropriate where a claimant is only seeking to establish a point of principle. For example, in Meade-Hill and anor v British Council 1995 ICR 847, CA, the Court of Appeal made a declaration that a mobility clause in a contract of employment that required employees of the British Council to serve in such parts of the United Kingdom as the Council required was prima facie unenforceable on the ground of unlawful indirect sex discrimination. More women than men are the secondary earners in their households and consequently a smaller proportion of women than men would be willing or able to move to another part of the country if required to do so.

As mentioned under 'Void and unenforceable terms' above, the EqA contains provisions that render void or unenforceable provisions in collective agreements or rules of undertakings (covering employers, trade unions and qualifications bodies) that constitute, promote or provide for discriminatory treatment that is prohibited by the Act. To this end, S.146(3) EqA provides that an employment tribunal must make a declaration that a term in a collective agreement is void, or a rule of an undertaking is unenforceable, where an employee or would-be employee makes a well-founded claim that such a term or rule would in the future have the effect of discriminating against him or her.

34.83 Recommendations

Section 124(2) EqA states that an employment tribunal 'may... make an appropriate recommendation'. This simplifies and harmonises the provisions in previous discrimination legislation: the DDA provided that a tribunal could recommend that the respondent take, within a specified period, 'reasonable' action to obviate or reduce the adverse effect on the complainant of any matter to which the complaint relates; this differed from the equivalent provisions in the SDA and RRA, which required the action to be 'practicable'.

We anticipate that any circumstance in which a recommendation was made under the antecedent discrimination legislation would also entitle an employment tribunal to make a recommendation under the EqA – the new definition widens, rather than narrows, the scope of the power (of which more below). Five examples of recommendations under the old legislation:

- that an individual who had been sexually harassing the complainant be moved to a post elsewhere within the health authority and that he be suspended until such a move was practicable – Whittington v Morris and anor ET Case No.17846/89

- that an individual who had victimised the complainant contrary to the RRA by putting her application for a post on hold while her race discrimination complaint against a colleague was being investigated be sent for equal opportunities training – London Borough of Southwark v Ayton EAT 0515/03

- that an expired caution and related disciplinary documents, disclosed by the employer's solicitors in preparation for a preliminary hearing of the claimant's race discrimination claim and found to have constituted victimisation under the RRA, be destroyed by the employer and his legal representatives within ten weeks of the promulgation of the decision – Muhammad v Governing Body of Acland Burghley School ET Case No.2204096/03

- that continuity of employment be preserved as far as possible and back-pay given in the case of an employee who was re-engaged after resigning because his supervisor had racially insulted him – Savage v Liverpool City Council ET Case No.35225/86

- that the employment tribunal's liability and remedy judgments should be circulated to, and read and digested by, each member of the respondent school's governing board; that the school should secure the services of an appropriately qualified HR professional to conduct a review of its existing equality, disciplinary, grievance and recruitment policies and procedures, and amend or redraft them as necessary to ensure compliance with UK employment law; and that the school should undertake a programme of formal equality and diversity training on, among other things, recruitment and selection procedures, beginning with the governing board and highest management levels and 'cascading' down through the entire organisation – Lycée Français Charles de Gaulle v Delambre EAT 0563/10.

34.84 In sex and race discrimination cases, it was established that tribunals could not use the power to make recommendations as a way of requiring employers to engage in positive discrimination; for example, by making a recommendation that the applicant be offered the next available job (see North West Thames Regional Health Authority v Noone 1988 ICR 813, CA). However, in disability discrimination cases the duty to make reasonable adjustments may require the employer to treat the disabled person more favourably – see Archibald v Fife Council 2004 ICR 954, HL, considered in Chapter 21, 'Failure to make reasonable adjustments', under 'Common types of adjustment – redeployment'.

The major change introduced by the EqA in relation to recommendations is contained in S.124(3) EqA. Under previous discrimination legislation, tribunals could only make recommendations 'for the purpose of obviating or reducing the adverse effect on the complainant' – see, for example, S.17A(2)(c) DDA and

S.65(1)(c) SDA. So, a tribunal might make a recommendation that the employer organise equal opportunities training for senior employees. However, if the claimant had already left the organisation, then any such recommendation would not do anything at all for the claimant, and so such a recommendation could not be made.

34.85 In its response to consultation on the Equality Bill in July 2008, the Government recognised that 'around 70 per cent of employees involved in discrimination cases leave the organisation' and as a result this restriction on recommendations limited the power of tribunals to make recommendations that could prevent discrimination in that workplace in the future. To address this the EqA widens the scope for tribunals to make recommendations that will benefit the wider workforce and help to prevent future discrimination. An 'appropriate recommendation' is thus defined under S.124(3) as one for the purpose of obviating or reducing the adverse effect on the complainant or 'on any other person' of any matter to which the proceedings relate. The Explanatory Notes suggest that tribunals can now make recommendations such as that the employer publish selection criteria for promotion, improve harassment policy, or retrain staff, regardless of whether the complainant is still employed – para 406. (Stop press: the Government is consulting on repealing S.124(3) – see Introduction to this Handbook.)

However, the EqA does not appear to set out an enforcement mechanism for this more general power. Where a tribunal makes an appropriate recommendation that relates to the claimant, then S.124(7) provides that if the employer fails, without reasonable excuse, to comply with that recommendation, the tribunal can order an increase in compensation or, if no compensation was originally ordered, can order compensation to be paid. But this section only applies where the recommendation relates to the claimant, so where the recommendation relates to 'any other person' there would appear to be no way of enforcing it if the employer fails to comply.

34.86 Note that with regard to national security proceedings, the power to make recommendations affecting a person other than the claimant is restricted. S.125 EqA prohibits such recommendations if they would affect anything done by the Security Service, Secret Intelligence Service, Government Communications Headquarters (GCHQ) or a part of the armed forces that is assisting GCHQ. In such cases, recommendations by tribunals are limited to those that benefit the claimant.

In cases of indirect discrimination contrary to S.19 EqA, where discrimination in the application of a provision, criterion or practice was not intended to discriminate against the claimant, a tribunal can only order compensation once it has considered whether to make a declaration or recommendation – S.124(5).

In a case decided under the old provisions in the SDA, the Court of Appeal held that a tribunal's power to make a recommendation does not include the power to recommend that an employee's pay be increased. Future loss of wages should be covered by an award of compensation where appropriate – Irvine v Prestcold Ltd 1981 ICR 777, CA.

Costs

34.87

The 2004 Rules of Procedure made significant changes to the costs regime in employment tribunals. Historically, costs have rarely been awarded in employment cases. However, when the 2001 Rules came into force, rule 14(3) increased the maximum sum of unassessed costs that a tribunal has power to award from £500 to £10,000 (a limit maintained in the 2004 Rules at rule 41(1)) and this change has inevitably led to an increase in the average level of costs awards made by tribunals.

Tribunals have a discretion under rule 40 to award costs in whole or in part in any of the following circumstances:

- where a party has caused a hearing or a pre-hearing review to be postponed or adjourned

- where a party has failed to comply with an order or a practice direction

- where a party has acted 'vexatiously, abusively, disruptively or otherwise unreasonably' in bringing the proceedings

- where a party or a party's representative has acted 'vexatiously, abusively, disruptively or otherwise unreasonably' in conducting the proceedings

- where the bringing or conducting of the proceedings by a party has been misconceived.

The 2004 Rules introduced a power for tribunals to take into account the **34.88** parties' ability to pay when making an award under any of the above heads – rule 41(2). They also gave tribunals a new power to make preparation time orders in favour of unrepresented litigants in respect of their preparation time for a hearing. The calculation of such an order is based on evidence provided by the receiving party and the tribunal's assessment of what is a reasonable and proportionate amount of time to spend on preparatory work, having regard to matters such as the complexity of the proceedings and the number of witnesses and documentation required. That time is multiplied by an hourly rate set by rule 45(2), which increases by £1 on 6 April each year – as of 6 April 2012, the rate is £32 per hour.

The bringing or conducting of proceedings will be regarded as 'misconceived' for the purpose of rule 40 if the claim has no reasonable prospect of success. However, the EAT has recognised the difficulty faced by claimants in providing evidence, particularly in discrimination cases that rely on the drawing of inferences, and tribunals should take this difficulty into account before awarding costs in a discrimination claim on the basis that the claimant brought a hopeless case – see, for example, Jackson v East Sussex County Council EAT 1377/99.

The rules operating in the EAT are more or less in line with those in the employment tribunals. The costs regime in both the tribunals and the EAT is discussed in detail in IDS Employment Law Handbook, 'Employment Tribunal Practice and Procedure' (2006), Chapter 18.

34.89 Judicial review

Section 113(3)(a) EqA allows for a discrimination complaint to be advanced in the High Court by way of judicial review proceedings in appropriate cases. In addition, S.30 of the Equality Act 2006 expressly provides the Equality and Human Rights Commission (EHRC) with power to bring judicial review proceedings where they are relevant to a matter in connection with which the EHRC has a function (see Chapter 37, 'Equality and Human Rights Commission').

Judicial review proceedings are governed by Part 54 of the Civil Procedure Rules and can only proceed with the permission of the court – rule 54.4. Rule 54.5 requires a claim for judicial review to be filed 'promptly' and 'in any event not later than three months after the grounds to make the claim first arose'.

34.90 Since judicial review is a public law remedy, there must be some public law element to the claim. The High Court has held that judicial review is not an appropriate remedy for enforcing an employer's obligations to its employees – R v British Broadcasting Corporation ex parte Lavelle 1983 ICR 99, QBD. For example, in R v Derbyshire County Council ex parte Noble 1990 ICR 808, CA, a deputy police surgeon sought to challenge his dismissal. He applied for judicial review seeking an order quashing the decision to terminate his employment and a mandatory order seeking reinstatement. The Court of Appeal, upholding the Divisional Court below, held that there was not a sufficient public element to allow judicial review. The claimant's claim arose out of the termination of his private contract for services and did not relate to a breach of public duty by the Council in the exercise of its powers. In deciding to terminate his contract, the Council was not exercising a public function or performing a public duty.

Judicial review is, however, an appropriate forum for a court to determine whether a public body has complied with the public sector equality duty provided for in S.149 EqA (public sector equality duties are considered in Chapter 38, 'General public sector equality duty', and Chapter 39, 'Specific public sector equality duties').

In McLaren v Home Office 1990 ICR 824, CA, the Court of Appeal gave the **34.91** following guidance on the principles governing whether or not a public sector employee or office holder should bring proceedings by way of judicial review:

- where the complaint is in the nature of a personal claim against the employer, a public sector employee's position will normally be the same as that of any other employee. Judicial review will not be appropriate and the employee should bring proceedings for compensation and/or any other private law remedy in the normal way

- judicial review is available where a public sector employee seeks to challenge the decision of a disciplinary or other body set up under statute or the royal prerogative to determine disputes affecting his or her employment

- judicial review is appropriate where a public sector employee is adversely affected by a decision of general application by his or her employer (e.g. the policy of discharging lesbians and gay men from the armed forces – R v Ministry of Defence ex parte Smith and ors 1996 ICR 740, CA)

- where a disciplinary procedure is of a purely domestic nature, judicial review will not be available, even if the outcome of the procedure affects the public.

The grounds on which it is appropriate for a party to challenge a public body's **34.92** action by way of judicial review were categorised by the House of Lords in Council of Civil Service Unions and ors v Minister for the Civil Service 1985 ICR 14, HL, as 'illegality', 'irrationality' and 'procedural impropriety'. However, Lord Diplock acknowledged that further grounds may be added as case law develops, and his Lordship envisaged in particular that 'proportionality' may become one of them.

The specific remedies available on a successful application for judicial review are:

- a mandatory order (formerly known as 'mandamus') requiring the public body to carry out its legal duties

- a prohibiting order, restraining the public body from acting beyond its powers, and

- a quashing order (formerly 'certiorari'), quashing the decision of the public body.

In addition, claimants may also be able to claim the general remedies of a **34.93** declaration, stay or injunction, and damages. S.31(2) of the Senior Courts Act 1981 (formerly known as the Supreme Courts Act 1981) sets out the circumstances in which the court may grant a declaration or injunction in a claim for judicial review. Damages, restitution or the recovery of a sum due can only be sought if another remedy is also sought. S.31(4) of the 1981 Act sets out the circumstances in which they may be awarded. Where provisions in

1231

a domestic statute are challenged on the grounds that they are incompatible with European equal treatment law, the EHRC is the appropriate party to initiate judicial review proceedings, rather than an individual or individuals. In R v Secretary of State for Employment ex parte Equal Opportunities Commission and anor 1994 ICR 317, HL, the House of Lords held that the EOC's duty to 'work towards the elimination of discrimination' and 'to promote equality of opportunity between men and women generally' (now part of the EHRC's duties) gave it locus standi (i.e. standing) to bring proceedings challenging the compatibility with EU law of the longer service qualification required of part-time employees who brought claims of unfair dismissal. Their Lordships went on to hold that judicial review was not appropriate for an individual employee, who should instead pursue her case in an employment tribunal where her claims under the EU Equal Treatment Directive (No.2002/73) and EU Equal Pay Directive (No.75/117) (now consolidated into the recast Equal Treatment Directive (No.2006/54)) were directly enforceable against her public sector employer.

The potential impact of judicial review proceedings on discrimination legislation is ably demonstrated by R (Equal Opportunities Commission) v Secretary of State for Trade and Industry 2007 ICR 1234, QBD. There the EOC – shortly before its demise and replacement by the EHRC – successfully challenged the United Kingdom's implementation of various provisions of the EU Equal Treatment Amendment Directive (No.2002/73) relating to the rights to bring claims for harassment and for discrimination on the grounds of pregnancy or maternity leave. As a result, the High Court held that the Government would have to recast the relevant provisions of the SDA in order to remedy the situation. The changes were eventually effected by the Sex Discrimination Act 1975 (Amendment) Regulations 2008 SI 2008/656 – the provisions of which are now consolidated into the EqA.

34.94 Striking-out claims

Under Rule 18(7)(b) of the Rules of Procedure, an employment judge or tribunal may make an order at a pre-hearing review, striking out or amending all or any part of a claim or response on the ground that it is scandalous, vexatious or has no reasonable prospect of success. A full discussion of this power can be found in IDS Employment Law Handbook, 'Employment Tribunal Practice and Procedure' (2006), Chapter 8, 'Case management'. It is, however, worth noting here that special considerations arise if a tribunal is asked to strike out a claim of discrimination.

In Anyanwu and anor v South Bank Students' Union & anor 2001 ICR 391, HL, their Lordships held that it is a matter of public interest that discrimination cases are not struck out unless it is obvious that they will not succeed. The questions of law that require determination in discrimination cases are often highly fact-sensitive. It is important, in order to minimise the risk of injustice in such cases, that they proceed to trial so that the facts can be established. Subsequently, in Ezsias v North Glamorgan NHS Trust 2007 ICR 1126, CA, the Court of Appeal held that the same or a similar approach should generally inform whistleblowing cases, which have much in common with discrimination cases, in that they involve an investigation into why an employer took a particular step. The Court stressed that it will only be in an exceptional case that an application will be struck out as having no reasonable prospect of success when the central facts are in dispute. An example might be where the facts sought to be established by the applicant are totally and inexplicably inconsistent with the undisputed contemporaneous documentation.

In Shestak v Royal College of Nursing and ors EAT 0270/08 the claimant **34.95** appealed against the decision to strike out a multitude of claims arising out of the termination of her trainee nursing placement. Upholding the tribunal's decision, the EAT held that undisputed documentary evidence – in the form of e-mails which could not, taken at their highest, support the claimant's interpretation of events – justified a departure from the usual approach that discrimination claims should not be struck out at a preliminary stage. However, it should not be assumed that a wealth of documentary evidence will warrant a strike-out order. In A v B and anor, 2011 ICR D9, CA, the claimant alleged that she was unfairly dismissed, victimised and subjected to sex discrimination following her allegation of sexual assault against a senior colleague. During the grievance process, it emerged that the claimant had falsified her academic qualifications, and the employer sought to rely on the false qualifications when making an application to strike out the unfair dismissal claim that was before an employment tribunal. The tribunal struck out the claim, but the Court of Appeal held that it had been wrong to do so. Given the shifting burden of proof rule that applies to claims under the SDA (and now to the EqA), the Court considered that there was a 'more than fanciful' chance that the employer would be required to prove that the dismissal was not on grounds that would constitute unlawful discrimination.

35 Compensation: general principles

General principles of assessment

Awards against individuals and co-respondents

As we discuss in Chapter 34, 'Enforcing individual rights', there is a variety of **35.1** orders that an employment tribunal may make if it finds a claim of discrimination proved. The most commonly requested of these is an order requiring the respondent to pay compensation to the complainant. The amount of compensation available corresponds to the damages that could be ordered by a county court in England and Wales for a claim in tort, or by a sheriff court in Scotland in proceedings for reparation – S.124(2)(b) and (6) combined with S.119(2) and (3) of the Equality Act 2010 (EqA). This means that there is no upper limit on the amount of compensation that can be awarded for discrimination, unlike, for example, compensation for unfair dismissal.

In this chapter we look at some of the general principles that govern tribunals' discretion in deciding whether to order compensation, and the appropriate amount. We consider first some of the basic rules that define when an order of compensation may be made. We then look at some of the adjustments to compensation that tribunals may be required to make, either by statute or to reflect the circumstances of the case. Finally, we consider the scope for tribunals to order individual employees, rather than or in addition to employers, to pay compensation to a successful claimant.

The specific heads under which compensation is awarded, such as financial loss **35.2** and injury to feelings, are considered separately in Chapter 36, 'Compensation: heads of damage'. That chapter also deals with the specific adjustments and reductions that only apply to certain heads of compensation, such as deductions for accelerated receipt or failure to mitigate loss. Chapter 36 also covers the issues of interest on awards of compensation and taxation.

General principles of assessment
35.3

As noted in Chapter 34, 'Enforcing individual rights', there are three remedies that an employment tribunal can order once it has found discrimination proved: a declaration, a recommendation and compensation. Under the discrimination legislation in force before the Equality Act 2010 took effect, there was a slight restriction on tribunals' freedom to decide which remedy or remedies to order. The compensation provisions of the antecedent discrimination legislation – S.65

1235

of the Sex Discrimination Act 1975 (SDA) was typical in this regard – stated that, once a tribunal had decided that a complaint was well founded, it 'shall make such of the following as it considers just and equitable', going on to list the range of orders discussed in Chapter 34. Accordingly, whether a tribunal could order compensation at all depended on whether the tribunal thought it would be 'just and equitable' to do so.

Under S.124 EqA, which is the replacement for S.65 SDA and its equivalent provisions in the other antecedent equality legislation, there is no such reference to justice and equity. S.124(2) states simply that if a tribunal upholds a discrimination claim, it '*may* (a) make a declaration as to the rights of the complainant and the respondent in relation to the matters to which the proceedings relate; (b) order the respondent to pay compensation to the complainant; (c) make an appropriate recommendation' (our stress). S.124(6) retains the stipulation found in the previous equality legislation that the amount of compensation which may be awarded under subsection (2)(b) corresponds to the amount which could be awarded by a county court or the sheriff. But there is no longer any express restriction on when a tribunal, having found discrimination proved, may award compensation. In other words, it may order compensation *regardless* of whether it thinks it just and equitable to do so, at least on the straight wording of the Act.

35.4 It must be asked, then, whether this change of wording will make any difference in practice. The answer is almost certainly 'no'. The principal rationale for this is that, in practice, it was rare for a tribunal to refuse to award compensation on the basis that it would not be 'just and equitable' under the pre-EqA regime. If compensation was sought in respect of some provable loss, it was generally given, unless there were exceptional circumstances. Three examples of where such exceptional circumstances were found to exist:

- **Chief Constable of Greater Manchester Police and anor v Hope** 1999 ICR 338, EAT: the claimant was a white male police sergeant who formed a brief sexual relationship with a 17-year-old Asian female civilian trainee. He was served with a disciplinary notice alleging that the relationship might have compromised his authority. He successfully claimed that the questioning to which his employer subjected him amounted to both race and sex discrimination. But the EAT overturned the tribunal's finding that the claimant had suffered injury to his feelings and should be awarded compensation of £750. It held that although the police force's justifications for questioning the claimant as it did could not defend it against the claim of direct discrimination, they could be relevant to the issue of remedy. To award a remedy in a case where the claimant's behaviour was 'unattractive' was, in the EAT's view, 'fundamentally wrong' and a result that would not have been intended by Parliament. It should be noted, however, that the judicial member of the EAT, His Honour Judge Peter Clark, dissented from the majority view in this case. In his opinion, the employment tribunal 'permissibly considered and rejected the option of declining to make any award of compensation on the ground that it was just and equitable not to do so', particularly in the light of the tribunal's finding that the claimant did in fact suffer injury to his feelings as a result of the discriminatory questioning. In HHJ Clark's view, the tribunal's award of £750 could not be said to be perverse

- **Smith v Trico Products Ltd** ET Case Nos.3300107/01 and another: the employment tribunal concluded that the claimant had been subjected to race discrimination but it also made a number of adverse findings about his behaviour at work, including that he would touch people in an offensive way; would read sex magazines in the canteen and play with himself; and would deny making mistakes and allege that others were sabotaging his work. In the circumstances, the tribunal came to the unusual conclusion that it would not be just and equitable to award S compensation and instead made a number of recommendations to assist the company in the future to ensure equality of opportunity

- **Smith v The George Hotel and ors** ET Case No.2704562/10: S worked as a hotel cleaner. She suffered from asthma and cold urticaria. Her employer became concerned about two issues – that S was wearing a fleece over her uniform, and that she left various apparatus and medication that she needed on a trolley in a corridor. The employer raised with her the issue of the medication and S agreed to keep it in a room used only by staff. When the employer also raised the issue of the fleece, saying it was not appropriate for S to wear it when she was cleaning hotel rooms and bathrooms, S simply commented that she had to live with the condition for the rest of her life. She did not tell the employer that she took off the fleece while she was cleaning, as she later claimed. The employer decided to terminate S's employment, primarily because of the fleece. An employment tribunal found that S's dismissal was unlawful disability discrimination, but concluded that she had engineered her dismissal by leading the employer to think that she had to wear the fleece at all times with a view to pursuing a claim under the Disability Discrimination Act 1995. She did not act in good faith and therefore it was not just or equitable to make any award of compensation.

The facts of these cases are fairly unusual and there are few other examples **35.5** of tribunals finding that it would not be just and equitable to award compensation. Accordingly, even though S.124 EqA is, on a straight reading, less restrictive than the previous provisions under which tribunals could award compensation, little practical difference can be expected given that the old restrictions were rarely applied. The Explanatory Notes to the EqA do not indicate any intention to change the scope of tribunals' power to award compensation for discrimination – para 414 states that the intention behind S.124 is 'generally to replicate the effect of provisions in previous legislation'.

The question might arise whether, now that tribunals are not enjoined to consider whether it is 'just and equitable' to make an order for compensation, they will be precluded from reducing quantum to the point of extinguishing an award of compensation altogether in circumstances where previously they felt able to do this under the 'just and equitable' formula. The reality is that there are several reasons why an employment tribunal may make an award of compensation but reduce it to reflect the circumstances in which a particular loss arose. For example, it might find 'contributory conduct' where the claimant's actions have partially caused or aggravated the effects of the discrimination, which may lead to a proportionate reduction in compensation. In exceptional circumstances, such conduct might even merit a reduction of compensation to nil. In our view, nothing in the change of wording to tribunals' powers regarding remedy prevents such a course of action continuing to be adopted in an appropriate case. There is arguably little difference in practice between contributory conduct and conduct that makes an award of compensation 'not just and equitable'. We consider this in more detail under 'Contributory conduct' below.

35.6 Unintentional indirect discrimination

Between direct and indirect discrimination, indirect discrimination is commonly seen as the lesser of the two evils. Whereas direct discrimination, as defined by S.13 EqA, occurs only if the employer was motivated (consciously or subconsciously) to treat the claimant less favourably because of a protected characteristic, indirect discrimination, as defined by S.19, occurs where an employer's ostensibly neutral practices have an adverse effect on a group sharing a common characteristic. In other words, while direct discrimination requires some causative link with the protected characteristic, indirect discrimination may arise unexpectedly and unintentionally. This distinction has been reflected, to a limited extent, in the kinds of remedy available for each.

The Race Relations Act 1976 (RRA) used to provide a wide-ranging exemption from liability for compensation in cases of unintentional indirect discrimination. S.57(3) RRA provided that, in an indirect discrimination case, the employment tribunal could make no award of damages if the employer proved that the policy that gave rise to the indirect discrimination 'was not applied with the intention of treating the claimant unfavourably on racial grounds'. Since 19 July 2003, this limitation applied only in respect of race discrimination on the grounds of colour or nationality (and not discrimination on the grounds of race, ethnic or national origins), following amendments made by the Race Relations Act 1976 (Amendment) Regulations 2003 SI 2003/1626. Similar provision was made until 2001 in respect of indirect sex discrimination and indirect marital status discrimination by S.66(3) of the SDA. In JH Walker Ltd v Hussain 1996 ICR 291, EAT (a race discrimination case), the EAT clarified what was meant by 'intention' in this context. In that case the employer's policy of not allowing any holiday to be taken during a period that encompassed the Muslim festival of Eid had been found to indirectly discriminate against Asian employees, and the discrimination was found by an employment tribunal not to be objectively justified. On appeal, the EAT held that the employer could not rely on S.57(3) because it knew about the adverse effect of its policy on its Muslim employees. The EAT stated that 'intention' here refers to the employer's state of mind with regard to the consequences of his actions. So, the relevant intention would be present if, at the time the act complained of was done, the employer (a) wanted to bring about a state of affairs that constituted the prohibited result of unfavourable treatment on racial grounds, and (b) knew that that prohibited result would follow. Thus, although the employer introduced the policy for genuine business reasons, and not as the result of any animus towards employees of a particular race, its decision to apply the policy regardless of the detriment it knew it would cause meant that it had applied the policy with the intention of treating the complainants unfavourably on racial grounds.

This explanation was helpful, in that it made it clear that intention to treat a **35.7** claimant unfavourably on racial grounds, for the purpose of old S.57(3) RRA, was something distinct from direct race discrimination. However, in shifting the focus from 'intention' to 'knowledge', the EAT inadvertently raised new problematic questions. For a start, was actual knowledge required, or would constructive knowledge suffice? If actual knowledge was required, then an employer who did not even consider the potentially discriminatory impact of a new policy would arguably be in a better position than one who consulted and made a considered decision, since only the latter employer would actually 'know' of a policy's discriminatory effect. This would be a counter-intuitive outcome, which tends to suggest that constructive knowledge must have been intended to be covered by the use of word 'intention' in the previous equality legislation – in other words, if an employer reasonably ought to have known of the unfavourable outcome, then he might be deemed to have intended it. However, this interpretation was expressly doubted by the Court of Appeal in British Medical Association v Chaudhary 2007 IRLR 800, CA, albeit in obiter dicta, the appeal having been decided on other grounds. The employment tribunal in that case had found that the BMA was 'at best reckless' as to the indirectly discriminatory impact of its policy of not providing legal assistance in discrimination claims brought by its members against the Royal College of Surgeons. The tribunal stated that the BMA knew, had it 'cared to consider it', that the policy had a disproportionate adverse effect on its Asian members. In the Court of Appeal, Lord Justice Mummery doubted whether the tribunal was correct to equate turning a blind eye with actual knowledge. In his view, S.57(3) RRA required 'actual knowledge or conscious realisation' on the employer's

1239

part that a policy would have a disparate impact on one racial group, and that he positively wished it to have that effect. Mummery LJ went on to suggest that showing lack of intention under S.57(3) should be a lower hurdle for a respondent to clear than rebutting a claim of direct discrimination.

It was also unclear from the EAT's decision in Hussain whether the employer was expected to know just that the unfavourable outcome would result, or whether he had to know that the unfavourable outcome would result *and that the outcome was prohibited*. Limb (b) of the test was that the employer knew that the 'prohibited result' would follow. This suggested that the employer must have known that the result would actually be prohibited – i.e. that the indirect discrimination was not objectively justified. So, an employer who properly consulted on a policy, considered its necessity, and weighed his business reasons against the policy's impact on employees, might reasonably argue that, although he knew of the impact that would result, he reasonably believed that the impact was justified and so he did not *know* that it was prohibited.

35.8 It can be seen that this approach resulted in a potentially confusing blurring of the boundary between direct and indirect discrimination. From a purely practical point of view, then, it is fortunate that the approach was abandoned for most forms of race discrimination in 2003, and sex and marital status discrimination in 2001, and that the religion or belief, sexual orientation and age discrimination legislation that followed in 2003 and 2006 did not adopt it. Having said that, the compensation provisions contained within the antecedent equality legislation continued to gesture towards the 'no fault' perception of indirect discrimination in another way. This was because they provided that, in cases of indirect discrimination, if the tribunal were to be satisfied that the discriminatory effect of the relevant policy or practice was unintentional, then it would first have to consider whether to make a declaration or recommendation before deciding whether to order compensation. It would also have to consider whether it was just and equitable to make an award of compensation on top of any declaration and/or recommendation. The wording of the Employment Equality (Age) Regulations 2006 SI 2006/1031 was typical in this regard. Reg 38(2) provided that, if the respondent proved that the unfavourable treatment resulting from indirect discrimination was unintentional, the tribunal could only award compensation if it 'makes such order under paragraph (1)(a) (if any) and such recommendation under paragraph (1)(c) (if any) as it would have made if it had no power [to award compensation]; and (where it makes an order under paragraph (1)(a) or a recommendation under paragraph (1)(c) or both) considers that it is just and equitable to [award compensation] as well'. Accordingly, in cases of unintentional indirect discrimination, the tribunal was required to think again about whether compensation would be just and equitable before making an award.

This restriction on tribunals' ability to award compensation in indirect discrimination cases has now been significantly watered down by the EqA, although the notion of whether an employer intended to indirectly discriminate has not been abandoned altogether. The relevant provisions are now to be found in S.124(4) and (5). These provide that if the tribunal '(a) finds that a contravention is established by virtue of S.19 [indirect discrimination], but (b) is satisfied that the provision, criterion or practice was not applied with the intention of discriminating against the complainant' (S.124(4)), then it 'must not make an order under subsection (2)(b) [compensation] unless it first considers whether to act under subsection (2)(a) [declaration] or (c) [recommendation]' – (S.124(5)). Thus, the tribunal no longer has to consider whether compensation, in addition to any declaration or recommendation, would be just and equitable. It merely has to consider a declaration and/or recommendation first.

35.9 The EqA retains the focus on 'intention' found in the earlier provisions, the meaning of which must still be informed by the EAT's decision in the Hussain case (above). Although the Equality and Human Rights Commission's Code of Practice on Employment ('the EHRC Employment Code') does not refer to Hussain, its guidance at para 15.45 on when 'intention' will be established is clearly inspired by the EAT's decision in that it stipulates: 'Indirect discrimination will be intentional where the respondent knew that certain consequences would follow from their actions and they wanted those consequences to follow. A motive, for example, of promoting business efficiency, does not mean that the act of indirect discrimination is unintentional.' Like the EAT in Hussain, the EHRC Employment Code thus takes the view that absence of discriminatory motive is not sufficient to prove absence of the relevant intention, and so the standard of proof on the employer is still relatively high. Given that proof of absence of intention no longer prevents a tribunal awarding compensation, nor even requires the tribunal to consider the justice and equity of making such an award, there seems little incentive on employers to invoke S.124(5) as a means of escaping liability to pay any compensation for proven indirect discrimination. Only if the tribunal has failed to consider a declaration or recommendation might the employer wish to rely on this provision, and even then, there is nothing to stop a tribunal reaffirming an award of compensation once it has gone through the formality of considering the alternatives.

Note that, although the burden of proving that the indirect discrimination was not intentional is not explicitly placed on the employer, an employer who wishes to rely on this section would be wise to raise the argument itself. Although it is open to a tribunal to consider whether there was an intention to discriminate, it would appear that it is not incumbent upon the tribunal to consider the question of its own motion – see Whitbread Walker Ltd v Jones EAT 1084/99 (a sex discrimination case).

35.10 Causation

As stated above, if an employment tribunal decides to award compensation, then it must be calculated in the same way as damages in tort (or in proceedings for reparation in Scotland) – S.124(6) in combination with S.119(2)(a) and (3)(a) EqA. The aim, as the EAT put it in Ministry of Defence v Cannock and ors 1994 ICR 918, EAT (a sex discrimination case), is that 'as best as money can do it, the applicant must be put into the position she [or he] would have been in *but for* the unlawful conduct' (our stress).

This means that tribunals must ascertain the position that the claimant would have been in had the discrimination not occurred. Another way of looking at it is to ask what loss has been caused by the discrimination in question. This principle can work for or against a claimant. For example, if a claimant is selected for redundancy for a disability-related reason, but it is established that he or she would have been selected for redundancy in any event, then he or she cannot recover for any financial loss flowing from the dismissal. He or she will, however, be able to claim for any injury to feelings caused by the treatment and, in exceptional cases where psychiatric illness results, damages for personal injury. Similar considerations apply when the discrimination relates to recruitment in circumstances where the tribunal considers that the claimant would not have got the job even if he or she had not been discriminated against. An example:

- **Greig v Initial Security Ltd** EATS 0036/05: G applied for a job as a security guard in May 2004. He stated on his application form that he had not worked since 1980, and that he suffered from depression. There was no indication on the form that he had any relevant experience and he was rejected without interview. When pressed for reasons, the respondent stated, among other things, that the nature of the job would not be suited to him because of his long-term depression. This was found to be direct discrimination on the ground of disability. However, the employment tribunal refused to award any compensation for financial loss, as there was little likelihood that the claimant would have been successful in his application, even if there had been no discrimination. He was nevertheless awarded £500 for injury to feelings. This relatively low sum was upheld on appeal by the EAT, which noted that the tribunal had found that the job application was not made 'wholly in good faith'.

35.11 Given that the issue of causation entails tribunals speculating about what would have happened, they may be required to consider many unpredictable factors. In Brash-Hall v Getty Images Ltd 2006 EWCA Civ 531, CA (a sex discrimination case), for example, B-H resigned while on maternity leave in August 2003 in circumstances that amounted to constructive dismissal and sex discrimination. However, in October GI Ltd undertook a genuine restructuring exercise and wrote to B-H offering her a choice of two posts or, in the event that she did not want to take up either, redundancy with enhanced severance pay. When an employment tribunal came to assess compensation for sex discrimination it found that B-H would have returned to work in August but only until the end of October, at which point she would have refused an alternative job offered under the restructuring and left. It further held that the job offered would have constituted suitable employment and that B-H's refusal would have been unreasonable, so she would not have been entitled to a statutory redundancy payment. The EAT rejected her appeal but the Court of Appeal allowed it in part. The Court accepted that B-H would have been offered the same redundancy package but did not think she would have been entitled to the enhanced severance pay contained in that offer, since it would have been conditional upon her signing a compromise agreement. Since B-H had neither proved nor sought to prove that she would have agreed to that, she was not entitled to the payment. She was, however, entitled to the first element of the severance package – the three months' pay in lieu of notice – as this was the basic minimum to which she was entitled under her contract of employment and was not conditional upon her signing the severance agreement.

35.12 Consideration of all these issues may require the tribunal to undertake quite strenuous mental gymnastics. The case of Ahsan v Labour Party EAT 0211/10 is a good illustration of this. It entailed consideration of the remedy for unlawful discrimination by a 'qualifying body' under S.12 of the Race Relations Act 1976 (RRA) (now Ss.53 and 54 EqA). The qualifying body in question was the Labour Party and the claimant sought compensation for its discriminatory actions between 1998 and 2000 that prevented him being selected as the Party's candidate to stand in local council elections. It was accepted by both sides before the employment tribunal that, if selected by the Party, the claimant would have gone on to be elected, and the tribunal accordingly awarded financial loss in respect of the allowances he would have received as a councillor between 1998 and 2004, at which point his term of office would have expired. However, for the period from 2004–08, the tribunal awarded only 25 per cent of the allowances usually paid to a councillor on the basis that there was only a 50 per cent chance that disciplinary proceedings taken against him in 2002 would not have prevented his standing again in 2004, and then only a 50 per cent chance that he would have succeeded in the election.

On appeal, the EAT overturned the award made in respect of 2004 onwards. The employment tribunal had failed to take into account that, by 2004, the claimant had been expelled from the Labour Party. The EAT thought it arguable that a candidate who failed to achieve selection in, say, year 5 as a result of a wrongful non-selection in year 1 could claim that that failure, and any financial consequences, were direct and natural consequences of the original wrong. However, it did not consider that the claimant here could establish the necessary causal link. He had an arguable case that his expulsion was the result of further discrimination by the Party, but since he had not lodged proceedings in respect

1243

of that alleged discrimination it could not be compensated as part of his current claim, which was concerned only with the acts of discrimination in the period 1998–2000. The claimant was in effect seeking to claim for the consequences of damage that might have caused loss in different circumstances, but did not do so in the events that actually happened.

35.13 It is worth noting that, in the course of argument in the Ahsan case, the claimant also sought to draw an analogy with the hypothetical case of an employee on a fixed-term contract who is discriminatorily dismissed. He argued that such a claimant would be entitled to compensation not only for earnings lost under that contract but also in subsequent contracts, if and to the extent that there was a chance that the original fixed-term contract would be renewed. The EAT did not expressly address this point but it must be thought worth exploring in cases involving discriminatory termination of a fixed-term contract.

The question of what loss is caused by a particular act of discrimination is very closely related to the question, in a discriminatory dismissal case, of whether the employee could or would been fairly dismissed were it not for the discrimination. This particular point, which is relevant to the assessment of future loss, is considered in detail in Chapter 36, 'Compensation: heads of damage', under 'Future loss – chance of non-discriminatory dismissal'.

35.14 **Breaking the chain of causation.** Certain events are said to 'break the chain of causation' – that is, a new cause or event 'takes over' as the cause of the claimant's loss. Case law on the tort of negligence commonly refers to a 'novus actus interveniens', i.e. a new intervening act. So, for example, in Horton v Taplin Contracts Ltd 2003 ICR 179, CA, an employer's arguable breach of statutory duty in failing to fit a tower scaffold with stabilisers was overtaken by the liability of an employee who deliberately toppled it over. The claimant, another employee who was working on the scaffold at the time, sought to recover compensation from the employer on the basis that the scaffold did not comply with health and safety regulations. The Court of Appeal did not accept that there was a breach, still less that any breach actually caused the claimant's injury, but held that, in any event, the employee's deliberate and unpredictable actions in toppling over the scaffold constituted a new intervening act, breaking the chain of causation.

This issue is less straightforward when the original liability and the event said to be a novus actus are closely related. In Bullimore v Pothecary Witham Weld and anor (No.2) 2011 IRLR 18, EAT, B successfully claimed for victimisation against PWW after it provided a negative reference to S, a company to which B later applied for a job. The negative reference mentioned tribunal proceedings that B had brought against PWW. On receipt of the reference, S withdrew the job offer it had made to B. The employment tribunal had no difficulty finding that the giving of the reference in these terms by PWW was an act of unlawful victimisation, but did not think that it should be liable to B for loss of earnings occasioned by S's withdrawal of the job offer. The tribunal found that S undoubtedly withdrew the offer because it did not want to employ a troublemaker, which was itself an act of unlawful victimisation. The tribunal took the view that S, of its own free choice, acted wrongfully and illegally, in a manner that would not be expected of a company in its position (a law firm). This meant that the withdrawal of the job offer was neither a foreseeable nor a natural consequence of PWW's original act of victimisation – in other words, the chain of causation had been broken. On appeal, the EAT disagreed with this analysis. It thought that it was entirely foreseeable that S might react to the reference provided by PWW in the way that it did. This was therefore a direct and natural consequence of PWW's unlawful act. The EAT went on to note that, as a matter of policy and fairness, PWW plainly ought to be liable. It would be unsatisfactory if a claimant who lost the opportunity of employment as the result of such a reference were unable to recover damages from the person giving it, especially as a remedy against the recipient of the reference would not always be available.

The Bullimore case indicates that another person's wrongful act will not **35.15** necessarily break the chain of causation. It is also clear that the liable employer's own wrongful act will not break the chain of causation. So, an employer cannot rely on its own wrongful act to limit the damages that would otherwise flow from its earlier act of discrimination. This point is underpinned by the decision in Prison Service v Beart (No.2) 2005 ICR 1206, CA. In that case the Prison Service discriminated against B on the ground of disability and then unfairly dismissed her. At the remedies hearing it argued that the unfair dismissal broke the chain of causation in respect of losses flowing from the discriminatory act and that all future losses should therefore be subject to the statutory cap on unfair dismissal compensation. The Court of Appeal ruled that the unlawful dismissal did not break the chain of causation. By way of contrast, in Ahsan v Labour Party EAT 0211/10 (discussed in some detail above) the EAT rejected the claimant's attempt to rely on the Beart decision in the absence of a finding that the intervening act was wrongful. The employment tribunal had found that the claimant's compensation for discrimination by the Labour Party should be limited up to the point at which he was expelled from the Party. He alleged that the expulsion was itself an act of discrimination and argued that the Party could not, therefore, rely on it to break the chain of causation. Rejecting that contention, the EAT distinguished Beart on the basis that the tribunal in the present case had made no finding that the Party's actions leading up to the exulsion were unlawful, whereas in Beart the employment tribunal had explicitly found the dismissal to be unfair. It was entirely understandable that in Beart the Court of Appeal was not prepared to regard the dismissal as notionally 'trumping' the established loss so as to break the chain of causation, but the same could not apply here in the absence of a finding of unlawfulness.

The employee who suffers the damage may, by his or her own actions, break the chain of causation between the employer's wrong and his or her loss. The House of Lords confirmed this in Corr v IBC Vehicles Ltd 2008 ICR 372, HL, where Lord Scott of Foscote referred to a passage in 'Clerk and Lindsell on Torts' 19th edition (2006), noting that a novus actus may take the form of conduct by the claimant. However, their Lordships in that case went on to hold that, in certain circumstances, the act of suicide may not break the chain of causation. There, the employer was held liable for the suicide of an employee who suffered severe depression after being seriously injured in an accident caused by the employer's negligence. The House of Lords held that the depression was a foreseeable consequence of that negligence and that it was not uncommon for someone so afflicted to take his or her own life, and that the suicide did not break the chain of causation between the employer's negligence and the damage suffered. It accordingly upheld the claim brought by the deceased employee's widow. Their Lordships rejected IBC Ltd's submission that the suicide had been a voluntary, independent act – it was not an informed decision taken by the employee as an adult of sound mind but the response of a man suffering from a severely depressive illness that impaired his capacity to make reasoned and informed judgements about his future, such illness being a consequence of the employer's tort. Lord Bingham noted that suicide could be a novus actus interveniens in cases where it is the result of a conscious decision, unrelated to the employer's tort, but that was not the case here.

35.16 Foreseeable loss

The calculation of loss under the law of tort is limited by the principle of foreseeability. Loss is foreseeable – and therefore recoverable – only if a reasonable person would have foreseen that loss of the type in question would have resulted from the wrongful act. Foreseeability relates to the nature of the loss, not its extent. So if it is reasonably foreseeable that an individual will suffer injury to feelings, then the fact that a particularly vulnerable individual suffers a complete breakdown does not mean the wrongdoer can escape liability: the *type* of loss was foreseeable, so the wrongdoer is liable for the full extent of that loss, no matter how extreme. This is the so-called 'eggshell skull' principle, explained further under '"Eggshell skull" principle' below.

There has been some uncertainty, however, as to whether this rule applies in the same way in discrimination cases. In Skyrail Oceanic Ltd v Coleman 1981 ICR 864, CA, Lord Justice Lawton observed that a claim for compensation under the SDA should be treated in the same way as a claim in tort in the county court, in that compensation should only be awarded for foreseeable types of damage. In Sheriff v Klyne Tugs (Lowestoft) Ltd 1999 ICR 1170, CA, on the other hand, Lord Justice Stuart-Smith, when commenting on the differences between suing for personal injury in the tort of negligence and suing for personal injury based on the statutory tort of race discrimination, concluded that the key difference was that in a claim based on race discrimination, there is no requirement that the claimant show that the damage he or she has suffered was reasonably foreseeable. In his Lordship's view, all that must be established is that the discrimination caused the damage.

This difference of opinion was resolved by the Court of Appeal in Essa v Laing **35.17** Ltd 2004 ICR 746, CA, in favour of the view expressed by Stuart-Smith LJ in the Sheriff case. The Court, by a majority, confirmed that compensation for an act of direct discrimination contrary to the RRA should cover all harm that arises directly and naturally from the act of discrimination. In the present case, the tribunal had erred in holding that the employee, who had suffered severe depression as a result of being racially abused at work and had been unable to work since, could only claim compensation for the loss that was a reasonably foreseeable consequence of the racial abuse. According to Lord Justice Pill, although there is a difference between physical or psychiatric injury on the one hand and injury to feelings on the other, the two are not so unlike as to be of a different kind for the purposes of the test of reasonable foreseeability. Thus, since injury to feelings was a reasonably foreseeable result of the discrimination, it followed that damages in respect of psychiatric injury were not too remote to be recoverable. Lord Justice Rix delivered a dissenting judgment, however, in which he contended that there was nothing in the RRA or the case law to require or suggest that a test of pure causation was the correct one to adopt in assessing the compensation to be awarded to claimants who have suffered discrimination. Rix LJ pointed out that liability in tort is generally limited by the concept of reasonable foreseeability and expressed the view that the same test should be applied to the statutory tort of discrimination. He also noted that there are various kinds of discrimination, ranging from the deliberate to the genuinely inadvertent, which meant that it would be inappropriate to apply a rule of compensation that would put discrimination on a par with deceitful or malicious torts.

The majority decision in Essa has clarified the law in this area, save in one respect. Pill LJ suggested the possibility that a different rule may apply to discriminatory acts of a different kind. Part of his reasoning was that the racial abuse suffered by the claimant was akin to assault and battery, in that it involved deliberate conduct, but he went on to note that 'it is possible that, where the discrimination takes other forms, different considerations will apply'. It is possible, therefore, that the principle is confined to racial abuse, or other forms of harassment. Lord Justice Clarke supported Pill LJ's ruling on the main issue but appears not to have explicitly endorsed this caveat. Rix LJ did not expressly refer to it either, but his observations to the effect that not all forms of discrimination are the same arguably touches on the same point. In a subsequent decision, Mr Justice Underhill, then President of the EAT, noted in Ahsan v Labour Party EAT 0211/10 that the issue had been left up in the air and that a test of reasonable foreseeability may still be appropriate in some factual situations, but did not offer a view on it. It is notable that in his judgment in the earlier case of Bullimore v Pothecary Witham Weld and anor (No.2) 2011 IRLR 18, EAT, Underhill P held that a respondent was liable for future loss of earnings caused by an act of victimisation on the basis that such loss was reasonably foreseeable. In so holding, he noted that the loss was also a 'direct and natural consequence' of the victimisation, 'if and in so far as this expresses a different concept'. This echoes the formulation adopted by the Court of Appeal in Essa when holding that compensation could be recovered for all damage arising 'directly and naturally' from the act of discrimination. In other words, Underhill P has given a strong hint that even in cases where the reasonable foreseeability test is applied, it may not produce a different outcome to the approach approved in Essa. All this uncertainty may therefore provide material for future appeals based on different factual situations, and indeed on different protected characteristics.

35.18 Whatever the final outcome, it is strongly arguable that in all discrimination cases, some injury to feelings is foreseeable, even inevitable, as a result of discriminatory behaviour, and the employer will in any event be liable for the full extent of any psychological injury suffered as a consequence according to the 'eggshell skull' principle. It is also important to note that, even if the Essa decision means that there is no requirement for loss to be reasonably foreseeable, there must still be direct causation between the unlawful act and the loss caused – see 'Causation' above.

35.19 'Eggshell skull' principle

As noted above, the 'eggshell skull' principle applies to loss arising from discrimination. The principle is alternatively expressed by saying that the discriminator must take the victim as he or she finds him or her. This means that even if the victim is unusually sensitive or susceptible, and the level of damage or loss sustained is therefore worse than it would have been for another individual, the discriminator will be liable for the full extent of the damage, loss or injury, so long as it can be shown that this flowed from the act of discrimination. So, depending upon the extent of an individual's vulnerability, employers may find themselves liable for damage that they consider far outweighs the seriousness of the acts of discrimination that occurred. However, particular complexities can arise where the discrimination exacerbates or accelerates the effect of a pre-existing condition. In such cases, awards for injury to feelings and personal injury should reflect only the exacerbation or acceleration. This can be particularly difficult to assess in cases of disability discrimination, for example, where the complainant necessarily has some mental or physical impairment to begin with in order to have the protected characteristic of disability. This matter is considered further in Chapter 36, 'Compensation: heads of damage', under 'Personal injury'.

Reductions from awards for injury to feelings and psychiatric injury because of pre-existing conditions should not be confused with contingency reductions from awards for *financial loss*. Employment tribunals will also reduce that part of an award of compensation which is for financial loss by a percentage to reflect contingencies – such as the likelihood that the claimant would have succumbed to a stress-related disorder in any event. Such adjustments are considered in Chapter 36, under 'Future loss'.

No upper limit   35.20

There are no upper limits on awards made under the EqA: employment tribunals can award full compensation for the loss suffered. This was emphasised by the EAT in Ministry of Defence v Hunt and ors 1996 ICR 554, EAT, a decision in a case brought under the SDA but one capable of setting down a general rule in all discrimination cases. There, the EAT said that the earlier guidance given in Ministry of Defence v Cannock and ors 1994 ICR 918, EAT, which included the suggestion that tribunals should maintain a sense of due proportion when arriving at the total compensation to be awarded to a claimant dismissed on the ground of sex discrimination, could not have been intended to introduce the notion of a judicial cap into an area of compensation in which there is no longer any statutory limit. In Waters v Griffin and ors EAT 706/00 (another sex discrimination case) the EAT held that a tribunal had erred in looking at the matter of compensation from the point of view of justice and equity, limiting both the loss of earnings and injury to feelings awards to a certain period of time. Tribunals are obliged to accept that all the consequences flowing directly from the discrimination should be reflected in damages, whether in relation to loss of earnings or injury to feelings, and any arbitrary cut-off point is wrong.

The employment tribunal statistics for the year 1 April 2010 to 31 March 2011 show that 16 discrimination complaints resulted in awards of £50,000 or more. The highest award in that year was £289,167 in a sex discrimination case. These figures were generally down on previous years, and awards in the hundreds of thousands of pounds are still relatively rare. However, given that the guiding principle is to compensate for all loss that flows from the discrimination, the occasional huge award does still occur. The compensation ordered in Michalak v Mid Yorkshire Hospitals NHS Trust and ors ET Case No.1810815/08 was reported to be the highest sum awarded by a tribunal for discrimination, totalling just under £4.5 million. M succeeded with claims for sex and race discrimination and unfair dismissal. She was awarded loss of earnings in respect of the entire remainder of her working life – a period of 15 years – amounting to just under £1 million. She received a further £650,000 for pension loss, £56,000 for psychiatric damage and £30,000 for injury to feelings, among other things. The tribunal also awarded a 15 per cent uplift in respect of the Trust's failure to comply with the statutory grievance procedure,

1249

which has since been repealed but was in force at the relevant time. Around half of the total represented 'grossing up', an additional amount awarded to ensure that the claimant is left with full compensation once she has paid the tax due on the award – see Chapter 36, 'Compensation: heads of damage', under 'Taxation'.

35.21 **No double recovery**

Where the employment tribunal complaint relates to a dismissal and the complainant claims that the dismissal was both unfair and discriminatory, the heads of compensation will largely overlap and, in this respect, cannot be awarded twice – S.126 Employment Rights Act 1996. In these circumstances, the EAT has stated that tribunals should order compensation under the discrimination legislation, thereby avoiding the cap on the unfair dismissal compensatory award (£72,300 from 1 February 2012) – D'Souza v London Borough of Lambeth 1997 IRLR 677, EAT. Such awards will also attract the more favourable rules on interest that apply to discrimination as opposed to unfair dismissal awards – see Chapter 36, 'Compensation: heads of damage', under 'Interest on awards'.

In certain cases, however, a tribunal may find it more appropriate to award damages under the unfair dismissal provisions than for discrimination. In Cooper and anor v Smith EAT 0452/03 the EAT approved an employment tribunal's reasoning that since damages for discrimination are paid net of social security benefits, and it did not have figures relating to any such benefits before it, compensation should be awarded under the unfair dismissal regime whereunder compensation is paid gross of certain statutory benefits and then subject to 'recoupment'. However, the claimant was not seriously disadvantaged by this approach, since the amount awarded was comfortably below the statutory cap on unfair dismissal compensation in any event.

35.22 **Failure to follow Acas Code of Practice**

Since April 2009, employment tribunals have had the power to increase or decrease awards by up to 25 per cent where there has been an unreasonable failure, by either party, to comply with the Acas Code of Practice on Disciplinary and Grievance Procedures (2009). The power is contained in S.207A of the Trade Union and Labour Relations (Consolidation) Act 1992 (TULR(C)A), which states at subsection (2): 'If, in the case of proceedings to which this section applies, it appears to the employment tribunal that (a) the claim to which the proceedings relate concerns a matter to which a relevant Code of Practice applies, (b) the employer has failed to comply with that Code in relation to that matter, and (c) that failure was unreasonable, the employment tribunal may, if it considers it just and equitable in all the circumstances to do so, increase any award it makes to the employee by no more than 25 per cent.' S.207A(3) goes on to make equivalent provision for the situation where the employee has unreasonably failed to comply with the Acas Code, in which case the tribunal may reduce the award by up to 25 per cent. These provisions apply to claims brought under any of the jurisdictions listed in Schedule A2 to the TULR(C)A, which includes proceedings brought under Ss.120 and 127 of the Equality Act 2010.

The Acas Code sets out minimum standards of reasonableness and fairness for handling disciplinary issues and employee grievances. The Code's recommendations are fairly general and should accord with most employers' standard practice. In summary, it suggests that:

- with regard to disciplinary matters, the employer should establish the facts of the case, inform the employee of the problem, hold a meeting with the employee, at which the employee may be accompanied, decide on appropriate action and give the employee an opportunity to appeal

- with regard to grievances, the employee should let the employer know the nature of the grievance, and the employer should hold a meeting at which the employee may be accompanied, decide on appropriate action and allow the employee to take the grievance further if it is not resolved at that stage.

The Code sets out some details of the considerations to be taken into account **35.23** at each stage of these procedures, such as questions of timing and the personnel involved. The majority of its recommendations are recognisable as common sense and good practice and so are not expected to require any great changes by employers and employees in the way such issues would usually be handled. The Code's requirements have not yet been considered in any great detail by the appellate courts. Furthermore, most of the tribunal judgments in which the Code has been considered involve complaints of unfair dismissal. However, the following are two examples of discrimination cases in which tribunals did consider the effect on compensation of breach of the Acas Code:

- **Rogan v Gunns International Transport and Shipping Ltd and ors** ET Case No.1102863/09: R, a woman, worked in an environment where sexual banter was common and she was frequently subjected to risqué remarks. In one incident, T, the operations manager of GITS Ltd, put written material on R's desk that was sexist and of a sexual nature, and which was degrading, humiliating and offensive towards women. Also, on occasions when R was standing by the photocopier, T would brush against her deliberately and put his arm round her body. Her complaint of sexual harassment was upheld by an employment tribunal, which noted that R had been subjected to unpleasant conduct by a senior member of the company, making her feel she could not complain. It awarded £10,000 for injury to feelings but reduced the award by 25 per cent to reflect R's complete and unreasonable failure to comply with the Acas grievance procedure. Although she felt unable to complain to T, or to the managing director, who was a friend of his, she could and should have made some complaint to someone else – for example, a colleague

- **Saxton v John Hollingworth Ltd** ET Case No.2339951/09: S succeeded in claims of disability discrimination and unfair dismissal, among other things. JH Ltd had failed to make reasonable adjustments to accommodate the back problems she suffered as a result of scoliosis, and was dismissive and hostile in response to S's legitimate concerns about matters such as having to lift heavy files. The employment tribunal awarded compensation for loss of earnings and injury to feelings, among other things, and applied an increase of 20 per cent because of JH Ltd's failure to comply with the Acas Code of Practice. In particular, it noted that paras 33 and 38, which require that employees be able to explain their grievance at the grievance meeting, and that the employer make a decision following the meeting, were not complied with. The manager conducting the grievance hearing had disregarded the claimant's detailed and lucid written explanation of her complaints, requiring her to set them out orally despite her distress. The tribunal was also unconvinced that the manager hearing the grievance had authority to make a decision on it, given that he was subordinate to a manager about whom the claimant was complaining.

35.24 For more detail on the Code's recommendations for each stage of the procedures, and the consequences of failure to abide by them, see IDS Employment Law Handbook, 'Unfair Dismissal' (2010), Chapter 3, 'Unfairness', under 'Fairness of internal procedure – the Acas Code of Practice'.

It ought to be stressed that the employment tribunal's power to adjust compensation is engaged only where the employee's or employer's failure to comply with the Code's recommendations is 'unreasonable' – S.207A TULR(C)A. The Code itself is couched in terms of reasonableness – for example, para 31 states that grievances should be raised 'without unreasonable delay' – and so S.207A's focus on whether non-adherence to the Code was reasonable in effect requires consideration of whether it was reasonable for the employer or employee to act unreasonably. This should give some idea of the breadth of the discretion that tribunals must be allowed when deciding whether to order an adjustment to compensation. This is, perhaps, particularly important in discrimination cases, where it may seem inappropriate to be prescriptive about how complaints should be handled, given that they often involve sensitive issues and raise personal conflicts.

35.25 **Size of adjustment.** As for the factors affecting the appropriateness and the size of any increase or reduction, it ought to be noted that S.207A(2) and (3) allow for an adjustment if the tribunal considers it 'just and equitable in all the circumstances'. This echoes the language of the statutory disciplinary and grievance procedures, which, under the Employment Act 2002 and the Employment Act 2002 (Dispute Resolution) Regulations 2004 SI 2004/752, were mandatory with regard to most workplace disputes before they were repealed and replaced by the current regime in April 2009. Under S.31 of the

1252

2002 Act, failure to follow the old statutory procedures would result in a minimum adjustment of 10 per cent, but up to 50 per cent if the tribunal considered it just and equitable. Some of the case law on the old procedures may therefore be relevant when tribunals come to assess the appropriate level of adjustment under S.207A TULR(C)A, at least in so far as the cases consider what is just and equitable.

One case law principle that ought to be carried over from the old regime to the new is that tribunals are entitled to have regard to the overall size of the compensatory award when deciding what size an adjustment to order. In Abbey National plc v Chagger 2010 ICR 397, CA, the Court of Appeal agreed with both the employment tribunal and the EAT that the size of C's compensatory award – almost £3 million – was capable of amounting to an 'exceptional circumstance' under S.31(4) of the 2002 Act, justifying an increase of less than the usual minimum 10 per cent. Then, in Wardle v Crédit Agricole Corporate and Investment Bank 2011 ICR 1290, CA, the Court went even further, holding that a tribunal's failure to have regard to the size of the award when considering the appropriate uplift was an error of law. The tribunal had increased an award of around £180,000 by 50 per cent. The Court of Appeal held that the maximum increase should be very exceptional indeed, reserved only for the most serious cases. It took the view that the intention behind the old legislation was that a tribunal should start with an uplift of 10 per cent and then consider whether it was just and equitable in the circumstances to increase that percentage. The mere fact that an employer has ignored procedures altogether would not justify an increase to the maximum, although it would often justify some increase beyond 10 per cent. On the facts of the present case, though there had been a wilful disregard of the disciplinary procedure at the first stage, an internal appeal hearing had been held and there was no suggestion that the appeal was conducted in bad faith. The Court thought that the appropriate uplift would ordinarily be in the region of 30 per cent, but even that would result in additional compensation of around £55,000. It left the final decision until after the parties had agreed on calculations for the various heads of damage and, in a later judgment, settled on an uplift of 15 per cent, which would be around £19,000 – Wardle v Crédit Agricole Corporate and Investment Bank (No.2) 2011 IRLR 819, CA. Lord Justice Elias noted that this was appropriate for the 'serious and cavalier' breaches found by the tribunal.

35.26 Given that the total size of award was a relevant factor under the old regime, which focused on whether an increase would be 'just and equitable', the same consideration will almost certainly be relevant for tribunals applying the 'just and equitable' test under S.207A TULR(C)A. Tribunals ought also to consider whether the adjustment should apply in respect of all of the grounds of claim. In Wardle (above), the Court held that the tribunal was wrong to apply the uplift to loss stemming from both the unfair dismissal and the discriminatory failure to promote. The employer's breach of the statutory procedures related

1253

only to the dismissal and so the uplift could not be applied to the injury to feelings award or to the loss resulting from the failure to promote W. The same consideration might arise when it comes to assessing adherence to the Acas Code – for example, if the employer properly observes the Code in relation to a grievance but disregards it when dismissing.

For a more detailed discussion of the level of adjustment for breach of the Acas Code and the general principles which govern this, see IDS Employment Law Handbook, 'Unfair Dismissal' (2010), Chapter 18, 'Compensatory awards: adjustments and reductions', under 'Adjustments for breach of Acas Code of Practice – increase/reduction in compensatory award'.

35.27 **Application to different heads of compensation.** The adjustment for failure to follow the Acas Code should apply to all heads of compensation. The power to make an adjustment under S.207A applies to 'any' award that the tribunal makes – S.207A(2) and (3). This is the same wording as was used by the 2002 Act. Thus, where there are several heads of claim – such as loss of earnings, injury to feelings and personal injury – there should be no need for the tribunal to differentiate between them when making an adjustment for failure to follow the Acas Code. This is indeed how tribunals have been applying S.207A in practice.

There is one exception to this. S.207A(6) provides that the Acas Code adjustment must be made *before* any award under S.38 of the Employment Act 2002 in respect of the employer's failure to provide written particulars of employment – see 'Failure to provide written particulars', below. Accordingly, the S.207A adjustment cannot affect the amount of an award under S.38 EA 2002.

35.28 One point that was unclear under the old statutory procedures regime was whether the adjustment should be applied before or after any adjustment made to take account of the claimant's liability to tax on the award. As explained in Chapter 36, 'Compensation: heads of damage', under 'Taxation', employment tribunals commonly decide what compensation the claimant should actually receive, then add an amount to offset the sum the claimant will have to pay to HM Revenue and Customs. In University of the Arts London v Rule EAT 0245/10 the EAT applied the uplift to the entire award, including the part that represented this tax indemnity. It noted that it was established that adjustments under the 2002 Act were designed to be punitive, not compensatory, and could see no reason for applying the adjustment to anything other than the whole award. If this might lead to injustice or inequity, that should be taken into account when considering the size of the adjustment. This is a logical approach but does not necessarily accord with common practice. In Wardle v Crédit Agricole Corporate and Investment Bank (No.2) 2011 IRLR 819, CA, for example, grossing up was done after the uplift had been applied. The Court of Appeal did not disagree with this approach, although it was not asked to consider it. Since the decision of the EAT in the Rule case is the only one to have considered this issue head-on, it must represent the current authority but, given the sums involved, the matter will almost certainly require further consideration by the higher courts in the near future.

Failure to provide written particulars

35.29

Section 38 of the Employment Act 2002 states that an employment tribunal must award compensation to an employee where a claim under any of the tribunal jurisdictions listed in Schedule 5 has succeeded, and the employer was in breach of his duty to provide full and accurate written particulars under S.1 of the Employment Rights Act 1996 – S.38(1)–(3) EA 2002. This duty is covered in full in IDS Employment Law Handbook, 'Contracts of Employment' (2009), Chapter 3, 'Written particulars', under 'Compensation under S.38 of the Employment Act 2002'.

The list of jurisdictions set out in Schedule 5 is fairly extensive and includes claims made under Ss.120 and 127 EqA, i.e. claims relating to discrimination in employment and failure to give equal pay. S.38 does not give employees a free-standing right to claim compensation for failure to provide full and accurate written particulars. The right to compensation is dependent upon a successful claim being brought by the employee under one of the jurisdictions listed in Schedule 5. However, an award under S.38 is not dependent on a claim having been brought under S.11 ERA, which would be the usual way in which an employer's breach of S.1 ERA would be established. It is sufficient for the tribunal to make a finding at the hearing that the employer was in breach of S.1 at the relevant time. The relevant time, for this purpose, is the date on which the main proceedings were begun by the employee – S.38(2)(b) and (3)(b) EA 2002.

Amount of award. The tribunal must award the 'minimum amount' of two 35.30 weeks' pay and may, if it considers it just and equitable in the circumstances, award the 'higher amount' of four weeks' pay – S.38(2), (3) and (4) EA 2002. In McDonnell v Macaraeg t/a Matson Mini Market ET Case No.1403128/10 M succeeded in a claim of indirect sex discrimination when she was dismissed from her part-time job in a shop. The employer accepted that no contract was ever provided to M, or to any other employee, at any time. The employment tribunal awarded the minimum two weeks' pay under S.38 – it noted that the respondent was a small employer with limited experience of employment, who had just taken over the business and who had since issued contracts to all employees.

The tribunal does not have to make any award under S.38 if there are exceptional circumstances that would make an award or increase unjust or inequitable – S.38(5). An award made under S.38 is on top of any award the tribunal may already have made in respect of the main claim, but is not dependent on the making of any such award. The tribunal can still make an award for failure to

1255

give written particulars where it has found in favour of the employee in the main claim but has not awarded compensation – S.38(2).

35.31 A 'week's pay' is calculated in accordance with Ss.220–229 ERA and is limited to the maximum under S.227 (£430 as from 1 February 2012, though this figure is adjusted annually) – S.38(6) EA 2002. The date of calculation is either the date on which main proceedings were commenced or, if the employee was no longer employed at that date, the effective date of termination of employment – S.38(7). For details of how to calculate a week's pay for these purposes, see IDS Employment Law Handbook, 'Wages' (2011), Chapter 10, 'A week's pay'.

35.32 Failure to follow tribunal recommendations

Section 124(7)(a) EqA gives employment tribunals the power to increase the amount of compensation to be paid where the respondent fails, without reasonable excuse, to comply with any recommendation that the tribunal has made in relation to the complainant. Failure to comply with a recommendation can also lead to an award of compensation where none was awarded at the time the recommendation was made – S.124(7)(b).

Note that where the tribunal has exercised the power under S.124(3)(b) to make a recommendation requiring the employer to take steps to reduce the adverse effects of discrimination on any other person (i.e. not the complainant) and the employer fails to comply, then compensation cannot be increased. This provision might be invoked where, for example, the claimant has left the job, but the tribunal makes a recommendation that the employer change its recruitment practices or enhance its harassment procedures. There does not appear to be any provision for a sanction if the employer fails to comply with a general recommendation. Recommendations are considered in detail in Chapter 34, 'Enforcing individual rights', under 'Remedies – recommendations'.

35.33 Contributory conduct

The common law has long recognised the possibility of reducing compensation for a tortious act to reflect the fact that the claimant's own conduct has contributed to his or her loss. It is clear that this principle applies to the assessment of compensation for discrimination. The EAT confirmed in Way and anor v Crouch 2005 ICR 1362, EAT, that the Law Reform (Contributory Negligence) Act 1945 applies to discrimination law, and employment tribunals can make a reduction from compensation to reflect contributory conduct. Two examples of deductions for contributory fault in discrimination cases:

- **Afriyie v Tripp t/a Kestrel Grove Nursing Home** ET Case No.3302266/10: A was employed as a healthcare assistant from January 2009 to March 2010. She became pregnant in August 2009. In February 2010 there was an incident in which A lost control with a service user and struck him, causing him minor injury. She was called to a disciplinary hearing and, after further investigation, she was summarily dismissed. She succeeded in a claim of pregnancy discrimination – the employment tribunal thought it clear that the employer had A's pregnancy in mind when it deliberated over whether it should dismiss. However, it reduced her compensation by 80 per cent for contributory fault in respect of the February 2010 incident

- **Olubanjoko v Yamaha Music (UK) Ltd and anor** ET Case No.3300231/10: O began working for YM Ltd in May 2008. Until March 2009 employees had been able to spend a certain amount of time working from home, but YM Ltd decided this policy was not working well and terminated it from 1 April. O became pregnant around that time. She also developed problems with back pain, which she believed to be caused by her chair at work. Over the next few months, she sought permission to work at home. She was initially allowed to do so for two days a week but YM Ltd became concerned about her performance and insisted on her working in the office. O raised grievances about this and other issues, including a complaint about a new office chair YM Ltd provided for her. During the course of various workplace disputes over home-working, the chair and YM Ltd's requirement that she provide written proof of antenatal appointments, YM Ltd accused her of threatening and aggressive behaviour and gave her a written warning. On 11 September, O's medical consultant wrote to YM Ltd asking that O be allowed to work from home and thereafter O simply started working at home without authorisation. In October, she was dismissed. She succeeded in a claim of sex discrimination. The employment tribunal noted that, from the outset, YM Ltd had treated O's concerns with scepticism and caution, although O's conduct fuelled that approach. YM Ltd's decision on the chair and on the issue of medical appointments was reasonable but it still treated O less favourably on grounds that, to a minor but nevertheless material extent, included a pregnancy-related condition. The tribunal reduced compensation for the unfair dismissal part of the claim by two thirds for contributory fault, taking into account O's aggressive and hostile behaviour to managers, and her being uncooperative and needlessly confrontational over the matter of her seating. It noted that a comparable reduction could, and should, be made to O's compensation for discrimination, to be decided at a later hearing.

If the discrimination claim covers the same ground as an unfair dismissal **35.34** claim, it might be expected that any deduction for contributory conduct will fall to be applied to both compensatory awards. However, although two different Appeal Tribunals have considered this issue, the point has not been definitively decided. In Fife Council v McPhee EAT 750/00 M, who had a serious visual impairment, kept £160 belonging to a client in his possession for ten days, in breach of the employer's procedures, and dissembled when questioned about it. He was subsequently dismissed. The employment tribunal found that M had not been able to read the employer's policies, and that

1257

overall the employer had failed to make reasonable adjustments. It reduced compensation for unfair dismissal by 50 per cent because of M's contributory conduct, but made no deduction in respect of disability discrimination. On appeal, the EAT indicated that this was wrong: where the two claims are inextricably intertwined, as here, in that it is the employee's conduct that leads to dismissal but the employer's failure to look after his interests that renders the dismissal unfair, deduction should be made from the compensation for discrimination as well. However, the point was not properly before the EAT and so this view is not strictly binding.

The issue came before the EAT again in Blackpool Fylde and Wyre Society for the Blind v Begg EAT 0035/05, which involved similar circumstances to McPhee. B, a blind man, was dismissed for having set up a company in competition with his employer. An employment tribunal concluded that B was unfairly dismissed, partly because of procedural failings that put him at a disadvantage owing to his disability. That same disadvantage amounted to disability discrimination. The tribunal made a 40 per cent reduction to B's compensation for unfair dismissal to reflect his contributory conduct, but no adjustment to the discrimination award. The employer was not allowed to challenge that approach on appeal since it had not raised the issue before the tribunal, and the EAT did not consider it right to allow the employer to take it as a new point on appeal. Nonetheless, it gave some consideration to the employer's argument. It accepted that, although the EAT's analysis in Fife Council v McPhee (above) was beside the point, its conclusion represented the Appeal Tribunal's 'firm view'. However, it was not convinced that the EAT was correct. It noted that the language of the Law Reform (Contributory Negligence) Act 1945 and that of the Employment Rights Act 1996 is different, and that 'it by no means follows where there is fault by way of contributory negligence that there will be culpable conduct by way of S.123 of the Employment Rights Act 1996'. The EAT observed that, were it to decide the matter, it would be helpful to have the assistance of the three statutory commissions – i.e. the Equal Opportunities Commission, the Disability Rights Commission and the Commission for Racial Equality, since subsumed into the Equality and Human Rights Commission.

35.35   As for the heads of damage that may be affected by a reduction for contributory fault, there is no direct authority on the point. If the McPhee analysis is to be followed then compensation for financial loss is certainly subject to reduction for contributory fault. There seems no reason why awards for non-pecuniary loss, such as injury to feelings and personal injury, should not be treated in the same way. The Law Reform (Contributory Negligence) Act 1945 does not differentiate between different heads of loss – indeed, it applies to the award of 'damages' and specifies in S.4 that 'damage' includes loss of life and personal injury.

Awards against individuals and co-respondents

35.36

Employers are liable for the discriminatory acts of their employees done in the course of their employment, whether or not those acts were done with the employer's knowledge or approval – S.109 EqA. However, an employer has a defence if it can show that it took such steps as were reasonably practicable to prevent the employee from doing that act or acts of that description – S.109(4): see Chapter 28, 'Liability of employers, employees and agents', under 'Employer's liability for acts of employees', for further details.

Under the antecedent discrimination statutes a victim of discrimination could claim directly against the perpetrator of the discriminatory act, as well as the employer, by alleging that the individual employee aided and abetted the unlawful act of the employer. This is still the case under the EqA, albeit that the language of the antecedent legislation has been simplified slightly. Now, an individual employee will be exposed to personal liability if he or she does something which, by virtue of S.109, is treated as being done by the employer and that thing amounts to a contravention by the employer of the EqA – S.110(1). It does not affect the employee's liability that the employer can rely upon the 'all reasonable steps' defence, but the employee's liability is still dependent upon the employer being otherwise liable, subject to that defence – S.110(2). Thus, a complainant cannot simply sue a fellow employee: he or she will need to bring a claim against both the fellow employee and the employer, although the employer may avoid liability if it successfully invokes the defence. A respondent employee has a defence in these circumstances if he or she reasonably relied on a statement by the employer that the act in question was not unlawful – S.110(3).

Awards against individuals as co-respondents are often sought in cases involving **35.37** allegations of harassment, where legal action is brought against both the employer and the alleged harasser. In such cases employment tribunals have often ordered individuals to pay quite substantial sums. Two examples:

- **Cox v Macklin Street Surgery and anor** ET Case No.2600517/00: J, a trainee GP, committed acts of sexual harassment against C that the employment tribunal described as 'wholly inappropriate, suggestive [and] very unpleasant' while both worked in the same surgery. The surgery and J admitted that J had sexually harassed C and that she was constructively dismissed owing to J's behaviour and the surgery's failure to respond properly to her complaints. The tribunal awarded damages for injury to feelings of £2,500 against the surgery and £3,500 against J personally

- **Crofton v Yeboah** EAT 475/00: an employment tribunal found that the individual respondent, C, had personally waged a three-year campaign against the complainant to undermine belief in his integrity. C's behaviour 'was "grossly offensive"... caused "great distress" over a length of time that was "severe" and... interfered with "home life, caused... serious public humiliation and damaged [the complainant's] reputation"'. The tribunal awarded £45,000 for injury to feelings against C personally, of which £10,000 represented aggravated damages. C successfully appealed to the EAT on the question of liability, but that decision was then overturned by the Court of Appeal (Yeboah v Crofton 2002 IRLR 634, CA). On consideration of a further appeal on remedies following the Court of Appeal's judgment, the EAT reduced the award for injury to feelings from £45,000 to £25,000, while upholding the award of £10,000 for aggravated damages in full. Neither the tribunal nor the Appeal Tribunal considered C's means when setting the award and the fact that C was an individual respondent did not appear to be a relevant consideration.

35.38 Joint and several awards

Employment tribunals are entitled to make awards on a joint and several basis. The effect of compensation being awarded on such a basis is that, where more than one respondent is found liable for the same act of unlawful discrimination, the claimant can take enforcement action against any one of the respondents for the full amount of the award. It is then up to the respondent to seek a contribution for the damages from the co-respondents. Thus, an individual employee who commits an act of unlawful discrimination can be liable to pay the full amount of the award, although he or she could then seek a contribution from the employer. Note, however, that the legal basis for seeking a contribution has recently been doubted by the EAT – see 'Apportionment' below.

The power to make joint and several awards in discrimination cases derives from the fact that employment tribunals are required to award compensation in the same way as in claims in tort (or proceedings for reparation in Scotland). The EAT gave the first express confirmation that joint and several awards for discrimination are possible in Way and anor v Crouch 2005 ICR 1362, EAT, a sex discrimination case. It had regard to the wording of Ss.65 and 66 SDA, which provided that the compensation available in a discrimination claim brought in the employment tribunal was the same as would be available in a claim brought in a county court in England and Wales, or the sheriff court in Scotland. (That same principle is maintained in the EqA by Ss.119 and 124(6).) Given that those civil courts are able to make awards on a joint and several basis, the EAT saw no reason why the tribunal should not be able to do likewise. However, it did not think that joint and several awards would often be appropriate and went on to set out some principles that tribunals must have regard to:

- in almost every case it will be unnecessary to make a joint and several award. The practice of apportioning liability (where appropriate) between individual employees and employers works well and does justice to the individual case

- if a tribunal considers it necessary to make a joint and several award of compensation then it should make clear its reasons for doing so

- if a tribunal does consider that it is appropriate to make a joint and several award, then it must have regard to the language of S.2(1) of the Civil Liability (Contribution) Act 1978, which requires that in proceedings for contribution, the court's attention is specifically directed to the extent of each person's responsibility for the damage in question. In other words, it is not appropriate in almost any case for an employment tribunal to make a joint and several award that allows for 100 per cent recovery from each respondent

- it is clear from S.2(1)(v) of the 1978 Act that it is not permissible for a tribunal to make a joint and several award of compensation because of the relative financial resources of the respondent. For example, a tribunal cannot make such an award simply because it believes that a company is more likely to be able to satisfy such an award than an individual or because a corporate respondent may be insolvent or in receivership

- the word 'responsibility' in S.2(1) refers both to the extent to which each tortfeasor caused the damage and to their relative culpability.

35.39 In short, the EAT in the Way case did two main things. First, it confirmed that joint and several awards are available in the employment tribunal. Secondly, it sought to restrict the use of such awards, stipulating that even when a joint and several award is appropriate, the tribunal should not provide for the entirety of the compensation to be recoverable from either respondent – it should still attempt to apportion the award, having regard to each respondent's responsibility. Since Way, later case law has confirmed the first aspect of the EAT's decision – that an employment tribunal may make an award against multiple respondents on a joint and several basis.

However, several cases have since doubted the second plank of the Way decision – that apportionment should be the default approach – to the extent that this part of the EAT's decision can no longer be considered correct. Uncertainty was first expressed by the EAT in Bullimore v Pothecary Witham Weld and anor (No.2) 2011 IRLR 18, EAT, which was concerned with two acts of victimisation under the SDA – the first by the claimant's ex-employer, which had given her a reference gratuitously referring to sex discrimination proceedings she had brought against it, and the second by a prospective employer, who withdrew a job offer from the claimant on receiving the reference. The employment tribunal, with the agreement of the parties, had proposed to apportion liability for compensation for the claimant's loss of earnings from the withdrawn job between the two employers, assessing each employer's culpability and degree of responsibility for the loss suffered. On appeal, Mr Justice Underhill, then

President of the EAT, commented (obiter) that it was doubtful that this approach was right in principle. The claimant's prospective loss of earnings was an indivisible loss for which apportionment would be inappropriate, at least according to the general principles governing concurrent liability in tort as described by the House of Lords in Barker v Corus UK Ltd 2006 UKHL 20, HL. Underhill P acknowledged the existence of conflicting guidance in Way but said that, even if it were correct, its relevance to the present case was doubtful. This was presumably because, whereas Way involved concurrent liability of employer and employee for the same act, Bullimore was concerned with separate acts of two separate employers, distinct in time, contributing to the same loss.

35.40 Doubts were also raised in Munchkins Restaurant Ltd and anor v Karmazyn and ors EAT 0359/09 and another. This time, the context was very similar to that in Way – i.e. an employer and a senior employee being found jointly liable for the employee's acts of discrimination against the claimant. The Appeal Tribunal, presided over by Mr Justice Langstaff, noted its 'very considerable doubts' about the suggestion in Way that the percentage of liability of each respondent in such cases is relevant. The EAT thought that, whenever there is an award of joint and several liability, the co-respondents or any one of them is individually liable for the full extent of the damages to the claimant in the ordinary way. As noted above, the 'ordinary way' is that the beneficiary of an award made on a joint and several basis can take enforcement action against any individual respondent, at his or her choice, for the full amount of the award. The EAT acknowledged that the respondents might, between themselves, each have a right to seek contribution from the other co-respondent(s), depending upon the relative contribution to and responsibility of each of them for the act or acts of discrimination in question. However, it did not think that this should affect the claimant, who is entitled to receive the full extent of his or her award from any of the respondents as he or she chooses.

The same view was forcefully restated by Underhill P when he returned to the issue in London Borough of Hackney v Sivanandan 2011 ICR 1374, EAT, a race discrimination case. Although he recognised that the practice of apportioning liability was not uncommon and had met with the approval of the EAT in Prison Service and ors v Johnson 1997 ICR 275, EAT, he nevertheless considered that it lacked any clear legal basis. In particular, he considered that the EAT's reference in Way to the Civil Liability (Contribution) Act 1978 was a 'red herring': the Act gives a person who is liable for a tortious act the right to seek a contribution from concurrent tortfeasors, but has no impact on the liability of any tortfeasor towards a claimant. In Underhill P's view, joint and several liability should be the norm when a claimant has suffered discrimination from multiple respondents and the damage caused by that discrimination is indivisible. If the employer and employee are jointly liable, there is, on ordinary principles, no basis for apportionment. Underhill P also thought that this approach made more practical sense, since it would be unjust if the claimant had to take the risk of the respondent employee being unable to meet the part of the liability that is apportioned to him or her.

While this would appear to settle the matter, establishing that it is no longer appropriate for tribunals to apportion indivisible loss for which employer(s) and employee(s) are concurrently liable, a caveat needs to be entered. In none of these cases has the issue of joint liability as between employer and employee been directly before the EAT – the doubts expressed in all three cases being merely obiter dicta. For this reason, Underhill P in Sivanandan noted that 'because the case of employer and employee respondents was not directly in issue before us, and was not specifically argued, we do not think that we should rule in terms that [Johnson] was wrongly decided or definitively disapprove the practice which it recognises'. He did, however, go on to state that tribunals should, in future, only make 'split awards' between respondents in respect of the same loss if such an order is positively sought by one of the parties and if the basis for such an award is clearly demonstrated. Underhill P did not think such cases would often arise. **35.41**

The state of the law on apportionment, then, is that it is almost certainly inappropriate but has not yet been definitively disapproved. Another division of the EAT, under Mr Justice Silber, had the opportunity to consider the state of the law in Bungay and anor v Saini and ors EAT 0331/10. It preferred the Karmazyn and Sivanandan approaches over Way, concurring with Underhill P's insight that Way was mistaken in treating the 1978 Act as governing the liability of concurrent tortfeasors to a claimant. The EAT therefore chose to follow the two later cases. However, even then, it did not state in terms that Way was wrongly decided, noting that 'the time *might well* have come when Way should no longer be relied on or even cited as accurately representing the law' (our stress). It should also be noted that this was not a case of employer and employee respondents either – the individual respondents were treated as 'agents' of the company respondent. Nonetheless, the principal-agent relationship is very closely analogous to the employer-employee relationship, and concurrent liability within each context arises in much the same way. For more detail see Chapter 28, 'Liability of employers, employees and agents', under 'Liability of principals for agents'.

In summary, the practicalities make it overwhelmingly likely that the practice of splitting up liability for loss between concurrently liable respondents to a discrimination claim will have to be abandoned. Employment tribunals ought to follow Mr Justice Underhill's direction, awarding compensation on a joint and several basis, and only apportioning loss when one of the parties has established that it is appropriate to do so. This recommended approach will in general serve the interests of claimants as they will normally have no interest in seeking an apportionment arrangement given that this would restrict the **35.42** options available when it comes to enforcement. And on the respondents' side, as Underhill P pointed out in Sivanandan, the co-respondents will commonly be represented by the same representative, for whom it would be a conflict of interest to argue for apportionment. It is therefore difficult to envisage situations in which a convincing argument may now be made for apportioning loss in cases of joint liability.

As for when a joint and several award will be appropriate as between employer and employee, Underhill P in Sivanandan made it clear that his analysis applied to cases of 'indivisible' damage – i.e. those where it is not possible to identify distinct elements of loss caused by individual tortfeasors. This will be the case in most claims brought against an employer and employee jointly, where the employee's actions are the true source of the employer's liability – i.e. the employee is the actual 'doer' of the harm and the employer is liable by virtue of S.109.

35.43 Two examples:

- **Munchkins Restaurant Ltd and anor v Karmazyn and ors** EAT 0359/09 and another: the claimants had been subjected to sex discrimination and sexual harassment by the owner of the restaurant in which they worked. The EAT considered that, where there are several respondents, an employment tribunal will have to decide whether to make a joint and several award. In some cases the reason for doing so will be obvious and need very little elaboration, and this was one such case. In essence, the owner *was* the company – none of the incidents complained of involved any other person, save for one passing reference to another employee

- **Miles v Gilbank and anor** 2006 ICR 1297, CA: G was employed by a hairdressing salon as a senior hair designer and trainee manager. There was a friendly atmosphere in the salon until February 2004 when G informed M, the salon manager and a major shareholder in the company, that she was pregnant. Thereafter, the atmosphere changed. An employment tribunal found that the company conducted no risk assessment and made no adjustments to working practices to accommodate G's condition. In particular, she was still required to administer bleach, which, as a pregnant woman, caused her concern. She was also ignored and made the subject of unsympathetic remarks. The tribunal concluded that there had been an 'inhumane and sustained campaign of bullying and discrimination' against G by M and her other managers. The company, which was liable for the actions of M and the other managers, had therefore discriminated against G by subjecting her to a detriment. Moreover, M was personally liable for her own discriminatory acts and also for the other managers' discriminatory acts because she had aided them to commit an unlawful act. The tribunal awarded the then maximum possible amount for injury to feelings, £25,000, and £3,550 in unpaid maternity pay, for all of which M and the company were jointly and severally liable. Both the EAT and the Court of Appeal dismissed M's appeal against this decision. (It should be noted that in this case the individual respondent was effectively the owner of the respondent company, and that the company had been voluntarily dissolved by M at the time of the tribunal hearing. Accordingly, if a joint and several award had not been made, G would not have been able to recover any compensation.)

Apportionment   35.44

It should be clear from the case analysis set out under 'Joint and several awards', above, that there is now unlikely to be any scope for apportionment in cases of indivisible damage caused by discrimination. Where the employer and an employee (or several employees) are jointly liable for the same injury or loss suffered by the claimant – such as injury to feelings, or loss of earnings caused by a discriminatory constructive dismissal – then all respondents are potentially liable for the full total of the tribunal award. However, there are two situations in which apportionment, in some sense of the word, may still be appropriate in discrimination cases. These two situations were explained by Mr Justice Underhill, then President of the EAT, in London Borough of Hackney v Sivanandan 2011 ICR 1374, EAT (discussed under 'Joint and several awards' above).

The first is where loss caused by different acts of discrimination is divisible. Underhill P gave as an example the situation where employers contribute at successive stages to the development of a progressive industrial disease, such as deafness. In such cases, each separate employer is liable only for the damage attributable to each, and the claimant must proceed against each individually to recover the total. Underhill P did not offer an example of how divisible loss might arise in a discrimination context. One example might be where an employee or employees subject an individual to harassment, which the individual complains about, and the employer dismisses rather than dealing with the problem and thus exacerbates the original discriminatory conduct and/or extent of the injury to feelings. If the employee suffers psychiatric damage from the harassment, that might be said to be the employee's liability, whereas liability for financial loss flowing from the discriminatory dismissal most properly attaches to the employer. However, this seems an artificial and unattractive approach.

The second is where there are claims of contribution as between the respondents.   35.45
It was confirmed by the Court of Appeal in Ross v Ryanair Ltd 2005 1 WLR 2447, CA (a claim of disability discrimination in the provision of facilities or services), that the Civil Liability (Contribution) Act 1978 applies to liabilities under the discrimination legislation. If this includes discrimination in employment, it would mean that an employer could seek a contribution from a jointly liable employee in respect of compensation it had paid out to a successful

claimant. However, when Underhill P came back to this topic in Brennan and ors v Sunderland City Council and ors and another case EAT 0286/11 and another he held that neither the 1978 Act nor the EqA (or the antecedent discrimination legislation) give tribunals jurisdiction to hear a claim for contribution. More significantly, he went on to give the obiter view that the 1978 Act does not even apply to liability for discrimination in employment. The wording and the legislative history of the 1978 Act indicate that it is only intended to apply to liabilities falling for determination in the High Court or county court, and it creates no right to contribution in relation to liabilities assessed by an employment tribunal. (Note that this analysis does not affect Ross v Ryanair Ltd (above), which remains authority for the proposition that the 1978 Act applies to discrimination claims in which the civil courts have jurisdiction, such as discrimination in the provision of services to the public.)

Note too that 'apportionment' also describes the situation where harm suffered by the claimant is partially caused by extraneous factors other than the discrimination for which the respondent, or respondents, have been found liable. For example, in Thaine v London School of Economics 2010 ICR 1422, EAT, the EAT endorsed a tribunal's decision to reduce an award for personal injury by 60 per cent to reflect the fact that there were a number of concurrent causes of the claimant's psychiatric ill-health, only one of which was the sex discrimination of which she complained. This case, and the concept of apportionment in this context, is discussed further in Chapter 36, 'Compensation: heads of damage', under 'Personal injury'.

36 Compensation: heads of damage

Past loss

Future loss

Pension loss

Injury to feelings

Aggravated damages

Personal injury

Exemplary damages

Interest on awards

Taxation

The kinds of loss for which compensation is available as a remedy for **36.1** discrimination can be divided into two broad categories – financial and non-financial. Financial loss covers all the things most readily given a monetary value, including earnings and pension benefits, bonuses, allowances and fringe benefits. Non-financial loss covers such things as personal injury, both physical and psychological, injury to feelings, aggravated damages and exemplary damages. Each of these individual sub-categories of loss can be referred to as a 'head' of damage, and for each different head there will be different principles governing whether compensation is available, how it should be calculated, and the extent to which compensation should be reduced to reflect various contingencies.

In this chapter, we begin by considering three kinds of financial loss. First, past loss and future loss, i.e. loss incurred by the date of the remedies hearing and loss that will continue to mount up after it. Of course, these are only general headings, since both refer to the same kinds of financial loss (i.e. loss of earnings and benefits), but there are differences in the way that adjustments and deductions are applied to each. We then focus on a specific kind of financial loss: pension loss. Such loss can be incurred both up to and beyond the date of the hearing, and so pension loss is both past and future, but the special rules for calculating it mean it deserves separate consideration. Next we examine the various kinds of non-financial loss, being injury to feelings, aggravated damages, personal injury, and exemplary damages, before turning to deal with the general issues of interest on compensation awards and tax implications.

————————————————————————**1267**

36.2 ## Past loss

Calculating past loss is generally relatively simple. Where the claimant has been dismissed, the tangible losses will be assessed in much the same way as the compensatory award in cases of unfair dismissal – see IDS Employment Law Handbook, 'Unfair Dismissal' (2010), Chapter 16, 'Compensatory awards: types of loss', under 'Immediate loss' – except, of course, that there will be no upper limit on the amount of compensation that can be awarded. Where the complainant claims that a dismissal is both unfair and discriminatory, the heads of compensation will largely overlap and, in this respect, cannot be awarded twice – S.126 Employment Rights Act 1996 (ERA). This point is discussed in Chapter 35, 'Compensation: general principles', under 'General principles of assessment – no double recovery'.

The main reason that past loss is simpler to calculate is that it does not generally involve speculation as to what might happen in future. Under this head, it is the losses that have already flowed from the act of discrimination that fall to be compensated. However, this may still involve argument over whether a particular loss does indeed flow from the discriminatory act. For example, in Watt v Transco plc EAT 0116/03 the claimant accepted voluntary redundancy, with an enhanced redundancy payment, when her employer failed to respond to her request to work part time. When an employment tribunal found that that failure was discriminatory, it reduced compensation for financial loss by an amount corresponding to 50 per cent of the enhanced redundancy payment. The EAT allowed an appeal against that approach, holding that it had no basis in law: either the whole redundancy payment was deductible or none of it was. Applying the normal rules of compensation, the entire enhanced redundancy payment should have been deducted. There was a causal connection between the redundancy payment and the discrimination in that, but for the discrimination, the redundancy would not have occurred. If the redundancy would have occurred in any event, then it might have been arguable that the redundancy payment was not deductible, but that was not the situation in this case.

36.3 The most obvious cases of past loss will be those where there has been a discriminatory dismissal, in which case lost earnings will be one of the most substantial heads of claim. Acts of discrimination other than dismissal may also cause financial loss before the remedy hearing – for example, where the discriminatory act was the withholding of a payment or benefit. In Berhane v Kurdish Housing Association ET Case No.3205158/09 the relationship between the managing director of KHA, B, and the management committee broke down and B was eventually dismissed. He sought to appeal but was told he could not do so because he had less than one year's service. He then wrote to KHA complaining of race discrimination and other matters. His grievance was rejected on 21 December. In the meantime, KHA had told B that he would be paid a bonus of £5,000 as a goodwill gesture. When KHA received a race relations questionnaire it cancelled payment of the bonus pending further legal advice. An employment tribunal later found that there was no race discrimination but that, in withdrawing the offer to pay the bonus, KHA victimised B. He was awarded £5,000 in respect of the withdrawal of the bonus (although this was under the heading of unlawful deduction from wages, as the tribunal considered that B had a contractual right to the payment), plus £2,000 injury to feelings.

Social security benefits

36.4

In cases of unfair dismissal, among others, the Employment Protection (Recoupment of Jobseeker's Allowance and Income Support) Regulations 1996 SI 1996/2349 ('the Recoupment Regulations') apply. They have the effect that if, as a result of being dismissed, the claimant becomes entitled to unemployment benefits such as Jobseeker's Allowance, income-related Employment and Support Allowance or Income Support, the value of these payments will not be taken into account by the employment tribunal in calculating the claimant's net loss. Instead, the Secretary of State may, under the Regulations, recoup the value of those payments from the employer, who deducts it from the amount he eventually pays to the employee.

These Regulations do not apply to discrimination cases – Reg 3 and Schedule 1 to the Regulations set out an exhaustive list of the tribunal payments and proceedings to which the Regulations apply and this list does not include the Equality Act 2010 (EqA) (or the antecedent discrimination legislation). Accordingly, successful claimants ought to give credit for such payments in the normal way – that is, the value of the payments is deducted when assessing the claimant's compensation. One of the governing principles in any assessment of compensation for tort is that a claimant should not receive more compensation than would put him or her in the same financial position as he or she would have been in had the discrimination not occurred. So, incapacity benefit received as a result of a discriminatory dismissal should be taken into account in calculating net loss. This was established in relation to unfair dismissal in Morgans v Alpha Plus Security Ltd 2005 ICR 525, EAT, which noted that the Recoupment Regulations as they then were did not cover incapacity benefit and so held that the general principle as described above ought to apply. And in Chan v Hackney London Borough Council 1997 ICR 1014, EAT – a race discrimination case – the EAT held that 'where a benefit is paid only because of incapacity to earn a wage, such payment ending immediately such incapacity is removed, it cannot... be right in assessing compensation to allow both the lost earnings and that benefit'. It ruled that the employment tribunal had therefore not erred in deducting invalidity benefit (the forerunner to incapacity benefit) from the employee's compensation for discrimination. (Note that, since 31 January 2011,

1269

incapacity benefit is in the process of being replaced by Employment and Support Allowance, to which exactly the same reasoning ought to apply.)

36.5 In Sheffield Forgemasters International Ltd v Fox; Telindus Ltd v Brading 2009 ICR 333, EAT, the issue was whether employees who had succeeded in claims for unfair dismissal and disability discrimination could be compensated for lost earnings at all in respect of periods when they were claiming incapacity benefit. The employers claimed that the employees' receipt of the benefit indicated that they were incapable of working, and so should not be compensated for loss of earnings during that period. The EAT dismissed this argument. In a detailed examination of the relevant statutory provisions, it concluded that during the first 28 weeks of entitlement to incapacity benefit, the special deeming provisions in the Social Security (Incapacity for Work) (General Regulations) 1995 SI 1995/311 – which deem a person who actually works as incapable of work – 'mean that the fact that an individual claims and receives incapacity benefit in the first [28 weeks] does not automatically and necessarily mean that he or she is incapable of working'. Furthermore, during the remainder of the period of incapacity, a person is entitled to the benefit if he or she scores sufficient points on the system set out in the Regulations, but many people who score sufficient points to be entitled to incapacity benefit still work. In conclusion, the EAT held that it was clear that eligibility for incapacity benefit did not mean that someone was incapable of working, and he or she was therefore not precluded from claiming compensation for lost earnings. However, the EAT stated that tribunals should be careful to consider all the evidence, including the basis of any application for incapacity benefit, before deciding whether the claimant would actually have earned any money during the relevant period. A similar analysis of the eligibility requirements for Employment and Support Allowance would need to be conducted for relevant cases after 31 January 2011.

For the purpose of assessing lost earnings, elements of social security benefits that a claimant receives in respect of children and/or household are not distinguished from benefits paid in respect of the claimant him or herself. In Chief Constable of West Yorkshire Police v Vento (No.2) 2002 IRLR 177, EAT, the EAT upheld an employment tribunal's decision to discount from the claimant's compensation for lost earnings those sums she later received as income support, including the elements of benefit provided in respect of her children and mortgage interest payments. There would be an element of double recovery were the claimant not required to give credit for the benefits relating to her children and mortgage when calculating the financial losses resulting from her discriminatory dismissal. (It should be noted that the EAT's decision in Vento was subsequently appealed to the Court of Appeal in relation to other aspects of that decision. These are discussed later in this chapter. However, the recoupment aspect of the EAT's decision was not the subject of appeal, which means that it remains authoritative and binding on employment tribunals.)

Delayed receipt

As shall be seen below, under 'Accelerated receipt', it has long been established practice for employment tribunals to discount awards made for future financial loss to reflect the fact that the claimant receives his or her lost earnings much earlier than he or she would have otherwise have done. In Melia v Magna Kansei Ltd 2006 ICR 410, CA (a non-discrimination case), the possibility of the converse being applied to an award for past financial loss was raised for the first time. The Court endorsed the EAT's decision to award £600 on top of loss of earnings of around £8,000 to compensate for the delayed payment. In the view of Lord Justice Chadwick, where loss sustained in consequence of dismissal includes past earnings as well as future earnings, as here, it is just and equitable to treat the two losses consistently. If future loss is discounted to reflect early receipt, so loss of past earnings should be increased to reflect delayed receipt.

The EAT termed this kind of award a 'premium for decelerated payment', but in reality such loss represents pre-judgment interest. The issue only arose in Melia because the claim was one of protected disclosure, brought under the ERA. Although the principles that apply to compensation awarded under the protected disclosure regime are more or less the same as those that apply to compensation for discrimination, there is no ERA equivalent of the Employment Tribunals (Interest on Awards in Discrimination Cases) Regulations 1996 SI 1996/2803, which allow for interest to be awarded in discrimination cases. The Court in Melia was therefore filling a gap in the legislation, and so its judgment is not authority for applying a similar premium in discrimination cases. Any delay in payment of incurred loss should only be reflected in an award of interest – see under 'Interest on awards' below.

Future loss

Future loss is typically far more complicated to calculate than past loss. An employment tribunal has to use its judgement to try to predict how long the claimant's losses will continue. If the discrimination relates to a dismissal and, at the time of the hearing, the claimant is unemployed, the tribunal will have to consider the period of time it is likely to take him or her to get another job and whether such new employment is likely to command the same, worse or better remuneration as the job from which the claimant was dismissed. This will mean considering issues such as the local job market and factors related to the individual, such as age and skills. If the employee has found other work on a lower rate of pay then the tribunal will need to consider whether the new job has potential for promotion or whether the claimant will at some stage find a job on better terms and conditions. If the tribunal fails to give reasons for its calculations, its decision will be open to challenge on appeal – see, for example, Silva and ors v Harrison (formerly Noble) EAT 0128/03.

1271

The EAT in Atos Origin IT Services UK Ltd v Haddock 2005 ICR 277, EAT, summarised the main principles governing the assessment of future loss. They are:

- unless a future loss is certain to occur or a chance that it will not is so small that it can be disregarded, the chance that it will not occur must be allowed for

- as in personal injury cases, the ordinary contingencies of life must be allowed for

- credit must be given for acceleration of receipt

- compensation will be assessed on the footing that the claimant or applicant will take reasonable steps to mitigate his or her loss. The award will be abated by the amount by which the loss would be reduced if he or she were to do so

- subject to two well-established exceptions, the claimant is not entitled to compensation for a loss which will in fact be avoided. The exceptions are that payments resulting from the benevolence of third parties and from an insurance policy for which the claimant, or applicant, has paid or contributed to the premiums are not to be taken into account

- to the extent that it is uncertain that a loss will be avoided, the chance that it will be must be estimated and appropriate credit given.

We consider all of these issues below.

36.8 As shall be seen in this chapter, the most complex calculations of future loss arise when the discrimination consists of dismissal and the employment tribunal must speculate as to how much the claimant has lost by way of earnings, and his or her chances of finding a replacement income. However, it is not just loss of salary that may sound in damages for future financial loss. All of the financial benefits associated with the lost employment fall to be considered under this heading, including things such as the value of private health insurance, gym membership and travel perks. For example, in Booth v Network Rail Infrastructure Ltd ET Case No.1801322/05 the claimant enjoyed unlimited first-class rail travel. When assessing compensation for discriminatory dismissal, the tribunal valued that perk at £500 per year, taking into account that it would likely have been subject to a charge as a taxable benefit. It went on to find that the claimant would have remained in employment for at least a further six years, which would have entitled her to free rail travel for life. It therefore made an award in respect of the value of free rail travel for life, less a 30 per cent deduction for uncertainty, which gave a total of just under £10,000. (Note that some aspects of the remedy decision were appealed against in Network Rail Infrastructure Ltd v Booth EAT 0071/06 but the award under this head of compensation was unaffected.)

Some other fringe benefits and bonuses not necessarily related to the employment may also be taken into account. In Mulford v Environment Agency ET Case No.1402617/06, for example, M developed a moderately severe depressive illness as a result of bullying and was then dismissed because of her resulting absence. Her compensation for financial loss included £10,000 as compensation for the loss of a contract to write a book: the tribunal held that had there been no discrimination, it was highly likely she would have been well enough to write the book, with an advance of £5,000 and projected royalties of £5,000.

Issues associated with specific protected characteristics. Certain kinds of **36.9** discrimination case may pose particular problems for tribunals in estimating future losses. For example, in disability discrimination cases, speculation on the claimant's future employment prospects can involve consideration of issues – such as the future effects of the disability – of which the tribunal members have little or no experience. The difficulty is illustrated by Buxton v Equinox Design Ltd 1999 ICR 269, EAT. B was diagnosed as having multiple sclerosis and advice received by the employer from the Employment Medical Advisory Service suggested that it should carry out a risk assessment in relation to B and other workers. The employer responded by dismissing B. The employment tribunal held that this amounted to disability discrimination and awarded future losses for one year. On appeal, the EAT held that to calculate future loss the tribunal had to ask itself the question: what would have been the outcome of the risk assessment? To do this the tribunal would need to hear medical evidence, which it had not done, with the result that there was no evidential basis for the tribunal's decision. The EAT remitted the case to the tribunal to reassess the award for future loss.

The difficulties faced by disabled people in seeking employment were also recognised in British Sugar plc v Kirker 1998 IRLR 624, EAT. There, K, who worked as a shift chemist at a sugar factory, had very poor eyesight and even though he wore special glasses his impairment was such that he qualified as disabled. After being selected for redundancy K successfully claimed that he had been discriminated against for a reason related to his disability. The employment tribunal awarded £103,000 compensation. When determining his future loss of earnings, the tribunal took account of a report by the Royal National Institute for the Blind which highlighted the barriers that visually impaired people face in securing and retaining paid work.

Similar considerations might apply in cases of age discrimination against older **36.10** people. Although age discrimination has been unlawful in Great Britain since 2006, an exemption for retirement at 65 remained in force until April 2011, subject to transitional provisions – see Chapter 5, 'Age', under 'Scope of protection under the Equality Act – abolition of the statutory retirement regime'. There was also an exemption allowing employers to refuse to employ job applicants who were within six months of the default retirement age. This

1273

means that the stereotypical assumption that employees will retire at 65 is still very strong, and is likely still to influence employers making recruitment decisions. In other words, older people are still likely to face more difficulties finding new employment than younger people. Tribunals ought to be able to take account of an older claimant's diminished employment prospects. Support for this approach can be derived from the approach adopted by courts to so-called 'stigma damage', which represents the extra difficulty a discrimination claimant may face in finding future employment because of the fact that he or she has brought a discrimination claim. As will be seen under 'Stigma damages' below, the Court of Appeal, in Abbey National plc v Chagger 2010 ICR 397, CA, has indicated that the fact that such damage results from the unlawful actions of a third party does not necessarily mean that it is not caused by the original act of discrimination – in that case, a discriminatory dismissal. So, when assessing how long a dismissed claimant is likely to be out of work, a tribunal might wish to consider the extent to which a 60-year-old will find it harder to secure new employment than a 30-year-old, for example.

36.11 Potential career-long loss

When the claim relates to a discriminatory dismissal, the employment tribunal, in calculating future loss of earnings, will have to consider the likely chance that the claimant, but for his or her dismissal, would have continued in his or her employment until retirement. The correct approach for determining this issue was set out by the Court of Appeal in Vento v Chief Constable of West Yorkshire Police (No.2) 2003 ICR 318, CA (a sex discrimination case). In that case, the question was: what were V's chances of remaining in the police force until the age of retirement at 55 if she had not been discriminated against and dismissed? The Court of Appeal confirmed that this requires an assessment of a chance, based on material available to the tribunal, including the use of statistical information as to the probability of an employee remaining in the service of the employer on a long-term basis. However, the Court emphasised that such statistical evidence is not determinative, and that, since such an assessment of chance involves a forecast about the course of future events, it should not be approached as if the tribunal were making a finding of fact based on a balance of probabilities.

In the Vento case the employment tribunal concluded that, had V not been discriminated against on the ground of her sex, she would have completed her probation, qualified as a police officer, and would then have had a 75 per cent chance of working in the police force for the rest of her career. Although the tribunal was provided with statistics showing that only 9 per cent of women police officers serve for more than 18 years, it was impressed by V's determination to be a police officer and her desire to provide for her children. It also took into account the fact that the police force had introduced family-friendly policies to encourage working mothers, and noted that V was unable to have any more children. On appeal, the Court of Appeal ruled that the tribunal had been entitled to approach the statistical evidence with circumspection. Quite apart from its findings as to V's ambition, dedication and determination in the face of adversity and its predictions of her future career based on those factors, the tribunal had relevant evidence which showed that future social and working conditions in the police force would differ from those prevailing in the decade covered by the statistics. This included evidence about the anticipated need to retain more female officers and the introduction of family-friendly working policies. There were also a number of factors specific to V that considerably lessened the relevance of the statistics to her particular case. In particular, V's inability to have any more children was important, as the high incidence of women officers failing to complete police careers was attributable to their leaving in order to have children. Although the Court doubted whether it would have assessed V's chances as being as high as 75 per cent, this was an option reasonably open to the tribunal and should not have been overturned by the EAT on the ground of perversity.

36.12 Once an employment tribunal is satisfied that the claimant would have remained with the employer for the entirety of his or her career it must then consider the claimant's chances of finding alternative employment. Only if those chances are slight or non-existent will an award of career-long loss be appropriate. In Abbey National plc v Chagger 2010 ICR 397, CA, the Court of Appeal confirmed that career-long loss is recoverable in appropriate cases – this case is discussed in more detail below under 'Chances of non-discriminatory dismissal' and 'Stigma damages'. However, a later Court of Appeal decision emphasised how exceptional such awards must be. In Wardle v Crédit Agricole Corporate and Investment Bank 2011 ICR 1290, CA, Lord Justice Elias (who also sat in Chagger) held that future loss should only be assessed over a career lifetime in rare cases – where a tribunal considers that an employee has no prospect of ever finding an equivalent job. In most cases it will be fair to assess loss up to the point where an employee would be likely to obtain an equivalent job. The tribunal in the instant case appeared to have awarded damages until the point at which it was sure the claimant would find an equivalent job, which was wrong. Given that the tribunal had found a 70 per cent chance that the claimant would return to a comparable job by the end of 2011, it was wrong to award any compensation for financial loss after that date (assessed at 30 per cent by the tribunal). Furthermore, it was arguable that the cut-off date should have been some time sooner, when the prospects of an equivalent job would have been greater than 50 per cent. On the basis of the tribunal's findings, the Court of Appeal considered that this was June 2011. Therefore, the tribunal should only have awarded the claimant compensation for future loss up to this date.

It is axiomatic that the shorter the length of time between the termination of the claimant's employment and the point at which the claimant would have retired in any event, the easier it is to predict the losses the claimant will have sustained by the discriminatory act. So, in cases where the claimant is within 10 to 15 years of retirement, an award of career-long loss may be more likely. An example:

- **Newsome v Sunderland City Council** ET Case No.6403592/99: N was a 48-year-old accountant who was dismissed in circumstances that amounted to disability discrimination. At the remedies hearing, the employment tribunal found that she would have worked until she was 65, in relatively secure public sector employment, and that it was most unlikely that she would work again. N was awarded £32,031 for past loss and £195,923 for future lost earnings, plus a further £28,985 pension loss.

36.13 Of course, considering loss over a long career presents significant problems when it comes to quantification. This is considered below under 'Calculation of future loss'. Note that, in assessing the chance of career-long loss, tribunals may also have to make allowances for the possibility that the claimant might have been promoted in the future had he or she remained in post. However, in Ministry of Defence v Cannock and ors 1994 ICR 918, EAT, the EAT warned that tribunals should be wary of assessing promotion chances on the high side as this was a question of 'chance' not 'fact'.

36.14 **Chance of non-discriminatory dismissal**
In cases of discriminatory dismissal, employment tribunals may also need to consider whether, were it not for the discriminatory dismissal, there could have been a non-discriminatory dismissal at the same time, or whether there would have been a non-discriminatory dismissal at some definable point in the future. The chance that the claimant could or would have been dismissed in any event, with no discrimination, can be recognised by making a proportionate reduction in compensation for future loss.

This principle is well established in the context of unfair dismissal. In Polkey v AE Dayton Services Ltd 1988 ICR 142, HL, the House of Lords established that where a dismissal was procedurally unfair, but the employer could show that there was a significant chance that, had it followed a fair procedure, it would have dismissed anyway, compensation could be reduced accordingly. It was initially thought that Polkey was limited to the situation where the dismissal was unfair purely as a matter of procedural failings, rather than a matter of substance (i.e. relating to the validity of the employer's reason for dismissal). The rationale for a Polkey reduction was understood to be that the lack of a fair procedure made no practical difference to the decision to dismiss. However, a wealth of subsequent case law considering Polkey has widened that principle, to the extent that it can now be regarded as merely an application of tribunals' obligation to determine compensation for unfair dismissal by reference to what is 'just and equitable'. So, even where the employer's reason for dismissal is flawed, it may invoke Polkey to argue for a reduction in compensation on the

1276

basis that a fair dismissal was likely at some point in the future. For a full discussion of the Polkey principle and 'just and equitable' compensation for unfair dismissal, see IDS Employment Law Handbook, 'Unfair Dismissal' (2010), Chapter 18, 'Compensatory awards: adjustments and reductions', under '"Polkey reductions"'.

The application of the so-called 'Polkey principle' in discrimination cases has **36.15** been recognised. In O'Donoghue v Redcar and Cleveland Borough Council 2001 IRLR 615, CA, the Court of Appeal held that an employment tribunal, having found an employee to have been unfairly dismissed on sex discriminatory grounds, was entitled to deploy Polkey-type reasoning to limit the period of loss. On the evidence, the tribunal concluded that the employee would have been lawfully dismissed within six months in any event by reason of her antagonistic and intransigent attitude. It accordingly limited the future loss for which the employer was liable to this period. However, it should be noted that this was still an assessment of compensation under the unfair dismissal regime – the tribunal and the EAT focused on what compensation it would be 'just and equitable' to award, which is the guiding principle under the ERA. Thus, this was not a direct transposition of the Polkey approach to discrimination compensation.

Polkey principles have, nonetheless, influenced the approach to compensation for discrimination. In Abbey National plc v Chagger 2010 ICR 397, CA, the Court of Appeal had to consider a claim for career-long loss. C successfully claimed unfair dismissal and race discrimination on the basis of his selection for redundancy by AN plc. The employment tribunal awarded him almost £3 million in compensation, accepting his submission that he would never again be able to obtain employment in the financial services industry. It declined to make a Polkey-type reduction to reflect the chance that, had no discrimination occurred, C would have been dismissed in any event. The tribunal took the view that, while the basis for making such a reduction is well established in unfair dismissal cases, the same principle should not apply to discrimination. On appeal, the EAT disagreed with that view and, on further appeal, so did the Court of Appeal. Lord Justice Elias, giving judgment for the Court, stated that if there was a chance that, apart from the discrimination, C would have been dismissed in any event, that possibility had to be factored into the measure of loss. Clearly, on the facts of the case, there was such a chance. The claimant was unlawfully dismissed in the context of a genuine redundancy situation, which affected only two candidates, one of whom had to be selected. Thus there was plainly a realistic prospect that C would have been dismissed even if the selection procedure had been conducted on a non-discriminatory basis. The Court remitted the case to enable the employment tribunal to assess that prospect.

Apart from the Polkey issue, the other significant aspect of the Court of Appeal's **36.16** decision in Chagger was that tribunals can recognise 'stigma damage' in

1277

assessing compensation. In short, this means that some account can be taken of other employers' likely reluctance to employ someone who has brought discrimination proceedings against a previous employer (unlawful though this would be). Stigma damage will normally be factored into the award for ongoing financial loss. However, it is worth noting here that Elias LJ suggested one exceptional circumstance in which stigma damage may itself be a free-standing head of loss – namely, where this is the only head of future loss. The example Elias LJ gave was that of an employee who would have been dismissed even if there had been no discrimination, for whom a Polkey-type reduction would reduce compensation for future loss to zero. Such an employee would be on the labour market at exactly the same time and in the same circumstances as he would have been had he been dismissed lawfully. Accordingly, the damage to his employment prospects from the stigma of taking proceedings would be the only potentially recoverable head of future loss. Elias LJ acknowledged that such damage would be difficult to prove and to quantify and suggested that a modest lump sum might be appropriate. The issue of compensation for stigma is discussed more fully under 'Stigma damages' below.

The Chagger case therefore makes it clear that a reduction in compensation along Polkey lines might serve to reduce future loss all the way down to zero. The circumstances justifying such an approach must, though, be regarded as rare. The following is an example (pre-dating Chagger) of a discriminatory dismissal from which no future loss was found to flow:

- **Mitchell and anor v Graff Diamonds Ltd** ET Case No.2200725/09: B suffered from psoriasis, a condition that the employment tribunal accepted constituted a disability for the purposes of the Disability Discrimination Act 1995 (DDA). On four occasions, his attendance at medical appointments related to his condition made him late for work. When GD Ltd had to make redundancies, one of the selection criteria it applied was punctuality, penalising employees with more than ten instances of lateness. B, who had 23 incidents of lateness, was selected and dismissed. The tribunal upheld B's claim of disability discrimination, finding that, as a result of his disability-related lateness, he was 'allowed' only six incidents of lateness compared to ten for non-disabled employees. However, the tribunal decided to limit compensation to a small award for injury to feelings, finding that even if B's disability-related lateness had been excluded from consideration he would still have been dismissed. Thus, no financial loss was attributable to the discriminatory dismissal.

36.17 An employment tribunal might also find that, because of the claimant's attitude, there was little prospect of him or her remaining in employment in any event. In Singh v Ahmed t/a Herberts Bakery ET Case No.1402240/10 S, who was disabled by a knee condition, went off work sick in August 2009 and was dismissed in May 2010 when he had exhausted his right to sick pay but was incapable of returning to work. He successfully claimed disability discrimination by way of failure to make reasonable adjustments, since no adjustments were attempted or even mooted by the employer. However, the tribunal found that there was only a 10 per cent chance of his avoiding dismissal in any event. The only realistic adjustment would have been for S to work part time and, on the evidence, it was unlikely that he would have been willing or able to work under such an arrangement.

Failure to recruit/promote   36.18

When a tribunal complaint relates to a failure to recruit or promote an individual because of a protected characteristic, future loss should be calculated on the basis that it represents compensation for the loss of a valuable chance to obtain work. Tribunals must try to attach a value to the loss, which is not always easy because this requires an assessment of the claimant's chances of being offered the job if the discrimination had not occurred. As is the case with compensation for discriminatory dismissal, the tribunal members will be expected to use their knowledge and experience and to perform a necessarily speculative role in assessing as accurately as possible the losses that have been caused by the employer's unlawful act of discrimination. Two examples:

- **Bernard v Merseyside Immigration Advice Unit** ET Case No.68127/94: an employment tribunal decided that, but for the employer's discrimination, B would have been offered the job she had applied for. Instead she had been forced to remain in her old job, from which she was eventually dismissed. The tribunal held that she was entitled to recover the whole of the difference between the pay she actually received in her job up to her dismissal and the pay that she would have received in the new job. It also held that she was entitled to recover the whole of the salary she would have received in the new job from the date of her dismissal to a date three months after the tribunal hearing

- **Williams v Newport Borough Council** ET Case No.5494/87: W was not promoted because of unlawful sex discrimination but the employment tribunal decided that she had only a one-in-four chance of gaining promotion in any event. However, it believed that she would attain promotion in two years and awarded a sum representing 25 per cent of her net salary loss over a two-year period, together with a sum for injury to feelings.

As the Williams case demonstrates, tribunals very often base their assessment of losses on the probability that the claimant would have been selected if the discrimination had not occurred. However, they have a wide discretion in this area. In some cases tribunals may simply award loss of earnings on the basis that the complainant would have got the job were it not for the discrimination. In others, where the individual's chances of obtaining the job were slim irrespective of any unlawful discrimination, the tribunal may prefer to award little or nothing for loss of opportunity, or to award a 'global' sum that combines loss of opportunity with other sub-heads of intangible losses such as 'injury to feelings'. In Greig v Initial Security Ltd EATS 0036/05, for example, the EAT dismissed G's appeal against a tribunal's award of £500 compensation for injury to feelings for disability discrimination relating to a failed job application. It noted that the tribunal had decided upon the figure of £500 on the basis that G had admitted that he was not very well qualified for the post and there was no doubt that he did not really expect his application to be successful.

36.19 Similarly, in Niyukuri v Premier Placement Services Ltd ET Case No.1308476/10, N suffered race discrimination when an employment agency delayed in accepting his registration. The agency refused to process his application until it had checked his immigration status with the Home Office, but that was a mere pretext since N had produced acceptable documentation and the agency was well aware that the Home Office would not provide specific confirmation. An employment tribunal found that the reason for the agency's hesitation, which delayed N's application for several weeks, was race. However, it made no award of financial loss. It had regard to the fact that the agency had 2,000 workers on its books and that, over the previous 12 months, only 10 per cent had worked. Taking into account the economic climate and the fact that the local area had particularly high unemployment, the tribunal thought the chances of N finding work through the agency were too remote for there to be any quantifiable financial loss.

The effect of a discriminatory rejection on the claimant's career can also be taken into account when assessing compensation. In Lockwood v West Group Engineering ET Case No.23329/86 the claimant was refused a job as a trainee machine operator on account of her sex. The tribunal awarded £750 for 'lost opportunity', even though she had since obtained better-paid employment elsewhere, because she would have preferred the trainee position on account of the better long-term prospects it afforded.

36.20 **Calculating future loss**
The longer the period for which future loss is awarded, the more complicated the calculation of the total becomes. This is particularly so in cases of discriminatory dismissal. As already noted in this chapter, where a claimant has no prospect, or only limited prospects, of securing employment equivalent to that from which he or she has been unlawfully dismissed, the employment tribunal may make an award of compensation covering the whole of the claimant's working life. Such cases demand consideration of a wide variety of variables, such as the chances of the claimant dying before he or she would otherwise have retired, or the claimant becoming unable to work through ill health.

In Kingston Upon Hull City Council v Dunnachie (No.3) 2003 IRLR 843, EAT, the EAT considered the extent to which tribunals are entitled to rely on the

'Ogden Tables' in making such calculations. These are issued by the Government Actuary's Department and allow for an actuarial adjustment of compensation for future loss in personal injury cases. The 7th edition was published in October 2011. The EAT concluded that reliance on such tables is appropriate only where it is established that the claimant is likely to suffer a career-long future loss of earnings. That caution was repeated by a later EAT in Birmingham City Council v Jaddoo EAT 0448/04 – the EAT's then President, Mr Justice Burton, remarking that tribunals should be wary of finding lifelong loss where the claimant is as young as 31 or 32, as was the position in that particular case.

36.21 The EAT in Dunnachie also held that the Ogden Tables are relevant only once the employment tribunal has determined a figure for estimated annual future loss and an estimated period of loss lasting until retirement. It is unlikely that a tribunal will arrive at a single annual figure for estimated loss. In some cases one figure in respect of the first one or two years and then a lower figure in respect of later periods will be appropriate. Whenever it is appropriate to use the Ogden Tables, the tribunal should adopt the discount rate in force under the Damages Act 1996 (currently 2.5 per cent) to take account of accelerated receipt of compensation (see 'Accelerated receipt' below). Once the tribunal has applied the Ogden Table multipliers, it is generally inappropriate for it then to apply a large percentage discount for contingencies, since these should have been taken into account at the outset in order to arrive at the multiplicand (the figure for estimated annual loss) and period of loss.

Although both the Dunnachie and Jaddoo cases considered compensation for unfair dismissal – which is awarded under a different compensation regime to that which prevails under the EqA – it has since been confirmed that the Ogden Tables can apply in discrimination cases also. In Abbey National plc v Chagger 2009 ICR 624, EAT, the Appeal Tribunal made some comments on the appropriateness of using the tables in a case where career-long loss was considered under the Race Relations Act 1976 (RRA). In fact, on other grounds of appeal, the EAT established that the instant case was not one where compensation should be awarded in respect of the claimant's entire career, and so its comments on the Ogden Tables must be regarded as obiter. It should also be noted that the EAT's decision was the subject of a further appeal but the Court of Appeal, in Abbey National plc v Chagger 2010 ICR 397, CA, was not required to consider the EAT's particular views on the Ogden Tables.

36.22 In Chagger the EAT approved the use of the Ogden Tables in a discrimination context, but only as a starting-point. It noted that even in a case where it is appropriate to use the tables, it will never be right to use the multiplier taken from the main tables without considering certain contingencies that those tables do not reflect. The Ogden Tables only take into account the possibility of death over the relevant period – they do not factor in, for example, that the employer might go out of business, that the employee might be dismissed for good cause, that the employee might leave voluntarily, or that he or she might otherwise become incapable of work. These other contingencies must be properly reflected in the ultimate multiplier used. This means the multiplier given by the tables will usually need to be reduced, although there may be cases where the tribunal believes that the contingencies in question are balanced by 'upside' contingencies, such as the possibility of promotion. The EAT went on to point out that, although the main Ogden Tables do not take account of contingencies other than mortality, section B of the Explanatory Notes that accompany the tables does suggest ways in which allowances may be made for certain other risks such as ill health and unemployment, and the way these may vary according to geography and the nature of the claimant's occupation.

Even when the Explanatory Notes are utilised, the tribunal must still consider whether the factors they take into account are relevant to the particular case before the tribunal. In Rudd v Eagle Place Services Ltd EAT 0151/09 – a disability discrimination case – the EAT allowed an appeal against an employment tribunal's decision to reduce the multiplier from 16.92 to 9.64 based on contingencies set out in section B. The tribunal had applied the reduction suggested by Table B, which is designed to apply to a man with a disability, without considering the appropriateness of those contingencies to the claimant's actual circumstances. The tribunal had also erred by failing to account for the value of the permanent health insurance (PHI) that the claimant lost when he was dismissed by the respondent. In his schedule of loss, the claimant asserted that the PHI would have paid him two thirds of his salary if his disability rendered him incapable of work. The EAT held that it was an error of law not to factor this into the calculation of the claimant's ongoing loss. Since the tribunal had discounted the multiplier based on Table B to reflect the chance that he would have become unemployed in any event as a result of his disability, it should have taken into account the corresponding increase in the chance of his thereby being disadvantaged by no longer having the benefit of the PHI.

36.23 Given that the Ogden Tables only fully consider mortality, and leave a lot of other considerations to the tribunal's own initiative, the EAT's suggestion in Chagger that they be used as a starting point and nothing more is a sensible one. Furthermore, the EAT went on to express doubts over whether, in the employment field, it is right to assess contingencies only on the basis of the kind of discounting factors used in section B of the Ogden Tables – particularly in view of the fact that those factors are based on general population figures and make no allowance for the possibility of the claimant leaving his employment voluntarily. This is another consideration that the tribunal will have to assess on a case-specific basis. Accordingly, while tribunals are free to use the Ogden Tables in calculating compensation for discrimination, the tables are of limited use, leaving much of the speculation and prediction to the tribunal's own judgement.

Permanent health insurance

The principle underlying many of the deductions that an employment tribunal may apply to a compensation award is that a claimant must not be compensated twice for the same loss – in other words, there must be no double recovery. This applies in respect of any payments made under a permanent health insurance scheme. In Atos Origin IT Services UK Ltd v Haddock 2005 ICR 277, EAT, H suffered two nervous breakdowns, resulting in a severe depressive illness which left him unable to work. The employer was found liable for direct disability discrimination and failure to make reasonable adjustments. However, H continued to be an employee, and the employer had a permanent health insurance policy, whereby it recouped 75 per cent of H's salary from the insurance company, and would continue to do so, as long as H continued to be unable to work. H had no contractual right to the payment from the insurance company and so could not recover any payment from it directly, save in exceptional circumstances. The employment tribunal, in attempting to assess the lump sum payable for future loss, concluded that compensation should be assessed on the basis that the employer was liable for 100 per cent of H's salary and declined to take account of the fact that H was covered under the insurance scheme.

On appeal, the EAT held that the same deductions had to be made from an award of compensation to victims of disability discrimination as would be made in personal injury cases, in respect of which payments made by the underwriters of a health insurance policy for which premiums are paid by the tortfeasor without contribution from the claimant fall to be deducted. Accordingly, any lump sum for future loss in the instant case should have been assessed on the basis of 25 per cent loss of salary, rather than 100 per cent. However, the EAT found another way of ensuring that H would receive, and the employer pay, all that H should receive but no more. It suggested that the tribunal make a recommendation under what was then S.8(2)(c) DDA (now S.124(2)(b) EqA) that the company continue to employ H until retirement age, and pay him all his contractual benefits (including full salary), so long as he continued to comply with the insurance company's conditions. Should the company fail to comply, then H could come back to the tribunal for an award of additional compensation, as provided for by S.8(5) DDA (now S.124(7) EqA). (For a full explanation of 'recommendations' as a remedy for discrimination, see Chapter 34, 'Enforcing individual rights', under 'Remedies – recommendations'.)

The availability of a PHI scheme may have to be taken into account by the tribunal when considering what would have happened but for the discrimination. In Smith v Waterman Boreham Ltd ET Case No.3202777/09 S suffered from Huntingdon's disease, a degenerative and incurable condition. An employment tribunal found that WB Ltd had failed to make reasonable adjustments when it dismissed S as redundant instead of considering the option of retaining him in employment pending investigation into the possibility of making a PHI claim. It considered that, had S remained in employment, then within a year to 18 months his condition would have progressed to the stage where he would have been eligible for PHI benefits. The tribunal therefore awarded compensation for the value of the salary S would have been paid over those 12 to 18 months, plus the value of PHI benefits over the 12 years from his dismissal to the date he would have retired. This came to nearly £140,000 in total, including £8,000 for injury to feelings.

36.26 ## Stigma damages

In Abbey National plc v Chagger 2010 ICR 397, CA, the Court of Appeal held that an employer who discriminated against an employee by dismissing him or her could be liable for the consequences of the stigma that might attach to the employee as a result of taking legal action for unlawful discrimination. The issue arose when the claimant was selected for redundancy under a procedure that an employment tribunal later found to be discriminatory on the ground of race. It awarded compensation of almost £3 million for career-long loss of earnings. Various points on appeal were taken to the EAT by both sides. Among other things, C argued that the compensation should reflect his decreased chances of finding other employment after leaving AN plc due to the stigma of having brought race discrimination proceedings. The EAT rejected that argument, holding that the immediate cause of such loss would be the unlawful act of a third party – refusing to employ someone on the basis that he or she had brought a race discrimination claim would be victimisation under S.2 RRA (now S.27 EqA).

On further appeal, however, the Court of Appeal agreed with the claimant's submission. It held that the mere fact that the immediate cause of his loss would be the actions of a third party did not relieve AN plc of liability for that loss. It drew authority for this proposition from the House of Lords' decision in Malik and anor v Bank of Credit and Commerce International SA (in compulsory liquidation) 1997 ICR 606, HL, which considered whether stigma damage was recoverable as loss flowing from a breach of contract. The Court of Appeal thought it clear from Malik that, if a stigma attaches to an employee from the unlawful way in which the employer runs his business, the employer will be liable for losses that flow from the fact that other employers will not want to recruit the employee. The case indicated that the mere fact that a third party is the immediate cause of the loss does not of itself break the chain of causation between the original employer's unlawful actions and the employee's loss.

36.27 Lord Justice Elias, giving the only judgment of a unanimous court in Chagger, identified several public policy considerations that supported the result. He noted that it can be difficult for a claimant to prove victimisation and should not be criticised for being reluctant to expend time, money and stress on a further claim. Furthermore, it was doubtful that Parliament, in passing the

1284

victimisation provisions, intended to curtail the protection a victim of discrimination would have against his own employer. It was also relevant that a third party employer could lawfully refuse to recruit an employee who had brought unfair dismissal proceedings against his or her former employer. In Elias LJ's view, it would be 'unsatisfactory and somewhat artificial if tribunals were obliged to discount stigma loss in the context of discrimination law but not in other contexts'.

Having found that stigma loss was, in principle, recoverable, the Court stated **36.28** that, in most cases, it would not need to be dealt with as a separate head of loss. On the contrary, it will be a factor for the tribunal to consider in determining the future period during which the claimant suffers loss of earnings. Elias LJ stated that it would be wrong for a tribunal to infer that an employee will suffer widespread stigma purely from his or her assertion to that effect, or from his or her suspicions that this might be so. However, where there is extensive evidence of a claimant's unsuccessful attempts to find new employment, a tribunal would be entitled to conclude that, for whatever reason, the claimant is unlikely to find further employment in his or her chosen industry. In the instant case, the claimant had made over 100 job applications, and used 26 recruitment agencies, but failed to find any job in financial services. In those circumstances, it was unnecessary for the tribunal to reach a conclusive view on the contribution that stigma played in his difficulties in finding fresh employment. Rather, the claimant's loss should be assessed on the basis that he would have remained with AN plc until he was 65, taking into account his likely earnings in his new career as a teacher.

Elias LJ did observe, however, that there is one exceptional case where it could **36.29** be necessary for a tribunal to award compensation specifically to reflect the impact of stigma on a claimant's future job prospects – namely, where this is the only head of future loss. The example Elias LJ gave was that of an employee who would have been dismissed even if there had been no discrimination. He would be on the labour market at exactly the same time and in the same circumstances as he would have been had he been dismissed lawfully. Accordingly, the damage to his employment prospects from the stigma of taking proceedings would be the only potentially recoverable head of future loss. Here, however, the employee would be asserting that this is a head of loss, and the onus would be on him to prove it. In practice this would be a difficult task.

Even if the employee were to establish such a loss, the tribunal would be faced with the almost impossible task of having to assess it. The tribunal would have to determine how far difficulties in obtaining employment result from general market considerations and how far they result from the stigma. In the unlikely event that the evidence of the stigma difficulties was sufficiently strong, it would be open to the tribunal to make an award of future loss for a specific period. But, in the more likely scenario that the evidence showed that stigma was only one of the claimant's difficulties, it may be that a modest lump sum would be appropriate to compensate him or her for the stigma element in his employment difficulties. Such an approach, suggested Elias LJ, would be analogous to the lump sum awards made in personal injury cases to compensate an injured claimant for the risks of future disadvantage on the labour market.

36.30 There is one example of an employment tribunal making a free-standing award in respect of disadvantage on the labour market – Kapoor v ICIC Bank UK plc ET Case No.2202061/09. Although this was not a discrimination case but rather involved the statutory protection for making a 'protected disclosure' under Part IVA of the ERA, the tribunal's decision is informative since it has been recognised in several cases that the protected disclosure and discrimination regimes are analogous and that the same principles govern compensation: see, for example, Virgo Fidelis Senior School v Boyle 2004 ICR 1210, EAT. In the Kapoor case K began working for ICIC plc in Mumbai in September 2007 and in April 2008 transferred to London. His contract stated that he would work in London for 22 months but could be repatriated at any time. In January 2009, K and a colleague made a protected disclosure that a manager had falsified profit and loss figures. ICIC plc carried out an investigation but did not uphold the allegations. K and his colleague then complained to the Financial Services Authority, which carried out its own investigation. ICIC plc had to bear the cost of this investigation, some £100,000. In April, K was transferred back to Mumbai and the colleague was made redundant. An employment tribunal upheld K's claim that he had been subjected to a detriment for having made a protected disclosure – the transfer to Mumbai was a detriment to K and the tribunal was in no doubt that the reason for it was K's complaint to the FSA.

When it came to remedy, the tribunal found that K would have been transferred to India by the end of June 2009 in any event. Nonetheless, he suffered considerable hurt, distress and shock and so it was right to award him £10,000 for injury to feelings. The tribunal also awarded a 'modest lump sum', following Elias LJ's guidance in Chagger, of £8,000, to compensate him for future disadvantage in the labour market. It noted that K was seeking work in the United Kingdom and that there had been considerable publicity in his case. The tribunal thought it very likely that potential employers would discover such information about prospective candidates, it being more readily available nowadays owing to the internet. The tribunal also readily accepted that employers in the financial services sector would be reluctant to employ someone known to be both a whistleblower and willing to bring legal proceedings against his employer.

36.31 Accelerated receipt
As any award for financial loss in future years results in a payment that is paid up front in a single lump sum, a discount rate is usually applied (unless the

1286

award is very small) to take into account the benefit of receiving the monetary sum early, on the assumption that the money can then be invested to yield growth. The Court of Appeal confirmed in Bentwood Bros (Manchester) Ltd v Shepherd 2003 ICR 1000, CA, that employment tribunals should not ignore the fact that the complainant has the benefit of immediately receiving money that he or she would otherwise have had to wait for. However, in this particular case, the tribunal applied a single deduction of 5 per cent of the total compensation designed to compensate for two and a half years' future earnings and ten years' pension payments. The Court of Appeal held that, in so doing, the tribunal had failed to recognise that the conventional investment rate referred to in legal textbooks of 5 per cent was intended to be an annual rate. The Court also held that, arguably, 5 per cent was on the high side, given that the statutory discount rate applicable in personal injury cases had recently been reduced to 2.5 per cent. The question of the appropriate rate to apply as a discount for accelerated receipt was therefore remitted to the tribunal for reconsideration. The tribunal subsequently confirmed that the appropriate discount for accelerated receipt was 3 per cent.

In Benchmark Dental Laboratories Group Ltd v Perfitt EAT 0304/04 the EAT considered two matters of general interest with regard to discount for accelerated receipt. The first concerned the appropriate discount rate. The EAT pointed out that the rate prescribed for use in personal injury cases is set by the Lord Chancellor pursuant to S.1 of the Damages Act 1996. The Damages (Personal Injury) Order 2001 SI 2001/2301 currently prescribes 2.5 per cent as the assumed rate of return on investment of awards of personal injury damages. Although employment tribunals are not bound by this discount, the EAT observed that it will be good practice for them to adopt it.

36.32 The second issue concerned the application of that rate to the particular circumstances of the case. The employment tribunal found that the employee had been unfairly dismissed and subject to disability discrimination. It further found that, at the age of 57, the period of the employee's loss would be likely to continue until his retirement age, i.e. eight years. It calculated his actual financial loss as being £121,864 and then applied a 2.5 per cent discount for accelerated payment to that entire sum, resulting in an award of £118,818. On appeal, the EAT ruled that the tribunal had erred by applying the 2.5 per cent discount to the entire period of loss. That was because receipt of the entire sum was not accelerated to the same extent equally across the whole period: the benefit to the employee of early receipt was far greater in respect of that part of the award for lost earnings at the end of the period. Taking a broad brush approach, the EAT held that one appropriate way of calculating the discount for accelerated receipt in the instant case was to apply a total discount of 10 per cent to half the award, since it was the second half of the award in respect of which early receipt was most accelerated. This represented a discount of 2.5 per cent multiplied by half the number of years covered by the compensation

1287

award (in this case, four). In the event of greater sophistication being required, the EAT suggested that parties should refer the tribunal to appropriate compensation tables, such as the Ogden Tables (see under 'Calculating future loss' above, and IDS Employment Law Handbook, 'Unfair Dismissal' (2010), Chapter 16, 'Compensatory awards: types of loss', under 'Future loss – career-long loss'). However, the EAT made it clear that in the absence of a more sophisticated approach, a tribunal would not err in law by applying a discount for accelerated receipt on the basis of the broad considerations set out above. Where a multiplier is being used (as may be the case where career-long loss is being claimed on account of personal injury caused by the act of discrimination), the standard formula may already incorporate a discount for accelerated receipt.

It is possible that some kinds of financial loss other than loss of earnings might attract a higher discount for accelerated receipt. In Network Rail Infrastructure Ltd v Booth EAT 0071/06 an employment tribunal awarded compensation for, among other things, the private health insurance the claimant lost on dismissal. It assessed the value of the insurance at £900 per year for five years, totalling £4,500, but reduced that by 25 per cent for accelerated receipt. The reduction was suggested by the claimant and accepted by the tribunal and so it did not set out any reasons for such a high discount rate. It is possible that benefits like health insurance can be bought more cheaply when a number of years are paid for in advance. On appeal, the EAT accepted NRI Ltd's challenge to the tribunal's fixing of the period of loss at five years – the tribunal had not given sufficient reasons for this calculation – and remitted this issue for the tribunal to reconsider, but it made no comment on the discount for accelerated receipt.

36.33 Mitigation of loss

At common law, claimants are under a duty to mitigate their loss. An equivalent duty arises in all discrimination claims, whereby compensation may be decreased if a claimant has reduced, or could reasonably have been expected to reduce, his or her losses. The most obvious way he or she might do this following a dismissal is by obtaining alternative employment.

It is for the employer to show that the complainant has failed to mitigate his or her loss. In Ministry of Defence v Hunt and ors 1996 ICR 554, EAT, the EAT stressed that the employer must adduce evidence in relation to mitigation and that a vague assertion of failure to mitigate unsupported by any evidence is unlikely to succeed. In the first instance, compensation will be assessed on the basis that the employee took all reasonable steps to reduce his or her loss. If the employee in fact failed to take such steps – for example, by turning down suitable new employment – the award will be reduced to reflect only those losses that would have been incurred if the employee had taken the appropriate steps. Whether an employee has mitigated his or her loss is a question of fact and tribunals will judge the matter on the particular circumstances of the case. They must apply the law properly, however: the question is not whether the

employee has behaved reasonably in general terms but whether he or she has taken reasonable steps to mitigate. The difference between the two is illustrated by the following examples:

- **Ministry of Defence v Cannock and ors** 1994 ICR 918, EAT: the employment tribunal found that one of the claimants, H, decided no longer actively to seek work nine months after the birth of her first child not because of an unwillingness to return to work but on 'a reasonable assessment of the position in which she found herself following her compulsory discharge from the Navy'. On that basis, the tribunal found that there had been no breach by H of the duty to mitigate. However, on appeal the EAT held that the tribunal had misdirected itself. H was under a duty to mitigate her loss by continuing to look for work. If she chose not to do so, then she could not continue to accrue compensation for loss of her career. The fact that a decision not to pursue a career was reasonable did not mean that she had taken all reasonable steps to mitigate her loss. The case was remitted to the tribunal for proper consideration of this point

- **Warlow v Clarion Community Newspapers Ltd** ET Case No.1700326/99: W discovered she was pregnant and informed her employer about a week later. The employer subsequently commented that she was 'plodding' because of her pregnancy, and dismissed her. She brought a number of claims, including for sex discrimination, which the employment tribunal upheld. W stated that the dismissal was a severe blow to her morale and she felt extremely low for two months. By the time she was ready to look for new work, there was no point because in her field – advertising sales – it takes time to build up contacts, and by the time she could have done so she would have had to leave to have her baby. The tribunal accepted her evidence that she had taken such steps as were reasonable and awarded her compensation for loss of earnings to the date she would have begun her maternity leave.

36.34 In general, claimants will be in a better position to answer any charge of failing to mitigate their loss if they can show that they made efforts to find alternative employment straight away following dismissal. Tribunals may scrutinise a claimant's reasons for not seeking alternative work immediately. In Live Nation (Venues) Ltd v Hussain and other cases EAT 0234–6/08 – a case decided in the context of compensation for unfair dismissal – the EAT held that an employment tribunal was entitled to find that a claimant who had not taken immediate steps to find alternative employment following his dismissal had not unreasonably failed to mitigate his loss. The tribunal had observed that the claimant was 'certainly employable' and had 'influential friends', and noted that he had admitted that he had not yet started looking seriously for a job and that he ought to have done so. The EAT held that while a claimant must take reasonable steps to mitigate his or her loss, it is not necessarily unreasonable for an employee who is suddenly faced with dismissal after 26 years, as in the instant case, to take stock of his situation and consider what steps he should take thereafter. The claimant had told the tribunal that he was severely damaged and distressed by the experience. Although the EAT thought that the tribunal had been generous in its analysis of the claimant's situation, it noted that the discretion given to tribunals to deal with the question of mitigation is very wide and so declined to interfere with the tribunal's decision.

It will often be relevant to consider the kind of work that is available to a dismissed claimant when considering whether the claimant has taken reasonable steps in mitigation. In particular, it may not be considered reasonable for a senior employee to take the first available job, no matter how lowly it is. The EAT pointed out in Hibiscus Housing Association v McIntosh Ltd EAT 0534/08, an unfair dismissal case, that 'it is not reasonable to expect a dismissed employee to lower her sights immediately in the kind of job for which she applies. A dismissed manager, for example, may be able to work as a cleaner, but it is not reasonable to expect him or her to do so immediately. It may become reasonable to expect the dismissed employee to accept a lesser paid job with lesser status after a period of time, but that is a matter of fact and degree for the tribunal.' In certain circumstances it may even be reasonable for the claimant to give up his or her job search entirely and focus on retraining for a different career – see under 'Retraining' below.

36.35 **Non-dismissal cases.** As will be clear from the decisions cited in this section, most mitigation of loss cases arise in the context of dismissal. However, there might equally be a reduction if the claimant fails to take all reasonable steps to minimise financial loss in respect of discrimination occurring during the currency of the employment relationship. For example, in Manning v Southern Vectis Commercial ET Case No.3101058/10, M suffered from a back problem that amounted to a disability under the DDA (now S.6 EqA). She went off work sick in 2007 and did not return, except for very short periods, although her employment continued. Between 2007 and March 2009 M tried several times to persuade SVC to allow her to return to work on a phased or part-time basis, but SVC persistently refused. It made it clear in a meeting in March 2009 that there would be no halfway house – either she returned full time or not at all. M eventually brought a claim of failure to make reasonable adjustments. The employment tribunal upheld her claim, finding that it would have been reasonable for SVC to arrange a phased return to work. As to remedy, it calculated M's financial loss as beginning in March 2009, being the earliest date, on the balance of probabilities, that SVC's policy of requiring full-time work was applied to her, and ending in March 2010, being the date that M decided that she could no longer work for SVC and lodged her tribunal claim. The tribunal decided not to award full loss of earnings for that period, finding that M was at fault in failing to follow up and query the situation after March 2009. It deducted 50 per cent for what it called 'contributory conduct', but which it also described as a failure to take reasonable steps to mitigate loss. The

1290

tribunal applied a further 25 per cent reduction to reflect the chance that, even if M had returned to work, the arrangement would not have worked out.

Refusal of offer of re-employment. In cases of discriminatory dismissal, an **36.36** unreasonable refusal of an offer of re-employment from the dismissing employer may amount to a failure to mitigate. It should be borne in mind that, in relation to a dismissal, the duty to mitigate only arises after dismissal, so refusing offers made before employment was terminated cannot amount to a failure to mitigate – Savoia v Chiltern Herb Farms Ltd 1981 IRLR 65, EAT. A refusal is more likely to be reasonable if the employee has been badly treated by the employer – Fyfe v Scientific Furnishings Ltd 1989 ICR 648, EAT. This may be an important consideration in discrimination cases, given that discrimination is inherently likely to lead to hurt feelings.

In Wilding v British Telecommunications plc 2002 ICR 1079, CA – a disability discrimination case – BT plc offered W re-employment on a part-time basis shortly after lodging an appeal against an employment tribunal's finding that it had discriminated against W on the ground of disability. W rejected the offer of re-employment and set out a number of grounds for so doing, including the fact that he viewed BT's appeal as inconsistent with its offer of re-employment; the manner of his dismissal; the injury to feelings he had suffered; and the way in which his appeal against dismissal had been conducted, along with various other grounds. The tribunal concluded that W had acted unreasonably in refusing BT's offer and had therefore failed to mitigate his loss. The EAT agreed, as did the Court of Appeal, which rejected the notion that the test for mitigation is a purely objective one. In the Court's view, it also requires the tribunal to look at all the circumstances of the case, including the subjective reasons that the claimant has given for turning down the offer. Where the claimant has given a full explanation as to why he or she turned down the offer, the ultimate question for the tribunal is whether he or she acted unreasonably in doing so. The answer to this should be determined after taking into account the history and all the circumstances of the case, including the claimant's state of mind, and remembering that the burden of proof and the standard of reasonableness to be applied is not too high.

As is apparent from the Wilding decision, the question of reasonableness is **36.37** directed at the employee's actions, not those of the employer. In Debique v Ministry of Defence EAT 0075/11 the EAT observed that the question is 'not whether it was reasonable for the employer to make the offer in question, but whether it was unreasonable for the employee to refuse it'. In that case, which concerned compensation for sex and race discrimination, the EAT upheld an employment tribunal's decision that D, a soldier, had been unreasonable to refuse an offer of redeployment. The discrimination had occurred in the MoD's failure to accommodate D's childcare commitments. Once she had commenced tribunal proceedings, the MoD offered her an alternative role that would be

1291

compatible with her childcare arrangements. The posting would have been for five years and the senior officer who outlined the offer stated that it came with a guarantee of non-deployment, i.e. that D would not be sent into active service during that time. In assessing whether D was reasonable to reject the offer on the basis of her doubts over that guarantee, the tribunal took into account that, as a matter of strict military law, there could be no absolute guarantee of non-deployment. However, it accepted that it was highly unlikely that D would in fact be deployed during the five-year posting, and was satisfied that the offer – and the explanation of the steps that had been taken to ensure that it was secure – should have given her sufficient assurances about her future. The EAT held that that was a permissible finding of fact. It therefore rejected D's appeal against the tribunal's decision to reduce compensation.

36.38 **Retraining.** It may be reasonable for a claimant to seek to mitigate his or her loss by retraining, where he or she has failed to find suitable alternative employment – see, for example, Orthet Ltd v Vince-Cain 2005 ICR 374, EAT, and BMB Recruitment v Hunter EATS 0056/05 (both sex discrimination cases). In fact, it may well be appropriate for the employment tribunal to add the cost to the claimant of attending such a training course to the compensation award because of its mitigating and ameliorative effects.

In Hibiscus Housing Association v McIntosh Ltd EAT 0534/08, an unfair dismissal case, the EAT had to consider the claimant's decision to apply for a university course. The EAT noted that whether this was itself something that disqualified the claimant from a compensatory award was a question of fact for the tribunal. The law is neither that, where an employee seeks higher or further education following a dismissal, this of itself constitutes a failure to mitigate, nor that such a course, once applied for, may necessarily be followed to a conclusion however many years distant at the employer's expense. In the present case, the tribunal had found that it was not unreasonable for the claimant to apply to university in order to improve her employment prospects, especially in view of the circumstances of her dismissal and her inability to obtain a favourable reference. The EAT refused to interfere with that conclusion on appeal.

36.39 **Setting up a new business.** It may be a reasonable step for a claimant to set up his or her own business in seeking to mitigate his or her loss. In AON Training Ltd v Dore 2005 IRLR 891, CA, D, who had dyslexia, set up his own business following his dismissal on the ground of disability. The Court of Appeal held that it was reasonable for him, following his unpleasant experiences as an employee of AON Ltd and the likely difficulty of obtaining another appropriate job, to set up his own business. The Court went on to advise that, once it is established that this is a reasonable way to mitigate loss, then damages should be calculated as follows: 'The [tribunal] should, first, calculate what sum represents loss of remuneration. It should then consider the costs incurred in mitigating loss and such a sum, if reasonably incurred, should be added to the loss. From that sum should be deducted e earnings from the new business.' So while interest payable on the loan to rt up the business was recoverable, the tribunal had erred in failing to take it up the business loss of earnings from the old job, and any income ea account both the business. For further consideration of the principles of mi from the new IDS Employment Law Handbook, 'Unfair Dismissal' (2\n of loss, see 'Compensatory awards: adjustments and reductions', Chapter 18, mitigate losses'. Failure to

Order of adjustments and deductions

Two of the most significant compensation adjustments made
future loss are the adjustment for the chance that an employ **36.40**
have continued in employment if it were not for the act of discrin for
reduction because of the claimant's failure to mitigate his or h t
question then arises as to which deduction should be made fu
period of doubt arising from contradictory EAT decisions, the
Appeal has held that the percentage deduction should be app
mitigation has been taken into account, not least because of the absu
that would ensue if the calculation were made the other way round – l
of Defence v Wheeler and ors 1998 ICR 242, CA. To illustrate the ap
sanctioned by the Court of Appeal in Wheeler, take the example of a cl
who earned £500 per week prior to her discriminatory dismissal.
employment tribunal finds that: (i) she would have had only a 40 per cent
chance of remaining in employment had no discrimination occurred; and
(ii) acting reasonably to mitigate her loss, she could have earned £250 per
week following her dismissal. The mitigation deduction is made first –
i.e. £250 is subtracted from £500, leaving £250. Reducing that amount to
40 per cent leaves a weekly loss of £100.

Although not dealt with in the Wheeler case, it is likely that any deduction for
contributory conduct should be made last of all the deductions that fall to be
made. This reflects the position under unfair dismissal law where, apart from
any deduction of enhanced redundancy pay and the application of the statutory
cap (neither of which are relevant here), a reduction for contributory fault is
applied after all other deductions have been made. The reduction for
contributory conduct, which potentially applies to all heads of compensation,
not just future loss, is considered in Chapter 35, 'Compensation: general
principles', under 'General principles of assessment – contributory conduct'.
For a full discussion of the issues that arise when there are several deductions
and adjustments to be made, see IDS Employment Law Handbook, 'Unfair
Dismissal' (2010), Chapter 18, 'Compensatory awards: adjustments and
reductions', under 'Order of adjustments and deductions'.

1293

36.41 Harassment

It is unlikely that a ~~mplainant~~ who has been the victim of harassment related to a protected ch~~ristic~~ will have suffered financial loss as a direct result of the harassmen~~t~~, ~~un~~less, of course, the employee has resigned or been dismissed as a result. ~~Th~~e ~~bulk~~ of compensation awards for harassment are usually made up of pay~~ments~~ ~~for~~ injury to feelings and aggravated damages, dealt with below.

Similar~~ly~~, ~~where~~ discrimination consists of a detriment applied to the claimant during ~~employ~~ment, unless the detriment consists of the withholding of a pay~~ment or~~ benefit, the question of compensation will focus on injury to fe~~elings~~. ~~In~~ ~~C~~ommissioner of Police of the Metropolis v Shaw EAT 0125/11, for ~~example, w~~here the prosecution of disciplinary proceedings against the claimant ~~was held~~ to be an unlawful detriment, the claimant suffered no financial loss ~~but was~~ awarded £30,000 for injury to feelings and aggravated damages alone. ~~This cas~~e is discussed fully under 'Aggravated damages' below.

~~In sev~~ere cases of harassment (or serious detrimental treatment) it may be that ~~the c~~laimant sustains such serious psychiatric injury that he or she is unable to ~~wo~~rk for a considerable amount of time and will need financial compensation ~~to~~ cover this period. Depending on the circumstances, this may even be the rest ~~o~~f the claimant's working life. In such cases, the claimant will be entitled to claim compensation for personal injury in addition to any other head of damages awardable for the act of discriminatory harassment; for example, injury to feelings. Where the loss covers the remainder of the claimant's career, a tribunal should apply the methods used to calculate future loss in personal injury cases, basing its calculation on the Ogden Tables but having regard to the caveats as to the reliability of these tables noted under 'Calculating future loss' above. Other issues that arise when calculating loss for personal injury are discussed under 'Personal injury' below.

36.42 Pension loss

One of the most significant losses an employee may sustain as a result of being discriminatorily dismissed is that of pension rights, particularly where the claimant has a final salary (defined benefit) pension. Although in one sense pension loss is partly past and partly future, the main cost to the employer is whatever it will take to secure to the claimant the benefits he or she has lost under the scheme. So, although pension loss may cover unpaid contributions between the date of dismissal and the date of the hearing, the main part of the award will be forward-looking.

In Ministry of Defence v Cannock and ors 1994 ICR 918, EAT, the EAT endorsed the guidelines on compensation for loss of pension rights produced by a committee of employment tribunal chairmen in consultation with the Government Actuary's Department. The committee's booklet, entitled 'Employment Tribunals – Compensation for Loss of Pension Rights' (3rd edition, 2003), suggests that in assessing pension loss, tribunals should adopt one of two approaches. The 'simplified approach', appropriate in most cases, involves a calculation based largely on the pension contributions that would have been made by the employer had the dismissal not occurred. The second and more complicated is the 'substantial loss approach', which involves the use of actuarial tables.

It is not compulsory to use the guidance, but if tribunals adopt a different **36.43** approach, they must explain what that approach is, and why they adopted it. In Chief Constable of West Midlands Police v Gardner EAT 0174/11 and another – a disability case – the employment tribunal awarded just under £34,000 for pension loss, having found that the claimant would not find new employment with a final salary scheme equivalent to that which he enjoyed in his employment with the police. When it came to setting the appropriate multiplier for future pension loss the tribunal stated that it would apply the 2003 guidance, but noted that some of the economic assumptions underlying that guidance were out of date. For example, it assumed that money can be invested to earn an average annual return of 6.5 per cent, which was no longer realistic in 2011. The tribunal therefore adopted actuarial data from the more up-to-date Ogden Tables (see 'Calculating future loss' above). The tribunal's decision was subject to a successful liability appeal and so the question of its approach to remedy did not strictly arise before the EAT. Nonetheless, the EAT offered its view, noting that while this 'pick and mix' approach seemed ill-advised in general, on the particular facts of the case it was permissible. It noted that the tribunal is not bound, as a matter of law, to adopt the methodology set out in either the Ogden Tables or the substantial or simplified approach from the 2003 booklet.

In Greenhoff v Barnsley Metropolitan Borough Council 2006 ICR 1514, EAT – another disability discrimination case – the EAT suggested that tribunals dealing with cases involving lost pension rights should take the following five steps 'in this logical sequence':

- identify all possible benefits that the employee could obtain under the pension scheme

- set out the terms of the pension scheme relevant to each possible benefit

- consider in respect of each benefit the advantages and disadvantages of applying the 'simplified approach', the 'substantial loss' approach or any other approach which the tribunal or parties consider appropriate

- explain why it has adopted a particular approach and rejected any other possible approach

- set out its conclusions and explain the amount of compensation for each head of the claim.

36.44   This five-step process, said the EAT, is not mandatory, but it noted that the problems that arose in the Greenhoff case (above) would not have occurred had the tribunal in the instant case followed it.

Even where the employment tribunal does set out its reasoning for choosing a particular approach, it may still fall into error if it fails to set out the assumptions on which it has based its calculations. In Bone v Mayor and Burgesses of the London Borough of Newham and ors EAT 0075/08 the EAT remitted a tribunal's assessment of pension loss under the simplified approach. While the tribunal had attempted to set out its reasoning, it had not set out the evidence on which it based its assertion that the claimant would benefit from significant salary increases in the private sector job she had found following dismissal by her public sector employer, nor adequate reasoning for finding that she would return to local government employment within four years.

36.45   It is also incumbent on tribunals to consider the prospect of the claimant becoming entitled to pension benefits in any new employment – Network Rail Infrastructure Ltd v Booth EAT 0071/06. In that case, compensation for pension benefits made up a significant portion of the overall award, the claimant having been dismissed from employment with a final salary pension scheme. The EAT rejected a challenge to the tribunal's choice of the simplified approach but held that it had erred in failing to make a reduction to reflect the pension benefits to which the claimant would be entitled when she found new employment. The tribunal had made findings on when she would be likely to find equivalent employment, and had noted that the new employment would be likely to offer only a less-generous money purchase scheme. It was an error of law for it not then to adjust compensation for pension loss to reflect the value of that prospective scheme.

Tribunals can take into account current conditions in the pension market in assessing loss. In Cuerden v Yorkshire Housing Ltd ET Case No.1803654/08, for example, the claimant resigned from her job because of disability discrimination. The employment tribunal, when assessing her future pension loss, noted that it was 'highly unlikely' that she would find a new job with a final salary pension scheme, as 'many such schemes were closed to new entrants and many employers were even looking to change arrangements for existing members'. Adopting the 'substantial loss' approach, the tribunal awarded her £59,263.82 for loss of pension rights. (The employer appealed to the EAT in this case and was partially successful, but the tribunal's approach to quantifying pension loss was not criticised by the Appeal Tribunal –Yorkshire Housing Ltd v Cuerden EAT 0397/09.)

For a full discussion of the guidelines, and analysis of the different types of pension loss, see IDS Employment Law Handbook, 'Unfair Dismissal' (2010), Chapter 17, 'Compensatory awards: pension loss'.

Injury to feelings

The availability of an award for injury to feelings is given statutory foundation by S.119(4) EqA, which specifically provides that tribunals may award compensation for injury to feelings, whether or not they award compensation under any other head. This introduces consistency across all of the protected characteristics. Whereas, for example, S.57(4) RRA made the same provision with regard to race discrimination, there was no equivalent provision in the Employment Equality (Age) Regulations 2006 SI 2006/1031 in respect of age. Having said that, it was never doubted under the antecedent equality legislation that injury to feelings awards were available as a remedy for all kinds of discrimination in employment.

This head of damage is of great importance in discrimination cases, whether the discrimination occurs in the context of recruitment, during employment, harassment, or in the form of a dismissal. Employment tribunals have a broad discretion as to the amount to award for injury to feelings, and their awards will only be overturned on appeal if they are wholly erroneous. In Prison Service and ors v Johnson 1997 ICR 275, EAT (a race discrimination case), the EAT summarised the general principles that underlie awards for injury to feelings:

- awards for injury to feelings are designed to compensate the injured party fully but not to punish the guilty party

- an award should not be inflated by feelings of indignation at the guilty party's conduct

- awards should not be so low as to diminish respect for the policy of the discrimination legislation. On the other hand, awards should not be so excessive that they might be regarded as untaxed riches

- awards should be broadly similar to the range of awards in personal injury cases

- tribunals should bear in mind the value in everyday life of the sum they are contemplating

- tribunals should bear in mind the need for public respect for the level of the awards made.

Since the Johnson case was decided, tribunals have been given a helping hand **36.47** in applying these principles as they relate to the level of the award. In Vento v Chief Constable of West Yorkshire Police (No.2) 2003 ICR 318, CA, the Court of Appeal set down three bands of injury to feelings award, indicating the range of award that is appropriate depending on the seriousness of the discrimination in question. These bands are discussed under 'Quantum: the Vento guidelines' below. The Court also described some of the elements that can be compensated under the head of injury to feelings. According to Lord

1297

Justice Mummery, injury to feelings encompasses 'subjective feelings of upset, frustration, worry, anxiety, mental distress, fear, grief, anguish, humiliation, unhappiness, stress, depression'.

36.48 **Awards for different acts of discrimination.** In Al Jumard v Clywd Leisure Ltd and ors 2008 IRLR 345, EAT, the EAT ruled that where unlawful discrimination has occurred in respect of two or more different grounds (i.e. protected characteristics), the compensatory award for injury to feelings should be assessed with respect to each discriminatory act. Each act is a separate wrong for which damages should be provided. In that case the claimant succeeded with claims for race discrimination and disability discrimination. There was some overlap between the two claims. For example, he had been given a written warning for setting off the alarm at the leisure centre where he worked. He had set the alarm properly but failed to get off the premises quickly enough because his disability impaired his mobility. The employment tribunal found that the warning was an act of race discrimination (white employees had not been similarly disciplined) and of disability discrimination (non-disabled employees had been treated more favourably). However, some of the acts and detriments about which the claimant complained fell into one category or the other. He had been accused of aggressive conduct and placed under surveillance, which were specifically acts of race discrimination; and the employer had failed to make reasonable adjustments, which was a specific act of disability discrimination. The tribunal proposed to make an award of £13,000 in respect of injury to feelings and stress suffered from both race and disability discrimination. It also made an award of £5,000 for personal injury, in respect of pain and suffering caused specifically by the failure to make reasonable adjustments. The claimant's main objection to this composite approach to the two kinds of discrimination was that it had led the tribunal to make a smaller award than it would have done if the incidents were considered separately. He therefore appealed.

The EAT noted that the tribunal's approach would have been appropriate had the discriminatory acts overlapped in the sense of having arisen entirely out of the same set of facts. But where, as here, certain acts of discrimination fall into one category or the other, injury to feelings must be considered separately in respect of those acts. The EAT derived support for this approach from the earlier decision of the Appeal Tribunal in Birmingham City Council v Jaddoo EAT 0448/04, which also involved injury to feelings in respect of both race and disability discrimination. Had the correct approach been adopted in the instant case, it would, said the EAT, have helped focus the tribunal's mind on the compensatory nature of the award for injured feelings. The EAT thought that the 'offence, humiliation or upset resulting from a deliberate act of race discrimination may quite understandably cause greater injury to feelings than, say, a thoughtless failure to make an adjustment under the Disability Discrimination Act'. The EAT did add, however, that where more than one form of discrimination arises out of the same facts, asking to what extent each discrete head of discrimination has contributed to the injured feelings can be an artificial exercise, and that it will not be an error of law where the tribunal fails to do that.

Remitting the case to the employment tribunal, the EAT did note that adopting **36.49** the correct approach would not necessarily result in the tribunal ordering an increased award. As the Court of Appeal had emphasised in Vento v Chief Constable of West Yorkshire Police (No.2) (above), after making an award for injury to feelings, the tribunal must stand back and have regard to the overall compensation figure to ensure that it is proportionate and not subject to double-counting.

Compensation, not punishment   **36.50**
The need to focus on compensating the claimant rather than on punishing the wrongdoer influenced the EAT's decision to reduce the complainant's award for injury to feelings in Corus Hotels plc v Woodward and anor EAT 0536/05. In that case, the injury to feelings award made by an employment tribunal to an unsuccessful job applicant who suffered unlawful sex discrimination was reduced by the EAT from £5,000 to £4,000. The tribunal had found that, as one-off incidents go, this incident was serious. However, on appeal the EAT held that although the tribunal had been entitled to take into account its 'deep concern' at the complete failure of the employer's equal opportunities policy in deciding the liability issue, it had erred in taking this factor into account in assessing compensation for injury to feelings. In the EAT's view, the tribunal appeared to have allowed its feelings of indignation at the employer's conduct to inflate the award by way of punishment.

Similarity to personal injury awards   **36.51**
It is sometimes observed that the damages available for injury to feelings can occasionally outstrip those available for catastrophic personal injury. That observation may carry the implied criticism that this would not seem right to the 'man on the Clapham omnibus'. On this point, the EAT in Corus Hotels plc v Woodward and anor EAT 0536/05 considered the extent to which an appeal to what the reasonable man or woman would conclude was the appropriate level of award for injury to feelings is relevant in assessing the level of compensation. The EAT rejected the employer's contention that the tribunal had erred by not taking into account the fact that the hypothetical man or woman in the street would have considered the award of £5,000 too high when compared with awards in personal injury cases. In the EAT's view, it was clear from the guidelines in Vento v Chief Constable of West Yorkshire Police (No.2) 2003 ICR 318, CA (discussed under 'Quantum: the Vento guidelines' below), that a tribunal is required to take into account the broad level of awards in personal injury cases as a whole, rather than specific hypothetical comparators.

1299

The EAT went on to note that Vento had largely dealt with the problem of excessive personal injury awards by setting out bands and limits, and that the ordinary person's opinion of those authoritative guidelines was not the tribunal's concern.

36.52 No deductions for future contingencies

Where a claimant is dismissed on discriminatory grounds, evidence that he or she would subsequently have been dismissed in any event may properly be taken into account to establish a cut-off point in respect of any claim for future loss of earnings. This is discussed under 'Future loss' above. No such cut-off point may be applied in respect of an award of damages for injury to feelings, however. Such an award is designed to compensate the claimant for those feelings of anger, upset and humiliation arising from the knowledge that it was an act of discrimination that brought about the dismissal, and it cannot be discounted or reduced in order to reflect a separate and notional future event such as lawful dismissal. In O'Donoghue v Redcar and Cleveland Borough Council 2001 IRLR 615, CA, the Court of Appeal confirmed that an employment tribunal erred when, having established that an employee's dismissal constituted an act of victimisation, it reduced her award for injury to feelings to reflect its finding that she would in any event have been lawfully dismissed within six months on account of her unacceptable attitude towards colleagues.

36.53 Gradated awards

Employment tribunals may find it helpful to break down their calculation of an injury to feelings award into stages, to reflect a claimant's stages of recovery. For example, in Kavanagh v Royal College of Psychiatrists ET Case No.2301717/99, the tribunal upheld the claimant's claim that she had suffered unlawful victimisation. It decided that she had suffered serious injury to her feelings for some five months, until she found another job, and it was a further three months before she fully recovered. The tribunal awarded a total of £6,500 compensation for injury to feelings, comprising £1,000 a month in respect of the first five months, and £500 a month in respect of the next three. Although this is not typical of how tribunals approach the matter of assessing injury to feelings, it does show a sensitivity to the fact that the degree of injury can reduce over time once the acuteness of the act of discrimination begins to fade and/or the detrimental consequences that flow from the discriminatory act diminish as a result of, for example, the claimant finding alternative employment.

36.54 When will an injury to feelings award be made?

Contrary to widespread belief, an award for injury to feelings is not automatic in every case where discrimination is established. The onus remains on the claimant to establish the nature and extent of such injury. However, it is apparent that, as a head of loss, injury to feelings is a crucial element in most cases and that such an award is virtually inevitable to reflect the fact that any act of discrimination is likely to cause hurt to feelings at the very least to some minor degree. This is so whether the discrimination occurs in the context of recruitment, during employment, or in the form of dismissal. It is important to bear in mind that a claimant can recover compensation for injury to feelings regardless of whether he or she has suffered any financial loss as a result of the discrimination. So, for example, in Murphy v Sheffield Hallam University EAT 006/99, the employment tribunal concluded that the claimant would not have been offered the job even if there had been no discrimination on the ground of his disability, but nonetheless awarded him £2,500 for injury to feelings.

In Murray v Powertech (Scotland) Ltd 1992 IRLR 257, EAT, the discrimination took the form of a pregnancy dismissal. The employment tribunal in that case did not add an award for injury to feelings to its award for loss of wages because, it said, there was no evidence before it of the claimant's feelings having been hurt. On appeal, the EAT confirmed that it was for the claimant to establish the heads of claim but added that a claim for injury to feelings is so fundamental to a discrimination case that it is almost inevitable that a claim under this head will arise for the tribunal to consider. All that is required, said the EAT, is that the matter of injury to feelings be stated. In this case the tribunal had found that the claimant had been shocked by her dismissal. The EAT said that this alone might well have been enough to raise the question of injury to feelings, and it remitted the case for the tribunal to examine that question more closely.

36.55 The EAT reiterated that injury must actually be proved in Ministry of Defence v Cannock and ors 1994 ICR 918, EAT, but took the view that this may not be difficult as 'no tribunal will take much persuasion that the anger, distress and affront caused by the act of discrimination has injured the claimant's feelings'. And in Ministry of Defence v Sullivan 1994 ICR 193, EAT, Mr Justice Tuckey observed that while there was no automatic right to recover compensation for injured feelings, it would be surprising if such an award were not made. In practice, a claimant should always claim injury to feelings on his or her claim form and produce evidence directed towards showing the nature and extent of the injury suffered, particularly if more than a nominal award is being sought.

36.56 **Evidence.** A claimant does not need to produce medical evidence of injury to feelings. As Lord Justice Mummery in the Court of Appeal acknowledged in Vento v Chief Constable of West Yorkshire Police (No.2) 2003 ICR 318, CA, injury to feelings is not a medical term: 'It is self evident that the assessment of compensation for an injury or loss, which is neither physical nor financial, presents special problems for the judicial process, which aims to produce results objectively justified by evidence, reason and precedent. Subjective feelings of upset, frustration, worry, anxiety, mental distress, fear, grief, anguish, humiliation, unhappiness, stress, depression and so on and the degree of their intensity are incapable of objective proof or of measurement in monetary terms.

1301

Translating hurt feelings into hard currency is bound to be an artificial exercise... Although they are incapable of objective proof or measurement in monetary terms, hurt feelings are none the less real in human terms. The courts and tribunals have to do the best they can on the available material to make a sensible assessment, accepting that it is impossible to justify or explain a particular sum with the same kind of solid evidential foundation and persuasive practical reasoning available in the calculation of financial loss or compensation for bodily injury.' However, medical evidence is likely to be needed where the non-pecuniary award includes an element for personal injury – whether physical or psychiatric (see under 'Personal injury' below).

36.57 **Relevance of victim's knowledge of discrimination**
It has been suggested that the availability of damages for injury to feelings depends on that injury being caused by the claimant's knowledge that he or she is being subjected to discrimination. In Skyrail Oceanic Ltd v Coleman 1981 ICR 864, CA, C married a man who worked for one of her employer's competitors. During the engagement, confidential information was leaked to the competitor and, two months after the marriage, C was dismissed because of concerns about conflict of interest. C brought a claim of unfair dismissal but amended it to include one of sex discrimination after she learned that the two companies had discussed the matter and decided that she should be dismissed rather than her husband because he was the breadwinner. She succeeded in her claim and the employment tribunal awarded £1,000 for injury to feelings. When the case came before the Court of Appeal, it reduced that sum to £100. Lord Justice Lawton noted: 'Any injury to feelings must result from the knowledge that it was an act of sex discrimination that brought about a dismissal. Injury to feelings unrelated to sex discrimination, such as, in this case, the circumstance that leakages of information had taken place in July 1978 and that others might reasonably have suspected the appellant to have been responsible for them, is not properly attributable to an unlawful act of sex discrimination. The [employment] tribunal thought that the circumstances in which the appellant had been dismissed might have damaged her reputation. That would not have been a consequence of sex discrimination and should have been disregarded.'

Coleman thus appeared to suggest that, if the claimant did not know that his or her treatment was discriminatory at the time, he or she could not claim injury to feelings in respect of it. That was certainly how the employment tribunal in Taylor v XLN Telecom Ltd and anor 2010 ICR 656, EAT, read the Coleman case. In that case, T, a black man employed by XLNT Ltd, was the subject of concerns about his performance. In 2008 he lodged a grievance and, while this was in the process of being heard, complained about racially offensive conduct by one of his managers. The grievance was rejected and, following a probation review, T was suspended and eventually dismissed for poor performance. He brought claims of unfair dismissal and victimisation under the RRA. The employment tribunal held that, while the decision to dismiss was partly made on performance grounds, XLNT Ltd was also influenced by the fact that T had complained of race discrimination. It awarded compensation for financial loss but rejected T's claims for injury to feelings, injury to health and aggravated damages. It considered that, following the Coleman case, T was required to show that these injuries were attributable to the knowledge (whenever it was acquired) that his dismissal amounted to an act of unlawful victimisation. Instead, all the evidence pointed to his being aggrieved by the employer's failure to comply with the (now repealed) statutory disciplinary and grievance procedures.

On appeal, the EAT held that the employment tribunal's reading of Coleman **36.58** was incorrect. The calculation of a remedy under the RRA (now under the EqA) is governed by the same principles as a claim in tort, where the victim is compensated for the direct and natural consequences of the wrongful act. This is so irrespective of his or her knowledge of the facts that constituted the tort. Although no common law tort is precisely equivalent to the statutory tort of discrimination, the EAT observed that there are torts which require a mental element – generally characterised as malice – on the part of the wrongdoer, and yet no authority suggests that a person pursuing such a claim can only recover compensation to the extent that his or her injury is attributable to knowledge that the act in question was tortious. The claimant simply recovers for the injury caused by the wrongful act. The EAT noted that one purpose of the discrimination legislation is to provide compensation for the distress caused by overtly discriminatory conduct. Such distress can also be caused by conduct that is not overtly discriminatory. If such conduct was on the ground of a protected characteristic, then it would seem artificial and arbitrary to withhold compensation for it because the victim was not aware of his or her employer's discriminatory motives at the time. The injury is still attributable to the discriminatory conduct.

The EAT observed in passing that, as a general rule, 'the distress and humiliation suffered by the victim will be greater where the discrimination is overt, or where, even in the absence of overt signs, the victim understands the motivation at the time to be discriminatory; and in such cases the compensation may be correspondingly higher. But that is a different point and does not justify the conclusion that there should be no compensation in other cases.'

Quantum: the Vento guidelines **36.59**
The size of the award for injury to feelings can vary enormously depending on the facts of each case and the degree of hurt, distress and humiliation caused to the complainant by the discrimination. However, in Vento v Chief Constable of West Yorkshire Police (No.2) 2003 ICR 318, CA, the Court of Appeal gave specific guidance on how employment tribunals should approach the issue. The

1303

case concerned a probationary police constable who brought a claim of sex discrimination after she was dismissed at the end of her probationary period. She alleged that, following the breakdown of her marriage, her fellow officers had shown an unwarranted interest in her private life and she became the victim of bullying, undue scrutiny and undeserved criticism. An employment tribunal upheld her claim and awarded compensation in the sum of £257,844. This included £50,000 for injury to feelings, £15,000 aggravated damages, £9,000 for personal injury and £18,015 interest. The case ended up before the Court of Appeal, which decided that the tribunal award of £74,000 for injury to feelings, aggravated damages and personal injury was clearly excessive and constituted an error of law.

In the Court's view, the award was out of line with EAT rulings, with the Judicial Studies Board Guidelines for the Assessment of General Damages in Personal Injury Cases ('the JSB Guidelines'), and with personal injury cases in respect of which general damages are awarded for pain, suffering, disability and loss of amenity. In particular, the total award of £74,000 was in excess of the JSB Guidelines for the award of general damages for moderate brain damage. On the facts of the case, the Court of Appeal concluded that a fair award for non-pecuniary losses was £32,000 – made up of £18,000 for injury to feelings, £5,000 for aggravated damages and £9,000 for personal injury of a psychiatric nature, which took the form of clinical depression and adjustment disorder lasting for three years.

36.60 The most useful aspect of the Court of Appeal's decision in Vento was Lord Justice Mummery's identification of three broad bands of compensation for injury to feelings, as distinct from compensation for psychiatric or similar personal injury. These comprised:

- a top band of between £15,000–25,000: this should apply only to the most serious cases, such as where there has been a lengthy campaign of discriminatory harassment. Only in very exceptional cases should an award of compensation for injury to feelings exceed £25,000

- a middle band of between £5,000–15,000: this should be used for serious cases that do not merit an award in the highest band

- a lower band of between £500–5,000: this is appropriate for less serious cases, such as where the act of discrimination is an isolated or one-off occurrence. In general, awards of less than £500 should be avoided, as they risk being regarded as so low as not to be a proper recognition of injury to feelings.

The Court added that there would be considerable flexibility within each band, allowing tribunals to fix what they considered to be fair, reasonable and just compensation in the particular circumstances of each case. Furthermore, common sense required that regard should be had to the 'overall magnitude of the sum total of the awards of compensation for non-pecuniary loss made under the various headings of injury to feelings, psychiatric damage and aggravated damage'.

Effect of inflation. The Vento guidelines were laid down in December 2002. **36.61** Since then employment tribunals have taken differing views as to the effect of inflation on the bands, but in Da'Bell v National Society for Prevention of Cruelty to Children 2010 IRLR 19, EAT, the EAT issued a formal revision of the figures. It endorsed a 20 per cent increase to each of the limits, so that:

- the top band is now £18,000–30,000

- the middle band is now £6,000–18,000

- the lower band is now £600–6,000.

Top band: £18,000–30,000. A clear example of the kind of serious case **36.62** attracting an injury to feelings award at the upper limit of the highest band is Miles v Gilbank and anor 2006 ICR 1297, CA (also discussed in Chapter 35, 'Compensation: general principles', under 'Awards against individuals and co-respondents – joint and several awards'). In that case the Court of Appeal upheld an employment tribunal's award of £25,000 (which was the very top of the upper 'Vento' band at the time) for injury to feelings to a pregnant employee who had suffered unlawful sex discrimination. The tribunal had found that, once it became known that that claimant, a hairdresser, was pregnant, there had been an 'inhumane and sustained campaign of bullying and discrimination' against her by the manager of the salon and her other managers. This campaign was 'targeted, deliberate, repeated and consciously inflicted' and 'not only demonstrated... a total lack of concern for the welfare of the claimant herself, but a callous disregard... for the life of her unborn child'.

Similarly, in Driscoll v News Group Newspapers ET Case Nos.3202077/07 and another the claimant, a sports writer on the *News of the World*, was subjected to many acts of disability discrimination and harassment, which caused him 'a considerable amount of hurt and anguish; damaged his confidence and self-esteem; [and] caused a depressive illness to someone without any previous history of depression'. Both sides were agreed that injury to feelings should be within the top band of the Vento guidance and the tribunal awarded £25,000 for injury to feelings.

It is also important, however, that tribunals do not lose sight of the overall level **36.63** of the award for non-pecuniary loss, as noted in Vento (above). This point was emphasised in Scott v Commissioners of Inland Revenue 2004 ICR 1410, CA (see also under 'Aggravated damages' below), where the Court of Appeal observed that the top band did not incorporate elements of aggravation but dealt solely with the kinds of treatment that may make the injury to a person's feelings even graver than it would otherwise have been – for example, a lengthy campaign of discriminatory treatment. This exacerbation was separate from aggravated damages, which are intended to deal with cases where the injury was inflicted by conduct that was high-handed, malicious, insulting or oppressive. The Court went on to dismiss the claimant's appeal against a tribunal's award of £15,000 for injury to feelings, notwithstanding that he had been seriously discriminated against on the grounds of sex and disability, and victimised for complaining about his treatment. In reaching its conclusion, the tribunal found that allegations of sexual harassment made by a colleague against the claimant had been upheld without justification by the employer, and that details of the employer's financial settlement with his accuser were made public before the claimant was finally dismissed on ill-health grounds after he became depressed as a result of his treatment. In the Court of Appeal's view, given the tribunal's finding that the claimant had 'suffered, continuously, enormous injury to his feelings', there was no doubt that a markedly higher award for injury to feelings would have been unappealable. But the actual award of £15,000 – although it lay at the bottom end of the higher Vento band – could not be said to be so low as to be perverse.

One further example of a top band award:

- **Sullivan v Contal Plant (in administration)** ET Case No.3301375/08: S, an employee with almost ten years' service, informed his employer that he had been diagnosed with cancer of the gum and was going into hospital for an emergency operation. While he was in hospital, the company sent him his P45, with no warning or consultation. The tribunal awarded him £20,000 for injury to feelings, describing this as 'a particularly devastating and capricious way to deal with any employee'.

36.64 **Middle band: £6,000–18,000.** Two employment tribunal awards that fell into the middle band:

- **Grant v Northumberland County Council** ET Case No.2505048/08: G had bipolar disorder and had had substantial periods of time off work on three occasions. During the last absence, the Council began a sickness procedure that was in effect a disciplinary procedure. This exacerbated her condition, delaying her recovery by some three years. The employment tribunal made an award of £17,500, at the top end of the middle Vento band. In doing so, it took into account the fact that the Council's failure to make reasonable adjustments had substantially delayed G's return to work, and that 'work, as well as being a potential stressor... was also a source of some comfort for her. Without it she had little enjoyment of life and was to some extent isolated'

- **Wade-Jones v CJ Upton and Sons Ltd** ET Case No.1901127/09: the employment tribunal upheld W-J's claim that she was sexually harassed. On one occasion, comments were made about her legs – she normally wore trousers to work but on that day had worn a skirt and a colleague pulled her chair back to expose her legs and said: 'Let's have a look then'. On another occasion, when she described a client as being like Richard Gere, her manager said: 'So you shagged him then.' After she had given in her notice she was required to be present at an advisory meeting, where she was threatened with disciplinary action. The tribunal held that the meeting would not have taken place had W-J not complained of sex discrimination, and the threat amounted to victimisation and harassment. It awarded £15,000 for injury to feelings – it ruled out an award in the highest band as there was no lengthy campaign, but noted that there were certainly serious incidents that caused W-J distress.

Lower band: £600–6,000. Three employment tribunal awards that fell into **36.65** the lowest band:

- **Kellie v Izmaylova Ltd** ET Case No.2200442/11: K suffered from sickle cell anaemia. From the age of 20 she had been hospitalised once or twice a year because of the condition, but between August 2010 and March 2011 she was admitted to hospital four times, and required treatment by daily injections between hospital admissions. She applied for a post with I Ltd as international relations assistant and was interviewed in early November 2010. She was offered and accepted the post and began work on Monday 8 November. That afternoon, she sent an e-mail to I Ltd saying that, having read the company rules, she was informing it of her condition. On Thursday she became ill and called an ambulance. She told I Ltd that she hoped to be back at work by the following Monday. At 4.55 pm that day I Ltd e-mailed her to say that she should take care of her health before beginning a new job and terminated her employment. An employment tribunal found unfair dismissal and disability discrimination – K was dismissed because of the health crisis she suffered. It awarded £5,000 for injury to feelings. It accepted that K was devastated by her dismissal, but noted that she had only had the job for a short period. It considered that the loss of a short-lived job would not cause as great a degree of injury to feelings as would the loss of a long-held job, and so decided that an award in the lower Vento band was appropriate

- **Williams v Central Manchester University Hospitals NHS Trust** ET Case No.2408486/10: during a meeting to discuss her return to work, an associate director of HR said to W, who is Jewish: 'You wouldn't expect a Jew to take up a post with the Gestapo, would you, because after all, they wouldn't fit – it wouldn't work.' The Trust offered no apology at the time but admitted at the employment tribunal hearing that the remark constituted race discrimination. The tribunal found that the remark was deeply offensive and vindictive, but noted that it was a one-off. It awarded W £4,500 for injury to feelings

- **Johnson v JD Wetherspoon plc and anor** ET Case No.3202854/08: the employment tribunal held that J had suffered sex discrimination when a colleague called her a 'slag'. It was a derogatory comment, related to her sex – a man would not have been called the same thing – and it could reasonably be considered to have the effect of violating J's dignity. The tribunal awarded £1,500 for injury to feelings.

36.66 **Minimum awards.** The Court of Appeal in Vento directed that awards of less than £500 should be avoided, as they risk being regarded as being so low as not to be a proper recognition of injury to feelings. This has had the result that, in practice, £500 has been the minimum level for an injury to feelings award (now £600 following the uprating in the Da'Bell case (above)). Three examples of cases where employment tribunals have felt justified limiting awards to the very lowest end of the scale:

- **Niyukuri v Premier Placement Services Ltd** ET Case No.1308476/10: N approached PPS Ltd, an employment agency, to register for work in April 2010. He provided the necessary documentation to prove that he had the right to work in the United Kingdom but the responsible manager at PPS Ltd was uneasy about him, having formed the impression that N was aggressive. The manager told N he wished to check his right to work with the Home Office, although he knew that there was no real procedure for doing so. Eventually, N's registration was processed but only after some weeks had passed. He brought a claim of race discrimination, alleging that PPS Ltd put unnecessary hurdles in the way of his registration and did so because of his race. The employment tribunal upheld the claim, finding that N had probably failed to observe the usual social niceties and spoken loudly, but that this was more likely to reflect language and racial differences than aggression. It therefore concluded that a white British person who had produced the appropriate documents would have immediately been offered an interview. The tribunal accepted that N suffered hurt but believed the greatest hurt related to his lack of work. It awarded £600 for injury to feelings

- **Abdulle v River Island Clothing Company** ET Case No.2346023/10: the employment tribunal upheld A's claim of religious discrimination. The claim related to an occasion when the shop at which A worked was short-staffed and a manager refused to allow A to take time off work in the middle of the day to attend Muslim prayers. The tribunal awarded £500 for injury to feelings, noting that this was a one-off incident about which A had not formally complained, but which the employer's HR department had not troubled to acknowledge

- **McDonnell v Macaraeg t/a Matson Mini Market** ET Case No.1403128/10: M began working for the employer in December 2009 for 16 hours a week, working two shifts of 1 pm to 6 pm and one shift of noon to 6 pm. Her partner started working for the same employer in May 2010 for a trial period, working three afternoon shifts. Their hours fitted well with their childcare arrangements – they had two children under school age. However, in August, the employer terminated M's partner's employment and asked M to change her hours to work six evening shifts. When M refused she was told that if she couldn't work the evening shifts, there was no longer a job for her. M succeeded in a claim of indirect sex discrimination – the employment tribunal accepted that a requirement to work six evening shifts per week is likely to put women at a disadvantage because of childcare responsibilities. It was not proportionate for the employer to change M's shifts given that it did not enquire whether any other employee would be willing to work evening shifts. M said that she was 'a bit annoyed' at her treatment. The tribunal awarded £500 for injury to feelings.

No award. As noted above, most successful discrimination complaints result in **36.67** an award for injury to feelings. There are cases where no award is made, even where discrimination has been proved, but these are rare. One example is Pinches v Sopranos Pizza Ltd ET Case No.1300824/10. In that case P brought claims of, inter alia, racial harassment and sex discrimination. The racial harassment claim centred on P being called an 'English idiot', which the employment tribunal found involved a specific reference to nationality and, although it did not particularly offend P, it did amount to a detriment. The sex discrimination complaint was rather more serious and involved sexual harassment. The tribunal gave a provisional view on the compensation it would award. While it was prepared to make an award at the lower-to-middle end of the lowest Vento band for sex discrimination, it did not think the racial harassment element warranted an injury to feelings award, having regard to the fact that P did not particularly take offence. The tribunal considered that its declaration of unlawful conduct should suffice as a remedy in this regard.

Appealing against level of compensation   36.68

As the Vento guidelines make clear, employment tribunals have a wide discretion when deciding on the level of award to make for injury to feelings and appeals against the amount awarded will succeed only in very limited circumstances. According to the Court of Appeal in Skyrail Oceanic Ltd v Coleman 1981 ICR 864, CA, the appellate tribunal should only interfere with an award (for any head of damages, not just injury to feelings) if the employment tribunal 'acted on a wrong principle of law or... misapprehended the facts or... made a wholly erroneous estimate of the damage suffered'. Similarly, in Vento v Chief Constable of West Yorkshire Police (No.2) 2003 ICR 318, CA, the Court of Appeal formulated what is sometimes referred to as the 'perversity test' as follows: 'The decision of the employment tribunal... ought only to be overturned if it is shown to be a perverse conclusion, that is a decision which no reasonable tribunal, properly directing itself on the law and on the materials before it, could reasonably have reached.' In other words, an appellate court cannot interfere with the amount awarded by a tribunal for injury to feelings simply because it would have awarded a greater or smaller sum.

One example of the EAT stepping in to correct an employment tribunal's assessment of injury to feelings is Governing Body of St Andrew's Catholic Primary School and ors v Blundell EAT 0330/09, which concerned a claim of victimisation under the Sex Discrimination Act 1975. In that case B, a teacher, had brought a claim of sex discrimination in relation to her treatment before and following maternity leave. The tribunal rejected all her grounds of claim and the EAT rejected an appeal, save in one respect. B later complained that the headmistress of the school ostracised her from the time that her tribunal claim was concluded, and that this escalated to bullying and harassment after the lodging of her appeal to the EAT. The treatment culminated in a 'feedback' meeting, following a classroom observation of her teaching, when the headmistress told B that everything she had seen during the observation was inadequate, that she had very grave concerns, and that B's future as a teacher was under review. B went off sick with a stress-related illness soon after that meeting. She was later dismissed after she told some of the parents that she was being bullied by the school management.

36.69 When B succeeded in a second tribunal claim, this time for victimisation, she was awarded almost £300,000, of which £22,000 was for injury to feelings. On the school's appeal, the EAT agreed that the injury to feelings award was too high. It accepted the school's argument that the tribunal ought to have had regard to cases such as HM Prison Service v Salmon 2001 IRLR 425, EAT, where £20,000 for an extremely lengthy and vile campaign against the claimant was said to be on the high side. The EAT noted that the treatment in the present case was serious and undoubtedly had deeply unpleasant consequences for B but that, had the tribunal used cases like Salmon as a benchmark, it could not have concluded that this case fell within the top Vento band, nor that it merited an award of £22,000. In the EAT's view, it was a serious case falling fairly and squarely within the middle band. It substituted the sum of £14,000 for the original award. (Note that this decision was the subject of a further appeal – see Governing Body of St Andrew's Catholic Primary School v Blundell 2012 ICR 295, CA – but the Court of Appeal did not have to reconsider the injury to feelings award.)

36.70 **Other issues affecting quantum of injury to feelings award**
Tribunals seldom give detailed reasons for deciding on a particular award, often making only a general comment on whether they regard the case as falling at the bottom, middle or top end of the scale. It is possible, however, to identify particular factors or trends that appear to influence the size of awards made for injury to feelings.

Personal characteristics. An award for injury to feelings is intended to **36.71**
compensate for the hurt and humiliation suffered by the claimant. This means
that, in theory, the award depends not on the seriousness of the discrimination
but on the nature of the claimant's reaction to that discrimination. If, because
he or she is of a sensitive disposition, a claimant is extremely upset and
humiliated by behaviour that others would have found merely annoying, then
the employment tribunal should reflect this fact in the award for injury to
feelings (see Chapter 35, 'Compensation: general principles' under 'General
principles of assessment – "eggshell skull" principle'). The discriminator will be
liable for the full extent of the injury, in so far as it can be shown that this
flowed from the act of discrimination. It follows that, in deciding on the level
of award to make, the tribunal's main task will be to determine what effect the
discrimination has had on the life of the claimant. Key factors will be whether
the discrimination has led to any medical condition – such as depression, panic
attacks, or any stress-related illness; whether the claimant has suffered a loss of
confidence; how the discrimination has affected the claimant's personal
relationships; and whether the claimant continues to suffer as a result of the
discrimination. Factors such as the age of the claimant, his or her experience
and length of time in the job can also provide a useful indication of the effect
that the discrimination has had. First-hand evidence of such matters from the
claimant will clearly be important to enable the tribunal to judge the level of
hurt and humiliation suffered.

Two sex discrimination cases in which the claimant's personal characteristics
increased the level of injury to feelings:

* **Cox v Macklin Street Surgery and anor** ET Case No.2600517/00:
J, a trainee GP, committed acts of sexual harassment against C that the
employment tribunal described as 'wholly inappropriate, suggestive [and]
very unpleasant'. Both the surgery and J admitted that J had sexually
harassed C and that C was constructively dismissed as a result of J's
behaviour and the surgery's failure to respond properly to her complaints.
In assessing compensation, the tribunal awarded damages for injury to
feelings of £2,500 against the surgery and £3,500 against J. His behaviour
in the context of sexual harassment as a whole was towards the lower end
of the scale but C had just started to take part in an IVF scheme. The stress
she suffered caused her to haemorrhage and she was taken off the scheme,
and this consequence was therefore reflected in the quantum of the awards
for injury to feelings made against both respondents

* **Bainbridge v Mosey** ET Case No.6402140/01: B worked for M as a sales
representative. An employment tribunal found that M sexually harassed
her verbally and physically, and that after she made complaints she was
dismissed. In assessing compensation for injury to feelings the tribunal
noted that B had suffered sexual abuse by a babysitter as a child and M's

1311

conduct had triggered severe effects related to this prior trauma. She had become withdrawn and distressed and had taken an overdose. The tribunal decided that the award should be at the upper end of the middle Vento band, which recognised the injury to her ability to cope with life and work and her future vulnerability, while also reflecting an apparent improvement shown by the fact that she was no longer receiving medical treatment. It accordingly awarded £10,000 for injury to feelings.

36.72 The converse of the eggshell skull principle also holds true: an award for injury to feelings may be reduced in circumstances where the employment tribunal finds that the claimant was more than usually resilient and therefore suffered less or would recover more quickly. A tribunal is also likely to take into account the claimant's demeanour at the hearing in assessing the extent of injury caused to his or her feelings. In Wade v James Stuart and Co Ltd ET Case No.1802204/06, for example, the employment tribunal was influenced by the fact that the claimant was 'substantially distressed' when she gave evidence. However, being reduced to tears in court is not guaranteed to increase the level of an award of compensation. In Etheridge v Chief Constable of West Midlands Police and anor ET Case Nos.1307015/04 and others the employment tribunal noted: 'We have had to be careful about attaching too much weight to outward manifestations of [the claimant's] distress. She becomes tearful quite easily; she did so at several points in the history of events, and also while giving evidence to us. On the other hand, there is no expert evidence that she has an "eggshell personality" or anything approaching it. A victim of discrimination who cries easily should not necessarily receive higher compensation than one who suppresses and bottles up her suffering, which may in principle be as great as or greater than that of the victim who cries easily. As in the case of any tort, there should be no premium on a long face.'

36.73 **Nature of job.** In Orlando v Didcot Power Station Sports and Social Club 1996 IRLR 262, EAT, the EAT held that an employment tribunal was permitted to find that the loss of a part-time job could result in a lower level of compensation for injury to feelings than would be the case following the loss of a full-time career. The rationale behind such a distinction was that losing a full-time career was more disruptive to an individual's life than losing a part-time job. The EAT stressed, however, that such a finding would depend upon the facts of the particular case. Tribunals should not make generalised assumptions about the importance that individuals attach to part-time jobs.

Applying the same rationale, it is also open to tribunals to consider the nature of the job itself in fixing the award for injury to feelings. Loss of a rewarding and enjoyable career may cause more distress than loss of boring and repetitive work. Everything depends on the facts of the case, however, and tribunals should avoid making generalised assumptions about how the loss of a particular job might affect someone.

1312

Nature of complaint. Although, strictly speaking, the nature of the complaint **36.74** is not something that employment tribunals should consider when awarding compensation for injury to feelings – it is the effect of the discrimination on the claimant that matters – common sense dictates that they will be more prepared to accept that feelings have been seriously injured when the discrimination is of a serious nature than when it takes only a mild form. Tribunals often look at the seriousness or otherwise of the discrimination to help determine how severely the claimant's feelings have been injured.

Handling of complaint. The manner in which an employer handles a complaint **36.75** of discrimination is likely to be relevant to the level of an award for injury to feelings. For example, a delay in investigating an allegation of discriminatory abuse may lead to an increase in the award. Serious failings in the handling of a grievance may even lead to an award of aggravated damages – see 'Aggravated damages' below.

In British Telecommunications plc v Reid and anor 2004 IRLR 327, CA, the Court of Appeal upheld an employment tribunal's award of £6,000 for injury to feelings for race discrimination awarded to a claimant who suffered racial abuse from a colleague. The Court rejected the employer's argument that the tribunal had erred in taking into account subsequent events, such as the fact that the complainant had suffered the indignity of a 'totally unjustified' disciplinary investigation for having left work early after suffering the discriminatory abuse complained of; the stress associated with his transfer to another site to avoid contact with the colleague who was the subject of his complaint; and the length of time he had to wait (14 months) for the employer to investigate his grievance against the offending colleague. In the Court of Appeal's view, if all those matters arose out of the discrimination and were consequent upon it, then they were relevant to the inquiry into the extent of injury to the complainant's feelings. In particular, the Court noted that if a grievance procedure about a discrimination complaint is completed quickly by an employer, this may help to limit the extent of the injury to the complainant's feelings. Conversely, if it takes a considerable time, the injury to feelings may well be greater because the injury is prolonged.

Size of employer's business. It has been held that the size and resources of an **36.76** employer's business should not be taken into account by tribunals when assessing the appropriate level of an injury to feelings award – see Evans v Oakland Nursing Home Group Ltd EAT 0331/99 (a pre-Vento disability discrimination case).

Aggravated damages **36.77**

Compensation for non-financial loss may include an added element of aggravated damages in particularly serious cases of discrimination. Aggravated damages are not specifically mentioned in the EqA (nor were they in any of

1313

the antecedent equality legislation) but the power of employment tribunals to award such damages is now well established – see, for example, Prison Service and ors v Johnson 1997 ICR 275, EAT. The power derives from the general principles applicable to the award of compensation for other torts where the behaviour of the defendant may aggravate the injury caused to the plaintiff.

36.78 **Relationship with injury to feelings award**

There has been some confusion over whether awards for injury to feelings and awards for aggregated damages should be dealt with separately in employment tribunal judgments. Are aggravated damages a standalone head of compensation or merely a sub-heading of an injury to feelings award? The distinction may be important to avoid over-compensating a complainant, such as might happen if the aggravating features of the employer's conduct are already reflected in an injury to feelings award. It is notable that in Scottish law, aggravated damages are not recognised as a separate head of damages – D Watt (Shetland) Ltd v Reid EAT 424/01. Instead, damages for injury to feelings can include an element to reflect the way the victim was treated.

The position in England and Wales is rather less clear-cut. The EAT in Tchoula v ICTS (UK) Ltd 2000 ICR 1191, EAT, held that it was a matter of form, rather than substance, as to whether a tribunal included aggravated damages as part of its award for injury to feelings or expressed the award separately, but in Scott v Commissioners of Inland Revenue 2004 ICR 1410, CA, the Court of Appeal was of the view that the two awards should be expressed separately. Then, in Martins v Choudhary 2007 EWCA Civ 1379, CA, Lady Justice Smith stated that in harassment or discrimination cases, 'where damages fall to be awarded for injury to feelings, the quantum of damage should reflect the aggravating features of the defendant's conduct as they have affected the claimant. As "aggravated damages" are supposed to be compensatory, that seems to me to be the most satisfactory way of dealing with them. If a separate award of "aggravated damages" is made, it looks like a punishment; in other words it looks like exemplary damages.' Smith LJ recognised that different views had been expressed by the Court of Appeal on this point, and explicitly stated that her view was obiter (i.e. non-binding).

36.79 The issue was revisited by the then President of the EAT, Mr Justice Underhill, in Commissioner of Police of the Metropolis v Shaw EAT 0125/11. He was firmly of the view that aggravated damages are an aspect of injury to feelings and should be dealt with as a sub-heading under the same head of loss to avoid over-compensation. He noted that aggravated damages are compensatory only and should not be awarded to punish the respondent. Punition is a feature of exemplary damages, which may only be awarded in a very limited class of cases – see under 'Exemplary damages' below. Aggravated damages are a part of injury to feelings and, as such, the dividing line between the two will often be blurred. Thus, tribunals should avoid compensating claimants under both heads for the same loss. The ultimate question, according to Underhill P, is whether the overall award is proportionate to the totality of the claimant's suffering. This being so, tribunals ought to be wary of focusing on the *quality* of the respondent's conduct – i.e. assuming that the more heinous the conduct, the more devastating its impact on the claimant. Although that is not necessarily an illegitimate assumption, as a matter of broad common sense, the danger is that this approach can easily lead a tribunal into fixing compensation by reference to what it thinks is appropriate by way of punishment, or 'in order to give vent to its indignation'. Tribunals must not lose sight of the ultimate purpose of aggravated damages, which is to compensate for the additional distress caused to the claimant by the aggravating features in question.

Applying this reasoning to the particular case before him, Underhill P held that the employment tribunal had wrongly made an award for aggravated damages to reflect the seriousness of the conduct itself rather than aggravation of injury to feelings. The claimant, S, was a police officer who reported dishonest conduct by a colleague. As a result, he was suspended on unfounded disciplinary charges, which were collusively supported by a more senior officer. Although the charges were eventually dropped, S moved to a new role having suffered lasting distress and disillusionment at his treatment. A tribunal held that S was subjected to an unlawful detriment by reason of his having made a protected disclosure. (Note that protection from detriment for having made a protected disclosure is established by the ERA, and so is not, strictly speaking, a ground of 'discrimination', but it is accepted that the general principles governing compensation are the same.) At the remedy hearing the tribunal awarded £37,000 in compensation, comprising £17,000 for injury to feelings and £20,000 for aggravated damages. The EAT allowed an appeal against that award. Although £37,000 was not so manifestly excessive as to constitute an error of law, the tribunal had made an award for aggravated damages that reflected the seriousness of the conduct itself rather than the aggravation to S's feelings. In Underhill P's view, the appropriate overall amount for S's injury to feelings was £30,000. If it were necessary to specify, he indicated that he would split that award between a 'core' award of £22,500 and £7,500 for aggravating factors, such as the lack of an apology.

36.80 Significantly, Underhill P went on to doubt whether the practice of making separate injury to feelings and aggravated damages awards is a good thing. He identified several imperfections in this approach. First, it is an artificial exercise to attempt to distinguish between hurt caused by a 'core' wrongful act, and that caused by exceptional features. Secondly, and related to that first point, there is a real risk of double recovery. Thirdly, there is the danger that compartmentalising aggravated damages might tempt tribunals, if only subconsciously, to see them as punitive. And finally, the separate approaches lead to unnecessary complication and technicality. Underhill P thought it would be preferable if a single award for injury to feelings were made, taking into account aggravating

1315

features. However, he noted that, although the question has never been addressed head-on, separate awards of aggravated damages have been approved by the Court of Appeal too many times for him to be able to say that this is the wrong approach. Nevertheless, he recommended that an award for aggravated damages should be formulated as a sub-heading of injury to feelings rather than a distinct head of loss in future.

36.81 **Whether total award subject to the Vento limit.** Any move towards treating aggravated damages as a subset of injury to feelings will inevitably raise the question of whether the overall total ought to be subject to the 'limits' on injury to feelings awards set down in Vento v Chief Constable of West Yorkshire Police (No.2) 2003 ICR 318, CA – see under 'Injury to feelings – quantum: the Vento guidelines' above. There are several examples of aggravated damages awards taking the total sum for hurt feelings above what the Court of Appeal in Vento indicated should be the maximum. For example, in Driscoll v News Group Newspapers ET Case Nos.3202077/07 and another, an employment tribunal found that there had been high-handed and oppressive behaviour justifying an aggravated damages award of £10,000, in addition to an award for 'ordinary' injury to feelings of £25,000. The total of these awards was therefore above the top Vento band of £25,000 (since uprated, by case law, to £30,000). The practice of making a separate award for aggravated damages has meant that the Vento ceiling could still be respected as regards 'ordinary' injury to feelings alone, and indeed the Court of Appeal in Vento appeared to endorse this practice.

When doubting the wisdom of separating 'ordinary' injury to feelings and aggravated damages in Commissioner of Police of the Metropolis v Shaw (above), Mr Justice Underhill noted that he did not think that Vento specifically considered the practice of awarding aggravated damages on top of injury to feelings – that was merely the way the employment tribunal in that case had approached compensation. Instead, the Court of Appeal in Vento appeared to emphasise the importance of considering the award for non-pecuniary loss as a total. However, Underhill P did not wish to add extra complication by directing that tribunals abandon the practice of 'putting any sufficiently serious aggravating features in a separate box'. Accordingly, it seems that tribunals may still award aggravated damages over and above the limits set down for 'ordinary' injury to feelings awards. However, tribunals ought to bear in mind the general principle that the total award for non-pecuniary loss must be fair and proportionate.

36.82 **Circumstances where aggravated damages may be awarded**
The classic statement of when aggravated damages are available was made by the Court of Appeal in Alexander v Home Office 1988 ICR 685, CA, where it held that aggravated damages can be awarded in a discrimination case where the defendants have behaved 'in a high-handed, malicious, insulting or

oppressive manner in committing the act of discrimination'. That quotation has been cited and applied by courts and tribunals ever since and remains a sound statement of general principle. However, Mr Justice Underhill, then President of the EAT, gave a more detailed exposition in Commissioner of Police of the Metropolis v Shaw EAT 0125/11, identifying three broad categories of case:

- where the manner in which the wrong was committed was particularly upsetting. This is what the Court of Appeal in Alexander meant when referring to acts done in a 'high-handed, malicious, insulting or oppressive manner'

- where there was a discriminatory motive, i.e. the conduct was evidently based on prejudice or animosity, or was spiteful, vindictive or intended to wound. Where such motive is evident, the discrimination will be likely to cause more distress than the same acts would cause if done inadvertently; for example, through ignorance or insensitivity. However, this will only be the case if the claimant was aware of the motive in question – an unknown motive could not cause aggravation of the injury to feelings

- where subsequent conduct adds to the injury – for example, where the employer conducts tribunal proceedings in an unnecessarily offensive manner, or 'rubs salt in the wound' by plainly showing that he does not take the claimant's complaint of discrimination seriously.

We do not suppose that Underhill P intended these headings to be exhaustive and, in any event, these categories are likely to overlap in practice. Nonetheless, the decided cases that have included aggravated damages awards more or less fit into these headings. We consider some examples of each.

Manner in which the wrong was committed. Such cases generally involve **36.83** discriminatory acts committed at a high level within the organisation. For example, in Driscoll v News Group Newspapers ET Case Nos.3202077/07 and another, the employment tribunal found that a number of individuals at the top level of management at the *News of the World* had behaved in a bullying manner towards the claimant over a long period of time, and there were acts of disability harassment. All of this amounted to high-handed and oppressive behaviour, justifying an aggravated damages award of £10,000, in addition to an award for injury to feelings of £25,000. And in British Telecommunications plc v Reid and anor 2004 IRLR 327, CA, the Court of Appeal confirmed that an employment tribunal had been entitled to treat the promotion of an employee, E, whom the claimant had accused of race discrimination, as high-handed conduct by the employer. The tribunal took into account the fact that E had gone unpunished and had remained in his job and the Court found it 'striking' that E had been promoted, given the circumstances.

The facts of Commissioner of Police of the Metropolis v Shaw (above), in which Underhill P set out categories of different aggravated behaviour, provide

1317

an example of aggravating conduct in the manner in which the wrong was committed. The claimant in that case reported dishonest conduct by a colleague and, as a result, was suspended on unfounded disciplinary charges, which were collusively supported by a more senior officer. The employment tribunal found that the instigation of those disciplinary proceedings was an unlawful act, being a detriment to which the claimant was subjected for having made a protected disclosure. It awarded £17,000 for injury to feelings and £20,000 aggravated damages. The EAT allowed an appeal against that award, but agreed that there were aggravating factors, and so substituted a total award of £30,000 for injury to feelings including aggravated damages. One of the aggravating features it thought relevant was that the very officer about whom the claimant had made the protected disclosure escorted him from the building when the disciplinary proceedings were brought against him. It also had regard to the absence of any subsequent apology or of any action against the colleague or the senior officer who had supported him.

36.84 **Motive.** Express findings of discriminatory motive seem to be fairly rare – aggravating factors are more commonly found in the employer's unwillingness to tackle discrimination, or preference to punish the complainant rather than the wrongdoer. One example is Simpson v BAA Airports Ltd ET Case No.2703460/09. In that case S, a black British woman, suffered several racially offensive comments from her line manager, G. Among other things, he told her that if he ever needed a blood transplant, under no circumstances would he accept black blood as it had germs. He also told a number of racist jokes about black people and called another black employee a 'nigger'. When S complained again, a formal grievance was instigated against G and his line manager investigated, but after six months the latter decided that there was insufficient evidence to uphold the grievance. An employment tribunal found racial harassment and race discrimination. It condemned the way in which the employer had dealt with the grievance, initially suggesting that S tackle G herself, and later setting up a 'facilitation meeting' between them. It concluded that the employer was aware that there was a climate of racist abuse, which it allowed to continue while trying to minimise its effects by conducting half-hearted investigations. The tribunal awarded S £18,000 for injury to feelings, £10,000 for psychiatric injury and £10,000 aggravated damages. Among other things, it noted that S's line manager's comments were malicious and that he intended them so be so.

Note that the clear *absence* of motive may well save an employer from an award of aggravated damages. In Griffin v Plymouth Hospitals NHS Trust ET Case No.1701040/09 G succeeded in a claim of failure to make reasonable adjustments in relation to difficulty she experienced in manual handling. She repeatedly asked for help but none was provided. She lodged a grievance, but resigned when she despaired of the Trust providing her with the help she required. The tribunal found that there were a number of reasonable adjustments that the Trust could have made to obviate the need for manual handling and lifting, but failed to do so. It noted that G suffered considerable stress and awarded £10,000 for injury to feelings. However, it concluded that the Trust's failings were due to incompetence rather than high-handedness, and so refused to make any award of aggravated damages.

Subsequent conduct. This third category clearly covers both the situation **36.85** where the employer's response to the discrimination in the workplace is aggravating (e.g. by not treating a grievance seriously) and where the employer's response to tribunal proceedings is unnecessarily aggressive or retaliatory. Three examples of the former:

● **HM Prison Service v Salmon** 2001 IRLR 425, EAT: a female prison officer was subjected to a humiliating working environment in which male colleagues openly read pornographic magazines and engaged in unacceptable sexual banter. An employment tribunal found that there was an anti-female culture where unsolicited remarks about women in the prison service would be made, along with sexist jokes designed to provoke a reaction. One prison officer, D, wrote wholly offensive and sexually degrading comments about S in a court dock book that would be seen by prison officers only. The stress and humiliation caused S psychiatric damage. The tribunal awarded £20,000 injury to feelings, of which £5,000 related to aggravated damages. This was to reflect the tribunal's view that the manner in which the prison service had dealt with the incident suggested that it perceived the matter as trivial and this perception was communicated to S. It was obvious that the senior officer at the court had attempted an on-the-spot cover-up by blanking out the entries in the dock book with a felt-tip pen. Furthermore, D had not been disciplined swiftly or decisively after admitting responsibility for the dock book incident. The overall picture was of high-handedness and arrogance

● **Desousa v Barrow t/a Southbourne Parts Garage** ET Case No.310329/08: D was an MOT assistant who had a mental impairment and was being supported by the local council through the Work Step programme. He was harassed and bullied by other mechanics working at the garage, but an employment tribunal found that the employer seemed to abdicate all management responsibility. In particular, the tribunal noted the failure to respond either in a timely manner, or at all, to the conduct complained of, and the trivialisation of the whole affair. Furthermore, certain incidents should have led to immediate disciplinary action against the responsible employees. Nor had any explanation or apology been offered. The tribunal awarded £5,000 aggravated damages, in addition to an award for injury to feelings of £20,000

● **Bungay and anor v Saini and ors** EAT 0331/10: S and C succeeded in claims of direct discrimination and harassment contrary to the former

1319

Employment Equality (Religion or Belief) Regulations 2003 SI 2003/1660. These claims arose out of an anti-Hindu campaign conducted by the advice centre at which they worked and its directors. Two directors in particular, B and P, were prominent in the campaign against them. Among other things, they made false accusations to the police about C and S, causing them to be arrested following their dismissal and later released without charge. The employment tribunal awarded compensation, making B and P jointly and severally liable, and including a sum for aggravated damages. It took account of the high-handed manner in which B and P had conducted the disciplinary hearings that led to C's and S's dismissals, and their subsequent unfounded and malicious accusation to the police. The EAT rejected B and P's appeal against the tribunal's award of aggravated damages in respect of post-dismissal conduct.

36.86 As for aggravating features in the conduct of tribunal proceedings, the EAT in Zaiwalla and Co and anor v Walia 2002 IRLR 697, EAT, confirmed for the first time that damages are available. In that case the EAT upheld an award of £7,500 for aggravated damages in a case where the employment tribunal found that the employer's solicitors had put a 'monumental amount of effort' into defending the proceedings to an 'inappropriate' extent. It further found that the defence of the proceedings was 'deliberately designed… to be intimidatory and cause the maximum unease and distress to the claimant'.

The EAT rejected the respondent's argument that the only appropriate response to misconduct in the defence of proceedings was for the tribunal to make an order for costs. The EAT observed that costs orders are limited to reflecting the costs reasonably incurred by the party, and are not related to the victim's feelings. It thought that there was a very good public policy reason for allowing such a claim in an appropriate discrimination case, since the alternative would be for the claimant to bring further proceedings for victimisation, increasing the employment tribunals' already considerable workload. It followed, in the EAT's view, that it would be preferable for the tribunal hearing the case, which would be best placed to judge the seriousness of the misconduct and its effect on the complainant, to compensate him or her by way of aggravated damages.

36.87 The EAT stressed in Zaiwalla that its decision should not be taken as a 'green light' to claimants to claim for aggravated damages in respect of the alleged misconduct of proceedings as a matter of course. This was an exceptional case, and cases where an award of aggravated damages will be made in respect of such behaviour would be few and far between. However, there have been several further examples, two of which are outlined below:

- **Kirby v Quality Electrical Supplies and Technology Ltd and ors** ET Case No.2412616/09: K began working for QEST Ltd in October 2006. She entered into a civil partnership in August 2007 and by February 2008 her sexuality was generally known in the office. A colleague called her an offensive name related to sexuality and K complained, but nothing was done. Thereafter her manager began a campaign of discrimination and harassment against her based on her sexual orientation. Among other things, he called her a 'slag', a 'slut' and a 'whore' and made comments related to her sexuality. She lodged a formal grievance but received a cursory response from QEST Ltd, offering no apology and stating that the manager had left the company. An employment tribunal upheld her claim of harassment and awarded £20,000 injury to feelings plus £2,000 aggravated damages. It noted that, among other things, QEST Ltd persisted in calling witnesses to suggest that K's motivation in pursuing the claim was purely financial

• **Wade-Jones v CJ Upton and Sons Ltd** ET Case No.1901127/09: an employment tribunal upheld W-J's claim that she was sexually harassed. It awarded £15,000 for injury to feelings, taking account of the fact that W-J suffered from depression and the employer did not apologise for its conduct. It also awarded £5,000 to reflect the aggressive manner in which the employer's legal adviser had treated W-J in relation to the proceedings. The employer gave him free rein to act as he saw fit. Among other things, he had contacted one of W-J's possible future employers to make enquiries about her, and this caused her great distress.

Employment tribunals must be careful to distinguish between unnecessarily aggressive conduct and unobjectionable ways of conducting a defence. In Newcastle Upon Tyne Hospitals NHS Foundation Trust v Bagley EAT 0417/11 – which concerned a reasonable adjustments case brought under the DDA – the employment tribunal based its decision to award aggravated damages on a number of factors related to the employer's conduct in litigation. It noted that the employer's case included the 'insulting' suggestions that the claimant sought to stay at home, rather than return to work part time, because it was more profitable for her to do so; that administrative convenience was more important than the claimant's health and her career; and that the claimant was the author of her own misfortune and unwilling to return to work. The tribunal also considered the employer's failure to admit the fact of the claimant's disability until six months after her ET1 was lodged to be oppressive, given the medical knowledge at its disposal. On appeal, the EAT held that the tribunal should not have awarded aggravated damages (although it also overturned the decision on liability and so this point did not strictly arise for determination). The employment tribunal had incorrectly focused upon the manner of the employer's behaviour rather than upon its impact upon the claimant. Furthermore, the delay in admitting disability could not be considered oppressive given that the employer did not have access to the relevant occupational health report until after proceedings were commenced, and indeed after disclosure. **36.88**

36.89 **Causal link between conduct and loss**

The presence of high-handed conduct will not necessarily be enough, on its own, to lead to an award of aggravated damages. As the authorities cited above make clear, aggravated damages are compensatory, not punitive. This means that there must be some causal link between the conduct and the damage suffered if compensation is to be available. In HM Prison Service v Salmon 2001 IRLR 425, EAT, the EAT made it clear that 'aggravated damages are awarded only on the basis, and to the extent, that the aggravating features have increased the impact of the discriminatory act or conduct on the applicant and thus the injury to his or her feelings'.

36.90 # Personal injury

The principle that employment tribunals have jurisdiction to award compensation for personal injury caused by unlawful discrimination, whether physical or psychiatric, was confirmed by the Court of Appeal in Sheriff v Klyne Tugs (Lowestoft) Ltd 1999 ICR 1170, CA. Accordingly, claimants can claim damages relating to psychological (or physical) injury for discrimination as a separate head of loss in its own right. It will not be possible to claim twice in respect of the same injury under two different heads of loss, however, so tribunals must be clear about what is compensated as injury to feelings and what amounts to personal injury.

The Court of Appeal also made it clear in Sheriff that a complainant who has suffered a personal injury as a result of discrimination must ensure that he or she expressly claims for personal injury in the discrimination proceedings. Otherwise, there is a risk that he or she will lose the chance to litigate the issue later in the form of a claim for damages based on tort and/or breach of contract in the High Court or county court, because of the doctrines of res judicata (or 'cause of action estoppel'), issue estoppel and/or the rule in Henderson v Henderson 1843–60 All ER Rep 378, Ch D.

36.91 **Causation**

Some discrimination cases may involve bodily injury resulting from physical assaults and, in these relatively rare cases, proving causation should not be problematic for the claimant. However, it is much more likely that, in the context of discrimination claims, the type of personal injury at issue is psychiatric injury, particularly in harassment cases.

The specific causes of psychiatric illness, such as clinical depression, are often unclear. Nor is it necessarily obvious to what extent such a condition may have been influenced by external home or work pressures that have nothing to do with the discrimination suffered. This means that the claimant will need to demonstrate that the discriminatory acts actually caused the psychiatric damage in order to prove liability and claim compensation. Similar problems of causation arise where a physical condition (such as a heart attack) is said to have resulted from the stress caused by the acts of discrimination in question. In Sheriff v Klyne Tugs (Lowestoft) Ltd 1999 ICR 1170, CA, Lord Justice Stuart-Smith suggested in obiter remarks that any claimant in a discrimination case where personal injury is alleged may wish to obtain a medical report to support his or her claim. In cases of psychiatric injury, this is likely to necessitate the report of a psychiatrist, who may also be required to give evidence to the tribunal.

In Thaine v London School of Economics 2010 ICR 1422, EAT – a sex **36.92** discrimination case – the employment tribunal awarded compensation for psychiatric ill health as well as for injury to feelings and loss of earnings. However, it went on to discount the award by 60 per cent to reflect the fact that there had been a number of 'concurrent causes' for the claimant's ill health for which the employer was not liable – namely, issues in her personal life and incidents of sexual harassment that she had suffered, or perceived herself to have suffered, but for which LSE was not responsible. The claimant challenged that discount on appeal but the EAT endorsed the tribunal's approach. It held that an employer should not have to compensate a claimant for his injury in its entirety when the harm for which it was responsible was just one of many causes of the ill health. In so holding, the EAT had regard to obiter guidance on the issue of apportionment in psychiatric ill health cases given in Sutherland (Chairman of the Governors of St Thomas Becket RC High School) v Hatton 2002 ICR 613, CA. There, Lady Justice Hale suggested that where there are multiple causes of psychiatric illness, the court should make a sensible attempt at apportionment between them. Lady Justice Smith and Lord Justice Sedley in Dickins v O2 plc 2009 IRLR 58, CA, took a different approach and concluded that, although in such cases it may be appropriate to make a reduction to some of the heads of damage to reflect future risks of non-tortious loss, there should not be a rule that a judge should apportion the damages across the board merely because one non-tortious cause has been in play. Taking all the case law into account, the EAT in Thaine concluded that it would be unfair to expect the employer to compensate the claimant for her psychiatric ill health and its consequences in its entirety when the unlawful discrimination for which it was responsible, though materially contributing to her ill health, was just one of many causes. Accordingly the tribunal had been entitled to reduce the claimant's compensation by 60 per cent.

It is important to note that the Court of Appeal in the Sheriff case ruled that a claimant seeking damages for personal injury arising from the statutory tort of discrimination does not need to show that the injury was reasonably foreseeable, as would be the case if he or she were suing under the common law tort of negligence in the county court or the High Court. An old Court of Appeal case – Skyrail Oceanic Ltd v Coleman 1981 ICR 864, CA – had suggested otherwise, but the Court of Appeal in Essa v Laing Ltd 2004 ICR 746, CA, confirmed that compensation for an act of direct discrimination

1323

contrary to the Race Relations Act 1976 was available in respect of all harm arising naturally and directly from the act of discrimination. In other words, no test of reasonable foreseeability need be applied. It is generally assumed that this principle extends to all kinds of discrimination compensation awarded under what would now be S.124(2)(b) and (6) combined with S.119(2) and (3) EqA, not just race discrimination, although other cases have expressed doubt about this. For a full analysis of this issue see Chapter 35, 'Compensation: general principles', under 'General principles of assessment – causation'.

36.93 Quantifying personal injury damages
There are two types of damages to consider with regard to compensation awards in discrimination cases under the head of personal injury: 'general damages' for pain, suffering or loss of amenity, and 'special damages', covering the financial losses that flow directly from the psychiatric injury caused by the discrimination.

36.94 General damages. The Judicial Studies Board Guidelines for the Assessment of General Damages in Personal Injury Cases ('the JSB Guidelines') provide guidance on the appropriate levels of awards for pain, suffering and loss of amenity. In the context of psychiatric injury, the JSB Guidelines draw a distinction between psychiatric damage generally (giving categories of appropriate levels of awards for 'Severe', 'Moderately Severe' and 'Moderate') and post-traumatic stress disorder (for which the relevant categories are 'Severe', 'Moderately Severe', 'Moderate' and 'Minor'). Two discrimination cases in which these guidelines were considered:

- **Grant v Northumberland County Council** ET Case No.2505048/08: G suffered from bipolar effective disorder and had several lengthy absences from work. After one of these absences, the employer began an investigation under its absence procedures – a disciplinary measure – and as a result of this, G's health suffered greatly. An employment tribunal found this to be a failure to make a reasonable adjustment contrary to the DDA. G claimed for personal injury as a separate head of damages, and the tribunal noted that she already had a pre-existing psychiatric illness, but on the evidence available, the employer's failure to make reasonable adjustments delayed her ability to return to work by a period of three years. She had also attempted suicide and as a result had been hospitalised for 18 weeks. The tribunal assessed the appropriate award as £12,000, at the upper end of the moderately severe bracket

- **Faithful v AXA PPP Healthcare plc** ET Case No.1100218/09: an employment tribunal upheld F's claim for race discrimination. She was a Brazilian woman who was mimicked by a number of colleagues (including her line manager) and was called nicknames relating to her nationality. The tribunal awarded £22,000 for injury to feelings, £10,000 aggravated damages and £25,000 for personal injury. There was medical evidence showing that F's perception of her treatment had caused a moderate-to-severe depressive illness. The medical report found no pre-existing condition and specifically excluded F's brother's death, which occurred around the same time, as a contributing factor. The tribunal noted that the guidance required it to have regard to the injured person's ability to cope with life and work and observed that F's medical report indicated that she could not carry out even the simplest of household tasks without help from her husband. It also took account of the fact that F's illness left her withdrawn and unable to socialise in her usual manner, something else referred to in the JSB Guidelines.

Special damages. In severe cases of discrimination or harassment, it may be **36.95** that the complainant has sustained such serious psychiatric injury that he or she is unable to work for a considerable period and will need financial compensation to cover this period, which, depending on the circumstances, may even be the rest of his or her working life. In an orthodox negligence claim for personal injuries (resulting from a car accident, for example), an approach is used whereby a 'multiplicand' is multiplied by a 'multiplier'. The multiplicand is arrived at in the same way as calculating past financial loss (see under 'Past loss' above), resulting in an estimated figure representing annual net loss. A multiplier is then applied to the multiplicand. The multiplier represents the full number of years that the individual will not be able to work, minus built-in deductions to take into account varying levels of mortality and other contingencies according to the individual's age at the time the award of compensation is made. To perform this calculation, a set of actuarial tables is used (the Ogden Tables). These contain tables of multipliers for different situations, with particular tables to be applied in cases of life-long loss.

In a discrimination claim in an employment tribunal, however, where personal injury is claimed as a head of loss, one of two different approaches might apply. If the case is not one of career-long loss, future financial losses are to be assessed using the usual discrimination/unfair dismissal law approach (see under 'Future loss' above). Where the loss covers the remainder of the complainant's career, a tribunal should apply the methods used to calculate future loss in personal injury cases, using the Ogden Tables. In Kingston Upon Hull City Council v Dunnachie (No.3) and another case 2003 IRLR 843, EAT, the EAT approved the use of the Ogden Tables to provide the multiplier for this purpose – but only where the future loss being calculated is in respect of claimants who will be unable to work again for the rest of their working lives. The EAT specifically discouraged the use of multipliers based on the Ogden Tables to calculate unfair dismissal compensation (and, by extension, discrimination damages) in cases where the extent of loss falls short of the remainder of the claimant's career. For further discussion of the use of these tables in a discrimination context, see under 'Future loss – calculating future loss' above.

1325

36.96 **Overlap and danger of double recovery**

As with aggravated damages and injury to feelings, employment tribunals may, but need not, make separate awards for injury to feelings and personal injury. Where separate awards are made, tribunals must be careful to avoid double recovery: the aim of compensatory damages is not to reward the claimant or provide a windfall. There is clearly a danger in discrimination cases of an overlap between an award for pain, suffering and loss of amenity arising from psychiatric injury and an award for injury to feelings resulting from the same discriminatory act(s).

This danger was recognised by the EAT in HM Prison Service v Salmon 2001 IRLR 425, EAT, where it acknowledged that, although the two awards are distinct in principle, they are not easily separable in practice because it is not always possible to identify when the distress and humiliation suffered as a result of unlawful discrimination becomes a recognised psychiatric illness. The concept of 'injury to feelings' is wide enough to cover anything from minor upset caused by one-off incidents at the lower end of the scale to serious and prolonged feelings of humiliation and depression at the upper end. The EAT saw nothing wrong in practice with tribunals treating the personal injury as having been compensated for under the heading of injury to feelings, so long as the tribunal identifies those aspects of the victim's medical condition that the injury to feelings award is also intended to cover. Moreover, where separate awards are made, a tribunal must be aware of the risk of compensating the victim twice for the same suffering.

36.97 In Vento v Chief Constable of West Yorkshire Police (No.2) 2003 ICR 318, CA, the Court of Appeal reiterated that tribunals should take due account of any overlap between individual heads of damage to prevent double compensation. So, for example, in Cuerden v Yorkshire Housing ET Case No.1803654/08 the claimant suffered an exacerbation of an existing depressive disorder as a result of the employer's failure to make reasonable adjustments. An employment tribunal concluded that the exacerbation of her condition would have lasted for about two years and made an award of £7,500 for psychiatric injury. It also awarded £9,000 for injury to feelings, but stressed that it took great care to ensure there was no double recovery. (There was a partially successful appeal in this case – see Yorkshire Housing Ltd v Cuerden EAT 0397/09 – but the tribunal's approach to personal injury and injury to feelings was not challenged.)

Note that it is possible for claimants to seek injury to feelings and financial compensation in the employment tribunal but seek compensation for personal injury separately in the civil courts, subject to the issues of estoppel, noted above. This occurred in Commissioner of Police of the Metropolis v Shaw EAT 0125/11. In that case the EAT did not explore the reasons why the claimant had proceeded in that way but did observe that it was very unusual. It pointed

1326

out that employment tribunals have jurisdiction to make awards for personal injury caused by unlawful discrimination and that 'it will almost always be better if claims for such injury are dealt with in the same forum as the other losses for which compensation is sought – not least because, even though injury to feelings and injury to mental health are formally distinct, there is in practice an overlap between them and it will be difficult for the tribunal hearing whichever claim is decided second to assess to what extent the claimant has already received compensation for what is in substance the same suffering'.

Exemplary damages

36.98

Exemplary damages are damages that are aimed at *punishing* the wrongdoer rather than compensating the victim. The House of Lords, in Rookes v Barnard 1964 AC 1129, HL, confirmed that exemplary damages were justified in three categories of case as follows:

- conduct by servants of Government that is oppressive, arbitrary or unconstitutional

- conduct of a respondent designed to be self-profiting (for example, not taking disciplinary action against an alleged discriminator because he or she is a profitable employee)

- damages specifically authorised by statute (which is not the case so far as discrimination legislation is concerned).

When the Court of Appeal analysed Rooke v Barnard and subsequent case law in AB v South West Water Services Ltd 1993 QB 507, CA, it came to the conclusion that the House of Lords' decision could only apply to torts recognised by law at the time that that judgment was handed down, i.e. in 1964. Thus, for some while, the view prevailed that exemplary damages could not be awarded in discrimination cases, since discrimination in employment was not established as a statutory tort until well after 1964. However, the House of Lords revisited the matter in Kuddus v Chief Constable of Leicestershire Constabulary 2002 2 AC 122, HL, and found both as a matter of law and of principle that exemplary damages should not be restricted to torts in existence prior to 1964. The Law Lords were divided, however, on the question of whether exemplary damages were available for the statutory discrimination torts.

Support for the view that exemplary damages are available for statutory torts **36.99** such as those created by the discrimination legislation was put forward by the EAT in Virgo Fidelis Senior School v Boyle 2004 ICR 1210, EAT – a whistleblowing case. The claimant, a schoolteacher, was dismissed and suffered a detriment for making a public interest disclosure. He was awarded total compensation of £47,755, which included an award of £45,000 for injury to feelings. The school appealed to the EAT against the level of the award, and the claimant cross appealed on the basis, partly, that the tribunal should have made an award of exemplary damages in respect of the local authority's involvement in the dismissal process. The local authority was not a party to the proceedings but the claimant argued that damages could be awarded on the basis that the school was a servant of the Government. The EAT held that there was no reason in principle why exemplary damages could not be awarded under the discrimination legislation, provided the relevant conditions were met. However, on the facts of the case, in exercising its disciplinary powers the school had not acted as a servant or agent exercising executive power derived from the Government. Nor was there sufficient evidence to say that there had been oppressive, arbitrary, or unconstitutional action. The EAT therefore refused to interfere with the tribunal's decision not to award exemplary damages.

Further guidance on the role and nature of exemplary damages in discrimination law was given by the EAT in Ministry of Defence v Fletcher 2010 IRLR 25, EAT, where an employment tribunal awarded the claimant damages in respect of sex discrimination and harassment, including £20,000 aggravated damages and £50,000 exemplary damages. The Ministry of Defence appealed and the EAT overturned the award of exemplary damages. It accepted that certain 'ordinary' employment law functions performed under statute by an official of a public body of sufficient seniority may, subject to other conditions, be capable of supporting an award of exemplary damages. However, the MoD was not abusing any special power available to it by virtue of its status as a public body. Thus, the first of the three categories identified in Rookes v Barnard (above) was not in play. Although the tribunal had characterised the MoD's failure to provide redress for the claimant's claims as 'oppressive, arbitrary and unconstitutional', it did not cross the high threshold warranting an award of exemplary damages.

36.100 Even had the MoD's conduct crossed that threshold, the EAT was of the view that the award of £50,000 would still have been unsustainable: the tribunal had awarded the aggregate of the award for injury to feelings and aggravated damages, but there was no rationale for this, and such an approach was likely to lead to double recovery. Only if the amount of compensatory and aggravated damages was insufficient to show disapproval of the perpetrator's conduct and to provide a proportionate punitive element would exemplary damages be justified. The EAT noted that, where an award is appropriate, the Court of Appeal's decision in Thompson v Commissioner of Police of the Metropolis and another case 1998 QB 498, CA, is authority for a lower limit of £5,000, since uprated to £6,000 in line with inflation. Had exemplary damages been appropriate here, the EAT would have put the award at the lower end of the scale and not awarded more than £7,500.

In Scanlon v Redcar and Cleveland Borough Council ET Case No.2510997/04 the employment tribunal awarded S £20,000 in aggravated damages for sex discrimination, part of a total award of £442,466. The tribunal considered that the oppressive conduct of the Council, together with its abuse of power exercised in its capacity as a public body, brought it 'well within the ambit of an award for exemplary damages' but that such an award would not be appropriate, as the award of aggravated damages was sufficient in the circumstances. But the tribunal went on to say that if it were to make separate awards, then £7,500 as aggravated damages and £12,500 as exemplary damages would be appropriate. The exemplary damages would have been in relation to the fact that the Council, through the actions of a Councillor, made extremely damaging and false public statements about the claimant.

The tribunal's approach in Scanlon seems questionable in the light of more **36.101** recent case law. Several cases, such as Martins v Choudhary 2007 EWCA Civ 1379, CA, and Commissioner of Police of the Metropolis v Shaw EAT 0125/11, have emphasised that aggravated damages are intended to *compensate* the claimant, not punish the respondent. It therefore seems inappropriate to suggest that aggravated and exemplary damages are interchangeable grounds, as the tribunal did in Scanlon. However, there is higher authority for the suggestion that the need for exemplary damages may be eclipsed by compensation awarded under other heads. In Hackney London Borough Council v Sivanandan and ors 2011 ICR 1374, EAT, the EAT held that there were no grounds on which to award exemplary damages, rejecting the claimant's assertion that the respondent Council would not 'learn any lessons' unless punished. The EAT observed in passing that, if the Council may be taught a lesson by a large award, the £421,000 awarded to the claimant under other heads might be thought sufficient for that purpose. It was hard to see how a further £6,000 in exemplary damages would make an appreciable difference.

Interest on awards

36.102

The Employment Tribunals (Interest on Awards in Discrimination Cases) Regulations 1996 SI 1996/2803 give tribunals the power to award interest on awards made in discrimination cases. Under Reg 2(1) an employment tribunal is required to consider whether to award interest even if the applicant does not specifically apply for it. The parties can agree the amount of interest to be awarded – Reg 2(2). If they do not agree, interest is calculated under the rules set out in Reg 3. In general terms, interest is to be calculated as simple interest which accrues from day to day – Reg 3(1).

Under Reg 3(2), the rate of interest is that which applies to the special investment account established by the Court Funds Office for the purpose of holding monies related to cases in the Court of Protection, among other things. This is described in Reg 3(2) as the rate set under S.27(1) of the Court Funds Rules 1987 SI 1987/821. This was the appropriate statutory reference until 2 October 2011. However, on 3 October, the 1987 Rules were revoked in their entirety and replaced by the Court Funds Rules 2011 SI 2011/1734. Reg 3(2) has not been updated to refer to the new Rules. The applicable interest rate, which is set by the Ministry of Justice, has remained the same since 2009 and it is presumably intended that the rate as at 2 October, namely 0.5 per cent, still applies.

36.103 More generally, it should be noted that the 1996 Regulations have not been updated to refer to the EqA. The Regulations still contain references to the enforcement provisions of the antecedent discrimination legislation and so, on their face, do not apply to claims brought under the EqA since 1 October 2010. However, the Equality Act 2010 (Commencement No.4, Savings, Consequential, Transitional, Transitory and Incidental Provisions and Revocation) Order 2010 SI 2010/2317 makes the necessary adjustments in this regard. Article 21(1) and Schedule 7 together provide that specified provisions of subordinate legislation are treated as if made under the equivalent power in the EqA. In this way, the 1996 Regulations are to be treated as if made under S.139 EqA, which allows for the enactment of subordinate legislation to regulate the payment of interest in discrimination cases. Thus, the 1996 Regulations can be taken to apply in relation to discriminatory acts occurring after 1 October 2010 as they did previously.

36.104 **Dates for calculating interest.** The relevant date for the purpose of calculating interest differs according to whether the interest relates to a sum for injury to feelings or to arrears of remuneration, and whether there would be serious injustice caused by an application of the normal rules. For injury to feelings awards, Reg 6(1)(a) provides that the period of the award of interest starts on the date of the act of discrimination complained of and ends on the day on which the employment tribunal calculates the amount of interest – the 'day of calculation'. It must be presumed that where discrimination extends over a period, the tribunal will be afforded some discretion to decide when the discrimination can be said to start. In Al Jumard v Clwyd Leisure Ltd and ors 2008 IRLR 345, EAT, one of several grounds of appeal was that the tribunal had erred in taking December 2003 as the start point when it had made a finding of a discriminatory act in May 2002. The EAT noted that the tribunal appeared to have forgotten about the earlier incident when fixing the date under Reg 6, although it was right to say that the claimant's more substantial complaints only started in December 2003. The EAT stated that it would have been reluctant to refer this issue alone back to the tribunal, had it been the only complaint, but since other grounds of appeal had succeeded the tribunal should consider this point too and see what difference, if any, it made to their analysis.

For all other awards, interest is awarded for the period beginning on the 'mid-point date' and ending on the day of calculation – Reg 6(1)(b). The 'mid-point date' is the date halfway through the period beginning on the date of the act of unlawful discrimination and ending on the day of calculation – Reg 4(2). No award of interest can be made in relation to losses which will arise after the day of calculation, such as future loss of earnings – Reg 5. The EAT confirmed in Ministry of Defence v Cannock and ors 1994 ICR 918, EAT (a sex discrimination case), that this meant that no interest could be awarded on pension losses.

Regulation 6(3) permits tribunals to calculate interest for periods other than those specified in Reg 6(1) where there would be 'serious injustice' if different dates were not used. In the Cannock case, the EAT upheld an employment tribunal's decision to award interest over a longer period than normal in a case where the losses being compensated had occurred many years previously.

Statement of interest. The employment tribunal's decision must contain a **36.105** statement of the total amount of interest awarded and, where the amount has not been agreed by the parties, a table setting out how it has been calculated or a description of the method of calculation – Reg 7(1). If no award of interest has been made, the tribunal must set out its reasons for this – Reg 7(2).

Late payment of compensation **36.106**

If an employer pays the full amount of an award within 14 days of the date of the decision, no additional interest will be payable – Reg 8(2). However, under the Employment Tribunals (Interest) Order 1990 SI 1990/479, if the full amount is not paid within 14 days, interest will be payable on the total award from and including the day after the award was made until payment. The applicable interest rate is currently 8 per cent – Article 4 of the 1990 Order, applying S.17 of the Judgments Act 1838.

Taxation **36.107**

Financial loss is generally calculated net of tax, the claimant being awarded an amount based on his or her take-home pay. This practice has been applied by the employment tribunals and endorsed by the EAT on numerous occasions – for a recent example see Governing Body of St Andrew's Catholic Primary School and ors v Blundell EAT 0330/09.

The practice avoids the need for both sides to account for income tax and National Insurance contributions on what would otherwise be earnings. However, some kinds of tribunal award, including awards for future loss of earnings consequent on dismissal, are taxable in themselves under S.401 of the Income Tax (Earnings and Pensions) Act 2003 in so far as they exceed £30,000. When this happens, the standard practice is for tribunals to 'gross up' the award. This means increasing the amount of compensation so that, once the appropriate amount has been paid to HM Revenue and Customs, the claimant is left with the figure the tribunal originally intended to award. Thus, in British Sugar plc v Kirker 1998 IRLR 624, EAT, the employment tribunal initially awarded £103,000 for future loss of earnings, but subsequently reviewed the award and increased it to £167,000 to take account

1331

of the tax that was payable on the award to the extent that it exceeded £30,000. This increase ensured that Mr Kirker retained £103,000, the extra £64,000 being payable to the Inland Revenue.

36.108 The question of whether awards in respect of injury to feelings require grossing up has proven rather more difficult to answer. In Orthet Ltd v Vince-Cain 2005 ICR 374, EAT, the EAT held that an employment tribunal had been entitled to make an award of £15,000 for injury to feelings without reference to the tax implications of the award. The EAT stated that it had not been referred to any authority, nor any authoritative commentary, which holds or asserts that tax is payable on such an award. It also had regard to the Income and Corporation Taxes Act 1988, then in force, which exempted from employment taxation any amount paid on account of injury to, or the disability of, the employee. (The same exemption has been re-enacted at S.406 of the Income Tax (Earnings and Pensions) Act 2003, which currently governs the position.) The tribunal had therefore not fallen into error by failing to gross up the award. In giving the EAT's judgment, His Honour Judge McMullen QC observed that, if it is unclear whether tax is payable on an award, the problem can be resolved by the employer giving an indemnity in the claimant's favour agreeing to pay any tax in the event that the Inland Revenue subsequently attacks the award. Alternatively, a review of the tribunal's remedies decision could be sought.

The decision in Vince-Cain might seem to settle the issue. However, in a subsequent decision in Yorkshire Housing Ltd v Cuerden EAT 0397/09, the EAT did not think it quite so clear-cut. The Appeal Tribunal there referred to HHJ McMullen's suggestion in Vince-Cain that all injury to feelings awards are exempt from taxation as 'controversial'. It did not, though, need to decide whether that was correct. The particular appeal related to compensation awarded for disability discrimination in respect of the employer's failure to make reasonable adjustments during the currency of the employment relationship. The EAT was satisfied that awards for pre-termination discrimination, at least, are not subject to tax, and so decided the case on this basis. The question of whether injury to feelings awards relating to discriminatory dismissals require grossing up is therefore undecided.

36.109 A further point considered in Cuerden was the rate at which grossing up should be applied. The employment tribunal there had added an amount representing 40 per cent tax to the claimant's award, on the basis that this was the claimant's marginal tax rate. The EAT held that that was the wrong approach, since not all of the award over £30,000 would fall to be taxed at that rate. The tribunal should have taken account of the claimant's personal allowance and basic rate of tax for the year in which she received the award of compensation.

37 Equality and Human Rights Commission

Composition and structure

Duties

Powers

Inquiries

Investigation of unlawful acts

Enforcement

Codes of Practice

Help for complainants

Judicial review and other legal proceedings

The Equality and Human Rights Commission (EHRC) was established by the **37.1** Equality Act 2006 (EqA 2006) as the first single equality commission in Great Britain to assume overall responsibility for combating unlawful discrimination in employment and other fields and promoting equality of opportunity. It opened its doors on 1 October 2007 when it took over the role and functions of the three existing equality commissions – the Equal Opportunities Commission (EOC), the Commission for Racial Equality (CRE) and the Disability Rights Commission (DRC) – and assumed responsibility for promoting equality and combating unlawful discrimination in the 'new' discrimination strands of sexual orientation, religion or belief, and age, as well as for the promotion of human rights – see the Equality Act 2006 (Dissolution of Commissions and Consequential and Transitional Provisions) Order 2007 SI 2007/2602. According to the Government's White Paper, 'Fairness for All: A New Commission for Equality and Human Rights', published in May 2004, the rationale for establishing the EHRC was to have 'a strong and authoritative champion for equality and human rights' to benefit individuals and organisations alike by providing a single access point on all discrimination issues.

The creation of a single equality commission was not without controversy. One of the main points of criticism was that, since it must monitor all the strands of equality law, the EHRC cannot devote the same level of specialist attention to the needs of people with disabilities as the DRC once did. To an extent, these concerns are borne out by the content of the EHRC's Statutory Code of Practice on Employment, which, in its attempt to cover all the employment issues arising under the Equality Act 2010 (EqA 2010), goes into less detail on issues of disability discrimination than the old DRC Code. (Stop press: the Government is considering major reforms to the EHRC – see Introduction to this Handbook.)

37.2 Upon coming to power in May 2010, the Coalition Government announced that it was to review the status and future of all non-departmental bodies, including the EHRC. A document entitled 'Public Bodies Reform – Proposals for Change', published by the Cabinet Office in October 2010, indicated that while the EHRC survived the threat of abolition, it would be subject to reform in order to provide 'better focus on its core regulatory functions and improved use of taxpayers' money'. A consultation on the Government's plans for reform, 'Building a fairer Britain: Reform of the Equality and Human Rights Commission', opened on 22 March 2011 and ran until 15 June 2011 but concrete proposals to amend the role, powers and duties of the EHRC, as set out in the EqA 2006, have not been forthcoming. In the meantime, however, the EHRC, like many Government departments and non-departmental bodies, has undergone a substantial cut in its budget, which has impacted on both its ability to produce statutory and non-statutory guidance and its capacity to investigate alleged discrimination.

In this chapter we start by giving a brief outline of the EHRC's composition and structure and then go on to describe its duties and powers. We also consider the Codes of Practice that the EHRC issues; the help it gives to complainants; and its involvement in judicial review cases and other legal proceedings. While this chapter deals with the role played by the EHRC in enforcing the public sector equality duties provided for under the EqA 2010, reference should be made to Chapter 38, 'General public sector equality duty', and Chapter 39, 'Specific public sector duties', for details of the duties themselves.

37.3 Composition and structure

Sections 1 and 94(1) EqA 2006 establish the EHRC as the single equality commission for England, Scotland and Wales, operating out of offices in London, Manchester, Cardiff, Edinburgh and Glasgow. The EHRC's composition, structure and functions are governed by Schedule 1 to the 2006 Act. (Note that a different set-up applies in Northern Ireland, where for some time there has been a separate, single Equality Commission for Northern Ireland, established under the Northern Ireland Act 1998.)

The EHRC is a non-departmental public body, funded by the Government Equalities Office (part of the Home Office) but independent of Government – paras 38 and 42, Sch 1 EqA 2006. It comprises between ten and 15 individuals – known as Commissioners – who are appointed by the Secretary of State – para 1(1), Sch 1. At the time of publication of this Handbook, there are 14 Commissioners and the Secretary of State in charge under the 2006 Act is the

Home Secretary and Minister for Women and Equalities, Theresa May, who has responsibility for appointing the Commissioners.

37.4 In appointing Commissioners, the Secretary of State must only choose individuals who have 'experience or knowledge relating to' discrimination (whether on grounds of age, disability, gender, gender reassignment, race, religion or belief, sexual orientation or otherwise) and human rights, unless they are suitable for some other special reason. It is also important that the Commissioners collectively have the necessary experience and knowledge to carry out their functions – para 2(1) and (2), Sch 1. The EqA 2006 makes further specific provision for having at least one Commissioner who is (or has been) disabled, one who has knowledge of conditions in Scotland, and one who has knowledge of conditions in Wales – para 2(3) and (4).

Commissioners are appointed for a specified period of between two and four years, and may be reappointed when their term expires – para 3(2) and (3), Sch 1. They may resign from their post by giving written notice to the Secretary of State, or face dismissal if the Secretary of State is of the opinion that they are unable, unfit or unwilling to perform their functions – para 3(4) and (5).

37.5 Apart from selecting Commissioners, the Secretary of State also appoints a Commissioner as Chairman and one or more as deputy Chairman – para 4(1). The Chairman, or if unavailable a deputy Chairman, presides over meetings and performs such functions as may be specified in the terms of appointment or assigned by the Commission – para 4(2) and (3), Sch 1. On its launch, Trevor Phillips, the former head of the CRE, became the first, and thus far only, Chairman of the EHRC. The Commission appoints a Chief Executive – with the consent of the Secretary of State – who is also a Commissioner by virtue of holding that office – paras 7(1)(a) and 1(2). The Commission is further allowed to appoint any other staff it needs to carry out its functions, but the Secretary of State must approve the overall number of staff and their terms and conditions of appointment – para 7(1)(b) and (3).

The Commission has the power to regulate its own proceedings – para 5, Sch 1. It can also establish advisory and decision-making committees, made up of Commissioners, staff and non-Commissioners – paras 11 and 12. It can therefore draw on external expertise where it considers this appropriate. Decision-making committees must be chaired by a Commissioner and can have any function delegated to them – para 15.

Duties
37.6

Section 3 EqA 2006 sets out the *general duty* of the EHRC and provides the context in which it must exercise its specific duties (see below). The general duty is a very broad statement of principle, reflecting the wide remit of the EHRC's responsibilities and setting out the results that the Commission must

1335

work towards. It states that the 'Commission shall exercise its functions... with a view to encouraging and supporting the development of a society in which –

(a) people's ability to achieve their potential is not limited by prejudice or discrimination,

(b) there is respect for and protection of each individual's human rights,

(c) there is respect for the dignity and worth of each individual,

(d) each individual has an equal opportunity to participate in society, and

(e) there is mutual respect between groups based on understanding and valuing of diversity and on shared respect for equality and human rights'.

37.7 In furtherance of these objectives, the EqA 2006 sets out a number of *specific* duties, contained in Ss.8–12, in respect of equality and diversity, human rights, groups, and monitoring of both the law and the progress being made towards developing the kind of society envisaged above. The specific duties are described below.

Note that the consultation paper, 'Building a fairer Britain: Reform of the Equality and Human Rights Commission' (March 2011), proposed repealing the EHRC's general duty in S.3 EqA 2006. At the time of publication of this Handbook, the Government has not put forward any amending legislation, nor given any firm indication as to whether it intends to proceed with the reforms proposed in the consultation document.

37.8 **Equality and diversity**
Under S.8(1) EqA 2006, the EHRC has specific duties to:

- promote understanding of the importance of equality and diversity

- encourage good practice in relation to equality and diversity

- promote equality of opportunity

- promote awareness and understanding of rights under the EqA 2010

- enforce the EqA 2010

- work towards the elimination of unlawful discrimination

- work towards the elimination of unlawful harassment.

'Equality' is defined as 'equality between individuals' and 'diversity' as 'the fact that individuals are different' – S.8(2). Both are defined in broad terms so as to encompass areas not yet regulated by the existing discrimination statutes.

37.9 Section 8(3) further provides that in promoting equality of opportunity between disabled people and others, the EHRC may 'promote the favourable treatment' of disabled people.

As with the general duty in S.3, the specific duties were highlighted as an area in need of reform by the consultation document, 'Building a fairer Britain'. The document proposed a move from the current situation where S.8 lists broad duties such as 'promoting equality of opportunity' and 'promoting understanding of the importance of equality and diversity', to a set of more specific duties such as promoting awareness of equality legislation. At the time of publication of this Handbook no amending legislation has been put before Parliament.

Human rights
37.10

Section 9(1) EqA 2006 sets out the EHRC's duties in respect of human rights, which are to promote understanding of the importance of human rights, to encourage good practice in relation to them, and to promote the awareness, understanding and protection of them. In addition, it must encourage public authorities to comply with their duty under S.6 of the Human Rights Act 1998 to act in a way compatible with the rights derived from the European Convention on Human Rights as set out in Schedule 1 to that Act. Note that the Commission will not generally undertake independent enforcement of human rights – apart from its power to seek judicial review, its functions in respect of human rights are largely promotional. It will, however, take account of relevant human rights, whether Convention rights or otherwise, when fulfilling its duties under Ss.8 and 10 EqA 2006 (that is, in respect of equality and diversity, and groups) – S.9(4) EqA 2006.

Groups
37.11

By virtue of S.10 EqA 2006, the EHRC is also under specific duties to promote understanding of the importance of good relations and encourage good practice in respect of relations between members of different groups and between members of groups and others. It must further work towards the elimination of prejudice against, hatred of and hostility towards members of groups, and work towards enabling members of groups to participate in society by, for example, challenging sexism in the media. 'Group', for this purpose, is defined as a group sharing a common attribute in respect of age; disability; gender; proposed, commenced or completed reassignment of gender; race; religion or belief; and sexual orientation – S.10(2). However, it may also be a smaller group within a group of persons who share a common attribute (in addition to the attribute by which the larger group is defined) – S.10(3). According to the Explanatory Notes to the 2006 Act, examples of such groups are Muslim women or black and ethnic minority lesbians and gay men.

Monitoring of the law and of society
37.12

Section 11(1) EqA 2006 requires the EHRC to keep the effectiveness of the equality and human rights enactments under review. An important element of this specific duty is its advisory role in respect of any proposed or existing enactments. It may advise the Government on their effectiveness and effect and

1337

make recommendations where it considers it necessary to amend, repeal or consolidate any legislation – S.11(2).

In furtherance of its general duty to encourage the development of a society that achieves the goals set out in S.3 of the 2006 Act (see above), the EHRC is also required to identify relevant changes in society that have occurred or are expected to occur; the outcomes at which to aim for the purpose of encouraging and supporting the development of the society envisaged in S.3; and the indicators by which progress towards those outcomes can be tracked – S.12. Furthermore, within three years of this part of the EqA 2006 coming into operation – i.e. 1 October 2007 – and every three years thereafter, the EHRC must publish a 'state of the nation' report on progress towards the identified outcomes – S.12(4). The first such report, entitled 'How fair is Britain?', was published slightly late, on 11 October 2010.

37.13 Powers

To carry out its specific duties, the EHRC has a wide range of powers – both general and enforcement – available to it.

37.14 General powers

The general powers given to the EHRC broadly replicate those of the DRC, but are framed in slightly wider terms. An additional power, previously only available to the CRE, is the power to make grants. We outline these general powers below.

37.15 Information and advice. The EHRC has general powers to publish or otherwise disseminate ideas or information, undertake research, provide education or training, and give advice or guidance, although this does not include the preparation of documents to be used for the purpose of legal proceedings – S.13 EqA 2006. With regard to the latter, the EHRC has separate powers to provide such advice in respect of particular legal proceedings under S.28 (see 'Help for complainants' below).

37.16 Codes of Practice. Under S.14 EqA 2006 the EHRC may issue statutory Codes of Practice in the areas of discrimination and equal pay, among others. One such example is cited extensively throughout this Handbook – the EHRC Statutory Code of Practice on Employment (for further details, see 'Codes of Practice' below).

37.17 Grants. In furtherance of its duties under Ss.8–10 EqA 2006, the EHRC has the power to make grants to others – S.17. Previously, only the CRE had this power. According to Meg Munn (Secretary of State for Women and Equality at the time of the Bill's passage through Parliament), this 'will enable it to provide financial assistance to a wide range of voluntary and other organisations,

1338

including those that operate at a local level' (Hansard (HC) 1.12.05, col.98). S.17(2) allows the Commission to attach conditions, including as to payment, to the financial assistance it provides.

Inquiries. Section 16(1) EqA 2006 gives the EHRC the power to conduct **37.18** inquiries into any matter relating to its specific duties in respect of equality and diversity, groups and human rights. The conduct of these inquiries is regulated by Schedule 2 to the 2006 Act. In contrast to investigations, inquiries do not form part of the EHRC's enforcement powers. Inquiries and investigations are considered in further detail under 'Inquiries' and 'Investigation of unlawful acts' below.

Enforcement powers   37.19
Under the EqA 2006, the EHRC is vested with important enforcement powers, including authority to:

- carry out investigations – S.20

- issue unlawful act notices with or without an action plan – Ss.21 and 22

- enter into an agreement with the alleged discriminator to prevent an unlawful act – S.23

- apply to the courts for an injunction (or interdict in Scotland) to restrain persistent or likely discrimination – S.24

- make arrangements for conciliation in civil proceedings brought in respect of claims under Parts III, IV, VI and VII EqA 2010 (public functions, the provision of goods and services, education and associations are covered in these Parts of the 2010 Act and can result in civil proceedings) – S.27

- provide legal assistance – S.28.

Details of each of these powers, with the exception of conciliation – which only applies to non-employment cases – are given later in this chapter.

Inquiries   37.20

Section 16(1) EqA 2006 gives the EHRC the power to conduct inquiries into any matter relating to its specific duties in respect of equality and diversity, groups and human rights. The conduct of these inquiries is regulated by Schedule 2 to the Act. The old Commissions used to have similar inquiry powers, though – unlike those Commissions – it is possible for the EHRC to examine more than one strand of equality concern in the same inquiry. Thus, for example, the Commission could conduct an inquiry into the employment prospects of disabled women.

In contrast to investigations, which we consider below, inquiries do not form part of the EHRC's enforcement powers. According to the Government's response to consultation on the 2006 Bill/Act, such inquiries are intended to enable the Commission to conduct general inquiries into problem areas in equality, diversity and human rights (except where the human rights matters relate to the Secret Intelligence Service – para 20, Sch 2), often in partnership with the bodies concerned, and provide recommendations for improved employment policy and practice. As the Explanatory Notes to the EqA 2006 make clear, inquiries can be conducted in relation to one or more named parties, or they can be thematic (e.g. looking at causes of unequal outcomes) or sectoral (e.g. examining the employment of disabled people in the retail sector).

37.21 Terms of reference

Before conducting an inquiry, the EHRC is required to publish the terms of reference in a manner likely to bring it to the attention of anyone affected by or interested in it. In particular, the Commission must always give notice of the terms of reference to any persons specified in them – para 2, Sch 2 EqA 2006.

37.22 Representations

The EHRC must give any person specified in the terms of reference an opportunity to make written or oral representations in relation to the inquiry – paras 6(2) and 7, Sch 2 EqA 2006. It may similarly hear representations from any other person, but the Commission is entitled, where it thinks it appropriate, to refuse to consider representations that are not made by or on behalf of the person specified in the terms of reference or representations that are made on behalf of such a person but not by a barrister or solicitor (or advocate in Scotland) – paras 6(1) and 8(2). If the Commission makes such a refusal, it must give written notice of its decision and the reasons for it to the person who made the representations – para 8(3).

37.23 Evidence

Subject to some exceptions relating to the Secret Intelligence Service, the EHRC may, in the course of the inquiry, serve a notice on any person requiring him or her to provide information, produce documents or give oral evidence in connection with the inquiry – paras 9, 10(1) and 14, Sch 2 EqA 2006. However, it cannot require production of any documents that the person is prohibited from disclosing by virtue of an enactment or which could not have been required in litigation before the High Court (or Court of Session in Scotland), and witnesses may only be required to attend if their travel expenses are reimbursed – para 10(3).

It is open to a person to object to giving evidence in an inquiry by applying to a county court (or sheriff court in Scotland) to have the notice cancelled on the ground that the requirement imposed in the notice is unnecessary having regard to the purpose of the inquiry or is otherwise unreasonable – para 11, Sch 2 EqA 2006. The Commission, likewise, can apply to the county court (or sheriff court in Scotland) to enforce the notice – para 12. In order to ensure that any evidence requested by the Commission is forthcoming, para 13 of Schedule 2 makes it a criminal offence to ignore a notice or order for compliance, to provide falsified documents or to give false evidence. If found guilty a person is liable, on summary conviction, to a fine not exceeding level 5 on the standard scale (currently £5,000).

Reports and recommendations   37.24

An inquiry concludes with the EHRC publishing a report of its findings, usually followed by recommendations – paras 15 and 16, Sch 2 EqA 2006. The report may not refer to the activities of a person in terms that will harm that person unless it is necessary in order for the report adequately to reflect the results of the inquiry – S.16(3)(b) EqA 2006. Where the report records findings of an adverse nature in relation to a person, the Commission is required first to send a draft report to that person and give him or her 28 days to make written representations which it has to consider – S.16(5). A court or tribunal may have regard to a finding of the report but must not treat it as conclusive – para 17.

Overlap with investigations   37.25

If, during the course of its inquiry, the Commission begins to suspect that the person who is the subject of the inquiry may have committed an unlawful act – for example, a breach of the EqA 2010 – it should not, so far as possible, continue to consider that act as part of its inquiry – S.16(2)(a) EqA 2006. The inquiry report must similarly be silent on whether a specified or identifiable person has committed an unlawful act – S.16(3)(a).

The suspicion, however, may warrant instigating an investigation under S.20 EqA 2006 in respect of the person – S.16(2)(b). If this were to happen, the inquiry in relation to the person being investigated, or the part which needs his or her involvement, must be suspended or aborted while the investigation is ongoing – S.16(2)(d). Any information or evidence acquired as a result of the inquiry, on the other hand, may be used in the subsequent investigation – S.16(2)(c). Investigations are discussed immediately below.

Investigation of unlawful acts   37.26

Under S.20 EqA 2006, the EHRC has power to carry out an investigation into whether or not a person has –

- committed an unlawful act

- complied with a requirement imposed by an unlawful act notice under S.21 (see 'Enforcement – unlawful act notices' below), or

1341

- complied with an undertaking given in accordance with an agreement made with the Commission under S.23 (agreements under S.23 are discussed under 'Enforcement – agreements in lieu of enforcement action' below) – S.20(1).

Following the consolidation of the various discrimination enactments into one statute, 'unlawful' in this context now means 'contrary to a provision of the EqA 2010' – S.34(1) of the 2006 Act. However, unlawful acts for these purposes do not include breaches of Part 12 (which concerns disabled people and transport) or S.190 (which concerns disability-related improvements to let dwelling houses) of the 2010 Act – S.34(2) of the 2006 Act.

37.27 Crucially, the EHRC cannot investigate the commission of an unlawful act under S.20 EqA 2006 unless it suspects that the person concerned may have committed the act in question – S.20(2) EqA 2006. In other words, the EHRC cannot conduct 'fishing expeditions'. Without there being a reasonable belief that unlawful acts of discrimination or harassment have occurred or are occurring, only a general inquiry can be instigated (see above). Commenting on the standard of suspicion required before the EHRC can carry out an investigation, Baroness Ashton of Upholland (Parliamentary Under-Secretary at the Department for Constitutional Affairs at the time of the 2006 Act/Bill's passage through Parliament) said: 'The Commission cannot form a suspicion without the grounds to do so. Combined with its public law duty to act reasonably, the word "suspect" suffices to imply a reasonable suspicion based on specific grounds... it does not equate to a belief as high as a civil burden of proof, but there must be material before the Commission sufficient to raise a reasonable suspicion that the named person may have committed acts of the kind that it is proposed to investigate. The Commission must be able to justify its decision to investigate as reasonable and fair, and it would be required to produce the evidence it based the decision on if challenged.' Such evidence would 'include such things as material that flows from an inquiry; material that has been put before a court or a tribunal that may have led to a decision, or the case may have settled and the proceedings withdrawn; information that is brought to the attention of the Commission through help-line or advice services. A suspicion based on a single unsubstantiated complaint, for example, would be unlikely to be defensible, but a number of complainants over a long period of time, combined for example with a number of settled cases of which the Commission is aware, is likely to be sufficient' (Hansard (HL) 11.7.05, col.941). It follows that while it may be helpful to conduct a general inquiry first (in terms of collecting material to substantiate a belief that an unlawful act is occurring or has occurred), it is in no way a prerequisite for commencing an investigation.

In Chapter 24, 'Recruitment', under 'Pre-employment health questions', we explain how S.60 EqA 2010 sets out new provisions that make it unlawful for an employer, other than in specified circumstances, to ask a job applicant questions about health or disability. An infringement of the primary provision – S.60(1) – is enforceable only as an unlawful act by the EHRC and not by individuals in employment tribunals. Given the prevalence of health questions in the recruitment process, it is likely that the EHRC will be undertaking more investigations as allegations of employers breaching S.60(1) arise.

Stages of an investigation   37.28
Once a decision has been made to launch an investigation, matters will proceed as follows:

- the EHRC draws up the terms of reference for the investigation

- the EHRC gives notice of the investigation

- the EHRC holds a preliminary inquiry

- the investigation itself begins. The 2006 Act does not lay down any specific procedure for the investigation, and this remains a matter for the EHRC's discretion. However, the rules of 'natural justice' must be observed

- the EHRC publishes a report of its findings, usually with recommendations.

Terms of reference   37.29
Before embarking on an investigation, the EHRC must prepare the terms of reference, specifying the person to be investigated and the nature of the unlawful act the Commission suspects – para 3(a), Sch 2 EqA 2006. However, it cannot single-handedly decide the scope of the investigation. It is under a duty to inform the person to be investigated of the proposed terms of reference of the investigation, give him or her an opportunity to make representations, and then consider them – para 3(b)–(d). The Commission must then publish the terms of reference, once settled – para 3(e). If the terms of reference are subsequently revised – perhaps after evidence comes to light during representations made to the Commission (see below) – the same procedure of agreeing the terms of reference must be gone through again – para 5.

When conducting an investigation into an unlawful act, it is important to confine it to the Commission's belief as stated in the terms of reference. If it goes beyond the terms of reference or the terms of reference are wider than are justified by the belief, the investigation may be challenged and quashed on the ground that the Commission has acted ultra vires (outside its powers). In London Borough of Hillingdon v Commission for Racial Equality 1982 IRLR 424, HL, the House of Lords upheld the High Court's ruling quashing the CRE's decision to embark on a formal investigation into the housing of homeless persons by Hillingdon Borough. The CRE's belief was that there might have been racial discrimination against homeless applicants newly arrived from overseas – yet the terms of reference went wider and allowed an investigation into the Borough's treatment of any homeless applicants.

1343

37.30 Preliminary inquiry

The EHRC must give any person specified in the terms of reference an opportunity to make written or oral representations in relation to the investigation – paras 6(2) and 7, Sch 2 EqA 2006. It may similarly hear representations from any other person, but it is entitled, where it thinks it appropriate, to refuse to consider representations where they are not made by or on behalf of the person specified in the terms of reference or they are made on behalf of such a person but not by a barrister or solicitor (or advocate in Scotland) – paras 6(1) and 8(2). If the Commission makes such a refusal, it must give written notice of its decision and the reasons for it to the person who made the representations – para 8(3).

Following these representations, the Commission may, if it still believes that unlawful discrimination or harassment has occurred, go ahead with the investigation, or it may amend the terms of reference. However, if the terms of reference are changed, the Commission must start again from scratch – giving notice and agreeing the terms of reference – para 5, Sch 2 EqA 2006.

37.31 Conducting an investigation

Although there is no set procedure for investigations, they must comply with the requirements of natural justice. Thus, accused persons must know the charges, be allowed to put their case, and be allowed to appeal to another party (for the last of these, see the section 'Enforcement', under 'Unlawful act notices – appeal against unlawful act notice' below). The rules of natural justice applicable to investigations are not, however, as strict as, say, the rules that must be followed in criminal proceedings. There is, for example, no entitlement to call witnesses or adduce evidence or cross-examine witnesses – R v Commission for Racial Equality ex parte Cottrell and anor 1980 IRLR 279, Div Ct.

37.32 Power to obtain information

Once the investigation is under way, the EHRC has power to serve a notice on any person requiring information to be given, documents to be produced or witnesses to attend to give oral evidence – paras 9 and 10(1), Sch 2 EqA 2006. The notice may specify the form in which the relevant information or evidence should be given as well as the timing – para 10(2). However, a notice may not require a person to provide information that he or she is prohibited from disclosing by virtue of an enactment, or to do anything that he or she could not be compelled to do in proceedings before the High Court (or Court of Session), and may not require a person to attend as a witness unless the Commission pays for the travel expenses – para 10(3). Similarly, a person may disregard a notice if it would require the disclosure of information prejudicial to national security – para 14.

It is open to a person to object to giving evidence in an investigation by applying to a county court (or sheriff court in Scotland) to have the notice cancelled on the ground that the requirement imposed in it is unnecessary having regard to the purpose of the investigation or is otherwise unreasonable – para 11, Sch 2 EqA 2006. The EHRC, likewise, can, if it believes that a person has failed (or is likely to fail) to comply with a notice without reasonable excuse, apply to the county court (or sheriff court in Scotland) to enforce the notice by court order – para 12.

It is an offence, punishable on summary conviction by a fine not exceeding level **37.33** 5 on the standard scale (currently £5,000), without reasonable excuse, to fail to comply with a notice or court order enforcing the notice, falsify anything provided or produced in accordance with a notice, or make a false statement in giving oral evidence in accordance with a notice – para 13.

Recommendations and reports

37.34

An investigation concludes with the EHRC publishing a report of its findings, usually together with recommendations that may be addressed to 'any class of person' and may relate to any matter arising during the investigation – paras 15 and 16, Sch 2 EqA 2006. A person to whom a recommendation is addressed must have regard to it – para 18.

There is no timetable for preparing the report and in the context of similar reports under the RRA the Court of Appeal has accepted that the findings of an investigation need not be published or made available as soon as the report is concluded – Commission for Racial Equality v Amari Plastics Ltd 1982 ICR 304, CA. In practice, the timing of the report can be something of a problem and it is often delayed until an unlawful act notice has been issued and the time limit for bringing an appeal against it has expired (see 'Enforcement – unlawful act notices' below). Otherwise, there is the risk of publishing a report that condemns the employer as an unlawful discriminator even though the finding of unlawful discrimination is subsequently overturned on appeal.

In any event, the EHRC must not publish a report that records a finding that **37.35** the person concerned has committed an unlawful act unless it has sent him or her a draft of the report and allowed at least 28 days in which to make written representations, and considered any representations made – S.20(4) EqA 2006.

A court or tribunal may have regard to the finding of an investigation but shall not treat it as conclusive – para 17, Sch 2 EqA 2006.

Enforcement

37.36

The EHRC's Enforcement and Compliance Policy, published in May 2009 and available on the Commission's website, states that 'the Commission will usually only take formal enforcement action where attempts to encourage compliance have failed'. Thus, where an inquiry or investigation turns up evidence of an unlawful act having taken place, the Commission will generally seek to remedy the issue through informal action and secure a change in the offending institution, employer or individual's discriminatory practices (see 'Agreements in lieu of enforcement action' below). It will be much rarer for the Commission to serve an unlawful act notice or proceed to direct enforcement through litigation. The EHRC's Policy states that in deciding which of its powers to use, the Commission will have regard to the following factors:

- value for money – is legal enforcement action the best use of the Commission's public funds?

- the extent and severity of any breach of legislation and the reasons given for such a breach

- the extent and severity of any departure from Codes of Practice and whether this was deliberate or reckless

- the impact, likelihood and severity of impact on the affected group or individual

- the size and resources of the organisation involved

- the financial burden to be imposed on an organisation as a consequence of enforcement action

- the extent and outcome of any previous communication with the Commission in situations where the Commission has repeatedly expressed its concerns

- the steps taken or agreements made to remedy the breach and to reduce risks of recurrence

- the priorities of the Commission as set out in its Business Plan and Legal Strategy

- any other relevant considerations.

We now consider the means of enforcement available to the Commission, beginning with unlawful act notices.

37.37 Unlawful act notices

If in the course of an investigation the EHRC is satisfied that a person has committed an unlawful act of discrimination or harassment, the Commission may issue an unlawful act notice – S.21(1) EqA 2006. The notice must give details of the unlawful act that has been committed and of the provision of the EqA 2010 that makes the act unlawful – S.21(2). The notice may also require the person concerned to prepare an 'action plan' (see 'Action plans' below) for the purpose of avoiding a repetition or continuation of the unlawful act, and may recommend action to be taken by the person for that purpose – S.21(4).

1346

Furthermore, the notice must set out the details of the appeal procedure against the notice as well as inform the person of the Commission's further enforcement powers of investigating non-compliance with an unlawful act notice (see below) and applying for an injunction (or an interdict in Scotland) restraining the person from committing an unlawful act (discussed under 'Injunctions to restrain discrimination' below) – S.21(3).

Appeal against unlawful act notice. If an unlawful act notice is served, the **37.38** person on whom it is served may appeal against it to a county court (or sheriff court in Scotland) or an employment tribunal no later than six weeks after the notice has been served on the grounds that he or she has not committed the unlawful act specified in it or that a requirement for the preparation of an action plan is unreasonable – S.21(5) and (7) EqA 2006. This is in addition to the power available in all administrative cases to seek a judicial review of the Commission's decision in the High Court where it has allegedly acted perversely or unreasonably in exercising its powers (see 'Judicial review and other legal proceedings' below.) Once an appeal has been heard, the court or tribunal may affirm, annul or vary a notice or requirement or make an order for costs (or expenses in Scotland) – S.21(6).

Note that special tribunal rules of procedure (the Employment Tribunals (Unlawful Act Notices Appeals) Rules of Procedure) set out the procedural rules in relation to an appeal against an unlawful act notice in detail. These are contained in Schedule 5 to the Employment Tribunals (Constitution and Rules of Procedure) Regulations 2004 SI 2004/1861.

Follow-up investigation. The EHRC can mount a follow-up investigation to **37.39** check that the requirements of an unlawful act notice are being complied with – S.20(1)(b) EqA 2006. The same rules for giving notice, obtaining information and documents, etc, apply as in any other investigation (see above under 'Investigation of unlawful acts'). Furthermore, the Commission must not publish a report that records a finding that the person concerned has failed to comply with a requirement imposed by an unlawful act notice unless it has sent him or her a draft of the report and allowed him or her at least 28 days in which to make written representations, and considered any representations made – S.20(4).

Action plans
37.40

An unlawful act notice may require the person concerned to propose an action plan with a view to securing compliance with a requirement not to commit further unlawful acts – S.22(1) EqA 2006. An action plan is therefore intended to change practices, policies, procedures or other arrangements that caused or contributed to the commission of the unlawful act of discrimination or harassment. In order to be accepted by the EHRC, the action plan must be 'adequate' – i.e. the action specified in it must be sufficient to prevent any

—**1347**

further unlawful acts from occurring. The Commission has the power to obtain information from any person for the purpose of determining whether a proposed action plan is adequate – S.22(8). The power only covers information in writing or copies of documents and does not extend to requiring a person to give oral evidence. To obtain the information, the Commission must issue a notice. If the person does not comply with the notice, the Commission may apply for a court order to obtain the information – paras 10 and 12, Sch 2. It is open to the Commission to order revision of the draft plan until it is satisfied it meets its objective – S.22(4).

Where an unlawful act notice requires a person to propose an action plan, it will specify a date by which the person must provide the Commission with a first draft of that plan – S.22(2) EqA 2006. Upon receipt, the Commission may approve the draft plan – S.22(3)(a). If the person fails to provide a plan, the Commission may apply to a county court (or sheriff court in Scotland) for an order directing him or her to serve a draft action plan – S.22(6)(a). If the person serves the action plan on the Commission by either of these routes it will come into force six weeks after service unless the Commission gives notice to the person that it is not 'adequate' – S.22(5)(a)(i).

37.41 If the Commission considers that a proposed action plan is not adequate, it may give notice to the person concerned stating its view and requiring him or her to provide a revised action plan. This notice may include recommendations as to action that the Commission considers might be included in an action plan that would be adequate. It will also specify a time by which the revised plan must be served on the Commission – S.22(3)(b) EqA 2006. If the revised draft plan is served, it will come into force six weeks after it is given to the Commission unless the Commission considers that this plan is also not adequate and seeks a court order under S.22(6)(b) (see below). If no revised plan is served on the Commission, the original plan will come into force six weeks after service unless the Commission seeks an order under S.22(6)(b) to compel the service of a revised plan.

If a person has served a revised draft plan but the Commission considers that it too is inadequate, the Commission may apply to a county court (or sheriff court in Scotland) for an order requiring the person to provide a further revised draft plan – S.22(6)(b) EqA 2006. The order must specify the time by which the additional revised draft plan must be served and may also contain such directions as the court considers appropriate as to the actions that should be specified in that action plan.

37.42 If the court refuses to grant an order requiring a person to serve a further revised draft plan under S.22(6)(b), the original revised plan given to the Commission will come into force – S.22(5)(b).

Enforcement of the action plan. The EHRC may, during a period of five years **37.43** beginning on the date on which the action plan comes into force, apply to the county court (or sheriff court in Scotland) for an order requiring the person concerned to act in accordance with the action plan or to take specified action for a similar purpose – S.22(6)(c) EqA 2006.

Where a person fails, without reasonable excuse, to comply with a court order either to produce or to implement an action plan, he or she will be guilty of an offence that is punishable on summary conviction by a fine not exceeding level 5 on the standard scale (currently £5,000) – S.22(9) EqA 2006. S.22(7) permits an action plan to be varied by agreement between the Commission and the person who prepared it.

Agreements in lieu of enforcement action
If the EHRC has reason to believe that a person has committed an unlawful act, it may enter into an agreement with that person under which:

37.44

- the person concerned undertakes not to commit an unlawful act of a specified kind and to take, or refrain from taking, other specified action (which may include the preparation of a plan for the purpose of avoiding an unlawful act), and

- the Commission undertakes not to proceed against the person under Ss.20 or 21 (i.e. conducting an investigation or taking any steps with a view to the issue of an unlawful act notice) in respect of any unlawful act – S.23(1) EqA 2006.

An agreement under S.23 may be entered into regardless of whether the person **37.45** is or has been the subject of an investigation under S.20 – S.23(4)(a). However, the Commission must be of the opinion that the person has committed an unlawful act – S.23(2). The mere fact that the person is entering into an agreement is not to be treated as an admission that an unlawful act has been committed – S.23(3).

The Commission can also enter into an agreement under S.23 with a public authority in respect of a breach of any of the public sector duties set out in S.34(2) in lieu of issuing a public sector compliance notice (see 'Enforcing public sector duties' below) – S.23(5) EqA 2006. The agreement may cover incidental or supplementary matters, such as action that may be taken in the event of a breakdown of the agreement or the circumstances in which either party may terminate the agreement. Although binding on the parties, an agreement may be consensually varied or terminated by the parties – S.23(4)(b) and (c).

Follow-up investigation. The EHRC may subsequently investigate whether or **37.46** not a person has complied with an undertaking given under S.23 EqA 2006 – S.20(1)(c). The same rules for giving notice, obtaining information and

1349

documents, etc, apply as in any other investigation (see 'Investigation of unlawful acts' above). The Commission must not publish a report that records a finding that the person concerned has failed to comply with an undertaking unless it has sent him or her a draft of the report and allowed the individual concerned at least 28 days in which to make written representations, and considered any representations made – S.20(4).

37.47 **Enforcement of agreement.** Where the Commission thinks that a party to the agreement has failed to comply, or is unlikely to comply, with an undertaking under the agreement, the Commission may apply to the county court (or sheriff court in Scotland) for an order requiring the person to comply with the undertaking and to take such other action as the court (or sheriff) may specify – S.24(2) and (3) EqA 2006.

37.48 **Injunctions to restrain discrimination**

If the Commission believes that a person, unless restrained, is likely to commit an unlawful act of discrimination or harassment, it has the power under S.24(1) EqA 2006 to apply to a county court for an injunction (or to a sheriff court in Scotland for an interdict) prohibiting the person from committing the act.

This provision marks an extension of the power to tackle persistent discrimination that could previously only be invoked where it had been shown that the person had already discriminated. Accordingly, the DRC, CRE and EOC could only seek an injunction to restrain unlawful discriminatory acts where they had already conducted an investigation and issued a non-discrimination notice (the predecessor of the unlawful act notice), or had obtained a finding by a tribunal that the person had committed an unlawful act. S.24(1) omits these preliminary steps and, according to Baroness Ashton, commenting on the provision during the Bill's Report Stage in the House of Lords, the major advantage of widening this power is that it enables the Commission 'to bring proceedings directly and immediately once there is sufficient evidence that, unless restrained, a person is likely to discriminate' (Hansard (HL) 19.10.05, col.798). Although this makes the power a more flexible tool than previously, Baroness Ashton nevertheless stressed that the process of applying for an injunction will remain rigorous, emphasising that it is 'an evidence-based process, where only evidence of real substance will convince a court that an injunction is necessary to prevent an unlawful act. The [EHRC] would be very unwise to launch a case unless it had strong evidence on which to rely. If it were to do so, it would risk costs being awarded against it, as well as damaging its reputation' (Hansard (HL) 19.10.05, col.798).

37.49 **Discriminatory advertisements, instructions and pressure to discriminate**

Prior to the EqA 2010 coming into force, the EHRC had a power under S.25(3) EqA 2006 to institute legal proceedings specifically in relation to unlawful advertising. However, Ss.25 and 26 were abolished by the amendments

1350

contained in Schedule 26 to the EqA 2010. It is unclear why these sections have been repealed, but it appears that such action will be allowed by the remaining enforcement provisions contained in S.24A EqA 2006 (a provision newly inserted by Schedule 26). In this regard, para 1024 of the Explanatory Notes that accompanied the 2010 Act states that 'the substantive prohibition against discriminatory practices and advertisements is no longer required as it is covered elsewhere in the Act'. The Notes go on to point out that the amendment extends enforcement by the EHRC to cover both direct and indirect discrimination on account of any of the protected characteristics as well as discrimination arising from disability.

Section 25(3) EqA 2006 – which, as noted above, was repealed by Schedule 26 to the EqA 2010 – also allowed the EHRC to institute legal proceedings in relation to instructions or pressure to discriminate. The relevant substantive provisions in the previous equality enactments have been replaced by S.111 EqA 2010 – see Chapter 28, 'Liability of employers, employees and agents', under 'Instructing, causing and inducing discrimination'. S.111(5)(c) confers on the EHRC the power to bring enforcement proceedings under the EqA 2006 in relation to this provision.

Enforcing public sector duties 37.50

Sections 31 and 32 EqA 2006 confer on the EHRC two specific powers of enforcement in respect of the public sector equality duty set out in Ss.149 and 153 EqA 2010 – assessment, and compliance notices. For details of the public sector equality duty, see Chapter 38, 'General public sector equality duty', and Chapter 39, 'Specific public sector equality duties'. The powers in Ss.31 and 32 EqA 2006 also apply in respect of the socio-economic duty contained in S.154 EqA 2010; however, that duty is not expected to be brought into force – see Chapter 40, 'Socio-economic duty'.

Assessments. Section 31 EqA 2006 provides that the Commission may assess **37.51** the extent to which a public authority has complied with a duty under or by virtue of Ss.149, 153 or 154 EqA 2010 – i.e. the general public sector equality duty, a specific duty provided for in secondary legislation or the socio-economic duty. In conducting an assessment, the Commission has the same powers and obligations that it has in relation to inquiries and investigations (see 'Inquiries' and 'Investigation of unlawful acts' above) in terms of giving notice, representations, evidence, reports and recommendations, etc – S.31(2) and para 4, Sch 2 EqA 2006.

Compliance notices. If the EHRC thinks that a public authority has failed to **37.52** comply with a duty under Ss.149, 153 or 154 EqA 2010, it may give the authority a notice requiring two things: first, that the authority comply with the duty; and secondly, that it give the Commission, within the period of 28 days beginning with the date on which it receives the notice, written information of steps taken or proposed for the purpose of complying with the duty – S.32(2) EqA 2006. The Commission must undertake an assessment before issuing a compliance notice in respect of the general public sector equality duty in S.149 – S.39(4) EqA 2006. However, there is no such mandatory requirement in respect of the specific duties under S.153 or S.154 EqA 2010.

As part of a compliance notice, the Commission is entitled to require that the authority concerned provide it with information for the purposes of assessing compliance with the duty. If this is the case, the notice must specify the period within which the information is to be given (which shall begin with the date on which the notice is received and shall not exceed three months), and the manner and form in which the information is to be given – S.32(3) EqA 2006. However, a public authority is not required to provide information that it is prohibited from disclosing by virtue of an enactment or could not be compelled to give in proceedings before the High Court (or Court of Session in Scotland) – S.32(6). The rules regarding witnesses set out in paras 11–14 of Schedule 2 apply in these circumstances (see under 'Investigation of unlawful acts' above) – S.32(7).

37.53 The Commission may seek enforcement of the compliance notice by a court order – the High Court (or Court of Session) in respect of a general duty and the county (or sheriff) court in respect of any specific duty – S.32(8) and (9) EqA 2006. However, the EHRC will not apply to a court for enforcement of a compliance notice prior to the expiry of a time limit specified in the notice – S.32(10).

Note that as an alternative to issuing a compliance notice the Commission can enter into an agreement under S.23 EqA 2006 whereby it undertakes not to proceed with enforcement action in return for the public authority promising to undertake not to commit a specified unlawful act (see 'Agreements in lieu of enforcement action' above) – S.23(5).

37.54 **Application of enforcement powers**
New S.24A EqA 2006, added by Schedule 26 to the EqA 2010, makes further provision for the exercise by the EHRC of the range of enforcement powers contained in Ss.20–24 EqA 2006 – i.e. inquiries, investigations, unlawful act notices, action plans, agreements in lieu of enforcement action and injunctions (S.24A does not apply to the EHRC's enforcement of the public sector equality duties under Ss.31 and 32). Unfortunately, S.24A is not a felicitously drafted provision, but its general meaning seems to be reasonably clear. Subsection (1) sets out a list of unlawful acts to which the supplementary provisions set out elsewhere in S.24A (apparently) apply. These include acts of direct discrimination, enquiries about disability and health contrary to S.60(1) EqA 2010, and indirect discrimination. In relation to these unlawful acts, the EHRC may, by virtue of S.24A(2), use all or any of the enforcement powers previously discussed whether or not it knows or suspects that an individual has been affected by the

discrimination under scrutiny. For these purposes, an unlawful act 'includes making arrangements to act in a particular way which would, if applied to an individual, amount to' direct discrimination – S.24A(3).

For the avoidance of doubt, S.24A(4) EqA 2006 makes it clear that none of the **37.55** provisions contained in the 2006 Act – and, in particular, the statutory enforcement rights of the EHRC – affect an individual's right to bring a claim under the EqA 2010.

It should be noted that the EHRC also has a specific power under S.111(5)(c) EqA 2010 to bring enforcement proceedings in respect of instructing, causing or inducing discrimination – see 'Discriminatory advertisements, instructions and pressure to discriminate' above.

Codes of Practice
37.56

Under S.14(1) EqA 2006, the Commission may issue a statutory Code of Practice in connection with any matter addressed by the EqA 2010. Such Codes shall contain provisions designed to ensure or facilitate compliance with the 2010 Act, or to promote equality of opportunity – S.14(2) EqA 2006.

Before issuing a Code, the EHRC will publish and consult on proposals and submit a draft to the Secretary of State who, if he or she approves it, will notify the Commission and lay a copy before Parliament – S.14(6) and (7)(a) EqA 2006. If neither House passes a resolution disapproving the draft within 40 days (the 'negative resolution procedure'), the Code will come into force on a day specified by order of the Secretary of State – S.14(8). If, and in so far as, the Code relates to a duty imposed on public authorities – for example, by virtue of S.149 EqA 2010 (see Chapter 38, 'General public sector equality duty') – the Secretary of State must consult the Scottish Ministers and the National Assembly for Wales before approving the draft or commencement order – S.14(9). Where the Secretary of State rejects the proposed Code he or she must not do so without giving the Commission written reasons for the decision – S.14(7)(b).

Once in force, the Code may be revised by the Commission or, at its request, **37.57** revoked by an order made by the Secretary of State – S.15(1) and (3). According to the Explanatory Notes to the EqA 2006, the order to revoke the Code will be subject to the negative resolution procedure.

Three Codes of Practice were laid before Parliament by the EHRC on 12 October 2010 and came into effect on 6 April 2011. These are:

- Code of Practice on Employment: this Code, which is cited extensively throughout this Handbook, addresses all the strands of discrimination covered in the EqA 2010 as they arise in employment and occupation

1353

- Code of Practice on Equal Pay: this Code covers the equal pay provisions in the EqA 2010 and provides advice on good pay practice

- Code of Practice on Services, Public Functions and Associations: this Code covers some of the non-employment areas of the EqA 2010.

By virtue of S.15(4) EqA 2006, a failure to comply with a provision of a Code will not itself give rise to criminal or civil proceedings but the Code will be admissible in such proceedings and must be taken into account by a court or tribunal if the court or tribunal considers it to be relevant.

37.58 Help for complainants

The EHRC may assist an individual who is or may become a party to legal proceedings if the proceedings relate or may relate (wholly or partly) to a provision of the EqA 2010, and the individual alleges that he or she has been the victim of behaviour contrary to a provision of the Act – S.28(1) EqA 2006. The criteria according to which the legal assistance is granted are determined by the Commission. Furthermore, there is no express duty on the EHRC to consider every application it receives. However, in practice it is likely that the Commission will be required to consider every application in order to identify any that it wishes to support.

The type of assistance the EHRC may provide or arrange for comprises legal advice, legal representation, facilities for the resolution of a dispute, or any other form of assistance – S.28(4) EqA 2006. The same assistance may also be given in respect of any provision of European Community law relating to discrimination on grounds of sex (including gender reassignment), racial origin, ethnic origin, religion, belief, disability, age or sexual orientation, or which confers rights on individuals – S.28(12). This extends to any allegation by an individual that he or she is disadvantaged by a statutory provision in UK domestic law that is contrary to a provision of EU law or a failure to implement a right required by EU law into UK domestic law – S.28(13).

37.59 The Government's consultation paper, 'Building a fairer Britain: Reform of the Equality and Human Rights Commission', published in March 2011, set out proposals for new arrangements for providing equality information, advice and support following the Government's decision to cease funding for the EHRC's helpline and legal grants programme in 2012. In December 2011 the Government Equalities Office announced the creation of a new Equality Advisory and Support Service to provide support to vulnerable and disadvantaged individuals facing discrimination.

37.60 Costs

When a person who has been assisted by the EHRC becomes entitled to have some or all of the costs (or expenses in Scotland) in the proceedings from another party, S.29(1) and (2)(a) EqA 2006 provides that the EHRC will recover its expenses (the amount of which may be determined by regulations made by the Secretary of State) in providing the assistance out of costs awarded or paid by agreement. The EHRC is able to enforce the reimbursement as a debt, although the debt ranks after any obligation on the person to pay money to the Legal Services Commission in England or Wales and to the Scottish Legal Aid Board in Scotland – S.29(2)(b) and (3).

The award of costs in discrimination claims is addressed in Chapter 34, 'Enforcing individual rights', under 'Costs'. The issue of costs generally is explored in greater detail in IDS Employment Law Handbook, 'Employment Tribunal Practice and Procedure' (2006), Chapter 18, 'Costs and allowances'.

Judicial review and other legal proceedings 37.61

Section 30 EqA 2006 gives the EHRC capacity to institute or intervene in judicial review or other legal proceedings where the proceedings are relevant to any of its functions, subject to any limitations imposed under legislation or by rules of court – S.30(1) and (4)(b). By virtue of S.30(2) the EHRC also has the necessary title and interest in relation to any such legal proceedings in Scotland.

For details of the circumstances in which judicial review can arise in relation to discrimination, see Chapter 34, 'Enforcing individual rights', under 'Judicial review'.

Part 9

Public sector equality duties

38 General public sector equality duty

Scope of the general duty

Eliminating prohibited conduct

Advancing equality of opportunity

Fostering good relations

Favourable treatment

Compliance

Who is subject to the general duty?

Enforcement

A key element of the Equality Act 2010 (EqA) is the 'public sector equality **38.1** duty', which is intended to ensure that public authorities and other bodies or persons exercising public functions consider the need to maintain standards of equality, equal opportunities and good relations between different groups. The principle behind the need for such a duty is that while equality law in general provides redress in individual cases, it has a limited effect on more deep-seated or systemic causes of discrimination, such as 'institutional racism'. The equality duty is intended to ensure that public authorities actively pursue equality objectives in exercising their functions.

In this regard, S.149 EqA brings the pre-existing public sector equality duties on race, gender and disability together under one umbrella, replacing S.71 of the Race Relations Act 1976 (RRA), S.76A of the Sex Discrimination Act 1975 (SDA), and S.49A of the Disability Discrimination Act 1995 (DDA) respectively, while also extending the duty to other protected characteristics – see 'Scope of the general duty – "relevant protected characteristic"' below. Although the duty is not identical to its precursors, it contains similar concepts, and much of the case law decided under the old equality duties is likely to be relevant to its interpretation, as we shall see later in this chapter.

The public sector equality duty, which has been in force since 5 April 2011, **38.2** applies across all segments of activity. It covers policy formulation and implementation and decision-making in the spheres of service provision, public procurement and education, as well as in relation to employment. The bulk of the case law on the duty is related to the provision of public services, such as libraries, social care and housing. While such subject matters are outside the scope of this Handbook, we discuss the key principles decided by such authorities in so far as they are pertinent to employment. (Stop press: the Government is currently reviewing the operation of the public duty – see Introduction to this Handbook.)

38.3 **Mandatory duty.** The public sector equality duty is mandatory for those to whom it applies, although there are certain exceptions in terms of which of a body's functions are and are not covered – see 'Who is subject to the general duty?' below for further detail. This means that compliance is not excused because of financial exigencies; in fact, the High Court has observed that 'even where the context of decision-making is financial resources in a tight budget, that does not excuse compliance [sic] with the [equality duties] and indeed there is much to be said for the proposition that even in [such] times the need for clear, well-informed decision-making when assessing the impacts on less advantaged members of society is as great, if not greater' – R (on the application of Rahman) v Birmingham City Council 2011 EWHC 944, QBD. Furthermore, public authorities may not delegate their duty – see 'Who is subject to the general duty? – a non-delegable duty' below.

38.4 **Relationship with specific duties.** The EqA confers on ministers a power to impose specific duties, i.e. legal requirements over and above the public sector equality duty, that are designed to ensure that public bodies meet their obligations under that duty. These duties, which are imposed by secondary legislation on most but not all of the public bodies which are subject to the public sector equality duty, are discussed in Chapter 39, 'Specific public sector equality duties'. There are two currently applicable to public bodies in England: the duty to publish information and the duty to set and publish objectives.

The public sector equality duty is commonly known as the 'general equality duty' or simply the 'general duty', to distinguish it from the specific duties, and that is how we shall refer to it hereafter. Although not all public authorities or bodies exercising public functions are required to comply with the specific duties, they may wish to consider at least partial voluntary compliance as this may assist them to comply with the general duty.

38.5 **Code of Practice and guidance.** As explained in Chapter 1, 'UK discrimination law', the Equality and Human Rights Commission (EHRC) has issued two statutory Codes of Practice in relation to the employment provisions of the EqA, as it is empowered to do by S.14 of the Equality Act 2006. Work began on a draft Code of Practice to cover the general equality duty but the Government subsequently took the view that a further statutory Code might place too much of a burden on public bodies. Thus, the EHRC has indicated on its website its intention to issue the draft Code as a 'non-statutory' code instead, to 'give a formal, authoritative, and comprehensive legal interpretation' of Part 11, Chapter 1 EqA, which covers the public sector equality duty, specific duties, and related powers.

In any event, the EHRC has published extensive non-statutory guidance on the general and specific duties, as it is empowered to do under S.13 of the 2006 Act. While this guidance is non-statutory, it is likely to assist those involved in implementing the equality duties and their advisers to ensure proper compliance. We refer to it where relevant in this chapter and in Chapter 39, 'Specific public sector equality duties'. The guidance currently consists of 'The essential guide to the public sector equality duty' (January 2012); 'Meeting the equality duty in policy and decision-making' (January 2012); 'Engagement and the equality duty: a guide for public authorities' (December 2011); 'Objectives and the equality duty: a guide for public authorities' (December 2011); and 'Equality information and the equality duty: a guide for public authorities' (December 2011). These guides cover England and non-devolved public authorities in Scotland and Wales; separate guidance is available for devolved public authorities in Scotland and Wales.

Scope of the general duty 38.6

The general public sector equality duty requires public authorities to have 'due regard' to the need to achieve the following three aims when exercising their functions:

- the elimination of 'discrimination, harassment, victimisation and any other conduct' prohibited by the EqA – S.149(1)(a) EqA

- the advancement of 'equality of opportunity between persons who share a relevant protected characteristic and persons who do not share it' – S.149(1)(b) EqA

- the fostering of 'good relations between persons who share a relevant protected characteristic and persons who do not share it' – S.149(1)(c) EqA.

In order to comply with the duty, public authorities must have the necessary regard to the need to achieve all of these aims. It is not enough simply to avoid discriminating: the duty requires a more proactive approach, particularly in relation to the second and third aims. We discuss the three aims in more detail below (see 'Eliminating prohibited conduct', 'Advancing equality of opportunity' and 'Fostering good relations').

'Relevant protected characteristic' 38.7
The relevant protected characteristics referred to in the second and third limbs of the general duty are age; disability; gender reassignment; pregnancy and maternity; race; religion or belief; sex; and sexual orientation – S.149(7) EqA.

When exercising the public sector equality duty, it will not usually be sufficient to treat the relevant protected groups homogenously, as this will not address such issues as are unique to a particular protected characteristic. In R (on the

1361

application of Hurley and anor) v Secretary of State for Business, Innovation and Skills 2012 EWHC 201, QBD, the High Court considered a challenge to the Government's decision to increase university tuition fees based on an equality impact assessment which considered the equality implications for individuals in lower socio-economic groups. The Court noted that 'specific and different issues need to be considered with respect to each protected characteristic'. While there was 'significant correlation between the socially disadvantaged and those from disabled households or from ethnic minorities, clearly they are not the same thing'. However, on the facts of the case, given that the decision under challenge was essentially financial, the Court found that the Secretary of State's full engagement with the implications for the economically disadvantaged necessarily covered any disproportionate economic disadvantage for protected groups (although he was found to have failed to comply with the general duty for another reason).

38.8 **Marriage and civil partnership.** It is evident from S.149(7) EqA that the second and third limbs of the general equality duty do *not* apply to the protected characteristic of marriage and civil partnership, whereas the first limb does, since discrimination on grounds of marriage or civil partnership is prohibited by the EqA generally. There was some discussion during the progress of the Equality Bill as to whether protection against discrimination on grounds of marriage or civil partnership should be retained in the EqA – see Chapter 8, 'Marriage and civil partnership', under 'Scope of protection under the Equality Act'. The original rationale for providing protection from marital discrimination in the Sex Discrimination Act 1975 (SDA) was that at the time the SDA was enacted it was a requirement in some types of employment that a woman resign when she got married. Thus, a female civil servant or a teacher, for example, would automatically lose her job if she married. The protection was extended to civil partners by the Civil Partnership Act 2004. Taking the view that the 'marriage bar' to employment no longer persists, the Government considered it unnecessary to require public authorities to consider the need to 'advance equality of opportunity' for married people or civil partners or to 'foster good relations' between them and those who are unmarried or not in a civil partnership.

As noted above, the first limb of the equality duty – the need to eliminate discrimination, harassment, victimisation and any other conduct prohibited by the Act – applies to marriage and civil partnership to the extent that discrimination on this ground is prohibited elsewhere in the EqA. In this regard, note that the EqA does *not* protect against harassment on the ground of marriage or civil partnership, and nor does it provide any protection on this ground in areas other than that of work – see Chapter 8, 'Marriage and civil partnership', under 'Scope of protection under the Equality Act', and Chapter 14, 'Prohibited conduct: general principles', under 'Potential claims under each protected characteristic'.

Equal pay. The first limb of the general equality duty extends to matters **38.9** concerning equal pay, since S.149(8) EqA provides that the reference in S.149(1)(a) to 'conduct that is prohibited by or under this Act' includes a breach of an equality clause or rule or non-discrimination rule. In other words, public authorities must, in the exercise of their functions, have due regard to the need to eliminate breaches of the law on equal pay. Equal pay law is outside the scope of this Handbook but is considered in IDS Employment Law Handbook, 'Equal Pay' (2011).

Eliminating prohibited conduct   38.10

The first limb of the public sector equality duty provides that public authorities must, in the exercise of their functions, have due regard to the need to eliminate discrimination, harassment, victimisation and any other conduct that is prohibited by or under the EqA – S.149(1)(a). This covers not only the elimination of more overt forms of prohibited conduct, such as direct discrimination and harassment, but also any risk of indirect discrimination.

This aim appears to be intended to cover the prevention of potential discriminatory conduct, as well as the elimination of existing discriminatory conduct. However, it seems unlikely that a public authority would be expected to introduce measures to combat potential prohibited conduct if there was no evidence of any risk of it occurring; the requirement is to have due regard to the *need* to eliminate prohibited conduct.

One effect of this aim is that a public authority must consider whether a proposed policy or decision may have a discriminatory impact. If so, the authority will need to decide whether to discontinue the policy or alter the decision, or whether it can mitigate the discriminatory effect of its consequences. If there is a risk that a policy or decision will have indirectly discriminatory effects, the public authority will need to ensure that it is able to justify any such discrimination before proceeding. In addition, the aim may involve public authorities giving thought to what active steps they may need to take in order to eliminate discriminatory conduct, such as introducing anti-harassment training. The Explanatory Notes to the EqA state, by way of example, that the duty 'could lead a police authority to review its recruitment procedures to ensure they do not unintentionally deter applicants from ethnic minorities, with the aim of eliminating unlawful discrimination' (para 484).

Advancing equality of opportunity   38.11

The second limb of the general duty provides that public authorities must, in the exercise of their functions, have due regard to the need to advance equality of opportunity between persons who share a relevant protected characteristic and persons who do not share it – S.149(1)(b) EqA.

This aim is potentially broader than the first aim of eliminating prohibited conduct. It is not fulfilled simply by ensuring that in performing its functions a public authority commits no unlawful discrimination – Hereward and Foster LLP and anor v Legal Services Commission 2010 EWHC 3370, QBD (a case decided under S.76A SDA). Positive steps are required.

Section 149(3) EqA explains in more detail what S.149(1)(b) requires. It specifies that the aim involves, in particular, the need to:

- 'remove or minimise disadvantages suffered' by persons who share a relevant protected characteristic where those disadvantages are 'connected to that characteristic'

- 'take steps to meet the needs of' persons who share a relevant protected characteristic where those needs are different from the needs of persons who do not share it

- encourage those who share a relevant protected characteristic to 'participate in public life or in any other activity' in which their participation is 'disproportionately low'.

These matters are discussed further below.

38.12 It is important to recognise that this aim is to do with the advancement of *equality*, and not the promotion of the interests of a minority. Indeed, promoting the interests of a minority may very well mean that other groups are proportionally disadvantaged, and the aim of advancing equality between different groups is *not* thereby fulfilled. In R (on the application of Harris) v London Borough of Haringey 2010 EWCA Civ 703, CA, the Court of Appeal held that S.71 RRA did not require the promotion of the interests of a racial minority or minorities. The aims of paying due regard to the need to promote equality of opportunity and good relations between persons of different racial groups were not necessarily achieved by a proposal 'which may promote the economic interests of a particular racial group, even a deprived group'. Note, however, that favourable treatment is expressly permitted by the EqA in the context of the general equality duty so long as it is not discriminatory – S.149(6) (discussed under 'Favourable treatment' below).

A common misconception about the aim of advancing equality of opportunity is that it requires the elimination of difference. This is not the intention, as the Government Equalities Office (GEO) takes pains to point out in its guidance 'Equality Act 2010: Public Sector Equality Duty – What do I need to know? A quick start guide for public sector organisations' (June 2011) ('the Quick Start Guide'). It emphasises that the equality duty 'does not require public bodies to treat everyone the same' but rather 'to think about people's different needs and how these can be met'. Thus, it may very well be appropriate to provide services that are aimed at specific sectors, or provided by particular sector-related organisations on behalf of the public authority. The guide says that the duty 'does not require public bodies to treat all religions as being equal or to treat all religious festivals equally' and suggests that 'a public body displaying a Christmas tree every year in its reception area' would not be in breach.

Section 149(1)(b) EqA does not require that equality of opportunity is actually **38.13** advanced, so long as due regard is paid to the aim – R (on the application of Gill) v Secretary of State for Justice 2010 EWHC 364, QBD (decided under S.49A DDA). In other words, it is possible that no action will be taken and no results demonstrated, and the aim still be fulfilled. The meaning of 'due regard' is discussed in detail under 'Compliance – "due regard"' below. However, if particular steps towards advancing equality of opportunity are not taken when they should have been taken, the public authority will find it difficult to claim later to have had due regard to the aim – Pieretti v London Borough of Enfield 2010 EWCA Civ 1104, CA (also decided under S.49A DDA).

Removing/minimising characteristic-related disadvantages   **38.14**
As noted above, S.149(3) EqA provides that having due regard to the need to advance equality of opportunity between persons with a relevant protected characteristic and persons without it involves having due regard, in particular, to the need to do three different things. The first is to remove or minimise disadvantages suffered by persons who share a relevant protected characteristic that are connected to that characteristic – S.149(3)(a). Such disadvantages may not always be apparent. It follows that this aim may well involve obtaining specific information about adverse impact – R (on the application of JM and anor) v Isle of Wight Council 2011 EWHC 2911, QBD.

A report submitted to the EHRC, 'Making practice happen: Practitioners' views on the most effective specific equality duties' (January 2009), contains a number of accounts of how various public bodies have removed or minimised characteristic-related disadvantages under previous equality duties in the employment context. For example:

- the Mental Health Act Commission made changes to its recruitment process to encourage more women to apply for area commissioner positions. It simplified job descriptions and person specifications to remove non-essential content that might discourage people with less experience from applying. It also moved temporarily to internal recruitment rather than open competition, which saw several women move from being local to area commissioners

- Hertfordshire Fire and Rescue Service instigated 'positive action days' before the start of its recruitment process, to allow potential recruits to test their strength and use simulation to experience working at height and in confined spaces, and to go through some of the required written work. The aim was to address diversity barriers for women (who disproportionately

1365

failed on upper body strength) and for black and ethnic minority recruits (who disproportionately failed on written tests)

- a review of the Metropolitan Police's workforce revealed women to be under-represented in the specialist firearms operational command unit. Action to overcome the barriers to recruitment included the development of a scheme whereby female firearms officers were trained to mentor female applicants and support them through the application process. Given the difference between men's and women's physiologies, bespoke training programmes were introduced to equip women to pass the job-related fitness test. Coaching was provided on how to complete application forms in accordance with the national competencies. Personal development courses were arranged to show the women how to compile and follow a personal action plan. This resulted in an increase in the number of women in the firearms team from ten to 25 over a two-year period.

38.15 ## Taking steps to meet different needs

Secondly, S.149(3)(b) EqA provides that having due regard to the need to advance equality of opportunity involves having due regard to the need to take steps to meet the needs of persons who share a relevant protected characteristic where those needs are different from those of persons who do not share it.

It should always be remembered that the duty is to pay due regard to the need, rather than to take positive steps – see under 'Advancing equality of opportunity' above. Frequently, where a public authority is responding to a reduction in its budget, it will decide to take steps that negatively impact upon groups which share a particular relevant protected characteristic. This does not necessarily mean that the public authority is thereby failing to comply with its duty. Where it can demonstrate that it has properly considered possible steps to mitigate the probable or potential adverse effects of a decision or change in policy, this will enable it to show that it has had 'due regard' to the need to advance equality of opportunity – R (on the application of JG and anor) v Lancashire County Council 2011 EWHC 2295, QBD. In that case the High Court held that a local authority had complied with its disability equality duty under S.49A DDA when it made various changes to its provision of adult social care services in order to achieve savings. The authority had undertaken significant consultation and prepared a mitigation plan as to how to minimise the adverse impact of implementing the changes.

38.16 By contrast, in R (on the application of W) v Birmingham City Council and another case 2011 EWHC 1147, QBD, a local authority was held to have failed to comply with the disability equality duty when it changed the eligibility criteria which determined whether it would provide care support for people with disabilities. It had failed to consider whether the impact on disabled people was so serious that a less draconian alternative should be identified and funded to the extent necessary by making savings elsewhere. There had been no attempt to evaluate the practical impact of the change and no assessment of the extent to which certain mitigating factors would reduce its potential severity.

Needs of disabled persons. The steps involved in meeting the needs of disabled **38.17** persons that are different from the needs of persons who are not disabled include, in particular, steps to take account of disabled persons' disabilities – S.149(4) EqA. It should be noted that this is one respect in which a relevant protected group may receive more favourable treatment than others. This is permitted by S.149(6) EqA – see 'Favourable treatment' below.

In its Quick Start Guide, the GEO explains that public bodies should take account of disabled people's impairments when making decisions about policies or services, which 'might mean making reasonable adjustments or treating disabled people better than non-disabled people in order to meet their needs'. It provides the following example, which we have adapted to the employment context:

- a university might decide to provide car-parking spaces for disabled staff so that those who cannot use public transport because of their impairment have equality of opportunity in coming to work. Although non-disabled staff might also want a parking space, they will not suffer the same degree of disadvantage without one.

Another example, in the education context, is drawn from a study by the **38.18** disability network RADAR, 'Lights, Camera, Action: Promoting Disability Equality in the Public Sector' (published on the EHRC's website):

- in order to support learners with autistic spectrum disorders to access further education, City College Norwich built a dedicated centre known as 'the RUG (Really Useful Group) room'. The RUG room, which was designed with learners, is a safe haven for students with autism as well as a social learning space. Learners with autism often find small, enclosed spaces very calming and so the computers have 'sails' over them, which helps the students feel safe while keeping the space open. Learners were also allowed to design a social seating area. Many students with autism find socialising difficult but they designed a space that made them feel comfortable talking to each other and staff.

There is evidently considerable overlap between this aspect of complying with the general equality duty, and the duty to make reasonable adjustments. This duty is discussed fully in Chapter 21, 'Failure to make reasonable adjustments'.

Encouraging participation in public life, etc   38.19
The third specific matter to which due regard must be had, in order to meet the second aim of having due regard to advancing equality of opportunity, is the need to encourage persons who share a relevant protected characteristic to

1367

participate in public life or in any other activity in which participation by such persons is disproportionately low – S.149(3)(c) EqA. An example given in the Explanatory Notes to the EqA:

- the duty could lead a local authority to target training and mentoring schemes at disabled people to enable them to stand as local councillors, with the aim of advancing equality of opportunity for different groups of people who have the same disability, and in particular encouraging their participation in public life (para 484).

While the need to encourage participation in public life is unlikely to be relevant in an employment context, there may well be circumstances in which a public sector employer perceives a need to encourage persons who share a relevant protected characteristic to participate in an 'activity' in which participation for that characteristic is low. For example, where the employer has a predominantly white male staff association, it may actively need to encourage women and people who are black or from ethnic minorities to consider putting themselves forward in order to ensure that the body is more representative of the workforce. It should be borne in mind that the aim is not to ensure that such bodies consist entirely of people with minority protected characteristics, but that participation is proportionate to the make-up of the workforce or community.

38.20 Fostering good relations

The third and final limb of the general duty is that a public authority must, in the exercise of its functions, have due regard to the need to 'foster good relations' between persons who share a relevant protected characteristic and persons who do not share it – S.149(1)(c) EqA.

Again, the EqA sets out the particular constituents of this aim: S.149(5) provides that having due regard to this aim involves having due regard, in particular, to the need to (a) tackle prejudice, and (b) promote understanding.

38.21 The Explanatory Notes to the EqA give the following example of action that could be taken to promote this aim in the employment context:

- the duty could lead a large government department, in its capacity as an employer, to provide staff with education and guidance, with the aim of fostering good relations between its transsexual staff and its non-transsexual staff (para 484).

Again, it is important to appreciate, as with advancing equality of opportunity, that this aim is not necessarily fulfilled by promoting minority interests. It is the health of the relationships between different groups of people that is the focus – see R (on the application of Harris) v London Borough of Haringey 2010 EWCA Civ 703, CA, discussed under 'Advancing equality of opportunity' above.

Tackling prejudice

Having due regard to the need to foster good relations between persons who share a relevant protected characteristic and persons who do not share it involves having due regard to the need to tackle prejudice – S.149(5)(a) EqA. The Explanatory Notes to the EqA give an example of action that could be taken as a result of having due regard to the need to tackle prejudice, which we have adapted to the employment context:

- the duty could lead a public authority to review its anti-bullying strategy to ensure that it addresses the issue of homophobic bullying, with the aim of fostering good relations, and in particular tackling prejudice against gay and lesbian people (para 484).

Another example could be running 'mental health first aid' training and awareness schemes in the workplace, to address the stigma frequently attached to mental illnesses.

Promoting understanding

Having due regard to the need to foster good relations between persons who share a relevant protected characteristic and persons who do not share it involves having due regard to the need to promote understanding – S.149(5)(b) EqA. By implication, this means understanding between persons who share a relevant protected characteristic and persons who do not share it.

This can have application to all relevant protected characteristics, though the need to promote understanding of people with mental health disabilities, those practising less mainstream religions, and people who are undergoing or have undergone gender reassignment frequently stand out. The EHRC-commissioned document 'Public bodies and the public sector duties relating to transsexual and transgender people: Report of findings and case studies' (Summer 2010) contains a number of examples of action that can be taken to demonstrate due regard to the need to promote understanding of gender reassignment, two of which we summarise below:

- the Metropolitan Police Service's trans staff association includes people with a number of different gender identities. Through this association staff are consulted on relevant policies, such as transitioning at work. The Service also introduced trans awareness training, including both face-to-face events (for example, a two-day 'listening' event on gender identity) and a section in the mandatory computer-based training programme. This is supplemented with more in-depth training for LGBT liaison officers

- Wrexham County Borough Council engaged with a local trans group and embedded staff training on trans issues within existing staff training structures. The training delivery takes the form of two transgender awareness events per year open to all staff and elected members. More detailed sessions are provided on request to departments and teams. Trans awareness is also addressed within the wider gender equality training. The training has enabled staff to become more comfortable and skilled in assisting trans service users, and has assisted the Council in mainstreaming trans equality within a range of policies.

38.24 Favourable treatment

When pursuing the three aims that comprise the general equality duty, a public authority is entitled to treat some people more favourably than others, so long as this does not involve conduct that is prohibited by the Act – S.149(6) EqA. For example, a public authority may treat a disabled person more favourably than a non-disabled person when taking steps to meet the disabled person's needs. Reasonable adjustments for people with disabilities are discussed in Chapter 21, 'Failure to make reasonable adjustments'.

Alternatively, a public authority may make use of the specific exceptions in the EqA which permit different treatment. These are explained in Chapter 30, 'General exceptions', and Chapter 31, 'Specific exceptions'. For example, favourable treatment of a particular protected group may be permitted by an occupational requirement (see Chapter 30 under 'Occupational requirements').

38.25   Finally, public authorities may use the 'positive action' provisions of the EqA in appropriate circumstances. S.158 EqA allows the use of positive action measures to alleviate disadvantage experienced by people who share a protected characteristic, reduce their under-representation in relation to particular activities, and meet their particular needs. For example, this would cover training courses targeted at particular disadvantaged groups, such as the bespoke training programmes provided for women to enable them to pass the fitness test for a police firearms unit, cited above under 'Advancing equality of opportunity – removing/minimising characteristic-related disadvantages'. Alternatively, computer training courses could be targeted at staff aged over 60, who may tend to have lower IT literacy levels. Targeted advertising and open days would also be permitted by S.158.

Section 159 EqA entitles employers to take a protected characteristic into account when deciding who to recruit or promote where people having the protected characteristic are at a disadvantage or are under-represented. This provision is subject to a number of important conditions, including that it can be relied on only where the candidates are as qualified as each other. It does not permit employers to adopt a blanket policy of treating candidates who share a particular protected characteristic more favourably than others who do not. It would not, for example, be lawful for a woman to be promoted in preference to a man in order to improve the gender balance of more senior appointments, if the man were the better candidate.

1370

Positive action is discussed fully in Chapter 30, 'General exceptions', under 'Positive action', and the Code of Practice on Employment issued by the EHRC provides guidance and examples of permitted action.

Compliance 38.26

What is required for a public authority to comply with the general equality duty is fact-sensitive and 'inevitably varies considerably from situation to situation, from time to time and from stage to stage' – R (on the application of Bailey and ors) v London Borough of Brent Council and another case 2011 EWCA Civ 1586, CA. There is no requirement to devise policies to achieve the equality aims: a public authority has a degree of latitude in how it approaches its consideration of various needs – R (on the application of Green) v Gloucestershire County Council and another case 2011 EWHC 2687, QBD.

This has not prevented the question of what observance of the duty requires of decision-makers being the subject of detailed analysis by the courts, and there are clear principles to which public authorities must adhere in order to comply. The High Court in R (on the application of the Equality and Human Rights Commission) v Secretary of State for Justice 2010 EWHC 147, QBD (a case on the race and disability equality duties in S.71 RRA and S.49A DDA concerning the treatment of foreign national prisoners) provided a useful summary: 'The duty to have due regard is a duty which is mandatory; it is also an important duty and one which must be fulfilled prior to the adoption or implementation of the decision, function or policy in question. The duty requires the decision-maker to embark upon a sufficient and proper decision-making process so as to discharge the duty with an open mind. The question in every case is whether the decision-maker has in substance had due regard to the relevant statutory need.' We shall now discuss in more detail what this requires.

'Due regard' 38.27

Precisely what is meant by having 'due regard' to the need to fulfil the equality aims is not defined in the EqA or in the Explanatory Notes to the Act but has merited considerable judicial consideration, both under S.149(1) EqA and under the precursors to the general equality duty in the RRA, SDA and DDA. It is clear from these authorities that the general equality duty does not require public authorities to eliminate discrimination, advance equality of opportunity, and foster good relations in the exercise of their functions. It requires them to have 'due regard' to the need to do those things; in other words, 'to bring these important considerations relating to discrimination into consideration' – R (on the application of Brown) v Secretary of State for Work and Pensions and anor 2008 EWHC 3158, QBD (a case on S.49A DDA). Lord Justice Dyson in R (on the application of Baker and ors) v Secretary of State for Communities and Local Government and anor 2008 EWCA Civ 141, CA, stressed (in the context of S.71 RRA) that the equality duty is not a duty to achieve results, but rather to have due regard to the need to achieve the identified goals.

Thus the concept of 'due regard' in theory permits public authorities to exercise their functions in a way that is neutral or even has the opposite effect to eliminating discrimination, advancing equality of opportunity, or fostering good relations, so long as proper consideration has been paid to the need to pursue these aims. Counterintuitive as this may seem, in a time of acute economic difficulty it is not inconceivable that public authorities may find their choice limited to disadvantaging one group or disadvantaging another. On the other hand, if no due regard has been paid to the relevant needs, then the public authority will have failed in its duty even if ultimately it would have made the same decision had it had due regard.

38.28 Nevertheless, if due regard is had to the prescribed needs, the decision-maker should thereby be enabled to address potential inequalities; and if inequalities are not addressed, this may evidence a failure to have had due regard to the need to address them. In R (on the application of Luton Borough Council and ors) v Secretary of State for Education 2011 EWHC 217, QBD, the High Court found a 'clear tie-in' between the Secretary of State's complete failure to have regard to the duties under the SDA, RRA and DDA and his lack of consultation with the applicants. If he had consulted them, they would have been able to draw his attention to the special equality considerations relevant to schools in their particular areas which would be affected by his decision to cancel school-building projects.

38.29 **Balancing exercise.** In R (on the application of Baker and ors) v Secretary of State for Communities and Local Government and anor 2008 EWCA Civ 141, CA, Lord Justice Dyson defined 'due regard' as 'the regard that is appropriate in all the circumstances' in which the public authority concerned is carrying out its function as a public authority. He intimated that this involves a balancing act between considering the effects of the disadvantage to the affected group and the factors relevant to the authority's functions, which include the financial constraints under which it operates.

Lord Justice Scott Baker in R (on the application of Brown) v Secretary of State for Work and Pensions and anor 2008 EWHC 3158, QBD, elaborated on this definition, stating that there must be a proper regard for all the identified goals in the context of the function that is being exercised at the time by the public authority; but at the same time, the public authority must also pay regard to any countervailing factors which, in the context of the function being exercised, it is proper and reasonable for it to consider. What the relevant countervailing factors are will depend on the function being exercised and all the circumstances that impinge upon it. Clearly, economic and practical factors will often be important. According to Scott Baker LJ, the public authority's task is to 'balance all, and bring all to mind before it makes its decision on what it is going to do in carrying out the particular function or policy in question'.

As can be seen from these comments, the considerations relevant to a public **38.30** authority's duty under S.149 EqA are not necessarily decisive. The fact that, for example, an employer's decision to cut spending on adult social care will result in a diminished service for certain disabled people does not necessarily mean that a public authority is prohibited from taking that decision. The weight to be given to the need to fulfil the equality aims is for the decision-maker to determine.

These principles were applied by the High Court in the context of the general equality duty in R (on the application of D and anor) v Manchester City Council 2011 EWHC 17, QBD. In that case, which concerned a challenge by two disabled elderly people to a local authority's budget-setting and consultation processes in relation to adult social care services, the High Court confirmed that the S.149 duty does not involve the taking of any prescribed step or the achievement of a result. The substantive obligation imposed by the equality duty is to have such regard to the relevant needs as is 'appropriate in all the circumstances'. The Court explained that there are two interrelated aspects to that obligation: (a) how far to investigate what impact (if any) the decision to be made may have on the needs to which regard must be had, and (b) what weight to give to any anticipated impact on those needs relative to other material considerations.

As the Court indicated in the above case, what may be 'appropriate' in each **38.31** respect is a matter of judgement for the relevant public authority. How much weight is to be given to each of the factors in play is a matter for the authority concerned, not the court. This was confirmed by the High Court in R (on the application of Hurley and anor) v Secretary of State for Business, Innovation and Skills 2012 EWHC 201, QBD, which involved a challenge to the Government's increase of university tuition fees. The Court held that 'provided the court is satisfied that there has been a rigorous consideration of the duty, so that there is a proper appreciation of the potential impact of the decision on equality objectives... it is for the decision-maker to decide how much weight should be given to the various factors informing the decision. The concept of "due regard" requires the court to ensure that there has been a proper and conscientious focus on the statutory criteria, but if that is done, the court cannot interfere with the decision simply because it would have given greater weight to the equality implications of the decision than did the decision-maker.' To hold otherwise would be to 'allow unelected judges to review on substantive merits grounds almost all aspects of public decision-making'. Note, however, that decisions may still be challenged on the ground that the assessment reached is unreasonable or irrational (see under 'Enforcement – judicial review' below).

1373

38.32 **Question of substance.** In R (on the application of Brown) v Secretary of State for Work and Pensions and anor 2008 EWHC 3158, QBD, Scott Baker LJ suggested six general principles governing what is intended by 'due regard', which are often cited in cases and literature concerning the exercise of the public sector equality duty. The third of these is that 'the duty must be exercised in substance, with rigour and with an open mind... It is not a question of "ticking boxes".'

Performing the duty substantively means, in effect, that the thought processes required by S.149 EqA must be properly incorporated into the decision-making process. In Brown, Scott Baker LJ said that the duty has to be 'integrated within the discharge of the public functions of the authority', and referred to the remarks of Lord Justice Moses in R (on the application of Kaur and anor) v London Borough of Ealing 2008 EWHC 2062, QBD, that a racial equality impact assessment 'should be an integral part of the formation of a proposed policy, not justification for its adoption'. The Court of Appeal applied this principle in the context of S.149 EqA in R (on the application of Bailey and ors) v London Borough of Brent Council and another case 2011 EWCA Civ 1586, CA, in holding that a local authority had not acted unlawfully in deciding to close half of its public libraries. The Court held that the S.149 duty should be 'embedded in the process' though it can have 'no fixed content, bearing in mind the range of potential factors and situations'.

38.33 Having said that, it is worth noting the Court's qualification in Bailey (above) that public authorities cannot be expected to apply, and indeed are to be discouraged from applying, 'the degree of forensic analysis for the purpose of an [equality impact assessment] and of consideration of their duties under S.149 which a QC might deploy in court'. As the High Court commented in R (on the application of Hurley and anor) v Secretary of State for Business, Innovation and Skills 2012 EWHC 201, QBD, there is no failure to comply simply because 'it is possible to point to one or other piece of evidence which might be considered relevant which was not specifically identified in the [equality impact assessment]... [V]irtually every decision could be challenged on that basis.'

38.34 *Not a box-ticking exercise.* An element of performing the duty 'in substance' is that it is not, as Scott Baker LJ put it in R (on the application of Brown) v Secretary of State for Work and Pensions and anor 2008 EWHC 3158, QBD, a question of 'ticking boxes'. Referring to the duty, and even conducting an equality impact assessment, does not necessarily mean that the duty has been fulfilled. The High Court in R (on the application of Rahman) v Birmingham City Council 2011 EWHC 944, QBD, stressed (in the context of the old equality duties) that the duty is not merely to have regard to any equality impact assessment, but to have due regard to the equality duties: 'The equality impact assessment is not an end in itself but a tool to decision-making that meets the standards set by the statutory duties.'

If an equality impact assessment is to be used, therefore, it must be sufficiently substantial in terms of its content and rigorous in its analysis. In R (on the application of Green) v Gloucestershire County Council and another case 2011 EWHC 2687, QBD, a library-closure case, the High Court found that it could not fairly be said that the defendant local authorities had had no regard at all to their respective statutory duties, in light of the fact that they had both produced a number of equality impact assessments. However, the Court found that the local authorities had failed in their duties in that they had neither undertaken 'a sufficiently thorough information-gathering exercise' nor properly analysed that information. Although, as the High Court pointed out in Green, carrying out an equality impact assessment is 'not an invariable necessity for conformity with the public sector equality duty', public authorities should beware that whatever information-gathering, monitoring, analysis or objective-setting they do carry out is both sufficiently rigorous in its analysis, and taken into account in their decision-making and not left to gather dust.

Failure to refer to duty not determinative. On the other hand, a failure to refer **38.35** explicitly to S.149 EqA is not, by itself, determinative of whether or not the duty has been fulfilled. As Lord Justice Dyson put it in R (on the application of Baker and ors) v Secretary of State for Communities and Local Government and anor 2008 EWCA Civ 141, CA, 'so to hold would be to sacrifice substance to form.' In R (on the application of McDonald) v Royal Borough of Kensington and Chelsea 2011 UKSC 33, SC, the Supreme Court addressed this point in holding that a local authority had not failed to have regard to the disability equality duty under S.49A DDA despite the fact that it had not expressly referred to the duty in considering what care it was required to provide to a disabled person. The Court held that where a public authority is discharging its functions under statutes that expressly direct its attention to the needs of disabled persons, 'it may be entirely superfluous to make express reference to S.49A and absurd to infer from an omission to do so a failure on the authority's part to have regard to their general duty under the section... The question is one of substance, not of form.'

Needless to say, however – and as Scott Baker LJ indicated in R (on the application of Brown) v Secretary of State for Work and Pensions and anor 2008 EWHC 3158, QBD – it is good practice for the policy- or decision-maker to refer to S.149 EqA and even to relevant non-statutory guidance in all cases where the duty is in play. In that way the policy- or decision-maker is 'more likely to ensure that the relevant factors are taken into account and the scope for argument as to whether the duty has been performed will be reduced' – Dyson LJ in Baker (above). For example, in R (on the application of Luton Borough Council and ors) v Secretary of State for Education 2011 EWHC 217,

QBD, the High Court considered that although the fact that the equality duty is not specifically mentioned is not determinative of whether it has been performed, in that case the absence of such references or records was 'glaring and very telling'. There was no satisfactory evidence that any regard was had to the relevant duties at all, let alone the necessary rigorous regard. For further discussion, see under 'Record-keeping' below.

38.36 **Consciousness of duty.** Those within a public authority who take decisions that might affect people who share a particular relevant protected characteristic must be conscious of the equality duty's requirements, and how these are engaged, at the time that they are fulfilling their functions. The need to ensure that decision-makers are aware of their duty to have 'due regard' to the identified goals was Scott Baker LJ's first general principle in R (on the application of Brown) v Secretary of State for Work and Pensions and anor (above). An incomplete or erroneous appreciation of the duties will mean that 'due regard' is not given to them. These principles were applied in R (on the application of Bailey and ors) v London Borough of Brent Council and another case 2011 EWCA Civ 1586, CA, in which the Court of Appeal held that the thought-processes of decision-makers need to have regard to the S.149 duty, and this 'must be kept in mind by decision-makers throughout the decision-making process'. Material must be analysed 'with the specific statutory consideration in mind'.

A failure to ensure that decision-makers were conscious of the duty rendered a local authority's decision to restrict adult care services unlawful in R (on the application of Chavda and ors) v London Borough of Harrow 2007 EWHC 3064, QBD. The High Court commented: 'There is no evidence that this legal duty and its implications were drawn to the attention of the decision-takers who should have been informed not just of the disabled as an issue but of the particular obligations which the law imposes. It was not enough to refer obliquely in the attached summary to "potential conflict with the DDA" – this would not give a busy councillor any idea of the serious duties imposed upon the Council by the Act.' Similarly, in the later case of R (on the application of Rahman) v Birmingham City Council 2011 EWHC 944, QBD, the High Court held that a Council's decision to terminate funding for legal advice services was unlawful, in part because there was 'no evidence to suggest that each of the decision-makers [was] aware of the duty and how it was engaged... at the time they took the decision'. The inference from the absence of any reference to the equality impact needs assessment in the reports relied upon by the decision-makers was that it was not materially considered even if individual councillors were aware that one had been undertaken.

It may be worth noting, however, the High Court's qualifications in R (on the application of Staff Side of the Police Negotiating Board and ors) v Secretary of State for Work and Pensions and ors 2011 EWHC 3175, QBD, in relation to the old gender equality duty in S.76A SDA, to the effect that 'a minister may rely on workings and a review of effects carried out within his department to satisfy the "due regard" requirement… without having personally to read an impact assessment, so long as the task has been assigned to officials at an appropriate level of seniority or expertise. Equally… the "due regard" duty can be discharged by a minister if he can be satisfied that the relevant equality assessment had been carried out by another Government department as well or better placed than his own to undertake the task, particularly where that other department has policy responsibility in relation to the effects under review.' (Note that other aspects of this case were subsequently considered by the Court of Appeal – 2012 EWCA Civ 332.)

Advance consideration. The case authorities stress that 'due regard' must be **38.37** given in advance of a decision or policy being made; the duty will not be fulfilled by retrospective justification. As Scott Baker LJ put it, as his second general principle in R (on the application of Brown) v Secretary of State for Work and Pensions and anor 2008 EWHC 3158, QBD: '[T]he "due regard" duty must be fulfilled before and at the time that a particular policy that will or might affect disabled people is being considered by the public authority in question. It involves a conscious approach and state of mind… Attempts to justify a decision as being consistent with the exercise of the duty when it was not, in fact, considered before the decision, are not enough to discharge the duty.'

Proportionality. The degree of regard that should be given is the regard that is **38.38** 'due'. In other words, 'regard' is proportionate. It is possible that the degree of regard required may vary depending on the size of the public body and the range of functions it performs, simply in the sense that there may be fewer issues to which a smaller organisation can have regard (although note that decreased resources will *not* lessen the degree of regard that is due – see R (on the application of Rahman) v Birmingham City Council 2011 EWHC 944, QBD, mentioned in the introduction to this chapter).

More importantly, however, the degree of regard due will vary depending on the extent to which those functions are relevant to equality. The GEO's Quick Start Guide explains that a proportionate approach involves 'giving greater consideration to the equality duty where a function or policy has the potential to have a substantial effect on discrimination or equality of opportunity for the public or the public body's employees, and less consideration where the potential effect on equality is slight'.

The number of people affected by a decision or policy may mean less regard is **38.39** due, but this is not necessarily the case. For example, where a substantial part of the workforce is Muslim, the employer may need to give greater consideration to the need to provide a prayer room or to consider scheduling work at times to allow for employees to pray, than if only a small minority of employees is potentially affected. However, even if there is only one member of staff who is of a particular protected characteristic, harassment of that employee could have a significant effect on him or her, and proportionately greater regard may need to be paid to the equality aims in relation to that employee.

Due regard may even mean *no* regard, depending on the factual circumstances, according to the High Court in Hereward and Foster LLP and anor v Legal Services Commission 2010 EWHC 3370, QBD. The GEO's Quick Start Guide states that: 'Where it is clear from initial consideration that a policy will not have any effect on equality for any of the protected characteristics, no further analysis or action is necessary. For example, if a public body is conducting a review in relation to an issue which has no implications for equality – such as an evaluation of the effect of coastal pollution on marine life – undertaking a formal consultation or analysis addressing equality issues where it is evident that the equality duty is not relevant would be pointless and is not required.' In R (on the application of Bailey and ors) v London Borough of Brent Council and another case 2011 EWCA Civ 1586, CA, the Court of Appeal considered that if, in an appropriate case, 'due regard' legitimately involves no regard, it then becomes 'empty semantics' to distinguish between giving no consideration in the first place and giving consideration and then ruling a matter out as irrelevant or insignificant. In that case the Court found that there was 'simply no basis' for thinking that a decision to close libraries could give rise to unlawful harassment or victimisation. The High Court in R (on the application of Hurley and anor) v Secretary of State for Business, Innovation and Skills 2012 EWHC 201, QBD, also stressed this, commenting that 'there must be some reason to think that the exercise of the functions might in some way relate to a particular aspect of the duty under consideration'.

38.40 Care should be taken, however. In Hurley (above) the Court accepted that 'if there is any doubt about whether a particular statutory objective is engaged, the issue needs to be explored before any conclusion can be safely reached that it is not'. In that case, the Court held that the Secretary of State had not appeared to do this, and had to that extent failed to comply with the equality duties to which he was subject. Similarly, in Hereward and Foster LLP and anor v Legal Services Commission (above), the Court held that even though a criterion was not indirectly discriminatory, it was capable of having an impact on part-time supervisors. A potential impact on the activities of part-time workers, even tangential, called for some consideration of the application of the equality duty. Thus, where there is a potential impact, even if small, some regard must be given to the need to achieve the equality aims.

38.41 **Relevance of objections.** Note that in R (on the application of Bailey and ors) v London Borough of Brent Council and another case 2011 EWCA Civ 1586, CA (above), one of the factors the Court took into account was that no objections, prior to the Council's decision, were made about the possibility of discrimination arising from library closures. The Court considered that although the S.149 duty is mandatory, the failure in a particular case to advance such objections prior to a decision 'is at least capable of being relevant' when considering whether due regard was given. This is slightly surprising, as there is no such legislative qualification, but indicates that the failure to raise an equality issue when there is opportunity to do so may affect the degree of regard that the authority is required to pay to it.

'In the exercise of its functions'   38.42
Section 149(1) EqA requires a public authority to have due regard to the need to fulfil the three equality aims 'in the exercise of its functions'. As we discuss under 'Who is subject to the general duty?' below, public authorities are required to apply the general equality duty in relation to *all* their functions; other bodies and persons who exercise public functions are required to apply the duty in relation only to those functions by virtue of S.149(2).

Affected functions. It follows from what has been said immediately above that **38.43** public authorities need to be alert to applying the duty in respect of any sphere of their activities, not only in respect of those activities that they are required by legislation to carry out. In Barnsley Metropolitan Borough Council v Norton and ors 2011 EWCA Civ 834, CA, the Court of Appeal held that the duty under S.49A DDA was not something that had to be considered only when a public authority was exercising functions that bore on the rights of a disabled person under some other legislation. The duty was general, and applied to the carrying out of any function of any public authority. The Council in that case breached its duty by commencing proceedings to obtain an order for possession of a caretaker's house without having due regard to the need to take steps to take account of the caretaker's daughter's disabilities.

Public authorities must continue to apply the duty in relation to functions which are in practice carried out by a contractor – see 'Who is subject to the general duty? – a non-delegable duty' below.

However, it may well be the case that equality implications simply do not arise **38.44** in connection with the exercise of certain of a public authority's functions. If this is the case, the public authority is entitled to have no regard to the duty in respect of that function, because the degree of regard required is proportionate to the relevance to equality of the decision or policy in question – see further under '"Due regard" – proportionality' above. In the Barnsley case (above) Lord Justice Lloyd noted that 'it does not necessarily follow that whenever a public authority is considering or exercising any function, whatever it may be and in whatever circumstances, it must give conscious thought to how it might affect a disabled person'. In Mayor and Burgesses of the London Borough of Brent v Corcoran and anor 2010 EWCA Civ 774, CA, the Court of Appeal held that the requirement under S.71 RRA to have 'due regard' to the need to eliminate unlawful racial discrimination did not mean that whenever a public authority takes any decision whatever it must give advance consideration to issues of race discrimination. There were decisions which clearly had nothing to do with race, still less racial discrimination. In such circumstances the S.71 duty did not arise.

38.45 **Continuing duty.** The requirement on a public authority to have due regard 'in the exercise of its functions' means that the duty must be complied with on a continuous basis. This is the fifth of Scott Baker LJ's general principles in R (on the application of Brown) v Secretary of State for Work and Pensions and anor 2008 EWHC 3158, QBD. In other words, due regard must be had to the need to fulfil the equality aims at every stage of the process: at the inquiry stage; when a decision or policy is formulated; when it is implemented and applied; whenever it is subject to review; and, again, as circumstances change which might alter its impact in relation to the equality aims. This was emphasised in Pieretti v London Borough of Enfield 2010 EWCA Civ 1104, CA, in which the Court of Appeal held that the disability equality duty in S.49A DDA applied to local authorities in carrying out all of their functions associated with providing housing. The Court stated that the duty applied both to formulation of policy, such as when the local authority was drawing up its criteria, and to the application of that policy in an individual case: both were aspects of it carrying out its functions.

This is subject to the qualification that it may be appropriate for a public authority to wait until facts have emerged or a budget is decided before applying the duty. In R (on the application of Green) v Gloucestershire County Council and another case 2011 EWHC 2687, QBD, the High Court held that in relation to the decision of two Councils significantly to reduce their public library provision, the formative stage at which the duty was to be performed was not at the early stage when officers were contemplating policy options but as part of the decision-making process. And in R (on the application of JG and anor) v Lancashire County Council 2011 EWHC 2295, QBD, the High Court held that a Council had complied with its duty under S.49A DDA when it made changes to social care services in order to comply with significant budgetary constraints. The Court held that it was sensible and lawful for a Council first to formulate its budget proposals and then, at the time of developing the policies, to consider the specific impact of proposed policies that might be implemented within the budgetary framework. The potential impact of the policy proposals on those affected was specifically identified for further investigation involving a series of meaningful consultations; and the Council did not commit itself to the implementation of specific policies within the budgetary framework until it had carried out a full and detailed assessment of their likely effect.

38.46 The High Court adopted a similar approach in R (on the application of Fawcett Society) v Chancellor of the Exchequer and ors 2010 EWHC 3522, QBD, a case involving a high-profile challenge by the Fawcett Society to the Government's

1380

2010 Budget. The Society argued that the Government had failed to comply with the gender equality duty in S.76A SDA in setting the Budget, in that it had failed to have due regard to the need to eliminate discrimination and promote equality of opportunity between men and women. However, the High Court held that it was perfectly sensible for the Government to wait until policy was adequately formulated for there to be a clear basis on which its gender equality impact could be assessed. In two areas, however, the Government admitted that it ought to have carried out a gender equality impact assessment at an earlier stage than it did.

Sufficient information

The duty to have due regard requires public authorities to be sufficiently informed before taking a decision. If the relevant material is not available, there is a duty to acquire it and this may mean that further consultation with appropriate groups is required. In R (on the application of Brown) v Secretary of State for Work and Pensions and anor 2008 EWHC 3158, QBD, in the context of complying with the disability equality duty under S.49A DDA, the Court considered that a public authority would 'have to have due regard to the need to take steps to gather relevant information in order that it can properly take steps to take into account disabled persons' disabilities'. The degree of pro-activity required in gathering information will depend on the circumstances: in Pieretti v London Borough of Enfield 2010 EWCA Civ 1104, CA, the Court of Appeal acknowledged that a disabled person may not be 'adept at proclaiming his disability'. On the facts of that case, the Court held that if some feature of the evidence raised a real possibility that the person subject to a potential decision was disabled such as to affect the decision, further inquiry should be made. However, as the High Court pointed out in R (on the application of Hurley and anor) v Secretary of State for Business, Innovation and Skills 2012 EWHC 201, QBD, 'none of this is necessary if the public body properly considers that it can exercise its duty with the material it has'.

Public bodies subject to the specific public sector equality duties are required to publish equality-related information to demonstrate their compliance with the general duty – see Chapter 39, 'Specific public sector equality duties', under 'Publication of information'. However, whether or not a public body is subject to this specific duty, it will still need to gather and take into consideration information about who is going to be affected by potential decisions if it is properly to comply with the general duty, ensuring that the information is sufficient to enable it to assess the impact on people with different protected characteristics and the relations between them. If there is evidence of possible negative impact, the public body can then give proper consideration to the extent, nature and duration of the potential impact, and whether this can be eliminated, mitigated or justified. Although public bodies are no longer required to undertake formal equality impact assessments, under either the general or specific duties, they should consider whether that or another means of gathering information is appropriate when a proposed decision or policy may have an impact on equality – see the Brown case (above).

38.48 However, there is a limit to the level of investigation required. As the Court of Appeal has pointed out, public authorities are not required to undertake highly forensic analyses – R (on the application of Bailey and ors) v London Borough of Brent Council and another case 2011 EWCA Civ 1586, CA. What is needed is *sufficient* information about the likely impact of their decisions to enable public authorities to comply with their duty – Child Poverty Action Group v Secretary of State for Work and Pensions 2011 EWHC 2616, QBD. In R (on the application of Rahman) v Birmingham City Council 2011 EWHC 944, QBD, a Council's information was found to be insufficient to enable it to have due regard to the equality aims in deciding to terminate funding for legal advice services. The High Court criticised the Council's impact assessment for being 'driven by the hopes of the advantages to be derived from a new policy rather than focusing upon the assessment of the degree of disadvantage to existing users of terminating funding arrangements until new arrangements [could] be put in place'.

In this respect, note that *consultations* also need to be sufficient in order to ensure the sufficiency of information gathered through them: in R (on the application of JM and anor) v Isle of Wight Council 2011 EWHC 2911, QBD, the High Court held that a consultation document provided insufficient information to allow those consulted to give intelligent consideration to the proposals and to provide an intelligent response, in that, for example, it did not give information about the effect of the changes on disabled people, the costs and potential savings, the numbers of people likely to be affected or the nature of the services that would or would not be included in the revised criteria. Because of the deficiencies in the consultation process, Council members were deprived of important information as to the potential impact of the proposed changes, which meant that they had insufficient information when they were discharging their disability equality duty.

38.49 Record-keeping
The general equality duty does not require decisions to be documented. A breach of the duty will not necessarily be inferred from a failure to keep records – R (on the application of McDonald) v Royal Borough of Kensington and Chelsea 2011 UKSC 33, SC. Nevertheless, it is clearly good practice for a public body to keep records of its consideration of the general duty's aims, as this will enable it to provide evidence of its consideration of the duty in the course of exercising its functions. This is the sixth of the general principles put forward by Scott Baker LJ in R (on the application of Brown) v Secretary of State for Work and Pensions and anor 2008 EWHC 3158, QBD: 'Proper

record-keeping encourages transparency and will discipline those carrying out the relevant function to undertake their disability equality duties conscientiously.'

Local authority contracts

38.50

Section 17 of the Local Government Act 1988 prohibits local authorities and other specified public authorities from taking into account non-commercial matters when entering into public supply or works contracts. This was amended by the EqA to specify that it does not prevent those authorities from taking into account non-commercial matters to the extent that they consider it necessary or expedient to do so to enable or facilitate compliance with the general or specific public sector equality duties – S.17(10).

Who is subject to the general duty?

38.51

The general equality duty applies, primarily, to public authorities – S.149(1) EqA. A person or body is a 'public authority' for this purpose if it is listed in Schedule 19 to the Act – S.150(1). Part 1 of the Schedule sets out the 'general' public authorities. These include:

- ministers and government departments (other than the Security Service, Secret Intelligence Service or Government Communications Headquarters (GCHQ))
- the armed forces (except for any part required to assist GCHQ)
- certain broadcasting corporations
- the EHRC and the Information Commissioner
- various court and legal services
- the Crown Prosecution Service and other criminal justice services
- environment, housing and development agencies
- NHS trusts and other bodies involved in the provision of health and social care and social security
- various industry and business bodies including Acas and the Bank of England
- local government authorities
- other educational bodies
- Parliamentary and devolved bodies
- police authorities
- regulators, and
- the Office for Budget Responsibility.

Parts 2 and 3 list the relevant Welsh and Scottish authorities respectively. Part 4 lists cross-border authorities. Currently there are four listed, which are exclusively cross-border Welsh authorities such as the Environment Agency and NHS Blood and Transplant.

38.52 The other group of persons subject to the general duty consists of those who are not public authorities, but who exercise 'public functions' – S.149(2) EqA. These bodies are subject to the duty in respect of the exercise of those functions only. The question of which bodies exercise public functions within the meaning of S.149(2) is discussed under 'Bodies carrying out public functions' below.

Section 151(1) EqA confers on Ministers of the Crown the power to amend Schedule 19 in order to specify other bodies to which the equality duty applies. This power is subject to a duty to consult the EHRC, the Welsh Ministers or the Scottish Ministers as relevant, according to the provisions set out in S.152(1). Similarly, the Welsh and Scottish Ministers are empowered by S.151(2) and (3) to amend Schedule 19 Parts 2 and 3, as relevant, but must obtain the consent of a Minister of the Crown and consult the EHRC before making an order for amendment – Ss.152(2) and (3). However, persons may only be added to the list in Schedule 19 if the minister making the order considers that they exercise at least one public function – S.151(8). Nor may Schedule 19 be amended to apply the duty to certain of the public bodies or functions expressly excluded from the application of the public sector equality duty by Schedule 18. These include the exercise of judicial functions, Parliament, the Scottish Parliament, the National Assembly for Wales and the General Synod – S.151(9) (see 'Exceptions' below).

38.53 **A non-delegable duty**
The question arises as to whether the duty continues to apply to a public authority in respect of functions it has outsourced or contracted out to a different provider. The law is clear that the duty does continue to apply in full to the public authority. S.150(3) EqA provides that a public authority named in Schedule 19 is subject to the equality duty in respect of *all* of its functions, subject to the limited exceptions in Schedule 18 (discussed under 'Exceptions' below), and unless it is listed in Schedule 19 as being subject to the duty in respect of certain functions only, in which case the duty applies only in respect of the exercise of those functions (see 'Certain specified functions' below) – S.150(4). Thus, while an authority may choose to delegate some of its functions, it may not delegate or subcontract its duty under S.149.

This raises implications for outsourcing and public procurement processes. The contracting public authority will need to ensure that the contractor applies the duty. In R (on the application of Brown) v Secretary of State for Work and Pensions and anor 2008 EWHC 3158, QBD, a case on the disability equality duty in S.49A DDA, the High Court stressed that the duty is non-delegable and always remains on the public authority charged with it, even where the authority delegates the performance of a policy or programme that it has promulgated (this was the fourth general principle expounded by Lord Justice Scott Baker). However, the Court noted that the nature of what the public authority has to do to fulfil its duty may well change in such situations. It held that where another body is charged with fulfilling in practice a policy promulgated by a public authority, the duty to have 'due regard' to the needs identified will only be fulfilled by the public authority if:

- it appoints a third party that is *capable* of fulfilling the general duty and is *willing* to do so; and

- it maintains *proper supervision* of the third party to ensure it carries out its duty.

In this regard, the EHRC provides some practical guidance on procurement **38.54** and commissioning for public authorities. In 'The essential guide to the public sector equality duty' (January 2012) it advises authorities to consider the extent to which equality considerations are relevant and proportionate to the subject matter of the contract, and to build such considerations into the appropriate stages of the procurement process. Where an external body undertakes public functions, it should be reminded of its responsibilities under the general equality duty. The guide suggests including conditions in the contract that prohibit the contractor from unlawfully discriminating under the EqA and require it to take all reasonable steps to ensure that staff, suppliers and subcontractors meet their obligations under the Act.

It is worth noting, however, that public contracts should not be awarded on the basis of equality-related criteria to the extent that public authorities thereby find themselves in breach of other relevant legislation. Reg 30 of the Public Contracts Regulations 2006 SI 2006/5 specifies that public contracts be awarded on the basis of economic advantage or lowest price.

Note that a private or voluntary-sector body which provides a public service on **38.55** behalf of a public authority will *also* become subject to the equality duty – see 'Bodies carrying out public functions' below. Conversely, if the contracted-out service is not a public function, the public authority is the only party subject to the duty. While (as emphasised above) the public authority remains subject to the duty in either situation, the nature of the duty will differ if the contractor is also personally subject to it. For example, where public functions are contracted out, the procuring public authority will go some way towards meeting the duty to which it is subject by reminding the contractor of his own responsibilities. Where, on the other hand, the duty does not directly apply to the contractor, the procuring public authority may need to include obligations relating to equality in the contract in order to comply with its own obligations.

1385

38.56 **Overseas outsourcing.** Note that where a public authority outsources its functions overseas, it still remains subject to the equality duty in respect of those functions. In the Public Bill Committee on the Equality Bill in the House of Commons, the Solicitor-General noted: 'In such cases, we would have to ensure that public bodies used their procurement processes to ensure that anything outsourced abroad was subject to strict contractual terms that required the delivery of equalities, and that would be enforceable on a contractual basis, even though we are talking about things across the sea' (Hansard, HC Public Bill Committee, 15th Sitting, col.550 (30 June 2009)).

38.57 **Certain specified functions**

A public authority named in Schedule 19 to the EqA is subject to the equality duty in respect of all of its functions unless it is listed in respect of certain functions only – S.150(3). If that is the case, then the duty applies to the exercise of those specified functions only – S.150(4). These public authorities are:

- BBC, Channel Four Television Corporation and Welsh Authority – the duty does not apply, inter alia, in respect of functions relating to the provision of a content service

- Health Service Commissioner for England – the duty applies only in respect of specified statutory functions and its public procurement functions

- Bank of England – the duty applies only in respect of its public functions

- Common Council of the City of London – the duty applies to it in its capacity as a local authority or port health authority, and as a police authority

- Sub-Treasurer of the Inner Temple or Under-Treasurer of the Middle Temple – the duty applies to that person in his or her capacity as a local authority

- a Local Commissioner in England – the duty applies only in respect of specified statutory functions and public procurement functions

- Parliamentary Commissioner for Administration – the duty applies only in respect of specified statutory functions and public procurement functions

- most of the regulators, including the General Council of the Bar, the General Dental Council, the General Medical Council, and the Law Society of England and Wales – the duty applies only in respect of their public functions.

38.58 Thus, functions of such bodies that fall outside those specified areas will not be subject to the general duty. To take as an example the Common Council of the City of London, there are few such excluded functions. The Council qualifies as an 'English local authority' by virtue of S.162(6) of the Education and Inspections Act 2006 and is thus subject to the general equality duty in respect of the educational establishments that it maintains. However, the general duty would not apply to the Council's exercise of its functions in relation to its governance of the independent Christ's Hospital, for example.

Bodies carrying out public functions   38.59

As mentioned above, it is not only public authorities that are subject to the public sector equality duty. The duty is also imposed on persons, not being public authorities, as and when they exercise 'public functions' – S.149(2) EqA. This potentially covers both private and voluntary sector providers.

In this context, a 'public function' is defined by S.150(5) as 'a function of a public nature for the purposes of the Human Rights Act 1998'. The Human Rights Act 1998 (HRA) does not itself define a public function, although it provides that 'public authority' includes 'any person certain of whose functions are functions of a public nature' – S.6(3)(b) HRA – and that such a person is not to be considered a 'public authority' in relation to an act that is of a private nature – S.6(5). Ultimately, whether or not a public function is being exercised will be a matter for the courts to decide. The question of what amounts to a public authority for the purposes of the HRA has received an enormous amount of judicial and academic attention, and the case law decided under it will also be germane to the interpretation of S.149(2) EqA. A number of factors are likely to be relevant to the question of whether a function is a public function within the meaning of S.149(2). These will include whether the function is publicly funded; whether it involves the exercise of statutory powers; and whether it is taking the place of central or local government, or is offered as an alternative to a government service. Other factors include whether its structures and work are closely linked with the delegating state body.

In this regard, we know, for example, that the HRA has been interpreted as   38.60
applying to the privatised utilities companies in so far as they exercise public utility functions, which means that they will therefore be regarded as exercising public functions for the purposes of S.149(2) EqA, and, as such, will be required to comply with the public sector equality duty in relation to the exercise of those functions. However, the meaning of 'public function' for the purposes of the HRA has been restrictively interpreted elsewhere. In YL v Birmingham City Council and ors 2007 UKHL 27, HL, in a judgment from which two of their Lordships dissented, the House of Lords held that the provision of care and accommodation by a private company under a commercial contract with a local authority (as opposed to by public subsidy), to enable the authority to fulfil its statutory duties, was not an inherently public function and fell outside S.6(3)(b) HRA.

Note that where a private person exercises a public function, it is only in respect of the exercise of that function that it will be subject to the equality duty – S.149(2) EqA. The duty does not apply to its non-public functions. This is also made explicit for some of the public authorities listed in Schedule 19 – for example, the Bank of England and various professional regulatory bodies – which have a dual role.

38.61 In 'The essential guide to the public sector equality duty' (January 2012) the EHRC gives the following additional example of a dual-function body:

- a private company running a prison on behalf of the government. The company would be covered by the general equality duty with regard to its public functions, but not with regard to other work, such as providing security services for a supermarket.

38.62 **Employment functions.** While public authorities are, subject to limited exceptions, covered by the general equality duty in respect of all their functions, including employment-related functions, it may be unclear whether non-public bodies exercising public functions are covered by the duty in the employment context. A proposed amendment to the Equality Bill would have created an exception 'in relation to matters of employment' to the application of the duty to non-public bodies exercising public functions. In response, in the Public Bill Committee in the House of Commons, the Solicitor-General noted: 'It seems to us that employment is part and parcel of the way in which public functions are delivered, because it is difficult to deliver that if one cannot consider the technical abilities of the people one employs to do it. How could a private contractor be required to make arrangements for advancing equality in all the aspects of running a prison but not in relation to the people it employs or how it employs them? Employment functions have not been excluded from the current duties' (Hansard, HC Public Bill Committee, 15th Sitting, col.550 (30 June 2009)). The employment policies and decisions of a contractor carrying out public functions may thus be caught by the duty, if there is sufficient connection between those employment matters and the delivery of the public service.

38.63 **Territorial jurisdiction.** We have already mentioned (in the section 'Who is subject to the general duty?', under 'A non-delegable duty – overseas outsourcing' above) the phenomenon of certain 'back-office' functions being delegated by public authorities to overseas contractors. This raises the question of whether such overseas contractors are covered by the duty. Clearly, if the outsourced functions are not 'public functions' within the meaning of the EqA – and few are likely to be – they will not be covered by S.149. In the unlikely event that a public function is carried out by an overseas company, then the question of the territorial jurisdiction of Part 11, Chapter 1 of the EqA would come into play. In this regard, in the Public Bill Committee on the Equality Bill in the House of Commons, the Solicitor-General asserted: 'The duty will, of course, only impact on bodies carrying out public functions within Great Britain' (Hansard, HC Public Bill Committee, 15th Sitting, col.550 (30 June 2009)). A full examination of the territorial aspects of public law is outside the scope of this chapter, but see Chapter 34, 'Enforcing individual rights', under

'Jurisdiction of tribunals – territorial jurisdiction', for a discussion of the territorial scope of the EqA in respect of individual civil claims.

Exceptions   38.64

Schedule 18 to the EqA (which is given effect by S.149(9)) sets out a number of exceptions to the application of the public sector equality duty. Para 1 of Schedule 18 disapplies the duty in respect of age to functions relating to the provision of education to pupils in schools; benefits, facilities or services to pupils in schools; and accommodation, benefits, facilities or services in relation to children's homes or other accommodation. This means, for example, that schools will not have to consider advancing equality between pupils of different ages. However, they will still need to have due regard to the need to eliminate discrimination, advance equality of opportunity, and foster good relations between pupils in respect of the other protected characteristics; and, as age is not disapplied in the context of work, it continues to be a relevant protected characteristic with regard to staff working at schools and children's homes.

Paragraph 2 of Schedule 18 to the EqA stipulates that the second aim of the general equality duty, which requires a public body to have regard to the need to advance equality of opportunity (S.149(1)(b)), does not apply in relation to the exercise of immigration and nationality functions to the protected characteristics of age, race (meaning, for this purpose, only nationality or ethnic or national origins) or religion or belief.

Schedule 18 also provides that S.149 does not apply to the exercise of a judicial   38.65 function, or to functions exercised on behalf of, or on the instructions of, a person exercising a judicial function – para 3, Sch 18.

Finally, para 4 of Schedule 18 contains certain exemptions from S.149(2). It exempts from the general equality duty specified bodies which are not public authorities but would otherwise be caught by the general duty in their exercise of public functions. These specified bodies are the House of Commons, the House of Lords, the Scottish Parliament, the National Assembly for Wales, the General Synod of the Church of England, the Security Service, the Secret Intelligence Service, the Government Communications Headquarters (GCHQ), and any part of the armed forces assisting GCHQ. Para 4 also exempts specified related functions from S.149(2), being functions in connection with proceedings in the House of Commons or the House of Lords; in the Scottish Parliament (other than a function of the Scottish Parliamentary Corporate Body); and in the National Assembly for Wales (other than a function of the Assembly Commission) – para 4(3).

Paragraph 5 of Schedule 18 gives Ministers of the Crown power to amend the   38.66 Schedule, so as to add, vary or omit an exception to S.149. However, this power is limited by para 5(2) to the effect that judicial functions and parliamentary proceedings can never be made subject to the general equality duty.

38.67 Enforcement

A failure to comply with the general or specific public sector equality duties does not confer any cause of action under private law – S.156 EqA. Thus, employees cannot bring claims in an employment tribunal alleging discrimination on the basis of a breach of the general equality duty. The Explanatory Notes to the Act state that the duties are, however, enforceable by way of judicial review (para 507) – see 'Judicial review' below.

38.68 Background to discrimination claim

Although a breach of S.149 EqA does not in itself confer a cause of action at private law, it is arguable that a failure to comply with the duty may form part of the evidential background to a discrimination claim under the Act. This is most likely to be relevant with respect to the question of whether a public body can justify, under S.19(2)(d) EqA, a policy that is potentially indirectly discriminatory (see Chapter 17, 'Indirect discrimination: objective justification').

This was considered in G v Head Teacher and Governors of St Gregory's Catholic Science College 2011 EWHC 1452, QBD. In that case, the High Court ruled that it was indirect race discrimination for a school to impose a policy which prevented a boy of African-Caribbean ethnicity from having his hair in cornrows. The school sought to justify the policy, which it alleged was imposed to prevent gang culture infiltrating the school. Mr Justice Collins, giving the judgment of the High Court, noted that the purpose of the duty is 'to require public bodies to whom it applies to give advance consideration to issues of race discrimination before making any policy decision that may be affected by them'. He quoted Lady Justice Arden in R (on the application of Elias) v Secretary of State for Defence and anor 2006 IRLR 934, CA, where she talked about the race equality duty under S.71 RRA as 'an integral and important part of the mechanisms for ensuring the fulfilment of the aims of anti-discrimination legislation'. In the same case, Lord Justice Mummery considered that the employer's failure to perform that duty added to his difficulties in attempting to justify an act of discrimination committed in carrying out his functions: 'He has to justify something which he did not even consider required any justification. In these circumstances the court should consider with great care the ex post facto justifications advanced at the hearing.' However, in G's case, Collins J observed that although the equality duty was not fulfilled, that did not of itself mean that the policy was not a proportionate means of achieving a legitimate aim.

38.69 Formal assessments by the EHRC

Sections 31 and 32 EqA 2006 confer on the EHRC two specific powers of enforcement in respect of the public sector equality duty – a power of assessment and a power to issue compliance notices. These are discussed in

1390

Chapter 37, 'Equality and Human Rights Commission', under 'Enforcement – enforcing public sector duties'.

Judicial review

38.70

Public law regulates the exercise of statutory powers by public bodies, and the equality duty is enforceable under public law by way of judicial review. Any individual or group of people with an interest may make an application for judicial review, although S.30 EqA 2006 gives the EHRC specific capacity to institute or intervene in judicial review or other legal proceedings where the proceedings are relevant to any of its functions, subject to any limitations imposed under legislation or by rules of court – S.30(1) and (4)(b).

Judicial review proceedings are governed by Part 54 of the Civil Procedure Rules. Application is made to the Administrative Court, a division of the High Court, usually at the Royal Courts of Justice in London or at the Law Courts in Cardiff. There are commonly three grounds on which it is appropriate for a party to challenge a public body's action by way of judicial review, as categorised by the House of Lords in Council of Civil Service Unions and ors v Minister for the Civil Service 1985 ICR 14, HL: 'illegality', 'irrationality' and 'procedural impropriety'. Judicial review is concerned not with the merits of a decision, but with whether the public body has acted lawfully.

Remedies. Under rule 54.2 of the Civil Procedure Rules, specified remedies are available on a successful application for judicial review. These are: **38.71**

- a mandatory order (formerly known as 'mandamus') requiring the public body to carry out its legal duties

- a prohibiting order, restraining the public body from acting beyond its powers, and

- a quashing order (formerly 'certiorari'), quashing the decision of the public body.

In addition, under rule 54.3 applicants may claim a declaration of rights as they may under private law. An award of damages can – rarely – also be made, but judicial review should not be used if damages are the only remedy being sought – see rule 54.3(2).

Note that the remedies available under judicial review are discretionary. Usually **38.72** in applications related to the public sector equality duty the applicants will be seeking a quashing order, revoking the relevant decision on the ground that the public body did not comply with the equality duty in making it. The public body would then have to make the decision again, but with due regard to the equality aims. However, a Court will consider whether it would be proportionate to grant such an order. In R (on the application of Hurley and anor) v Secretary of State for Business, Innovation and Skills 2012 EWHC 201, QBD, the High

1391

Court refused to quash regulations increasing university tuition fees, despite having found that the Secretary of State had breached his equality duties. The Court emphasised that 'administrative chaos' and 'significant economic implications' would not, of themselves, 'begin to justify a refusal to quash the orders if the breach was sufficiently significant'. However, in that case it was not appropriate to quash the orders given that there was very substantial compliance with the duties and an adequate analysis of the implications on protected groups of the fee structure which was the main object of the challenge.

For further details of judicial review, including the circumstances in which it can arise in relation to discrimination claims, see Chapter 34, 'Enforcing individual rights', under 'Judicial review'.

39 Specific public sector equality duties

Regulatory framework

Scope of the specific duties

Publication of information

Equality objectives

Manner of publication

Who is subject to the specific duties?

Enforcement

The purpose of the specific public sector equality duties, as set out in the **39.1** Explanatory Note to the Equality Act 2010 (Specific Duties) Regulations 2011 SI 2011/2260, is 'to ensure better performance by the public authorities concerned of their duty to have due regard to the matters set out in S.149(1) of the Equality Act 2010'. In other words, the specific public sector equality duties are intended to help those public authorities to which they apply to comply with the general equality duty, discussed in Chapter 38, 'General public sector equality duty'. The specific duties do not replace the general duty: authorities subject to the specific duties must ensure that they comply with the general duty as well. (Stop press: the Government is currently reviewing the operation of the public duty – see Introduction to this Handbook.)

As indicated in Chapter 38, the general duty set out in S.149 of the Equality Act 2010 (EqA) consolidates the pre-existing public sector equality duties on race, gender and disability, while also extending the duty to other protected characteristics. Secondary legislation made under the old equality statutes put certain public authorities under specific duties which were intended to ensure that the respective general equality duties were complied with. For example, the Race Relations Act 1976 (Statutory Duties) Order 2001 SI 2001/3458 required certain public authorities to publish a 'race equality scheme' explaining how they would fulfil their equality duties. The order set out in considerable detail what the scheme had to include by way of arrangements for assessing and consulting on the likely impact of proposed policies on the promotion of race equality, monitoring such policies, publishing results, ensuring public access to information and services, and training staff in relation to the duties. A further specific duty required public bodies to monitor staff and applicants

──**1393**

by racial group, while for public authorities over a certain size these monitoring requirements were more extensive.

39.2 The specific duties under the Equality Act 2010 (Specific Duties) Regulations 2011 SI 2011/2260 are noticeably less prescriptive than their precursors. As we explain under 'Scope of the specific duties' below, the specific public sector equality duties require public authorities to publish equality-related information and objectives, but leave the detail of what this involves up to the public authority. Some concern was expressed that removing the requirement to publish equality schemes would dilute the effect of the specific duties. In consultation, however, the Government indicated its desire to focus on 'outcomes' rather than prescribing 'processes' to avoid placing 'unnecessary burdens' on public services ('Equality Bill: Making it work – Policy proposals for specific duties' (June 2009)). The primary aims of the specific duties are to improve public bodies' focus on the equality aims, and to encourage transparency and accountability.

39.3 **Guidance.** As indicated in the introduction to Chapter 38, 'General public sector equality duty', under 'Code of Practice and guidance', there is no statutory Code of Practice in relation to the public sector equality duty, but the Equality and Human Rights Commission (EHRC) has published extensive non-statutory guidance on the general and specific duties, as it is empowered to do under S.13 of the Equality Act 2006 (EqA 2006). All of this guidance is relevant to enable compliance with the specific duties, but the following three guides are particularly pertinent: 'Equality information and the equality duty: a guide for public authorities' (December 2011); 'Objectives and the equality duty: a guide for public authorities' (December 2011) ('the Objectives Guide'); and 'The essential guide to the public sector equality duty' (January 2012) ('the Essential Guide'). These guides cover England and non-devolved public authorities in Scotland and Wales; separate guidance is available for devolved public authorities in Scotland and in Wales. The Government Equalities Office's 'Equality Act 2010: Specific duties to support the equality duty – What do I need to know? A quick start guide for public sector organisations' (October 2011) ('the GEO's Quick Start Guide') is a useful, briefer guide to the specific duties. We refer to these guides, as appropriate, in the course of this chapter.

39.4 ## Regulatory framework

The Equality Act 2010 (Specific Duties) Regulations 2011 SI 2011/2260, which set out the specific public sector equality duties in England, are made under S.153 EqA. S.153 gives Ministers of the Crown, Welsh Ministers and Scottish Ministers the power to impose specific duties on the public authorities listed in Parts 1, 2 and 3 of Schedule 19 respectively for the purpose of enabling the better performance of the general equality duty. Before such specific duties are imposed, the relevant minister must consult the EHRC – S.153(4).

Section 154 EqA gives power to ministers to impose similar specific duties on certain cross-border authorities listed in Part 4 of Schedule 19. Currently, these cross-border authorities are limited to the Environment Agency, NHS Blood and Transplant, the NHS Business Services Authority, and the Student Loans Company. An alphabetical code next to the names of the authorities in the Schedule, linked to a table in S.154(3), indicates that Ministers of the Crown have the power to impose specific duties on these authorities, and that they must consult Welsh Ministers before making regulations imposing such duties – S.154(2). Ministers must also consult the EHRC – S.154(4).

39.5 The powers in Ss.153 and 154 EqA are supplemented by S.155, which provides that regulations made under S.153 or S.154 may require public authorities to consider matters set out elsewhere from time to time by a minister. The Explanatory Notes to the EqA give the following example:

- a person exercising the power may decide to impose a specific duty that requires specified public bodies to take into account particular national priorities set out in a public service agreement when setting their equality objectives (para 506).

No such duties have as yet been imposed.

Section 155(5) EqA gives ministers power to modify or remove specific duties imposed under S.153 or S.154.

Public procurement

39.6

Section 155 EqA specifies that regulations made under S.153 or S.154 may impose duties on a public authority in connection with its public procurement functions, where the public authority is a contracting authority within the meaning of the EU Public Sector Directive (No.2004/18) – Ss.155(2) and (3). The term 'public procurement' covers buying goods and services from the private sector.

The effect of this provision is that public authorities may be made subject to specific duties in relation to functions that are regulated by the EU public procurement regime, in addition to whatever other specific duties they are under in relation to the public sector equality duty. The Explanatory Notes to the EqA give the following example:

- a person exercising the power may decide to impose a specific duty which requires contracting authorities to set out how they will use their procurement functions to better meet the requirements of the public sector equality duty (para 506).

39.7 No such duties have as yet been imposed. However, the example from the Explanatory Notes given above suggests that advancement of equality in public procurement is in any event likely to be by reference to the general equality duty, rather than by the imposition of extensive independent duties.

1395

It should be noted, too, that regardless of whether any specific procurement-related duties are imposed, public authorities are required to comply with the general public sector equality duty in relation to the commissioning and procurement of services, as these are part of their functions – see Chapter 38, 'General public sector equality duty', under 'Who is subject to the general duty? – a non-delegable duty'.

39.8 Scope of the specific duties

While the general equality duty set out in S.149(1) EqA (and discussed in Chapter 38, 'General public sector equality duty') is the same for England, Scotland and Wales, the specific duties differ between those jurisdictions.

In England, and for non-devolved public authorities in Scotland and Wales, the specific duties are set out in the Equality Act 2010 (Specific Duties) Regulations 2011 SI 2011/2260 ('the Specific Duties Regulations'), which came into force on 10 September 2011. Specific duties for Wales are set out in the Equality Act 2010 (Statutory Duties) (Wales) Regulations 2011 SI 2011/1064, which came into force on 6 April 2011. The Scottish Ministers published the draft Equality Act 2010 (Specific Duties) (Scotland) Regulations 2012 in March 2012, and these are due to come into force on 27 May 2012. Full discussion of the Welsh and Scottish specific duties is outside the scope of this Handbook, but it is notable that both the Welsh and the draft Scottish duties are considerably more prescriptive than those applicable to public authorities in England and to non-devolved public authorities.

In this chapter, we consider the specific duties in the 2011 Regulations applicable in England and to non-devolved public authorities in Scotland and Wales. There are two: the duty to publish equality information, and the duty to set and publish equality objectives.

39.9 Publication of information

The first specific duty is that public authorities to which the Specific Duties Regulations apply (see 'Who is subject to the specific duties?' below) must 'publish information' to demonstrate their compliance with the general duty – Reg 2(1). This information must include, in particular, information relating to:

- its employees who share a relevant protected characteristic (subject to an exemption for small public authorities) – Reg 2(4)(a) (see 'Exemption for small public authorities' and 'What information should be published? – information about employees' below), and

- other persons affected by its policies and practices who share a relevant protected characteristic – Reg 2(4)(b) (see 'What information should be published? – information about people affected by policies and practices' below).

According to the GEO's Quick Start Guide, publishing relevant equality information 'will make public bodies transparent about their decision-making processes, and accountable to their service users. It will give the public the information they need to hold public bodies to account for their performance on equality.' The important point is that publication of information is directed at demonstrating compliance with the general duty: in other words, as the EHRC puts it, 'publishing information is not simply a matter of demonstrating the sufficiency of your equality evidence base. More importantly, it is about demonstrating how you have used your evidence base to have due regard to the aims of the general equality duty (i.e. how you have used it in making a particular decision or in the way you have delivered your work)' ('Equality information and the equality duty: a guide for public authorities' (December 2011)).

Relevant protected characteristic   39.10

As noted above, Reg 2(4) of the Specific Duties Regulations requires a relevant public authority to publish information relating to its employees, and other persons affected by its policies and practices, 'who share a relevant protected characteristic'. The Regulations do not define 'relevant protected characteristic'. However, expressions used in subordinate legislation have the same meaning as in the enabling Act, unless a contrary intention appears – S.11 Interpretation Act 1978. So 'relevant protected characteristic' has the same meaning as it does in S.149(7) EqA in the context of the general equality duty – as to which, see Chapter 38, 'General public sector equality duty', under 'Scope of the general duty – "relevant protected characteristic"'.

Effectively, this means that public authorities are required to publish information in relation to employees and affected persons who share any of the characteristics protected by the EqA, apart from that of marriage and civil partnership, which is not listed in S.149(7) as a 'relevant protected characteristic'. The practical effect is that it is unnecessary to publish information on marriage or civil partnership status, or to include questions on it in monitoring surveys, for the purpose of complying with the specific or general duties.

Exemption for small public authorities   39.11

Public authorities with fewer than 150 employees are exempted from the requirement in Reg 2(4)(a) to publish information relating to employees who share a relevant protected characteristic – Reg 2(5). However, the EHRC notes in the Essential Guide that such public authorities 'may still need to collect workforce information to be able to understand the impact of their policies and practices on their workforce. They may also need to publish some information about the impact of their employment functions on people with the different

1397

protected characteristics in order to demonstrate compliance with the general equality duty.' This might include, for example, an assessment of the impact on equality of the public body's recruitment procedures.

39.12 What information should be published?

The Specific Duties Regulations provide little guidance as to the content of the information which should be published, beyond the requirements set out under 'Publication of information' above to include information relating to employees and other affected persons who share a relevant protected characteristic (see further under 'Information about employees' and 'Information about people affected by policies and practices' below). Authorities concerned as to what information should be published may find it helpful to remember that the purpose of the specific duties is to enable compliance with the general duty, so information to assist compliance and to demonstrate that it has fulfilled its duty is likely to be the kind of information that it should publish under Reg 2.

The GEO's Quick Start Guide says that public bodies must publish information 'to show that they consciously thought about the three aims of the equality duty as part of the process of decision-making'. It suggests that for most public bodies, it will be sensible to start by looking at what equality information they publish already, and 'consider whether that gives a reasonable picture of progress on equality issues affecting its employees and service users'.

39.13 In the Essential Guide the EHRC suggests that the information to be published will usually fall into two main categories:

- *information to identify equality issues* (such as equality monitoring information about employees or service users, or information about the effect of activities on people with different protected characteristics), and

- *information about steps taken to have due regard to the aims of the general duty* (such as records of applying due regard in making certain decisions, information that was considered in that decision-making, consideration of steps to mitigate adverse impacts, or details of policies to address equality concerns).

39.14 Format. There is no prescribed format for the publication of information: it is up to each public body to decide how to arrange the information it decides to publish, so long as it is 'accessible to the public' – Reg 4(1) (see 'Manner of publication' below). What the Specific Duties Regulations do *not* require is the creation of equality impact assessments, equality schemes or action plans, as were imposed under the old characteristic-specific equality duties. Public bodies may continue to publish information in whatever formats they have been used to, but they will need to ensure that this information demonstrates that they have complied with the current general duty. For example, the public body could include details of any analysis it has carried out on the information it holds when considering a new policy or programme.

Proportionality. Proportionality is a key principle of the EqA. The extent of **39.15** the requirements imposed by the Specific Duties Regulations is intended to vary depending on the size of the public body, the range of functions it performs, and the extent to which those functions could affect equality. In the Essential Guide the EHRC suggests, by way of example, that whereas small organisations like primary schools may only need to publish 'a short evidenced account of their equality priorities and work, with an indication of key trends and issues', larger organisations like government departments will need to publish 'a more detailed account of their equality considerations and performance across a wider range of functions'. What is needed is relevant, proportionate information which is broad enough to give a full picture of performance across all the public body's functions, in so far as equality issues are relevant to those functions.

Information about employees. Regulation 2(4)(a) of the Specific Duties **39.16** Regulations requires a relevant public authority to publish information, in particular, relating to its employees who share a relevant protected characteristic (subject to an exemption for small public authorities – see 'Publication of information – exemption for small public authorities' above). The information that different authorities will need to collect to ensure that they have enough evidence to inform their decisions in relation to employment is likely to vary widely between different sectors and organisations. The GEO's Quick Start Guide suggests that this could include information relating to:

- the make-up of the overall workforce
- the gender pay gap and pay equality issues more generally for the public body
- recruitment and retention rates for staff with different protected characteristics
- applications for flexible working and their outcomes for different protected characteristics
- applications for learning and development opportunities and their outcomes for staff with different protected characteristics
- grievances and disciplinary issues for staff with different protected characteristics.

It also suggests that published information could include details of policies and programmes that have been put in place to address equality concerns within the workforce, and information from staff surveys.

The EHRC's list of information about employment it would normally expect to **39.17** see published (taken from 'Equality information and the equality duty: a guide

1399

for public authorities' (December 2011)) is considerably more comprehensive. It suggests the following:

- the race, disability, gender and age distribution of the workforce at different grades, and whether they are full or part time

- an indication of the likely representation on sexual orientation and religion and belief, provided that no one can be identified as a result

- an indication of any issues for transsexual staff, based on engagement with transsexual staff or equality organisations

- gender pay gap information

- information about occupational segregation (that is, staff with certain protected characteristics being over-represented in particular roles; for example, women as cleaners, or at certain grades)

- grievance and dismissal information for people with relevant protected characteristics

- complaints about discrimination and other prohibited conduct from staff

- details and feedback concerning engagement with staff and trade unions

- quantitative and qualitative research with employees, e.g. staff surveys

- records of how authorities have had due regard to the aims of the duty in decision-making with regard to employment, including any assessments of impact on equality and any evidence used, and

- details of policies and programmes that have been put in place to address equality concerns raised by staff and trade unions.

39.18 The guide also suggests that it would be useful to publish disaggregated information on the following matters ('disaggregated' meaning separated out according to protected characteristics):

- return-to-work rates after maternity leave

- success rates of job applicants

- take-up of training opportunities

- applications for promotion and success rates

- applications for flexible working and success rates

- other reasons for termination, like redundancy and retirement

- length of service/time on pay grade, and

- pay gap for other protected groups.

Information about people affected by policies and practices. For the majority **39.19** of public bodies, complying with the equality duty will primarily require consideration not of their decisions and policies in relation to their workforce, but of how their decisions and policies affect members of the public, particularly in terms of service delivery. This important aspect of the general and specific duties is outside the scope of this Handbook. For completeness, however, note that Reg 2(4)(b) requires the published information to include, specifically, information relating to persons other than employees of the public authority who are affected by its policies and practices and who share a relevant protected characteristic. According to the GEO's Quick Start Guide, this could include information relating to:

- the number of people with different protected characteristics who access and use services in different ways

- customer satisfaction levels and informal feedback from service users with different protected characteristics and results of consultations

- complaints about discrimination and complaints from people with different protected characteristics, and

- service outcomes for people with different protected characteristics.

It could also include details of policies and programmes that have been put in place to address equality concerns in service delivery.

Other information. The Quick Start Guide suggests that public bodies may **39.20** also find it helpful to consider what equality information is published by similar bodies; and whether there are any topical equality issues – such as the gender pay gap – that are relevant to their activities, and how these have been considered.

Monitoring. It is evident from the lists of possible information above that, to **39.21** some extent, public authorities will need to monitor their employees in order to gather the appropriate information. Having said that, as the Quick Start Guide notes, 'it will be for individual public bodies to decide whether such information is necessary for them to demonstrate their compliance with the equality duty'.

Monitoring and sensitive information. The Quick Start Guide suggests that **39.22** 'the specific duties do not require public bodies to ask every member of staff about such issues as their age, sexual orientation, or religious beliefs'. Collecting information in relation to some such protected characteristics can be sensitive, so this should only be done where the information is relevant and the public body is sure it will be used appropriately. Referring to national reports, such as those available from the Office for National Statistics, and engaging with equality organisations may be more appropriate than monitoring in some cases. The EHRC's 'Equality information and the equality duty: a guide for public authorities' (December 2011) suggests considering whether the information

1401

needed is already available from other sources; taking account of how its potential accuracy and completeness will affect its usefulness; and considering the process used to gather information and how to ensure the data remains confidential and anonymous.

Further specific advice as to the practicalities of monitoring and appropriate questions is available from the EHRC. Public bodies need to exercise particular caution with regard to asking job applicants disability-related questions. S.60(1) EqA provides that employers must not ask job applicants questions about their health before offering them work. However, this is subject to a number of exceptions, including that such questions can be asked if necessary for the purpose of monitoring diversity among job applicants – S.60(6)(c). Care should be taken that any such disability-related questions are properly directed, and that any information gathered in this way is stored anonymously, without reference to the relevant application forms. See Chapter 24, 'Recruitment', under 'Pre-employment health questions', for a full discussion of S.60.

39.23 Regularity of publication

Public authorities listed in Schedule 1 to the Specific Duties Regulations (see 'Who is subject to the specific duties?' below) were required to publish the relevant information by 31 January 2012, and after that they must publish information at annual intervals beginning with the date of last publication. They may publish information at more frequent intervals if they wish to do so – Reg 2(2).

Public authorities listed in Schedule 2 to the Regulations – effectively, schools and pupil referral units – were required to publish the relevant information by 6 April 2012, and after that they must publish information at annual intervals beginning with the date of last publication. Again, they may publish information at more frequent intervals – Reg 2(3).

39.24 In the Essential Guide the EHRC recommends that although the regulatory requirement is to publish equality information at least annually, 'it is good practice to publish information when it is available to keep it up-to-date'. In this regard, note that there is no requirement that all available information be published in one go: individual sets of information may be released as and when they are ready for publication. If information is published before the deadline, it does not then need to be published again, although its location should be signposted, at least, to ensure that it can be accessed (see 'Manner of publication' below). The GEO's Quick Start Guide suggests that it may be convenient to publish information 'to fit in with planning cycles or to coincide with a particular policy announcement or service change. If information or data sets are incomplete, it may be helpful to publish the information available with an explanation of how the data gap will be filled in future.'

Equality objectives   39.25

The second specific duty is that public authorities to which the Specific Duties Regulations apply must 'prepare and publish one or more objectives' they think they should achieve in order to fulfil any of the three aims of the general duty set out in S.149(1) EqA – Reg 3(1). As discussed in Chapter 38, 'General public sector equality duty', under 'Scope of the general duty', these aims are:

- the elimination of 'discrimination, harassment, victimisation and any other conduct' prohibited by the EqA – S.149(1)(a) EqA

- the advancement of 'equality of opportunity between persons who share a relevant protected characteristic and persons who do not share it' – S.149(1)(b) EqA

- the fostering of 'good relations between persons who share a relevant protected characteristic and persons who do not share it' – S.149(1)(c) EqA.

There is no exemption from this specific duty for small public authorities.

Specific and measurable   39.26
Regulation 3(3) of the Specific Duties Regulations provides that an objective published by a public authority in compliance with Reg 3(1) must be 'specific and measurable'. According to the EHRC's Objectives Guide, 'specific and measurable' objectives are explicit about:

- the policy, function or practice they relate to

- the people that are affected

- the outcome they seek to achieve

- why they have been selected, and

- how success will be measured (e.g. by how much or by how many).

Although not a legislative requirement, the Objectives Guide suggests that objectives should be S.M.A.R.T. (Specific, Measurable, Achievable, Realistic and Time-bound) in order to ensure their effectiveness. An example of a SMART objective, adapted from the Objectives Guide to fit the employment context:

- a police force identifies that the number of white employees achieving promotion is proportionately six times higher than the number of black employees. The police force sets an objective to reduce the difference by at least 50 per cent over the next four-year period.

Some examples of vague, non-SMART objectives drawn from the Objectives **39.27** Guide, which should be avoided in order to ensure compliance with Reg 3(3):

- we will give more attention to gender issues

1403

- we will ensure we meet all our legal obligations relating to equality
- we will continue to train our staff on equality
- we will continue to engage with diverse groups.

39.28 **Regularity of publication**
All public authorities covered by the Regulations, including schools and pupil referral units, were required to publish their objectives by 6 April 2012. Thereafter, they must publish objectives at four-yearly intervals beginning with the date of last publication. They may, however, publish them at more frequent intervals if they wish to do so – Reg 3(2). For example, objectives might be published more frequently where they have shorter timescales for implementation, or to fit in with an organisation's usual planning processes.

39.29 **Setting objectives**
As with publishing information under the first specific duty, the Regulations allow authorities considerable latitude in setting objectives. Aside from the requirement in Reg 3(3) that objectives be specific and measurable (see 'Specific and measurable' above), there are no specific legislative conditions attached to the content of the equality objectives, and nor is any fixed number of objectives required.

Nevertheless, certain essential principles can be established. First, and obviously, as the objectives are meant to assist public bodies to fulfil the three general equality aims set out in S.149(1) EqA, consideration should be given to the aims in setting them. In addition, objective-setters need to ensure that they have regard to the key issues affecting staff with each of the relevant protected characteristics, and that no relevant protected characteristic is overlooked.

39.30 Beyond this, it is important that objectives are developed according to actual and relevant needs. As the Objectives Guide puts it, 'objectives should be based on robust information and evidence of need, rather than merely being a collection of ideas from colleagues across your organisation'. Basing objectives on evidence taken from the equality information published under the first specific duty, and in respect of the public body's functions, should ensure that they are appropriate and relevant.

Interestingly, the Objectives Guide also suggests that 'objectives that are too narrow in scope, or which fail to address the most significant equality issues in your sector and your organisation could potentially leave you open to question by the public or legal challenge by the Commission'. Clearly, objectives that cover an organisation's primary equality challenges are more likely to facilitate improvements in equality and demonstrate to employees and to the public that the organisation in question is fulfilling its general equality duty under S.149(1) EqA. Conversely, a failure to address these

1404

challenges in setting objectives can be seen as evidence of a failure to pay due regard to the need to fulfil the equality aims.

It is also interesting that the EHRC encourages organisations to set targets that **39.31** are ambitious in their scope. If an objective is too narrow, it could indicate that whatever regard is being paid to the need in question is insufficient and therefore does not constitute 'due' regard (see Chapter 38, 'General public sector equality duty', under 'Compliance – "due regard"' for a comprehensive discussion of what this term means). As discussed under 'Achieving objectives' below, there is no automatic penalty for a failure to achieve objectives, so in that sense nothing is lost by making them ambitious. However, we suggest that it would nevertheless be sensible for organisations to adopt objectives that remain within the confines of what is realistically achievable, without sidestepping or minimising the breadth of the equality challenges and issues that they face. In this regard, it may be appropriate to set interim objectives that are achievable but which contribute towards medium and longer term goals.

Proportionality. The objectives set should be proportionate, in terms of **39.32** number and content, to the public body's size, the relevance of equality to its functions, and the evidence that such objectives are needed. The EHRC's Essential Guide suggests that 'larger public authorities like government departments are likely to set a greater number of equality objectives, across a broader range of issues, than a smaller public body with a narrower area of influence, such as a primary school'. When setting objectives, public authorities should consider to what extent a function or policy affects discrimination, equality of opportunity and good relations, and the extent of any disadvantage that needs to be addressed.

Achieving objectives. Notwithstanding the emphasis upon setting and **39.33** publishing objectives in the Regulations, there is no explicit requirement that public authorities actually achieve them, and no set punishment for a failure to do so. The primary aim of this specific duty is to focus the public authority's corporate mind on the equality challenges which it faces; to demonstrate compliance with the general equality duty and further progress towards achieving the equality aims; and to assist staff and the public to assess its equality performance. Nevertheless, the progress made towards its objectives is of course likely to be an important piece of evidence to demonstrate compliance with the general equality duty. Substantial or repeated failures to achieve set objectives could lead to reduced morale or lack of confidence on the part of a body's staff and stakeholders, and even lead to intervention by the EHRC. See 'Enforcement' below and Chapter 37, 'Equality and Human Rights Commission', under 'Enforcement – enforcing public sector duties', for a summary of the EHRC's powers to conduct assessments and issue compliance notices with regard to the specific duties.

39.34 # Manner of publication

Public authorities subject to the specific duties have considerable latitude with respect to how they are to publish the required information and objectives. The only legislative requirement is that publication 'in such a manner that the information is accessible to the public' – Reg 4(1) Specific Duties Regulations. Publication could be on a dedicated page on the authority's website, for example.

Regulation 4(2) clarifies that a public authority may publish the information and/or objectives within another published document. For example, equality information and objectives could be included in an annual report or business plan.

39.35 Although Reg 4(1) simply states that the information must be published in such a manner that it is publicly 'accessible', the GEO's Quick Start Guide states that information must be published in a way 'which makes it *easy* for people to access it' (our emphasis). It suggests:

> 'Public bodies should publish information in a place and format that is easy to access for both internal and external users. If some information is published periodically over the year, public bodies may want to consider how to link to all the relevant information together... In addition to publishing [information and objectives] electronically on their website, they should consider making them available in other formats. They should also consider whether the information is provided in a way which makes it easy for the public to understand and use, to enable public accountability... [I]nformation should be easily found; published as quickly as possible after its collection; be as detailed as possible; and be freely available for re-use by the public.'

This is also the interpretation adopted by the EHRC. The Essential Guide emphasises that 'it will be easier for you to demonstrate compliance with the specific duties if your information is clearly labelled, easy to find, and in one place on your website'. It suggests as a minimum standard that public bodies publish their objectives in PDF and in Word on their websites. While acknowledging that the specific duties do not require background information, 'your objectives are likely to be more transparent and easy to understand if you publish a short narrative to introduce them, setting out what information (including engagement) you used to reach your decisions and what you hope to achieve through them'.

39.36 It is debatable whether the Regulations require information and objectives to be readily accessible, as opposed to simply being able to be accessed by the public. Nevertheless, it is certainly good practice to follow the EHRC's advice in this regard, and would assist an authority to demonstrate compliance and

1406

ensure the published information is kept up to date and renewed at the required minimum intervals.

Furthermore, public authorities need to ensure that they comply with the duty to make reasonable adjustments for disabled people in considering how to make their published information accessible, and should consider producing information in alternative formats where relevant. S.20(6) EqA specifies that, in relation to the provision of information under the reasonable adjustments duty, the steps which it is reasonable to have to take include steps for ensuring that information is provided 'in an accessible format'. For a full discussion of the duty to make reasonable adjustments, see Chapter 21, 'Failure to make reasonable adjustments', and, with specific regard to S.20(6), under 'Duty to make reasonable adjustments – requirement for information to be in an accessible format'.

Data protection issues   39.37

It is important to note that the EqA is not the only piece of legislation to regulate the publication of information. When processing and publishing equality information, the privacy and compliance implications of the Data Protection Act 1998 must be taken into account. For information on the Act's requirements, see IDS Employment Law Supplement, 'Data Protection Act 1998' (2000), and the website of the Information Commissioner's Office.

The EHRC's 'Equality information and the equality duty: a guide for public authorities' (December 2011) advises that 'where the number of staff or service users with a particular protected characteristic is fewer than ten, and the information is "sensitive personal information" that might lead to individuals being identified, it is good practice to replace the number with an asterisk. Where you do this, check that it is not possible to work out this missing data from the other information that you publish. Other ways to prevent individuals from being identified include, for example, using ranges or bands, or by disaggregating your published information less.'

Who is subject to the specific duties?   39.38

The public authorities subject to the specific duties are set out in Schedules 1 and 2 to the Specific Duties Regulations. They include most public bodies in England, most of those operating across Great Britain, such as government departments (except in relation to devolved functions), and a small number of cross-border bodies. The few public authorities not specifically listed are not subject to the specific duties, although if listed in Schedule 19 to the EqA they will be subject to the general equality duty.

Schedule 1 to the Regulations contains a long list of public authorities, including the following:

- the armed forces (other than any part of the armed forces which is required to assist the Government Communications Headquarters (GCHQ))

- the BBC, Channel Four Television Corporation and Welsh Authority (except in respect of functions relating to the provision of a 'content service')

- the EHRC and the Information Commissioner

- court and legal services, such as the Legal Services Board and Legal Services Commission

- bodies responsible for criminal justice, such as HM Chief Inspector of Constabulary and HM Chief Inspector of the Crown Prosecution Service

- authorities responsible for environment, housing and development, such as the Environment Agency and the Homes and Communities Agency

- bodies concerned with health, social care and social security, such as the Care Quality Commission, the Child Maintenance and Enforcement Commission, NHS trusts and primary care trusts

- industry/business-related authorities, such as Acas, the Bank of England (in respect of its public functions), the Civil Aviation Authority, the Financial Services Authority and the National Audit Office

- local government authorities, including county councils and district councils, the Greater London Authority, London borough councils, the London Development Agency, fire and rescue authorities, National Park authorities, Passenger Transport Executives and regional development agencies

- Ministers of the Crown and government departments (other than the Security Service, the Secret Intelligence Service or GCHQ)

- the governing bodies of further and higher education institutions, the Higher Education Funding Council for England and the Student Loans Company

- the National Assembly for Wales Commission and the Scottish Parliamentary Corporate Body

- police-related bodies including the British Transport Police Force, the Independent Police Complaints Commission, police authorities and the Serious Organised Crime Agency, and

- the General Council of the Bar (in respect of its public functions), the Health and Safety Executive, and the Law Society of England and Wales (in respect of its public functions).

39.39 Note that some of the authorities listed above are covered by the specific duties in respect of specified functions only. The specified functions of those particular authorities correspond to those covered by the general equality duty, which are listed in Chapter 38, 'General public sector equality duty', under 'Who is

1408

subject to the general duty? – certain specified functions'. With respect to the specific duties, these public authorities are:

- BBC, Channel Four Television Corporation and Welsh Authority – the duty does not apply, inter alia, in respect of functions relating to the provision of a content service

- Bank of England – the duty applies only in respect of its public functions

- Common Council of the City of London – the duty applies to it in its capacity as a local authority or port health authority, and as a police authority

- the General Council of the Bar and the Law Society of England and Wales – the duty applies only in respect of their public functions.

Schedule 2 to the Specific Duties Regulations covers schools: namely, the governing bodies of English local authority-maintained educational establishments; local authorities with respect to the pupil referral units they establish and maintain; and the proprietors of City Technology Colleges, City Colleges for Technology or the Arts, and Academies. **39.40**

Whereas the general duty applies to non-public bodies exercising 'public functions' (see Chapter 38, 'General public sector equality duty', under 'Who is subject to the general duty? – bodies carrying out public functions'), the specific duties do not.

As noted under 'Scope of the specific duties' above, separate specific duties apply under different secondary legislation to certain Welsh and Scottish public bodies.

Enforcement
39.41

As with the general public sector equality duty, S.156 EqA clarifies that a breach of the specific duties gives rise to no cause of action under private law. No other sanction is specified in the legislation. It is, however, clear that the EHRC has powers of assessment and powers to issue compliance notices in relation to the specific duties just as it has in relation to the general duty – see Chapter 38, 'General public sector equality duty', under 'Enforcement – formal assessments by the EHRC', and, more particularly, Chapter 37, 'Equality and Human Rights Commission', under 'Enforcement – enforcing public sector duties'.

Judicial review
39.42
There is some confusion with respect to the position regarding judicial review of compliance with the specific public sector equality duties. The Explanatory Notes to S.156 EqA state: 'This section is designed to make it clear that the duties imposed by or under Chapter 1 of Part 11 do not create any private law rights for individuals. These duties are, however, enforceable by way of judicial

1409

review' (para 507). Thus, so far as the Explanatory Notes are concerned, the specific duties are amenable to judicial review.

However, the GEO's Quick Start Guide states, without further explanation: 'Unlike the [general] equality duty, the specific duties cannot be enforced by judicial review.' This is an interesting discrepancy, given that both the Explanatory Notes and the Quick Start Guide are Government publications. The answer is probably that a stand-alone application for judicial review of the specific duties is unlikely to be made: they are ancillary to the general duty and fulfilment of the specific duties is intended to encourage and demonstrate compliance with the general duty. A failure to publish the requisite information or objectives when required is unlikely to be of sufficient gravity to merit a judicial review application. However, we suggest that if a public body breaches those specific duties, and subsequently makes a decision that is perceived to be in breach of the general duty to have due regard to the equality aims, the failure to comply with the specific duties is likely to form an important part of the case against the public body upon judicial review.

40 Socio-economic duty

In an attempt to address the inequality that arises from a person's social class **40.1** or family background, the previous Labour Government introduced a 'socio-economic duty'. The provisions setting out this duty form Part 1 of the Equality Act 2010 (EqA), and require certain public bodies to consider socio-economic disadvantage when deciding how to exercise their functions. The Explanatory Notes to the EqA state that the duty requires those public bodies, 'when making strategic decisions such as deciding priorities and setting objectives, to consider how their decisions might help to reduce the inequalities associated with socio-economic disadvantage' (para 23). *The socio-economic duty has, however, never been implemented.* The current Coalition Government has indicated that it will not bring the duty into effect, and until such time as it is brought into force, for practical purposes it can effectively be ignored. Nevertheless, in the awareness that political administrations change, we provide a brief outline of the duty in this chapter. (Stop press: the Government has announced its intention to repeal the socio-economic duty – see Introduction to this Handbook.)

The socio-economic duty is similar to the general public sector equality duty explained in Chapter 38, but is more specific and therefore limited in scope. While the general equality duty applies in relation to the exercise of all the functions of a relevant public authority, the socio-economic duty applies only to the strategic decisions of a smaller number of public authorities – see 'Scope of the duty – decisions of a strategic nature' below. It should also be noted that the socio-economic duty applies primarily to strategic matters outside the sphere of employment. However, it is capable of influencing the decisions of relevant public authorities.

Guidance. In January 2010 the Government Equalities Office published a **40.2** 45-page guide – 'The Equality Bill: Duty to reduce socio-economic inequalities' (the 'GEO guide') – explaining the background to the duty and how it might operate for the different types of public body that it covers. While the guide has no legal status, and is no longer available on the Home Office website (although it can be traced on the internet), it is nonetheless a useful source of information

1411

as to how the duty might be expected to operate in practice and how compliance with it would be monitored, if the relevant provisions were brought into force. We refer to the contents of the guide as relevant in the course of this chapter.

40.3 Scope of the duty

The socio-economic duty requires a relevant authority, when 'making decisions of a strategic nature about how to exercise its functions', to 'have due regard to the desirability of exercising them in a way that is designed to reduce the inequalities of outcome which result from socio-economic disadvantage' – S.1(1) EqA.

It should be noted that S.1 does not attempt to introduce a new protected characteristic. It does not make it unlawful to discriminate against someone on the ground that they live in a council house, or were state-educated, or were brought up by a single parent, for example. It is rather a matter of requiring public authorities to consider how they can better target their policies and resources to help those who are socio-economically disadvantaged, in the course of exercising their existing functions on a strategic level.

The wording of this duty introduces a number of concepts that are not defined by the EqA and which require further elaboration. We discuss these below.

40.4 Socio-economic disadvantage

The identification of socio-economic disadvantage is far from straightforward. The GEO guide defines it as 'the state of being disadvantaged in life – in terms of getting on, getting educated, getting a job, etc – by one or more of a range of external factors'. It suggests that of those 'external factors', poverty is the most important, but that 'it can also be about the complex interplay of factors such as health, housing, education, and family background, and the resulting lack of ambitions and expectations, that so often combine to keep people in poverty'. In other words, socio-economic disadvantage is the disadvantage that arises as a result of a combination of social and economic factors in the life of an individual or community.

The fact that the socio-economic duty is based on a notion of such complexity is likely to be one reason why it has not yet come into force. While the formulation of the duty is clearly well-intentioned, and the disadvantages it seeks to combat undoubtedly real, it is arguably problematic to base a legislative provision on a concept that is potentially so difficult to pin down: while disadvantage in relation to housing or educational attainment may be measurable, it is a more slippery task to determine lack of ambition or expectation, for example, objectively.

However, in this regard it should be noted that the Equality and Human Rights **40.5**
Commission (EHRC), in conjunction with other bodies, has produced a
substantial and ambitious 'Equality Measurement Framework', which is
intended to provide a 'baseline of evidence' for the evaluation of societal
inequalities. The framework can be used to monitor how individuals and
groups across the protected characteristics, by reference to social class, achieve
the 'central and valuable things in life', such as enjoying an adequate standard
of living, being healthy, having good opportunities for education and learning,
enjoying legal security, and being free from crime and the fear of crime.

Inequalities of outcome   **40.6**

The socio-economic duty is aimed at reducing 'inequalities of outcome'. Again,
this is not a phrase defined by the Act, but the GEO guide states that it is
intended to mean any measurable difference in outcomes associated with (but
not restricted to) the sort of socio-economic disadvantage to which the equality
duty is directed. The Explanatory Notes to the EqA suggest that such inequalities
could include 'inequalities in education, health, housing, crime rates, or other
matters associated with socio-economic disadvantage. It is for public bodies
subject to the duty to determine which socio-economic inequalities they are in
a position to influence' (para 23).

Although not mentioned in the above list, the need to reduce inequalities in
employment which result from socio-economic disadvantage could clearly fall
within the remit of the duty. The GEO guide envisages that the duty may have
some application in the employment field. It gives 'levels of unemployment' as
an example of an outcome related to life chances. More particularly, the guide
notes that central government departments – which are already trying to recruit
more women, people from ethnic minorities and disabled people to make sure
their workforce reflects the make-up of the population as a whole – may also
need to consider how they can attract people from different socio-economic
backgrounds. Inequalities in recruitment, then, would certainly be capable of
constituting 'inequalities of outcome'.

By extension, it is possible that should the duty come into force, the public **40.7**
bodies covered by it would also need to have regard to the socio-economic duty
in relation to staff training and development, for example. While inequalities of
outcome may well exist in these areas, however, decisions relating to such
matters would only come within the ambit of the duty if they were of a 'strategic
nature' – see 'Decisions of a strategic nature' below.

Decisions of a strategic nature   **40.8**

The socio-economic duty comes into play only when a relevant public authority
makes 'decisions of a strategic nature about how to exercise its functions' –
S.1(1) EqA. Such 'strategic decisions' are not defined further in the Act.
However, the Explanatory Notes give as examples 'deciding priorities and

1413

setting objectives' (para 23), and the GEO guide states that they are the 'key, high-level decisions' that determine how an organisation goes about its business, including setting priorities and targets, allocating resources, and commissioning services. It suggests that a key aspect of fulfilling the duty will be for each of the public bodies covered by the duty to 'identify the decisions of a strategic nature that it takes, and which (if any) socio-economic inequalities that they can have a significant influence on'. Such inequalities may be the result of a particular strategy or policy or practice, or related to the absence of such a strategy or policy.

For present purposes, note the GEO guide's suggestion that a local authority's employment strategy may well involve strategic decisions, especially with regard to those furthest from the job market. As discussed under 'Scope of the duty – inequalities of outcome' above, policy decisions in central government as to recruitment may well fall within the scope of the duty: the guide suggests that central government may make strategic decisions in relation to 'overarching HR strategies'. However, we suggest that the duty is much more likely to be relevant to decisions made in central and local government that relate to getting people into work generally, rather than to direct recruitment.

40.9 Due regard

As to the meaning of 'due regard' in the context of the requirement in S.1(1) EqA to 'have due regard to the desirability of exercising [functions] in a way that is designed to reduce... inequalities of outcome', the GEO guide states that this equates to 'giving weight to a particular issue in proportion to its relevance'. The guide cites with approval Lord Justice Dyson's interpretation of the same words in the context of the old public sector race equality duty in R (on the application of Baker and ors) v Secretary of State for Communities and Local Government and anor 2008 EWCA Civ 141, CA. There, his Lordship observed that 'due regard' means 'the regard that is appropriate in all the circumstances. These include on the one hand the importance of the areas of life of the members of the disadvantaged... group that are affected by the inequality of opportunity and the extent of the inequality; and on the other hand, such countervailing factors as are relevant to the function which the decision-maker is performing.' Applying the same approach to the socio-economic duty, a relevant public authority would be expected to balance the requirement to consider the desirability of reducing the unequal outcomes resulting from socio-economic disadvantage against other relevant factors and objectives (including, for example, the financial constraints within which the authority operates).

For further analysis of this established legal concept, see Chapter 38, 'General public sector equality duty', under 'Compliance – "due regard"'.

Exception: inequalities related to immigration control

40.10

The socio-economic duty does not apply to inequalities that result from an individual being subject to immigration control, within the meaning of S.115(9) of the Immigration and Asylum Act 1999 – S.1(6) EqA.

In the Public Bill Committee on the Equality Bill in the House of Commons, the Solicitor-General explained that the reason for this exception was in order not to impose an additional duty on those public authorities that already have a statutory duty of care towards people who are subject to immigration control (see Hansard, HC Public Bill Committee, 6th Sitting, col.161 (11 June 2009)).

Compliance

40.11

Section 1(2) EqA provides that in deciding how to fulfil the socio-economic duty, the relevant authority 'must take into account any guidance issued by a Minister of the Crown'. No such guidance has been issued, and in its absence it is not entirely clear how the duty is intended to operate, particularly given the problems in defining socio-economic disadvantage and inequalities of outcome outlined above.

The GEO guide acknowledges that different organisations will need to apply the duty in different ways. Nevertheless, it suggests the following basic approach as one that all public bodies covered by the duty would be expected to adopt:

- when making key strategic decisions affecting spending and public services, relevant public authorities should take account of the impact those decisions may have on narrowing the gaps in outcomes experienced by different socio-economic groups

- the above should be achieved by examining the evidence which the particular public authority holds on the inequalities relevant to the decision or issue, and the role of socio-economic factors in driving these inequalities

- where this evidence suggests that taking a particular decision or course of action would reduce outcome gaps, the authority should give appropriate weight to the desirability of taking that course of action, and balance this against other policy objectives and available resources

- each public authority should be able to demonstrate how it has fulfilled this duty and should take account of this in its existing monitoring and reporting mechanisms.

The Explanatory Notes to the EqA give the following three examples of how the socio-economic duty might be applied in practice:

40.12

1415

- the Department of Health decides to improve the provision of primary care services. It finds evidence that people suffering socio-economic disadvantage are less likely to access such services during working hours, owing to their conditions of employment. The Department therefore advises that such services should be available at other times of the day

- under the duty, a Regional Development Agency (RDA), when reviewing its funding programmes, could decide to amend the selection criteria for a programme designed to promote business development, to encourage more successful bids from deprived areas. The same RDA could also decide to continue a programme aimed at generating more jobs in the IT sector, which, while not contributing to a reduction in socio-economic inequalities, has wider economic benefits in attracting more well-paid jobs to the region. This decision would comply with the duty, because the RDA would have given due consideration to reducing socio-economic inequalities

- the duty could lead a local education authority, when conducting a strategic review of its school applications process, to analyse the impact of its campaign to inform parents about the applications process, looking particularly at different neighbourhoods. If the results suggest that parents in more deprived areas are less likely to access or make use of the information provided, the authority could decide to carry out additional work in those neighbourhoods in future campaigns, to ensure that children from deprived areas have a better chance of securing a place at their school of choice.

40.13 Evidence

The examples cited above, and the compliance pointers set out in the GEO guide, indicate that public authorities subject to the socio-economic duty would need to have regard to evidence in order to see what inequalities of outcome they might be in a position to redress. The EqA does not impose any specific duties on public authorities to collect or collate evidence; rather, they would be expected to have recourse to relevant available data, and analyse this to determine whether their strategic decisions could have a positive impact in reducing inequalities. The guide suggests that the evidence a public body should consider when taking strategic decisions would vary depending on the decision in question. In some cases, data collected and reported at a national level might be appropriate, such as the Labour Market Survey, the British Crime Survey, the Index of Multiple Deprivation, and so on. But appropriate evidence might also be obtained from data collected at a local or regional level. The guide suggests that evidence from research studies, surveys of local people, and feedback from public consultations might all be useful, although 'hard' data and statistics would be necessary 'to monitor the success of different approaches'.

1416

Who is subject to the duty?

As the socio-economic duty applies to strategic decisions only, the public authorities to which it would apply, if brought into force, are 'high-level strategic bodies taking key decisions', as the Solicitor-General put it in the Public Bill Committee on the Equality Bill in the House of Commons (Hansard, HC Public Bill Committee, 5th Sitting, col.145 (11 June 2009)).

Section 1(3) EqA lists which public authorities are subject to the socio-economic duty. They are:

- Ministers of the Crown

- government departments other than the Security Service, the Secret Intelligence Service or the Government Communications Headquarters

- county councils and district councils in England

- the Greater London Authority

- London borough councils

- the Common Council of the City of London in its capacity as a local authority

- the Council of the Isles of Scilly

- strategic health authorities established under S.13 of the National Health Service Act 2006 (NHSA), or continued in existence by virtue of that section

- primary care trusts established under S.18 NHSA, or continued in existence by virtue of that section

- regional development agencies established by the Regional Development Agencies Act 1998

- police authorities established for particular areas in England.

The duty also applies to 'partner authorities' of a 'responsible local authority' **40.15** in relation to their participation in the preparation or modification of a 'sustainable community strategy' – S.1(4) EqA. A 'partner authority' and 'responsible local authority' are defined in Ss.104 and 103 respectively of the Local Government and Public Involvement in Health Act 2007; a 'sustainable community strategy' is a strategy prepared under S.4 of the Local Government Act 2000 – S.1(5) EqA.

Under S.2(1) EqA, a Minister of the Crown has the power to add or remove public authorities that are subject to the duty; to restrict the application of the duty in respect of a particular public authority to certain functions; or to remove or alter such a restriction. For the purposes of this provision, a public authority is defined as one that 'has functions of a public nature' – S.2(2).

40.16 However, a Minister of the Crown is not entitled under S.2(1) EqA to impose a duty on an authority in relation to any devolved Scottish or Welsh functions – S.2(3). Powers in relation to devolved functions similar to those under S.2(1) are reserved to the Scottish and Welsh Ministers as relevant, subject to consultation with a Minister of the Crown – S.2(4)–(7). Regulations made under S.2(1) or (4) may make any consequential amendments that are necessary or expedient to S.1 – S.2(8). In particular, Scottish or Welsh ministers may use S.2(8) to amend S.1 so as to give them power to issue new guidance in relation to a Scottish or Welsh authority, thereby replacing guidance already issued by a minister under S.1(2) – S.2(9). Any new guidance must take account of any such existing guidance and a Minister of the Crown must be consulted – S.2(10).

40.17 ## Monitoring and enforcement

The GEO guide indicates that, should the socio-economic duty come into force, public authorities would be monitored in its implementation by inspectorates such as Ofsted through existing mechanisms. The Government and other interested parties would be able to use the information made available through the monitoring process to assess a body's compliance with the duty.

Section 3 EqA provides that '[a] failure in respect of the performance of a duty under S.1 does not confer a cause of action at private law'. This means that an individual or company would not be entitled to commence civil proceedings against a relevant public authority in his, her or its own name, claiming damages for breach of statutory duty. The Explanatory Notes to the EqA give the following example:

- an individual feels that the socio-economic disadvantages he faces should entitle him to a flat in a new social housing development, ahead of those whom he judges to be less disadvantaged. However, there is no provision in this Act for him to bring a case against the local council or other public body in such circumstances (para 33).

40.18 The socio-economic duty would be enforceable only by way of judicial review. This would entitle an individual or interest group whose interests were affected by the decisions of a public authority to bring judicial review proceedings against the authority if there was evidence that it had failed to comply with the duty. For details of judicial review, see Chapter 38, 'General public sector equality duty', under 'Enforcement – judicial review'.

The GEO guide points out that, in addition, organisations such as charities, residents' associations, pressure groups and local businesses could have a role in holding public bodies to account by challenging decisions through the public bodies' feedback and engagement procedures.

Case list

(Note that employment tribunal cases are not included in this list.)

A

1420

1422

Chief Constable of West Yorkshire v Vento (No.1) 2001 IRLR 124, EAT   15.49
Child Poverty Action Group v Secretary of State for Work and Pensions
   2011 EWHC 2616, QBD   38.48
Chondol v Liverpool City Council EAT 0298/08   11.52, 15.55, 25.88, 26.41
Choux v Royal College of Veterinary Surgeons EAT 668/95   15.46, 15.48
Church of Scientology and anor v Sweden 1979 ECC 511, ECtHR   11.6
City of Edinburgh Council v Dickson EAT 0038/09   15.80, 20.7
CJ O'Shea Construction Ltd v Bassi 1998 ICR 1130, EAT   28.49
Clarke and anor v Eley (IMI) Kynoch Ltd 1983 ICR 165, EAT   16.24, 16.37, 26.7
Clarke v Hampshire Electro-Plating Co Ltd 1992 ICR 312, EAT   34.24
Clark v TDG Ltd t/a Novacold 1999 ICR 951, CA   1.18, 20.3, 20.4, 21.79
Clymo v Wandsworth London Borough Council 1989 ICR 250, EAT   24.77
Cobb and ors v Secretary of State for Employment and anor 1989
   ICR 506, EAT   17.46, 17.92
Coca Cola Enterprises Ltd v Shergill EAT 0003/02   6.98
Coleman v Attridge Law and anor 2008 ICR 1128, ECJ   2.16, 2.18, 15.100, 15.107,
   15.108, 18.49, 18.55, 18.56 ,22.13, 31.19
College of Ripon and York St John v Hobbs 2002 IRLR 185, EAT   6.21, 6.23
Commissioner of Police of the Metropolis and anor v Osinaike EAT 0373/09 32.73, 33.10
Commissioner of Police of the Metropolis v Hendricks 2003 ICR 530, CA   34.21
Commissioner of Police of the Metropolis v Shaw EAT 0125/11   36.41, 36.79, 36.81,
   36.82, 36.83, 36.101, 39.97
Commissioner of Police of the Metropolis v Virdi 2009 EWCA Civ 477, CA   6.70, 33.11
Commissioner of Police of the Metropolis v Virdi EAT 0598/07   33.11
Commissioners of Inland Revenue and anor v Morgan 2002 IRLR 776, EAT   19.64
Commission for Racial Equality v Amari Plastics Ltd 1982 ICR 304, CA   37.34
Commission for Racial Equality v Dutton 1989 IRLR 8, CA   10.23, 16.37
Community Law Clinic Solicitors Ltd and ors v Methuen EAT 0024/11   33.22
Conteh v Parking Partners Ltd 2011 ICR 341, EAT   18.74, 25.93. 25.118, 28.102
Cooper and anor v Smith EAT 0452/03   35.21
Coote v Granada Hospitality Ltd 1999 ICR 100, ECJ   19.16, 19.44, 27.3, 27.10, 30.82
Copal Castings Ltd v Hinton EAT 0903/04   21.44
Copsey v WBB Devon Clays Ltd 2005 ICR 1789, CA   3.5, 11.47
Coral Squash Clubs Ltd v Matthews and anor 1979 ICR 607, EAT   33.36
Cordell v Foreign and Commonwealth Office 2012 ICR 280, EAT   15.34, 15.55, 21.67,
   21.68, 25.53
Cornelius v University College of Swansea 1987 IRLR 141, CA   19.5
Corr v IBC Vehicles Ltd 2008 ICR 372, HL   35.15
Corus Hotels plc v Woodward and anor EAT 0536/05   36.50, 36.51
Cosgrove v Caesar and Howie 2001 IRLR 653, EAT   21.17, 21.76
Council of Civil Service Unions and ors v Minister for the Civil Service 1985
   ICR 14, HL   34.92, 38.70
Country Style Foods Ltd v Bouzir 2011 EWCA Civ 1519, CA   32.20, 32.53
Coutinho v Rank Nemo (DMS) Ltd and ors 2009 ICR 1296, CA   19.7, 27.27
Cox v General Medical Council EAT 0076/01   29.9, 29.10, 29.17
Coyne v Home Office 2000 ICR 1443, CA   18.76
Craddock v Cornwall County Council and anor EAT 0367/05   17.42
Crofton v Yeboah EAT 475/00   35.37

1423

E

EB v BA 2006 IRLR 471, CA   32.56

Eagle Place Services Ltd and ors v Rudd 2010 IRLR 486, EAT   15.42, 20.6, 20.8,
                                                                                   33.13, 33.16

Ealing, Hammersmith and Hounslow Family Health Services Authority v
    Shukla 1993 ICR 710, EAT   28.11

Eastern and Coastal Kent Primary Care Trust v Grey 2009 IRLR 429, EAT   21.54

EBR Attridge LLP (formerly Attridge Law) and anor v Coleman 2010
    ICR 242, EAT   1.14, 2.16, 15.99, 15.100, 18.55

Edmund Nuttall Ltd v Butterfield 2006 ICR 77, EAT   6.60

Edozie v Group 4 Securicor plc and anor EAT 0124/09   32.9

Eke v Commissioners of Customs and Excise 1981 IRLR 334, EAT   25.93

Ekpe v Commissioner of Police of the Metropolis 2001 ICR 1084, EAT   6.71, 6.79, 6.92

Enderby v Frenchay Health Authority and anor 1994 ICR 112, ECJ   16.109, 17.44

English v Thomas Sanderson Blinds Ltd 2009 ICR 543, CA   13.14, 18.11, 18.16, 18.18,
                                                                                   18.37, 18.59, 25.116

Environment Agency v Rowan 2008 ICR 218, EAT   21.15, 21.28, 21.42, 25.42

Equal Opportunities Commission v Secretary of State for Trade and Industry
    2007 ICR 1234, QBD   2.18, 20.17

Essa v Laing Ltd 2004 ICR 746, CA   35.17, 36.92

Evans v Oakland Nursing Home Group Ltd EAT 0331/99   36.76

Eversheds Legal Services Ltd v De Belin 2011 ICR 1137, EAT   15.30, 26.61

Eweida v British Airways plc 2009 ICR 303, EAT   16.83, 16.161, 20.14, 20.32

Eweida v British Airways plc 2010 ICR 890, CA   3.20, 3.27, 11.43, 11.45, 11.55, 11.56,
                                                       11.57, 11.60, 16.45, 16.83, 16.95, 16.137,
                                                       16.161, 16.165, 17.69, 20.32, 25.102

Ezsias v North Glamorgan NHS Trust 2007 ICR 1126, CA   33.22, 34.94

F

FTATU v Modgill and ors and other cases 1980 IRLR 142, EAT   15.17

F v G 2012 ICR 246, EAT   34.55, 34.56, 34.59

Fareham College Corporation v Walters 2009 IRLR 991, EAT   21.45, 21.79, 25.27, 26.1

Faulkner v Chief Constable of Hampshire Constabulary EAT 0505/05   17.65

Federal Republic of Nigeria v Ogbonna 2012 ICR 32, EAT   30.78

Fife Council v McPhee EAT 750/00   35.34

Fitzpatrick v British Railways Board 1992 ICR 221, CA   24.75

Foster and ors v British Gas plc 1991 ICR 84, ECJ   2.12

Fox v Ocean City Recruitment Ltd EAT 0035/11   28.90

Francis and ors v British Airways Engineering Overhaul Ltd 1982 IRLR 10, EAT   16.32

Francovich and ors v Italian Republic 1995 ICR 722, ECJ   2.24

Fuchs and anor v Land Hessen 2012 ICR 93, ECJ   15.86, 17.94, 26.85, 26.89

Fulton and ors v Strathclyde Regional Council EAT 949/83   16.56

Fyfe v Scientific Furnishings Ltd 1989 ICR 648, EAT   36.36

G

GMB Union v Fenton EAT 0798/02 and others   19.29

GMB v Allen and ors 2007 IRLR 752, EAT   19.36

GMB v Allen and ors 2008 ICR 1407, CA   17.52, 19.36

L

McDougall v Richmond Adult Community College 2007
  ICR 1567, EAT   6.12, 6.40
McFarlane v Relate Avon Ltd 2010 ICR 507, EAT   3.20, 11.50, 11.52, 11.57, 11.59,
                                                     13.26, 16.167, 17.50, 17.73 26.41
McFarlane v Relate Avon Ltd 2010 IRLR 872, CA   11.51, 16.167, 17.73
McKechnie Plastic Components v Grant EAT 0284/08   6.10, 6.119, 6.146
McLaren v Home Office 1990 ICR 824, CA   34.91
McNicol v Balfour Beatty Rail Maintenance Ltd 2002 ICR 1498, CA   6.13, 6.23
McNicol v Balfour Beatty Rail Maintenance Ltd; Rugamer v Sony Music
  Entertainment UK Ltd 2002 ICR 381, EAT   6.13, 6.23
McRoberts v Adams EAT 499/92   34.37
Madarassy v Nomura International plc 2007 ICR 867, CA   32.33, 32.39, 32.42, 32.48,
                                                         32.52, 33.11, 33.16, 33.28
Mahon v Accuread Ltd EAT 0081/08   6.144
Mahood v Irish Centre Housing Ltd EAT 0228/10   28.90, 28.106
Majrowski v Guy's and St Thomas's NHS Trust 2006 ICR 1199, HL   28.97
Malik and anor v Bank of Credit and Commerce International SA
  (in compulsory liquidation) 1997 ICR 606, HL   36.26
Mandla and anor v Dowell Lee and ors 1983 ICR 385, HL   10.17, 10.19, 10.20, 10.25,
                                    10.26, 10.27, 10.29, 10.30, 10.38, 16.11, 17.54
Mangold v Helm 2006 IRLR 143, ECJ   2.19, 2.21, 2.23, 5.4, 5.5, 5.6, 5.9,
                                                       12.3, 28.13, 34.10
Mankoo v British School of Motoring Ltd EAT 657/82   28.24
Marleasing SA v La Comercial Internacional de Alimentación SA, 1992 1
  CMLR 305, ECJ   2.14, 2.15, 11.3, 13.3
Marschall v Land Nordrhein-Westfalen 2001 ICR 45, ECJ   30.57
Marshall v Southampton and South West Hampshire Area Health Authority
  (Teaching) 1986 ICR 335, ECJ   2.12, 5.5
Martins v Choudhary 2007 EWCA Civ 1379, CA   36.78, 36.101
Martin v Devonshires Solicitors 2011 ICR 352, EAT   19.30, 19.46, 19.58, 26.107,
                                      26.108, 26.109, 32.17, 32.25
Martin v Lancehawk Ltd t/a European Telecom Solutions EAT 0525/03   15.66
Mayor and Burgesses of the London Borough of Brent v Corcoran and anor
  2010 EWCA Civ 774, CA   38.44
Mayor and Burgesses of the London Borough of Lewisham v Malcolm 2008
  IRLR 700, HL   1.18, 1.19, 6.3, 16.131, 20.4, 20.7, 20.9, 20.13, 20.16, 20.27, 25.36
Meade-Hill and anor v British Council 1995 ICR 847, CA   16.38, 16.40, 16.88, 16.95,
                                                             16.117, 34.82
Medical Protection Society and ors v Sadek 2004 ICR 1263, CA   29.7
Meikle v Nottinghamshire County Council 2005 ICR 1, CA   21.104, 21.106,
                                                          26.100, 34.18
Meister v Speech Design Carrier Systems GmbH Case C-415/10, ECJ   32.5, 32.28, 32.36,
                                      32.40, 32.46, 32.51, 32.65, 32.69 33.29
Melia v Magna Kansei Ltd 2006 ICR 410, CA   36.6
Metropolitan Church of Bessarabia v Moldova 2002 35 EHRR 13, ECtHR   11.10
Metropolitan Police Service v Shoebridge 2004 ICR 1690, EAT   27.17, 27.21
Mid Staffordshire General Hospitals NHS Trust v Cambridge 2003 IRLR 566, EAT 21.12
Miles v Gilbank and anor 2006 ICR 1297, CA   35.43, 36.62

Index

IDS Handbook • Discrimination at Work

1443

1495

1507